COMPILATION OF THE SOCIAL SECURITY LAWS

United States Congress House of Representatives Committee on Ways and Means

The BiblioGov Project is an effort to expand awareness of the public documents and records of the U.S. Government via print publications. In broadening the public understanding of government and its work, an enlightened democracy can grow and prosper. Ranging from historic Congressional Bills to the most recent Budget of the United States Government, the BiblioGov Project spans a wealth of government information. These works are now made available through an environmentally friendly, print-on-demand basis, using only what is necessary to meet the required demands of an interested public. We invite you to learn of the records of the U.S. Government, heightening the knowledge and debate that can lead from such publications.

Included are the following Collections:

Budget of The United States Government
Presidential Documents
United States Code
Education Reports from ERIC
GAO Reports
History of Bills
House Rules and Manual
Public and Private Laws

Code of Federal Regulations
Congressional Documents
Economic Indicators
Federal Register
Government Manuals
House Journal
Privacy act Issuances
Statutes at Large

| 111TH CONGRESS 1st Session | COMMITTEE PRINT | WMCP 111–2 |

COMPILATION

OF THE

SOCIAL SECURITY LAWS

INCLUDING THE SOCIAL SECURITY ACT,
AS AMENDED, AND RELATED ENACTMENTS
THROUGH JANUARY 1, 2009

VOLUME I—PART 1

PRINTED FOR THE USE OF THE
COMMITTEE ON WAYS AND MEANS BY ITS STAFF

COMPILATION OF THE SOCIAL SECURITY LAWS THROUGH JANUARY 1, 2009—Vol. I—PART 1

111TH CONGRESS 1st Session	COMMITTEE PRINT	WMCP 111–2

COMPILATION

OF THE

SOCIAL SECURITY LAWS

INCLUDING THE SOCIAL SECURITY ACT,
AS AMENDED, AND RELATED ENACTMENTS
THROUGH JANUARY 1, 2009

VOLUME I—PART 1

PRINTED FOR THE USE OF THE

COMMITTEE ON WAYS AND MEANS BY ITS STAFF

U.S. GOVERNMENT PRINTING OFFICE

52–528

WASHINGTON : 2009

For sale by the Superintendent of Documents, U.S. Government Printing Office
Internet: bookstore.gpo.gov   Phone: toll free (866) 512–1800;   DC area (202) 512–1800
Fax: (202) 512–2104 Mail: Stop IDCC, Washington, DC 20402–0001

ISBN 978-0-16-084289-4

COMMITTEE ON WAYS AND MEANS

CHARLES B. RANGEL, New York, *Chairman*

FORTNEY PETE STARK, California
SANDER M. LEVIN, Michigan
JIM McDERMOTT, Washington
JOHN LEWIS, Georgia
RICHARD E. NEAL, Massachusetts
JOHN S. TANNER, Tennessee
XAVIER BECERRA, California
LLOYD DOGGETT, Texas
EARL POMEROY, North Dakota
MIKE THOMPSON, California
JOHN B. LARSON, Connecticut
EARL BLUMENAUER, Oregon
RON KIND, Wisconsin
BILL PASCRELL JR., New Jersey
SHELLEY BERKLEY, Nevada
JOSEPH CROWLEY, New York
CHRIS VAN HOLLEN, Maryland
KENDRICK B. MEEK, Florida
ALLYSON Y. SCHWARTZ, Pennsylvania
ARTUR DAVIS, Alabama
DANNY K. DAVIS, Illinois
BOB ETHERIDGE, North Carolina
LINDA T. SANCHEZ, California
BRIAN HIGGINS, New York
JOHN A. YARMUTH, Kentucky

DAVE CAMP, Michigan
WALLY HERGER, California
SAM JOHNSON, Texas
KEVIN BRADY, Texas
PAUL RYAN, Wisconsin
ERIC CANTOR, Virginia
JOHN LINDER, Georgia
DEVIN NUNES, California
PATRICK J. TIBERI, Ohio
GINNY BROWN-WAITE, Florida
GEOFF DAVIS, Kentucky
DAVE G. REICHERT, Washington
CHARLES W. BOUSTANY JR., LOUISIANA
DEAN HELLER, Nevada
PETER J. ROSKAM, Illinois

JANICE MAYS, *Chief Counsel and Staff Director*
JON TRAUB, *Minority Staff Director*

(II)

PREFACE

The Social Security Act

The original Social Security Act is P.L. 74-271 (49 Stat. 620), approved August 14, 1935. The Social Security Act (SSAct) has been amended significantly since 1935. A list of laws which have amended the SSAct may be found in Volume II, Appendix G.

Administration of the Social Security Act

The Social Security Board was responsible for administration of the original Social Security Act except for parts 1, 2, 3, and 5 of Title V (which were administered by the Children's Bureau, then in the Department of Labor); part 4 of Title V which increased the appropriations authorized for carrying out the Act of June 2, 1920 and Title VI which authorized grants to the States for public health work.

The Social Security Board was transferred to the Federal Security Agency by Reorganization Plan No. 1 of 1939 and the Board's functions were to be carried on under the direction and supervision of the Federal Security Administrator. Reorganization Plan No. 2 of 1946 transferred the functions of the Children's Bureau and the functions of the Secretary of Labor under Title V of the Act to the Federal Security Administrator and the Board was abolished.

The Bureau of Employment Security, with its unemployment compensation and employment service function, was transferred from the Federal Security Agency to the Department of Labor by Reorganization Plan No. 2 of 1949.

The Department of Health, Education, and Welfare was established by Reorganization Plan No. 1 of 1953 with a Secretary of Health, Education, and Welfare as the head of the Department. All functions of the Federal Security Agency, which was abolished, were transferred to the Department of Health, Education, and Welfare. The functions of the Federal Security Administrator were transferred to the Secretary of Health, Education and Welfare.

The Department of Health, Education, and Welfare was redesignated the Department of Health and Human Services, and the Secretary of Health, Education, and Welfare was redesignated the Secretary of Health and Human Services by P.L. 96-88, §509, approved October 17, 1979. The Department of Health and Human Services redesignation was effective May 4, 1980 (45 Federal Register 29642; May 5, 1980). The Department of Education which was established by P.L. 96–88 was activated May 4, 1980 (Executive Order 12212 of May 2, 1980; 45 Federal Register 29557; May 5, 1980).

Effective March 31, 1995, the Social Security Administration was established as an independent agency by P.L. 103-296, §101, approved August 15, 1994, with a Commissioner of Social Security responsible for the exercise of all powers and the discharge of all duties of the Administration.

Compilation of the Social Security Laws

This Compilation currently consists of 2 volumes:

Volume I
Table of Contents
The Social Security Act
PART 1 - Titles I through XVII
PART 2 - Titles XVIII through XXI and an
Index

Volume II
Table of Contents
Provisions from other laws
—cited in the SSAct

—affecting programs administered under the SSAct and Appendixes

Effect of Compilation

The Compilation of the Social Security Laws is not prima facie evidence of the provisions of the Social Security Act or other laws or statutes which are included, but has been prepared for convenient reference purposes.

Citations in Volume I

Citations have been included to enable the reader to locate the SSAct provisions in the United States Code (U.S.C.). These U.S.C. citations are shown within brackets after the SSAct section.

For example: Social Security Act - Sec.201. [42 U.S.C. 401]

SSAct section 201 may be found in Title 42 of the U.S.C. at section 401.

COMPILED BY

THE SOCIAL SECURITY ADMINISTRATION
OFFICE OF RETIREMENT AND DISABILITY POLICY
OFFICE OF POLICYNET AND PROGRAM SUPPORT
DIVISION OF POLICYNET MANAGEMENT
TECHNICAL DOCUMENTS BRANCH
6401 SECURITY BOULEVARD
BALTIMORE, MARYLAND 21235–6401

This volume is available online at http://www.socialsecurity.gov under "Other Useful Links", "Our Program Rules".

TABLE OF CONTENTS[1]

VOLUME I

Page

SOCIAL SECURITY ACT

Title I	[Grants to States for Old–Age Assistance for the Aged]	1
Title II	Federal Old–Age, Survivors, and Disability Insurance Benefits	7
Title III	Grants to States for Unemployment Compensation Administration	251
Title IV	Grants to States for Aid and Services to Needy Families with Children and for Child–Welfare Services	263
Title V	Maternal and Child Health Services Block Grant	531
Title VI	[Temporary State Fiscal Relief]	549
Title VII	Administration	551
Title VIII	Special Benefits for Certain World War II Veterans	565
Title IX	Miscellaneous Provisions Relating to Employment Security	581
Title X	[Grants to States for Aid to the Blind]	599
Title XI	General Provisions, Peer Review, and Administrative Simplification	605
Title XII	Advances to State Unemployment Funds	755
Title XIII	[Reconversion Unemployment Benefits for Seamen]	761
Title XIV	[Grants to States for Aid to the Permanently and Totally Disabled]	763
Title XV	[Unemployment Compensation for Federal Employees]	769
Title XVI	[Grants to States for Aid to the Aged, Blind, or Disabled]	771
Title XVI	Supplemental Security Income for the Aged, Blind, and Disabled	779
Title XVII	Grants for Planning Comprehensive Action to Combat Mental Retardation	857
Title XVIII	Health Insurance for the Aged and Disabled	859
Title XIX	Grants to States for Medical Assistance Programs	1709
Title XX	Block Grants to States for Social Services	2027
Title XXI	State Children's Health Insurance Program	2037

INDEX TO SOCIAL SECURITY ACT 2073

---

[1] This table of contents does not appear in the law.

vii

SOCIAL SECURITY ACT[1]

(As Amended through January 1, 2009)

AN ACT

To provide for the general welfare by establishing a system of Federal old-age benefits, and by enabling the several States to make more adequate provision for aged persons, blind persons, dependent and crippled children, maternal and child welfare, public health, and the administration of their unemployment compensation laws; to establish a Social Security Board; to raise revenue; and for other purposes.

Be it enacted by the Senate and House of Representatives of the United States of America in Congress assembled,

[TITLE I—GRANTS TO STATES FOR OLD–AGE ASSISTANCE FOR THE AGED[2]]

TABLE OF CONTENTS OF TITLE[3]

		Page
Sec. 1.	Appropriation	1
Sec. 2.	State old-age plans	2
Sec. 3.	Payment to States	4
Sec. 4.	Operation of State plans	5
[Sec. 5.	Repealed.]	5
Sec. 6.	Definition	5

APPROPRIATION

SEC. 1. [42 U.S.C. 301] For the purpose of enabling each State, as far as practicable under the conditions in such State, to furnish financial assistance to aged needy individuals, there is hereby authorized to be appropriated for each fiscal year a sum sufficient to carry out the purposes of this title. The sums made available under this section shall be used for making payments to States which have submitted, and had approved by the Secretary of Health, Education, and Welfare[4]

---

[1] P.L. 74-271, approved August 14, 1935, 49 Stat. 620.

[2] Title I of the Social Security Act is administered by the Department of Health and Human Services. The Office of Family Assistance administers benefit payments under Title I. The Administration for Public Services, Office of Human Development Services, administers social services under Title I.

Title I appears in the United States Code as §§301-306, subchapter I, chapter 7, Title 42.

Regulations relating to Title I are contained in subtitle A and chapter XIII, Title 45, Code of Federal Regulations.

P.L. 92-603, §303, *repealed* Title I effective January 1, 1974, *except* with respect to Puerto Rico, Guam, and the Virgin Islands. The Commonwealth of the Northern Marianas may elect to initiate a Title I social services program if it chooses; see Vol. II, P.L. 94-241, approved March 24, 1976, 90 Stat. 263, [Covenant to Establish Northern Mariana Islands].

See Vol. II, 31 U.S.C. 6504-6505, with respect to intergovernmental cooperation and 31 U.S.C. 7501-7507, with respect to uniform audit requirements for State and local governments receiving Federal financial assistance.

See Vol. II, P.L. 82-183, §618, for the "Jenner Amendment", which prohibits denial of grants-in-aid under certain conditions.

See Vol. II, P.L. 88-352, §601, for prohibition against discrimination in Federally assisted programs.

See Vol. II, P.L. 89-97, §121(b), with respect to restrictions on payment to a State receiving payments under Title XIX.

See Vol. II, P.L. 90-248, §234(c), with respect to nursing homes which do not meet all requirements of a State for licensure.

[3] This table of contents does not appear in the law.

[4] This was deemed a reference to the Secretary of Health and Human Services under section 509 of the "Department of Education Organization Act" (P.L. 96-88, 93 Stat. 695), effective May 4, 1980.

2 SOCIAL SECURITY ACT—§ 1(cont)

(hereinafter referred to as the "Secretary"), State plans for old-age assistance.

STATE OLD-AGE PLANS

SEC. 2. [42 U.S.C. 302] (a) A State plan for old-age assistance must—

(1) except to the extent permitted by the Secretary with respect to services, provide that it shall be in effect in all political subdivisions of the State, and, if administered by them, be mandatory upon them;

(2) provide for financial participation by the State;

(3) either provide for the establishment or designation of a single State agency to administer the plan, or provide for the establishment or designation of a single State agency to supervise the administration of the plan;

(4) provide (A) for granting an opportunity for a fair hearing before the State agency to any individual whose claim for assistance under the plan is denied or is not acted upon with reasonable promptness, and (B) that if the State plan is administered in each of the political subdivisions of the State by a local agency and such local agency provides a hearing at which evidence may be presented prior to a hearing before the State agency, such local agency may put into effect immediately upon issuance its decision upon the matter considered at such hearing;

(5) provide (A) such methods of administration (including methods relating to the establishment and maintenance of personnel standards on a merit basis, except that the Secretary shall exercise no authority with respect to the selection, tenure of office, and compensation of any individual employed in accordance with such methods) as are found by the Secretary[5] to be necessary for the proper and efficient operation of the plan, and (B) for the training and effective use of paid subprofessional staff, with particular emphasis on the full-time or part-time employment of recipients and other persons of low income, as community service aides, in the administration of the plan and for the use of nonpaid or partially paid volunteers in a social service volunteer program in providing services to applicants and recipients and in assisting any advisory committees established by the State agency;

(6) provide that the State agency will make such reports, in such form and containing such information, as the Secretary may from time to time require, and comply with such provisions as the Secretary may from time to time find necessary to assure the correctness and verification of such reports;

(7) provide safeguards which permit the use or disclosure of information concerning applicants or recipients only (A) to public officials who require such information in connection with their official duties, or (B) to other persons for purposes directly connected with the administration of the State plan;

(8) provide that all individuals wishing to make application for assistance under the plan shall have opportunity to do so, and

---

[5] P.L. 91-648, §208(a)(3)(D), transferred to the U.S. Civil Service Commission, effective March 6, 1971, all powers, functions, and duties of the Secretary under subparagraph (A). Functions of the Commission were transferred, effective January 1, 1979, to the Director of the Office of Personnel Management by section 102 of Reorganization Plan No. 2 of 1978.

that such assistance shall be furnished with reasonable promptness to all eligible individuals;

(9) provide, if the plan includes assistance for or on behalf of individuals in private or public institutions, for the establishment or designation of a State authority or authorities which shall be responsible for establishing and maintaining standards for such institutions;

(10) if the State plan includes old-age assistance—

(A) provide that the State agency shall, in determining need for such assistance, take into consideration any other income and resources of an individual claiming old-age assistance, as well as any expenses reasonably attributable to the earning of any such income; except that, in making such determination, (i) the State agency may disregard not more than $7.50 per month of any income and (ii) of the first $80 per month of additional income which is earned the State agency may disregard not more than the first $20 thereof plus one-half of the remainder;[6]

(B) include reasonable standards, consistent with the objectives of this title, for determining eligibility for and the extent of such assistance; and

(C) provide a description of the services (if any) which the State agency makes available (using whatever internal organizational arrangement it finds appropriate for this purpose) to applicants for and recipients of such assistance to help them attain self-care, including a description of the steps taken to assure, in the provision of such services, maximum utilization of other agencies providing similar or related services; and

(11) provide that information is requested and exchanged for purposes of income and eligibility verification in accordance with a State system which meets the requirements of section 1137 of this Act.

(b) The Secretary shall approve any plan which fulfills the conditions specified in subsection (a), except that he shall not approve any plan which imposes, as a condition of eligibility for assistance under the plan—

(1) an age requirement of more than sixty-five years; or

(2) any residence requirement which (A) in the case of applicants for old-age assistance, excludes any resident of the State who has resided therein five years during the nine years immediately preceding the application for old-age assistance and has resided therein continuously for one year immediately preceding the application, and (B) in the case of applicants for medical assistance for the aged, excludes any individual who resides in the State; or

(3) any citizenship requirement which excludes any citizen of the United States.

At the option of the State, the plan may provide that manuals and other policy issuances will be furnished to persons without charge for the reasonable cost of such materials, but such provision shall not be

---

[6] See Vol. II, Appendix K, Income and Resource Exclusions, for a list of provisions from Federal laws regarding exclusions from income and resources.

4 SOCIAL SECURITY ACT—§ 2(b)(3)(cont)

required by the Secretary as a condition for the approval of such plan under this title.

(c) Nothing in this title shall be construed to permit a State to have in effect with respect to any period more than one State plan approved under this title.

PAYMENT TO STATES

SEC. 3. [42 U.S.C. 303] (a) From the sums appropriated therefor, the Secretary of the Treasury shall pay to each State which has a plan approved under this title, for each quarter, beginning with the quarter commencing October 1, 1960—

(1) [Stricken.[7]]

(2) in the case of Puerto Rico, the Virgin Islands, and Guam, an amount equal to one-half of the total of the sums expended during such quarter as old-age assistance under the State plan, not counting so much of any expenditure with respect to any month as exceeds $37.50 multiplied by the total number of recipients of old-age assistance for such month; plus

(3) [Stricken.[8]]

(4) in the case of any State, an amount equal to 50 percent of the total amounts expended during such quarter as found necessary by the Secretary for the proper and efficient administration of the State plan.

(b) The method of computing and paying such amounts shall be as follows:

(1) The Secretary of Health, Education, and Welfare shall, prior to the beginning of each quarter, estimate the amount to be paid to the State for such quarter under the provisions of subsection(a), such estimate to be based on (A) a report filed by the State containing its estimate of the total sum to be expended in such quarter in accordance with the provisions of such subsection, and stating the amount appropriated or made available by the State and its political subdivisions for such expenditures in such quarter, and if such amount is less than the State's proportionate share of the total sum of such estimated expenditures, the source or sources from which the difference is expected to be derived, (B) records showing the number of aged individuals in the State, and (C) such other investigation as the Secretary may find necessary.

(2) The Secretary of Health, Education, and Welfare shall then certify to the Secretary of the Treasury the amount so estimated by the Secretary of Health, Education, and Welfare, (A) reduced or increased, as the case may be, by any sum by which he finds that his estimate for any prior quarter was greater or less than the amount which should have been paid to the State under subsection (a) for such quarter, and (B) reduced by a sum equivalent to the pro rata share to which the United States is equitably entitled, as determined by the Secretary of Health, Education, and Welfare, of the net amount recovered during any prior quarter by the State or any political subdivision thereof with respect to assistance furnished under the State plan; except that such increases or reductions shall not be made to the extent that such sums have

[7] P.L. 97-35, §2184(a)(4)(A); 95 Stat. 816.
[8] P.L. 97-35, §2184(a)(4)(A); 95 Stat. 816.

SOCIAL SECURITY ACT—§ 6(a)   5

been applied to make the amount certified for any prior quarter greater or less than the amount estimated by the Secretary for such prior quarter: *Provided,* That any part of the amount recovered from the estate of a deceased recipient which is not in excess of the amount expended by the State or any political subdivision thereof for the funeral expenses of the deceased shall not be considered as a basis for reduction under clause (B) of this paragraph.

(3) The Secretary of the Treasury shall thereupon, through the Division of Disbursement[9] of the Treasury Department and prior to audit or settlement by the General Accounting Office[10], pay to the State, at the time or times fixed by the Secretary of Health, Education, and Welfare, the amount so certified.

OPERATION OF STATE PLANS

SEC. 4. [42 U.S.C. 304] In the case of any State plan which has been approved under this title by the Secretary of Health, Education, and Welfare, if the Secretary, after reasonable notice and opportunity for hearing to the State agency administering or supervising the administration of such plan, finds—

(1) that the plan has been so changed as to impose any age, residence, or citizenship requirement prohibited by section 2(b), or that in the administration of the plan any such prohibited requirement is imposed, with the knowledge of such State agency, in a substantial number of cases; or

(2) that in the administration of the plan there is a failure to comply substantially with any provision required by section 2(a) to be included in the plan;

the Secretary shall notify such State agency that further payments will not be made to the State (or, in his discretion, that payments will be limited to categories under or parts of the State plan not affected by such failure) until the Secretary is satisfied that such prohibited requirement is no longer so imposed, and that there is no longer any such failure to comply. Until he is so satisfied he shall make no further payments to such State (or shall limit payments to categories under or parts of the State plan not affected by such failure).

SEC. 5.   [Repealed.[11]]

DEFINITION[12]

SEC. 6. [42 U.S.C. 306] (a)[13] For the purposes of this title, the term "old-age assistance" means money payments to, or (if provided in or after the third month before the month in which the recipient makes application for assistance) medical care in behalf of or any type of remedial care recognized under State law in behalf of, needy individuals who are 65 years of age or older, but does not include any such pay-

---

[9] As in original. The Division of Disbursement was consolidated in the Fiscal Service of the Treasury Department by Reorganization Plan No. III, §1(a), effective June 30, 1940 [54 Stat. 1231].

[10] P.L. 108-271, §8(b), provided that "Any reference to the General Accounting Office in any law, rule, regulation, certificate, directive, instruction, or other official paper in force on the date of enactment [July 7, 2004] of this Act shall be considered to refer and apply to the Government Accountability Office."

[11] P.L. 92-603, §303(a); 86 Stat. 1484.

The P.L. 92-603, §303(b), repeal exception is deemed not applicable to §5 because it was executed with expenditure of the appropriation for the fiscal year ending June 30, 1936, and never became applicable to Puerto Rico, Guam, or the Virgin Islands.

[12] As in original. P.L. 86-778, §601(f)(2), [74 Stat. 991], did not amend the catchline.

[13] As in original; "(a)" should be stricken.

6   SOCIAL SECURITY ACT—§ 6(a)(cont)

ments to or care in behalf of any individual who is an inmate of a public institution (except as a patient in a medical institution). Such term also includes payments which are not included within the meaning of such term under the preceding sentence, but which would be so included except that they are made on behalf of such a needy individual to another individual who (as determined in accordance with standards prescribed by the Secretary) is interested in or concerned with the welfare of such needy individual, but only with respect to a State whose State plan approved under section 2 includes provision for—

(1) determination by the State agency that such needy individual has, by reason of his physical or mental condition, such inability to manage funds that making payments to him would be contrary to his welfare and, therefore, it is necessary to provide such assistance through payments described in this sentence;

(2) making such payments only in cases in which such payments will, under the rules otherwise applicable under the State plan for determining need and the amount of old-age assistance to be paid (and in conjunction with other income and resources), meet all the need[14] of the individuals with respect to whom such payments are made;

(3) undertaking and continuing special efforts to protect the welfare of such individual and to improve, to the extent possible, his capacity for self-care and to manage funds;

(4) periodic review by such State agency of the determination under paragraph (1) to ascertain whether conditions justifying such determination still exist, with provision for termination of such payments if they do not and for seeking judicial appointment of a guardian or other legal representative, as described in section 1111, if and when it appears that such action will best serve the interests of such needy individual; and

(5) opportunity for a fair hearing before the State agency on the determination referred to in paragraph (1) for any individual with respect to whom it is made.

At the option of a State (if its plan approved under this title so provides), such term (i) need not include money payments to an individual who has been absent from such State for a period in excess of 90 consecutive days (regardless of whether he has maintained his residence in such State during such period) until he has been present in such State for 30 consecutive days in the case of such an individual who has maintained his residence in such State during such period or 90 consecutive days in the case of any other such individual, and (ii) may include rent payments made directly to a public housing agency on behalf of a recipient or a group or groups of recipients of assistance under such plan.

---

[14] As in original. Should be "needs".

TITLE II—FEDERAL OLD–AGE, SURVIVORS, AND DISABILITY INSURANCE BENEFITS[1]

TABLE OF CONTENTS OF TITLE[2]

		Page
Sec. 201.	Federal old-age and survivors insurance trust fund and federal disability insurance trust fund	8
Sec. 202.	Old-age and survivors insurance benefit payments	21
Sec. 203.	Reduction of insurance benefits	61
Sec. 204.	Overpayments and underpayments	79
Sec. 205.	Evidence, procedure, and certification for payment	82
Sec. 206.	Representation of claimants	109
Sec. 207.	Assignment	114
Sec. 208.	Penalties	114
Sec. 209.	Definition of wages	118
Sec. 210.	Definition of employment	125
Sec. 211.	Self-employment	142
Sec. 212.	Crediting of self-employment income to calendar years	152
Sec. 213.	Quarter and quarter of coverage	153
Sec. 214.	Insured status for purposes of old-age and survivors insurance benefits	156
Sec. 215.	Computation of primary insurance amount	157
Sec. 216.	Other definitions	177
Sec. 217.	Benefits in case of veterans	189
Sec. 218.	Voluntary agreements for coverage of State and local employees	195
[Sec. 219.	Repealed.]	208
Sec. 220.	Disability provisions inapplicable if benefit rights impaired	208
Sec. 221.	Disability determinations	208
Sec. 222.	Rehabilitation services	214
Sec. 223.	Disability insurance benefit payments	217
Sec. 224.	Reduction of benefits based on disability	228
Sec. 225.	Additional rules relating to benefits based on disability	231
Sec. 226.	Entitlement to hospital insurance benefits	232

---

[1] Title II of the Social Security Act is administered by the Social Security Administration. Title II appears in the United States Code as §§401-433, subchapter II, chapter 7, Title 42.

Regulations relating to Title II are contained in chapter III, Title 20, Code of Federal Regulations.

See Vol. II, 31 U.S.C. 3720 and 3720A with respect to collection of payments due to Federal agencies; and §3803(c)(2)(C) with respect to benefits not affected by P.L. 100-383.

See Vol. II, P.L. 88-352, §601, for prohibition against discrimination in Federally assisted programs.

See Vol. II, P.L. 94-566, §503, with respect to preservation of medicaid eligibility for individuals who cease to be eligible for supplemental security income benefits on account of cost-of-living increases in social security benefits.

See Vol. II, P.L. 95-608, §§201-204, with respect to Indian child and family programs.

See Vol. II, P.L. 98-21, §101(e), with respect to the effect of amendments made by that law on benefits under the Federal Retirement System.

See Vol. II, P.L. 99-177, §255, with respect to exemption of certain benefits from budget reductions.

See Vol. II, P.L. 100-204, §724(d), with respect to furnishing information to the United States Commission on Improving the Effectiveness of the United Nations; and §725(b), with respect to the detailing of Government personnel.

See Vol. II, P.L. 100-235, §§5-8, with respect to responsibilities of each Federal agency for computer systems security and privacy.

See Vol. II, P.L. 100-383, §§105(f)(2) and 206(d)(2), with respect to exclusion from income and resources of certain payments to certain individuals.

See Vol. II, P.L. 100-690, §5301(a)(1)(C) and (d)(1)(B), with respect to benefits of drug traffickers and possessors.

See Vol. II, P.L. 101-508, §§13301 and 13302, with respect to OASDI Trust Funds.

See Vol. II, P.L. 104-193, §435, with respect to qualifying quarters for aliens.

See Vol. II, P.L. 106-170, §302, with respect to demonstration projects providing for reductions in disability insurance benefits based on earnings.

[2] This table of contents does not appear in the law.

Sec. 226A.	Special provisions relating to coverage under medicare program for end stage renal disease	236
Sec. 227.	Transitional insured status	238
Sec. 228.	Benefits at age 72 for certain uninsured individuals	239
Sec. 229.	Benefits in case of members of the uniformed services	242
Sec. 230.	Adjustment of the contribution and benefit base	242
Sec. 231.	Benefits in case of certain individuals interned during World War II	244
Sec. 232.	Processing of tax data	245
Sec. 233.	International agreements	246
Sec. 234.	Demonstration project authority	248

FEDERAL OLD-AGE AND SURVIVORS INSURANCE TRUST FUND AND FEDERAL DISABILITY INSURANCE TRUST FUND[3]

SEC. 201. [42 U.S.C. 401] (a) There is hereby created on the books of the Treasury of the United States a trust fund to be known as the "Federal Old-Age and Survivors Insurance Trust Fund". The Federal Old-Age and Survivors Insurance Trust Fund shall consist of the securities held by the Secretary of the Treasury for the Old-Age Reserve Account and the amount standing to the credit of the Old-Age Reserve Account on the books of the Treasury on January 1, 1940, which securities and amount the Secretary of the Treasury is authorized and directed to transfer to the Federal Old-Age and Survivors Insurance Trust Fund, and, in addition, such gifts and bequests as may be made as provided in subsection (i)(1), and such amounts as may be appropriated to, or deposited in, the Federal Old-Age and Survivors Insurance Trust Fund as hereinafter provided. There is hereby appropriated to the Federal Old-Age and Survivors Insurance Trust Fund for the fiscal year ending June 30, 1941, and for each fiscal year thereafter, out of any moneys in the Treasury not otherwise appropriated, amounts equivalent to 100 per centum of—

(1) the taxes (including interest, penalties, and additions to the taxes) received under subchapter A of chapter 9 of the Internal Revenue Code of 1939[4] (and covered into the Treasury) which are deposited into the Treasury by collectors of internal revenue before January 1, 1951; and

(2) the taxes certified each month by the Commissioner of Internal Revenue as taxes received under subchapter A of chapter 9 of such Code which are deposited into the Treasury by collectors of internal revenue after December 31, 1950, and before January 1, 1953, with respect to assessments of such taxes made before January 1, 1951; and

(3) the taxes imposed by subchapter A of chapter 9 of such Code with respect to wages (as defined in section 1426 of such Code), and by chapter 21 (other than sections 3101(b) and 3111(b)) of

---

[3] See Vol. II, 14 U.S.C. 707(e)(3) with respect to the requirement for certification to the Secretary of Labor of an individual's insured status.

See Vol. II, P.L. 98-21, §121(e), with respect to transfers of funds from the Secretary of the Treasury to the Trust Fund.

See Vol. II, P.L. 98-168, §§201-208, with respect to certain Federal employees covered under both the Social Security Act and a Federal retirement system.

See Vol. II, P.L. 107-134, §301, with respect to the impact on the Trust Funds of the amendments by this Victims of Terrorism Tax Relief Act of 2001.

See Vol. II, P.L. 110-246, §15361, with respect to a provision for the protection of Social Security.

[4] P.L. 76-1.

SOCIAL SECURITY ACT—§ 201(a)(4)

the Internal Revenue Code of 1954[5] with respect to wages (as defined in section 3121 of such Code[6]) reported to the Commissioner of Internal Revenue pursuant to section 1420(c) of the Internal Revenue Code of 1939 after December 31, 1950, or to the Secretary of the Treasury or his delegates pursuant to subtitle F of the Internal Revenue Code of 1954 after December 31, 1954, as determined by the Secretary of the Treasury by applying the applicable rates of tax under such subchapter or chapter 21 (other than sections 3101(b) and 3111(b)) to such wages, which wages shall be certified by the Commissioner of Social Security on the basis of the records of wages established and maintained by such Commissioner in accordance with such reports, less the amounts specified in clause (1) of subsection (b) of this section; and

(4) the taxes imposed by subchapter E of chapter 1 of the Internal Revenue Code of 1939, with respect to self-employment income (as defined in section 481 of such Code), and by chapter 2 (other than section 1401(b)) of the Internal Revenue Code of 1954[7] with respect to self-employment income (as defined in section 1402 of such Code[8]) reported to the Commissioner of Internal Revenue on tax returns under such subchapter or to the Secretary of the Treasury or his delegate on tax returns under subtitle F of such Code, as determined by the Secretary of the Treasury by applying the applicable rate of tax under such subchapter or chapter (other than section 1401(b)) to such self-employment income, which self-employment income shall be certified by the Commissioner of Social Security on the basis of the records of self-employment income established and maintained by the Commissioner of Social Security in accordance with such returns, less the amounts specified in clause (2) of subsection (b) of this section.

The amounts appropriated by clauses (3) and (4) shall be transferred from time to time from the general fund in the Treasury to the Federal Old-Age and Survivors Insurance Trust Fund, and the amounts appropriated by clauses (1) and (2) of subsection (b) shall be transferred from time to time from the general fund in the Treasury to the Federal Disability Insurance Trust Fund, such amounts to be determined on the basis of estimates by the Secretary of the Treasury of the taxes, specified in clauses (3) and (4) of this subsection, paid to or deposited into the Treasury; and proper adjustments shall be made in amounts subsequently transferred to the extent prior estimates were in excess of or were less than the taxes specified in such clauses (3) and (4) of this subsection. All amounts transferred to either Trust Fund under the preceding sentence shall be invested by the Managing Trustee in the same manner and to the same extent as the other assets of such Trust Fund. Notwithstanding the preceding sentence, in any case in which the Secretary of the Treasury determines that the assets of either such Trust Fund would otherwise be inadequate to meet such Fund's obligations for any month, the Secretary of the Treasury shall transfer to such Trust Fund on the first day of such month the amount

---

[5] See Vol. II, P.L. 83-591, Chapter 21.

[6] See Vol. II, P.L. 83-591, §3121.

P.L. 99-514, §2, provides, except when inappropriate, any reference to the Internal Revenue Code of 1954 shall include a reference to the Internal Revenue Code of 1986.

[7] See Vol. II, P.L. 83-591, Chapter 2.

[8] See Vol. II, P.L. 83-591, §1402.

10   SOCIAL SECURITY ACT—§ 201(a)(4)(cont)

which would have been transferred to such Fund under this section as in effect on October 1, 1990; and such Trust Fund shall pay interest to the general fund on the amount so transferred on the first day of any month at a rate (calculated on a daily basis, and applied against the difference between the amount so transferred on such first day and the amount which would have been transferred to the Trust Fund up to that day under the procedures in effect on January 1, 1983) equal to the rate earned by the investments of such Fund in the same month under subsection (d).

(b) There is hereby created on the books of the Treasury of the United States a trust fund to be known as the "Federal Disability Insurance Trust Fund". The Federal Disability Insurance Trust Fund shall consist of such gifts and bequests as may be made as provided in subsection (i)(1), and such amounts as may be appropriated to, or deposited in, such fund as provided in this section. There is hereby appropriated to the Federal Disability Insurance Trust Fund for the fiscal year ending June 30, 1957, and for each fiscal year thereafter, out of any moneys in the Treasury not otherwise appropriated, amounts equivalent to 100 per centum of—

(1)(A) 1/2 of 1 per centum of the wages (as defined in section 3121 of the Internal Revenue Code of 1954[9]) paid after December 31, 1956, and before January 1, 1966, and reported to the Secretary of the Treasury or his delegate pursuant to subtitle F of the Internal Revenue Code of 1954, (B) 0.70 of 1 per centum of the wages (as so defined) paid after December 31, 1965, and before January 1, 1968, and so reported, (C) 0.95 of 1 per centum of the wages (as so defined) paid after December 31, 1967, and before January 1, 1970, and so reported, (D) 1.10 per centum of the wages (as so defined) paid after December 31, 1969, and before January 1, 1973, and so reported, (E) 1.1 per centum of the wages (as so defined) paid after December 31, 1972, and before January 1, 1974, and so reported, (F) 1.15 per centum of the wages (as so defined) paid after December 31, 1973, and before January 1, 1978, and so reported, (G) 1.55 per centum of the wages (as so defined) paid after December 31, 1977, and before January 1, 1979, and so reported, (H) 1.50 per centum of the wages (as so defined) paid after December 31, 1978, and before January 1, 1980, and so reported, (I) 1.12 per centum of the wages (as so defined) paid after December 31, 1979, and before January 1, 1981, and so reported, (J) 1.30 per centum of the wages (as so defined) paid after December 31, 1980, and before January 1, 1982, and so reported, (K) 1.65 per centum of the wages (as so defined) paid after December 31, 1981, and before January 1, 1983, and so reported, (L) 1.25 per centum of the wages (as so defined) paid after December 31, 1982, and before January 1, 1984, and so reported, (M) 1.00 per centum of the wages (as so defined) paid after December 31, 1983, and before January 1, 1988, and so reported, (N) 1.06 per centum of the wages (as so defined) paid after December 31, 1987, and before January 1, 1990, and so reported, (O) 1.20 per centum of the wages (as so defined) paid after December 31, 1989, and before January 1, 1994, and so reported, (P) 1.88 per centum of the wages (as

---

[9] See Vol. II, P.L. 83-591, §3121.

SOCIAL SECURITY ACT—§ 201(b)(2)(A)   11

so defined) paid after December 31, 1993, and before January 1, 1997, and so reported, (Q) 1.70 per centum of the wages (as so defined) paid after December 31, 1996, and before January 1, 2000, and so reported, and (R) 1.80 per centum of the wages (as so defined) paid after December 31, 1999, and so reported, which wages shall be certified by the Commissioner of Social Security on the basis of the records of wages established and maintained by such Commissioner in accordance with such reports; and

(2)(A) 3/8 of 1 per centum of the amount of self-employment income (as defined in section 1402 of the Internal Revenue Code of 1954[10]) reported to the Secretary of the Treasury or his delegate on tax returns under subtitle F of the Internal Revenue Code of 1954 for any taxable year beginning after December 31, 1956, and before January 1, 1966, (B) 0.525 of 1 per centum of the amount of self-employment income (as so defined) so reported for any taxable year beginning after December 31, 1965, and before January 1, 1968, (C) 0.7125 of 1 per centum of the amount of self-employment income (as so defined) so reported for any taxable year beginning after December 31, 1967, and before January 1, 1970, (D) 0.825 of 1 per centum of the amount of self-employment income (as so defined) so reported for any taxable year beginning after December 31, 1969, and before January 1, 1973, (E) 0.795 of 1 per centum of the amount of self-employment income (as so defined) so reported for any taxable year beginning after December 31, 1972, and before January 1, 1974, (F) 0.815 of 1 per centum of the amount of self-employment income (as so defined) as reported for any taxable year beginning after December 31, 1973, and before January 1, 1978, (G) 1.090 per centum of the amount of self-employment income (as so defined) so reported for any taxable year beginning after December 31, 1977, and before January 1, 1979, (H) 1.0400 per centum of the amount of self-employment income (as so defined) so reported for any taxable year beginning after December 31, 1978, and before January 1, 1980, (I) 0.7775 per centum of the amount of self-employment income (as so defined) so reported for any taxable year beginning after December 31, 1979, and before January 1, 1981, (J) 0.9750 per centum of the amount of self-employment income (as so defined) so reported for any taxable year beginning after December 31, 1980, and before January 1, 1982, (K) 1.2375 per centum of the amount of self-employment income (as so defined) so reported for any taxable year beginning after December 31, 1981, and before January 1, 1983, (L) 0.9375 per centum of the amount of self-employment income (as so defined) so reported for any taxable year beginning after December 31, 1982, and before January 1, 1984, (M) 1.00 per centum of the amount of self-employment income (as so defined) so reported for any taxable year beginning after December 31, 1983, and before January 1, 1988, (N) 1.06 per centum of the self-employment income (as so defined) so reported for any taxable year beginning after December 31, 1987, and before January 1, 1990, (O)

---

[10] See Vol. II, P.L. 83-591, §1402.

12   SOCIAL SECURITY ACT—§ 201(b)(2)(A)(cont)

1.20 per centum of the amount of self-employment income (as so defined) so reported for any taxable year beginning after December 31, 1989, and before January 1, 1994, (P) 1.88 per centum of the amount of self-employment income (as so defined) so reported for any taxable year beginning after December 31, 1993, and before January 1, 1997, (Q) 1.70 per centum of the amount of self-employment income (as so defined) so reported for any taxable year beginning after December 31, 1996, and before January 1, 2000, and (R) 1.80 per centum of the amount of self-employment income (as so defined) so reported for any taxable year beginning after December 31, 1999, which self-employment income shall be certified by the Commissioner of Social Security on the basis of the records of self-employment income established and maintained by the Commissioner of Social Security in accordance with such returns.

(c) With respect to the Federal Old-Age and Survivors Insurance Trust Fund and the Federal Disability Insurance Trust Fund (hereinafter in this title called the "Trust Funds") there is hereby created a body to be known as the Board of Trustees of the Trust Funds (hereinafter in this title called the "Board of Trustees") which Board of Trustees shall be composed of the Commissioner of Social Security, the Secretary of the Treasury, the Secretary of Labor, and the Secretary of Health and Human Services, all ex officio, and of two members of the public (both of whom may not be from the same political party), who shall be nominated by the President for a term of four years and subject to confirmation by the Senate. A member of the Board of Trustees serving as a member of the public and nominated and confirmed to fill a vacancy occurring during a term shall be nominated and confirmed only for the remainder of such term. An individual nominated and confirmed as a member of the public may serve in such position after the expiration of such member's term until the earlier of the time at which the member's successor takes office or the time at which a report of the Board is first issued under paragraph (2) after the expiration of the member's term. The Secretary of the Treasury shall be the Managing Trustee of the Board of Trustees (hereinafter in this title called the "Managing Trustee"). The Deputy Commissioner of Social Security shall serve as Secretary of the Board of Trustees. The Board of Trustees shall meet not less frequently than once each calendar year. It shall be the duty of the Board of Trustees to—

(1) Hold the Trust Funds;

(2)[11] Report to the Congress not later than the first day of April of each year on the operation and status of the Trust Funds during the preceding fiscal year and on their expected operation and status during the next ensuing five fiscal years;

(3) Report immediately to the Congress whenever the Board of Trustees is of the opinion that the amount of either of the Trust Funds is unduly small;

(4) Recommend improvements in administrative procedures and policies designed to effectuate the proper coordination of the

---

[11] See Vol. II, P.L. 108-203, §413, with respect to the reinstatement of certain reporting requirements.

SOCIAL SECURITY ACT—§ 201(d)   13

old-age and survivors insurance and Federal-State unemployment compensation program; and

(5) Review the general policies followed in managing the Trust Funds, and recommend changes in such policies, including necessary changes in the provisions of the law which govern the way in which the Trust Funds are to be managed.

The report provided for in paragraph (2) above shall include a statement of the assets of, and the disbursements made from, the Trust Funds during the preceding fiscal year, an estimate of the expected future income to, and disbursements to be made from, the Trust Funds during each of the next ensuing five fiscal years, and a statement of the actuarial status of the Trust Funds. Such statement shall include a finding by the Board of Trustees as to whether the Federal Old-Age and Survivors Insurance Trust Fund and the Federal Disability Insurance Trust Fund, individually and collectively, are in close actuarial balance (as defined by the Board of Trustees). Such report shall include an actuarial opinion by the Chief Actuary of the Social Security Administration certifying that the techniques and methodologies used are generally accepted within the actuarial profession and that the assumptions and cost estimates used are reasonable. Such report shall also include an actuarial analysis of the benefit disbursements made from the Federal Old-Age and Survivors Insurance Trust Fund with respect to disabled beneficiaries. Such report shall be printed as a House document of the session of the Congress to which the report is made. A person serving on the Board of Trustees shall not be considered to be a fiduciary and shall not be personally liable for actions taken in such capacity with respect to the Trust Funds.

(d) It shall be the duty of the Managing Trustee to invest such portion of the Trust Funds as is not, in his judgment, required to meet current withdrawals. Such investments may be made only in interest-bearing obligations of the United States or in obligations guaranteed as to both principal and interest by the United States. For such purpose such obligations may be acquired (1) on original issue at the issue price, or (2) by purchase of outstanding obligations at the market price. The purposes for which obligations of the United States may be issued under chapter 31 of title 31, United States Code[12], are hereby extended to authorize the issuance at par of public-debt obligations for purchase by the Trust Funds. Such obligations issued for purchase by the Trust Funds shall have maturities fixed with due regard for the needs of the Trust Funds and shall bear interest at a rate equal to the average market yield (computed by the Managing Trustee on the basis of market quotations as of the end of the calendar month next preceding the date of such issue) on all marketable interest-bearing obligations of the United States then forming a part of the public debt which are not due or callable until after the expiration of four years from the end of such calendar month; except that where such average market yield is not a multiple of one-eighth of 1 per centum, the rate of interest of such obligations shall be the multiple of one-eighth of 1 per centum nearest such market yield. Each obligation issued for purchase by the Trust Funds under this subsection shall be evidenced by a paper instrument in the form of a bond, note, or certificate of indebtedness issued by the Secretary of the Treasury setting forth the

---

[12] See Vol. II, 31 U.S.C. 3111.

14 SOCIAL SECURITY ACT—§ 201(d)(cont)

principal amount, date of maturity, and interest rate of the obligation, and stating on its face that the obligation shall be incontestable in the hands of the Trust Fund to which it is issued, that the obligation is supported by the full faith and credit of the United States, and that the United States is pledged to the payment of the obligation with respect to both principal and interest. The Managing Trustee may purchase other interest-bearing obligations of the United States or obligations guaranteed as to both principal and interest by the United States, on original issue or at the market price, only where he determines that the purchase of such other obligations is in the public interest.

(e) Any obligations acquired by the Trust Funds (except public-debt obligations issued exclusively to the Trust Funds) may be sold by the Managing Trustee at the market price, and such public-debt obligations may be redeemed at par plus accrued interest.

(f) The interest on, and the proceeds from the sale or redemption of, any obligations held in the Federal Old-Age and Survivors Insurance Trust Fund and the Federal Disability Insurance Trust Fund shall be credited to and form a part of the Federal Old-Age and Survivors Insurance Trust Fund and the Disability Insurance Trust Fund, respectively. Payment from the general fund of the Treasury to either of the Trust Funds of any such interest or proceeds shall be in the form of paper checks drawn on such general fund to the order of such Trust Fund.[13]

(g)(1)(A) The Managing Trustee of the Trust Funds (which for purposes of this paragraph shall include also the Federal Hospital Insurance Trust Fund and the Federal Supplementary Medical Insurance Trust Fund established by title XVIII) is directed to pay from the Trust Funds into the Treasury—

(i) the amounts estimated by the Managing Trustee, the Commissioner of Social Security, and the Secretary of Health and Human Services which will be expended, out of moneys appropriated from the general fund in the Treasury, during a three-month period by the Department of Health and Human Services for the administration of title XVIII of this Act, and by the Department of the Treasury for the administration of titles II and XVIII of this Act and chapters 2 and 21 of the Internal Revenue Code of 1986, less

(ii) the amounts estimated (pursuant to the applicable method prescribed under paragraph (4) of this subsection) by the Commissioner of Social Security which will be expended, out of moneys made available for expenditures from the Trust Funds, during such three-month period to cover the cost of carrying out the functions of the Social Security Administration, specified in section 232, which relate to the administration of provisions of the Internal Revenue Code of 1986 other than those referred to in clause (i) and the functions of the Social Security Administration in connection with the withholding of taxes from benefits, as described in section 207(c), pursuant to requests by persons entitled to such benefits or such persons' representative payee.[14]

Such payments shall be carried into the Treasury as the net amount of repayments due the general fund account for reimbursement of ex-

---

[13] For treatment of outstanding obligations, see Vol. II, P.L. 103-296, §301(c)(2).
[14] See Vol. II, P.L. 94-202, §8(f), with respect to making the estimates required under this clause.

SOCIAL SECURITY ACT—§ 201(g)(1)(B)(i)(I)   15

penses incurred in connection with the administration of titles II and XVIII of this Act and chapters 2 and 21 of the Internal Revenue Code of 1986.[15] A final accounting of such payments for any fiscal year shall be made at the earliest practicable date after the close thereof. There are hereby authorized to be made available for expenditure, out of any or all of the Trust Funds, such amounts as the Congress may deem appropriate to pay the costs of the part of the administration of this title, title VIII, title XVI, and title XVIII for which the Commissioner of Social Security is responsible, the costs of title XVIII for which the Secretary of Health and Human Services is responsible, and the costs of carrying out the functions of the Social Security Administration, specified in section 232, which relate to the administration of provisions of the Internal Revenue Code of 1986 other than those referred to in clause (i) of the first sentence of this subparagraph and the functions of the Social Security Administration in connection with the withholding of taxes from benefits, as described in section 207(c), pursuant to requests by persons entitled to such benefits or such persons' representative payee. Of the amounts authorized to be made available out of the Federal Old–Age and Survivors Insurance Trust Fund and the Federal Disability Insurance Trust Fund under the preceding sentence, there are hereby authorized to be made available from either or both of such Trust Funds for continuing disability reviews—

(i) for fiscal year 1996, $260,000,000;
(ii) for fiscal year 1997, $360,000,000;
(iii) for fiscal year 1998, $570,000,000;
(iv) for fiscal year 1999, $720,000,000;
(v) for fiscal year 2000, $720,000,000;
(vi) for fiscal year 2001, $720,000,000; and
(vii) for fiscal year 2002, $720,000,000.

For purposes of this subparagraph, the term "continuing disability review" means a review conducted pursuant to section 221(i) and a review or disability eligibility redetermination conducted to determine the continuing disability and eligibility of a recipient of benefits under the supplemental security income program under title XVI, including any review or redetermination conducted pursuant to section 207 or 208 of the Social Security Independence and Program Improvements Act of 1994 (Public Law 103-296).

(B) After the close of each fiscal year—

(i) the Commissioner of Social Security shall determine—

(I) the portion of the costs, incurred during such fiscal year, of administration of this title, title VIII, title XVI, and title XVIII for which the Commissioner is responsible and of carrying out the functions of the Social Security Administration, specified in section 232, which relate to the administration of provisions of the Internal Revenue Code of 1986 (other than those referred to in clause (i) of the first sentence of subparagraph (A)) and the functions of the Social Security Administration in connection with the withholding of taxes from benefits, as described in section 207(c), pursuant to requests by persons entitled to such

---

[15] See Vol. II, P.L. 92-603, §305(b), with respect to repayment of expenditures made from OASDI Trust Funds for costs of administration of title XVI of the Social Security Act.

16   SOCIAL SECURITY ACT—§ 201(g)(1)(B)(i)(I)(cont)

benefits or such persons' representative payee, which should have been borne by the general fund of the Treasury,

(II) the portion of such costs which should have been borne by the Federal Old-Age and Survivors Insurance Trust Fund,

(III) the portion of such costs which should have been borne by the Federal Disability Insurance Trust Fund,

(IV) the portion of such costs which should have been borne by the Federal Hospital Insurance Trust Fund, and

(V) the portion of such costs which should have been borne by the Federal Supplementary Medical Insurance Trust Fund (and, of such portion, the portion of such costs which should have been borne by the Medicare Prescription Drug Account in such Trust Fund), and

(ii) the Secretary of Health and Human Services shall determine—

(I) the portion of the costs, incurred during such fiscal year, of the administration of title XVIII for which the Secretary is responsible, which should have been borne by the general fund of the Treasury,

(II) the portion of such costs which should have been borne by the Federal Hospital Insurance Trust Fund, and

(III) the portion of such costs which should have been borne by the Federal Supplementary Medical Insurance Trust Fund (and, of such portion, the portion of such costs which should have been borne by the Medicare Prescription Drug Account in such Trust Fund).

(C) After the determinations under subparagraph (B) have been made for any fiscal year, the Commissioner of Social Security and the Secretary shall each certify to the Managing Trustee the amounts, if any, which should be transferred from one to any of the other such Trust Funds and the amounts, if any, which should be transferred between the Trust Funds (or one of the Trust Funds) and the general fund of the Treasury, in order to ensure that each of the Trust Funds and the general fund of the Treasury have borne their proper share of the costs, incurred during such fiscal year, for—

(i) the parts of the administration of this title, title VIII, title XVI, and title XVIII for which the Commissioner of Social Security is responsible,

(ii) the parts of the administration of title XVIII for which the Secretary is responsible, and

(iii) carrying out the functions of the Social Security Administration, specified in section 232, which relate to the administration of provisions of the Internal Revenue Code of 1986 (other than those referred to in clause (i) of the first sentence of subparagraph (A)) and the functions of the Social Security Administration in connection with the withholding of taxes from benefits, as described in section 207(c), pursuant to requests by persons entitled to such benefits or such persons' representative payee.

The Managing Trustee shall transfer any such amounts in accordance with any certification so made.

(D) The determinations required under subclauses (IV) and (V) of subparagraph (B)(i) shall be made in accordance with the cost allocation methodology in existence on the date of the enactment of the Social Security Independence and Program Improvements Act of 1994, until such time as the methodology for making the determinations required under such subclauses is revised by agreement of the Commissioner and the Secretary, except that the determination of the amounts to be borne by the general fund of the Treasury with respect to expenditures incurred in carrying out the functions of the Social Security Administration specified in section 232 and the functions of the Social Security Administration in connection with the withholding of taxes from benefits as described in section 207(c) shall be made pursuant to the applicable method prescribed under paragraph (4).

(2) The Managing Trustee is directed to pay from time to time from the Trust Funds into the Treasury the amount estimated by him as taxes imposed under section 3101(a) of the Internal Revenue Code of 1986 which are subject to refund under section 6413(c) of such Code with respect to wages (as defined in section 3121 of such Code). Such taxes shall be determined on the basis of the records of wages maintained by the Commissioner of Social Security in accordance with the wages reported to the Secretary of the Treasury or his delegate pursuant to subtitle F of such Code, and the Commissioner of Social Security shall furnish the Managing Trustee such information as may be required by the Trustee for such purpose. The payments by the Managing Trustee shall be covered into the Treasury as repayments to the account for refunding internal revenue collections. Payments pursuant to the first sentence of this paragraph shall be made from the Federal Old-Age and Survivors Insurance Trust Fund and the Federal Disability Insurance Trust Fund in the ratio in which amounts were appropriated to such Trust Funds under clause (3) of subsection (a) of this section and clause (1) of subsection (b) of this section.

(3) Repayments made under paragraph (1) or (2) shall not be available for expenditures but shall be carried to the surplus fund of the Treasury. If it subsequently appears that the estimates under either such paragraph in any particular period were too high or too low, appropriate adjustments shall be made by the Managing Trustee in future payments.

(4) The Commissioner of Social Security shall utilize the method prescribed pursuant to this paragraph, as in effect immediately before the date of the enactment of the Social Security Independence and Program Improvements Act of 1994, for determining the costs which should be borne by the general fund of the Treasury of carrying out the functions of the Commissioner, specified in section 232, which relate to the administration of provisions of the Internal Revenue Code of 1986 (other than those referred to in clause (i) of the first sentence of paragraph (1)(A)). The Board of Trustees of such Trust Funds shall prescribe the method of determining the costs which should be borne by the general fund in the Treasury of carrying out the functions of the Social Security Administration in connection with the withholding of taxes from benefits, as described in section 207(c), pursuant to requests by persons entitled to such benefits or such persons' representative payee. If at any time or times thereafter the Boards of Trustees of such Trust Funds consider such action advisable, they may modify the method of determining such costs.[16]

---

[16] See Vol. II, P.L. 94-202, §8(e), with respect to employment of assistants.

18 SOCIAL SECURITY ACT—§ 201(g)(4)(cont)

(h) Benefit payments required to be made under section 223, and benefit payments required to be made under subsection (b), (c), or (d) of section 202 to individuals entitled to benefits on the basis of the wages and self-employment income of an individual entitled to disability insurance benefits, shall be made only from the Federal Disability Insurance Trust Fund. All other benefit payments required to be made under this title (other than section 226) shall be made only from the Federal Old-Age and Survivors Insurance Trust Fund.

(i)(1) The Managing Trustee may accept on behalf of the United States money gifts and bequests made unconditionally to the Federal Old-Age and Survivors Insurance Trust Fund, the Federal Disability Insurance Trust Fund, the Federal Hospital Insurance Trust Fund, or the Federal Supplementary Medical Insurance Trust Fund (and for the Medicare Prescription Drug Account and the Transitional Assistance Account in such Trust Fund) or to the Social Security Administration, the Department of Health and Human Services, or any part or officer thereof, for the benefit of any of such Funds or any activity financed through such Funds.[17]

(2) Any such gift accepted pursuant to the authority granted in paragraph (1) of this subsection shall be deposited in—

(A) the specific trust fund designated by the donor or

(B) if the donor has not so designated, the Federal Old-Age and Survivors Insurance Trust Fund.

(j) There are authorized to be made available for expenditure, out of the Federal Old-Age and Survivors Insurance Trust Fund, or the Federal Disability Insurance Trust Fund (as determined appropriate by the Commissioner of Social Security), such amounts as are required to pay travel expenses, either on an actual cost or commuted basis, to individuals for travel incident to medical examinations requested by the Commissioner of Social Security in connection with disability determinations under this title, and to parties, their representatives, and all reasonably necessary witnesses for travel within the United States (as defined in section 210(i)) to attend reconsideration interviews and proceedings before administrative law judges with respect to any determination under this title. The amount available under the preceding sentence for payment for air travel by any person shall not exceed the coach fare for air travel between the points involved unless the use of first-class accommodations is required (as determined under regulations of the Commissioner of Social Security) because of such person's health condition or the unavailability of alternative accommodations; and the amount available for payment for other travel by any person shall not exceed the cost of travel (between the points involved) by the most economical and expeditious means of transportation appropriate to such person's health condition, as specified in such regulations. The amount available for payment under this subsection for travel by a representative to attend an administrative proceeding before an administrative law judge or other adjudicator shall not exceed the maximum amount allowable under this subsection for such travel originating within the geographic area of the office having jurisdiction over such proceeding.

---

[17] See Vol. II, P.L. 92-603, §132(g), with respect to tax treatment of gifts or bequests to the Trust Funds.

(k) Expenditures made for experiments and demonstration projects under section 234 shall be made from the Federal Disability Insurance Trust Fund and the Federal Old-Age and Survivors Insurance Trust Fund, as determined appropriate by the Commissioner of Social Security.

(l)(1) If at any time prior to January 1988 the Managing Trustee determines that borrowing authorized under this subsection is appropriate in order to best meet the need for financing the benefit payments from the Federal Old-Age and Survivors Insurance Trust Fund or the Federal Disability Insurance Trust Fund, the Managing Trustee may borrow such amounts as he determines to be appropriate from the other such Trust Fund, or, subject to paragraph (5), from the Federal Hospital Insurance Trust Fund established under section 1817, for transfer to and deposit in the Trust Fund whose need for financing is involved.

(2) In any case where a loan has been made to a Trust Fund under paragraph (1), there shall be transferred on the last day of each month after such loan is made, from the borrowing Trust Fund to the lending Trust Fund, the total interest accrued to such day with respect to the unrepaid balance of such loan at a rate equal to the rate which the lending Trust Fund would earn on the amount involved if the loan were an investment under subsection (d) (even if such an investment would earn interest at a rate different than the rate earned by investments redeemed by the lending fund in order to make the loan).

(3)(A) If in any month after a loan has been made to a Trust Fund under paragraph (1), the Managing Trustee determines that the assets of such Trust Fund are sufficient to permit repayment of all or part of any loans made to such Fund under paragraph (1), he shall make such repayments as he determines to be appropriate.

(B)(i) If on the last day of any year after a loan has been made under paragraph (1) by the Federal Hospital Insurance Trust Fund to the Federal Old-Age and Survivors Insurance Trust Fund or the Federal Disability Insurance Trust Fund, the Managing Trustee determines that the OASDI trust fund ratio exceeds 15 percent, he shall transfer from the borrowing Trust Fund to the Federal Hospital Insurance Trust Fund an amount that—

(I) together with any amounts transferred from another borrowing Trust Fund under this paragraph for such year, will reduce the OASDI trust fund ratio to 15 percent; and

(II) does not exceed the outstanding balance of such loan.

(ii) Amounts required to be transferred under clause (i) shall be transferred on the last day of the first month of the year succeeding the year in which the determination described in clause (i) is made.

(iii) For purposes of this subparagraph, the term "OASDI trust fund ratio" means, with respect to any calendar year, the ratio of—

(I) the combined balance in the Federal Old-Age and Survivors Insurance Trust Fund and the Federal Disability Insurance Trust Fund, as of the last day of such calendar year, to

(II) the amount estimated by the Commissioner of Social Security to be the total amount to be paid from the Federal Old-Age and Survivors Insurance Trust Fund and the Federal Disability Insurance Trust Fund during the calendar year following such calendar year for all purposes authorized by section 201 (other than payments of interest on, and repayments

20 SOCIAL SECURITY ACT—§ 201(l)(3)(B)(iii)(II)(cont)

of, loans from the Federal Hospital Insurance Trust Fund under paragraph (1), but excluding any transfer payments between such trust funds and reducing the amount of any transfer to the Railroad Retirement Account by the amount of any transfers into either such trust fund from that Account).

(C)(i) The full amount of all loans made under paragraph (1) (whether made before or after January 1, 1983) shall be repaid at the earliest feasible date and in any event no later than December 31, 1989.

(ii) For the period after December 31, 1987, and before January 1, 1990, the Managing Trustee shall transfer each month to the Federal Hospital Insurance Trust Fund from any Trust Fund with any amount outstanding on a loan made from the Federal Hospital Insurance Trust Fund under paragraph (1) an amount not less than an amount equal to (I) the amount owed to the Federal Hospital Insurance Trust Fund by such Trust Fund at the beginning of such month (plus the interest accrued on the outstanding balance of such loan during such month), divided by (II) the number of months elapsing after the preceding month and before January 1990. The Managing Trustee may, during this period, transfer larger amounts than prescribed by the preceding sentence.

(4) The Board of Trustees shall make a timely report to the Congress of any amounts transferred (including interest payments) under this subsection.

(5)(A) No amounts may be borrowed from the Federal Hospital Insurance Trust Fund under paragraph (1) during any month if the Hospital Insurance Trust Fund ratio for such month is less than 10 percent.

(B) For purposes of this paragraph, the term "Hospital Insurance Trust Fund ratio" means, with respect to any month, the ratio of—

(i) the balance in the Federal Hospital Insurance Trust Fund, reduced by the outstanding amount of any loan (including interest thereon) theretofore made to such Trust Fund under this subsection, as of the last day of the second month preceding such month, to

(ii) the amount obtained by multiplying by twelve the total amount which (as estimated by the Secretary) will be paid from the Federal Hospital Insurance Trust Fund during the month for which such ratio is to be determined (other than payments of interest on, or repayments of loans from another Trust Fund under this subsection), and reducing the amount of any transfers to the Railroad Retirement Account by the amount of any transfer into the Hospital Insurance Trust Fund from that Account.

(m)(1) The Secretary of the Treasury shall implement procedures to permit the identification of each check issued for benefits under this title that has not been presented for payment by the close of the sixth month following the month of its issuance.

(2) The Secretary of the Treasury shall, on a monthly basis, credit each of the Trust Funds for the amount of all benefit checks (including interest thereon) drawn on such Trust Fund more than 6 months previously but not presented for payment and not previously credited to such Trust Fund, to the extent provided in advance in appropriation Acts.

SOCIAL SECURITY ACT—§ 202(a)(3)(B)

(3) If a benefit check is presented for payment to the Treasury and the amount thereof has been previously credited pursuant to paragraph (2) to one of the Trust Funds, the Secretary of the Treasury shall nevertheless pay such check, if otherwise proper, recharge such Trust Fund, and notify the Commissioner of Social Security.

(4) A benefit check bearing a current date may be issued to an individual who did not negotiate the original benefit check and who surrenders such check for cancellation if the Secretary of the Treasury determines it is necessary to effect proper payment of benefits.

(n) Not later than July 1, 2004, the Secretary of the Treasury shall transfer, from amounts in the general fund of the Treasury that are not otherwise appropriated—

(1) $624,971,854 to the Federal Old-Age and Survivors Insurance Trust Fund;

(2) $105,379,671 to the Federal Disability Insurance Trust Fund; and

(3) $173,306,134 to the Federal Hospital Insurance Trust Fund.

Amounts transferred in accordance with this subsection shall be in satisfaction of certain outstanding obligations for deemed wage credits for 2000 and 2001.

OLD-AGE AND SURVIVORS INSURANCE BENEFIT PAYMENTS[18]

Old-Age Insurance Benefits

SEC. 202. [42 U.S.C. 402] (a) Every individual who—

(1) is a fully insured individual (as defined in section 214(a)),

(2) has attained age 62, and

(3) has filed application for old-age insurance benefits or was entitled to disability insurance benefits for the month preceding the month in which he attained retirement age (as defined in section 216(l)),

shall be entitled to an old-age insurance benefit for each month, beginning with—

(A) in the case of an individual who has attained retirement age (as defined in section 216(l)), the first month in which such individual meets the criteria specified in paragraphs (1), (2), and (3), or

(B) in the case of an individual who has attained age 62, but has not attained retirement age (as defined in section 216(l)), the first month throughout which such individual meets the criteria specified in paragraphs (1) and (2) (if in that month he meets the criterion specified in paragraph (3)),

and ending with the month preceding the month in which he dies. Except as provided in subsection (q) and subsection (w), such individual's

---

[18] See Vol. II, P.L. 83-591, §1402(a)(1), with respect to certain payments under the Food Security Act of 1985 excluded from net earnings from self-employment.

See Vol. II, P.L. 88-525, §11(i) and (j), with respect to applications for food stamps.

See Vol. II, P.L. 97-377, §156(d), with respect to information furnished for determination of payments to surviving spouses of members of the Armed Forces.

See Vol. II, P.L. 98-21, §131(d)(2), with respect to the application requirement for individuals not entitled to benefits for December 1993.

See Vol. II, P.L. 106-170, §302, with respect to demonstration projects providing for reductions in disability benefits based on earnings.

22 SOCIAL SECURITY ACT—§ 202(a)(3)(B)(cont)

old-age insurance benefit for any month shall be equal to his primary insurance amount (as defined in section 215(a)) for such month.

Wife's Insurance Benefits

(b)(1) The wife (as defined in section 216(b)) and every divorced wife (as defined in section 216(d)) of an individual entitled to old-age or disability insurance benefits, if such wife or such divorced wife—

(A) has filed application for wife's insurance benefits,

(B) has attained age 62 or (in the case of a wife) has in her care (individually or jointly with such individual) at the time of filing such application a child entitled to a child's insurance benefit on the basis of the wages and self-employment income of such individual,

(C) in the case of a divorced wife, is not married, and

(D) is not entitled to old-age or disability insurance benefits, or is entitled to old-age or disability insurance benefits based on a primary insurance amount which is less than one-half of the primary insurance amount of such individual,

shall (subject to subsection (s)) be entitled to a wife's insurance benefit for each month, beginning with—

(i) in the case of a wife or divorced wife (as so defined) of an individual entitled to old-age benefits, if such wife or divorced wife has attained retirement age (as defined in section 216(l)), the first month in which she meets the criteria specified in subparagraphs (A), (B), (C), and (D), or

(ii) in the case of a wife or divorced wife (as so defined) of—

(I) an individual entitled to old-age insurance benefits, if such wife or divorced wife has not attained retirement age (as defined in section 216(l)), or

(II) an individual entitled to disability insurance benefits, the first month throughout which she is such a wife or divorced wife and meets the criteria specified in subparagraphs (B), (C), and (D) (if in such month she meets the criterion specified in subparagraph (A)),

whichever is earlier, and ending with the month preceding the month in which any of the following occurs—

(E) she dies,

(F) such individual dies,

(G) in the case of a wife, they are divorced and either (i) she has not attained age 62, or (ii) she has attained age 62 but has not been married to such individual for a period of 10 years immediately before the date the divorce became effective,

(H) in the case of a divorced wife, she marries a person other than such individual,

(I) in the case of a wife who has not attained age 62, no child of such individual is entitled to a child's insurance benefit,

(J) she becomes entitled to an old-age or disability insurance benefit based on a primary insurance amount which is equal to or exceeds one-half of the primary insurance amount of such individual, or

(K) such individual is not entitled to disability insurance benefits and is not entitled to old-age insurance benefits.

SOCIAL SECURITY ACT—§ 202(c)(1)(D) 23

(2) Except as provided in subsections (k)(5) and (q), such wife's insurance benefit for each month shall be equal to one-half of the primary insurance amount of her husband (or, in the case of a divorced wife, her former husband) for such month.

(3) In the case of any divorced wife who marries—

(A) an individual entitled to benefits under subsection (c), (f), (g), or (h) of this section, or

(B) an individual who has attained the age of 18 and is entitled to benefits under subsection (d),

such divorced wife's entitlement to benefits under this subsection shall, notwithstanding the provisions of paragraph (1) (but subject to subsection (s)), not be terminated by reason of such marriage.

(4)(A) Notwithstanding the preceding provisions of this subsection, except as provided in subparagraph (B), the divorced wife of an individual who is not entitled to old-age or disability insurance benefits, but who has attained age 62 and is a fully insured individual (as defined in section 214), if such divorced wife—

(i) meets the requirements of subparagraphs (A) through (D) of paragraph (1), and

(ii) has been divorced from such insured individual for not less than 2 years,

shall be entitled to a wife's insurance benefit under this subsection for each month, in such amount, and beginning and ending with such months, as determined (under regulations of the Commissioner of Social Security) in the manner otherwise provided for wife's insurance benefits under this subsection, as if such insured individual had become entitled to old-age insurance benefits on the date on which the divorced wife first meets the criteria for entitlement set forth in clauses (i) and (ii).

(B) A wife's insurance benefit provided under this paragraph which has not otherwise terminated in accordance with subparagraph (E), (F), (H), or (J) of paragraph (1) shall terminate with the month preceding the first month in which the insured individual is no longer a fully insured individual.

Husband's Insurance Benefits

(c)(1) The husband (as defined in section 216(f)) and every divorced husband (as defined in section 216(d)) of an individual entitled to old-age or disability insurance benefits, if such husband or such divorced husband—

(A) has filed application for husband's insurance benefits,

(B) has attained age 62 or (in the case of a husband) has in his care (individually or jointly with such individual) at the time of filing such application a child entitled to child's insurance benefits on the basis of the wages and self-employment income of such individual,

(C) in the case of a divorced husband, is not married, and

(D) is not entitled to old-age or disability insurance benefits, or is entitled to old-age or disability insurance benefits based on a primary insurance amount which is less than one-half of the primary insurance amount of such individual,

24 SOCIAL SECURITY ACT—§ 202(c)(1)(D)(i)

shall (subject to subsection (s)) be entitled to a husband's insurance benefit for each month, beginning with—

(i) in the case of a husband or divorced husband (as so defined) of an individual who is entitled to an old-age insurance benefit, if such husband or divorced husband has attained retirement age (as defined in section 216(l)), the first month in which he meets the criteria specified in subparagraphs (A), (B), (C), and (D), or

(ii) in the case of a husband or divorced husband (as so defined) of—

(I) an individual entitled to old-age insurance benefits, if such husband or divorced husband has not attained retirement age (as defined in section 216(l)), or

(II) an individual entitled to disability insurance benefits,

the first month throughout which he is such a husband or divorced husband and meets the criteria specified in subparagraphs (B), (C), and (D) (if in such month he meets the criterion specified in subparagraph (A)),

whichever is earlier, and ending with the month preceding the month in which any of the following occurs:

(E) he dies,

(F) such individual dies,

(G) in the case of a husband, they are divorced and either (i) he has not attained age 62, or (ii) he has attained age 62 but has not been married to such individual for a period of 10 years immediately before the divorce became effective,

(H) in the case of a divorced husband, he marries a person other than such individual,

(I) in the case of a husband who has not attained age 62, no child of such individual is entitled to a child's insurance benefit,

(J) he becomes entitled to an old-age or disability insurance benefit based on a primary insurance amount which is equal to or exceeds one-half of the primary insurance amount of such individual, or

(K) such individual is not entitled to disability insurance benefits and is not entitled to old-age insurance benefits.

(2) Except as provided in subsections (k)(5) and (q), such husband's insurance benefit for each month shall be equal to one-half of the primary insurance amount of his wife (or, in the case of a divorced husband, his former wife) for such month.

(3) In the case of any divorced husband who marries—

(A) an individual entitled to benefits under subsection (b), (e), (g), or (h) of this section, or

(B) an individual who has attained the age of 18 and is entitled to benefits under subsection (d), by reason of paragraph (1)(B)(ii) thereof,

such divorced husband's entitlement to benefits under this subsection, notwithstanding the provisions of paragraph (1) (but subject to subsection (s)), shall not be terminated by reason of such marriage.

(4)(A) Notwithstanding the preceding provisions of this subsection, except as provided in subparagraph (B), the divorced husband of an individual who is not entitled to old-age or disability insurance benefits, but who has attained age 62 and is a fully insured individual (as defined in section 214), if such divorced husband—

SOCIAL SECURITY ACT—§ 202(d)(1)(D)   25

(i) meets the requirements of subparagraphs (A) through (D) of paragraph (1), and

(ii) has been divorced from such insured individual for not less than 2 years,

shall be entitled to a husband's insurance benefit under this subsection for each month, in such amount, and beginning and ending with such months, as determined (under regulations of the Commissioner of Social Security) in the manner otherwise provided for husband's insurance benefits under this subsection, as if such insured individual had become entitled to old-age insurance benefits on the date on which the divorced husband first meets the criteria for entitlement set forth in clauses (i) and (ii).

(B) A husband's insurance benefit provided under this paragraph which has not otherwise terminated in accordance with subparagraph (E), (F), (H), or (J) of paragraph (1) shall terminate with the month preceding the first month in which the insured individual is no longer a fully insured individual.

Child's Insurance Benefits

(d)(1) Every child (as defined in section 216(e)) of an individual entitled to old-age or disability insurance benefits, or of an individual who dies a fully or currently insured individual, if such child—

(A) has filed application for child's insurance benefits,

(B) at the time such application was filed was unmarried and (i) either had not attained the age of 18 or was a full-time elementary or secondary school student and had not attained the age of 19, or (ii) is under a disability (as defined in section 223(d)) which began before he attained the age of 22, and

(C) was dependent upon such individual—

(i) if such individual is living, at the time such application was filed,

(ii) if such individual has died, at the time of such death, or

(iii) if such individual had a period of disability which continued until he became entitled to old-age or disability insurance benefits, or (if he has died) until the month of his death, at the beginning of such period of disability or at the time he became entitled to such benefits,

shall be entitled to a child's insurance benefit for each month, beginning with—

(i) in the case of a child (as so defined) of such an individual who has died, the first month in which such child meets the criteria specified in subparagraphs (A), (B), and (C), or

(ii) in the case of a child (as so defined) of an individual entitled to an old-age insurance benefit or to a disability insurance benefit, the first month throughout which such child is a child (as so defined) and meets the criteria specified in subparagraphs (B) and (C) (if in such month he meets the criterion specified in subparagraph (A)),

whichever is earlier, and ending with the month preceding whichever of the following first occurs—

(D) the month in which such child dies, or marries,

26 SOCIAL SECURITY ACT—§ 202(d)(1)(E)

(E) the month in which such child attains the age of 18, but only if he (i) is not under a disability (as so defined) at the time he attains such age, and (ii) is not a full-time elementary or secondary school student during any part of such month,

(F) if such child was not under a disability (as so defined) at the time he attained the age of 18, the earlier of—

(i) the first month during no part of which he is a full-time elementary or secondary school student, or

(ii) the month in which he attains the age of 19,

but only if he was not under a disability (as so defined) in such earlier month;

(G) if such child was under a disability (as so defined) at the time he attained the age of 18 or if he was not under a disability (as so defined) at such time but was under a disability (as so defined) at or prior to the time he attained (or would attain) the age of 22—

(i) the termination month, subject to section 223(e) (and for purposes of this subparagraph, the termination month for any individual shall be the third month following the month in which his disability ceases; except that, in the case of an individual who has a period of trial work which ends as determined by application of section 222(c)(4)(A), the termination month shall be the earlier of (I) the third month following the earliest month after the end of such period of trial work with respect to which such individual is determined to no longer be suffering from a disabling physical or mental impairment, or (II) the third month following the earliest month in which such individual engages or is determined able to engage in substantial gainful activity, but in no event earlier than the first month occurring after the 36 months following such period of trial work in which he engages or is determined able to engage in substantial gainful activity),

or (if later) the earlier of—

(ii) the first month during no part of which he is a full-time elementary or secondary school student, or

(iii) the month in which he attains the age of 19,

but only if he was not under a disability (as so defined) in such earlier month; or

(H) if the benefits under this subsection are based on the wages and self–employment income of a stepparent who is subsequently divorced from such child's natural parent, the month after the month in which such divorce becomes final.

Entitlement of any child to benefits under this subsection on the basis of the wages and self-employment income of an individual entitled to disability insurance benefits shall also end with the month before the first month for which such individual is not entitled to such benefits unless such individual is, for such later month, entitled to old-age insurance benefits or unless he dies in such month. No payment under this paragraph may be made to a child who would not meet the definition of disability in section 223(d) except for paragraph (1)(B) thereof for any month in which he engages in substantial gainful activity.

(2) Such child's insurance benefit for each month shall, if the individual on the basis of whose wages and self-employment income the child is entitled to such benefit has not died prior to the end of such

month, be equal to one-half of the primary insurance amount of such individual for such month. Such child's insurance benefit for each month shall, if such individual has died in or prior to such month, be equal to three-fourths of the primary insurance amount of such individual.

(3) A child shall be deemed dependent upon his father or adopting father or his mother or adopting mother at the time specified in paragraph (1)(C) unless, at such time, such individual was not living with or contributing to the support of such child and—

(A) such child is neither the legitimate nor adopted child of such individual, or

(B) such child has been adopted by some other individual.

For purposes of this paragraph, a child deemed to be a child of a fully or currently insured individual pursuant to section 216(h)(2)(B) or section 216(h)(3) shall be deemed to be the legitimate child of such individual.

(4) A child shall be deemed dependent upon his stepfather or stepmother at the time specified in paragraph (1)(C) if, at such time, the child was receiving at least one-half of his support from such stepfather or stepmother.

(5) In the case of a child who has attained the age of eighteen and who marries—

(A) an individual entitled to benefits under subsection (a), (b), (c), (e), (f), (g), or (h) of this section or under section 223(a), or

(B) another individual who has attained the age of eighteen and is entitled to benefits under this subsection,

such child's entitlement to benefits under this subsection shall, notwithstanding the provisions of paragraph (1) but subject to subsection (s), not be terminated by reason of such marriage.

(6) A child whose entitlement to child's insurance benefits on the basis of the wages and self-employment income of an insured individual terminated with the month preceding the month in which such child attained the age of 18, or with a subsequent month, may again become entitled to such benefits (provided no event specified in paragraph (1)(D) has occurred) beginning with the first month thereafter in which he—

(A)(i) is a full-time elementary or secondary school student and has not attained the age of 19, or (ii) is under a disability (as defined in section 223(d)) and has not attained the age of 22, or

(B) is under a disability (as so defined) which began (i) before the close of the 84th month following the month in which his most recent entitlement to child's insurance benefits terminated because he ceased to be under such disability, or (ii) after the close of the 84th month following the month in which his most recent entitlement to child's insurance benefits terminated because he ceased to be under such disability due to performance of substantial gainful activity,

but only if he has filed application for such reentitlement. Such reentitlement shall end with the month preceding whichever of the following first occurs:

(C) the first month in which an event specified in paragraph (1)(D) occurs;

(D) the earlier of (i) the first month during no part of which he is a full-time elementary or secondary school student or (ii)

28 SOCIAL SECURITY ACT—§ 202(d)(6)(D)(cont)

the month in which he attains the age of 19, but only if he is not under a disability (as so defined) in such earlier month; or

(E) if he was under a disability (as so defined), the termination month (as defined in paragraph (1)(G)(i)), subject to section 223(e), or (if later) the earlier of—

(i) the first month during no part of which he is a full-time elementary or secondary school student, or

(ii) the month in which he attains the age of 19.

(7) For the purposes of this subsection—

(A) A "full-time elementary or secondary school student" is an individual who is in full-time attendance as a student at an elementary or secondary school, as determined by the Commissioner of Social Security (in accordance with regulations prescribed by the Commissioner) in the light of the standards and practices of the schools involved, except that no individual shall be considered a "full-time elementary or secondary school student" if he is paid by his employer while attending an elementary or secondary school at the request, or pursuant to a requirement, of his employer. An individual shall not be considered a "full-time elementary or secondary school student" for the purpose of this section while that individual is confined in a jail, prison, or other penal institution or correctional facility, pursuant to his conviction of an offense (committed after the effective date of this sentence[19]) which constituted a felony under applicable law. An individual who is determined to be a full-time elementary or secondary school student shall be deemed to be such a student throughout the month with respect to which such determination is made.

(B) Except to the extent provided in such regulations, an individual shall be deemed to be a full-time elementary or secondary school student during any period of nonattendance at an elementary or secondary school at which he has been in full-time attendance if (i) such period is 4 calendar months or less, and (ii) he shows to the satisfaction of the Commissioner of Social Security that he intends to continue to be in full-time attendance at an elementary or secondary school immediately following such period. An individual who does not meet the requirement of clause (ii) with respect to such period of nonattendance shall be deemed to have met such requirement (as of the beginning of such period) if he is in full-time attendance at an elementary or secondary school immediately following such period.

(C)(i) An "elementary or secondary school" is a school which provides elementary or secondary education, respectively, as determined under the law of the State or other jurisdiction in which it is located.

(ii) For the purpose of determining whether a child is a "full-time elementary or secondary school student" or "intends to continue to be in full-time attendance at an elementary or secondary school", within the meaning of this subsection, there shall be disregarded any education provided, or to be provided, beyond grade 12.

---

[19] October 1, 1980 [P.L. 96-473, §5(b); 94 Stat. 2265].

SOCIAL SECURITY ACT—§ 202(d)(9)(A)

(D) A child who attains age 19 at a time when he is a full-time elementary or secondary school student (as defined in subparagraph (A) of this paragraph and without application of subparagraph (B) of such paragraph) but has not (at such time) completed the requirements for, or received, a diploma or equivalent certificate from a secondary school (as defined in subparagraph (C)(i)) shall be deemed (for purposes of determining whether his entitlement to benefits under this subsection has terminated under paragraph (1)(F) and for purposes of determining his initial entitlement to such benefits under clause (i) of paragraph (1)(B)) not to have attained such age until the first day of the first month following the end of the quarter or semester in which he is enrolled at such time (or, if the elementary or secondary school (as defined in this paragraph) in which he is enrolled is not operated on a quarter or semester system, until the first day of the first month following the completion of the course in which he is so enrolled or until the first day of the third month beginning after such time, whichever first occurs).

(8) In the case of—

(A) an individual entitled to old-age insurance benefits (other than an individual referred to in subparagraph (B)), or

(B) an individual entitled to disability insurance benefits, or an individual entitled to old-age insurance benefits who was entitled to disability insurance benefits for the month preceding the first month for which he was entitled to old-age insurance benefits, a child of such individual adopted after such individual became entitled to such old-age or disability insurance benefits shall be deemed not to meet the requirements of clause (i) or (iii) of paragraph (1)(C) unless such child—

(C) is the natural child or stepchild of such individual (including such a child who was legally adopted by such individual), or

(D)(i) was legally adopted by such individual in an adoption decreed by a court of competent jurisdiction within the United States, and

(ii) in the case of a child who attained the age of 18 prior to the commencement of proceedings for adoption, the child was living with or receiving at least one-half of the child's support from such individual for the year immediately preceding the month in which the adoption is decreed.

(9)(A) A child who is a child of an individual under clause (3) of the first sentence of section 216(e) and is not a child of such individual under clause (1) or (2) of such first sentence shall be deemed not to be dependent on such individual at the time specified in subparagraph (1)(C) of this subsection unless (i) such child was living with such individual in the United States and receiving at least one-half of his support from such individual (I) for the year immediately before the month in which such individual became entitled to old-age insurance benefits or disability insurance benefits or died, or (II) if such individual had a period of disability which continued until he had become entitled to old-age insurance benefits, or disability insurance benefits, or died, for the year immediately before the month in which such period of disability began, and (ii) the period during which such child was living with such individual began before the child attained age 18.

(B) In the case of a child who was born in the one-year period during which such child must have been living with and receiving at least one-half of his support from such individual, such child shall be deemed to meet such requirements for such period if, as of the close of such period, such child has lived with such individual in the United States and received at least one-half of his support from such individual for substantially all of the period which begins on the date of such child's birth.

(10) For purposes of paragraph (1)(H)—

(A) each stepparent shall notify the Commissioner of Social Security of any divorce upon such divorce becoming final; and

(B) the Commissioner shall annually notify any stepparent of the rule for termination described in paragraph (1)(H) and of the requirement described in subparagraph (A).

Widow's Insurance Benefits

(e)(1) The widow (as defined in section 216(c)) and every surviving divorced wife (as defined in section 216(d)) of an individual who died a fully insured individual, if such widow or such surviving divorced wife—

(A) is not married,

(B)(i) has attained age 60, or (ii) has attained age 50 but has not attained age 60 and is under a disability (as defined in section 223(d)) which began before the end of the period specified in paragraph (4),

(C)(i) has filed application for widow's insurance benefits,

(ii) was entitled to wife's insurance benefits, on the basis of the wages and self-employment income of such individual, for the month preceding the month in which such individual died, and—

(I) has attained retirement age (as defined in section 216(l)),

(II) is not entitled to benefits under subsection (a) or section 223, or

(III) has in effect a certificate (described in paragraph (8)) filed by her with the Commissioner of Social Security, in accordance with regulations prescribed by the Commissioner of Social Security, in which she elects to receive widow's insurance benefits (subject to reduction as provided in subsection (q)), or

(iii) was entitled, on the basis of such wages and self-employment income, to mother's insurance benefits for the month preceding the month in which she attained retirement age (as defined in section 216(l)), and

(D) is not entitled to old-age insurance benefits or is entitled to old-age insurance benefits each of which is less than the primary insurance amount (as determined after application of subparagraphs (B) and (C) of paragraph (2)) of such deceased individual, shall be entitled to a widow's insurance benefit for each month, beginning with—

(E) if she satisfies subparagraph (B) by reason of clause (i) thereof, the first month in which she becomes so entitled to such insurance benefits, or

SOCIAL SECURITY ACT—§ 202(e)(2)(B)(i)(III)   31

(F) if she satisfies subparagraph (B) by reason of clause (ii) thereof—

(i) the first month after her waiting period (as defined in paragraph (5)) in which she becomes so entitled to such insurance benefits, or

(ii) the first month during all of which she is under a disability and in which she becomes so entitled to such insurance benefits, but only if she was previously entitled to insurance benefits under this subsection on the basis of being under a disability and such first month occurs (I) in the period specified in paragraph (4) and (II) after the month in which a previous entitlement to such benefits on such basis terminated,

and ending with the month preceding the first month in which any of the following occurs: she remarries, dies, becomes entitled to an old-age insurance benefit equal to or exceeding the primary insurance amount (as determined after application of subparagraphs (B) and (C) of paragraph (2)) of such deceased individual, or, if she became entitled to such benefits before she attained age 60, subject to section 223(e), the termination month (unless she attains retirement age (as defined in section 216(l)) on or before the last day of such termination month). For purposes of the preceding sentence, the termination month for any individual shall be the third month following the month in which her disability ceases; except that, in the case of an individual who has a period of trial work which ends as determined by application of section 222(c)(4)(A), the termination month shall be the earlier of (I) the third month following the earliest month after the end of such period of trial work with respect to which such individual is determined to no longer be suffering from a disabling physical or mental impairment, or (II) the third month following the earliest month in which such individual engages or is determined able to engage in substantial gainful activity, but in no event earlier than the first month occurring after the 36 months following such period of trial work in which she engages or is determined able to engage in substantial gainful activity.

(2)(A) Except as provided in subsection (k)(5), subsection (q), and subparagraph (D) of this paragraph, such widow's insurance benefit for each month shall be equal to the primary insurance amount (as determined for purposes of this subsection after application of subparagraphs (B) and (C)) of such deceased individual.

(B)(i) For purposes of this subsection, in any case in which such deceased individual dies before attaining age 62 and section 215(a)(1) (as in effect after December 1978) is applicable in determining such individual's primary insurance amount—

(I) such primary insurance amount shall be determined under the formula set forth in section 215(a)(1)(B)(i) and (ii) which is applicable to individuals who initially become eligible for old-age insurance benefits in the second year after the year specified in clause (ii),

(II) the year specified in clause (ii) shall be substituted for the second calendar year specified in section 215(b)(3)(A)(ii)(I), and

(III) such primary insurance amount shall be increased under section 215(i) as if it were the primary insurance amount referred to in section 215(i)(2)(A)(ii)(II), except that it shall be

32   SOCIAL SECURITY ACT—§ 202(e)(2)(B)(i)(III)(cont)

increased only for years beginning after the first year after the year specified in clause (ii).

(ii) The year specified in this clause is the earlier of—

(I) the year in which the deceased individual attained age 60, or would have attained age 60 had he lived to that age, or

(II) the second year preceding the year in which the widow or surviving divorced wife first meets the requirements of paragraph (1)(B) or the second year preceding the year in which the deceased individual died, whichever is later.

(iii) This subparagraph shall apply with respect to any benefit under this subsection only to the extent its application does not result in a primary insurance amount for purposes of this subsection which is less than the primary insurance amount otherwise determined for such deceased individual under section 215.

(C) If such deceased individual was (or upon application would have been) entitled to an old-age insurance benefit which was increased (or subject to being increased) on account of delayed retirement under the provisions of subsection (w), then, for purposes of this subsection, such individual's primary insurance amount, if less than the old-age insurance benefit (increased, where applicable, under section 215(f)(5), 215(f)(6), or 215(f)(9)(B) and under section 215(i) as if such individual were still alive in the case of an individual who has died) which he was receiving (or would upon application have received) for the month prior to the month in which he died, shall be deemed to be equal to such old-age insurance benefit, and (notwithstanding the provisions of paragraph (3) of such subsection (w)) the number of increment months shall include any month in the months of the calendar year in which he died, prior to the month in which he died, which satisfy the conditions in paragraph (2) of such subsection (w).

(D) If the deceased individual (on the basis of whose wages and self-employment income a widow or surviving divorced wife is entitled to widow's insurance benefits under this subsection) was, at any time, entitled to an old-age insurance benefit which was reduced by reason of the application of subsection (q), the widow's insurance benefit of such widow or surviving divorced wife for any month shall, if the amount of the widow's insurance benefit of such widow or surviving divorced wife (as determined under subparagraph (A) and after application of subsection (q)) is greater than—

(i) the amount of the old-age insurance benefit to which such deceased individual would have been entitled (after application of subsection (q)) for such month if such individual were still living and section 215(f)(5), 215(f)(6), or 215(f)(9)(B) were applied, where applicable, and

(ii) 82 ½ percent of the primary insurance amount (as determined without regard to subparagraph (C)) of such deceased individual,

be reduced to the amount referred to in clause (i), or (if greater) the amount referred to in clause (ii).

(3) For purposes of paragraph (1), if—

(A) a widow or surviving divorced wife marries after attaining age 60 (or after attaining age 50 if she was entitled before such marriage occurred to benefits based on disability under this subsection), or

SOCIAL SECURITY ACT—§ 202(e)(7)(B)   33

(B) a disabled widow or disabled surviving divorced wife described in paragraph (1)(B)(ii) marries after attaining age 50, such marriage shall be deemed not to have occurred.

(4) The period referred to in paragraph (1)(B)(ii), in the case of any widow or surviving divorced wife, is the period beginning with whichever of the following is the latest:

(A) the month in which occurred the death of the fully insured individual referred to in paragraph (1) on whose wages and self-employment income her benefits are or would be based, or

(B) the last month for which she was entitled to mother's insurance benefits on the basis of the wages and self-employment income of such individual, or

(C) the month in which a previous entitlement to widow's insurance benefits on the basis of such wages and self-employment income terminated because her disability had ceased,

and ending with the month before the month in which she attains age 60, or, if earlier, with the close of the eighty-fourth month following the month with which such period began.

(5)(A) The waiting period referred to in paragraph (1)(F), in the case of any widow or surviving divorced wife, is the earliest period of five consecutive calendar months—

(i) throughout which she has been under a disability, and

(ii) which begins not earlier than with whichever of the following is the later: (I) the first day of the seventeenth month before the month in which her application is filed, or (II) the first day of the fifth month before the month in which the period specified in paragraph (4) begins.

(B) For purposes of paragraph (1)(F)(i), each month in the period commencing with the first month for which such widow or surviving divorced wife is first eligible for supplemental security income benefits under title XVI, or State supplementary payments of the type referred to in section 1616(a) (or payments of the type described in section 212(a) of Public Law 93-66) which are paid by the Commissioner of Social Security under an agreement referred to in section 1616(a) (or in section 212(b) of Public Law 93-66), shall be included as one of the months of such waiting period for which the requirements of subparagraph (A) have been met.

(6) In the case of an individual entitled to monthly insurance benefits payable under this section for any month prior to January 1973 whose benefits were not redetermined under section 102(g) of the Social Security Amendments of 1972[20], such benefits shall not be redetermined pursuant to such section, but shall be increased pursuant to any general benefit increase (as defined in section 215(i)(3)) or any increase in benefits made under or pursuant to section 215(i), including for this purpose the increase provided effective for March 1974, as though such redetermination had been made.

(7) Any certificate filed pursuant to paragraph (1)(C)(ii)(III) shall be effective for purposes of this subsection—

(A) for the month in which it is filed and for any month thereafter, and

(B) for months, in the period designated by the individual filing such certificate, of one or more consecutive months (not exceeding

---

[20] See Vol. II, P.L. 92-603.

34   SOCIAL SECURITY ACT—§ 202(e)(7)(B)(cont)

12) immediately preceding the month in which such certificate is filed;

except that such certificate shall not be effective for any month before the month in which she attains age 62.

(8) An individual shall be deemed to be under a disability for purposes of paragraph (1)(B)(ii) if such individual is eligible for supplemental security income benefits under title XVI, or State supplementary payments of the type referred to in section 1616(a) (or payments of the type described in section 212(a) of Public Law 93-66[21]) which are paid by the Commissioner of Social Security under an agreement referred to in section 1616(a) (or in section 212(b) of Public Law 93-66), for the month for which all requirements of paragraph (1) for entitlement to benefits under this subsection (other than being under a disability) are met.

Widower's Insurance Benefits

(f)(1) The widower (as defined in section 216(g)) and every surviving divorced husband (as defined in section 216(d)) of an individual who died a fully insured individual, if such widower or such surviving divorced husband

(A) is not married,

(B)(i) has attained age 60, or (ii) has attained age 50 but has not attained age 60 and is under a disability (as defined in section 223(d)) which began before the end of the period specified in paragraph (4),

(C)(i) has filed application for widower's insurance benefits,

(ii) was entitled to husband's insurance benefits, on the basis of the wages and self-employment income of such individual, for the month preceding the month in which such individual died, and—

(I) has attained retirement age (as defined in section 216(l)),

(II) is not entitled to benefits under subsection (a) or section 223, or

(III) has in effect a certificate (described in paragraph (8)) filed by him with the Commissioner of Social Security, in accordance with regulations prescribed by the Commissioner of Social Security, in which he elects to receive widower's insurance benefits (subject to reduction as provided in subsection (q)), or

(iii) was entitled, on the basis of such wages and self-employment income, to father's insurance benefits for the month preceding the month in which he attained retirement age (as defined in section 216(l)), and

(D) is not entitled to old-age insurance benefits, or is entitled to old-age insurance benefits each of which is less than the primary insurance amount (as determined after application of subparagraphs (B) and (C) of paragraph (3)) of such deceased individual, shall be entitled to a widower's insurance benefit for each month, beginning with—

---

[21] See Vol. II, P.L. 93-66, §212(a).

SOCIAL SECURITY ACT—§ 202(f)(2)(B)(i)(III)   35

(E) if he satisfies subparagraph (B) by reason of clause (i) thereof, the first month in which he becomes so entitled to such insurance benefits, or

(F) if he satisfies subparagraph (B) by reason of clause (ii) thereof—

(i) the first month after his waiting period (as defined in paragraph (5)) in which he becomes so entitled to such insurance benefits, or

(ii) the first month during all of which he is under a disability and in which he becomes so entitled to such insurance benefits, but only if he was previously entitled to insurance benefits under this subsection on the basis of being under a disability and such first month occurs (I) in the period specified in paragraph (4) and (II) after the month in which a previous entitlement to such benefits on such basis terminated,

and ending with the month preceding the first month in which any of the following occurs: he remarries, dies, or becomes entitled to an old-age insurance benefit equal to or exceeding the primary insurance amount (as determined after application of subparagraphs (B) and (C) of paragraph (3)) of such deceased individual, or, if he became entitled to such benefits before he attained age 60, subject to section 223(e), the termination month (unless he attains retirement age (as defined in section 216(l)) on or before the last day of such termination month). For purposes of the preceding sentence, the termination month for any individual shall be the third month following the month in which his disability ceases; except that, in the case of an individual who has a period of trial work which ends as determined by application of section 222(c)(4)(A), the termination month shall be the earlier of (I) the third month following the earliest month after the end of such period of trial work with respect to which such individual is determined to no longer be suffering from a disabling physical or mental impairment, or (II) the third month following the earliest month in which such individual engages or is determined able to engage in substantial gainful activity, but in no event earlier than the first month occurring after the 36 months following such period of trial work in which he engages or is determined able to engage in substantial gainful activity.

(2)(A) Except as provided in subsection (k)(5), subsection (q), and subparagraph (D) of this paragraph, such widower's insurance benefit for each month shall be equal to the primary insurance amount (as determined for purposes of this subsection after application of subparagraphs (B) and (C)) of such deceased individual.

(B)(i) For purposes of this subsection, in any case in which such deceased individual dies before attaining age 62 and section 215(a)(1) (as in effect after December 1978) is applicable in determining such individual's primary insurance amount—

(I) such primary insurance amount shall be determined under the formula set forth in section 215(a)(1)(B)(i) and (ii) which is applicable to individuals who initially become eligible for old-age insurance benefits in the second year after the year specified in clause (ii),

(II) the year specified in clause (ii) shall be substituted for the second calendar year specified in section 215(b)(3)(A)(ii)(I), and

(III) such primary insurance amount shall be increased under section 215(i) as if it were the primary insurance amount

36 SOCIAL SECURITY ACT—§ 202(f)(2)(B)(i)(III)(cont)

referred to in section 215(i)(2)(A)(ii)(II), except that it shall be increased only for years beginning after the first year after the year specified in clause (ii).

(ii) The year specified in this clause is the earlier of—

(I) the year in which the deceased individual attained age 60, or would have attained age 60 had she lived to that age, or

(II) the second year preceding the year in which the widower or surviving divorced husband first meets the requirements of paragraph (1)(B) or the second year preceding the year in which the deceased individual died, whichever is later.

(iii) This subparagraph shall apply with respect to any benefit under this subsection only to the extent its application does not result in a primary insurance amount for purposes of this subsection which is less than the primary insurance amount otherwise determined for such deceased individual under section 215.

(C) If such deceased individual was (or upon application would have been) entitled to an old-age insurance benefit which was increased (or subject to being increased) on account of delayed retirement under the provisions of subsection (w), then, for purposes of this subsection, such individual's primary insurance amount, if less than the old-age insurance benefit (increased, where applicable, under section 215(f)(5), 215(f)(6), or 215(f)(9)(B) and under section 215(i) as if such individual were still alive in the case of an individual who has died) which she was receiving (or would upon application have received) for the month prior to the month in which she died, shall be deemed to be equal to such old-age insurance benefit, and (notwithstanding the provisions of paragraph (3) of such subsection (w)) the number of increment months shall include any month in the months of the calendar year in which she died, prior to the month in which she died, which satisfy the conditions in paragraph (2) of such subsection (w).

(D) If the deceased individual (on the basis of whose wages and self-employment income a widower or surviving divorced husband is entitled to widower's insurance benefits under this subsection) was, at any time, entitled to an old-age insurance benefit which was reduced by reason of the application of subsection (q), the widower's insurance benefit of such widower or surviving divorced husband for any month shall, if the amount of the widower's insurance benefit of such widower or surviving divorced husband (as determined under subparagraph (A) and after application of subsection (q)) is greater than—

(i) the amount of the old-age insurance benefit to which such deceased individual would have been entitled (after application of subsection (q)) for such month if such individual were still living and section 215(f)(5), 215(f)(6), or 215(f)(9)(B) were applied, where applicable, and

(ii) 82 1/2 percent of the primary insurance amount (as determined without regard to subparagraph (C)) of such deceased individual;

be reduced to the amount referred to in clause (i), or (if greater) the amount referred to in clause (ii).

(3) For purposes of paragraph (1), if—

(A) a widower or surviving divorced husband marries after attaining age 60 (or after attaining age 50 if he was entitled before such marriage occurred to benefits based on disability under this subsection), or

SOCIAL SECURITY ACT—§ 202(f)(7)(A)   37

(B) a disabled widower or surviving divorced husband described in paragraph (1)(B)(ii) marries after attaining age 50,
such marriage shall be deemed not to have occurred.

(4) The period referred to in paragraph (1)(B)(ii), in the case of any widower or surviving divorced husband, is the period beginning with whichever of the following is the latest:

(A) the month in which occurred the death of the fully insured individual referred to in paragraph (1) on whose wages and self-employment income his benefits are or would be based,

(B) the last month for which he was entitled to father's insurance benefits on the basis of the wages and self-employment income of such individual, or

(C) the month in which a previous entitlement to widower's insurance benefits on the basis of such wages and self-employment income terminated because his disability had ceased,

and ending with the month before the month in which he attains age 60, or, if earlier, with the close of the eighty-fourth month following the month with which such period began.

(5)(A) The waiting period referred to in paragraph (1)(F), in the case of any widower or surviving divorced husband, is the earliest period of five consecutive calendar months—

(i) throughout which he has been under a disability, and

(ii) which begins not earlier than with whichever of the following is the later: (I) the first day of the seventeenth month before the month in which his application is filed, or (II) the first day of the fifth month before the month in which the period specified in paragraph (4) begins.

(B) For purposes of paragraph (1)(F)(i), each month in the period commencing with the first month for which such widower or surviving divorced husband is first eligible for supplemental security income benefits under title XVI, or State supplementary payments of the type referred to in section 1616(a) (or payments of the type described in section 212(a) of Public Law 93-66[22]) which are paid by the Commissioner of Social Security under an agreement referred to in section 1616(a) (or in section 212(b) of Public Law 93-66), shall be included as one of the months of such waiting period for which the requirements of subparagraph (A) have been met.

(6) In the case of an individual entitled to monthly insurance benefits payable under this section for any month prior to January 1973 whose benefits were not redetermined under section 102(g) of the Social Security Amendments of 1972[23], such benefits shall not be redetermined pursuant to such section, but shall be increased pursuant to any general benefit increase (as defined in section 215(i)(3)) or any increase in benefits made under or pursuant to section 215(i), including for this purpose the increase provided effective for March 1974, as though such redetermination had been made.

(7) Any certificate filed pursuant to paragraph (1)(C)(ii)(III) shall be effective for purposes of this subsection—

(A) for the month in which it is filed and for any month thereafter, and

---

[22] See Vol. II, P.L. 93-66, §212.
[23] See Vol. II, P.L. 92-603, §102(g).

38 SOCIAL SECURITY ACT—§ 202(f)(7)(B)

(B) for months, in the period designated by the individual filing such certificate, of one or more consecutive months (not exceeding 12) immediately preceding the month in which such certificate is filed;

except that such certificate shall not be effective for any month before the month in which he attains age 62.

(8) An individual shall be deemed to be under a disability for purposes of paragraph (1)(B)(ii) if such individual is eligible for supplemental security income benefits under title XVI, or State supplementary payments of the type referred to in section 1616(a) (or payments of the type described in section 212(a) of Public Law 93-66) which are paid by the Commissioner of Social Security under an agreement referred to in such section 1616(a) (or in section 212(b) of Public Law 93-66), for the month for which all requirements of paragraph (1) for entitlement to benefits under this subsection (other than being under a disability) are met.

Mother's and Father's Insurance Benefits

(g)(1) The surviving spouse and every surviving divorced parent (as defined in section 216(d)) of an individual who died a fully or currently insured individual, if such surviving spouse or surviving divorced parent—

(A) is not married,

(B) is not entitled to a surviving spouse's insurance benefit,

(C) is not entitled to old-age insurance benefits, or is entitled to old-age insurance benefits each of which is less than three-fourths of the primary insurance amount of such individual,

(D) has filed application for mother's or father's insurance benefits, or was entitled to a spouse's insurance benefit on the basis of the wages and self-employment income of such individual for the month preceding the month in which such individual died,

(E) at the time of filing such application has in his or her care a child of such individual entitled to a child's insurance benefit, and

(F) in the case of a surviving divorced parent—

(i) the child referred to in subparagraph (E) is his or her son, daughter, or legally adopted child, and

(ii) the benefits referred to in such subparagraph are payable on the basis of such individual's wages and self-employment income,

shall (subject to subsection (s)) be entitled to a mother's or father's insurance benefit for each month, beginning with the first month in which he or she becomes so entitled to such insurance benefits and ending with the month preceding the first month in which any of the following occurs: no child of such deceased individual is entitled to a child's insurance benefit, such surviving spouse or surviving divorced parent becomes entitled to an old-age insurance benefit equal to or exceeding three-fourths of the primary insurance amount of such deceased individual, he or she becomes entitled to a surviving spouse's insurance benefit, he or she remarries, or he or she dies. Entitlement to such benefits shall also end, in the case of a surviving divorced parent, with the month immediately preceding the first month in which

SOCIAL SECURITY ACT—§ 202(h)(2)(A)   39

no son, daughter, or legally adopted child of such surviving divorced parent is entitled to a child's insurance benefit on the basis of the wages and self-employment income of such deceased individual.

(2) Such mother's or father's insurance benefit for each month shall be equal to three-fourths of the primary insurance amount of such deceased individual.

(3) In the case of a surviving spouse or surviving divorced parent who marries—

> (A) an individual entitled to benefits under this subsection or subsection (a), (b), (c), (e), (f), or (h), or under section 223(a), or
>
> (B) an individual who has attained the age of eighteen and is entitled to benefits under subsection (d),

the entitlement of such surviving spouse or surviving divorced parent to benefits under this subsection shall, notwithstanding the provisions of paragraph (1) but subject to subsection (s), not be terminated by reason of such marriage.

Parent's Insurance Benefits

(h)(1) Every parent (as defined in this subsection) of an individual who died a fully insured individual, if such parent—

> (A) has attained age 62,
>
> (B)(i) was receiving at least one-half of his support from such individual at the time of such individual's death or, if such individual had a period of disability which did not end prior to the month in which he died, at the time such period began or at the time of such death, and (ii) filed proof of such support within two years after the date of such death, or, if such individual had such a period of disability, within two years after the month in which such individual filed application with respect to such period of disability or two years after the date of such death, as the case may be,
>
> (C) has not married since such individual's death,
>
> (D) is not entitled to old-age insurance benefits, or is entitled to old-age insurance benefits each of which is less than 82 1/2 percent of the primary insurance amount of such deceased individual if the amount of the parent's insurance benefit for such month is determinable under paragraph (2)(A) (or 75 percent of such primary insurance amount in any other case), and
>
> (E) has filed application for parent's insurance benefits,

shall be entitled to a parent's insurance benefit for each month beginning with the first month after August 1950 in which such parent becomes so entitled to such parent's insurance benefits and ending with the month preceding the first month in which any of the following occurs: such parent dies, marries, or becomes entitled to an old-age insurance benefit equal to or exceeding 82 1/2 percent of the primary insurance amount of such deceased individual if the amount of the parent's insurance benefit for such month is determinable under paragraph (2)(A) (or 75 percent of such primary insurance amount in any other case).

(2)(A) Except as provided in subparagraphs (B) and (C), such parent's insurance benefit for each month shall be equal to 82 1/2 percent of the primary insurance amount of such deceased individual.

40 SOCIAL SECURITY ACT—§ 202(h)(2)(B)

(B) For any month for which more than one parent is entitled to parent's insurance benefits on the basis of such deceased individual's wages and self-employment income, such benefit for each such parent for such month shall (except as provided in subparagraph (C)) be equal to 75 percent of the primary insurance amount of such deceased individual.

(C) In any case in which—

(i) any parent is entitled to a parent's insurance benefit for a month on the basis of a deceased individual's wages and self-employment income, and

(ii) another parent of such deceased individual is entitled to a parent's insurance benefit for such month on the basis of such wages and self-employment income, and on the basis of an application filed after such month and after the month in which the application for the parent's benefits referred to in clause (i) was filed,

the amount of the parent's insurance benefit of the parent referred to in clause (i) for the month referred to in such clause shall be determined under subparagraph (A) instead of subparagraph (B) and the amount of the parent's insurance benefit of a parent referred to in clause (ii) for such month shall be equal to 150 percent of the primary insurance amount of the deceased individual minus the amount (before the application of section 203(a)) of the benefit for such month of the parent referred to in clause (i).

(3) As used in this subsection, the term "parent" means the mother or father of an individual, a stepparent of an individual by a marriage contracted before such individual attained the age of sixteen, or an adopting parent by whom an individual was adopted before he attained the age of sixteen.

(4) In the case of a parent who marries—

(A) an individual entitled to benefits under this subsection or subsection (b), (c), (e), (f), or (g), or

(B) an individual who has attained the age of eighteen and is entitled to benefits under subsection (d),

such parent's entitlement to benefits under this subsection shall, notwithstanding the provisions of paragraph (1) but subject to subsection (s), not be terminated by reason of such marriage.

Lump-Sum Death Payments

(i) Upon the death, after August 1950, of an individual who died a fully or currently insured individual, an amount equal to three times such individual's primary insurance amount (as determined without regard to the amendments made by section 2201 of the Omnibus Budget Reconciliation Act of 1981[24], relating to the repeal of the minimum benefit provisions), or an amount equal to $255, whichever is the smaller, shall be paid in a lump sum to the person, if any, determined by the Commissioner of Social Security to be the widow or widower of the deceased and to have been living in the same household with the deceased at the time of death. If there is no such person, or

---

[24] P.L. 97-35.

SOCIAL SECURITY ACT—§ 202(j)(1)

if such person dies before receiving payment, then such amount shall be paid—

(1) to a widow (as defined in section 216(c)) or widower (as defined in section 216(g)) who is entitled (or would have been so entitled had a timely application been filed), on the basis of the wages and self-employment income of such insured individual, to benefits under subsection (e), (f), or (g) of this section for the month in which occurred such individual's death; or

(2) if no person qualifies for payment under paragraph (1), or if such person dies before receiving payment, in equal shares to each person who is entitled (or would have been so entitled had a timely application been filed), on the basis of the wages and self-employment income of such insured individual, to benefits under subsection (d) of this section for the month in which occurred such individual's death.

No payment shall be made to any person under this subsection unless application therefor shall have been filed, by or on behalf of such person (whether or not legally competent), prior to the expiration of two years after the date of death of such insured individual, or unless such person was entitled to wife's or husband's insurance benefits, on the basis of the wages and self-employment income of such insured individual, for the month preceding the month in which such individual died. In the case of any individual who died outside the forty-eight States and the District of Columbia after December 1953 and before January 1, 1957, whose death occurred while he was in the active military or naval service of the United States, and who is returned to any of such States, the District of Columbia, Alaska, Hawaii, the Commonwealth of Puerto Rico, the Virgin Islands, Guam, or American Samoa for interment or reinterment, the provisions of the preceding sentence shall not prevent payment to any person under the second sentence of this subsection if application for a lump-sum death payment with respect to such deceased individual is filed by or on behalf of such person (whether or not legally competent) prior to the expiration of two years after the date of such interment or reinterment. In the case of any individual who died outside the fifty States and the District of Columbia after December 1956 while he was performing service, as a member of a uniformed service, to which the provisions of section 210(l)(1) are applicable, and who is returned to any State, or to any Territory or possession of the United States, for interment or reinterment, the provisions of the third sentence of this subsection shall not prevent payment to any person under the second sentence of this subsection if application for a lump-sum death payment with respect to such deceased individual is filed by or on behalf of such person (whether or not legally competent) prior to the expiration of two years after the date of such interment or reinterment.

Application for Monthly Insurance Benefits

(j)(1) Subject to the limitations contained in paragraph (4), an individual who would have been entitled to a benefit under subsection (a), (b), (c), (d), (e), (f), (g), or (h) for any month after August 1950 had he filed application therefor prior to the end of such month shall be

42 SOCIAL SECURITY ACT—§ 202(j)(1)(cont)

entitled to such benefit for such month if he files application therefor prior to—

(A) the end of the twelfth month immediately succeeding such month in any case where the individual (i) is filing application for a benefit under subsection (e) or (f), and satisfies paragraph (1)(B) of such subsection by reason of clause (ii) thereof, or (ii) is filing application for a benefit under subsection (b), (c), or (d) on the basis of the wages and self-employment income of a person entitled to disability insurance benefits, or

(B) the end of the sixth month immediately succeeding such month in any case where subparagraph (A) does not apply.

Any benefit under this title for a month prior to the month in which application is filed shall be reduced, to any extent that may be necessary, so that it will not render erroneous any benefit which, before the filing of such application, the Commissioner of Social Security has certified for payment for such prior month.

(2) An application for any monthly benefits under this section filed before the first month in which the applicant satisfies the requirements for such benefits shall be deemed a valid application (and shall be deemed to have been filed in such first month) only if the applicant satisfies the requirements for such benefits before the Commissioner of Social Security makes a final decision on the application and no request under section 205(b) for notice and opportunity for a hearing thereon is made or, if such a request is made, before a decision based upon the evidence adduced at the hearing is made (regardless of whether such decision becomes the final decision of the Commissioner of Social Security).

(3) Notwithstanding the provisions of paragraph (1), an individual may, at his option, waive entitlement to any benefit referred to in paragraph (1) for any one or more consecutive months (beginning with the earliest month for which such individual would otherwise be entitled to such benefit) which occur before the month in which such individual files application for such benefit; and, in such case, such individual shall not be considered as entitled to such benefits for any such month or months before such individual filed such application. An individual shall be deemed to have waived such entitlement for any such month for which such benefit would, under the second sentence of paragraph (1), be reduced to zero.

(4)(A) Except as provided in subparagraph (B), no individual shall be entitled to a monthly benefit under subsection (a), (b), (c), (e), or (f) for any month prior to the month in which he or she files an application for benefits under that subsection if the amount of the monthly benefit to which such individual would otherwise be entitled for any such month would be subject to reduction pursuant to subsection (q).

(B)(i) If the individual applying for retroactive benefits is a widow, surviving divorced wife, or widower and is under a disability (as defined in section 223(d)), and such individual would, except for subparagraph (A), be entitled to retroactive benefits as a disabled widow or widower or disabled surviving divorced wife for any month before attaining the age of 60, then subparagraph (A) shall not apply with respect to such month or any subsequent month.

(ii) Subparagraph (A) does not apply to a benefit under subsection (e) or (f) for the month immediately preceding the month of application, if the insured individual died in that preceding month.

SOCIAL SECURITY ACT—§ 202(k)(2)(B)   43

(iii) As used in this subparagraph, the term "retroactive benefits" means benefits to which an individual becomes entitled for a month prior to the month in which application for such benefits is filed.

(5) In any case in which it is determined to the satisfaction of the Commissioner of Social Security that an individual failed as of any date to apply for monthly insurance benefits under this title by reason of misinformation provided to such individual by any officer or employee of the Social Security Administration relating to such individual's eligibility for benefits under this title, such individual shall be deemed to have applied for such benefits on the later of—

(A) the date on which such misinformation was provided to such individual, or

(B) the date on which such individual met all requirements for entitlement to such benefits (other than application therefor).

Simultaneous Entitlement to Benefits

(k)(1) A child, entitled to child's insurance benefits on the basis of the wages and self-employment income of an insured individual, who would be entitled, on filing application, to child's insurance benefits on the basis of the wages and self-employment income of some other insured individual, shall be deemed entitled, subject to the provisions of paragraph (2) hereof, to child's insurance benefits on the basis of the wages and self-employment income of such other individual if an application for child's insurance benefits on the basis of the wages and self-employment income of such other individual has been filed by any other child who would, on filing application, be entitled to child's insurance benefits on the basis of the wages and self-employment income of both such insured individuals.

(2)(A) Any child who under the preceding provisions of this section is entitled for any month to child's insurance benefits on the wages and self-employment income of more than one insured individual shall, notwithstanding such provisions, be entitled to only one of such child's insurance benefits for such month. Such child's insurance benefits for such month shall be the benefit based on the wages and self-employment income of the insured individual who has the greatest primary insurance amount, except that such child's insurance benefits for such month shall be the largest benefit to which such child could be entitled under subsection (d) (without the application of section 203(a)) or subsection (m) if entitlement to such benefit would not, with respect to any person, result in a benefit lower (after the application of section 203(a)) than the benefit which would be applicable if such child were entitled on the wages and self-employment income of the individual with the greatest primary insurance amount. Where more than one child is entitled to child's insurance benefits pursuant to the preceding provisions of this paragraph, each such child who is entitled on the wages and self-employment income of the same insured individuals shall be entitled on the wages and self-employment income of the same such insured individual.

(B) Any individual (other than an individual to whom subsection (e)(3) or (f)(3) applies) who, under the preceding provisions of this section and under the provisions of section 223, is entitled for any month to more than one monthly insurance benefit (other than an old-age or

44 SOCIAL SECURITY ACT—§ 202(k)(2)(B)(cont)

disability insurance benefit) under this title shall be entitled to only one such monthly benefit for such month, such benefit to be the largest of the monthly benefits to which he (but for this subparagraph (B)) would otherwise be entitled for such month. Any individual who is entitled for any month to more than one widow's or widower's insurance benefit to which subsection (e)(3) or (f)(3) applies shall be entitled to only one such benefit for such month, such benefit to be the largest of such benefits.

(3)(A) If an individual is entitled to an old-age or disability insurance benefit for any month and to any other monthly insurance benefit for such month, such other insurance benefit for such month, after any reduction under subsection (q), subsection (e)(2) or (f)(2), and any reduction under section 203(a), shall be reduced, but not below zero, by an amount equal to such old-age or disability insurance benefit (after reduction under such subsection (q)).

(B) If an individual is entitled for any month to a widow's or widower's insurance benefit to which subsection (e)(3) or (f)(3) applies and to any other monthly insurance benefit under section 202 (other than an old-age insurance benefit), such other insurance benefit for such month, after any reduction under subparagraph (A), any reduction under subsection (q), and any reduction under section 203(a), shall be reduced, but not below zero, by an amount equal to such widow's or widower's insurance benefit after any reduction or reductions under such subparagraph (A) and such section 203(a).

(4) Any individual who, under this section and section 223, is entitled for any month to both an old-age insurance benefit and a disability insurance benefit under this title shall be entitled to only the larger of such benefits for such month, except that, if such individual so elects, he shall instead be entitled to only the smaller of such benefits for such month.

(5)(A) The amount of a monthly insurance benefit of any individual for each month under subsection (b), (c), (e), (f), or (g) (as determined after application of the provisions of subsection (q) and the preceding provisions of this subsection) shall be reduced (but not below zero) by an amount equal to two-thirds of the amount of any monthly periodic benefit payable to such individual for such month which is based upon such individual's earnings while in the service of the Federal Government or any State (or political subdivision thereof, as defined in section 218(b)(2)) if, during any portion of the last 60 months of such service ending with the last day such individual was employed by such entity—

(i) such service did not constitute "employment" as defined in section 210, or

(ii) such service was being performed while in the service of the Federal Government, and constituted "employment" as so defined solely by reason of—

(I) clause (ii) or (iii) of subparagraph (G) of section 210(a)(5), where the lump-sum payment described in such clause (ii) or the cessation of coverage described in such clause (iii) (whichever is applicable) was received or occurred on or after January 1, 1988, or

(II) an election to become subject to the Federal Employees' Retirement System provided in chapter 84 of title 5, United States Code, or the Foreign Service Pension

SOCIAL SECURITY ACT—§ 202(n)(1)(A)

System provided in subchapter II of chapter 8 of title I of the Foreign Service Act of 1980[25] made pursuant to law after December 31, 1987,

unless subparagraph (B) applies. The amount of the reduction in any benefit under this subparagraph, if not a multiple of $0.10, shall be rounded to the next higher multiple of $0.10.

(B)(i) Subparagraph (A)(i) shall not apply with respect to monthly periodic benefits based wholly on service as a member of a uniformed service (as defined in section 210(m)).

(ii) Subparagraph (A)(ii) shall not apply with respect to monthly periodic benefits based in whole or in part on service which constituted "employment" as defined in section 210 if such service was performed for at least 60 months in the aggregate during the period beginning January 1, 1988, and ending with the close of the first calendar month as of the end of which such individual is eligible for benefits under this subsection and has made a valid application for such benefits.

(C) For purposes of this paragraph, any periodic benefit which otherwise meets the requirements of subparagraph (A), but which is paid on other than a monthly basis, shall be allocated on a basis equivalent to a monthly benefit (as determined by the Commissioner of Social Security) and such equivalent monthly benefit shall constitute a monthly periodic benefit for purposes of subparagraph (A). For purposes of this subparagraph, the term "periodic benefit" includes a benefit payable in a lump sum if it is a commutation of, or a substitute for, periodic payments.

Entitlement to Survivor Benefits Under Railroad Retirement Act

(l) If any person would be entitled, upon filing application therefor to an annuity under section 2 of the Railroad Retirement Act of 1974[26], or to a lump–sum payment under section 6(b) of such Act, with respect to the death of an employee (as defined in such Act) no lump–sum death payment, and no monthly benefit for the month in which such employee died or for any month thereafter, shall be paid under this section to any person on the basis of the wages and self–employment income of such employee.

(m)   [Repealed.[27]]

Termination of Benefits Upon Removal of Primary Beneficiary

(n)(1) If any individual is (after the date of enactment of this subsection[28]) removed under section 237(a) of the Immigration and Nationality Act (other than under paragraph (1)(C) of such section) or under section 212(a)(6)(A) of such Act, then, notwithstanding any other provisions of this title—

(A) no monthly benefit under this section or section 223 shall be paid to such individual, on the basis of his wages and self-employment income, for any month occurring (i) after the month in which

---

[25] See Vol. II, P.L. 96-465, Title I, Chapter 8.
[26] See Vol. II, P.L. 75-162 [as amended by P.L. 93-445].
[27] P.L. 97-35, §2201(b)(10); 95 Stat. 831; P.L. 97-123, §2(j)(1); 95 Stat. 1661.
[28] September 1, 1954 [P.L. 83-761, §107; 68 Stat. 1083.

46   SOCIAL SECURITY ACT—§ 202(n)(1)(A)(cont)

the Commissioner of Social Security is notified by the Attorney General or the Secretary of Homeland Security that such individual has been so removed, and (ii) before the month in which such individual is thereafter lawfully admitted to the United States for permanent residence,

(B) if no benefit could be paid to such individual (or if no benefit could be paid to him if he were alive) for any month by reason of subparagraph (A), no monthly benefit under this section shall be paid, on the basis of his wages and self-employment income, for such month to any other person who is not a citizen of the United States and is outside the United States for any part of such month, and

(C) no lump-sum death payment shall be made on the basis of such individual's wages and self-employment income if he dies (i) in or after the month in which such notice is received, and (ii) before the month in which he is thereafter lawfully admitted to the United States for permanent residence.

Section 203(b), (c), and (d) of this Act shall not apply with respect to any such individual for any month for which no monthly benefit may be paid to him by reason of this paragraph.

(2) As soon as practicable after the removal of any individual under any of the paragraphs of section 237(a) of the Immigration and Nationality Act (other than under paragraph (1)(C) of such section) or under section 212(a)(6)(A) of such Act[29], the Attorney General or the Secretary of Homeland Security shall notify the Commissioner of Social Security of such removal.

(3) For purposes of paragraphs (1) and (2) of this subsection, an individual against whom a final order of removal has been issued under paragraph (4)(D) of section 237(a) of the Immigration and Nationality Act (relating to participating in Nazi persecutions or genocide) shall be considered to have been removed under such paragraph (4)(D) as of the date on which such order became final.

Application for Benefits by Survivors of Members and Former Members of the Uniformed Services

(o) In the case of any individual who would be entitled to benefits under subsection (d), (e), (g), or (h) upon filing proper application therefor, the filing with the Administrator of Veterans' Affairs by or on behalf of such individual of an application for such benefits, on the form described in section 3005 of title 38, United States Code[30], shall satisfy the requirement of such subsection (d), (e), (g), or (h) that an application for such benefits be filed.

Extension of Period for Filing Proof of Support and Applications for Lump-Sum Death Payment

(p) In any case in which there is a failure—

(1) to file proof of support under subparagraph (B) of subsection (h)(1), or under clause (B) of subsection (f)(1) of this section as

---

[29] See Vol. II, P.L. 82-414, §§212(a)(6)(A)and 237(a).
[30] See Vol. II, 38 U.S.C. 3005.

in effect prior to the Social Security Act Amendments of 1950[31], within the period prescribed by such subparagraph or clause, or

(2) to file, in the case of a death after 1946, application for a lump-sum death payment under subsection (i), or under subsection (g) of this section as in effect prior to the Social Security Act Amendments of 1950, within the period prescribed by such subsection,

any such proof or application, as the case may be, which is filed after the expiration of such period shall be deemed to have been filed within such period if it is shown to the satisfaction of the Commissioner of Social Security that there was good cause for failure to file such proof or application within such period. The determination of what constitutes good cause for purposes of this subsection shall be made in accordance with regulations of the Commissioner of Social Security.

Reduction of Benefit Amounts for Certain Beneficiaries

(q)(1) Subject to paragraph (9), if the first month for which an individual is entitled to an old-age, wife's, husband's, widow's, or widower's insurance benefit is a month before the month in which such individual attains retirement age, the amount of such benefit for such month and for any subsequent month shall, subject to the succeeding paragraphs of this subsection, be reduced by—

(A) $5/9$ of 1 percent of such amount if such benefit is an old-age insurance benefit, $25/36$ of 1 percent of such amount if such benefit is a wife's or husband's insurance benefit, or $19/40$ of 1 percent of such amount if such benefit is a widow's or widower's insurance benefit, multiplied by

(B)(i) the number of months in the reduction period for such benefit (determined under paragraph (6)), if such benefit is for a month before the month in which such individual attains retirement age, or

(ii) if less, the number of such months in the adjusted reduction period for such benefit (determined under paragraph (7)), if such benefit is (I) for the month in which such individual attains age 62, or (II) for the month in which such individual attains retirement age.

(2) If an individual is entitled to a disability insurance benefit for a month after a month for which such individual was entitled to an old-age insurance benefit, such disability insurance benefit for each month shall be reduced by the amount such old-age insurance benefit would be reduced under paragraphs (1) and (4) for such month had such individual attained retirement age (as defined in section 216(l)) in the first month for which he most recently became entitled to a disability insurance benefit.

(3)(A) If the first month for which an individual both is entitled to a wife's, husband's, widow's, or widower's insurance benefit and has attained age 62 (in the case of a wife's or husband's insurance benefit) or age 50 (in the case of a widow's or widower's insurance benefit) is a month for which such individual is also entitled to—

---

[31] P.L. 81-734.

48 SOCIAL SECURITY ACT—§ 202(q)(3)(A)(i)

(i) an old-age insurance benefit (to which such individual was first entitled for a month before he attains retirement age (as defined in section 216(l))), or

(ii) a disability insurance benefit,

then in lieu of any reduction under paragraph (1) (but subject to the succeeding paragraphs of this subsection) such wife's, husband's, widow's, or widower's insurance benefit for each month shall be reduced as provided in subparagraph (B), (C), or (D).

(B) For any month for which such individual is entitled to an old-age insurance benefit and is not entitled to a disability insurance benefit, such individual's wife's or husband's insurance benefit shall be reduced by the sum of—

(i) the amount by which such old-age insurance benefit is reduced under paragraph (1) for such month, and

(ii) the amount by which such wife's or husband's insurance benefit would be reduced under paragraph (1) for such month if it were equal to the excess of such wife's or husband's insurance benefit (before reduction under this subsection) over such old-age insurance benefit (before reduction under this subsection).

(C) For any month for which such individual is entitled to a disability insurance benefit, such individual's wife's, husband's, widow's, or widower's insurance benefit shall be reduced by the sum of—

(i) the amount by which such disability insurance benefit is reduced under paragraph (2) for such month (if such paragraph applied to such benefit), and

(ii) the amount by which such wife's, husband's, widow's, or widower's insurance benefit would be reduced under paragraph (1) for such month if it were equal to the excess of such wife's, husband's, widow's, or widower's insurance benefit (before reduction under this subsection) over such disability insurance benefit (before reduction under this subsection).

(D) For any month for which such individual is entitled neither to an old-age insurance benefit nor to a disability insurance benefit, such individual's wife's, husband's, widow's, or widower's insurance benefit shall be reduced by the amount by which it would be reduced under paragraph (1).

(E) Notwithstanding subparagraph (A) of this paragraph, if the first month for which an individual is entitled to a widow's or widower's insurance benefit is a month for which such individual is also entitled to an old-age insurance benefit to which such individual was first entitled for that month or for a month before she or he became entitled to a widow's or widower's benefit, the reduction in such widow's or widower's insurance benefit shall be determined under paragraph (1).

(4) If—

(A) an individual is or was entitled to a benefit subject to reduction under paragraph (1) or (3) of this subsection, and

(B) such benefit is increased by reason of an increase in the primary insurance amount of the individual on whose wages and self-employment income such benefit is based,

then the amount of the reduction of such benefit (after the application of any adjustment under paragraph (7)) for each month beginning with the month of such increase in the primary insurance amount shall be computed under paragraph (1) or (3), whichever applies, as though the increased primary insurance amount had been in effect for and after the month for which the individual first became entitled to such monthly benefit reduced under such paragraph (1) or (3).

(5)(A) No wife's or husband's insurance benefit shall be reduced under this subsection—

(i) for any month before the first month for which there is in effect a certificate filed by him or her with the Commissioner of Social Security, in accordance with regulations prescribed by the Commissioner of Social Security, in which he or she elects to receive wife's or husband's insurance benefits reduced as provided in this subsection, or

(ii) for any month in which he or she has in his or her care (individually or jointly with the person on whose wages and self-employment income the wife's or husband's insurance benefit is based) a child of such person entitled to child's insurance benefits.

(B) Any certificate described in subparagraph (A)(i) shall be effective for purposes of this subsection (and for purposes of preventing deductions under section 203(c)(2))—

(i) for the month in which it is filed and for any month thereafter, and

(ii) for months, in the period designated by the individual filing such certificate, of one or more consecutive months (not exceeding 12) immediately preceding the month in which such certificate is filed;

except that such certificate shall not be effective for any month before the month in which he or she attains age 62, nor shall it be effective for any month to which subparagraph (A)(ii) applies.

(C) If an individual does not have in his or her care a child described in subparagraph (A)(ii) in the first month for which he or she is entitled to a wife's or husband's insurance benefit, and if such first month is a month before the month in which he or she attains retirement age (as defined in section 216(l)), he or she shall be deemed to have filed in such first month the certificate described in subparagraph (A)(i).

(D) No widow's or widower's insurance benefit for a month in which he or she has in his or her care a child of his or her deceased spouse (or deceased former spouse) entitled to child's insurance benefits shall be reduced under this subsection below the amount to which he or she would have been entitled had he or she been entitled for such month to mother's or father's insurance benefits on the basis of his or her deceased spouse's (or deceased former spouse's) wages and self-employment income.

(6) For purposes of this subsection, the "reduction period" for an individual's old-age, wife's, husband's, widow's, or widower's insurance benefit is the period—

(A) beginning—

(i) in the case of an old-age insurance benefit, with the first day of the first month for which such individual is entitled to such benefit,

(ii) in the case of a wife's or husband's insurance benefit, with the first day of the first month for which a certificate described in paragraph (5)(A)(i) is effective, or

(iii) in the case of a widow's or widower's insurance benefit, with the first day of the first month for which such individual is entitled to such benefit or the first day of the month in which such individual attains age 60, whichever is the later, and

(B) ending with the last day of the month before the month in which such individual attains retirement age.

(7) For purposes of this subsection, the "adjusted reduction period" for an individual's old-age, wife's, husband's, widow's, or widower's insurance benefit is the reduction period prescribed in paragraph (6) for such benefit, excluding—

(A) any month in which such benefit was subject to deductions under section 203(b), 203(c)(1), 203(d)(1), or 222(b),

(B) in the case of wife's or husband's insurance benefits, any month in which such individual had in his or her care (individually or jointly with the person on whose wages and self-employment income such benefit is based) a child of such person entitled to child's insurance benefits,

(C) in the case of wife's or husband's insurance benefits, any month for which such individual was not entitled to such benefits because of the occurrence of an event that terminated her or his entitlement to such benefits,

(D) in the case of widow's or widower's insurance benefits, any month in which the reduction in the amount of such benefit was determined under paragraph (5)(D),

(E) in the case of widow's or widower's insurance benefits, any month before the month in which she or he attained age 62, and also for any later month before the month in which she or he attained retirement age, for which she or he was not entitled to such benefit because of the occurrence of an event that terminated her or his entitlement to such benefits, and

(F) in the case of old-age insurance benefits, any month for which such individual was entitled to a disability insurance benefit.

(8) This subsection shall be applied after reduction under section 203(a) and before application of section 215(g). If the amount of any reduction computed under paragraph (1), (2), or (3) is not a multiple of $0.10, it shall be increased to the next higher multiple of $0.10.

(9) The amount of the reduction for early retirement specified in paragraph (1)—

(A) for old-age insurance benefits, wife's insurance benefits, and husband's insurance benefits, shall be the amount specified in such paragraph for the first 36 months of the reduction period (as defined in paragraph (6)) or adjusted reduction period (as defined in paragraph (7)), and five-twelfths of 1 percent for any additional months included in such periods; and

(B) for widow's insurance benefits and widower's insurance benefits, shall be periodically revised by the Commissioner of Social Security such that—

(i) the amount of the reduction at early retirement age as defined in section 216(l) shall be 28.5 percent of the full benefit; and

(ii) the amount of the reduction for each month in the reduction period (specified in paragraph (6)) or the adjusted reduction period (specified in paragraph (7)) shall be established by linear interpolation between 28.5 percent at the

SOCIAL SECURITY ACT—§ 202(q)(11)   51

month of attainment of early retirement age and 0 percent at the month of attainment of retirement age.

(10) For purposes of applying paragraph (4), with respect to monthly benefits payable for any month after December 1977 to an individual who was entitled to a monthly benefit as reduced under paragraph (1) or (3) prior to January 1978, the amount of reduction in such benefit for the first month for which such benefit is increased by reason of an increase in the primary insurance amount of the individual on whose wages and self-employment income such benefit is based and for all subsequent months (and similarly for all subsequent increases) shall be increased by a percentage equal to the percentage increase in such primary insurance amount (such increase being made in accordance with the provisions of paragraph (8)). In the case of an individual whose reduced benefit under this section is increased as a result of the use of an adjusted reduction period (in accordance with paragraphs (1) and (3) of this subsection), then for the first month for which such increase is effective, and for all subsequent months, the amount of such reduction (after the application of the previous sentence, if applicable) shall be determined—

(A) in the case of old-age, wife's, and husband's insurance benefits, by multiplying such amount by the ratio of (i) the number of months in the adjusted reduction period to (ii) the number of months in the reduction period,

(B) in the case of widow's and widower's insurance benefits for the month in which such individual attains age 62, by multiplying such amount by the ratio of (i) the number of months in the reduction period beginning with age 62 multiplied by $19/40$ of 1 percent, plus the number of months in the adjusted reduction period prior to age 62 multiplied by $19/40$ of 1 percent to (ii) the number of months in the reduction period multiplied by $19/40$ of 1 percent, and

(C) in the case of widow's and widower's insurance benefits for the month in which such individual attains retirement age (as defined in section 216(l)), by multiplying such amount by the ratio of (i) the number of months in the adjusted reduction period multiplied by $19/40$ of 1 percent to (ii) the number of months in the reduction period beginning with age 62 multiplied by $19/40$ of 1 percent, plus the number of months in the adjusted reduction period prior to age 62 multiplied by $19/40$ of 1 percent,

such determination being made in accordance with the provisions of paragraph (8).

(11) When an individual is entitled to more than one monthly benefit under this title and one or more of such benefits are reduced under this subsection, paragraph (10) shall apply separately to each such benefit reduced under this subsection before the application of subsection (k) (pertaining to the method by which monthly benefits are offset when an individual is entitled to more than one kind of benefit) and the application of this paragraph shall operate in conjunction with paragraph (3).

Presumed Filing of Application by Individuals Eligible for Old-Age Insurance Benefits and for Wife's or Husband's Insurance Benefits

(r)(1) If the first month for which an individual is entitled to an old-age insurance benefit is a month before the month in which such individual attains retirement age (as defined in section 216(l)), and if such individual is eligible for a wife's or husband's insurance benefit for such first month, such individual shall be deemed to have filed an application in such month for wife's or husband's insurance benefits.

(2) If the first month for which an individual is entitled to a wife's or husband's insurance benefit reduced under subsection (q) is a month before the month in which such individual attains retirement age (as defined in section 216(l)), and if such individual is eligible (but for section 202(k)(4)) for an old-age insurance benefit for such first month, such individual shall be deemed to have filed an application for old-age insurance benefits—

(A) in such month, or

(B) if such individual is also entitled to a disability insurance benefit for such month, in the first subsequent month for which such individual is not entitled to a disability insurance benefit.

(3) For purposes of this subsection, an individual shall be deemed eligible for a benefit for a month if, upon filing application therefor in such month, he would be entitled to such benefit for such month.

Child Over Specified Age to be Disregarded for Certain Benefit Purposes Unless Disabled

(s)(1) For the purposes of subsections (b)(1), (c)(1), (g)(1), (q)(5), and (q)(7) of this section and paragraphs (2), (3), and (4) of section 203(c), a child who is entitled to child's insurance benefits under subsection (d) for any month, and who has attained the age of 16 but is not in such month under a disability (as defined in section 223(d)), shall be deemed not entitled to such benefits for such month, unless he was under such a disability in the third month before such month.

(2) So much of subsections (b)(3), (c)(4), (d)(5), (g)(3), and (h)(4) of this section as precedes the semicolon, shall not apply in the case of any child unless such child, at the time of the marriage referred to therein, was under a disability (as defined in section 223(d)) or had been under such a disability in the third month before the month in which such marriage occurred.

(3) The last sentence of subsection (c) of section 203, subsection (f)(1)(C) of section 203, and subsections (b)(3)(B), (c)(6)(B), (f)(3)(B), and (g)(6)(B) of section 216 shall not apply in the case of any child with respect to any month referred to therein unless in such month or the third month prior thereto such child was under a disability (as defined in section 223(d)).

Suspension of Benefits of Aliens Who Are Outside the United States; Residency Requirements for Dependents and Survivors

(t)(1) Notwithstanding any other provision of this title, no monthly benefits shall be paid under this section or under section 223 to any

SOCIAL SECURITY ACT—§ 202(t)(4)(D)   53

individual who is not a citizen or national of the United States for any month which is—

(A) after the sixth consecutive calendar month during all of which the Commissioner of Social Security finds, on the basis of information furnished to the Commissioner by the Attorney General or information which otherwise comes to the Commissioner's attention, that such individual is outside the United States, and

(B) prior to the first month thereafter for all of which such individual has been in the United States.

For purposes of the preceding sentence, after an individual has been outside the United States for any period of thirty consecutive days he shall be treated as remaining outside the United States until he has been in the United States for a period of thirty consecutive days.

(2) Subject to paragraph (11), paragraph (1) shall not apply to any individual who is a citizen of a foreign country which the Commissioner of Social Security finds has in effect a social insurance or pension system which is of general application in such country and under which—

(A) periodic benefits, or the actuarial equivalent thereof, are paid on account of old age, retirement, or death, and

(B) individuals who are citizens of the United States but not citizens of such foreign country and who qualify for such benefits are permitted to receive such benefits or the actuarial equivalent thereof while outside such foreign country without regard to the duration of the absence.

(3) Paragraph (1) shall not apply in any case where its application would be contrary to any treaty obligation of the United States in effect on the date of the enactment of this subsection[32].

(4) Subject to paragraph (11), paragraph (1) shall not apply to any benefit for any month if—

(A) not less than forty of the quarters elapsing before such month are quarters of coverage for the individual on whose wages; and self-employment income such benefit is based, or

(B) the individual on whose wages and self-employment income such benefit is based has, before such month, resided in the United States for a period or periods aggregating ten years or more, or

(C) the individual entitled to such benefit is outside the United States while in the active military or naval service of the United States, or

(D) the individual on whose wages and self-employment income such benefit is based died, before such month, either (i) while on active duty or inactive duty training (as those terms are defined in section 210(l)(2) and (3)) as a member of a uniformed service (as defined in section 210(m)), or (ii) as the result of a disease or injury which the Secretary of Veterans Affairs determines was incurred or aggravated in line of duty while on active duty (as defined in section 210(l)(2)), or an injury which he determines was incurred or aggravated in line of duty while on inactive duty training (as defined in section 210(l)(3)), as a member of a uniformed service (as defined in section 210(m)), if the Secretary of Veterans Affairs determines that such individual was discharged or released from

---

[32] August 1, 1956 [P.L. 84-880, §118(a); 70 Stat. 835, 856].

54   SOCIAL SECURITY ACT—§ 202(t)(4)(D)(cont)

the period of such active duty or inactive duty training under conditions other than dishonorable, and if the Secretary of Veterans Affairs certifies to the Commissioner of Social Security his determinations with respect to such individual under this clause, or

(E) the individual on whose employment such benefit is based had been in service covered by the Railroad Retirement Act of 1937 or 1974[33] which was treated as employment covered by this Act pursuant to the provisions of section 5(k)(1) of the Railroad Retirement Act of 1937 or section 18(2) of the Railroad Retirement Act of 1974[34];

except that subparagraphs (A) and (B) of this paragraph shall not apply in the case of any individual who is a citizen of a foreign country that has in effect a social insurance or pension system which is of general application in such country and which satisfies subparagraph (A) but not subparagraph (B) of paragraph (2), or who is a citizen of a foreign country that has no social insurance or pension system of general application if at any time within five years prior to the month in which the Social Security Amendments of 1967 are enacted[35] (or the first month thereafter for which his benefits are subject to suspension under paragraph (1)) payments to individuals residing in such country were withheld by the Treasury Department under the first section of the Act of October 9, 1940 (31 U.S.C. 123)[36].

(5) No person who is, or upon application would be, entitled to a monthly benefit under this section for December 1956 shall be deprived, by reason of paragraph (1), of such benefit or any other benefit based on the wages and self-employment income of the individual on whose wages and self-employment income such monthly benefit for December 1956 is based.

(6) If an individual is outside the United States when he dies and no benefit may, by reason of paragraph (1) or (10), be paid to him for the month preceding the month in which he dies, no lump-sum death payment may be made on the basis of such individual's wages and self-employment income.

(7) Subsections (b), (c), and (d) of section 203 shall not apply with respect to any individual for any month for which no monthly benefit may be paid to him by reason of paragraph (1) of this subsection.

(8) The Attorney General shall certify to the Commissioner of Social Security such information regarding aliens who depart from the United States to any foreign country (other than a foreign country which is territorially contiguous to the continental United States) as may be necessary to enable the Commissioner of Social Security to carry out the purposes of this subsection and shall otherwise aid, assist, and cooperate with the Commissioner of Social Security in obtaining such other information as may be necessary to enable the Commissioner of Social Security to carry out the purposes of this subsection.

(9) No payments shall be made under part A of title XVIII with respect to items or services furnished to an individual in any month for which the prohibition in paragraph (1) against payment of benefits to him is applicable (or would be if he were entitled to any such benefits).

---

[33] P.L. 75-162.
[34] See Vol. II, P.L. 75-162, §18(2).
[35] January 2, 1968 [P.L. 90-248; 81 Stat. 821].
[36] P.L. 97-258, §5(b), repealed the Act of October 9, 1940. See, instead, Vol. II, 31 U.S.C. 3329.

SOCIAL SECURITY ACT—§ 202(t)(11)(C)(ii)(II) 55

(10) Notwithstanding any other provision of this title, no monthly benefits shall be paid under this section or under section 223, for any month beginning after June 30, 1968, to an individual who is not a citizen or national of the United States and who resides during such month in a foreign country if payments for such month to individuals residing in such country are withheld by the Treasury Department under the first section of the Act of October 9, 1940 (31 U.S.C. 123)[37].

(11)(A) Paragraph (2) and subparagraphs (A), (B), (C), and (E) of paragraph (4) shall apply with respect to an individual's monthly benefits under subsection (b), (c), (d), (e), (f), (g), or (h) only if such individual meets the residency requirements of this paragraph with respect to those benefits.

(B) An individual entitled to benefits under subsection (b), (c), (e), (f), or (g) meets the residency requirements of this paragraph with respect to those benefits only if such individual has resided in the United States, and while so residing bore a spousal relationship to the person on whose wages and self-employment income such entitlement is based, for a total period of not less than 5 years. For purposes of this subparagraph, a period of time for which an individual bears a spousal relationship to another person consists of a period throughout which the individual has been, with respect to such other person, a wife, a husband, a widow, a widower, a divorced wife, a divorced husband, a surviving divorced wife, a surviving divorced husband, a surviving divorced mother, a surviving divorced father, or (as applicable in the course of such period) any two or more of the foregoing.

(C) An individual entitled to benefits under subsection (d) meets the residency requirements of this paragraph with respect to those benefits only if—

(i)(I) such individual has resided in the United States (as the child of the person on whose wages and self-employment income such entitlement is based) for a total period of not less than 5 years, or

(II) the person on whose wages and self-employment income such entitlement is based, and the individual's other parent (within the meaning of subsection (h)(3)), if any, have each resided in the United States for a total period of not less than 5 years (or died while residing in the United States), and

(ii) in the case of an individual entitled to such benefits as an adopted child, such individual was adopted within the United States by the person on whose wages and self-employment income such entitlement is based, and has lived in the United States with such person and received at least one-half of his or her support from such person for a period (beginning before such individual attained age 18) consisting of—

(I) the year immediately before the month in which such person became eligible for old-age insurance benefits or disability insurance benefits or died, whichever occurred first, or

(II) if such person had a period of disability which continued until he or she became entitled to old-age insurance benefits or disability insurance benefits or died,

---

[37] P.L. 97-258, §5(b), repealed the Act of October 9, 1940. See, instead, Vol. II, 31 U.S.C. 3329.

56 SOCIAL SECURITY ACT—§ 202(t)(11)(C)(ii)(II)(cont)

the year immediately before the month in which such period of disability began.

(D) An individual entitled to benefits under subsection (h) meets the residency requirements of this paragraph with respect to those benefits only if such individual has resided in the United States, and while so residing was a parent (within the meaning of subsection (h)(3)) of the person on whose wages and self-employment income such entitlement is based, for a total period of not less than 5 years.

(E) This paragraph shall not apply with respect to any individual who is a citizen or resident of a foreign country with which the United States has an agreement in force concluded pursuant to section 233, except to the extent provided by such agreement.

Conviction of Subversive Activities, Etc.

(u)(1) If any individual is convicted of any offense (committed after the date of the enactment of this subsection[38]) under—

(A) chapter 37 (relating to espionage and censorship), chapter 105 (relating to sabotage), or chapter 115 (relating to treason, sedition, and subversive activities) of title 18 of the United States Code[39], or

(B) section 4 of the Internal Security Act of 1950[40], as amended, then the court may, in addition to all other penalties provided by law, impose a penalty that in determining whether any monthly insurance benefit under this section or section 223 is payable to such individual for the month in which he is convicted or for any month thereafter, in determining the amount of any such benefit payable to such individual for any such month, and in determining whether such individual is entitled to insurance benefits under part A of title XVIII for any such month, there shall not be taken into account—

(C) any wages paid to such individual or to any other individual in the calendar year in which such conviction occurs or in any prior calendar year, and

(D) any net earnings from self-employment derived by such individual or by any other individual during a taxable year in which such conviction occurs or during any prior taxable year.

(2) As soon as practicable after an additional penalty has, pursuant to paragraph (1), been imposed with respect to any individual, the Attorney General shall notify the Commissioner of Social Security of such imposition.

(3) If any individual with respect to whom an additional penalty has been imposed pursuant to paragraph (1) is granted a pardon of the offense by the President of the United States, such additional penalty shall not apply for any month beginning after the date on which such pardon is granted.

Waiver of Benefits

(v)(1) Notwithstanding any other provisions of this title, and subject to paragraph (3), in the case of any individual who files a waiver pur-

---

[38] August 1, 1956 [P.L. 84-880, §121(a); 70 Stat. 838, 856].
[39] See Vol. II, 18 U.S.C. chapters 37, 105, and 115.
[40] See Vol. II, P.L. 81-831, §4.

suant to section 1402(g) of the Internal Revenue Code of 1986[41] and is granted a tax exemption thereunder, no benefits or other payments shall be payable under this title to him, no payments shall be made on his behalf under part A of title XVIII, and no benefits or other payments under this title shall be payable on the basis of his wages and self-employment income to any other person, after the filing of such waiver.

(2) Notwithstanding any other provision of this title, and subject to paragraph (3), in the case of any individual who files a waiver pursuant to section 3127 of the Internal Revenue Code of 1986 and is granted a tax exemption thereunder, no benefits or other payments shall be payable under this title to him, no payments shall be made on his behalf under part A of title XVIII, and no benefits or other payments under this title shall be payable on the basis of his wages and self-employment income to any other person, after the filing of such waiver.

(3) If, after an exemption referred to in paragraph (1) or (2) is granted to an individual, such exemption ceases to be effective, the waiver referred to in such paragraph shall cease to be applicable in the case of benefits and other payments under this title and part A of title XVIII to the extent based on—

(A) his wages for and after the calendar year following the calendar year in which occurs the failure to meet the requirements of section 1402(g) or 3127 of the Internal Revenue Code of 1986[42] on which the cessation of such exemption is based, and

(B) his self-employment income for and after the taxable year in which occurs such failure.

Increase in Old-Age Insurance Benefit Amounts on Account of Delayed Retirement

(w)(1) The amount of an old-age insurance benefit (other than a benefit based on a primary insurance amount determined under section 215(a)(3) as in effect in December 1978 or section 215(a)(1)(C)(i) as in effect thereafter) which is payable without regard to this subsection to an individual shall be increased by—

(A) the applicable percentage (as determined under paragraph (6)) of such amount, multiplied by

(B) the number (if any) of the increment months for such individual.

(2) For purposes of this subsection, the number of increment months for any individual shall be a number equal to the total number of the months—

(A) which have elapsed after the month before the month in which such individual attained retirement age (as defined in section 216(l)) or (if later) December 1970 and prior to the month in which such individual attained age 70, and

(B) with respect to which—

(i) such individual was a fully insured individual (as defined in section 214(a)),

---

[41] See Vol. II, P.L. 83-591, §1402(g).
[42] See Vol. II, P.L. 83-591, §§1402(g) and 3127.

(ii) such individual either was not entitled to an old-age insurance benefit or, if so entitled, did not receive benefits pursuant to a request by such individual that benefits not be paid, and

(iii) such individual was not subject to a penalty imposed under section 1129A.

(3) For purposes of applying the provisions of paragraph (1), a determination shall be made under paragraph (2) for each year, beginning with 1972, of the total number of an individual's increment months through the year for which the determination is made and the total so determined shall be applicable to such individual's old-age insurance benefits beginning with benefits for January of the year following the year for which such determination is made; except that the total number applicable in the case of an individual who attains age 70 after 1972 shall be determined through the month before the month in which he attains such age and shall be applicable to his old-age insurance benefit beginning with the month in which he attains such age.

(4) This subsection shall be applied after reduction under section 203(a).

(5) If an individual's primary insurance amount is determined under paragraph (3) of section 215(a) as in effect in December 1978, or section 215(a)(1)(C)(i) as in effect thereafter, and, as a result of this subsection, he would be entitled to a higher old-age insurance benefit if his primary insurance amount were determined under section 215(a) (whether before, in, or after December 1978) without regard to such paragraph, such individual's old-age insurance benefit based upon his primary insurance amount determined under such paragraph shall be increased by an amount equal to the difference between such benefit and the benefit to which he would be entitled if his primary insurance amount were determined under such section without regard to such paragraph.

(6) For purposes of paragraph (1)(A), the "applicable percentage" is—

(A) $1/12$ of 1 percent in the case of an individual who first becomes eligible for an old-age insurance benefit in any calendar year before 1979;

(B) $1/4$ of 1 percent in the case of an individual who first becomes eligible for an old-age insurance benefit in any calendar year after 1978 and before 1987;

(C) in the case of an individual who first becomes eligible for an old-age insurance benefit in a calendar year after 1986 and before 2005, a percentage equal to the applicable percentage in effect under this paragraph for persons who first became eligible for an old-age insurance benefit in the preceding calendar year (as increased pursuant to this subparagraph), plus $1/24$ of 1 percent if the calendar year in which that particular individual first becomes eligible for such benefit is not evenly divisible by 2; and

(D) $2/3$ of 1 percent in the case of an individual who first becomes eligible for an old-age insurance benefit in a calendar year after 2004.

Limitation on Payments to Prisoners, Certain Other Inmates of Publicly Funded Institutions, Fugitives, Probationers, and Parolees

(x)(1)(A) Notwithstanding any other provision of this title, no monthly benefits shall be paid under this section or under section 223 to any individual for any month ending with or during or beginning with or during a period of more than 30 days throughout all of which such individual—

(i) is confined in a jail, prison, or other penal institution or correctional facility pursuant to his conviction of a criminal offense,

(ii) is confined by court order in an institution at public expense in connection with—

(I) a verdict or finding that the individual is guilty but insane, with respect to a criminal offense,

(II) a verdict or finding that the individual is not guilty of such an offense by reason of insanity,

(III) a finding that such individual is incompetent to stand trial under an allegation of such an offense, or

(IV) a similar verdict or finding with respect to such an offense based on similar factors (such as a mental disease, a mental defect, or mental incompetence),

(iii) immediately upon completion of confinement as described in clause (i) pursuant to conviction of a criminal offense an element of which is sexual activity, is confined by court order in an institution at public expense pursuant to a finding that the individual is a sexually dangerous person or a sexual predator or a similar finding,

(iv) is fleeing to avoid prosecution, or custody or confinement after conviction, under the laws of the place from which the person flees, for a crime, or an attempt to commit a crime, which is a felony under the laws of the place from which the person flees, or, in jurisdictions that do not define crimes as felonies, is punishable by death or imprisonment for a term exceeding 1 year regardless of the actual sentence imposed, or

(v) is violating a condition of probation or parole imposed under Federal or State law.

(B)(i) For purposes of clause (i) of subparagraph (A), an individual shall not be considered confined in an institution comprising a jail, prison, or other penal institution or correctional facility during any month throughout which such individual is residing outside such institution at no expense (other than the cost of monitoring) to such institution or the penal system or to any agency to which the penal system has transferred jurisdiction over the individual.

(ii) For purposes of clause (ii) of subparagraph (A), an individual confined in an institution as described in such clause (ii) shall be treated as remaining so confined until—

(I) he or she is released from the care and supervision of such institution, and

(II) such institution ceases to meet the individual's basic living needs.

(iii) Notwithstanding subparagraph (A), the Commissioner shall, for good cause shown, pay the individual benefits that have been withheld or would otherwise be withheld pursuant to clause (iv) or (v) of subparagraph (A) if the Commissioner determines that—

60   SOCIAL SECURITY ACT—§ 202(x)(1)(B)(iii)(I)

(I) a court of competent jurisdiction has found the individual not guilty of the criminal offense, dismissed the charges relating to the criminal offense, vacated the warrant for arrest of the individual for the criminal offense, or issued any similar exonerating order (or taken similar exonerating action), or

(II) the individual was erroneously implicated in connection with the criminal offense by reason of identity fraud.

(iv) Notwithstanding subparagraph (A), the Commissioner may, for good cause shown based on mitigating circumstances, pay the individual benefits that have been withheld or would otherwise be withheld pursuant to clause (iv) or (v) of subparagraph (A) if the Commissioner determines that—

(I) the offense described in clause (iv) or underlying the imposition of the probation or parole described in clause (v) was nonviolent and not drug-related, and

(II) in the case of an individual from whom benefits have been withheld or otherwise would be withheld pursuant to subparagraph (A)(v), the action that resulted in the violation of a condition of probation or parole was nonviolent and not drug-related.

(2) Benefits which would be payable to any individual (other than a confined individual to whom benefits are not payable by reason of paragraph (1)) under this title on the basis of the wages and self-employment income of such a confined individual but for the provisions of paragraph (1), shall be payable as though such confined individual were receiving such benefits under this section or section 223.

(3)(A) Notwithstanding the provisions of section 552a of title 5, United States Code[43], or any other provision of Federal or State law, any agency of the United States Government or of any State (or political subdivision thereof) shall make available to the Commissioner of Social Security, upon written request, the name and social security account number of any individual who is confined as described in paragraph (1) if the confinement is under the jurisdiction of such agency and the Commissioner of Social Security requires such information to carry out the provisions of this section.

(B)(i) The Commissioner shall enter into an agreement under this subparagraph with any interested State or local institution comprising a jail, prison, penal institution, or correctional facility, or comprising any other institution a purpose of which is to confine individuals as described in paragraph (1)(A)(ii). Under such agreement—

(I) the institution shall provide to the Commissioner, on a monthly basis and in a manner specified by the Commissioner, the names, Social Security account numbers, dates of birth, confinement commencement dates, and, to the extent available to the institution, such other identifying information concerning the individuals confined in the institution as the Commissioner may require for the purpose of carrying out paragraph (1) and other provisions of this title; and

(II) the Commissioner shall pay to the institution, with respect to information described in subclause (I) concerning each individual who is confined therein as described in paragraph (1)(A), who receives a benefit under this title for the month

---

[43] See Vol. II, 5 U.S.C. 552a.

SOCIAL SECURITY ACT—§ 203(a)(1)   61

preceding the first month of such confinement, and whose benefit under this title is determined by the Commissioner to be not payable by reason of confinement based on the information provided by the institution, $400 (subject to reduction under clause (ii)) if the institution furnishes the information to the Commissioner within 30 days after the date such individual's confinement in such institution begins, or $200 (subject to reduction under clause (ii)) if the institution furnishes the information after 30 days after such date but within 90 days after such date.

(ii) The dollar amounts specified in clause (i)(II) shall be reduced by 50 percent if the Commissioner is also required to make a payment to the institution with respect to the same individual under an agreement entered into under section 1611(e)(1)(I).

(iii) There are authorized to be transferred from the Federal Old-Age and Survivors Insurance Trust Fund and the Federal Disability Insurance Trust Fund, as appropriate, such sums as may be necessary to enable the Commissioner to make payments to institutions required by clause (i)(II).

(iv) The Commissioner shall maintain, and shall provide on a reimbursable basis, information obtained pursuant to agreements entered into under this paragraph to any agency administering a Federal or federally-assisted cash, food, or medical assistance program for eligibility and other administrative purposes under such program.

(C) Notwithstanding the provisions of section 552a of title 5, United States Code[44], or any other provision of Federal or State law (other than section 6103 of the Internal Revenue Code of 1986[45] and section 1106(c) of this Act), the Commissioner shall furnish any Federal, State, or local law enforcement officer, upon the written request of the officer, with the current address, Social Security number, and photograph (if applicable) of any beneficiary under this title, if the officer furnishes the Commissioner with the name of the beneficiary, and other identifying information as reasonably required by the Commissioner to establish the unique identity of the beneficiary, and notifies the Commissioner that—

(i) the beneficiary is described in clause (iv) or (v) of paragraph (1)(A); and

(ii) the location or apprehension of the beneficiary is within the officer's official duties.

(y) Notwithstanding any other provision of law, no monthly benefit under this title shall be payable to any alien in the United States for any month during which such alien is not lawfully present in the United States as determined by the Attorney General.

REDUCTION OF INSURANCE BENEFITS

Maximum Benefits

SEC. 203. [42 U.S.C. 403] (a)(1) In the case of an individual whose primary insurance amount has been computed or recomputed under section 215(a)(1) or (4), or section 215(d), as in effect after December 1978, the total monthly benefits to which beneficiaries may be entitled

---

[44] See Vol. II, 5 U.S.C. 552a.
[45] See Vol. II, P.L. 83-591, §6103.

62 SOCIAL SECURITY ACT—§ 203(a)(1)(cont)

under section 202 or 223 for a month on the basis of the wages and self-employment income of such individual shall, except as provided by paragraphs (3) and (6) (but prior to any increases resulting from the application of paragraph (2)(A)(ii)(III) of section 215(i)), be reduced as necessary so as not to exceed—

(A) 150 percent of such individual's primary insurance amount to the extent that it does not exceed the amount established with respect to this subparagraph by paragraph (2),

(B) 272 percent of such individual's primary insurance amount to the extent that it exceeds the amount established with respect to subparagraph (A) but does not exceed the amount established with respect to this subparagraph by paragraph (2),

(C) 134 percent of such individual's primary insurance amount to the extent that it exceeds the amount established with respect to subparagraph (B) but does not exceed the amount established with respect to this subparagraph by paragraph (2), and

(D) 175 percent of such individual's primary insurance amount to the extent that it exceeds the amount established with respect to subparagraph (C).

Any such amount that is not a multiple of $0.10 shall be decreased to the next lower multiple of $0.10.

(2)(A) For individuals who initially become eligible for old-age or disability insurance benefits, or who die (before becoming so eligible for such benefits), in the calendar year 1979, the amounts established with respect to subparagraphs (A), (B), and (C) of paragraph (1) shall be $230, $332, and $433, respectively.

(B) For individuals who initially become eligible for old-age or disability insurance benefits, or who die (before becoming so eligible for such benefits), in any calendar year after 1979, each of the amounts so established shall equal the product of the corresponding amount established for the calendar year 1979 by subparagraph (A) of this paragraph and the quotient obtained under subparagraph (B)(ii) of section 215(a)(1), with such product being rounded in the manner prescribed by section 215(a)(1)(B)(iii).

(C) In each calendar year after 1978 the Commissioner of Social Security shall publish in the Federal Register, on or before November 1, the formula which (except as provided in section 215(i)(2)(D)) is to be applicable under this paragraph to individuals who become eligible for old-age or disability insurance benefits, or who die (before becoming eligible for such benefits), in the following calendar year.

(D) A year shall not be counted as the year of an individual's death or eligibility for purposes of this paragraph or paragraph (8) in any case where such individual was entitled to a disability insurance benefit for any of the 12 months immediately preceding the month of such death or eligibility (but there shall be counted instead the year of the individual's eligibility for the disability insurance benefits to which he was entitled during such 12 months).

(3)(A) When an individual who is entitled to benefits on the basis of the wages and self-employment income of any insured individual and to whom this subsection applies would (but for the provisions of section 202(k)(2)(A)) be entitled to child's insurance benefits for a month on the basis of the wages and self-employment income of one or more other insured individuals, the total monthly benefits to which all beneficiaries are entitled on the basis of such wages and self-employment income shall not be reduced under this subsection to less than the smaller of—

(i) the sum of the maximum amounts of benefits payable on the basis of the wages and self-employment income of all such insured individuals, or

(ii) an amount (I) initially equal to the product of 1.75 and the primary insurance amount that would be computed under section 215(a)(1), for January of the year determined for purposes of this clause under the following two sentences, with respect to average indexed monthly earnings equal to one-twelfth of the contribution and benefit base determined for that year under section 230, and (II) thereafter increased in accordance with the provisions of section 215(i)(2)(A)(ii).

The year established for purposes of clause (ii) shall be 1983 or, if it occurs later with respect to any individual, the year in which occurred the month that the application of the reduction provisions contained in this subparagraph began with respect to benefits payable on the basis of the wages and self-employment income of the insured individual. If for any month subsequent to the first month for which clause (ii) applies (with respect to benefits payable on the basis of the wages and self-employment income of the insured individual) the reduction under this subparagraph ceases to apply, then the year determined under the preceding sentence shall be redetermined (for purposes of any subsequent application of this subparagraph with respect to benefits payable on the basis of such wages and self-employment income) as though this subparagraph had not been previously applicable.

(B) When two or more persons were entitled (without the application of section 202(j)(1) and section 223(b)) to monthly benefits under section 202 or 223 for January 1971 or any prior month on the basis of the wages and self-employment income of such insured individual and the provisions of this subsection as in effect for any such month were applicable in determining the benefit amount of any persons on the basis of such wages and self-employment income, the total of benefits for any month after January 1971 shall not be reduced to less than the largest of—

(i) the amount determined under this subsection without regard to this subparagraph,

(ii) the largest amount which has been determined for any month under this subsection for persons entitled to monthly benefits on the basis of such insured individual's wages and self-employment income, or

(iii) if any persons are entitled to benefits on the basis of such wages and self-employment income for the month before the effective month (after September 1972) of a general benefit increase under this title (as defined in section 215(i)(3)) or a benefit increase under the provisions of section 215(i), an amount equal to the sum of amounts derived by multiplying the benefit amount determined under this title (excluding any part thereof determined under section 202(w)) for the month before such effective month (including this subsection, but without the application of section 222(b), section 202(q), and subsections (b), (c), and (d) of this section), for each such person for such month, by a percentage equal to the percentage of the increase provided under such benefit in-

64   SOCIAL SECURITY ACT—§ 203(a)(3)(B)(iii)(cont)

crease (with any such increased amount which is not a multiple of $0.10 being rounded to the next lower multiple of $0.10);
but in any such case (I) subparagraph (A) of this paragraph shall not be applied to such total of benefits after the application of clause (ii) or (iii), and (II) if section 202(k)(2)(A) was applicable in the case of any such benefits for a month, and ceases to apply for a month after such month, the provisions of clause (ii) or (iii) shall be applied, for and after the month in which section 202(k)(2)(A) ceases to apply, as though subparagraph (A) of this paragraph had not been applicable to such total of benefits for the last month for which clause (ii) or (iii) was applicable.

(C) When any of such individuals is entitled to monthly benefits as a divorced spouse under section 202(b) or (c) or as a surviving divorced spouse under section 202(e) or (f) for any month, the benefit to which he or she is entitled on the basis of the wages and self-employment income of such insured individual for such month shall be determined without regard to this subsection, and the benefits of all other individuals who are entitled for such month to monthly benefits under section 202 on the wages and self-employment income of such insured individual shall be determined as if no such divorced spouse or surviving divorced spouse were entitled to benefits for such month.

(D) In any case in which—

(i) two or more individuals are entitled to monthly benefits for the same month as a spouse under subsection (b) or (c) of section 202, or as a surviving spouse under subsection (e), (f), or (g) of section 202,

(ii) at least one of such individuals is entitled by reason of subparagraph (A)(ii) or (B) of section 216(h)(1), and

(iii) such entitlements are based on the wages and self-employment income of the same insured individual,

the benefit of the entitled individual whose entitlement is based on a valid marriage (as determined without regard to subparagraphs (A)(ii) and (B) of section 216(h)(1)) to such insured individual shall, for such month and all months thereafter, be determined without regard to this subsection, and the benefits of all other individuals who are entitled, for such month or any month thereafter, to monthly benefits under section 202 based on the wages and self-employment income of such insured individual shall be determined as if such entitled individual were not entitled to benefits for such month.

(4) In any case in which benefits are reduced pursuant to the provisions of this subsection, the reduction shall be made after any deductions under this section and after any deductions under section 222(b). Notwithstanding the preceding sentence, any reduction under this subsection in the case of an individual who is entitled to a benefit under subsection (b), (c), (d), (e), (f), (g), or (h) of section 202 for any month on the basis of the same wages and self-employment income as another person—

(A) who also is entitled to a benefit under subsection (b), (c), (d), (e), (f), (g), or (h) of section 202 for such month,

(B) who does not live in the same household as such individual, and

(C) whose benefit for such month is suspended (in whole or in part) pursuant to subsection (h)(3) of this section,

SOCIAL SECURITY ACT—§ 203(a)(7)   65

shall be made before the suspension under subsection (h)(3). Whenever a reduction is made under this subsection in the total of monthly benefits to which individuals are entitled for any month on the basis of the wages and self-employment income of an insured individual, each such benefit other than the old-age or disability insurance benefit shall be proportionately decreased.

(5) Notwithstanding any other provision of law, when—

(A) two or more persons are entitled to monthly benefits for a particular month on the basis of the wages and self-employment income of an insured individual and (for such particular month) the provisions of this subsection are applicable to such monthly benefits, and

(B) such individual's primary insurance amount is increased for the following month under any provision of this title,

then the total of monthly benefits for all persons on the basis of such wages and self-employment income for such particular month, as determined under the provisions of this subsection, shall for purposes of determining the total monthly benefits for all persons on the basis of such wages and self-employment income for months subsequent to such particular month be considered to have been increased by the smallest amount that would have been required in order to assure that the total of monthly benefits payable on the basis of such wages and self-employment income for any such subsequent month will not be less (after the application of the other provisions of this subsection and section 202(q)) than the total of monthly benefits (after the application of the other provisions of this subsection and section 202(q)) payable on the basis of such wages and self-employment income for such particular month.

(6) Notwithstanding any of the preceding provisions of this subsection other than paragraphs (3)(A), (3)(C), (3)(D), (4), and (5) (but subject to section 215(i)(2)(A)(ii)), the total monthly benefits to which beneficiaries may be entitled under sections 202 and 223 for any month on the basis of the wages and self-employment income of an individual entitled to disability insurance benefits shall be reduced (before the application of section 224) to the smaller of—

(A) 85 percent of such individual's average indexed monthly earnings (or 100 percent of his primary insurance amount, if larger), or

(B) 150 percent of such individual's primary insurance amount.

(7) In the case of any individual who is entitled for any month to benefits based upon the primary insurance amounts of two or more insured individuals, one or more of which primary insurance amounts were determined under section 215(a) or 215(d) as in effect (without regard to the table contained therein) prior to January 1979 and one or more of which primary insurance amounts were determined under section 215(a)(1) or (4), or section 215(d), as in effect after December 1978, the total benefits payable to that individual and all other individuals entitled to benefits for that month based upon those primary insurance amounts shall be reduced to an amount equal to the amount determined in accordance with the provisions of paragraph (3)(A)(ii) of this subsection, except that for this purpose the references to subparagraph (A) in the last two sentences of paragraph (3)(A) shall be deemed to be references to paragraph (7).

66   SOCIAL SECURITY ACT—§ 203(a)(8)

(8) Subject to paragraph (7) and except as otherwise provided in paragraph (10)(C), this subsection as in effect in December 1978 shall remain in effect with respect to a primary insurance amount computed under section 215(a) or (d), as in effect (without regard to the table contained therein) in December 1978 and as amended by section 5117 of the Omnibus Budget Reconciliation Act of 1990[46], except that a primary insurance amount so computed with respect to an individual who first becomes eligible for an old-age or disability insurance benefit, or dies (before becoming eligible for such a benefit), after December 1978, shall instead be governed by this section as in effect after December 1978. For purposes of the preceding sentence, the phrase "rounded to the next higher multiple of $0.10", as it appeared in subsection (a)(2)(C) of this section as in effect in December 1978, shall be deemed to read "rounded to the next lower multiple of $0.10".

(9) When—
    (A) one or more persons were entitled (without the application of section 202(j)(1)) to monthly benefits under section 202 for May 1978 on the basis of the wages and self-employment income of an individual,
    (B) the benefit of at least one such person for June 1978 is increased by reason of the amendments made by section 204 of the Social Security Amendments of 1977[47]; and
    (C) the total amount of benefits to which all such persons are entitled under such section 202 are reduced under the provisions of this subsection (or would be so reduced except for the first sentence of section 203(a)(4)),
then the amount of the benefit to which each such person is entitled for months after May 1978 shall be increased (after such reductions are made under this subsection) to the amount such benefits would have been if the benefit of the person or persons referred to in subparagraph (B) had not been so increased.

(10)(A) Subject to subparagraphs (B) and (C)—
    (i) the total monthly benefits to which beneficiaries may be entitled under sections 202 and 223 for a month on the basis of the wages and self-employment income of an individual whose primary insurance amount is computed under section 215(a)(2)(B)(i) shall equal the total monthly benefits which were authorized by this section with respect to such individual's primary insurance amount for the last month of his prior entitlement to disability insurance benefits, increased for this purpose by the general benefit increases and other increases under section 215(i) that would have applied to such total monthly benefits had the individual remained entitled to disability insurance benefits until the month in which he became entitled to old-age insurance benefits or reentitled to disability insurance benefits or died, and
    (ii) the total monthly benefits to which beneficiaries may be entitled under sections 202 and 223 for a month on the basis of the wages and self-employment income of an individual whose primary insurance amount is computed under section 215(a)(2)(C) shall equal the total monthly benefits which were authorized by this section with respect to such individual's primary insurance

---

[46] P.L. 101-508.
[47] P.L. 95-216.

amount for the last month of his prior entitlement to disability insurance benefits.

(B) In any case in which—

(i) the total monthly benefits with respect to such individual's primary insurance amount for the last month of his prior entitlement to disability insurance benefits was computed under paragraph (6), and

(ii) the individual's primary insurance amount is computed under subparagraph (B)(i) or (C) of section 215(a)(2) by reason of the individual's entitlement to old-age insurance benefits or death,

the total monthly benefits shall equal the total monthly benefits that would have been authorized with respect to the primary insurance amount for the last month of his prior entitlement to disability insurance benefits if such total monthly benefits had been computed without regard to paragraph (6).

(C) This paragraph shall apply before the application of paragraph (3)(A), and before the application of section 203(a)(1) of this Act as in effect in December 1978.

Deductions on Account of Work

(b)(1) Deductions, in such amounts and at such time or times as the Commissioner of Social Security shall determine, shall be made from any payment or payments under this title to which an individual is entitled, and from any payment or payments to which any other persons are entitled on the basis of such individual's wages and self-employment income, until the total of such deductions equals—

(A) such individual's benefit or benefits under section 202 for any month, and

(B) if such individual was entitled to old-age insurance benefits under section 202(a) for such month, the benefit or benefits of all other persons for such month under section 202 based on such individual's wages and self-employment income,

if for such month he is charged with excess earnings, under the provisions of subsection (f) of this section, equal to the total of benefits referred to in clauses (A) and (B). If the excess earnings so charged are less than such total of benefits, such deductions with respect to such month shall be equal only to the amount of such excess earnings. If a child who has attained the age of 18 and is entitled to child's insurance benefits, or a person who is entitled to mother's or father's insurance benefits, is married to an individual entitled to old-age insurance benefits under section 202(a), such child or such person, as the case may be, shall, for the purposes of this subsection and subsection (f), be deemed to be entitled to such benefits on the basis of the wages and self-employment income of such individual entitled to old-age insurance benefits. If a deduction has already been made under this subsection with respect to a person's benefit or benefits under section 202 for a month, he shall be deemed entitled to payments under such section for such month for purposes of further deductions under this subsection, and for purposes of charging of each person's excess earnings under subsection (f), only to the extent of the total of his benefits remaining after such earlier deductions have been made. For purposes of this subsection and subsection (f)—

(i) an individual shall be deemed to be entitled to payments under section 202 equal to the amount of the benefit or benefits to which he is entitled under such section after the application of subsection (a) of this section, but without the application of the first sentence of paragraph (4) thereof; and

(ii) if a deduction is made with respect to an individual's benefit or benefits under section 202 because of the occurrence in any month of an event specified in subsection (c) or (d) of this section or in section 222(b), such individual shall not be considered to be entitled to any benefits under such section 202 for such month.

(2)(A) Except as provided in subparagraph (B), in any case in which—

(i) any of the other persons referred to in paragraph (1)(B) is entitled to monthly benefits as a divorced spouse under section 202(b) or (c) for any month, and

(ii) such person has been divorced for not less than 2 years,

the benefit to which he or she is entitled on the basis of the wages and self-employment income of the individual referred to in paragraph (1) for such month shall be determined without regard to deductions under this subsection as a result of excess earnings of such individual, and the benefits of all other individuals who are entitled for such month to monthly benefits under section 202 on the basis of the wages and self-employment income of such individual referred to in paragraph (1) shall be determined as if no such divorced spouse were entitled to benefits for such month.

(B) Clause (ii) of subparagraph (A) shall not apply with respect to any divorced spouse in any case in which the individual referred to in paragraph (1) became entitled to old-age insurance benefits under section 202(a) before the date of the divorce.

Deductions on Account of Noncovered Work Outside the United States or Failure to Have Child in Care

(c) Deductions, in such amounts and at such time or times as the Commissioner of Social Security shall determine, shall be made from any payment or payments under this title to which an individual is entitled, until the total of such deductions equals such individual's benefits or benefit under section 202 for any month—

(1) in which such individual is under retirement age (as defined in section 216(l)) and for more than forty-five hours of which such individual engaged in noncovered remunerative activity outside the United States;

(2) in which such individual, if a wife or husband under retirement age (as defined in section 216(l)) entitled to a wife's or husband's insurance benefit, did not have in his or her care (individually or jointly with his or her spouse) a child of such spouse entitled to a child's insurance benefit and such wife's or husband's insurance benefit for such month was not reduced under the provisions of section 202(q);

(3) in which such individual, if a widow or widower entitled to a mother's or father's insurance benefit, did not have in his or her care a child of his or her deceased spouse entitled to a child's insurance benefit; or

SOCIAL SECURITY ACT—§ 203(d)(2)

(4) in which such an individual, if a surviving divorced mother or father entitled to a mother's or father's insurance benefit, did not have in his or her care a child of his or her deceased former spouse who (A) is his or her son, daughter, or legally adopted child and (B) is entitled to a child's insurance benefit on the basis of the wages and self-employment income of such deceased former spouse.

For purposes of paragraphs (2), (3), and (4) of this subsection, a child shall not be considered to be entitled to a child's insurance benefit for any month in which paragraph (1) of section 202(s) applies or an event specified in section 222(b) occurs with respect to such child. Subject to paragraph (3) of such section 202(s), no deduction shall be made under this subsection from any child's insurance benefit for the month in which the child entitled to such benefit attained the age of eighteen or any subsequent month; nor shall any deduction be made under this subsection from any widow's or widower's insurance benefit if the widow, surviving divorced wife, widower, or surviving divorced husband involved became entitled to such benefit prior to attaining age 60.

Deductions From Dependents' Benefits on Account of Noncovered Work Outside the United States by Old–Age Insurance Beneficiary

(d)(1)(A) Deductions shall be made from any wife's, husband's, or child's insurance benefit, based on the wages and self-employment income of an individual entitled to old-age insurance benefits, to which a wife, divorced wife, husband, divorced husband, or child is entitled, until the total of such deductions equals such wife's, husband's, or child's insurance benefit or benefits under section 202 for any month in which such individual is under retirement age (as defined in section 216(l)) and for more than forty-five hours of which such individual engaged in noncovered remunerative activity outside the United States.

(B)(i) Except as provided in clause (ii), in any case in which—

(I) a divorced spouse is entitled to monthly benefits under section 202(b) or (c) for any month, and

(II) such divorced spouse has been divorced for not less than 2 years,

the benefit to which he or she is entitled for such month on the basis of the wages and self-employment income of the individual entitled to old-age insurance benefits referred to in subparagraph (A) shall be determined without regard to deductions under this paragraph as a result of excess earnings of such individual, and the benefits of all other individuals who are entitled for such month to monthly benefits under section 202 on the basis of the wages and self-employment income of such individual referred to in subparagraph (A) shall be determined as if no such divorced spouse were entitled to benefits for such month.

(ii) Subclause (II) of clause (i) shall not apply with respect to any divorced spouse in any case in which the individual entitled to old-age insurance benefits referred to in subparagraph (A) became entitled to such benefits before the date of the divorce.

(2) Deductions shall be made from any child's insurance benefit to which a child who has attained the age of eighteen is entitled, or from

70 SOCIAL SECURITY ACT—§ 203(d)(2)(cont)

any mother's or father's insurance benefit to which a person is entitled, until the total of such deductions equals such child's insurance benefit or benefits or mother's or father's insurance benefit or benefits under section 202 for any month in which such child or person entitled to mother's or father's insurance benefits is married to an individual under retirement age (as defined in section 216(l)), who is entitled to old-age insurance benefits and for more than forty-five hours of which such individual engaged in noncovered remunerative activity outside the United States.

Occurrence of More Than One Event

(e) If more than one of the events specified in subsections (c) and (d) and section 222(b) occurs in any one month which would occasion deductions equal to a benefit for such month, only an amount equal to such benefit shall be deducted.

Months to Which Earnings Are Charged

(f) For purposes of subsection (b)—

(1) The amount of an individual's excess earnings (as defined in paragraph (3)) shall be charged to months as follows: There shall be charged to the first month of such taxable year an amount of his excess earnings equal to the sum of the payments to which he and all other persons (excluding divorced spouses referred to in subsection (b)(2)) are entitled for such month under section 202 on the basis of his wages and self-employment income (or the total of his excess earnings if such excess earnings are less than such sum), and the balance, if any, of such excess earnings shall be charged to each succeeding month in such year to the extent, in the case of each such month, of the sum of the payments to which such individual and all such other persons are entitled for such month under section 202 on the basis of his wages and self-employment income, until the total of such excess has been so charged. Where an individual is entitled to benefits under section 202(a) and other persons (excluding divorced spouses referred to in subsection (b)(2)) are entitled to benefits under section 202(b), (c), or (d) on the basis of the wages and self-employment income of such individual, the excess earnings of such individual for any taxable year shall be charged in accordance with the provisions of this subsection before the excess earnings of such persons for a taxable year are charged to months in such individual's taxable year. Notwithstanding the preceding provisions of this paragraph but subject to section 202(s), no part of the excess earnings of an individual shall be charged to any month (A) for which such individual was not entitled to a benefit under this title, (B) in which such individual was at or above retirement age (as defined in section 216(l)), (C) in which such individual, if a child entitled to child's insurance benefits, has attained the age of 18, (D) for which such individual is entitled to widow's or widower's insurance benefits if such individual became so entitled prior to attaining age 60, (E) in which such individual did not engage in self-employment and did not render services for wages

SOCIAL SECURITY ACT—§ 203(f)(4)(A) 71

(determined as provided in paragraph (5) of this subsection) of more than the applicable exempt amount as determined under paragraph (8), if such month is in the taxable year in which occurs the first month after December 1977 that is both (i) a month for which the individual is entitled to benefits under subsection (a), (b), (c), (d), (e), (f), (g), or (h) of section 202 (without having been entitled for the preceding month to a benefit under any other of such subsections), and (ii) a month in which the individual did not engage in self-employment and did not render services for wages (determined as provided in paragraph (5)) of more than the applicable exempt amount as determined under paragraph (8), or (F) in which such individual did not engage in self-employment and did not render services for wages (determined as provided in paragraph (5) of this subsection) of more than the applicable exempt amount as determined under paragraph (8), in the case of an individual entitled to benefits under section 202(b) or (c) (but only by reason of having a child in his or her care within the meaning of paragraph (1)(B) of subsection (b) or (c), as may be applicable) or under section 202(d) or (g), if such month is in a year in which such entitlement ends for a reason other than the death of such individual, and such individual is not entitled to any benefits under this title for the month following the month during which such entitlement under section 202(b), (d), or (g) ended.

(2) As used in paragraph (1), the term "first month of such taxable year" means the earliest month in such year to which the charging of excess earnings described in such paragraph is not prohibited by the application of clauses (A), (B), (C), (D), (E), and (F) thereof.

(3) For purposes of paragraph (1) and subsection (h), an individual's excess earnings for a taxable year shall be 33 1/3 percent of his earnings for such year in excess of the product of the applicable exempt amount as determined under paragraph (8) in the case of an individual who has attained (or, but for the individual's death, would have attained) retirement age (as defined in section 216(l)) before the close of such taxable year, or 50 percent of his earnings for such year in excess of such product in the case of any other individual, multiplied by the number of months in such year, except that, in determining an individual's excess earnings for the taxable year in which he attains retirement age (as defined in section 216(l)), there shall be excluded any earnings of such individual for the month in which he attains such age and any subsequent month (with any net earnings or net loss from self-employment in such year being prorated in an equitable manner under regulations of the Commissioner of Social Security). For purposes of the preceding sentence, notwithstanding section 211(e), the number of months in the taxable year in which an individual dies shall be 12. The excess earnings as derived under the first sentence of this paragraph, if not a multiple of $1, shall be reduced to the next lower multiple of $1.

(4) For purposes of clause (E) of paragraph (1)—

(A) An individual will be presumed, with respect to any month, to have been engaged in self-employment in such month until it is shown to the satisfaction of the Commis-

72 SOCIAL SECURITY ACT—§ 203(f)(4)(A)(cont)

sioner of Social Security that such individual rendered no substantial services in such month with respect to any trade or business the net income or loss of which is includible in computing (as provided in paragraph (5) of this subsection) his net earnings or net loss from self-employment for any taxable year. The Commissioner of Social Security shall by regulations prescribe the methods and criteria for determining whether or not an individual has rendered substantial services with respect to any trade or business.

(B) An individual will be presumed, with respect to any month, to have rendered services for wages (determined as provided in paragraph (5) of this subsection) of more than the applicable exempt amount as determined under paragraph (8) until it is shown to the satisfaction of the Commissioner of Social Security that such individual did not render such services in such month for more than such amount.

(5)(A) An individual's earnings for a taxable year shall be (i) the sum of his wages for services rendered in such year and his net earnings from self-employment for such year, minus (ii) any net loss from self-employment for such year.

(B) For purposes of this section—

(i) an individual's net earnings from self-employment for any taxable year shall be determined as provided in section 211, except that paragraphs (1), (4), and (5) of section 211(c) shall not apply and the gross income shall be computed by excluding the amounts provided by subparagraph (D), and

(ii) an individual's net loss from self-employment for any taxable year is the excess of the deductions (plus his distributive share of loss described in section 702(a)(8) of the Internal Revenue Code of 1986[48] taken into account under clause (i) over the gross income (plus his distributive share of income so described) taken into account under clause (i).

(C) For purposes of this subsection, an individual's wages shall be computed without regard to the limitations as to amounts of remuneration specified in paragraphs (1), (6)(B), (6)(C), (7)(B), and (8) of section 209(a); and in making such computation services which do not constitute employment as defined in section 210, performed within the United States by the individual as an employee or performed outside the United States in the active military or naval service of the United States, shall be deemed to be employment as so defined if the remuneration for such services is not includible in computing his net earnings or net loss from self-employment. The term "wages" does not include—

(i) the amount of any payment made to, or on behalf of, an employee or any of his dependents (including any amount paid by an employer for insurance or annuities, or into a fund, to provide for any such payment) on account of retirement, or

(ii) any payment or series of payments by an employer to an employee or any of his dependents upon or after the termination of the employee's employment relationship because of retirement after attaining an age specified in a plan re-

---

[48] See Vol. II, P.L. 83-591, §702(a)(8).

SOCIAL SECURITY ACT—§ 203(f)(7)　　　73

ferred to in section 209(a)(11)(B) or in a pension plan of the employer.

(D) In the case of—

(i) an individual who has attained retirement age (as defined in section 216(l)) on or before the last day of the taxable year, and who shows to the satisfaction of the Commissioner of Social Security that he or she is receiving royalties attributable to a copyright or patent obtained before the taxable year in which he or she attained such age and that the property to which the copyright or patent relates was created by his or her own personal efforts, or

(ii) an individual who has become entitled to insurance benefits under this title, other than benefits under section 223 or benefits payable under section 202(d) by reason of being under a disability, and who shows to the satisfaction of the Commissioner of Social Security that he or she is receiving, in a year after his or her initial year of entitlement to such benefits, any other income not attributable to services performed after the month in which he or she initially became entitled to such benefits,

there shall be excluded from gross income any such royalties or other income.

(E) For purposes of this section, any individual's net earnings from self-employment which result from or are attributable to the performance of services by such individual as a director of a corporation during any taxable year shall be deemed to have been derived (and received) by such individual in that year, at the time the services were performed, regardless of when the income, on which the computation of such net earnings from self-employment is based, is actually paid to or received by such individual (unless such income was actually paid and received prior to that year).

(6) For purposes of this subsection, wages (determined as provided in paragraph (5)(C)) which, according to reports received by the Commissioner of Social Security, are paid to an individual during a taxable year shall be presumed to have been paid to him for services performed in such year until it is shown to the satisfaction of the Commissioner of Social Security that they were paid for services performed in another taxable year. If such reports with respect to an individual show his wages for a calendar year, such individual's taxable year shall be presumed to be a calendar year for purposes of this subsection until it is shown to the satisfaction of the Commissioner of Social Security that his taxable year is not a calendar year.

(7) Where an individual's excess earnings are charged to a month and the excess earnings so charged are less than the total of the payments (without regard to such charging) to which all persons (excluding divorced spouses referred to in subsection (b)(2)) are entitled under section 202 for such month on the basis of his wages and self-employment income, the difference between such total and the excess so charged to such month shall be paid (if it is otherwise payable under this title) to such individual and other persons in the proportion that the benefit to which each of them is entitled (without regard to such charging, without the

application of section 202(k)(3), and prior to the application of section 203(a)) bears to the total of the benefits to which all of them are entitled.

(8)(A) Whenever the Commissioner of Social Security pursuant to section 215(i) increases benefits effective with the month of December following a cost-of-living computation quarter he shall also determine and publish in the Federal Register on or before November 1 of the calendar year in which such quarter occurs the new exempt amounts (separately stated for individuals described in subparagraph (D) and for other individuals) which are to be applicable (unless prevented from becoming effective by subparagraph (C)) with respect to taxable years ending in (or with the close of) the calendar year after the calendar year in which such benefit increase is effective (or, in the case of an individual who dies during the calendar year after the calendar year in which the benefit increase is effective, with respect to such individual's taxable year which ends, upon his death, during such year).

(B) Except as otherwise provided in subparagraph (D), the exempt amount which is applicable to individuals described in such subparagraph and the exempt amount which is applicable to other individuals, for each month of a particular taxable year, shall each be whichever of the following is the larger—

(i) the corresponding exempt amount which is in effect with respect to months in the taxable year in which the determination under subparagraph (A) is made, or

(ii) the product of the corresponding exempt amount which is in effect with respect to months in the taxable year ending after 2001 and before 2003 (with respect to individuals described in subparagraph (D)) or the taxable year ending after 1993 and before 1995 (with respect to other individuals), and the ratio of—

(I) the national average wage index (as defined in section 209(k)(1)) for the calendar year before the calendar year in which the determination under subparagraph (A) is made, to

(II) the national average wage index (as so defined) for 2000 (with respect to individuals described in subparagraph (D)) or 1992 (with respect to other individuals),

with such product, if not a multiple of $10, being rounded to the next higher multiple of $10 where such product is a multiple of $5 but not of $10 and to the nearest multiple of $10 in any other case. Whenever the Commissioner of Social Security determines that an exempt amount is to be increased in any year under this paragraph, he shall notify the House Committee on Ways and Means and the Senate Committee on Finance within 30 days after the close of the base quarter (as defined in section 215(i)(1)(A)) in such year of the estimated amount of such increase, indicating the new exempt amount, the actuarial estimates of the effect of the increase, and the actuarial assumptions and methodology used in preparing such estimates.

(C) Notwithstanding the determination of a new exempt amount by the Commissioner of Social Security under subparagraph (A) (and notwithstanding any publication thereof under

SOCIAL SECURITY ACT—§ 203(g)(2)   75

such subparagraph or any notification thereof under the last sentence of subparagraph (B)), such new exempt amount shall not take effect pursuant thereto if during the calendar year in which such determination is made a law increasing the exempt amount is enacted.

(D) Notwithstanding any other provision of this subsection, the exempt amount which is applicable to an individual who has attained retirement age (as defined in section 216(l)) before the close of the taxable year involved shall be—

(i) for each month of any taxable year ending after 1995 and before 1997, $1,041.66 2/3,

(ii) for each month of any taxable year ending after 1996 and before 1998, $1,125.00,

(iii) for each month of any taxable year ending after 1997 and before 1999, $1,208.33 1/3,

(iv) for each month of any taxable year ending after 1998 and before 2000, $1,291.66 2/3,

(v) for each month of any taxable year ending after 1999 and before 2001, $1,416.66 2/3,

(vi) for each month of any taxable year ending after 2000 and before 2002, $2,083.33 1/3,

(vii) for each month of any taxable year ending after 2001 and before 2003, $2,500.00.

(E) Notwithstanding subparagraph (D), no deductions in benefits shall be made under subsection (b) with respect to the earnings of any individual in any month beginning with the month in which the individual attains retirement age (as defined in section 216(l)).

(9) For purposes of paragraphs (3), (5)(D)(i), (8)(D), and (8)(E), the term "retirement age (as defined in section 216(l))", with respect to any individual entitled to monthly insurance benefits under section 202, means the retirement age (as so defined) which is applicable in the case of old-age insurance benefits, regardless of whether or not the particular benefits to which the individual is entitled (or the only such benefits) are old-age insurance benefits.

Penalty for Failure To Report Certain Events

(g) Any individual in receipt of benefits subject to deduction under subsection (c), (or who is in receipt of such benefits on behalf of another individual), because of the occurrence of an event specified therein, who fails to report such occurrence to the Commissioner of Social Security prior to the receipt and acceptance of an insurance benefit for the second month following the month in which such event occurred, shall suffer deductions in addition to those imposed under subsection (c) as follows:

(1) if such failure is the first one with respect to which an additional deduction is imposed by this subsection, such additional deduction shall be equal to his benefit or benefits for the first month of the period for which there is a failure to report even though such failure is with respect to more than one month;

(2) if such failure is the second one with respect to which an additional deduction is imposed by this subsection, such additional

deduction shall be equal to two times his benefit or benefits for the first month of the period for which there is a failure to report even though such failure is with respect to more than two months; and

(3) if such failure is the third or a subsequent one for which an additional deduction is imposed under this subsection, such additional deduction shall be equal to three times his benefit or benefits for the first month of the period for which there is a failure to report even though the failure to report is with respect to more than three months;

except that the number of additional deductions required by this subsection shall not exceed the number of months in the period for which there is a failure to report. As used in this subsection, the term "period for which there is a failure to report" with respect to any individual means the period for which such individual received and accepted insurance benefits under section 202 without making a timely report and for which deductions are required under subsection (c).

Report of Earnings to Commissioner of Social Security

(h)(1)(A) If an individual is entitled to any monthly insurance benefit under section 202 during any taxable year in which he has earnings or wages, as computed pursuant to paragraph (5) of subsection (f), in excess of the product of the applicable exempt amount as determined under subsection (f)(8) times the number of months in such year, such individual (or the individual who is in receipt of such benefit on his behalf) shall make a report to the Commissioner of Social Security of his earnings (or wages) for such taxable year. Such report shall be made on or before the fifteenth day of the fourth month following the close of such year, and shall contain such information and be made in such manner as the Commissioner of Social Security may by regulations prescribe. Such report need not be made for any taxable year—

(i) beginning with or after the month in which such individual attained retirement age (as defined in section 216(l)), or

(ii) if benefit payments for all months (in such taxable year) in which such individual is under retirement age (as defined in section 216(l)) have been suspended under the provisions of the first sentence of paragraph (3) of this subsection, unless—

(I) such individual is entitled to benefits under subsection (b), (c), (d), (e), (f), (g), or (h) of section 202,

(II) such benefits are reduced under subsection (a) of this section for any month in such taxable year, and

(III) in any such month there is another person who also is entitled to benefits under subsection (b), (c), (d), (e), (f), (g), or (h) of section 202 on the basis of the same wages and self-employment income and who does not live in the same household as such individual.

The Commissioner of Social Security may grant a reasonable extension of time for making the report of earnings required in this paragraph if the Commissioner finds that there is valid reason for a delay, but in no case may the period be extended more than four months.

(B) If the benefit payments of an individual have been suspended for all months in any taxable year under the provisions of the first

SOCIAL SECURITY ACT—§ 203(h)(3)   77

sentence of paragraph (3) of this subsection, no benefit payment shall be made to such individual for any such month in such taxable year after the expiration of the period of three years, three months, and fifteen days following the close of such taxable year unless within such period the individual, or some other person entitled to benefits under this title on the basis of the same wages and self-employment income, files with the Commissioner of Social Security information showing that a benefit for such month is payable to such individual.

(2) If an individual fails to make a report required under paragraph (1), within the time prescribed by or in accordance with such paragraph, for any taxable year and any deduction is imposed under subsection (b) by reason of his earnings for such year, he shall suffer additional deductions as follows:

(A) if such failure is the first one with respect to which an additional deduction is imposed under this paragraph, such additional deduction shall be equal to his benefit or benefits for the last month of such year for which he was entitled to a benefit under section 202, except that if the deduction imposed under subsection (b) by reason of his earnings for such year is less than the amount of his benefit (or benefits) for the last month of such year for which he was entitled to a benefit under section 202, the additional deduction shall be equal to the amount of the deduction imposed under subsection (b) but not less than $10;

(B) if such failure is the second one for which an additional deduction is imposed under this paragraph, such additional deduction shall be equal to two times his benefit or benefits for the last month of such year for which he was entitled to a benefit under section 202;

(C) if such failure is the third or a subsequent one for which an additional deduction is imposed under this paragraph, such additional deduction shall be equal to three times his benefit or benefits for the last month of such year for which he was entitled to a benefit under section 202;

except that the number of the additional deductions required by this paragraph with respect to a failure to report earnings for a taxable year shall not exceed the number of months in such year for which such individual received and accepted insurance benefits under section 202 and for which deductions are imposed under subsection (b) by reason of his earnings. In determining whether a failure to report earnings is the first or a subsequent failure for any individual, all taxable years ending prior to the imposition of the first additional deduction under this paragraph, other than the latest one of such years, shall be disregarded.

(3) If the Commissioner of Social Security determines, on the basis of information obtained by or submitted to him, that it may reasonably be expected that an individual entitled to benefits under section 202 for any taxable year will suffer deductions imposed under subsection (b) by reason of his earnings for such year, the Commissioner of Social Security may, before the close of such taxable year, suspend the total or less than the total payment for each month in such year (or for only such months as the Commissioner of Social Security may specify) of the benefits payable on the basis of such individual's wages and self-employment income; and such suspension shall remain in effect with respect to the benefits for any month until the Commissioner

78 SOCIAL SECURITY ACT—§ 203(h)(3)(cont)

of Social Security has determined whether or not any deduction is imposed for such month under subsection (b). The Commissioner of Social Security is authorized, before the close of the taxable year of an individual entitled to benefits during such year, to request of such individual that he make, at such time or times as the Commissioner of Social Security may specify, a declaration of his estimated earnings for the taxable year and that he furnish to the Commissioner of Social Security such other information with respect to such earnings as the Commissioner of Social Security may specify. A failure by such individual to comply with any such request shall in itself constitute justification for a determination under this paragraph that it may reasonably be expected that the individual will suffer deductions imposed under subsection (b) by reason of his earnings for such year. If, after the close of a taxable year of an individual entitled to benefits under section 202 for such year, the Commissioner of Social Security requests such individual to furnish a report of his earnings (as computed pursuant to paragraph (5) of subsection (f)) for such taxable year or any other information with respect to such earnings which the Commissioner of Social Security may specify, and the individual fails to comply with such request, such failure shall in itself constitute justification for a determination that such individual's benefits are subject to deductions under subsection (b) for each month in such taxable year (or only for such months thereof as the Commissioner of Social Security may specify) by reason of his earnings for such year.

(4) The Commissioner of Social Security shall develop and implement procedures in accordance with this subsection to avoid paying more than the correct amount of benefits to any individual under this title as a result of such individual's failure to file a correct report or estimate of earnings or wages. Such procedures may include identifying categories of individuals who are likely to be paid more than the correct amount of benefits and requesting that they estimate their earnings or wages more frequently than other persons subject to deductions under this section on account of earnings or wages.

(i) [Repealed.[49]]

Attainment of Retirement Age

(j) For the purposes of this section, an individual shall be considered as having attained retirement age (as defined in section 216(l)) during the entire month in which he attains such age.

Noncovered Remunerative Activity Outside the United States

(k) An individual shall be considered to be engaged in noncovered remunerative activity outside the United States if he performs services outside the United States as an employee and such services do not constitute employment as defined in section 210 and are not performed in the active military or naval service of the United States, or if he carries on a trade or business outside the United States (other than the performance of service as an employee) the net income or loss of which (1) is not includible in computing his net earnings from

---

[49] P.L. 103-296, §309(a); 108 Stat. 1523.

SOCIAL SECURITY ACT—§ 204(a)(1)(A)

self-employment for a taxable year and (2) would not be excluded from net earnings from self-employment, if carried on in the United States, by any of the numbered paragraphs of section 211(a). When used in the preceding sentence with respect to a trade or business (other than the performance of service as an employee), the term "United States" does not include the Commonwealth of Puerto Rico, the Virgin Islands, Guam, or American Samoa in the case of an alien who is not a resident of the United States (including the Commonwealth of Puerto Rico, the Virgin Islands, Guam, and American Samoa); and the term "trade or business" shall have the same meaning as when used in section 162 of the Internal Revenue Code of 1986[50].

Good Cause for Failure To Make Reports Required

(l) The failure of an individual to make any report required by subsection (g) or (h)(1)(A) within the time prescribed therein shall not be regarded as such a failure if it is shown to the satisfaction of the Commissioner of Social Security that he had good cause for failing to make such report within such time. The determination of what constitutes good cause for purposes of this subsection shall be made in accordance with regulations of the Commissioner of Social Security, except that in making any such determination, the Commissioner of Social Security shall specifically take into account any physical, mental, educational, or linguistic limitation such individual may have (including any lack of facility with the English language).

OVERPAYMENTS AND UNDERPAYMENTS[51]

SEC. 204. [42 U.S.C. 404] (a)(1) Whenever the Commissioner of Social Security finds that more or less than the correct amount of payment has been made to any person under this title, proper adjustment or recovery shall be made, under regulations prescribed by the Commissioner of Social Security, as follows:

(A) With respect to payment to a person of more than the correct amount, the Commissioner of Social Security shall decrease any payment under this title to which such overpaid person is entitled, or shall require such overpaid person or his estate to refund the amount in excess of the correct amount, or shall decrease any payment under this title payable to his estate or to any other person on the basis of the wages and self-employment income which were the basis of the payments to such overpaid person, or shall obtain recovery by means of reduction in tax refunds based on notice to the Secretary of the Treasury as permitted under section 3720A of title 31, United States Code[52], or shall apply any combination of the foregoing. A payment made under this title on the basis of an erroneous report of death by the Department of Defense of an individual in the line of duty while he is a member of the uniformed services (as defined in section 210(m)) on active duty (as defined in section 210(l)) shall not be considered an incorrect payment for any month prior to the month such Department

---

[50] See Vol. II, P.L. 83-591, §162.

[51] See §1870 with respect to adjustment of Title XVIII overpayments against payment of benefits under Title II.

[52] See Vol. II, 31 U.S.C. 3720A.

80 SOCIAL SECURITY ACT—§ 204(a)(1)(A)(cont)

notifies the Commissioner of Social Security that such individual is alive.

(B) With respect to payment to a person of less than the correct amount, the Commissioner of Social Security shall make payment of the balance of the amount due such underpaid person, or, if such person dies before payments are completed or before negotiating one or more checks representing correct payments, disposition of the amount due shall be made in accordance with subsection (d).

(2) Notwithstanding any other provision of this section, when any payment of more than the correct amount is made to or on behalf of an individual who has died, and such payment—

(A) is made by direct deposit to a financial institution;

(B) is credited by the financial institution to a joint account of the deceased individual and another person; and

(C) such other person was entitled to a monthly benefit on the basis of the same wages and self-employment income as the deceased individual for the month preceding the month in which the deceased individual died,

the amount of such payment in excess of the correct amount shall be treated as a payment of more than the correct amount to such other person. If any payment of more than the correct amount is made to a representative payee on behalf of an individual after the individual's death, the representative payee shall be liable for the repayment of the overpayment, and the Commissioner of Social Security shall establish an overpayment control record under the social security account number of the representative payee.

(b) In any case in which more than the correct amount of payment has been made, there shall be no adjustment of payments to, or recovery by the United States from, any person who is without fault if such adjustment or recovery would defeat the purpose of this title or would be against equity and good conscience. In making for purposes of this subsection any determination of whether any individual is without fault, the Commissioner of Social Security shall specifically take into account any physical, mental, educational, or linguistic limitation such individual may have (including any lack of facility with the English language).

(c) No certifying or disbursing officer shall be held liable for any amount certified or paid by him to any person where the adjustment or recovery of such amount is waived under subsection (b), or where adjustment under subsection (a) is not completed prior to the death of all persons against whose benefits deductions are authorized.

(d) If an individual dies before any payment due him under this title is completed, payment of the amount due (including the amount of any unnegotiated checks) shall be made—

(1) to the person, if any, who is determined by the Commissioner of Social Security to be the surviving spouse of the deceased individual and who either (i) was living in the same household with the deceased at the time of his death or (ii) was, for the month in which the deceased individual died, entitled to a monthly benefit on the basis of the same wages and self-employment income as was the deceased individual;

(2) if there is no person who meets the requirements of paragraph (1), or if the person who meets such requirements dies be-

SOCIAL SECURITY ACT—§ 204(f)(2)   81

fore the payment due him under this title is completed, to the child or children, if any, of the deceased individual who were, for the month in which the deceased individual died, entitled to monthly benefits on the basis of the same wages and self-employment income as was the deceased individual (and, in case there is more than one such child, in equal parts to each such child);

(3) if there is no person who meets the requirements of paragraph (1) or (2), or if each person who meets such requirements dies before the payment due him under this title is completed, to the parent or parents, if any, of the deceased individual who were, for the month in which the deceased individual died, entitled to monthly benefits on the basis of the same wages and self-employment income as was the deceased individual (and, in case there is more than one such parent, in equal parts to each such parent);

(4) if there is no person who meets the requirements of paragraph (1), (2), or (3), or if each person who meets such requirements dies before the payment due him under this title is completed, to the person, if any, determined by the Commissioner of Social Security to be the surviving spouse of the deceased individual;

(5) if there is no person who meets the requirements of paragraph (1), (2), (3), or (4), or if each person who meets such requirements dies before the payment due him under this title is completed, to the person or persons, if any, determined by the Commissioner of Social Security to be the child or children of the deceased individual (and, in case there is more than one such child, in equal parts to each such child);

(6) if there is no person who meets the requirements of paragraph (1), (2), (3), (4), or (5), or if each person who meets such requirements dies before the payment due him under this title is completed, to the parent or parents, if any, of the deceased individual (and, in case there is more than one such parent, in equal parts to each such parent); or

(7) if there is no person who meets the requirements of paragraph (1), (2), (3), (4), (5), or (6), or if each person who meets such requirements dies before the payment due him under this title is completed, to the legal representative of the estate of the deceased individual, if any.

(e) For payments which are adjusted by reason of payment of benefits under the supplemental security income program established by title XVI, see section 1127.

(f)(1) With respect to any deliquent[53] amount, the Commissioner of Social Security may use the collection practices described in sections 3711(f), 3716, 3717, and 3718 of title 31, United States Code[54], and in section 5514 of title 5, United States Code[55], all as in effect immediately after the enactment of the Debt Collection Improvement Act of 1996[56].

(2) For purposes of paragraph (1), the term "delinquent amount" means an amount—

---

[53] As in original.
[54] See Vol. II, 31 U.S.C. 3711(f), 3716, 3717, and 3718.
[55] See Vol. II, 5 U.S.C. 5514.
[56] P.L. 104-134 was enacted April 26, 1996.

82　　SOCIAL SECURITY ACT—§ 204(f)(2)(A)

(A) in excess of the correct amount of payment under this title;

(B) paid to a person after such person has attained 18 years of age; and

(C) determined by the Commissioner of Social Security, under regulations, to be otherwise unrecoverable under this section after such person ceases to be a beneficiary under this title.

(g) For provisions relating to the cross-program recovery of overpayments made under programs administered by the Commissioner of Social Security, see section 1147.

EVIDENCE, PROCEDURE, AND CERTIFICATION FOR PAYMENT[57]

SEC. 205. [42 U.S.C. 405] (a) The Commissioner of Social Security shall have full power and authority to make rules and regulations and to establish procedures, not inconsistent with the provisions of this title, which are necessary or appropriate to carry out such provisions, and shall adopt reasonable and proper rules and regulations to regulate and provide for the nature and extent of the proofs and evidence and the method of taking and furnishing the same in order to establish the right to benefits hereunder.

(b)(1) The Commissioner of Social Security is directed to make findings of fact, and decisions as to the rights of any individual applying for a payment under this title. Any such decision by the Commissioner of Social Security which involves a determination of disability and which is in whole or in part unfavorable to such individual shall contain a statement of the case, in understandable language, setting forth a discussion of the evidence, and stating the Commissioner's determination and the reason or reasons upon which it is based. Upon request by any such individual or upon request by a wife, divorced wife, widow, surviving divorced wife, surviving divorced mother, surviving divorced father, husband, divorced husband, widower, surviving divorced husband, child, or parent who makes a showing in writing that his or her rights may be prejudiced by any decision the Commissioner of Social Security has rendered, the Commissioner shall give such applicant and such other individual reasonable notice and opportunity for a hearing with respect to such decision, and, if a hearing is held, shall, on the basis of evidence adduced at the hearing, affirm, modify, or reverse the Commissioner's findings of fact and such decision. Any such request with respect to such a decision must be filed within sixty days after notice of such decision is received by the individual making such request. The Commissioner of Social Security is further authorized, on the Commissioner's own motion, to hold such hearings and

---

[57] See Vol. II, P.L. 84-885, §33, with respect to evidence of United States citizenship.

See Vol. II, P.L. 90-321, §913(2), with respect to electronic fund transfers.

See Vol. II, P.L. 95-630, §§1101-1121, with respect to an individual's right to financial privacy.

See Vol. II, P.L. 97-455, §5, with respect to conduct of face-to-face reconsiderations in disability cases.

See Vol. II, P.L. 98-473, §1212, with respect to the requirement for printed notices regarding the commission of forgery in conjunction with the cashing or attempted cashing of title II checks.

See Vol. II, P.L. 103-296, §206(g), with respect to annual reports on reviews of OASDI and SSI cases.

See Vol. II, P.L. 104-193, §111, with respect to the requirement for development of a prototype of a counterfeit-resistant social security card.

See Vol. II, P.L. 108-203, §103(a) with respect to a report evaluating existing procedures and reviews for qualification of representative payees.

See Vol. II, P.L. 108-458, §7213, with respect to security enhancements and other improvements with respect to social security cards and numbers.

SOCIAL SECURITY ACT—§ 205(b)(3)(B) 83

to conduct such investigations and other proceedings as the Commissioner may deem necessary or proper for the administration of this title. In the course of any hearing, investigation, or other proceeding, the Commissioner may administer oaths and affirmations, examine witnesses, and receive evidence. Evidence may be received at any hearing before the Commissioner of Social Security even though inadmissible under rules of evidence applicable to court procedure.

(2) In any case where—

(A) an individual is a recipient of disability insurance benefits, or of child's, widow's, or widower's insurance benefits based on disability,

(B) the physical or mental impairment on the basis of which such benefits are payable is found to have ceased, not to have existed, or to no longer be disabling, and

(C) as a consequence of the finding described in subparagraph (B), such individual is determined by the Commissioner of Social Security not to be entitled to such benefits,

any reconsideration of the finding described in subparagraph (B), in connection with a reconsideration by the Commissioner of Social Security (before any hearing under paragraph (1) on the issue of such entitlement) of the Commissioner's determination described in subparagraph (C), shall be made only after opportunity for an evidentiary hearing, with regard to the finding described in subparagraph (B), which is reasonably accessible to such individual. Any reconsideration of a finding described in subparagraph (B) may be made either by the State agency or the Commissioner of Social Security where the finding was originally made by the State agency, and shall be made by the Commissioner of Social Security where the finding was originally made by the Commissioner of Social Security. In the case of a reconsideration by a State agency of a finding described in subparagraph (B) which was originally made by such State agency, the evidentiary hearing shall be held by an adjudicatory unit of the State agency other than the unit that made the finding described in subparagraph (B). In the case of a reconsideration by the Commissioner of Social Security of a finding described in subparagraph (B) which was originally made by the Commissioner of Social Security, the evidentiary hearing shall be held by a person other than the person or persons who made the finding described in subparagraph (B).

(3)(A) A failure to timely request review of an initial adverse determination with respect to an application for any benefit under this title or an adverse determination on reconsideration of such an initial determination shall not serve as a basis for denial of a subsequent application for any benefit under this title if the applicant demonstrates that the applicant, or any other individual referred to in paragraph (1), failed to so request such a review acting in good faith reliance upon incorrect, incomplete, or misleading information, relating to the consequences of reapplying for benefits in lieu of seeking review of an adverse determination, provided by any officer or employee of the Social Security Administration or any State agency acting under section 221.

(B) In any notice of an adverse determination with respect to which a review may be requested under paragraph (1), the Commissioner of Social Security shall describe in clear and specific language the effect

84 SOCIAL SECURITY ACT—§ 205(b)(3)(B)(cont)

on possible entitlement to benefits under this title of choosing to reapply in lieu of requesting review of the determination.

(c)(1) For the purposes of this subsection—

(A) The term "year" means a calendar year when used with respect to wages and a taxable year when used with respect to self-employment income.

(B) The term "time limitation" means a period of three years, three months, and fifteen days.

(C) The term "survivor" means an individual's spouse, surviving divorced wife, surviving divorced husband, surviving divorced mother, surviving divorced father, child, or parent, who survives such individual.

(D) The term "period" when used with respect to self-employment income means a taxable year and when used with respect to wages means—

(i) a quarter if wages were reported or should have been reported on a quarterly basis on tax returns filed with the Secretary of the Treasury or his delegate under section 6011 of the Internal Revenue Code of 1986[58] or regulations thereunder (or on reports filed by a State under section 218(e) (as in effect prior to December 31, 1986) or regulations thereunder),

(ii) a year if wages were reported or should have been reported on a yearly basis on such tax returns or reports, or

(iii) the half year beginning January 1 or July 1 in the case of wages which were reported or should have been reported for calendar year 1937.

(2)(A) On the basis of information obtained by or submitted to the Commissioner of Social Security, and after such verification thereof as the Commissioner deems necessary, the Commissioner of Social Security shall establish and maintain records of the amounts of wages paid to, and the amounts of self-employment income derived by, each individual and of the periods in which such wages were paid and such income was derived and, upon request, shall inform any individual or his survivor, or the legal representative of such individual or his estate, of the amounts of wages and self-employment income of such individual and the periods during which such wages were paid and such income was derived, as shown by such records at the time of such request.

(B)(i) In carrying out the Commissioner's duties under subparagraph (A) and subparagraph (F), the Commissioner of Social Security shall take affirmative measures to assure that social security account numbers will, to the maximum extent practicable, be assigned to all members of appropriate groups or categories of individuals by assigning such numbers (or ascertaining that such numbers have already been assigned):

(I) to aliens at the time of their lawful admission to the United States either for permanent residence or under other authority of law permitting them to engage in employment in the United States and to other aliens at such time as their status is so changed as to make it lawful for them to engage in such employment;

---

[58] See Vol. II, P.L. 83-591, §6011.

SOCIAL SECURITY ACT—§ 205(c)(2)(C)(ii)

(II) to any individual who is an applicant for or recipient of benefits under any program financed in whole or in part from Federal funds including any child on whose behalf such benefits are claimed by another person; and

(III) to any other individual when it appears that he could have been but was not assigned an account number under the provisions of subclauses (I) or (II) but only after such investigation as is necessary to establish to the satisfaction of the Commissioner of Social Security, the identity of such individual, the fact that an account number has not already been assigned to such individual, and the fact that such individual is a citizen or a noncitizen who is not, because of his alien status, prohibited from engaging in employment;

and, in carrying out such duties, the Commissioner of Social Security is authorized to take affirmative measures to assure the issuance of social security numbers:

(IV) to or on behalf of children who are below school age at the request of their parents or guardians; and

(V) to children of school age at the time of their first enrollment in school.

(ii) The Commissioner of Social Security shall require of applicants for social security account numbers such evidence as may be necessary to establish the age, citizenship, or alien status, and true identity of such applicants, and to determine which (if any) social security account number has previously been assigned to such individual. With respect to an application for a social security account number for an individual who has not attained the age of 18 before such application, such evidence shall include the information described in subparagraph (C)(ii).

(iii) In carrying out the requirements of this subparagraph, the Commissioner of Social Security shall enter into such agreements as may be necessary with the Attorney General and other officials and with State and local welfare agencies and school authorities (including nonpublic school authorities).

(C)(i)[59] It is the policy of the United States that any State (or political subdivision thereof) may, in the administration of any tax, general public assistance, driver's license, or motor vehicle registration law within its jurisdiction, utilize the social security account numbers issued by the Commissioner of Social Security for the purpose of establishing the identification of individuals affected by such law, and may require any individual who is or appears to be so affected to furnish to such State (or political subdivision thereof) or any agency thereof having administrative responsibility for the law involved, the social security account number (or numbers, if he has more than one such number) issued to him by the Commissioner of Social Security.

(ii) In the administration of any law involving the issuance of a birth certificate, each State shall require each parent to furnish to such State (or political subdivision thereof) or any agency thereof having

---

[59] See Vol. II, P.L. 80-759, §12(e), with respect to disclosure of the social security number for individuals required to submit to registration.

See Vol. II, P.L. 83-591, §6109, with respect to use of a social security number as a "taxpayer identifying number" as that term is used in the "Debt Collection Act of 1982" [P.L. 97-365].

See Vol. II, P.L. 88-525, §16(e), with respect to use of the social security number for participation in the food stamp program.

administrative responsibility for the law involved, the social security account number (or numbers, if the parent has more than one such number) issued to the parent unless the State (in accordance with regulations prescribed by the Commissioner of Social Security) finds good cause for not requiring the furnishing of such number. The State shall make numbers furnished under this subclause available to the Commissioner of Social Security and the agency administering the State's plan under part D of title IV in accordance with Federal or State law and regulation. Such numbers shall not be recorded on the birth certificate. A State shall not use any social security account number, obtained with respect to the issuance by the State of a birth certificate, for any purpose other than for the enforcement of child support orders in effect in the State, unless section 7(a) of the Privacy Act of 1974[60] does not prohibit the State from requiring the disclosure of such number, by reason of the State having adopted, before January 1, 1975, a statute or regulation requiring such disclosure.

(iii)(I) In the administration of section 9 of the Food and Nutrition Act of 2008[61] (7 U.S.C. 2018) involving the determination of the qualifications of applicants under such Act, the Secretary of Agriculture may require each applicant retail store or wholesale food concern to furnish to the Secretary of Agriculture the social security account number of each individual who is an officer of the store or concern and, in the case of a privately owned applicant, furnish the social security account numbers of the owners of such applicant. No officer or employee of the Department of Agriculture shall have access to any such number for any purpose other than the establishment and maintenance of a list of the names and social security account numbers of such individuals for use in determining those applicants who have been previously sanctioned or convicted under section 12 or 15 of such Act (7 U.S.C. 2021 or 2024).

(II) The Secretary of Agriculture may share any information contained in any list referred to in subclause (I) with any other agency or instrumentality of the United States which otherwise has access to social security account numbers in accordance with this subsection or other applicable Federal law, except that the Secretary of Agriculture may share such information only to the extent that such Secretary determines such sharing would assist in verifying and matching such information against information maintained by such other agency or instrumentality. Any such information shared pursuant to this subclause may be used by such other agency or instrumentality only for the purpose of effective administration and enforcement of the Food and Nutrition Act of 2008[62] or for the purpose of investigation of violations of other Federal laws or enforcement of such laws.

(III) The Secretary of Agriculture, and the head of any other agency or instrumentality referred to in this subclause, shall restrict, to the satisfaction of the Commissioner of Social Security, access to social security account numbers obtained pursuant to this clause only to of-

---

[60] See Vol. II, P.L. 93-579, §7(a) .

[61] P.L. 110-246, §4002(b)(1)(B), struck out "Food Stamp Act of 1977" and substituted "Food and Nutrition Act of 2008", effective October 1, 2008. P.L. 110-234, §4002(b)(1)(B), which made the same amendment, was repealed, effective May 22, 2008 pursuant to P.L. 110-246, §4(a).

[62] P.L. 110-246, §4002(b)(1)(B), struck out "Food Stamp Act of 1977" and substituted "Food and Nutrition Act of 2008", effective October 1, 2008. P.L. 110-234, §4002(b)(1)(B), which made the same amendment, was repealed, effective May 22, 2008 pursuant to P.L. 110-246, §4(a).

ficers and employees of the United States whose duties or responsibilities require access for the purposes described in subclause (II).

(IV) The Secretary of Agriculture, and the head of any agency or instrumentality with which information is shared pursuant to clause (II), shall provide such other safeguards as the Commissioner of Social Security determines to be necessary or appropriate to protect the confidentiality of the social security account numbers.

(iv) In the administration of section 506 of the Federal Crop Insurance Act, the Federal Crop Insurance Corporation may require each policyholder and each reinsured company to furnish to the insurer or to the Corporation the social security account number of such policyholder, subject to the requirements of this clause. No officer or employee of the Federal Crop Insurance Corporation shall have access to any such number for any purpose other than the establishment of a system of records necessary for the effective administration of such Act. The Manager of the Corporation may require each policyholder to provide to the Manager, at such times and in such manner as prescribed by the Manager, the social security account number of each individual that holds or acquires a substantial beneficial interest in the policyholder. For purposes of this clause, the term "substantial beneficial interest" means not less than 5 percent of all beneficial interest in the policyholder. The Secretary of Agriculture shall restrict, to the satisfaction of the Commissioner of Social Security, access to social security account numbers obtained pursuant to this clause only to officers and employees of the United States or authorized persons whose duties or responsibilities require access for the administration of the Federal Crop Insurance Act. The Secretary of Agriculture shall provide such other safeguards as the Commissioner of Social Security determines to be necessary or appropriate to protect the confidentiality of such social security account numbers. For purposes of this clause the term "authorized person" means an officer or employee of an insurer whom the Manager of the Corporation designates by rule, subject to appropriate safeguards including a prohibition against the release of such social security account number (other than to the Corporation) by such person.

(v) If and to the extent that any provision of Federal law heretofore enacted is inconsistent with the policy set forth in clause (i), such provision shall, on and after the date of the enactment of this subparagraph[63] , be null, void, and of no effect. If and to the extent that any such provision is inconsistent with the requirement set forth in clause (ii), such provision shall, on and after the date of the enactment of such subclause[64], be null, void, and of no effect.

(vi)(I) For purposes of clause of this subparagraph, an agency of a State (or political subdivision thereof) charged with the administration of any general public assistance, driver's license, or motor vehicle registration law which did not use the social security account number for identification under a law or regulation adopted before January 1, 1975, may require an individual to disclose his or her social security number to such agency solely for the purpose of administering the laws referred to in clause above and for the purpose of responding to requests for information from an agency administering a program

---

[63] October 4, 1976 [P.L. 94-455, §1211(b); 90 Stat. 1711].

[64] Subclause (II) of clause (i) was enacted in October 13, 1988. [P.L. 100-485; 102 Stat. 2353].

88   SOCIAL SECURITY ACT—§ 205(c)(2)(C)(vi)(I)(cont)

funded under part A of title IV or an agency operating pursuant to the provisions of part D of such title.

(II) Any State or political subdivision thereof (and any person acting as an agent of such an agency or instrumentality), in the administration of any driver's license or motor vehicle registration law within its jurisdiction, may not display a social security account number issued by the Commissioner of Social Security (or any derivative of such number) on any driver's license, motor vehicle registration, or personal identification card (as defined in section 7212(a)(2) of the 9/11 Commission Implementation Act of 2004), or include, on any such license, registration, or personal identification card, a magnetic strip, bar code, or other means of communication which conveys such number (or derivative thereof).

(vii) For purposes of this subparagraph, the term "State" includes the District of Columbia, the Commonwealth of Puerto Rico, the Virgin Islands, Guam, the Commonwealth of the Northern Marianas, and the Trust Territory of the Pacific Islands.

(viii)(I) Social security account numbers and related records that are obtained or maintained by authorized persons pursuant to any provision of law enacted on or after October 1, 1990, shall be confidential, and no authorized person shall disclose any such social security account number or related record.

(II) Paragraphs (1), (2), and (3) of section 7213(a) of the Internal Revenue Code of 1986[65] shall apply with respect to the unauthorized willful disclosure to any person of social security account numbers and related records obtained or maintained by an authorized person pursuant to a provision of law enacted on or after October 1, 1990, in the same manner and to the same extent as such paragraphs apply with respect to unauthorized disclosures of return and return information described in such paragraphs. Paragraph (4) of section 7213(a) of such Code shall apply with respect to the willful offer of any item of material value in exchange for any such social security account number or related record in the same manner and to the same extent as such paragraph applies with respect to offers (in exchange for any return or return information) described in such paragraph.

(III) For purposes of this clause, the term "authorized person" means an officer or employee of the United States, an officer or employee of any State, political subdivision of a State, or agency of a State or political subdivision of a State, and any other person (or officer or employee thereof), who has or had access to social security account numbers or related records pursuant to any provision of law enacted on or after October 1, 1990. For purposes of this subclause, the term "officer or employee" includes a former officer or employee.

(IV) For purposes of this clause, the term "related record" means any record, list, or compilation that indicates, directly or indirectly, the identity of any individual with respect to whom a social security account number or a request for a social security account number is maintained pursuant to this clause.

(ix) In the administration of the provisions of chapter 81 of title 5, United States Code, and the Longshore and Harbor Workers' Compensation Act (33 U.S.C. 901 et seq.), the Secretary of Labor may require by regulation that any person filing a notice of injury or a claim

---

[65] Subclause (II) of clause (i) was enacted in October 13, 1988. [P.L. 100-485; 102 Stat. 2353].

SOCIAL SECURITY ACT—§ 205(c)(2)(E)(ii)(I) 89

for benefits under such provisions provide as part of such notice or claim such person's social security account number, subject to the requirements of this clause. No officer or employee of the Department of Labor shall have access to any such number for any purpose other than the establishment of a system of records necessary for the effective administration of such provisions. The Secretary of Labor shall restrict, to the satisfaction of the Commissioner of Social Security, access to social security account numbers obtained pursuant to this clause to officers and employees of the United States whose duties or responsibilities require access for the administration or enforcement of such provisions. The Secretary of Labor shall provide such other safeguards as the Commissioner of Social Security determines to be necessary or appropriate to protect the confidentiality of the social security account numbers.

(D)(i) It is the policy of the United States that—

(I) any State (or any political subdivision of a State) and any authorized blood donation facility may utilize the social security account numbers issued by the Commissioner of Social Security for the purpose of identifying blood donors, and

(II) any State (or political subdivision of a State) may require any individual who donates blood within such State (or political subdivision) to furnish to such State (or political subdivision), to any agency thereof having related administrative responsibility, or to any authorized blood donation facility the social security account number (or numbers, if the donor has more than one such number) issued to the donor by the Commissioner of Social Security.

(ii) If and to the extent that any provision of Federal law enacted before the date of the enactment of this subparagraph[66] is inconsistent with the policy set forth in clause, such provision shall, on and after such date, be null, void, and of no effect.

(iii) For purposes of this subparagraph—

(I) the term "authorized blood donation facility" means an entity described in section 1141(h)(1)(B), and

(II) the term "State" includes the District of Columbia, the Commonwealth of Puerto Rico, the Virgin Islands, Guam, the Commonwealth of the Northern Marianas, and the Trust Territory of the Pacific Islands.

(E)(i) It is the policy of the United States that—

(I) any State (or any political subdivision of a State) may utilize the social security account numbers issued by the Commissioner of Social Security for the additional purposes described in clause (ii) if such numbers have been collected and are otherwise utilized by such State (or political subdivision) in accordance with applicable law, and

(II) any district court of the United States may use, for such additional purposes, any such social security account numbers which have been so collected and are so utilized by any State.

(ii) The additional purposes described in this clause are the following:

(I) Identifying duplicate names of individuals on master lists used for jury selection purposes.

---

[66] This subparagraph was enacted November 10, 1988.

90   SOCIAL SECURITY ACT—§ 205(c)(2)(E)(ii)(II)

(II) Identifying on such master lists those individuals who are ineligible to serve on a jury by reason of their conviction of a felony.

(iii) To the extent that any provision of Federal law enacted before the date of the enactment of this subparagraph[67] is inconsistent with the policy set forth in clause, such provision shall, on and after that date, be null, void, and of no effect.

(iv) For purposes of this subparagraph, the term "State" has the meaning such term has in subparagraph (D).

(F) The Commissioner of Social Security shall require, as a condition for receipt of benefits under this title, that an individual furnish satisfactory proof of a social security account number assigned to such individual by the Commissioner of Social Security or, in the case of an individual to whom no such number has been assigned, that such individual make proper application for assignment of such a number.

(G) The Commissioner of Social Security shall issue a social security card to each individual at the time of the issuance of a social security account number to such individual. The social security card shall be made of banknote paper, and (to the maximum extent practicable) shall be a card which cannot be counterfeited.

(H) The Commissioner of Social Security shall share with the Secretary of the Treasury the information obtained by the Commissioner pursuant to the second sentence of subparagraph (B)(ii) and to subparagraph (C)(ii) for the purpose of administering those sections of the Internal Revenue Code of 1986 which grant tax benefits based on support or residence of children.

(3) The Commissioner's record shall be evidence for the purpose of proceedings before the Commissioner of Social Security or any court of the amounts of wages paid to, and self-employment income derived by, an individual and of the periods in which such wages were paid and such income was derived. The absence of an entry in such records as to wages alleged to have been paid to, or as to self-employment income alleged to have been derived by, an individual in any period shall be evidence that no such alleged wages were paid to, or that no such alleged income was derived by, such individual during such period.

(4) Prior to the expiration of the time limitation following any year the Commissioner of Social Security may, if it is brought to the Commissioner's attention that any entry of wages or self-employment income in the Commissioner's records for such year is erroneous or that any item of wages or self-employment income for such year has been omitted from such records, correct such entry or include such omitted item in his records, as the case may be. After the expiration of the time limitation following any year—

(A) the Commissioner's records (with changes, if any, made pursuant to paragraph (5)) of the amounts of wages paid to, and self-employment income derived by, an individual during any period in such year shall be conclusive for the purposes of this title;

(B) the absence of an entry in the Commissioner's records as to the wages alleged to have been paid by an employer to an individual during any period in such year shall be presumptive evidence for the purposes of this title that no such alleged wages were paid to such individual in such period; and

---

[67] August 15, 1994 [P.L. 103-296, §304; 108 Stat. 1520].

SOCIAL SECURITY ACT—§ 205(c)(5)(F)(i)

(C) the absence of an entry in the Commissioner's records as to the self-employment income alleged to have been derived by an individual in such year shall be conclusive for the purposes of this title that no such alleged self-employment income was derived by such individual in such year unless it is shown that he filed a tax return of his self-employment income for such year before the expiration of the time limitation following such year, in which case the Commissioner of Social Security shall include in the Commissioner's records the self-employment income of such individual for such year.

(5) After the expiration of the time limitation following any year in which wages were paid or alleged to have been paid to, or self-employment income was derived or alleged to have been derived by, an individual, the Commissioner of Social Security may change or delete any entry with respect to wages or self-employment income in the Commissioner's records of such year for such individual or include in the Commissioner's records of such year for such individual any omitted item of wages or self-employment income but only—

(A) if an application for monthly benefits or for a lump-sum death payment was filed within the time limitation following such year; except that no such change, deletion, or inclusion may be made pursuant to this subparagraph after a final decision upon the application for monthly benefits or lump-sum death payment;

(B) if within the time limitation following such year an individual or his survivor makes a request for a change or deletion, or for an inclusion of an omitted item, and alleges in writing that the Commissioner's records of the wages paid to, or the self-employment income derived by, such individual in such year are in one or more respects erroneous; except that no such change, deletion, or inclusion may be made pursuant to this subparagraph after a final decision upon such request. Written notice of the Commissioner's decision on any such request shall be given to the individual who made the request;

(C) to correct errors apparent on the face of such records;

(D) to transfer items to records of the Railroad Retirement Board if such items were credited under this title when they should have been credited under the Railroad Retirement Act of 1937 or 1974[68], or to enter items transferred by the Railroad Retirement Board which have been credited under the Railroad Retirement Act of 1937 or 1974 when they should have been credited under this title;

(E) to delete or reduce the amount of any entry which is erroneous as a result of fraud;

(F) to conform the Commissioner's records to—

(i) tax returns or portions thereof (including information returns and other written statements) filed with the Commissioner of Internal Revenue under title VIII of the Social

---

[68] P.L. 75-162 [as amended by P.L. 93-445].

92   SOCIAL SECURITY ACT—§ 205(c)(5)(F)(i)(cont)

Security Act[69], under subchapter E of chapter 1 or subchapter A of chapter 9 of the Internal Revenue Code of 1939[70], under chapter 2 or 21 of the Internal Revenue Code of 1954 or the Internal Revenue Code of 1986[71], or under regulations made under authority of such title, subchapter, or chapter;

(ii) wage reports filed by a State pursuant to an agreement under section 218 or regulations of the Commissioner of Social Security thereunder; or

(iii) assessments of amounts due under an agreement pursuant to section 218 (as in effect prior to December 31, 1986), if such assessments are made within the period specified in subsection (q) of such section (as so in effect), or allowances of credits or refunds of overpayments by a State under an agreement pursuant to such section;

except that no amount of self-employment income of an individual for any taxable year (if such return or statement was filed after the expiration of the time limitation following the taxable year) shall be included in the Commissioner's records pursuant to this subparagraph;

(G) to correct errors made in the allocation, to individuals or periods, of wages or self-employment income entered in the records of the Commissioner of Social Security;

(H) to include wages paid during any period in such year to an individual by an employer;

(I) to enter items which constitute remuneration for employment under subsection (o), such entries to be in accordance with certified reports of records made by the Railroad Retirement Board pursuant to section 5(k)(3) of the Railroad Retirement Act of 1937 or section 7(b)(7) of the Railroad Retirement Act of 1974[72]; or

(J) to include self-employment income for any taxable year, up to, but not in excess of, the amount of wages deleted by the Commissioner of Social Security as payments erroneously included in such records as wages paid to such individual, if such income (or net earnings from self-employment), not already included in such records as self-employment income, is included in a return or statement (referred to in subparagraph (F)) filed before the expiration of the time limitation following the taxable year in which such deletion of wages is made.

(6) Written notice of any deletion or reduction under paragraph (4) or (5) shall be given to the individual whose record is involved or to his survivor, except that (A) in the case of a deletion or reduction with respect to any entry of wages such notice shall be given to such individual only if he has previously been notified by the Commissioner of Social Security of the amount of his wages for the period involved,

---

[69] The reference to Title VIII of the Social Security Act refers to the Title VIII-Taxes with Respect to Employment-that was omitted from the Act as superseded by the provisions of the Internal Revenue code of 1939 and the Internal Revenue code of 1986. However, the provisions of §205 still apply with regard to tax return information provided under Title VIII of the Act prior to its repeal.
P.L. 76-1, §4, 53 Stat.1 repealed the former Title VIII, effective February 11, 1939. The substance of Title VIII was then included in the Internal Revenue Code of 1039 at §§1400-1425. Currently, the substance of the former Title VIII may be found at §§3101-3126 (Subtitle C-Employment Taxes; Chapter 21-Federal Insurance Contributions Act). See Vol. II, P.L. 83-591, §§3101-3126.
[70] P.L. 76-1.
[71] See Vol. II, P.L. 83-591.
[72] See Vol. II, P.L. 75-162, §7(b)(7).

and (B) such notice shall be given to such survivor only if he or the individual whose record is involved has previously been notified by the Commissioner of Social Security of the amount of such individual's wages and self-employment income for the period involved.

(7) Upon request in writing (within such period, after any change or refusal of a request for a change of the Commissioner's records pursuant to this subsection, as the Commissioner of Social Security may prescribe), opportunity for hearing with respect to such change or refusal shall be afforded to any individual or his survivor. If a hearing is held pursuant to this paragraph the Commissioner of Social Security shall make findings of fact and a decision based upon the evidence adduced at such hearing and shall include any omitted items, or change or delete any entry, in the Commissioner's records as may be required by such findings and decision.

(8) A translation into English by a third party of a statement made in a foreign language by an applicant for or beneficiary of monthly insurance benefits under this title shall not be regarded as reliable for any purpose under this title unless the third party, under penalty or perjury—

    (A) certifies that the translation is accurate; and

    (B) discloses the nature and scope of the relationship between the third party and the applicant or recipient, as the case may be.

(9) Decisions of the Commissioner of Social Security under this subsection shall be reviewable by commencing a civil action in the United States district court as provided in subsection (g).

(d) For the purpose of any hearing, investigation, or other proceeding authorized or directed under this title, or relative to any other matter within the Commissioner's jurisdiction hereunder, the Commissioner of Social Security shall have power to issue subpoenas requiring the attendance and testimony of witnesses and the production of any evidence that relates to any matter under investigation or in question before the Commissioner of Social Security. Such attendance of witnesses and production of evidence at the designated place of such hearing, investigation, or other proceeding may be required from any place in the United States or in any Territory or possession thereof. Subpoenas of the Commissioner of Social Security shall be served by anyone authorized by the Commissioner (1) by delivering a copy thereof to the individual named therein, or (2) by registered mail or by certified mail addressed to such individual at his last dwelling place or principal place of business. A verified return by the individual so serving the subpena setting forth the manner of service, or, in the case of service by registered mail or by certified mail, the return post-office receipt therefor signed by the individual so served, shall be proof of service. Witnesses so subpoenaed shall be paid the same fees and mileage as are paid witnesses in the district courts of the United States.

(e) In case of contumacy by, or refusal to obey a subpena duly served upon, any person, any district court of the United States for the judicial district in which said person charged with contumacy or refusal to obey is found or resides or transacts business, upon application by the Commissioner of Social Security, shall have jurisdiction to issue an order requiring such person to appear and give testimony, or to appear and produce evidence, or both; any failure to obey such order of the court may be punished by said court as contempt thereof.

94   SOCIAL SECURITY ACT—§ 205(e)(cont)

(f)   [Repealed.[73]]

(g) Any individual, after any final decision of the Commissioner of Social Security made after a hearing to which he was a party, irrespective of the amount in controversy, may obtain a review of such decision by a civil action commenced within sixty days after the mailing to him of notice of such decision or within such further time as the Commissioner of Social Security may allow. Such action shall be brought in the district court of the United States for the judicial district in which the plaintiff resides, or has his principal place of business, or, if he does not reside or have his principal place of business within any such judicial district, in the United States District Court for the District of Columbia. As part of the Commissioner's answer the Commissioner of Social Security shall file a certified copy of the transcript of the record including the evidence upon which the findings and decision complained of are based. The court shall have power to enter, upon the pleadings and transcript of the record, a judgment affirming, modifying, or reversing the decision of the Commissioner of Social Security, with or without remanding the cause for a rehearing. The findings of the Commissioner of Social Security as to any fact, if supported by substantial evidence, shall be conclusive, and where a claim has been denied by the Commissioner of Social Security or a decision is rendered under subsection (b) hereof which is adverse to an individual who was a party to the hearing before the Commissioner of Social Security, because of failure of the claimant or such individual to submit proof in conformity with any regulation prescribed under subsection (a) hereof, the court shall review only the question of conformity with such regulations and the validity of such regulations. The court may, on motion of the Commissioner of Social Security made for good cause shown before the Commissioner files the Commissioner's answer, remand the case to the Commissioner of Social Security for further action by the Commissioner of Social Security, and it may at any time order additional evidence to be taken before the Commissioner of Social Security, but only upon a showing that there is new evidence which is material and that there is good cause for the failure to incorporate such evidence into the record in a prior proceeding; and the Commissioner of Social Security shall, after the case is remanded, and after hearing such additional evidence if so ordered, modify or affirm the Commissioner's findings of fact or the Commissioner's decision, or both, and shall file with the court any such additional and modified findings of fact and decision and, in any case in which the Commissioner has not made a decision fully favorable to the individual, a transcript of the additional record and testimony upon which the Commissioner's action in modifying or affirming was based. Such additional or modified findings of fact and decision shall be reviewable only to the extent provided for review of the original findings of fact and decision. The judgment of the court shall be final except that it shall be subject to review in the same manner as a judgment in other civil actions. Any action instituted in accordance with this subsection shall survive notwithstanding any change in the person occupying the office of Commissioner of Social Security or any vacancy in such office.

(h) The findings and decision of the Commissioner of Social Security after a hearing shall be binding upon all individuals who were parties

---

[73] P.L. 91-452, §236; 84 Stat. 930.

to such hearing. No findings of fact or decision of the Commissioner of Social Security shall be reviewed by any person, tribunal, or governmental agency except as herein provided. No action against the United States, the Commissioner of Social Security or any officer or employee thereof shall be brought under section 1331 or 1346 of title 28, United States Code[74], to recover on any claim arising under this title.

(i) Upon final decision of the Commissioner of Social Security, or upon final judgment of any court of competent jurisdiction, that any person is entitled to any payment or payments under this title, the Commissioner of Social Security shall certify to the Managing Trustee the name and address of the person so entitled to receive such payment or payments, the amount of such payment or payments, and the time at which such payment or payments should be made, and the Managing Trustee, through the Fiscal Service of the Department of the Treasury, and prior to any action thereon by the General Accounting Office[75], shall make payment in accordance with the certification of the Commissioner of Social Security (except that in the case of (A) an individual who will have completed ten years of service (or five or more years of service, all of which accrues after December 31, 1995) creditable under the Railroad Retirement Act of 1937 or the Railroad Retirement Act of 1974[76], (B) the wife or husband of such an individual, (C) any survivor of such an individual if such survivor is entitled, or could upon application become entitled, to an annuity under section 2 of the Railroad Retirement Act of 1974, and (D) any other person entitled to benefits under section 202 of this Act on the basis of the wages and self-employment income of such an individual (except a survivor of such an individual where such individual did not have a current connection with the railroad industry, as defined in the Railroad Retirement Act of 1974, at the time of his death), such certification shall be made to the Railroad Retirement Board which shall provide for such payment or payments to such person on behalf of the Managing Trustee in accordance with the provisions of the Railroad Retirement Act of 1974): *Provided,* That where a review of the Commissioner's decision is or may be sought under subsection (g) the Commissioner of Social Security may withhold certification of payment pending such review. The Managing Trustee shall not be held personally liable for any payment or payments made in accordance with a certification by the Commissioner of Social Security.

Representative Payees

(j)(1)(A) If the Commissioner of Social Security determines that the interest of any individual under this title would be served thereby, certification of payment of such individual's benefit under this title may be made, regardless of the legal competency or incompetency of the individual, either for direct payment to the individual, or for his or her use and benefit, to another individual, or an organization, with

---

[74] See Vol. II, 28 U.S.C. 1331 and 1346.

[75] P.L. 108-271, §8(b), provided that "Any reference to the General Accounting Office in any law, rule, regulation, certificate, directive, instruction, or other official paper in force on the date of enactment [July 7, 2004] of this Act shall be considered to refer and apply to the Government Accountability Office."

[76] P.L. 75-162 [as amended by P.L. 93-445].

96   SOCIAL SECURITY ACT—§ 205(j)(1)(A)(cont)

respect to whom the requirements of paragraph (2) have been met (hereinafter in this subsection referred to as the individual's "representative payee"). If the Commissioner of Social Security or a court of competent jurisdiction determines that a representative payee has misused any individual's benefit paid to such representative payee pursuant to this subsection or section 807 or 1631(a)(2), the Commissioner of Social Security shall promptly revoke certification for payment of benefits to such representative payee pursuant to this subsection and certify payment to an alternative representative payee or, if the interest of the individual under this title would be served thereby, to the individual.

(B) In the case of an individual entitled to benefits based on disability, the payment of such benefits shall be made to a representative payee if the Commissioner of Social Security determines that such payment would serve the interest of the individual because the individual also has an alcoholism or drug addiction condition (as determined by the Commissioner) and the individual is incapable of managing such benefits.

(2)(A) Any certification made under paragraph (1) for payment of benefits to an individual's representative payee shall be made on the basis of—

(i) an investigation by the Commissioner of Social Security of the person to serve as representative payee, which shall be conducted in advance of such certification and shall, to the extent practicable, include a face-to-face interview with such person, and

(ii) adequate evidence that such certification is in the interest of such individual (as determined by the Commissioner of Social Security in regulations).

(B)(i) As part of the investigation referred to in subparagraph (A), the Commissioner of Social Security shall—

(I) require the person being investigated to submit documented proof of the identity of such person, unless information establishing such identity has been submitted with an application for benefits under this title, title VIII, or title XVI,

(II) verify such person's social security account number (or employer identification number),

(III) determine whether such person has been convicted of a violation of section 208, 811, or 1632,

(IV) obtain information concerning whether such person has been convicted of any other offense under Federal or State law which resulted in imprisonment for more than 1 year,

(V) obtain information concerning whether such person is a person described in section 202(x)(1)(A)(iv), and

(VI) determine whether certification of payment of benefits to such person has been revoked pursuant to this subsection or, the designation of such person as a representative payee has been revoked pursuant to section 807(a), payment of benefits to such person has been terminated pursuant to section 1631(a)(2)(A)(iii) by reason of misuse of funds paid as benefits under this title or title XVI.

(ii) The Commissioner of Social Security shall establish and maintain a centralized file, which shall be updated periodically and which shall be in a form which renders it readily retrievable by each servicing office of the Social Security Administration. Such file shall consist of—

(I) a list of the names and social security account numbers (or employer identification numbers) of all persons with respect to whom certification of payment of benefits has been revoked on or after January 1, 1991, pursuant to this subsection, whose designation as a representative payee has been revoked pursuant to section 807(a), or with respect to whom payment of benefits has been terminated on or after such date pursuant to section 1631(a)(2)(A)(iii), by reason of misuse of funds paid as benefits under this title, title VIII, or title XVI, and

(II) a list of the names and social security account numbers (or employer identification numbers) of all persons who have been convicted of a violation of section 208, 811, or 1632.

(iii) Notwithstanding the provisions of section 552a of title 5, United States Code[77], or any other provision of Federal or State law (other than section 6103 of the Internal Revenue Code of 1986[78] and section 1106(c) of this Act), the Commissioner shall furnish any Federal, State, or local law enforcement officer, upon the written request of the officer, with the current address, social security account number, and photograph (if applicable) of any person investigated under this paragraph, if the officer furnishes the Commissioner with the name of such person and such other identifying information as may reasonably be required by the Commissioner to establish the unique identity of such person, and notifies the Commissioner that—

(I) such person is described in section 202(x)(1)(A)(iv),

(II) such person has information that is necessary for the officer to conduct the officer's official duties, and

(III) the location or apprehension of such person is within the officer's official duties.

(C)(i) Benefits of an individual may not be certified for payment to any other person pursuant to this subsection if—

(I) such person has previously been convicted as described in subparagraph (B)(III),

(II) except as provided in clause (ii), certification of payment of benefits to such person under this subsection has previously been revoked as described in subparagraph (B)(VI), the designation of such person as a representative payee has been revoked pursuant to section 807(a), or payment of benefits to such person pursuant to section 1631(a)(2)(A)(ii) has previously been terminated as described in section 1631(a)(2)(B)(ii)(V),

(III) except as provided in clause (iii), such person is a creditor of such individual who provides such individual with goods or services for consideration,

(IV) such person has previously been convicted as described in subparagraph (B)(i)(IV), unless the Commissioner determines that such certification would be appropriate notwithstanding such conviction, or

(V) such person is a person described in section 202(x)(1)(A)(iv).

(ii) The Commissioner of Social Security shall prescribe regulations under which the Commissioner of Social Security may grant exemp-

---

[77] See Vol. II, 5 U.S.C. 552a.
[78] See Vol. II, P.L. 83-591, §6103.

98 SOCIAL SECURITY ACT—§ 205(j)(2)(C)(ii)(cont)

tions to any person from the provisions of clause (II) on a case-by-case basis if such exemption is in the best interest of the individual whose benefits would be paid to such person pursuant to this subsection.

(iii) Clause (III) shall not apply with respect to any person who is a creditor referred to therein if such creditor is—

(I) a relative of such individual if such relative resides in the same household as such individual,

(II) a legal guardian or legal representative of such individual,

(III) a facility that is licensed or certified as a care facility under the law of a State or a political subdivision of a State,

(IV) a person who is an administrator, owner, or employee of a facility referred to in subclause (III) if such individual resides in such facility, and the certification of payment to such facility or such person is made only after good faith efforts have been made by the local servicing office of the Social Security Administration to locate an alternative representative payee to whom such certification of payment would serve the best interests of such individual, or

(V) an individual who is determined by the Commissioner of Social Security, on the basis of written findings and under procedures which the Commissioner of Social Security shall prescribe by regulation, to be acceptable to serve as a representative payee.

(iv) The procedures referred to in clause (iii)(V) shall require the individual who will serve as representative payee to establish, to the satisfaction of the Commissioner of Social Security, that—

(I) such individual poses no risk to the beneficiary,

(II) the financial relationship of such individual to the beneficiary poses no substantial conflict of interest, and

(III) no other more suitable representative payee can be found.

(v) In the case of an individual described in paragraph (1)(B), when selecting such individual's representative payee, preference shall be given to—

(I) a community-based nonprofit social service agency certified (as defined in paragraph (10)),

(II) a Federal, State, or local government agency whose mission is to carry out income maintenance, social service, or health care-related activities,

(III) a State or local government agency with fiduciary responsibilities, or

(IV) a designee of an agency (other than of a Federal agency) referred to in the preceding subclauses of this clause, if the Commissioner of Social Security deems it appropriate, unless the Commissioner of Social Security determines that selection of a family member would be appropriate.

(D)(i) Subject to clause (ii), if the Commissioner of Social Security makes a determination described in the first sentence of paragraph (1) with respect to any individual's benefit and determines that direct payment of the benefit to the individual would cause substantial harm to the individual, the Commissioner of Social Security may defer (in the case of initial entitlement) or suspend (in the case of existing entitlement) direct payment of such benefit to the individual, until such time as the selection of a representative payee is made pursuant to this subsection.

(ii)(I) Except as provided in subclause (II), any deferral or suspension of direct payment of a benefit pursuant to clause shall be for a period of not more than 1 month.

(II) Subclause shall not apply in any case in which the individual is, as of the date of the Commissioner's determination, legally incompetent, under the age of 15 years, or described in paragraph (1)(B).

(iii) Payment pursuant to this subsection of any benefits which are deferred or suspended pending the selection of a representative payee shall be made to the individual or the representative payee as a single sum or over such period of time as the Commissioner of Social Security determines is in the best interest of the individual entitled to such benefits.

(E)(i) Any individual who is dissatisfied with a determination by the Commissioner of Social Security to certify payment of such individual's benefit to a representative payee under paragraph (1) or with the designation of a particular person to serve as representative payee shall be entitled to a hearing by the Commissioner of Social Security to the same extent as is provided in subsection (b), and to judicial review of the Commissioner's final decision as is provided in subsection (g).

(ii) In advance of the certification of payment of an individual's benefit to a representative payee under paragraph (1), the Commissioner of Social Security shall provide written notice of the Commissioner's initial determination to certify such payment. Such notice shall be provided to such individual, except that, if such individual—

(I) is under the age of 15,

(II) is an unemancipated minor under the age of 18, or

(III) is legally incompetent,

then such notice shall be provided solely to the legal guardian or legal representative of such individual.

(iii) Any notice described in clause (ii) shall be clearly written in language that is easily understandable to the reader, shall identify the person to be designated as such individual's representative payee, and shall explain to the reader the right under clause of such individual or of such individual's legal guardian or legal representative—

(I) to appeal a determination that a representative payee is necessary for such individual,

(II) to appeal the designation of a particular person to serve as the representative payee of such individual, and

(III) to review the evidence upon which such designation is based and submit additional evidence.

(3)(A) In any case where payment under this title is made to a person other than the individual entitled to such payment, the Commissioner of Social Security shall establish a system of accountability monitoring whereby such person shall report not less often than annually with respect to the use of such payments. The Commissioner of Social Security shall establish and implement statistically valid procedures for reviewing such reports in order to identify instances in which such persons are not properly using such payments.

(B) Subparagraph (A) shall not apply in any case where the other person to whom such payment is made is a State institution. In such cases, the Commissioner of Social Security shall establish a system of accountability monitoring for institutions in each State.

100 SOCIAL SECURITY ACT—§ 205(j)(3)(C)

(C) Subparagraph (A) shall not apply in any case where the individual entitled to such payment is a resident of a Federal institution and the other person to whom such payment is made is the institution.

(D) Notwithstanding subparagraphs (A), (B), and (C), the Commissioner of Social Security may require a report at any time from any person receiving payments on behalf of another, if the Commissioner of Social Security has reason to believe that the person receiving such payments is misusing such payments.

(E) In any case in which the person described in subparagraph (A) or (D) receiving payments on behalf of another fails to submit a report required by the Commissioner of Social Security under subparagraph (A) or (D), the Commissioner may, after furnishing notice to such person and the individual entitled to such payment, require that such person appear in person at a field office of the Social Security Administration serving the area in which the individual resides in order to receive such payments.

(F) The Commissioner of Social Security shall maintain a centralized file, which shall be updated periodically and which shall be in a form which will be readily retrievable by each servicing office of the Social Security Administration, of—

(i) the address and the social security account number (or employer identification number) of each representative payee who is receiving benefit payments pursuant to this subsection, section 807, or section 1631(a)(2), and

(ii) the address and social security account number of each individual for whom each representative payee is reported to be providing services as representative payee pursuant to this subsection, section 807, or section 1631(a)(2).

(G) Each servicing office of the Administration shall maintain a list, which shall be updated periodically, of public agencies and certified community-based nonprofit social service agencies (as defined in paragraph (10) which are qualified to serve as representative payees pursuant to this subsection or 807 or section 1631(a)(2) and which are located in the area served by such servicing office.

(4)(A)(i) Except as provided in the next sentence, a qualified organization may collect from an individual a monthly fee for expenses (including overhead) incurred by such organization in providing services performed as such individual's representative payee pursuant to this subsection if such fee does not exceed the lesser of—

(I) 10 percent of the monthly benefit involved, or

(II) $25.00 per month ($50.00 per month in any case in which the individual is described in paragraph(1)(B).

A qualified organization may not collect a fee from an individual for any month with respect to which the Commissioner of Social Security or a court of competent jurisdiction has determined that the organization misused all or part of the individual's benefit, and any amount so collected by the qualified organization for such month shall be treated as a misused part of the individual's benefit for purposes of paragraphs (5) and (6). The Commissioner shall adjust annually (after 1995) each dollar amount set forth in subclause (II) under procedures providing for adjustments in the same manner and to the same extent as adjustments are provided for under the procedures used to adjust benefit amounts under section 215(2)(A), except that any amount so

SOCIAL SECURITY ACT—§ 205(j)(5)(B)   101

adjusted that is not a multiple of $1.00 shall be rounded to the nearest multiple of $1.00.

(ii) In the case of an individual who is no longer currently entitled to monthly insurance benefits under this title but to whom all past-due benefits have not been paid, for purposes of clause (i), any amount of such past-due benefits payable in any month shall be treated as a monthly benefit referred to in clause (i) (I).

Any agreement providing for a fee in excess of the amount permitted under this subparagraph shall be void and shall be treated as misuse by such organization of such individual's benefits.

(B) For purposes of this paragraph, the term "qualified organization" means any State or local government agency whose mission is to carry out income maintenance, social service, or health care-related activities, any State or local government agency with fiduciary responsibilities, or any certified community-based nonprofit social service agency (as defined in paragraph (10)), if such agency, in accordance with any applicable regulations of the Commissioner of Social Security—

(i) regularly provides services as the representative payee, pursuant to this subsection or 807 or section 1631(a)(2), concurrently to 5 or more individuals,

(ii) demonstrates to the satisfaction of the Commissioner of Social Security that such agency is not otherwise a creditor of any such individual.

The Commissioner of Social Security shall prescribe regulations under which the Commissioner of Social Security may grant an exception from clause (ii) for any individual on a case-by-case basis if such exception is in the best interests of such individual.

(C) Any qualified organization which knowingly charges or collects, directly or indirectly, any fee in excess of the maximum fee prescribed under subparagraph (A) or makes any agreement, directly or indirectly, to charge or collect any fee in excess of such maximum fee, shall be fined in accordance with title 18, United States Code, or imprisoned not more than 6 months, or both.

(5) In cases where the negligent failure of the Commissioner of Social Security to investigate or monitor a representative payee results in misuse of benefits by the representative payee, the Commissioner of Social Security shall certify for payment to the beneficiary or the beneficiary's alternative representative payee an amount equal to such misused benefits. In any case in which a representative payee that—

(A) is not an individual (regardless of whether it is a "qualified organization" within the meaning of paragraph (4)(B)); or

(B) is an individual who, for any month during a period when misuse occurs, serves 15 or more individuals who are beneficiaries under this title, title VIII, title XVI, or any combination of such titles;

misuses all or part of an individual's benefit paid to such representative payee, the Commissioner of Social Security shall certify for payment to the beneficiary or the beneficiary's alternative representative payee an amount equal to the amount of such benefit so misused. The provisions of this paragraph are subject to the limitations of paragraph (7)(B). The Commissioner of Social Security shall make a good faith effort to obtain restitution from the terminated representative payee.

102 SOCIAL SECURITY ACT—§ 205(j)(6)

(6)(A) In addition to such other reviews of representative payees as the Commissioner of Social Security may otherwise conduct, the Commissioner shall provide for the periodic onsite review of any person or agency located in the United States that receives the benefits payable under this title (alone or in combination with benefits payable under title VIII or title XVI) to another individual pursuant to the appointment of such person or agency as a representative payee under this subsection, section 807, or section 1631(a)(2) in any case in which—

(i) the representative payee is a person who serves in that capacity with respect to 15 or more such individuals;

(ii) the representative payee is a certified community-based nonprofit social service agency (as defined in paragraph (10) of this subsection or section 1631(a)(2)(I)); or

(iii) the representative payee is an agency (other than an agency described in clause (ii)) that serves in that capacity with respect to 50 or more such individuals.

(B) Within 120 days after the end of each fiscal year, the Commissioner shall submit to the Committee on Ways and Means of the House of Representatives and the Committee on Finance of the Senate a report on the results of periodic onsite reviews conducted during the fiscal year pursuant to subparagraph (A) and of any other reviews of representative payees conducted during such fiscal year in connection with benefits under this title. Each such report shall describe in detail all problems identified in such reviews and any corrective action taken or planned to be taken to correct such problems, and shall include—

(i) the number of such reviews;

(ii) the results of such reviews;

(iii) the number of cases in which the representative payee was changed and why;

(iv) the number of cases involving the exercise of expedited, targeted oversight of the representative payee by the Commissioner conducted upon receipt of an allegation of misuse of funds, failure to pay a vendor, or a similar irregularity;

(v) the number of cases discovered in which there was a misuse of funds;

(vi) how any such cases of misuse of funds were dealt with by the Commissioner;

(vii) the final disposition of such cases of misuse of funds, including any criminal penalties imposed; and

(viii) such other information as the Commissioner deems appropriate.

(7)(A) If the Commissioner of Social Security or a court of competent jurisdiction determines that a representative payee that is not a Federal, State, or local government agency has misused all or part of an individual's benefit that was paid to such representative payee under this subsection, the representative payee shall be liable for the amount misused, and such amount (to the extent not repaid by the representative payee) shall be treated as an overpayment of benefits under this title to the representative payee for all purposes of this Act and related laws pertaining to the recovery of such overpayments. Subject to subparagraph (B), upon recovering all or any part of such amount, the Commissioner shall certify an amount equal to the re-

SOCIAL SECURITY ACT—§ 205(n)   103

covered amount for payment to such individual or such individual's alternative representative payee.

(B) The total of the amount certified for payment to such individual or such individual's alternative representative payee under subparagraph (A) and the amount certified for payment under paragraph (5) may not exceed the total benefit amount misused by the representative payee with respect to such individual.

(8) For purposes of this subsection, the term "benefit based on disability" of an individual means a disability insurance benefit of such individual under section 223 or a child's, widow's, or widower's insurance benefit of such individual under section 202 based on such individual's disability.

(9) For purposes of this subsection, misuse of benefits by a representative payee occurs in any case in which the representative payee receives payment under this title for the use and benefit of another person and converts such payment, or any part thereof, to a use other than for the use and benefit of such other person. The Commissioner of Social Security may prescribe by regulation the meaning of the term "use and benefit" for purposes of this paragraph.

(10) For purposes of this subsection, the term "certified community-based nonprofit social service agency" means a community-based nonprofit social service agency which is in compliance with requirements, under regulations which shall be prescribed by the Commissioner, for annual certification to the Commissioner that it is bonded in accordance with requirements specified by the Commissioner and that it is licensed in each State in which it serves as a representative payee (if licensing is available in the State) in accordance with requirements specified by the Commissioner. Any such annual certification shall include a copy of any independent audit on the agency which may have been performed since the previous certification.

(k) Any payment made after December 31, 1939, under conditions set forth in subsection (j), any payment made before January 1, 1940, to, or on behalf of, a legally incompetent individual, and any payment made after December 31, 1939, to a legally incompetent individual without knowledge by the Commissioner of Social Security of incompetency prior to certification of payment, if otherwise valid under this title, shall be a complete settlement and satisfaction of any claim, right, or interest in and to such payment.

(l) The Commissioner of Social Security is authorized to delegate to any member, officer, or employee of the Social Security Administration designated by him any of the powers conferred upon him by this section, and is authorized to be represented by his own attorneys in any court in any case or proceeding arising under the provisions of subsection (e).

(m)   [Repealed.[79]]

(n) The Commissioner of Social Security may, in the Commissioner's discretion, certify to the Managing Trustee any two or more individuals of the same family for joint payment of the total benefits payable to such individuals for any month, and if one of such individuals dies before a check representing such joint payment is negotiated, payment of the amount of such unnegotiated check to the surviving individual or individuals may be authorized in

---

[79] P.L. 81-734, §101(b)(2); 64 Stat. 488. See, instead, §202(j)(2).

104 SOCIAL SECURITY ACT—§ 205(n)(cont)

accordance with regulations of the Secretary of the Treasury; except that appropriate adjustment or recovery shall be made under section 204(a) with respect to so much of the amount of such check as exceeds the amount to which such surviving individual or individuals are entitled under this title for such month.

Crediting of Compensation Under the Railroad Retirement Act

(o) If there is no person who would be entitled, upon application therefor, to an annuity under section 2 of the Railroad Retirement Act of 1974[80], or to a lump-sum payment under section 6(b) of such Act, with respect to the death of an employee (as defined in such Act), then, notwithstanding section 210(a)(9)[81] of this Act, compensation (as defined in such Railroad Retirement Act, but excluding compensation attributable as having been paid during any month on account of military service creditable under section 3 of such Act if wages are deemed to have been paid to such employee during such month under subsection (a) or (e) of section 217 of this Act) of such employee shall constitute remuneration for employment for purposes of determining (A) entitlement to and the amount of any lump–sum death payment under this title on the basis of such employee's wages and self–employment income and (B) entitlement to and the amount of any monthly benefit under this title, for the month in which such employee died or for any month thereafter, on the basis of such wages and self–employment income. For such purposes, compensation (as so defined) paid in a calendar year before 1978 shall, in the absence of evidence to the contrary, be presumed to have been paid in equal proportions with respect to all months in the year in which the employee rendered services for such compensation.

Special Rules in Case of Federal Service

(p)(1) With respect to service included as employment under section 210 which is performed in the employ of the United States or in the employ of any instrumentality which is wholly owned by the United States, including service, performed as a member of a uniformed service, to which the provisions of subsection (l)(1) of such section are applicable, and including service, performed as a volunteer or volunteer leader within the meaning of the Peace Corps Act[82], to which the provisions of section 210(o) are applicable, the Commissioner of Social Security shall not make determinations as to the amounts of remuneration for such service, or the periods in which or for which such remuneration was paid, but shall accept the determinations with respect thereto of the head of the appropriate Federal agency or instrumentality, and of such agents as such head may designate, as evidenced by returns filed in accordance with the provisions of section 3122 of the Internal Revenue Code of 1954[83] and certifications made pursuant to this subsection. Such determinations shall be final and conclusive. Nothing in this paragraph shall be construed to affect the Commis-

---

[80] See Vol. II, P.L. 75-162 [as amended by P.L. 93-445], §2.
[81] P.L. 83-761, §101(a)(5), redesignated §210(a)(9) as §201(a)(10).
[82] See Vol. II, P.L. 87-293.
[83] See Vol. II, P.L. 83-591, §3122.

sioner's authority to determine under sections 209 and 210 whether any such service constitutes employment, the periods of such employment, and whether remuneration paid for any such service constitutes wages.

(2) The head of any such agency or instrumentality is authorized and directed, upon written request of the Commissioner of Social Security, to make certification to the Commissioner with respect to any matter determinable for the Commissioner of Social Security by such head or his agents under this subsection, which the Commissioner of Social Security finds necessary in administering this title.

(3) The provisions of paragraphs (1) and (2) shall be applicable in the case of service performed by a civilian employee, not compensated from funds appropriated by the Congress, in the Army and Air Force Exchange Service, Army and Air Force Motion Picture Service, Navy Exchanges, Marine Corps Exchanges, or other activities, conducted by an instrumentality of the United States subject to the jurisdiction of the Secretary of Defense, at installations of the Department of Defense for the comfort, pleasure, contentment, and mental and physical improvement of personnel of such Department; and for purposes of paragraphs (1) and (2) the Secretary of Defense shall be deemed to be the head of such instrumentality. The provisions of paragraphs (1) and (2) shall be applicable also in the case of service performed by a civilian employee, not compensated from funds appropriated by the Congress, in the Coast Guard Exchanges or other activities, conducted by an instrumentality of the United States subject to the jurisdiction of the Secretary of Homeland Security, at installations of the Coast Guard for the comfort, pleasure, contentment, and mental and physical improvement of personnel of the Coast Guard; and for purposes of paragraphs (1) and (2) the Secretary of Homeland Security shall be deemed to be the head of such instrumentality.

Expedited Benefit Payments

(q)(1) The Commissioner of Social Security shall establish and put into effect procedures under which expedited payment of monthly insurance benefits under this title will, subject to paragraph (4) of this subsection, be made as set forth in paragraphs (2) and (3) of this subsection.

(2) In any case in which—

(A) an individual makes an allegation that a monthly benefit under this title was due him in a particular month but was not paid to him, and

(B) such individual submits a written request for the payment of such benefit—

(i) in the case of an individual who received a regular monthly benefit in the month preceding the month with respect to which such allegation is made, not less than 30 days after the 15th day of the month with respect to which such allegation is made (and in the event that such request is submitted prior to the expiration of such 30-day period, it shall be deemed to have been submitted upon the expiration of such period), and

106 SOCIAL SECURITY ACT—§ 205(q)(2)(B)(ii)

(ii) in any other case, not less than 90 days after the later of (I) the date on which such benefit is alleged to have been due, or (II) the date on which such individual furnished the last information requested by the Commissioner of Social Security (and such written request will be deemed to be filed on the day on which it was filed, or the ninetieth day after the first day on which the Commissioner of Social Security has evidence that such allegation is true, whichever is later),

the Commissioner of Social Security shall, if he finds that benefits are due, certify such benefits for payment, and payment shall be made within 15 days immediately following the date on which the written request is deemed to have been filed.

(3) In any case in which the Commissioner of Social Security determines that there is evidence, although additional evidence might be required for a final decision, that an allegation described in paragraph (2)(A) is true, he may make a preliminary certification of such benefit for payment even though the 30-day or 90-day periods described in paragraph (2)(B)(i) and (B)(ii) have not elapsed.

(4) Any payment made pursuant to a certification under paragraph (3) of this subsection shall not be considered an incorrect payment for purposes of determining the liability of the certifying or disbursing officer.

(5) For purposes of this subsection, benefits payable under section 228 shall be treated as monthly insurance benefits payable under this title. However, this subsection shall not apply with respect to any benefit for which a check has been negotiated, or with respect to any benefit alleged to be due under either section 223, or section 202 to a wife, husband, or child of an individual entitled to or applying for benefits under section 223, or to a child who has attained age 18 and is under a disability, or to a widow or widower on the basis of being under a disability.

Use of Death Certificates to Correct Program Information

(r)(1) The Commissioner of Social Security shall undertake to establish a program under which—

(A) States (or political subdivisions thereof) voluntarily contract with the Commissioner of Social Security to furnish the Commissioner of Social Security periodically with information (in a form established by the Commissioner of Social Security in consultation with the States) concerning individuals with respect to whom death certificates (or equivalent documents maintained by the States or subdivisions) have been officially filed with them; and

(B) there will be (i) a comparison of such information on such individuals with information on such individuals in the records being used in the administration of this Act, (ii) validation of the results of such comparisons, and (iii) corrections in such records to accurately reflect the status of such individuals.

(2) Each State (or political subdivision thereof) which furnishes the Commissioner of Social Security with information on records of deaths in the State or subdivision under this subsection may be paid by the Commissioner of Social Security from amounts available for adminis-

tration of this Act the reasonable costs (established by the Commissioner of Social Security in consultations with the States) for transcribing and transmitting such information to the Commissioner of Social Security.

(3) In the case of individuals with respect to whom federally funded benefits are provided by (or through) a Federal or State agency other than under this Act, the Commissioner of Social Security shall to the extent feasible provide such information through a cooperative arrangement with such agency, for ensuring proper payment of those benefits with respect to such individuals if—

(A) under such arrangement the agency provides reimbursement to the Commissioner of Social Security for the reasonable cost of carrying out such arrangement, and

(B) such arrangement does not conflict with the duties of the Commissioner of Social Security under paragraph (1).

(4) The Commissioner of Social Security may enter into similar agreements with States to provide information for their use in programs wholly funded by the States if the requirements of subparagraphs (A) and (B) of paragraph (3) are met.

(5) The Commissioner of Social Security may use or provide for the use of such records as may be corrected under this section, subject to such safeguards as the Commissioner of Social Security determines are necessary or appropriate to protect the information from unauthorized use or disclosure, for statistical and research activities conducted by Federal and State agencies.

(6) Information furnished to the Commissioner of Social Security under this subsection may not be used for any purpose other than the purpose described in this subsection and is exempt from disclosure under section 552 of title 5, United States Code, and from the requirements of section 552a of such title[84].

(7) The Commissioner of Social Security shall include information on the status of the program established under this section and impediments to the effective implementation of the program in the 1984 report required under section 704 of this Act.

(8)(A) The Commissioner of Social Security shall, upon the request of the official responsible for a State driver's license agency pursuant to the Help America Vote Act of 2002[85]—

(i) enter into an agreement with such official for the purpose of verifying applicable information, so long as the requirements of subparagraphs (A) and (B) of paragraph (3) are met; and

(ii) include in such agreement safeguards to assure the maintenance of the confidentiality of any applicable information disclosed and procedures to permit such agency to use the applicable information for the purpose of maintaining its records.

(B) Information provided pursuant to an agreement under this paragraph shall be provided at such time, in such place, and in such manner as the Commissioner determines appropriate.

(C) The Commissioner shall develop methods to verify the accuracy of information provided by the agency with respect to applications for voter registration, for whom the last 4 digits of a social security number are provided instead of a driver's license number.

---

[84] See Vol. II, Title 5, §552 and 552a.
[85] P.L. 107-252.

108   SOCIAL SECURITY ACT—§ 205(r)(8)(D)

(D) For purposes of this paragraph—

(i) the term "applicable information" means information regarding whether—

(I) the name (including the first name and any family forename or surname), the date of birth (including the month, day, and year), and social security number of an individual provided to the Commissioner match the information contained in the Commissioner's records, and

(II) such individual is shown on the records of the Commissioner as being deceased; and

(ii) the term "State driver's license agency" means the State agency which issues driver's licenses to individuals within the State and maintains records relating to such licensure.

(E) Nothing in this paragraph may be construed to require the provision of applicable information with regard to a request for a record of an individual if the Commissioner determines there are exceptional circumstances warranting an exception (such as safety of the individual or interference with an investigation).

(F) Applicable information provided by the Commission pursuant to an agreement under this paragraph or by an individual to any agency that has entered into an agreement under this paragraph shall be considered as strictly confidential and shall be used only for the purposes described in this paragraph and for carrying out an agreement under this paragraph. Any officer or employee or former officer or employee of a State, or any officer or employee or former officer or employee of a contractor of a State who, without the written authority of the Commissioner, publishes or communicates any applicable information in such individual's possession by reason of such employment or position as such an officer, shall be guilty of a felony and upon conviction thereof shall be fined or imprisoned, or both, as described in section 208.

Notice Requirements

(s) The Commissioner of Social Security shall take such actions as are necessary to ensure that any notice to one or more individuals issued pursuant to this title by the Commissioner of Social Security or by a State agency—

(1) is written in simple and clear language, and

(2) includes the address and telephone number of the local office of the Social Security Administration which serves the recipient.

In the case of any such notice which is not generated by a local servicing office, the requirements of paragraph (2) shall be treated as satisfied if such notice includes the address of the local office of the Social Security Administration which services the recipient of the notice and a telephone number through which such office can be reached.

Same-Day Personal Interviews at Field Offices In Cases Where Time Is of The Essence

(t) In any case in which an individual visits a field office of the Social Security Administration and represents during the visit to an officer

SOCIAL SECURITY ACT—§ 206(a)(1) 109

or employee of the Social Security Administration in the office that the individual's visit is occasioned by—

(1) the receipt of a notice from the Social Security Administration indicating a time limit for response by the individual, or

(2) the theft, loss, or nonreceipt of a benefit payment under this title,

the Commissioner of Social Security shall ensure that the individual is granted a face-to-face interview at the office with an officer or employee of the Social Security Administration before the close of business on the day of the visit.

(u)(1)(A) The Commissioner of Social Security shall immediately redetermine the entitlement of individuals to monthly insurance benefits under this title if there is reason to believe that fraud or similar fault was involved in the application of the individual for such benefits, unless a United States attorney, or equivalent State prosecutor, with jurisdiction over potential or actual related criminal cases, certifies, in writing, that there is a substantial risk that such action by the Commissioner of Social Security with regard to beneficiaries in a particular investigation would jeopardize the criminal prosecution of a person involved in a suspected fraud.

(B) When redetermining the entitlement, or making an initial determination of entitlement, of an individual under this title, the Commissioner of Social Security shall disregard any evidence if there is reason to believe that fraud or similar fault was involved in the providing of such evidence.

(2) For purposes of paragraph (1), similar fault is involved with respect to a determination if—

(A) an incorrect or incomplete statement that is material to the determination is knowingly made; or

(B) information that is material to the determination is knowingly concealed.

(3) If, after redetermining pursuant to this subsection the entitlement of an individual to monthly insurance benefits, the Commissioner of Social Security determines that there is insufficient evidence to support such entitlement, the Commissioner of Social Security may terminate such entitlement and may treat benefits paid on the basis of such insufficient evidence as overpayments.

REPRESENTATION OF CLAIMANTS[86]

Sec. 206. [42 U.S.C. 406] (a)(1) The Commissioner of Social Security may prescribe rules and regulations governing the recognition of agents or other persons, other than attorneys as hereinafter provided, representing claimants before the Commissioner of Social Security, and may require of such agents or other persons, before being recognized as representatives of claimants that they shall show that they are of good character and in good repute, possessed of the necessary qualifications to enable them to render such claimants valuable service, and otherwise competent to advise and assist such claimants in the presentation of their cases. An attorney in good standing who is admitted to practice before the highest court of the State, Territory,

---

[86] See Vol. II, P.L. 108-203, §303, with respect to a nationwide demonstration project providing for extension of fee withholding procedures to non-attorney representatives and §304, with respect to a GAO study regarding the fee payment process for claimant representatives.

110   SOCIAL SECURITY ACT—§ 206(a)(1)(cont)

District, or insular possession of his residence or before the Supreme Court of the United States or the inferior Federal courts, shall be entitled to represent claimants before the Commissioner of Social Security. Notwithstanding the preceding sentences, the Commissioner, after due notice and opportunity for hearing, (A) may refuse to recognize as a representative, and may disqualify a representative already recognized, any attorney who has been disbarred or suspended from any court or bar to which he or she was previously admitted to practice or who has been disqualified from participating in or appearing before any Federal program or agency, and (B) may refuse to recognize, and may disqualify, as a non-attorney representative any attorney who has been disbarred or suspended from any court or bar to which he or she was previously admitted to practice. A representative who has been disqualified or suspended pursuant to this section from appearing before the Social Security Administration as a result of collecting or receiving a fee in excess of the amount authorized shall be barred from appearing before the Social Security Administration as a representative until full restitution is made to the claimant and, thereafter, may be considered for reinstatement only under such rules as the Commissioner may prescribe. The Commissioner of Social Security may, after due notice and opportunity for hearing, suspend or prohibit from further practice before the Commissioner any such person, agent, or attorney who refuses to comply with the Commissioner's rules and regulations or who violates any provision of this section for which a penalty is prescribed. The Commissioner of Social Security may, by rule and regulation, prescribe the maximum fees which may be charged for services performed in connection with any claim before the Commissioner of Social Security under this title, and any agreement in violation of such rules and regulations shall be void. Except as provided in paragraph (2)(A), whenever the Commissioner of Social Security, in any claim before the Commissioner for benefits under this title, makes a determination favorable to the claimant, the Commissioner shall, if the claimant was represented by an attorney in connection with such claim, fix (in accordance with the regulations prescribed pursuant to the preceding sentence) a reasonable fee to compensate such attorney for the services performed by him in connection with such claim.

(2)(A) In the case of a claim of entitlement to past-due benefits under this title, if—

(i) an agreement between the claimant and another person regarding any fee to be recovered by such person to compensate such person for services with respect to the claim is presented in writing to the Commissioner of Social Security prior to the time of the Commissioner's determination regarding the claim,

(ii) the fee specified in the agreement does not exceed the lesser of—

(I) 25 percent of the total amount of such past-due benefits (as determined before any applicable reduction under section 1127(a)), or

(II) $4,000, and

(iii) the determination is favorable to the claimant,

then the Commissioner of Social Security shall approve that agreement at the time of the favorable determination, and (subject to paragraph (3)) the fee specified in the agreement shall be the maximum fee.

The Commissioner of Social Security may from time to time increase the dollar amount under clause (ii)(II) to the extent that the rate of increase in such amount, as determined over the period since January 1, 1991, does not at any time exceed the rate of increase in primary insurance amounts under section 215(i) since such date. The Commissioner of Social Security shall publish any such increased amount in the Federal Register.

(B) For purposes of this subsection, the term "past-due benefits" excludes any benefits with respect to which payment has been continued pursuant to subsection (g) or (h) of section 223.

(C) In any case involving—

(i) an agreement described in subparagraph (A) with any person relating to both a claim of entitlement to past-due benefits under this title and a claim of entitlement to past-due benefits under title XVI, and

(ii) a favorable determination made by the Commissioner of Social Security with respect to both such claims,

the Commissioner of Social Security may approve such agreement only if the total fee or fees specified in such agreement does not exceed, in the aggregate, the dollar amount in effect under subparagraph (A)(ii)(II).

(D) In the case of a claim with respect to which the Commissioner of Social Security has approved an agreement pursuant to subparagraph (A), the Commissioner of Social Security shall provide the claimant and the person representing the claimant a written notice of—

(i) the dollar amount of the past-due benefits (as determined before any applicable reduction under section 1127(a)) and the dollar amount of the past-due benefits payable to the claimant,

(ii) the dollar amount of the maximum fee which may be charged or recovered as determined under this paragraph, and

(iii) a description of the procedures for review under paragraph (3).

(3)(A) The Commissioner of Social Security shall provide by regulation for review of the amount which would otherwise be the maximum fee as determined under paragraph (2) if, within 15 days after receipt of the notice provided pursuant to paragraph (2)(D)—

(i) the claimant, or the administrative law judge or other adjudicator who made the favorable determination, submits a written request to the Commissioner of Social Security to reduce the maximum fee, or

(ii) the person representing the claimant submits a written request to the Commissioner of Social Security to increase the maximum fee.

Any such review shall be conducted after providing the claimant, the person representing the claimant, and the adjudicator with reasonable notice of such request and an opportunity to submit written information in favor of or in opposition to such request. The adjudicator may request the Commissioner of Social Security to reduce the maximum fee only on the basis of evidence of the failure of the person representing the claimant to represent adequately the claimant's interest or on the basis of evidence that the fee is clearly excessive for services rendered.

(B)(i) In the case of a request for review under subparagraph (A) by the claimant or by the person representing the claimant, such re-

112   SOCIAL SECURITY ACT—§ 206(a)(3)(B)(i)(cont)

view shall be conducted by the administrative law judge who made the favorable determination or, if the Commissioner of Social Security determines that such administrative law judge is unavailable or if the determination was not made by an administrative law judge, such review shall be conducted by another person designated by the Commissioner of Social Security for such purpose.

(ii) In the case of a request by the adjudicator for review under subparagraph (A), the review shall be conducted by the Commissioner of Social Security or by an administrative law judge or other person (other than such adjudicator) who is designated by the Commissioner of Social Security.

(C) Upon completion of the review, the administrative law judge or other person conducting the review shall affirm or modify the amount which would otherwise be the maximum fee. Any such amount so affirmed or modified shall be considered the amount of the maximum fee which may be recovered under paragraph (2). The decision of the administrative law judge or other person conducting the review shall not be subject to further review.

(4) Subject to subsection (d), if the claimant is determined to be entitled to past-due benefits under this title and the person representing the claimant is an attorney, the Commissioner of Social Security shall, notwithstanding section 205(i), certify for payment out of such past-due benefits (as determined before any applicable reduction under section 1127(a)) to such attorney an amount equal to so much of the maximum fee as does not exceed 25 percent of such past-due benefits (as determined before any applicable reduction under section 1127(a)).

(5) Any person who shall, with intent to defraud, in any manner willfully and knowingly deceive, mislead, or threaten any claimant or prospective claimant or beneficiary under this title by word, circular, letter or advertisement, or who shall knowingly charge or collect directly or indirectly any fee in excess of the maximum fee, or make any agreement directly or indirectly to charge or collect any fee in excess of the maximum fee, prescribed by the Commissioner of Social Security shall be deemed guilty of a misdemeanor and, upon conviction thereof, shall for each offense be punished by a fine not exceeding $500 or by imprisonment not exceeding one year, or both. The Commissioner of Social Security shall maintain in the electronic information retrieval system used by the Social Security Administration a current record, with respect to any claimant before the Commissioner of Social Security, of the identity of any person representing such claimant in accordance with this subsection.

(b)(1)(A) Whenever a court renders a judgment favorable to a claimant under this title who was represented before the court by an attorney, the court may determine and allow as part of its judgment a reasonable fee for such representation, not in excess of 25 percent of the total of the past-due benefits to which the claimant is entitled by reason of such judgment, and the Commissioner of Social Security may, notwithstanding the provisions of section 205(i), but subject to subsection (d) of this section, certify the amount of such fee for payment to such attorney out of, and not in addition to, the amount of such past-due benefits. In case of any such judgment, no other fee may be payable or certified for payment for such representation except as provided in this paragraph.

SOCIAL SECURITY ACT—§ 206(d)(2)(B)(ii)   113

(B) For purposes of this paragraph—
  (i) the term "past-due benefits" excludes any benefits with respect to which payment has been continued pursuant to subsection (g) or (h) of section 223, and
  (ii) amounts of past-due benefits shall be determined before any applicable reduction under section 1127(a).

(2) Any attorney who charges, demands, receives, or collects for services rendered in connection with proceedings before a court to which paragraph (1) is applicable any amount in excess of that allowed by the court thereunder shall be guilty of a misdemeanor and upon conviction thereof shall be subject to a fine of not more than $500, or imprisonment for not more than one year, or both.[87]

(c) The Commissioner of Social Security shall notify each claimant in writing, together with the notice to such claimant of an adverse determination, of the options for obtaining attorneys to represent individuals in presenting their cases before the Commissioner of Social Security. Such notification shall also advise the claimant of the availability to qualifying claimants of legal services organizations which provide legal services free of charge.

(d) ASSESSMENT ON ATTORNEYS.—
  (1) IN GENERAL.—Whenever a fee for services is required to be certified for payment to an attorney from a claimant's past-due benefits pursuant to subsection (a)(4) or (b)(1), the Commissioner shall impose on the attorney an assessment calculated in accordance with paragraph (2).
  (2) AMOUNT.—
    (A) The amount of an assessment under paragraph (1) shall be equal to the product obtained by multiplying the amount of the representative's fee that would be required to be so certified by subsection (a)(4) or (b)(1) before the application of this subsection, by the percentage specified in subparagraph (B), except that the maximum amount of the assessment may not exceed the greater of $75 or the adjusted amount as provided pursuant to the following two sentences. In the case of any calendar year beginning after the amendments made by section 301 of the Social Security Protection Act of 2003 take effect, the dollar amount specified in the preceding sentence (including a previously adjusted amount) shall be adjusted annually under the procedures used to adjust benefit amounts under section 215(i)(2)(A)(ii), except such adjustment shall be based on the higher of $75 or the previously adjusted amount that would have been in effect for December of the preceding year, but for the rounding of such amount pursuant to the following sentence. Any amount so adjusted that is not a multiple of $1 shall be rounded to the next lowest multiple of $1, but in no case less than $75.
    (B) The percentage specified in this subparagraph is—
      (i) for calendar years before 2001, 6.3 percent, and
      (ii) for calendar years after 2000, such percentage rate as the Commissioner determines is necessary in order to achieve full recovery of the costs of determining and

---

[87] See Vol. II, P.L. 96-481, with respect to an award of attorney fees and other expenses.

114 SOCIAL SECURITY ACT—§ 206(d)(2)(B)(ii)(cont)

certifying fees to attorneys from the past-due benefits of claimants, but not in excess of 6.3 percent.

(3) COLLECTION.—The Commissioner may collect the assessment imposed on an attorney under paragraph (1) by offset from the amount of the fee otherwise required by subsection (a)(4) or (b)(1) to be certified for payment to the attorney from a claimant's past-due benefits.

(4) PROHIBITION ON CLAIMANT REIMBURSEMENT.—An attorney subject to an assessment under paragraph (1) may not, directly or indirectly, request or otherwise obtain reimbursement for such assessment from the claimant whose claim gave rise to the assessment.

(5) DISPOSITION OF ASSESSMENTS.—Assessments on attorneys collected under this subsection shall be credited to the Federal Old-Age and Survivors Insurance Trust Fund and the Federal Disability Insurance Trust Fund, as appropriate.

(6) AUTHORIZATION OF APPROPRIATIONS.—The assessments authorized under this section shall be collected and available for obligation only to the extent and in the amount provided in advance in appropriations Acts. Amounts so appropriated are authorized to remain available until expended, for administrative expenses in carrying out this title and related laws.

ASSIGNMENT[88]

SEC. 207. [42 U.S.C. 407] (a) The right of any person to any future payment under this title shall not be transferable or assignable, at law or in equity, and none of the moneys paid or payable or rights existing under this title shall be subject to execution, levy, attachment, garnishment, or other legal process, or to the operation of any bankruptcy or insolvency law.

(b) No other provision of law, enacted before, on, or after the date of the enactment of this section[89], may be construed to limit, supersede, or otherwise modify the provisions of this section except to the extent that it does so by express reference to this section.

(c) Nothing in this section shall be construed to prohibit withholding taxes from any benefit under this title, if such withholding is done pursuant to a request made in accordance with section 3402(p)(1) of the Internal Revenue Code of 1986[90] by the person entitled to such benefit or such person's representative payee.

PENALTIES[91]

SEC. 208. [42 U.S.C. 408] (a) Whoever—

(1) for the purpose of causing an increase in any payment authorized to be made under this title, or for the purpose of causing any payment to be made where no payment is authorized under this title, shall make or cause to be made any false statement or representation (including any false statement or representation in connection with any matter arising under subchapter E

---

[88] See Vol. II, P.L. 83-591, §§86, 861, and 871, with respect to income subject to taxes.
[89] This section was enacted August 10, 1939, [P.L. 76-379, §207].
This subsection was enacted April 20, 1983, [P.L. 98-21, §335(a)(2)].
[90] See Vol. II, P.L. 83-591, § 3402(p)(1).
[91] See Vol. II, 18 U.S.C. 1028 and 1738, with respect to penalties relating to use of identification documents.

SOCIAL SECURITY ACT—§ 208(a)(7)(A)   115

of chapter 1, or subchapter A or E of chapter 9 of the Internal Revenue Code of 1939[92], or chapter 2 or 21 or subtitle F of the Internal Revenue Code of 1954[93]) as to—

(A) whether wages were paid or received for employment (as said terms are defined in this title and the Internal Revenue Code), or the amount of wages or the period during which paid or the person to whom paid; or

(B) whether net earnings from self-employment (as such term is defined in this title and in the Internal Revenue Code) were derived, or as to the amount of such net earnings or the period during which or the person by whom derived; or

(C) whether a person entitled to benefits under this title had earnings in or for a particular period (as determined under section 203(f) of this title for purposes of deductions from benefits), or as to the amount thereof; or

(2) makes or causes to be made any false statement or representation of a material fact in any application for any payment or for a disability determination under this title; or

(3) at any time makes or causes to be made any false statement or representation of a material fact for use in determining rights to payment under this title; or

(4) having knowledge of the occurrence of any event affecting (1) his initial or continued right to any payment under this title, or (2) the initial or continued right to any payment of any other individual in whose behalf he has applied for or is receiving such payment, conceals or fails to disclose such event with an intent fraudulently to secure payment either in a greater amount than is due or when no payment is authorized; or

(5) having made application to receive payment under this title for the use and benefit of another and having received such a payment, knowingly and willfully converts such a payment, or any part thereof, to a use other than for the use and benefit of such other person; or

(6) willfully, knowingly, and with intent to deceive the Commissioner of Social Security as to his true identity (or the true identity of any other person) furnishes or causes to be furnished false information to the Commissioner of Social Security with respect to any information required by the Commissioner of Social Security in connection with the establishment and maintenance of the records provided for in section 205(c)(2); or

(7) for the purpose of causing an increase in any payment authorized under this title (or any other program financed in whole or in part from Federal funds), or for the purpose of causing a payment under this title (or any such other program) to be made when no payment is authorized thereunder, or for the purpose of obtaining (for himself or any other person) any payment or any other benefit to which he (or such other person) is not entitled, or for the purpose of obtaining anything of value from any person, or for any other purpose—

(A) willfully, knowingly, and with intent to deceive, uses a social security account number, assigned by the

---

[92] P.L. 76-1.
[93] See Vol. II, P.L. 83-591, Chapter 2.

116 SOCIAL SECURITY ACT—§ 208(a)(7)(A)(cont)

Commissioner of Social Security (in the exercise of the Commissioner's authority under section 205(c)(2) to establish and maintain records) on the basis of false information furnished to the Commissioner of Social Security by him or by any other person; or

(B) with intent to deceive, falsely represents a number to be the social security account number assigned by the Commissioner of Social Security to him or to another person, when in fact such number is not the social security account number assigned by the Commissioner of Social Security to him or to such other person; or

(C) knowingly alters a social security card issued by the Commissioner of Social Security, buys or sells a card that is, or purports to be, a card so issued, counterfeits a social security card, or possesses a social security card or counterfeit social security card with intent to sell or alter it; or

(8) discloses, uses, or compels the disclosure of the social security number of any person in violation of the laws of the United States;

shall be guilty of a felony and upon conviction thereof shall be fined under title 18, United States Code, or imprisoned for not more than five years, or both.

(b)(1) Any Federal court, when sentencing a defendant convicted of an offense under subsection (a), may order, in addition to or in lieu of any other penalty authorized by law, that the defendant make restitution to the victims of such offense specified in paragraph (4).

(2) Sections 3612, 3663, and 3664 of title 18, United States Code[94], shall apply with respect to the issuance and enforcement of orders of restitution to victims of such offense under this subsection.

(3) If the court does not order restitution, or orders only partial restitution, under this subsection, the court shall state on the record the reasons therefor.

(4) For purposes of paragraphs (1) and (2), the victims of an offense under subsection (a) are the following:

(A) Any individual who suffers a financial loss as a result of the defendant's violation of subsection (a).

(B) The Commissioner of Social Security, to the extent that the defendant's violation of subsection (a) results in—

(i) the Commissioner of Social Security making a benefit payment that should not have been made; or

(ii) an individual suffering a financial loss due to the defendant's violation of subsection (a) in his or her capacity as the individual's representative payee appointed pursuant to section 205(j).

(5)(A) Except as provided in subparagraph (B), funds paid to the Commissioner of Social Security as restitution pursuant to a court order shall be deposited in the Federal Old-Age and Survivors Insurance Trust Fund, or the Federal Disability Insurance Trust Fund, as appropriate.

(B) In the case of funds paid to the Commissioner of Social Security pursuant to paragraph (4)(B)(ii), the Commissioner of Social Security

---

[94] See Vol. II, 18 U.S.C. 3612, 3663 and 3664, with respect to penalties relating to use of identification documents.

SOCIAL SECURITY ACT—§ 208(e)(3) 117

shall certify for payment to the individual described in such paragraph an amount equal to the lesser of the amount of the funds so paid or the individual's outstanding financial loss, except that such amount may be reduced by the amount of any overpayments of benefits owed under this title, title VIII, or title XVI by the individual.

(c) Any person or other entity who is convicted of a violation of any of the provisions of this section, if such violation is committed by such person or entity in his role as, or in applying to become, a certified payee under section 205(j) on behalf of another individual (other than such person's spouse), upon his second or any subsequent such conviction shall, in lieu of the penalty set forth in the preceding provisions of this section, be guilty of a felony and shall be fined under title 18, United States Code, or imprisoned for not more than five years, or both.

(d) Any individual or entity convicted of a felony under this section or under section 1632(b) may not be certified as a payee under section 205(j). For the purpose of subsection (a)(7), the terms "social security number" and "social security account number" mean such numbers as are assigned by the Commissioner of Social Security under section 205(c)(2) whether or not, in actual use, such numbers are called social security numbers.

(e)(1) Except as provided in paragraph (2), an alien—

(A) whose status is adjusted to that of lawful temporary resident under section 210 or 245A of the Immigration and Nationality Act[95] or under section 902 of the Foreign Relations Authorization Act, Fiscal Years 1988 and 1989[96],

(B) whose status is adjusted to that of permanent resident—

(i) under section 202 of the Immigration Reform and Control Act of 1986[97], or

(ii) pursuant to section 249 of the Immigration and Nationality Act[98], or

(C) who is granted special immigrant status under section 101(a)(27)(I) of the Immigration and Nationality Act[99],

shall not be subject to prosecution for any alleged conduct described in paragraph (6) or (7) of subsection (a) if such conduct is alleged to have occurred prior to 60 days after the date of the enactment of the Omnibus Budget Reconciliation Act of 1990[100].

(2) Paragraph (1) shall not apply with respect to conduct (described in subsection (a)(7)(C)) consisting of—

(A) selling a card that is, or purports to be, a social security card issued by the Commissioner of Social Security,

(B) possessing a social security card with intent to sell it, or

(C) counterfeiting a social security card with intent to sell it.

(3) Paragraph (1) shall not apply with respect to any criminal conduct involving both the conduct described in subsection (a)(7) to which paragraph (1) applies and any other criminal conduct if such other conduct would be criminal conduct if the conduct described in subsection (a)(7) were not committed.

---

[95] See Vol. II, P.L. 82-414, §§210 and 245A.
[96] See Vol. II, P.L. 100-204, §902.
[97] P.L. 99-603.
[98] P.L. 82-414, §249.
[99] See Vol. II, P.L. 82-414, §101(a)(27)(I).
[100] November 5, 1990 [P.L. 101-508; 104 Stat. 143].

118   SOCIAL SECURITY ACT—§ 208(e)(3)(cont)

DEFINITION OF WAGES

SEC. 209. [42 U.S.C. 409] (a) For the purposes of this title, the term "wages" means remuneration paid prior to 1951 which was wages for the purposes of this title under the law applicable to the payment of such remuneration, and remuneration paid after 1950 for employment, including the cash value of all remuneration (including benefits) paid in any medium other than cash; except that, in the case of remuneration paid after 1950, such term shall not include—

(1)(A) That part of remuneration which, after remuneration (other than remuneration referred to in the succeeding subsections of this section) equal to $3,600 with respect to employment has been paid to an individual during any calendar year prior to 1955, is paid to such individual during such calendar year;

(B) That part of remuneration which, after remuneration (other than remuneration referred to in the succeeding subsections of this section) equal to $4,200 with respect to employment has been paid to an individual during any calendar year after 1954 and prior to 1959, is paid to such individual during such calendar year;

(C) That part of remuneration which, after remuneration (other than remuneration referred to in the succeeding subsections of this section) equal to $4,800 with respect to employment has been paid to an individual during any calendar year after 1958 and prior to 1966, is paid to such individual during such calendar year;

(D) That part of remuneration which, after remuneration (other than remuneration referred to in the succeeding subsections of this section) equal to $6,600 with respect to employment has been paid to an individual during any calendar year after 1965 and prior to 1968, is paid to such individual during such calendar year;

(E) That part of remuneration which, after remuneration (other than remuneration referred to in the succeeding subsections of this section) equal to $7,800 with respect to employment has been paid to an individual during any calendar year after 1967 and prior to 1972, is paid to such individual during such calendar year;

(F) That part of remuneration which, after remuneration (other than remuneration referred to in the succeeding subsections of this section) equal to $9,000 with respect to employment has been paid to an individual during any calendar year after 1971 and prior to 1973, is paid to such individual during any such calendar year;

(G) That part of remuneration which, after remuneration (other than remuneration referred to in the succeeding subsections of this section) equal to $10,800 with respect to employment has been paid to an individual during any calendar year after 1972 and prior to 1974, is paid to such individual during such calendar year;

(H) That part of remuneration which, after remuneration (other than remuneration referred to in the succeeding subsections of this section) equal to $13,200 with respect to employment has been paid to an individual during any calendar year after 1973 and prior to 1975, is paid to such individual during such calendar year;

(I) That part of remuneration which, after remuneration (other than remuneration referred to in the succeeding subsections of

SOCIAL SECURITY ACT—§ 209(a)(4)   119

this section) equal to the contribution and benefit base (determined under section 230) with respect to employment has been paid to an individual during any calendar year after 1974 with respect to which such contribution and benefit base is effective, is paid to such individual during such calendar year;

(2) The amount of any payment (including any amount paid by an employer for insurance or annuities, or into a fund, to provide for any such payment) made to, or on behalf of, an employee or any of his dependents under a plan or system established by an employer which makes provision for his employees generally (or for his employees generally and their dependents) or for a class or classes of his employees (or for a class or classes of his employees and their dependents), on account of (A) sickness or accident disability (but, in the case of payments made to an employee or any of his dependents, this clause shall exclude from the term "wages" only payments which are received under a workmen's compensation law), or[101] (B) medical or hospitalization expenses in connection with sickness or accident disability, or (C) death, except that this subsection does not apply to a payment for group-term life insurance to the extent that such payment is includible in the gross income of the employee under the Internal Revenue Code of 1986;

(3) Any payment on account of sickness or accident disability, or medical or hospitalization expenses in connection with sickness or accident disability, made by an employer to, or on behalf of, an employee after the expiration of six calendar months following the last calendar month in which the employee worked for such employer;

(4) Any payment made to, or on behalf of, an employee or his beneficiary (A) from or to a trust exempt from tax under section 165(a) of the Internal Revenue Code of 1939[102] at the time of such payment or, in the case of a payment after 1954, under sections 401 and 501(a) of the Internal Revenue Code of 1954 or the Internal Revenue Code of 1986[103], unless such payment is made to an employee of the trust as remuneration for services rendered as such employee and not as a beneficiary of the trust, or (B) under or to an annuity plan which, at the time of such payment, meets the requirements of section 165(a)(3), (4), (5), and (6) of the Internal Revenue Code of 1939 or, in the case of a payment after 1954 and prior to 1963, the requirements of section 401(a)(3), (4), (5), and (6) of the Internal Revenue Code of 1954, or (C) under or to an annuity plan which, at the time of any such payment after 1962, is a plan described in section 403(a) of the Internal Revenue Code of 1986[104], or (D) under or to a bond purchase plan which, at the time of any such payment after 1962, is a qualified bond purchase plan described in section 405(a) of the Internal Revenue Code of 1954 (as in effect before the enactment of the Tax Reform Act of 1984), or (E) under or to an annuity contract described in section 403(b) of the Internal Revenue Code of 1986[105], other than

---

[101] See Vol. II, P.L. 97-123, §3(e), with respect to treatment of payments under a State temporary disability law.

[102] P.L. 76-1.

[103] See Vol. II, P.L. 83-591, §§401 and 501(a).

[104] See Vol. II, P.L. 83-591, §403(a).

[105] See Vol. II, P.L. 83-591, §403(b).

120   SOCIAL SECURITY ACT—§ 209(a)(4)(cont)

a payment for the purchase of such contract which is made by reason of a salary reduction agreement (whether evidenced by a written instrument or otherwise), or (F) under or to an exempt governmental deferred compensation plan (as defined in section 3121(v)(3) of such Code[106]), or (G) to supplement pension benefits under a plan or trust described in any of the foregoing provisions of this subsection to take into account some portion or all of the increase in the cost of living (as determined by the Secretary of Labor) since retirement but only if such supplemental payments are under a plan which is treated as a welfare plan under section 3(2)(B)(ii) of the Employee Retirement Income Security Act of 1974[107], or (H) under a simplified employee pension (as defined in section 408(k)(1) of such Code), other than any contributions described in section 408(k)(6) of such Code, or (I) under a cafeteria plan (within the meaning of section 125 of the Internal Revenue Code of 1986) if such payment would not be treated as wages without regard to such plan and it is reasonable to believe that (if section 125 applied for purposes of this section) section 125 would not treat any wages as constructively received; or (J) under an arrangement to which section 408(p) of such Code applies, other than any elective contributions under paragraph (2)(A)(i) thereof; or (K) under a plan described in section 457(e)(11)(A)(ii) of the Internal Revenue Code of 1986 and maintained by an eligible employer (as defined in section 457(e)(1) of such Code);

(5) The payment by an employer (without deduction from the remuneration of the employee)—

    (A) of the tax imposed upon an employee under section 3101 of the Internal Revenue Code of 1986[108], or

    (B) of any payment required from an employee under a State unemployment compensation law,

with respect to remuneration paid to an employee for domestic service in a private home of the employer or for agricultural labor;

(6)(A) Remuneration paid in any medium other than cash to an employee for service not in the course of the employer's trade or business or for domestic service in a private home of the employer;

(B) Cash remuneration paid by an employer in any calendar year to an employee for domestic service in a private home of the employer (including domestic service on a farm operated for profit), if the cash remuneration paid in such year by the employer to the employee for such service is less than the applicable dollar threshold (as defined in section 3121(x) of the Internal Revenue Code of 1986[109]) for such year;

(C) Cash remuneration paid by an employer in any calendar year to an employee for service not in the course of the employer's trade or business, if the cash remuneration paid in such year by the employer to the employee for such service is less than $100. As used in this paragraph, the term "service not in the course of the employer's trade or business" does not include domestic

---

[106] See Vol. II, P.L. 83-591, §3121(v).
[107] See Vol. II, P.L. 93-406, §3(2)(B)(ii).
[108] See Vol. II, P.L. 83-591, §3101.
[109] See Vol. II, P.L. 83-591, §3121(x).

service in a private home of the employer and does not include service described in section 210(f)(5);

(7)(A) Remuneration paid in any medium other than cash for agricultural labor;

(B) Cash remuneration paid by an employer in any calendar year to an employee for agricultural labor unless—

(i) the cash remuneration paid in such year by the employer to the employee for such labor is $150 or more, or

(ii) the employer's expenditures for agricultural labor in such year equal or exceed $2,500,

except that clause (ii) shall not apply in determining whether remuneration paid to an employee constitutes "wages" under this section if such employee (I) is employed as a hand harvest laborer and is paid on a piece rate basis in an operation which has been, and is customarily and generally recognized as having been, paid on a piece rate basis in the region of employment, (II) commutes daily from his permanent residence to the farm on which he is so employed, and (III) has been employed in agriculture less than 13 weeks during the preceding calendar year;

(8) Remuneration paid by an employer in any year to an employee for service described in section 210(j)(3)(C) (relating to home workers), if the cash remuneration paid in such year by the employer to the employee for such service is less than $100;

(9) Remuneration paid to or on behalf of an employee if (and to the extent that) at the time of the payment of such remuneration it is reasonable to believe that a corresponding deduction is allowable under section 217 of the Internal Revenue Code of 1986 (determined without regard to section 274(n) of such Code[110]);

(10)(A) Tips paid in any medium other than cash;

(B) Cash tips received by an employee in any calendar month in the course of his employment by an employer unless the amount of such cash tips is $20 or more;

(11) Any payment or series of payments by an employer to an employee or any of his dependents which is paid—

(A) upon or after the termination of an employee's employment relationship because of (A) death, or (B) retirement for disability, and

(B) under a plan established by the employer which makes provision for his employees generally or a class or classes of his employees (or for such employees or class or classes of employees and their dependents),

other than any such payment or series of payments which would have been paid if the employee's employment relationship had not been so terminated;

(12) Any payment made by an employer to a survivor or the estate of a former employee after the calendar year in which such employee died;

(13) Any payment made by an employer to an employee, if at the time such payment is made such employee is entitled to disability insurance benefits under section 223(a) and such entitlement commenced prior to the calendar year in which such payment is

---

[110] See Vol. II, P.L. 83-591, §§217 and 274(n).

122   SOCIAL SECURITY ACT—§ 209(a)(13)(cont)

made, and if such employee did not perform any services for such employer during the period for which such payment is made;

(14)(A) Remuneration paid by an organization exempt from income tax under section 501 of the Internal Revenue Code of 1986[111] in any calendar year to an employee for service rendered in the employ of such organization, if the remuneration paid in such year by the organization to the employee for such service is less than $100;

(B) Any contribution, payment, or service, provided by an employer which may be excluded from the gross income of an employee, his spouse, or his dependents, under the provisions of section 120 of the Internal Revenue Code of 1986[112] (relating to amounts received under qualified group legal services plans);

(15) Any payment made, or benefit furnished, to or for the benefit of an employee if at the time of such payment or such furnishing it is reasonable to believe that the employee will be able to exclude such payment or benefit from income under section 127 or 129 of the Internal Revenue Code of 1986[113];

(16) The value of any meals or lodging furnished by or on behalf of the employer if at the time of such furnishing it is reasonable to believe that the employee will be able to exclude such items from income under section 119 of the Internal Revenue Code of 1986[114];

(17) Any benefit provided to or on behalf of an employee if at the time such benefit is provided it is reasonable to believe that the employee will be able to exclude such benefit from income under section 74(c), 108(f)(4), 117, or 132 of the Internal Revenue Code of 1986[115];

(18) Remuneration consisting of income excluded from taxation under section 7873 of the Internal Revenue Code of 1986 (relating to income derived by Indians from exercise of fishing rights);[116]

(19) Remuneration on account of—

(A) a transfer of a share of stock to any individual pursuant to an exercise of an incentive stock option (as defined in section 422(b) of the Internal Revenue Code of 1986) or under an employee stock purchase plan (as defined in section 423(b) of such Code), or

(B) any disposition by the individual of such stock or[117]

(20)[118] Any benefit or payment which is excludable from the gross income of the employee under section 139B(b) of the Internal Revenue Code of 1986)[119].

(b) Nothing in the regulations prescribed for purposes of chapter 24 of the Internal Revenue Code of 1986[120] (relating to income tax withholding) which provides an exclusion from "wages" as used in such

---

[111] See Vol. II, P.L. 83-591, §501.
[112] See Vol. II, P.L. 83-591, §120.
[113] See Vol. II, P.L. 83-591, §§127 and 129.
[114] See Vol. II, P.L. 83-591, §119.
[115] See Vol. II, P.L. 83-591, §§74(c), 117 and 132.
[116] P.L. 110-245, §115(a)(2), struck out "or".
[117] P.L. 110-245, §115(a)(2), struck out the period and substituted "or".
[118] P.L. 110-245, §115(a)(2), added paragraph (20), effective as if included in P.L. 110-142, §5, applicable to taxable years beginning after December 31, 2007.
[119] See Vol. II, P.L. 83-591, §139B(b).
[120] See Vol. II, P.L. 83-591, chapter 24.

SOCIAL SECURITY ACT—§ 209(g) 123

chapter shall be construed to require a similar exclusion from "wages" in the regulations prescribed for purposes of this title.

(c) For purposes of this title, in the case of domestic service described in subsection (a)(6)(B), any payment of cash remuneration for such service which is more or less than a whole-dollar amount shall, under such conditions and to such extent as may be prescribed by regulations made under this title, be computed to the nearest dollar. For the purpose of the computation to the nearest dollar, the payment of a fractional part of a dollar shall be disregarded unless it amounts to one-half dollar or more, in which case it shall be increased to $1. The amount of any payment of cash remuneration so computed to the nearest dollar shall, in lieu of the amount actually paid, be deemed to constitute the amount of cash remuneration for purposes of subsection (a)(6)(B).

(d) For purposes of this title, in the case of an individual performing service, as a member of a uniformed service, to which the provisions of section 210(l)(1) are applicable, the term "wages" shall, subject to the provisions of subsection (a)(1) of this section, include as such individual's remuneration for such service only (1) his basic pay as described in chapter 3 and section 1009 of title 37, United States Code[121], in the case of an individual performing service to which subparagraph (A) of such section 210(l)(1) applies, or (2) his compensation for such service as determined under section 206(a) of title 37, United States Code[122], in the case of an individual performing service to which subparagraph (B) of such section 210(l)(1) applies.

(e) For purposes of this title, in the case of an individual performing service, as a volunteer or volunteer leader within the meaning of the Peace Corps Act[123], to which the provisions of section 210(o) are applicable, (1) the term "wages" shall, subject to the provisions of subsection (a) of this section, include as such individual's remuneration for such service only amounts certified as payable pursuant to section 5(c) or 6(1) of the Peace Corps Act, and (2) any such amount shall be deemed to have been paid to such individual at the time the service, with respect to which it is paid, is performed.

(f) For purposes of this title, tips received by an employee in the course of his employment shall be considered remuneration for employment. Such remuneration shall be deemed to be paid at the time a written statement including such tips is furnished to the employer pursuant to section 6053(a) of the Internal Revenue Code of 1986[124] or (if no statement including such tips is so furnished) at the time received.

(g) For purposes of this title, in any case where an individual is a member of a religious order (as defined in section 3121(r)(2) of the Internal Revenue Code of 1986[125]) performing service in the exercise of duties required by such order, and an election of coverage under section 3121(r) of such Code is in effect with respect to such order or with respect to the autonomous subdivision thereof to which such member belongs, the term "wages" shall, subject to the provisions of subsection (a) of this section, include as such individual's remuneration for

---

[121] See Vol. II, 37 U.S.C. 1009.
[122] See Vol. II, 37 U.S.C. 206(a).
[123] See Vol. II, P.L. 87-293, §§5(c) and 6(1) .
[124] See Vol. II, P.L. 83-591, §6053(a).
[125] See Vol. II, P.L. 83-591, §6053(a).

124 SOCIAL SECURITY ACT—§ 209(g)(cont)

such service the fair market value of any board, lodging, clothing, and other perquisites furnished to such member by such order or subdivision thereof or by any other person or organization pursuant to an agreement with such order or subdivision, except that the amount included as such individual's remuneration under this paragraph shall not be less than $100 a month.

(h) For purposes of this title, in the case of an individual performing service under the provisions of section 294 of title 28, United States Code[126] (relating to assignment of retired justices and judges to active duty), the term "wages" shall not include any payment under section 371(b) of such title 28 which is received during the period of such service.

(i) Nothing in any of the foregoing provisions of this section (other than subsection (a)) shall exclude from the term "wages"—

(1) Any employer contribution under a qualified cash or deferred arrangement (as defined in section 401(k) of the Internal Revenue Code of 1986[127]) to the extent not included in gross income by reason of section 402(a)(8) of such Code[128], or

(2) Any amount which is treated as an employer contribution under section 414(h)(2) of such Code where the pickup referred to in such section is pursuant to a salary reduction agreement (whether evidenced by a written instrument or otherwise).

(j) Any amount deferred under a nonqualified deferred compensation plan (within the meaning of section 3121(v)(2)(C) of the Internal Revenue Code of 1986[129]) shall be taken into account for purposes of this title as of the later of when the services are performed, or when there is no substantial risk of forfeiture of the rights to such amount. Any amount taken into account as wages by reason of the preceding sentence (and the income attributable thereto) shall not thereafter be treated as wages for purposes of this title.

(k)(1) For purposes of sections 203(f)(8)(B)(ii), 213(d)(2)(B), 215(a)(1)(B)(ii), 215(a)(1)(C)(ii), 215(a)(1)(D), 215(b)(3)(A)(ii), 215(i)(1)(E), 215(i)(2)(C)(ii), 224(f)(2)(B), and 230(b)(2) (and 230(b)(2) as in effect immediately prior to the enactment of the Social Security Amendments of 1977), the term "national average wage index" for any particular calendar year means, subject to regulations of the Commissioner of Social Security under paragraph (2), the average of the total wages for such particular calendar year.

(2) The Commissioner of Social Security shall prescribe regulations under which the national average wage index for any calendar year shall be computed—

(A) on the basis of amounts reported to the Secretary of the Treasury or his delegate for such year,

(B) by disregarding the limitation on wages specified in subsection (a)(1),

(C) with respect to calendar years after 1990, by incorporating deferred compensation amounts and factoring in for such years the rate of change from year to year in such amounts, in a manner

---

[126] See Vol. II, 28 U.S.C. 294.
[127] See Vol. II, P.L. 83-591, §401(k).
[128] As in original. Reference should be to §402(e)(3). (P.L. 102-318, §521(a) amended §402(a) through (c).)
[129] See Vol. II, P.L. 83-591, §3121(v).

SOCIAL SECURITY ACT—§ 210(a)(1) 125

consistent with the requirements of section 10208 of the Omnibus Budget Reconciliation Act of 1989, and

(D) with respect to calendar years before 1978, in a manner consistent with the manner in which the average of the total wages for each of such calendar years was determined as provided by applicable law as in effect for such years.

(3) For purposes of this subsection, the term "deferred compensation amount" means—

(A) any amount excluded from gross income under chapter 1 of the Internal Revenue Code of 1986 by reason of section 402(a)(8)[130], 402(h)(1)(B), or 457(a) of such Code or by reason of a salary reduction agreement under section 403(b) of such Code,

(B) any amount with respect to which a deduction is allowable under chapter 1 of such Code by reason of a contribution to a plan described in section 501(c)(18) of such Code[131], and

(C) to the extent provided in regulations of the Commissioner of Social Security, deferred compensation provided under any arrangement, agreement, or plan referred to in subsection (i) or (j).

DEFINITION OF EMPLOYMENT

SEC. 210. [42 U.S.C. 410] For the purposes of this title—

Employment

(a) The term "employment" means any service performed after 1936 and prior to 1951 which was employment for the purposes of this title under the law applicable to the period in which such service was performed, and any service, of whatever nature, performed after 1950 (A) by an employee for the person employing him, irrespective of the citizenship or residence of either, (i) within the United States, or (ii) on or in connection with an American vessel or American aircraft under a contract of service which is entered into within the United States or during the performance of which and while the employee is employed on the vessel or aircraft it touches at a port in the United States, if the employee is employed on and in connection with such vessel or aircraft when outside the United States, or (B) outside the United States by a citizen or resident of the United States as an employee (i) of an American employer (as defined in subsection (e) of this section), or (ii) of a foreign affiliate (as defined in section 3121(l)(6) of the Internal Revenue Code of 1986[132]) of an American employer during any period for which there is in effect an agreement, entered into pursuant to section 3121(l) of such Code, with respect to such affiliate, or (C) if it is service, regardless of where or by whom performed, which is designated as employment or recognized as equivalent to employment under an agreement entered into under section 233; except that, in the case of service performed after 1950, such term shall not include—

(1) Service performed by foreign agricultural workers lawfully admitted to the United States from the Bahamas, Jamaica, and the other British West Indies, or from any other foreign country or

---

[130] As in original. Reference should be to §402(e)(3). (P.L. 102-318, §521(a) amended §402(a) through (c).)

[131] See Vol. II, P.L. 83-591, §501(c)(18).

[132] See Vol. II, P.L. 83-591, §3121.

126 SOCIAL SECURITY ACT—§ 210(a)(1)(cont)

possession thereof, on a temporary basis to perform agricultural labor;

(2) Domestic service performed in a local college club, or local chapter of a college fraternity or sorority, by a student who is enrolled and is regularly attending classes at a school, college, or university;

(3)(A) Service performed by a child under the age of 18 in the employ of his father or mother;

(B) Service not in the course of the employer's trade or business, or domestic service in a private home of the employer, performed by an individual under the age of 21 in the employ of his father or mother, or performed by an individual in the employ of his spouse or son or daughter; except that the provisions of this subparagraph shall not be applicable to such domestic service performed by an individual in the employ of his son or daughter if—

(i) the employer is a surviving spouse or a divorced individual and has not remarried, or has a spouse living in the home who has a mental or physical condition which results in such spouse's being incapable of caring for a son, daughter, stepson, or stepdaughter (referred to in clause (ii)) for at least 4 continuous weeks in the calendar quarter in which the service is rendered, and

(ii) a son, daughter, stepson, or stepdaughter of such employer is living in the home, and

(iii) the son, daughter, stepson, or stepdaughter (referred to in clause (ii)) has not attained age 18 or has a mental or physical condition which requires the personal care and supervision of an adult for at least 4 continuous weeks in the calendar quarter in which the service is rendered;

(4) Service performed by an individual on or in connection with a vessel not an American vessel, or on or in connection with an aircraft not an American aircraft, if (A) the individual is employed on and in connection with such vessel or aircraft when outside the United States and (B)(i) such individual is not a citizen of the United States or (ii) the employer is not an American employer;

(5) Service performed in the employ of the United States or any instrumentality of the United States, if such service—

(A) would be excluded from the term "employment" for purposes of this title if the provisions of paragraphs (5) and (6) of this subsection as in effect in January 1983 had remained in effect, and

(B) is performed by an individual who—

(i) has been continuously performing service described in subparagraph (A) since December 31, 1983, and for purposes of this clause—

(I) if an individual performing service described in subparagraph (A) returns to the performance of such service after being separated therefrom for a period of less than 366 consecutive days, regardless of whether the period began before, on, or after December 31, 1983, then such service shall be considered continuous,

(II) if an individual performing service described in subparagraph (A) returns to the performance of

SOCIAL SECURITY ACT—§ 210(a)(5)(D)(i)

such service after being detailed or transferred to an international organization as described under section 3343 of subchapter III of chapter 33 of title 5, United States Code, or under section 3581 of chapter 35 of such title, then the service performed for that organization shall be considered service described in subparagraph (A),

(III) if an individual performing service described in subparagraph (A) is reemployed or reinstated after being separated from such service for the purpose of accepting employment with the American Institute of Taiwan as provided under section 3310 of chapter 48 of title 22, United States Code[133], then the service performed for that Institute shall be considered service described in subparagraph (A),

(IV) if an individual performing service described in subparagraph (A) returns to the performance of such service after performing service as a member of a uniformed service (including, for purposes of this clause, service in the National Guard and temporary service in the Coast Guard Reserve) and after exercising restoration or reemployment rights as provided under chapter 43 of title 38, United States Code[134], then the service so performed as a member of a uniformed service shall be considered service described in subparagraph (A), and

(V) if an individual performing service described in subparagraph (A) returns to the performance of such service after employment (by a tribal organization) to which section 104(e)(2) of the Indian Self-Determination Act[135] applies, then the service performed for that tribal organization shall be considered service described in subparagraph (A); or

(ii) is receiving an annuity from the Civil Service Retirement and Disability Fund, or benefits (for service as an employee) under another retirement system established by a law of the United States for employees of the Federal Government (other than for members of the uniformed services);

except that this paragraph shall not apply with respect to any such service performed on or after any date on which such individual performs—

(C) service performed as the President or Vice President of the United States,

(D) service performed—

(i) in a position placed in the Executive Schedule under sections 5312 through 5317 of title 5, United States Code,

---

[133] See Vol. II, 22 U.S.C. 3310.
[134] See Vol. II, 38 U.S.C. Chapter 43.
[135] See Vol. II, P.L. 93-638, §104(e)(2).

128   SOCIAL SECURITY ACT—§ 210(a)(5)(D)(ii)

(ii) as a noncareer appointee in the Senior Executive Service or a noncareer member of the Senior Foreign Service, or

(iii) in a position to which the individual is appointed by the President (or his designee) or the Vice President under section 105(a)(1), 106(a)(1), or 107(a)(1) or (b)(1) of title 3, United States Code[136], if the maximum rate of basic pay for such position is at or above the rate for level V of the Executive Schedule,

(E) service performed as the Chief Justice of the United States, an Associate Justice of the Supreme Court, a judge of a United States court of appeals, a judge of a United States district court (including the district court of a territory), a judge of the United States Claims Court[137], a judge of the United States Court of International Trade, a judge[138] of the United States Tax Court, a United States magistrate, or a referee in bankruptcy or United States bankruptcy judge,

(F) service performed as a Member, Delegate, or Resident Commissioner of or to the Congress,

(G)[139] any other service in the legislative branch of the Federal Government if such service—

(i) is performed by an individual who was not subject to subchapter III of chapter 83 of title 5, United States Code, or to another retirement system established by a law of the United States for employees of the Federal Government (other than for members of the uniformed services), on December 31, 1983, or

(ii) is performed by an individual who has, at any time after December 31, 1983, received a lump-sum payment under section 8342(a) of title 5, United States Code, or under the corresponding provision of the law establishing the other retirement system described in clause (i), or

(iii) is performed by an individual after such individual has otherwise ceased to be subject to subchapter III of chapter 83 of title 5, United States Code (without having an application pending for coverage under such subchapter), while performing service in the legislative branch (determined without regard to the provisions of subparagraph (B) relating to continuity of employment), for any period of time after December 31, 1983,

and for purposes of this subparagraph (G) an individual is subject to such subchapter III or to any such other retirement system at any time only if (a) such individual's pay is subject to deductions, contributions, or similar payments (concurrent with the service being performed at that time) under section 8334(a) of such title 5 or the corresponding provision

---

[136] See Vol. II, 3 U.S.C. 105(a)(1), 106(a)(1), or 107(a)(1) or (b)(1).

[137] P.L. 102-572, §902(b)(1), provided that "the United States Claims Court" shall be deemed to refer to "the United States Court of Federal Claims", effective October 29, 1992.

[138] P.L. 110-458, §108(k)(2), struck out "or special judge", effective December 23, 2008.

[139] See Vol. II, P.L 98-369, §2601(c), with respect to the applicability of subchapter III, chapter 83, of Title 5, United States Code, to service performed after December 31, 1983; and §2601(e)(1), with respect to employees of certain nonprofit organizations who are considered to be performing services in the employ of an instrumentality of the United States.

SOCIAL SECURITY ACT—§ 210(a)(7)(C) 129

of the law establishing such other system, or (in a case to which section 8332(k)(1) of such title applies) such individual is making payments of amounts equivalent to such deductions, contributions, or similar payments while on leave without pay, or (b) such individual is receiving an annuity from the Civil Service Retirement and Disability Fund, or is receiving benefits (for service as an employee) under another retirement system established by a law of the United States for employees of the Federal Government (other than for members of the uniformed services), or

(H) service performed by an individual—

(i) on or after the effective date of an election by such individual, under section 301 of the Federal Employees' Retirement System Act of 1986[140], section 307 of the Central Intelligence Agency Retirement Act (50 U.S.C. 2157)[141], or the Federal Employees' Retirement System Open Enrollment Act of 1997 to become subject to the Federal Employees' Retirement System provided in chapter 84 of title 5, United States Code[142], or

(ii) on or after the effective date of an election by such individual, under regulations issued under section 860 of the Foreign Service Act of 1980[143], to become subject to the Foreign Service Pension System provided in subchapter II of chapter 8 of title I of such Act;

(6) Service performed in the employ of the United States or any instrumentality of the United States if such service is performed—

(A) in a penal institution of the United States by an inmate thereof;

(B) by any individual as an employee included under section 5351(2) of title 5, United States Code[144] (relating to certain interns, student nurses, and other student employees of hospitals of the Federal Government), other than as a medical or dental intern or a medical or dental resident in training; or

(C) by any individual as an employee serving on a temporary basis in case of fire, storm, earthquake, flood, or other similar emergency;

(7) Service performed in the employ of a State, or any political subdivision thereof, or any instrumentality of any one or more of the foregoing which is wholly owned thereby, except that this paragraph shall not apply in the case of—

(A) service included under an agreement under section 218,

(B) service which, under subsection (k), constitutes covered transportation service,

(C) service in the employ of the Government of Guam or the Government of American Samoa or any political subdivision thereof, or of any instrumentality of any one or more of the foregoing which is wholly owned thereby, performed

---

[140] See Vol. II, P.L. 99-335, §301.
[141] See Vol. II, 50 U.S.C. 2157.
[142] See Vol. II, 5 U.S.C. Chapter 84.
[143] See Vol. II, P.L. 96-465, §860.
[144] See Vol. II, 5 U.S.C. 5351(2).

by an officer or employee thereof (including a member of the legislature of any such Government or political subdivision), and, for purposes of this title—

(i) any person whose service as such an officer or employee is not covered by a retirement system established by a law of the United States shall not, with respect to such service, be regarded as an officer or employee of the United States or any agency or instrumentality thereof, and

(ii) the remuneration for service described in clause (i) (including fees paid to a public official) shall be deemed to have been paid by the Government of Guam or the Government of American Samoa or by a political subdivision thereof or an instrumentality of any one or more of the foregoing which is wholly owned thereby, whichever is appropriate,

(D) service performed in the employ of the District of Columbia or any instrumentality which is wholly owned thereby, if such service is not covered by a retirement system established by a law of the United States (other than the Federal Employees Retirement System provided in chapter 84 of title 5, United States Code[145]); except that the provisions of this subparagraph shall not be applicable to service performed—

(i) in a hospital or penal institution by a patient or inmate thereof;

(ii) by any individual as an employee included under section 5351(2) of title 5, United States Code (relating to certain interns, student nurses, and other student employees of hospitals of the District of Columbia Government), other than as a medical or dental intern or as a medical or dental resident in training;

(iii) by any individual as an employee serving on a temporary basis in case of fire, storm, snow, earthquake, flood, or other similar emergency; or

(iv) by a member of a board, committee, or council of the District of Columbia, paid on a per diem, meeting, or other fee basis,

(E) service performed in the employ of the Government of Guam (or any instrumentality which is wholly owned by such Government) by an employee properly classified as a temporary or intermittent employee, if such service is not covered by a retirement system established by a law of Guam; except that (i) the provisions of this subparagraph shall not be applicable to services performed by an elected official or a member of the legislature or in a hospital or penal institution by a patient or inmate thereof, and (ii) for purposes of this subparagraph, clauses (i) and (ii) of subparagraph (C) shall apply, or

(F) service in the employ of a State (other than the District of Columbia, Guam, or American Samoa), of any political subdivision thereof, or of any instrumentality of any one or more of the foregoing which is wholly owned thereby, by

---

[145] See Vol. II, 5 U.S.C. Chapter 84.

SOCIAL SECURITY ACT—§ 210(a)(10)(B) 131

an individual who is not a member of a retirement system of such State, political subdivision, or instrumentality, except that the provisions of this subparagraph shall not be applicable to service performed—

(i) by an individual who is employed to relieve such individual from unemployment;

(ii) in a hospital, home, or other institution by a patient or inmate thereof;

(iii) by any individual as an employee serving on a temporary basis in case of fire, storm, snow, earthquake, flood, or other similar emergency;

(iv) by an election official or election worker if the remuneration paid in a calendar year for such service is less than $1,000 with respect to service performed during any calendar year commencing on or after January 1, 1995, ending on or before December 31, 1999, and the adjusted amount determined under section 218(c)(8)(B) for any calendar year commencing on or after January 1, 2000, with respect to service performed during such calendar year; or

(v) by an employee in a position compensated solely on a fee basis which is treated pursuant to section 211(c)(2)(E) as a trade or business for purposes of inclusion of such fees in net earnings from self employment;

for purposes of this subparagraph, except as provided in regulations prescribed by the Secretary of the Treasury, the term "retirement system" has the meaning given such term by section 218(b)(4).

(8)(A) Service performed by a duly ordained, commissioned, or licensed minister of a church in the exercise of his ministry or by a member of a religious order in the exercise of duties required by such order, except that this subparagraph shall not apply to service performed by a member of such an order in the exercise of such duties, if an election of coverage under section 3121(r) of the Internal Revenue Code of 1986[146] is in effect with respect to such order, or with respect to the autonomous subdivision thereof to which such member belongs;

(B) Service performed in the employ of a church or qualified church-controlled organization if such church or organization has in effect an election under section 3121(w) of the Internal Revenue Code of 1986[147], other than service in an unrelated trade or business (within the meaning of section 513(a) of such Code);

(9) Service performed by an individual as an employee or employee representative as defined in section 3231 of the Internal Revenue Code of 1986[148];

(10) Service performed in the employ of—

(A) a school, college, or university, or

(B) an organization described in section 509(a)(3) of the Internal Revenue Code of 1986[149] if the organization is or-

---

[146] See Vol. II, P.L. 83-591, §3121(r).
[147] See Vol. II, P.L. 83-591, §3121(w).
[148] See Vol. II, P.L. 83-591, §3231.
[149] See Vol. II, P.L. 83-591, §509(a)(3).

132 SOCIAL SECURITY ACT—§ 210(a)(10)(B)(cont)

ganized, and at all times thereafter is operated, exclusively for the benefit of, to perform the functions of, or to carry out the purposes of a school, college, or university and is operated, supervised, or controlled by or in connection with such school, college, or university, unless it is a school, college, or university of a State or a political subdivision thereof and the services in its employ performed by a student referred to in section 218(c)(5) are covered under the agreement between the Commissioner of Social Security and such State entered into pursuant to section 218;

if such service is performed by a student who is enrolled and regularly attending classes at such school, college, or university;

(11) Service performed in the employ of a foreign government (including service as a consular or other officer or employee or a Nonduplication representative);

(12) Service performed in the employ of an instrumentality wholly owned by a foreign government—

(A) If the service is of a character similar to that performed in foreign countries by employees of the United States Government or of an instrumentality thereof; and

(B) If the Secretary of State shall certify to the Secretary of the Treasury that the foreign government, with respect to whose instrumentality and employees thereof exemption is claimed, grants an equivalent exemption with respect to similar service performed in the foreign country by employees of the United States Government and of instrumentalities thereof;

(13) Service performed as a student nurse in the employ of a hospital or a nurses' training school by an individual who is enrolled and is regularly attending classes in a nurses' training school chartered or approved pursuant to State law;

(14)(A) Service performed by an individual under the age of eighteen in the delivery or distribution of newspapers or shopping news, not including delivery or distribution to any point for subsequent delivery or distribution;

(B) Service performed by an individual in, and at the time of, the sale of newspapers or magazines to ultimate consumers, under an arrangement under which the newspapers or magazines are to be sold by him at a fixed price, his compensation being based on the retention of the excess of such price over the amount at which the newspapers or magazines are charged to him, whether or not he is guaranteed a minimum amount of compensation for such service, or is entitled to be credited with the unsold newspapers or magazines turned back;

(15) Service performed in the employ of an international organization entitled to enjoy privileges, exemptions, and immunities as an international organization under the International Organizations Immunities Act[150] (59 Stat. 669), except service which constitutes "employment" under subsection (r);

(16) Service performed by an individual under an arrangement with the owner or tenant of land pursuant to which—

---

[150] See Vol. II, P.L. 79-291.

SOCIAL SECURITY ACT—§ 210(a)(20)(C)   133

(A) such individual undertakes to produce agricultural or horticultural commodities (including livestock, bees, poultry, and fur-bearing animals and wildlife) on such land,

(B) the agricultural or horticultural commodities produced by such individual, or the proceeds therefrom, are to be divided between such individual and such owner or tenant, and

(C) the amount of such individual's share depends on the amount of the agricultural or horticultural commodities produced;

(17) Service in the employ of any organization which is performed (A) in any year during any part of which such organization is registered, or there is in effect a final order of the Subversive Activities Control Board requiring such organization to register, under the Internal Security Act of 1950[151], as amended, as a Communist-action organization, a Communist-front organization, or a Communist-infiltrated organization, and (B) after June 30, 1956;

(18) Service performed in Guam by a resident of the Republic of the Philippines while in Guam on a temporary basis as a nonimmigrant alien admitted to Guam pursuant to section 101(a)(15)(H)(ii) of the Immigration and Nationality Act[152] (8 U.S.C. 1101(a)(15)(H)(ii));

(19) Service which is performed by a nonresident alien individual for the period he is temporarily present in the United States as a nonimmigrant under subparagraph (F), (J), (M), or (Q) of section 101(a)(15) of the Immigration and Nationality Act, as amended, and which is performed to carry out the purpose specified in subparagraph (F), (J), (M), or (Q) as the case may be;

(20) Service (other than service described in paragraph (3)(A)) performed by an individual on a boat engaged in catching fish or other forms of aquatic animal life under an arrangement with the owner or operator of such boat pursuant to which—

(A) such individual does not receive any additional compensation other than as provided in subparagraph (B) and other than case remuneration—

(i) which does not exceed $100 per trip;

(ii) which is contingent on a minimum catch; and

(iii) which is paid solely for additional duties (such as mate, engineer, or cook) for which additional cash remuneration is traditional in the industry,

(B) such individual receives a share of the boat's (or the boats' in the case of a fishing operation involving more than one boat) catch of fish or other forms of aquatic animal life or a share of the proceeds from the sale of such catch, and

(C) the amount of such individual's share depends on the amount of the boat's (or boats' in the case of a fishing operation involving more than one boat) catch of fish or other forms of aquatic animal life,

but only if the operating crew of such boat (or each boat from which the individual receives a share in the case of a fishing oper-

---

[151] See Vol. II, P.L. 81-831.
[152] See Vol. II, P.L. 82-414, §101(a)(15)(H)(ii).

134 SOCIAL SECURITY ACT—§ 210(a)(21)

ation involving more than one boat) is normally made up of fewer than 10 individuals; or

(21) Domestic service in a private home of the employer which—

(A) is performed in any year by an individual under the age of 18 during any portion of such year; and

(B) is not the principal occupation of such employee.

For purposes of paragraph (20), the operating crew of a boat shall be treated as normally made up of fewer than 10 individuals if the average size of the operating crew on trips made during the preceding 4 calendar quarters consisted of fewer than 10 individuals.

Included and Excluded Service

(b) If the services performed during one-half or more of any pay period by an employee for the person employing him constitute employment, all the services of such employee for such period shall be deemed to be employment; but if the services performed during more than one-half of any such pay period by an employee for the person employing him do not constitute employment, then none of the services of such employee for such period shall be deemed to be employment. As used in this subsection, the term "pay period" means a period (of not more than thirty-one consecutive days) for which a payment of remuneration is ordinarily made to the employee by the person employing him. This subsection shall not be applicable with respect to services performed in a pay period by an employee for the person employing him, where any of such service is excepted by paragraph (9) of subsection (a).

American Vessel

(c) The term "American vessel" means any vessel documented or numbered under the laws of the United States; and includes any vessel which is neither documented or numbered under the laws of the United States nor documented under the laws of any foreign country, if its crew is employed solely by one or more citizens or residents of the United States or corporations organized under the laws of the United States or of any State.

American Aircraft

(d) The term "American aircraft" means an aircraft registered under the laws of the United States.

American Employer

(e)(1) The term[153] "American employer" means an employer which is (A)[154] the United States or any instrumentality thereof, (B)[155] a State or any political subdivision thereof, or any instrumentality of any one

---

[153] P.L. 110-245, §302(b)(1), struck out "(e) The term" and substituted "(e)(1) The term".

[154] P.L. 110-245, §302(b)(2), redesignated clause (1) as clause (A).

[155] P.L. 110-245, §302(b)(2), redesignated clause (2) as clause (B).

or more of the foregoing, (C)[156] an individual who is a resident of the United States, (D)[157] a partnership, if two-thirds or more of the partners are residents of the United States, (E)[158] a trust, if all of the trustees are residents of the United States, or (F)[159] a corporation organized under the laws of the United States or of any State.

(2)[160](A) If any employee of a foreign person is performing services in connection with a contract between the United States Government (or any instrumentality thereof) and any member of any domestically controlled group of entities which includes such foreign person, such foreign person shall be treated as an American employer with respect to such services performed by such employee..

(B) For purposes of this paragraph—

(i) The term "domestically controlled group of entities" means a controlled group of entities the common parent of which is a domestic corporation.,

(ii) The term "controlled group of entities" means a controlled group of corporations as defined in section 1563(a)(1) of the Internal Revenue Code of 1986[161], except that—

(I) "more than 50 percent" shall be substituted for "at least 80 percent" each place it appears therein, and

(II) the determination shall be made without regard to subsections (a)(4) and (b)(2) of section 1563 of such Code.

A partnership or any other entity (other than a corporation) shall be treated as a member of a controlled group of entities if such entity is controlled (within the meaning of section 954(d)(3) of such Code[162]) by members of such group (including any entity treated as a member of such group by reason of this sentence).

(C) Subparagraph (A) shall not apply to any services to which paragraph (1) of section 3121(z) of the Internal Revenue Code of 1986[163] does not apply by reason of paragraph (4) of such section.

Agricultural Labor

(f) The term "agricultural labor" includes all service performed—

(1) On a farm, in the employ of any person, in connection with cultivating the soil, or in connection with raising or harvesting any agricultural or horticultural commodity, including the raising, shearing, feeding, caring for, training, and management of livestock, bees, poultry, and fur-bearing animals and wildlife.

(2) In the employ of the owner or tenant or other operator of a farm, in connection with the operation, management, conservation, improvement, or maintenance of such farm and its tools and equipment, or in salvaging timber or clearing land of brush and

---

[156] P.L. 110-245, §302(b)(2), redesignated clause (3) as clause (C).
[157] P.L. 110-245, §302(b)(2), redesignated clause (4) as clause (D).
[158] P.L. 110-245, §302(b)(2), redesignated clause (5) as clause (E).
[159] P.L. 110-245, §302(b)(2), redesignated clause (6) as clause (F).
[160] P.L. 110-245, §302(b)(3), added paragraph (2), applicable to services performed in calendar months beginning more than 30 days after June 17, 2008.
[161] See Vol. II, P.L. 83-591, §1563(a).
[162] See Vol. II, P.L. 83-591, §954(d).
[163] See Vol. II, P.L. 83-591, §3121(z).

136   SOCIAL SECURITY ACT—§ 210(f)(2)(cont)

other debris left by a hurricane, if the major part of such service is performed on a farm.

(3) In connection with the production or harvesting of any commodity defined as an agricultural commodity in section 15(g) of the Agricultural Marketing Act[164], as amended, or in connection with the ginning of cotton, or in connection with the operation or maintenance of ditches, canals, reservoirs, or waterways, not owned or operated for profit, used exclusively for supplying and storing water for farming purposes.

(4)(A) In the employ of the operator of a farm in handling, planting, drying, packing, packaging, processing, freezing, grading, storing, or delivering to storage or to market or to a carrier for transportation to market, in its unmanufactured state, any agricultural or horticultural commodity; but only if such operator produced more than one-half of the commodity with respect to which such service is performed.

(B) In the employ of a group of operators of farms (other than a cooperative organization) in the performance of service described in subparagraph (A), but only if such operators produced all of the commodity with respect to which such service is performed. For the purposes of this subparagraph, any unincorporated group of operators shall be deemed a cooperative organization if the number of operators comprising such group is more than twenty at any time during the calendar year in which such service is performed.

(5) On a farm operated for profit if such service is not in the course of the employer's trade or business.

The provisions of subparagraphs (A) and (B) of paragraph (4) shall not be deemed to be applicable with respect to service performed in connection with commercial canning or commercial freezing or in connection with any agricultural or horticultural commodity after its delivery to a terminal market for distribution for consumption.

Farm

(g) The term "farm" includes stock, dairy, poultry, fruit, fur-bearing animal, and truck farms, plantations, ranches, nurseries, ranges, greenhouses or other similar structures used primarily for the raising of agricultural or horticultural commodities, and orchards.

State

(h) The term "State" includes the District of Columbia, the Commonwealth of Puerto Rico, the Virgin Islands, Guam, and American Samoa.

United States

(i) The term "United States" when used in a geographical sense means the States, the District of Columbia, the Commonwealth of Puerto Rico, the Virgin Islands, Guam, and American Samoa.

---

[164] See Vol. II, P.L. 71-10, §15(g).

Employee

(j) The term "employee" means—

(1) any officer of a corporation; or

(2) any individual who, under the usual common law rules applicable in determining the employer-employee relationship, has the status of an employee; or

(3) any individual (other than an individual who is an employee under paragraph (1) or (2) of this subsection) who performs services for remuneration for any person—

(A) as an agent-driver or commission-driver engaged in distributing meat products, vegetable products, fruit products, bakery products, beverages (other than milk), or laundry or dry-cleaning services, for his principal;

(B) as a full-time life insurance salesman;

(C) as a home worker performing work, according to specifications furnished by the person for whom the services are performed, on materials or goods furnished by such person which are required to be returned to such person or a person designated by him; or

(D) as a traveling or city salesman, other than as an agent-driver or commission-driver, engaged upon a full-time basis in the solicitation on behalf of, and the transmission to, his principal (except for side-line sales activities on behalf of some other person) of orders from wholesalers, retailers, contractors, or operators of hotels, restaurants, or other similar establishments for merchandise for resale or supplies for use in their business operations;

if the contract of service contemplates that substantially all of such services are to be performed personally by such individual; except that an individual shall not be included in the term "employee" under the provisions of this paragraph if such individual has a substantial investment in facilities used in connection with the performance of such services (other than in facilities for transportation), or if the services are in the nature of a single transaction not part of a continuing relationship with the person for whom the services are performed.

Covered Transportation Service

(k)(1) Except as provided in paragraph (2), all service performed in the employ of a State or political subdivision in connection with its operation of a public transportation system shall constitute covered transportation service if any part of the transportation system was acquired from private ownership after 1936 and prior to 1951.

(2) Service performed in the employ of a State or political subdivision in connection with the operation of its public transportation system shall not constitute covered transportation service if—

(A) any part of the transportation system was acquired from private ownership after 1936 and prior to 1951, and substantially all service in connection with the operation of the transportation system is, on December 31, 1950, covered under a general retire-

138 SOCIAL SECURITY ACT—§ 210(k)(2)(A)(cont)

ment system providing benefits which, by reason of a provision of the State constitution dealing specifically with retirement systems of the State or political subdivisions thereof, cannot be diminished or impaired; or

(B) no part of the transportation system operated by the State or political subdivision on December 31, 1950, was acquired from private ownership after 1936 and prior to 1951;

except that if such State or political subdivision makes an acquisition after 1950 from private ownership of any part of its transportation system, then, in the case of any employee who—

(C) became an employee of such State or political subdivision in connection with and at the time of its acquisition after 1950 of such part, and

(D) prior to such acquisition rendered service in employment in connection with the operation of such part of the transportation system acquired by the State or political subdivision,

the service of such employee in connection with the operation of the transportation system shall constitute covered transportation service, commencing with the first day of the third calendar quarter following the calendar quarter in which the acquisition of such part took place, unless on such first day such service of such employee is covered by a general retirement system which does not, with respect to such employee, contain special provisions applicable only to employees described in subparagraph (C).

(3) All service performed in the employ of a State or political subdivision thereof in connection with its operation of a public transportation system shall constitute covered transportation service if the transportation system was not operated by the State or political subdivision prior to 1951 and, at the time of its first acquisition (after 1950) from private ownership of any part of its transportation system, the State or political subdivision did not have a general retirement system covering substantially all service performed in connection with the operation of the transportation system.

(4) For the purposes of this subsection—

(A) The term "general retirement system" means any pension, annuity, retirement, or similar fund or system established by a State or by a political subdivision thereof for employees of the State, political subdivision, or both; but such term shall not include such a fund or system which covers only service performed in positions connected with the operation of its public transportation system.

(B) A transportation system or a part thereof shall be considered to have been acquired by a State or political subdivision from private ownership if prior to the acquisition service performed by employees in connection with the operation of the system or part thereof acquired constituted employment under this title, and some of such employees became employees of the State or political subdivision in connection with and at the time of such acquisition.

(C) The term "political subdivision" includes an instrumentality of (i) a State, (ii) one or more political subdivisions of a State, or (iii) a State and one or more of its political subdivisions.

Service in the Uniformed Services

(l)(1) Except as provided in paragraph (4), the term "employment" shall, notwithstanding the provisions of subsection (a) of this section, include—

(A) service performed after December 1956 by an individual as a member of a uniformed service on active duty, but such term shall not include any such service which is performed while on leave without pay, and

(B) service performed after December 1987 by an individual as a member of a uniformed service on inactive duty training.

(2) The term "active duty" means "active duty" as described in paragraph (21) of section 101 of title 38, United States Code[165], except that it shall also include "active duty for training" as described in paragraph (22) of such section.

(3) The term "inactive duty training" means "inactive duty training" as described in paragraph (23) of such section 101.

(4)(A) Paragraph (1) of this subsection shall not apply in the case of any service, performed by an individual as a member of a uniformed service, which is creditable under section 3(i) of the Railroad Retirement Act of 1974[166]. The Railroad Retirement Board shall notify the Commissioner of Social Security, with respect to all such service which is so creditable.

(B) In any case where benefits under this title are already payable on the basis of such individual's wages and self-employment income at the time such notification (with respect to such individual) is received by the Commissioner of Social Security, the Commissioner of Social Security shall certify no further benefits for payment under this title on the basis of such individual's wages and self-employment income, or shall recompute the amount of any further benefits payable on the basis of such wages and self-employment income, as may be required as a consequence of subparagraph (A) of this paragraph. No payment of a benefit to any person on the basis of such individual's wages and self-employment income, certified by the Commissioner of Social Security prior to the end of the month in which the Commissioner receives such notification from the Railroad Retirement Board, shall be deemed by reason of this subparagraph to have been an erroneous payment or a payment to which such person was not entitled. The Commissioner of Social Security shall, as soon as possible after the receipt of such notification from the Railroad Retirement Board, advise such Board whether or not any such benefit will be reduced or terminated by reason of subparagraph (A), and if any such benefit will be so reduced or terminated, specify the first month with respect to which such reduction or termination will be effective.

Member of a Uniformed Service

(m) The term "member of a uniformed service" means any person appointed, enlisted, or inducted in a component of the Army, Navy, Air Force, Marine Corps, or Coast Guard (including a reserve compo-

---

[165] See Vol. II, 38 U. S.C. 101 and see P.L. 95-202, §401, with respect to the Women's Air Forces Service Pilots.

[166] See Vol. II, P.L. 75-162, §3(i) [as amended by P.L. 93-445].

140 SOCIAL SECURITY ACT—§ 210(m)(cont)

nent as defined in section 101(27) of title 38, United States Code[167]), or in one of those services without specification of component, or as a commissioned officer of the Coast and Geodetic Survey, the National Oceanic and Atmospheric Administration Corps, or the Regular or Reserve Corps of the Public Health Service, and any person serving in the Army or Air Force under call or conscription. The term includes—

(1) a retired member of any of those services;

(2) a member of the Fleet Reserve or Fleet Marine Corps Reserve;

(3) a cadet at the United States Military Academy, a midshipman at the United States Naval Academy, and a cadet at the United States Coast Guard Academy or United States Air Force Academy;

(4) a member of the Reserve Officers' Training Corps, the Naval Reserve Officers' Training Corps, or the Air Force Reserve Officers' Training Corps, when ordered to annual training duty for fourteen days or more, and while performing authorized travel to and from that duty; and

(5) any person while en route to or from, or at, a place for final acceptance or for entry upon active duty in the military, naval, or air service—

(A) who has been provisionally accepted for such duty; or

(B) who, under the Military Selective Service Act[168], has been selected for active military, naval, or air service;

and has been ordered or directed to proceed to such place. The term does not include a temporary member of the Coast Guard Reserve.

Crew Leader

(n) The term "crew leader" means an individual who furnishes individuals to perform agricultural labor for another person, if such individual pays (either on his own behalf or on behalf of such person) the individuals so furnished by him for the agricultural labor performed by them and if such individual has not entered into a written agreement with such person whereby such individual has been designated as an employee of such person; and such individuals furnished by the crew leader to perform agricultural labor for another person shall be deemed to be the employees of such crew leader. A crew leader shall, with respect to services performed in furnishing individuals to perform agricultural labor for another person and service performed as a member of the crew, be deemed not to be an employee of such other person.

Peace Corps Volunteer Service

(o) The term "employment" shall, notwithstanding the provisions of subsection (a), include service performed by an individual as a volunteer or volunteer leader within the meaning of the Peace Corps Act[169].

---

[167] See Vol. II, 38 U.S.C. 101(27).
[168] P.L. 80-759.
[169] See Vol. II, P.L. 87-293.

SOCIAL SECURITY ACT—§ 210(p)(3)(C)   141

Medicare Qualified Government Employment

(p)(1) For purposes of sections 226 and 226A, the term "medicare qualified government employment" means any service which would constitute "employment" as defined in subsection (a) of this section but for the application of the provisions of—

(A) subsection (a)(5), or

(B) subsection (a)(7), except as provided in paragraphs (2) and (3).

(2) Service shall not be treated as employment by reason of paragraph (1)(B) if the service is performed—

(A) by an individual who is employed by a State or political subdivision thereof to relieve him from unemployment,

(B) in a hospital, home, or other institution by a patient or inmate thereof as an employee of a State or political subdivision thereof or of the District of Columbia,

(C) by an individual, as an employee of a State or political subdivision thereof or of the District of Columbia, serving on a temporary basis in case of fire, storm, snow, earthquake, flood or other similar emergency,

(D) by any individual as an employee included under section 5351(2) of title 5, United States Code[170] (relating to certain interns, student nurses, and other student employees of hospitals of the District of Columbia Government), other than as a medical or dental intern or a medical or dental resident in training, or

(E) by an election official or election worker if the remuneration paid in a calendar year for such service is less than $1,000 with respect to service performed during any calendar year commencing on or after January 1, 1995, ending on or before December 31, 1999, and the adjusted amount determined under section 218(c)(8)(B) for any calendar year commencing on or after January 1, 2000, with respect to service performed during such calendar year.

As used in this paragraph, the terms "State" and "political subdivision" have the meanings given those terms in section 218(b).

(3) Service performed for an employer shall not be treated as employment by reason of paragraph (1)(B) if—

(A) such service would be excluded from the term "employment" for purposes of this section if paragraph (1)(B) did not apply;

(B) such service is performed by an individual—

(i) who was performing substantial and regular service for remuneration for that employer before April 1, 1986,

(ii) who is a bona fide employee of that employer on March 31, 1986, and

(iii) whose employment relationship with that employer was not entered into for purposes of meeting the requirements of this subparagraph; and

(C) the employment relationship with that employer has not been terminated after March 31, 1986.

---

[170] See Vol. II, 5 U.S.C. 5351(2).

142 SOCIAL SECURITY ACT—§ 210(p)(4)

(4) For purposes of paragraph (3), under regulations (consistent with regulations established under section 3121(u)(2)(D) of the Internal Revenue Code of 1954[171])—

(A) all agencies and instrumentalities of a State (as defined in section 218(b)) or of the District of Columbia shall be treated as a single employer, and

(B) all agencies and instrumentalities of a political subdivision of a State (as so defined) shall be treated as a single employer and shall not be treated as described in subparagraph (A).

Treatment of Real Estate Agents and Direct Sellers

(q) Notwithstanding any other provision of this title, the rules of section 3508 of the Internal Revenue Code of 1986[172] shall apply for purposes of this title.

Service in the Employ of International Organizations by Certain Transferred Federal Employees

(r)(1) For purposes of this title, service performed in the employ of an international organization by an individual pursuant to a transfer of such individual to such international organization pursuant to section 3582 of title 5, United States Code, shall constitute "employment" if—

(A) immediately before such transfer, such individual performed service with a Federal agency which constituted "employment" as defined in subsection (a), and

(B) such individual would be entitled, upon separation from such international organization and proper application, to reemployment with such Federal agency under such section 3582.

(2) For purposes of this subsection:

(A) The term "Federal agency" means an agency, as defined in section 3581(1) of title 5, United States Code.

(B) The term "international organization" has the meaning provided such term by section 3581(3) of title 5, United States Code[173].

SELF-EMPLOYMENT

SEC. 211. [42 U.S.C. 411] For the purposes of this title—

Net Earnings From Self-Employment[174]

(a) The term "net earnings from self-employment" means the gross income, as computed under subtitle A of the Internal Revenue Code of 1986, derived by an individual from any trade or business carried on by such individual, less the deductions allowed under such subtitle which are attributable to such trade or business, plus his distributive share (whether or not distributed) of the ordinary net income or loss,

---

[171] See Vol. II, P.L. 83-591, §3121(u).

[172] See Vol. II, P.L. 83-591, §3508.

[173] See Vol. II, 5 U.S.C. 3581 and 3582.

[174] See Vol. II, P.L. 83-591, §1402(a)(1), with respect to certain payments under the Food Security Act of 1985 excluded from net earnings from self-employment.

SOCIAL SECURITY ACT—§ 211(a)(3)   143

as computed under section 702(a)(8) of such Code, from any trade or business carried on by a partnership of which he is a member; except that in computing such gross income and deductions and such distributive share of partnership ordinary net income or loss—

(1) There shall be excluded rentals from real estate and from personal property leased with the real estate (including such rentals paid in crop shares, and including payments under section 1233(2) of the Food Security Act of 1985 (16 U.S.C. 3833(2)) to individuals receiving benefits under section 202 or 223[175]), together with the deductions attributable thereto, unless such rentals are received in the course of a trade or business as a real estate dealer; except that the preceding provisions of this paragraph shall not apply to any income derived by the owner or tenant of land if (A) such income is derived under an arrangement, between the owner or tenant and another individual, which provides that such other individual shall produce agricultural or horticultural commodities (including livestock, bees, poultry, and fur-bearing animals and wildlife) on such land, and that there shall be material participation by the owner or tenant (as determined without regard to any activities of an agent of such owner or tenant) in the production or the management of the production of such agricultural or horticultural commodities, and (B) there is material participation by the owner or tenant (as determined without regard to any activities of an agent of such owner or tenant) with respect to any such agricultural or horticultural commodity;

(2) There shall be excluded dividends on any share of stock, and interest on any bond, debenture, note, or certificate, or other evidence of indebtedness, issued with interest benefits[176] or in registered form by any corporation (including one issued by a government or political subdivision thereof), unless such dividends and interest are received in the course of a trade or business as a dealer in stocks or securities;

(3) There shall be excluded any gain or loss (A) which is considered under subtitle A of the Internal Revenue Code of 1986 as gain or loss from the sale or exchange of a capital asset, (B) from the cutting of timber, or the disposal of timber, coal, or iron ore, if section 631 of the Internal Revenue Code of 1954[177] applies to such gain or loss, or (C) from the sale, exchange, involuntary conversion, or other disposition of property if such property is neither (i) stock in trade or other property of a kind which would properly be includible in inventory if on hand at the close of the taxable year, nor (ii) property held primarily for sale to customers in the ordinary course of the trade or business;

---

[175] P.L. 110-246, §15301(b), inserted "', and including payments under section 1233(2) of the Food Security Act of 1985 (16 U.S.C. 3833(2)) to individuals receiving benefits under section 202 or 223", applicable to payments made after December 31, 2007.

P.L. 110-234, §15301(b), which made the same amendment was repealed, effective May 22, 2008 pursuant to P.L. 110–246, §4(a).

[176] P.L. 110-246, §4115(c)(1)(A)(i), struck out "coupons" and substituted "benefits", effective October 1, 2008.

P.L. 110-234, §4115(c)(1)(A)(i), which made the same amendment was repealed, effective May 22, 2008 pursuant to P.L. 110-246, §4(a).

[177] See Vol. II, P.L. 83-591, §631.

144   SOCIAL SECURITY ACT—§ 211(a)(4)

(4) The deduction for net operating losses provided in section 172 of the Internal Revenue Code of 1986[178] shall not be allowed;

(5)(A) If any of the income derived from a trade or business (other than a trade or business carried on by a partnership) is community income under community property laws applicable to such income, the gross income and deductions attributable to such trade or business shall be treated as the gross income and deductions of the spouse carrying on such trade or business or, if such trade or business is jointly operated, treated as the gross income and deductions of each spouse on the basis of their respective distributive share of the gross income and deductions;

(B) If any portion of a partner's distributive share of the ordinary net income or loss from a trade or business carried on by a partnership is community income or loss under the community property laws applicable to such share, all of such distributive share shall be included in computing the net earnings from self-employment of such partner, and no part of such share shall be taken into account in computing the net earnings from self-employment of the spouse of such partner;

(6) A resident of the Commonwealth of Puerto Rico shall compute his net earnings from self-employment in the same manner as a citizen of the United States but without regard to the provisions of section 933 of the Internal Revenue Code of 1986[179];

(7) An individual who is a duly ordained, commissioned, or licensed minister of a church or a member of a religious order shall compute his net earnings from self-employment derived from the performance of service described in subsection (c)(4) without regard to section 107 (relating to rental value of parsonages), section 119 (relating to meals and lodging furnished for the convenience of the employer), and section 911 (relating to earned income from sources without the United States) of the Internal Revenue Code of 1986, but shall not include in any such net earnings from self-employment the rental value of any parsonage or any parsonage allowance (whether or not excluded under section 107 of the Internal Revenue Code of 1986) provided after the individual retires, or any other retirement benefit received by such individual from a church plan (as defined in section 414(e) of such Code) after the individual retires;

(8) The exclusion from gross income provided by section 931 of the Internal Revenue Code of 1986 shall not apply;

(9) There shall be excluded amounts received by a partner pursuant to a written plan of the partnership, which meets such requirements as are prescribed by the Secretary of the Treasury or his delegate, and which provides for payments on account of retirement, on a periodic basis, to partners generally or to a class or classes of partners, such payments to continue at least until such partner's death, if—

(A) such partner rendered no services with respect to any trade or business carried on by such partnership (or its successors) during the taxable year of such partnership (or its

[178] See Vol. II, P.L. 83-591, §172.
[179] See Vol. II, P.L. 83-591, §933.

SOCIAL SECURITY ACT—§ 211(a)(16)   145

successors), ending within or with his taxable year, in which such amounts were received, and

(B) no obligation exists (as of the close of the partnership's taxable year referred to in subparagraph (A)) from the other partners to such partner except with respect to retirement payments under such plan, and

(C) such partner's share, if any, of the capital of the partnership has been paid to him in full before the close of the partnership's taxable year referred to in subparagraph (A);

(10) The exclusion from gross income provided by section 911(a)(1) of the Internal Revenue Code of 1954[180] shall not apply;

(11) In lieu of the deduction provided by section 164(f) of the Internal Revenue Code of 1986[181] (relating to deduction for one-half of self-employment taxes), there shall be allowed a deduction equal to the product of—

(A) the taxpayer's net earnings from self-employment for the taxable year (determined without regard to this paragraph), and

(B) one-half of the sum of the rates imposed by subsections (a) and (b) of section 1401 of such Code[182] for such year;

(12) There shall be excluded the distributive share of any item of income or loss of a limited partner, as such, other than guaranteed payments described in section 707(c) of the Internal Revenue Code of 1986[183] to that partner for services actually rendered to or on behalf of the partnership to the extent that those payments are established to be in the nature of remuneration for those services;

(13) In the case of church employee income, the special rules of subsection (i)(1) shall apply;

(14) There shall be excluded income excluded from taxation under section 7873 of the Internal Revenue Code of 1986[184] (relating to income derived by Indians from exercise of fishing rights);[185]

(15) The deduction under section 162(l)[186] (relating to health insurance costs of self-employed individuals) shall not be allowed; and[187]

(16)[188] Notwithstanding the preceding provisions of this subsection, each spouse's share of income or loss from a qualified joint venture shall be taken into account as provided in section 761(f) of the Internal Revenue Code of 1986 in determining net earnings from self-employment of such spouse.

If the taxable year of a partner is different from that of the partnership, the distributive share which he is required to include in computing his net earnings from self-employment shall be based upon the ordinary net income or loss of the partnership for any taxable year of the partnership (even though beginning prior to 1951) ending within

---

[180] See Vol. II, P.L. 83-591, §911.
[181] See Vol. II, P.L. 83-591, §164(f).
[182] See Vol. II, P.L. 83-591, §1401.
[183] See Vol. II, P.L. 83-591, §707(c).
[184] See Vol. II, P.L. 83-591, §7873.
[185] P.L. 110-28, §8215(b)(2), struck out "and".
[186] See Vol. II, P.L. 83-591, §162(l).
[187] P.L. 110-28 §8215(b)(2), struck out the period and substituted "; and".
[188] P.L. 110-28, §8215(b)(2), added paragraph (16), applicable to taxable years beginning after December 31, 2006.

146 SOCIAL SECURITY ACT—§ 211(a)(16)(i)

or with his taxable year. In the case of any trade or business which is carried on by an individual or by a partnership and in which, if such trade or business were carried on exclusively by employees, the major portion of the services would constitute agricultural labor as defined in section 210(f)—

(i) in the case of an individual, if the gross income derived by him from such trade or business is not more than the upper limit[189], the net earnings from self-employment derived by him from such trade or business may, at his option, be deemed to be 66 2/3 percent of such gross income; or

(ii) in the case of an individual, if the gross income derived by him from such trade or business is more than the upper limit[190] and the net earnings from self-employment derived by him from such trade or business (computed under this subsection without regard to this sentence) are less than the lower limit[191], the net earnings from self-employment derived by him from such trade or business may, at his option, be deemed to be the lower limit[192]; and

(iii) in the case of a member of a partnership, if his distributive share of the gross income of the partnership derived from such trade or business (after such gross income has been reduced by the sum of all payments to which section 707(c) of the Internal Revenue Code of 1986[193] applies) is not more than the upper limit[194], his distributive share of income described in section 702(a)(8) of such Code derived from such trade or business may, at his option, be deemed to be an amount equal to 66 2/3 percent of his distributive share of such gross income (after such gross income has been so reduced); or

(iv) in the case of a member of a partnership, if his distributive share of the gross income of the partnership derived from such trade or business (after such gross income has been reduced by the sum of all payments to which section 707(c) of the Internal Revenue Code of 1986 applies) is more than the upper limit[195] and his distributive share (whether or not distributed) of income described in section 702(a)(8) of such Code derived from such trade

---

[189] P.L. 110-246, §15352(b)(1)(A), struck out "$2,400" and substituted "the upper limit", applicable to taxable years beginning after December 31, 2007.
P.L. 110-234, §15352(b)(1)(A), which made the same amendment was repealed, effective May 22, 2008 pursuant to P.L. 110-246, §4(a).
[190] P.L. 110-246, §15352(b)(1)(A), struck out "$2,400" and substituted "the upper limit", applicable to taxable years beginning after December 31, 2007.
P.L. 110-234, §15352(b)(1)(A), which made the same amendment was repealed, effective May 22, 2008 pursuant to P.L. 110-246, §4(a).
[191] P.L. 110-246, §15352(b)(1)(B), struck out "$1,600" and substituted "the lower limit", applicable to taxable years beginning after December 31, 2007.
P.L. 110-234, §15352(b)(1)(B), which made the same amendment was repealed, effective May 22, 2008 pursuant to P.L. 110-246, §4(a).
[192] P.L. 110-246, §15352(b)(1)(B), struck out "$1,600" and substituted "the lower limit", applicable to taxable years beginning after December 31, 2007.
P.L. 110-234, §15352(b)(1)(B), which made the same amendment was repealed, effective May 22, 2008 pursuant to P.L. 110-246, §4(a).
[193] See Vol. II, P.L. 83-591, §707(c).
[194] P.L. 110-246, §15352(b)(1)(A), struck out "$2,400" and substituted "the upper limit", applicable to taxable years beginning after December 31, 2007.
P.L. 110-234, §15352(b)(1)(A), which made the same amendment was repealed, effective May 22, 2008 pursuant to P.L. 110-246, §4(a).
[195] P.L. 110-246, §15352(b)(1)(A), struck out "$2,400" and substituted "the upper limit", applicable to taxable years beginning after December 31, 2007.
P.L. 110-234, §15352(b)(1)(A), which made the same amendment was repealed, effective May 22, 2008 pursuant to P.L. 110-246, §4(a).

SOCIAL SECURITY ACT—§ 211(a)(16)(vi) 147

or business (computed under this subsection without regard to this sentence) is less than the lower limit[196], his distributive share of income described in such section 702(a)(8) derived from such trade or business may, at his option, be deemed to be the lower limit[197].

For purposes of the preceding sentence, gross income means—

(v) in the case of any such trade or business in which the income is computed under a cash receipts and disbursements method, the gross receipts from such trade or business reduced by the cost or other basis of property which was purchased and sold in carrying on such trade or business, adjusted (after such reduction) in accordance with the provisions of paragraphs (1) through (6) and paragraph (8) of this subsection; and

(vi) in the case of any such trade or business in which the income is computed under an accrual method, the gross income from such trade or business, adjusted in accordance with the provisions of paragraphs (1) through (6) and paragraph (8) of this subsection;

and, for purposes of such sentence, if an individual (including a member of a partnership) derives gross income from more than one such trade or business, such gross income (including his distributive share of the gross income of any partnership derived from any such trade or business) shall be deemed to have been derived from one trade or business.

The preceding sentence and clauses (i) through (iv) of the second preceding sentence shall also apply in the case of any trade or business (other than a trade or business specified in such second preceding sentence) which is carried on by an individual who is self-employed on a regular basis as defined in subsection (g), or by a partnership of which an individual is a member on a regular basis as defined in subsection (g), but only if such individual's net earnings from self-employment in the taxable year as determined without regard to this sentence are less than the lower limit[198] and less than 66 2/3 percent of the sum (in such taxable year) of such individual's gross income derived from all trades or businesses carried on by him and his distributive share of the income or loss from all trades or businesses carried on by all the partnerships of which he is a member; except that this sentence shall not apply to more than 5 taxable years in the case of any individual, and in no case in which an individual elects to determine the amount of his net earnings from self-employment for a taxable year under the provisions of the two preceding sentences with respect to a trade or business to which the second preceding sentence applies and with

---

[196] P.L. 110-246, §15352(b)(1)(B), struck out "$1,600" and substituted "the lower limit", applicable to taxable years beginning after December 31, 2007.

P.L. 110-234, §15352(b)(1)(B), which made the same amendment was repealed, effective May 22, 2008 pursuant to P.L. 110-246, §4(a).

[197] P.L. 110-246, §15352(b)(1)(B), struck out "$1,600" and substituted "the lower limit", applicable to taxable years beginning after December 31, 2007.

P.L. 110-234, §15352(b)(1)(B), which made the same amendment was repealed, effective May 22, 2008 pursuant to P.L. 110-246, §4(a).

[198] P.L. 110-246, §15352(b)(1)(B), struck out "$1,600" and substituted "the lower limit", applicable to taxable years beginning after December 31, 2007.

P.L. 110-234, §15352(b)(1)(B), which made the same amendment was repealed, effective May 22, 2008 pursuant to P.L. 110-246, §4(a).

148 SOCIAL SECURITY ACT—§ 211(a)(16)(vi)(cont)

respect to a trade or business to which this sentence applies shall such net earnings for such year exceed the lower limit[199].

Self-Employment Income

(b) The term "self-employment income" means the net earnings from self-employment derived by an individual (other than a nonresident alien individual, except as provided by an agreement under section 233) during any taxable year beginning after 1950; except that such term shall not include—

(1) That part of the net earnings from self-employment which is in excess of—

(A) For any taxable year ending prior to 1955, (i) $3,600, minus (ii) the amount of the wages paid to such individual during the taxable year; and

(B) For any taxable year ending after 1954 and prior to 1959, (i) $4,200, minus (ii) the amount of the wages paid to such individual during the taxable year; and

(C) For any taxable year ending after 1958 and prior to 1966, (i) $4,800, minus (ii) the amount of the wages paid to such individual during the taxable year; and

(D) For any taxable year ending after 1965 and prior to 1968, (i) $6,600, minus (ii) the amount of the wages paid to such individual during the taxable year; and

(E) For any taxable year ending after 1967 and beginning prior to 1972, (i) $7,800, minus (ii) the amount of the wages paid to such individual during the taxable year; and

(F) For any taxable year beginning after 1971 and prior to 1973, (i) $9,000, minus (ii) the amount of the wages paid to such individual during the taxable year; and

(G) For any taxable year beginning after 1972 and prior to 1974, (i) $10,800, minus (ii) the amount of the wages paid to such individual during the taxable year; and

(H) For any taxable year beginning after 1973 and prior to 1975, (i) $13,200, minus (ii) the amount of the wages paid to such individual during the taxable year; and

(I) For any taxable year beginning in any calendar year after 1974, (i) an amount equal to the contribution and benefit base (as determined under section 230) which is effective for such calendar year, minus (ii) the amount of the wages paid to such individual during such taxable year; or

(2) The net earnings from self-employment, if such net earnings for the taxable year are less than $400.

An individual who is not a citizen of the United States but who is a resident of the Commonwealth of Puerto Rico, the Virgin Islands, Guam, or American Samoa shall not, for the purposes of this subsection, be considered to be a nonresident alien individual. In the case of church employee income, the special rules of subsection (i)(2) shall apply for purposes of paragraph (2).

---

[199] P.L. 110-246, §15352(b)(1)(B), struck out "$1,600" and substituted "the lower limit", applicable to taxable years beginning after December 31, 2007.

P.L. 110-234, §15352(b)(1)(B), which made the same amendment was repealed, effective May 22, 2008 pursuant to P.L. 110-246, §4(a).

Trade or Business

(c) The term "trade or business", when used with reference to self-employment income or net earnings from self-employment, shall have the same meaning as when used in section 162 of the Internal Revenue Code of 1986[200], except that such term shall not include—

(1) The performance of the functions of a public office, other than the functions of a public office of a State or a political subdivision thereof with respect to fees received in any period in which the functions are performed in a position compensated solely on a fee basis and in which such functions are not covered under an agreement entered into by such State and the Commissioner of Social Security pursuant to section 218;

(2) The performance of service by an individual as an employee, other than—

(A) service described in section 210(a)(14)(B) performed by an individual who has attained the age of eighteen,

(B) service described in section 210(a)(16),

(C) service described in section 210(a)(11), (12), or (15) performed in the United States by a citizen of the United States, except service which constitutes "employment" under section 210(r),

(D) service described in paragraph (4) of this subsection,

(E) service performed by an individual as an employee of a State or a political subdivision thereof in a position compensated solely on a fee basis with respect to fees received in any period in which such service is not covered under an agreement entered into by such State and the Commissioner of Social Security pursuant to section 218,

(F) service described in section 210(a)(20), and

(G) service described in section 210(a)(8)(B);

(3) The performance of service by an individual as an employee or employee representative as defined in section 3231 of the Internal Revenue Code of 1986[201];

(4) The performance of service by a duly ordained, commissioned, or licensed minister of a church in the exercise of his ministry or by a member of a religious order in the exercise of duties required by such order;

(5) The performance of service by an individual in the exercise of his profession as a Christian Science practitioner; or

(6) The performance of service by an individual during the period for which an exemption under section 1402(g) of the Internal Revenue Code of 1986[202] is effective with respect to him.

The provisions of paragraph (4) or (5) shall not apply to service (other than service performed by a member of a religious order who has taken a vow of poverty as a member of such order) performed by an individual unless an exemption under section 1402(e) of the Internal Revenue Code of 1986 is effective with respect to him.

---

[200] See Vol. II, P.L. 83-591, §162.
[201] See Vol. II, P.L. 83-591, §3231.
[202] See Vol. II, P.L. 83-591, §1402(g).

Partnership and Partner

(d) The term "partnership" and the term "partner" shall have the same meaning as when used in subchapter K of chapter 1 of the Internal Revenue Code of 1986.

Taxable Year

(e) The term "taxable year" shall have the same meaning as when used in subtitle A of the Internal Revenue Code of 1986; and the taxable year of any individual shall be a calendar year unless he has a different taxable year for the purposes of subtitle A of such Code, in which case his taxable year for the purposes of this title shall be the same as his taxable year under such subtitle A.

Partner's Taxable Year Ending as Result of Death

(f) In computing a partner's net earnings from self-employment for his taxable year which ends as a result of his death (but only if such taxable year ends within, and not with, the taxable year of the partnership), there shall be included so much of the deceased partner's distributive share of the partnership's ordinary income or loss for the partnership taxable year as is not attributable to an interest in the partnership during any period beginning on or after the first day of the first calendar month following the month in which such partner died. For purposes of this subsection—

(1) in determining the portion of the distributive share which is attributable to any period specified in the preceding sentence, the ordinary income or loss of the partnership shall be treated as having been realized or sustained ratably over the partnership taxable year; and

(2) the term "deceased partner's distributive share" includes the share of his estate or of any other person succeeding, by reason of his death, to rights with respect to his partnership interest.

Regular Basis

(g) An individual shall be deemed to be self-employed on a regular basis in a taxable year, or to be a member of a partnership on a regular basis in such year, if he had net earnings from self-employment, as defined in the first sentence of subsection (a), of not less than $400 in at least two of the three consecutive taxable years immediately preceding such taxable year from trades or businesses carried on by such individual or such partnership.

(h)(1) In determining the net earnings from self-employment of any options dealer or commodities dealer—

(A) notwithstanding subsection (a)(3)(A), there shall not be excluded any gain or loss (in the normal course of the taxpayer's activity of dealing in or trading section 1256 contracts) from section 1256 contracts or property related to such contracts, and

(B) the deduction provided by section 1202 of the Internal Revenue Code of 1986 shall not apply.

(2) For purposes of this subsection—

SOCIAL SECURITY ACT—§ 211(j)(4)(B)   151

(A) The term "options dealer" has the meaning given such term by section 1256(g)(8) of such Code[203].

(B) The term "commodities dealer" means a person who is actively engaged in trading section 1256 contracts and is registered with a domestic board of trade which is designated as a contract market by the Commodities Futures Trading Commission.

(C) The term "section 1256 contracts" has the meaning given to such term by section 1256(b) of such Code.

(i)(1) In applying subsection (a)—

(A) church employee income shall not be reduced by any deduction;

(B) church employee income and deductions attributable to such income shall not be taken into account in determining the amount of other net earnings from self-employment.

(2)(A) Subsection (b)(2) shall be applied separately—

(i) to church employee income, and

(ii) to other net earnings from self-employment.

(B) In applying subsection (b)(2) to church employee income, "$100" shall be substituted for "$400".

(3) Paragraph (1) shall not apply to any amount allowable as a deduction under subsection (a)(11), and paragraph (1) shall be applied before determining the amount so allowable.

(4) For purposes of this section, the term "church employee income" means gross income for services which are described in section 210(a)(8)(B) (and are not described in section 210(a)(8)(A)).

Codification of Treatment of Certain Termination Payments Received by Former Insurance Salesmen

(j) Nothing in subsection (a) shall be construed as including in the net earnings from self-employment of an individual any amount received during the taxable year from an insurance company on account of services performed by such individual as an insurance salesman for such company if—

(1) such amount is received after termination of such individual's agreement to perform such services for such company,

(2) such individual performs no services for such company after such termination and before the close of such taxable year,

(3) such individual enters into a covenant not to compete against such company which applies to at least the 1-year period beginning on the date of such termination, and

(4) the amount of such payment—

(A) depends primarily on policies sold by or credited to the account of such individual during the last year of such agreement or the extent to which such policies remain in force for some period after such termination, or both, and

(B) does not depend to any extent on length of service or overall earnings from services performed for such company (without regard to whether eligibility for payment depends on length of service).

---

[203] See Vol. II, P.L. 83-591, §1256.

152   SOCIAL SECURITY ACT—§ 211(j)(4)(B)(cont)

(k) [204] UPPER AND LOWER LIMITS.—For purposes of subsection (a)—

(1) The lower limit for any taxable year is the sum of the amounts required under section 213(d) for a quarter of coverage in effect with respect to each calendar quarter ending with or within such taxable year.

(2) The upper limit for any taxable year is the amount equal to 150 percent of the lower limit for such taxable year.

CREDITING OF SELF-EMPLOYMENT INCOME TO CALENDAR YEARS

SEC. 212. [42 U.S.C. 412] (a) For the purposes of determining average monthly wage and quarters of coverage the amount of self-employment income derived during any taxable year which begins before 1978 shall—

(1) in the case of a taxable year which is a calendar year, be credited equally to each quarter of such calendar year; and

(2) in the case of any other taxable year, be credited equally to the calendar quarter in which such taxable year ends and to each of the next three or fewer preceding quarters any part of which is in such taxable year.

(b) Except as provided in subsection (c), for[205] the purposes of determining average indexed monthly earnings, average monthly wage, and quarters of coverage the amount of self-employment income derived during any taxable year which begins after 1977 shall—

(1) in the case of a taxable year which is a calendar year or which begins with or during a calendar year and ends with or during such year, be credited to such calendar year; and

(2) in the case of any other taxable year, be allocated proportionately to the two calendar years, portions of which are included within such taxable year, on the basis of the number of months in each such calendar year which are included completely within the taxable year.

For purposes of clause (2), the calendar month in which a taxable year ends shall be treated as included completely within that taxable year.

(c)[206] For the purpose of determining average indexed monthly earnings, average monthly wage, and quarters of coverage in the case of any individual who elects the option described in clause (ii) or (iv) in the matter following section 211(a)(16) for any taxable year that does not begin with or during a particular calendar year and end with or during such year, the self-employment income of such individual deemed to be derived during such taxable year shall be allocated to the two calendar years, portions of which are included within such taxable year, in the same proportion to the total of such deemed self-employment income as the sum of the amounts applicable under section 213(d) for the calendar quarters ending with or within each

---

[204] P.L. 110-246, §15352(b)(2),added subsection (k), applicable to taxable years beginning after December 31, 2007.
P.L. 110-234, §15352(b)(2), which made the same amendment was repealed, effective May 22, 2008 pursuant to P.L. 110-246, §4(a).
[205] P.L. 110-246, §15352(b)(3)(A), struck out "For" and substituted " Except as provided in subsection (c), for".
P.L. 110-234, §15352(b)(3)(A), which made the same amendment was repealed, effective May 22, 2008 pursuant to P.L. 110-246, §4(a).
[206] P.L. 110-246, §15352(b)(3)(B), added subsection (c), applicable to taxable years beginning after December 31, 2007.
P.L. 110-234, §15352(b)(3)(B), which made the same amendment was repealed, effective May 22, 2008 pursuant to P.L. 110-246, §4(a).

SOCIAL SECURITY ACT—§ 213(a)(2)(B)(iii)   153

such calendar year bears to the lower limit for such taxable year specified in section 211(k)(1).

QUARTER AND QUARTER OF COVERAGE

Definitions

SEC. 213. [42 U.S.C. 413] (a) For the purposes of this title—
    (1) The term "quarter", and the term "calendar quarter", mean a period of three calendar months ending on March 31, June 30, September 30, or December 31.
    (2)(A) The term "quarter of coverage" means—
        (i) for calendar years before 1978, and subject to the provisions of subparagraph (B), a quarter in which an individual has been paid $50 or more in wages (except wages for agricultural labor paid after 1954) or for which he has been credited (as determined under section 212) with $100 or more of self-employment income; and
        (ii) for calendar years after 1977, and subject to the provisions of subparagraph (B), each portion of the total of the wages paid and the self-employment income credited (pursuant to section 212) to an individual in a calendar year which equals the amount required for a quarter of coverage in that calendar year (as determined under subsection (d)), with such quarter of coverage being assigned to a specific calendar quarter in such calendar year only if necessary in the case of any individual who has attained age 62 or died or is under a disability and the requirements for insured status in subsection (a) or (b) of section 214, the requirements for entitlement to a computation or recomputation of his primary insurance amount, or the requirements of paragraph (3) of section 216(i) would not otherwise be met.
    (B) Notwithstanding the provisions of subparagraph (A)—
        (i) no quarter after the quarter in which an individual dies shall be a quarter of coverage, and no quarter any part of which is included in a period of disability (other than the initial quarter and the last quarter of such period) shall be a quarter of coverage;
        (ii) if the wages paid to an individual in any calendar year equal $3,000 in the case of a calendar year before 1951, or $3,600 in the case of a calendar year after 1950 and before 1955, or $4,200 in the case of a calendar year after 1954 and before 1959, or $4,800 in the case of a calendar year after 1958 and before 1966, or $6,600 in the case of a calendar year after 1965 and before 1968, or $7,800 in the case of a calendar year after 1967 and before 1972, or $9,000 in the case of the calendar year 1972, or $10,800 in the case of the calendar year 1973, or $13,200 in the case of the calendar year 1974, or an amount equal to the contribution and benefit base (as determined under section 230) in the case of any calendar year after 1974 and before 1978 with respect to which such contribution and benefit base is effective, each quarter of such year shall (subject to clauses (i) and (v)) be a quarter of coverage;
        (iii) if an individual has self-employment income for a taxable year, and if the sum of such income and the wages paid

154 SOCIAL SECURITY ACT—§ 213(a)(2)(B)(iii)(cont)

to him during such year equals $3,600 in the case of a taxable year beginning after 1950 and ending before 1955, or $4,200 in the case of a taxable year ending after 1954 and before 1959, or $4,800 in the case of a taxable year ending after 1958 and before 1966, or $6,600 in the case of a taxable year ending after 1965 and before 1968, or $7,800 in the case of a taxable year ending after 1967 and before 1972, or $9,000 in the case of a taxable year beginning after 1971 and before 1973, or $10,800 in the case of a taxable year beginning after 1972 and before 1974, or $13,200 in the case of a taxable year beginning after 1973 and before 1975, or an amount equal to the contribution and benefit base (as determined under section 230) which is effective for the calendar year in the case of any taxable year beginning in any calendar year after 1974 and before 1978, each quarter any part of which falls in such year shall (subject to clauses (i) and (v)) be a quarter of coverage;

(iv) if an individual is paid wages for agricultural labor in a calendar year after 1954 and before 1978, then, subject to clauses (i) and (v), (I) the last quarter of such year which can be but is not otherwise a quarter of coverage shall be a quarter of coverage if such wages equal or exceed $100 but are less than $200; (II) the last two quarters of such year which can be but are not otherwise quarters of coverage shall be quarters of coverage if such wages equal or exceed $200 but are less than $300; (III) the last three quarters of such year which can be but are not otherwise quarters of coverage shall be quarters of coverage if such wages equal or exceed $300 but are less than $400; and (IV) each quarter of such year which is not otherwise a quarter of coverage shall be a quarter of coverage if such wages are $400 or more;

(v) no quarter shall be counted as a quarter of coverage prior to the beginning of such quarter;

(vi) not more than one quarter of coverage may be credited to a calendar quarter; and

(vii) no more than four quarters of coverage may be credited to any calendar year after 1977.

If in the case of an individual who has attained age 62 or died or is under a disability and who has been paid wages for agricultural labor in a calendar year after 1954 and before 1978, the requirements for insured status in subsection (a) or (b) of section 214, the requirements for entitlement to a computation or recomputation of his primary insurance amount, or the requirements of paragraph (3) of section 216(i) are not met after assignment of quarters of coverage to quarters in such year as provided in clause (iv) of the preceding sentence, but would be met if such quarters of coverage were assigned to different quarters in such year, then such quarters of coverage shall instead be assigned, for purposes only of determining compliance with such requirements, to such different quarters. If, in the case of an individual who did not die prior to January 1, 1955, and who attained age 62 (if a woman) or age 65 (if a man) or died before July 1, 1957, the requirements for insured status in section 214(a)(3) are not met because of his having too few quarters of coverage but would be met if his quarters of coverage in the first calendar year in which he had any covered employment had been determined on the basis of the period during which wages were earned rather than on the basis of the period during which wages were paid (any such wages paid that are reallocated on an earned basis shall not be used in determining quarters of coverage for subsequent calendar years), then upon application filed by the individual or his survivors and satisfactory proof of his record of wages earned being furnished by such individual or his survivors, the quarters of coverage in such calendar year may be determined on the basis of the periods during which wages were earned.

Crediting of Wages Paid in 1937

(b) With respect to wages paid to an individual in the six-month periods commencing either January 1, 1937, or July 1, 1937; (A) if wages of not less than $100 were paid in any such period, one-half of the total amount thereof shall be deemed to have been paid in each of the calendar quarters in such period; and (B) if wages of less than $100 were paid in any such period, the total amount thereof shall be deemed to have been paid in the latter quarter of such period, except that if in any such period, the individual attained age sixty-five, all of the wages paid in such period shall be deemed to have been paid before such age was attained.

Alternative Method for Determining Quarters of Coverage With Respect to Wages in the Period from 1937 to 1950

(c) For purposes of sections 214(a) and 215(d), an individual shall be deemed to have one quarter of coverage for each $400 of his total wages prior to 1951 (as defined in section 215(d)(1)(C)), except where such individual is not a fully insured individual on the basis of the number of quarters of coverage so derived plus the number of quarters of coverage derived from the wages and self-employment income credited to such individual for periods after 1950.

Amount Required for a Quarter of Coverage

(d)(1) The amount of wages and self-employment income which an individual must have in order to be credited with a quarter of coverage in any year under subsection (a)(2)(A)(ii) shall be $250 in the calendar year 1978 and the amount determined under paragraph (2) of this subsection for years after 1978.

(2) The Commissioner of Social Security shall, on or before November 1 of 1978 and of every year thereafter, determine and publish in the Federal Register the amount of wages and self-employment income which an individual must have in order to be credited with a quarter of coverage in the succeeding calendar year. The amount required for a quarter of coverage shall be the larger of—

    (A) the amount in effect in the calendar year in which the determination under this subsection is made, or

    (B) the product of the amount prescribed in paragraph (1) which is required for a quarter of coverage in 1978 and the ratio of the national average wage index (as defined in section 209(k)(1)) for

156   SOCIAL SECURITY ACT—§ 213(d)(2)(B)(cont)

the calendar year before the year in which the determination under this paragraph is made to the national average wage index (as so defined) for 1976,

with such product, if not a multiple of $10, being rounded to the next higher multiple of $10 where such amount is a multiple of $5 but not of $10 and to the nearest multiple of $10 in any other case.

INSURED STATUS FOR PURPOSES OF OLD-AGE AND SURVIVORS INSURANCE BENEFITS

SEC. 214. [42 U.S.C. 414] For the purposes of this title—

Fully Insured Individual

(a) The term "fully insured individual" means any individual who had not less than—

(1) one quarter of coverage (whenever acquired) for each calendar year elapsing after 1950 (or, if later, the year in which he attained age 21) and before the year in which he died or (if earlier) the year in which he attained age 62, except that in no case shall an individual be a fully insured individual unless he has at least 6 quarters of coverage; or

(2) 40 quarters of coverage; or

(3) in the case of an individual who died before 1951, 6 quarters of coverage;

not counting as an elapsed year for purposes of paragraph (1) any year any part of which was included in a period of disability (as defined in section 216(i)), and who satisfies the criterion specified in subsection (c).

Average Indexed Monthly Earnings; Average Monthly Wage

(b) The term "currently insured individual" means any individual who had not less than six quarters of coverage during the thirteen-quarter period ending with (1) the quarter in which he died, (2) the quarter in which he became entitled to old-age insurance benefits, (3) the quarter in which he became entitled to primary insurance benefits under this title as in effect prior to the enactment of this section[207], or (4) in the case of any individual entitled to disability insurance benefits, the quarter in which he most recently became entitled to disability insurance benefits, not counting as part of such thirteen-quarter period any quarter any part of which was included in a period of disability unless such quarter was a quarter of coverage, and who satisfies the criterion specified in subsection (c).

(c) For purposes of subsections (a) and (b), the criterion specified in this subsection is that the individual, if not a United States citizen or national—

(1) has been assigned a social security account number that was, at the time of assignment, or at any later time, consistent with the requirements of subclause (I) or (III) of section 205(c)(2)(B)(i); or

(2) at the time any such quarters of coverage are earned—

---

[207] August 28, 1950 [P.L. 81-734, §104(a); 64 Stat. 477, 505].

SOCIAL SECURITY ACT—§ 215(a)(1)(B)(iii)   157

(A) is described in subparagraph (B) or (D) of section 101(a)(15) of the Immigration and Nationality Act[208],

(B) is lawfully admitted temporarily to the United States for business (in the case of an individual described in such subparagraph (B)) or the performance as a crewman (in the case of an individual described in such subparagraph (D)), and

(C) the business engaged in or service as a crewman performed is within the scope of the terms of such individual's admission to the United States.

COMPUTATION OF PRIMARY INSURANCE AMOUNT

SEC. 215. [42 U.S.C. 415] For the purposes of this title—

Primary Insurance Amount

(a)(1)(A) The primary insurance amount of an individual shall (except as otherwise provided in this section) be equal to the sum of—

(i) 90 percent of the individual's average indexed monthly earnings (determined under subsection (b)) to the extent that such earnings do not exceed the amount established for purposes of this clause by subparagraph (B),

(ii) 32 percent of the individual's average indexed monthly earnings to the extent that such earnings exceed the amount established for purposes of clause (i) but do not exceed the amount established for purposes of this clause by subparagraph (B), and

(iii) 15 percent of the individual's average indexed monthly earnings to the extent that such earnings exceed the amount established for purposes of clause (ii),

rounded, if not a multiple of $0.10, to the next lower multiple of $0.10, and thereafter increased as provided in subsection (i).

(B)(i) For individuals who initially become eligible for old-age or disability insurance benefits, or who die (before becoming eligible for such benefits), in the calendar year 1979, the amount established for purposes of clause (i) and (ii) of subparagraph (A) shall be $180 and $1,085, respectively.

(ii) For individuals who initially become eligible for old-age or disability insurance benefits, or who die (before becoming eligible for such benefits), in any calendar year after 1979, each of the amounts so established shall equal the product of the corresponding amount established with respect to the calendar year 1979 under clause (i) of this subparagraph and the quotient obtained by dividing—

(I) the national average wage index (as defined in section 209(k)(1)) for the second calendar year preceding the calendar year for which the determination is made, by

(II) the national average wage index (as so defined) for 1977.

(iii) Each amount established under clause (ii) for any calendar year shall be rounded to the nearest $1, except that any amount so established which is a multiple of $0.50 but not of $1 shall be rounded to the next higher $1.

---

[208] See P.L. 82-414, §101(a)(15).

158 SOCIAL SECURITY ACT—§ 215(a)(1)(C)

(C)(i) No primary insurance amount computed under subparagraph (A) may be less than an amount equal to $11.50 multiplied by the individual's years of coverage in excess of 10, or the increased amount determined for purposes of this clause under subsection (i).

(ii) For purposes of clause (i), the term "years of coverage" with respect to any individual means the number (not exceeding 30) equal to the sum of (I) the number (not exceeding 14 and disregarding any fraction) determined by dividing (a) the total of the wages credited to such individual (including wages deemed to be paid prior to 1951 to such individual under section 217, compensation under the Railroad Retirement Act of 1937[209] prior to 1951 which is creditable to such individual pursuant to this title, and wages deemed to be paid prior to 1951 to such individual under section 231) for years after 1936 and before 1951 by (b) $900, plus (II) the number equal to the number of years after 1950 each of which is a computation base year (within the meaning of subsection (b)(2)(B)(ii)) and in each of which he is credited with wages (including wages deemed to be paid to such individual under section 217, compensation under the Railroad Retirement Act of 1937 or 1974[210] which is creditable to such individual pursuant to this title, and wages deemed to be paid to such individual under section 229) and self-employment income of not less than 25 percent (in the case of a year after 1950 and before 1978) of the maximum amount which (pursuant to subsection (e)) may be counted for such year, or 25 percent (in the case of a year after 1977 and before 1991) or 15 percent (in the case of a year after 1990) of the maximum amount which (pursuant to subsection (e)) could be counted for such year if section 230 as in effect immediately prior to the enactment of the Social Security Amendments of 1977[211] had remained in effect without change (except that, for purposes of subsection (b)(2)(A) of such section 230 as so in effect, the reference therein to the average of the wages of all employees as reported to the Secretary of the Treasury for any calendar year shall be deemed a reference to the national average wage index (within the meaning of section 209(k)(1)) for such calendar year).

(D) In each calendar year the Commissioner of Social Security shall publish in the Federal Register, on or before November 1, the formula for computing benefits under this paragraph and for adjusting wages and self-employment income under subsection (b)(3) in the case of an individual who becomes eligible for an old-age insurance benefit, or (if earlier) becomes eligible for a disability insurance benefit or dies, in the following year, and the national average wage index (as defined in section 209(k)(1)) on which that formula is based.

(2)(A) A year shall not be counted as the year of an individual's death or eligibility for purposes of this subsection or subsection (i) in any case where such individual was entitled to a disability insurance benefit for any of the 12 months immediately preceding the month of such death or eligibility (but there shall be counted instead the year of the individual's eligibility for the disability insurance benefit or benefits to which he was entitled during such 12 months).

(B) In the case of an individual who was entitled to a disability insurance benefit for any of the 12 months before the month in which he

---

[209] P.L. 75-162.
[210] P.L. 75-162 [as amended by P.L. 93-445].
[211] December 20, 1977 [P.L. 95-216, 91 Stat. 1509].

became entitled to an old-age insurance benefit, became reentitled to a disability insurance benefit, or died, the primary insurance amount for determining any benefit attributable to that entitlement, reentitlement, or death is the greater of—

(i) the primary insurance amount upon which such disability insurance benefit was based, increased by the amount of each general benefit increase (as defined in subsection (i)(3)), and each increase provided under subsection (i)(2), that would have applied to such primary insurance amount had the individual remained entitled to such disability insurance benefit until the month in which he became so entitled or reentitled or died, or

(ii) the amount computed under paragraph (1)(C).

(C) In the case of an individual who was entitled to a disability insurance benefit for any month, and with respect to whom a primary insurance amount is required to be computed at any time after the close of the period of the individual's disability (whether because of such individual's subsequent entitlement to old-age insurance benefits or to a disability insurance benefit based upon a subsequent period of disability, or because of such individual's death), the primary insurance amount so computed may in no case be less than the primary insurance amount with respect to which such former disability insurance benefit was most recently determined.

(3)(A) Paragraph (1) applies only to an individual who was not eligible for an old-age insurance benefit prior to January 1979 and who in that or any succeeding month—

(i) becomes eligible for such a benefit,

(ii) becomes eligible for a disability insurance benefit, or

(iii) dies, and (except for subparagraph (C)(i) thereof) it applies to every such individual except to the extent otherwise provided by paragraph (4).

(B) For purposes of this title, an individual is deemed to be eligible—

(i) for old-age insurance benefits, for months beginning with the month in which he attains age 62, or

(ii) for disability insurance benefits, for months beginning with the month in which his period of disability began as provided under section 216(i)(2)(C),

except as provided in paragraph (2)(A) in cases where fewer than 12 months have elapsed since the termination of a prior period of disability.

(4) Paragraph (1) (except for subparagraph (C)(i) thereof) does not apply to the computation or recomputation of a primary insurance amount for—

(A) an individual who was eligible for a disability insurance benefit for a month prior to January 1979 unless, prior to the month in which occurs the event described in clause (i), (ii), or (iii) of paragraph (3)(A), there occurs a period of at least 12 consecutive months for which he was not entitled to a disability insurance benefit, or

(B) an individual who had wages or self-employment income credited for one or more years prior to 1979, and who was not eligible for an old-age or disability insurance benefit, and did not die, prior to January 1979, if in the year for which the computation or recomputation would be made the individual's primary insurance amount would be greater if computed or recomputed—

160 SOCIAL SECURITY ACT—§ 215(a)(4)(B)(i)

(i) under section 215(a) as in effect in December 1978, for purposes of old-age insurance benefits in the case of an individual who becomes eligible for such benefits prior to 1984, or

(ii) as provided by section 215(d), in the case of an individual to whom such section applies.

In determining whether an individual's primary insurance amount would be greater if computed or recomputed as provided in subparagraph (B), (I) the table of benefits in effect in December 1978, as modified by paragraph (6), shall be applied without regard to any increases in that table which may become effective (in accordance with subsection (i)(4)) for years after 1978 (subject to clause (iii) of subsection (i)(2)(A)) and (II) such individual's average monthly wage shall be computed as provided by subsection (b)(4).

(5)(A) Subject to subparagraphs (B), (C), (D) and (E), for purposes of computing the primary insurance amount (after December 1978) of an individual to whom paragraph (1) does not apply (other than an individual described in paragraph (4)(B)), this section as in effect in December 1978 shall remain in effect, except that, effective for January 1979, the dollar amount specified in paragraph (3) of subsection (a) shall be increased to $11.50.

(B)(i) Subject to clauses (ii), (iii), and (iv), and notwithstanding any other provision of law, the primary insurance amount of any individual described in subparagraph (C) shall be, in lieu of the primary insurance amount as computed pursuant to any of the provisions referred to in subparagraph (D), the primary insurance amount computed under subsection (a) of section 215 as in effect in December 1978, without regard to subsections (b)(4) and (c) of such section as so in effect.

(ii) The computation of a primary insurance amount under this subparagraph shall be subject to section 104(j)(2) of the Social Security Amendments of 1972[212] (relating to the number of elapsed years under section 215(b)).

(iii) In computing a primary insurance amount under this subparagraph, the dollar amount specified in paragraph (3) of section 215(a) (as in effect in December 1978) shall be increased to $11.50.

(iv) In the case of an individual to whom section 215(d) applies, the primary insurance amount of such individual shall be the greater of—

(I) the primary insurance amount computed under the preceding clauses of this subparagraph, or

(II) the primary insurance amount computed under section 215(d).

(C) An individual is described in this subparagraph if—

(i) paragraph (1) does not apply to such individual by reason of such individual's eligibility for an old-age or disability insurance benefit, or the individual's death, prior to 1979, and

(ii) such individual's primary insurance amount computed under this section as in effect immediately before the date of the enactment of the Omnibus Budget Reconciliation Act of 1990[213]

---

[212] See Vol. II, P.L. 92-603, §104(j)(2).
[213] P.L. 101-508 was enacted November 5, 1990.

SOCIAL SECURITY ACT—§ 215(a)(7)(B)(i)   161

would have been computed under the provisions described in sub-paragraph (D).

(D) The provisions described in this subparagraph are—

(i) the provisions of this subsection as in effect prior to the enactment of the Social Security Amendments of 1965[214], if such provisions would preclude the use of wages prior to 1951 in the computation of the primary insurance amount,

(ii) the provisions of section 209 as in effect prior to the enactment of the Social Security Act Amendments of 1950, and

(iii) the provisions of section 215(d) as in effect prior to the enactment of the Social Security Amendments of 1977[215].

(E) For purposes of this paragraph, the table for determining primary insurance amounts and maximum family benefits contained in this section in December 1978 shall be revised as provided by subsection (i) for each year after 1978.

(6)(A) In applying the table of benefits in effect in December 1978 under this section for purposes of the last sentence of paragraph (4), such table, revised as provided by subsection (i), as applicable, shall be extended for average monthly wages of less than $76.00 and primary insurance benefits (as determined under subsection (d)) of less than $16.20.

(B) The Commissioner of Social Security shall determine and promulgate in regulations the methodology for extending the table under subparagraph (A).

(7)(A) In the case of an individual whose primary insurance amount would be computed under paragraph (1) of this subsection, who—

(i) attains age 62 after 1985 (except where he or she became entitled to a disability insurance benefit before 1986 and remained so entitled in any of the 12 months immediately preceding his or her attainment of age 62), or

(ii) would attain age 62 after 1985 and becomes eligible for a disability insurance benefit after 1985,

and who first becomes eligible after 1985 for a monthly periodic payment (including a payment determined under subparagraph (C), but excluding (I) a payment under the Railroad Retirement Act of 1974[216] or 1937[217], (II) a payment by a social security system of a foreign country based on an agreement concluded between the United States and such foreign country pursuant to section 233, and (III) a payment based wholly on service as a member of a uniformed service (as defined in section 210(m)) which is based in whole or in part upon his or her earnings for service which did not constitute "employment" as defined in section 210 for purposes of this title (hereafter in this paragraph and in subsection (d)(3) referred to as "noncovered service"), the primary insurance amount of that individual during his or her concurrent entitlement to such monthly periodic payment and to old-age or disability insurance benefits shall be computed or recomputed under subparagraph (B).

(B)(i) If paragraph (1) of this subsection would apply to such an individual (except for subparagraph (A) of this paragraph), there shall

---

[214] P.L. 89-97 was enacted July 30, 1965.
[215] P.L. 95-216 was enacted December 20, 1977.
[216] P.L. 75-162 [as amended by P.L. 93-445].
[217] P.L. 75-162.

162 SOCIAL SECURITY ACT—§ 215(a)(7)(B)(i)(cont)

first be computed an amount equal to the individual's primary insurance amount under paragraph (1) of this subsection, except that for purposes of such computation the percentage of the individual's average indexed monthly earnings established by subparagraph (A)(i) of paragraph (1) shall be the percent specified in clause (ii). There shall then be computed (without regard to this paragraph) a second amount, which shall be equal to the individual's primary insurance amount under paragraph (1) of this subsection, except that such second amount shall be reduced by an amount equal to one-half of the portion of the monthly periodic payment which is attributable to noncovered service performed after 1956 (with such attribution being based on the proportionate number of years of such noncovered service) and to which the individual is entitled (or is deemed to be entitled) for the initial month of his or her concurrent entitlement to such monthly periodic payment and old-age or disability insurance benefits. The individual's primary insurance amount shall be the larger of the two amounts computed under this subparagraph (before the application of subsection (i)) and shall be deemed to be computed under paragraph (1) of this subsection for the purpose of applying other provisions of this title.

(ii) For purposes of clause (i), the percent specified in this clause is—

(I) 80.0 percent with respect to individuals who become eligible (as defined in paragraph (3)(B)) for old-age insurance benefits (or became eligible as so defined for disability insurance benefits before attaining age 62) in 1986;

(II) 70.0 percent with respect to individuals who so become eligible in 1987;

(III) 60.0 percent with respect to individuals who so become eligible in 1988;

(IV) 50.0 percent with respect to individuals who so become eligible in 1989; and

(V) 40.0 percent with respect to individuals who so become eligible in 1990 or thereafter.

(C)(i) Any periodic payment which otherwise meets the requirements of subparagraph (A), but which is paid on other than a monthly basis, shall be allocated on a basis equivalent to a monthly payment (as determined by the Commissioner of Social Security), and such equivalent monthly payment shall constitute a monthly periodic payment for purposes of this paragraph.

(ii) In the case of an individual who has elected to receive a periodic payment that has been reduced so as to provide a survivor's benefit to any other individual, the payment shall be deemed to be increased (for purposes of any computation under this paragraph or subsection (d)(3) by the amount of such reduction.

(iii) For purposes of this paragraph, the term "periodic payment" includes a payment payable in a lump sum if it is a commutation of, or a substitute for, periodic payments.

(D) This paragraph shall not apply in the case of an individual who has 30 years or more of coverage. In the case of an individual who has more than 20 years of coverage but less than 30 years of coverage (as so defined), the percent specified in the applicable subdivision of subparagraph (B)(ii) shall (if such percent is smaller than the applicable

SOCIAL SECURITY ACT—§ 215(b)(1)(B) 163

percent specified in the following table) be deemed to be the applicable percent specified in the following table:

If the number of such individual's years of coverage (as so defined) is:	The applicable percent is:
29	85 percent
28	80 percent
27	75 percent
26	70 percent
25	65 percent
24	60 percent
23	55 percent
22	50 percent
21	45 percent

For purposes of this subparagraph, the term "year of coverage" shall have the meaning provided in paragraph (1)(C)(ii), except that the reference to "15 percent" therein shall be deemed to be a reference to "25 percent".

(E) This paragraph shall not apply in the case of an individual whose eligibility for old-age or disability insurance benefits is based on an agreement concluded pursuant to section 233 or an individual who on January 1, 1984—

(i) is an employee performing service to which social security coverage is extended on that date solely by reason of the amendments made by section 101 of the Social Security Amendments of 1983[218]; or

(ii) is an employee of a nonprofit organization which (on December 31, 1983) did not have in effect a waiver certificate under section 3121(k) of the Internal Revenue Code of 1954[219] and to the employees of which social security coverage is extended on that date solely by reason of the amendments made by section 102 of that Act, unless social security coverage had previously extended to service performed by such individual as an employee of that organization under a waiver certificate which was subsequently (prior to December 31, 1983) terminated.

Average Indexed Monthly Earnings; Average Monthly Wage

(b)(1) An individual's average indexed monthly earnings shall be equal to the quotient obtained by dividing—

(A) the total (after adjustment under paragraph (3)) of his wages paid in and self-employment income credited to his benefit computation years (determined under paragraph (2)), by

(B) the number of months in those years.

---

[218] P.L. 98-21.
[219] P.L. 83-591; however, §3121(k) was repealed by P.L. 98-21, §102(b)(2).

164 SOCIAL SECURITY ACT—§ 215(b)(2)

(2)(A) The number of an individual's benefit computation years equals the number of elapsed years reduced—

(i) in the case of an individual who is entitled to old-age insurance benefits (except as provided in the second sentence of this subparagraph), or who has died, by 5 years, and

(ii) in the case of an individual who is entitled to disability insurance benefits, by the number of years equal to one-fifth of such individual's elapsed years (disregarding any resulting fractional part of a year), but not by more than 5 years.

Clause (ii), once applicable with respect to any individual, shall continue to apply for purposes of determining such individual's primary insurance amount for purposes of any subsequent eligibility for disability or old-age insurance benefits unless prior to the month in which such eligibility begins there occurs a period of at least 12 consecutive months for which he was not entitled to a disability or an old-age insurance benefit. If an individual described in clause (ii) is living with a child (of such individual or his or her spouse) under the age of 3 in any calendar year which is included in such individual's computation base years, but which is not disregarded pursuant to clause (ii) or to subparagraph (B) (in determining such individual's benefit computation years) by reason of the reduction in the number of such individual's elapsed years under clause (ii), the number by which such elapsed years are reduced under this subparagraph pursuant to clause (ii) shall be increased by one (up to a combined total not exceeding 3) for each such calendar year; except that (I) no calendar year shall be disregarded by reason of this sentence (in determining such individual's benefit computation years) unless the individual was living with such child substantially throughout the period in which the child was alive and under the age of 3 in such year and the individual had no earnings as described in section 203(f)(5) in such year, (II) the particular calendar years to be disregarded under this sentence (in determining such benefit computation years) shall be those years (not otherwise disregarded under clause (ii)) which, before the application of section 215(f), meet the conditions of subclause (I), and (III) this sentence shall apply only to the extent that its application would not result in a lower primary insurance amount. The number of an individual's benefit computation years as determined under this subparagraph shall in no case be less than 2.

(B) For purposes of this subsection with respect to any individual—

(i) the term "benefit computation years" means those computation base years, equal in number to the number determined under subparagraph (A), for which the total of such individual's wages and self-employment income, after adjustment under paragraph (3), is the largest;

(ii) the term "computation base years" means the calendar years after 1950 and before—

(I) in the case of an individual entitled to old-age insurance benefits, the year in which occurred (whether by reason of section 202(j)(1) or otherwise) the first month of that entitlement; or

(II) in the case of an individual who has died (without having become entitled to old-age insurance benefits), the year succeeding the year of his death;

SOCIAL SECURITY ACT—§ 215(b)(4) 165

except that such term excludes any calendar year entirely included in a period of disability; and

(iii) the term "number of elapsed years" means (except as otherwise provided by section 104(j)(2) of the Social Security Amendments of 1972[220]) the number of calendar years after 1950 (or, if later, the year in which the individual attained age 21) and before the year in which the individual died, or, if it occurred earlier (but after 1960), the year in which he attained age 62; except that such term excludes any calendar year any part of which is included in a period of disability.

(3)(A) Except as provided by subparagraph (B), the wages paid in and self-employment income credited to each of an individual's computation base years for purposes of the selection therefrom of benefit computation years under paragraph (2) shall be deemed to be equal to the product of—

(i) the wages and self-employment income paid in or credited to such year (as determined without regard to this subparagraph), and

(ii) the quotient obtained by dividing—

(I) the national average wage index (as defined in section 209(k)(1)) for the second calendar year preceding the earliest of the year of the individual's death, eligibility for an old-age insurance benefit, or eligibility for a disability insurance benefit (except that the year in which the individual dies, or becomes eligible, shall not be considered as such year if the individual was entitled to disability insurance benefits for any month in the 12-month period immediately preceding such death or eligibility, but there shall be counted instead the year of the individual's eligibility for the disability insurance benefit to which he was entitled in such 12-month period), by

(II) the national average wage index (as so defined) for the computation base year for which the determination is made.

(B) Wages paid in or self-employment income credited to an individual's computation base year which—

(i) occurs after the second calendar year specified in subparagraph (A)(ii)(I), or

(ii) is a year treated under subsection (f)(2)(C) as though it were the last year of the period specified in paragraph (2)(B)(ii), shall be available for use in determining an individual's benefit computation years, but without applying subparagraph (A) of this paragraph.

(4) For purposes of determining the average monthly wage of an individual whose primary insurance amount is computed (after 1978) under section 215(a) or 215(d) as in effect (except with respect to the table contained therein) in December 1978, by reason of subsection (a)(4)(B), this subsection as in effect in December 1978 shall remain in effect, except that paragraph (2)(C) (as then in effect) shall be deemed to provide that "computation base years" include only calendar years in the period after 1950 (or 1936, if applicable) and prior to the year in which occurred the first month for which the individual was eligible (as defined in subsection (a)(3)(B) as in effect in January 1979) for

---

[220] See Vol. II, P.L. 92-603, §104(j)(2).

166   SOCIAL SECURITY ACT—§ 215(b)(4)(cont)

an old-age or disability insurance benefit, or, if earlier, the year in which he died. Any calendar year all of which is included in a period of disability shall not be included as a computation base year for such purposes.

Application of Prior Provisions in Certain Cases

(c) Subject to the amendments made by section 5117 of the Omnibus Budget Reconciliation Act of 1990[221], this subsection as in effect in December 1978 shall remain in effect with respect to an individual to whom subsection (a)(1) does not apply by reason of the individual's eligibility for an old-age or disability insurance benefit, or the individual's death, prior to 1979.

Primary Insurance Benefit Under 1939 Act

(d)(1) For purposes of column I of the table appearing in subsection (a), as that subsection was in effect in December 1977, an individual's primary insurance benefit shall be computed as follows:

(A) The individual's average monthly wage shall be determined as provided in subsection (b), as in effect in December 1977 (but without regard to paragraph (4) thereof and subject to section 104(j)(2) of the Social Security Amendments of 1972[222]), except that for purposes of paragraphs (2)(C) and (3) of that subsection (as so in effect) 1936 shall be used instead of 1950.

(B) For purposes of subparagraphs (B) and (C) of subsection (b)(2) (as so in effect)—

(i) the total wages prior to 1951 (as defined in subparagraph (C) of this paragraph) of an individual—

(I) shall, in the case of an individual who attained age 21 prior to 1950, be divided by the number of years (hereinafter in this subparagraph referred to as the "divisor") elapsing after the year in which the individual attained age 20, or 1936 if later, and prior to the earlier of the year of death or 1951, except that such divisor shall not include any calendar year entirely included in a period of disability, and in no case shall the divisor be less than one, and

(II) shall, in the case of an individual who died before 1950 and before attaining age 21, be divided by the number of years (hereinafter in this subparagraph referred to as the "divisor") elapsing after the second year prior to the year of death, or 1936 if later, and prior to the year of death, and in no case shall the divisor be less than one; and

(ii) the total wages prior to 1951 (as defined in subparagraph (C) of this paragraph) of an individual who either attained age 21 after 1949 or died after 1949 before attaining age 21, shall be divided by the number of years (hereinafter

---

[221] P.L. 101-508.
[222] See Vol. II, P.L. 92-603, §104(j)(2).

SOCIAL SECURITY ACT—§ 215(d)(2)(C)(ii) 167

in this subparagraph referred to as the "divisor") elapsing after 1949 and prior to 1951.

The quotient so obtained shall be deemed to be the individual's wages credited to each of the years which were used in computing the amount of the divisor, except that—

(iii) if the quotient exceeds $3,000, only $3,000 shall be deemed to be the individual's wages for each of the years which were used in computing the amount of the divisor, and the remainder of the individual's total wages prior to 1951 (I) if less than $3,000, shall be deemed credited to the computation base year (as defined in subsection (b)(2) as in effect in December 1977) immediately preceding the earliest year used in computing the amount of the divisor, of (II) if $3,000 or more, shall be deemed credited, in $3,000 increments, to the computation base year (as so defined) immediately preceding the earliest year used in computing the amount of the divisor and to each of the computation base years (as so defined) consecutively preceding that year, with any remainder less than $3,000 being credited to the computation base year (as so defined) immediately preceding the earliest year to which a full $3,000 increment was credited; and

(iv) no more than $42,000 may be taken into account, for purposes of this subparagraph, as total wages after 1936 and prior to 1951.

(C) For the purposes of subparagraph (B), "total wages prior to 1951" with respect to an individual means the sum of (i) remuneration credited to such individual prior to 1951 on the records of the Commissioner of Social Security, (ii) wages deemed paid prior to 1951 to such individual under section 217, (iii) compensation under the Railroad Retirement Act of 1937[223] prior to 1951 creditable to him pursuant to this title, and (iv) wages deemed paid prior to 1951 to such individual under section 231.

(D) The individual's primary insurance benefit shall be 40 percent of the first $50 of his average monthly wage as computed under this subsection, plus 10 percent of the next $200 of his average monthly wage, increased by 1 percent for each increment year. The number of increment years is the number, not more than 14 nor less than 4, that is equal to the individual's total wages prior to 1951 divided by $1,650 (disregarding any fraction).

(2) The provisions of this subsection shall be applicable only in the case of an individual—

(A) with respect to whom at least one of the quarters elapsing prior to 1951 is a quarter of coverage;

(B) who attained age 22 after 1950 and with respect to whom less than six of the quarters elapsing after 1950 are quarters of coverage, or who attained such age before 1951; and

(C)(i) who becomes entitled to benefits under section 202(a) or 223 or who dies, or

(ii) whose primary insurance amount is required to be recomputed under paragraph (2), (6), or (7) of subsection (f) or under section 231.

---

[223] P.L. 75-162.

168   SOCIAL SECURITY ACT—§ 215(d)(3)

(3) In the case of an individual whose primary insurance amount is not computed under paragraph (1) of subsection (a) by reason of paragraph (4)(B)(ii) of that subsection, who—

(A) attains age 62 after 1985 (except where he or she became entitled to a disability insurance benefit before 1986, and remained so entitled in any of the 12 months immediately preceding his or her attainment of age 62), or

(B) would attain age 62 after 1985 and becomes eligible for a disability insurance benefit after 1985,

and who first becomes eligible after 1985 for a monthly periodic payment (including a payment determined under subsection (a)(7)(C), but excluding (I) a payment under the Railroad Retirement Act of 1974[224] or 1937), (II) a payment by a social security system of a foreign country based on an agreement concluded between the United States and such foreign country pursuant to section 233, and (III) a payment based wholly on service as a member of a uniformed service (as defined in section 210(m)) which is based (in whole or in part) upon his or her earnings in noncovered service, the primary insurance amount of such individual during his or her concurrent entitlement to such monthly periodic payment and to old-age or disability insurance benefits shall be the primary insurance amount computed or recomputed under this subsection (without regard to this paragraph and before the application of subsection (i)) reduced by an amount equal to the smaller of—

(i) one-half of the primary insurance amount (computed without regard to this paragraph and before the application of subsection (i)), or

(ii) one-half of the portion of the monthly periodic payment (or payment determined under subsection (a)(7)(C)) which is attributable to noncovered service performed after 1956 (with such attribution being based on the proportionate number of years of such noncovered service) and to which that individual is entitled (or is deemed to be entitled) for the initial month of such concurrent entitlement.

This paragraph shall not apply in the case of any individual to whom subsection (a)(7) would not apply by reason of subparagraph (E) or the first sentence of subparagraph (D) thereof.

Certain Wages and Self-Employment Income Not To Be Counted

(e) For the purposes of subsections (b) and (d)—

(1) in computing an individual's average indexed monthly earnings or, in the case of an individual whose primary insurance amount is computed under section 215(a) as in effect prior to January 1979, average monthly wage, there shall not be counted the excess over $3,600 in the case of any calendar year after 1950 and before 1955, the excess over $4,200 in the case of any calendar year after 1954 and before 1959, the excess over $4,800 in the case of any calendar year after 1958 and before 1966, the excess over $6,600 in the case of any calendar year after 1965 and before 1968, the excess over $7,800 in the case of any calendar year

---

[224] P.L. 75-162 [as amended by P.L. 93-445].

SOCIAL SECURITY ACT—§ 215(f)(2)(D)(i)   169

after 1967 and before 1972, the excess over $9,000 in the case of any calendar year after 1971 and before 1973, the excess over $10,800 in the case of any calendar year after 1972 and before 1974, the excess over $13,200 in the case of any calendar year after 1973 and before 1975, and the excess over an amount equal to the contribution and benefit base (as determined under section 230) in the case of any calendar year after 1974 with respect to which such contribution and benefit base is effective, (before the application, in the case of average indexed monthly earnings, of subsection (b)(3)(A)) of (A) the wages paid to him in such year, plus (B) the self-employment income credited to such year (as determined under section 212); and

(2) if an individual's average indexed monthly earnings or, in the case of an individual whose primary insurance amount is computed under section 215(a) as in effect prior to January 1979, average monthly wage, computed under subsection (b) or for the purposes of subsection (d) is not a multiple of $1, it shall be reduced to the next lower multiple of $1.

Recomputation of Benefits

(f)(1) After an individual's primary insurance amount has been determined under this section, there shall be no recomputation of such individual's primary insurance amount except as provided in this subsection or, in the case of a World War II veteran who died prior to July 27, 1954, as provided in section 217(b).

(2)(A) If an individual has wages or self-employment income for a year after 1978 for any part of which he is entitled to old-age or disability insurance benefits, the Commissioner of Social Security shall, at such time or times and within such period as the Commissioner may by regulation prescribe, recompute the individual's primary insurance amount for that year.

(B) For the purpose of applying subparagraph (A) of subsection (a)(1) to the average indexed monthly earnings of an individual to whom that subsection applies and who receives a recomputation under this paragraph, there shall be used, in lieu of the amounts established by subsection (a)(1)(B) for purposes of clauses (i) and (ii) of subsection (a)(1)(A), the amounts so established that were (or, in the case of an individual described in subsection (a)(4)(B), would have been) used in the computation of such individual's primary insurance amount prior to the application of this subsection.

(C) A recomputation of any individual's primary insurance amount under this paragraph shall be made as provided in subsection (a)(1) as though the year with respect to which it is made is the last year of the period specified in subsection (b)(2)(B)(ii); and subsection (b)(3)(A) shall apply with respect to any such recomputation as it applied in the computation of such individual's primary insurance amount prior to the application of this subsection.

(D) A recomputation under this paragraph with respect to any year shall be effective—

(i) in the case of an individual who did not die in that year, for monthly benefits beginning with benefits for January of the following year; or

170   SOCIAL SECURITY ACT—§ 215(f)(2)(D)(ii)

(ii) in the case of an individual who died in that year, for monthly benefits beginning with benefits for the month in which he died.

(3) [Repealed.[225]]

(4) A recomputation shall be effective under this subsection only if it increases the primary insurance amount by at least $1.

(5) In the case of a man who became entitled to old-age insurance benefits and died before the month in which he attained retirement age (as defined in section 216(l)), the Commissioner of Social Security shall recompute his primary insurance amount as provided in subsection (a) as though he became entitled to old-age insurance benefits in the month in which he died; except that (i) his computation base years referred to in subsection (b)(2) shall include the year in which he died, and (ii) his elapsed years referred to in subsection (b)(3) shall not include the year in which he died or any year thereafter. Such recomputation of such primary insurance amount shall be effective for and after the month in which he died.

(6) Upon the death after 1967 of an individual entitled to benefits under section 202(a) or section 223, if any person is entitled to monthly benefits or a lump-sum death payment, on the wages and self-employment income of such individual, the Commissioner of Social Security shall recompute the decedent's primary insurance amount, but only if the decedent during his lifetime was paid compensation which was treated under section 205(o) as remuneration for employment.

(7) This subsection as in effect in December 1978 shall continue to apply to the recomputation of a primary insurance amount computed under subsection (a) or (d) as in effect (without regard to the table in subsection (a)) in that month, and, where appropriate, under subsection (d) as in effect in December 1977, including a primary insurance amount computed under any such subsection whose operation is modified as a result of the amendments made by section 5117 of the Omnibus Budget Reconciliation Act of 1990. For purposes of recomputing a primary insurance amount determined under subsection (a) or (d) (as so in effect) in the case of an individual to whom those subsections apply by reason of subsection (a)(4)(B) as in effect after December 1978, no remuneration shall be taken into account for the year in which the individual initially became eligible for an old-age or disability insurance benefit or died, or for any year thereafter, and (effective January 1982) the recomputation shall be modified by the application of subsection (a)(6) where applicable.

(8) The Commissioner of Social Security shall recompute the primary insurance amounts applicable to beneficiaries whose benefits are based on a primary insurance amount which was computed under subsection (a)(3) effective prior to January 1979, or would have been so computed if the dollar amount specified therein were $11.50. Such recomputation shall be effective January 1979, and shall include the effect of the increase in the dollar amount provided by subsection (a)(1)(C)(i). Such primary insurance amount shall be deemed to be provided under such section for purposes of subsection (i).

(9)(A) In the case of an individual who becomes entitled to a periodic payment determined under subsection (a)(7)(A) (including a pay-

---

[225] P.L. 95-216, §201(f)(2); 91 Stat. 1521.

ment determined under subsection (a)(7)(C)) in a month subsequent to the first month in which he or she becomes entitled to an old-age or disability insurance benefit, and whose primary insurance amount has been computed without regard to either such subsection or subsection (d)(3), such individual's primary insurance amount shall be recomputed (notwithstanding paragraph (4) of this subsection), in accordance with either such subsection or subsection (d)(3), as may be applicable, effective with the first month of his or her concurrent entitlement to such benefit and such periodic payment.

(B) If an individual's primary insurance amount has been computed under subsection (a)(7) or (d)(3), and it becomes necessary to recompute that primary insurance amount under this subsection—

(i) so as to increase the monthly benefit amount payable with respect to such primary insurance amount (except in the case of the individual's death), such increase shall be determined as though the recomputed primary insurance amount were being computed under subsection (a)(7) or (d)(3), or

(ii) by reason of the individual's death, such primary insurance amount shall be recomputed without regard to (and as though it had never been computed with regard to) subsection (a)(7) or (d)(3).

Rounding of Benefits

(g) The amount of any monthly benefit computed under section 202 or 223 which (after any reduction under sections 203(a) and 224 and any deduction under section 203(b), and after any deduction under section 1840(a)(1)) is not a multiple of $1 shall be rounded to the next lower multiple of $1.

Service of Certain Public Health Service Officers

(h)(1) Notwithstanding the provisions of subchapter III of chapter 83 of title 5, United States Code[226], remuneration paid for service to which the provisions of section 210(l)(1) of this Act are applicable and which is performed by an individual as a commissioned officer of the Reserve Corps of the Public Health Service prior to July 1, 1960, shall not be included in computing entitlement to or the amount of any monthly benefit under this title, on the basis of his wages and self-employment income, for any month after June 1960 and prior to the first month with respect to which the Director of the Office of Personnel Management certifies to the Commissioner of Social Security that, by reason of a waiver filed as provided in paragraph (2), no further annuity will be paid to him, his wife, and his children, or, if he has died, to his widow and children, under subchapter III of chapter 83 of title 5, United States Code, on the basis of such service.

(2) In the case of a monthly benefit for a month prior to that in which the individual, on whose wages and self-employment income such benefit is based, dies, the waiver must be filed by such individual; and such waiver shall be irrevocable and shall constitute a waiver on behalf of himself, his wife, and his children. If such individual did not

---

[226] See Vol. II, 5 U.S.C. Chapter 83.

172 SOCIAL SECURITY ACT—§ 215(h)(2)(cont)

file such a waiver before he died, then in the case of a benefit for the month in which he died or any month thereafter, such waiver must be filed by his widow, if any, and by or on behalf of all his children, if any; and such waivers shall be irrevocable. Such a waiver by a child shall be filed by his legal guardian or guardians, or, in the absence thereof, by the person (or persons) who has the child in his care.

Cost-of-Living Increases in Benefits

(i)(1) For purposes of this subsection—

(A) the term "base quarter" means (i) the calendar quarter ending on September 30 in each year after 1982, or (ii) any other calendar quarter in which occurs the effective month of a general benefit increase under this title;

(B) the term "cost-of-living computation quarter" means a base quarter, as defined in subparagraph (A)(i), with respect to which the applicable increase percentage is greater than zero; except that there shall be no cost-of-living computation quarter in any calendar year if in the year prior to such year a law has been enacted providing a general benefit increase under this title or if in such prior year such a general benefit increase becomes effective;

(C) the term "applicable increase percentage" means—

(i) with respect to a base quarter or cost-of-living computation quarter in any calendar year before 1984, or in any calendar year after 1983 and before 1989 for which the OASDI fund ratio is 15.0 percent or more, or in any calendar year after 1988 for which the OASDI fund ratio is 20.0 percent or more, the CPI increase percentage; and

(ii) with respect to a base quarter or cost-of-living computation quarter in any calendar year after 1983 and before 1989 for which the OASDI fund ratio is less than 15.0 percent, or in any calendar year after 1988 for which the OASDI fund ratio is less than 20.0 percent, the CPI increase percentage or the wage increase percentage, whichever (with respect to that quarter) is the lower;

(D) the term "CPI increase percentage", with respect to a base quarter or cost-of-living computation quarter in any calendar year, means the percentage (rounded to the nearest one-tenth of 1 percent) by which the Consumer Price Index for that quarter (as prepared by the Department of Labor) exceeds such index for the most recent prior calendar quarter which was a base quarter under subparagraph (A)(ii) or, if later, the most recent cost-of-living computation quarter under subparagraph (B);

(E) the term "wage increase percentage", with respect to a base quarter or cost-of-living computation quarter in any calendar year, means the percentage (rounded to the nearest one-tenth of 1 percent) by which the national average wage index (as defined in section 209(k)(1)) for the year immediately preceding such calendar year exceeds such index for the year immediately preceding the most recent prior calendar year which included a base quarter under subparagraph (A)(ii) or, if later, which included a cost-of-living computation quarter;

SOCIAL SECURITY ACT—§ 215(i)(2)(A)(ii)(III)   173

(F) the term "OASDI fund ratio", with respect to any calendar year, means the ratio of—

(i) the combined balance in the Federal Old-Age and Survivors Insurance Trust Fund and the Federal Disability Insurance Trust Fund as of the beginning of such year, including the taxes transferred under section 201(a) on the first day of such year and reduced by the outstanding amount of any loan (including interest thereon) theretofore made to either such Fund from the Federal Hospital Insurance Trust Fund under section 201(l), to

(ii) the total amount which (as estimated by the Commissioner of Social Security) will be paid from the Federal Old-Age and Survivors Insurance Trust Fund and the Federal Disability Insurance Trust Fund during such calendar year for all purposes authorized by section 201 (other than payments of interest on, or repayments of, loans from the Federal Hospital Insurance Trust Fund under section 201(l)), but excluding any transfer payments between such trust funds and reducing the amount of any transfers to the Railroad Retirement Account by the amount of any transfers into either such trust fund from that Account;

(G) the Consumer Price Index for a base quarter, a cost-of-living computation quarter, or any other calendar quarter shall be the arithmetical mean of such index for the 3 months in such quarter.

(2)(A)(i) The Commissioner of Social Security shall determine each year beginning with 1975 (subject to the limitation in paragraph (1)(B)) whether the base quarter (as defined in paragraph (1)(A)(i)) in such year is a cost-of-living computation quarter.

(ii) If the Commissioner of Social Security determines that the base quarter in any year is a cost–of–living computation quarter, the Commissioner shall, effective with the month of December of that year as provided in subparagraph (B), increase—

(I) the benefit amount to which individuals are entitled for that month under section 227 or 228,

(II) the primary insurance amount of each other individual on which benefit entitlement is based under this title, and

(III) the amount of total monthly benefits based on any primary insurance amount which is permitted under section 203 (and such total shall be increased, unless otherwise so increased under another provision of this title, at the same time as such primary insurance amount) or, in the case of a primary insurance amount computed under subsection (a) as in effect (without regard to the table contained therein) prior to January 1979, the amount to which the beneficiaries may be entitled under section 203 as in effect in December 1978, except as provided by section 203(a)(7) and (8) as in effect after December 1978.

The increase shall be derived by multiplying each of the amounts described in subdivisions (I), (II), and (III) (including each of those amounts as previously increased under this subparagraph) by the applicable increase percentage; and any amount so increased that is not a multiple of $0.10 shall be decreased to the next lower multiple of $0.10. Any increase under this subsection in a primary insurance amount determined under subparagraph (C)(i) of subsection (a)(1) shall be applied after the initial determination of such primary insurance amount under that subparagraph (with the amount of such increase, in the case of an individual who becomes eligible for old-age or disability insurance benefits or dies in a calendar year after 1979, being determined from the range of possible primary insurance amounts published by the Commissioner of Social Security under the last sentence of subparagraph (D)).

(iii) In the case of an individual who becomes eligible for an old-age or disability insurance benefit, or who dies prior to becoming so eligible, in a year in which there occurs an increase provided under clause (ii), the individual's primary insurance amount (without regard to the time of entitlement to that benefit) shall be increased (unless otherwise so increased under another provision of this title and, with respect to a primary insurance amount determined under subsection (a)(1)(C)(i)(I) in the case of an individual to whom that subsection (as in effect in December 1981) applied, subject to the provisions of subsection (a)(1)(C)(i) and clauses (iv) and (v) of this subparagraph (as then in effect)) by the amount of that increase and subsequent applicable increases, but only with respect to benefits payable for months after November of that year.

(B) The increase provided by subparagraph (A) with respect to a particular cost-of-living computation quarter shall apply in the case of monthly benefits under this title for months after November of the calendar year in which occurred such cost-of-living computation quarter, and in the case of lump-sum death payments with respect to deaths occurring after November of such calendar year.

(C)(i) Whenever the Commissioner of Social Security determines that a base quarter in a calendar year is also a cost-of-living computation quarter, the Commissioner shall notify the House Committee on Ways and Means and the Senate Committee on Finance of such determination within 30 days after the close of such quarter, indicating the amount of the benefit increase to be provided, the Commissioner's estimate of the extent to which the cost of such increase would be met by an increase in the contribution and benefit base under section 230 and the estimated amount of the increase in such base, the actuarial estimates of the effect of such increase, and the actuarial assumptions and methodology used in preparing such estimates.

(ii) The Commissioner of Social Security shall determine and promulgate the OASDI fund ratio for the current calendar year on or before November 1 of the current calendar year, based upon the most recent data then available. The Commissioner of Social Security shall include a statement of the fund ratio and the national average wage index (as defined in section 209(k)(1)) and a statement of the effect such ration and the level of such index may have upon benefit increases under this subsection in any notification made under clause (i) and any determination published under subparagraph (D).

(D) If the Commissioner of Social Security determines that a base quarter in a calendar year is also a cost-of-living computation quarter, the Commissioner shall publish in the Federal Register within 45 days after the close of such quarter a determination that a benefit increase is resultantly required and the percentage thereof. The Commissioner shall also publish in the Federal Register at that time (i) a revision of the range of the primary insurance amounts which are possible after the application of this subsection based on the dollar amount specified in subparagraph (C)(i) of subsection (a)(1) (with such revised primary insurance amounts constituting the increased amounts determined for purposes of such subparagraph (C)(i) under this subsection), or specified in subsection (a)(3) as in effect prior to 1979, and (ii) a revision of the range of maximum family benefits which correspond to such primary insurance amounts (with such maximum benefits being effective notwithstanding section 203(a) except for paragraph (3)(B) thereof (or paragraph (2) thereof as in effect prior to 1979)). Notwithstanding the preceding sentence, such revision of maximum family benefits shall be subject to paragraph (6) of section 203(a) (as added by section 101(a)(3) of the Social Security Disability Amendments of 1980[227]).

(3) As used in this subsection, the term "general benefit increase under this title" means an increase (other than an increase under this subsection) in all primary insurance amounts on which monthly insurance benefits under this title are based.

(4) This subsection as in effect in December 1978, and as amended by sections 111(a)(6), 111(b)(2), and 112 of the Social Security Amendments of 1983[228] and by section 9001 of the Omnibus Budget Reconciliation Act of 1986[229], shall continue to apply to subsections (a) and (d), as then in effect and as amended by section 5117 of the Omnibus Budget Reconciliation Act of 1990[230], for purposes of computing the primary insurance amount of an individual to whom subsection (a), as in effect after December 1978, does not apply (including an individual to whom subsection (a) does not apply in any year by reason of paragraph (4)(B) of that subsection (but the application of this subsection in such cases shall be modified by the application of subdivision (I) in the last sentence of paragraph (4) of that subsection)), except that for this purpose, in applying paragraphs (2)(A)(ii), (2)(D)(iv), and (2)(D)(v) of this subsection as in effect in December 1978, the phrase "increased to the next higher multiple of $0.10" shall be deemed to read "decreased to the next lower multiple of $0.10". For purposes of computing primary insurance amounts and maximum family benefits (other than primary insurance amounts and maximum family benefits for individuals to whom such paragraph (4)(B) applies), the Commissioner of Social Security shall revise the table of benefits contained in subsection (a), as in effect in December 1978, in accordance with the requirements of paragraph (2)(D) of this subsection as then in effect, except that the requirement in such paragraph (2)(D) that the Commissioner of Social Security publish such revision of the table of benefits in the Federal Register shall not apply.

(5)(A) If—

(i) with respect to any calendar year the "applicable increase percentage" was determined under clause (ii) of paragraph (1)(C) rather than under clause (i) of such paragraph, and the increase becoming effective under paragraph (2) in such year was accordingly determined on the basis of the wage increase percentage rather than the CPI increase percentage (or there was no such increase becoming effective under paragraph (2) in that year be-

---

[227] P.L. 96-265.
[228] P.L. 98-21.
[229] P.L. 99-509.
[230] P.L. 101-508.

176 SOCIAL SECURITY ACT—§ 215(i)(5)(A)(i)(cont)

cause there was no wage increase percentage greater than zero), and

(ii) for any subsequent calendar year in which an increase under paragraph (2) becomes effective the OASDI fund ratio is greater than 32.0 percent,

then each of the amounts described in subdivisions (I), (II), and (III) of paragraph (2)(A)(ii), as increased under paragraph (2) effective with the month of December in such subsequent calendar year, shall be further increased (effective with such month) by an additional percentage, which shall be determined under subparagraph (B) and shall apply as provided in subparagraph (C). Any amount so increased that is not a multiple of $0.10 shall be decreased to the next lower multiple of $0.10.

(B) The applicable additional percentage by which the amounts described in subdivisions (I), (II), and (III) of paragraph (2)(A)(ii) are to be further increased under subparagraph (A) in the subsequent calendar year involved shall be the amount derived by—

(i) subtracting (I) the compounded percentage benefit increases that were actually paid under paragraph (2) and this paragraph from (II) the compounded percentage benefit increases that would have been paid if all increases under paragraph (2) had been made on the basis of the CPI increase percentage,

(ii) dividing the difference by the sum of the compounded percentage in clause (i)(I) and 100 percent, and

(iii) multiplying such quotient by 100 so as to yield such applicable additional percentage (which shall be rounded to the nearest one-tenth of 1 percent),

with the compounded increases referred to in clause (i) being measured—

(iv) in the case of amounts described in subdivision (I) of paragraph (2)(A)(ii), over the period beginning with the calendar year in which monthly benefits described in such subdivision were first increased on the basis of the wage increase percentage and ending with the year before such subsequent calendar year, and

(v) in the case of amounts described in subdivisions (II) and (III) of paragraph (2)(A)(ii), over the period beginning with the calendar year in which the individual whose primary insurance amount is increased under such subdivision (II) became eligible (as defined in subsection (a)(3)(B)) for the old-age or disability insurance benefit that is being increased under this subsection, or died before becoming so eligible, and ending with the year before such subsequent calendar year;

except that if the Commissioner of Social Security determines in any case that the application (in accordance with subparagraph (C)) of the additional percentage as computed under the preceding provisions of this subparagraph would cause the OASDI fund ratio to fall below 32.0 percent in the calendar year immediately following such subsequent year, the Commissioner shall reduce such applicable additional percentage to the extent necessary to ensure that the OASDI fund ratio will remain at or above 32.0 percent through the end of such following year.

(C) Any applicable additional percentage increase in an amount described in subdivision (I), (II), or (III) of paragraph (2)(A)(ii), made under this paragraph in any calendar year, shall thereafter be treated

SOCIAL SECURITY ACT—§ 216(c)(1)

for all the purposes of this Act as a part of the increase made in such amount under paragraph (2) for that year.

OTHER DEFINITIONS

SEC. 216. [42 U.S.C. 416] For the purposes of this title—

Spouse; Surviving Spouse

(a)(1) The term "spouse" means a wife as defined in subsection (b) or a husband as defined in subsection (f).

(2) The term "surviving spouse" means a widow as defined in subsection (c) or a widower as defined in subsection (g).

Wife

(b) The term "wife" means the wife of an individual, but only if she (1) is the mother of his son or daughter, (2) was married to him for a period of not less than one year immediately preceding the day on which her application is filed, or (3) in the month prior to the month of her marriage to him (A) was entitled to, or on application therefor and attainment of age 62 in such prior month would have been entitled to, benefits under subsection (b), (e), or (h) of section 202, (B) had attained age eighteen and was entitled to, or on application therefor would have been entitled to, benefits under subsection (d) of such section (subject, however, to section 202(s)), or (C) was entitled to, or upon application therefor and attainment of the required age (if any) would have been entitled to, a widow's, child's (after attainment of age 18), or parent's insurance annuity under section 2 of the Railroad Retirement Act of 1974[231], as amended. For purposes of clause (2), a wife shall be deemed to have been married to an individual for a period of one year throughout the month in which occurs the first anniversary of her marriage to such individual. For purposes of subparagraph (C) of section 202(b)(1), a divorced wife shall be deemed not to be married throughout the month in which she becomes divorced.

Widow

(c)(1) The term "widow" (except when used in the first sentence of section 202(i)) means the surviving wife of an individual, but only if (A) she is the mother of his son or daughter, (B) she legally adopted his son or daughter while she was married to him and while such son or daughter was under the age of eighteen, (C) he legally adopted her son or daughter while she was married to him and while such son or daughter was under the age of eighteen, (D) she was married to him at the time both of them legally adopted a child under the age of eighteen, (E) except as provided in paragraph (2), she was married to him for a period of not less than nine months immediately prior to the day on which he died, or (F) in the month prior to the month of her marriage to him (i) she was entitled to, or on application therefor and attainment of age 62 in such prior month would have been entitled to, benefits under subsection (b), (e), or (h) of section 202, (ii) she had

---

[231] See Vol. II, P.L. 75-162 [as amended by P.L. 93-445].

178 SOCIAL SECURITY ACT—§ 216(c)(1)(cont)

attained age eighteen and was entitled to, or on application therefor would have been entitled to, benefits under subsection (d) of such section (subject, however, to section 202(s)), or (iii) she was entitled to, or upon application therefor and attainment of the required age (if any) would have been entitled to, a widow's, child's (after attainment of age 18), or parent's insurance annuity under section 2 of the Railroad Retirement Act of 1974, as amended[232].

(2) The requirements of paragraph (1)(E) in connection with the surviving wife of an individual shall be treated as satisfied if—

(A) the individual had been married prior to the individual's marriage to the surviving wife,

(B) the prior wife was institutionalized during the individual's marriage to the prior wife due to mental incompetence or similar incapacity,

(C) during the period of the prior wife's institutionalization, the individual would have divorced the prior wife and married the surviving wife, but the individual did not do so because such divorce would have been unlawful, by reason of the prior wife's institutionalization, under the laws of the State in which the individual was domiciled at the time (as determined based on evidence satisfactory to the Commissioner of Social Security),

(D) the prior wife continued to remain institutionalized up to the time of her death, and

(E) the individual married the surviving wife within 60 days after the prior wife's death.

Divorced Spouses; Divorce

(d)(1) The term "divorced wife" means a woman divorced from an individual, but only if she had been married to such individual for a period of 10 years immediately before the date the divorce became effective.

(2) The term "surviving divorced wife" means a woman divorced from an individual who has died, but only if she had been married to the individual for a period of 10 years immediately before the date the divorce became effective.

(3) The term "surviving divorced mother" means a woman divorced from an individual who has died, but only if (A) she is the mother of his son or daughter, (B) she legally adopted his son or daughter while she was married to him and while such son or daughter was under the age of 18, (C) he legally adopted her son or daughter while she was married to (him and while such son or daughter was under the age of 18, or (D) she was married to him at the time both of them legally adopted a child under the age of 18.

(4) The term "divorced husband" means a man divorced from an individual, but only if he had been married to such individual for a period of 10 years immediately before the date the divorce became effective.

(5) The term "surviving divorced husband" means a man divorced from an individual who has died, but only if he had been married to

---

[232] See Vol. II, P.L. 75-162, §2.

SOCIAL SECURITY ACT—§ 216(e)   179

the individual for a period of 10 years immediately before the divorce became effective.

(6) The term "surviving divorced father" means a man divorced from an individual who has died, but only if (A) he is the father of her son or daughter, (B) he legally adopted her son or daughter while he was married to her and while such son or daughter was under the age of 18, (C) she legally adopted his son or daughter while he was married to her and while such son or daughter was under the age of 18, or (D) he was married to her at the time both of them legally adopted a child under the age of 18.

(7) The term "surviving divorced parent" means a surviving divorced mother as defined in paragraph (3) of this subsection or a surviving divorced father as defined in paragraph (6).

(8) The terms "divorce" and "divorced" refer to a divorce a vinculo matrimonii.

Child

(e) The term "child" means (1) the child or legally adopted child of an individual, (2) a stepchild who has been such stepchild for not less than one year immediately preceding the day on which application for child's insurance benefits is filed or (if the insured individual is deceased) not less than nine months immediately preceding the day on which such individual died, and (3) a person who is the grandchild or stepgrandchild of an individual or his spouse, but only if (A) there was no natural or adoptive parent (other than such a parent who was under a disability, as defined in section 223(d)) of such person living at the time (i) such individual became entitled to old-age insurance benefits or disability insurance benefits or died, or (ii) if such individual had a period of disability which continued until such individual (became entitled to old-age insurance benefits or disability insurance benefits, or died, at the time such period of disability began, or (B) such person was legally adopted after the death of such individual by such individual's surviving spouse in an adoption that was decreed by a court of competent jurisdiction within the United States and such person's natural or adopting parent or stepparent was not living in such individual's household and making regular contributions toward such person's support at the time such individual died. For purposes of clause (1), a person shall be deemed, as of the date of death of an individual, to be the legally adopted child of such individual if such person was either living with or receiving at least one-half of his support from such individual at the time of such individual's death and was legally adopted by such individual's surviving spouse after such individual's death but only if (A) proceedings for the adoption of the child had been instituted by such individual before his death, or (B) such child was adopted by such individual's surviving spouse before the end of two years after (i) the day on which such individual died or (ii) the date of enactment of the Social Security Amendments of 1958[233]. For purposes of clause (2), a person who is not the stepchild of an individual shall be deemed the stepchild of such individual if such individual was not the mother or adopting mother or the father

---

[233] August 28, 1958 [P.L. 85-840; 72 Stat. 1013].

or adopting father of such person and such individual and the mother or adopting mother, or the father or adopting father, as the case may be, of such person went through a marriage ceremony resulting in a purported marriage between them which, but for a legal impediment described in the last sentence of subsection (h)(1)(B), would have been a valid marriage. For purposes of clause (2), a child shall be deemed to have been the stepchild of an individual for a period of one year throughout the month in which occurs the expiration of such one year. For purposes of clause (3), a person shall be deemed to have no natural or adoptive parent living (other than a parent who was under a disability) throughout the most recent month in which a natural or adoptive parent (not under a disability) dies.

Husband

(f) The term "husband" means the husband of an individual, but only if (1) he is the father of her son or daughter, (2) he was married to her for a period of not less than one year immediately preceding the day on which his application is filed, or (3) in the month prior to the month of his marriage to her (A) he was entitled to, or on application (therefor and attainment of age 62 in such prior month would have been entitled to, benefits under subsection (c), (f) or (h) of section 202, (B) he had attained age eighteen and was entitled to, or on application therefor would have been entitled to, benefits under subsection (d) of such section (subject, however, to section 202(s)), or (C) he was entitled to, or upon application therefor and attainment of the required age (if any) he would have been entitled to, a widower's, child's (after attainment of age 18), or parent's insurance annuity under section 2 of the Railroad Retirement Act of 1974[234], as amended. For purposes of clause (2), a husband shall be deemed to have been married to an individual for a period of one year throughout the month in which occurs the first anniversary of his marriage to her. For purposes of subparagraph (C) of section 202(c)(1), a divorced husband shall be deemed not to be married throughout the month which he becomes divorced.

Widower

(g)(1) The term "widower" (except when used in the first sentence of section 202(i)) means the surviving husband of an individual, but only if (A) he is the father of her son or daughter, (B) he legally adopted her son or daughter while he was married to her and while such son or daughter was under the age of eighteen, (C) she legally adopted his son or daughter while he was married to her and while such son or daughter was under the age of eighteen, (D) he was married to her at the time both of them legally adopted a child under the age of eighteen, (E) except as provided in paragraph (2), he was married to her for a period of not less than nine months immediately prior to the day on which she died, or (F) in the month before the month of his marriage to her (i) he was entitled to, or on application therefor and attainment of age 62 in such prior month would have been entitled to, benefits under subsection (c), (f) or (h) of section 202, (ii) he had attained age

---

[234] See Vol. II, P.L. 75-162, §2 [as amended by P.L. 93-445].

SOCIAL SECURITY ACT—§ 216(h)(1)(B)(i)   181

eighteen and was entitled to, or on application therefor would have been entitled to, benefits under subsection (d) of such section (subject, however, to section 202(s)), or (iii) he was entitled to, or on application therefor and attainment of the required age (if any) he would have been entitled to, a widower's, child's (after attainment of age 18), or parent's insurance annuity under section 2 of the Railroad Retirement Act of 1974[235], as amended.

(2) The requirements of paragraph (1)(E) in connection with the surviving husband of an individual shall be treated as satisfied if—

(A) the individual had been married prior to the individual's marriage to the surviving husband,

(B) the prior husband was institutionalized during the individual's marriage to the prior husband due to mental incompetence or similar incapacity,

(C) during the period of the prior husband's institutionalization, the individual would have divorced the prior husband and married the surviving husband, but the individual did not do so because such divorce would have been unlawful, by reason of the prior husband's institutionalization, under the laws of the State in which the individual was domiciled at the time (as determined based on evidence satisfactory to the Commissioner of Social Security),

(D) the prior husband continued to remain institutionalized up to the time of his death, and

(E) the individual married the surviving husband within 60 days after the prior husband's death.

Determination of Family Status

(h)(1)(A)(i) An applicant is the wife, husband, widow, or widower of a fully or currently insured individual for purposes of this title if the courts of the State in which such insured individual is domiciled at the time such applicant files an application, or, if such insured individual is dead, the courts of the State in which he was domiciled at the time of death, or, if such insured individual is or was not so domiciled in any State, the courts of the District of Columbia, would find that such applicant and such insured individual were validly married at the time such applicant files such application or, if such insured individual is dead, at the time he died.

(ii) If such courts would not find that such applicant and such insured individual were validly married at such time, such applicant shall, nevertheless be deemed to be the wife, husband, widow, or widower, as the case may be, of such insured individual if such applicant would, under the laws applied by such courts in determining the devolution of intestate personal property, have the same status with respect to the taking of such property as a wife, husband, widow, or widower of such insured individual.

(B)(i) In any case where under subparagraph (A) an applicant is not (and is not deemed to be) the wife, widow, husband, or widower of a fully or currently insured individual, or where under subsection (b), (c), (d), (f), or (g) such applicant is not the wife, divorced wife, widow,

---

[235] See Vol. II, P.L. 75-162, §2 [as amended by P.L. 93-445].

surviving divorced wife, husband, divorced husband, widower, or surviving divorced husband of such individual, but it is established to the satisfaction of the Commissioner of Social Security that such applicant in good faith went through a marriage ceremony with such individual resulting in a purported marriage between them which, but for a legal impediment not known to the applicant at the time of such ceremony, would have been a valid marriage, then, for purposes of subparagraph (A) and subsections (b), (c), (d), (f), and (g), such purported marriage shall be deemed to be a valid marriage. Notwithstanding the preceding sentence, in the case of any person who would be deemed under the preceding sentence a wife, widow, husband, or widower of the insured individual, such marriage shall not be deemed to be a valid marriage unless the applicant and the insured individual were living in the same household at the time of the death of (the insured individual or (if the insured individual is living) at the time the applicant files the application. A marriage that is deemed to be a valid marriage by reason of the preceding sentence shall continue to be deemed a valid marriage if the insured individual and the person entitled to benefits as the wife or husband of the insured individual are no longer living in the same household at the time of the death of such insured individual.

(ii) The provisions of clause (i) shall not apply if the Commissioner of Social Security determines, on the basis of information brought to the Commissioner's attention, that such applicant entered into such purported marriage with such insured individual with knowledge that it would not be a valid marriage.

(iii) The entitlement to a monthly benefit under subsection (b) or (c) of section 202, based on the wages and self-employment income of such insured individual, of a person who would not be deemed to be a wife or husband of such insured individual but for this subparagraph, shall end with the month before the month in which such person enters into a marriage, valid without regard to this subparagraph, with a person other than such insured individual.

(iv) For purposes of this subparagraph, a legal impediment to the validity of a purported marriage includes only an impediment (I) resulting from the lack of dissolution of a previous marriage or otherwise arising out of such previous marriage or its dissolution, or (II) resulting from a defect in the procedure followed in connection with such purported marriage.

(2)(A) In determining whether an applicant is the child or parent of a fully or currently insured individual for purposes of this title, the Commissioner of Social Security shall apply such law as would be applied in determining the devolution of intestate personal property by the courts of the State in which such insured individual is domiciled at the time such applicant files application, or, if such insured individual is dead, by the courts of the State in which he was domiciled at the time of his death, or, if such insured individual is or was not so domiciled in any State, by the courts of the District of Columbia. Applicants who according to such law would have the same status relative to taking intestate personal property as a child or parent shall be deemed such.

(B) If an applicant is a son or daughter of a fully or currently insured individual but is not (and is not deemed to (be) the child of such insured individual under subparagraph (A), such applicant shall nev-

SOCIAL SECURITY ACT—§ 216(h)(3)(C)(i)(I)   183

ertheless be deemed to be the child of such insured individual if such insured individual and the mother or father, as the case may be, of such applicant went through a marriage ceremony resulting in a purported marriage between them which, but for a legal impediment described in the last sentence of paragraph (1)(B), would have been a valid marriage.

(3) An applicant who is the son or daughter of a fully or currently insured individual, but who is not (and is not deemed to be) the child of such insured individual under paragraph (2), shall nevertheless be deemed to be the child of such insured individual if:

(A) in the case of an insured individual entitled to old-age insurance benefits (who was not, in the month preceding such entitlement, entitled to disability insurance benefits)—

(i) such insured individual—

(I) has acknowledged in writing that the applicant is his or her son or daughter,

(II) has been decreed by a court to be the mother or father of the applicant, or

(III) has been ordered by a court to contribute to the support of the applicant because the applicant is his or her son or daughter,

and such acknowledgment, court decree, or court order was made not less than one year before such insured individual became entitled to old-age insurance benefits or attained retirement age (as defined in subsection (l)), whichever is earlier; or

(ii) such insured individual is shown by evidence satisfactory to the Commissioner of Social Security to be the mother or father of the applicant and was living with or contributing to the support of the applicant at the time such applicant's application for benefits was filed;

(B) in the case of an insured individual entitled to disability insurance benefits, or who was entitled to such benefits in the month preceding the first month for which he or she was entitled to old-age insurance benefits—

(i) such insured individual—

(I) has acknowledged in writing that the applicant is his or her son or daughter,

(II) has been decreed by a court to be the mother or father of the applicant, or

(III) has been ordered by a court to contribute to the support of the applicant because the applicant is his or her son or daughter,

and such acknowledgment, court decree, or court order was made before such insured individual's most recent period of disability began; or

(ii) such insured individual is shown by evidence satisfactory to the Commissioner of Social Security to be the mother or father of the applicant and was living with or contributing to the support of that applicant at the time such applicant's application for benefits was filed;

(C) in the case of a deceased individual—

(i) such insured individual—

(I) had acknowledged in writing that the applicant is his or her son or daughter,

184   SOCIAL SECURITY ACT—§ 216(h)(3)(C)(i)(II)

(II) had been decreed by a court to be the mother or father of the applicant, or

(III) had been ordered by a court to contribute to the support of the applicant because the applicant was his or her son or daughter,

and such acknowledgment, court decree, or court order was made before the death of such insured individual, or

(ii) such insured individual is shown by evidence satisfactory to the Commissioner of Social Security to have been the mother or father of the applicant, and such insured individual was living with or contributing to the support of the applicant at the time such insured individual died.

For purposes of subparagraphs (A)(i) and (B)(i), an acknowledgement, court decree, or court order shall be deemed to have occurred on the first day of the month in which it actually occurred.

Disability; Period of Disability

(i)(1) Except for purposes of sections 202(d), 202(e), 202(f), 223, and 225, the term "disability" means (A) inability to engage in any substantial gainful activity by reason of any medically determinable physical or mental impairment which can be expected to result in death or has lasted or can be expected to last for a continuous period of not less than 12 months, or (B) blindness; and the term "blindness" means central visual acuity of $20/200$ or less in the better eye with the use of a correcting lens. An eye which is accompanied by a limitation in the fields of vision such that the widest diameter of the visual field subtends an angle no greater than 20 degrees shall be considered for purposes of this paragraph as having a central visual acuity of $20/200$ or less. The provisions of paragraphs (2)(A),(2)(B),(3), (4), (5), and (6) of section 223(d) shall be applied for purposes of determining whether an individual is under a disability within the meaning of the first sentence of this paragraph in the same manner as they are applied for purposes of paragraph (1) of such section. Nothing in this title shall be construed as authorizing the Commissioner or any other officer or employee of the United States to interfere in any way with the practice of medicine or with relationships between practitioners of medicine and their patients, or to exercise any supervision or control over the administration or operation of any hospital.

(2)(A) The term "period of disability" means a continuous period (beginning and ending as hereinafter provided in this subsection) during which an individual was under a disability (as defined in paragraph (1)), but only if such period is of not less than five full calendar months' duration or such individual was entitled to benefits under section 223 for one or more months in such period.

(B) No period of disability shall begin as to any individual unless such individual files an application for a disability determination with respect to such period; and no such period shall begin as to any individual after such individual attains retirement age (as defined in subsection (l)). In the case of a deceased individual, the requirement of an application under the preceding sentence may be satisfied by an application for a disability determination filed with respect to such individual within 3 months after the month in which he died.

(C) A period of disability shall begin—
(i) on the day the disability began, but only if the individual satisfies the requirements of paragraph (3) on such day; or
(ii) if such individual does not satisfy the requirements of paragraph (3) on such day, then on the first day of the first quarter thereafter in which he satisfies such requirements.

(D) A period of disability shall end with the close of whichever of the following months is the earlier: (i) the month preceding the month in which the individual attains retirement age (as defined in subsection (l)), or (ii) the month preceding (I) the termination month (as defined in section 223(a)(1)), or, if earlier (II) the first month for which no benefit is payable by reason of section 223(e), where no benefit is payable for any of the succeeding months during the 36–month period referred to in such section. The provisions set forth in section 223(f) with respect to determinations of whether entitlement to benefits under this title or title XVIII based on the disability of any individual is terminated (on the basis of a finding that the physical or mental impairment on the basis of which such benefits are provided has ceased, does not exist, or is not disabling) shall apply in the same manner and to the same extent with respect to determinations of whether a period of disability has ended (on the basis of a finding that the physical or mental impairment on the basis of which the finding of disability was made has ceased, does not exist, or is not disabling).

(E) Except as is otherwise provided in subparagraph (F), no application for a disability determination which is filed more than 12 months after the month prescribed by subparagraph (D) as the month in which the period of disability ends (determined without regard to subparagraph (B) and this subparagraph) shall be accepted as an application for purposes of this paragraph.

(F) An application for a disability determination which is filed more than 12 months after the month prescribed by subparagraph (D) as the month in which the period of disability ends (determined without regard to subparagraphs (B) and (E)) shall be accepted as an application for purposes of this paragraph if—
(i) in the case of an application filed by or on behalf of an individual with respect to a disability which ends after the month in which the Social Security Amendments of 1967 is enacted[236], such application is filed not more than 36 months after the month in which such disability ended, such individual is alive at the time the application is filed, and the Commissioner of Social Security finds in accordance with (regulations prescribed by the Commissioner that the failure of such individual to file an application for a disability determination within the time specified in subparagraph (E) was attributable to a physical or mental condition of such individual which rendered him incapable of executing such an application, and
(ii) in the case of an application filed by or on behalf of an individual with respect to a period of disability which ends in or before the month in which the Social Security Amendments of 1967 is enacted—

---

[236] January 1968 [P.L. 90-248; 81 Stat. 821].

186   SOCIAL SECURITY ACT—§ 216(i)(2)(F)(ii)(I)

(I) such application is filed not more than 12 months after the month in which the Social Security Amendments of 1967 is enacted,

(II) a previous application for a disability determination has been filed by or on behalf of such individual (1) in or before the month in which the Social Security Amendments of 1967 is enacted[237], and (2) not more than 36 months after the month in which his disability ended, and

(III) the Commissioner of Social Security finds in accordance with regulations prescribed by the Commissioner, that the failure of such individual to file an application within the then specified time period was attributable to a physical or mental condition of such individual which rendered him incapable of executing such an application.

In making a determination under this subsection, with respect to the disability or period of disability of any individual whose application for a determination thereof is accepted solely by reason of the provisions of this subparagraph (F), the provisions of this subsection (other than the provisions of this subparagraph) shall be applied as such provisions are in effect at the time such determination is made.

(G) An application for a disability determination filed before the first day on which the applicant satisfies the requirements for a period of disability under this subsection shall be deemed a valid application (and shall be deemed to have been filed on such first day) only if the applicant satisfies the requirements for a period of disability before the Commissioner of Social Security makes a final decision on the application and no request under section 205(b) for notice and opportunity (for a hearing thereon is made or, if such a request is made, before a decision based upon the evidence adduced at the hearing is made (regardless of whether such decision becomes the final decision of the Commissioner of Social Security).

(3) The requirements referred to in clauses (i) and (ii) of paragraph (2)(C) are satisfied by an individual with respect to any quarter only if—

(A) he would have been a fully insured individual (as defined in section 214) had he attained age 62 and filed application for benefits under section 202(a) on the first day of such quarter; and

(B)(i) he had not less than 20 quarters of coverage during the 40-quarter period which ends with such quarter, or

(ii) if such quarter ends before he attains (or would attain) age 31, not less than one-half (and not less than 6) of the quarters during the period ending with such quarter and beginning after he attained the age of 21 were quarters of coverage, or (if the number of quarters in such period is less than 12) not less than 6 of the quarters in the 12-quarter period ending with such quarter were quarters of coverage, or

(iii) in the case of an individual (not otherwise insured under clause (i)) who, by reason of clause (ii), had a prior period of disability that began during a period before the quarter in which he or she attained age 31, not less than one-half of the quarters beginning after such individual attained age 21 and ending with

---

[237] January 1968 [P.L. 90-248; 81 Stat. 821].

such quarter are quarters of coverage, or (if the number of quarters in such period is less than 12) not less than 6 of the quarters in the 12-quarter period ending with such quarter are quarters of coverage;

except that the provisions of subparagraph (B) of this paragraph shall not apply in the case of an individual who is blind (within the meaning of "blindness" as defined in paragraph (1)). For purposes of subparagraph (B) of this paragraph, when the number of quarters in any period is an odd number, such number shall be reduced by one, and a quarter shall not be counted as part of any period if any part of such quarter was included in a prior period of disability unless such quarter was a quarter of coverage.

Periods of Limitation Ending on Nonwork Days

(j) Where this title, any provision of another law of the United States (other than the Internal Revenue Code of 1986) relating to or changing the effect of this title, or any regulation issued by the Commissioner of Social Security pursuant thereto provides for a period within which an act is required to be done which affects eligibility for or the amount of any benefit or payment under this title or is necessary to establish or protect any rights under this title, and such period ends on a Saturday, Sunday, or legal holiday, or on any other day all or part of which is declared to be a nonwork day for Federal employees by statute or Executive order, then such act shall be considered as done within such period if it is done on the first day thereafter which is not a Saturday, Sunday, or legal holiday or any other day all or part of which is declared to be a nonwork day for Federal employees by statute or Executive order. For purposes of this subsection, the day on which a period ends shall include the day on which an extension of such period, as authorized by law or by the Commissioner of Social Security pursuant to law, ends. The provisions of this subsection shall not extend the period during which benefits under this title may (pursuant to section 202(j)(1) or 223(b)) be paid for months prior to the day application for such benefits is filed, or during which an application for benefits under this title may (pursuant to section 202(j)(2) or 223(b)) be accepted as such.

Waiver of Nine-Month Requirement for Widow, Stepchild, or Widower in Case of Accidental Death or in Case of Serviceman Dying in Line of Duty, or in Case of Remarriage to the Same Individual

(k) The requirement in clause (E) of subsection (c)(1) or clause (E) of subsection (g)(1) that the surviving spouse of an individual have been married to such individual for a period of not less than nine months immediately prior to the day on which such individual died in order to qualify as such individual's widow or widower, and the requirement in subsection (e) that the stepchild of a deceased individual have been such stepchild for not less than nine months immediately preceding the day on which such individual died in order to qualify as such individual's child, shall be deemed to be satisfied, where such individual dies within the applicable nine-month period, if—

(1) his death—

(A) is accidental, or

(B) occurs in line of duty while he is a member of a uniformed (service serving on active duty (as defined in section 210(l)(2)),

unless the Commissioner of Social Security determines that at the time of the marriage involved the individual could not have reasonably been expected to live for nine months, or

(2)(A) the widow or widower of such individual had been previously married to such individual and subsequently divorced and such requirement would have been satisfied at the time of such divorce if such previous marriage had been terminated by the death of such individual at such time instead of by divorce; or

(B) the stepchild of such individual had been the stepchild of such individual during a previous marriage of such stepchild's parent to such individual which ended in divorce and such requirement would have been satisfied at the time of such divorce if such previous marriage had been terminated by the death of such individual at such time instead of by divorce;

except that paragraph (2) of this subsection shall not apply if the Commissioner of Social Security determines that at the time of the marriage involved the individual could not have reasonably been expected to live for nine months. For purposes of paragraph (1)(A) of this subsection, the death of an individual is accidental if he receives bodily injuries solely through violent, external, and accidental means and, as a direct result of the bodily injuries and independently of all other causes, loses his life not later than three months after the day on which he receives such bodily injuries.

Retirement Age

(l)(1) The term "retirement age" means—

(A) with respect to an individual who attains early retirement age (as defined in paragraph (2)) before January 1, 2000, 65 years of age;

(B) with respect to an individual who attains early retirement age after December 31, 1999, and before January 1, 2005, 65 years of age plus the number of months in the age increase factor (as determined under paragraph (3)) for the calendar year in which such individual attains early retirement age;

(C) with respect to an individual who attains early retirement age after December 31, 2004, and before January 1, 2017, 66 (years of age;

(D) with respect to an individual who attains early retirement age after December 31, 2016, and before January 1, 2022, 66 years of age plus the number of months in the age increase factor (as determined under paragraph (3)) for the calendar year in which such individual attains early retirement age; and

(E) with respect to an individual who attains early retirement age after December 31, 2021, 67 years of age.

(2) The term "early retirement age" means age 62 in the case of an old-age, wife's, or husband's insurance benefit, and age 60 in the case of a widow's or widower's insurance benefit.

SOCIAL SECURITY ACT—§ 217(a)(2) 189

(3) The age increase factor for any individual who attains early retirement age in a calendar year within the period to which subparagraph (B) or (D) of paragraph (1) applies shall be determined as follows:

(A) With respect to an individual who attains early retirement age in the 5-year period consisting of the calendar years 2000 through 2004, the age increase factor shall be equal to two-twelfths of the number of months in the period beginning with January 2000 and ending with December of the year in which the individual attains early retirement age.

(B) With respect to an individual who attains early retirement age in the 5-year period consisting of the calendar years 2017 through 2021, the age increase factor shall be equal to two-twelfths of the number of months in the period beginning with January 2017 and ending with December of the year in which the individual attains early retirement age.

BENEFITS IN CASE OF VETERANS

SEC. 217. [42 U.S.C. 417] (a)(1) For purposes of determining entitlement to and the amount of any monthly benefit for any month after August 1950, or entitlement to and the amount of any lump-sum death payment in case of a death after such month, payable under this title on the basis of the wages and self-employment income of any World War II veteran, and for purposes of section 216(i)(3), such veteran shall be deemed to have been paid wages (in addition to the wages, if any, actually paid to him) of $160 in each month during any part of which he served in the active military or naval service of the United States during World War II. This subsection shall not be applicable in the case of any monthly benefit or lump-sum death payment if—

(A) a larger such benefit or payment, as the case may be, would be payable without its application; or

(B) a benefit (other than a benefit payable in a lump sum unless it is a commutation of, or a substitute for, periodic payments) which is based, in whole or in part, upon the active military or naval service of such veteran during World War II is determined by any agency or wholly owned instrumentality of the United States (other than the Department of Veterans Affairs) to be payable by it under any other law of the United States or under a system established by such agency or instrumentality.

The provisions of clause (B) shall not apply in the case of any monthly benefit or lump-sum death payment under this title if its application would reduce by $0.50 or less the primary insurance amount (as computed under section 215 prior to any recomputation thereof pursuant to subsection (f) of such section) of the individual on whose wages and self-employment income such benefit or payment is based. The provisions of clause (B) shall also not apply for purposes of section 216(i)(3).

(2) Upon application for benefits or a lump-sum death payment on the basis of the wages and self-employment income of any World War II veteran, the Commissioner of Social Security shall make a decision without regard to clause (B) of paragraph (1) of this subsection unless the Commissioner has been notified by some other agency or instrumentality of the United States that, on the basis of the military or naval service of such veteran during World War II, a benefit described in clause (B) of paragraph (1) has been determined by such

190 SOCIAL SECURITY ACT—§ 217(a)(2)(cont)

agency or instrumentality to be payable by it. If the Commissioner has not been so notified, the Commissioner of Social Security shall then ascertain whether some other agency or wholly owned instrumentality of the United States has decided that a benefit described in clause (B) of paragraph (1) is payable by it. If any such agency or instrumentality has decided, or thereafter decides, that such a benefit is payable by it, it shall so notify the Commissioner of Social Security, and the Commissioner of Social Security shall certify no further benefits for payment or shall recompute the amount of any further benefits payable, as may be required by paragraph (1) of this subsection.

(3) Any agency or wholly owned instrumentality of the United States which is authorized by any law of the United States to pay benefits, or has a system of benefits which are based, in whole or in part, on military or naval service during World War II shall, at the request of the Commissioner of Social Security, certify to the Commissioner, with respect to any veteran, such information as the Commissioner of Social Security deems necessary to carry out the Commissioner's functions under paragraph (2) of this subsection.

(b)(1) Subject to paragraph (3), any World War II veteran who died during the period of three years immediately following his separation from the active military or naval service of the United States shall be deemed to have died a fully insured individual whose primary insurance amount is the amount determined under section 215(c) as in effect in December 1978. Notwithstanding section 215(d) as in effect in December 1978, the primary insurance benefit (for purposes of section 215(c) as in effect in December 1978) of such veteran shall be determined as provided in this title as in effect prior to the enactment of this section[238], except that the 1 per centum addition provided for in section 209(a)(4)(B) of this Act as in effect prior to the enactment of this section shall be applicable only with respect to calendar years prior to 1951. This subsection shall not be applicable in the case of any monthly benefit or lump-sum death payment if—

(A) a larger such benefit or payment, as the case may be, would be payable without its application;

(B) any pension or compensation is determined by the Secretary of Veterans Affairs to be payable by him on the basis of the death of such veteran;

(C) the death of the veteran occurred while he was in the active military or naval service of the United States; or

(D) such veteran has been discharged or released from the active military or naval service of the United States subsequent to July 26, 1951.

(2) Upon an application for benefits or a lump-sum death payment on the basis of the wages and self-employment income of any World War II veteran, the Commissioner of Social Security shall make a decision without regard to paragraph (1)(B) of this subsection unless the Commissioner has been notified by the Secretary of Veterans Affairs that pension or compensation is determined to be payable by that Commissioner of Social Security by reason of the death of such veteran. The Commissioner of Social Security shall thereupon report such decision to the Secretary of Veterans Affairs. If the Secretary of Veterans Affairs in any such case has made an adjudication or

---

[238] August 28, 1950 [P.L. 81-734; 64 Stat. 477].

SOCIAL SECURITY ACT—§ 217(e)(1) 191

thereafter makes an adjudication that any pension or compensation is payable under any law administered by it, the Secretary of Veterans Affairs shall notify the Commissioner of Social Security, and the Commissioner of Social Security shall certify no further benefits for payment, or shall recompute the amount of any further benefits payable, as may be required by paragraph (1) of this subsection. Any payments theretofore certified by the Commissioner of Social Security on the basis of paragraph (1) of this subsection to any individual, not exceeding the amount of any accrued pension or compensation payable to him by the Secretary of Veterans Affairs, shall (notwithstanding the provisions of section 3101 of title 38, United States Code[239]) be deemed to have been paid to him by that Secretary on account of such accrued pension or compensation. No such payment certified by the Commissioner of Social Security, and no payment certified by the Commissioner for any month prior to the first month for which any pension or compensation is paid by the Secretary of Veterans Affairs shall be deemed by reason of this subsection to have been an erroneous payment.

(3)(A) The preceding provisions of this subsection shall apply for purposes of determining the entitlement to benefits under section 202, based on the primary insurance amount of the deceased World War II veteran, of any surviving individual only if such surviving individual makes application for such benefits before the end of the 18-month period after the month in which the Omnibus Budget Reconciliation Act of 1990 was enacted[240].

(B) Subparagraph (A) shall not apply if any person is entitled to benefits under section 202 based on the primary insurance amount of such veteran for the month preceding the month in which such application is made.

(c) In the case of any World War II veteran to whom subsection (a) is applicable, proof of support required under section 202(h) may be filed by a parent at any time prior to July 1951 or prior to the expiration of two years after the date of the death of such veteran, whichever is the later.

(d) For the purposes of this section—

(1) The term "World War II" means the period beginning with September 16, 1940, and ending at the close of July 24, 1947.

(2) The term "World War II veteran" means any individual who served in the active military or naval service of the United States at any time during World War II and who, if discharged or released therefrom, was so discharged or released under conditions other than dishonorable after active service of ninety days or more or by reason of a disability or injury incurred or aggravated in service in line of duty; but such term shall not include any individual who died while in the active military or naval service of the United States if his death was inflicted (other than by an enemy of the United States) as lawful punishment for a military or naval offense.

(e)(1) For purposes of determining entitlement to and the amount of any monthly benefit or lump-sum death payment payable under this title on the basis of wages and self-employment income of any veteran

---

[239] See Vol. II, Title 38. P.L. 102-40 redesignated §3101 as §5301.
[240] P.L. 101-508 was enacted in November 1990.

192 SOCIAL SECURITY ACT—§ 217(e)(1)(cont)

(as defined in paragraph (4)), and for purposes of section 216(i)(3), such veteran shall be deemed to have been paid wages (in addition to the wages, if any, actually paid to him) of $160 in each month during any part of which he served in the active military or naval service of the United States on or after July 25, 1947, and prior to January 1, 1957. This subsection shall not be applicable in the case of any monthly benefit or lump-sum death payment if—

(A) a larger such benefit or payment, as the case may be, would be payable without its application; or

(B) a benefit (other than a benefit payable in a lump sum unless it is a commutation of, or a substitute for, periodic payments) which is based, in whole or in part, upon the active military or naval service of such veteran on or after July 25, 1947, and prior to January 1, 1957, is determined by any agency or wholly owned instrumentality of the United States (other than the Department of Veterans Affairs) to be payable by it under any other law of the United States or under a system established by such agency or instrumentality.

The provisions of clause (B) shall not apply in the case of any monthly benefit or lump-sum death payment under this title if its application would reduce by $0.50 or less the primary insurance amount (as computed under section 215 prior to any recomputation thereof pursuant to subsection (f) of such section) of the individual on whose wages and self-employment income such benefit or payment is based. The provisions of clause (B) shall also not apply for purposes of section 216(i)(3). In the case of monthly benefits under this title for months after December 1956 (and any lump-sum death payment under this title with respect to a death occurring after December 1956) based on the wages and self-employment income of a veteran who performed service (as a member of a uniformed service) to which the provisions of section 210(l)(1) are applicable, wages which would, but for the provisions of clause (B), be deemed under this subsection to have been paid to such veteran with respect to his active military or naval service performed after December 1950 shall be deemed to have been paid to him with respect to such service notwithstanding the provisions of such clause, but only if the benefits referred to in such clause which are based (in whole or in part) on such service are payable solely by the Army, Navy, Air Force, Marine Corps, Coast Guard, Coast and Geodetic Survey, National Oceanic and Atmospheric Administration Corps, or Public Health Service.

(2) Upon application for benefits or a lump-sum death payment on the basis of the wages and self-employment income of any veteran, the Commissioner of Social Security shall make a decision without regard to clause (B) of paragraph (1) of this subsection unless the Commissioner has been notified by some other agency or instrumentality of the United States that, on the basis of the military or naval service of such veteran on or after July 25, 1947, and prior to January 1, 1957, a benefit described in clause (B) of paragraph (1) has been determined by such agency or instrumentality to be payable by it. If the Commissioner has not been so notified, the Commissioner of Social Security shall then ascertain whether some other agency or wholly owned instrumentality of the United States has decided that a benefit described in clause (B) of paragraph (1) is payable by it. If any such agency or instrumentality has decided, or thereafter decides,

that such a benefit is payable by it, it shall so notify the Commissioner of Social Security, and the Commissioner of Social Security shall certify no further benefits for payment or shall recompute the amount of any further benefits payable, as may be required by paragraph (1) of this subsection.

(3) Any agency or wholly owned instrumentality of the United States which is authorized by any law of the United States to pay benefits, or has a system of benefits which are based, in whole or in part, on military or naval service on or after July 25, 1947, and prior to January 1, 1957, shall, at the request of the Commissioner of Social Security, certify to the Commissioner, with respect to any veteran, such information as the Commissioner of Social Security deems necessary to carry out the Commissioner's functions under paragraph (2) of this subsection.

(4) For the purposes of this subsection, the term "veteran" means any individual who served in the active military or naval service of the United States at any time on or after July 25, 1947, and prior to January 1, 1957, and who, if discharged or released therefrom, was so discharged or released under conditions other than dishonorable after active service of ninety days or more or by reason of a disability or injury incurred or aggravated in service in line of duty; but such term shall not include any individual who died while in the active military or naval service of the United States if his death was inflicted (other than by an enemy of the United States) as lawful punishment for a military or naval offense.

(f)(1) In any case where a World War II veteran (as defined in subsection (d)(2)) or a veteran (as defined in subsection (e)(4)) has died or shall hereafter die, and his or her surviving spouse or child is entitled under subchapter III of chapter 83 of title 5, United States Code, to an annuity in the computation of which his or her active military or naval service was included, clause (B) of subsection (a)(1) or clause (B) of subsection (e)(1) shall not operate (solely by reason of such annuity) to make such subsection inapplicable in the case of any monthly benefit under section 202 which is based on his or her wages and self-employment income; except that no such surviving spouse or child shall be entitled under section 202 to any monthly benefit in the computation of which such service is included by reason of this subsection (A) unless such surviving spouse or child after December 1956 waives his or her right to receive such annuity, or (B) for any month prior to the first month with respect to which the Director of the Office of Personnel Management certifies to the Commissioner of Social Security that (by reason of such waiver) no further annuity will be paid to such surviving spouse or child under such subchapter III on the basis of such veteran's military or civilian service. Any such waiver shall be irrevocable.

(2) Whenever a surviving spouse waives his or her right to receive such annuity such waiver shall constitute a waiver on his or her own behalf; a waiver by a legal guardian or guardians, or, in the absence of a legal guardian, the person (or persons) who has the child in his or her care, of the child's right to receive such annuity shall constitute a waiver on behalf of such child. Such a waiver with respect to an annuity based on a veteran's service shall be valid only if the surviving spouse and all children, or, if there is no surviving spouse, all the children, waive their rights to receive annuities under subchapter III

194   SOCIAL SECURITY ACT—§ 217(f)(2)(cont)

of chapter 83 of title 5, United States Code, based on such veteran's military or civilian service.

Appropriation to Trust Funds

(g)(1) Within thirty days after the date of the enactment of the Social Security Amendments of 1983[241], the Commissioner of Social Security shall determine the amount equal to the excess of—

(A) the actuarial present value as of such date of enactment of the past and future benefit payments from the Federal Old-Age and Survivors Insurance Trust Fund, the Federal Disability Insurance Trust Fund, and the Federal Hospital Insurance Trust Fund under this title and title XVIII, together with associated administrative costs, resulting from the operation of this section (other than this subsection) and section 210 of this Act as in effect before the enactment of the Social Security Amendments of 1950[242], over

(B) any amounts previously transferred from the general fund of the Treasury to such Trust Funds pursuant to the provisions of this subsection as in effect immediately before the date of the enactment of the Social Security Amendments of 1983[243].

Such actuarial present value shall be based on the relevant actuarial assumptions set forth in the report of the Board of Trustees of each such Trust Fund for 1983 under sections 201(c) and 1817(b). Within thirty days after the date of the enactment of the Social Security Amendments of 1983, the Secretary of the Treasury shall transfer the amount determined under this paragraph with respect to each such Trust Fund to such Trust Fund from amounts in the general fund of the Treasury not otherwise appropriated.

(2) The Commissioner of Social Security shall revise the amount determined under paragraph (1) with respect to each such Trust Fund in 1985 and each fifth year thereafter, as determined appropriate by the Commissioner of Social Security from data which becomes available to the Commissioner after the date of the determination under paragraph (1) on the basis of the amount of benefits and administrative expenses actually paid from such Trust Fund under this title or title XVIII and the relevant actuarial assumptions set forth in the report of the Board of Trustees of such Trust Fund for such year under section 201(c) or 1817(b). Within 30 days after any such revision, the Secretary of the Treasury, to the extent provided in advance in appropriation Acts, shall transfer to such Trust Fund, from amounts in the general fund of the Treasury not otherwise appropriated, or from such Trust Fund to the general fund of the Treasury, such amounts as the Secretary of the Treasury determines necessary to take into account such revision.

(h)(1) For the purposes of this section, any individual who the Commissioner of Social Security finds—

(A) served during World War II (as defined in subsection (d)(1)) in the active military or naval service of a country which was on

---

[241] April 20, 1983 [P.L. 98-21; 97 Stat. 65].
[242] August 28, 1950 [P.L. 81-734; 64 Stat. 477].
[243] April 20, 1983 [P.L. 98-21; 97 Stat. 65].

SOCIAL SECURITY ACT—§ 218(b)(2)

September 16, 1940, at war with a country with which the United States was at war during World War II;

(B) entered into such active service on or before December 8, 1941;

(C) was a citizen of the United States throughout such period of service or lost his United States citizenship solely because of his entrance into such service;

(D) had resided in the United States for a period or periods aggregating four years during the five-year period ending on the day of, and was domiciled in the United States on the day of, such entrance into such active service; and

(E)(i) was discharged or released from such service under conditions other than dishonorable after active service of ninety days or more or by reason of a disability or injury incurred or aggravated in service in line of duty, or

(ii) died while in such service,

shall be considered a World War II veteran (as defined in subsection (d)(2)) and such service shall be considered to have been performed in the active military or naval service of the United States.

(2) In the case of any individual to whom paragraph (1) applies, proof of support required under section 202(f) or (h) may be filed at any time prior to the expiration of two years after the date of such individual's death or the date of the enactment of this subsection[244], whichever is the later.

VOLUNTARY AGREEMENTS FOR COVERAGE OF STATE AND LOCAL EMPLOYEES[245]

Purpose of Agreement

SEC. 218. [42 U.S.C. 418] (a)(1) The Commissioner of Social Security shall, at the request of any State, enter into an agreement with such State for the purpose of extending the insurance system established by this title to services performed by individuals as employees of such State or any political subdivision thereof. Each such agreement shall contain such provisions, not inconsistent with the provisions of this section, as the State may request.

(2) Notwithstanding section 210(a), for the purposes of this title the term "employment" includes any service included under an agreement entered into under this section.

Definitions

(b) For the purposes of this section—

(1) The term "State" does not include the District of Columbia, Guam, or American Samoa.

(2) The term "political subdivision" includes an instrumentality of (A) a State, (B) one or more political subdivisions of a State, or (C) a State and one or more of its political subdivisions.

---

[244] August 28, 1958 [P.L. 85-840; 72 Stat. 1013].

[245] See Vol. II, P.L. 99-272, §12114, with respect to coverage of Connecticut State Police.

See Vol. II, P.L. 100-203, §9008, with respect to modification of the agreement with Iowa to provide coverage for certain policemen and firemen.

196 SOCIAL SECURITY ACT—§ 218(b)(3)

(3) The term "employee" includes an officer of a State or political subdivision.

(4) The term "retirement system" means a pension, annuity, retirement, or similar fund or system established by a State or by a political subdivision thereof.

(5) The term "coverage group" means (A) employees of the State other than those engaged in performing service in connection with a proprietary function; (B) employees of a political subdivision of a State other than those engaged in performing service in connection with a proprietary function; (C) employees of a State engaged in performing service in connection with a single proprietary function; or (D) employees of a political subdivision of a State engaged in performing service in connection with a single proprietary function. If under the preceding sentence an employee would be included in more than one coverage group by reason of the fact that he performs service in connection with two or more proprietary functions or in connection with both a proprietary function and a nonproprietary function, he shall be included in only one such coverage group. The determination of the coverage group in which such employee shall be included shall be made in such manner as may be specified in the agreement. Persons employed under section 709 of title 32, United States Code[246], who elected under section 6 of the National Guard Technicians Act of 1968[247] to remain covered by an employee retirement system of, or plan sponsored by, a State or the Commonwealth of Puerto Rico, shall, for the purposes of this Act, be employees of the State or the Commonwealth of Puerto Rico and (notwithstanding the preceding provisions of this paragraph), shall be deemed to be a separate coverage group. For purposes of this section, individuals employed pursuant to an agreement, entered into pursuant to section 205 of the Agricultural Marketing Act of 1946[248] (7 U.S.C. 1624) or section 14 of the Perishable Agricultural Commodities Act, 1930[249] (7 U.S.C. 499n), between a State and the United States Department of Agriculture to perform services as inspectors of agricultural products may be deemed, at the option of the State, to be employees of the State and (notwithstanding the preceding provisions of this paragraph) shall be deemed to be a separate coverage group.

Services Covered

(c)(1) An agreement under this section shall be applicable to any one or more coverage groups designated by the State.

(2) In the case of each coverage group to which the agreement applies, the agreement must include all services (other than services excluded by or pursuant to subsection (d) or paragraph (3), (5), or (6) of this subsection) performed by individuals as members of such group.

(3) Such agreement shall, if the State requests it, exclude (in the case of any coverage group) any one or more of the following:

---

[246] See Vol. II, 32 U.S.C. 709.
[247] See Vol. II, P.L. 90-486, §6.
[248] See Vol. II, P.L. 79-733, §205.
[249] See Vol. II, P.L. 71-325, §14.

SOCIAL SECURITY ACT—§ 218(c)(7)   197

(A) All services in any class or classes of (i) elective positions, (ii) part-time positions, or (iii) positions the compensation for which is on a fee basis;

(B) All services performed by individuals as members of a coverage group in positions covered by a retirement system on the date such agreement is made applicable to such coverage group, but only in the case of individuals who, on such date (or, if later, the date on which they first occupy such positions), are not eligible to become members of such system and whose services in such positions have not already been included under such agreement pursuant to subsection (d)(3).

(4) The Commissioner of Social Security shall, at the request of any State, modify the agreement with such State so as to (A) include any coverage group to which the agreement did not previously apply, or (B) include, in the case of any coverage group to which the agreement applies, services previously excluded from the agreement; but the agreement as so modified may not be inconsistent with the provisions of this section applicable in the case of an original agreement with a State. A modification of an agreement pursuant to clause (B) of the preceding sentence may apply to individuals to whom paragraph (3)(B) is applicable (whether or not the previous exclusion of the service of such individuals was pursuant to such paragraph), but only if such individuals are, on the effective date specified in such modification, ineligible to be members of any retirement system or if the modification with respect to such individuals is pursuant to subsection (d)(3).

(5) Such agreement shall, if the State requests it, exclude (in the case of any coverage group) any agricultural labor, or service performed by a student, designated by the State. This paragraph shall apply only with respect to service which is excluded from employment by any provision of section 210(a) other than paragraph (7) of such section and service the remuneration for which is excluded from wages by subparagraph (B) of section 209(a)(7).

(6) Such agreement shall exclude—

(A) service performed by an individual who is employed to relieve him from unemployment,

(B) service performed in a hospital, home, or other institution by a patient or inmate thereof,

(C) covered transportation service (as determined under section 210(k)),

(D) service (other than agricultural labor or service performed by a student) which is excluded from employment by any provision of section 210(a) other than paragraph (7) of such section,

(E) service performed by an individual as an employee serving on a temporary basis in case of fire, storm, snow, earthquake, flood, or other similar emergency, and

(F) service described in section 210(a)(7)(F) which is included as "employment" under section 210(a).

(7) No agreement may be made applicable (either in the original agreement or by any modification thereof) to service performed by any individual to whom paragraph (3)(B) is applicable unless such agreement provides (in the case of each coverage group involved) either that the service of any individual to whom such paragraph is applicable and who is a member of such coverage group shall continue to be cov-

198   SOCIAL SECURITY ACT—§ 218(c)(7)(cont)

ered by such agreement in case he thereafter becomes eligible to be a member of a retirement system, or that such service shall cease to be so covered when he becomes eligible to be a member of such a system (but only if the agreement is not already applicable to such system pursuant to subsection (d)(3)), whichever may be desired by the State.

(8)(A) Notwithstanding any other provision of this section, the agreement with any State entered into under this section may at the option of the State be modified at any time to exclude service performed by election officials or election workers if the remuneration paid in a calendar year for such service is less than $1,000 with respect to service performed during any calendar year commencing on or after January 1, 1995, ending on or before December 31, 1999, and the adjusted amount determined under subparagraph (B) for any calendar year commencing on or after January 1, 2000, with respect to service performed during such calendar year. Any modification of an agreement pursuant to this paragraph shall be effective with respect to services performed in and after the calendar year in which the modification is mailed or delivered by other means to the Commissioner of Social Security.

(B) For each year after 1999, the Commissioner of Social Security shall adjust the amount referred to in subparagraph (A) at the same time and in the same manner as is provided under section 215(a)(1)(B)(ii) with respect to the amounts referred to in section 215(a)(1)(B)(i), except that—

(i) for purposes of this subparagraph, 1997 shall be substituted for the calendar year referred to in section 215(a)(1)(B)(ii)(II), and

(ii) such amount as so adjusted, if not a multiple of $100, shall be rounded to the next higher multiple of $100 where such amount is a multiple of $50 and to the nearest multiple of $100 in any other case.

The Commissioner of Social Security shall determine and publish in the Federal Register each adjusted amount determined under this subparagraph not later than November 1 preceding the year for which the adjustment is made.

Positions Covered By Retirement Systems

(d)(1) No agreement with any State may be made applicable (either in the original agreement or by any modification thereof) to any service performed by employees as members of any coverage group in positions covered by a retirement system either (A) on the date such agreement is made applicable to such coverage group, or (B) on the date of enactment of the succeeding paragraph of this subsection[250] (except in the case of positions which are, by reason of action by such State or political subdivision thereof, as may be appropriate, taken prior to the date of enactment of such succeeding paragraph, no longer covered by a retirement system on the date referred to in clause (A), and except in the case of positions excluded by paragraph (5)(A)). The preceding sentence shall not be applicable to any service performed by an employee as a member of any coverage group in a position (other than a position excluded by paragraph (5)(A)) covered by a retirement

---

[250] September 1, 1954 [P.L. 83-761; 68 Stat. 1056].

system on the date an agreement is made applicable to such coverage group if, on such date (or, if later, the date on which such individual first occupies such position), such individual is ineligible to be a member of such system.

(2) It is hereby declared to be the policy of the Congress in enacting the succeeding paragraphs of this subsection that the protection afforded employees in positions covered by a retirement system on the date an agreement under this section is made applicable to service performed in such positions, or receiving periodic benefits under such retirement system at such time, will not be impaired as a result of making the agreement so applicable or as a result of legislative enactment in anticipation thereof.

(3) Notwithstanding paragraph (1), an agreement with a State may be made applicable (either in the original agreement or by any modification thereof) to service performed by employees in positions covered by a retirement system (including positions specified in paragraph (4) but not including positions excluded by or pursuant to paragraph (5)), if the governor of the State, or an official of the State designated by him for the purpose, certifies to the Commissioner of Social Security that the following conditions have been met:

(A) A referendum by secret written ballot was held on the question of whether service in positions covered by such retirement system should be excluded from or included under an agreement under this section;

(B) An opportunity to vote in such referendum was given (and was limited) to eligible employees;

(C) Not less than ninety days' notice of such referendum was given to all such employees;

(D) Such referendum was conducted under the supervision of the governor or an agency or individual designated by him; and

(E) A majority of the eligible employees voted in favor of including service in such positions under an agreement under this section.

An employee shall be deemed an "eligible employee" for purposes of any referendum with respect to any retirement system if, at the time such referendum was held, he was in a position covered by such retirement system and was a member of such system, and if he was in such a position at the time notice of such referendum was given as required by clause (C) of the preceding sentence; except that he shall not be deemed an "eligible employee" if, at the time the referendum was held, he was in a position to which the State agreement already applied, or if he was in a position excluded by or pursuant to paragraph (5). No referendum with respect to a retirement system shall be valid for purposes of this paragraph unless held within the two-year period which ends on the date of execution of the agreement or modification which extends the insurance system established by this title to such retirement system, nor shall any referendum with respect to a retirement system be valid for purposes of this paragraph if held less than one year after the last previous referendum held with respect to such retirement system.

(4) For the purposes of subsection (c) of this section, the following employees shall be deemed to be a separate coverage group—

(A) all employees in positions which were covered by the same retirement system on the date the agreement was made applica-

200 SOCIAL SECURITY ACT—§ 218(d)(4)(A)(cont)

ble to such system (other than employees to whose services the agreement already applied on such date);

(B) all employees in positions which became covered by such system at any time after such date; and

(C) all employees in positions which were covered by such system at any time before such date and to whose services the insurance system established by this title has not been extended before such date because the positions were covered by such retirement system (including employees to whose services the agreement was not applicable on such date because such services were excluded pursuant to subsection (c)(3)(B)).

(5)(A) Nothing in paragraph (3) of this subsection shall authorize the extension of the insurance system established by this title to service in any policeman's or fireman's position.

(B) At the request of the State, any class or classes of positions covered by a retirement system which may be excluded from the agreement pursuant to paragraph (3) or (5) of subsection (c), and to which the agreement does not already apply, may be excluded from the agreement at the time it is made applicable to such retirement system; except that, notwithstanding the provisions of paragraph (3)(B) of such subsection, such exclusion may not include any services to which such paragraph (3)(B) is applicable. In the case of any such exclusion, each such class so excluded shall, for purposes of this subsection, constitute a separate retirement system in case of any modification of the agreement thereafter agreed to.

(6)(A) If a retirement system covers positions of employees of the State and positions of employees of one or more political subdivisions of the State, or covers positions of employees of two or more political subdivisions of the State, then, for purposes of the preceding paragraphs of this subsection, there shall, if the State so desires, be deemed to be a separate retirement system with respect to any one or more of the political subdivisions concerned and, where the retirement system covers positions of employees of the State, a separate retirement system with respect to the State or with respect to the State and any one or more of the political subdivisions concerned. Where a retirement system covering positions of employees of a State and positions of employees of one or more political subdivisions of the State, or covering positions of employees of two or more political subdivisions of the State, is not divided into separate retirement systems pursuant to the preceding sentence or pursuant to subparagraph (C), then the State may, for purposes of subsection (e) only, deem the system to be a separate retirement system with respect to any one or more of the political subdivisions concerned and, where the retirement system covers positions of employees of the State, a separate retirement system with respect to the State or with respect to the State and any one or more of the political subdivisions concerned.

(B) If a retirement system covers positions of employees of one or more institutions of higher learning, then, for purposes of such preceding paragraphs there shall, if the State so desires, be deemed to be a separate retirement system for the employees of each such institution of higher learning. For the purposes of this subparagraph, the term "institutions of higher learning" includes junior colleges and teachers colleges. If a retirement system covers positions of employees of a hospital which is an integral part of a political subdivision, then,

SOCIAL SECURITY ACT—§ 218(d)(6)(D)(ii)   201

for purposes of the preceding paragraphs there shall, if the State so desires, be deemed to be a separate retirement system for the employees of such hospital.

(C) For the purposes of this subsection, any retirement system established by the State of Alaska, California, Connecticut, Florida, Georgia, Illinois, Kentucky, Louisiana, Massachusetts, Minnesota, Nevada, New Jersey, New Mexico, New York, North Dakota, Pennsylvania, Rhode Island, Tennessee, Texas, Vermont, Washington, Wisconsin, or Hawaii, or any political subdivision of any such State, which, on, before, or after the date of enactment of this subparagraph[251], is divided into two divisions or parts, one of which is composed of positions of members of such system who desire coverage under an agreement under this section and the other of which is composed of positions of members of such system who do not desire such coverage, shall, if the State so desires and if it is provided that there shall be included in such division or part composed of members desiring such coverage the positions of individuals who become members of such system after such coverage is extended, be deemed to be a separate retirement system with respect to each such division or part. If, in the case of a separate retirement system which is deemed to exist by reason of subparagraph (A) and which has been divided into two divisions or parts pursuant to the first sentence of this subparagraph, individuals become members of such system by reason of action taken by a political subdivision after coverage under an agreement under this section has been extended to the division or part thereof composed of positions of individuals who desire such coverage, the positions of such individuals who become members of such retirement system by reason of the action so taken shall be included in the division or part of such system composed of positions of members who do not desire such coverage if (i) such individuals, on the day before becoming such members, were in the division or part of another separate retirement system (deemed to exist by reason of subparagraph (A)) composed of positions of members of such system who do not desire coverage under an agreement under this section, and (ii) all of the positions in the separate retirement system of which such individuals so become members and all of the positions in the separate retirement system referred to in clause (i) would have been covered by a single retirement system if the State had not taken action to provide for separate retirement systems under this paragraph.

(D)(i) The position of any individual which is covered by any retirement system to which subparagraph (C) is applicable shall, if such individual is ineligible to become a member of such system on August 1, 1956, or, if later, the day he first occupies such position, be deemed to be covered by the separate retirement system consisting of the positions of members of the division or part who do not desire coverage under the insurance system established under this title.

(ii) Notwithstanding clause (i), the State may, pursuant to subsection (c)(4)(B) and subject to the conditions of continuation or termination of coverage provided for in subsection (c)(7), modify its agreement under this section to include services performed by all individuals de-

---

[251] P.L. 84-880, §104(e), enacted this sentence August 1, 1956.
P.L. 85-840, §315(a)(1), enacted this subparagraph August 28, 1958.

scribed in clause (i) other than those individuals to whose services the agreement already applies. Such individuals shall be deemed (on and after the effective date of the modification) to be in positions covered by the separate retirement system consisting of the positions of members of the division or part who desire coverage under the insurance system established under this title.

(E) An individual who is in a position covered by a retirement system to which subparagraph (C) is applicable and who is not a member of such system but is eligible to become a member thereof shall, for purposes of this subsection (other than paragraph (8)), be regarded as a member of such system; except that, in the case of any retirement system a division or part of which is covered under the agreement (either in the original agreement or by a modification thereof), which coverage is agreed to prior to 1960, the preceding provisions of this subparagraph shall apply only if the State so requests and any such individual referred to in such preceding provisions shall, if the State so requests, be treated, after division of the retirement system pursuant to such subparagraph (C), the same as individuals in positions referred to in subparagraph (F).

(F) In the case of any retirement system divided pursuant to subparagraph (C), the position of any member of the division or part composed of positions of members who do not desire coverage may be transferred to the separate retirement system composed of positions of members who desire such coverage if it is so provided in a modification of such agreement which is mailed, or delivered by other means, to the Commissioner of Social Security prior to 1970 or, if later, the expiration of two years after the date on which such agreement, or the modification thereof making the agreement applicable to such separate retirement system, as the case may be, is agreed to, but only if, prior to such modification or such later modification, as the case may be, the individual occupying such position files with the State a written request for such transfer. Notwithstanding subsection (e)(1), any such modification or later modification, providing for the transfer of additional positions within a retirement system previously divided pursuant to subparagraph (C) to the separate retirement system composed of positions of members who desire coverage, shall be effective with respect to services performed after the same effective date as that which was specified in the case of such previous division.

(G) For the purposes of this subsection, in the case of any retirement system of the State of Florida, Georgia, Minnesota, North Dakota, Pennsylvania, Washington, or Hawaii which covers positions of employees of such State who are compensated in whole or in part from grants made to such State under title III, there shall be deemed to be, if such State so desires, a separate retirement system with respect to any of the following:

(i) the positions of such employees;

(ii) the positions of all employees of such State covered by such retirement system who are employed in the department of such State in which the employees referred to in clause (i) are employed; or

(iii) employees of such State covered by such retirement system who are employed in such department of such State in positions other than those referred to in clause (i).

(7) The certification by the governor (or an official of the State designated by him for the purpose) required under paragraph (3) shall be deemed to have been made, in the case of a division or part (created under subparagraph (C) of paragraph (6) or the corresponding provision of prior law) consisting of the positions of members of a retirement system who desire coverage under the agreement under this section, if the governor (or the official so designated) certifies to the Commissioner of Social Security that—

(A) an opportunity to vote by written ballot on the question of whether they wish to be covered under an agreement under this section was given to all individuals who were members of such system at the time the vote was held;

(B) not less than ninety days' notice of such vote was given to all individuals who were members of such system on the date the notice was issued;

(C) the vote was conducted under the supervision of the governor or an agency or individual designated by him; and

(D) such system was divided into two parts or divisions in accordance with the provisions of subparagraphs (C) and (D) of paragraph (6) or the corresponding provision of prior law.

For purposes of this paragraph, an individual in a position to which the State agreement already applied or in a position excluded by or pursuant to paragraph (5) shall not be considered a member of the retirement system.

(8)(A) Notwithstanding paragraph (1), if under the provisions of this subsection an agreement is, after December 31, 1958, made applicable to service performed in positions covered by a retirement system, service performed by an individual in a position covered by such a system may not be excluded from the agreement because such position is also covered under another retirement system.

(B) Subparagraph (A) shall not apply to service performed by an individual in a position covered under a retirement system if such individual, on the day the agreement is made applicable to service performed in positions covered by such retirement system, is not a member of such system and is a member of another system.

(C) If an agreement is made applicable, prior to 1959, to service in positions covered by any retirement system, the preceding provisions of this paragraph shall be applicable in the case of such system if the agreement is modified to so provide.

(D) Except in the case of State agreements modified as provided in subsection (l) and agreements with interstate instrumentalities, nothing in this paragraph shall authorize the application of an agreement to service in any policeman's or fireman's position.

Effective Date of Agreement

(e)(1) Any agreement or modification of an agreement under this section shall be effective with respect to services performed after an effective date specified in such agreement or modification; except that such date may not be earlier than the last day of the sixth calendar year preceding the year in which such agreement or modification, as the case may be, is mailed or delivered by other means to the Commissioner of Social Security.

(2) In the case of service performed by members of any coverage group—

> (A) to which an agreement under this section is made applicable, and

> (B) with respect to which the agreement, or modification thereof making the agreement so applicable, specifies an effective date earlier than the date of execution of such agreement and such modification, respectively,

the agreement shall, if so requested by the State, be applicable to such services (to the extent the agreement was not already applicable) performed before such date of execution and after such effective date by any individual as a member of such coverage group if he is such a member on a date, specified by the State, which is earlier than such date of execution, except that in no case may the date so specified be earlier than the date such agreement or such modification, as the case may be, is mailed, or delivered by other means, to the Commissioner of Social Security.

(3) Notwithstanding the provisions of paragraph (2) of this subsection, in the case of services performed by individuals as members of any coverage group to which an agreement under this section is made applicable, and with respect to which there were timely paid in good faith to the Secretary of the Treasury amounts equivalent to the sum of the taxes which would have been imposed by sections 3101 and 3111 of the Internal Revenue Code of 1986[252] had such services constituted employment for purposes of chapter 21 of such Code[253] at the time they were performed, and with respect to which refunds were not obtained, such individuals may, if so requested by the State, be deemed to be members of such coverage group on the date designated pursuant to paragraph (2).

Duration of Agreement

(f) No agreement under this section may be terminated, either in its entirety or with respect to any coverage group, on or after the date of the enactment of the Social Security Amendments of 1983[254].

Instrumentalities of Two or More States

(g)(1) The Commissioner of Social Security may, at the request of any instrumentality of two or more States, enter into an agreement with such instrumentality for the purpose of extending the insurance system established by this title to services performed by individuals as employees of such instrumentality. Such agreement, to the extent practicable, shall be governed by the provisions of this section applicable in the case of an agreement with a State.

(2) In the case of any instrumentality of two or more States, if—

> (A) employees of such instrumentality are in positions covered by a retirement system of such instrumentality or of any of such States or any of the political subdivisions thereof, and

---

[252] See Vol. II, P.L. 83-591, §§3101 and 3111.
[253] See Vol. II, P.L. 83-591, Chapter 21.
[254] April 20, 1983 [P.L. 98-21; 97 Stat. 65].

SOCIAL SECURITY ACT—§ 218(g)(3) 205

(B) such retirement system is (on, before, or after the date of enactment of this paragraph[255]) divided into two divisions or parts, one of which is composed of positions of members of such system who are employees of such instrumentality and who desire coverage under an agreement under this section and the other of which is composed of positions of members of such system who are employees of such instrumentality and who do not desire such coverage, and

(C) it is provided that there shall be included in such division or part composed of the positions of members desiring such coverage the positions of employees of such instrumentality who become members of such system after such coverage is extended,

then such retirement system shall, if such instrumentality so desires, be deemed to be a separate retirement system with respect to each such division or part. An individual who is in a position covered by a retirement system divided pursuant to the preceding sentence and who is not a member of such system but is eligible to become a member thereof shall, for purposes of this subsection, be regarded as a member of such system. Coverage under the agreement of any such individual shall be provided under the same conditions, to the extent practicable, as are applicable in the case of the States to which the provisions of subsection (d)(6)(C) apply. The position of any employee of any such instrumentality which is covered by any retirement system to which the first sentence of this paragraph is applicable shall, if such individual is ineligible to become a member of such system on the date of enactment of this paragraph[256] or, if later, the day he first occupies such position, be deemed to be covered by the separate retirement system consisting of the positions of members of the division or part who do not desire coverage under the insurance system established under this title. Services in positions covered by a separate retirement system created pursuant to this subsection (and consisting of the positions of members who desire coverage under an agreement under this section) shall be covered under such agreement on compliance, to the extent practicable, with the same conditions as are applicable to coverage under an agreement under this section of services in positions covered by a separate retirement system created pursuant to subparagraph (C) of subsection (d)(6) or the corresponding provision of prior law (and consisting of the positions of members who desire coverage under such agreement).

(3) Any agreement with any instrumentality of two or more States entered into pursuant to this Act may, notwithstanding the provisions of subsection (d)(5)(A) and the references thereto in subsections (d)(1) and (d)(3), apply to service performed by employees of such instrumentality in any policeman's or fireman's position covered by a retirement system, but only upon compliance, to the extent practicable, with the requirements of subsection (d)(3). For the purpose of the preceding sentence, a retirement system which covers positions of policemen or firemen or both, and other positions shall, if the instrumentality concerned so desires, be deemed to be a separate retirement system with respect to the positions of such policemen or firemen, or both, as the case may be.

---

[255] August 30, 1957 [P.L. 85-226; 71 Stat. 511].
[256] August 30, 1957 [P.L. 85-226; 71 Stat. 511].

Delegation of Functions

(h) The Commissioner of Social Security is authorized, pursuant to agreement with the head of any Federal agency, to delegate any of the Commissioner's functions under this section to any officer or employee of such agency and otherwise to utilize the services and facilities of such agency in carrying out such functions, and payment therefor shall be in advance or by way of reimbursement, as may be provided in such agreement.

Wisconsin Retirement Fund

(i)(1) Notwithstanding paragraph (1) of subsection (d), the agreement with the State of Wisconsin may, subject to the provisions of this subsection, be modified so as to apply to service performed by employees in positions covered by the Wisconsin retirement fund or any successor system.

(2) All employees in positions covered by the Wisconsin retirement fund at any time on or after January 1, 1951, shall, for the purposes of subsection (c) only, be deemed to be a separate coverage group; except that there shall be excluded from such separate coverage group all employees in positions to which the agreement applies without regard to this subsection.

(3) The modification pursuant to this subsection shall exclude (in the case of employees in the coverage group established by paragraph (2) of this subsection) service performed by any individual during any period before he is included under the Wisconsin retirement fund.

(4) The modification pursuant to this subsection shall, if the State of Wisconsin requests it, exclude (in the case of employees in the coverage group established by paragraph (2) of this subsection) all service performed in policemen's positions, all service performed in firemen's positions, or both.

Certain Positions No Longer Covered By Retirement Systems

(j) Notwithstanding subsection (d), an agreement with any State entered into under this section prior to the date of the enactment of this subsection[257] may, prior to January 1, 1958, be modified pursuant to subsection (c)(4) so as to apply to services performed by employees, as members of any coverage group to which such agreement already applies (and to which such agreement applied on such date of enactment), in positions (1) to which such agreement does not already apply, (2) which were covered by a retirement system on the date such agreement was made applicable to such coverage group, and (3) which, by reason of action by such State or political subdivision thereof, as may be appropriate, taken prior to the date of the enactment of this subsection, are no longer covered by a retirement system on the date such agreement is made applicable to such services.

---

[257] September 1, 1954 [P.L. 83-761; 68 Stat. 1058].

Certain Employees of the State of Utah

(k) Notwithstanding the provisions of subsection (d), the agreement with the State of Utah entered into pursuant to this section may be modified pursuant to subsection (c)(4) so as to apply to services performed for any of the following, the employees performing services for each of which shall constitute a separate coverage group: Weber Junior College, Carbon Junior College, Dixie Junior College, Central Utah Vocational School, Salt Lake Area Vocational School, Center for the Adult Blind, Union High School (Roosevelt, Utah), Utah High School Activities Association, State Industrial School, State Training School, State Board of Education, and Utah School Employees Retirement Board. Any modification agreed to prior to January 1, 1955, may be made effective with respect to services performed by employees as members of any of such coverage groups after an effective date specified therein, except that in no case may any such date be earlier than December 31, 1950. Coverage provided for in this subsection shall not be affected by a subsequent change in the name of a group.

Policemen and Firemen in Certain States

(l) Any agreement with a State entered into pursuant to this section may, notwithstanding the provisions of subsection (d)(5)(A) and the references thereto in subsections (d)(1) and (d)(3), be modified pursuant to subsection (c)(4) to apply to service performed by employees of such State or any political subdivision thereof in any policeman's or fireman's position covered by a retirement system in effect on or after the date of the enactment of this subsection, but only upon compliance with the requirements of subsection (d)(3). For the purposes of the preceding sentence, a retirement system which covers positions of policemen or firemen, or both, and other positions shall, if the State concerned so desires, be deemed to be a separate retirement system with respect to the positions of such policemen or firemen, or both, as the case may be.

Positions Compensated Solely on a Fee Basis

(m)(1) Notwithstanding any other provision in this section, an agreement entered into under this section may be made applicable to service performed after 1967 in any class or classes of positions compensated solely on a fee basis to which such agreement did not apply prior to 1968 only if the State specifically requests that its agreement be made applicable to such service in such class or classes of positions.

(2) Notwithstanding any other provision in this section, an agreement entered into under this section may be modified, at the option of the State, at any time after 1967, so as to exclude services performed in any class or classes of positions compensation for which is solely on a fee basis.

(3) Any modification made under this subsection shall be effective with respect to services performed after the last day of the calendar year in which the modification is mailed or delivered by other means to the Commissioner of Social Security.

208   SOCIAL SECURITY ACT—§ 218(m)(4)

(4) If any class or classes of positions have been excluded from coverage under the State agreement by a modification agreed to under this subsection, the Commissioner of Social Security and the State may not thereafter modify such agreement so as to again make the agreement applicable with respect to such class or classes of positions.

(n)(1) The Commissioner of Social Security shall, at the request of any State, enter into or modify an agreement with such State under this section for the purpose of extending the provisions of title XVIII, and sections 226 and 226A, to services performed by employees of such State or any political subdivision thereof who are described in paragraph (2).

(2) This subsection shall apply only with respect to employees—

(A) whose services are not treated as employment as that term applies under section 210(p) by reason of paragraph (3) of such section; and

(B) who are not otherwise covered under the State's agreement under this section.

(3) For purposes of sections 226 and 226A of this Act, services covered under an agreement pursuant to this subsection shall be treated as "medicare qualified government employment".

(4) Except as otherwise provided in this subsection, the provisions of this section shall apply with respect to services covered under the agreement pursuant to this subsection.

SEC. 219.   [Repealed.[258]]

DISABILITY PROVISIONS INAPPLICABLE IF BENEFIT RIGHTS IMPAIRED

SEC. 220. [42 U.S.C. 420] None of the provisions of this title relating to periods of disability shall apply in any case in which their application would result in the denial of monthly benefits or a lump-sum death payment which would otherwise be payable under this title; nor shall they apply in the case of any monthly benefit or lump-sum death payment under this title if such benefit or payment would be greater without their application.

DISABILITY DETERMINATIONS[259]

SEC. 221. [42 U.S.C. 421] (a)(1) In the case of any individual, the determination of whether or not he is under a disability (as defined in section 216(i) or 223(d)) and of the day such disability began, and the determination of the day on which such disability ceases, shall be made by a State agency, notwithstanding any other provision of law, in any State that notifies the Commissioner of Social Security in writing that it wishes to make such disability determinations commencing with such month as the Commissioner of Social Security and the State agree upon, but only if (A) the Commissioner of Social Security has not found, under subsection (b)(1), that the State agency has substantially failed to make disability determinations in accordance with the applicable provisions of this section or rules issued thereunder, and (B) the State has not notified the Commissioner of Social Security, under subsection (b)(2), that it does not wish to make such determinations. If the Commissioner of Social Security once makes

---

[258] P.L. 86-778, §103(j)(1); 74 Stat. 937.

[259] See Vol. II, P.L. 108-203, §413, with respect to the reinstatement of reporting requirements under §221(c)(3)(C) and (i)(3).

the finding described in clause (A) of the preceding sentence, or the State gives the notice referred to in clause (B) of such sentence, the Commissioner of Social Security may thereafter determine whether (and, if so, beginning with which month and under what conditions) the State may again make disability determinations under this paragraph.

(2) The disability determinations described in paragraph (1) made by a State agency shall be made in accordance with the pertinent provisions of this title and the standards and criteria contained in regulations or other written guidelines of the Commissioner of Social Security pertaining to matters such as disability determinations, the class or classes of individuals with respect to which a State may make disability determinations (if it does not wish to do so with respect to all individuals in the State), and the conditions under which it may choose not to make all such determinations. In addition, the Commissioner of Social Security shall promulgate regulations specifying, in such detail as the Commissioner deems appropriate, performance standards and administrative requirements and procedures to be followed in performing the disability determination function in order to assure effective and uniform administration of the disability insurance program throughout the United States. The regulations may, for example, specify matters such as—

    (A) the administrative structure and the relationship between various units of the State agency responsible for disability determinations,

    (B) the physical location of and relationship among agency staff units, and other individuals or organizations performing tasks for the State agency, and standards for the availability to applicants and beneficiaries of facilities for making disability determinations,

    (C) State agency performance criteria, including the rate of accuracy of decisions, the time periods within which determinations must be made, the procedures for and the scope of review by the Commissioner of Social Security, and, as the Commissioner finds appropriate, by the State, of its performance in individual cases and in classes of cases, and rules governing access of appropriate Federal officials to State offices and to State records relating to its administration of the disability determination function,

    (D) fiscal control procedures that the State agency may be required to adopt, and

    (E) the submission of reports and other data, in such form and at such time as the Commissioner of Social Security may require, concerning the State agency's activities relating to the disability determination.

Nothing in this section shall be construed to authorize the Commissioner of Social Security to take any action except pursuant to law or to regulations promulgated pursuant to law.

(b)(1) If the Commissioner of Social Security finds, after notice and opportunity for a hearing, that a State agency is substantially failing to make disability determinations in a manner consistent with the Commissioner's regulations and other written guidelines, the Commissioner of Social Security shall, not earlier than 180 days following the Commissioner's finding, and after the Commissioner has complied

210 SOCIAL SECURITY ACT—§ 221(b)(1)(cont)

with the requirements of paragraph (3), make the disability determinations referred to in subsection (a)(1).

(2) If a State, having notified the Commissioner of Social Security of its intent to make disability determinations under subsection (a)(1), no longer wishes to make such determinations, it shall notify the Commissioner of Social Security in writing of that fact, and, if an agency of the State is making disability determinations at the time such notice is given, it shall continue to do so for not less than 180 days, or (if later) until the Commissioner of Social Security has complied with the requirements of paragraph (3). Thereafter, the Commissioner of Social Security shall make the disability determinations referred to in subsection (a)(1).

(3)(A) The Commissioner of Social Security shall develop and initiate all appropriate procedures to implement a plan with respect to any partial or complete assumption by the Commissioner of Social Security of the disability determination function from a State agency, as provided in this section, under which employees of the affected State agency who are capable of performing duties in the disability determination process for the Commissioner of Social Security shall, notwithstanding any other provision of law, have a preference over any other individual in filling an appropriate employment position with the Commissioner of Social Security (subject to any system established by the Commissioner of Social Security for determining hiring priority among such employees of the State agency) unless any such employee is the administrator, the deputy administrator, or assistant administrator (or his equivalent) of the State agency, in which case the Commissioner of Social Security may accord such priority to such employee.

(B) The Commissioner of Social Security shall not make such assumption of the disability determination function until such time as the Secretary of Labor determines that, with respect to employees of such State agency who will be displaced from their employment on account of such assumption by the Commissioner of Social Security and who will not be hired by the Commissioner of Social Security to perform duties in the disability determination process, the State has made fair and equitable arrangements to protect the interests of employees so displaced. Such protective arrangements shall include only those provisions which are provided under all applicable Federal, State and local statutes including, but not limited to, (i) the preservation of rights, privileges, and benefits (including continuation of pension rights and benefits) under existing collective-bargaining agreements; (ii) the continuation of collective-bargaining rights; (iii) the assignment of affected employees to other jobs or to retraining programs; (iv) the protection of individual employees against a worsening of their positions with respect to their employment; (v) the protection of health benefits and other fringe benefits; and (vi) the provision of severance pay, as may be necessary.

(c)(1) The Commissioner of Social Security may on the Commissioner's own motion or as required under paragraphs (2) and (3) review a determination, made by a State agency under this section, that an individual is or is not under a disability (as defined in section 216(i) or 223(d)) and, as a result of such review, may modify such agency's determination and determine that such individual either is or is not under a disability (as so defined) or that such individual's disability began on a day earlier or later than that determined by such agency, or that such disability ceased on a day earlier or later than that determined by such agency. A review by the Commissioner of Social Security on the Commissioner's own motion of a State agency determination under this paragraph may be made before or after any action is taken to implement such determination.

(2) The Commissioner of Social Security (in accordance with paragraph (3)) shall review determinations, made by State agencies pursuant to this section, that individuals are under disabilities (as defined in section 216(i) or 223(d)). Any review by the Commissioner of Social Security of a State agency determination under this paragraph shall be made before any action is taken to implement such determination.

(3)(A) In carrying out the provisions of paragraph (2) with respect to the review of determinations made by State agencies pursuant to this section that individuals are under disabilities (as defined in section 216(i) or 223(d)), the Commissioner of Social Security shall review—

> (i) at least 50 percent of all such determinations made by State agencies on applications for benefits under this title, and
>
> (ii) other determinations made by State agencies pursuant to this section to the extent necessary to assure a high level of accuracy in such other determinations.

(B) In conducting reviews pursuant to subparagraph (A), the Commissioner of Social Security shall, to the extent feasible, select for review those determinations which the Commissioner of Social Security identifies as being the most likely to be incorrect.

(C) Not later than April 1, 1992, and annually thereafter, the Commissioner of Social Security shall submit to the Committee on Ways and Means of the House of Representatives and the Committee on Finance of the Senate a written report setting forth the number of reviews conducted under subparagraph (A)(ii) during the preceding fiscal year and the findings of the Commissioner of Social Security based on such reviews of the accuracy of the determinations made by State agencies pursuant to this section.

(d) Any individual dissatisfied with any determination under subsection (a), (b), (c), or (g) shall be entitled to a hearing thereon by the Commissioner of Social Security to the same extent as is provided in section 205(b) with respect to decisions of the Commissioner of Social Security, and to judicial review of the Commissioner's final decision after such hearing as is provided in section 205(g).

(e) Each State which is making disability determinations under subsection (a)(1) shall be entitled to receive from the Trust Funds, in advance or by way of reimbursement, as determined by the Commissioner of Social Security, the cost to the State of making disability determinations under subsection (a)(1). The Commissioner of Social Security shall from time to time certify such amount as is necessary for this purpose to the Managing Trustee, reduced or increased, as the case may be, by any sum (for which adjustment hereunder has not previously been made) by which the amount certified for any prior period was greater or less than the amount which should have been paid to the State under this subsection for such period; and the Managing Trustee, prior to audit or settlement by the General Account-

212   SOCIAL SECURITY ACT—§ 221(e)(cont)

ing Office[260], shall make payment from the Trust Funds at the time or times fixed by the Commissioner of Social Security, in accordance with such certification. Appropriate adjustments between the Federal Old-Age and Survivors Insurance Trust Fund and the Federal Disability Insurance Trust Fund with respect to the payments made under this subsection shall be made in accordance with paragraph (1) of subsection (g) of section 201 (but taking into account any refunds under subsection (f) of this section) to insure that the Federal Disability Insurance Trust Fund is charged with all expenses incurred which are attributable to the administration of section 223 and the Federal Old-Age and Survivors Insurance Trust Fund is charged with all other expenses.

(f) All money paid to a State under this section shall be used solely for the purposes for which it is paid; and any money so paid which is not used for such purposes shall be returned to the Treasury of the United States for deposit in the Trust Funds.

(g) In the case of individuals in a State which does not undertake to perform disability determinations under subsection (a)(1), or which has been found by the Commissioner of Social Security to have substantially failed to make disability determinations in a manner consistent with the Commissioner's regulations and guidelines, in the case of individuals outside the United States, and in the case of any class or classes of individuals for whom no State undertakes to make disability determinations, the determinations referred to in subsection (a) shall be made by the Commissioner of Social Security in accordance with regulations prescribed by the Commissioner.

(h) An initial determination under subsection (a), (c), (g), or (i) that an individual is not under a disability, in any case where there is evidence which indicates the existence of a mental impairment, shall be made only if the Commissioner of Social Security has made every reasonable effort to ensure that a qualified psychiatrist or psychologist has completed the medical portion of the case review and any applicable residual functional capacity assessment.

(i)(1) In any case where an individual is or has been determined to be under a disability, the case shall be reviewed by the applicable State agency or the Commissioner of Social Security (as may be appropriate), for purposes of continuing eligibility, at least once every 3 years, subject to paragraph (2); except that where a finding has been made that such disability is permanent, such reviews shall be made at such times as the Commissioner of Social Security determines to be appropriate. Reviews of cases under the preceding sentence shall be in addition to, and shall not be considered as a substitute for, any other reviews which are required or provided for under or in the administration of this title.

(2) The requirement of paragraph (1) that cases be reviewed at least every 3 years shall not apply to the extent that the Commissioner of Social Security determines, on a State-by-State basis, that such requirement should be waived to insure that only the appropriate number of such cases are reviewed. The Commissioner of Social Security

---

[260] P.L. 108-271, §8(b), provided that "Any reference to the General Accounting Office in any law, rule, regulation, certificate, directive, instruction, or other official paper in force on the date of enactment [July 7, 2004] of this Act shall be considered to refer and apply to the Government Accountability Office.''rce on July 7, 2004, shall be considered to refer and apply to the Government Accountability Office."

shall determine the appropriate number of cases to be reviewed in each State after consultation with the State agency performing such reviews, based upon the backlog of pending reviews, the projected number of new applications for disability insurance benefits, and the current and projected staffing levels of the State agency, but the Commissioner of Social Security shall provide for a waiver of such requirement only in the case of a State which makes a good faith effort to meet proper staffing requirements for the State agency and to process case reviews in a timely fashion. The Commissioner of Social Security shall report annually to the Committee on Finance of the Senate and the Committee on Ways and Means of the House of Representatives with respect to the determinations made by the Commissioner of Social Security under the preceding sentence.

(3) The Commissioner of Social Security shall report annually to the Committee on Finance of the Senate and the Committee on Ways and Means of the House of Representatives with respect to the number of reviews of continuing disability carried out under paragraph (1), the number of such reviews which result in an initial termination of benefits, the number of requests for reconsideration of such initial termination or for a hearing with respect to such termination under subsection (d), or both, and the number of such initial terminations which are overturned as the result of a reconsideration or hearing.

(4) In any case in which the Commissioner of Social Security initiates a review under this subsection of the case of an individual who has been determined to be under a disability, the Commissioner of Social Security shall notify such individual of the nature of the review to be carried out, the possibility that such review could result in the termination of benefits, and the right of the individual to provide medical evidence with respect to such review.

(5) For suspension of reviews under this subsection in the case of an individual using a ticket to work and self-sufficiency, see section 1148(i).

(j) The Commissioner of Social Security shall prescribe regulations which set forth, in detail—

> (1) the standards to be utilized by State disability determination services and Federal personnel in determining when a consultative examination should be obtained in connection with disability determinations;

> (2) standards for the type of referral to be made; and

> (3) procedures by which the Commissioner of Social Security will monitor both the referral processes used and the product of professionals to whom cases are referred.

Nothing in this subsection shall be construed to preclude the issuance, in accordance with section 553(b)(A) of title 5, United States Code, of interpretive rules, general statements of policy, and rules of agency organization relating to consultative examinations if such rules and statements are consistent with such regulations.

(k)(1) The Commissioner of Social Security shall establish by regulation uniform standards which shall be applied at all levels of determination, review, and adjudication in determining whether individuals are under disabilities as defined in section 216(i) or 223(d).

214 SOCIAL SECURITY ACT—§ 221(k)(2)

(2) Regulations promulgated under paragraph (1) shall be subject to the rulemaking procedures established under section 553 of title 5, United States Code[261].

(l)(1) In any case where an individual who is applying for or receiving benefits under this title on the basis of disability by reason of blindness is entitled to receive notice from the Commissioner of Social Security of any decision or determination made or other action taken or proposed to be taken with respect to his or her rights under this title, such individual shall at his or her election be entitled either (A) to receive a supplementary notice of such decision, determination, or action, by telephone, within 5 working days after the initial notice is mailed, (B) to receive the initial notice in the form of a certified letter, or (C) to receive notification by some alternative procedure established by the Commissioner of Social Security and agreed to by the individual.

(2) The election under paragraph (1) may be made at any time, but an opportunity to make such an election shall in any event be given, to every individual who is an applicant for benefits under this title on the basis of disability by reason of blindness, at the time of his or her application. Such an election, once made by an individual, shall apply with respect to all notices of decisions, determinations, and actions which such individual may thereafter be entitled to receive under this title until such time as it is revoked or changed.

(m)(1) In any case where an individual entitled to disability insurance benefits under section 223 or to monthly insurance benefits under section 202 based on such individual's disability (as defined in section 223(d)) has received such benefits for at least 24 months—

(A) no continuing disability review conducted by the Commissioner may be scheduled for the individual solely as a result of the individual's work activity;

(B) no work activity engaged in by the individual may be used as evidence that the individual is no longer disabled; and

(C) no cessation of work activity by the individual may give rise to a presumption that the individual is unable to engage in work.

(2) An individual to which paragraph (1) applies shall continue to be subject to—

(A) continuing disability reviews on a regularly scheduled basis that is not triggered by work; and

(B) termination of benefits under this title in the event that the individual has earnings that exceed the level of earnings established by the Commissioner to represent substantial gainful activity.

REHABILITATION SERVICES

SEC. 222. [42 U.S.C. 422] (a)   [Repealed.[262]]

(b)   [Repealed.[263]]

---

[261] See Vol. II, 5 U.S.C. 553.
[262] P.L. 106-170, §101(b)(1)(B); 113 Stat.1873.
[263] P.L. 106-170, §101(b)(1)(C); 113 Stat.1873.

Period of Trial Work

(c)(1) The term "period of trial work", with respect to an individual entitled to benefits under section 223, 202(d), 202(e), or 202(f), means a period of months beginning and ending as provided in paragraphs (3) and (4).

(2) For purposes of sections 216(i) and 223, any services rendered by an individual during a period of trial work shall be deemed not to have been rendered by such individual in determining whether his disability has ceased in a month during such period. For purposes of this subsection the term "services" means activity (whether legal or illegal) which is performed for remuneration or gain or is determined by the Commissioner of Social Security to be of a type normally performed for remuneration or gain.

(3) A period of trial work for any individual shall begin with the month in which he becomes entitled to disability insurance benefits, or, in the case of an individual entitled to benefits under section 202(d) who has attained the age of eighteen, with the month in which he becomes entitled to such benefits or the month in which he attains the age of eighteen, whichever is later, or, in the case of an individual entitled to widow's or widower's insurance benefits under section 202(e) or (f) who became entitled to such benefits prior to attaining age 60, with the month in which such individual becomes so entitled. Notwithstanding the preceding sentence, no period of trial work may begin for any individual prior to the beginning of the month following the month in which this paragraph is enacted[264]; and no such period may begin for an individual in a period of disability of such individual in which he had a previous period of trial work.

(4) A period of trial work for any individual shall end with the close of whichever of the following months is the earlier:

(A) the ninth month, in any period of 60 consecutive months, in which the individual renders services (whether or not such nine months are consecutive); or

(B) the month in which his disability (as defined in section 223(d)) ceases (as determined after application of paragraph (2) of this subsection).

(5) Upon conviction by a Federal court that an individual has fraudulently concealed work activity during a period of trial work from the Commissioner of Social Security by—

(A) providing false information to the Commissioner of Social Security as to whether the individual had earnings in or for a particular period, or as to the amount thereof;

(B) receiving disability insurance benefits under this title while engaging in work activity under another identity, including under another social security account number or a number purporting to be a social security account number; or

(C) taking other actions to conceal work activity with an intent fraudulently to secure payment in a greater amount than is due or when no payment is authorized,

no benefit shall be payable to such individual under this title with respect to a period of disability for any month before such conviction dur-

---

[264] The month is October 1960; the paragraph was enacted on September 13, 1960, as part of P.L. 86-778 [74 Stat. 968].

216   SOCIAL SECURITY ACT—§ 222(c)(5)(C)(cont)

ing which the individual rendered services during the period of trial work with respect to which the fraudulently concealed work activity occurred, and amounts otherwise due under this title as restitution, penalties, assessments, fines, or other repayments shall in all cases be in addition to any amounts for which such individual is liable as overpayments by reason of such concealment.

Costs of Rehabilitation Services From Trust Funds

(d)(1) For purposes of making vocational rehabilitation services more readily available to disabled individuals who are—
   (A) entitled to disability insurance benefits under section 223,
   (B) entitled to child's insurance benefits under section 202(d) after having attained age 18 (and are under a disability),
   (C) entitled to widow's insurance benefits under section 202(e) prior to attaining age 60, or
   (D) entitled to widower's insurance benefits under section 202(f) prior to attaining age 60,
to the end that savings will accrue to the Trust Funds as a result of rehabilitating such individuals, there are authorized to be transferred from the Federal Old-Age and Survivors Insurance Trust Fund and the Federal Disability Insurance Trust Fund each fiscal year such sums as may be necessary to enable the Commissioner of Social Security to reimburse the State for the reasonable and necessary costs of vocational rehabilitation services furnished such individuals (including services during their waiting periods), under a State plan for vocational rehabilitation services approved under title I of the Rehabilitation Act of 1973[265] (29 U.S.C. 701 et seq.), (i) in cases where the furnishing of such services results in the performance by such individuals of substantial gainful activity for a continuous period of nine months, (ii) in cases where such individuals receive benefits as a result of section 225(b) (except that no reimbursement under this paragraph shall be made for services furnished to any individual receiving such benefits for any period after the close of such individual's ninth consecutive month of substantial gainful activity or the close of the month in which his or her entitlement to such benefits ceases, whichever first occurs), and (iii) in cases where such individuals, without good cause, refuse to continue to accept vocational rehabilitation services or fail to cooperate in such a manner as to preclude their successful rehabilitation. The determination that the vocational rehabilitation services contributed to the successful return of an individual to substantial gainful activity, the determination that an individual, without good cause, refused to continue to accept vocational rehabilitation services or failed to cooperate in such a manner as to preclude successful rehabilitation, and the determination of the amount of costs to be reimbursed under this subsection shall be made by the Commissioner of Social Security in accordance with criteria formulated by the Commissioner.

(2) In the case of any State which is unwilling to participate or does not have a plan which meets the requirements of paragraph (1), the Commissioner of Social Security may provide such services in such

---

[265] P.L. 93-112.

State by agreement or contract with other public or private agencies, organizations, institutions, or individuals. The provision of such services shall be subject to the same conditions as otherwise apply under paragraph (1).

(3) Payments under this subsection shall be made in advance or by way of reimbursement, with necessary adjustments for overpayments and underpayments.

(4) Money paid from the Trust Funds under this subsection for the reimbursement of the costs of providing services to individuals who are entitled to benefits under section 223 (including services during their waiting periods), or who are entitled to benefits under section 202(d) on the basis of the wages and self-employment income of such individuals, shall be charged to the Federal Disability Insurance Trust Fund, and all other money paid from the Trust Funds under this subsection shall be charged to the Federal Old-Age and Survivors Insurance Trust Fund. The Commissioner of Social Security shall determine according to such methods and procedures as the Commissioner may deem appropriate—

(A) the total amount to be reimbursed for the cost of services under this subsection, and

(B) subject to the provisions of the preceding sentence, the amount which should be charged to each of the Trust Funds.

(5) For purposes of this subsection the term "vocational rehabilitation services" shall have the meaning assigned to it in title I of the Rehabilitation Act of 1973[266] (29 U.S.C. 701 et seq.), except that such services may be limited in type, scope, or amount in accordance with regulations of the Commissioner of Social Security designed to achieve the purpose of this subsection.

Treatment Referrals for Individuals With An Alcoholism or Drug Addiction Condition

(e) In the case of any individual whose benefits under this title are paid to a representative payee pursuant to section 205(j)(1)(B), the Commissioner of Social Security shall refer such individual to the appropriate State agency administering the State plan for substance abuse treatment services approved under subpart II of part B of title XIX of the Public Health Service Act (42 U.S.C. 300x-21 et seq.).

DISABILITY INSURANCE BENEFIT PAYMENTS

Disability Insurance Benefits

SEC. 223. [42 U.S.C. 423] (a)(1) Every individual who—

(A) is insured for disability insurance benefits (as determined under subsection (c)(1)),

(B) has not attained retirement age (as defined in section 216(l)),

(C) if not a United States citizen or national—

(i) has been assigned a social security account number that was, at the time of assignment, or at any later time, consis-

---

[266] P.L. 93-112.

218   SOCIAL SECURITY ACT—§ 223(a)(1)(C)(i)(cont)

tent with the requirements of subclause (I) or (III) of section 205(c)(2)(B)(i); or

(ii) at the time any quarters of coverage are earned—

(I) is described in subparagraph (B) or (D) of section 101(a)(15) of the Immigration and Nationality Act[267],

(II) is lawfully admitted temporarily to the United States for business (in the case of an individual described in such subparagraph (B)) or the performance as a crewman (in the case of an individual described in such subparagraph (D)), and

(III) the business engaged in or service as a crewman performed is within the scope of the terms of such individual's admission to the United States.

(D) has filed application for disability insurance benefits, and

(E) is under a disability (as defined in subsection (d))

shall be entitled to a disability insurance benefit (i) for each month beginning with the first month after his waiting period (as defined in subsection (c)(2)) in which he becomes so entitled to such insurance benefits, or (ii) for each month beginning with the first month during all of which he is under a disability and in which he becomes so entitled to such insurance benefits, but only if he was entitled to disability insurance benefits which terminated, or had a period of disability (as defined in section 216(i)) which ceased, within the 60-month period preceding the first month in which he is under such disability, and ending with the month preceding whichever of the following months is the earliest: the month in which he dies, the month in which he attains retirement age (as defined in section 216(l)), or, subject to subsection (e), the termination month. For purposes of the preceding sentence, the termination month for any individual shall be the third month following the month in which his disability ceases; except that, in the case of an individual who has a period of trial work which ends as determined by application of section 222(c)(4)(A), the termination month shall be the earlier of (I) the third month following the earliest month after the end of such period of trial work with respect to which such individual is determined to no longer be suffering from a disabling physical or mental impairment, or (II) the third month following the earliest month in which such individual engages or is determined able to engage in substantial gainful activity, but in no event earlier than the first month occurring after the 36 months following such period of trial work in which he engages or is determined able to engage in substantial gainful activity. No payment under this paragraph may be made to an individual who would not meet the definition of disability in subsection (d) except for paragraph (1)(B) thereof for any month in which he engages in substantial gainful activity, and no payment may be made for such month under subsection (b), (c), or (d) of section 202 to any person on the basis of the wages and self-employment income of such individual. In the case of a deceased individual, the requirement of subparagraph (C) may be satisfied by

---

[267] See Vol. II, P.L. 97-248, §278(d), with respect to deemed entitlement for hospital insurance benefits purposes.

See Vol. II, P.L. 106-170, §302, with respect to demonstration projects providing for reductions in disability benefits based on earnings.

SOCIAL SECURITY ACT—§ 223(c)(1)(B)(ii)   219

an application for benefits filed with respect to such individual within 3 months after the month in which he died.

(2) Except as provided in section 202(q) and section 215(b)(2)(A)(ii), such individual's disability insurance benefit for any month shall be equal to his primary insurance amount for such month determined under section 215 as though he had attained age 62 in—

(A) the first month of his waiting period, or

(B) in any case in which clause (ii) of paragraph (1) of this subsection is applicable, the first month for which he becomes entitled to such disability insurance benefits,

and as though he had become entitled to old-age insurance benefits in the month in which the application for disability insurance benefits was filed and he was entitled to an old-age insurance benefit for each month for which (pursuant to subsection (b)) he was entitled to a disability insurance benefit. For the purposes of the preceding sentence, in the case of an individual who attained age 62 in or before the first month referred to in subparagraph (A) or (B) of such sentence, as the case may be, the elapsed years referred to in section 215(b)(3) shall not include the year in which he attained age 62, or any year thereafter.

Filing of Application

(b) An application for disability insurance benefits filed before the first month in which the applicant satisfies the requirements for such benefits (as prescribed in subsection (a)(1)) shall be deemed a valid application (and shall be deemed to have been filed in such first month) only if the applicant satisfies the requirements for such benefits before the Commissioner of Social Security makes a final decision on the application and no request under section 205(b) for notice and opportunity for a hearing thereon is made, or if such a request is made, before a decision based upon the evidence adduced at the hearing is made (regardless of whether such decision becomes the final decision of the Commissioner of Social Security). An individual who would have been entitled to a disability insurance benefit for any month had he filed application therefor before the end of such month shall be entitled to such benefit for such month if such application is filed before the end of the 12th month immediately succeeding such month.

Definitions of Insured Status and Waiting Period

(c) For purposes of this section—

(1) An individual shall be insured for disability insurance benefits in any month if—

(A) he would have been a fully insured individual (as defined in section 214) had he attained age 62 and filed application for benefits under section 202(a) on the first day of such month, and

(B)(i) he had not less than 20 quarters of coverage during the 40-quarter period which ends with the quarter in which such month occurred, or

(ii) if such month ends before the quarter in which he attains (or would attain) age 31, not less than one-half (and not less than 6) of the quarters during the period ending with the quarter in which such month occurred and beginning after he attained the age of 21 were quarters of coverage, or (if the number of quarters in such period is less than 12) not less than 6 of the quarters in the 12-quarter period ending with such quarter were quarters of coverage, or

(iii) in the case of an individual (not otherwise insured under clause (i)) who, by reason of section 216(i)(3)(B)(ii), had a prior period of disability that began during a period before the quarter in which he or she attained age 31, not less than one-half of the quarters beginning after such individual attained age 21 and ending with the quarter in which such month occurs are quarters of coverage, or (if the number of quarters in such period is less than 12) not less than 6 of the quarters in the 12-quarter period ending with such quarter are quarters of coverage;

except that the provisions of subparagraph (B) of this paragraph shall not apply in the case of an individual who is blind (within the meaning of "blindness" as defined in section 216(i)(1)). For purposes of subparagraph (B) of this paragraph, when the number of quarters in any period is an odd number, such number shall be reduced by one, and a quarter shall not be counted as part of any period if any part of such quarter was included in a period of disability unless such quarter was a quarter of coverage.

(2) The term "waiting period" means, in the case of any application for disability insurance benefits, the earliest period of five consecutive calendar months—

(A) throughout which the individual with respect to whom such application is filed has been under a disability, and

(B)(i) which begins not earlier than with the first day of the seventeenth month before the month in which such application is filed if such individual is insured for disability insurance benefits in such seventeenth month, or (ii) if he is not so insured in such month, which begins not earlier than with the first day of the first month after such seventeenth month in which he is so insured.

Notwithstanding the preceding provisions of this paragraph, no waiting period may begin for any individual before January 1, 1957.

Definition of Disability

(d)(1) The term "disability" means—

(A) inability to engage in any substantial gainful activity by reason of any medically determinable physical or mental impairment which can be expected to result in death or which has lasted or can be expected to last for a continuous period of not less than 12 months; or

(B) in the case of an individual who has attained the age of 55 and is blind (within the meaning of "blindness" as defined in section 216(i)(1)), inability by reason of such blindness to engage in substantial gainful activity requiring skills or abilities compara-

SOCIAL SECURITY ACT—§ 223(d)(4)(A)   221

ble to those of any gainful activity in which he has previously engaged with some regularity and over a substantial period of time.

(2) For purposes of paragraph (1)(A)—

(A) An individual shall be determined to be under a disability only if his physical or mental impairment or impairments are of such severity that he is not only unable to do his previous work but cannot, considering his age, education, and work experience, engage in any other kind of substantial gainful work which exists in the national economy, regardless of whether such work exists in the immediate area in which he lives, or whether a specific job vacancy exists for him, or whether he would be hired if he applied for work. For purposes of the preceding sentence (with respect to any individual), "work which exists in the national economy" means work which exists in significant numbers either in the region where such individual lives or in several regions of the country.

(B) In determining whether an individual's physical or mental impairment or impairments are of a sufficient medical severity that such impairment or impairments could be the basis of eligibility under this section, the Commissioner of Social Security shall consider the combined effect of all of the individual's impairments without regard to whether any such impairment, if considered separately, would be of such severity. If the Commissioner of Social Security does find a medically severe combination of impairments, the combined impact of the impairments shall be considered throughout the disability determination process.

(C) An individual shall not be considered to be disabled for purposes of this title if alcoholism or drug addiction would (but for this subparagraph) be a contributing factor material to the Commissioner's determination that the individual is disabled.

(3) For purposes of this subsection, a "physical or mental impairment" is an impairment that results from anatomical, physiological, or psychological abnormalities which are demonstrable by medically acceptable clinical and laboratory diagnostic techniques.

(4)(A) The Commissioner of Social Security shall by regulations prescribe the criteria for determining when services performed or earnings derived from services demonstrate an individual's ability to engage in substantial gainful activity. No individual who is blind shall be regarded as having demonstrated an ability to engage in substantial gainful activity on the basis of earnings that do not exceed an amount equal to the exempt amount which would be applicable under section 203(f)(8), to individuals described in subparagraph (D) thereof, if section 102 of the Senior Citizens' Right to Work Act of 1996[268] had not been enacted. Notwithstanding the provisions of paragraph (2), an individual whose services or earnings meet such criteria shall, except for purposes of section 222(c), be found not to be disabled. In determining whether an individual is able to engage in substantial gainful activity by reason of his earnings, where his disability is sufficiently severe to result in a functional limitation requiring assistance in order for him to work, there shall be excluded from such earnings an amount equal to the cost (to such individual) of any attendant care services, medical devices, equipment, prostheses, and similar items

---

[268] Title I of P.L. 104-121, the Contract with America Advancement Act of 1996.

222 SOCIAL SECURITY ACT—§ 223(d)(4)(A)(cont)

and services (not including routine drugs or routine medical services unless such drugs or services are necessary for the control of the disabling condition) which are necessary (as determined by the Commissioner of Social Security in regulations) for that purpose, whether or not such assistance is also needed to enable him to carry out his normal daily functions; except that the amount to be excluded shall be subject to such reasonable limits as the Commissioner of Social Security may prescribe.

(B) In determining under subparagraph (A) when services performed or earnings derived from services demonstrate an individual's ability to engage in substantial gainful activity, the Commissioner of Social Security shall apply the criteria described in subparagraph (A) with respect to services performed by any individual without regard to the legality of such services.

(5)(A) An individual shall not be considered to be under a disability unless he furnishes such medical and other evidence of the existence thereof as the Commissioner of Social Security may require. An individual's statement as to pain or other symptoms shall not alone be conclusive evidence of disability as defined in this section; there must be medical signs and findings, established by medically acceptable clinical or laboratory diagnostic techniques, which show the existence of a medical impairment that results from anatomical, physiological, or psychological abnormalities which could reasonably be expected to produce the pain or other symptoms alleged and which, when considered with all evidence required to be furnished under this paragraph (including statements of the individual or his physician as to the intensity and persistence of such pain or other symptoms which may reasonably be accepted as consistent with the medical signs and findings), would lead to a conclusion that the individual is under a disability. Objective medical evidence of pain or other symptoms established by medically acceptable clinical or laboratory techniques (for example, deteriorating nerve or muscle tissue) must be considered in reaching a conclusion as to whether the individual is under a disability. Any non-Federal hospital, clinic, laboratory, or other provider of medical services, or physician not in the employ of the Federal Government, which supplies medical evidence required and requested by the Commissioner of Social Security under this paragraph shall be entitled to payment from the Commissioner of Social Security for the reasonable cost of providing such evidence.

(B) In making any determination with respect to whether an individual is under a disability or continues to be under a disability, the Commissioner of Social Security shall consider all evidence available in such individual's case record, and shall develop a complete medical history of at least the preceding twelve months for any case in which a determination is made that the individual is not under a disability. In making any determination the Commissioner of Social Security shall make every reasonable effort to obtain from the individual's treating physician (or other treating health care provider) all medical evidence, including diagnostic tests, necessary in order to properly make such determination, prior to evaluating medical evidence obtained from any other source on a consultative basis.

(6)(A) Notwithstanding any other provision of this title, any physical or mental impairment which arises in connection with the commission by an individual (after the date of the enactment of this paragraph[269]) of an offense which constitutes a felony under applicable law and for which such individual is subsequently convicted, or which is aggravated in connection with such an offense (but only to the extent so aggravated), shall not be considered in determining whether an individual is under a disability.

(B) Notwithstanding any other provision of this title, any physical or mental impairment which arises in connection with an individual's confinement in a jail, prison, or other penal institution or correctional facility pursuant to such individual's conviction of an offense (committed after the date of the enactment of this paragraph) constituting a felony under applicable law, or which is aggravated in connection with such a confinement (but only to the extent so aggravated), shall not be considered in determining whether such individual is under a disability for purposes of benefits payable for any month during which such individual is so confined.

(e)(1) No benefit shall be payable under subsection (d)(1)(B)(ii), (d)(6)(A)(ii), (d)(6)(B), (e)(1)(B)(ii), or (f)(1)(B)(ii) of section 202 or under subsection (a)(1) of this section to an individual for any month, after the third month, in which he engages in substantial gainful activity during the 36-month period following the end of his trial work period determined by application of section 222(c)(4)(A).

(2) No benefit shall be payable under section 202 on the basis of the wages and self-employment income of an individual entitled to a benefit under subsection (a)(1) of this section for any month for which the benefit of such individual under subsection (a)(1) is not payable under paragraph (1).

Standard of Review for Termination of Disability Benefits

(f) A recipient of benefits under this title or title XVIII based on the disability of any individual may be determined not to be entitled to such benefits on the basis of a finding that the physical or mental impairment on the basis of which such benefits are provided has ceased, does not exist, or is not disabling only if such finding is supported by—

(1) substantial evidence which demonstrates that—

(A) there has been any medical improvement in the individual's impairment or combination of impairments (other than medical improvement which is not related to the individual's ability to work), and

(B) the individual is now able to engage in substantial gainful activity; or

(2) substantial evidence which—

(A) consists of new medical evidence and a new assessment of the individual's residual functional capacity, and demonstrates that—

(i) although the individual has not improved medically, he or she is nonetheless a beneficiary of advances in medical or vocational therapy or technology (related to the individual's ability to work), and

(ii) the individual is now able to engage in substantial gainful activity, or

---

[269] October 19, 1980 [P.L. 96-473; 94 Stat. 2263].

224 SOCIAL SECURITY ACT—§ 223(f)(2)(B)

(B) demonstrates that—

(i) although the individual has not improved medically, he or she has undergone vocational therapy (related to the individual's ability to work), and

(ii) the individual is now able to engage in substantial gainful activity; or

(3) substantial evidence which demonstrates that, as determined on the basis of new or improved diagnostic techniques or evaluations, the individual's impairment or combination of impairments is not as disabling as it was considered to be at the time of the most recent prior decision that he or she was under a disability or continued to be under a disability, and that therefore the individual is able to engage in substantial gainful activity; or

(4) substantial evidence (which may be evidence on the record at the time any prior determination of the entitlement to benefits based on disability was made, or newly obtained evidence which relates to that determination) which demonstrates that a prior determination was in error.

Nothing in this subsection shall be construed to require a determination that a recipient of benefits under this title or title XVIII based on an individual's disability is entitled to such benefits if the prior determination was fraudulently obtained or if the individual is engaged in substantial gainful activity, cannot be located, or fails, without good cause, to cooperate in a review of the entitlement to such benefits or to follow prescribed treatment which would be expected to restore his or her ability to engage in substantial gainful activity. In making for purposes of the preceding sentence any determination relating to fraudulent behavior by any individual or failure by any individual without good cause to cooperate or to take any required action, the Commissioner of Social Security shall specifically take into account any physical, mental, educational, or linguistic limitation such individual may have (including any lack of facility with the English language). Any determination under this section shall be made on the basis of all the evidence available in the individual's case file, including new evidence concerning the individual's prior or current condition which is presented by the individual or secured by the Commissioner of Social Security. Any determination made under this section shall be made on the basis of the weight of the evidence and on a neutral basis with regard to the individual's condition, without any initial inference as to the presence or absence of disability being drawn from the fact that the individual has previously been determined to be disabled. For purposes of this subsection, a benefit under this title is based on an individual's disability if it is a disability insurance benefit, a child's, widow's, or widower's insurance benefit based on disability, or a mother's or father's insurance benefit based on the disability of the mother's or father's child who has attained age 16.

Continued Payment of Disability Benefits During Appeal

(g)(1) In any case where—

SOCIAL SECURITY ACT—§ 223(h)(1)   225

(A) an individual is a recipient of disability insurance benefits, or of child's, widow's, or widower's insurance benefits based on disability,

(B) the physical or mental impairment on the basis of which such benefits are payable is found to have ceased, not to have existed, or to no longer be disabling, and as a consequence such individual is determined not to be entitled to such benefits, and

(C) a timely request for a hearing under section 221(d), or for an administrative review prior to such hearing, is pending with respect to the determination that he is not so entitled,

such individual may elect (in such manner and form and within such time as the Commissioner of Social Security shall by regulations prescribe) to have the payment of such benefits, the payment of any other benefits under this title based on such individual's wages and self-employment income, the payment of mother's or father's insurance benefits to such individual's mother or father based on the disability of such individual as a child who has attained age 16, and the payment of benefits under title XVIII based on such individual's disability, continued for an additional period beginning with the first month beginning after the date of the enactment of this subsection[270] for which (under such determination) such benefits are no longer otherwise payable, and ending with the earlier of (i) the month preceding the month in which a decision is made after such a hearing, or (ii) the month preceding the month in which no such request for a hearing or an administrative review is pending.

(2)(A) If an individual elects to have the payment of his benefits continued for an additional period under paragraph (1), and the final decision of the Commissioner of Social Security affirms the determination that he is not entitled to such benefits, any benefits paid under this title pursuant to such election (for months in such additional period) shall be considered overpayments for all purposes of this title, except as otherwise provided in subparagraph (B).

(B) If the Commissioner of Social Security determines that the individual's appeal of his termination of benefits was made in good faith, all of the benefits paid pursuant to such individual's election under paragraph (1) shall be subject to waiver consideration under the provisions of section 204. In making for purposes of this subparagraph any determination of whether any individual's appeal is made in good faith, the Commissioner of Social Security shall specifically take into account any physical, mental, educational, or linguistic limitation such individual may have (including any lack of facility with the English language).

Interim Benefits in Cases of Delayed Final Decisions

(h)(1) In any case in which an administrative law judge has determined after a hearing as provided under section 205(b) that an individual is entitled to disability insurance benefits or child's, widow's, or widower's insurance benefits based on disability and the Commissioner of Social Security has not issued the Commissioner's final decision in such case within 110 days after the date of the administrative

---

[270] January 12, 1983 [P.L. 97-455; 96 Stat. 2497].

226 SOCIAL SECURITY ACT—§ 223(h)(1)(cont)

law judge's determination, such benefits shall be currently paid for the months during the period beginning with the month preceding the month in which such 110–day period expires and ending with the month preceding the month in which such final decision is issued.

(2) For purposes of paragraph (1), in determining whether the 110-day period referred to in paragraph (1) has elapsed, any period of time for which the action or inaction of such individual or such individual's representative without good cause results in the delay in the issuance of the Commissioner's final decision shall not be taken into account to the extent that such period of time exceeds 20 calendar days.

(3) Any benefits currently paid under this title pursuant to this subsection (for the months described in paragraph (1)) shall not be considered overpayments for any purpose of this title (unless payment of such benefits was fraudulently obtained), and such benefits shall not be treated as past-due benefits for purposes of section 206(b)(1).

Reinstatement of Entitlement

(i)(1)(A) Entitlement to benefits described in subparagraph (B)(i)(I) shall be reinstated in any case where the Commissioner determines that an individual described in subparagraph (B) has filed a request for reinstatement meeting the requirements of paragraph (2)(A) during the period prescribed in subparagraph (C). Reinstatement of such entitlement shall be in accordance with the terms of this subsection.

(B) An individual is described in this subparagraph if—
> (i) prior to the month in which the individual files a request for reinstatement—
>> (I) the individual was entitled to benefits under this section or section 202 on the basis of disability pursuant to an application filed therefor; and
>> (II) such entitlement terminated due to the performance of substantial gainful activity;
> (ii) the individual is under a disability and the physical or mental impairment that is the basis for the finding of disability is the same as (or related to) the physical or mental impairment that was the basis for the finding of disability that gave rise to the entitlement described in clause (i); and
> (iii) the individual's disability renders the individual unable to perform substantial gainful activity.

(C)(i) Except as provided in clause (ii), the period prescribed in this subparagraph with respect to an individual is 60 consecutive months beginning with the month following the most recent month for which the individual was entitled to a benefit described in subparagraph (B)(i)(I) prior to the entitlement termination described in subparagraph (B)(i)(II).

(ii) In the case of an individual who fails to file a reinstatement request within the period prescribed in clause (i), the Commissioner may extend the period if the Commissioner determines that the individual had good cause for the failure to so file.

(2)(A)(i) A request for reinstatement shall be filed in such form, and containing such information, as the Commissioner may prescribe.

SOCIAL SECURITY ACT—§ 223(i)(6)   227

(ii) A request for reinstatement shall include express declarations by the individual that the individual meets the requirements specified in clauses (ii) and (iii) of paragraph (1)(B).

(B) A request for reinstatement filed in accordance with subparagraph (A) may constitute an application for benefits in the case of any individual who the Commissioner determines is not entitled to reinstated benefits under this subsection.

(3) In determining whether an individual meets the requirements of paragraph (1)(B)(ii), the provisions of subsection (f) shall apply.

(4)(A)(i) Subject to clause (ii), entitlement to benefits reinstated under this subsection shall commence with the benefit payable for the month in which a request for reinstatement is filed.

(ii) An individual whose entitlement to a benefit for any month would have been reinstated under this subsection had the individual filed a request for reinstatement before the end of such month shall be entitled to such benefit for such month if such request for reinstatement is filed before the end of the twelfth month immediately succeeding such month.

(B)(i) Subject to clauses (ii) and (iii), the amount of the benefit payable for any month pursuant to the reinstatement of entitlement under this subsection shall be determined in accordance with the provisions of this title.

(ii) For purposes of computing the primary insurance amount of an individual whose entitlement to benefits under this section is reinstated under this subsection, the date of onset of the individual's disability shall be the date of onset used in determining the individual's most recent period of disability arising in connection with such benefits payable on the basis of an application.

(iii) Benefits under this section or section 202 payable for any month pursuant to a request for reinstatement filed in accordance with paragraph (2) shall be reduced by the amount of any provisional benefit paid to such individual for such month under paragraph (7).

(C) No benefit shall be payable pursuant to an entitlement reinstated under this subsection to an individual for any month in which the individual engages in substantial gainful activity.

(D) The entitlement of any individual that is reinstated under this subsection shall end with the benefits payable for the month preceding whichever of the following months is the earliest:

(i) The month in which the individual dies.

(ii) The month in which the individual attains retirement age.

(iii) The third month following the month in which the individual's disability ceases.

(5) Whenever an individual's entitlement to benefits under this section is reinstated under this subsection, entitlement to benefits payable on the basis of such individual's wages and self–employment income may be reinstated with respect to any person previously entitled to such benefits on the basis of an application if the Commissioner determines that such person satisfies all the requirements for entitlement to such benefits except requirements related to the filing of an application. The provisions of paragraph (4) shall apply to the reinstated entitlement of any such person to the same extent that they apply to the reinstated entitlement of such individual.

(6) An individual to whom benefits are payable under this section or section 202 pursuant to a reinstatement of entitlement under this sub-

section for 24 months (whether or not consecutive) shall, with respect to benefits so payable after such twenty–fourth month, be deemed for purposes of paragraph (1)(B)(i)(I) and the determination, if appropriate, of the termination month in accordance with subsection (a)(1) of this section, or subsection (d)(1), (e)(1), or (f)(1) of section 202, to be entitled to such benefits on the basis of an application filed therefor.

(7)(A) An individual described in paragraph (1)(B) who files a request for reinstatement in accordance with the provisions of paragraph (2)(A) shall be entitled to provisional benefits payable in accordance with this paragraph, unless the Commissioner determines that the individual does not meet the requirements of paragraph (1)(B)(i) or that the individual's declaration under paragraph (2)(A)(ii) is false. Any such determination by the Commissioner shall be final and not subject to review under subsection (b) or (g) of section 205.

(B) The amount of a provisional benefit for a month shall equal the amount of the last monthly benefit payable to the individual under this title on the basis of an application increased by an amount equal to the amount, if any, by which such last monthly benefit would have been increased as a result of the operation of section 215(i).

(C)(i) Provisional benefits shall begin with the month in which a request for reinstatement is filed in accordance with paragraph (2)(A).

(ii) Provisional benefits shall end with the earliest of—

(I) the month in which the Commissioner makes a determination regarding the individual's entitlement to reinstated benefits;

(II) the fifth month following the month described in clause (i);

(III) the month in which the individual performs substantial gainful activity; or

(IV) the month in which the Commissioner determines that the individual does not meet the requirements of paragraph (1)(B)(i) or that the individual's declaration made in accordance with paragraph (2)(A)(ii) is false.

(D) In any case in which the Commissioner determines that an individual is not entitled to reinstated benefits, any provisional benefits paid to the individual under this paragraph shall not be subject to recovery as an overpayment unless the Commissioner determines that the individual knew or should have known that the individual did not meet the requirements of paragraph (1)(B).

Limitation on Payments to Prisoners

(j) For provisions relating to limitation on payments to prisoners, see section 202(x).

REDUCTION OF BENEFITS BASED ON DISABILITY

SEC. 224. [42 U.S.C. 424a] (a) If for any month prior to the month in which an individual attains the age of 65—

(1) such individual is entitled to benefits under section 223, and

(2) such individual is entitled for such month to—

(A) periodic benefits on account of his or her total or partial disability (whether or not permanent) under a workmen's compensation law or plan of the United States or a State, or

(B) periodic benefits on account of his or her total or partial disability (whether or not permanent) under any other law or plan of the United States, a State, a political subdivision (as that term is used in section 218(b)(2)), or an instrumentality of two or more States (as that term is used in section 218(g)), other than (i) benefits payable under title 38, United States Code, (ii) benefits payable under a program of assistance which is based on need, (iii) benefits based on service all or substantially all of which was included under an agreement entered into by a State and the Commissioner of Social Security under section 218, and (iv) benefits under a law or plan of the United States based on service all or substantially all of which is employment as defined in section 210,

the total of his benefits under section 223 for such month and of any benefits under section 202 for such month based on his wages and self-employment income shall be reduced (but not below zero) by the amount by which the sum of—

(3) such total of benefits under sections 223 and 202 for such month, and

(4) such periodic benefits payable (and actually paid) for such month to such individual under such laws or plans,

exceeds the higher of—

(5) 80 per centum of his "average current earnings", or

(6) the total of such individual's disability insurance benefits under section 223 for such month and of any monthly insurance benefits under section 202 for such month based on his wages and self-employment income, prior to reduction under this section.

In no case shall the reduction in the total of such benefits under sections 223 and 202 for a month (in a continuous period of months) reduce such total below the sum of—

(7) the total of the benefits under sections 223 and 202, after reduction under this section, with respect to all persons entitled to benefits on the basis of such individual's wages and self-employment income for such month which were determined for such individual and such persons for the first month for which reduction under this section was made (or which would have been so determined if all of them had been so entitled in such first month), and

(8) any increase in such benefits with respect to such individual and such persons, before reduction under this section, which is made effective for months after the first month for which reduction under this section is made.

For purposes of clause (5), an individual's average current earnings means the largest of (A) the average monthly wage (determined under section 215(b) as in effect prior to January 1979) used for purposes of computing his benefits under section 223, (B) one-sixtieth of the total of his wages and self-employment income (computed without regard to the limitations specified in sections 209(a)(1) and 211(b)(1)) for the five consecutive calendar years after 1950 for which such wages and self-employment income were highest, or (C) one-twelfth of the total of his wages and self-employment income (computed without regard to the limitations specified in sections 209(a)(1) and 211(b)(1)) for the calendar year in which he had the highest such wages and income during the period consisting of the calendar year in which he became disabled (as defined in section 223(d)) and the five years preceding that year.

230 SOCIAL SECURITY ACT—§ 224(a)(8)(cont)

(b) If any periodic benefit for a total or partial disability under a law or plan described in subsection (a)(2) is payable on other than a monthly basis (excluding a benefit payable as a lump sum except to the extent that it is a commutation of, or a substitute for, periodic payments), the reduction under this section shall be made at such time or times and in such amounts as the Commissioner of Social Security finds will approximate as nearly as practicable the reduction prescribed by subsection (a).

(c) Reduction of benefits under this section shall be made after any reduction under subsection (a) of section 203, but before deductions under such section and under section 222(b).

(d) The reduction of benefits required by this section shall not be made if the law or plan described in subsection (a)(2) under which a periodic benefit is payable provides for the reduction thereof when anyone is entitled to benefits under this title on the basis of the wages and self-employment income of an individual entitled to benefits under section 223, and such law or plan so provided on February 18, 1981.

(e) If it appears to the Commissioner of Social Security that an individual may be eligible for periodic benefits under a law or plan which would give rise to reduction under this section, he may require, as a condition of certification for payment of any benefits under section 223 to any individual for any month and of any benefits under section 202 for such month based on such individual's wages and self-employment income, that such individual certify (i) whether he has filed or intends to file any claim for such periodic benefits, and (ii) if he has so filed, whether there has been a decision on such claim. The Commissioner of Social Security may, in the absence of evidence to the contrary, rely upon such a certification by such individual that he has not filed and does not intend to file such a claim, or that he has so filed and no final decision thereon has been made, in certifying benefits for payment pursuant to section 205(i).

(f)(1) In the second calendar year after the year in which reduction under this section in the total of an individual's benefits under section 223 and any benefits under section 202 based on his wages and self-employment income was first required (in a continuous period of months), and in each third year thereafter, the Commissioner of Social Security shall redetermine the amount of such benefits which are still subject to reduction under this section; but such redetermination shall not result in any decrease in the total amount of benefits payable under this title on the basis of such individual's wages and self-employment income. Such redetermined benefit shall be determined as of, and shall become effective with, the January following the year in which such redetermination was made.

(2) In making the redetermination required by paragraph (1), the individual's average current earnings (as defined in subsection (a)) shall be deemed to be the product of—

(A) his average current earnings as initially determined under subsection (a); and

(B) the ratio of (i) the national average wage index (as defined in section 209(k)(1)) for the calendar year before the year in which such redetermination is made to (ii) the national average wage index (as so defined) for the calendar year before the year in which

SOCIAL SECURITY ACT—§ 225(a) 231

the reduction was first computed (but not counting any reduction made in benefits for a previous period of disability).
Any amount determined under this paragraph which is not a multiple of $1 shall be reduced to the next lower multiple of $1.

(g) Whenever a reduction in the total of benefits for any month based on an individual's wages and self-employment income is made under this section, each benefit, except the disability insurance benefit, shall first be proportionately decreased, and any excess of such reduction over the sum of all such benefits other than the disability insurance benefits shall then be applied to such disability insurance benefit.

(h)(1) Notwithstanding any other provision of law, the head of any Federal agency shall provide such information within its possession as the Commissioner of Social Security may require for purposes of making a timely determination of the amount of the reduction, if any, required by this section in benefits payable under this title, or verifying other information necessary in carrying out the provisions of this section.

(2) The Commissioner of Social Security is authorized to enter into agreements with States, political subdivisions, and other organizations that administer a law or plan subject to the provisions of this section, in order to obtain such information as he may require to carry out the provisions of this section.

ADDITIONAL RULES RELATING TO BENEFITS BASED ON DISABILITY

Suspension of Benefits

SEC. 225. [42 U.S.C. 425] (a) If the Commissioner of Social Security, on the basis of information obtained by or submitted to him, believes that an individual entitled to benefits under section 223, or that a child who has attained the age of eighteen and is entitled to benefits under section 202(d), or that a widow or surviving divorced wife who has not attained age 60 and is entitled to benefits under section 202(e), or that a widower or surviving divorced husband who has not attained age 60 and is entitled to benefits under section 202(f), may have ceased to be under a disability, the Commissioner of Social Security may suspend the payment of benefits under such section 202(d), 202(e), 202(f), or 223 until it is determined (as provided in section 221) whether or not such individual's disability has ceased or until the Commissioner of Social Security believes that such disability has not ceased. In the case of any individual whose disability is subject to determination under an agreement with a State under section 221(b), the Commissioner of Social Security shall promptly notify the appropriate State of his action under this subsection and shall request a prompt determination of whether such individual's disability has ceased. For purposes of this subsection, the term "disability" has the meaning assigned to such term in section 223(d). Whenever the benefits of an individual entitled to a disability insurance benefit are suspended for any month, the benefits of any individual entitled thereto under subsection (b), (c), or (d) of section 202, on the basis of the wages and self-employment income of such individual, shall be suspended for such month. The first sentence of this subsection shall not apply to any child entitled to benefits under section 202(d), if he has attained the age of 18 but has not attained the age of 22, for any

232   SOCIAL SECURITY ACT—§ 225(a)(cont)

month during which he is a full-time student (as defined and determined under section 202(d)).

Continued Payments During Rehabilitation Program

(b) Notwithstanding any other provision of this title, payment to an individual of benefits based on disability (as described in the first sentence of subsection (a)) shall not be terminated or suspended because the physical or mental impairment, on which the individual's entitlement to such benefits is based, has or may have ceased, if—

(1) such individual is participating in a program consisting of the Ticket to Work and Self-Sufficiency Program under section 1148 or another program of vocational rehabilitation services, employment services, or other support services approved by the Commissioner of Social Security, and

(2) the Commissioner of Social Security determines that the completion of such program, or its continuation for a specified period of time, will increase the likelihood that such individual may (following his participation in such program) be permanently removed from the disability benefit rolls.

ENTITLEMENT TO HOSPITAL INSURANCE BENEFITS

SEC. 226. [42 U.S.C. 426] (a) Every individual who—

(1) has attained age 65, and

(2)(A) is entitled to monthly insurance benefits under section 202, would be entitled to those benefits except that he has not filed an application therefor (or application has not been made for a benefit the entitlement to which for any individual is a condition of entitlement therefor), or would be entitled to such benefits but for the failure of another individual, who meets all the criteria of entitlement to monthly insurance benefits, to meet such criteria throughout a month, and, in conformity with regulations of the Secretary, files an application for hospital insurance benefits under part A of title XVIII,

(B) is a qualified railroad retirement beneficiary, or

(C)(i) would meet the requirements of subparagraph (A) upon filing application for the monthly insurance benefits involved if medicare qualified government employment (as defined in section 210(p)) were treated as employment (as defined in section 210(a)) for purposes of this title, and (ii) files an application, in conformity with regulations of the Secretary, for hospital insurance benefits under part A of title XVIII,

shall be entitled to hospital insurance benefits under part A of title XVIII for each month for which he meets the condition specified in paragraph (2), beginning with the first month after June 1966 for which he meets the conditions specified in paragraphs (1) and (2).

(b) Every individual who—

(1) has not attained age 65, and

(2)(A) is entitled to, and has for 24 calendar months been entitled to, (i) disability insurance benefits under section 223 or (ii) child's insurance benefits under section 202(d) by reason of a disability (as defined in section 223(d)) or (iii) widow's insurance benefits under section 202(e) or widower's insurance benefits un-

SOCIAL SECURITY ACT—§ 226(b)(2)(C)(ii)(II)   233

der section 202(f) by reason of a disability (as defined in section 223(d)), or

(B) is, and has been for not less than 24 months, a disabled qualified railroad retirement beneficiary, within the meaning of section 7(d) of the Railroad Retirement Act of 1974[271], or

(C)(i) has filed an application, in conformity with regulations of the Secretary, for hospital insurance benefits under part A of title XVIII pursuant to this subparagraph, and

(ii) would meet the requirements of subparagraph (A) (as determined under the disability criteria, including reviews, applied under this title), including the requirement that he has been entitled to the specified benefits for 24 months, if—

(I) medicare qualified government employment (as defined in section 210(p)) were treated as employment (as defined in section 210(a)) for purposes of this title, and

(II) the filing of the application under clause (i) of this subparagraph were deemed to be the filing of an application for the disability-related benefits referred to in clause (i), (ii), or (iii) of subparagraph (A),

shall be entitled to hospital insurance benefits under part A of title XVIII for each month beginning with the later of (I) July 1973 or (II) the twenty-fifth month of his entitlement or status as a qualified railroad retirement beneficiary described in paragraph (2), and ending (subject to the last sentence of this subsection) with the month following the month in which notice of termination of such entitlement to benefits or status as a qualified railroad retirement beneficiary described in paragraph (2) is mailed to him, or if earlier, with the month before the month in which he attains age 65. In applying the previous sentence in the case of an individual described in paragraph (2)(C), the "twenty-fifth month of his entitlement" refers to the first month after the twenty-fourth month of entitlement to specified benefits referred to in paragraph (2)(C) and "notice of termination of such entitlement" refers to a notice that the individual would no longer be determined to be entitled to such specified benefits under the conditions described in that paragraph. For purposes of this subsection, an individual who has had a period of trial work which ended as provided in section 222(c)(4)(A), and whose entitlement to benefits or status as a qualified railroad retirement beneficiary as described in paragraph (2) has subsequently terminated, shall be deemed to be entitled to such benefits or to occupy such status (notwithstanding the termination of such entitlement or status) for the period of consecutive months throughout all of which the physical or mental impairment, on which such entitlement or status was based, continues, and throughout all of which such individual would have been entitled to monthly insurance benefits under title II or as a qualified railroad retirement beneficiary had such individual been unable to engage in substantial gainful activity, but not in excess of 78 such months. In determining when an individual's entitlement or status terminates for purposes of the preceding sentence, the term "36 months" in the second sentence of section 223(a)(1), in section 202(d)(1)(G)(i), in the last sentence of section 202(e)(1), and in the last sentence of section 202(f)(1) shall be applied as though it read "15 months".

---

[271] See Vol. II, P.L. 75-162 [as amended by P.L. 93-445].

234 SOCIAL SECURITY ACT—§ 226(b)(2)(C)(ii)(II)(cont)

(c) For purposes of subsection (a)—

(1) entitlement of an individual to hospital insurance benefits for a month shall consist of entitlement to have payment made under, and subject to the limitations in, part A of title XVIII on his behalf for inpatient hospital services, post-hospital extended care services, and home health services (as such terms are defined in part C[272] of title XVIII) furnished him in the United States (or outside the United States in the case of inpatient hospital services furnished under the conditions described in section 1814(f)) during such month; except that (A) no such payment may be made for post-hospital extended care services furnished before January 1967, and (B) no such payment may be made for post-hospital extended care services unless the discharge from the hospital required to qualify such services for payment under part A of title XVIII occurred (i) after June 30, 1966, or on or after the first day of the month in which he attains age 65, whichever is later, or (ii) if he was entitled to hospital insurance benefits pursuant to subsection (b), at a time when he was so entitled; and

(2) an individual shall be deemed entitled to monthly insurance benefits under section 202 or section 223, or to be a qualified railroad retirement beneficiary, for the month in which he died if he would have been entitled to such benefits, or would have been a qualified railroad retirement beneficiary, for such month had he died in the next month.

(d) For purposes of this section, the term "qualified railroad retirement beneficiary" means an individual whose name has been certified to the Secretary by the Railroad Retirement Board under section 7(d) of the Railroad Retirement Act of 1974[273]. An individual shall cease to be a qualified railroad retirement beneficiary at the close of the month preceding the month which is certified by the Railroad Retirement Board as the month in which he ceased to meet the requirements of section 7(d) of the Railroad Retirement Act of 1974.

(e)(1)(A) For purposes of determining entitlement to hospital insurance benefits under subsection (b) in the case of widows and widowers described in paragraph (2)(A)(iii) thereof—

(i) the term "age 60" in sections 202(e)(1)(B)(ii), 202(e)(4), 202(f)(1)(B)(ii), and 202(f)(4) shall be deemed to read "age 65"; and

(ii) the phrase "before she attained age 60" in the matter following subparagraph (F) of section 202(e)(1) and the phrase "before he attained age 60" in the matter following subparagraph (F) of section 202(f)(1) shall each be deemed to read "based on a disability".

(B) For purposes of subsection (b)(2)(A)(iii), each month in the period commencing with the first month for which an individual is first eligible for supplemental security income benefits under title XVI, or State supplementary payments of the type referred to in section 1616(a) of this Act (or payments of the type described in section 212(a) of Public Law 93-66) which are paid by the Secretary under an agree-

---

[272] P.L. 105-33, §4002(f)(1), provided that any reference to part C of title XVIII is deemed a reference to part D of title XVIII as of August 5, 1997.

P.L. 108-173, §101(e)(1), provides that any reference to part D of title XVIII is deemed a reference to part E of title XVIII.

[273] See Vol. II, P.L. 75-162, §7(d) [as amended by P.L. 93-445].

ment referred to in section 1616(a) (or in section 212(b) of Public Law 93-66), shall be included as one of the 24 months for which such individual must have been entitled to widow's or widower's insurance benefits on the basis of disability in order to become entitled to hospital insurance benefits on that basis.

(2) For purposes of determining entitlement to hospital insurance benefits under subsection (b) in the case of an individual under age 65 who is entitled to benefits under section 202, and who was entitled to widow's insurance benefits or widower's insurance benefits based on disability for the month before the first month in which such individual was so entitled to old-age insurance benefits (but ceased to be entitled to such widow's or widower's insurance benefits upon becoming entitled to such old-age insurance benefits), such individual shall be deemed to have continued to be entitled to such widow's insurance benefits or widower's insurance benefits for and after such first month.

(3) For purposes of determining entitlement to hospital insurance benefits under subsection (b), any disabled widow aged 50 or older who is entitled to mother's insurance benefits (and who would have been entitled to widow's insurance benefits by reason of disability if she had filed for such widow's benefits), and any disabled widower aged 50 or older who is entitled to father's insurance benefits (and who would have been entitled to widower's insurance benefits by reason of disability if he had filed for such widower's benefits), shall, upon application for such hospital insurance benefits be deemed to have filed for such widow's or widower's insurance benefits.

(4) For purposes of determining entitlement to hospital insurance benefits under subsection (b) in the case of an individual described in clause (iii) of subsection (b)(2)(A), the entitlement of such individual to widow's or widower's insurance benefits under section 202(e) or (f) by reason of a disability shall be deemed to be the entitlement to such benefits that would result if such entitlement were determined without regard to the provisions of section 202(j)(4).

(f) For purposes of subsection (b) (and for purposes of section 1837(g)(1) of this Act and section 7(d)(2)(ii) of the Railroad Retirement Act of 1974[274]), the 24 months for which an individual has to have been entitled to specified monthly benefits on the basis of disability in order to become entitled to hospital insurance benefits on such basis effective with any particular month (or to be deemed to have enrolled in the supplementary medical insurance program, on the basis of such entitlement, by reason of section 1837(f)), where such individual had been entitled to specified monthly benefits of the same type during a previous period which terminated—

    (1) more than 60 months before the month in which his current disability began in any case where such monthly benefits were of the type specified in clause (A)(i) or (B) of subsection (b)(2), or

    (2) more than 84 months before the month in which his current disability began in any case where such monthly benefits were of the type specified in clause (A)(ii) or (A)(iii) of such subsection,

shall not include any month which occurred during such previous period, unless the physical or mental impairment which is the basis for disability is the same as (or directly related to) the physical or mental

---

[274] See Vol. II, P.L. 75-162, §7(d)(2)(ii) [as amended by P.L. 93-445].

236 SOCIAL SECURITY ACT—§ 226(f)(2)(cont)

impairment which served as the basis for disability in such previous period.

(g) The Secretary and Director of the Office of Personnel Management shall jointly prescribe and carry out procedures designed to assure that all individuals who perform medicare qualified government employment by virtue of service described in section 210(a)(5) are fully informed with respect to (1) their eligibility or potential eligibility for hospital insurance benefits (based on such employment) under part A of title XVIII, (2) the requirements for and conditions of such eligibility, and (3) the necessity of timely application as a condition of entitlement under subsection (b)(2)(C), giving particular attention to individuals who apply for an annuity under chapter 83 of title 5, United States Code[275], or under another similar Federal retirement program, and whose eligibility for such an annuity is or would be based on a disability.

(h) For purposes of applying this section in the case of an individual medically determined to have amyotrophic lateral sclerosis (ALS), the following special rules apply:

(1) Subsection (b) shall be applied as if there were no requirement for any entitlement to benefits, or status, for a period longer than 1 month.

(2) The entitlement under such subsection shall begin with the first month (rather than twenty-fifth month) of entitlement or status.

(3) Subsection (f) shall not be applied.

(i) For purposes of this section, each person whose monthly insurance benefit for any month is terminated or is otherwise not payable solely by reason of paragraph (1) or (7) of section 225(c) shall be treated as entitled to such benefit for such month.

(j) For entitlement to hospital insurance benefits in the case of certain uninsured individuals, see section 103 of the Social Security Amendments of 1965[276].

SPECIAL PROVISIONS RELATING TO COVERAGE UNDER MEDICARE
PROGRAM FOR END STAGE RENAL DISEASE

SEC. 226A. [42 U.S.C. 426-1] (a) Notwithstanding any provision to the contrary in section 226 or title XVIII, every individual who—

(1)(A) is fully or currently insured (as such terms are defined in section 214), or would be fully or currently insured if (i) his service as an employee (as defined in the Railroad Retirement Act of 1974[277]) after December 31, 1936, were included within the meaning of the term "employment" for purposes of this title, and (ii) his medicare qualified government employment (as defined in section 210(p)) were included within the meaning of the term "employment" for purposes of this title;

(B)(i) is entitled to monthly insurance benefits under this title, (ii) is entitled to an annuity under the Railroad Retirement Act of 1974, or (iii) would be entitled to a monthly insurance benefit under this title if medicare qualified government employment (as

---

[275] See Vol. II, 5 U.S.C. chapter 83.
[276] See Vol. II, P.L. 89-97, §103.
[277] P.L. 75-162 [as amended by P.L. 93-445].

defined in section 210(p)) were included within the meaning of the term "employment" for purposes of this title; or

(C) is the spouse or dependent child (as defined in regulations) of an individual described in subparagraph (A) or (B);

(2) is medically determined to have end stage renal disease; and

(3) has filed an application for benefits under this section;

shall, in accordance with the succeeding provisions of this section, be entitled to benefits under part A and eligible to enroll under part B of title XVIII, subject to the deductible, premium, and coinsurance provisions of that title.

(b) Subject to subsection (c), entitlement of an individual to benefits under part A and eligibility to enroll under part B of title XVIII by reasons of this section on the basis of end stage renal disease—

(1) shall begin with—

(A) the third month after the month in which a regular course of renal dialysis is initiated, or

(B) the month in which such individual receives a kidney transplant, or (if earlier) the first month in which such individual is admitted as an inpatient to an institution which is a hospital meeting the requirements of section 1861(e) (and such additional requirements as the Secretary may prescribe under section 1881(b) for such institutions) in preparation for or anticipation of kidney transplantation, but only if such transplantation occurs in that month or in either of the next two months,

whichever first occurs (but no earlier than one year preceding the month of the filing of an application for benefits under this section); and

(2) shall end, in the case of an individual who receives a kidney transplant, with the thirty-sixth month after the month in which such individual receives such transplant or, in the case of an individual who has not received a kidney transplant and no longer requires a regular course of dialysis, with the twelfth month after the month in which such course of dialysis is terminated.

(c) Notwithstanding the provisions of subsection (b)—

(1) in the case of any individual who participates in a self-care dialysis training program prior to the third month after the month in which such individual initiates a regular course of renal dialysis in a renal dialysis facility or provider of services meeting the requirements of section 1881(b), entitlement to benefits under part A and eligibility to enroll under part B of title XVIII shall begin with the month in which such regular course of renal dialysis is initiated;

(2) in any case in which a kidney transplant fails (whether during or after the thirty-six-month period specified in subsection (b)(2)) and as a result the individual who received such transplant initiates or resumes a regular course of renal dialysis, entitlement to benefits under part A and eligibility to enroll under part B of title XVIII shall begin with the month in which such course is initiated or resumed; and

(3) in any case in which a regular course of renal dialysis is resumed subsequent to the termination of an earlier course, entitlement to benefits under part A and eligibility to enroll under

238 SOCIAL SECURITY ACT—§ 226A(c)(3)(cont)

part B of title XVIII shall begin with the month in which such regular course of renal dialysis is resumed.

(c)[278] For purposes of this section, each person whose monthly insurance benefit for any month is terminated or is otherwise not payable solely by reason of paragraph (1) or (7) of section 225(c) shall be treated as entitled to such benefit for such month.

TRANSITIONAL INSURED STATUS[279]

SEC. 227. [42 U.S.C. 427] (a) In the case of any individual who attains the age of 72 before 1969 but who does not meet the requirements of section 214(a), the 6 quarters of coverage referred to in paragraph (1) of section 214(a) shall, instead, be 3 quarters of coverage for purposes of determining entitlement of such individual to benefits under section 202(a), and of the spouse to benefits under section 202(b) or section 202(c), but, in the case of such spouse, only if he or she attains the age of 72 before 1969 and only with respect to spouse's insurance benefits under section 202(b) or section 202(c) for and after the month in which he or she attains such age. For each month before the month in which any such individual meets the requirements of section 214(a), the amount of the old-age insurance benefit shall, notwithstanding the provisions of section 202(a), be the larger of $64.40 or the amount most recently established in lieu thereof under section 215(i) and the amount of the spouse's insurance benefit of the spouse shall, notwithstanding the provisions of section 202(b) or section 202(c), be the larger of $32.20 or the amount most recently established in lieu thereof under section 215(i).

(b) In the case of any individual who has died, who does not meet the requirements of section 214(a), and whose surviving spouse attains age 72 before 1969, the 6 quarters of coverage referred to in paragraph (3) of section 214(a) and in paragraph (1) thereof shall, for purposes of determining the entitlement to surviving spouse's insurance benefits under section 202(e) or section 202(f), instead be—

(1) 3 quarters of coverage if such surviving spouse attains the age of 72 in or before 1966,

(2) 4 quarters of coverage if such surviving spouse attains the age of 72 in 1967, or

(3) 5 quarters of coverage if such surviving spouse attains the age of 72 in 1968.

The amount of the surviving spouse's insurance benefit for each month shall, notwithstanding the provisions of section 202(e) or section 202(f) (and section 202(m)), be the larger of $64.40 or the amount most recently established in lieu thereof under section 215(i).

(c) In the case of any individual who becomes, or upon filing application therefor would become, entitled to benefits under section 202(a) by reason of the application of subsection (a) of this section, who dies, and whose surviving spouse attains the age of 72 before 1969, such deceased individual shall be deemed to meet the requirements of subsection (b) of this section for purposes of determining entitlement of such surviving spouse to surviving spouse's insurance benefits under section 202(e) or section 202(f).

---

[278] As in original. P.L. 103-296, §201(a)(3)(D)(ii), added a second subsection (c).

[279] See Vol. II, Appendices A and B, Cost-of-Living Increase and Other Determinations, with respect to flat-rate benefits to workers age 72 and not insured under usual requirements.

SOCIAL SECURITY ACT—§ 228(c)(3) 239

BENEFITS AT AGE 72 FOR CERTAIN UNINSURED INDIVIDUALS[280]

Eligibility

SEC. 228. [42 U.S.C. 428] (a) Every individual who—
(1) has attained the age of 72,
(2)(A) attained such age before 1968, or (B) (i) attained such age after 1967 and before 1972, and (ii) has not less than 3 quarters of coverage, whenever acquired, for each calendar year elapsing after 1966 and before the year in which he or she attained such age,
(3) is a resident of the United States (as defined in subsection (e)), and is (A) a citizen of the United States or (B) an alien lawfully admitted for permanent residence who has resided in the United States (as defined in section 210(i)) continuously during the 5 years immediately preceding the month in which he or she files application under this section, and
(4) has filed application for benefits under this section,
shall (subject to the limitations in this section) be entitled to a benefit under this section for each month beginning with the first month after September 1966 in which he or she becomes so entitled to such benefits and ending with the month preceding the month in which he or she dies. No application under this section which is filed by an individual more than 3 months before the first month in which he or she meets the requirements of paragraphs (1), (2), and (3) shall be accepted as an application for purposes of this section.

Benefit Amount

(b) The benefit amount to which an individual is entitled under this section for any month shall be the larger of $64.40 or the amount most recently established in lieu thereof under section 215(i).

Reduction for Governmental Pension System Benefits

(c)(1) The benefit amount of any individual under this section for any month shall be reduced (but not below zero) by the amount of any periodic benefit under a governmental pension system for which he or she is eligible for such month.
(2) In the case of a husband and wife only one of whom is entitled to benefits under this section for any month, the benefit amount, after any reduction under paragraph (1), shall be further reduced (but not below zero) by the excess (if any) of (A) the total amount of any periodic benefits under governmental pension systems for which the spouse who is not entitled to benefits under this section is eligible for such month, over (B) the benefit amount as determined without regard to this subsection.
(3) In the case of a husband or wife both of whom are entitled to benefits under this section for any month, the benefit amount of each spouse, after any reduction under paragraph (1), shall be further

---

[280] See Vol. II, Appendices A and B, Cost-of-Living Increase and Other Determinations, with respect to flat-rate benefits at age 72 for certain uninsured persons.
See Vol. II, P.L. 98-21, §305(e), with respect to changes in payment amounts under this section.

240 SOCIAL SECURITY ACT—§ 228(c)(3)(cont)

reduced (but not below zero) by the excess (if any) of (A) the total amount of any periodic benefits under governmental pension systems for which the other spouse is eligible for such month, over (B) the benefit amount of such other spouse as determined without regard to this subsection.

(4) For purposes of this subsection, in determining whether an individual is eligible for periodic benefits under a governmental pension system—

(A) such individual shall be deemed to have filed application for such benefits,

(B) to the extent that entitlement depends on an application by such individual's spouse, such spouse shall be deemed to have filed application, and

(C) to the extent that entitlement depends on such individual or his or her spouse having retired, such individual and his or her spouse shall be deemed to have retired before the month for which the determination of eligibility is being made.

(5) For purposes of this subsection, if any periodic benefit is payable on any basis other than a calendar month, the Commissioner of Social Security shall allocate the amount of such benefit to the appropriate calendar months.

(6) If, under the foregoing provisions of this section, the amount payable for any month would be less than $1, such amount shall be reduced to zero. In the case of a husband and wife both of whom are entitled to benefits under this section for the month, the preceding sentence shall be applied with respect to the aggregate amount so payable for such month.

(7) If any benefit amount computed under the foregoing provisions of this section is not a multiple of $0.10, it shall be raised to the next higher multiple of $0.10.

(8) Under regulations prescribed by the Commissioner of Social Security, benefit payments under this section to an individual (or aggregate benefit payments under this section in the case of a husband and wife) of less than $5 may be accumulated until they equal or exceed $5.

Suspension for Months in Which Cash Payments Are Made Under Public Assistance

(d) The benefit to which any individual is entitled under this section for any month shall not be paid for such month if—

(1) such individual receives aid or assistance in the form of money payments in such month under a State plan approved under title I, X, XIV, or XVI, or under a State program funded under part A of title IV, or

(2) such individual's husband or wife receives such aid or assistance in such month, and under the State plan the needs of such individual were taken into account in determining eligibility for (or amount of) such aid or assistance,

unless the State agency administering or supervising the administration of such plan notifies the Commissioner of Social Security, at such time and in such manner as may be prescribed in accordance with regulations of the Commissioner of Social Security, that such payments

SOCIAL SECURITY ACT—§ 228(h) 241

to such individual (or such individual's husband or wife) under such plan are being terminated with the payment or payments made in such month and such individual is not an individual with respect to whom supplemental security income benefits are payable pursuant to title XVI or section 211 of Public Law 93-66[281] for the following month, nor shall such benefit be paid for such month if such individual is an individual with respect to whom supplemental security income benefits are payable pursuant to title XVI or section 211 of Public Law 93-66 for such month, unless the Commissioner of Social Security determines that such benefits are not payable with respect to such individual for the month following such month.

Suspension Where Individual Is Residing Outside the United States

(e) The benefit to which any individual is entitled under this section for any month shall not be paid if, during such month, such individual is not a resident of the United States. For purposes of this subsection, the term "United States" means the 50 States and the District of Columbia.

Treatment as Monthly Insurance Benefits

(f) For purposes of subsections (t) and (u) of section 202, and of section 1840, a monthly benefit under this section shall be treated as a monthly insurance benefit payable under section 202.

Annual Reimbursement of Federal Old-Age and Survivors Insurance Trust Fund

(g) There are authorized to be appropriated to the Federal Old-Age and Survivors Insurance Trust Fund for the fiscal year ending June 30, 1969, and for each fiscal year thereafter, such sums as the Commissioner of Social Security deems necessary on account of—
> (1) payments made under this section during the second preceding fiscal year and all fiscal years prior thereto to individuals who, as of the beginning of the calendar year in which falls the month for which payment was made, had less than 3 quarters of coverage,
> (2) the additional administrative expenses resulting from the payments described in paragraph (1), and
> (3) any loss in interest to such Trust Fund resulting from such payments and expenses,

in order to place such Trust Fund in the same position at the end of such fiscal year as it would have been in if such payments had not been made.

Definitions

(h) For purposes of this section—

---

[281] See Vol. II, P.L. 93-66, §211.

242   SOCIAL SECURITY ACT—§ 228(h)(1)

(1) The term "quarter of coverage" includes a quarter of coverage as defined in section 5(l) of the Railroad Retirement Act of 1937[282].

(2) The term "governmental pension system" means the insurance system established by this title or any other system or fund established by the United States, a State, any political subdivision of a State, or any wholly owned instrumentality of any one or more of the foregoing which provides for payment of (A) pensions, (B) retirement or retired pay, or (C) annuities or similar amounts payable on account of personal services performed by any individual (not including any payment under any workmen's compensation law or any payment by the Secretary of Veterans Affairs as compensation for service-connected disability or death).

(3) The term "periodic benefit" includes a benefit payable in a lump sum if it is a commutation of, or a substitute for, periodic payments.

(4) The determination of whether an individual is a husband or wife for any month shall be made under subsection (h) of section 216 without regard to subsections (b) and (f) of section 216.

BENEFITS IN CASE OF MEMBERS OF THE UNIFORMED SERVICES[283]

SEC. 229. [42 U.S.C. 429] For purposes of determining entitlement to and the amount of any monthly benefit for any month after December 1972, or entitlement to and the amount of any lump-sum death payment in case of a death after such month, payable under this title on the basis of the wages and self-employment income of any individual, and for purposes of section 216(i)(3), such individual, if he was paid wages for service as a member of a uniformed service (as defined in section 210(m)) which was included in the term "employment" as defined in section 210(a) as a result of the provisions of section 210(l)(1)(A), shall be deemed to have been paid—

(1) in each calendar quarter occurring after 1956 and before 1978 in which he was paid such wages, additional wages of $300, and

(2) in each calendar year occurring after 1977 and before 2002 in which he was paid such wages, additional wages of $100 for each $300 of such wages, up to a maximum of $1,200 of additional wages for any calendar year.

ADJUSTMENT OF THE CONTRIBUTION AND BENEFIT BASE

SEC. 230. [42 U.S.C. 430] (a) Whenever the Commissioner of Social Security pursuant to section 215(i) increases benefits effective with the December following a cost-of-living computation quarter, the Commissioner shall also determine and publish in the Federal Register on or before November 1 of the calendar year in which such quarter occurs the contribution and benefit base determined under subsection (b) or (c) which shall be effective with respect to remuneration paid after the calendar year in which such quarter occurs and taxable years beginning after such year.

---

[282] P.L. 75-162. P.L. 93-445, §101, amended the Railroad Retirement Act of 1937 in its entirety, effective January 1, 1975. See Vol. II, P.L. 75-162, §2, instead.

[283] See Vol. II, 38 U.S.C. 5303A.

SOCIAL SECURITY ACT—§ 230(d)   243

(b) The amount of such contribution and benefit base shall (subject to subsection (c)) be the amount of the contribution and benefit base in effect in the year in which the determination is made or, if larger, the product of—

(1) $60,600, and

(2) the ratio of (A) the national average wage index (as defined in section 209(k)(1)) for the calendar year before the calendar year in which the determination under subsection (a) is made to (B) the national average wage index (as so defined) for 1992,

with such product, if not a multiple of $300, being rounded to the next higher multiple of $300 where such product is a multiple of $150 but not of $300 and to the nearest multiple of $300 in any other case.

(c) For purposes of this section, and for purposes of determining wages and self-employment income under sections 209, 211, 213, and 215 of this Act and sections 1402, 3121, 3122, 3125, 6413, and 6654 of the Internal Revenue Code of 1986[284], (1) the "contribution and benefit base" with respect to remuneration paid in (and taxable years beginning in) any calendar year after 1973 and prior to the calendar year with the June of which the first increase in benefits pursuant to section 215(i) of this Act becomes effective shall be $13,200 or (if applicable) such other amount as may be specified in a law enacted subsequent to the law which added this section, and (2) the "contribution and benefit base" with respect to remuneration paid (and taxable years beginning)—

(A) in 1978 shall be $17,700,

(B) in 1979 shall be $22,900,

(C) in 1980 shall be $25,900, and

(D) in 1981 shall be $29,700.

For purposes of determining under subsection (b) the "contribution and benefit base" with respect to remuneration paid (and taxable years beginning) in 1982 and subsequent years, the dollar amounts specified in clause (2) of the preceding sentence shall be considered to have resulted from the application of such subsection (b) and to be the amount determined (with respect to the years involved) under that subsection.

(d) Notwithstanding any other provision of law, the contribution and benefit base determined under this section for any calendar year after 1976 for purposes of section 4022(b)(3)(B) of Public Law 93-406[285], with respect to any plan, shall be the contribution and benefit base that would have been determined for such year if this section as in effect immediately prior to the enactment of the Social Security Amendments of 1977[286] had remained in effect without change (except that, for purposes of subsection (b) of such section 230 as so in effect, the reference to the contribution and benefit base in paragraph (1) of such subsection (b) shall be deemed a reference to an amount equal to $45,000, each reference in paragraph (2) of such subsection (b) to the average of the wages of all employees as reported to the Secretary of Treasury shall be deemed a reference to the national average wage index (as defined in section 209(k)(1)), the reference to a preceding calendar year in paragraph (2)(A) of such

---

[284] See Vol. II, P.L. 83-591, §§1402, 3121, 3122, 3125, 6413, and 6654.

[285] See Vol. II, P.L. 93-406, §4022(b)(3)(B).

[286] December 20, 1977 [P.L. 95-216, 91 Stat. 1509].

244 SOCIAL SECURITY ACT—§ 230(d)(cont)

subsection (b) shall be deemed a reference to the calendar year before the calendar year in which the determination under subsection (a) of such section 230 is made, and the reference to a calendar year in paragraph (2)(B) of such subsection (b) shall be deemed a reference to 1992).

BENEFITS IN CASE OF CERTAIN INDIVIDUALS INTERNED DURING WORLD WAR II

SEC. 231. [42 U.S.C. 431] (a) For the purposes of this section the term "internee" means an individual who was interned during any period of time from December 7, 1941, through December 31,1946, at a place within the United States operated by the Government of the United States for the internment of United States citizens of Japanese ancestry.

(b)(1) For purposes of determining entitlement to and the amount of any monthly benefit for any month after December 1972, or entitlement to and the amount of any lump-sum death payment in the case of a death after such month, payable under this title on the basis of the wages and self-employment income of any individual, and for purposes of section 216(i)(3), such individual shall be deemed to have been paid during any period after he attained age 18 and for which he was an internee, wages (in addition to any wages actually paid to him) at a weekly rate of basic pay during such period as follows—

(A) in the case such individual was not employed prior to the beginning of such period, 40 multiplied by the minimum hourly rate or rates in effect at any such time under section 206(a)(1) of title 29, United States Code, for each full week during such period; and

(B) in the case such individual who was employed prior to the beginning of such period, 40 multiplied by the greater of (i) the highest hourly rate received during any such employment, or (ii) the minimum hourly rate or rates in effect at any such time under section 206(a)(1) of title 29, United States Code[287], for each full week during such period.

(2) This subsection shall not be applicable in the case of any monthly benefit or lump-sum death payment if—

(A) a larger such benefit or payment, as the case may be, would be payable without its application; or

(B) a benefit (other than a benefit payable in a lump-sum unless it is a commutation of, or a substitute for, periodic payments) which is based, in whole or in part, upon internment during any period from December 7, 1941, through December 31, 1946, at a place within the United States operated by the Government of the United States for the internment of United States citizens of Japanese ancestry, is determined by any agency or wholly owned instrumentality of the United States to be payable by it under any other law of the United States or under a system established by such agency or instrumentality.

The provisions of clause (B) shall not apply in the case of any monthly benefit or lump-sum death payment under this title if its application would reduce by $0.50 or less the primary insurance amount (as computed under section 215 prior to any recomputation thereof pursuant

---

[287] See Vol. II, 29 U.S.C. 206(a)(1).

SOCIAL SECURITY ACT—§ 232 245

to subsection (f) of such section) of the individual on whose wages and self-employment income such benefit or payment is based. The provisions of clause (B) shall also not apply for purposes of section 216(i)(3).

(3) Upon application for benefits, a recalculation of benefits (by reason of this section), or a lump-sum death payment on the basis of the wages and self-employment income of any individual who was an internee, the Commissioner of Social Security shall accept the certification of the Secretary of Defense or his designee concerning any period of time for which an internee is to receive credit under paragraph (1) and shall make a decision without regard to clause (B) of paragraph (2) of this subsection unless the Commissioner has been notified by some other agency or instrumentality of the United States that, on the basis of the period for which such individual was an internee, a benefit described in clause (B) of paragraph (2) has been determined by such agency or instrumentality to be payable by it. If the Commissioner of Social Security has not been so notified, the Commissioner shall then ascertain whether some other agency or wholly owned instrumentality of the United States has decided that a benefit described in clause (B) of paragraph (2) is payable by it. If any such agency or instrumentality has decided, or thereafter decides, that such a benefit is payable by it, it shall so notify the Commissioner of Social Security, and the Commissioner of Social Security shall certify no further benefits for payment or shall recompute the amount of any further benefits payable, as may be required by this section.

(4) Any agency or wholly owned instrumentality of the United States which is authorized by any law of the United States to pay benefits, or has a system of benefits which are based, in whole or in part, on any period for which any individual was an internee shall, at the request of the Commissioner of Social Security, certify to the Commissioner, with respect to any individual who was an internee, such information as the Commissioner of Social Security deems necessary to carry out the Commissioner's functions under paragraph (3) of this subsection.

(c) There are authorized to be appropriated to the Trust Funds and the Federal Hospital Insurance Trust Fund for the fiscal year ending June 30, 1978, such sums as the Commissioner of Social Security and the Secretary jointly determine would place the Trust Funds and the Federal Hospital Insurance Trust Fund in the position in which they would have been if the preceding provisions of this section had not been enacted.

PROCESSING OF TAX DATA[288]

Sec. 232. [42 U.S.C. 432] The Secretary of the Treasury shall make available information returns filed pursuant to part III of subchapter A of chapter 61 of subtitle F of the Internal Revenue Code of 1954, to the Commissioner of Social Security for the purposes of this title and title XI. The Commissioner of Social Security and the Secretary of the Treasury are authorized to enter into an agreement for the processing by the Commissioner of Social Security of information contained in re-

---

[288] See Vol. II, P.L. 83-591, §6103(l), with respect to disclosure of returns and return information by the Secretary of the Treasury to the Social Security Administration, and §7213(a)(1) with respect to the penalty for unauthorized disclosure of that tax return information.

See Vol. II, P.L. 88-525, §11(e)(19), with respect to requesting and exchanging information for purposes of verifying income and eligibility for supplemental nutrition assistance.

246 SOCIAL SECURITY ACT—§ 232(cont)

turns filed pursuant to part III of subchapter A of chapter 61 of subtitle F of the Internal Revenue Code of 1986. Notwithstanding the provisions of section 6103(a) of the Internal Revenue Code of 1986[289], the Secretary of the Treasury shall make available to the Commissioner of Social Security such documents as may be agreed upon as being necessary for purposes of such processing. The Commissioner of Social Security shall process any withholding tax statements or other documents made available to the Commissioner by the Secretary of the Treasury pursuant to this section. Any agreement made pursuant to this section shall remain in full force and effect until modified or otherwise changed by mutual agreement of the Commissioner of Social Security and the Secretary of the Treasury.

INTERNATIONAL AGREEMENTS

Purpose of Agreement

SEC. 233. [42 U.S.C. 433] (a) The President is authorized (subject to the succeeding provisions of this section) to enter into agreements establishing totalization arrangements between the social security system established by this title and the social security system of any foreign country, for the purposes of establishing entitlement to and the amount of old-age, survivors, disability, or derivative benefits based on a combination of an individual's periods of coverage under the social security system established by this title and the social security system of such foreign country.

Definitions

(b) For the purposes of this section—
(1) the term "social security system" means, with respect to a foreign country, a social insurance or pension system which is of general application in the country and under which periodic benefits, or the actuarial equivalent thereof, are paid on account of old age, death, or disability; and
(2) the term "period of coverage" means a period of payment of contributions or a period of earnings based on wages for employment or on self-employment income, or any similar period recognized as equivalent thereto under this title or under the social security system of a country which is a party to an agreement entered into under this section.

Crediting Periods of Coverage; Conditions of Payment of Benefits

(c)(1) Any agreement establishing a totalization arrangement pursuant to this section shall provide—
(A) that in the case of an individual who has at least 6 quarters of coverage as defined in section 213 of this Act and periods of coverage under the social security system of a foreign country which is a party to such agreement, periods of coverage of such individual under such social security system of such foreign country may be combined with periods of coverage under this title and

---

[289] See Vol. II, P.L. 83-591, §6103(a).

otherwise considered for the purposes of establishing entitlement to and the amount of old-age, survivors, and disability insurance benefits under this title;

(B)(i) that employment or self-employment, or any service which is recognized as equivalent to employment or self-employment under this title or the social security system of a foreign country which is a party to such agreement, shall, on or after the effective date of such agreement, result in a period of coverage under the system established under this title or under the system established under the laws of such foreign country, but not under both, and (ii) the methods and conditions for determining under which system employment, self-employment, or other service shall result in a period of coverage; and

(C) that where an individual's periods of coverage are combined, the benefit amount payable under this title shall be based on the proportion of such individual's periods of coverage which was completed under this title.

(2) Any such agreement may provide that an individual who is entitled to cash benefits under this title shall, notwithstanding the provisions of section 202(t), receive such benefits while he resides in a foreign country which is a party to such agreement.

(3) Section 226 shall not apply in the case of any individual to whom it would not be applicable but for this section or any agreement or regulation under this section.

(4) Any such agreement may contain other provisions which are not inconsistent with the other provisions of this title and which the President deems appropriate to carry out the purposes of this section.

Regulations

(d) The Commissioner of Social Security shall make rules and regulations and establish procedures which are reasonable and necessary to implement and administer any agreement which has been entered into in accordance with this section.

Reports to Congress; Effective Date of Agreements

(e)(1) Any agreement to establish a totalization arrangement entered into pursuant to this section shall be transmitted by the President to the Congress together with a report on the estimated number of individuals who will be affected by the agreement and the effect of the agreement on the estimated income and expenditures of the programs established by this Act.

(2) Such an agreement shall become effective on any date, provided in the agreement, which occurs after the expiration of the period (following the date on which the agreement is transmitted in accordance with paragraph (1)) during which at least one House of the Congress has been in session on each of 60 days; except that such agreement shall not become effective if, during such period, either House of the Congress adopts a resolution of disapproval of the agreement.

248   SOCIAL SECURITY ACT—§ 233(e)(2)(cont)

DEMONSTRATION PROJECT AUTHORITY[290]

SEC. 234. [42 U.S.C. 434] (a) AUTHORITY.—

(1) IN GENERAL.—The Commissioner of Social Security (in this section referred to as the "Commissioner") shall develop and carry out experiments and demonstration projects designed to determine the relative advantages and disadvantages of—

(A) various alternative methods of treating the work activity of individuals entitled to disability insurance benefits under section 223 or to monthly insurance benefits under section 202 based on such individual's disability (as defined in section 223(d)), including such methods as a reduction in benefits based on earnings, designed to encourage the return to work of such individuals;

(B) altering other limitations and conditions applicable to such individuals (including lengthening the trial work period (as defined in section 222(c)), altering the 24-month waiting period for hospital insurance benefits under section 226, altering the manner in which the program under this title is administered, earlier referral of such individuals for rehabilitation, and greater use of employers and others to develop, perform, and otherwise stimulate new forms of rehabilitation); and

(C) implementing sliding scale benefit offsets using variations in—

(i) the amount of the offset as a proportion of earned income;

(ii) the duration of the offset period; and

(iii) the method of determining the amount of income earned by such individuals, to the end that savings will accrue to the Trust Funds, or to otherwise promote the objectives or facilitate the administration of this title.

(2) AUTHORITY FOR EXPANSION OF SCOPE.—The Commissioner may expand the scope of any such experiment or demonstration project to include any group of applicants for benefits under the program established under this title with impairments that reasonably may be presumed to be disabling for purposes of such demonstration project, and may limit any such demonstration project to any such group of applicants, subject to the terms of such demonstration project which shall define the extent of any such presumption.

(b) REQUIREMENTS.—The experiments and demonstration projects developed under subsection (a) shall be of sufficient scope and shall be carried out on a wide enough scale to permit a thorough evaluation of the alternative methods under consideration while giving assurance that the results derived from the experiments and projects will obtain generally in the operation of the disability insurance program under this title without committing such program to the adoption of any particular system either locally or nationally.

---

[290] See Vol. II, P.L. 106-170, §302(c), with respect to expansion of waiver authority available in connection with demonstration projects providing for reductions in disability insurance benefits based on earnings and §302(f), with respect to funding of such demonstration projects.

SOCIAL SECURITY ACT—§ 234(d)(2)   249

(c) AUTHORITY TO WAIVE COMPLIANCE WITH BENEFITS REQUIREMENTS.—In the case of any experiment or demonstration project initiated under subsection (a) on or before December 17, 2005, the Commissioner may waive compliance with the benefit requirements of this title and the requirements of section 1148 as they relate to the program established under this title, and the Secretary may (upon the request of the Commissioner) waive compliance with the benefits requirements of title XVIII, insofar as is necessary for a thorough evaluation of the alternative methods under consideration. No such experiment or project shall be actually placed in operation unless at least 90 days prior thereto a written report, prepared for purposes of notification and information only and containing a full and complete description thereof, has been transmitted by the Commissioner to the Committee on Ways and Means of the House of Representatives and to the Committee on Finance of the Senate. Periodic reports on the progress of such experiments and demonstration projects shall be submitted by the Commissioner to such committees. When appropriate, such reports shall include detailed recommendations for changes in administration or law, or both, to carry out the objectives stated in subsection (a).

(d) REPORTS.—

(1) INTERIM REPORTS.—On or before June 9 of each year, the Commissioner shall submit to the Committee on Ways and Means of the House of Representatives and to the Committee on Finance of the Senate an annual interim report on the progress of the experiments and demonstration projects carried out under this subsection together with any related data and materials that the Commissioner may consider appropriate.

(2) TERMINATION AND FINAL REPORT.—The authority to initiate projects under the preceding provisions of this section shall terminate on December 18, 2005. Not later than 90 days after the termination of any experiment or demonstration project carried out under this section, the Commissioner shall submit to the Committee on Ways and Means of the House of Representatives and to the Committee on Finance of the Senate a final report with respect to that experiment or demonstration project.

TITLE III—GRANTS TO STATES FOR UNEMPLOYMENT COMPENSATION ADMINISTRATION[1]

TABLE OF CONTENTS OF TITLE[2]

		Page
Sec. 301.	Appropriations	251
Sec. 302.	Payments to States	251
Sec. 303.	Provisions of State laws	252
Sec. 304.	Judicial review	262

APPROPRIATIONS

SEC. 301. [42 U.S.C. 501] The amounts made available pursuant to section 901(c)(1)(A) for the purpose of assisting the States in the administration of their unemployment compensation laws shall be used as hereinafter provided.

PAYMENTS TO STATES

SEC. 302. [42 U.S.C. 502] (a) The Secretary of Labor shall from time to time certify to the Secretary of the Treasury for payment to each State which has an unemployment compensation law approved by the Secretary of Labor under the Federal Unemployment Tax Act[3], such amounts as the Secretary of Labor determines to be necessary for the proper and efficient administration of such law during the fiscal year for which such payment is to be made, including 100 percent of so much of the reasonable expenditures of the State as are attributable to the costs of the implementation and operation of the immigration status verification system described in section 1137(d). The Secretary of Labor's determination shall be based on (1) the population of the State; (2) an estimate of the number of persons covered by the State law and of the cost of proper and efficient administration of such law; and (3) such other factors as the Secretary of Labor finds relevant. The Secretary of Labor shall not certify for payment under this section in any fiscal year a total amount in excess of the amount appropriated therefor for such fiscal year.

(b) Out of the sums appropriated therefor, the Secretary of the Treasury shall, upon receiving a certification under subsection (a),

---

[1] The President's Reorganization Plan No. 2 of 1949, §1 (14 FR 5225, 63 Stat. 1065), transferred the Bureau of Employment Security, including the United States Employment Service, from the Federal Security Agency to the Department of Labor, effective August 20, 1949.

Title III of the Social Security Act is administered by the Department of Labor.

Title III appears in the United States Code as §§501-504 of subchapter III, chapter 7, Title 42.

Regulations of the Secretary of Labor relating to Title III are contained in chapter V, Title 20, and subtitle A, Title 29, Code of Federal Regulations. Regulations of the Secretary of Health and Human Services relating to Title III are contained in subtitle A, Title 45, Code of Federal Regulations.

See Vol. II, P.L. 88-352, §601, for prohibition against discrimination in Federally assisted programs.

See Vol. II, P.L. 97-248, §604(c), with respect to an appropriation of funds to assist States in meeting administrative costs.

See Vol. II, P.L. 100-628, §904(c)(2) and (3), with respect to access to State employment records.

See Vol. II, P.L. 109-91, §202, with respect to flexibility in unemployment compensation administration to address Hurricane Katrina and §203, with respect to any necessary operating instructions and regulations.

[2] This table of contents does not appear in the law.

[3] The "Federal Unemployment Tax Act" is in §§3301-3311 of P.L. 83-591.

See Vol. II, P.L. 83-591, §§3301-3311.

252   SOCIAL SECURITY ACT—§ 302(b)(cont)

pay, through the Fiscal Service of the Department of the Treasury and prior to audit or settlement by the General Accounting Office[4], to the State agency charged with the administration of such law the amount so certified.

(c) No portion of the cost of mailing a statement under section 6050B(b) of the Internal Revenue Code of 1986[5] (relating to unemployment compensation) shall be treated as not being a cost for the proper and efficient administration of the State unemployment compensation law by reason of including with such statement information about the earned income credit provided by section 32 of the Internal Revenue Code of 1986[6]. The preceding sentence shall not apply if the inclusion of such information increases the postage required to mail such statement.

PROVISIONS OF STATE LAWS

SEC. 303. [42 U.S.C. 503] (a) The Secretary of Labor shall make no certification for payment to any State unless he finds that the law of such State, approved by the Secretary of Labor under the Federal Unemployment Tax Act[7], includes provision for—

(1) Such methods of administration (including after January 1, 1940, methods relating to the establishment and maintenance of personnel standards on a merit basis, except that the Secretary of Labor shall exercise no authority with respect to the selection, tenure of office, and compensation of any individual employed in accordance with such methods) as are found by the Secretary of Labor to be reasonably calculated to insure full payment of unemployment compensation when due[8]; and

(2) Payment of unemployment compensation solely through public employment offices or such other agencies as the Secretary of Labor may approve; and

(3) Opportunity for a fair hearing, before an impartial tribunal, for all individuals whose claims for unemployment compensation are denied; and

(4) The payment of all money received in the unemployment fund of such State (except for refunds of sums erroneously paid into such fund and except for refunds paid in accordance with the provisions of section 3305(b) of the Federal Unemployment Tax Act), immediately upon such receipt, to the Secretary of the Treasury to the credit of the unemployment trust fund established by section 904; and

(5) Expenditure of all money withdrawn from an unemployment fund of such State, in the payment of unemployment compensation, exclusive of expenses of administration, and for refunds of sums erroneously paid into such fund and refunds paid in accordance with the provisions of section 3305(b) of the Fed-

---

[4] P.L. 108-271, §8(b), provided that "Any reference to the General Accounting Office in any law, rule, regulation, certificate, directive, instruction, or other official paper in force on the date of enactment to this Act [July 7, 2004] shall be considered to refer and apply to the Government Accountability Office."

[5] See Vol. II, P.L. 83-591, §6050B(b).

[6] See Vol. II, P.L. 83-591, §32.

[7] See Vol. II, P.L. 83-591, §§3301-3311.

[8] P.L. 91-648, §208(a)(2)(B), transferred to the U.S. Civil Service Commission, effective March 6, 1971, all functions, powers, and duties of the Secretary of Labor under paragraph (1).

SOCIAL SECURITY ACT—§ 303(a)(10)(A) 253

eral Unemployment Tax Act[9]: *Provided,*That an amount equal to the amount of employee payments in to the unemployment fund of a State may be used in the payment of cash benefits to individuals with respect to their disability, exclusive of expenses of administration: *Provided further,* That the amounts 903(c)(2) or 903(d)(4) may, subject to the conditions prescribed in such section, be used for expenses incurred by the State for administration of its unemployment compensation law and public employment offices: *Provided further,* That nothing in this paragraph shall be construed to prohibit deducting an amount from unemployment compensation otherwise payable to an individual and using the amount so deducted to pay for health insurance, or the withholding of Federal, State, or local individual income tax, if the individual elected to have such deduction made and such deduction was made under a program approved by the Secretary of Labor: *Provided further,* That amounts may be deducted from unemployment benefits and used to repay overpayments as provided in subsection (g): *Provided further,* That amounts may be withdrawn for the payment of short-time compensation under a plan approved by the Secretary of Labor: *Provided further,* That amounts may be withdrawn for the payment of allowances under a self-employment assistance program (as defined in section 3306(t) of the Internal Revenue Code of 1986[10]); and

(6) The making of such reports, in such form and containing such information, as the Secretary of Labor may from time to time require, and compliance with such provisions as the Secretary of Labor may from time to time find necessary to assure the correctness and verification of such reports; and

(7) Making available upon request to any agency of the United States charged with the administration of public works or assistance through public employment, the name, address, ordinary occupation and employment status of each recipient of unemployment compensation, and a statement of such recipient's rights to further compensation under such law; and

(8) Effective July 1, 1941, the expenditure of all moneys received pursuant to section 302 of this title solely for the purposes and in the amounts found necessary by the Secretary of Labor for the proper and efficient administration of such State law; and

(9) Effective July 1, 1941, the replacement, within a reasonable time, of any moneys received pursuant to section 302 of this title, which, because of any action or contingency, have been lost or have been expended for purposes other than, or in amounts in excess of, those found necessary by the Secretary of Labor for the proper administration of such State law; and

(10) A requirement that, as a condition of eligibility for regular compensation for any week, any claimant who has been referred to reemployment services pursuant to the profiling system under subsection (j)(1)(B) participate in such services or in similar services unless the State agency charged with the administration of the State law determines—

(A) such claimant has completed such services; or

---

[9] See Vol. II, P.L. 83-591, §3305(b).
[10] See Vol. II, P.L. 83-591, §3306(t).

254 SOCIAL SECURITY ACT—§ 303(a)(10)(B)

(B) there is justifiable cause for such claimant's failure to participate in such services.

(b) Whenever the Secretary of Labor, after reasonable notice and opportunity for hearing to the State agency charged with the administration of the State law, finds that in the administration of the law there is—

(1) a denial, in a substantial number of cases, of unemployment compensation to individuals entitled thereto under such law; or

(2) a failure to comply substantially with any provision specified in subsection (a);

the Secretary of Labor shall notify such State agency that further payments will not be made to the State until the Secretary of Labor is satisfied that there is no longer any such denial or failure to comply. Until he is so satisfied he shall make no further certification to the Secretary of the Treasury with respect to such State: *Provided,* That there shall be no finding under clause (1) until the question of entitlement shall have been decided by the highest judicial authority given jurisdiction under such State law: *Provided further,* That any costs may be paid with respect to any claimant by a State and included as costs of administration of its law.

(c) The Secretary of Labor shall make no certification for payment to any State if he finds, after reasonable notice and opportunity for hearing to the State agency charged with the administration of the State law—

(1) that such State does not make its records available to the Railroad Retirement Board, and furnish to the Railroad Retirement Board at the expense of the Railroad Retirement Board such copies thereof as the Railroad Retirement Board deems necessary for its purposes;

(2) that such State is failing to afford reasonable cooperation with every agency of the United States charged with the administration of any unemployment insurance law; or

(3) that any interest required to be paid on advances under title XII of this Act has not been paid by the date on which such interest is required to be paid or has been paid directly or indirectly (by an equivalent reduction in State unemployment taxes or otherwise) by such State from amounts in such State's unemployment fund, until such interest is properly paid.

(d)(1) The State agency charged with the administration of the State law—

(A) shall disclose, upon request and on a reimbursable basis, to officers and employees of the Department of Agriculture and to officers or employees of any State supplemental nutrition assistance program benefits[11] agency any of the following information contained in the records of such State agency—

(i) wage information,

(ii) whether an individual is receiving, has received, or has made application for, unemployment compensation, and the

---

[11] P.L. 110-246, §4002(b)(1)(D), struck out "food stamp" and substituted "supplemental nutrition assistance program benefits", effective October 1, 2008.

P.L. 110-234, §4002(b)(1)(D), which made the same amendment was repealed, effective May 22, 2008 pursuant to P.L. 110-246, §4(a).

SOCIAL SECURITY ACT—§ 303(d)(2)(B)(iii)(I)   255

amount of any such compensation being received (or to be received) by such individual,

(iii) the current (or most recent) home address of such individual, and

(iv) whether an individual has refused an offer of employment and, if so, a description of the employment so offered and the terms, conditions, and rate of pay therefor, and

(B) shall establish such safeguards as are necessary (as determined by the Secretary of Labor in regulations) to insure that information disclosed under subparagraph (A) is used only for purposes of determining an individual's eligibility for benefits, or the amount of benefits, under the supplemental nutrition assistance program[12] established under the Food and Nutrition Act of 2008[13].

(2)(A) For purposes of this paragraph, the term "unemployment compensation" means any unemployment compensation payable under the State law (including amounts payable pursuant to an agreement under a Federal unemployment compensation law).

(B) The State agency charged with the administration of the State law—

(i) may require each new applicant for unemployment compensation to disclose whether the applicant owes an uncollected overissuance (as defined in section 13(c)(1) of the Food and Nutrition Act of 2008[14]) of supplemental nutrition assistance program benefits[15],

(ii) may notify the State supplemental nutrition assistance program benefits[16] agency to which the uncollected overissuance is owed that the applicant has been determined to be eligible for unemployment compensation if the applicant discloses under clause (i) that the applicant owes an uncollected overissuance and the applicant is determined to be so eligible,

(iii) may deduct and withhold from any unemployment compensation otherwise payable to an individual—

(I) the amount specified by the individual to the State agency to be deducted and withheld under this clause,

---

[12] P.L. 110-246, §4002(b)(1)(A), struck out "food stamp program" and substituted "supplemental nutrition assistance program", effective October 1, 2008.

P.L. 110-234, §4002(b)(1)(A), which made the same amendment was repealed, effective May 22, 2008 pursuant to P.L. 110-246, §4(a).

[13] P.L. 110-246, §4002(b)(1)(B), struck out "Food Stamp Act" and substituted "Food and Nutrition Act of 2008", effective October 1, 2008.

P.L. 110-234, §4002(b)(1)(B), which made the same amendment was repealed, effective May 22, 2008 pursuant to P.L. 110-246, §4(a).

[14] P.L. 110-246, §4002(b)(1)(B), struck out "Food Stamp Act" and substituted "Food and Nutrition Act of 2008", effective October 1, 2008.

P.L. 110-234, §4002(b)(1)(B), which made the same amendment was repealed, effective May 22, 2008 pursuant to P.L. 110-246, §4(a).

[15] P.L. 110-246, §4002(b)(1)(D), struck out "food stamp" and substituted "supplemental nutrition assistance program benefits", effective October 1, 2008.

P.L. 110-234, §4002(b)(1)(D), which made the same amendment was repealed, effective May 22, 2008 pursuant to P.L. 110-246, §4(a).

P.L. 110-246, §4115(c)(1)(A)(i), struck out "coupons"; and substituted "benefits", effective October 1, 2008. Effectuated as if this change was included in §4002(b)(1)(D), so as not to duplicate "benefits".

P.L. 110-234, §4115(c)(1)(A)(i), which made the same amendment was repealed, effective May 22, 2008 pursuant to P.L. 110-246, §4(a).

[16] P.L. 110-246, §4002(b)(1)(D), struck out "food stamp" and substituted "supplemental nutrition assistance program benefits", effective October 1, 2008.

P.L. 110-234, §4002(b)(1)(D), which made the same amendment was repealed, effective May 22, 2008 pursuant to P.L. 110-246, §4(a).

256   SOCIAL SECURITY ACT—§ 303(d)(2)(B)(iii)(II)

(II) the amount (if any) determined pursuant to an agreement submitted to the State supplemental nutrition assistance program benefits[17] agency under section 13(c)(3)(A) of the Food and Nutrition Act of 2008[18], or

(III) any amount otherwise required to be deducted and withheld from the unemployment compensation pursuant to section 13(c)(3)(B) of such Act, and

(iv) shall pay any amount deducted and withheld under clause (iii) to the appropriate State supplemental nutrition assistance program benefits[19] agency.

(C) Any amount deducted and withheld under subparagraph (B)(iii) shall for all purposes be treated as if it were paid to the individual as unemployment compensation and paid by the individual to the State supplemental nutrition assistance program benefits[20] agency to which the uncollected overissuance is owed as repayment of the individual's uncollected overissuance.

(D) A State supplemental nutrition assistance program benefits[21] agency to which an uncollected overissuance is owed shall reimburse the State agency charged with the administration of the State unemployment compensation law for the administrative costs incurred by the State agency under this paragraph that are attributable to repayment of uncollected overissuance to the State supplemental nutrition assistance program benefits[22] agency to which the uncollected overissuance is owed.

(3) Whenever the Secretary of Labor, after reasonable notice and opportunity for hearing to the State agency charged with the administration of the State law, finds that there is a failure to comply substantially with the requirements of paragraph (1), the Secretary of Labor shall notify such State agency that further payments will not be made to the State until he is satisfied that there is no longer any such failure. Until the Secretary of Labor is so satisfied, he shall make no further certification to the Secretary of the Treasury with respect to such State.

---

[17] P.L. 110-246, §4002(b)(1)(D), struck out "food stamp" and substituted "supplemental nutrition assistance program benefits", effective October 1, 2008.
   P.L. 110-234, §4002(b)(1)(D), which made the same amendment was repealed, effective May 22, 2008 pursuant to P.L. 110-246, §4(a).
[18] See Vol. II, P.L. 88-525, §13(c).
   P.L. 110-246, §4002(b)(1)(B), struck out "Food Stamp Act" and substituted "Food and Nutrition Act of 2008", effective October 1, 2008.
   P.L. 110-234, §4002(b)(1)(B), which made the same amendment was repealed, effective May 22, 2008 pursuant to P.L. 110-246, §4(a).
[19] P.L. 110-246, §4002(b)(1)(D), struck out "food stamp" and substituted "supplemental nutrition assistance program benefits", effective October 1, 2008.
   P.L. 110-234, §4002(b)(1)(D), which made the same amendment was repealed, effective May 22, 2008 pursuant to P.L. 110-246, §4(a).
[20] P.L. 110-246, §4002(b)(1)(D), struck out "food stamp" and substituted "supplemental nutrition assistance program benefits", effective October 1, 2008.
   P.L. 110-234, §4002(b)(1)(D), which made the same amendment was repealed, effective May 22, 2008 pursuant to P.L. 110-246, §4(a).
[21] P.L. 110-246, §4002(b)(1)(D), struck out "food stamp" and substituted "supplemental nutrition assistance program benefits", effective October 1, 2008.
   P.L. 110-234, §4002(b)(1)(D), which made the same amendment was repealed, effective May 22, 2008 pursuant to P.L. 110-246, §4(a).
[22] P.L. 110-246, §4002(b)(1)(D), struck out "food stamp" and substituted "supplemental nutrition assistance program benefits", effective October 1, 2008.
   P.L. 110-234, §4002(b)(1)(D), which made the same amendment was repealed, effective May 22, 2008 pursuant to P.L. 110-246, §4(a).

SOCIAL SECURITY ACT—§ 303(e)(2)(A)(iii)(II)   257

(4) For purposes of this subsection, the term "State supplemental nutrition assistance program benefits[23] agency" means any agency described in section 3(t)(1)[24] of the Food and Nutrition Act of 2008[25] which administers the supplemental nutrition assistance program[26] established under such Act.

(e)(1) The State agency charged with the administration of the State law—

> (A) shall disclose, upon request and on a reimbursable basis, directly to officers or employees of any State or local child support enforcement agency any wage information contained in the records of such State agency, and

> (B) shall establish such safeguards as are necessary (as determined by the Secretary of Labor in regulations) to insure that information disclosed under subparagraph (A) is used only for purposes of establishing and collecting child support obligations from, and locating, individuals owing such obligations.

For purposes of this subsection, the term "child support obligations" only includes obligations which are being enforced pursuant to a plan described in section 454 of this Act which has been approved by the Secretary of Health and Human Services under part D of title IV of this Act.

(2)(A) The State agency charged with the administration of the State law—

> (i) shall require each new applicant for unemployment compensation to disclose whether or not such applicant owes child support obligations (as defined in the last sentence of paragraph (1)),

> (ii) shall notify the State or local child support enforcement agency enforcing such obligations, if any applicant discloses under clause (i) that he owes child support obligations and he is determined to be eligible for unemployment compensation, that such applicant has been so determined to be eligible,

> (iii) shall deduct and withhold from any unemployment compensation otherwise payable to an individual—

>> (I) the amount specified by the individual to the State agency to be deducted and withheld under this clause,

>> (II) the amount (if any) determined pursuant to an agreement submitted to the State agency under section 454(19)(B)(i) of this Act, or

---

[23] P.L. 110-246, §4002(b)(1)(D), struck out "food stamp" and substituted "supplemental nutrition assistance program benefits", effective October 1, 2008.
P.L. 110-234, §4002(b)(1)(D), which made the same amendment was repealed, effective May 22, 2008 pursuant to P.L. 110-246, §4(a).
[24] P.L. 110-246, §4115(c)(2)(F), struck out "3(n)(1)" and substituted "3(t)(1)", effective October 1, 2008.
P.L. 110-234, §4115(c)(2)(F), which made the same amendment was repealed, effective May 22, 2008 pursuant to P.L. 110-246, §4(a).
[25] See Vol. II, P.L. 88-525, §3(t)(1).
See Vol. II, P.L. 88-525, §11(e)(19), with respect to requesting and exchanging information for verifying income and eligibility for food stamps.
P.L. 110-246, §4002(b)(1)(B), struck out "Food Stamp Act" and substituted "Food and Nutrition Act of 2008", effective October 1, 2008.
P.L. 110-234, §4002(b)(1)(B), which made the same amendment was repealed, effective May 22, 2008 pursuant to P.L. 110-246, §4(a).
[26] P.L. 110-246, §4002(b)(1)(A), struck out "food stamp program" and substituted "supplemental nutrition assistance program", effective October 1, 2008.
P.L. 110-234, §4002(b)(1)(A), which made the same amendment was repealed, effective May 22, 2008 pursuant to P.L. 110-246, §4(a).

258 SOCIAL SECURITY ACT—§ 303(e)(2)(A)(iii)(III)

(III) any amount otherwise required to be so deducted and withheld from such unemployment compensation through legal process (as defined in section 462(e)), and

(iv) shall pay any amount deducted and withheld under clause (iii) to the appropriate State or local child support enforcement agency.

Any amount deducted and withheld under clause (iii) shall for all purposes be treated as if it were paid to the individual as unemployment compensation and paid by such individual to the State or local child support enforcement agency in satisfaction of his child support obligations.

(B) For purposes of this paragraph, the term "unemployment compensation" means any compensation payable under the State law (including amounts payable pursuant to agreements under any Federal unemployment compensation law).

(C) Each State or local child support enforcement agency shall reimburse the State agency charged with the administration of the State unemployment compensation law for the administrative costs incurred by such State agency under this paragraph which are attributable to child support obligations being enforced by the State or local child support enforcement agency.

(3)[27] Whenever the Secretary of Labor, after reasonable notice and opportunity for hearing to the State agency charged with the administration of the State law, finds that there is a failure to comply substantially with the requirements of paragraph (1) or (2), the Secretary of Labor shall notify such State agency that further payments will not be made to the State until he is satisfied that there is no longer any such failure. Until the Secretary of Labor is so satisfied, he shall make no further certification to the Secretary of the Treasury with respect to such State.

(4) For purposes of this subsection, the term "State or local child support enforcement agency" means any agency of a State or political subdivision thereof operating pursuant to a plan described in the last sentence of paragraph (1).

(5) A State or local child support enforcement agency may disclose to any agent of the agency that is under contract with the agency to carry out the purposes described in paragraph (1)(B) wage information that is disclosed to an officer or employee of the agency under paragraph (1)(A). Any agent of a State or local child support agency that receives wage information under this paragraph shall comply with the safeguards established pursuant to paragraph (1)(B).

(f) The State agency charged with the administration of the State law shall provide that information shall be requested and exchanged for purposes of income and eligibility verification in accordance with a State system which meets the requirements of section 1137 of this Act.

(g)(1) A State may deduct from unemployment benefits otherwise payable to an individual an amount equal to any overpayment made to such individual under an unemployment benefit program of the United States or of any other State, and not previously recovered. The amount so deducted shall be paid to the jurisdiction under whose pro-

---

[27] See Vol. II, P.L. 96-499, §1025, with respect to withholding certification of State unemployment laws.

gram such overpayment was made. Any such deduction shall be made only in accordance with the same procedures relating to notice and opportunity for a hearing as apply to the recovery of overpayments of regular unemployment compensation paid by such State.

(2) Any State may enter into an agreement with the Secretary of Labor under which—

(A) the State agrees to recover from unemployment benefits otherwise payable to an individual by such State any overpayments made under an unemployment benefit program of the United States to such individual and not previously recovered, in accordance with paragraph (1), and to pay such amounts recovered to the United States for credit to the appropriate account, and

(B) the United States agrees to allow the State to recover from unemployment benefits otherwise payable to an individual under an unemployment benefit program of the United States any overpayments made by such State to such individual under a State unemployment benefit program and not previously recovered, in accordance with the same procedures as apply under paragraph (1).

(3) For purposes of this subsection, "unemployment benefits" means unemployment compensation, trade adjustment allowances, and other unemployment assistance.

(h)(1) The State agency charged with the administration of the State law shall, on a reimbursable basis—

(A) disclose quarterly, to the Secretary of Health and Human Services, wage and claim information, as required pursuant to section 453(i)(1), contained in the records of such agency;

(B) ensure that information provided pursuant to subparagraph (A) meets such standards relating to correctness and verification as the Secretary of Health and Human Services, with the concurrence of the Secretary of Labor, may find necessary; and

(C) establish such safeguards as the Secretary of Labor determines are necessary to insure that information disclosed under subparagraph (A) is used only for purposes of subsections (i)(1), (i)(3), and (j) of section 453.

(2) Whenever the Secretary of Labor, after reasonable notice and opportunity for hearing to the State agency charged with the administration of the State law, finds that there is a failure to comply substantially with the requirements of paragraph (1), the Secretary of Labor shall notify such State agency that further payments will not be made to the State until the Secretary of Labor is satisfied that there is no longer any such failure. Until the Secretary of Labor is so satisfied, such Secretary shall make no future certification to the Secretary of the Treasury with respect to the State.

(3) For purposes of this subsection—

(A) the term "wage information" means information regarding wages paid to an individual, the social security account number of such individual, and the name, address, State, and the Federal employer identification number of the employer paying such wages to such individual; and

(B) the term "claim information" means information regarding whether an individual is receiving, has received, or has made ap-

260 SOCIAL SECURITY ACT—§ 303(h)(3)(B)(cont)

plication for, unemployment compensation, the amount of any such compensation being received (or to be received by such individual), and the individual's current (or most recent) home address.

(i)(1) The State agency charged with the administration of the State law—

(A) shall disclose, upon request and on a reimbursable basis, only to officers and employees of the Department of Housing and Urban Development and to representatives of a public housing agency, any of the following information contained in the records of such State agency with respect to individuals applying for or participating in any housing assistance program administered by the Department who have signed an appropriate consent form approved by the Secretary of Housing and Urban Development—

(i) wage information, and

(ii) whether an individual is receiving, has received, or has made application for, unemployment compensation, and the amount of any such compensation being received (or to be received) by such individual, and

(B) shall establish such safeguards as are necessary (as determined by the Secretary of Labor in regulations) to ensure that information disclosed under subparagraph (A) is used only for purposes of determining an individual's eligibility for benefits, or the amount of benefits, under a housing assistance program of the Department of Housing and Urban Development.

(2) The Secretary of Labor shall prescribe regulations governing how often and in what form information may be disclosed under paragraph (1)(A).

(3) Whenever the Secretary of Labor, after reasonable notice and opportunity for hearing to the State agency charged with the administration of the State law, finds that there is a failure to comply substantially with the requirements of paragraph (1), the Secretary of Labor shall notify such State agency that further payments will not be made to the State until he or she is satisfied that there is no longer any such failure. Until the Secretary of Labor is so satisfied, he or she shall make no future certification to the Secretary of the Treasury with respect to such State.

(4) For purposes of this subsection, the term "public housing agency" means any agency described in section 3(b)(6) of the United States Housing Act of 1937[28].

(j)(1) The State agency charged with the administration of the State law shall establish and utilize a system of profiling all new claimants for regular compensation that—

(A) identifies which claimants will be likely to exhaust regular compensation and will need job search assistance services to make a successful transition to new employment;

(B) refers claimants identified pursuant to subparagraph (A) to reemployment services, such as job search assistance services, available under any State or Federal law;

(C) collects follow-up information relating to the services received by such claimants and the employment outcomes for such claimants subsequent to receiving such services and utilizes such

[28] See Vol. II, P.L. 75-412, §3(b).

information in making identifications pursuant to subparagraph (A); and

(D) meets such other requirements as the Secretary of Labor determines are appropriate.

(2) Whenever the Secretary of Labor, after reasonable notice and opportunity for hearing to the State agency charged with the administration of the State law, finds that there is a failure to comply substantially with the requirements of paragraph (1), the Secretary of Labor shall notify such State agency that further payments will not be made to the State until he is satisfied that there is no longer any such failure. Until the Secretary of Labor is so satisfied, he shall make no further certification to the Secretary of the Treasury with respect to such State.

(k)(1) For purposes of subsection (a), the unemployment compensation law of a State must provide—

(A) that if an employer transfers its business to another employer, and both employers are (at the time of transfer) under substantially common ownership, management, or control, then the unemployment experience attributable to the transferred business shall also be transferred to (and combined with the unemployment experience attributable to) the employer to whom such business is so transferred,

(B) that unemployment experience shall not, by virtue of the transfer of a business, be transferred to the person acquiring such business if—

(i) such person is not otherwise an employer at the time of such acquisition, and

(ii) the State agency finds that such person acquired the business solely or primarily for the purpose of obtaining a lower rate of contributions,

(C) that unemployment experience shall (or shall not) be transferred in accordance with such regulations as the Secretary of Labor may prescribe to ensure that higher rates of contributions are not avoided through the transfer or acquisition of a business,

(D) that meaningful civil and criminal penalties are imposed with respect to—

(i) persons that knowingly violate or attempt to violate those provisions of the State law which implement subparagraph (A) or (B) or regulations under subparagraph (C), and

(ii) persons that knowingly advise another person to violate those provisions of the State law which implement subparagraph (A) or (B) or regulations under subparagraph (C), and

(E) for the establishment of procedures to identify the transfer or acquisition of a business for purposes of this subsection.

(2) For purposes of this subsection—

(A) the term "unemployment experience", with respect to any person, refers to such person's experience with respect to unemployment or other factors bearing a direct relation to such person's unemployment risk;

(B) the term "employer" means an employer as defined under the State law;

(C) the term "business" means a trade or business (or a part thereof);

262 SOCIAL SECURITY ACT—§ 303(k)(2)(D)

(D) the term "contributions" has the meaning given such term by section 3306(g) of the Internal Revenue Code of 1986[29];

(E) the term "knowingly" means having actual knowledge of or acting with deliberate ignorance of or reckless disregard for the prohibition involved; and

(F) the term "person" has the meaning given such term by section 7701(a)(1) of the Internal Revenue Code of 1986[30].

JUDICIAL REVIEW

SEC. 304. [42 U.S.C. 504] (a) Whenever the Secretary of Labor—

(1) finds that a State law does not include any provision specified in section 303(a), or

(2) makes a finding with respect to a State under subsection (b), (c), (d), (e), (h), (i), or (j) of section 303,

such State may, within 60 days after the Governor of the State has been notified of such action, file with the United States court of appeals for the circuit in which such State is located or with the United States Court of Appeals for the District of Columbia, a petition for review of such action. A copy of the petition shall be forthwith transmitted by the clerk of the court to the Secretary of Labor. The Secretary of Labor thereupon shall file in the court the record of the proceedings on which he based his action as provided in section 2112 of title 28, United States Code[31].

(b) The findings of fact by the Secretary of Labor, if supported by substantial evidence, shall be conclusive; but the court, for good cause shown, may remand the case to the Secretary of Labor to take further evidence and the Secretary of Labor may thereupon make new or modified findings of fact and may modify his previous action, and shall certify to the court the record of the further proceedings. Such new or modified findings of fact shall likewise be conclusive if supported by substantial evidence.

(c) The court shall have jurisdiction to affirm the action of the Secretary of Labor or to set it aside, in whole or in part. The judgment of the court shall be subject to review by the Supreme Court of the United States upon certiorari or certification as provided in section 1254 of title 28 of the United States Code[32].

(d)(1) The Secretary of Labor shall not withhold any certification for payment to any State under section 302 until the expiration of 60 days after the Governor of the State has been notified of the action referred to in paragraph (1) or (2) of subsection (a) or until the State has filed a petition for review of such action, whichever is earlier.

(2) The commencement of judicial proceedings under this section shall stay the Secretary's action for a period of 30 days, and the court may thereafter grant interim relief if warranted, including a further stay of the Secretary's action and including such other relief as may be necessary to preserve status or rights.

---

[29] See Vol. II, P.L. 83-591, §3306(g).
[30] See Vol. II, P.L. 83-591, §7701(a)(1).
[31] See Vol. II, 28 U.S.C. 2112.
[32] See Vol. II, 28 U.S.C. 1254.

TITLE IV—GRANTS TO STATES FOR AID AND SERVICES TO NEEDY FAMILIES WITH CHILDREN AND FOR CHILD–WELFARE SERVICES[1]

TABLE OF CONTENTS OF TITLE[2]

Page

Part A—BLOCK GRANTS TO STATES FOR TEMPORARY ASSISTANCE FOR NEEDY FAMILIES

Sec. 401.	Purpose	265
Sec. 402.	Eligible States; State plan	265
Sec. 403.	Grants to States	268
Sec. 404.	Use of grants	292
Sec. 405.	Administrative provisions	297
Sec. 406.	Federal loans for State welfare programs	298
Sec. 407.	Mandatory work requirements	298
Sec. 408.	Prohibitions; Requirements	305
Sec. 409.	Penalties	315
Sec. 410.	Appeal of adverse decision	323
Sec. 411.	Data collection and reporting	324
Sec. 411A.	State required to provide certain information	327
Sec. 412.	Direct funding and administration by Indian tribes	327
Sec. 413.	Research, evaluations, and national studies	331
Sec. 414.	Study by the census bureau	335
Sec. 415.	Waivers	336
Sec. 416.	Administration	337
Sec. 417.	Limitation on Federal authority	338
Sec. 418.	Funding for child care	338
Sec. 419.	Definitions	340

Part B—CHILD AND FAMILY SERVICES

---

[1] Title IV of the Social Security Act is administered by the Department of Health and Human Services. The Office of Family Assistance administers benefit payments under Title IV, Parts A and C. The Administration for Public Services, Office of Human Development Services, administers social services under Title IV, Parts B and E. The Office of Child Support Enforcement administers the child support program under Title IV, Part D.

Title IV appears in the United States Code as §§601–687, subchapter IV, chapter 7, Title 42.

Regulations of the Secretary of Health and Human Services relating to Title IV are contained in chapters II, III, and XIII, Title 45, Code of Federal Regulations. Regulations of the Secretary of Labor relating to Title IV are contained in subtitle A, Title 29, and chapter 29, Title 41, Code of Federal Regulations.

See Vol. II, 31 U.S.C. 3720 and 3720A, with respect to collection of payments due to Federal agencies; 6504–6505, with respect to intergovernmental cooperation; 7501–7507, with respect to uniform audit requirements for State and local governments receiving Federal financial assistance.

See Vol. II, P.L. 82-183, §618, which prohibits denial of grants-in-aid under certain conditions.

See Vol. II, P.L. 88-352, §601, for prohibition against discrimination in federally assisted programs.

See Vol. II, P.L. 89-73, §213, with respect to eligibility for Federal surplus property.

See Vol. II, P.L. 89-97, §121(b), with respect to restrictions on payment to a State receiving payments under Title XIX.

See Vol. II, Appendix I, P.L. 94-241, §1, for §502(a)(1) of H.J. Res. 549, with respect to participation by the Commonwealth of the Northern Mariana Islands on the same basis as Guam.

See Vol. II, P.L. 100-204, §724(d), with respect to furnishing information to the United States Commission on Improving the Effectiveness of the United Nations; and §725(b), with respect to the detailing of Government personnel.

See Vol. II, P.L. 100-235, §§5–8, with respect to responsibilities of each Federal agency for computer systems security and privacy.

See Vol. II, P.L. 100-690, §5301(a)(1)(C) and (d)(1)(B), with respect to benefits of drug traffickers and possessors.

See Vol. II, P.L. 101-508, §§13301 and 13302, with respect to the OASDI Trust Funds.

[2] This table of contents does not appear in the law.

264 SOCIAL SECURITY ACT—TITLE IV(cont)

Subpart 1—Stephanie Tubbs Jones Child Welfare Services Program

[Sec. 420. Repealed.] 341
Sec. 421. Purpose 341
Sec. 422. State plans for child welfare services 342
Sec. 423. Allotments to States 345
Sec. 424. Payment to States 346
Sec. 425. Limitations on authorization of appropriations 348
Sec. 426. Research, training, or demonstration projects 348
Sec. 427. Family connection grants 349
Sec. 428. Payments to Indian tribal organizations 352
Sec. 429. National random sample study of child welfare 352

Subpart 2—Promoting Safe and Stable Families

Sec. 430. Findings and Purpose 353
Sec. 431. Definitions 353
Sec. 432. State plans 355
Sec. 433. Allotments to States 357
Sec. 434. Payments to States 359
Sec. 435. Evaluations; Research; Technical Assistance 360
Sec. 436. Authorization of appropriations; Reservation of certain
amounts 361
Sec. 437. Discretionary and Targeted Grants 362
Sec. 438. Entitlement funding for State courts to assess and improve
handling of proceedings relating to foster care and
adoption 368
Sec. 439. Grants for programs for mentoring children of prisoners 370

[Part C—Repealed.]

Part D—Child Support and Establishment of Paternity

Sec. 451. Appropriation 378
Sec. 452. Duties of the Secretary 378
Sec. 453. Federal parent locator service 387
Sec. 453A. State directory of new hires 402
Sec. 454. State plan for child and spousal support 405
Sec. 454A. Automated data processing 415
Sec. 454B. Collection and disbursement of support payments 418
Sec. 455. Payments to States 420
Sec. 456. Support obligations 425
Sec. 457. Distribution of collected support 425
Sec. 458. Incentive payments to States 431
Sec. 459. Consent by the United States to income withholding,
garnishment, and similar proceedings for enforcement of child
support and alimony obligations 440
Sec. 459A. International support enforcement 444
Sec. 460. Civil actions to enforce support obligations 446
[Sec. 461. Repealed.] 446
[Sec. 462. Repealed.] 446
Sec. 463. Use of Federal Parent Locator Service in connection with the
enforcement or determination of child custody and in cases of
parental kidnaping of a child 446
Sec. 464. Collection of past-due support from Federal tax refunds 447
Sec. 465. Allotments from pay for child and spousal support owed by
members of the uniformed services on active duty 450
Sec. 466. Requirement of statutorily prescribed procedures to improve
effectiveness of child support enforcement 451
Sec. 467. State guidelines for child support awards 468
Sec. 468. Encouragement of States to adopt simple civil process for
voluntarily acknowledging paternity and a civil procedure for
establishing paternity in contested cases 469
Sec. 469. Collection and reporting of child support enforcement
data 469
Sec. 469A. Nonliability for financial institutions providing financial records
to State child support enforcement agencies in child support
cases 469

SOCIAL SECURITY ACT—§ 402(a)(1)(A) 265

| Sec. 469B. | Grants to States for access and visitation programs | 470 |

Part E—Federal Payments for Foster Care and Adoption Assistance
Sec. 470.	Purpose: appropriation	471
Sec. 471.	State plan for foster care and adoption assistance	472
Sec. 472.	Foster care maintenance payments program	481
Sec. 473.	Adoption and Guardianship assistance program	485
Sec. 473A.	Adoption incentive payments	493
Sec. 473B..	Timely interstate home study incentive payments	498
Sec. 474.	Payments to States; Allotments to States	500
Sec. 475.	Definitions	505
Sec. 476.	Technical assistance; Data collection and evaluation	512
Sec. 477.	John H. Chafee foster care independence program	514
Sec. 478.	Rule of construction	521
Sec. 479.	Collection of data relating to adoption and foster care	521
Sec. 479A.	Annual report	523
Sec. 479B.	Programs operated by Indian tribal organizations	524

Part A—BLOCK GRANTS TO STATES FOR TEMPORARY ASSISTANCE FOR NEEDY FAMILIES[3]

PURPOSE

SEC. 401. [42 U.S.C. 601] (a) IN GENERAL.—The purpose of this part is to increase the flexibility of States in operating a program designed to—

(1) provide assistance to needy families so that children may be cared for in their own homes or in the homes of relatives;

(2) end the dependence of needy parents on government benefits by promoting job preparation, work, and marriage;

(3) prevent and reduce the incidence of out-of-wedlock pregnancies and establish annual numerical goals for preventing and reducing the incidence of these pregnancies; and

(4) encourage the formation and maintenance of two-parent families.

(b) NO INDIVIDUAL ENTITLEMENT.—This part shall not be interpreted to entitle any individual or family to assistance under any State program funded under this part.

ELIGIBLE STATES; STATE PLAN

SEC. 402. [42 U.S.C. 602] (a) IN GENERAL.—As used in this part, the term "eligible State" means, with respect to a fiscal year, a State that, during the 27–month period ending with the close of the 1st quarter of the fiscal year, has submitted to the Secretary a plan that the Secretary has found includes the following:

(1) OUTLINE OF FAMILY ASSISTANCE PROGRAM.—

(A) GENERAL PROVISIONS.—A written document that outlines how the State intends to do the following:

---

[3] See Vol. II, P.L. 104-193, §115, with respect to denial of assistance and benefits for certain drug-related convictions; §402, with respect to limited eligibility of qualified aliens for certain Federal programs; §422, with respect to authority for States to provide for attribution of sponsors income and resources to the alien with respect to State programs; and §911, with respect to fraud under means-tested welfare and public assistance programs.

See Vol. II, P.L. 109-68, §8, with respect to availability of additional unspent TANF funds for families affected by Hurricane Katrina.

See Vol. II, P.L. 109-171, §7101(a), with respect to Temporary Assistance for Needy Families and Related Programs Funding.

266   SOCIAL SECURITY ACT—§ 402(a)(1)(A)(i)

(i) Conduct a program, designed to serve all political subdivisions in the State (not necessarily in a uniform manner), that provides assistance to needy families with (or expecting) children and provides parents with job preparation, work and support services to enable them to leave the program and become self-sufficient.

(ii) Require a parent or caretaker receiving assistance under the program to engage in work (as defined by the State) once the State determines the parent or caretaker is ready to engage in work, or once the parent or caretaker has received assistance under the program for 24 months (whether or not consecutive), whichever is earlier, consistent with section 407(e)(2).

(iii) Ensure that parents and caretakers receiving assistance under the program engage in work activities in accordance with section 407.

(iv) Take such reasonable steps as the State deems necessary to restrict the use and disclosure of information about individuals and families receiving assistance under the program attributable to funds provided by the Federal Government.

(v) Establish goals and take action to prevent and reduce the incidence of out-of-wedlock pregnancies, with special emphasis on teenage pregnancies, and establish numerical goals for reducing the illegitimacy ratio of the State (as defined in section 403(a)(2)(C)(iii)).

(vi) Conduct a program, designed to reach State and local law enforcement officials, the education system, and relevant counseling services, that provides education and training on the problem of statutory rape so that teenage pregnancy prevention programs may be expanded in scope to include men.

(B) SPECIAL PROVISIONS.—

(i) The document shall indicate whether the State intends to treat families moving into the State from another State differently than other families under the program, and if so, how the State intends to treat such families under the program.

(ii) The document shall indicate whether the State intends to provide assistance under the program to individuals who are not citizens of the United States, and if so, shall include an overview of such assistance.

(iii) The document shall set forth objective criteria for the delivery of benefits and the determination of eligibility and for fair and equitable treatment, including an explanation of how the State will provide opportunities for recipients who have been adversely affected to be heard in a State administrative or appeal process.

(iv) Not later than 1 year after the date of enactment of this section, unless the chief executive officer of the State opts out of this provision by notifying the Secretary, a State shall, consistent with the exception provided in section 407(e)(2), require a parent or caretaker receiving assistance under the program who, after receiving such

SOCIAL SECURITY ACT—§ 402(a)(7)(A)(i)   267

assistance for 2 months is not exempt from work requirements and is not engaged in work, as determined under section 407(c), to participate in community service employment, with minimum hours per week and tasks to be determined by the State.

(2) CERTIFICATION THAT THE STATE WILL OPERATE A CHILD SUPPORT ENFORCEMENT PROGRAM.—A certification by the chief executive officer of the State that, during the fiscal year, the State will operate a child support enforcement program under the State plan approved under part D.

(3) CERTIFICATION THAT THE STATE WILL OPERATE A FOSTER CARE AND ADOPTION ASSISTANCE PROGRAM.—A certification by the chief executive officer of the State that, during the fiscal year, the State will operate a foster care and adoption assistance program under the State plan approved under part E, and that the State will take such actions as are necessary to ensure that children receiving assistance under such part are eligible for medical assistance under the State plan under title XIX.

(4) CERTIFICATION OF THE ADMINISTRATION OF THE PROGRAM.—A certification by the chief executive officer of the State specifying which State agency or agencies will administer and supervise the program referred to in paragraph (1) for the fiscal year, which shall include assurances that local governments and private sector organizations—

(A) have been consulted regarding the plan and design of welfare services in the State so that services are provided in a manner appropriate to local populations; and

(B) have had at least 45 days to submit comments on the plan and the design of such services.

(5) CERTIFICATION THAT THE STATE WILL PROVIDE INDIANS WITH EQUITABLE ACCESS TO ASSISTANCE.—A certification by the chief executive officer of the State that, during the fiscal year, the State will provide each member of an Indian tribe, who is domiciled in the State and is not eligible for assistance under a tribal family assistance plan approved under section 412, with equitable access to assistance under the State program funded under this part attributable to funds provided by the Federal Government.

(6) CERTIFICATION OF STANDARDS AND PROCEDURES TO ENSURE AGAINST PROGRAM FRAUD AND ABUSE.—A certification by the chief executive officer of the State that the State has established and is enforcing standards and procedures to ensure against program fraud and abuse, including standards and procedures concerning nepotism, conflicts of interest among individuals responsible for the administration and supervision of the State program, kickbacks, and the use of political patronage.

(7) OPTIONAL CERTIFICATION OF STANDARDS AND PROCEDURES TO ENSURE THAT THE STATE WILL SCREEN FOR AND IDENTIFY DOMESTIC VIOLENCE.—

(A) IN GENERAL.—At the option of the State, a certification by the chief executive officer of the State that the State has established and is enforcing standards and procedures to—

(i) screen and identify individuals receiving assistance under this part with a history of domestic violence while maintaining the confidentiality of such individuals;

268 SOCIAL SECURITY ACT—§ 402(a)(7)(A)(ii)

(ii) refer such individuals to counseling and supportive services; and

(iii) waive, pursuant to a determination of good cause, other program requirements such as time limits (for so long as necessary) for individuals receiving assistance, residency requirements, child support cooperation requirements, and family cap provisions, in cases where compliance with such requirements would make it more difficult for individuals receiving assistance under this part to escape domestic violence or unfairly penalize such individuals who are or have been victimized by such violence, or individuals who are at risk of further domestic violence.

(B) DOMESTIC VIOLENCE DEFINED.—For purposes of this paragraph, the term "domestic violence" has the same meaning as the term "battered or subjected to extreme cruelty", as defined in section 408(a)(7)(C)(iii).

(b) PLAN AMENDMENTS.—Within 30 days after a State amends a plan submitted pursuant to subsection (a), the State shall notify the Secretary of the amendment.

(c) PUBLIC AVAILABILITY OF STATE PLAN SUMMARY.—The State shall make available to the public a summary of any plan or plan amendment section.

GRANTS TO STATES

SEC. 403. [42 U.S.C. 603] (a) GRANTS.—

(1) FAMILY ASSISTANCE GRANT.—

(A) IN GENERAL.—Each eligible State shall be entitled to receive from the Secretary, for each of fiscal years 1996, 1997, 1998, 1999, 2000, 2001, 2002, and 2003, a grant in an amount equal to the State family assistance grant.

(B) STATE FAMILY ASSISTANCE GRANT.—The State family assistance grant payable to a State for a fiscal year shall be the amount that bears the same ratio to the amount specified in subparagraph (C) of this paragraph as the amount required to be paid to the State under this paragraph for fiscal year 2002 (determined without regard to any reduction pursuant to section 409 or 412(a)(1)) bears to the total amount required to be paid under this paragraph for fiscal year 2002 (as so determined).

(C) APPROPRIATION.—Out of any money in the Treasury of the United States not otherwise appropriated, there are appropriated for fiscal year 2003 $16,566, 542,000 for grants under this paragraph.

(2) HEALTHY MARRIAGE PROMOTION AND RESPONSIBLE FATHERHOOD GRANTS.—

(A) IN GENERAL.—

(i) USE OF FUNDS.—Subject to subparagraphs (B) and (C), the Secretary may use the funds made available under subparagraph (D) for the purpose of conducting and supporting research and demonstration projects by public or private entities, and providing technical assistance to States, Indian tribes and tribal organizations, and such other entities as the Secretary may specify that are receiving a grant under another provision of this part.

(ii) LIMITATIONS.—The Secretary may not award funds made available under this paragraph on a non-competitive basis, and may not provide any such funds to an entity for the purpose of carrying out healthy marriage promotion activities or for the purpose of carrying out activities promoting responsible fatherhood unless the entity has submitted to the Secretary an application which—

(I) describes—

(aa) how the programs or activities proposed in the application will address, as appropriate, issues of domestic violence; and

(bb) what the applicant will do, to the extent relevant, to ensure that participation in the programs or activities is voluntary, and to inform potential participants that their participation is voluntary; and

(II) contains a commitment by the entity—

(aa) to not use the funds for any other purpose; and

(bb) to consult with experts in domestic violence or relevant community domestic violence coalitions in developing the programs and activities.

(iii) HEALTHY MARRIAGE PROMOTION ACTIVITIES.—In clause (i), the term "healthy marriage promotion activities" means the following:

(I) Public advertising campaigns on the value of marriage and the skills needed to increase marital stability and health.

(II) Education in high schools on the value of marriage, relationship skills, and budgeting.

(III) Marriage education, marriage skills, and relationship skills programs, that may include parenting skills, financial management, conflict resolution, and job and career advancement, for non-married pregnant women and non-married expectant fathers.

(IV) Pre-marital education and marriage skills training for engaged couples and for couples or individuals interested in marriage.

(V) Marriage enhancement and marriage skills training programs for married couples.

(VI) Divorce reduction programs that teach relationship skills.

(VII) Marriage mentoring programs which use married couples as role models and mentors in at-risk communities.

(VIII) Programs to reduce the disincentives to marriage in means-tested aid programs, if offered in conjunction with any activity described in this subparagraph.

(B) LIMITATION ON USE OF FUNDS FOR DEMONSTRATION PROJECTS FOR COORDINATION OF CHILD WELFARE AND TANF SERVICES TO TRIBAL FAMILIES AT RISK OF CHILD ABUSE OR NEGLECT.—

(i) IN GENERAL.—Of the amounts made available under subparagraph (D) for a fiscal year, the Secretary may not award more than $2,000,000 on a competitive basis to fund demonstration projects designed to test the effectiveness of tribal governments or tribal consortia in coordinating the provision to tribal families at risk of child abuse or neglect of child welfare services and services under tribal programs funded under this part.

(ii) LIMITATION ON USE OF FUNDS.—

(I) to improve case management for families eligible for assistance from such a tribal program;

(II) for supportive services and assistance to tribal children in out-of-home placements and the tribal families caring for such children, including families who adopt such children; and

(III) for prevention services and assistance to tribal families at risk of child abuse and neglect.

(iii) REPORTS.—The Secretary may require a recipient of funds awarded under this subparagraph to provide the Secretary with such information as the Secretary deems relevant to enable the Secretary to facilitate and oversee the administration of any project for which funds are provided under this subparagraph.

(C) LIMITATION ON USE OF FUNDS FOR ACTIVITIES PROMOTING RESPONSIBLE FATHERHOOD.—

(i) IN GENERAL.—Of the amounts made available under subparagraph (D) for a fiscal year, the Secretary may not award more than $50,000,000 on a competitive basis to States, territories, Indian tribes and tribal organizations, and public and nonprofit community entities, including religious organizations, for activities promoting responsible fatherhood.

(ii) ACTIVITIES PROMOTING RESPONSIBLE FATHERHOOD.—In this paragraph, the term "activities promoting responsible fatherhood" means the following:

(I) Activities to promote marriage or sustain marriage through activities such as counseling, mentoring, disseminating information about the benefits of marriage and 2-parent involvement for children, enhancing relationship skills, education regarding how to control aggressive behavior, disseminating information on the causes of domestic violence and child abuse, marriage preparation programs, premarital counseling, marital inventories, skills-based marriage education, financial planning seminars, including improving a family's ability to effectively manage family business affairs by means such as education, counseling, or mentoring on matters related to family finances, including household management, budgeting, banking, and handling of financial transactions and home maintenance, and divorce education and reduction programs, including mediation and counseling.

(II) Activities to promote responsible parenting through activities such as counseling, mentoring, and mediation, disseminating information about good parenting practices, skills-based parenting education, encouraging child support payments, and other methods.

(III) Activities to foster economic stability by helping fathers improve their economic status by providing activities such as work first services, job search, job training, subsidized employment, job retention, job enhancement, and encouraging education, including career-advancing education, dissemination of employment materials, coordination with existing employment services such as welfare-to-work programs, referrals to local employment training initiatives, and other methods.

(IV) Activities to promote responsible fatherhood that are conducted through a contract with a nationally recognized, nonprofit fatherhood promotion organization, such as the development, promotion, and distribution of a media campaign to encourage the appropriate involvement of parents in the life of any child and specifically the issue of responsible fatherhood, and the development of a national clearinghouse to assist States and communities in efforts to promote and support marriage and responsible fatherhood.

(D) APPROPRIATION.—Out of any money in the Treasury of the United States not otherwise appropriated, there are appropriated $150,000,000 for each of fiscal years 2006 through 2010, for expenditure in accordance with this paragraph.

(3) SUPPLEMENTAL GRANT FOR POPULATION INCREASES IN CERTAIN STATES.—

(A) IN GENERAL.—Each qualifying State shall, subject to subparagraph (F), be entitled to receive from the Secretary—

(i) for fiscal year 1998 a grant in an amount equal to 2.5 percent of the total amount required to be paid to the State under former section 403 (as in effect during fiscal year 1994) for fiscal year 1994; and

(ii) for each of fiscal years 1999, 2000, and 2001, a grant in an amount equal to the sum of—

(I) the amount (if any) required to be paid to the State under this paragraph for the immediately preceding fiscal year; and

(II) 2.5 percent of the sum of—

(aa) the total amount required to be paid to the State under former section 403 (as in effect during fiscal year 1994) for fiscal year 1994; and

272 SOCIAL SECURITY ACT—§ 403(a)(3)(A)(ii)(II)(cont)

(bb) the amount (if any) required to be paid to the State under this paragraph for the fiscal year preceding the fiscal year for which the grant is to be made.

(B) PRESERVATION OF GRANT WITHOUT INCREASES FOR STATES FAILING TO REMAIN QUALIFYING STATES.—Each State that is not a qualifying State for a fiscal year specified in subparagraph (A)(ii) but was a qualifying State for a prior fiscal year shall, subject to subparagraph (F), be entitled to receive from the Secretary for the specified fiscal year, a grant in an amount equal to the amount required to be paid to the State under this paragraph for the most recent fiscal year for which the State was a qualifying State.

(C) QUALIFYING STATE.—

(i) IN GENERAL.—For purposes of this paragraph, a State is a qualifying State for a fiscal year if—

(I) the level of welfare spending per poor person by the State for the immediately preceding fiscal year is less than the national average level of State welfare spending per poor person for such preceding fiscal year; and

(II) the population growth rate of the State (as determined by the Bureau of the Census) for the most recent fiscal year for which information is available exceeds the average population growth rate for all States (as so determined) for such most recent fiscal year.

(ii) STATE MUST QUALIFY IN FISCAL YEAR 1998.—Notwithstanding clause (i), a State shall not be a qualifying State for any fiscal year after 1998 by reason of clause (i) if the State is not a qualifying State for fiscal year 1998 by reason of clause (i).

(iii) CERTAIN STATES DEEMED QUALIFYING STATES.—For purposes of this paragraph, a State is deemed to be a qualifying State for fiscal years 1998, 1999, 2000, and 2001 if—

(I) the level of welfare spending per poor person by the State for fiscal year 1994 is less than 35 percent of the national average level of State welfare spending per poor person for fiscal year 1994; or

(II) the population of the State increased by more than 10 percent from April 1, 1990 to July 1, 1994, according to the population estimates in publication CB94–204 of the Bureau of the Census.

(D) DEFINITIONS.—As used in this paragraph:

(i) LEVEL OF WELFARE SPENDING PER POOR PERSON.—The term "level of State welfare spending per poor person" means, with respect to a State and a fiscal year—

(I) the sum of—

(aa) the total amount required to be paid to the State under former section 403 (as in effect

SOCIAL SECURITY ACT—§ 403(a)(3)(H)(iii)   273

during fiscal year 1994) for fiscal year 1994; and

(bb) the amount (if any) paid to the State under this paragraph for the immediately preceding fiscal year; divided by

(II) the number of individuals, according to the 1990 decennial census, who were residents of the State and whose income was below the poverty line.

(ii) NATIONAL AVERAGE LEVEL OF STATE WELFARE SPENDING PER POOR PERSON.—The term "national average level of State welfare spending per poor person" means, with respect to a fiscal year, an amount equal to—

(I) the total amount required to be paid to the States under former section 403 (as in effect during fiscal year 1994) for fiscal year 1994; divided by

(II) the number of individuals, according to the 1990 decennial census, who were residents of any State and whose income was below the poverty line.

(iii) STATE.—The term "State" means each of the 50 States of the United States and the District of Columbia.

(E) APPROPRIATION.—Out of any money in the Treasury of the United States not otherwise appropriated, there are appropriated for fiscal years 1998, 1999, 2000, and 2001 such sums as are necessary for grants under this paragraph, in a total amount not to exceed $800,000,000.

(F) GRANTS REDUCED PRO RATA IF INSUFFICIENT APPROPRIATIONS.—If the amount appropriated pursuant to this paragraph for a fiscal year is less than the total amount of payments otherwise required to be made under this paragraph for the fiscal year, then the amount otherwise payable to any State for the fiscal year under this paragraph shall be reduced by a percentage equal to the amount so appropriated divided by such total amount.

(G) BUDGET SCORING.—Notwithstanding section 257(b)(2) of the Balanced Budget and Emergency Deficit Control Act of 1985, the baseline shall assume that no grant shall be made under this paragraph after fiscal year 2001.

(H) REAUTHORIZATION.—Notwithstanding any other provision of this paragraph—

(i) any State that was a qualifying State under this paragraph for fiscal year 2001 or any prior fiscal year shall be entitled to receive from the Secretary for each of fiscal years 2002 and 2003 a grant in an amount equal to the amount required to be paid to the State under this paragraph for the most recent fiscal year in which the State was a qualifying State;

(ii)[4] subparagraph (G) shall be applied as if "fiscal year 2009" were substituted for "fiscal year 2001"; and

(iii) out of any money in the Treasury of the United States not otherwise appropriated, there are appropri-

---

[4] P.L. 110-275, §301(b), amended clause (ii) in its entirety, effective July 15, 2008. For clause (ii) as it formerly read, see Vol. II, Appendix J, Superseded Provisions, P.L. 110-275.

274 SOCIAL SECURITY ACT—§ 403(a)(3)(H)(iii)(cont)

ated for each of fiscal years 2002 and 2003 such sums as are necessary for grants under this subparagraph.

(4) BONUS TO REWARD HIGH PERFORMANCE STATES.—

(A) IN GENERAL.—The Secretary shall make a grant pursuant to this paragraph to each State for each bonus year for which the State is a high performing State.

(B) AMOUNT OF GRANT.—

(i) IN GENERAL.—Subject to clause (ii) of this subparagraph, the Secretary shall determine the amount of the grant payable under this paragraph to a high performing State for a bonus year, which shall be based on the score assigned to the State under subparagraph (D)(i) for the fiscal year that immediately precedes the bonus year.

(ii) LIMITATION.—The amount payable to a State under this paragraph for a bonus year shall not exceed 5 percent of the State family assistance grant.

(C) FORMULA FOR MEASURING STATE PERFORMANCE.—Not later than 1 year after the date of the enactment of the Personal Responsibility and Work Opportunity Reconciliation Act of 1996[5], the Secretary, in consultation with the National Governors' Association and the American Public Welfare Association, shall develop a formula for measuring State performance in operating the State program funded under this part so as to achieve the goals set forth in section 401(a).

(D) SCORING OF STATE PERFORMANCE; SETTING OF PERFORMANCE THRESHOLDS.—For each bonus year, the Secretary shall—

(i) use the formula developed under subparagraph (C) to assign a score to each eligible State for the fiscal year that immediately precedes the bonus year; and

(ii) prescribe a performance threshold in such a manner so as to ensure that—

(I) the average annual total amount of grants to be made under this paragraph for each bonus year equals $200,000,000; and

(II) the total amount of grants to be made under this paragraph for all bonus years equals $1,000,000,000.

(E) DEFINITIONS.—As used in this paragraph:

(i) BONUS YEAR.—The term "bonus year" means fiscal years 1999, 2000, 2001, 2002, and 2003.

(ii) HIGH PERFORMING STATE.—The term "high performing State" means, with respect to a bonus year, an eligible State whose score assigned pursuant to subparagraph (D)(i) for the fiscal year immediately preceding the bonus year equals or exceeds the performance threshold prescribed under subparagraph (D)(ii) for such preceding fiscal year.

(F) APPROPRIATION.—Out of any money in the Treasury of the United States not otherwise appropriated, there are ap-

---

[5] P.L. 104-193 was enacted August 22, 1996 [P.L. 104-193; 110 Stat. 2105].

propriated for fiscal years 1999 through 2003 $1,000,000,000 for grants under this paragraph.

(5) WELFARE-TO-WORK GRANTS.—

(A) FORMULA GRANTS.—

(i) ENTITLEMENT.—A State shall be entitled to receive from the Secretary of Labor a grant for each fiscal year specified in subparagraph (H) of this paragraph for which the State is a welfare-to-work State, in an amount that does not exceed the lesser of—

(I) 2 times the total of the expenditures by the State (excluding qualified State expenditures (as defined in section 409(a)(7)(B)(i)) and any expenditure described in subclause (I), (II), or (IV) of section 409(a)(7)(B)(iv)) during the period permitted under subparagraph (C)(vii) of this paragraph for the expenditure of funds under the grant for activities described in subparagraph (C)(i) of this paragraph; or

(II) the allotment of the State under clause (iii) of this subparagraph for the fiscal year.

(ii) WELFARE–TO–WORK STATE.—A State shall be considered a welfare-to-work State for a fiscal year for purposes of this paragraph if the Secretary of Labor determines that the State meets the following requirements:

(I) The State has submitted to the Secretary of Labor and the Secretary of Health and Human Services (in the form of an addendum to the State plan submitted under section 402) a plan which—

(aa) describes how, consistent with this subparagraph, the State will use any funds provided under this subparagraph during the fiscal year;

(bb) specifies the formula to be used pursuant to clause (vi) to distribute funds in the State, and describes the process by which the formula was developed;

(cc) contains evidence that the plan was developed in consultation and coordination with appropriate entities in sub-State areas;

(dd) contains assurances by the Governor of the State that the private industry council (and any alternate agency designated by the Governor under item (ee)) for a service delivery area in the State will coordinate the expenditure of any funds provided under this subparagraph for the benefit of the service delivery area with the expenditure of the funds provided to the State under section 403(a)(1);

(ee) if the Governor of the State desires to have an agency other than a industry council administer the funds provided under this subparagraph for the benefit of 1 or more service delivery areas in the State, contains an application to the Secretary of Labor for a

276   SOCIAL SECURITY ACT—§ 403(a)(5)(A)(ii)(I)(cont)

waiver of clause (vii)(I) with respect to the area or areas in order to permit an alternate agency designated by the Governor to so administer the funds; and

(ff) describes how the State will ensure that a private industry council to which information is disclosed pursuant to section 403(a)(5)(K) or 454A(f)(5) has procedures for safeguarding the information and for ensuring that the information is used solely for the purpose described in that section.

(II) The State has provided to the Secretary of Labor an estimate of the amount that the State intends to expend during the period permitted under subparagraph (C)(vii) of this paragraph for the expenditure of funds under the grant (excluding expenditures described in section 409(a)(7)(B)(iv) (other than subclause (III) thereof)) pursuant to this paragraph.

(III) The State has agreed to negotiate in good faith with the Secretary of Health and Human Services with respect to the substance and funding of any evaluation under section 413(j), and to cooperate with the conduct of any such evaluation.

(IV) The State is an eligible State for the fiscal year.

(V) The State certifies that qualified State expenditures (within the meaning of section 409(a)(7)) for the fiscal year will be not less than the applicable percentage of historic State expenditures (within the meaning of section 409(a)(7)) with respect to the fiscal year.

(iii) ALLOTMENTS TO WELFARE-TO-WORK STATES.—

(I) IN GENERAL.—Subject to this clause, the allotment of a welfare-to-work State for a fiscal year shall be the available amount for the fiscal year, multiplied by the State percentage for the fiscal year.

(II) MINIMUM ALLOTMENT.—The allotment of a welfare-to-work State (other than Guam, the Virgin Islands, or American Samoa) for a fiscal year shall not be less than 0.25 percent of the available amount for the fiscal year.

(III) PRO RATA REDUCTION.—Subject to subclause (II), the Secretary of Labor shall make pro rata reductions in the allotments to States under this clause for a fiscal year as necessary to ensure that the total of the allotments does not exceed the available amount for the fiscal year.

(iv) AVAILABLE AMOUNT.—As used in this subparagraph, the term "available amount" means, for a fiscal year, the sum of—

(I) 75 percent of the sum of—

SOCIAL SECURITY ACT—§ 403(a)(5)(A)(vi)(I) 277

(aa) the amount specified in subparagraph (H) for the fiscal year, minus the total of the amounts reserved pursuant to subparagraphs (E), (F), and (G) for the fiscal year; and

(bb) any amount reserved pursuant to subparagraph (E) for the immediately preceding fiscal year that has not been obligated; and

(II) any available amount for the immediately preceding fiscal year that has not been obligated by a State, other than funds reserved by the State for distribution under clause (vi)(III) and funds distributed pursuant to clause (vi)(I) in any State in which the service delivery area is the State.

(v) STATE PERCENTAGE.—As used in clause (iii), the term "State percentage" means, with respect to a fiscal year, $1/2$ of the sum of—

(I) the percentage represented by the number of individuals in the State whose income is less than the poverty line divided by the number of such individuals in the United States; and

(II) the percentage represented by the number of adults who are recipients of assistance under the State program funded under this part divided by the number of adults in the United States who are recipients of assistance under any State program funded under this part.

(vi) PROCEDURE FOR DISTRIBUTION OF FUNDS WITHIN STATES.—

(I) ALLOCATION FORMULA.—A State to which a grant is made under this subparagraph shall devise a formula for allocating not less than 85 percent of the amount of the grant among the service delivery areas in the State, which—

(aa) determines the amount to be allocated for the benefit of a service delivery area in proportion to the number (if any) by which the population of the area with an income that is less than the poverty line exceeds 7.5 percent of the total population of the area, relative to such number for all such areas in the State with such an excess, and accords a weight of not less than 50 percent to this factor;

(bb) may determine the amount to be allocated for the benefit of such an area in proportion to the number of adults residing in the area who have been recipients of assistance under the State program funded under this part (whether in effect before or after the amendments made by section 103(a) of the Personal Responsibility and Work Opportunity Reconciliation Act of 1996[6] first applied to the

---

[6] P.L. 104-193, §103; 110 Stat. 2112.

278   SOCIAL SECURITY ACT—§ 403(a)(5)(A)(vi)(I)(cont)

State) for at least 30 months (whether or not consecutive) relative to the number of such adults residing in the State; and

(cc) may determine the amount to be allocated for the benefit of such an area in proportion to the number of unemployed individuals residing in the area relative to the number of such individuals residing in the State.

(II) DISTRIBUTION OF FUNDS.—

(aa) IN GENERAL.—If the amount allocated by the formula to a service delivery area is at least $100,000, the State shall distribute the amount to the entity administering the grant in the area.

(bb) SPECIAL RULE.—If the amount allocated by the formula to a service delivery area is less than $100,000, the sum shall be available for distribution in the State under subclause (III) during the fiscal year.

(III) PROJECTS TO HELP LONG-TERM RECIPIENTS OF ASSISTANCE ENTER UNSUBSIDIZED JOBS.—The Governor of a State to which a grant is made under this subparagraph may distribute not more than 15 percent of the grant funds (plus any amount required to be distributed under this subclause by reason of subclause (II)(bb)) to projects that appear likely to help long-term recipients of assistance under the State program funded under this part (whether in effect before or after the amendments made by section 103(a) of the Personal Responsibility and Work Opportunity Reconciliation Act of 1996[7] first applied to the State) enter unsubsidized employment.

(vii) ADMINISTRATION.—

(I) PRIVATE INDUSTRY COUNCILS.—The private industry council for a service delivery area in a State shall have sole authority, in coordination with the chief elected official (as defined in section 101 of the Workforce Investment Act of 1998[8]) of the area, to expend the amounts distributed under clause (vi)(II)(aa) for the benefit of the service delivery area, in accordance with the assurances described in clause (ii)(I)(dd) provided by the Governor of the State.

(II) ENFORCEMENT OF COORDINATION OF EXPENDITURES WITH OTHER EXPENDITURES UNDER THIS PART.—Notwithstanding subclause (I) of this clause, on a determination by the Governor of a State that a private industry council (or an alternate agency described in clause (ii)(I)(dd)) has

---

[7] P.L. 104-193, §103; 110 Stat. 2112.
[8] See Vol. II, P.L. 105-220, §101.

used funds provided under this subparagraph in a manner inconsistent with the assurances described in clause (ii)(I)(dd)—

(aa) the private industry council (or such alternate agency) shall remit the funds to the Governor; and

(bb) the Governor shall apply to the Secretary of Labor for a waiver of subclause (I) of this clause with respect to the service delivery area or areas involved in order to permit an alternate agency designated by the Governor to administer the funds in accordance with the assurances.

(III) AUTHORITY TO PERMIT USE OF ALTERNATE ADMINISTERING AGENCY.—The Secretary of Labor shall approve an application submitted under clause (ii)(I)(ee) or subclause (II)(bb) of this clause to waive subclause (I) of this clause with respect to 1 or more service delivery areas if the Secretary determines that the alternate agency designated in the application would improve the effectiveness or efficiency of the administration of amounts distributed under clause (vi)(II)(aa) for the benefit of the area or areas.

(viii) DATA TO BE USED IN DETERMINING THE NUMBER OF ADULT TANF RECIPIENTS.—For purposes of this subparagraph, the number of adult recipients of assistance under a State program funded under this part for a fiscal year shall be determined using data for the most recent 12-month period for which such data is available before the beginning of the fiscal year.

(ix) REVERSION OF UNALLOTTED FORMULA FUNDS.—If at the end of any fiscal year any funds available under this subparagraph have not been allotted due to a determination by the Secretary that any State has not met the requirements of clause (ii), such funds shall be transferred to the General Fund of the Treasury of the United States.

(B) COMPETITIVE GRANTS.—

(i) IN GENERAL.—The Secretary of Labor shall award grants in accordance with this subparagraph, in fiscal years 1998 and 1999, for projects proposed by eligible applicants, based on the following:

(I) The effectiveness of the proposal in—

(aa) expanding the base of knowledge about programs aimed at moving recipients of assistance under State programs funded under this part who are least job ready into unsubsidized employment.

(bb) moving recipients of assistance under State programs funded under this part who are least job ready into unsubsidized employment; and

280 SOCIAL SECURITY ACT—§ 403(a)(5)(B)(i)(I)(cont)

(cc) moving recipients of assistance under State programs funded under this part who are least job ready into unsubsidized employment, even in labor markets that have a shortage of low-skill jobs.

(II) At the discretion of the Secretary of Labor, any of the following:

(aa) The history of success of the applicant in moving individuals with multiple barriers into work.

(bb) Evidence of the applicant's ability to leverage private, State, and local resources.

(cc) Use by the applicant of State and local resources beyond those required by subparagraph (A).

(dd) Plans of the applicant to coordinate with other organizations at the local and State level.

(ee) Use by the applicant of current or former recipients of assistance under a State program funded under this part as mentors, case managers, or service providers.

(ii) ELIGIBLE APPLICANTS.—As used in clause (i), the term "eligible applicant" means a private industry council for a service delivery area in a State, a political subdivision of a State, or a private entity applying in conjunction with the private industry council for such a service delivery area or with such a political subdivision, that submits a proposal developed in consultation with the Governor of the State.

(iii) DETERMINATION OF GRANT AMOUNT.—In determining the amount of a grant to be made under this subparagraph for a project proposed by an applicant, the Secretary of Labor shall provide the applicant with an amount sufficient to ensure that the project has a reasonable opportunity to be successful, taking into account the number of long–term recipients of assistance under a State program funded under this part, the level of unemployment, the job opportunities and job growth, the poverty rate, and such other factors as the Secretary of Labor deems appropriate, in the area to be served by the project.

(iv) CONSIDERATION OF NEEDS OF RURAL AREAS AND CITIES WITH LARGE CONCENTRATIONS OF POVERTY.—In making grants under this subparagraph, the Secretary of Labor shall consider the needs of rural areas and cities with large concentrations of residents with an income that is less than the poverty line.

(v) FUNDING.—For grants under this subparagraph for each fiscal year specified in subparagraph (H), there shall be available to the Secretary of Labor an amount equal to the sum of—

(I) 25 percent of the sum of—

(aa) the amount specified in subparagraph (H) for the fiscal year, minus the total of the

SOCIAL SECURITY ACT—§ 403(a)(5)(C)(ii)(II)   281

amounts reserved pursuant to subparagraphs (E), (F) and (G) for the fiscal year; and

(bb) any amount reserved pursuant to subparagraph (E) for the immediately preceding fiscal year that has not been obligated; and

(II) any amount available for grants under this subparagraph for the immediately preceding fiscal year that has not been obligated.

(C) LIMITATIONS ON USE OF FUNDS.—

(i) ALLOWABLE ACTIVITIES.—An entity to which funds are provided under this paragraph shall use the funds to move individuals into and keep individuals in lasting unsubsidized employment by means of any of the following:

(I) The conduct and administration of community service or work experience programs.

(II) Job creation through public or private sector employment wage subsidies.

(III) On-the-job training.

(IV) Contracts with public or private providers of readiness, placement, and post-employment services or if the entity is not a private industry council or workforce investment board, the direct provision of such services.

(V) Job vouchers for placement, readiness, and post-employment services.

(VI) Job retention or support services if such services are not otherwise available. Contracts or vouchers for job placement services supported by such funds must require that at least $1/2$ of the payment occur after an eligible individual placed into the workforce has been in the workforce for 6 months.

(VII) Not more than 6 months of vocational educational or job training.

(ii) GENERAL ELIGIBILITY.—An entity that operates a project with funds provided under this paragraph may expend funds provided to the project for the benefit of recipients of assistance under the program funded under this part of the State in which the entity is located who—

(I) has received assistance under the State program funded under this part (whether in effect before or after the amendments made by section 103 of the Personal Responsibility and Work Opportunity Reconciliation Act of 1996[9] first apply to the State) for at least 30 months (whether or not consecutive); or

(II) within 12 months, will become ineligible for assistance under the State program funded under this part by reason of a durational limit on such assistance, without regard to any exemption

---

[9] P.L. 104-193, §103; 110 Stat. 2112.

282 SOCIAL SECURITY ACT—§ 403(a)(5)(C)(ii)(II)(cont)

provided pursuant to section 408(a)(7)(C) that may apply to the individual.

(iii) NONCUSTODIAL PARENTS.—An entity that operates a project with funds provided under this paragraph may use the funds to provide services in a form described in clause (i) to noncustodial parents with respect to whom the requirements of the following subclauses are met:

(I) The noncustodial parent is unemployed, underemployed, or having difficulty in paying child support obligations.

(II) At least 1 of the following applies to a minor child of the noncustodial parent (with preference in the determination of the noncustodial parents to be provided services under this paragraph to be provided by the entity to those noncustodial parents with minor children who meet, or who have custodial parents who meet, the requirements of item (aa)):

(aa) The minor child or the custodial parent of the minor child meets the requirements of subclause (I) or (II) of clause (ii).

(bb) The minor child is eligible for, or is receiving, benefits under the program funded under this part.

(cc) The minor child received benefits under the program funded under this part in the 12-month period preceding the date of the determination but no longer receives such benefits.

(dd) The minor child is eligible for, or is receiving, assistance under the Food and Nutrition Act of 2008[10], benefits under the supplemental security income program under title XVI of this Act, medical assistance under title XIX of this Act, or child health assistance under title XXI of this Act.

(III) In the case of a noncustodial parent who becomes enrolled in the project on or after the date of the enactment of this clause, the noncustodial parent is in compliance with the terms of an oral or written personal responsibility contract entered into among the noncustodial parent, the entity, and (unless the entity demonstrates to the Secretary that the entity is not capable of coordinating with such agency) the agency responsible for administering the State plan under part D, which was developed taking into account the employment and child support status of the noncustodial parent,

---

[10] P.L. 88-525.

P.L. 110-246, §4002(b)(1)(B), struck out "Food Stamp Act of 1977" and substituted "Food and Nutrition Act of 2008", effective October 1, 2008. P.L. 110-234, §4002(b)(1)(B), which made the same amendment, was repealed, effective May 22, 2008 pursuant to P.L. 110-246, §4(a).

SOCIAL SECURITY ACT—§ 403(a)(5)(C)(iii)(III) 283

which was entered into not later than 30 (or, at the option of the entity, not later than 90) days after the noncustodial parent was enrolled in the project, and which, at a minimum, includes the following:

(aa) A commitment by the noncustodial parent to cooperate, at the earliest opportunity, in the establishment of the paternity of the minor child, through voluntary acknowledgement or other procedures, and in the establishment of a child support order.

(bb) A commitment by the noncustodial parent to cooperate in the payment of child support for the minor child, which may include a modification of an existing support order to take into account the ability of the noncustodial parent to pay such support and the participation of such parent in the project.

(cc) A commitment by the noncustodial parent to participate in employment or related activities that will enable the noncustodial parent to make regular child support payments, and if the noncustodial parent has not attained 20 years of age, such related activities may include completion of high school, a general equivalency degree, or other education directly related to employment.

(dd) A description of the services to be provided under this paragraph, and a commitment by the noncustodial parent to participate in such services, that are designed to assist the noncustodial parent obtain and retain employment, increase earnings, and enhance the financial and emotional contributions to the well-being of the minor child.

In order to protect custodial parents and children who may be at risk of domestic violence, the preceding provisions of this subclause shall not be construed to affect any other provision of law requiring a custodial parent to cooperate in establishing the paternity of a child or establishing or enforcing a support order with respect to a child, or entitling a custodial parent to refuse, for good cause, to provide such cooperation as a condition of assistance or benefit under any program, shall not be construed to require such cooperation by the custodial parent as a condition of participation of either parent in the program authorized under this paragraph, and shall not be construed to require a custodial parent to cooperate with or participate in any activity under this clause. The entity operating a project under this clause with funds provided under this paragraph shall consult with domestic

284   SOCIAL SECURITY ACT—§ 403(a)(5)(C)(iv)

violence prevention and intervention organizations in the development of the project.

(iv) TARGETING OF HARD TO EMPLOY INDIVIDUALS WITH CHARACTERISTICS ASSOCIATED WITH LONG-TERM WELFARE DEPENDENCE.—An entity that operates a project with funds provided under this paragraph may expend not more than 30 percent of all funds provided to the project for programs that provide assistance in a form described in clause (i)—

(I) to recipients of assistance under the program funded under this part of the State in which the entity is located who have characteristics associated with long-term welfare dependence (such as school dropout, teen pregnancy, or poor work history), including, at the option of the State, by providing assistance in such form as a condition of receiving assistance under the State program funded under this part;

(II) to children—

(aa) who have attained 18 years of age but not 25 years of age; and

(bb) who, before attaining 18 years of age, were recipients of foster care maintenance payments (as defined in section 475(4)) under part E or were in foster care under the responsibility of a State;

(III) to recipients of assistance under the State program funded under this part, determined to have a significant barriers to self-sufficiency, pursuant to criteria established by the local private industry council; or

(IV) to custodial parents with incomes below 100 percent of the poverty line (as defined in section 673(2) of the Omnibus Budget Reconciliation Act of 1981[11], including any revision required by such section, applicable to a family of the size involved).

To the extent that the entity does not expend such funds in accordance with the preceding sentence, the entity shall expend such funds in accordance with clauses (ii) and (iii) and, as appropriate, clause (v).

(v) AUTHORITY TO PROVIDE WORK-RELATED SERVICES TO INDIVIDUALS WHO HAVE REACHED THE 5 YEAR LIMIT.—An entity that operates a project with funds provided under this paragraph may use the funds to provide assistance in a form described in clause (i) of this subparagraph to, or for the benefit of, individuals who (but for section 408(a)(7)) would be eligible for assistance under the program funded under this part of the State in which the entity is located.

(vi) RELATIONSHIP TO OTHER PROVISIONS OF THIS PART.—

---

[11] See Vol. II, P.L. 97-35, §673(2).

(I) RULES GOVERNING USE OF FUNDS.—The rules of section 404, other than subsections (b), (f), and (h) of section 404, shall not apply to a grant made under this paragraph.

(II) RULES GOVERNING PAYMENTS TO STATES.—The Secretary of Labor shall carry out the functions otherwise assigned by section 405 to the Secretary of Health and Human Services with respect to the grants payable under this paragraph.

(III) ADMINISTRATION.—Section 416 shall not apply to the programs under this paragraph.

(vii) PROHIBITION AGAINST USE OF GRANT FUNDS FOR ANY OTHER FUND MATCHING REQUIREMENT.—An entity to which funds are provided under this paragraph shall not use any part of the funds, nor any part of State expenditures made to match the funds, to fulfill any obligation of any State, political subdivision, or private industry council to contribute funds under section 403(b) or 418 or any other provision of this Act or other Federal law.

(viii) DEADLINE FOR EXPENDITURE.—An entity to which funds are provided under this paragraph shall remit to the Secretary of Labor any part of the funds that are not expended within 5 years after the date the funds are so provided.

(ix) REGULATIONS.—Within 90 days after the date of the enactment of this paragraph, the Secretary of Labor, after consultation with the Secretary of Health and Human Services and the Secretary of Housing and Urban Development, shall prescribe such regulations as may be necessary to implement this paragraph.

(x) REPORTING REQUIREMENTS.—The Secretary of Labor, in consultation with the Secretary of Health and Human Services, States, and organizations that represent State or local governments, shall establish requirements for the collection and maintenance of financial and participant information and the reporting of such information by entities carrying out activities under this paragraph.

(D) DEFINITIONS.—

(i) INDIVIDUALS WITH INCOME LESS THAN THE POVERTY LINE.—For purposes of this paragraph, the number of individuals with an income that is less than the poverty line shall be determined for a fiscal year—

(I) based on the methodology used by the Bureau of the Census to produce and publish intercensal poverty data for States and counties (or, in the case of Puerto Rico, the Virgin Islands, Guam, and American Samoa, other poverty data selected by the Secretary of Labor); and

(II) using data for the most recent year for which such data is available before the beginning of the fiscal year.

(ii) PRIVATE INDUSTRY COUNCIL.—As used in this paragraph, the term "private industry council" means, with

286 SOCIAL SECURITY ACT—§ 403(a)(5)(D)(ii)(cont)

respect to a service delivery area, the private industry council or local workforce investment board established for the service delivery area pursuant to title I of the Workforce Investment Area[12] of 1998[13], as appropriate.

(iii) SERVICE DELIVERY AREA.—As used in this paragraph, the term "service delivery area" shall have the meaning given such term for purposes of the Job Training Partnership Act or[14].

(E) FUNDING FOR INDIAN TRIBES.—1 percent of the amount specified in subparagraph (H) for fiscal year 1998 and $15,000,000 of the amount so specified for fiscal year 1999 shall be reserved for grants to Indian tribes under section 412(a)(3).

(F) FUNDING FOR EVALUATIONS OF WELFARE-TO-WORK PROGRAMS.—0.6 percent $9,000,000 of the amount specified in subparagraph (H) for fiscal year 1998 and of the amount so specified for fiscal year 1999 shall be reserved for use by the Secretary to carry out section 413(j).

(G) FUNDING FOR EVALUATION OF ABSTINENCE EDUCATION PROGRAMS.—

(i) IN GENERAL.—0.2 percent $3,000,000 of the amount specified in subparagraph (H) for fiscal year 1998 and of the amount so specified for fiscal year 1999 shall be reserved for use by the Secretary to evaluate programs under section 510, directly or through grants, contracts, or interagency agreements.

(ii) AUTHORITY TO USE FUNDS FOR EVALUATIONS OF WELFARE-TO-WORK PROGRAMS.—Any such amount not required for such evaluations shall be available for use by the Secretary to carry out section 413(j).

(iii) DEADLINE FOR OUTLAYS.—Outlays from funds used pursuant to clause (i) for evaluation of programs under section 510 shall not be made after fiscal year 2005.

(iv) INTERIM REPORT.—Not later than January 1, 2002, the Secretary shall submit to the Congress an interim report on the evaluations referred to in clause (i).

(H) APPROPRIATIONS.—

(i) IN GENERAL.—Out of any money in the Treasury of the United States not otherwise appropriated, there are appropriated for grants under this paragraph—

(I) $1,500,000,000 for fiscal years 1998; and

(II) $1,4000,000 for fiscal year 1999.

(ii) AVAILABILITY.—The amounts made available pursuant to clause (i) shall remain available for such period as is necessary to make the grants provided for in this paragraph.

(I) WORKER PROTECTIONS.—

(i) NONDISPLACEMENT IN WORK ACTIVITIES.—

---

[12] As in original. Probably should be "Act".
[13] P.L. 105-220; 112 Stat. 936.
[14] As in original.

(I) GENERAL PROHIBITION.—Subject to this clause, an adult in a family receiving assistance attributable to funds provided under this paragraph may fill a vacant employment position in order to engage in a work activity.

(II) PROHIBITION AGAINST VIOLATION OF CONTRACTS.—A work activity engaged in under a program operated with funds provided under this paragraph shall not violate an existing contract for services or a collective bargaining agreement, and such a work activity that would violate a collective bargaining agreement shall not be undertaken without the written concurrence of the labor organization and employer concerned.

(III) OTHER PROHIBITIONS.—An adult participant in a work activity engaged in under a program operated with funds provided under this paragraph shall not be employed or assigned—

(aa) when any other individual is on layoff from the same or any substantially equivalent job;

(bb) if the employer has terminated the employment of any regular employee or otherwise caused an involuntary reduction in its workforce with the intention of filling the vacancy so created with the participant; or

(cc) if the employer has caused an involuntary reduction to less than full time in hours of any employee in the same or a substantially equivalent job.

(ii) HEALTH AND SAFETY.—Health and safety standards established under Federal and State law otherwise applicable to working conditions of employees shall be equally applicable to working conditions of other participants engaged in a work activity under a program operated with funds provided under this paragraph.

(iii) NONDISCRIMINATION.—In addition to the protections provided under the provisions of law specified in section 408(c), an individual may not be discriminated against by reason of gender with respect to participation in work activities engaged in under a program operated with funds provided under this paragraph.

(iv) GRIEVANCE PROCEDURE.—

(I) IN GENERAL.—Each State to which a grant is made under this paragraph shall establish and maintain a procedure for grievances or complaints from employees alleging violations of clause (i) and participants in work activities alleging violations of clause (i), (ii), or (iii).

(II) HEARING.—The procedure shall include an opportunity for a hearing.

(III) REMEDIES.—The procedure shall include remedies for violation of clause (i), (ii), or (iii),

288 SOCIAL SECURITY ACT—§ 403(a)(5)(I)(iv)(III)(cont)

which may continue during the pendency of the procedure, and which may include—

(aa) suspension or termination of payments from funds provided under this paragraph;

(bb) prohibition of placement of a participant with an employer that has violated clause (i), (ii), or (iii);

(cc) where applicable, reinstatement of an employee, payment of lost wages and benefits, and reestablishment of other relevant terms, conditions and privileges of employment; and

(dd) where appropriate, other equitable relief.

(IV) APPEALS.—

(aa) FILING.—Not later than 30 days after a grievant or complainant receives an adverse decision under the procedure established pursuant to subclause (I), the grievant or complainant may appeal the decision to a State agency designated by the State which shall be independent of the State or local agency that is administering the programs operated with funds provided under this paragraph and the State agency administering, or supervising the administration of, the State program funded under this part.

(bb) FINAL DETERMINATION.—Not later than 120 days after the State agency designated under item (aa) receives a grievance or complaint made under the procedure established by a State pursuant to subclause (I), the State agency shall make a final determination on the appeal.

(v) RULE OF INTERPRETATION.—This subparagraph shall not be construed to affect the authority of a State to provide or require workers' compensation.

(vi) NONPREEMPTION OF STATE LAW.—The provisions of this subparagraph shall not be construed to preempt any provision of State law that affords greater protections to employees or to other participants engaged in work activities under a program funded under this part than is afforded by such provisions of this subparagraph.

(J) INFORMATION DISCLOSURE.—If a State to which a grant is made under section 403 establishes safeguards against the use or disclosure of information about applicants or recipients of assistance under the State program funded under this part, the safeguards shall not prevent the State agency administering the program from furnishing to a private industry council the names, addresses, telephone numbers, and identifying case number information in the State program funded under this part, of noncustodial parents residing in the service delivery area of the private industry council, for the purpose of identifying and contacting noncustodial par-

SOCIAL SECURITY ACT—§ 403(b)(5)(B)   289

ents regarding participation in the program under this paragraph.

(b) CONTINGENCY FUND.—

(1) ESTABLISHMENT.—There is hereby established in the Treasury of the United States a fund which shall be known as the "Contingency Fund for State Welfare Programs" (in this section referred to as the "Fund").

(2) DEPOSITS INTO FUND.—Out of any money in the Treasury of the United States not otherwise appropriated, there are appropriated for fiscal years 1997, 1998, 1999, 2000, 2001, 2002, and 2003 such sums as are necessary for payment to the Fund in a total amount not to exceed $2,000,000,000, reduced by the sum of the dollar amounts specified in paragraph (6)(C)(ii).

(3) GRANTS.—

(A) PROVISIONAL PAYMENTS.—If an eligible State submits to the Secretary a request for funds under this paragraph during an eligible month, the Secretary shall, subject to this paragraph, pay to the State, from amounts appropriated pursuant to paragraph (2), an amount equal to the amount of funds so requested.

(B) PAYMENT PRIORITY.—The Secretary shall make payments under subparagraph (A) in the order in which the Secretary receives requests for such payments.

(C) LIMITATIONS.—

(i) MONTHLY PAYMENT TO A STATE.—The total amount paid to a single State under subparagraph (A) during a month shall not exceed $1/12$ of 20 percent of the State family assistance grant.

(ii) PAYMENTS TO ALL STATES.—The total amount paid to all States under subparagraph (A) during fiscal years 1997 through 2010 shall not exceed the total amount appropriated pursuant to paragraph (2).

(4) ELIGIBLE MONTH.—As used in paragraph (3)(A), the term "eligible month" means, with respect to a State, a month in the 2-month period that begins with any month for which the State is a needy State.

(5) NEEDY STATE.—For purposes of paragraph (4), a State is a needy State for a month if—

(A) the average rate of—

(i) total unemployment in such State (seasonally adjusted) for the period consisting of the most recent 3 months for which data for all States are published equals or exceeds 6.5 percent; and

(ii) total unemployment in such State (seasonally adjusted) for the 3-month period equals or exceeds 110 percent of such average rate for either (or both) of the corresponding 3-month periods ending in the 2 preceding calendar years; or

(B) as determined by the Secretary of Agriculture (in the discretion of the Secretary of Agriculture), the monthly average number of individuals (as of the last day of each month) participating in the supplemental nutrition assistance pro-

290   SOCIAL SECURITY ACT—§ 403(b)(5)(B)(cont)

gram[15] in the State in the then most recently concluded 3-month period for which data are available exceeds by not less than 10 percent the less or of—

(i) the monthly average number of individuals (as of the last day of each month) in the State that would have participated in the supplemental nutrition assistance program[16] in the corresponding 3-month period in fiscal year 1994 if the amendments made by titles IV and VIII of the Personal Responsibility and Work Opportunity Reconciliation Act of 1996[17] had been in effect throughout fiscal year 1994; or

(ii) the monthly average number of individuals (as of the last day of each month) in the State that would have participated in the supplemental nutrition assistance program[18] in the corresponding 3-month period in fiscal year 1995 if the amendments made by titles IV and VIII of the Personal Responsibility and Work Opportunity Reconciliation Act of 1996 had been in effect throughout fiscal year 1995.

(6) ANNUAL RECONCILIATION.—

(A) IN GENERAL.—Notwithstanding paragraph (3), if the Secretary makes a payment to a State under this subsection in a fiscal year, then the State shall remit to the Secretary, within 1 year after the end of the first subsequent period of 3 consecutive months for which the State is not a needy State, an amount equal to the amount (if any) by which—

(i) the total amount paid to the State under paragraph (3) of this subsection in the fiscal year; exceeds

(ii) the product of—

(I) the Federal medical assistance percentage for the State (as defined in section 1905(b), as such section was in effect on September 30, 1995);

(II) the State's reimbursable expenditures for the fiscal year; and

(III) $1/12$ times the number of months during the fiscal year for which the Secretary made a payment to the State under such paragraph (3).

(B) DEFINITIONS.—As used in subparagraph (A);

(i) REIMBURSABLE EXPENDITURES.—The term "reimbursable expenditures" means, with respect to a State and a fiscal year, the amount (if any) by which—

(I) countable State expenditures for the fiscal year; exceeds

(II) historic State expenditures (as defined in section 409(a)(7)(B)(iii)), excluding any amount

---

[15] P.L. 110-246, §4002(b)(1)(A), struck out "food stamp program" and substituted "supplemental nutrition assistance program", effective October 1, 2008. P.L. 110-234, §4002(b)(1)(A), which made the same amendment, was repealed, effective May 22, 2008 pursuant to P.L. 110-246, §4(a).

[16] P.L. 110-246, §4002(b)(1)(A), struck out "food stamp program" and substituted "supplemental nutrition assistance program", effective October 1, 2008. P.L. 110-234, §4002(b)(1)(A), which made the same amendment, was repealed, effective May 22, 2008 pursuant to P.L. 110-246, §4(a).

[17] P.L. 104-193; 110 Stat. 2260 and 2308.

[18] P.L. 110-246, §4002(b)(1)(A), struck out "food stamp program" and substituted "supplemental nutrition assistance program", effective October 1, 2008. P.L. 110-234, §4002(b)(1)(A), which made the same amendment, was repealed, effective May 22, 2008 pursuant to P.L. 110-246, §4(a).

SOCIAL SECURITY ACT—§ 403(b)(8)   291

expended by the State for child care under subsection (g) or (i) of section 402 (as in effect during fiscal year 1994) for fiscal year 1994.

(ii) COUNTABLE STATE EXPENDITURES.—The term "countable expenditures" means, with respect to a State and a fiscal year—

(I) the qualified State expenditures (as defined in section 409(a)(7)(B)(i) (other than the expenditures described in subclause (I)(bb) of such section)) under the State program funded under this part for the fiscal year; plus

(II) any amount paid to the State under paragraph (3) during the fiscal year that is expended by the State under the State program funded under this part.

(C) ADJUSTMENT OF STATE REMITTANCES.—

(i) IN GENERAL.—The amount otherwise required by subparagraph (A) to be remitted by a State for a fiscal year shall be increased by the lesser of—

(I) the total adjustment for the fiscal year, multiplied by the adjustment percentage for the State for the fiscal year; or

(II) the unadjusted net payment to the State for the fiscal year.

(ii) TOTAL ADJUSTMENT.—As used in clause (i), the term "total adjustment" means—

(I) in the case of fiscal year 1998, $2,000,000;

(II) in the case of fiscal year 1999, $9,000,000;

(III) in the case of fiscal year 2001, $13,000,000.

(iii) ADJUSTMENT PERCENTAGE.—As used in clause (i), the term "adjustment percentage" means, with respect to a State and a fiscal year—

(I) the unadjusted net payment to the State for the fiscal year; divided by

(II) the sum of the unadjusted net payments to all States for the fiscal year.

(iv) UNADJUSTED NET PAYMENT.—As used in this subparagraph, the term, "unadjusted net payment" means with respect to a State and a fiscal year—

(I) the total amount paid to the State under paragraph (3) in the fiscal year; minus

(II) the amount that, in the absence of this subparagraph, would be required by subparagraph (A) or by section 409(a)(10) to be remitted by the State in respect of the payment.

(7) OTHER TERMS DEFINED.—As used in this subsection:

(A) STATE.—The term "State" means each of the 50 States of the United States and the District of Columbia.

(B) SECRETARY.—The term "Secretary" means the Secretary of the Treasury.

(8) ANNUAL REPORTS.—The Secretary shall annually report to the Congress on the status of the Fund.

USE OF GRANTS

SEC. 404. [42 U.S.C. 604] (a) GENERAL RULES.—Subject to this part, a State to which a grant is made under section 403 may use the grant—

(1) in any manner that is reasonably calculated to accomplish the purpose of this part, including to provide low income households with assistance in meeting home heating and cooling costs; or

(2) in any manner that the State was authorized to use amounts received under part A or F, as such parts were in effect on September 30, 1995, or (as the option of the State) August 21, 1996.

(b) LIMITATION ON USE OF GRANT FOR ADMINISTRATIVE PURPOSES.—

(1) LIMITATION.—A State to which a grant is made under section 403 shall not expend more than 15 percent of the grant for administrative purposes.

(2) EXCEPTION.—Paragraph (1) shall not apply to the use of a grant for information technology and computerization needed for tracking or monitoring required by or under this part.

(c) AUTHORITY TO TREAT INTERSTATE IMMIGRANTS UNDER RULES OF FORMER STATE.—A State operating a program funded under this part may apply to a family the rules (including benefit amounts) of the program funded under this part of another State if the family has moved to the State from the other State and has resided in the State for less than 12 months.

(d) AUTHORITY TO USE PORTION OF GRANT FOR OTHER PURPOSES.—

(1) IN GENERAL.—Subject to paragraph (2), a State may use not more than 30 percent of the amount of any grant made to the State under section 403(a) for a fiscal year to carry out a State program pursuant to any or all of the following provisions of law:

(A) Title XX of this Act.

(B) The Child Care and Development Block Grant Act of 1990[19].

(2) LIMITATION ON AMOUNT TRANSFERABLE TO TITLE XX PROGRAMS.—

(A) IN GENERAL.—A State may use not more than the applicable percent of the amount of any grant made to the State under section 403(a) for a fiscal year to carry out State programs pursuant to title XX.

(B) APPLICABLE PERCENT.—For purposes of subparagraph (A), the applicable percent is 4.25 percent in the case of fiscal year 2001 and each succeeding fiscal year.

(3) APPLICABLE RULES.—

(A) IN GENERAL.—Except as provided in subparagraph (B) of this paragraph, any amount paid to a State under this part that is used to carry out a State program pursuant to a provision of law specified in paragraph (1) shall not be subject to the requirements of this part, but shall be subject to the requirements that apply to Federal funds provided directly under the provision of law to carry out the program, and the

---

[19] P.L. 101-508, §5082; 42 U.S.C. 9858-9858(q).

SOCIAL SECURITY ACT—§ 404(h)(2)(B)(ii)   293

expenditure of any amount so used shall not be considered to be an expenditure under this part.

(B) EXCEPTION RELATING TO TITLE XX PROGRAMS.—All amounts paid to a State under this part that are used to carry out State programs pursuant to title XX shall be used only for programs and services to children or their families whose income is less than 200 percent of the income official poverty line (as defined by the Office of Management and Budget, and revised annually in accordance with section 673(2) of the Omnibus Budget Reconciliation Act of 1981[20]) applicable to a family of the size involved.

(e) AUTHORITY TO RESERVE CERTAIN AMOUNTS FOR ASSISTANCE.—A State or tribe may reserve amounts paid to the State or tribe under this part for any fiscal year for the purpose of providing, without fiscal year limitation, assistance under the State or tribal program funded under this part.

(f) AUTHORITY TO OPERATE EMPLOYMENT PLACEMENT PROGRAM.—A State to which a grant is made under section 403 may use the grant to make payments (or provide job placement vouchers) to State–approved public and private job placement agencies that provide employment placement services to individuals who receive assistance under the State program funded under this part.

(g) IMPLEMENTATION OF ELECTRONIC BENEFIT TRANSFER SYSTEM.—A State to which a grant is made under section 403 is encouraged to implement an electronic benefit transfer system for providing assistance under the State program funded under this part, and may use the grant for such purpose.

(h) USE OF FUNDS FOR INDIVIDUAL DEVELOPMENT ACCOUNTS.—

(1) IN GENERAL.—A State to which a grant is made under section 403 may use the grant to carry out a program to fund individual development accounts (as defined in paragraph (2)) established by individuals eligible for assistance under the State program funded under this part.

(2) INDIVIDUAL DEVELOPMENT ACCOUNTS.—

(A) ESTABLISHMENT.—Under a State program carried out under paragraph (1), an individual development account may be established by or on behalf of an individual eligible for assistance under the State program operated under this part for the purpose of enabling the individual to accumulate funds for a qualified purpose described in subparagraph (B).

(B) QUALIFIED PURPOSE.—A qualified purpose described in this subparagraph is 1 or more of the following, as provided by the qualified entity providing assistance to the individual under this subsection:

(i) POSTSECONDARY EDUCATIONAL EXPENSES.—Postsecondary educational expenses paid from an individual development account directly to an eligible educational institution.

(ii) FIRST HOME PURCHASE.—Qualified acquisition costs with respect to a qualified principal residence for a qualified first-time homebred, if paid from an individual

---

[20] See Vol. II, P.L. 97-35, §673(2).

294   SOCIAL SECURITY ACT—§ 404(h)(2)(B)(iii)

development account directly to the persons to whom the amounts are due.

(iii) BUSINESS CAPITALIZATION.—Amounts paid from an individual development account directly to a business capitalization account which is established in a federally insured financial institution and is restricted to use solely for qualified business capitalization expenses.

(C) CONTRIBUTIONS TO BE FROM EARNED INCOME.—An individual may only contribute to an individual development account such amounts as are derived from earned income, as defined in section 911(d)(2) of the Internal Revenue Code of 1986[21].

(D) WITHDRAWAL OF FUNDS.—The Secretary shall establish such regulations as may be necessary to ensure that funds held in an individual development account are not withdrawn except for 1 or more of the qualified purposes described in subparagraph (B).

(3) REQUIREMENTS.—

(A) IN GENERAL.—An individual development account established under this subsection shall be a trust created or organized in the United States and funded through periodic contributions by the establishing individual and matched by or through a qualified entity for a qualified purpose (as described in paragraph (2)(B)).

(B) QUALIFIED ENTITY.—As used in this subsection, the term "qualified entity" means—

(i) a not-for-profit organization described in section 501(c)(3) of the Internal Revenue Code of 1986 and exempt from taxation under section 501(a) of such Code[22]; or

(ii) a State or local government agency acting in cooperation with an organization described in clause (i).

(4) NO REDUCTION IN BENEFITS.—Notwithstanding any other provision of Federal law (other than the Internal Revenue Code of 1986) that requires consideration of 1 or more financial circumstances of an individual, for the purpose of determining eligibility to receive, or the amount of, any assistance or benefit authorized by such law to be provided to or for the benefit of such individual, funds (including interest accruing) in an individual development account under this subsection shall be disregarded for such purpose with respect to any period during which such individual maintains or makes contributions into such an account.

(5) DEFINITIONS.—As used in this subsection—

(A) ELIGIBLE EDUCATIONAL INSTITUTION.—The term "eligible educational institution" means the following:

(i) An institution described in section 481(a)(1) or 1201(a) of the Higher Education Act of 1965[23] (20 U.S.C. 1088(a)(1) or 1141(a)), as such sections are in effect on the date of the enactment of this subsection.

---

[21] See Vol. II, P.L. 83-591, §911(d).
[22] See Vol. II, P.L. 83-591, §501(a) and (c)(3).
[23] See Vol. II, P.L. 89-329, §481(a) and §1201(a).

SOCIAL SECURITY ACT—§ 404(h)(5)(I)   295

(ii) An area vocational education school (as defined in subparagraph (C) or (D) of section 521(4) of the Carl D. Perkins Vocational and Applied Technology Education Act[24] (20 U.S.C. 2471(4))) which is in any State (as defined in section 521(33) of such Act), as such sections are in effect on the date of the enactment of this subsection.

(B) POST-SECONDARY EDUCATIONAL EXPENSES.—The term "post-secondary educational expenses" means—

(i) tuition and fees required for the enrollment or attendance of a student at an eligible educational institution, and

(ii) fees, books, supplies, and equipment required for courses of instruction at an eligible educational institution.

(C) QUALIFIED ACQUISITION COSTS.—The term "qualified acquisition costs" means the costs of acquiring, constructing, or reconstructing a residence. The term includes any usual or reasonable settlement, financing, or other closing costs.

(D) QUALIFIED BUSINESS.—The term "qualified business" means any business that does not contravene any law or public policy (as determined by the Secretary).

(E) QUALIFIED BUSINESS CAPITALIZATION EXPENSES.—The term "qualified business capitalization expenses" means qualified expenditures for the capitalization of a qualified business pursuant to a qualified plan.

(F) QUALIFIED EXPENDITURES.—The term "qualified expenditures" means expenditures included in a qualified plan, including capital, plant, equipment, working capital, and inventory expenses.

(G) QUALIFIED FIRST-TIME HOMEBUYER.—

(i) IN GENERAL.—The term "qualified first-time homebuyer" means a taxpayer (and, if married, the taxpayer's spouse) who has no present ownership interest in a principal residence during the 3-year period ending on the date of acquisition of the principal residence to which this subsection applies.

(ii) DATE OF ACQUISITION.—The term "date of acquisition" means the date on which a binding contract to acquire, construct, or reconstruct the principal residence to which this subparagraph applies is entered into.

(H) QUALIFIED PLAN.—The term "qualified plan" means a business plan which—

(i) is approved by a financial institution, or by a nonprofit loan fund having demonstrated fiduciary integrity,

(ii) includes a description of services or goods to be sold, a marketing plan, and projected financial statements, and

(iii) may require the eligible individual to obtain the assistance of an experienced entrepreneurial advisor.

(I) QUALIFIED PRINCIPAL RESIDENCE.—The term "qualified principal residence" means a principal residence (within the meaning of section 1034 of the Internal Revenue Code of

---

[24] See Vol. II, P.L. 88-210, §521(4).

296 SOCIAL SECURITY ACT—§ 404(h)(5)(I)(cont)

1986[25]), the qualified acquisition costs of which do not exceed 100 percent of the average area purchase price applicable to such residence (determined in accordance with paragraphs (2) and (3) of section 143(e) of such Code[26]).

(i) SANCTION WELFARE RECIPIENTS FOR FAILING TO ENSURE THAT MINOR DEPENDENT CHILDREN ATTEND SCHOOL.—A State to which a grant is made under section 403 shall not be prohibited from sanctioning a family that includes an adult who has received assistance under any State program funded under this part attributable to funds provided by the Federal Government or under the supplemental nutrition assistance program[27], as defined in section 3(l)[28] of the Food and Nutrition Act of 2008[29], if such adult fails to ensure that the minor dependent children of such adult attend school as required by the law of the State in which the minor children reside.

(j) REQUIREMENT FOR HIGH SCHOOL DIPLOMA OR EQUIVALENT.—A State to which a grant is made under section 403 shall not be prohibited from sanctioning a family that includes an adult who is older than age 20 and younger than age 51 and who has received assistance under any State program funded under this part attributable to funds provided by the Federal Government or under the supplemental nutrition assistance program[30], as defined in section 3(l)[31] of the Food and Nutrition Act of 2008[32], if such adult does not have, or is not working toward attaining, a secondary school diploma or its recognized equivalent unless such adult has been determined in the judgment of medical, psychiatric, or other appropriate professionals to lack the requisite capacity to complete successfully a course of study that would lead to a secondary school diploma or its recognized equivalent.

(k) LIMITATIONS ON USE OF GRANT FOR MATCHING UNDER CERTAIN FEDERAL TRANSPORTATION PROGRAM.—

(1) USE LIMITATIONS.—A State to which a grant is made under section 403 may not use any part of the grant to match funds made available under section 3037 of the Transportation Equity Act for the 21st Century, unless—

(A) the grant is used for new or expanded transportation services (and not for construction) that benefit individuals

---

[25] See Vol. II, P.L. 83-591, §1034.

[26] See Vol. II, P.L. 83-591, §§143(e)(2) and (3).

[27] P.L. 110-246, §4002(b)(1)(A), struck out "food stamp program" and substituted "supplemental nutrition assistance program", effective October 1, 2008. P.L. 110-234, §4002(b)(1)(A), which made the same amendment, was repealed, effective May 22, 2008 pursuant to P.L. 110-246, §4(a).

[28] P.L. 110-246, §4115(c)(2)(G), struck out "3(h)" and substituted "3(l)", effective October 1, 2008. P.L. 110-234, §4115(c)(2)(G), which made the same amendment, was repealed, effective May 22, 2008 pursuant to P.L. 110-246, §4(a).

[29] See Vol. II, P.L. 88-525, §3(l).

P.L. 110-246, §4002(b)(1)(B), struck out "Food Stamp Act of 1977" and substituted "Food and Nutrition Act of 2008", effective October 1, 2008. P.L. 110-234, §4002(b)(1)(B), which made the same amendment, was repealed, effective May 22, 2008 pursuant to P.L. 110-246, §4(a).

[30] P.L. 110-246, §4002(b)(1)(A), struck out "food stamp program" and substituted "supplemental nutrition assistance program", effective October 1, 2008. P.L. 110-234, §4002(b)(1)(A), which made the same amendment, was repealed, effective May 22, 2008 pursuant to P.L. 110-246, §4(a).

[31] P.L. 110-246, §4115 (c)(2)(G), struck out "3(h)" and substituted "3(l)", effective October 1, 2008. P.L. 110-234, §4115 (c)(2)(G), which made the same amendment, was repealed, effective May 22, 2008 pursuant to P.L. 110-246, §4(a).

[32] See Vol.II, P.L. 88-525, §3(l).

P.L. 110-246, §4002(b)(1)(B), struck out "Food Stamp Act of 1977" and substituted "Food and Nutrition Act of 2008", effective October 1, 2008. P.L. 110-234, §4002(b)(1)(B), which made the same amendment, was repealed, effective May 22, 2008 pursuant to P.L. 110-246, §4(a).

SOCIAL SECURITY ACT—§ 405(c)(2)   297

described in subparagraph (C), and not to subsidize current operating costs;

(B) the grant is used to supplement and not supplant other State expenditures on transportation;

(C) the preponderance of the benefits derived from such use of the grant accrues to individuals who are—

(i) recipients of assistance under the State program funded under this part;

(ii) former recipients of such assistance;

(iii) noncustodial parents who are described in section 403(a)(5)(C)(iii); and

(iv) low-income individuals who are at risk of qualifying for such assistance; and

(D) the services provided through such use of the grant promote the ability of such recipients to engage in work activities (as defined in section 407(d)).

(2) AMOUNT LIMITATION.—From a grant made to a State under section 403(a), the amount that a State uses to match funds described in paragraph (1) of this subsection shall not exceed the amount (if any) by which 30 percent of the total amount of the grant exceeds the amount (if any) of the grant that is used by the State to carry out any State program described in subsection (d)(1) of this section.

(3) RULE OF INTERPRETATION.—The provision by a State of a transportation benefit under a program conducted under section 3037 of the Transportation Equity Act for the 21st Century, to an individual who is not otherwise a recipient of assistance under the State program funded under this part, using funds from a grant made under section 403(a) of this Act, shall not be considered to be the provision of assistance to the individual under the State program funded under this part.

ADMINISTRATIVE PROVISIONS

SEC. 405. [42 U.S.C. 605] (a) QUARTERLY.—The Secretary shall pay each grant payable to a State under section 403 in quarterly installments, subject to this section.

(b) NOTIFICATION.—Not later than 3 months before the payment of any such quarterly installment to a State, the Secretary shall notify the State of the amount of any reduction determined under section 412(a)(1)(B) with respect to the State.

(c) COMPUTATION AND CERTIFICATION OF PAYMENTS TO STATES.—

(1) COMPUTATION.—The Secretary shall estimate the amount to be paid to each eligible State for each quarter under this part, such estimate to be based on a report filed by the State containing an estimate by the State of the total sum to be expended by the State in the quarter under the State program funded under this part and such other information as the Secretary may find necessary.

(2) CERTIFICATION.—The Secretary of Health and Human Services shall certify to the Secretary of the Treasury the amount estimated under paragraph (1) with respect to a State, reduced or increased to the extent of any overpayment or underpayment which the Secretary of Health and Human Services determines was made under this part to the State for any prior quarter and

298 SOCIAL SECURITY ACT—§ 405(c)(2)(cont)

with respect to which adjustment has not been made under this paragraph.

(d) PAYMENT METHOD.—Upon receipt of a certification under subsection (c)(2) with respect to a State, the Secretary of the Treasury shall, through the Fiscal Service of the Department of the Treasury and before audit or settlement by the General Accounting Office[33], pay to the State, at the time or times fixed by the Secretary of Health and Human Services, the amount so certified.

FEDERAL LOANS FOR STATE WELFARE PROGRAMS

SEC. 406. [42 U.S.C. 606] (a) LOAN AUTHORITY.—

(1) IN GENERAL.—The Secretary shall make loans to any loan-eligible State, for a period to maturity of not more than 3 years.

(2) LOAN-ELIGIBLE STATE.—As used in paragraph (1), the term "loan-eligible State" means a State against which a penalty has not been imposed under section 409(a)(1).

(b) RATE OF INTEREST.—The Secretary shall charge and collect interest on any loan made under this section at a rate equal to the current average market yield on outstanding marketable obligations of the United States with remaining periods to maturity comparable to the period to maturity of the loan.

(c) USE OF LOAN.—A State shall use a loan made to the State under this section only for any purpose for which grant amounts received by the State under section 403(a) may be used, including—

(1) welfare anti-fraud activities, and

(2) the provision of assistance under the State program to Indian families that have moved from the service area of an Indian tribe with a tribal family assistance plan approved under section 412.

(d) LIMITATION ON TOTAL AMOUNT OF LOANS TO A STATE.—The cumulative dollar amount of all loans made to a State under this section during fiscal years 1997 through 2003 shall not exceed 10 percent of the State family assistance grant.

(e) LIMITATION ON TOTAL AMOUNT OF OUTSTANDING LOANS.—The total dollar amount of loans outstanding under this section may not exceed $1,700,000,000.

(f) APPROPRIATION.—Out of any money in the Treasury of the United States not otherwise appropriated, there are appropriated such sums as may be necessary for the cost of loans under this section.

MANDATORY WORK REQUIREMENTS

SEC. 407. [42 U.S.C. 607] (a) PARTICIPATION RATE REQUIREMENTS.—

(1) A State to which a grant is made under section 403 for a fiscal year shall achieve the minimum participation rate specified in the following table for the fiscal year with respect to all families receiving assistance under the State program funded under this part or any other State program funded with qualified State expenditures (as defined in section 409(a)(7)(B)(i)):

---

[33] P.L. 108-271, §8(b), provided that "Any reference to the General Accounting Office in any law, rule, regulation, certificate, directive, instruction, or other official paper in force on the date of enactment [July 7, 2004] of this Act shall be considered to refer and apply to the Government Accountability Office."

SOCIAL SECURITY ACT—§ 407(b)(1)(B)(ii)(II)   299

If the fiscal year is:	The minimum participation rate is:
1997	25
1998	30
1999	35
2000	40
2001	45
2002 or thereafter	50.

(2) A State to which a grant is made under section 403 for a fiscal year shall achieve the minimum participation rate specified in the following table for the fiscal year with respect to 2-parent families receiving assistance under the State program funded under this part or any other State program funded with qualified State expenditures (as defined in section 409(a)(7)(B)(i)):

If the fiscal year is:	The minimum participation rate is:
1997	75
1998	75
1999 or thereafter	90.

(b) CALCULATION OF PARTICIPATION RATES.—

    (1) ALL FAMILIES.—

        (A) AVERAGE MONTHLY RATE.—For purposes of subsection (a)(1), the participation rate for all families of a State for a fiscal year is the average of the participation rates for all families of the State for each month in the fiscal year.

        (B) MONTHLY PARTICIPATION RATES.—The participation rate of a State for all families of the State for a month, expressed as a percentage, is—

            (i) the number of families receiving assistance under the State program funded under this part or any other State program funded with qualified State expenditures (as defined in section 409(a)(7)(B)(i)) that include an adult or a minor child head of household who is engaged in work for the month; divided by

            (ii) the amount by which—

                (I) the number of families receiving such assistance during the month that include an adult or a minor child head of household receiving such assistance; exceeds

                (II) the number of families receiving such assistance that are subject in such month to a penalty described in subsection (e)(1) but have not been subject to such penalty for more than

300   SOCIAL SECURITY ACT—§ 407(b)(1)(B)(ii)(II)(cont)

3 months within the preceding 12-month period (whether or not consecutive).

(2) 2-PARENT FAMILIES.—

(A) AVERAGE MONTHLY RATE.—For purposes of subsection (a)(2), the participation rate for 2-parent families of a State for a fiscal year is the average of the participation rates for 2-parent families of the State for each month in the fiscal year.

(B) MONTHLY PARTICIPATION RATES.—The participation rate of a State for 2-parent families of the State for a month shall be calculated by use of the formula set forth in paragraph (1)(B), except that in the formula the term "number of 2-parent families" shall be substituted for the term "number of families" each place such latter term appears.

(C) FAMILY WITH A DISABLED PARENT NOT TREATED AS A 2-PARENT FAMILY.—A family that includes a disabled parent shall not be considered a 2-parent family for purposes of subsections (a) and (b) of this section.

(3) PRO RATA REDUCTION OF PARTICIPATION RATE DUE TO CASELOAD REDUCTIONS NOT REQUIRED BY FEDERAL LAW AND NOT RESULTING FROM CHANGES IN STATE ELIGIBILITY CRITERIA.—

(A) IN GENERAL.—The Secretary shall prescribe regulations for reducing the minimum participation rate otherwise required by this section for a fiscal year by the number of percentage points equal to the number of percentage points (if any) by which—

(i) the average monthly number of families receiving assistance during the immediately preceding fiscal year under the State program funded under this part or any other State program funded with qualified State expenditures (as defined in section 409(a)(7)(B)(i)) is less than

(ii) the average monthly number of families that received assistance under the State program referred to in clause (i) during fiscal year 2005.

The minimum participation rate shall not be reduced to the extent that the Secretary determines that the reduction in the number of families receiving such assistance is required by Federal law.

(B) ELIGIBILITY CHANGES NOT COUNTED.—The regulations required by subparagraph (A) shall not take into account families that are diverted from a State program funded under this part as a result of differences in eligibility criteria under a State program funded under this part and the eligibility criteria in effect during fiscal year 2005. Such regulations shall place the burden on the Secretary to prove that such families were diverted as a direct result of differences in such eligibility criteria.

(4) STATE OPTION TO INCLUDE INDIVIDUALS RECEIVING ASSISTANCE UNDER A TRIBAL FAMILY ASSISTANCE PLAN OR TRIBAL WORK PROGRAM.—For purposes of paragraph (1)(B) and (2)(B), a State may, at its option, include families in the State that are receiving assistance under a tribal family assistance plan approved under section 412 or under a tribal work program to which funds are provided under this part.

SOCIAL SECURITY ACT—§ 407(c)(2)(A)(i) 301

(5) STATE OPTION FOR PARTICIPATION REQUIREMENT EXEMPTIONS.—For any fiscal year, a State may, at its option, not require an individual who is single custodial parent caring for a child who has not attained 12 months of age to engage in work, and may disregard such an individual in determining the participation rates under subsection (a) for not more than 12 months.

(c) ENGAGED IN WORK.—

(1) GENERAL RULES.—

(A) For purposes of subsection (b)(1)(B)(i), a recipient is engaged in work for a month in a fiscal year if the recipient is participating in work activities for at least the minimum average number of hours per week specified in the following table during the month, not fewer than 20 hours per week of which are attributable to an activity described in paragraph (1), (2), (3), (4), (5), (6), (7), (8), or (12) of subsection (d), subject to this subsection:

If the month is in fiscal year:	The minimum average number of hours per week is:
1997	20
1998	20
1999	25
2000 or thereafter	30.

(B) 2-PARENT FAMILIES.—For purposes of subsection (b)(2)(B), an individual is engaged in work for a month in a fiscal year if—

(i) the individual and the other parent in the family are participating in work activities for a total of at least 35 hours per week during the month, not fewer than 30 hours per week of which are attributable to an activity described in paragraph (1), (2), (3), (4), (5), (6), (7), (8), or (12) of subsection (d), subject to this subsection; and

(ii) if the family of the individual receives federally-funded child care assistance and an adult in the family is not disabled or caring for a severely disabled child, the individual and the other parent in the family are participating in work activities for a total of at least 55 hours per week during the month, not fewer than 50 hours per week of which are attributable to an activity described in paragraph (1), (2), (3), (4), (5), (6), (7), (8), or (12) of subsection (d).

(2) LIMITATIONS AND SPECIAL RULES.—

(A) NUMBER OF WEEKS FOR WHICH JOB SEARCH COUNTS AS WORK.—

(i) LIMITATION.—Notwithstanding paragraph (1) of this subsection, an individual shall not be considered to be engaged in work by virtue of participation in an activity described in subsection (d)(6) of a State program funded under this part or any other State

302 SOCIAL SECURITY ACT—§ 407(c)(2)(A)(ii)

program funded with qualified State expenditures (as defined in section 409(a)(7)(B)(i)), after the individual has participated in such an activity for 6 weeks (or, if the unemployment rate of the State is at least 50 percent greater than the unemployment rate of the United States or the State is a needy State within the meaning of section 403(b)(6)), 12 weeks), or if the participation is for a week that immediately follows 4 consecutive weeks of such participation.

(ii) LIMITED AUTHORITY TO COUNT LESS THAN FULL WEEK OF PARTICIPATION.—For purposes of clause (i) of this subparagraph, on not more than 1 occasion per individual, the State shall consider participation of the individual in an activity described in subsection (d)(6) for 3 or 4 days during a week as a week of participation in the activity by the individual.

(B) SINGLE PARENT OR RELATIVE WITH CHILD UNDER AGE 6 DEEMED TO BE MEETING WORK PARTICIPATION REQUIREMENTS IF PARENT OR RELATIVE IS ENGAGED IN WORK FOR 20 HOURS PER WEEK.—For purposes of determining monthly participation rates under subsection (b)(1)(B)(i), a recipient who is the only parent or caretaker relative in the family of a child who has not attained 6 years of age is deemed to be engaged in work for a month if the recipient is engaged in work for an average of at least 20 hours per week during the month.

(C) SINGLE TEEN HEAD OF HOUSEHOLD OR MARRIED TEEN WHO MAINTAINS SATISFACTORY SCHOOL ATTENDANCE DEEMED TO BE MEETING WORK PARTICIPATION REQUIREMENTS.—For purposes of determining monthly participation rates under subsection (b)(1)(B)(i), a recipient who is married or a head of household and has not attained 20 years of age is deemed to be engaged in work for a month in a fiscal year if the recipient—

(i) maintains satisfactory attendance at secondary school or the equivalent during the month; or

(ii) participates in education directly related to employment for an average of at least 20 hours per week during the month.

(D) LIMITATION ON NUMBER OF PERSONS WHO MAY BE TREATED AS ENGAGED IN WORK BY REASON OF PARTICIPATION IN EDUCATIONAL ACTIVITIES.—For purposes of determining monthly participation rates under paragraphs (1)(B)(i) and (2)(B) of subsection (b), not more than 30 percent of the number of individuals in all families and in 2-parent families, respectively, in a State who are treated as engaged in work for a month may consist of individuals who are determined to be engaged in work for the month by reason of participation in vocational educational training, or (if the month is in fiscal year 2000 or thereafter) deemed to be engaged in work for the month by reason of subparagraph (C) of this paragraph.

(d) WORK ACTIVITIES DEFINED.—As used in this section, the term "work activities" means—

(1) unsubsidized employment;

(2) subsidized private sector employment;

(3) subsidized public sector employment;

(4) work experience (including work associated with the refurbishing of publicly assisted housing) if sufficient private sector employment is not available;

(5) on-the-job training;

(6) job search and job readiness assistance;

(7) community service programs;

(8) vocational educational training (not to exceed 12 months with respect to any individual);

(9) job skills training directly related to employment;

(10) education directly related to employment, in the case of a recipient who has not received a high school diploma or a certificate of high school equivalency;

(11) satisfactory attendance at secondary school or in a course of study leading to a certificate of general equivalence, in the case of a recipient who has not completed secondary school or received such a certificate; and

(12) the provision of child care services to an individual who is participating in a community service program.

(e) PENALTIES AGAINST INDIVIDUALS.—

(1) IN GENERAL.—Except as provided in paragraph (2), if an individual in a family receiving assistance under the State program funded under this part or any other State program funded with qualified State expenditures (as defined in section 409(a)(7)(B)(i)) refuses to engage in work required in accordance with this section, the State shall—

(A) reduce the amount of assistance otherwise payable to the family pro rata (or more, at the option of the State) with respect to any period during a month in which the individual so refuses; or

(B) terminate such assistance,

subject to such good cause and other exceptions as the State may establish.

(2) EXCEPTION.—Notwithstanding paragraph (1), a State may not reduce or terminate assistance under the State program funded under this part or any other State program funded with qualified State expenditures (as defined in section 409(a)(7)(B)(i)) based on a refusal of an individual to engage in work required in accordance with this section if the individual is a single custodial parent caring for a child who has not attained 6 years of age, and the individual proves that the individual has a demonstrated inability (as determined by the State) to obtain needed child care, for 1 or more of the following reasons:

(A) Unavailability of appropriate child care within a reasonable distance from the individual's home or work site.

(B) Unavailability or unsuitability of informal child care by a relative or under other arrangements.

(C) Unavailability of appropriate and affordable formal child care arrangements.

(f) NONDISPLACEMENT IN WORK ACTIVITIES.—

(1) IN GENERAL.—Subject to paragraph (2), an adult in a family receiving assistance under a State program funded under this part attributable to funds provided by the Federal Government

304   SOCIAL SECURITY ACT—§ 407(f)(2)

may fill a vacant employment position in order to engage in a work activity described in subsection (d).

(2) NO FILLING OF CERTAIN VACANCIES.—No adult in a work activity described in subsection (d) which is funded, in whole or in part, by funds provided by the Federal Government shall be employed or assigned—

(A) when any other individual is on layoff from the same or any substantially equivalent job; or

(B) if the employer has terminated the employment of any regular employee or otherwise caused an involuntary reduction of its workforce in order to fill the vacancy so created with an adult described in paragraph (1).

(3) GRIEVANCE PROCEDURE.—A State with a program funded under this part shall establish and maintain a grievance procedure for resolving complaints of alleged violations of paragraph (2).

(4) NO PREEMPTION.—Nothing in this subsection shall preempt or supersede any provision of State or local law that provides greater protection for employees from displacement.

(g) SENSE OF THE CONGRESS.—It is the sense of the Congress that in complying with this section, each State that operates a program funded under this part is encouraged to assign the highest priority to requiring adults in 2-parent families and adults in single-parent families that include older preschool or school-age children to be engaged in work activities.

(h) SENSE OF THE CONGRESS THAT STATES SHOULD IMPOSE CERTAIN REQUIREMENTS ON NONCUSTODIAL, NONSUPPORTING MINOR PARENTS.—It is the sense of the Congress that the States should require noncustodial, nonsupporting parents who have not attained 18 years of age to fulfill community work obligations and attend appropriate parenting or money management classes after school.

(i) VERIFICATION OF WORK AND WORK-ELIGIBLE INDIVIDUALS IN ORDER TO IMPLEMENT REFORMS.—

(1) SECRETARIAL DIRECTION AND OVERSIGHT.—

(A) Regulations for determining whether activities may be counted as "work activities", how to count and verify reported hours of work, and determining who is a work-eligible individual—

(i) IN GENERAL.—Not later than June 30, 2006, the Secretary shall promulgate regulations to ensure consistent measurement of work participation rates under State programs funded under this part and State programs funded with qualified State expenditures (as defined in section 409(a)(7)(B)(i)), which shall include information with respect to—

(I) determining whether an activity of a recipient of assistance may be treated as a work activity under subsection (d);

(II) uniform methods for reporting hours of work by a recipient of assistance;

(III) the type of documentation needed to verify reported hours of work by a recipient of assistance; and

SOCIAL SECURITY ACT—§ 408(a)(2)(A)   305

(IV) the circumstances under which a parent who resides with a child who is a recipient of assistance should be included in the work participation rates.

(ii) ISSUANCE OF REGULATIONS ON AN INTERIM FINAL BASIS.—The regulations referred to in clause (i) may be effective and final immediately on an interim basis as of the date of publication of the regulations. If the Secretary provides for an interim final regulation, the Secretary shall provide for a period of public comment on the regulation after the date of publication. The Secretary may change or revise the regulation after the public comment period.

(B) OVERSIGHT OF STATE PROCEDURES.—The Secretary shall review the State procedures established in accordance with paragraph (2) to ensure that such procedures are consistent with the regulations promulgated under subparagraph (A) and are adequate to ensure an accurate measurement of work participation under the State programs funded under this part and any other State programs funded with qualified State expenditures (as so defined).

(2) REQUIREMENT FOR STATES TO ESTABLISH AND MAINTAIN WORK PARTICIPATION VERIFICATION PROCEDURES.—Not later than September 30, 2006, a State to which a grant is made under section 403 shall establish procedures for determining, with respect to recipients of assistance under the State program funded under this part or under any State programs funded with qualified State expenditures (as so defined), whether activities may be counted as work activities, how to count and verify reported hours of work, and who is a work-eligible individual, in accordance with the regulations promulgated pursuant to paragraph (1)(A)(i) and shall establish internal controls to ensure compliance with the procedures.

PROHIBITIONS; REQUIREMENTS

SEC. 408. [42 U.S.C. 608] (a) IN GENERAL.—

(1) NO ASSISTANCE FOR FAMILIES WITHOUT A MINOR CHILD.—A State to which a grant is made under section 403 shall not use any part of the grant to provide assistance to a family unless the family includes a minor child who resides with the family (consistent with paragraph (10)) or a pregnant individual.

(2) REDUCTION OR ELIMINATION OF ASSISTANCE FOR NONCOOPERATION IN ESTABLISHING PATERNITY OR OBTAINING CHILD SUPPORT.—If the agency responsible for administering the State plan approved under part D determines that an individual is not cooperating with the State in establishing paternity or in establishing, modifying, or enforcing a support order with respect to a child of the individual, and the individual does not qualify for any good cause or other exception established by the State pursuant to section 454(29), then the State—

(A) shall deduct from the assistance that would otherwise be provided to the family of the individual under the State program funded under this part an amount equal to not less than 25 percent of the amount of such assistance; and

306 SOCIAL SECURITY ACT—§ 408(a)(2)(B)

(B) may deny the family any assistance under the State program.

(3)[34] NO ASSISTANCE FOR FAMILIES NOT ASSIGNING CERTAIN SUPPORT RIGHTS TO THE STATE.—

(A) IN GENERAL.—A State to which a grant is made under section 403 shall require, as a condition of providing assistance to a family under the State program funded under this part, that a member of the family assign to the State any rights the family member may have (on behalf of the family member or of any other person for whom the family member has applied for or is receiving such assistance) to support from any other person, not exceeding the total amount of assistance so provided to the family, which accrue (or have accrued) before the date the family ceases to receive assistance under the program, which assignment, on and after such date, shall not apply with respect to any support (other than support collected pursuant to section 464) which accrued before the family received such assistance and which the State has not collected by—

(i)(I) September 30, 2000, if the assignment is executed on or after October 1, 1997, and before October 1, 2000; or

(II) the date the family ceases to receive assistance under the program, if the assignment is executed on or after October 1, 2000; or

(ii) If the State elects to distribute collections under section 457(a)(6), the date the family ceases to receive assistance under the program, if the assignment is executed on or after October 1, 1998.

(B) LIMITATION.—A State to which a grant is made under section 403 shall not require, as a condition of providing assistance to any family under the State program funded under this part, that a member of the family assign to the State any rights to support described in subparagraph (A) which accrue after the date the family ceases to receive assistance under the program.

(4) NO ASSISTANCE FOR TEENAGE PARENTS WHO DO NOT ATTEND HIGH SCHOOL OR OTHER EQUIVALENT TRAINING PROGRAM.—A State to which a grant is made under section 403 shall not use any part of the grant to provide assistance to an individual who has not attained 18 years of age, is not married, has a minor child at least 12 weeks of age in his or her care, and has not successfully completed a high-school education (or its equivalent), if the individual does not participate in—

(A) educational activities directed toward the attainment of a high school diploma or its equivalent; or

(B) an alternative educational or training program that has been approved by the State.

(5) NO ASSISTANCE FOR TEENAGE PARENTS NOT LIVING IN ADULT-SUPERVISED SETTINGS.—

---

[34] P.L. 109-171, §7301, amends subsection (3) in its entirety, **to be effective on October 1, 2009.** For applicability of the amendment and allowance for a State option to accelerate the effective date to October 1, 2008, at the earliest, see Vol. II, P.L. 109-171, §7301(e).

SOCIAL SECURITY ACT—§ 408(a)(5)(B)(ii)(III) 307

(A) IN GENERAL.—

(i) REQUIREMENT.—Except as provided in subparagraph (B), a State to which a grant is made under section 403 shall not use any part of the grant to provide assistance to an individual described in clause (ii) of this subparagraph if the individual and the minor child referred to in clause (ii)(II) do not reside in a place of residence maintained by a parent, legal guardian, or other adult relative of the individual as such parent's, guardian's, or adult relative's own home.

(ii) INDIVIDUAL DESCRIBED.—For purposes of clause (i), an individual described in this clause is an individual who—

(I) has not attained 18 years of age; and

(II) is not married, and has a minor child in his or her care.

(B) EXCEPTION.—

(i) PROVISION OF, OR ASSISTANCE IN LOCATING, ADULT-SUPERVISED LIVING ARRANGEMENT.—In the case of an individual who is described in clause (ii), the State agency referred to in section 402(a)(4) shall provide, or assist the individual in locating, a second chance home, maternity home, or other appropriate adult-supervised supportive living arrangement, taking into consideration the needs and concerns of the individual, unless the State agency determines that the individual's current living arrangement is appropriate, and thereafter shall require that the individual and the minor child referred to in subparagraph (A)(ii)(II) reside in such living arrangement as a condition of the continued receipt of assistance under the State program funded under this part attributable to funds provided by the Federal Government (or in an alternative appropriate arrangement, should circumstances change and the current arrangement cease to be appropriate).

(ii) INDIVIDUAL DESCRIBED.—For purposes of clause (i), an individual is described in this clause if the individual is described in subparagraph (A)(ii), and—

(I) the individual has no parent, legal guardian, or other appropriate adult relative described in subclause (II) of his or her own who is living or whose whereabouts are known;

(II) no living parent, legal guardian, or other appropriate adult relative, who would otherwise meet applicable State criteria to act as the individual's legal guardian, of such individual allows the individual to live in the home of such parent, guardian, or relative;

(III) the State agency determines that—

(aa) the individual or the minor child referred to in subparagraph (A)(ii)(II) is being or has been subjected to serious physical or emotional harm, sexual abuse, or exploitation in the residence of the individual's own parent or legal guardian; or

(bb) substantial evidence exists of an act or failure to act that presents an imminent or serious harm if the individual and the minor child lived in the same residence with the individual's own parent or legal guardian; or

(IV) the State agency otherwise determines that it is in the best interest of the minor child to waive the requirement of subparagraph (A) with respect to the individual or the minor child.

(iii) SECOND-CHANCE HOME.—For purposes of this subparagraph, the term "second-chance home" means an entity that provides individuals described in clause (ii) with a supportive and supervised living arrangement in which such individuals are required to learn parenting skills, including child development, family budgeting, health and nutrition, and other skills to promote their long-term economic independence and the well-being of their children.

(6) NO MEDICAL SERVICES.—

(A) IN GENERAL.—A State to which a grant is made under section 403 shall not use any part of the grant to provide medical services.

(B) EXCEPTION FOR PREPREGNANCY FAMILY PLANNING SERVICES.—As used in subparagraph (A), the term "medical services" does not include prepregnancy family planning services.

(7) NO ASSISTANCE FOR MORE THAN 5 YEARS.—

(A) IN GENERAL.—A State to which a grant is made under section 403 shall not use any part of the grant to provide assistance to a family that includes an adult who has received assistance under any State program funded under this part attributable to funds provided by the Federal Government, for 60 months (whether or not consecutive) after the date the State program funded under this part commences, subject to this paragraph.

(B) MINOR CHILD EXCEPTION.—In determining the number of months for which an individual who is a parent or pregnant has received assistance under the State program funded under this part, the State shall disregard any month for which such assistance was provided with respect to the individual and during which the individual was—

(i) a minor child; and

(ii) not the head of a household or married to the head of a household.

(C) HARDSHIP EXCEPTION.—

(i) IN GENERAL.—The State may exempt a family from the application of subparagraph (A) by reason of hardship or if the family includes an individual who has been battered or subjected to extreme cruelty.

(ii) LIMITATION.—The average monthly number of families with respect to which an exemption made by a State under clause (i) is in effect for a fiscal year shall

SOCIAL SECURITY ACT—§ 408(a)(7)(G) 309

not exceed 20 percent of the average monthly number of families to which assistance is provided under the State program funded under this part during the fiscal year or the immediately preceding fiscal year (but not both), as the State may elect.

(iii) BATTERED OR SUBJECT TO EXTREME CRUELTY DEFINED.—For purposes of clause (i), an individual has been battered or subjected to extreme cruelty if the individual has been subjected to—

(I) physical acts that resulted in, or threatened to result in, physical injury to the individual;

(II) sexual abuse;

(III) sexual activity involving a dependent child;

(IV) being forced as the caretaker relative of a dependent child to engage in nonconsensual sexual acts or activities;

(V) threats of, or attempts at, physical or sexual abuse;

(VI) mental abuse; or

(VII) neglect or deprivation of medical care.

(D) DISREGARD OF MONTHS OF ASSISTANCE RECEIVED BY ADULT WHILE LIVING IN INDIAN COUNTRY OR AN ALASKAN NATIVE VILLAGE WITH 50 PERCENT UNEMPLOYMENT.—

(i) IN GENERAL.—In determining the number of months for which an adult has received assistance under a State or tribal program funded under this part, the State or tribe shall disregard any month during which the adult lived in Indian country or an Alaskan Native village if the most reliable data available with respect to the month (or a period including the month) indicate that at least 50 percent of the adults living in Indian country or in the village were not employed.

(ii) INDIAN COUNTRY DEFINED.—As used in clause (i), the term "Indian country" has the meaning given such term in section 1151 of title 18, United States Code[35].

(E) RULE OF INTERPRETATION.—Subparagraph (A) shall not be interpreted to require any State to provide assistance to any individual for any period of time under the State program funded under this part.

(F) RULE OF INTERPRETATION.—This part shall not be interpreted to prohibit any State from expending State funds not originating with the Federal Government on benefits for children or families that have become ineligible for assistance under the State program funded under this part by reason of subparagraph (A).

(G) INAPPLICABILITY TO WELFARE-TO-WORK GRANTS AND ASSISTANCE.—For purposes of subparagraph (A) of this paragraph, a grant made under section 403(a)(5) shall not be considered a grant made under section 403, and noncash assistance from funds provided under section 403(a)(5) shall not be considered assistance.

---

[35] See Vol. II, 18 U.S.C. 1151.

310 SOCIAL SECURITY ACT—§ 408(a)(8)

(8) DENIAL OF ASSISTANCE FOR 10 YEARS TO A PERSON FOUND TO HAVE FRAUDULENTLY MISREPRESENTED RESIDENCE IN ORDER TO OBTAIN ASSISTANCE IN 2 OR MORE STATES.—A State to which a grant is made under section 403 shall not use any part of the grant to provide cash assistance to an individual during the 10-year period that begins on the date the individual is convicted in Federal or State court of having made a fraudulent statement or representation with respect to the place of residence of the individual in order to receive assistance simultaneously from 2 or more States under programs that are funded under this title, title XIX, or the Food and Nutrition Act of 2008[36], or benefits in 2 or more States under the supplemental security income program under title XVI. The preceding sentence shall not apply with respect to a conviction of an individual, for any month beginning after the President of the United States grants a pardon with respect to the conduct which was the subject of the conviction.

(9) DENIAL OF ASSISTANCE FOR FUGITIVE FELONS AND PROBATION AND PAROLE VIOLATORS.—

(A) IN GENERAL.—A State to which a grant is made under section 403 shall not use any part of the grant to provide assistance to any individual who is—

(i) fleeing to avoid prosecution, or custody or confinement after conviction, under the laws of the place from which the individual flees, for a crime, or an attempt to commit a crime, which is a felony under the laws of the place from which the individual flees, or which, in the case of the State of New Jersey, is a high misdemeanor under the laws of such State; or

(ii) violating a condition of probation or parole imposed under Federal or State law.

The preceding sentence shall not apply with respect to conduct of an individual, for any month beginning after the President of the United States grants a pardon with respect to the conduct.

(B) EXCHANGE OF INFORMATION WITH LAW ENFORCEMENT AGENCIES.—If a State to which a grant is made under section 403 establishes safeguards against the use or disclosure of information about applicants or recipients of assistance under the State program funded under this part, the safeguards shall not prevent the State agency administering the program from furnishing a Federal, State, or local law enforcement officer, upon the request of the officer, with the current address of any recipient if the officer furnishes the agency with the name of the recipient and notifies the agency that—

(i) the recipient—

(I) is described in subparagraph (A); or

---

[36] P.L. 88-525.

P.L. 110-246, §4002(b)(1)(B), struck out "Food Stamp Act of 1977" and substituted "Food and Nutrition Act of 2008", effective October 1, 2008. P.L. 110-234, §4002(b)(1)(B), which made the same amendment, was repealed, effective May 22, 2008 pursuant to P.L. 110-246, §4(a).

SOCIAL SECURITY ACT—§ 408(a)(11)(B)   311

    (II) has information that is necessary for the officer to conduct the official duties of the officer; and

    (ii) the location or apprehension of the recipient is within such official duties.

(10) DENIAL OF ASSISTANCE FOR MINOR CHILDREN WHO ARE ABSENT FROM THE HOME FOR A SIGNIFICANT PERIOD.—

    (A) IN GENERAL.—A State to which a grant is made under section 403 shall not use any part of the grant to provide assistance for a minor child who has been, or is expected by a parent (or other caretaker relative) of the child to be, absent from the home for a period of 45 consecutive days or, at the option of the State, such period of not less than 30 and not more than 180 consecutive days as the State may provide for in the State plan submitted pursuant to section 402.

    (B) STATE AUTHORITY TO ESTABLISH GOOD CAUSE EXCEPTIONS.—The State may establish such good cause exceptions to subparagraph (A) as the State considers appropriate if such exceptions are provided for in the State plan submitted pursuant to section 402.

    (C) DENIAL OF ASSISTANCE FOR RELATIVE WHO FAILS TO NOTIFY STATE AGENCY OF ABSENCE OF CHILD.—A State to which a grant is made under section 403 shall not use any part of the grant to provide assistance for an individual who is a parent (or other caretaker relative) of a minor child and who fails to notify the agency administering the State program funded under this part of the absence of the minor child from the home for the period specified in or provided for pursuant to subparagraph (A), by the end of the 5-day period that begins with the date that it becomes clear to the parent (or relative) that the minor child will be absent for such period so specified or provided for.

(11) MEDICAL ASSISTANCE REQUIRED TO BE PROVIDED FOR CERTAIN FAMILIES HAVING EARNINGS FROM EMPLOYMENT OR CHILD SUPPORT.—

    (A) EARNINGS FROM EMPLOYMENT.—A State to which a grant is made under section 403 and which has a State plan approved under title XIX shall provide that in the case of a family that is treated (under section 1931(b)(1)(A) for purposes of title XIX) as receiving aid under a State plan approved under this part (as in effect on July 16, 1996), that would become ineligible for such aid because of hours of or income from employment of the caretaker relative (as defined under this part as in effect on such date) or because of section 402(a)(8)(B)(ii)(II) (as so in effect), and that was so treated as receiving such aid in at least 3 of the 6 months immediately preceding the month in which such ineligibility begins, the family shall remain eligible for medical assistance under the State's plan approved under title XIX for an extended period or periods as provided in section 1925 or 1902(e)(1) (as applicable), and that the family will be appropriately notified of such extension as required by section 1925(a)(2).

    (B) CHILD SUPPORT.—A State to which a grant is made under section 403 and which has a State plan approved un-

312   SOCIAL SECURITY ACT—§ 408(a)(11)(B)(cont)

der title XIX shall provide that in the case of a family that is treated (under section 1931(b)(1)(A) for purposes of title XIX) as receiving aid under a State plan approved under this part (as in effect on July 16, 1996), that would become ineligible for such aid as a result (wholly or partly) of the collection of child or spousal support under part D and that was so treated as receiving such aid in at least 3 of the 6 months immediately preceding the month in which such ineligibility begins, the family shall remain eligible for medical assistance under the State's plan approved under title XIX for an extended period or periods as provided in section 1931(c)(1).

(b) INDIVIDUAL RESPONSIBILITY PLANS.—

(1) ASSESSMENT.—The State agency responsible for administering the State program funded under this part shall make an initial assessment of the skills, prior work experience, and employability of each recipient of assistance under the program who—

(A) has attained 18 years of age; or

(B) has not completed high school or obtained a certificate of high school equivalency, and is not attending secondary school.

(2) CONTENTS OF PLANS.—

(A) IN GENERAL.—On the basis of the assessment made under subsection (a) with respect to an individual, the State agency, in consultation with the individual, may develop an individual responsibility plan for the individual, which—

(i) sets forth an employment goal for the individual and a plan for moving the individual immediately into private sector employment;

(ii) sets forth the obligations of the individual, which may include a requirement that the individual attend school, maintain certain grades and attendance, keep school age children of the individual in school, immunize children, attend parenting and money management classes, or do other things that will help the individual become and remain employed in the private sector;

(iii) to the greatest extent possible is designed to move the individual into whatever private sector employment the individual is capable of handling as quickly as possible, and to increase the responsibility and amount of work the individual is to handle over time;

(iv) describes the services the State will provide the individual so that the individual will be able to obtain and keep employment in the private sector, and describe the job counseling and other services that will be provided by the State; and

(v) may require the individual to undergo appropriate substance abuse treatment.

(B) TIMING.—The State agency may comply with paragraph (1) with respect to an individual—

(i) within 90 days (or, at the option of the State, 180 days) after the effective date of this part, in the case of an individual who, as of such effective date, is a recipient

SOCIAL SECURITY ACT—§ 408(f)(1)(A)(i)(I)   313

of aid under the State plan approved under part A (as in effect immediately before such effective date); or

(ii) within 30 days (or, at the option of the State, 90 days) after the individual is determined to be eligible for such assistance, in the case of any other individual.

(3) PENALTY FOR NONCOMPLIANCE BY INDIVIDUAL.—In addition to any other penalties required under the State program funded under this part, the State may reduce, by such amount as the State considers appropriate, the amount of assistance otherwise payable under the State program to a family that includes an individual who fails without good cause to comply with a responsibility plan signed by the individual.

(4) STATE DISCRETION.—The exercise of the authority of this subsection shall be within the sole discretion of the State.

(c) SANCTIONS AGAINST RECIPIENTS NOT CONSIDERED WAGE REDUCTIONS.—A penalty imposed by a State against the family of an individual by reason of the failure of the individual to comply with a requirement under the State program funded under this part shall not be construed to be a reduction in any wage paid to the individual.

(d) NONDISCRIMINATION PROVISIONS.—The following provisions of law shall apply to any program or activity which receives funds provided under this part:

(1) The Age Discrimination Act of 1975[37] (42 U.S.C. 6101 et seq.).

(2) Section 504 of the Rehabilitation Act of 1973[38] (29 U.S.C. 794).

(3) The Americans with Disabilities Act of 1990 (42 U.S.C. 12101 et seq.).

(4) Title VI of the Civil Rights Act of 1964[39] (42 U.S.C. 2000d et seq.).

(e) SPECIAL RULES RELATING TO TREATMENT OF CERTAIN ALIENS.—For special rules relating to the treatment of certain aliens, see title IV of the Personal Responsibility and Work Opportunity Reconciliation Act of 1996[40].

(f) SPECIAL RULES RELATING TO THE TREATMENT OF NON-213A ALIENS.—The following rules shall apply if a State elects to take the income or resources of any sponsor of a non-213A alien into account in determining whether the alien is eligible for assistance under the State program funded under this part, or in determining the amount or types of such assistance to be provided to the alien:

(1) DEEMING OF SPONSOR'S INCOME AND RESOURCES.—For a period of 3 years after a non-213A alien enters the United States:

(A) INCOME DEEMING RULE.—The income of any sponsor of the alien and of any spouse of the sponsor is deemed to be income of the alien, to the extent that the total amount of the income exceeds the sum of—

(i) the lesser of—

(I) 20 percent of the total of any amounts received by the sponsor or any such spouse in the

---

[37] P.L. 94-135.
[38] See Vol. II, P.L. 93-112, §504.
[39] See Vol. II, P.L. 88-352, Title VI.
[40] See Vol. II, P.L. 104-193, §§411, 412, 421, 422, and 435.

314   SOCIAL SECURITY ACT—§ 408(f)(1)(A)(i)(I)(cont)

month as wages or salary or as net earnings from self-employment, plus the full amount of any costs incurred by the sponsor and any such spouse in producing self-employment income in such month; or

(II) $175;

(ii) the cash needs standard established by the State for purposes of determining eligibility for assistance under the State program funded under this part for a family of the same size and composition as the sponsor and any other individuals living in the same household as the sponsor who are claimed by the sponsor as dependents for purposes of determining the sponsor's Federal personal income tax liability but whose needs are not taken into account in determining whether the sponsor's family has met the cash needs standard;

(iii) any amounts paid by the sponsor or any such spouse to individuals not living in the household who are claimed by the sponsor as dependents for purposes of determining the sponsor's Federal personal income tax liability; and

(iv) any payments of alimony or child support with respect to individuals not living in the household.

(B) RESOURCE DEEMING RULE.—The resources of a sponsor of the alien and of any spouse of the sponsor are deemed to be resources of the alien to the extent that the aggregate value of the resources exceeds $1,500.

(C) SPONSORS OF MULTIPLE NON-213A ALIENS.—If a person is a sponsor of 2 or more non-213A aliens who are living in the same home, the income and resources of the sponsor and any spouse of the sponsor that would be deemed income and resources of any such alien under subparagraph (A) shall be divided into a number of equal shares equal to the number of such aliens, and the State shall deem the income and resources of each such alien to include 1 such share.

(2) INELIGIBILITY OF NON-213A ALIENS SPONSORED BY AGENCIES; EXCEPTION.—A non-213A alien whose sponsor is or was a public or private agency shall be ineligible for assistance under a State program funded under this part, during a period of 3 years after the alien enters the United States, unless the State agency administering the program determines that the sponsor either no longer exists or has become unable to meet the alien's needs.

(3) INFORMATION PROVISIONS.—

(A) DUTIES OF NON-213A ALIENS.—A non-213A alien, as a condition of eligibility for assistance under a State program funded under this part during the period of 3 years after the alien enters the United States, shall be required to provide to the State agency administering the program—

(i) such information and documentation with respect to the alien's sponsor as may be necessary in order for the State agency to make any determination required under this subsection, and to obtain any cooperation from the sponsor necessary for any such determination; and

SOCIAL SECURITY ACT—§ 409(a)(1)(B)   315

(ii) such information and documentation as the State agency may request and which the alien or the alien's sponsor provided in support of the alien's immigration application.

(B) DUTIES OF FEDERAL AGENCIES.—The Secretary shall enter into agreements with the Secretary of State and the Attorney General under which any information available to them and required in order to make any determination under this subsection will be provided by them to the Secretary (who may, in turn, make the information available, upon request, to a concerned State agency).

(4) NON-213A ALIEN DEFINED.—An alien is a non-213A alien for purposes of this subsection if the affidavit of support or similar agreement with respect to the alien that was executed by the sponsor of the alien's entry into the United States was executed other than pursuant to section 213A of the Immigration and Nationality Act[41].

(5) INAPPLICABILITY TO ALIEN MINOR SPONSORED BY A PARENT.—This subsection shall not apply to an alien who is a minor child if the sponsor of the alien or any spouse of the sponsor is a parent of the alien.

(6) INAPPLICABILITY TO CERTAIN CATEGORIES OF ALIENS.—This subsection shall not apply to an alien who is—

(A) admitted to the United States as a refugee under section 207 of the Immigration and Nationality Act;

(B) paroled into the United States under section 212(d)(5) of such Act for a period of at least 1 year; or

(C) granted political asylum by the Attorney General under section 208 of such Act[42].

(g) STATE REQUIRED TO PROVIDE CERTAIN INFORMATION.—Each State to which a grant is made under section 403 shall, at least 4 times annually and upon request of the Immigration and Naturalization Service, furnish the Immigration and Naturalization Service with the name and address of, and other identifying information on, any individual who the State knows is not lawfully present in the United States

PENALTIES

SEC. 409. [42 U.S.C. 609] (a) IN GENERAL.—Subject to this section:

(1) USE OF GRANT IN VIOLATION OF THIS PART.—

(A) GENERAL PENALTY.—If an audit conducted under chapter 75 of title 31, United States Code, finds that an amount paid to a State under section 403 for a fiscal year has been used in violation of this part, the Secretary shall reduce the grant payable to the State under section 403(a)(1) for the immediately succeeding fiscal year quarter by the amount so used.

(B) ENHANCED PENALTY FOR INTENTIONAL VIOLATIONS.—If the State does not prove to the satisfaction of the Secretary that the State did not intend to use the amount in violation of this part, the Secretary shall further reduce the grant

---

[41] See Vol. II., P.L. 82-414, §213A.
[42] See Vol. II., P.L. 82-414, §§207, 212(d)(5) and 208.

payable to the State under section 403(a)(1) for the immediately succeeding fiscal year quarter by an amount equal to 5 percent of the State family assistance grant.

(C) PENALTY FOR MISUSE OF COMPETITIVE WELFARE-TO-WORK FUNDS.—If the Secretary of Labor finds that an amount paid to an entity under section 403(a)(5)(B) has been used in violation of subparagraph (B) or (C) of section 403(a)(5), the entity shall remit to the Secretary of Labor an amount equal to the amount so used.

(2) FAILURE TO SUBMIT REQUIRED REPORT.—

(A) IN GENERAL.—If the Secretary determines that a State has not, within 45 days after the end of a fiscal quarter, submitted the report required by section 411(a) for the quarter, the Secretary shall reduce the grant payable to the State under section 403(a)(1) for the immediately succeeding fiscal year by an amount equal to 4 percent of the State family assistance grant.

(B) RESCISSION OF PENALTY.—The Secretary shall rescind a penalty imposed on a State under subparagraph (A) with respect to a report if the State submits the report before the end of the fiscal quarter that immediately succeeds the fiscal quarter for which the report was required.

(3) FAILURE TO SATISFY MINIMUM PARTICIPATION RATES.—

(A) IN GENERAL.—If the Secretary determines that a State to which a grant is made under section 403 for a fiscal year has failed to comply with section 407(a) for the fiscal year, the Secretary shall reduce the grant payable to the State under section 403(a)(1) for the immediately succeeding fiscal year by an amount equal to the applicable percentage of the State family assistance grant.

(B) APPLICABLE PERCENTAGE DEFINED.—As used in subparagraph (A), the term "applicable percentage" means, with respect to a State—

(i) if a penalty was not imposed on the State under subparagraph (A) for the immediately preceding fiscal year, 5 percent; or

(ii) if a penalty was imposed on the State under subparagraph (A) for the immediately preceding fiscal year, the lesser of—

(I) the percentage by which the grant payable to the State under section 403(a)(1) was reduced for such preceding fiscal year, increased by 2 percentage points; or

(II) 21 percent.

(C) PENALTY BASED ON SEVERITY OF FAILURE.—The Secretary shall impose reductions under subparagraph (A) with respect to a fiscal year based on the degree of noncompliance, and may reduce the penalty if the noncompliance is due to circumstances that caused the State to become a needy State (as defined in section 403(b)(6)) during the fiscal year or if the noncompliance is due to extraordinary circumstances such as a natural disaster or regional recession. The Secretary shall provide a written report to Congress to justify any waiver or penalty reduction due to such extraordinary circumstances.

(4) FAILURE TO PARTICIPATE IN THE INCOME AND ELIGIBILITY VERIFICATION SYSTEM.—If the Secretary determines that a State program funded under this part is not participating during a fiscal year in the income and eligibility verification system required by section 1137, the Secretary shall reduce the grant payable to the State under section 403(a)(1) for the immediately succeeding fiscal year by an amount equal to not more than 2 percent of the State family assistance grant.

(5) FAILURE TO COMPLY WITH PATERNITY ESTABLISHMENT AND CHILD SUPPORT ENFORCEMENT REQUIREMENTS UNDER PART D.—Notwithstanding any other provision of this Act, if the Secretary determines that the State agency that administers a program funded under this part does not enforce the penalties requested by the agency administering part D against recipients of assistance under the State program who fail to cooperate in establishing paternity or in establishing, modifying, or enforcing a child support order in accordance with such part and who do not qualify for any good cause or other exception established by the State under section 454(29), the Secretary shall reduce the grant payable to the State under section 403(a)(1) for the immediately succeeding fiscal year (without regard to this section) by not more than 5 percent.

(6) FAILURE TO TIMELY REPAY A FEDERAL LOAN FUND FOR STATE WELFARE PROGRAMS.—If the Secretary determines that a State has failed to repay any amount borrowed from the Federal Loan Fund for State Welfare Programs established under section 406 within the period of maturity applicable to the loan, plus any interest owed on the loan, the Secretary shall reduce the grant payable to the State under section 403(a)(1) for the immediately succeeding fiscal year quarter (without regard to this section) by the outstanding loan amount, plus the interest owed on the outstanding amount. The Secretary shall not forgive any outstanding loan amount or interest owed on the outstanding amount.

(7) FAILURE OF ANY STATE TO MAINTAIN CERTAIN LEVEL OF HISTORIC EFFORT.—

(A) IN GENERAL.—The Secretary shall reduce the grant payable to the State under section 403(a)(1) for fiscal year 1998, 1999, 2000, 2001, 2002, 2003, 2004, 2005, 2006, 2007, 2008, 2009, 2010, or 2011 by the amount (if any) by which qualified State expenditures for the then immediately preceding fiscal year are less that the applicable percentage of historic State expenditures with respect to such preceding fiscal year.

(B) DEFINITIONS.—As used in this paragraph:

(i) QUALIFIED STATE EXPENDITURES.—

(I) IN GENERAL.—The term "qualified State expenditures" means, with respect to a State and a fiscal year, the total expenditures by the State during the fiscal year, under all State programs, for any of the following with respect to eligible families:

(aa) Cash assistance, including any amount collected by the State as support pursuant to a plan approved under part D, on behalf of a family receiving assistance under the

318   SOCIAL SECURITY ACT—§ 409(a)(7)(B)(i)(I)(cont)

State program funded under this part, that is distributed to the family under section 457(a)(1)(B) and disregarded in determining the eligibility of the family for, and the amount of, such assistance.

(bb) Child care assistance.

(cc) Educational activities designed to increase self-sufficiency, job training, and work, excluding any expenditure for public education in the State except expenditures which involve the provision of services or assistance to a member of an eligible family which is not generally available to persons who are not members of an eligible family.

(dd) Administrative costs in connection with the matters described in items (aa), (bb), (cc), and (ee), but only to the extent that such costs do not exceed 15 percent of the total amount of qualified State expenditures for the fiscal year.

(ee) Any other use of funds allowable under section 404(a)(1).

(II) EXCLUSION OF TRANSFERS FROM OTHER STATE AND LOCAL PROGRAMS.—Such term does not include expenditures under any State or local program during a fiscal year, except to the extent that—

(aa) the expenditures exceed the amount expended under the State or local program in the fiscal year most recently ending before the date of the enactment of this section[43]; or

(bb) the State is entitled to a payment under former section 403 (as in effect immediately before such date of enactment) with respect to the expenditures.

(III) EXCLUSION OF AMOUNTS EXPENDED TO REPLACE PENALTY GRANT REDUCTIONS.—Such term does not include any amount expended in order to comply with paragraph (12).

(IV) ELIGIBLE FAMILIES.—As used in subclause (I), the term "eligible families" means families eligible for assistance under the State program funded under this part, families that would be eligible for such assistance but for the application of section 408(a)(7) of this Act, and families of aliens lawfully present in the United States that would be eligible for such assistance but for the application of title IV of the Personal Responsibility and Work Opportunity Reconciliation Act of 1996[44].

(V) COUNTING OF SPENDING ON CERTAIN PRO-FAMILY ACTIVITIES.—The term "qualified State expenditures" includes the total expenditures by the State during the fiscal year under all State

---

[43] July 1, 1997.
[44] P.L. 104-193; 110 Stat. 2260.

programs for a purpose described in paragraph (3) or (4) of section 401(a).

(ii) APPLICABLE PERCENTAGE.—The term "applicable percentage" means for fiscal years 1997 through 2010, 80 percent (or, if the State meets the requirements of section 407(a) for the fiscal year, 75 percent).

(iii) HISTORIC STATE EXPENDITURES.—The term "historic State expenditures" means, with respect to a State, the lesser of—

(I) the expenditures by the State under parts A and F (as in effect during fiscal year 1994) for fiscal year 1994; or

(II) the amount which bears the same ratio to the amount described in subclause (I) as—

(aa) the State family assistance grant, plus the total amount required to by paid to the State under former section 403 for fiscal year 1994 with respect to amounts expended by the State for child care under subsection (g) or (i) of section 402 (as in effect during fiscal year 1994); bears to

(bb) the total amount required to be paid to the State under former section 403 (as in effect during fiscal year 1994) for fiscal year 1994.

Such term does not include any expenditures under the State plan approved under part A (as so in effect) on behalf of individuals covered by a tribal family assistance plan approved under section 412, as determined by the Secretary.

(iv) EXPENDITURES BY THE STATE.—The term "expenditures by the State" does not include—

(I) any expenditure from amounts made available by the Federal Government;

(II) any State funds expended for the medicaid program under title XIX;

(III) any State funds which are used to match Federal funds provided under section 403(a)(5); or

(IV) any State funds which are expended as a condition of receiving Federal funds other than under this part.

Notwithstanding subclause (IV) of the preceding sentence, such term includes expenditures by a State for child care in a fiscal year to the extent that the total amount of the expenditures does not exceed the amount of State expenditures in fiscal year 1994 or 1995 (whichever is the greater) that equal the non-Federal share for the programs described in section 418(a)(1)(A).

(v) SOURCE OF DATA.—In determining expenditures by a State for fiscal years 1994 and 1995, the Secretary shall use information which was reported by the State on ACF Form 231 or (in the case of expenditures under part F) ACF Form 331, available as of the dates specified in clauses (ii) and (iii) of section 403(a)(1)(D).

320 SOCIAL SECURITY ACT—§ 409(a)(8)

(8) NONCOMPLIANCE OF STATE CHILD SUPPORT ENFORCEMENT PROGRAM WITH REQUIREMENTS OF PART D.—

(A) IN GENERAL.—If the Secretary finds, with respect to a State's program under part D, in a fiscal year beginning on or after October 1, 1997—

(i)(I) on the basis of data submitted by a State pursuant to section 454(15)(B), or on the basis of the results of a review conducted under section 452(a)(4), that the State program failed to achieve the paternity establishment percentages (as defined in section 452(g)(2)), or to meet other performance measures that may be established by the Secretary;

(II) on the basis of the results of an audit or audits conducted under section 452(a)(4)(C)(i) that the State data submitted pursuant to section 454(15)(B) is incomplete or unreliable; or

(III) on the basis of the results of an audit or audits conducted under section 452(a)(4)(C) that a State failed to substantially comply with 1 or more of the requirements of part D (other than paragraph (24) or subparagraph (A) or (B)(i) of paragraph (27), of section 454 and

(ii) that, with respect to the succeeding fiscal year—

(I) the State failed to take sufficient corrective action to achieve the appropriate performance levels or compliance as described in subparagraph (A)(i); or

(II) the data submitted by the State pursuant to section 454(15)(B) is incomplete or unreliable; the amounts otherwise payable to the State under this part for quarters following the end of such succeeding fiscal year, prior to quarters following the end of the first quarter throughout which the State program has achieved the paternity establishment percentages or other performance measures as described in subparagraph (A)(i)(I), or is in substantial compliance with 1 or more of the requirements of part D as described in subparagraph (A)(i)(III), as appropriate, shall be reduced by the percentage specified in subparagraph (B).

(B) AMOUNT OF REDUCTIONS.—The reductions required under subparagraph (A) shall be—

(i) not less than 1 nor more than 2 percent;

(ii) not less than 2 nor more than 3 percent, if the finding is the 2nd consecutive finding made pursuant to subparagraph (A); or

(iii) not less than 3 nor more than 5 percent, if the finding is the 3rd or a subsequent consecutive such finding.

(C) DISREGARD OF NONCOMPLIANCE WHICH IS OF A TECHNICAL NATURE.—For purposes of this section and section 452(a)(4), a State determined as a result of an audit—

(i) to have failed to have substantially complied with 1 or more of the requirements of part D shall be determined to have achieved substantial compliance only if

SOCIAL SECURITY ACT—§ 409(a)(12) 321

the Secretary determines that the extent of the noncompliance is of a technical nature which does not adversely affect the performance of the State's program under part D; or

(ii) to have submitted incomplete or unreliable data pursuant to section 454(15)(B) shall be determined to have submitted adequate data only if the Secretary determines that the extent of the incompleteness or unreliability of the data is of a technical nature which does not adversely affect the determination of the level of the State's paternity establishment percentages (as defined under section 452(g)(2)) or other performance measures that may be established by the Secretary.

(9) FAILURE TO COMPLY WITH 5-YEAR LIMIT ON ASSISTANCE.—If the Secretary determines that a State has not complied with section 408(a)(7) during a fiscal year, the Secretary shall reduce the grant payable to the State under section 403(a)(1) for the immediately succeeding fiscal year by an amount equal to 5 percent of the State family assistance grant.

(10) FAILURE OF STATE RECEIVING AMOUNTS FROM CONTINGENCY FUND TO MAINTAIN 100 PERCENT OF HISTORIC EFFORT.—If, at the end of any fiscal year during which amounts from the Contingency Fund for State Welfare Programs have been paid to a State, the Secretary finds that the qualified State expenditures (as defined in paragraph (7)(B)(i) (other than the expenditures described in subclause (I)(bb) of that paragraph)) under the State program funded under this part for the fiscal year are less than 100 percent of historic State expenditures (as defined in paragraph (7)(B)(iii) of this subsection), excluding any amount expended by the State for child care under subsection (g) or (i) of section 402 (as in effect during fiscal year 1994) for fiscal year 1994, the Secretary shall reduce the grant payable to the State under section 403(a)(1) for the immediately succeeding fiscal year by the total of the amounts so paid to the State that the State has not remitted under section 403(b)(6).

(11) FAILURE TO MAINTAIN ASSISTANCE TO ADULT SINGLE CUSTODIAL PARENT WHO CANNOT OBTAIN CHILD CARE FOR CHILD UNDER AGE 6.—

(A) IN GENERAL.—If the Secretary determines that a State to which a grant is made under section 403 for a fiscal year has violated section 407(e)(2) during the fiscal year, the Secretary shall reduce the grant payable to the State under section 403(a)(1) for the immediately succeeding fiscal year by an amount equal to not more than 5 percent of the State family assistance grant.

(B) PENALTY BASED ON SEVERITY OF FAILURE.—The Secretary shall impose reductions under subparagraph (A) with respect to a fiscal year based on the degree of noncompliance.

(12) REQUIREMENT TO EXPEND ADDITIONAL STATE FUNDS TO REPLACE GRANT REDUCTIONS; PENALTY FOR FAILURE TO DO SO.—If the grant payable to a State under section 403(a)(1) for a fiscal year is reduced by reason of this subsection, the State shall, during the immediately succeeding fiscal year, expend under the State program funded under this part an amount equal to the

total amount of such reductions. If the State fails during such succeeding fiscal year to make the expenditure required by the preceding sentence from its own funds, the Secretary may reduce the grant payable to the State under section 403(a)(1) for the fiscal year that follows such succeeding fiscal year by an amount equal to the sum of—

(A) not more than 2 percent of the State family assistance grant; and

(B) the amount of the expenditure required by the preceding sentence.

(13) PENALTY FOR FAILURE OF STATE TO MAINTAIN HISTORIC EFFORT DURING YEAR IN WHICH WELFARE-TO-WORK GRANT IS RECEIVED.—If a grant is made to a State under section 403(a)(5)(A) for a fiscal year and paragraph (7) of this subsection requires the grant payable to the State under section 403(a)(1) to be reduced for the immediately succeeding fiscal year, then the Secretary shall reduce the grant payable to the State under section 403(a)(1) for such succeeding fiscal year by the amount of the grant made to the State under section 403(a)(5)(A) for the fiscal year.

(14) PENALTY FOR FAILURE TO REDUCE ASSISTANCE FOR RECIPIENTS REFUSING WITHOUT GOOD CAUSE TO WORK.—

(A) IN GENERAL.—If the Secretary determines that a State to which a grant is made under section 403 in a fiscal year has violated section 407(e) during the fiscal year, the Secretary shall reduce the grant payable to the State under section 403(a)(1) for the immediately succeeding fiscal year by an amount equal to not less than 1 percent and not more than 5 percent of the State family assistance grant.

(B) PENALTY BASED ON SEVERITY OF FAILURE.—The Secretary shall impose reductions under subparagraph (A) with respect to a fiscal year based on the degree of noncompliance.

(15) PENALTY FOR FAILURE TO ESTABLISH OR COMPLY WITH WORK PARTICIPATION VERIFICATION PROCEDURES.—

(A) IN GENERAL.—If the Secretary determines that a State to which a grant is made under section 403 in a fiscal year has violated section 407(i)(2) during the fiscal year, the Secretary shall reduce the grant payable to the State under section 403(a)(1) for the immediately succeeding fiscal year by an amount equal to not less than 1 percent and not more than 5 percent of the State family assistance grant.

(B) PENALTY BASED ON SEVERITY OF FAILURE.—The Secretary shall impose reductions under subparagraph (A) with respect to a fiscal year based on the degree of noncompliance.

(b) REASONABLE CAUSE EXCEPTION.—

(1) IN GENERAL.—The Secretary may not impose a penalty on a State under subsection (a) with respect to a requirement if the Secretary determines that the State has reasonable cause for failing to comply with the requirement.

(2) EXCEPTION.—Paragraph (1) of this subsection shall not apply to any penalty under paragraph (6), (7), (8), (10), (12), or (13) of subsection (a).

(c) CORRECTIVE COMPLIANCE PLAN.—

(1) IN GENERAL.—

(A) NOTIFICATION OF VIOLATION.—Before imposing a penalty against a State under subsection (a) with respect to a violation of this part, the Secretary shall notify the State of the violation and allow the State the opportunity to enter into a corrective compliance plan in accordance with this subsection which outlines how the State will correct or discontinue, as appropriate the violation and how the State will insure continuing compliance with this part.

(B) 60-DAY PERIOD TO PROPOSE A CORRECTIVE COMPLIANCE PLAN.—During the 60-day period that begins on the date the State receives a notice provided under subparagraph (A) with respect to a violation, the State may submit to the Federal Government a corrective compliance plan to correct or discontinue, as appropriate the violation.

(C) CONSULTATION ABOUT MODIFICATIONS.—During the 60-day period that begins with the date the Secretary receives a corrective compliance plan submitted by a State in accordance with subparagraph (B), the Secretary may consult with the State on modifications to the plan.

(D) ACCEPTANCE OF PLAN.—A corrective compliance plan submitted by a State in accordance with subparagraph (B) is deemed to be accepted by the Secretary if the Secretary does not accept or reject the plan during 60-day period that begins on the date the plan is submitted.

(2) EFFECT OF CORRECTING OR DISCONTINUING VIOLATION.—The Secretary may not impose any penalty under subsection (a) with respect to any violation covered by a State corrective compliance plan accepted by the Secretary if the State corrects or discontinues, as appropriate the violation pursuant to the plan.

(3) EFFECT OF FAILING TO CORRECT OR DISCONTINUE VIOLATION.—The Secretary shall assess some or all of a penalty imposed on a State under subsection (a) with respect to a violation if the State does not, in a timely manner, correct or discontinue, as appropriate, the violation pursuant to a State corrective compliance plan accepted by the Secretary.

(4) INAPPLICABILITY TO CERTAIN PENALTIES.—This subsection shall not apply to the imposition of a penalty against a State under paragraph (6), (7), (8), (10), (12), or (13) of subsection (a).

(d) LIMITATION ON AMOUNT OF PENALTIES.—

(1) IN GENERAL.—In imposing the penalties described in subsection (a), the Secretary shall not reduce any quarterly payment to a State by more than 25 percent.

(2) CARRYFORWARD OF UNRECOVERED PENALTIES.—To the extent that paragraph (1) of this subsection prevents the Secretary from recovering during a fiscal year the full amount of penalties imposed on a State under subsection (a) of this section for a prior fiscal year, the Secretary shall apply any remaining amount of such penalties to the grant payable to the State under section 403(a)(1) for the immediately succeeding fiscal year.

APPEAL OF ADVERSE DECISION

SEC. 410. [42 U.S.C. 610] (a) IN GENERAL.—Within 5 days after the date the Secretary takes any adverse action under this part with

324   SOCIAL SECURITY ACT—§ 410(a)(cont)

respect to a State, the Secretary shall notify the chief executive officer of the State of the adverse action, including any action with respect to the State plan submitted under section 402 or the imposition of a penalty under section 409.

(b) ADMINISTRATIVE REVIEW.—

(1) IN GENERAL.—Within 60 days after the date a State receives notice under subsection (a) of an adverse action, the State may appeal the action, in whole or in part, to the Departmental Appeals Board established in the Department of Health and Human Services (in this section referred to as the "Board") by filing an appeal with the Board.

(2) PROCEDURAL RULES.—The Board shall consider an appeal filed by a State under paragraph (1) on the basis of such documentation as the State may submit and as the Board may require to support the final decision of the Board. In deciding whether to uphold an adverse action or any portion of such an action, the Board shall conduct a thorough review of the issues and take into account all relevant evidence. The Board shall make a final determination with respect to an appeal filed under paragraph (1) not less than 60 days after the date the appeal is filed.

(c) JUDICIAL REVIEW OF ADVERSE DECISION.—

(1) IN GENERAL.—Within 90 days after the date of a final decision by the Board under this section with respect to an adverse action taken against a State, the State may obtain judicial review of the final decision (and the findings incorporated into the final decision) by filing an action in—

(A) the district court of the United States for the judicial district in which the principal or headquarters office of the State agency is located; or

(B) the United States District Court for the District of Columbia.

(2) PROCEDURAL RULES.—The district court in which an action is filed under paragraph (1) shall review the final decision of the Board on the record established in the administrative proceeding, in accordance with the standards of review prescribed by subparagraphs (A) through (E) of section 706(2) of title 5, United States Code[45]. The review shall be on the basis of the documents and supporting data submitted to the Board.

DATA COLLECTION AND REPORTING

SEC. 411. [42 U.S.C. 611] (a) QUARTERLY REPORTS BY STATES.—

(1) GENERAL REPORTING REQUIREMENT.—

(A) CONTENTS OF REPORT.—Each eligible State shall collect on a monthly basis, and report to the Secretary on a quarterly basis, the following disaggregated case record information on the families receiving assistance under the State program funded under this part (except for information relating to activities carried out under section 403(a)(5)):

(i) The county of residence of the family.

(ii) Whether a child receiving such assistance or an adult in the family is receiving—

(I) Federal disability insurance benefits;

---

[45] See Vol. II, 5 U.S.C. 706(2) A through E.

SOCIAL SECURITY ACT—§ 411(a)(1)(A)(xiv)   325

(II) benefits based on Federal disability status;

(III) aid under a State plan approved under title XIV (as in effect without regard to the amendment made by section 301 of the Social Security Amendments of 1972[46]));

(IV) aid or assistance under a State plan approved under title XVI (as in effect without regard to such amendment) by reason of being permanently and totally disabled; or

(V) supplemental security income benefits under title XVI (as in effect pursuant to such amendment) by reason of disability.

(iii) The ages of the members of such families.

(iv) The number of individuals in the family, and the relation of each family member to the head of the family.

(v) The employment status and earnings of the employed adult in the family.

(vi) The marital status of the adults in the family, including whether such adults have never married, are widowed, or are divorced.

(vii) The race and educational level of each adult in the family.

(viii) The race and educational level of each child in the family.

(ix) Whether the family received subsidized housing, medical assistance under the State plan approved under title XIX, supplemental nutrition assistance program[47], or subsidized child care, and if the latter 2, the amount received.

(x) The number of months that the family has received each type of assistance under the program.

(xi) If the adults participated in, and the number of hours per week of participation in, the following activities:

(I) Education.

(II) Subsidized private sector employment.

(III) Unsubsidized employment.

(IV) Public sector employment, work experience, or community service.

(V) Job search.

(VI) Job skills training or on-the-job training.

(VII) Vocational education.

(xii) Information necessary to calculate participation rates under section 407.

(xiii) The type and amount of assistance received under the program, including the amount of and reason for any reduction of assistance (including sanctions).

(xiv) Any amount of unearned income received by any member of the family.

---

[46] P.L. 92-603; 86 Stat. 1465.

[47] P.L. 110-246, §4002(b)(1)(E), struck out "food stamps" and substituted "supplemental nutrition assistance program benefits", effective October 1, 2008. P.L. 110-234, §4002(b)(1)(E), which made the same amendment, was repealed, effective May 22, 2008 pursuant to P.L. 110-246, §4(a).

326   SOCIAL SECURITY ACT—§ 411(a)(1)(A)(xv)

(xv) The citizenship of the members of the family.

(xvi) From a sample of closed cases, whether the family left the program, and if so, whether the family left due to—

    (I) employment;

    (II) marriage;

    (III) the prohibition set forth in section 408(a)(7);

    (IV) sanction; or

    (V) State policy.

(xvii) With respect to each individual in the family who has not attained 20 years of age, whether the individual is a parent of a child in the family.

(B) USE OF SAMPLES.—

    (i) AUTHORITY.—A State may comply with subparagraph (A) by submitting disaggregated case record information on a sample of families selected through the use of scientifically acceptable sampling methods approved by the Secretary.

    (ii) SAMPLING AND OTHER METHODS.—The Secretary shall provide the States with such case sampling plans and data collection procedures as the Secretary deems necessary to produce statistically valid estimates of the performance of State programs funded under this part. The Secretary may develop and implement procedures for verifying the quality of data submitted by the States.

(2) REPORT ON USE OF FEDERAL FUNDS TO COVER ADMINISTRATIVE COSTS AND OVERHEAD.—The report required by paragraph (1) for a fiscal quarter shall include a statement of the percentage of the funds paid to the State under this part for the quarter that are used to cover administrative costs or overhead, with a separate statement of the percentage of such funds that are used to cover administrative costs or overhead incurred for programs operated with funds provided under section 403(a)(5).

(3) REPORT ON STATE EXPENDITURES ON PROGRAMS FOR NEEDY FAMILIES.—The report required by paragraph (1) for a fiscal quarter shall include a statement of the total amount expended by the State during the quarter on programs for needy families, with a separate statement of the total amount expended by the State during the quarter on programs operated with funds provided under section 403(a)(5).

(4) REPORT ON NONCUSTODIAL PARENTS PARTICIPATING IN WORK ACTIVITIES.—The report required by paragraph (1) for a fiscal quarter shall include the number of noncustodial parents in the State who participated in work activities (as defined in section 407(d)) during the quarter, with a separate statement of the number of such parents who participated in programs operated with funds provided under section 403(a)(5).

(5) REPORT ON TRANSITIONAL SERVICES.—The report required by paragraph (1) for a fiscal quarter shall include the total amount expended by the State during the quarter to provide transitional services to a family that has ceased to receive assistance under this part because of employment, along with a description of such services.

SOCIAL SECURITY ACT—§ 412(a)(1)(A) 327

(6) REPORT ON FAMILIES RECEIVING ASSISTANCE.—The report required by paragraph (1) for a fiscal quarter shall include for each month in the quarter—

(A) the number of families and individuals receiving assistance under the State program funded under this part (including the number of 2-parent and 1-parent families);

(B) the total dollar value of such assistance received by all families; and

(C) with respect to families and individuals participating in a program operated with funds provided under section 403(a)(5)—

(i) the total number of such families and individuals; and

(ii) the number of such families and individuals whose participation in such a program was terminated during a month.

(7) REGULATIONS.—The Secretary shall prescribe such regulations as may be necessary to define the data elements with respect to which reports are required by this subsection, and shall consult with the Secretary of Labor in defining the data elements with respect to programs operated with funds provided under section 403(a)(5).

(b) ANNUAL REPORTS TO THE CONGRESS BY THE SECRETARY.—Not later than 6 months after the end of fiscal year 1997, and each fiscal year thereafter, the Secretary shall transmit to the Congress a report describing—

(1) whether the States are meeting—

(A) the participation rates described in section 407(a); and

(B) the objectives of—

(i) increasing employment and earnings of needy families, and child support collections; and

(ii) decreasing out-of-wedlock pregnancies and child poverty;

(2) the demographic and financial characteristics of families applying for assistance, families receiving assistance, and families that become ineligible to receive assistance;

(3) the characteristics of each State program funded under this part; and

(4) the trends in employment and earnings of needy families with minor children living at home.

STATE REQUIRED TO PROVIDE CERTAIN INFORMATION

SEC. 411A. [42 U.S.C. 611a] Each State to which a grant is made under section 403 shall, at lease 4 times annually and upon request of the Immigration and Naturalization Service, furnish the Immigration and Naturalization Service with the name and address of, and other identifying information on, any individual who the State knows is unlawfully in the United States.

DIRECT FUNDING AND ADMINISTRATION BY INDIAN TRIBES

SEC. 412. [42 U.S.C. 612] (a) GRANTS FOR INDIAN TRIBES.—

(1) TRIBAL FAMILY ASSISTANCE GRANT.—

(A) IN GENERAL.—For each of fiscal years 1997, 1998, 1999, 2000, 2001, 2002 and 2003, the Secretary shall pay to each

328   SOCIAL SECURITY ACT—§ 412(a)(1)(B)

Indian tribe that has an approved tribal family assistance plan a tribal family assistance grant for the fiscal year in an amount equal to the amount determined under subparagraph (B), which shall be reduced for a fiscal year, on a pro rata basis for each quarter, in the case of a tribal family assistance plan approved during a fiscal year for which the plan is to be in effect, and shall reduce the grant payable under section 403(a)(1) to any State in which lies the service area or areas of the Indian tribe by that portion of the amount so determined that is attributable to expenditures by the State.

(B) AMOUNT DETERMINED.—

(i) IN GENERAL.—The amount determined under this subparagraph is an amount equal to the total amount of the Federal payments to a State or States under section 403 (as in effect during such fiscal year) for fiscal year 1994 attributable to expenditures (other than child care expenditures) by the State or States under parts A and F (as so in effect) for fiscal year 1994 for Indian families residing in the service area or areas identified by the Indian tribe pursuant to subsection (b)(1)(C) of this section.

(ii) USE OF STATE SUBMITTED DATA.—

(I) IN GENERAL.—The Secretary shall use State submitted data to make each determination under clause (i).

(II) DISAGREEMENT WITH DETERMINATION.—If an Indian tribe or tribal organization disagrees with State submitted data described under subclause (I), the Indian tribe or tribal organization may submit to the Secretary such additional information as may be relevant to making the determination under clause (i) and the Secretary may consider such information before making such determination.

(2) GRANTS FOR INDIAN TRIBES THAT RECEIVED JOBS FUNDS.—

(A) IN GENERAL.—For each of fiscal years 1997, 1998, 1999, 2000, 2001, 2002, and 2003 the Secretary shall pay to each eligible Indian tribe that proposes to operate a program described in subparagraph (C) a grant in an amount equal to the amount received by the Indian tribe in fiscal year 1994 under section 482(i) (as in effect during fiscal year 1994).

(B) ELIGIBLE INDIAN TRIBE.—For purposes of subparagraph (A), the term "eligible Indian tribe" means an Indian tribe or Alaska Native organization that conducted a job opportunities and basic skills training program in fiscal year 1995 under section 482(i) (as in effect during fiscal year 1995).

(C) USE OF GRANT.—Each Indian tribe to which a grant is made under this paragraph shall use the grant for the purpose of operating a program to make work activities available to such population and such service areas or areas as the tribe specifies.

(D) APPROPRIATION.—Out of any money in the Treasury of the United States not otherwise appropriated, there are appropriated $7,633,287 for each fiscal year specified in subparagraph (A) for grants under subparagraph (A).

SOCIAL SECURITY ACT—§ 412(b)

(3) WELFARE-TO-WORK GRANTS.—

(A) IN GENERAL.—The Secretary of Labor shall award a grant in accordance with this paragraph to an Indian tribe for each fiscal year specified in section 403(a)(5)(H) for which the Indian tribe is a welfare-to-work tribe, in such amount as the Secretary of Labor deems appropriate, subject to subparagraph (B) of this paragraph.

(B) WELFARE-TO-WORK TRIBE.—An Indian tribe shall be considered a welfare-to-work tribe for a fiscal year for purposes of this paragraph if the Indian tribe meets the following requirements:

(i) The Indian tribe has submitted to the Secretary of Labor a plan which describes how, consistent with section 403(a)(5), the Indian tribe will use any funds provided under this paragraph during the fiscal year. If the Indian tribe has a tribal family assistance plan, the plan referred to in the preceding sentence shall be in the form of an addendum to the tribal family assistance plan.

(ii) The Indian tribe is operating a program under a tribal family assistance plan approved by the Secretary of Health and Human Services, a program described in paragraph (2)(C), or an employment program funded through other sources under which substantial services are provided to recipients of assistance under a program funded under this part.

(iii) The Indian tribe has provided the Secretary of Labor with an estimate of the amount that the Indian tribe intends to expend during the fiscal year (excluding tribal expenditures described in section 409(a)(7)(B)(iv) (other than subclause (III) thereof)) pursuant to this paragraph.

(iv) The Indian tribe has agreed to negotiate in good faith with the Secretary of Health and Human Services with respect to the substance and funding of any evaluation under section 413(j), and to cooperate with the conduct of any such evaluation.

(C) LIMITATIONS ON USE OF FUNDS.—

(i) IN GENERAL.—Section 403(a)(5)(C) shall apply to funds provided to Indian tribes under this paragraph in the same manner in which such section applies to funds provided under section 403(a)(5).

(ii) WAIVER AUTHORITY.—The Secretary of Labor may waive or modify the application of a provision of section 403(a)(5)(C) (other than clause (viii) thereof) with respect to an Indian tribe to the extent necessary to enable the Indian tribe to operate a more efficient or effective program with the funds provided under this paragraph.

(iii) REGULATIONS.—Within 90 days after the date of the enactment of this paragraph, the Secretary of Labor, after consultation with the Secretary of Health and Human Services and the Secretary of Housing and Urban Development, shall prescribe such regulations as may be necessary to implement this paragraph.

(b) 3–YEAR TRIBAL FAMILY ASSISTANCE PLAN.—

330 SOCIAL SECURITY ACT—§ 412(b)(1)

(1) IN GENERAL.—Any Indian tribe that desires to receive a tribal family assistance grant shall submit to the Secretary a 3-year tribal family assistance plan that—

(A) outlines the Indian tribe's approach to providing welfare-related services for the 3-year period, consistent with this section;

(B) specifies whether the welfare-related services provided under the plan will be provided by the Indian tribe or through agreements, contracts, or compacts with intertribal consortia, States, or other entities;

(C) identifies the population and service area or areas to be served by such plan;

(D) provides that a family receiving assistance under the plan may not receive duplicative assistance from other State or tribal programs funded under this part;

(E) identifies the employment opportunities in or near the service area or areas of the Indian tribe and the manner in which the Indian tribe will cooperate and participate in enhancing such opportunities for recipients of assistance under the plan consistent with any applicable State standards; and

(F) applies the fiscal accountability provisions of section 5(f)(1) of the Indian Self-Determination and Education Assistance Act[48] (25 U.S.C. 450c(f)(1)), relating to the submission of a single-agency audit report required by chapter 75 of title 31, United States Code[49].

(2) APPROVAL.—The Secretary shall approve each tribal family assistance plan submitted in accordance with paragraph (1).

(3) CONSORTIUM OF TRIBES.—Nothing in this section shall preclude the development and submission of a single tribal family assistance plan by the participating Indian tribes of an intertribal consortium.

(c) MINIMUM WORK PARTICIPATION REQUIREMENTS AND TIME LIMITS.—The Secretary, with the participation of Indian tribes, shall establish for each Indian tribe receiving a grant under this section minimum work participation requirements, appropriate time limits for receipt of welfare-related services under the grant, and penalties against individuals—

(1) consistent with the purposes of this section;

(2) consistent with the economic conditions and resources available to each tribe; and

(3) similar to comparable provisions in section 407(e).

(d) EMERGENCY ASSISTANCE.—Nothing in this section shall preclude an Indian tribe from seeking emergency assistance from any Federal loan program or emergency fund.

(e) ACCOUNTABILITY.—Nothing in this section shall be construed to limit the ability of the Secretary to maintain program funding accountability consistent with—

(1) generally accepted accounting principles; and

(2) the requirements of the Indian Self-Determination and Education Assistance Act (25 U.S.C. 450 et seq.).

---

[48] P.L. 93-638.
[49] See Vol. II, 31 U.S.C. chapter 75.

SOCIAL SECURITY ACT—§ 413(c)   331

(f) ELIGIBILITY FOR FEDERAL LOANS.—Section 406 shall apply to an Indian tribe with an approved tribal assistance plan in the same manner as such section applies to a State, except that section 406(c) shall be applied by substituting "section 412(a)" for "section 403(a)".

(g) PENALTIES.—

(1) Subsections (a)(1), (a)(6), (b), and (c) of section 409, shall apply to an Indian tribe with an approved tribal assistance plan in the same manner as such subsections apply to a State.

(2) Section 409(a)(3) shall apply to an Indian tribe with an approved tribal assistance plan by substituting "meet minimum work participation requirements established under section 412(c)" for "comply with section 407(a)".

(h) DATA COLLECTION AND REPORTING.—Section 411 shall apply to an Indian tribe with an approved tribal family assistance plan.

(i) SPECIAL RULE FOR INDIAN TRIBES IN ALASKA.—

(1) IN GENERAL.—Notwithstanding any other provision of this section, and except as provided in paragraph (2), an Indian tribe in the State of Alaska that receives a tribal family assistance grant under this section shall use the grant to operate a program in accordance with requirements comparable to the requirements applicable to the program of the State of Alaska funded under this part. Comparability of programs shall be established on the basis of program criteria developed by the Secretary in consultation with the State of Alaska and such Indian tribes.

(2) WAIVER.—An Indian tribe described in paragraph (1) may apply to the appropriate State authority to receive a waiver of the requirement of paragraph (1).

RESEARCH, EVALUATIONS, AND NATIONAL STUDIES

SEC. 413. [42 U.S.C. 613] (a) RESEARCH.—The Secretary, directly or through grants, contracts, or interagency agreements, shall conduct research on the benefits, effects, and costs of operating different State programs funded under this part, including time limits relating to eligibility for assistance. The research shall include studies on the effects of different programs and the operation of such programs on welfare dependency, illegitimacy, teen pregnancy, employment rates, child well-being, and any other area the Secretary deems appropriate. The Secretary shall also conduct research on the costs and benefits of State activities under section 407.

(b) DEVELOPMENT AND EVALUATION OF INNOVATIVE APPROACHES TO REDUCING WELFARE DEPENDENCY AND INCREASING CHILD WELL-BEING.—

(1) IN GENERAL.—The Secretary may assist States in developing, and shall evaluate, innovative approaches for reducing welfare dependency and increasing the well-being of minor children living at home with respect to recipients of assistance under programs funded under this part. The Secretary may provide funds for training and technical assistance to carry out the approaches developed pursuant to this paragraph.

(2) EVALUATIONS.—In performing the evaluations under paragraph (1), the Secretary shall, to the maximum extent feasible, use random assignment as an evaluation methodology.

(c) DISSEMINATION OF INFORMATION.—The Secretary shall develop innovative methods of disseminating information on any research,

332   SOCIAL SECURITY ACT—§ 413(c)(cont)

evaluations, and studies conducted under this section, including the facilitation of the sharing of information and best practices among States and localities through the use of computers and other technologies.

(d) ANNUAL RANKING OF STATES AND REVIEW OF MOST AND LEAST SUCCESSFUL WORK PROGRAMS.—

(1) ANNUAL RANKING OF STATES.—The Secretary shall rank annually the States to which grants are paid under section 403 in the order of their success in placing recipients of assistance under the State program funded under this part into long-term private sector jobs, reducing the overall welfare caseload, and, when a practicable method for calculating this information becomes available, diverting individuals from formally applying to the State program and receiving assistance. In ranking States under this subsection, the Secretary shall take into account the average number of minor children living at home in families in the State that have incomes below the poverty line and the amount of funding provided each State for such families.

(2) ANNUAL REVIEW OF MOST AND LEAST SUCCESSFUL WORK PROGRAMS.—The Secretary shall review the programs of the 3 States most recently ranked highest under paragraph (1) and the 3 States most recently ranked lowest under paragraph (1) that provide parents with work experience, assistance in finding employment, and other work preparation activities and support services to enable the families of such parents to leave the program and become self-sufficient.

(e) ANNUAL RANKING OF STATES AND REVIEW OF ISSUES RELATING TO OUT-OF-WEDLOCK BIRTHS.—

(1) IN GENERAL.—The Secretary shall annually rank States to which grants are made under section 403 based on the following ranking factors:

(A) ABSOLUTE OUT-OF-WEDLOCK RATIOS.—The ratio represented by—

(i) the total number of out-of-wedlock births in families receiving assistance under the State program under this part in the State for the most recent year for which information is available; over

(ii) the total number of births in families receiving assistance under the State program under this part in the State for the year.

(B) NET CHANGES IN THE OUT-OF-WEDLOCK RATIO.—The difference between the ratio described in subparagraph (A) with respect to a State for the most recent year for which such information is available and the ratio with respect to the State for the immediately preceding year.

(2) ANNUAL REVIEW.—The Secretary shall review the programs of the 5 States most recently ranked highest under paragraph (1) and the 5 States most recently ranked the lowest under paragraph (1).

(f) STATE-INITIATED EVALUATIONS.—A State shall be eligible to receive funding to evaluate the State program funded under this part if—

(1) the State submits a proposal to the Secretary for the evaluation;

(2) the Secretary determines that the design and approach of the evaluation is rigorous and is likely to yield information that is credible and will be useful to other States; and

(3) unless otherwise waived by the Secretary, the State contributes to the cost of the evaluation, from non-Federal sources, an amount equal to at least 10 percent of the cost of the evaluation.

(g) REPORT ON CIRCUMSTANCES OF CERTAIN CHILDREN AND FAMILIES.—

(1) IN GENERAL.—Beginning 3 years after the date of the enactment of this section[50], the Secretary of Health and Human Services shall prepare and submit to the Committees on Ways and Means and on Education and the Workforce of the House of Representatives and to the Committees on Finance and on Labor and Resources of the Senate annual reports that examine in detail the matters described in paragraph (2) with respect to each of the following groups for the period after such enactment:

(A) Individuals who were children in families that have become ineligible for assistance under a State program funded under this part by reason of having reached a time limit on the provision of such assistance.

(B) Children born after such date of enactment to parents who, at the time of such birth, had not attained 20 years of age.

(C) Individuals who, after such date of enactment, became parents before attaining 20 years of age.

(2) MATTERS DESCRIBED.—The matters described in this paragraph are the following:

(A) The percentage of each group that has dropped out of secondary school (or the equivalent), and the percentage of each group at each level of educational attainment.

(B) The percentage of each group that is employed.

(C) The percentage of each group that has been convicted of a crime or has been adjudicated as a delinquent.

(D) The rate at which the members of each group are born, or have children, out-of-wedlock, and the percentage of each group that is married.

(E) The percentage of each group that continues to participate in State programs funded under this part.

(F) The percentage of each group that has health insurance provided by a private entity (broken down by whether the insurance is provided through an employer or otherwise), the percentage that has health insurance provided by an agency of government, and the percentage that does not have health insurance.

(G) The average income of the families of the members of each group.

(H) Such other matters as the Secretary deems appropriate.

(h) FUNDING OF STUDIES AND DEMONSTRATIONS.—

(1) IN GENERAL.—Out of any money in the Treasury of the United States not otherwise appropriated, there are appropriated

---

[50] The date of enactment of this section was August 22, 1996.

334   SOCIAL SECURITY ACT—§ 413(h)(1)(A)

$15,000,000 for each of fiscal years 1997 through 2002 for the purpose for paying—

(A) the cost of conducting the research described in subsection (a);

(B) the cost of developing and evaluating innovative approaches for reducing welfare dependency and increasing the well-being of minor children under subsection (b);

(C) the Federal share of any State-initiated study approved under subsection (f); and

(D) an amount determined by the Secretary to be necessary to operate and evaluate demonstration projects, relating to this part, that are in effect or approved under section 1115 as of August 22, 1996, and are continued after such date.

(2) ALLOCATION.—Of the amount appropriated under paragraph (1) for a fiscal year—

(A) 50 percent shall be allocated for the purposes described in subparagraphs (A) and (B) of paragraph (1), and

(B) 50 percent shall be allocated for the purposes described in subparagraphs (C) and (D) of paragraph (1).

(3) DEMONSTRATIONS OF INNOVATIVE STRATEGIES.—The Secretary may implement and evaluate demonstrations of innovative and promising strategies which—

(A) provide one-time capital funds to establish, expand, or replicate programs;

(B) test performance-based grant-to-loan financing in which programs meeting performance targets receive grants while programs not meeting such targets repay funding on a prorated basis; and

(C) test strategies in multiple States and types of communities.

(i) CHILD POVERTY RATES.—

(1) IN GENERAL.—Not later than May 31, 1998, and annually thereafter, the chief executive officer of each State shall submit to the Secretary a statement of the child poverty rate in the State as of such date of enactment or the date of the most recent prior statement under this paragraph.

(2) SUBMISSION OF CORRECTIVE ACTION PLAN.—Not later than 90 days after the date a State submits a statement under paragraph (1) which indicates that, as a result of the amendments made by section 103 of the Personal Responsibility and Work Opportunity Reconciliation Act of 1996[51], the child poverty rate of the State has increased by 5 percent or more since the most recent prior statement under paragraph (1), the State shall prepare and submit to the Secretary a corrective action plan in accordance with paragraph (3).

(3) CONTENTS OF PLAN.—A corrective action plan submitted under paragraph (2) shall outline the manner in which the State will reduce the child poverty rate in the State. The plan shall include a description of the actions to be taken by the State under such plan.

(4) COMPLIANCE WITH PLAN.—A State that submits a corrective action plan that the Secretary has found contains the information

---

[51] P.L. 104-193; 110 Stat. 2105.

required by this subsection shall implement the corrective action plan until the State determines that the child poverty rate in the State is less than the lowest child poverty rate on the basis of which the State was required to submit the corrective action plan.

(5) METHODOLOGY.—The Secretary shall prescribe regulations establishing the methodology by which a State shall determine the child poverty rate in the State. The methodology shall take into account factors including the number of children who receive free or reduced-price lunches, the number of supplemental nutrition assistance program benefits[52] households, and, to the extent available, county-by-county estimates of children in poverty as determined by the Census Bureau.

(j) EVALUATION OF WELFARE-TO-WORK PROGRAMS.—

(1) EVALUATION.—The Secretary, in consultation with the Secretary of Labor and the Secretary of Housing and Urban Development—

(A) shall develop a plan to evaluate how grants made under sections 403(a)(5) and 412(a)(3) have been used;

(B) may evaluate the use of such grants by such grantees as the Secretary deems appropriate, in accordance with an agreement entered into with the grantees after good-faith negotiations; and

(C) is urged to include the following outcome measures in the plan developed under subparagraph (A):

(i) Placements in unsubsidized employment, and placements in unsubsidized employment that last for at least 6 months.

(ii) Placements in the private and public sectors.

(iii) Earnings of individuals who obtain employment.

(iv) Average expenditures per placement.

(2) REPORTS TO THE CONGRESS.—

(A) IN GENERAL.—Subject to subparagraphs (B) and (C), the Secretary, in consultation with the Secretary of Labor and the Secretary of Housing and Urban Development, shall submit to the Congress reports on the projects funded under section 403(a)(5) and 412(a)(3) and on the evaluations of the projects.

(B) INTERIM REPORT.—Not later than January 1, 1999, the Secretary shall submit an interim report on the matter described in subparagraph (A).

(C) FINAL REPORT.—Not later than January 1, 2001, (or at a later date, if the Secretary informs the Committees of the Congress with jurisdiction over the subject matter of the report) the Secretary shall submit a final report on the matter described in subparagraph (A).

STUDY BY THE CENSUS BUREAU

SEC. 414. [42 U.S.C. 614] (a) IN GENERAL.—The Bureau of the Census shall continue to collect data on the 1992 and 1993 panels of the Survey of Income and Program Participation as necessary to obtain

---

[52] P.L. 110-246, §4002(b)(1)(D), struck out "food stamp" and substituted "supplemental nutrition assistance program benefits", effective October 1, 2008. P.L. 110-234, §4002(b)(1)(D), which made the same amendment, was repealed, effective May 22, 2008 pursuant to P.L. 110-246, §4(a).

336 SOCIAL SECURITY ACT—§ 414(a)(cont)

such information as will enable interested persons to evaluate the impact of the amendments made by title I of the Personal Responsibility and Work Opportunity Reconciliation Act of 1996[53] on a random national sample of recipients of assistance under State programs funded under this part and (as appropriate) other low-income families, and in doing so, shall pay particular attention to the issues of out-of-wedlock birth, welfare dependency, the beginning and end of welfare spells, and the causes of repeat welfare spells, and shall obtain information about the status of children participating in such panels.

(b) APPROPRIATION.—Out of any money in the Treasury of the United States not otherwise appropriated, there are appropriated $10,000,000 for each of fiscal years 1996, 1997, 1998, 1999, 2000, 2001, 2002, and 2003 for payment to the Bureau of the Census to carry out subsection (a).

WAIVERS

SEC. 415. [42 U.S.C. 615] (a) CONTINUATION OF WAIVERS.—

(1) WAIVERS IN EFFECT ON DATE OF ENACTMENT OF WELFARE REFORM.—

(A) IN GENERAL.—Except as provided in subparagraph (B), if any waiver granted to a State under section 1115 of this Act or otherwise which relates to the provision of assistance under a State plan under this part (as in effect on September 30, 1996) is in effect as of the date of the enactment August 22, 1996 of the Personal Responsibility and Work Opportunity Reconciliation Act of 1996[54], the amendments made by the Personal Responsibility and Work Opportunity Reconciliation Act of 1996 (other than by section 103(c) of the Personal Responsibility and Work Opportunity Reconciliation Act of 1996) shall not apply with respect to the State before the expiration (determined without regard to any extensions) of the waiver to the extent such amendments are inconsistent with the waiver.

(B) FINANCING LIMITATION.—Notwithstanding any other provision of law, beginning with fiscal year 1996, a State operating under a waiver described in subparagraph (A) shall be entitled to payment under section 403 for the fiscal year, in lieu of any other payment provided for in the waiver.

(2) WAIVERS GRANTED SUBSEQUENTLY.—

(A) IN GENERAL.—Except as provided in subparagraph (B), if any waiver granted to a State under section 1115 of this Act or otherwise which relates to the provision of assistance under a State plan under this part (as in effect on September 30, 1996) is submitted to the Secretary before the date of the enactment of the Personal Responsibility and Work Opportunity Reconciliation Act of 1996 and approved by the Secretary on or before July 1, 1997, and the State demonstrates to the satisfaction of the Secretary that the waiver will not result in Federal expenditures under title IV of this Act (as in effect without regard to the amendments made by the Personal Responsibility and Work Opportunity Reconcil-

---

[53] P.L. 104-193; 110 Stat. 2105.
[54] P.L. 104-193; 110 Stat. 2105.

SOCIAL SECURITY ACT—§ 416 337

iation Act of 1996) that are greater than would occur in the absence of the waiver, the amendments made by the Personal Responsibility and Work Opportunity Reconciliation Act of 1996 (other than by section 103(c) of the Personal Responsibility and Work Opportunity Reconciliation Act of 1996) shall not apply with respect to the State before the expiration (determined without regard to any extensions) of the waiver to the extent the amendments made by the Personal Responsibility and Work Opportunity Reconciliation Act of 1996 are inconsistent with the waiver.

(B) NO EFFECT ON NEW WORK REQUIREMENTS.—Notwithstanding subparagraph (A), a waiver granted under section 1115 or otherwise which relates to the provision of assistance under a State program funded under this part (as in effect on September 30, 1996) shall not affect the applicability of section 407 to the State.

(b) STATE OPTION TO TERMINATE WAIVER.—

(1) IN GENERAL.—A State may terminate a waiver described in subsection (a) before the expiration of the waiver.

(2) REPORT.—A State which terminates a waiver under paragraph (1) shall submit a report to the Secretary summarizing the waiver and any available information concerning the result or effect of the waiver.

(3) HOLD HARMLESS PROVISION.—

(A) IN GENERAL.—Notwithstanding any other provision of law, a State that, not later than the date described in subparagraph (B) of this paragraph, submits a written request to terminate a waiver described in subsection (a) shall be held harmless for accrued cost neutrality liabilities incurred under the waiver.

(B) DATE DESCRIBED.—The date described in this subparagraph is 90 days following the adjournment of the first regular session of the State legislature that begins after the date of the enactment[55] of the Personal Responsibility and Work Opportunity Reconciliation Act of 1996.

(c) SECRETARIAL ENCOURAGEMENT OF CURRENT WAIVERS.—The Secretary shall encourage any State operating a waiver described in subsection (a) to continue the waiver and to evaluate, using random sampling and other characteristics of accepted scientific evaluations, the result or effect of the waiver.

(d) CONTINUATION OF INDIVIDUAL WAIVERS.—A State may elect to continue 1 or more individual waivers described in subsection (a).

ADMINISTRATION

SEC. 416. [42 U.S.C. 616] The programs under this part and part D shall be administered by an Assistant Secretary for Family Support within the Department of Health and Human Services, who shall be appointed by the President, by and with the advice and consent of the Senate, and who shall be in addition to any other Assistant Secretary of Health and Human Services provided for by law, and the Secretary shall reduce the Federal workforce within the Department of Health and Human services by an amount equal to the sum

---

[55] August 22, 1996 [P.L 104-193; 110 Stat. 2105].

338   SOCIAL SECURITY ACT—§ 416(cont)

of 75 percent of the full-time equivalent positions at such Department that relate to any direct spending program, or any program funded through discretionary spending, that has been converted into a block grant program under the Personal Responsibility and Work Opportunity Reconciliation Act of 1996[56] and the amendments made by such Act, and by an amount equal to 75 percent of that portion of the total full-time equivalent departmental management positions at such Department that bears the same relationship to the amount appropriated for any direct spending program, or any program funded through discretionary spending, that has been converted into a block grant program under the Personal Responsibility and Work Opportunity Reconciliation Act of 1996 and the amendments made by such Act, as such amount relates to the total amount appropriated for use by such Department, and notwithstanding any other provision of law, the Secretary shall take such actions as may be necessary, including reductions in force actions, consistent with sections 3502 and 3595 of title 5, United States Code[57], to reduce the full-time equivalent positions within the Department of Health and Human Services by 245 full-time equivalent positions related to the program converted into a block grant under the amendments made by section 103 of the Personal Responsibility and Work Opportunity Reconciliation Act of 1996, and by 60 full-time equivalent managerial positions in the Department.

LIMITATION ON FEDERAL AUTHORITY

SEC. 417. [42 U.S.C. 617] No officer or employee of the Federal Government may regulate the conduct of States under this part or enforce any provision of this part, except to the extent expressly provided in this part.

FUNDING FOR CHILD CARE

SEC. 418. [42 U.S.C. 618] (a) GENERAL CHILD CARE ENTITLEMENT.—

(1) GENERAL ENTITLEMENT.—Subject to the amount appropriated under paragraph (3), each State shall, for the purpose of providing child care assistance, be entitled to payments under a grant under this subsection for a fiscal year in an amount equal to the greater of—

(A) the total amount required to be paid to the State under section 403 for fiscal year 1994 or 1995 (whichever is greater) with respect to expenditures for child care under subsections (g) and (i) of section 402 (as in effect before October 1, 1995); or

(B) the average of the total amounts required to be paid to the State for fiscal years 1992 through 1994 under the subsections referred to in subparagraph (A).

(2) REMAINDER.—

(A) GRANTS.—The Secretary shall use any amounts appropriated for a fiscal year under paragraph (3), and remaining after the reservation described in paragraph (4) and after

---

[56] P.L. 104-193; 110 Stat. 2105.
[57] See Vol. II, 5 U.S.C. 3502 and 3595.

SOCIAL SECURITY ACT—§ 418(a)(3)(B)   339

grants are awarded under paragraph (1), to make grants to States under this paragraph.

(B) ALLOTMENTS TO STATES.—The total amount available for payments to States under this paragraph, as determined under subparagraph (A), shall be allotted among the States based on the formula used for determining the amount of Federal payments to each State under section 403(n) (as in effect before October 1, 1995).

(C) FEDERAL MATCHING OF STATE EXPENDITURES EXCEEDING HISTORICAL EXPENDITURES.—The Secretary shall pay to each eligible State for a fiscal year an amount equal to the lesser of the State's allotment under subparagraph (B) or the Federal medical assistance percentage for the State for the fiscal year (as defined in section 1905(b), as such section was in effect on September 30, 1995) of so much of the State's expenditures for child care in that fiscal year as exceed the total amount of expenditures by the State (including expenditures from amounts made available from Federal funds) in fiscal year 1994 or 1995 (whichever is greater) for the programs described in paragraph (1)(A).

(D) REDISTRIBUTION.—

(i) IN GENERAL.—With respect to any fiscal year, if the Secretary determines (in accordance with clause (ii)) any amounts allotted to a State under this paragraph for such fiscal year will not be used by such State during such fiscal year for carrying out the purpose for which such amounts are allotted, the Secretary shall make such amounts available in the subsequent fiscal year for carrying out such purpose to one or more States which apply for such funds to the extent the Secretary determines that such States will be able to use such additional amounts for carrying out such purpose. Such available amounts shall be redistributed to a State pursuant to section 403(n) (as such section was in effect before October 1 1995) by substituting "the number of children residing in all States applying for such funds" for "the number of children residing in the United States in the second preceding fiscal year".

(ii) TIME OF DETERMINATION AND DISTRIBUTION.—The determination of the Secretary under clause (i) for a fiscal year shall be made not later than the end of the first quarter of the subsequent fiscal year. The redistribution of amounts under clause (i) shall be made as close as practicable to the date on which such determination is made. Any amount made available to a State from an appropriation for a fiscal year in accordance with this subparagraph shall, for purposes of this part, be regarded as part of such State's payment (as determined under this subsection) for the fiscal year in which the redistribution is made.

(3) APPROPRIATION.—For grants under this section, there are appropriated—

(A) $1,967,000,000 for fiscal year 1997;

(B) $2,067,000,000 for fiscal year 1998;

340 SOCIAL SECURITY ACT—§ 418(a)(3)(C)

(C) $2,167,000,000 for fiscal year 1999;

(D) $2,367,000,000 for fiscal year 2000;

(E) $2,567,000,000 for fiscal year 2001;

(F) $2,717,000,000 each of fiscal years 2002 and 2003;

(G) $2,917,000,000 for each of fiscal years 2006 through 2010.

(4) INDIAN TRIBES.—The Secretary shall reserve not less than 1 percent, and not more than 2 percent, of the aggregate amount appropriated to carry out this section in each fiscal year for payments to Indian tribes and tribal organizations.

(5) DATA USED TO DETERMINE STATE AND FEDERAL SHARES OF EXPENDITURES.—In making the determinations concerning expenditures required under paragraphs (1) and (2)(C), the Secretary shall use information that was reported by the State on ACF Form 231 and available as of the applicable dates specified in clauses (i)(I), (ii), and (iii)(III) of section 403(a)(1)(D).

(b) USE OF FUNDS.—

(1) IN GENERAL.—Amounts received by a State under this section shall only be used to provide child care assistance. Amounts received by a State under a grant under subsection (a)(1) shall be available for use by the State without fiscal year limitation.

(2) USE FOR CERTAIN POPULATIONS.—A State shall ensure that not less than 70 percent of the total amount of funds received by the State in a fiscal year under this section are used to provide child care assistance to families who are receiving assistance under a State program under this part, families who are attempting through work activities to transition off of such assistance program, and families who are at risk of becoming dependent on such assistance program.

(c) APPLICATION OF CHILD CARE AND DEVELOPMENT BLOCK GRANT ACT OF 1990.—Notwithstanding any other provision of law, amounts provided to a State under this section shall be transferred to the lead agency under the Child Care and Development Block Grant Act of 1990, integrated by the State into the programs established by the State under such Act, and be subject to requirements and limitations of such Act.

(d) DEFINITION.—As used in this section, the term "State" means each of the 50 States and the District of Columbia.

DEFINITIONS

SEC. 419. [42 U.S.C. 619] As used in this part:

(1) ADULT.—The term "adult" means an individual who is not a minor child.

(2) MINOR CHILD.—The term "minor child" means an individual who—

(A) has not attained 18 years of age; or

(B) has not attained 19 years of age and is a full-time student in a secondary school (or in the equivalent level of vocational or technical training).

(3) FISCAL YEAR.—The term "fiscal year" means any 12-month period ending on September 30 of a calendar year.

(4) INDIAN, INDIAN TRIBE, AND TRIBAL ORGANIZATION.—

(A) IN GENERAL.—Except as provided in subparagraph (B), the terms "Indian", "Indian tribe", and "tribal organization"

SOCIAL SECURITY ACT—§ 421(4) 341

have the meaning given such terms by section 4 of the Indian Self-Determination and Education Assistance Act (25 U.S.C. 450b)[58].

(B) SPECIAL RULE FOR INDIAN TRIBES IN ALASKA.—The term "Indian tribe" means, with respect to the State of Alaska, only the Metlakatla Indian Community of the Annette Islands Reserve and the following Alaska Native regional nonprofit corporations:

(i) Arctic Slope Native Association.

(ii) Kawerak, Inc.

(iii) Maniilaq Association.

(iv) Association of Village Council Presidents.

(v) Tanana Chiefs Conference.

(vi) Cook Inlet Tribal Council.

(vii) Bristol Bay Native Association.

(viii) Aleutian and Pribilof Island Association.

(ix) Chugachmuit.

(x) Tlingit Haida Central Council.

(xi) Kodiak Area Native Association.

(xii) Cooper River Native Association.

(5) STATE.—Except as otherwise specifically provided, the term "State" means the 50 States of the United States, the District of Columbia, the Commonwealth of Puerto Rico, the United States Virgin Islands, Guam, and American Samoa.

Part B—CHILD AND FAMILY SERVICES[59]

Subpart 1—Stephanie Tubbs Jones Child Welfare Services Program[60]

SEC. 420. [Repealed.[61]]

PURPOSE

SEC. 421. [42 U.S.C. 621] The purpose of this subpart is to promote State flexibility in the development and expansion of a coordinated child and family services program that utilizes community-based agencies and ensures all children are raised in safe, loving families, by—

(1) protecting and promoting the welfare of all children;

(2) preventing the neglect, abuse, or exploitation of children;

(3) supporting at-risk families through services which allow children, where appropriate, to remain safely with their families or return to their families in a timely manner;

(4) promoting the safety, permanence, and well-being of children in foster care and adoptive families; and

---

[58] See Vol. II, P.L. 94-437, §4.

[59] See Vol. II, P.L. 104-193, §403, with respect to five-year limited eligibility of qualified aliens for Federal means-tested public benefit.

[60] P.L. 110-351, §102(c), amended the heading for Subpart 1 in its entirety. For the heading as it formerly read, see Vol. II. Appendix J, Superseded Provisions, P.L. 110-351.See Vol. II, P.L. 100-409, §5, with respect to the effect of this Act on P.L. 92-203 or P.L. 96-487.

See Vol. II, P.L. 109-288, §2, with respect to Congressional findings with respect to child and family services.

[61] P.L. 109-288, §6(a); 120 Stat. 1233.

342 SOCIAL SECURITY ACT—§ 421(5)

(5) providing training, professional development and support to ensure a well-qualified child welfare workforce.

STATE PLANS FOR CHILD WELFARE SERVICES

SEC. 422. [42 U.S.C. 622] (a) In order to be eligible for payment under this subpart, a State must have a plan for child welfare services which has been developed jointly by the Secretary and the State agency designated pursuant to subsection (b)(1), and which meets the requirements of subsection (b).

(b) Each plan for child welfare services under this subpart shall—

(1)[62] provide that (A) the individual or agency that administers or supervises the administration of the State's services program under title XX will administer or supervise the administration of the plan (except as otherwise provided in section 103(d) of the Adoption Assistance and Child Welfare Act of 1980[63]), and (B) to the extent that child welfare services are furnished by the staff of the State agency or local agency administering the plan, a single organizational unit in such State or local agency, as the case may be, will be responsible for furnishing such child welfare services;

(2) provide for coordination between the services provided for children under the plan and the services and assistance provided under title XX, under the State program funded under part A, under the State plan approved under subpart 2 of this part, under the State plan approved under the State plan approved[64] under part E, and under other State programs having a relationship to the program under this subpart, with a view to provision of welfare and related services which will best promote the welfare of such children and their families;

(3) include a description of the services and activities which the State will fund under the State program carried out pursuant to this subpart, and how the services and activities will achieve the purpose of this subpart;

(4) contain a description of—

(A) the steps the State will take to provide child welfare services statewide and to expand and strengthen the range of existing services and develop and implement services to improve child outcomes; and

(B) the child welfare services staff development and training plans of the State;

(5) provide, in the development of services for children, for utilization of the facilities and experience of voluntary agencies in accordance with State and local programs and arrangements, as authorized by the State;

---

[62] P.L. 96-272, §103(a), amended §422 in its entirety effective June 17, 1980, except that in the case of Guam, Puerto Rico, the Virgin Islands, and the Commonwealth of the Northern Mariana Islands, §422(b)(1) shall be deemed to read as follows:

"(1) provide that (A) the State agency designated pursuant to section 402(a)(3) to administer or supervise the administration of the plan of the State approved under part A of this title will administer or supervise the administration of such plan for child welfare services, and (B) to the extent that child welfare services are furnished by the staff of the State agency or local agency administering such plan for child welfare services, the organizational unit in such State or local agency established pursuant to section 402(a)(15) will be responsible for furnishing such child welfare services;".

[63] See Vol. II, P.L. 96-272, §103(d).

[64] As in original. Second "under the State plan approved" should be stricken.

(6) provide that the agency administering or supervising the administration of the plan will furnish such reports, containing such information, and participate in such evaluations, as the Secretary may require;

(7) provide for the diligent recruitment of potential foster and adoptive families that reflect the ethnic and racial diversity of children in the State for whom foster and adoptive homes are needed;

(8) provide assurances that the State—

(A) is operating, to the satisfaction of the Secretary—

(i) a statewide information system from which can be readily determined the status, demographic characteristics, location, and goals for the placement of every child who is (or, within the immediately preceding 12 months, has been) in foster care;

(ii) a case review system (as defined in section 475(5)) for each child receiving foster care under the supervision of the State;

(iii) a service program designed to help children—

(I) where safe and appropriate, return to families from which they have been removed; or

(II) be placed for adoption, with a legal guardian, or, if adoption or legal guardianship is determined not to be appropriate for a child, in some other planned, permanent living arrangement, which may include a residential educational program; and

(iv) a preplacement preventive services program designed to help children at risk of foster care placement remain safely with their families; and

(B) has in effect policies and administrative and judicial procedures for children abandoned at or shortly after birth (including policies and procedures providing for legal representation of the children) which enable permanent decisions to be made expeditiously with respect to the placement of the children;

(9) contain a description, developed after consultation with tribal organizations (as defined in section 4 of the Indian Self-Determination and Education Assistance Act[65]) in the State, of the specific measures taken by the State to comply with the Indian Child Welfare Act;

(10) contain assurances that the State shall make effective use of cross-jurisdictional resources (including through contracts for the purchase of services), and shall eliminate legal barriers to facilitate timely adoptive or permanent placements for waiting children;

(11) contain a description of the activities that the State has undertaken for children adopted from other countries, including the provision of adoption and post-adoption services;

(12) provide that the State shall collect and report information on children who are adopted from other countries and who enter into State custody as a result of the disruption of a placement for adoption or the dissolution of an adoption, including the number

---

[65] See Vol. II, P.L. 94-437, §4.

344 SOCIAL SECURITY ACT—§ 422(b)(12)(cont)

of children, the agencies who handled the placement or adoption, the plans for the child, and the reasons for the disruption or dissolution;

(13) demonstrate substantial, ongoing, and meaningful collaboration with State courts in the development and implementation of the State plan under subpart 1, the State plan approved under subpart 2, and the State plan approved under part E, and in the development and implementation of any program improvement plan required under section 1123A;

(14) not later than October 1, 2007, include assurances that not more than 10 percent of the expenditures of the State with respect to activities funded from amounts provided under this subpart will be for administrative costs;

(15)[66](A) provides that the State will develop, in coordination and collaboration with the State agency referred to in paragraph (1) and the State agency responsible for administering the State plan approved under title XIX, and in consultation with pediatricians, other experts in health care, and experts in and recipients of child welfare services, a plan for the ongoing oversight and coordination of health care services for any child in a foster care placement, which shall ensure a coordinated strategy to identify and respond to the health care needs of children in foster care placements, including mental health and dental health needs, and shall include an outline of—

(i) a schedule for initial and follow-up health screenings that meet reasonable standards of medical practice;

(ii) how health needs identified through screenings will be monitored and treated;

(iii) how medical information for children in care will be updated and appropriately shared, which may include the development and implementation of an electronic health record;

(iv) steps to ensure continuity of health care services, which may include the establishment of a medical home for every child in care;

(v) the oversight of prescription medicines; and

(vi) how the State actively consults with and involves physicians or other appropriate medical or non-medical professionals in assessing the health and well-being of children in foster care and in determining appropriate medical treatment for the children; and

(B) subparagraph (A) shall not be construed to reduce or limit the responsibility of the State agency responsible for administering the State plan approved under title XIX to administer and provide care and services for children with respect to whom services are provided under the State plan developed pursuant to this subpart;

(16) provide that, not later than 1 year after the date of the enactment of this paragraph, the State shall have in place procedures providing for how the State programs assisted under this

---

[66] P.L. 110-351, §205, amended paragraph (15) in its entirety. For the effective date, see Vol. II, P.L. 110-351, §601. For paragraph (15) as it formerly read, see Vol. II, Appendix J, Superseded Provisions, P.L. 110-351.

SOCIAL SECURITY ACT—§ 423(b)   345

subpart, subpart 2 of this part, or part E would respond to a disaster, in accordance with criteria established by the Secretary which should include how a State would—

(A) identify, locate, and continue availability of services for children under State care or supervision who are displaced or adversely affected by a disaster;

(B) respond, as appropriate, to new child welfare cases in areas adversely affected by a disaster, and provide services in those cases;

(C) remain in communication with caseworkers and other essential child welfare personnel who are displaced because of a disaster;

(D) preserve essential program records; and

(E) coordinate services and share information with other States; and

(17)[67] not later than October 1, 2007, describe the State standards for the content and frequency of caseworker visits for children who are in foster care under the responsibility of the State, which, at a minimum, ensure that the children are visited on a monthly basis and that the caseworker visits are well-planned and focused on issues pertinent to case planning and service delivery to ensure the safety, permanency, and well-being of the children.

(c) DEFINITIONS.—In this subpart:

(1) ADMINISTRATIVE COSTS.—The term "administrative costs" means costs for the following, but only to the extent incurred in administering the State plan developed pursuant to this subpart: procurement, payroll management, personnel functions (other than the portion of the salaries of supervisors attributable to time spent directly supervising the provision of services by caseworkers), management, maintenance and operation of space and property, data processing and computer services, accounting, budgeting, auditing, and travel expenses (except those related to the provision of services by caseworkers or the oversight of programs funded under this subpart).

(2) OTHER TERMS.—For definitions of other terms used in this part, see section 475.

ALLOTMENTS TO STATES

SEC. 423. [42 U.S.C. 623] (a) IN GENERAL.—The sum appropriated pursuant to section 425 for each fiscal year shall be allotted by the Secretary for use by cooperating State public welfare agencies which have plans developed jointly by the State agency and the Secretary as follows: The Secretary shall first allot $70,000 to each State, and shall then allot to each State an amount which bears the same ratio to the remainder of such sum as the product of (1) the population of the State under the age of twenty-one and (2) the allotment percentage of the State (as determined under this section) bears to the sum of the corresponding products of all the States.

(b) DETERMINATION OF STATE ALLOTMENT PERCENTAGES.—The "allotment percentage" for any State shall be 100 percent less the State

---

[67] See Vol. II, P.L. 109-288, §7, with respect to a progress report regarding the monthly casework standards.

346 SOCIAL SECURITY ACT—§ 423(b)(cont)

percentage; and the State percentage shall be the percentage which bears the same ratio to 50 percent as the per capita income of such State bears to the per capita income of the United States; except that (1) the allotment percentage shall in no case be less than 30 percentor more than 70 percent, and (2) the allotment percentage shall be 70 percent in the case of Puerto Rico, the Virgin Islands, Guam, and American Samoa.

(c) PROMULGATION OF STATE ALLOTMENT PERCENTAGES.—The allotment percentage for each State shall be promulgated by the Secretary between October 1 and November 30 of each even-numbered year, on the basis of the average per capita income of each State and of the United States for the three most recent calendar years for which satisfactory data are available from the Department of Commerce. Such promulgation shall be conclusive for each of the two fiscal years in the period beginning October 1 next succeeding such promulgation.

(d) UNITED STATES DEFINED.—For purposes of this section, the term "United States" means the 50 States and the District of Columbia.

(e) REALLOTTMENT OF FUNDS.—

(1) IN GENERAL.—The amount of any allotment to a State for a fiscal year under the preceding provisions of this section which the State certifies to the Secretary will not be required for carrying out the State plan developed as provided in section 422 shall be available for reallotment from time to time, on such dates as the Secretary may fix, to other States which the Secretary determines—

(A) need sums in excess of the amounts allotted to such other States under the preceding provisions of this section, in carrying out their State plans so developed; and

(B) will be able to so use such excess sums during the fiscal year.

(2) IN GENERAL.—The Secretary shall make the reallotments on the basis of the State plans so developed, after taking into consideration—

(A) the population under 21 years of age;

(B) the per capita income of each of such other States as compared with the population under 21 years of age; and

(C) the per capita income of all such other States with respect to which such a determination by the Secretary has been made.

(3) AMOUNTS REALLOTTED TO A STATE DEEMED A PART OF STATE ALLOTMENT.—Any amount so reallotted to a State is deemed part of the allotment of the State under this section.

PAYMENT TO STATES

SEC. 424. [42 U.S.C. 624] (a) From the sums appropriated therefor and the allotment under this subpart, subject to the conditions set forth in this section, the Secretary shall from time to time pay to each State that has a plan developed in accordance with section 422 an amount equal to 75 per centum of the total sum expended under the plan (including the cost of administration of the plan) in meeting the costs of State, district, county, or other local child welfare services.

(b) The method of computing and making payments under this section shall be as follows:

SOCIAL SECURITY ACT—§ 424(e)(2)(A)   347

(1) The Secretary shall, prior to the beginning of each period for which a payment is to be made, estimate the amount to be paid to the State for such period under the provisions of this section.

(2) From the allotment available therefor, the Secretary shall pay the amount so estimated, reduced or increased, as the case may be, by any sum (not previously adjusted under this section) by which he finds that his estimate of the amount to be paid the State for any prior period under this section was greater or less than the amount which should have been paid to the State for such prior period under this section.

(c) LIMITATION ON USE OF FEDERAL FUNDS FOR CHILD CARE, FOSTER CARE MAINTENANCE PAYMENTS, OR ADOPTION ASSISTANCE PAYMENTS.—The total amount of Federal payments under this subpart for a fiscal year beginning after September 30, 2007, that may be used by a State for expenditures for child care, foster care maintenance payments, or adoption assistance payments shall not exceed the total amount of such payments for fiscal year 2005 that were so used by the State.

(d) LIMITATION ON USE BY STATES OF NON-FEDERAL FUNDS FOR FOSTER CARE MAINTENANCE PAYMENTS TO MATCH FEDERAL FUNDS.—For any fiscal year beginning after September 30, 2007, State expenditures of non-Federal funds for foster care maintenance payments shall not be considered to be expenditures under the State plan developed under this subpart for the fiscal year to the extent that the total of such expenditures for the fiscal year exceeds the total of such expenditures under the State plan developed under this subpart for fiscal year 2005.

(e)[68] LIMITATION ON REIMBURSEMENT FOR ADMINISTRATIVE COSTS.—A payment may not be made to a State under this section with respect to expenditures during a fiscal year for administrative costs, to the extent that the total amount of the expenditures exceeds 10 percent of the total expenditures of the State during the fiscal year for activities funded from amounts provided under this subpart.

(e)[69](1) The Secretary may not make a payment to a State under this subpart for a period in fiscal year 2008, unless the State has provided to the Secretary data which shows, for fiscal year 2007—

(A) the percentage of children in foster care under the responsibility of the State who were visited on a monthly basis by the caseworker handling the case of the child; and

(B) the percentage of the visits that occurred in the residence of the child.

(2)(A) Based on the data provided by a State pursuant to paragraph (1), the Secretary, in consultation with the State, shall establish, not later than June 30, 2008, an outline of the steps to be taken to ensure, by October 1, 2011, that at least 90 percent of the children in foster care under the responsibility of the State are visited by their caseworkers on a monthly basis, and that the majority of the visits occur in the residence of the child. The outline shall include target percentages to be reached each fiscal year, and should include a description of how the steps will be implemented. The steps may include activities

---

[68] P.L. 109-288, §6(e)(1), added this parargraph (e).
[69] As in original. P.L. 109-288, §7(b)(1), added this second paragraph (e).

348   SOCIAL SECURITY ACT—§ 424(e)(2)(A)(cont)

designed to improve caseworker retention, recruitment, training, and ability to access the benefits of technology.

(B) Beginning October 1, 2008, if the Secretary determines that a State has not made the requisite progress in meeting the goal described in subparagraph (A) of this paragraph, then the percentage that shall apply for purposes of subsection (a) of this section for the period involved shall be the percentage set forth in such subsection (a) reduced by—

(i) 1, if the number of full percentage points by which the State fell short of the target percentage established for the State for the period pursuant to such subparagraph is less than 10;

(ii) 3, if the number of full percentage points by which the State fell short, as described in clause (i), is not less than 10 and less than 20; or

(iii) 5, if the number of full percentage points by which the State fell short, as described in clause (i), is not less than 20.

LIMITATIONS ON AUTHORIZATION OF APPROPRIATIONS

SEC. 425. [42 U.S.C. 625] To carry out this this subpart (other than sections 426, 427, and 429)[70], there are authorized to be appropriated to the Secretary not more than $325,000,000 for each of fiscal years 2007 through 2011.

RESEARCH, TRAINING, OR DEMONSTRATION PROJECTS

SEC. 426. [42 U.S.C. 626] (a) There are hereby authorized to be appropriated for each fiscal year such sums as the Congress may determine—

(1) for grants by the Secretary—

(A) to public or other nonprofit institutions of higher learning, and to public or other nonprofit agencies and organizations engaged in research or child-welfare activities, for special research or demonstration projects in the field of child welfare which are of regional or national significance and for special projects for the demonstration of new methods or facilities which show promise of substantial contribution to the advancement of child welfare;

(B) to State or local public agencies responsible for administering, or supervising the administration of, the plan under this part, for projects for the demonstration of the utilization of research (including findings resulting there-from) in the field of child welfare in order to encourage experimental and special types of welfare services; and

(C) to public or other nonprofit institutions of higher learning for special projects for training personnel for work in the field of child welfare, including traineeships described in section 429 with such stipends and allowances as may be permitted by the Secretary; and

(2) for contracts or jointly financed cooperative arrangements with States and public and other organizations and agencies for the conduct of research, special projects, or demonstration projects relating to such matters.

---

[70] P.L. 110-351, §102(b), inserted "(other than sections 426,427, and 429)". For the effective date, see Vol. II, P. L. 110-351, §601.

SOCIAL SECURITY ACT—§ 427(a)

(b) Payments of grants or under contracts or cooperative arrangements under this section may be made in advance or by way of reimbursement, and in such installments, as the Secretary may determine; and shall be made on such conditions as the Secretary finds necessary to carry out the purposes of the grants, contracts, or other arrangements

(c) CHILD WELFARE TRAINEESHIPS.—The Secretary may approve an application for a grant to a public or nonprofit institution for higher learning to provide traineeships with stipends under section 426(a)(1)(C) only if the application—

(1) provides assurances that each individual who receives a stipend with such traineeship (in this section referred to as a "recipient") will enter into an agreement with the institution under which the recipient agrees—

(A) to participate in training at a public or private nonprofit child welfare agency on a regular basis (as determined by the Secretary) for the period of the traineeship;

(B) to be employed for a period of years equivalent to the period of the traineeship, in a public or private nonprofit child welfare agency in any State, within a period of time (determined by the Secretary in accordance with regulations) after completing the postsecondary education for which the traineeship was awarded;

(C) to furnish to the institution and the Secretary evidence of compliance with subparagraphs (A) and (B); and

(D) if the recipient fails to comply with subparagraph (A) or (B) and does not qualify for any exception to this subparagraph which the Secretary may prescribe in regulations, to repay to the Secretary all (or an appropriately prorated part) of the amount of the stipend, plus interest, and, if applicable, reasonable collection fees (in accordance with regulations promulgated by the Secretary);

(2) provides assurances that the institution will—

(A) enter into agreements with child welfare agencies for onsite training of recipients;

(B) permit an individual who is employed in the field of child welfare services to apply for a traineeship with a stipend if the traineeship furthers the progress of the individual toward the completion of degree requirements; and

(C) develop and implement a system that, for the 3-year period that begins on the date any recipient completes a child welfare services program of study, tracks the employment record of the recipient, for the purpose of determining the percentage of recipients who secure employment in the field of child welfare services and remain employed in the field.

FAMILY CONNECTION GRANTS[71]

SEC. 427. [42 U.S.C. 627] (a) IN GENERAL.—The Secretary of Health and Human Services may make matching grants to State, local, or tribal child welfare agencies, and private nonprofit organizations that have experience in working with foster children or children in kinship care arrangements, for the purpose of helping children who are in, or

---

[71] P.L. 110-351, §102(a), added this section. For the effective date, see Vol. II, P.L. 110-351, §601.

350   SOCIAL SECURITY ACT—§ 427(a) (1)

at risk of entering, foster care reconnect with family members through the implementation of—

(1) a kinship navigator program to assist kinship caregivers in learning about, finding, and using programs and services to meet the needs of the children they are raising and their own needs, and to promote effective partnerships among public and private agencies to ensure kinship caregiver families are served, which program—

(A) shall be coordinated with other State or local agencies that promote service coordination or provide information and referral services, including the entities that provide 2–1–1 or 3–1–1 information systems where available, to avoid duplication or fragmentation of services to kinship care families;

(B) shall be planned and operated in consultation with kinship caregivers and organizations representing them, youth raised by kinship caregivers, relevant government agencies, and relevant community-based or faithbased organizations;

(C) shall establish information and referral systems that link (via toll-free access) kinship caregivers, kinship support group facilitators, and kinship service providers to—

(i) each other;

(ii) eligibility and enrollment information for Federal, State, and local benefits;

(iii) relevant training to assist kinship caregivers in caregiving and in obtaining benefits and services; and

(iv) relevant legal assistance and help in obtaining legal services;

(D) shall provide outreach to kinship care families, including by establishing, distributing, and updating a kinship care website, or other relevant guides or outreach materials;

(E) shall promote partnerships between public and private agencies, including schools, community based or faith-based organizations, and relevant government agencies, to increase their knowledge of the needs of kinship care families to promote better services for those families;

(F) may establish and support a kinship care ombudsman with authority to intervene and help kinship caregivers access services; and

(G) may support any other activities designed to assist kinship caregivers in obtaining benefits and services to improve their caregiving;

(2) intensive family-finding efforts that utilize search technology to find biological family members for children in the child welfare system, and once identified, work to reestablish relationships and explore ways to find a permanent family placement for the children;

(3) family group decision-making meetings for children in the child welfare system, that—

(A) enable families to make decisions and develop plans that nurture children and protect them from abuse and neglect, and

(B) when appropriate, shall address domestic violence issues in a safe manner and facilitate connecting children exposed to domestic violence to appropriate services, including reconnection with the abused parent when appropriate; or

(4) residential family treatment programs that—

(A) enable parents and their children to live in a safe environment for a period of not less than 6 months; and

(B) provide, on-site or by referral, substance abuse treatment services, children's early intervention services, family counseling, medical, and mental health services, nursery and pre-school, and other services that are designed to provide comprehensive treatment that supports the family.

(b) APPLICATIONS.—An entity desiring to receive a matching grant under this section shall submit to the Secretary an application, at such time, in such manner, and containing such information as the Secretary may require, including—

(1) a description of how the grant will be used to implement 1 or more of the activities described in subsection (a);

(2) a description of the types of children and families to be served, including how the children and families will be identified and recruited, and an initial projection of the number of children and families to be served;

(3) if the entity is a private organization—

(A) documentation of support from the relevant local or State child welfare agency; or

(B) a description of how the organization plans to coordinate its services and activities with those offered by the relevant local or State child welfare agency; and

(4) an assurance that the entity will cooperate fully with any evaluation provided for by the Secretary under this section.

(c) LIMITATIONS.—

(1) GRANT DURATION.—The Secretary may award a grant under this section for a period of not less than 1 year and not more than 3 years.

(2) NUMBER OF NEW GRANTEES PER YEAR.—The Secretary may not award a grant under this section to more than 30 new grantees each fiscal year.

(d) FEDERAL CONTRIBUTION.—The amount of a grant payment to be made to a grantee under this section during each year in the grant period shall be the following percentage of the total expenditures proposed to be made by the grantee in the application approved by the Secretary under this section:

(1) 75 percent, if the payment is for the 1st or 2nd year of the grant period.

(2) 50 percent, if the payment is for the 3rd year of the grant period.

(e) FORM OF GRANTEE CONTRIBUTION.—A grantee under this section may provide not more than 50 percent of the amount which the grantee is required to expend to carry out the activities for which a grant is awarded under this section in kind, fairly evaluated, including plant, equipment, or services.

(f) USE OF GRANT.—A grantee under this section shall use the grant in accordance with the approved application for the grant.

(g) RESERVATIONS OF FUNDS.—

(1) KINSHIP NAVIGATOR PROGRAMS.—The Secretary shall reserve $5,000,000 of the funds made available under subsection

352   SOCIAL SECURITY ACT—§ 427(g)(2)

(h) for each fiscal year for grants to implement kinship navigator programs described in subsection (a)(1).

(2) EVALUATION.—The Secretary shall reserve 3 percent of the funds made available under subsection (h) for each fiscal year for the conduct of a rigorous evaluation of the activities funded with grants under this section.

(3) TECHNICAL ASSISTANCE.—The Secretary may reserve 2 percent of the funds made available under subsection (h) for each fiscal year to provide technical assistance to recipients of grants under this section.

(h) APPROPRIATION.—Out of any money in the Treasury of the United States not otherwise appropriated, there are appropriated to the Secretary for purposes of making grants under this section $15,000,000 for each of fiscal years 2009 through 2013.

PAYMENTS TO INDIAN TRIBAL ORGANIZATIONS[72]

SEC. 428. [42 U.S.C. 628] (a) The Secretary may, in appropriate cases (as determined by the Secretary) make payments under this subpart directly to an Indian tribal organization within any State which has a plan for child welfare services approved under this subpart. Such payments shall be made in such manner and in such amounts as the Secretary determines to be appropriate.

(b) Amounts paid under subsection (a) shall be deemed to be a part of the allotment (as determined under section 421) for the State in which such Indian tribal organization is located.

(c) For purposes of this section, the terms "Indian tribe" and "tribal organization" shall have the meanings given such terms by subsections (e) and (l) of section 4 of the Indian Self-Determination and Education Assistance Act (25 U.S.C. 450b), respectively.

NATIONAL RANDOM SAMPLE STUDY OF CHILD WELFARE

SEC. 429. [42 U.S.C. 628b] (a) IN GENERAL.—The Secretary shall conduct (directly, or by grant, contract, or interagency agreement) a national study based on random samples of children who are at risk of child abuse or neglect, or are determined by States to have been abused or neglected.

(b) REQUIREMENTS.—The study required by subsection (a) shall—

(1) have a longitudinal component; and

(2) yield data reliable at the State level for as many States as the Secretary determines is feasible.

(c) PREFERRED CONTENTS.—In conducting the study required by subsection (a), the Secretary should—

(1) carefully consider selecting the sample from cases of confirmed abuse or neglect; and

(2) follow each case for several years while obtaining information on, among other things—

(A) the type of abuse or neglect involved;

(B) the frequency of contact with State or local agencies;

(C) whether the child involved has been separated from the family, and, if so, under what circumstances;

(D) the number, type, and characteristics of out-of-home placements of the child; and

---

[72] See Vol. II, P.L. 95-608, Title II, with respect to Indian Child and Family Programs.

SOCIAL SECURITY ACT—§ 431(a)(1)(A)(ii)   353

(E) the average duration of each placement.
(d) REPORTS.—
(1) IN GENERAL.—From time to time, the Secretary shall prepare reports summarizing the results of the study required by subsection (a).
(2) AVAILABILITY.—The Secretary shall make available to the public any report prepared under paragraph (1), in writing or in the form of an electronic data tape.
(3) AUTHORITY TO CHARGE FEE.—The Secretary may charge and collect a fee for the furnishing of reports under paragraph (2).
(e) APPROPRIATION.—Out of any money in the Treasury of the United States not otherwise appropriated, there are appropriated to the Secretary for each of fiscal years 1996 through 2002 $6,000,000 to carry out this section.

Subpart 2—Promoting Safe and Stable Families[73]

FINDINGS AND PURPOSE

SEC. 430. [42 U.S.C. 629] The purpose of this program is to enable States to develop and establish, or expand, and to operate coordinated programs of community-based family support services, family preservation services, time-limited family reunification services, and adoption promotion and support services to accomplish the following objectives:
(1) To prevent child maltreatment among families at risk through the provision of supportive family services.
(2) To assure children's safety within the home and preserve intact families in which children have been maltreated, when the family's problems can be addressed effectively.
(3) To address the problems of families whose children have been placed in foster care so that reunification may occur in a safe and stable manner in accordance with the Adoption and Safe Families Act of 1997.
(4) To support adoptive families by providing support services as necessary so that they can make a lifetime commitment to their children.

DEFINITIONS

SEC. 431. [42 U.S.C. 629a] (a) IN GENERAL.—As used in this subpart:
(1) FAMILY PRESERVATION SERVICES.—The term "family preservation services" means services for children and families designed to help families (including adoptive and extended families) at risk or in crisis, including—
(A) service programs designed to help children—
(i) where safe and appropriate, return to families from which they have been removed; or
(ii) be placed for adoption, with a legal guardian, or, if adoption or legal guardianship is determined not to be

_____
[73] See Vol. II, P.L. 109-288, §3, with respect to reauthorization of the promoting safe and stable families program.

354 SOCIAL SECURITY ACT—§ 431(a)(1)(A)(ii)(cont)

safe and appropriate for a child, in some other planned, permanent living arrangement;

(B) preplacement preventive services programs, such as intensive family preservation programs, designed to help children at risk of foster care placement remain safely with their families;

(C) service programs designed to provide followup care to families to whom a child has been returned after a foster care placement;

(D) respite care of children to provide temporary relief for parents and other caregivers (including foster parents);

(E) services designed to improve parenting skills (by reinforcing parents' confidence in their strengths, and helping them to identify where improvement is needed and to obtain assistance in improving those skills) with respect to matters such as child development, family budgeting, coping with stress, health, and nutrition; and

(F) infant safe haven programs to provide a way for a parent to safely relinquish a newborn infant at a safe haven designated pursuant to a State law.

(2) FAMILY SUPPORT SERVICES.—The term "family support services" means community-based services to promote the safety and well-being of children and families designed to increase the strength and stability of families (including adoptive, foster, and extended families), to increase parents' confidence and competence in their parenting abilities, to afford children a safe, stable, and supportive family environment, to strengthen parental relationships and promote healthy marriages, and otherwise to enhance child development.

(3) STATE AGENCY.—The term "State agency" means the State agency responsible for administering the program under subpart 1.

(4) STATE.—The term "State" includes an Indian tribe or tribal organization, in addition to the meaning given such term for purposes of subpart 1.

(5) TRIBAL ORGANIZATION.—The term "tribal organization" means the recognized governing body of any Indian tribe.

(6) INDIAN TRIBE.—The term "Indian tribe" means any Indian tribe (as defined in section 482(i)(5), as in effect before August 22, 1996) and any Alaska Native organization (as defined in section 482(i)(7)(A), as so in effect).

(7) TIME–LIMITED FAMILY REUNIFICATION SERVICES.—

(A) IN GENERAL.—The term "time-limited family reunification services" means the services and activities described in subparagraph (B) that are provided to a child that is removed from the child's home and placed in a foster family home or a child care institution and to the parents or primary caregiver of such a child, in order to facilitate the reunification of the child safely and appropriately within a timely fashion, but only during the 15-month period that begins on the date that the child, pursuant to section 475(5)(F), is considered to have entered foster care.

SOCIAL SECURITY ACT—§ 432(a)(2)(C)(ii) 355

(B) SERVICES AND ACTIVITIES DESCRIBED.—The services and activities described in this subparagraph are the following:

(i) Individual, group, and family counseling.

(ii) Inpatient, residential, or outpatient substance abuse treatment services.

(iii) Mental health services.

(iv) Assistance to address domestic violence.

(v) Services designed to provide temporary child care and therapeutic services for families, including crisis nurseries.

(vi) Transportation to or from any of the services and activities described in this subparagraph.

(8) ADOPTION PROMOTION AND SUPPORT SERVICES.—The term "adoption promotion and support services" means services and activities designed to encourage more adoptions out of the foster care system, when adoptions promote the best interests of children, including such activities as pre- and post-adoptive services and activities designed to expedite the adoption process and support adoptive families.

(9) NON-FEDERAL FUNDS.—The term "non-Federal funds" means State funds, or at the option of a State, State and local funds.

(b) OTHER TERMS.—For other definitions of other terms used in this subpart, see section 475.

STATE PLANS

SEC. 432. [42 U.S.C. 629b] (a) PLAN REQUIREMENTS.—A State plan meets the requirements of this subsection if the plan—

(1) provides that the State agency shall administer, or supervise the administration of, the State program under this subpart;

(2)(A)(i) sets forth the goals intended to be accomplished under the plan by the end of the 5th fiscal year in which the plan is in operation in the State, and (ii) is updated periodically to set forth the goals intended to be accomplished under the plan by the end of each 5th fiscal year thereafter;

(B) describes the methods to be used in measuring progress toward accomplishment of the goals;

(C) contains assurances that the State—

(i) after the end of each of the 1st 4 fiscal years covered by a set of goals, will perform an interim review of progress toward accomplishment of the goals, and on the basis of the interim review will revise the statement of goals in the plan, if necessary, to reflect changed circumstances; and

(ii) after the end of the last fiscal year covered by a set of goals, will perform a final review of progress toward accomplishment of the goals, and on the basis of the final review (I) will prepare, transmit to the Secretary, and make available to the public a final report on progress toward accomplishment of the goals, and (II) will develop (in consultation with the entities required to be consulted pursuant to subsection (b)) and add to the plan a statement of the goals intended to be accomplished by the end of the 5th succeeding fiscal year;

356 SOCIAL SECURITY ACT—§ 432(a)(3)

(3) provides for coordination, to the extent feasible and appropriate, of the provision of services under the plan and the provision of services or benefits under other Federal or federally assisted programs serving the same populations;

(4) contains assurances that not more than 10 percent of expenditures under the plan for any fiscal year with respect to which the State is eligible for payment under section 434 for the fiscal year shall be for administrative costs, and that the remaining expenditures shall be for programs of family preservation services, community-based family support services, time-limited family reunification services, and adoption promotion and support services, with significant portions of such expenditures for each such program;

(5) contains assurances that the State will—

(A) annually prepare, furnish to the Secretary, and make available to the public a description (including separate descriptions with respect to family preservation services, community-based family support services time-limited family reunification services, and adoption promotion and support services) of—

(i) the service programs to be made available under the plan in the immediately succeeding fiscal year;

(ii) the populations which the programs will serve; and

(iii) the geographic areas in the State in which the services will be available; and

(B) perform the activities described in subparagraph (A)—

(i) in the case of the 1st fiscal year under the plan, at the time the State submits its initial plan; and

(ii) in the case of each succeeding fiscal year, by the end of the 3rd quarter of the immediately preceding fiscal year;

(6) provides for such methods of administration as the Secretary finds to be necessary for the proper and efficient operation of the plan;

(7)(A) contains assurances that Federal funds provided to the State under this subpart will not be used to supplant Federal or non-Federal funds for existing services and activities which promote the purposes of this subpart; and

(B) provides that the State will furnish reports to the Secretary, at such times, in such format, and containing such information as the Secretary may require, that demonstrate the State's compliance with the prohibition contained in subparagraph (A);

(8)(A) provides that the State agency will furnish such reports, containing such information, and participate in such evaluations, as the Secretary may require; and

(B) provides that, not later than June 30 of each year, the State will submit to the Secretary—

(i) copies of forms CFS 101-Part I and CFS 101-Part II (or any successor forms) that report on planned child and family services expenditures by the agency for the immediately succeeding fiscal year; and

(ii) copies of forms CFS 101-Part I and CFS 101-Part II (or any successor forms) that provide, with respect to the programs authorized under this subpart and subpart 1 and, at

SOCIAL SECURITY ACT—§ 433(a) 357

State option, other programs included on such forms, for the most recent preceding fiscal year for which reporting of actual expenditures is complete—

(I) the numbers of families and of children served by the State agency;

(II) the population served by the State agency;

(III) the geographic areas served by the State agency; and

(IV) the actual expenditures of funds provided to the State agency; and

(9) contains assurances that in administering and conducting service programs under the plan, the safety of the children to be served shall be of paramount concern.

(b) APPROVAL OF PLANS.—

(1) IN GENERAL.—The Secretary shall approve a plan that meets the requirements of subsection (a) only if the plan was developed jointly by the Secretary and the State, after consultation by the State agency with appropriate public and nonprofit private agencies and community-based organizations with experience in administering programs of services for children and families (including family preservation, family support, time-limited family reunification, and adoption promotion and support).

(2) PLANS OF INDIAN TRIBES OR TRIBAL CONSORTIA.—

(A) EXEMPTION FROM INAPPROPRIATE REQUIREMENTS.—The Secretary may exempt a plan submitted by an Indian tribe or tribal consortium from any requirement of this section that the Secretary determines would be inappropriate to apply to the Indian tribe or tribal consortium, taking into account the resources, needs, and other circumstances of the Indian tribe or tribal consortium.

(B) PLANS OF INDIAN TRIBES.—Notwithstanding subparagraph (A) of this paragraph, the Secretary may not approve a plan of an Indian tribe or tribal consortium under this subpart to which (but for this subparagraph) an allotment of less than $10,000 would be made under section 433(a) if allotments were made under section 433(a) to all Indian tribes and tribal consortia with plans approved under this subpart with the same or larger numbers of children.

(c) ANNUAL SUBMISSION OF STATE REPORTS TO CONGRESS.—The Secretary shall compile the reports required under subsection (a)(8)(B) and, not later than September 30 of each year, submit such compilation to the Committee on Ways and Means of the House of Representatives and the Committee on Finance of the Senate.

ALLOTMENTS TO STATES

SEC. 433. [42 U.S.C. 629c] (a) INDIAN TRIBES OR TRIBAL CONSORTIA.—From the amount reserved pursuant to section 436(b)(3) for any fiscal year, the Secretary shall allot to each Indian tribe with a plan approved under this subpart an amount that bears the same ratio to such reserved amount as the number of children in the Indian tribe bears to the total number of children in all Indian tribes with State plans so approved, as determined by the Secretary on the basis of the most current and reliable information available to the Secretary. If a consortium of Indian tribes submits a plan approved

358 SOCIAL SECURITY ACT—§ 433(a)(cont)

under this subpart, the Secretary shall allot to the consortium an amount equal to the sum of the allotments determined for each Indian tribe that is part of the consortium.

(b) TERRITORIES.—From the amount described in section 436(a) for any fiscal year that remains after applying section 436(b) for the fiscal year, the Secretary shall allot to each of the jurisdictions of Puerto Rico, Guam, the Virgin Islands, the Northern Mariana Islands, and American Samoa an amount determined in the same manner as the allotment to each of such jurisdictions is determined under section 423.

(c) OTHER STATES.—

(1) IN GENERAL.—From the amount described in section 436(a) for any fiscal year that remains after applying section 436(b) and subsection (b) of this section for the fiscal year, the Secretary shall allot to each State (other than an Indian tribe) which is not specified in subsection (b) of this section an amount equal to such remaining amount multiplied by the supplemental nutrition assistance program benefits[74] percentage of the State for the fiscal year.

(2) SUPPLEMENTAL NUTRITION ASSISTANCE PROGRAM BENEFITS[75] PERCENTAGE DEFINED.—

(A) IN GENERAL.—As used in paragraph (1) of this subsection, the term "supplemental nutrition assistance program benefits[76] percentage" means, with respect to a State and a fiscal year, the average monthly number of children receiving supplemental nutrition assistance program benefits[77] in the State for months in the 3 fiscal years referred to in subparagraph (B) of this paragraph, as determined from sample surveys made under section 16(c) of the Food and Nutrition Act of 2008[78], expressed as a percentage of the average monthly number of children receiving supplemental nutrition assistance program benefits[79] in the States described in such paragraph (1) for months in such 3 fiscal years, as so determined.

(B) FISCAL YEARS USED IN CALCULATION.—For purposes of the calculation pursuant to subparagraph (A), the Secretary shall use data for the 3 most recent fiscal years, preceding the fiscal year for which the State's allotment is calculated

---

[74] P.L. 110-246, §4002(b)(1)(D), struck out "food stamp" and substituted "supplemental nutrition assistance program benefits", effective October 1, 2008. P.L. 110-234, §4002(b)(1)(D), which made the same amendment, was repealed, effective May 22, 2008 pursuant to P.L. 110-246, §4(a).

[75] P.L. 110-246, §4002(b)(1)(D), struck out "food stamp" and substituted "supplemental nutrition assistance program benefits", effective October 1, 2008. P.L. 110-234, §4002(b)(1)(D), which made the same amendment, was repealed, effective May 22, 2008 pursuant to P.L. 110-246, §4(a).

[76] P.L. 110-246, §4002(b)(1)(D), struck out "food stamp" and substituted "supplemental nutrition assistance program benefits", effective October 1, 2008. P.L. 110-234, §4002(b)(1)(D), which made the same amendment, was repealed, effective May 22, 2008 pursuant to P.L. 110-246, §4(a).

[77] P.L. 110-246, §4002(b)(1)(D), struck out "food stamp" and substituted "supplemental nutrition assistance program benefits", effective October 1, 2008. P.L. 110-234, §4002(b)(1)(D), which made the same amendment, was repealed, effective May 22, 2008 pursuant to P.L. 110-246, §4(a). Executed as if duplication of the word "benefits" was not intended. Executed as if duplication of the word "benefits" was not intended.

[78] See Vol. II, P.L. 88-525, §16(c).
P.L. 110-246, §4002(b)(1)(B), struck out "Food Stamp Act of 1977" and substituted "Food and Nutrition Act of 2008", effective October 1, 2008. P.L. 110-234, §4002(b)(1)(B), which made the same amendment, was repealed, effective May 22, 2008 pursuant to P.L. 110-246, §4(a).

[79] P.L. 110-246, §4002(b)(1)(D), struck out "food stamp" and substituted "supplemental nutrition assistance program benefits", effective October 1, 2008. P.L. 110-234, §4002(b)(1)(D), which made the same amendment, was repealed, effective May 22, 2008 pursuant to P.L. 110-246, §4(a).

SOCIAL SECURITY ACT—§ 434(a)(2)(A)

under this subsection, for which such data are available to the Secretary.

(d) REALLOTMENTS.—The amount of any allotment to a State under subsection (a), (b), or (c) of this section for any fiscal year that the State certifies to the Secretary will not be required for carrying out the State plan under section 432 shall be available for reallotment using the allotment methodology specified in this section. Any amount so reallotted to a State is deemed part of the allotment of the State under the preceding provisions of subsection (a), (b), or (c) of this section.

(e) ALLOTMENT OF FUNDS RESERVED TO SUPPORT MONTHLY CASEWORKER VISITS.—

(1) TERRITORIES.—From the amount reserved pursuant to section 436(b)(4)(A) for any fiscal year, the Secretary shall allot to each jurisdiction specified in subsection (b) of this section, that has provided to the Secretary such documentation as may be necessary to verify that the jurisdiction has complied with section 436(b)(4)(B)(ii) during the fiscal year, an amount determined in the same manner as the allotment to each of such jurisdictions is determined under section 423 (without regard to the initial allotment of $70,000 to each State).

(2) OTHER STATES.—From the amount reserved pursuant to section 436(b)(4)(A) for any fiscal year that remains after applying paragraph (1) of this subsection for the fiscal year, the Secretary shall allot to each State (other than an Indian tribe) not specified in subsection (b) of this section, that has provided to the Secretary such documentation as may be necessary to verify that the State has complied with section 436(b)(4)(B)(ii) during the fiscal year, an amount equal to such remaining amount multiplied by the supplemental nutrition assistance program benefits[80] percentage of the State (as defined in subsection (c)(2) of this section) for the fiscal year, except that in applying subsection (c)(2)(A) of this section, "subsection (e)(2)" shall be substituted for "such paragraph (1)".

PAYMENTS TO STATES

SEC. 434. [42 U.S.C. 629d] (a) ENTITLEMENT.—Each State that has a plan approved under section 432 shall, subject to subsection (d) be entitled to payment of the sum of—

(1) the lesser of—

(A) 75 percent of the total expenditures by the State for activities under the plan during the fiscal year or the immediately succeeding fiscal year; or

(B) the allotment of the State under subsection (a), (b), or (c) of section 433, whichever is applicable, for the fiscal year; and

(2) the lesser of—

(A) 75 percent of the total expenditures by the State in accordance with section 436(b)(4)(B) during the fiscal year or the immediately succeeding fiscal year; or

---

[80] P.L. 110-246, §4002(b)(1)(D), struck out "food stamp" and substituted "supplemental nutrition assistance program benefits", effective October 1, 2008. P.L. 110-234, §4002(b)(1)(D), which made the same amendment, was repealed, effective May 22, 2008 pursuant to P.L. 110-246, §4(a).

360 SOCIAL SECURITY ACT—§ 434(a)(2)(B)

(B) the allotment of the State under section 433(e) for the fiscal year.

(b) PROHIBITIONS.—

(1) NO USE OF OTHER FEDERAL FUNDS FOR STATE MATCH.—Each State receiving an amount paid under subsection (a) may not expend any Federal funds to meet the costs of services under the State plan under section 432 not covered by the amount so paid.

(2) AVAILABILITY OF FUNDS.—A State may not expend any amount paid under subsection (a) for any fiscal year after the end of the immediately succeeding fiscal year.

(c)[81] DIRECT PAYMENTS TO TRIBAL ORGANIZATIONS OF INDIAN TRIBES OR TRIBAL CONSORTIA.—The Secretary shall pay any amount to which an Indian tribe or tribal consortium is entitled under this section directly to the tribal organization of the Indian tribe or in the case of a payment to a tribal consortium, such tribal organizations of, or entity established by, the Indian tribes that are part of the consortium as the consortium shall designate.

(d)[82] LIMITATION ON REIMBURSEMENT FOR ADMINISTRATIVE COSTS.—The Secretary shall not make a payment to a State under this section with respect to expenditures for administrative costs during a fiscal year, to the extent that the total amount of the expenditures exceeds 10 percent of the total expenditures of the State during the fiscal year under the State plan approved under section 432.

EVALUATIONS; RESEARCH; TECHNICAL ASSISTANCE

SEC. 435. [42 U.S.C. 629e] (a) EVALUATIONS.—

(1) IN GENERAL.—The Secretary shall evaluate and report to the Congress biennially on effectiveness of the programs carried out pursuant to this subpart in accomplishing the purposes of this subpart, and may evaluate any other Federal, State, or local program, regardless of whether federally assisted, that is designed to achieve the same purposes as the program under this subpart, in accordance with criteria established in accordance with paragraph (2).

(2) CRITERIA TO BE USED.—In developing the criteria to be used in evaluations under paragraph (1), the Secretary shall consult with appropriate parties, such as—

(A) State agencies administering programs under this part and part E;

(B) persons administering child and family services programs (including family preservation and family support programs) for private, nonprofit organizations with an interest in child welfare; and

(C) other persons with recognized expertise in the evaluation of child and family services programs (including family preservation and family support programs) or other related programs.

(3) TIMING OF REPORT.—Beginning in 2003, the Secretary shall submit the biennial report required by this subsection not later

---

[81] See Vol. II, P.L. 95-608, Title II, with respect to Indian Child and Family Programs.
[82] P.L. 109-288, §3(f)(1)(B), added subsection (d), applicable to expenditures made on or after October 1, 2007.

SOCIAL SECURITY ACT—§ 436(b)(1)   361

than April 1 of every other year, and shall include in each such report the funding level, the status of ongoing evaluations, findings to date, and the nature of any technical assistance provided to States under subsection (d).

(b) COORDINATION OF EVALUATIONS.—The Secretary shall develop procedures to coordinate evaluations under this section, to the extent feasible, with evaluations by the States of the effectiveness of programs under this subpart.

(c) EVALUATION, RESEARCH, AND TECHNICAL ASSISTANCE WITH RESPECT TO TARGETED PROGRAM RESOURCES.—Of the amount reserved under section 436(b)(1) for a fiscal year, the Secretary shall use not less than—

(1) $1,000,000 for evaluations, research, and providing technical assistance with respect to supporting monthly caseworker visits with children who are in foster care under the responsibility of the State, in accordance with section 436(b)(4)(B)(i); and

(2) $1,000,000 for evaluations, research, and providing technical assistance with respect to grants under section 437(f).

(d) TECHNICAL ASSISTANCE.—To the extent funds are available therefor, the Secretary shall provide technical assistance that helps States and Indian tribes or tribal consortia to—

(1) develop research-based protocols for identifying families at risk of abuse and neglect of use in the field;

(2) develop treatment models that address the needs of families at risk, particularly families with substance abuse issues;

(3) implement programs with well-articulated theories of how the intervention will result in desired changes among families at risk;

(4) establish mechanisms to ensure that service provision matches the treatment model; and

(5) establish mechanisms to ensure that postadoption services meet the needs of the individual families and develop models to reduce the disruption rates of adoption.

AUTHORIZATION OF APPROPRIATIONS; RESERVATION OF CERTAIN AMOUNTS[83]

SEC. 436. [42 U.S.C. 629f] (a) AUTHORIZATION.—In addition to any amount otherwise made available to carry out this subpart, there are authorized to be appropriated to carry out this subpart $345,000,000 for each of fiscal years 2007 through 2011[84]

(b) RESERVATION OF CERTAIN AMOUNTS.—From the amount specified in subsection (a) for a fiscal year, the Secretary shall reserve amounts as follows:

(1) EVALUATION, RESEARCH, TRAINING, AND TECHNICAL ASSISTANCE.—The Secretary shall reserve $6,000,000 for expenditure by the Secretary—

---

[83] See Vol. II, P.L. 109-288, §3(c), with respect to the reauthorization of the Promoting Safe and Stable Families Program.

[84] P.L. 109-288, §3(a), struck out "fiscal year 2006." and the next sentence and substituted "each of fiscal years 2007 through 2011*", effective October 1, 2006.

*As in original. Period is missing.

For subsection (a) as it formerly read, see Vol. II, Appendix J, Superseded Provisions, P.L. 109-288.

362 SOCIAL SECURITY ACT—§ 436(b)(1)(A)

(A) for research, training, and technical assistance costs related to the program under this subpart; and

(B) for evaluation of State programs based on the plans approved under section 432 and funded under this subpart, and any other Federal, State, or local program, regardless of whether federally assisted, that is designed to achieve the same purposes as the State programs.

(2) STATE COURT IMPROVEMENTS.—The Secretary shall reserve $10,000,000 for grants under section 438.

(3) INDIAN TRIBES OR TRIBAL CONSORTIA.—After applying paragraphs (4) and (5) (but before applying paragraphs (1) and (2), the Secretary shall reserve 3 percent for allotment to Indian tribes or tribal consortia in accordance with section 433(a).

(4) SUPPORT FOR MONTHLY CASEWORKER VISITS.—

(A) RESERVATION.—The Secretary shall reserve for allotment in accordance with section 433(e)—

(i) $5,000,000 for fiscal year 2008;

(ii) $10,000,000 for fiscal year 2009; and

(iii) $20,000,000 for each of fiscal years 2010 and 2011.

(B) USE OF FUNDS.—

(i) IN GENERAL.—A State to which an amount is paid from amounts reserved under subparagraph (A) shall use the amount to support monthly caseworker visits with children who are in foster care under the responsibility of the State, with a primary emphasis on activities designed to improve caseworker retention, recruitment, training, and ability to access the benefits of technology.

(ii) NONSUPPLEMENTATION.—A State to which an amount is paid from amounts reserved pursuant to subparagraph (A) shall not use the amount to supplant any Federal funds paid to the State under part E that could be used as described in clause (i).

(5) REGIONAL PARTNERSHIP GRANTS.—The Secretary shall reserve for awarding grants under section 437(f)—

(A) $40,000,000 for fiscal year 2007;

(B) $35,000,000 for fiscal year 2008;

(C) $30,000,000 for fiscal year 2009; and

(D) $20,000,000 for each of fiscal years 2010 and 2011.

DISCRETIONARY AND TARGETED GRANTS

SEC. 437. [42 U.S.C. 629g] (a) LIMITATIONS ON AUTHORIZATION OF APPROPRIATIONS.—In addition to any amount appropriated pursuant to section 436, there are authorized to be appropriated to carry out this section $200,000,000 for each of fiscal years 2007 through 2011.

(b) RESERVATION OF CERTAIN AMOUNTS.—From the amount (if any) appropriated pursuant to subsection (a) for a fiscal year, the Secretary shall reserve amounts as follows:

(1) EVALUATION, RESEARCH, TRAINING, AND TECHNICAL ASSISTANCE.—The Secretary shall reserve 3.3 percent for expenditure by the Secretary for the activities described in section 436(b)(1).

(2) STATE COURT IMPROVEMENTS.—The Secretary shall reserve 3.3 percent for grants under section 438.

SOCIAL SECURITY ACT—§ 437(f)(1)   363

(3) INDIAN TRIBES OR TRIBAL CONSORTIA.—The Secretary shall reserve 3 percent for allotment to Indian tribes or tribal consortia in accordance with subsection (c)(1).

(c) ALLOTMENTS.—

(1) INDIAN TRIBES OR TRIBAL CONSORTIA.—From the amount (if any) reserved pursuant to subsection (b)(3) for any fiscal year, the Secretary shall allot to each Indian tribe with a plan approved under this subpart an amount that bears the same ratio to such reserved amount as the number of children in the Indian tribe bears to the total number of children in all Indian tribes with State plans so approved, as determined by the Secretary on the basis of the most current and reliable information available to the Secretary. If a consortium of Indian tribes submits a plan approved under this subpart, the Secretary shall allot to the consortium an amount equal to the sum of the allotments determined for each Indian tribe that is part of the consortium.

(2) TERRITORIES.—From the amount (if any) appropriated pursuant to subsection (a) for any fiscal year that remains after applying subsection (b) for the fiscal year, the Secretary shall allot to each of the jurisdictions of Puerto Rico, Guam, the Virgin Islands, the Northern Mariana Islands, and American Samoa an amount determined in the same manner as the allotment to each of such jurisdictions is determined under section 423.

(3) OTHER STATES.—From the amount (if any) appropriated pursuant to subsection (a) for any fiscal year that remains after applying subsection (b) and paragraph (2) of this subsection for the fiscal year, the Secretary shall allot to each State (other than an Indian tribe) which is not specified in paragraph (2) of this subsection an amount equal to such remaining amount multiplied by the supplemental nutrition assistance program benefits[85] percentage (as defined in section 433(c)(2)) of the State for the fiscal year.

(d) GRANTS.—The Secretary may make a grant to a State which has a plan approved under this subpart in an amount equal to the lesser of—

(1) 75 percent of the total expenditures by the State for activities under the plan during the fiscal year or the immediately succeeding fiscal year; or

(2) the allotment of the State under subsection (c) for the fiscal year.

(e) APPLICABILITY OF CERTAIN RULES.—The rules of subsections (b) and (c) of section 434 shall apply in like manner to the amounts made available pursuant to subsection (a).

(f) TARGETED GRANTS TO INCREASE THE WELL-BEING OF, AND TO IMPROVE THE PERMANENCY OUTCOMES FOR, CHILDREN AFFECTED BY METHAMPHETAMINE OR OTHER SUBSTANCE ABUSE.—

(1) PURPOSE.—The purpose of this subsection is to authorize the Secretary to make competitive grants to regional partnerships to provide, through interagency collaboration and integration of programs and services, services and activities that are designed to in-

---

[85] P.L. 110-246, §4002(b)(1)(D), struck out "food stamp" and substituted "supplemental nutrition assistance program benefits", effective October 1, 2008. P.L. 110-234, §4002(b)(1)(D), which made the same amendment, was repealed, effective May 22, 2008 pursuant to P.L. 110-246, §4(a).

364 SOCIAL SECURITY ACT—§ 437(f)(2)

crease the well-being of, improve permanency outcomes for, and enhance the safety of children who are in an out-of-home placement or are at risk of being placed in an out-of-home placement as a result of a parent's or caretaker's methamphetamine or other substance abuse.

(2) REGIONAL PARTNERSHIP DEFINED.—

(A) IN GENERAL.—In this subsection, the term "regional partnership" means a collaborative agreement (which may be established on an interstate or intrastate basis) entered into by at least 2 of the following:

(i) The State child welfare agency that is responsible for the administration of the State plan under this part and part E.

(ii) The State agency responsible for administering the substance abuse prevention and treatment block grant provided under subpart II of part B of title XIX of the Public Health Service Act.

(iii) An Indian tribe or tribal consortium.

(iv) Nonprofit child welfare service providers.

(v) For-profit child welfare service providers.

(vi) Community health service providers.

(vii) Community mental health providers.

(viii) Local law enforcement agencies.

(ix) Judges and court personnel.

(x) Juvenile justice officials.

(xi) School personnel.

(xii) Tribal child welfare agencies (or a consortia of such agencies).

(xiii) Any other providers, agencies, personnel, officials, or entities that are related to the provision of child and family services under this subpart.

(B) REQUIREMENTS.—

(i) STATE CHILD WELFARE AGENCY PARTNER.—Subject to clause (ii)(I), a regional partnership entered into for purposes of this subsection shall include the State child welfare agency that is responsible for the administration of the State plan under this part and part E as 1 of the partners.

(ii) REGIONAL PARTNERSHIPS ENTERED INTO BY INDIAN TRIBES OR TRIBAL CONSORTIA.—If an Indian tribe or tribal consortium enters into a regional partnership for purposes of this subsection, the Indian tribe or tribal consortium—

(I) may (but is not required to) include such State child welfare agency as a partner in the collaborative agreement; and

(II) may not enter into a collaborative agreement only with tribal child welfare agencies (or a consortium of such agencies).

(iii) NO STATE AGENCY ONLY PARTNERSHIPS.—If a State agency described in clause (i) or (ii) of subparagraph (A) enters into a regional partnership for purposes of this subsection, the State agency may not enter into a collaborative agreement only with the other State agency described in such clause (i) or (ii).

(3) AUTHORITY TO AWARD GRANTS.—

(A) IN GENERAL.—In addition to amounts authorized to be appropriated to carry out this section, the Secretary shall award grants under this subsection, from the amounts reserved for each of fiscal years 2007 through 2011 under section 436(b)(5), to regional partnerships that satisfy the requirements of this subsection, in amounts that are not less than $500,000 and not more than $1,000,000 per grant per fiscal ear.

(B) REQUIRED MINIMUM PERIOD OF APPROVAL.—A grant shall be awarded under this subsection for a period of not less than 2, and not more than 5, fiscal years.

(4) APPLICATION REQUIREMENTS.—To be eligible for a grant under this subsection, a regional partnership shall submit to the Secretary a written application containing the following:

(A) Recent evidence demonstrating that methamphetamine or other substance abuse has had a substantial impact on the number of out-of-home placements for children, or the number of children who are at risk of being placed in an out-of-home placement, in the partnership region.

(B) A description of the goals and outcomes to be achieved during the funding period for the grant that will—

(i) enhance the well-being of children receiving services or taking part in activities conducted with funds provided under the grant;

(ii) lead to safety and permanence for such children; and

(iii) decrease the number of out-of-home placements for children, or the number of children who are at risk of being placed in an out-of-home placement, in the partnership region.

(C) A description of the joint activities to be funded in whole or in part with the funds provided under the grant, including the sequencing of the activities proposed to be conducted under the funding period for the grant.

(D) A description of the strategies for integrating programs and services determined to be appropriate for the child and where appropriate, the child's family.

(E) A description of the strategies for—

(i) collaborating with the State child welfare agency described in paragraph (2)(A)(i) (unless that agency is the lead applicant for the regional partnership); and

(ii) consulting, as appropriate, with—

(I) the State agency described in paragraph (2)(A)(ii); and

(II) the State law enforcement and judicial agencies.

To the extent the Secretary determines that the requirement of this subparagraph would be inappropriate to apply to a regional partnership that includes an Indian tribe, tribal consortium, or a tribal child welfare agency or a consortium of

366 SOCIAL SECURITY ACT—§ 437(f)(4)(F)

such agencies, the Secretary may exempt the regional partnership from the requirement.

(F) Such other information as the Secretary may require.

(5) USE OF FUNDS.—Funds made available under a grant made under this subsection shall only be used for services or activities that are consistent with the purpose of this subsection and may include the following:

(A) Family-based comprehensive long-term substance abuse treatment services.

(B) Early intervention and preventative services.

(C) Children and family counseling.

(D) Mental health services.

(E) Parenting skills training.

(F) Replication of successful models for providing family-based comprehensive long-term substance abuse treatment services.

(6) MATCHING REQUIREMENT.—

(A) FEDERAL SHARE.—A grant awarded under this subsection shall be available to pay a percentage share of the costs of services provided or activities conducted under such grant, not to exceed—

(i) 85 percent for the first and second fiscal years for which the grant is awarded to a recipient;

(ii) 80 percent for the third and fourth such fiscal years; and

(iii) 75 percent for the fifth such fiscal year.

(B) NON-FEDERAL SHARE.—The non-Federal share of the cost of services provided or activities conducted under a grant awarded under this subsection may be in cash or in kind. In determining the amount of the non-Federal share, the Secretary may attribute fair market value to goods, services, and facilities contributed from non-Federal sources.

(7) CONSIDERATIONS IN AWARDING GRANTS.—In awarding grants under this subsection, the Secretary shall—

(A) take into consideration the extent to which applicant regional partnerships—

(i) demonstrate that methamphetamine or other substance abuse by parents or caretakers has had a substantial impact on the number of out-of-home placements for children, or the number of children who are at risk of being placed in an out-of-home placement, in the partnership region;

(ii) have limited resources for addressing the needs of children affected by such abuse;

(iii) have a lack of capacity for, or access to, comprehensive family treatment services; and

(iv) demonstrate a plan for sustaining the services provided by or activities funded under the grant after the conclusion of the grant period; and

(B) after taking such factors into consideration, give greater weight to awarding grants to regional partnerships that propose to address methamphetamine abuse and addiction in the partnership region (alone or in combination with other drug abuse and addiction) and which demonstrate that methamphetamine abuse and addiction (alone or in combination with other drug abuse and addiction) is adversely affecting child welfare in the partnership region.

(8) PERFORMANCE INDICATORS.—

(A) IN GENERAL.—Not later than 9 months after the date of enactment of this subsection, the Secretary shall establish indicators that will be used to assess periodically the performance of the grant recipients under this subsection in using funds made available under such grants to achieve the purpose of this subsection.

(B) CONSULTATION REQUIRED.—In establishing the performance indicators required by subparagraph (A), the Secretary shall consult with the following:

(i) The Assistant Secretary for the Administration for Children and Families.

(ii) The Administrator of the Substance Abuse and Mental Health Services Administration.

(iii) Representatives of States in which a State agency described in clause (i) or (ii) of paragraph (2)(A) is a member of a regional partnership that is a grant recipient under this subsection.

(iv) Representatives of Indian tribes, tribal consortia, or tribal child welfare agencies that are members of a regional partnership that is a grant recipient under this subsection.

(9) REPORTS.—

(A) GRANTEE REPORTS.—

(i) ANNUAL REPORT.—Not later than September 30 of the first fiscal year in which a recipient of a grant under this subsection is paid funds under the grant, and annually thereafter until September 30 of the last fiscal year in which the recipient is paid funds under the grant, the recipient shall submit to the Secretary a report on the services provided or activities carried out during that fiscal year with such funds. The report shall contain such information as the Secretary determines is necessary to provide an accurate description of the services provided or activities conducted with such funds.

(ii) INCORPORATION OF INFORMATION RELATED TO PERFORMANCE INDICATORS.—Each recipient of a grant under this subsection shall incorporate into the first annual report required by clause (i) that is submitted after the establishment of performance indicators under paragraph (8), information required in relation to such indicators.

(B) REPORTS TO CONGRESS.—On the basis of the reports submitted under subparagraph (A), the Secretary annually shall submit to the Committee on Ways and Means of the House of Representatives and the Committee on Finance of the Senate a report on—

(i) the services provided and activities conducted with funds provided under grants awarded under this subsection;

(ii) the performance indicators established under paragraph (8); and

368　　SOCIAL SECURITY ACT—§ 437(f)(9)(B)(iii)

(iii) the progress that has been made in addressing the needs of families with methamphetamine or other substance abuse problems who come to the attention of the child welfare system and in achieving the goals of child safety, permanence, and family stability.

ENTITLEMENT FUNDING FOR STATE COURTS TO ASSESS AND IMPROVE HANDLING OF PROCEEDINGS RELATING TO FOSTER CARE AND ADOPTION

SEC. 438. [42 U.S.C. 629h] (a) IN GENERAL.—The Secretary shall make grants, in accordance with this section, to the highest State courts in States participating in the program under part E of title IV of the Social Security Act, for the purpose of enabling such courts—

(1) to conduct assessments, in accordance with such requirements as the Secretary shall publish, of the role, responsibilities, and effectiveness of State courts in carrying out State laws requiring proceedings (conducted by or under the supervision of the courts)—

(A) that implement parts B and E ;

(B) that determine the advisability or appropriateness of foster care placement;

(C) that determine whether to terminate parental rights;

(D) that determine whether to approve the adoption or other permanent placement of a child;

(E)[86] that determine the best strategy to use to expedite the interstate placement of children, including—

(i) requiring courts in different States to cooperate in the sharing of information;

(ii) authorizing courts to obtain information and testimony from agencies and parties in other States without requiring interstate travel by the agencies and parties; and

(iii) permitting the participation of parents, children, other necessary parties, and attorneys in cases involving interstate placement without requiring their interstate travel; and

(2) to implement improvements the highest state courts deem necessary as a result of the assessments, including—

(A) to provide for the safety, well-being, and permanence of children in foster care, as set forth in the Adoption and Safe Families Act of 1997 (Public Law 105-89); and

(B) to implement a corrective action plan, as necessary, resulting from reviews of child and family service programs under section 1123A of this Act;

(3) to ensure that the safety, permanence, and well-being needs of children are met in a timely and complete manner; and

(4) to provide for the training of judges, attorneys and other legal personnel in child welfare cases.

(b) APPLICATIONS.—

(1) IN GENERAL.—In order to be eligible to receive a grant under this section, a highest State court shall have in effect a rule requiring State courts to ensure that foster parents, pre-adoptive

---

[86] P.L. 109-239, §9(2), added subparagraph (E), effective October 1, 2006. See Vol. II, P.L. 109-239, §14, with respect to applicability and a possible delay permitted if State legislation is required.

parents, and relative caregivers of a child in foster care under the responsibility of the State are notified of any proceeding to be held with respect to the child, and shall submit to the Secretary an application at such time, in such form, and including such information and assurances as the Secretary may require, including—

(A) in the case of a grant for the purpose described in subsection (a)(3), a description of how courts and child welfare agencies on the local and State levels will collaborate and jointly plan for the collection and sharing of all relevant data and information to demonstrate how improved case tracking and analysis of child abuse and neglect cases will produce safe and timely permanency decisions;

(B) in the case of a grant for the purpose described in subsection (a)(4), a demonstration that a portion of the grant will be used for cross-training initiatives that are jointly planned and executed with the State agency or any other agency under contract with the State to administer the State program under the State plan under subpart 1, the State plan approved under section 434, or the State plan approved under part E; and

(C) in the case of a grant for any purpose described in subsection (a), a demonstration of meaningful and ongoing collaboration among the courts in the State, the State agency or any other agency under contract with the State who is responsible for administering the State program under part B or E, and, where applicable, Indian tribes.

(2) SEPARATE APPLICATIONS.—A highest State court desiring grants under this section for 2 or more purposes shall submit separate applications for the following grants:

(A) A grant for the purposes described in paragraphs (1) and (2) of subsection (a).

(B) A grant for the purpose described in subsection (a)(3).

(C) A grant for the purpose described in subsection (a)(4).

(c) ALLOTMENTS.—

(1) GRANTS TO ASSESS AND IMPROVE HANDLING OF COURT PROCEEDINGS RELATING TO FOSTER CARE AND ADOPTION.—

(A) IN GENERAL.—Each highest State court which has an application approved under subsection (b) of this section for a grant described in subsection (b)(2)(A) of this section, and is conducting assessment and improvement activities in accordance with this section, shall be entitled to payment, for each of fiscal years 2002 through 2011, from the amount reserved pursuant to section 436(b)(2) (and the amount, if any, reserved pursuant to section 437(b)(2)), of an amount equal to the sum of $85,000 plus the amount described in subparagraph (B) of this paragraph for the fiscal year.

(B) FORMULA.—The amount described in this subparagraph for any fiscal year is the amount that bears the same ratio to the amount reserved pursuant to section 436(b)(2) (and the amount, if any, reserved pursuant to section 437(b)(2)) for the fiscal year (reduced by the dollar amount specified in subparagraph (A) of this paragraph for the fiscal year) as the number of individuals in the State who have not attained 21 years of age bears to the total number of such

370 SOCIAL SECURITY ACT—§ 438(c)(2)

individuals in all States the highest State courts of which have approved applications under subsection (b) for such grant.

(2) GRANTS FOR IMPROVED DATA COLLECTION AND TRAINING.—

(A) IN GENERAL.—Each highest State court which has an application approved under subsection (b) of this section for a grant referred to in subparagraph (B) or (C) of subsection (b)(2) shall be entitled to payment, for each of fiscal years 2006 through 2010, from the amount made available under whichever of paragraph (1) or (2) of subsection (e) applies with respect to the grant, of an amount equal to the sum of $85,000 plus the amount described in subparagraph (B) of this paragraph for the fiscal year with respect to the grant.

(B) FORMULA.—The amount described in this subparagraph for any fiscal year with respect to a grant referred to in subparagraph (B) or (C) of subsection (b)(2) is the amount that bears the same ratio to the amount made available under subsection (e) for such a grant (reduced by the dollar amount specified in subparagraph (A) of this paragraph) as the number of individuals in the State who have not attained 21 years of age bears to the total number of such individuals in all States the highest State courts of which have approved applications under subsection (b) for such a grant.

(d) FEDERAL SHARE.—Each highest State court which receives funds paid under this section may use such funds to pay not more than 75 percent of the cost of activities under this section in each of fiscal years 2002 through 2011.

(e) FUNDING FOR GRANTS FOR IMPROVED DATA COLLECTION AND TRAINING.—Out of any money in the Treasury of the United States not otherwise appropriated, there are appropriated to the Secretary, for each of fiscal years 2006 through 2010—

(1) $10,000,000 for grants referred to in subsection (b)(2)(B); and

(2) $10,000,000 for grants referred to in subsection (b)(2)(C).

GRANTS FOR PROGRAMS FOR MENTORING CHILDREN OF PRISONERS

SEC. 439. [42 U.S.C. 629i] (a) FINDINGS AND PURPOSES.—

(1) FINDINGS.—

(A) In the period between 1991 and 1999, the number of children with a parent incarcerated in a Federal or State correctional facility increased by more than 100 percent, from approximately 900,000 to approximately 2,000,000. In 1999, 2.1 percent of all children in the United States had a parent in Federal or State prison.

(B) Prior to incarceration, 64 percent of female prisoners and 44 percent of male prisoners in State facilities lived with their children.

(C) Nearly 90 percent of the children of incarcerated fathers live with their mothers, and 79 percent of the children of incarcerated mothers live with a grandparent or other relative.

(D) Parental arrest and confinement lead stress, trauma, stigmatization, and separation problems for children. These problems are coupled with existing problems that include poverty, violence, parental substance abuse, high-crime environments, intrafamilial abuse, child abuse and neglect, multiple care givers, and/or prior separations. As a result, these children often exhibit a broad variety of behavioral, emotional, health, and educational problems that are often compounded by the pain of separation.

(E) Empirical research demonstrates that mentoring is a potent force for improving children's behavior across all risk behaviors affecting health. Quality, one-on-one relationships that provide young people with caring role models for future success have profound, life-changing potential. Done right, mentoring markedly advances youths' life prospects. A widely cited 1995 study by Public/Private Ventures measured the impact of one Big Brothers Big Sisters program and found significant effects in the lives of youth cutting first-time drug use by almost half and first-time alcohol use by about a third, reducing school absenteeism by half, cutting assaultive behavior by a third, improving parental and peer relationships, giving youth greater confidence in their school work, and improving academic performance.

(2) PURPOSES.—The purposes of this section are to authorize the Secretary—

(A) to make competitive grants to applicants in areas with substantial numbers of children of incarcerated parents, to support the establishment or expansion and operation of programs using a network of public and private community entities to provide mentoring services for children of prisoners; and

(B) to enter into on a competitive basis a cooperative agreement to conduct a service delivery demonstration project in accordance with the requirements of subsection (g).

(b) DEFINITIONS.—In this section:

(1) CHILDREN OF PRISONERS.—The term "children of prisoners" means children one or both of whose parents are incarcerated in a Federal, State, or local correctional facility. The term is deemed to include children who are in an ongoing mentoring relationship in a program under this section at the time of their parents' release from prison, for purposes of continued participation in the program.

(2) MENTORING.—The term "mentoring" means a structured, managed program in which children are appropriately matched with screened and trained adult volunteers for one–on–one relationships, involving meetings and activities on a regular basis, intended to meet, in part, the child's need for involvement with a caring and supportive adult who provides a positive role model.

(3) MENTORING SERVICES.—The term "mentoring services" means those services and activities that support a structured, managed program of mentoring, including the management by trained personnel of outreach to, and screening of, eligible children; outreach to, education and training of, and liaison with sponsoring local organizations; screening and training of adult volunteers; matching of children with suitable adult volunteer mentors; support and oversight of the mentoring relationship;

372   SOCIAL SECURITY ACT—§ 439(b)(3)(cont)

and establishment of goals and evaluation of outcomes for mentored children.

(c) PROGRAM AUTHORIZED.—From the amounts appropriated under subsection (i) for a fiscal year that remain after applying subsection (i)(2), the Secretary shall make grants under this section for each of fiscal years 2007 through 2011 to State or local governments, tribal governments or tribal consortia, faith-based organizations, and community-based organizations in areas that have significant numbers of children of prisoners and that submit applications meeting the requirements of this section, in amounts that do not exceed $5,000,000 per grant.

(d) APPLICATION REQUIREMENTS.—In order to be eligible for a grant under this section, the chief executive officer of the applicant must submit to the Secretary an application containing the following:

(1) PROGRAM DESIGN.—A description of the proposed program, including—

(A) a list of local public and private organizations and entities that will participate in the mentoring network;

(B) the name, description, and qualifications of the entity that will coordinate and oversee the activities of the mentoring network;

(C) the number of mentor-child matches proposed to be established and maintained annually under the program;

(D) such information as the Secretary may require concerning the methods to be used to recruit, screen support, and oversee individuals participating as mentors, (which methods shall include criminal background checks on the individuals), and to evaluate outcomes for participating children, including information necessary to demonstrate compliance with requirements established by the Secretary for the program; and

(E) such other information as the Secretary may require.

(2) COMMUNITY CONSULTATION; COORDINATION WITH OTHER PROGRAMS.—A demonstration that, in developing and implementing the program, the applicant will, to the extent feasible and appropriate—

(A) consult with public and private community entities, including religious organizations, and including, as appropriate, Indian tribal organizations and urban Indian organizations, and with family members of potential clients;

(B) coordinate the programs and activities under the program with other Federal, State, and local programs serving children and youth; and

(C) consult with appropriate Federal, State, and local corrections, workforce development, and substance abuse and mental health agencies.

(3) EQUAL ACCESS FOR LOCAL SERVICE PROVIDERS.—An assurance that public and private entities and community organizations, including religious organizations and Indian organizations, will be eligible to participate on an equal basis.

(4) RECORDS, REPORTS, AND AUDITS.—An agreement that the applicant will maintain such records, make such reports, and cooperate with such reviews or audits as the Secretary may find

necessary for purposes of oversight of project activities and expenditures.

(5) EVALUATION.—An agreement that the applicant will cooperate fully with the Secretary's ongoing and final evaluation of the program under the plan, by means including providing the Secretary access to the program and program-related records and documents, staff, and grantees receiving funding under the plan.

(e) FEDERAL SHARE.—

(1) IN GENERAL.—A grant for a program under this section shall be available to pay a percentage share of the costs of the program up to—

(A) 75 percent for the first and second fiscal years for which the grant is awarded; and

(B) 50 percent for the third and each succeeding such fiscal years.

(2) NON-FEDERAL SHARE.—The non-Federal share of the cost of projects under this section may be in cash or in kind. In determining the amount of the non-Federal share, the Secretary may attribute fair market value to goods, services, and facilities contributed from non-Federal sources.

(f) CONSIDERATIONS IN AWARDING GRANTS.—In awarding grants under this section, the Secretary shall take into consideration—

(1) the qualifications and capacity of applicants and networks of organizations to effectively carry out a mentoring program under this section;

(2) the comparative severity of need for mentoring services in local areas, taking into consideration data on the numbers of children (and in particular of low-income children) with an incarcerated parents (or parents) in the areas;

(3) evidence of consultation with existing youth and family service programs, as appropriate; and

(4) any other factors the Secretary may deem significant with respect to the need for or the potential success of carrying out a mentoring program under this section.

(g) SERVICE DELIVERY DEMONSTRATION PROJECT.—

(1) PURPOSE; AUTHORITY TO ENTER INTO COOPERATIVE AGREEMENT.—The Secretary shall enter into a cooperative agreement with an eligible entity that meets the requirements of paragraph (2) for the purpose of requiring the entity to conduct a demonstration project consistent with this subsection under which the entity shall—

(A) identify children of prisoners in need of mentoring services who have not been matched with a mentor by an applicant awarded a grant under this section, with a priority for identifying children who—

(i) reside in an area not served by a recipient of a grant under this section;

(ii) reside in an area that has a substantial number of children of prisoners;

(iii) reside in a rural area; or

(iv) are Indians;

(B) provide the families of the children so identified with—

(i) a voucher for mentoring services that meets the requirements of paragraph (5); and

374 SOCIAL SECURITY ACT—§ 439(g)(1)(B)(ii)

(ii) a list of the providers of mentoring services in the area in which the family resides that satisfy the requirements of paragraph (6); and

(C) monitor and oversee the delivery of mentoring services by providers that accept the vouchers.

(2) ELIGIBLE ENTITY.—

(A) IN GENERAL.—Subject to subparagraph (B), an eligible entity under this subsection is an organization that the Secretary determines, on a competitive basis—

(i) has substantial experience—

(I) in working with organizations that provide mentoring services for children of prisoners; and

(II) in developing quality standards for the identification and assessment of mentoring programs for children of prisoners; and

(ii) submits an application that satisfies the requirements of paragraph (3).

(B) LIMITATION.—An organization that provides mentoring services may not be an eligible entity for purposes of being awarded a cooperative agreement under this subsection.

(3) APPLICATION REQUIREMENTS.—To be eligible to be awarded a cooperative agreement under this subsection, an entity shall submit to the Secretary an application that includes the following:

(A) QUALIFICATIONS.—Evidence that the entity—

(i) meets the experience requirements of paragraph (2)(A)(i); and

(ii) is able to carry out—

(I) the purposes of this subsection identified in paragraph (1); and

(II) the requirements of the cooperative agreement specified in paragraph (4).

(B) SERVICE DELIVERY PLAN.—

(i) DISTRIBUTION REQUIREMENTS.—Subject to clause (iii), a description of the plan of the entity to ensure the distribution of not less than—

(I) 3,000 vouchers for mentoring services in the first year in which the cooperative agreement is in effect with that entity;

(II) 8,000 vouchers for mentoring services in the second year in which the agreement is in effect with that entity; and

(III) 13,000 vouchers for mentoring services in any subsequent year in which the agreement is in effect with that entity.

(ii) SATISFACTION OF PRIORITIES.—A description of how the plan will ensure the delivery of mentoring services to children identified in accordance with the requirements of paragraph (1)(A).

(iii) SECRETARIAL AUTHORITY TO MODIFY DISTRIBUTION REQUIREMENT.—The Secretary may modify the number of vouchers specified in subclauses (I) through (III) of clause (i) to take into account the availability of appropriations and the need to ensure that the vouchers distributed by the entity are for amounts that are adequate to ensure the provision of mentoring services for a 12-month period.

(C) COLLABORATION AND COOPERATION.—A description of how the entity will ensure collaboration and cooperation with other interested parties, including courts and prisons, with respect to the delivery of mentoring services under the demonstration project.

(D) OTHER.—Any other information that the Secretary may find necessary to demonstrate the capacity of the entity to satisfy the requirements of this subsection.

(4) COOPERATIVE AGREEMENT REQUIREMENTS.—A cooperative agreement awarded under this subsection shall require the eligible entity to do the following:

(A) IDENTIFY QUALITY STANDARDS FOR PROVIDERS.—To work with the Secretary to identify the quality standards that a provider of mentoring services must meet in order to participate in the demonstration project and which, at a minimum, shall include criminal records checks for individuals who are prospective mentors and shall prohibit approving any individual to be a mentor if the criminal records check of the individual reveals a conviction which would prevent the individual from being approved as a foster or adoptive parent under section 471(a)(20)(A).

(B) IDENTIFY ELIGIBLE PROVIDERS.—To identify and compile a list of those providers of mentoring services in any of the 50 States or the District of Columbia that meet the quality standards identified pursuant to subparagraph (A).

(C) IDENTIFY ELIGIBLE CHILDREN.—To identify children of prisoners who require mentoring services, consistent with the priorities specified in paragraph (1)(A).

(D) MONITOR AND OVERSEE DELIVERY OF MENTORING SERVICES.—To satisfy specific requirements of the Secretary for monitoring and overseeing the delivery of Mentoring services under the demonstration project, which shall include a requirement to ensure that providers of mentoring services under the project report data on the children served and the types of mentoring services provided.

(E) RECORDS, REPORTS, AND AUDITS.—To maintain any records, make any reports, and cooperate with any reviews and audits that the Secretary determines are necessary to oversee the activities of the entity in carrying out the demonstration project under this subsection.

(F) EVALUATIONS.—To cooperate fully with any evaluations of the demonstration project, including collecting and monitoring data and providing the Secretary or the Secretary's designee with access to records and staff related to the conduct of the project.

(G) LIMITATION ON ADMINISTRATIVE EXPENDITURES.—To ensure that administrative expenditures incurred by the entity in conducting the demonstration project with respect to a fiscal year do not exceed the amount equal to 10 percent of the amount awarded to carry out the project for that year.

376   SOCIAL SECURITY ACT—§ 439(g)(5)

(5) VOUCHER REQUIREMENTS.—A voucher for mentoring services provided to the family of a child identified in accordance with paragraph (1)(A) shall meet the following requirements:

(A) TOTAL PAYMENT AMOUNT; 12-MONTH SERVICE PERIOD.—The voucher shall specify the total amount to be paid a provider of mentoring services for providing the child on whose behalf the voucher is issued with mentoring services for a 12-month period.

(B) PERIODIC PAYMENTS AS SERVICES PROVIDED.—

(i) IN GENERAL.—The voucher shall specify that it may be redeemed with the eligible entity by the provider accepting the voucher in return for agreeing to provide mentoring services for the child on whose behalf the voucher is issued.

(ii) DEMONSTRATION OF THE PROVISION OF SERVICES.—A provider that redeems a voucher issued by the eligible entity shall receive periodic payments from the eligible entity during the 12-month period that the voucher is in effect upon demonstration of the provision of significant services and activities related to the provision of mentoring services to the child on whose behalf the voucher is issued.

(6) PROVIDER REQUIREMENTS.—In order to participate in the demonstration project, a provider of mentoring services shall—

(A) meet the quality standards identified by the eligible entity in accordance with paragraph (1);

(B) agree to accept a voucher meeting the requirements of paragraph (5) as payment for the provision of mentoring services to a child on whose behalf the voucher is issued;

(C) demonstrate that the provider has the capacity, and has or will have nonfederal resources, to continue supporting the provision of mentoring services to the child on whose behalf the voucher is issued, as appropriate, after the conclusion of the 12-month period during which the voucher is in effect; and

(D) if the provider is a recipient of a grant under this section, demonstrate that the provider has exhausted its capacity for providing mentoring services under the grant.

(7) 3-YEAR PERIOD; OPTION FOR RENEWAL.—

(A) IN GENERAL.—A cooperative agreement awarded under this subsection shall be effective for a 3-year period.

(B) RENEWAL.—The cooperative agreement may be renewed for an additional period, not to exceed 2 years and subject to any conditions that the Secretary may specify that are not inconsistent with the requirements of this subsection or subsection (i)(2)(B), if the Secretary determines that the entity has satisfied the requirements of the agreement and evaluations of the service delivery demonstration project demonstrate that the voucher service delivery method is effective in providing mentoring services to children of prisoners.

(8) INDEPENDENT EVALUATION AND REPORT.—

(A) IN GENERAL.—The Secretary shall enter into a contract with an independent, private organization to evaluate and prepare a report on the first 2 fiscal years in which the demonstration project is conducted under this subsection.

(B) DEADLINE FOR REPORT.—Not later than 90 days after the end of the second fiscal year in which the demonstration project is conducted under this subsection, the Secretary shall submit the report required under subparagraph (A) to the Committee on Ways and Means of the House of Representatives and the Committee on Finance of the Senate. The report shall include—

(i) the number of children as of the end of such second fiscal year who received vouchers for mentoring services; and

(ii) any conclusions regarding the use of vouchers for the delivery of mentoring services for children of prisoners.

(9) NO EFFECT ON ELIGIBILITY FOR OTHER FEDERAL ASSISTANCE.—A voucher provided to a family under the demonstration project conducted under this subsection shall be disregarded for purposes of determining the eligibility for, or the amount of, any other Federal or federally-supported assistance for the family.

(h) INDEPENDENT EVALUATION; REPORTS.—

(1) INDEPENDENT EVALUATION.—The Secretary shall conduct by grant, contract, or cooperative agreement an independent evaluation of the programs authorized under this section, including the service delivery demonstration project authorized under subsection (g).

(2) REPORTS.—Not later than 12 months after the date of enactment of this subsection, the Secretary shall submit a report to the Congress that includes the following:

(A) The characteristics of the mentoring programs funded under this section.

(B) The plan for implementation of the service delivery demonstration project authorized under subsection (g).

(C) A description of the outcome-based evaluation of the programs authorized under this section that the Secretary is conducting as of that date of enactment and how the evaluation has been expanded to include an evaluation of the demonstration project authorized under subsection (g).

(D) The date on which the Secretary shall submit a final report on the evaluation to the Congress.

(i) AUTHORIZATION OF APPROPRIATIONS; RESERVATIONS OF CERTAIN AMOUNTS.—

(1) LIMITATIONS ON AUTHORIZATION OF APPROPRIATIONS.—To carry out this section, there are authorized to be appropriated to the Secretary such sums as may be necessary for fiscal years 2007 through 2011.

(2) RESERVATIONS.—The Secretary shall reserve 4 percent of the amount appropriated for each fiscal year under paragraph (1) for expenditure by the Secretary for research, technical assistance, and evaluation related to programs under this section.

(A) RESEARCH, TECHNICAL ASSISTANCE, AND EVALUATION.—The Secretary shall enter into a contract with an independent, private organization to evaluate and prepare a

378   SOCIAL SECURITY ACT—§ 439(i)(2)(B)

report on the first 2 fiscal years in which the demonstration project is conducted under this subsection.
    (B) SERVICE DELIVERY DEMONSTRATION PROJECT.—
        (i) IN GENERAL.—Subject to clause (ii), for purposes of awarding a cooperative agreement to conduct the service delivery demonstration project authorized under subsection (g), the Secretary shall reserve not more than—
            (I) $5,000,000 of the amount appropriated under paragraph (1) for the first fiscal year in which funds are to be awarded for the agreement;
            (II) $10,000,000 of the amount appropriated under paragraph (1) for the second fiscal year in which funds are to be awarded for the agreement; and
            (III) $15,000,000 of the amount appropriated under paragraph (1) for the third fiscal year in which funds are to be awarded for the agreement.
        (ii) ASSURANCE OF FUNDING FOR GENERAL PROGRAM GRANTS.—With respect to any fiscal year, no funds may be awarded for a cooperative agreement under subsection (g), unless at least $25,000,000 of the amount appropriated under paragraph (1) for that fiscal year is used by the Secretary for making grants under this section for that fiscal year.

[Part C—Repealed.[87]]

Part D—Child Support and Establishment of Paternity[88]

APPROPRIATION

SEC. 451. [42 U.S.C. 651] For the purpose of enforcing the support obligations owed by noncustodial parents to their children and the spouse (or former spouse) with whom such children are living, locating noncustodial parents, establishing paternity, obtaining child and spousal support, and assuring that assistance in obtaining support will be available under this part to all children (whether or not eligible for assistance under a State program funded under part A) for whom such assistance is requested, there is hereby authorized to be appropriated for each fiscal year a sum sufficient to carry out the purposes of this part.

DUTIES OF THE SECRETARY

SEC. 452. [42 U.S.C. 652] (a) The Secretary shall establish, within the Department of Health and Human Services a separate organizational unit, under the direction of a designee of the Secretary, who shall report directly to the Secretary and who shall—

---

[87] P.L. 100-485, §202(a); 102 Stat. 2377.
[88] See Vol. II, P.L. 73-30, §3, for the requirement that State employment offices supply data in aid of administration of the child support programs.
    See Vol. II, P.L. 83-591, §6103(l)(1), with respect to disclosure of returns and return information by the Secretary of the Treasury to the Social Security Administration, and §7213(a)(1) with respect to the penalty for unauthorized disclosure of that tax return information.
    See Vol. II, P.L. 95-630, §§1101–1121, with respect to an individual's right to financial privacy.
    See Vol. II, P.L. 99-177, §256, with respect to treatment of the child support enforcement program.

(1) establish such standards for State programs for locating noncustodial parents, establishing paternity, and obtaining child support and support for the spouse (or former spouse) with whom the noncustodial parent's child is living as he determines to be necessary to assure that such programs will be effective;

(2) establish minimum organizational and staffing requirements for State units engaged in carrying out such programs under plans approved under this part;

(3) review and approve State plans for such programs;

(4)(A) review data and calculations transmitted by State agencies pursuant to section 454(15)(B) on State program accomplishments with respect to performance indicators for purposes of subsection (g) of this section and section 458;

(B) review annual reports submitted pursuant to section 454(15)(A) and, as appropriate, provide to the State comments, recommendations for additional or alternative corrective actions, and technical assistance; and

(C) conduct audits, in accordance with the Government auditing standards of the Comptroller General of the United States—

(i) at least once every 3 years (or more frequently, in the case of a State which fails to meet the requirements of this part concerning performance standards and reliability of program data) to assess the completeness, reliability, and security of the data and the accuracy of the reporting systems used in calculating performance indicators under subsection (g) of this section and section 458;

(ii) of the adequacy of financial management of the State program operated under the State plan approved under this part, including assessments of—

(I) whether Federal and other funds made available to carry out the State program are being appropriately expended, and are properly and fully accounted for; and

(II) whether collections and disbursements of support payments are carried out correctly and are fully accounted for; and

(iii) for such other purposes as the Secretary may find necessary;

(5) assist States in establishing adequate reporting procedures and maintain records of the operations of programs established pursuant to this part in each State, and establish procedures to be followed by States for collecting and reporting information required to be provided under this part, and establish uniform definitions (including those necessary to enable the measurement of State compliance with the requirements of this part relating to expedited processes) to be applied in following such procedures;

(6) maintain records of all amounts collected and disbursed under programs established pursuant to the provisions of this part and of the costs incurred in collecting such amounts;

(7) provide technical assistance to the States to help them establish effective systems for collecting child and spousal support and establishing paternity, and specify the minimum requirements of an affidavit to be used for the voluntary acknowledgment of paternity which shall include the social security number

380 SOCIAL SECURITY ACT—§ 452(a)(7)(cont)

of each parent and, after consultation with the States, other common elements as determined by such designee;

(8) receive applications from States for permission to utilize the courts of the United States to enforce court orders for support against noncustodial parents and, upon a finding that (A) another State has not undertaken to enforce the court order of the originating State against the noncustodial parent within a reasonable time, and (B) that utilization of the Federal courts is the only reasonable method of enforcing such order, approve such applications;

(9) operate the Federal Parent Locator Service established by section 453;

(10) not later than three months after the end of each fiscal year, beginning with the year 1977, submit to the Congress a full and complete report on all activities undertaken pursuant to the provisions of this part, which report shall include, but not be limited to, the following:

(A) total program costs and collections set forth in sufficient detail to show the cost to the States and the Federal Government, the distribution of collections to families, State and local governmental units, and the Federal Government; and an identification of the financial impact of the provisions of this part, including—

(i) the total amount of child support payments collected as a result of services furnished during the fiscal year to individuals receiving services under this part;

(ii) the cost to the States and to the Federal Government of so furnishing the services; and

(iii) the number of cases involving families—

(I) who became ineligible for assistance under State programs funded under part A during a month in the fiscal year; and

(II) with respect to whom a child support payment was received in the month;

(B) costs and staff associated with the Office of Child Support Enforcement;

(C) the following data, separately stated for cases where the child is receiving assistance under a State program funded under part A (or foster care maintenance payments under part E), or formerly received such assistance or payments and the State is continuing to collect support assigned to it pursuant to section 408(a)(3) or under section 471(a)(17) or 1912, and for all other cases under this part:

(i) the total number of cases in which a support obligation has been established in the fiscal year for which the report is submitted;

(ii) the total number of cases in which a support obligation has been established;

(iii) the number of cases in which support was collected during the fiscal year;

(iv) the total amount of support collected during such fiscal year and distributed as current support;

(v) the total amount of support collected during such fiscal year and distributed as arrearages;

SOCIAL SECURITY ACT—§ 452(b) 381

(vi) the total amount of support due and unpaid for all fiscal years; and

(vii) the number of child support cases filed in each State in such fiscal year, and the amount of the collections made in each State in such fiscal year, on behalf of children residing in another State or against parents residing in another State;

(D) the status of all State plans under this part as of the end of the fiscal year last ending before the report is submitted, together with an explanation of any problems which are delaying or preventing approval of State plans under this part;

(E) data, by State, on the use of the Federal Parent Locator Service, and the number of locate requests submitted without the noncustodial parent's social security account number;

(F) the number of cases, by State, in which an applicant for or recipient assistance under a State program funded under part A has refused to cooperate in identifying and locating the noncustodial parent and the number of cases in which refusal so to cooperate is based on good cause (as determined by the State);

(G) data, by State, on use of the Internal Revenue Service for collections, the number of court orders on which collections were made, the number of paternity determinations made and the number of parents located, in sufficient detail to show the cost and benefits to the States and to the Federal Government;

(H) the major problems encountered which have delayed or prevented implementation of the provisions of this part during the fiscal year last ending prior to the submission of such report; and

(I) compliance, by State, with the standards established pursuant to subsections (h) and (i); and

(11) not later than October 1, 1996, after consulting with the State directors of programs under this part, promulgate forms to be used by States in interstate cases for—

(A) collection of child support through income withholding;

(B) imposition of liens; and

(C) administrative subpoenas.

(b) The Secretary shall, upon the request of any State having in effect a State plan approved under this part, certify to the Secretary of the Treasury for collection pursuant to the provisions of section 6305 of the Internal Revenue Code of 1954[89] the amount of any child support obligation (including any support obligation with respect to the parent who is living with the child and receiving assistance under the State program funded under part A) which is assigned to such State or is undertaken to be collected by such State pursuant to section 454(4). No amount may be certified for collection under this subsection except the amount of the delinquency under a court or administrative order for support and upon a showing by the State that such State has made diligent and reasonable efforts to collect such amounts utilizing its own collection mechanisms, and upon an agreement that the State will reimburse the Secretary of the Treasury for any costs involved

---

[89] See Vol. II, P.L. 83-591, §6305.

382   SOCIAL SECURITY ACT—§ 452(b)(cont)

in making the collection. All reimbursements shall be credited to the appropriation accounts which bore all or part of the costs involved in making the collections. The Secretary after consultation with the Secretary of the Treasury may, by regulation, establish criteria for accepting amounts for collection and for making certification under this subsection including imposing such limitations on the frequency of making such certifications under this subsection.

(c) The Secretary of the Treasury shall from time to time pay to each State for distribution in accordance with the provisions of section 457 the amount of each collection made on behalf of such State pursuant to subsection (b).

(d)(1) Except as provided in paragraph (3), the Secretary shall not approve the initial and annually updated advance automated data processing planning document, referred to in section 454(16), unless he finds that such document, when implemented, will generally carry out the objectives of the management system referred to in such subsection, and such document—

(A) provides for the conduct of, and reflects the results of, requirements analysis studies, which include consideration of the program mission, functions, organization, services, constraints, and current support, of, in, or relating to, such system,

(B) contains a description of the proposed management system referred to in section 454(16), including a description of information flows, input data, and output reports and uses,

(C) sets forth the security and interface requirements to be employed in such management system,

(D) describes the projected resource requirements for staff and other needs, and the resources available or expected to be available to meet such requirements,

(E) contains an implementation plan and backup procedures to handle possible failures,

(F) contains a summary of proposed improvement of such management system in terms of qualitative and quantitative benefits, and

(G) provides such other information as the Secretary determines under regulation is necessary.

(2)(A) The Secretary shall through the separate organizational unit established pursuant to subsection (a), on a continuing basis, review, assess, and inspect the planning, design, and operation of, management information systems referred to in section 454(16), with a view to determining whether, and to what extent, such systems meet and continue to meet requirements imposed under paragraph (1) and the conditions specified under section 454(16).

(B) If the Secretary finds with respect to any statewide management information system referred to in section 454(16) that there is a failure substantially to comply with criteria, requirements, and other undertakings, prescribed by the advance automated data processing planning document theretofore approved by the Secretary with respect to such system, then the Secretary shall suspend his approval of such document until there is no longer any such failure of such system to comply with such criteria, requirements, and other undertakings so prescribed.

(3) The Secretary may waive any requirement of paragraph (1) or any condition specified under section 454(16), and shall waive the sin-

gle statewide system requirement under sections 454(16) and 454A, with respect to a State if—

(A) the State demonstrates to the satisfaction of the Secretary that the State has or can develop an alternative system or systems that enable the State—

(i) for purposes of section 409(a)(8), to achieve the paternity establishment percentages (as defined in section 452(g)(2)) and other performance measures that may be established by the Secretary;

(ii) to submit data under section 454(15)(B) that is complete and reliable;

(iii) to substantially comply with the requirements of this part; and

(iv) in the case of a request to waive the single statewide system requirement, to—

(I) meet all functional requirements of sections 454(16) and 454A;

(II) ensure that calculation of distributions meets the requirements of section 457 and accounts for distributions to children in different families or in different States or sub-State jurisdictions, and for distributions to other States;

(III) ensure that there is only one point of contact in the State which provides seamless case processing for all interstate case processing and coordinated, automated intrastate case management;

(IV) ensure that standardized data elements, forms, and definitions are used throughout the State;

(V) complete the alternative system in no more time than it would take to complete a single statewide system that meets such requirement and

(VI) process child support cases as quickly, efficiently, and effectively as such cases would be processed through a single statewide system that meets such requirement;

(B)(i) the waiver meets the criteria of paragraphs (1), (2), and (3) of section 1115(c); or

(ii) the State provides assurances to the Secretary that steps will be taken to otherwise improve the State's child support enforcement program; and

(C) in the case of a request to waive the single statewide system requirement, the State has submitted to the Secretary separate estimates of the total cost of a single statewide system that meets such requirement, and of any such alternative system or systems, which shall include estimates of the cost of developing and completing the system and of operating and maintaining the system for 5 years, and the Secretary has agreed with the estimates.

(e) The Secretary shall provide such technical assistance to States as he determines necessary to assist States to plan, design, develop, or install and provide for the security of, the management information systems referred to in section 454(16).

(f) The Secretary shall issue regulations to require that State agencies administering the child support enforcement program under this part petition enforce medical support included as part of a child sup-

384 SOCIAL SECURITY ACT—§ 452(f)(cont)

port order, whenever health care coverage is available to the noncustodial parent at a reasonable cost. A State agency administering the program under this part may enforce medical support against a custodial parent if health care coverage is available to the custodial parent at a reasonable cost, notwithstanding any other provision of this part. Such regulation shall also provide for improved information exchange between such State agencies and the State agencies administering the State medicaid programs under title XIX with respect to the availability of health insurance coverage. For purposes of this part, the term "medical support" may include health care coverage, such as coverage under a health insurance plan (including payment of costs of premiums, co-payments, and deductibles) and payment for medical expenses incurred on behalf of a child.

(g)(1) A State's program under this part shall be found, for purposes of section 409(a)(8), not to have complied substantially with the requirements of this part unless, for any fiscal year beginning on or after October 1, 1994, its paternity establishment percentage for such fiscal year is based on reliable data and (rounded to the nearest whole percentage point) equals or exceeds—

(A) 90 percent;

(B) for a State with a paternity establishment percentage of not less than 75 percent but less than 90 percent for such fiscal year, the paternity establishment percentage of the State for the immediately preceding fiscal year plus 2 percentage points;

(C) for a State with a paternity establishment percentage of not less than 50 percent but less than 75 percent for such fiscal year, the paternity establishment percentage of the State for the immediately preceding fiscal year plus 3 percentage points;

(D) for a State with a paternity establishment percentage of not less than 45 percent but less than 50 percent for such fiscal year, the paternity establishment percentage of the State for the immediately preceding fiscal year plus 4 percentage points;

(E) for a State with a paternity establishment percentage of not less than 40 percent but less than 45 percent for such fiscal year, the paternity establishment percentage of the State for the immediately preceding fiscal year plus 5 percentage points; or

(F) for a State with a paternity establishment percentage of less than 40 percent for such fiscal year, the paternity establishment percentage of the State for the immediately preceding fiscal year plus 6 percentage points.

In determining compliance under this section, a State may use as its paternity establishment percentage either the State's IV-D paternity establishment percentage (as defined in paragraph (2)(A)) or the State's statewide paternity establishment percentage (as defined in paragraph (2)(B)).

(2) For purposes of this section—

(A) the term "IV-D paternity establishment percentage" means, with respect to a State for a fiscal year, the ratio (expressed as a percentage) that the total number of children—

(i) who have been born out of wedlock,

(ii)(I) except as provided in the last sentence of this paragraph, with respect to whom assistance is being provided under the State program funded under part A in the fiscal year or, at the option of the State, as of the end of such year, or (II)

SOCIAL SECURITY ACT—§ 452(h)

with respect to whom services are being provided under the State's plan approved under this part in the fiscal year or, at the option of the State, as of the end of such year pursuant to an application submitted under section 454(4)(A)(ii), and

(iii) the paternity of whom has been established or acknowledged,

bears to the total number of children born out of wedlock and (except as provided in such last sentence) with respect to whom assistance was being provided under the State program funded under part A as of the end of the preceding fiscal year or with respect to whom services were being provided under the State's plan approved under this part as of the end of the preceding fiscal year pursuant to an application submitted under section 454(4)(A)(ii);

(B) the term "statewide paternity establishment percentage" means, with respect to a State for a fiscal year, the ratio (expressed as a percentage) that the total number of minor children—

(i) who have been born out of wedlock, and

(ii) the paternity of whom has been established or acknowledged during the fiscal year,

bears to the total number of children born out of wedlock during the preceding fiscal year; and

(C) the term "reliable data" means the most recent data available which are found by the Secretary to be reliable for purposes of this section.

For purposes of subparagraphs (A) and (B), the total number of children shall not include any child with respect to whom assistance is being provided under the State program funded under part A by reason of the death of a parent unless paternity is established for such child or any child with respect to whom an applicant or recipient is found by the State to qualify for a good cause or other exception to cooperation pursuant to section 454(29).

(3)(A) The Secretary may modify the requirements of this subsection to take into account such additional variables as the Secretary identifies (including the percentage of children in a State who are born out of wedlock or for whom support has not been established) that affect the ability of a State to meet the requirements of this subsection.

(B) The Secretary shall submit an annual report to the Congress that sets forth the data upon which the paternity establishment percentages for States for a fiscal year are based, lists any additional variables the Secretary has identified under subparagraph (A), and describes State performance in establishing paternity.[90]

(h) The standards required by subsection (a)(1) shall include standards establishing time limits governing the period or periods within which a State must accept and respond to requests (from States, jurisdictions thereof, or individuals who apply for services furnished by the State agency under this part or with respect to whom an assignment pursuant to section 408(a)(3) is in effect) for assistance in establishing and enforcing support orders, including requests to locate noncustodial parents, establish paternity, and initiate proceedings to establish and collect child support awards.

---

[90] See Vol. II, P.L. 100-485, §111(f)(3), with respect to the Secretary's collection of data necessary to implement the requirements of this subsection.

386 SOCIAL SECURITY ACT—§ 452(h)(cont)

(i) The standards required by subsection (a)(1) shall include standards establishing time limits governing the period or periods within which a State must distribute, in accordance with section 457, amounts collected as child support pursuant to the State's plan approved under this part.

(j) Out of any money in the Treasury of the United States not otherwise appropriated, there is hereby appropriated to the Secretary for each fiscal year an amount equal to 1 percent of the total amount paid to the Federal Government pursuant to a plan approved under this part during the immediately preceding fiscal year (as determined on the basis of the most recent reliable data available to the Secretary as of the end of the third calendar quarter following the end of such preceding fiscal year) or the amount appropriated under this paragraph for fiscal year 2002, whichever is greater, which shall be available for use by the Secretary, either directly or through grants, contracts, or interagency agreements, for—

(1) information dissemination and technical assistance to States, training of State and Federal staff, staffing studies, and related activities needed to improve programs under this part (including technical assistance concerning State automated systems required by this part); and

(2) research, demonstration, and special projects of regional or national significance relating to the operation of State programs under this part.

The amount appropriated under this subsection shall remain available until expended.

(k)(1) If the Secretary receives a certification by a State agency in accordance with the requirements of section 454(31) that an individual owes arrearages of child support in an amount exceeding $2,500, the Secretary shall transmit such certification to the Secretary of State for action (with respect to denial, revocation, or limitation of passports) pursuant to paragraph (2).

(2) The Secretary of State shall, upon certification by the Secretary transmitted under paragraph (1), refuse to issue a passport to such individual, and may revoke, restrict, or limit a passport issued previously to such individual.

(3) The Secretary and the Secretary of State shall not be liable to an individual for any action with respect to a certification by a State agency under this section.

(l) The Secretary, through the Federal Parent Locator Service, may aid State agencies providing services under State programs operated pursuant to this part and financial institutions doing business in two or more States in reaching agreements regarding the receipt from such institutions, and the transfer to the State agencies, of information that may be provided pursuant to section 466(a)(17)(A)(i), except that any State that, as of the date of the enactment of this subsection, is conducting data matches pursuant to section 466(a)(17)(A)(i) shall have until January 1, 2000, to allow the Secretary to obtain such information from such institutions that are operating in the State. For purposes of section 1113(d) of the Right to Financial Privacy Act of 1978[91], a disclosure pursuant to this subsection shall be considered a disclosure pursuant to a Federal statute.

---

[91] See Vol. II, P.L. 95-630, Title XI, §1113(d).

SOCIAL SECURITY ACT—§ 453(b)(1)   387

(l) COMPARISONS WITH INSURANCE INFORMATION.—

(1) IN GENERAL.—The Secretary, through the Federal Parent Locator Service, may—

(A) compare information concerning individuals owing past-due support with information maintained by insurers (or their agents) concerning insurance claims, settlements, awards, and payments; and

(B) furnish information resulting from the data matches to the State agencies responsible for collecting child support from the individuals.

(2) LIABILITY.—An insurer (including any agent of an insurer) shall not be liable under any Federal or State law to any person for any disclosure provided for under this subsection, or for any other action taken in good faith in accordance with this subsection.

FEDERAL PARENT LOCATOR SERVICE

SEC. 453. [42 U.S.C. 653] (a) ESTABLISHMENT; PURPOSE.—

(1) The Secretary shall establish and conduct a Federal Parent Locator Service, under the direction of the designee of the Secretary referred to in section 652(a) of this title, which shall be used for the purposes specified in paragraphs (2) and (3).

(2) For the purpose of establishing parentage or establishing, setting the amount of, modifying, or enforcing child support obligations, the Federal Parent Locator Service shall obtain and transmit to any authorized person specified in subsection (c)—

(A) information on, or facilitating the discovery of, the location of any individual—

(i) who is under an obligation to pay child support;

(ii) against whom such an obligation is sought;

(iii) to whom such an obligation is owed, including the individual's social security number (or numbers), most recent address, and the name, address, and employer identification number of the individual's employer; or

(iv) who has or may have parental rights with respect to a child,

(B) information on the individual's wages (or other income) from, and benefits of, employment (including rights to or enrollment in group health care coverage); and

(C) information on the type, status, location, and amount of any assets of, or debts owed by or to, any such individual.

(3) For the purpose of enforcing any Federal or State law with respect to the unlawful taking or restraint of a child, or making or enforcing a child custody or visitation determination, as defined in section 463(d)(1), the Federal Parent Locator Service shall be used to obtain and transmit the information specified in section 463(c) to the authorized persons specified in section 463(d)(2).

(b)(1) Upon request, filed in accordance with subsection (d), of any authorized person, as defined in subsection (c) for the information described in subsection (a)(2), or of any authorized person, as defined in section 463(d)(2) for the information described in section 463(c), the Secretary shall, notwithstanding any other provision of law, provide through the Federal Parent Locator Service such information to such person, if such information—

388 SOCIAL SECURITY ACT—§ 453(b)(1)(A)

(A) is contained in any files or records maintained by the Secretary or by the Department of Health and Human Services; or

(B) is not contained in such files or records, but can be obtained by the Secretary, under the authority conferred by subsection (e), from any other department, agency, or instrumentality of the United States or of any State, and is not prohibited from disclosure under paragraph (2).

(2) No information shall be disclosed to any person if the disclosure of such information would contravene the national policy or security interests of the United States or the confidentiality of census data. The Secretary shall give priority to requests made by any authorized person described in subsection (c)(1). No information shall be disclosed to any person if the State has notified the Secretary that the State has reasonable evidence of domestic violence or child abuse and the disclosure of such information could be harmful to the custodial parent or the child of such parent, provided that—

(A) in response to a request from an authorized person (as defined in subsection (c) of this section and section 463(d)(2)), the Secretary shall advise the authorized person that the Secretary has been notified that there is reasonable evidence of domestic violence or child abuse and that information can only be disclosed to a court or an agent of a court pursuant to subparagraph (B); and

(B) information may be disclosed to a court or an agent of a court described in subsection (c)(2) of this section or section 463(d)(2)(B), if—

(i) upon receipt of information from the Secretary, the court determines whether disclosure to any other person of that information could be harmful to the parent or the child; and

(ii) if the court determines that disclosure of such information to any other person could be harmful, the court and its agents shall not make any such disclosure.

(3) Information received or transmitted pursuant to this section shall be subject to the safeguard provisions contained in section 454(26).

(c) As used in subsection (a), the term "authorized person" means—

(1) any agent or attorney of any State having in effect a plan approved under this part, who has the duty or authority under such plans to seek to recover any amounts owed as child and spousal support or to seek to enforce orders providing child custody or visitation rights (including, when authorized under the State plan, any official of a political subdivision);

(2) the court which has authority to issue an order against a noncustodial parent for the support and maintenance of a child, or to issue an order against a resident parent for child custody or visitation rights, or any agent of such court;

(3) the resident parent, legal guardian, attorney, or agent of a child (other than a child receiving assistance under a State program funded under part A) (as determined by regulations prescribed by the Secretary) without regard to the existence of a court order against a noncustodial parent who has a duty to support and maintain any such child; and

SOCIAL SECURITY ACT—§ 453(g)   389

(4) a State agency that is administering a program operated under a State plan under subpart 1 of part B, or a State plan approved under subpart 2 of part B or under part E.

(d) A request for information under this section shall be filed in such manner and form as the Secretary shall by regulation prescribe and shall be accompanied or supported by such documents as the Secretary may determine to be necessary.

(e)(1) Whenever the Secretary receives a request submitted under subsection (b) which he is reasonably satisfied meets the criteria established by subsections (a), (b), and (c), he shall promptly undertake to provide the information requested from the files and records maintained by any of the departments, agencies, or instrumentalities of the United States or of any State.

(2) Notwithstanding any other provision of law, whenever the individual who is the head of any department, agency, or instrumentality of the United States receives a request from the Secretary for information authorized to be provided by the Secretary under this section, such individual shall promptly cause a search to be made of the files and records maintained by such department, agency, or instrumentality with a view to determining whether the information requested is contained in any such files or records. If such search discloses the information requested, such individual shall immediately transmit such information to the Secretary, except that if any information is obtained the disclosure of which would contravene national policy or security interests of the United States or the confidentiality of census data, such information shall not be transmitted and such individual shall immediately notify the Secretary. If such search fails to disclose the information requested, such individual shall immediately so notify the Secretary. The costs incurred by any such department, agency, or instrumentality of the United States or of any State in providing such information to the Secretary shall be reimbursed by him in an amount which the Secretary determines to be reasonable payment for the information exchange (which amount shall not include payment for the costs of obtaining, compiling, or maintaining the information). Whenever such services are furnished to an individual specified in subsection (c)(3), a fee shall be charged such individual. The fee so charged shall be used to reimburse the Secretary or his delegate for the expense of providing such services.

(3) The Secretary of Labor shall enter into an agreement with the Secretary to provide prompt access for the Secretary (in accordance with this subsection) to the wage and unemployment compensation claims information and data maintained by or for the Department of Labor or State employment security agencies.

(f) The Secretary, in carrying out his duties and functions under this section, shall enter into arrangements with State agencies administering State plans approved under this part for such State agencies to accept from resident parents, legal guardians, or agents of a child described in subsection (c)(3) and to transmit to the Secretary requests for information with regard to the whereabouts of noncustodial parents and otherwise to cooperate with the Secretary in carrying out the purposes of this section.

(g) REIMBURSEMENT FOR REPORTS BY STATE AGENCIES.—The Secretary may reimburse Federal and State agencies for the costs incurred by such entities in furnishing information requested by the

390   SOCIAL SECURITY ACT—§ 453(g)(cont)

Secretary under this section in an amount which the Secretary determines to be reasonable payment for the information exchange (which amount shall not include payment for the costs of obtaining, compiling, or maintaining the information).

(h) FEDERAL CASE REGISTRY OF CHILD SUPPORT ORDERS.—

(1) IN GENERAL.—Not later than October 1, 1998, in order to assist States in administering programs under State plans approved under this part and programs funded under part A, and for the other purposes specified in this section, the Secretary shall establish and maintain in the Federal Parent Locator Service an automated registry (which shall be known as the "Federal Case Registry of Child Support Orders"), which shall contain abstracts of support orders and other information described in paragraph (2) with respect to each case and order in each State case registry maintained pursuant to section 454A(e), as furnished (and regularly updated), pursuant to section 454A(f), by State agencies administering programs under this part.

(2) CASE AND ORDER INFORMATION.—The information referred to in paragraph (1) with respect to a case or an order shall be such information as the Secretary may specify in regulations (including the names, social security numbers or other uniform identification numbers, and State case identification numbers) to identify the individuals who owe or are owed support (or with respect to or on behalf of whom support obligations are sought to be established), and the State or States which have the case or order. Beginning not later than October 1, 1999, the information referred to in paragraph (1) shall include the names and social security numbers of the children of such individuals.

(3) ADMINISTRATION OF FEDERAL TAX LAWS.—The Secretary of the Treasury shall have access to the information described in paragraph (2) for the purpose of administering those sections of the Internal Revenue Code of 1986 which grant tax benefits based on support or residence of children.

(i) NATIONAL DIRECTORY OF NEW HIRES[92].—

(1) IN GENERAL.—In order to assist States in administering programs under State plans approved under this part and programs funded under part A, and for the other purposes specified in this section, the Secretary shall, not later than October 1, 1997, establish and maintain in the Federal Parent Locator Service an automated directory to be known as the National Directory of New Hires, which shall contain the information supplied pursuant to section 453A(g)(2).

(2) DATA ENTRY AND DELETION REQUIREMENTS.—

(A) IN GENERAL.—Information provided pursuant to section 453A(g)(2) shall be entered into the data base maintained by the National Directory of New Hires within two business days after receipt, and shall be deleted from the data base 24 months after the date of entry.

(B) 12-MONTH LIMIT ON ACCESS TO WAGE AND UNEMPLOYMENT COMPENSATION INFORMATION.—The Secretary shall not have access for child support enforcement purposes to

---

[92] See Vol. II, P.L. 104-193, §316(h), with respect to a requirement for cooperation in development of methods to access the various directories for new hires.

information in the National Directory of New Hires that is provided pursuant to section 453A(g)(2)(B), if 12 months has elapsed since the date the information is so provided and there has not been a match resulting from the use of such information in any information comparison under this subsection.

(C) RETENTION OF DATA FOR RESEARCH PURPOSES.—Notwithstanding subparagraphs (A) and (B), the Secretary may retain such samples of data entered in the National Directory of New Hires as the Secretary may find necessary to assist in carrying out subsection (j)(5).

(3) ADMINISTRATION OF FEDERAL TAX LAWS.—The Secretary of the Treasury shall have access to the information in the National Directory of New Hires for purposes of administering section 32 of the Internal Revenue Code of 1986, or the advance payment of the earned income tax credit under section 3507 of such Code, and verifying a claim with respect to employment in a tax return.

(4) LIST OF MULTISTATE EMPLOYERS.—The Secretary shall maintain within the National Directory of New Hires a list of multistate employers that report information regarding newly hired employees pursuant to section 453A(b)(1)(B), and the State which each such employer has designated to receive such information.

(j) INFORMATION COMPARISONS AND OTHER DISCLOSURES.—

(1) VERIFICATION BY SOCIAL SECURITY ADMINISTRATION.—

(A) IN GENERAL.—The Secretary shall transmit information on individuals and employers maintained under this section to the Social Security Administration to the extent necessary for verification in accordance with subparagraph (B).

(B) VERIFICATION BY SSA.—The Social Security Administration shall verify the accuracy of, correct, or supply to the extent possible, and report to the Secretary, the following information supplied by the Secretary pursuant to subparagraph (A):

(i) The name, social security number, and birth date of each such individual.

(ii) The employer identification number of each such employer.

(2) INFORMATION COMPARISONS.—For the purpose of locating individuals in a paternity establishment case or a case involving the establishment, modification, or enforcement of a support order, the Secretary shall—

(A) compare information in the National Directory of New Hires against information in the support case abstracts in the Federal Case Registry of Child Support Orders not less often than every 2 business days; and

(B) within 2 business days after such a comparison reveals a match with respect to an individual, report the information to the State agency responsible for the case.

(3) INFORMATION COMPARISONS AND DISCLOSURES OF INFORMATION IN ALL REGISTRIES FOR TITLE IV PROGRAM PURPOSES.—To the extent and with the frequency that the Secretary determines to be effective in assisting States to carry out their responsibilities

392 SOCIAL SECURITY ACT—§ 453(j)(3)(cont)

under programs operated under this part, part B, or part E[93] and programs funded under part A, the Secretary shall—

(A) compare the information in each component of the Federal Parent Locator Service maintained under this section against the information in each other such component (other than the comparison required by paragraph (2)), and report instances in which such a comparison reveals a match with respect to an individual to State agencies operating such programs; and

(B) disclose information in such components to such State agencies.

(4) PROVISION OF NEW HIRE INFORMATION TO THE SOCIAL SECURITY ADMINISTRATION.—The National Directory of New Hires shall provide the Commissioner of Social Security with all information in the National Directory.

(5) RESEARCH.—The Secretary may provide access to data in each component of the Federal Parent Locator Service maintained under this section to information reported by employers pursuant to section 453A(b) for research purposes found by the Secretary to be likely to contribute to achieving the purposes of part A or this part, but without personal identifiers.

(6) INFORMATION COMPARISONS AND DISCLOSURE FOR ENFORCEMENT OF OBLIGATIONS ON HIGHER EDUCATION ACT LOANS AND GRANTS.—

(A) FURNISHING OF INFORMATION BY THE SECRETARY OF EDUCATION.—The Secretary of Education shall furnish to the Secretary, on a quarterly basis or at such less frequent intervals as may be determined by the Secretary of Education, information in the custody of the Secretary of Education for comparison with information in the National Directory of New Hires, in order to obtain the information in such directory with respect to individuals who—

(i) are borrowers of loans made under title IV of the Higher Education Act of 1965[94] that are in default; or

(ii) owe an obligation to refund an overpayment of a grant awarded under such title.

(B) REQUIREMENT TO SEEK MINIMUM INFORMATION NECESSARY.—The Secretary of Education shall seek information pursuant to this section only to the extent essential to improving collection of the debt described in subparagraph (A).

(C) DUTIES OF THE SECRETARY.—

(i) INFORMATION COMPARISON; DISCLOSURE TO THE SECRETARY OF EDUCATION.—The Secretary, in cooperation with the Secretary of Education, shall compare information in the National Directory of New Hires with information in the custody of the Secretary of Education, and disclose information in that Directory to the Secretary of Education, in accordance with this paragraph, for the purposes specified in this paragraph.

(ii) CONDITION ON DISCLOSURE.—The Secretary shall make disclosures in accordance with clause (i) only to the

---

[93] P.L. 110-351, §105, inserted ", part B, or part E", effective October 7, 2008.
[94] See Vol. II, P.L. 89-329.

extent that the Secretary determines that such disclosures do not interfere with the effective operation of the program under this part. Support collection under section 466(b) shall be given priority over collection of any defaulted student loan or grant overpayment against the same income.

(D) USE OF INFORMATION BY THE SECRETARY OF EDUCATION.—The Secretary of Education may use information resulting from a data match pursuant to this paragraph only—

(i) for the purpose of collection of the debt described in subparagraph (A) owed by an individual whose annualized wage level (determined by taking into consideration information from the National Directory of New Hires) exceeds $16,000; and

(ii) after removal of personal identifiers, to conduct analyses of student loan defaults.

(E) DISCLOSURE OF INFORMATION BY THE SECRETARY OF EDUCATION.—

(i) DISCLOSURES PERMITTED.—The Secretary of Education may disclose information resulting from a data match pursuant to this paragraph only to—

(I) a guaranty agency holding a loan made under part B of title IV of the Higher Education Act of 1965 on which the individual is obligated;

(II) a contractor or agent of the guaranty agency described in subclause (I);

(III) a contractor or agent of the Secretary; and

(IV) the Attorney General.

(ii) PURPOSE OF DISCLOSURE.—The Secretary of Education may make a disclosure under clause (i) only for the purpose of collection of the debts owed on defaulted student loans, or overpayments of grants, made under title IV of the Higher Education Act of 1965.

(iii) RESTRICTION ON REDISCLOSURE.—An entity to which information is disclosed under clause (i) may use or disclose such information only as needed for the purpose of collecting on defaulted student loans, or overpayments of grants, made under title IV of the Higher Education Act of 1965[95].

(F) REIMBURSEMENT OF HHS COSTS.—The Secretary of Education shall reimburse the Secretary, in accordance with subsection (k)(3), for the additional costs incurred by the Secretary in furnishing the information requested under this subparagraph.

(7) INFORMATION COMPARISONS FOR HOUSING ASSISTANCE PROGRAMS.—

(A) FURNISHING OF INFORMATION BY HUD.—Subject to subparagraph (G), the Secretary of Housing and Urban Development shall furnish to the Secretary, on such periodic basis as determined by the Secretary of Housing and Urban Develop-

---

[95] See Vol. II, P.L. 89-329.

394 SOCIAL SECURITY ACT—§ 453(j)(7)(A)(i)

ment in consultation with the Secretary, information in the custody of the Secretary of Housing and Urban Development for comparison with information in the National Directory of New Hires, in order to obtain information in such Directory with respect to individuals who are participating in any program under—

(i) the United States Housing Act of 1937 (42 U.S.C. 1437 et seq.)[96];

(ii) section 202 of the Housing Act of 1959 (12 U.S.C. 1701q)[97];

(iii) section 221(d)(3), 221(d)(5), or 236 of the National Housing Act (12 U.S.C. 1715l(d) and 1715z-1)[98];

(iv) section 811 of the Cranston-Gonzalez National Affordable Housing Act (42 U.S.C. 8013)[99]; or

(v) section 101 of the Housing and Urban Development Act of 1965 (12 U.S.C. 1701s)[100].

(B) REQUIREMENT TO SEEK MINIMUM INFORMATION.—The Secretary of Housing and Urban Development shall seek information pursuant to this section only to the extent necessary to verify the employment and income of individuals described in subparagraph (A).

(C) DUTIES OF THE SECRETARY.—

(i) INFORMATION DISCLOSURE.—The Secretary, in cooperation with the Secretary of Housing and Urban Development, shall compare information in the National Directory of New Hires with information provided by the Secretary of Housing and Urban Development with respect to individuals described in subparagraph (A), and shall disclose information in such Directory regarding such individuals to the Secretary of Housing and Urban Development, in accordance with this paragraph, for the purposes specified in this paragraph.

(ii) CONDITION ON DISCLOSURE.—The Secretary shall make disclosures in accordance with clause (i) only to the extent that the Secretary determines that such disclosures do not interfere with the effective operation of the program under this part.

(D) USE OF INFORMATION BY HUD.—The Secretary of Housing and Urban Development may use information resulting from a data match pursuant to this paragraph only—

(i) for the purpose of verifying the employment and income of individuals described in subparagraph (A); and

(ii) after removal of personal identifiers, to conduct analyses of the employment and income reporting of individuals described in subparagraph (A).

(E) DISCLOSURE OF INFORMATION BY HUD.—

(i) PURPOSE OF DISCLOSURE.—The Secretary of Housing and Urban Development may make a disclosure under this subparagraph only for the purpose of verifying

---

[96] P.L. 75-412.
[97] See Vol. II, P.L. 86-372, §202.
[98] See Vol. II, P.L 73-479.
[99] See Vol. II, P.L. 101-625, §811.
[100] See Vol. II, P.L. 89-117, §101.

the employment and income of individuals described in subparagraph (A).

(ii) DISCLOSURES PERMITTED.—Subject to clause (iii), the Secretary of Housing and Urban Development may disclose information resulting from a data match pursuant to this paragraph only to a public housing agency, the Inspector General of the Department of Housing and Urban Development, and the Attorney General in connection with the administration of a program described in subparagraph (A). Information obtained by the Secretary of Housing and Urban Development pursuant to this paragraph shall not be made available under section 552 of title 5, United States Code.

(iii) CONDITIONS ON DISCLOSURE.—Disclosures under this paragraph shall be—

(I) made in accordance with data security and control policies established by the Secretary of Housing and Urban Development and approved by the Secretary;

(II) subject to audit in a manner satisfactory to the Secretary; and

(III) subject to the sanctions under subsection (l)(2).

(iv) ADDITIONAL DISCLOSURES.—

(I) DETERMINATION BY SECRETARIES.—The Secretary of Housing and Urban Development and the Secretary shall determine whether to permit disclosure of information under this paragraph to persons or entities described in subclause (II), based on an evaluation made by the Secretary of Housing and Urban Development (in consultation with and approved by the Secretary), of the costs and benefits of disclosures made under clause (ii) and the adequacy of measures used to safeguard the security and confidentiality of information so disclosed.

(II) PERMITTED PERSONS OR ENTITIES.—If the Secretary of Housing and Urban Development and the Secretary determine pursuant to subclause (I) that disclosures to additional persons or entities shall be permitted, information under this paragraph may be disclosed by the Secretary of Housing and Urban Development to a private owner, a management agent, and a contract administrator in connection with the administration of a program described in subparagraph (A), subject to the conditions in clause (iii) and such additional conditions as agreed to by the Secretaries.

(v) RESTRICTIONS ON REDISCLOSURE.—A person or entity to which information is disclosed under this subparagraph may use or disclose such information only as needed for verifying the employment and income of individuals described in subparagraph (A), subject to the conditions in clause (iii) and such additional conditions as agreed to by the Secretaries.

(F) REIMBURSEMENT OF HHS COSTS.—The Secretary of Housing and Urban Development shall reimburse the Secretary, in accordance with subsection (k)(3), for the costs incurred by the Secretary in furnishing the information requested under this paragraph.

(G) CONSENT.—The Secretary of Housing and Urban Development shall not seek, use, or disclose information under this paragraph relating to an individual without the prior written consent of such individual (or of a person legally authorized to consent on behalf of such individual).

(8) INFORMATION COMPARISONS AND DISCLOSURE TO ASSIST IN ADMINISTRATION OF UNEMPLOYMENT COMPENSATION PROGRAMS.—

(A) IN GENERAL.—If, for purposes of administering an unemployment compensation program under Federal or State law, a State agency responsible for the administration of such program transmits to the Secretary the names and social security account numbers of individuals, the Secretary shall disclose to such State agency information on such individuals and their employers maintained in the National Directory of New Hires, subject to this paragraph.

(B) CONDITION ON DISCLOSURE BY THE SECRETARY.—The Secretary shall make a disclosure under subparagraph (A) only to the extent that the Secretary determines that the disclosure would not interfere with the effective operation of the program under this part.

(C) USE AND DISCLOSURE OF INFORMATION BY STATE AGENCIES.—

(i) IN GENERAL.—A State agency may not use or disclose information provided under this paragraph except for purposes of administering a program referred to in subparagraph (A).

(ii) INFORMATION SECURITY.—The State agency shall have in effect data security and control policies that the Secretary finds adequate to ensure the security of information obtained under this paragraph and to ensure that access to such information is restricted to authorized persons for purposes of authorized uses and disclosures.

(iii) PENALTY FOR MISUSE OF INFORMATION.—An officer or employee of the State agency who fails to comply with this subparagraph shall be subject to the sanctions under subsection (l)(2) to the same extent as if such officer or employee was an officer or employee of the United States.

(D) PROCEDURAL REQUIREMENTS.—State agencies requesting information under this paragraph shall adhere to uniform procedures established by the Secretary governing information requests and data matching under this paragraph.

(E) REIMBURSEMENT OF COSTS.—The State agency shall reimburse the Secretary, in accordance with subsection (k)(3),

SOCIAL SECURITY ACT—§ 453(j)(9)(E)(i) 397

for the costs incurred by the Secretary in furnishing the information requested under this paragraph.

(9) INFORMATION COMPARISONS AND DISCLOSURE TO ASSIST IN FEDERAL DEBT COLLECTION.—

(A) FURNISHING OF INFORMATION BY THE SECRETARY OF THE TREASURY.—The Secretary of the Treasury shall furnish to the Secretary, on such periodic basis as determined by the Secretary of the Treasury in consultation with the Secretary, information in the custody of the Secretary of the Treasury for comparison with information in the National Directory of New Hires, in order to obtain information in such Directory with respect to persons—

(i) who owe delinquent nontax debt to the United States; and

(ii) whose debt has been referred to the Secretary of the Treasury in accordance with 31 U.S.C. 3711(g)[101].

(B) REQUIREMENT TO SEEK MINIMUM INFORMATION.—The Secretary of the Treasury shall seek information pursuant to this section only to the extent necessary to improve collection of the debt described in subparagraph (A).

(C) DUTIES OF THE SECRETARY.—

(i) INFORMATION DISCLOSURE.—The Secretary, in co-operation with the Secretary of the Treasury, shall compare information in the National Directory of New Hires with information provided by the Secretary of the Treasury with respect to persons described in subparagraph (A) and shall disclose information in such Directory regarding such persons to the Secretary of the Treasury in accordance with this paragraph, for the purposes specified in this paragraph. Such comparison of information shall not be considered a matching program as defined in 5 U.S.C. 552a[102].

(ii) CONDITION ON DISCLOSURE.—The Secretary shall make disclosures in accordance with clause (i) only to the extent that the Secretary determines that such disclosures do not interfere with the effective operation of the program under this part. Support collection under section 466(b) of this title shall be given priority over collection of any delinquent Federal nontax debt against the same income.

(D) USE OF INFORMATION BY THE SECRETARY OF THE TREASURY.—The Secretary of the Treasury may use information provided under this paragraph only for purposes of collecting the debt described in subparagraph (A).

(E) DISCLOSURE OF INFORMATION BY THE SECRETARY OF THE TREASURY.—

(i) PURPOSE OF DISCLOSURE.—The Secretary of the Treasury may make a disclosure under this subparagraph only for purposes of collecting the debt described in subparagraph (A).

---

[101] See Vol. II, 31 U.S.C. 3711(g).
[102] See Vol. II, 5 U.S.C. 552a.

(ii) DISCLOSURES PERMITTED.—Subject to clauses (iii) and (iv), the Secretary of the Treasury may disclose information resulting from a data match pursuant to this paragraph only to the Attorney General in connection with collecting the debt described in subparagraph (A).

(iii) CONDITIONS ON DISCLOSURE.—Disclosures under this subparagraph shall be—

(I) made in accordance with data security and control policies established by the Secretary of the Treasury and approved by the Secretary;

(II) subject to audit in a manner satisfactory to the Secretary; and

(III) subject to the sanctions under subsection (l)(2).

(iv) ADDITIONAL DISCLOSURES.—

(I) DETERMINATION BY SECRETARIES.—The Secretary of the Treasury and the Secretary shall determine whether to permit disclosure of information under this paragraph to persons or entities described in subclause (II), based on an evaluation made by the Secretary of the Treasury (in consultation with and approved by the Secretary), of the costs and benefits of such disclosures and the adequacy of measures used to safeguard the security and confidentiality of information so disclosed.

(II) PERMITTED PERSONS OR ENTITIES.—If the Secretary of the Treasury and the Secretary determine pursuant to subclause (I) that disclosures to additional persons or entities shall be permitted, information under this paragraph may be disclosed by the Secretary of the Treasury, in connection with collecting the debt described in subparagraph (A), to a contractor or agent of either Secretary and to the Federal agency that referred such debt to the Secretary of the Treasury for collection, subject to the conditions in clause (iii) and such additional conditions as agreed to by the Secretaries.

(v) RESTRICTIONS ON REDISCLOSURE.—A person or entity to which information is disclosed under this subparagraph may use or disclose such information only as needed for collecting the debt described in subparagraph (A), subject to the conditions in clause (iii) and such additional conditions as agreed to by the Secretaries.

(F) REIMBURSEMENT OF HHS COSTS.—The Secretary of the Treasury shall reimburse the Secretary, in accordance with subsection (k)(3), for the costs incurred by the Secretary in furnishing the information requested under this paragraph. Any such costs paid by the Secretary of the Treasury shall be considered costs of implementing 31 U.S.C. 3711(g) in accordance with 31 U.S.C. 3711(g)(6) and may be paid from the account established pursuant to 31 U.S.C. 3711(g)(7)[103].

---

[103] See Vol. II, 31 U.S.C. 3711(g).

SOCIAL SECURITY ACT—§ 453(j)(10)(E) 399

(10) INFORMATION COMPARISONS AND DISCLOSURE TO ASSIST IN ADMINISTRATION OF SUPPLEMENTAL NUTRITION ASSISTANCE PROGRAMS[104].—

(A) IN GENERAL.—If, for purposes of administering a supplemental nutrition assistance program[105] under the Food and Nutrition Act of 2008[106], a State agency responsible for the administration of the program transmits to the Secretary the names and social security account numbers of individuals, the Secretary shall disclose to the State agency information on the individuals and their employers maintained in the National Directory of New Hires, subject to this paragraph.

(B) CONDITION ON DISCLOSURE BY THE SECRETARY.—The Secretary shall make a disclosure under subparagraph (A) only to the extent that the Secretary determines that the disclosure would not interfere with the effective operation of the program under this part.

(C) USE AND DISCLOSURE OF INFORMATION BY STATE AGENCIES.—

(i) IN GENERAL.—A State agency may not use or disclose information provided under this paragraph except for purposes of administering a program referred to in subparagraph (A).

(ii) INFORMATION SECURITY.—The State agency shall have in effect data security and control policies that the Secretary finds adequate to ensure the security of information obtained under this paragraph and to ensure that access to such information is restricted to authorized persons for purposes of authorized uses and disclosures.

(iii) PENALTY FOR MISUSE OF INFORMATION.—An officer or employee of the State agency who fails to comply with this subparagraph shall be subject to the sanctions under subsection (l)(2) to the same extent as if the officer or employee were an officer or employee of the United States.

(D) PROCEDURAL REQUIREMENTS.—State agencies requesting information under this paragraph shall adhere to uniform procedures established by the Secretary governing information requests and data matching under this paragraph.

(E) REIMBURSEMENT OF COSTS.—The State agency shall reimburse the Secretary, in accordance with subsection (k)(3), for the costs incurred by the Secretary in furnishing the information requested under this paragraph.

---

[104] P.L. 110-246, §4002(b)(1)(A), struck out "FOOD STAMP PROGRAMS" and substituted "SUPPLEMENTAL NUTRITION ASSISTANCE PROGRAMS", effective October 1, 2008.", effective October 1, 2008. P.L. 110-234, §4002(b)(1)(A), which made the same amendment, was repealed, effective May 22, 2008 pursuant to P.L. 110-246, §4(a).
Executed as if "SUPPLEMENTAL NUTRITION ASSISTANCE PROGRAMS" was the intended substitution.
[105] P.L. 110-246, §4002(b)(1)(A), struck out "food stamp program" and substituted "supplemental nutrition assistance program", effective October 1, 2008. P.L. 110-234, §4002(b)(1)(A), which made the same amendment, was repealed, effective May 22, 2008 pursuant to P.L. 110-246, §4(a).
[106] P.L. 110-246, §4002(b)(1)(B), struck out "Food Stamp Act of 1977" and substituted "Food and Nutrition Act of 2008", effective October 1, 2008. P.L. 110-234, §4002(b)(1)(B), which made the same amendment, was repealed, effective May 22, 2008 pursuant to P.L. 110-246, §4(a).

400   SOCIAL SECURITY ACT—§ 453(j)(11)

(11)[107] INFORMATION COMPARISONS AND DISCLOSURES TO ASSIST IN ADMINISTRATION OF CERTAIN VETERANS BENEFITS.—

(A) FURNISHING OF INFORMATION BY SECRETARY OF VETERANS AFFAIRS.—Subject to the provisions of this paragraph, the Secretary of Veterans Affairs shall furnish to the Secretary, on such periodic basis as determined by the Secretary of Veterans Affairs in consultation with the Secretary, information in the custody of the Secretary of Veterans Affairs for comparison with information in the National Directory of New Hires, in order to obtain information in such Directory with respect to individuals who are applying for or receiving—

(i) needs-based pension benefits provided under chapter 15 of title 38, United States Code, or under any other law administered by the Secretary of Veterans Affairs;

(ii) parents' dependency and indemnity compensation provided under section 1315 of title 38, United States Code;

(iii) health care services furnished under subsections (a)(2)(G), (a)(3), or (b) of section 1710 of title 38, United States Code; or (iv) compensation paid under chapter 11 of title 38, United States Code, at the 100 percent rate based solely on unemployability and without regard to the fact that the disability or disabilities are not rated as 100 percent disabling under the rating schedule.

(B) REQUIREMENT TO SEEK MINIMUM INFORMATION.—The Secretary of Veterans Affairs shall seek information pursuant to this paragraph only to the extent necessary to verify the employment and income of individuals described in subparagraph (A).

(C) DUTIES OF THE SECRETARY.—

(i) INFORMATION DISCLOSURE.—The Secretary, in cooperation with the Secretary of Veterans Affairs, shall compare information in the National Directory of New Hires with information provided by the Secretary of Veterans Affairs with respect to individuals described in subparagraph (A), and shall disclose information in such Directory regarding such individuals to the Secretary of Veterans Affairs, in accordance with this paragraph, for the purposes specified in this paragraph.

(ii) CONDITION ON DISCLOSURE.—The Secretary shall make disclosures in accordance with clause (i) only to the extent that the Secretary determines that such disclosures do not interfere with the effective operation of the program under this part

(D) USE OF INFORMATION BY SECRETARY OF VETERANS AFFAIRS.—The Secretary of Veterans Affairs may use information resulting from a data match pursuant to this paragraph only—

(i) for the purposes specified in subparagraph (B); and

---

[107] P.L. 110-157, §301(a) added this paragraph, effective December 26, 2007.

SOCIAL SECURITY ACT—§ 453(m)(1) 401

(ii) after removal of personal identifiers, to conduct analyses of the employment and income reporting of individuals described in subparagraph (A).

(E) REIMBURSEMENT OF HHS COSTS.—The Secretary of Veterans Affairs shall reimburse the Secretary, in accordance with subsection (k)(3), for the costs incurred by the Secretary in furnishing the information requested under this paragraph.

(F) CONSENT.—The Secretary of Veterans Affairs shall not seek, use, or disclose information under this paragraph relating to an individual without the prior written consent of such individual (or of a person legally authorized to consent on behalf of such individual).

(G) EXPIRATION OF AUTHORITY.—The authority under this paragraph shall expire on September 30, 2011.

(k) FEES.—

(1) FOR SSA VERIFICATION.—The Secretary shall reimburse the Commissioner of Social Security, at a rate negotiated between the Secretary and the Commissioner, for the costs incurred by the Commissioner in performing the verification services described in subsection (j).

(2) FOR INFORMATION FROM STATE DIRECTORIES OF NEW HIRES.—The Secretary shall reimburse costs incurred by State directories of new hires in furnishing information as required by section 453A(g)(2), at rates which the Secretary determines to be reasonable (which rates shall not include payment for the costs of obtaining, compiling, or maintaining such information).

(3) FOR INFORMATION FURNISHED TO STATE AND FEDERAL AGENCIES.—A State or Federal agency that receives information from the Secretary pursuant to this section or section 452(l) shall reimburse the Secretary for costs incurred by the Secretary in furnishing the information, at rates which the Secretary determines to be reasonable (which rates shall include payment for the costs of obtaining, verifying, maintaining, and comparing the information).

(l) RESTRICTION ON DISCLOSURE AND USE.—

(1) IN GENERAL.—Information in the Federal Parent Locator Service, and information resulting from comparisons using such information, shall not be used or disclosed except as expressly provided in this section, subject to section 6103 of the Internal Revenue Code of 1986.

(2) PENALTY FOR MISUSE OF INFORMATION IN THE NATIONAL DIRECTORY OF NEW HIRES.—The Secretary shall require the imposition of an administrative penalty (up to and including dismissal from employment), and a fine of $1,000, for each act of unauthorized access to, disclosure of, or use of, information in the National Directory of New Hires established under subsection (i) by any officer or employee of the United States who knowingly and willfully violates this paragraph.

(m) INFORMATION INTEGRITY AND SECURITY.—The Secretary shall establish and implement safeguards with respect to the entities established under this section designed to—

(1) ensure the accuracy and completeness of information in the Federal Parent Locator Service; and

402 SOCIAL SECURITY ACT—§ 453(m)(2)

(2) restrict access to confidential information in the Federal Parent Locator Service to authorized persons, and restrict use of such information to authorized purposes.

(n) FEDERAL GOVERNMENT REPORTING.—Each department, agency, and instrumentality of the United States shall on a quarterly basis report to the Federal Parent Locator Service the name and social security number of each employee and the wages paid to the employee during the previous quarter, except that such a report shall not be filed with respect to an employee of a department, agency, or instrumentality performing intelligence or counter–intelligence functions, if the head of such department, agency, or instrumentality has determined that filing such a report could endanger the safety of the employee or compromise an ongoing investigation or intelligence mission.

(o) USE OF SET-ASIDE FUNDS.—Out of any money in the Treasury of the United States not otherwise appropriated, there is hereby appropriated to the Secretary for each fiscal year an amount equal to 2 percent of the total amount paid to the Federal government pursuant to a plan approved under this part during the immediately preceding fiscal year (as determined on the basis of the most recent reliable data available to the Secretary as of the end of the third calendar quarter following the end of such preceding fiscal year), or the amount appropriated under this paragraph for fiscal year 2002, whichever is greater which shall be available for use by the Secretary, either directly or through grants, contracts, or interagency agreements, for operation of the Federal Parent Locator Service under this section, to the extent such costs are not recovered through user fees. Amounts appropriated under this subsection shall remain available until expended.

(p) SUPPORT ORDER DEFINED.—As used in this part, the term "support order" means a judgment, decree, or order, whether temporary, final, or subject to modification, issued by a court or an administrative agency of competent jurisdiction, for the support and maintenance of a child, including a child who has attained the age of majority under the law of the issuing State, or of the parent with whom the child is living, which provides for monetary support, health care, arrearages, or reimbursement, and which may include related costs and fees, interest and penalties, income withholding, attorneys' fees, and other relief.

STATE DIRECTORY OF NEW HIRES[108]

SEC. 453A. [42 U.S.C. 653a] (a) ESTABLISHMENT.—
(1) IN GENERAL.—
(A) REQUIREMENT FOR STATES THAT HAVE NO DIRECTORY.—Except as provided in subparagraph (B), not later than October 1, 1997, each State shall establish an automated directory (to be known as the "State Directory of New Hires") which shall contain information supplied in accordance with subsection (b) by employers on each newly hired employee.
(B) STATES WITH NEW HIRE REPORTING LAW IN EXISTENCE.—A State which has a new hire reporting law in existence on the date of the enactment of this section may

---

[108] See Vol. II, P.L. 104-193, §316(h), with respect to a requirement for cooperation in development of methods to access the various directories of new hires.

SOCIAL SECURITY ACT—§ 453A(b)(1)(C)   403

continue to operate under the State law, but the State must meet the requirements of subsection (g)(2) not later than October 1, 1997, and the requirements of this section (other than subsection (g)(2)) not later than October 1, 1998.

(2) DEFINITIONS.—As used in this section:

(A) EMPLOYEES.—The term "employee"—

(i) means an individual who is an employee within the meaning of chapter 24 of the Internal Revenue Code of 1986; and

(ii) does not include an employee of a Federal or State agency performing intelligence or counterintelligence functions, if the head of such agency has determined that reporting pursuant to paragraph (1) with respect to the employee could endanger the safety of the employee or compromise an ongoing investigation or intelligence mission.

(B) EMPLOYER.—

(i) IN GENERAL.—The term "employer" has the meaning given such term in section 3401(d) of the Internal Revenue Code of 1986 and includes any governmental entity and any labor organization.

(ii) LABOR ORGANIZATION.—The term "labor organization" shall have the meaning given such term in section 2(5) of the National Labor Relations Act, and includes any entity (also known as a "hiring hall") which is used by the organization and an employer to carry out requirements described in section 8(f)(3) of such Act of an agreement between the organization and the employer.

(b) EMPLOYER INFORMATION.—

(1) REPORTING REQUIREMENT.—

(A) IN GENERAL.—Except as provided in subparagraphs (B) and (C), each employer shall furnish to the Directory of New Hires of the State in which a newly hired employee works, a report that contains the name, address, and social security number of the employee, and the name and address of, and identifying number assigned under section 6109 of the Internal Revenue Code of 1986[109] to, the employer.

(B) MULTISTATE EMPLOYERS.—An employer that has employees who are employed in 2 or more States and that transmits reports magnetically or electronically may comply with subparagraph (A) by designating 1 State in which such employer has employees to which the employer will transmit the report described in subparagraph (A), and transmitting such report to such State. Any employer that transmits reports pursuant to this subparagraph shall notify the Secretary in writing as to which State such employer designates for the purpose of sending reports.

(C) FEDERAL GOVERNMENT EMPLOYERS.—Any department, agency, or instrumentality of the United States shall comply with subparagraph (A) by transmitting the report described in subparagraph (A) to the National Directory of New Hires established pursuant to section 453.

---

[109] See Vol. II, P.L. 83-591, §6109.

404 SOCIAL SECURITY ACT—§ 453A(b)(2)

(2) TIMING OF REPORT.—Each State may provide the time within which the report required by paragraph (1) shall be made with respect to an employee, but such report shall be made—

(A) not later than 20 days after the date the employer hires the employee; or

(B) in the case of an employer transmitting reports magnetically or electronically, by 2 monthly transmissions (if necessary) not less than 12 days nor more than 16 days apart.

(c) REPORTING FORMAT AND METHOD.—Each report required by subsection (b) shall be made on a W–4 form or, at the option of the employer, an equivalent form, and may be transmitted by 1st class mail, magnetically, or electronically.

(d) CIVIL MONEY PENALTIES ON NONCOMPLYING EMPLOYERS.—The State shall have the option to set a State civil money penalty which shall not exceed—

(1) $25 per failure to meet the requirements of this section with respect to a newly hired employee; or

(2) $500 if, under State law, the failure is the result of a conspiracy between the employer and the employee to not supply the required report or to supply a false or incomplete report.

(e) ENTRY OF EMPLOYER INFORMATION.—Information shall be entered into the data base maintained by the State Directory of New Hires within 5 business days of receipt from an employer pursuant to subsection (b).

(f) INFORMATION COMPARISONS.—

(1) IN GENERAL.—Not later than May 1, 1998, an agency designated by the State shall, directly or by contract, conduct automated comparisons of the social security numbers reported by employers pursuant to subsection (b) and the social security numbers appearing in the records of the State case registry for cases being enforced under the State plan.

(2) NOTICE OF MATCH.—When an information comparison conducted under paragraph (1) reveals a match with respect to the social security number of an individual required to provide support under a support order, the State Directory of New Hires shall provide the agency administering the State plan approved under this part of the appropriate State with the name, address, and social security number of the employee to whom the social security number is assigned, and the name and address of, and identifying number assigned under section 6109 of the Internal Revenue Code of 1986[110] to, the employer.

(g) TRANSMISSION OF INFORMATION.—

(1) TRANSMISSION OF WAGE WITHHOLDING NOTICES TO EMPLOYERS.—Within 2 business days after the date information regarding a newly hired employee is entered into the State Directory of New Hires, the State agency enforcing the employee's child support obligation shall transmit a notice to the employer of the employee directing the employer to withhold from the income of the employee an amount equal to the monthly (or other periodic) child support obligation (including any past due support obligation) of

---

[110] See Vol. II, P.L. 83-591, §6109.

SOCIAL SECURITY ACT—§ 454(4)(A) 405

the employee, unless the employee's income is not subject to withholding pursuant to section 466(b)(3).

(2) TRANSMISSIONS TO THE NATIONAL DIRECTORY OF NEW HIRES.—

(A) NEW HIRE INFORMATION.—Within 3 business days after the date information regarding a newly hired employee is entered into the State Directory of New Hires, the State Directory of New Hires shall furnish the information to the National Directory of New Hires.

(B) WAGE AND UNEMPLOYMENT COMPENSATION INFORMATION.—The State Directory of New Hires shall, on a quarterly basis, furnish to the National Directory of New Hires information concerning the wages and unemployment compensation paid to individuals, by such dates, in such format, and containing such information as the Secretary of Health and Human Services shall specify in regulations.

(3) BUSINESS DAY DEFINED.—As used in this subsection, the term "business day" means a day on which State offices are open for regular business.

(h) OTHER USES OF NEW HIRE INFORMATION.—

(1) LOCATION OF CHILD SUPPORT OBLIGORS.—The agency administering the State plan approved under this part shall use information received pursuant to subsection (f)(2) to locate individuals for purposes of establishing paternity and establishing, modifying, and enforcing child support obligations, and may disclose such information to any agent of the agency that is under contract with the agency to carry out such purposes.

(2) VERIFICATION OF ELIGIBILITY FOR CERTAIN PROGRAMS.—A State agency responsible for administering a program specified in section 1137(b) shall have access to information reported by employers pursuant to subsection (b) of this section for purposes of verifying eligibility for the program.

(3) ADMINISTRATION OF EMPLOYMENT SECURITY AND WORKERS' COMPENSATION.—State agencies operating employment security and workers' compensation programs shall have access to information reported by employers pursuant to subsection (b) for the purposes of administering such programs.

STATE PLAN FOR CHILD AND SPOUSAL SUPPORT

SEC. 454. [42 U.S.C. 654] A State plan for child and spousal support must—

(1) provide that it shall be in effect in all political subdivisions of the State;

(2) provide for financial participation by the State;

(3) provide for the establishment or designation of a single and separate organizational unit, which meets such staffing and organizational requirements as the Secretary may by regulation prescribe, within the State to administer the plan;

(4) provide that the State will—

(A) provide services relating to the establishment of paternity or the establishment, modification, or enforcement of child support obligations, as appropriate, under the plan with respect to—

406   SOCIAL SECURITY ACT—§ 454(4)(A)(i)

(i) each child for whom (I) assistance is provided under the State program funded under part A of this title, (II) benefits or services for foster care maintenance are provided under the State program funded under part E of this title, (III) medical assistance is provided under the State plan approved under title XIX, or (IV) cooperation is required pursuant to section 6(l)(1) of the Food and Nutrition Act of 2008[111] (7 U.S.C. 2015(l)(1))[112], unless, in accordance with paragraph (29), good cause or other exceptions exist;

(ii) any other child, if an individual applies for such services with respect to the child; and

(B) enforce any support obligation established with respect to—

(i) a child with respect to whom the State provides services under the plan; or

(ii) the custodial parent of such a child;

(5) provide that (A) in any case in which support payments are collected for an individual with respect to whom an assignment pursuant to section 408(a)(3) is effective, such payments shall be made to the State for distribution pursuant to section 457 and shall not be paid directly to the family, and the individual will be notified on a monthly basis (or on a quarterly basis for so long as the Secretary determines with respect to a State that requiring such notice on a monthly basis would impose an unreasonable administrative burden) of the amount of the support payments collected, and (B) in any case in which support payments are collected for an individual pursuant to the assignment made under section 1912, such payments shall be made to the State for distribution pursuant to section 1912, except that this clause shall not apply to such payments for any month after the month in which the individual ceases to be eligible for medical assistance;

(6) provide that—

(A) services under the plan shall be made available to residents of other States on the same terms as to residents of the State submitting the plan;

(B)(i) an application fee for furnishing such services shall be imposed on an individual, other than an individual receiving assistance under a State program funded under part A or E, or under a State plan approved under title XIX, or who is required by the State to cooperate with the State agency administering the program under this part pursuant to subsection (l) or (m) of section 6 of the Food and Nutrition Act of 2008[113], and shall be paid by the individual applying for such services, or recovered from the absent parent, or paid by the State out of its own funds (the payment of which from State funds shall not be considered as an administrative cost

---

[111] P.L. 110-246, §4002(b)(1)(B), struck out "Food Stamp Act of 1977" and substituted "Food and Nutrition Act of 2008", effective October 1, 2008. P.L. 110-234, §4002(b)(1)(B), which made the same amendment, was repealed, effective May 22, 2008 pursuant to P.L. 110-246, §4(a).

[112] See Vol. II, P.L. 88-525, §6(l).

[113] P.L. 110-246, §4002(b)(1)(B), struck out "Food Stamp Act of 1977" and substituted "Food and Nutrition Act of 2008", effective October 1, 2008. P.L. 110-234, §4002(b)(1)(B), which made the same amendment, was repealed, effective May 22, 2008 pursuant to P.L. 110-246, §4(a).

of the State for the operation of the plan, and shall be considered income to the program), the amount of which (I) will not exceed $25 (or such higher or lower amount (which shall be uniform for all States) as the Secretary may determine to be appropriate for any fiscal year to reflect increases or decreases in administrative costs), and (II) may vary among such individuals on the basis of ability to pay (as determined by the State); and

(ii) in the case of an individual who has never received assistance under a State program funded under part A and for whom the State has collected at least $500 of support, the State shall impose an annual fee of $25 for each case in which services are furnished, which shall be retained by the State from support collected on behalf of the individual (but not from the first $500 so collected), paid by the individual applying for the services, recovered from the absent parent, or paid by the State out of its own funds (the payment of which from State funds shall not be considered as an administrative cost of the State for the operation of the plan, and the fees shall be considered income to the program);

(C) a fee of not more than $25 may be imposed in any case where the State requests the Secretary of the Treasury to withhold past-due support owed to or on behalf of such individual from a tax refund pursuant to section 464(a)(2);

(D) a fee (in accordance with regulations of the Secretary) for performing genetic tests may be imposed on any individual who is not a recipient of assistance under a State program funded under part A, and

(E) any costs in excess of the fees so imposed may be collected—

(i) from the parent who owes the child or spousal support obligation involved; or

(ii) at the option of the State, from the individual to whom such services are made available, but only if such State has in effect a procedure whereby all persons in such State having authority to order child or spousal support are informed that such costs are to be collected from the individual to whom such services were made available;[114]

(7) provide for entering into cooperative arrangements with appropriate courts and law enforcement officials and Indian tribes or tribal organizations (as defined in subsections (e) and (l) of section 4 of the Indian Self-Determination and Education Assistance Act (25 U.S.C. 450B)[115] (A) to assist the agency administering the plan, including the entering into of financial arrangements with such courts and officials in order to assure optimum results under such program, and (B) with respect to any other matters of common concern to such courts or officials and the agency administering the plan;

---

[114] See Vol. II, 31 U.S.C. 9701, with respect to fees and charges for Government services and things of value.
[115] See Vol. II, P.L. 94-437, §4.

408 SOCIAL SECURITY ACT—§ 454(8)

(8) provide that, for the purpose of establishing parentage, establishing, setting the amount of, modifying, or enforcing child support obligations, or making or enforcing a child custody or visitation determination, as defined in section 463(d)(1) the agency administering the plan will establish a service to locate parents utilizing—

(A) all sources of information and available records; and

(B) the Federal Parent Locator Service established under section 453,

and shall, subject to the privacy safeguards required under paragraph (26), disclose only the information described in sections 453 and 463 to the authorized persons specified in such sections for the purpose specified in such sections;

(9) provide that the State will, in accordance with standards prescribed by the Secretary, cooperate with any other State—

(A) in establishing paternity, if necessary,

(B) in locating a noncustodial parent residing in the State (whether or not permanently) against whom any action is being taken under a program established under a plan approved under this part in another State,

(C) in securing compliance by a noncustodial parent residing in such State (whether or not permanently) with an order issued by a court of competent jurisdiction against such parent for the support and maintenance of the child or children or the parent of such child or children with respect to whom aid is being provided under the plan of such other State;

(D) in carrying out other functions required under a plan approved under this part;

(E) not later than March 1, 1997, in using the forms promulgated pursuant to section 452(a)(11) for income withholding, imposition of liens, and issuance of administrative subpoenas in interstate child support cases;

(10) provide that the State will maintain a full record of collections and disbursements made under the plan and have an adequate reporting system;

(11)(A) provide that amounts collected as support shall be distributed as provided in section 457; and

(B) provide that any payment required to be made under section 456 or 457 to a family shall be made to the resident parent, legal guardian, or caretaker relative having custody of or responsibility for the child or children;

(12) provide for the establishment of procedures to require the State to provide individuals who are applying for or receiving services under the State plan, or who are parties to cases in which services are being provided under the State plan—

(A) with notice of all proceedings in which support obligations might be established or modified; and

(B) with a copy of any order establishing or modifying a child support obligation, or (in the case of a petition for modification) a notice of determination that there should be no change in the amount of the child support award, within 14 days after issuance of such order or determination;

(13) provide that the State will comply with such other requirements and standards as the Secretary determines to be necessary

to the establishment of an effective program for locating noncustodial parents, establishing paternity, obtaining support orders, and collecting support payments and provide that information requests by parents who are residents of other States be treated with the same priority as requests by parents who are residents of the State submitting the plan;

(14)(A) comply with such bonding requirements, for employees who receive, disburse, handle, or have access to, cash, as the Secretary shall by regulations prescribe;[116]

(B) maintain methods of administration which are designed to assure that persons responsible for handling cash receipts shall not participate in accounting or operating functions which would permit them to conceal in the accounting records the misuse of cash receipts (except that the Secretary shall by regulations provide for exceptions to this requirement in the case of sparsely populated areas where the hiring of unreasonable additional staff would otherwise be necessary);

(15) provide for—

(A) a process for annual reviews of and reports to the Secretary on the State program operated under the State plan approved under this part, including such information as may be necessary to measure State compliance with Federal requirements for expedited procedures, using such standards and procedures as are required by the Secretary, under which the State agency will determine the extent to which the program is operated in compliance with this part; and

(B) a process of extracting from the automated data processing system required by paragraph (16) and transmitting to the Secretary data and calculations concerning the levels of accomplishment (and rates of improvement) with respect to applicable performance indicators (including paternity establishment percentages) to the extent necessary for purposes of sections 452(g) and 458;

(16) provide for the establishment and operation by the State agency, in accordance with an (initial and annually updated) advance automated data processing planning document approved under section 452(d), of a statewide automated data processing and information retrieval system meeting the requirements of section 454A designed effectively and efficiently to assist management in the administration of the State plan, so as to control, account for, and monitor all the factors in the support enforcement collection and paternity determination process under such plan;

(17) provide that the State will have in effect an agreement with the Secretary entered into pursuant to section 463 for the use of the Parent Locator Service established under section 453 and, provide that the State will accept and transmit to the Secretary requests for information authorized under the provisions of the agreement to be furnished by such Service to authorized persons, will impose and collect (in accordance with regulations of the Secretary) a fee sufficient to cover the costs to the State and to the Secretary incurred by reason of such requests, will transmit to

---

[116] See Vol. II, 31 U.S.C. 9309, with respect to priority of sureties.

410 SOCIAL SECURITY ACT—§ 454(17)(cont)

the Secretary from time to time (in accordance with such regulations) so much of the fees collected as are attributable to such costs to the Secretary so incurred, and during the period that such agreement is in effect will otherwise comply with such agreement and regulations of the Secretary with respect thereto;

(18) provide that the State has in effect procedures necessary to obtain payment of past-due support from overpayments made to the Secretary of the Treasury as set forth in section 464, and take all steps necessary to implement and utilize such procedures;

(19) provide that the agency administering the plan—

(A) shall determine on a periodic basis, from information supplied pursuant to section 508 of the Unemployment Compensation Amendments of 1976[117], whether any individuals receiving compensation under the State's unemployment compensation law (including amounts payable pursuant to any agreement under any Federal unemployment compensation law) owe child support obligations which are being enforced by such agency; and

(B) shall enforce any such child support obligations which are owed by such an individual but are not being met—

(i) through an agreement with such individual to have specified amounts withheld from compensation otherwise payable to such individual and by submitting a copy of any such agreement to the State agency administering the unemployment compensation law;

(ii) in the absence of such an agreement, by bringing legal process (as defined in section 459(i)(5) of this Act) to require the withholding of amounts from such compensation;

(20) provide, to the extent required by section 466, that the State (A) shall have in effect all of the laws to improve child support enforcement effectiveness which are referred to in that section, and (B) shall implement the procedures which are prescribed in or pursuant to such laws;

(21)(A) at the option of the State, impose a late payment fee on all overdue support (as defined in section 466(e)) under any obligation being enforced under this part, in an amount equal to a uniform percentage determined by the State (not less than 3 percent nor more than 6 percent) of the overdue support, which shall be payable by the noncustodial parent owing the overdue support; and

(B) assure that the fee will be collected in addition to, and only after full payment of, the overdue support, and that the imposition of the late payment fee shall not directly or indirectly result in a decrease in the amount of the support which is paid to the child (or spouse) to whom, or on whose behalf, it is owed;

(22) in order for the State to be eligible to receive any incentive payments under section 458, provide that, if one or more political subdivisions of the State participate in the costs of carrying out activities under the State plan during any period, each such subdivision shall be entitled to receive an appropriate share (as determined by the State) of any such incentive payments made to

---

[117] See Vol II, P.L. 94-566, §508.

SOCIAL SECURITY ACT—§ 454(26)(D)   411

the State for such period, taking into account the efficiency and effectiveness of the activities carried out under the State plan by such political subdivision;

(23) provide that the State will regularly and frequently publicize, through public service announcements, the availability of child support enforcement services under the plan and otherwise, including information as to any application fees for such services and a telephone number or postal address at which further information may be obtained and will publicize the availability and encourage the use of procedures for voluntary establishment of paternity and child support by means the State deems appropriate;

(24) provide that the State will have in effect an automated data processing and information retrieval system—

(A) by October 1, 1997, which meets all requirements of this part which were enacted on or before the date of enactment of the Family Support Act of 1988,

(B) by October 1, 2000, which meets all requirements of this part enacted on or before the date of the enactment of the Personal Responsibility and Work Opportunity Reconciliation Act of 1996[118], except that such deadline shall be extended by 1 day for each day (if any) by which the Secretary fails to meet the deadline imposed by section 344(a)(3) of the Personal Responsibility and Work Opportunity Reconciliation Act of 1996;

(25) provide that if a family with respect to which services are provided under the plan ceases to receive assistance under the State program funded under part A, the State shall provide appropriate notice to the family and continue to provide such services, subject to the same conditions and on the same basis as in the case of other individuals to whom services are furnished under the plan, except that an application or other request to continue services shall not be required of such a family and paragraph (6)(B) shall not apply to the family;

(26) have in effect safeguards, applicable to all confidential information handled by the State agency, that are designed to protect the privacy rights of the parties, including—

(A) safeguards against unauthorized use or disclosure of information relating to proceedings or actions to establish paternity, or to establish, modify or enforce support, or to make or enforce a child custody determination;

(B) prohibitions against the release of information on the whereabouts of 1 party or the child to another party against whom a protective order with respect to the former party or the child has been entered;

(C) prohibitions against the release of information on the whereabouts of 1 party or the child to another person if the State has reason to believe that the release of the information may to that person result in physical or emotional harm to the party or the child;

(D) in cases in which the prohibitions under subparagraphs (B) and (C) apply, the requirement to notify the Secretary, for

---

[118] August 22, 1996 [P.L. 104-193, 110 Stat. 2105].

412 SOCIAL SECURITY ACT—§ 454(26)(D)(cont)

purposes of section 453(b)(2), that the State has reasonable evidence of domestic violence or child abuse against a party or the child and that the disclosure of such information could be harmful to the party or the child; and

(E) procedures providing that when the Secretary discloses information about a parent or child to a State court or an agent of a State court described in section 453(c)(2) or 463(d)(2)(B), and advises that court or agent that the Secretary has been notified that there is reasonable evidence of domestic violence or child abuse pursuant to section 453(b)(2), the court shall determine whether disclosure to any other person of information received from the Secretary could be harmful to the parent or child and, if the court determines that disclosure to any other person could be harmful, the court and its agents shall not make any such disclosure;

(27) provide that, on and after October 1, 1998, the State agency will—

(A) operate a State disbursement unit in accordance with section 454B; and

(B) have sufficient State staff (consisting of State employees) and (at State option) contractors reporting directly to the State agency to—

(i) monitor and enforce support collections through the unit in cases being enforced by the State pursuant to section 454(4) (including carrying out the automated data processing responsibilities described in section 454A(g)); and

(ii) take the actions described in section 466(c)(1) in appropriate cases;

(28) provide that, on and after October 1, 1997, the State will operate a State Directory of New Hires in accordance with section 453A;

(29) provide that the State agency responsible for administering the State plan—

(A) shall make the determination (and redetermination at appropriate intervals) as to whether an individual who has applied for or is receiving assistance under the State program funded under part A, the State program under part E, the State program under title XIX, or the supplemental nutrition assistance program[119], as defined under section 3(l)[120] of the Food and Nutrition Act of 2008[121] (7 U.S.C. 2012(l)[122]), is cooperating in good faith with the State in establishing the paternity of, or in establishing, modifying, or enforcing a support order for, any child of the individual by providing the

[119] P.L. 110-246, §4002(b)(1)(A), struck out "food stamp program" and substituted "supplemental nutrition assistance program", effective October 1, 2008. P.L. 110-234, §4002(b)(1)(A), which made the same amendment, was repealed, effective May 22, 2008 pursuant to P.L. 110-246, §4(a).
[120] P.L. 110-246, §4115(c)(2)(H), struck out "section 3(h)" and substituted "section 3(l)", effective October 1, 2008. P.L. 110-234, §4115(c)(2)(H), which made the same amendment, was repealed, effective May 22, 2008 pursuant to P.L. 110-246, §4(a).
[121] P.L. 110-246, §4002(b)(1)(B), struck out "Food Stamp Act of 1977" and substituted "Food and Nutrition Act of 2008", effective October 1, 2008. P.L. 110-234, §4002(b)(1)(B), which made the same amendment, was repealed, effective May 22, 2008 pursuant to P.L. 110-246, §4(a).
[122] See Vol. II, P.L. 88-525, §3(l).

State agency with the name of, and such other information as the State agency may require with respect to, the noncustodial parent of the child, subject to good cause and other exceptions which—

(i) in the case of the State program funded under part A, the State program under part E, or the State program under title XIX shall, at the option of the State, be defined, taking into account the best interests of the child, and applied in each case, by the State agency administering such program; and

(ii) in the case of the supplemental nutrition assistance program[123], as defined under section 3(l)[124] of the Food and Nutrition Act of 2008[125] (7 U.S.C. 2012(h)), shall be defined and applied in each case under that program in accordance with section 6(l)(2) of the Food and Nutrition Act of 2008[126] (7 U.S.C. 2015(l)(2))[127];

(B) shall require the individual to supply additional necessary information and appear at interviews, hearings, and legal proceedings;

(C) shall require the individual and the child to submit to genetic tests pursuant to judicial or administrative order;

(D) may request that the individual sign a voluntary acknowledgment of paternity, after notice of the rights and consequences of such an acknowledgment, but may not require the individual to sign an acknowledgment or otherwise relinquish the right to genetic tests as a condition of cooperation and eligibility for assistance under the State program funded under part A, the State program under part E, the State program under title XIX, or the supplemental nutrition assistance program[128], as defined under section 3(l)[129] of the Food and Nutrition Act of 2008[130] (7 U.S.C. 2012(h)); and

(E) shall promptly notify the individual and the State agency administering the State program funded under part A, the State agency administering the State program under part E, the State agency administering the State program under title XIX, or the State agency administering the

---

[123] P.L. 110-246, §4002(b)(1)(A), struck out "food stamp program" and substituted "supplemental nutrition assistance program", effective October 1, 2008. P.L. 110-234, §4002(b)(1)(A), which made the same amendment, was repealed, effective May 22, 2008 pursuant to P.L. 110-246, §4(a).

[124] P.L. 110-246, §4115(c)(2)(H), struck out "section 3(h)" and substituted "section 3(l)", effective October 1, 2008. P.L. 110-234, §4115(c)(2)(H), which made the same amendment, was repealed, effective May 22, 2008 pursuant to P.L. 110-246, §4(a).

[125] P.L. 110-246, §4002(b)(1)(B), struck out "Food Stamp Act of 1977" and substituted "Food and Nutrition Act of 2008", effective October 1, 2008. P.L. 110-234, §4002(b)(1)(B), which made the same amendment, was repealed, effective May 22, 2008 pursuant to P.L. 110-246, §4(a).

[126] P.L. 110-246, §4002(b)(1)(B), struck out "Food Stamp Act of 1977" and substituted "Food and Nutrition Act of 2008", effective October 1, 2008. P.L. 110-234, §4002(b)(1)(B), which made the same amendment, was repealed, effective May 22, 2008 pursuant to P.L. 110-246, §4(a).

[127] See Vol. II, P.L. 88-525, §6(l)(2).

[128] P.L. 110-246, §4002(b)(1)(A), struck out "food stamp program" and substituted "supplemental nutrition assistance program", effective October 1, 2008. P.L. 110-234, §4002(b)(1)(A), which made the same amendment, was repealed, effective May 22, 2008 pursuant to P.L. 110-246, §4(a).

[129] P.L. 110-246, §4115(c)(2)(H), struck out "section 3(h)" and substituted "section 3(l)", effective October 1, 2008. P.L. 110-234, §4115(c)(2)(H), which made the same amendment, was repealed, effective May 22, 2008 pursuant to P.L. 110-246, §4(a).

[130] P.L. 110-246, §4002(b)(1)(B), struck out "Food Stamp Act of 1977" and substituted "Food and Nutrition Act of 2008", effective October 1, 2008. P.L. 110-234, §4002(b)(1)(B), which made the same amendment, was repealed, effective May 22, 2008 pursuant to P.L. 110-246, §4(a).

414 SOCIAL SECURITY ACT—§ 454(29)(E)(cont)

supplemental nutrition assistance program[131], as defined under section 3(l)[132] of the Food and Nutrition Act of 2008[133] (7 U.S.C. 2012(h)), of each such determination, and if noncooperation is determined, the basis therefor;

(30) provide that the State shall use the definitions established under section 452(a)(5) in collecting and reporting information as required under this part;

(31) provide that the State agency will have in effect a procedure for certifying to the Secretary, for purposes of the procedure under section 452(k), determinations that individuals owe arrearages of child support in an amount exceeding $2,500, under which procedure—

(A) each individual concerned is afforded notice of such determination and the consequences thereof, and an opportunity to contest the determination; and

(B) the certification by the State agency is furnished to the Secretary in such format, and accompanied by such supporting documentation, as the Secretary may require;

(32)(A) provide that any request for services under this part by a foreign reciprocating country or a foreign country with which the State has an arrangement described in section 459A(d) shall be treated as a request by a State;

(B) provide, at State option, notwithstanding paragraph (4) or any other provision of this part, for services under the plan for enforcement of a spousal support order not described in paragraph (4)(B) entered by such a country (or subdivision); and

(C) provide that no applications will be required from, and no costs will be assessed for such services against, the foreign reciprocating country or foreign obligee (but costs may at State option be assessed against the obligor);[134]

(33) provide that a State that receives funding pursuant to section 428 and that has within its borders Indian country (as defined in section 1151 of title 18, United States Code[135]) may enter into cooperative agreements with an Indian tribe or tribal organization (as defined in subsections (e) and (l) of section 4 of the Indian Self-Determination and Education Assistance Act (25 U.S.C. 450b)), if the Indian tribe or tribal organization demonstrates that such tribe or organization has an established tribal court system or a Court of Indian Offenses with the authority to establish paternity, establish, modify, or enforce support orders or, and to enter support orders in accordance with child support guidelines established or adopted by such tribe or organization, under which the State and tribe or organization, under which the State and tribe or organization shall provide for the cooperative delivery of child support enforcement services in Indian country

---

[131] P.L. 110-246, §4002(b)(1)(A), struck out "food stamp program" and substituted "supplemental nutrition assistance program", effective October 1, 2008. P.L. 110-234, §4002(b)(1)(A), which made the same amendment, was repealed, effective May 22, 2008 pursuant to P.L. 110-246, §4(a).

[132] P.L. 110-246, §4115(c)(2)(H), struck out "section 3(h)" and substituted "section 3(l)", effective October 1, 2008. P.L. 110-234, §4115(c)(2)(H), which made the same amendment, was repealed, effective May 22, 2008 pursuant to P.L. 110-246, §4(a).

[133] P.L. 110-246, §4002(b)(1)(B), struck out "Food Stamp Act of 1977" and substituted "Food and Nutrition Act of 2008", effective October 1, 2008. P.L. 110-234, §4002(b)(1)(B), which made the same amendment, was repealed, effective May 22, 2008 pursuant to P.L. 110-246, §4(a).

[134] P.L. 109-171, §7301(b)(1)(C)(i), struck out "and".

[135] See Vol. II, 18 U.S.C. 1151.

SOCIAL SECURITY ACT—§ 454A(c)(1)(A)   415

and for the forwarding of all collections pursuant to the functions performed by the tribe or organization to the State agency, or conversely, by the State agency to the tribe or organization, which shall distribute such collections in accordance with such agreement; and[136]

(34)[137] include an election by the State to apply section 457(a)(2)(B) of this Act or former section 457(a)(2)(B) of this Act (as in effect for the State immediately before the date this paragraph first applies to the State) to the distribution of the amounts which are the subject of such sections and, for so long as the State elects to so apply such former section, the amendments made by subsection (b)(1) of section 7301 of the Deficit Reduction Act of 2005[138] shall not apply with respect to the State, notwithstanding subsection (e) of such section 7301.

The State may allow the jurisdiction which makes the collection involved to retain any application fee under paragraph (6)(B) or any late payment fee under paragraph (21). Nothing in paragraph (33) shall void any provision of any cooperative agreement entered into before the date of the enactment of such paragraph, nor shall such paragraph deprive any State of jurisdiction over Indian country (as so defined) that is lawfully exercised under section 402 of the Act entitled "An Act to prescribe penalties for certain acts of violence or intimidation, and for other purposes", approved April 11, 1968 (25 U.S.C. 1322).

AUTOMATED DATA PROCESSING

SEC. 454A. [42 U.S.C. 654a] (a) IN GENERAL.—In order for a State to meet the requirements of this section, the State agency administering the State program under this part shall have in operation a single statewide automated data processing and information retrieval system which has the capability to perform the tasks specified in this section with the frequency and in the manner required by or under this part.

(b) PROGRAM MANAGEMENT.—The automated system required by this section shall perform such functions as the Secretary may specify relating to management of the State program under this part, including—

(1) controlling and accounting for use of Federal, State, and local funds in carrying out the program; and

(2) maintaining the data necessary to meet Federal reporting requirements under this part on a timely basis.

(c) CALCULATION OF PERFORMANCE INDICATORS.—In order to enable the Secretary to determine the incentive payments and penalty adjustments required by sections 452(g) and 458, the State agency shall—

(1) use the automated system—

(A) to maintain the requisite data on State performance with respect to paternity establishment and child support enforcement in the State; and

---

[136] P.L. 109-171, §7301(b)(1)(C)(ii), struck out the period and substituted "; and".

[137] P.L. 109-171, §7301(b)(1)(C)(iii), adds paragraph (34), **to be effective on October 1, 2009**. For the applicability of, and State option to accelerate, the effective date, see Vol.II, P.L. 109-171, §7301(e).

[138] P.L. 109-171.

416   SOCIAL SECURITY ACT—§ 454A(c)(1)(B)

(B) to calculate the paternity establishment percentage for the State for each fiscal year; and

(2) have in place systems controls to ensure the completeness and reliability of, and ready access to, the data described in paragraph (1)(A), and the accuracy of the calculations described in paragraph (1)(B).

(d) INFORMATION INTEGRITY AND SECURITY.—The State agency shall have in effect safeguards on the integrity, accuracy, and completeness of, access to, and use of data in the automated system required by this section, which shall include the following (in addition to such other safeguards as the Secretary may specify in regulations):

(1) POLICIES RESTRICTING ACCESS.—Written policies concerning access to data by State agency personnel, and sharing of data with other persons, which—

(A) permit access to and use of data only to the extent necessary to carry out the State program under this part; and

(B) specify the data which may be used for particular program purposes, and the personnel permitted access to such data.

(2) SYSTEMS CONTROLS.—Systems controls (such as passwords or blocking of fields) to ensure strict adherence to the policies described in paragraph (1).

(3) MONITORING OF ACCESS.—Routine monitoring of access to and use of the automated system, through methods such as audit trails and feedback mechanisms, to guard against and promptly identify unauthorized access or use.

(4) TRAINING AND INFORMATION.—Procedures to ensure that all personnel (including State and local agency staff and contractors) who may have access to or be required to use confidential program data are informed of applicable requirements and penalties (including those in section 6103 of the Internal Revenue Code of 1986[139]), and are adequately trained in security procedures.

(5) PENALTIES.—Administrative penalties (up to and including dismissal from employment) for unauthorized access to, or disclosure or use of, confidential data.

(e) STATE CASE REGISTRY.—

(1) CONTENTS.—The automated system required by this section shall include a registry (which shall be known as the "State case registry") that contains records with respect to—

(A) each case in which services are being provided by the State agency under the State plan approved under this part; and

(B) each support order established or modified in the State on or after October 1, 1998.

(2) LINKING OF LOCAL REGISTRIES.—The State case registry may be established by linking local case registries of support orders through an automated information network, subject to this section.

(3) USE OF STANDARDIZED DATA ELEMENTS.—Such records shall use standardized data elements for both parents (such as names, social security numbers and other uniform identification numbers, dates of birth, and case identification numbers), and contain

---

[139] See Vol. II, P.L. 83-591, §6103.

SOCIAL SECURITY ACT—§ 454A(f)(2)   417

such other information (such as on case status) as the Secretary may require.

(4) PAYMENT RECORDS.—Each case record in the State case registry with respect to which services are being provided under the State plan approved under this part and with respect to which a support order has been established shall include a record of—

(A) the amount of monthly (or other periodic) support owed under the order, and other amounts (including arrearages, interest or late payment penalties, and fees) due or overdue under the order;

(B) any amount described in subparagraph (A) that has been collected;

(C) the distribution of such collected amounts;

(D) the birth date and, beginning not later than October 1, 1999, the social security number, of any child for whom the order requires the provision of support; and

(E) the amount of any lien imposed with respect to the order pursuant to section 466(a)(4).

(5) UPDATING AND MONITORING.—The State agency operating the automated system required by this section shall promptly establish and update, maintain, and regularly monitor, case records in the State case registry with respect to which services are being provided under the State plan approved under this part, on the basis of—

(A) information on administrative actions and administrative and judicial proceedings and orders relating to paternity and support;

(B) information obtained from comparison with Federal, State, or local sources of information;

(C) information on support collections and distributions; and

(D) any other relevant information.

(f) INFORMATION COMPARISONS AND OTHER DISCLOSURES OF INFORMATION.—The State shall use the automated system required by this section to extract information from (at such times, and in such standardized format or formats, as may be required by the Secretary), to share and compare information with, and to receive information from, other data bases and information necessary to enable the State agency (or the Secretary or other State or Federal agencies) to carry out this part, subject to section 6103 of the Internal Revenue Code of 1986[140]. Such information comparison activities shall include the following:

(1) FEDERAL CASE REGISTRY OF CHILD SUPPORT ORDERS.—Furnishing to the Federal Case Registry of Child Support Orders established under section 453(h) (and update as necessary, with information including notice of expiration of orders) the minimum amount of information on child support cases recorded in the State case registry that is necessary to operate the registry (as specified by the Secretary in regulations).

(2) FEDERAL PARENT LOCATOR SERVICE.—Exchanging information with the Federal Parent Locator Service for the purposes specified in section 453.

---

[140] See Vol. II, P.L. 83-591, §6103.

418 SOCIAL SECURITY ACT—§ 454A(f)(3)

(3) TEMPORARY FAMILY ASSISTANCE AND MEDICAID AGENCIES.—Exchanging information with State agencies (of the State and of other States) administering programs funded under part A, programs operated under a State plan approved under title XIX, and other programs designated by the Secretary, as necessary to perform State agency responsibilities under this part and under such programs.

(4) INTRASTATE AND INTERSTATE INFORMATION COMPARISONS.—Exchanging information with other agencies of the State, agencies of other States, and interstate information networks, as necessary and appropriate to carry out (or assist other States to carry out) the purposes of this part.

(5) PRIVATE INDUSTRY COUNCILS RECEIVING WELFARE–TO–WORK GRANTS.—Disclosing to a private industry council (as defined in section 403(a)(5)(D)(ii)) to which funds are provided under section 403(a)(5) the names, addresses, telephone numbers, and identifying case number information in the State program funded under part A, of noncustodial parents residing in the service delivery area of the private industry council, for the purpose of identifying and contacting noncustodial parents regarding participation in the program under section 403(a)(5).

(g) COLLECTION AND DISTRIBUTION OF SUPPORT PAYMENTS.—

(1) IN GENERAL.—The State shall use the automated system required by this section, to the maximum extent feasible, to assist and facilitate the collection and disbursement of support payments through the State disbursement unit operated under section 454B, through the performance of functions, including, at a minimum—

(A) transmission of orders and notices to employers (and other debtors) for the withholding of income—

(i) within 2 business days after receipt of notice of, and the income source subject to, such withholding from a court, another State, an employer, the Federal Parent Locator Service, or another source recognized by the State; and

(ii) using uniform formats prescribed by the Secretary;

(B) ongoing monitoring to promptly identify failures to make timely payment of support; and

(C) automatic use of enforcement procedures (including procedures authorized pursuant to section 466(c)) if payments are not timely made.

(2) BUSINESS DAY DEFINED.—As used in paragraph (1), the term "business day" means a day on which State offices are open for regular business.

(h) EXPEDITED ADMINISTRATIVE PROCEDURES.—The automated system required by this section shall be used, to the maximum extent feasible, to implement the expedited administrative procedures required by section 466(c).

COLLECTION AND DISBURSEMENT OF SUPPORT PAYMENTS

SEC. 454B. [42 U.S.C. 654b] (a) STATE DISBURSEMENT UNIT.—

(1) IN GENERAL.—In order for a State to meet the requirements of this section, the State agency must establish and operate a unit

SOCIAL SECURITY ACT—§ 454B(c)(1) 419

(which shall be known as the "State disbursement unit") for the collection and disbursement of payments under support orders—

(A) in all cases being enforced by the State pursuant to section 454(4); and

(B) in all cases not being enforced by the State under this part in which the support order is initially issued in the State on or after January 1, 1994, and in which the income of the noncustodial parent is subject to withholding pursuant to section 466(a)(8)(B).

(2) OPERATION.—The State disbursement unit shall be operated—

(A) directly by the State agency (or 2 or more State agencies under a regional cooperative agreement), or (to the extent appropriate) by a contractor responsible directly to the State agency; and

(B) except in cases described in paragraph (1)(B), in coordination with the automated system established by the State pursuant to section 454A.

(3) LINKING OF LOCAL DISBURSEMENT UNITS.—The State disbursement unit may be established by linking local disbursement units through an automated information network, subject to this section, if the Secretary agrees that the system will not costs more nor take more time to establish or operate than a centralized system. In addition, employers shall be given 1 location to which income withholding is sent.

(b) REQUIRED PROCEDURES.—The State disbursement unit shall use automated procedures, electronic processes, and computer-driven technology to the maximum extent feasible, efficient, and economical, for the collection and disbursement of support payments, including procedures—

(1) for receipt of payments from parents, employers, and other States, and for disbursements to custodial parents and other obligees, the State agency, and the agencies of other States;

(2) for accurate identification of payments;

(3) to ensure prompt disbursement of the custodial parent's share of any payment; and

(4) to furnish to any parent, upon request, timely information on the current status of support payments under an order requiring payments to be made by or to the parent, except that in cases described in subsection (a)(1)(B), the State disbursement unit shall not be required to convert and maintain in automated form records of payments kept pursuant to section 466(a)(8)(B)(iii) before the effective date of this section.

(c) TIMING OF DISBURSEMENTS.—

(1) IN GENERAL.—Except as provided in paragraph (2), the State disbursement unit shall distribute all amounts payable under section 457(a) within 2 business days after receipt from the employer or other source of periodic income, if sufficient information identifying the payee is provided. The date of collection for amounts collected and distributed under this part is the date of receipt by the State disbursement unit, except that if current support is withheld by an employer in the month when due and is received by the State disbursement unit in a month

420   SOCIAL SECURITY ACT—§ 454B(c)(2)

other than the month when due, the date of withholding may be deemed to be the date of collection.

(2) PERMISSIVE RETENTION OF ARREARAGES.—The State disbursement unit may delay the distribution of collections toward arrearages until the resolution of any timely appeal with respect to such arrearages.

(d) BUSINESS DAY DEFINED.—As used in this section, the term "business day" means a day on which State offices are open for regular business.

PAYMENTS TO STATES[141]

SEC. 455. [42 U.S.C. 655] (a)(1) From the sums appropriated therefor, the Secretary shall pay to each State for each quarter an amount—

(A) equal to the percent specified in paragraph (2) of the total amounts expended by such State during such quarter for the operation of the plan approved under section 454,

(B) equal to the percent specified in paragraph (3) of the sums expended during such quarter that are attributable to the planning, design, development, installation or enhancement of an automatic data processing and information retrieval system (including in such sums the full cost of the hardware components of such system), and

(C) equal to 66 percent of so much of the sums expended during such quarter as are attributable to laboratory costs incurred in determining paternity, and

(D) equal to 66 percent of the sums expended by the State during the quarter for an alternative statewide system for which a waiver has been granted under section 452(d)(3), but only to the extent that the total of the sums so expended by the State on or after the date of the enactment of this subparagraph does not exceed the least total cost estimate submitted by the State pursuant to section 452(d)(3)(C) in the request for the waiver;

except that no amount shall be paid to any State on account of amounts expended from amounts paid to the State under section 458 or to carry out an agreement which it has entered into pursuant to section 463. In determining the total amounts expended by any State during a quarter, for purposes of this subsection, there shall be excluded an amount equal to the total of any fees collected or other income resulting from services provided under the plan approved under this part.

(2) The percent applicable to quarters in a fiscal year for purposes of paragraph (1)(A) is—

(A) 70 percent for fiscal years 1984, 1985, 1986, and 1987,

(B) 68 percent for fiscal years 1988 and 1989, and

(C) 66 percent for fiscal year 1990 and each fiscal year thereafter.

(3)(A) The Secretary shall pay to each State, for each quarter in fiscal years 1996 and 1997, 90 percent of so much of the State expenditures described in paragraph (1)(B) as the Secretary finds are for a system meeting the requirements specified in section 454(16) (as in

---

[141] See Vol. II, P.L. 99-177, Title II, "Balanced Budget and Emergency Deficit Control Act of 1985", §256 [as amended by P.L. 100-119], with respect to treatment of child enforcement program; and §257(11), with respect to references to §401(c)(2) of the "Congressional Budget Act of 1974".

effect on September 30, 1995) but limited to the amount approved for States in the advance planning documents of such States submitted on or before September 30, 1995.

(B)(i) The Secretary shall pay to each State or system described in clause (iii), for each quarter in fiscal years 1996 through 2001, the percentage specified in clause (ii) of so much of the State or system expenditures described in paragraph (1)(B) as the Secretary finds are for a system meeting the requirements of sections 454(16) and 454A.

(ii) The percentage specified in this clause is 80 percent.

(iii) For purposes of clause (i), a system described in this clause is a system that has been approved by the Secretary to receive enhanced funding pursuant to the Family Support Act of 1988 (Public Law 100-485; 102 Stat. 2343) for the purpose of developing a system that meets the requirements of sections 454(16) (as in effect on and after September 30, 1995) and 454A, including systems that have received funding for such purpose pursuant to a waiver under section 1115(a).

(4)(A)(i) If—

(I) the Secretary determines that a State plan under section 454 would (in the absence of this paragraph) be disapproved for the failure of the State to comply with a particular subparagraph of section 454(24), and that the State has made and is continuing to make a good faith effort to so comply; and

(II) the State has submitted to the Secretary a corrective compliance plan that describes how, by when, and at what cost the State will achieve such compliance, which has been approved by the Secretary, then the Secretary shall not disapprove the State plan under section 454, and the Secretary shall reduce the amount otherwise payable to the State under paragraph (1)(A) of this subsection for the fiscal year by the penalty amount.

(ii) All failures of a State during a fiscal year to comply with any of the requirements referred to in the same subparagraph of section 454(24) shall be considered a single failure of the State to comply with that subparagraph during the fiscal year for purposes of this paragraph.

(B) In this paragraph:

(i) The term "penalty amount" means, with respect to a failure of a State to comply with a subparagraph of section 454(24)—

(I) 4 percent of the penalty base, in the case of the first fiscal year in which such a failure by the State occurs (regardless of whether a penalty is imposed under this paragraph with respect to the failure);

(II) 8 percent of the penalty base, in the case of the second such fiscal year;

(III) 16 percent of the penalty base, in the case of the third such fiscal year;

(IV) 25 percent of the penalty base, in the case of the fourth such fiscal year; or

(V) 30 percent of the penalty base, in the case of the fifth or any subsequent such fiscal year.

(ii) The term "penalty base" means, with respect to a failure of a State to comply with a subparagraph of section 454(24) during a fiscal year, the amount otherwise payable to the State under paragraph (1)(A) of this subsection for the preceding fiscal year.

(C)(i) The Secretary shall waive a penalty under this paragraph for any failure of a State to comply with section 454(24)(A) during fiscal year 1998 if—

(I) on or before August 1, 1998, the State has submitted to the Secretary a request that the Secretary certify the State as having met the requirements of such section;

(II) the Secretary subsequently provides the certification as a result of a timely review conducted pursuant to the request; and

(III) the State has not failed such a review.

(ii) If a State with respect to which a reduction is made under this paragraph for a fiscal year with respect to a failure to comply with a subparagraph of section 454(24) achieves compliance with such subparagraph by the beginning of the succeeding fiscal year, the Secretary shall increase the amount otherwise payable to the State under paragraph (1)(A) of this subsection for the succeeding fiscal year by an amount equal to 90 percent of the reduction for the fiscal year.

(iii) The Secretary shall reduce the amount of any reduction that, in the absence of this clause, would be required to be made under this paragraph by reason of the failure of a State to achieve compliance with section 454(24)(B) during the fiscal year, by an amount equal to 20 percent of the amount of the otherwise required reduction, for each State performance measure described in section 458(b)(4) with respect to which the applicable percentage under section 458(b)(6) for the fiscal year is 100 percent, if the Secretary has made the determination described in section 458(b)(5)(B) with respect to the State for the fiscal year.

(5)(A)(i) If—

(I) the Secretary determines that a State plan under section 454 would (in the absence of this paragraph) be disapproved for the failure of the State to comply with subparagraphs (A) and (B)(i) of section 454(27), and that the State has made and is continuing to make a good faith effort to so comply; and

(II) the State has submitted to the Secretary, not later than April 1, 2000, a corrective compliance plan that describes how, by when, and at what cost the State will achieve such compliance, which has been approved by the Secretary,

then the Secretary shall not disapprove the State plan under section 454, and the Secretary shall reduce the amount otherwise payable to the State under paragraph (1)(A) of this subsection for the fiscal year by the penalty amount.

(ii) All failures of a State during a fiscal year to comply with any of the requirements of section 454B shall be considered a single failure of the State to comply with subparagraphs (A) and (B)(i) of section 454(27) during the fiscal year for purposes of this paragraph.

(B) In this paragraph:

(i) The term "penalty amount" means, with respect to a failure of a State to comply with subparagraphs (A) and (B)(i) of section 454(27)—

(I) 4 percent of the penalty base, in the case of the 1st fiscal year in which such a failure by the State occurs (regardless of whether a penalty is imposed in that fiscal year under this paragraph with respect to the failure), except as provided in subparagraph (C)(ii) of this paragraph;

SOCIAL SECURITY ACT—§ 455(d) 423

(II) 8 percent of the penalty base, in the case of the 2nd such fiscal year;

(III) 16 percent of the penalty base, in the case of the 3rd such fiscal year;

(IV) 25 percent of the penalty base, in the case of the 4th such fiscal year; or

(V) 30 percent of the penalty base, in the case of the 5th or any subsequent such fiscal year.

(ii) The term "penalty base" means, with respect to a failure of a State to comply with subparagraphs (A) and (B)(i) of section 454(27) during a fiscal year, the amount otherwise payable to the State under paragraph (1)(A) of this subsection for the preceding fiscal year.

(C)(i) The Secretary shall waive all penalties imposed against a State under this paragraph for any failure of the State to comply with subparagraphs (A) and (B)(i) of section 454(27) if the Secretary determines that, before April 1, 2000, the State has achieved such compliance.

(ii) If a State with respect to which a reduction is required to be made under this paragraph with respect to a failure to comply with subparagraphs (A) and (B)(i) of section 454(27) achieves such compliance on or after April 1, 2000, and on or before September 30, 2000, then the penalty amount applicable to the State shall be 1 percent of the penalty base with respect to the failure involved.

(D) The Secretary may not impose a penalty under this paragraph against a State for a fiscal year for which the amount otherwise payable to the State under paragraph (1)(A) of this subsection is reduced under paragraph (4) of this subsection for failure to comply with section 454(24)(A).

(b)(1) Prior to the beginning of each quarter, the Secretary shall estimate the amount to which a State will be entitled under subsection (a) for such quarter, such estimates to be based on (A) a report filed by the State containing its estimate of the total sum to be expended in such quarter in accordance with the provisions of such subsection, and stating the amount appropriated or made available by the State and its political subdivisions for such expenditures in such quarter, and if such amount is less than the State's proportionate share of the total sum of such estimated expenditures, the source or sources from which the difference is expected to be derived, and (B) such other investigation as the Secretary may find necessary.

(2) Subject to subsection (d), the Secretary shall then pay, in such installments as he may determine, to the State the amount so estimated, reduced or increased to the extent of any overpayment or underpayment which the Secretary determines was made under this section to such State for any prior quarter and with respect to which adjustment has not already been made under this subsection.

(3) Upon the making of any estimate by the Secretary under this subsection, any appropriations available for payments under this section shall be deemed obligated.

(c) [Repealed.[142]]

(d) Notwithstanding any other provision of law, no amount shall be paid to any State under this section for any quarter, prior to the

---

[142] P.L. 97-248, §174(b); 96 Stat. 403.

424 SOCIAL SECURITY ACT—§ 455(d)(cont)

close of such quarter, unless for the period consisting of all prior quarters for which payment is authorized to be made to such State under subsection (a), there shall have been submitted by the State to the Secretary, with respect to each quarter in such period (other than the last two quarters in such period), a full and complete report (in such form and manner and containing such information as the Secretary shall prescribe or require) as to the amount of child support collected and disbursed and all expenditures with respect to which payment is authorized under subsection (a).

(e)(1) In order to encourage and promote the development and use of more effective methods of enforcing support obligations under this part in cases where either the children on whose behalf the support is sought or their noncustodial parents do not reside in the State where such cases are filed, the Secretary is authorized to make grants, in such amounts and on such terms and conditions as the Secretary determines to be appropriate, to States which propose to undertake new or innovative methods of support collection in such cases and which will use the proceeds of such grants to carry out special projects designed to demonstrate and test such methods.

(2) A grant under this subsection shall be made only upon a finding by the Secretary that the project involved is likely to be of significant assistance in carrying out the purpose of this subsection; and with respect to such project the Secretary may waive any of the requirements of this part which would otherwise be applicable, to such extent and for such period as the Secretary determines is necessary or desirable in order to enable the State to carry out the project.

(3) At the time of its application for a grant under this subsection the State shall submit to the Secretary a statement describing in reasonable detail the project for which the proceeds of the grant are to be used, and the State shall from time to time thereafter submit to the Secretary such reports with respect to the project as the Secretary may specify.

(4) Amounts expended by a State in carrying out a special project assisted under this section shall be considered, for purposes of section 458(b) (as amended by section 5(a) of the Child Support Enforcement Amendments of 1984[143]), to have been expended for the operation of the State's plan approved under section 454.

(5) There is authorized to be appropriated the sum of $7,000,000 for fiscal year 1985, $12,000,000 for fiscal year 1986, and $15,000,000 for each fiscal year thereafter, to be used by the Secretary in making grants under this subsection.

(f) The Secretary may make direct payments under this part to an Indian tribe or tribal organization that demonstrates to the satisfaction of the Secretary that it has the capacity to operate a child support enforcement program meeting the objectives of this part, including establishment of paternity, establishment, modification, and enforcement of support orders, and location of absent parents. The Secretary shall promulgate regulations establishing the requirements which must be met by an Indian tribe or tribal organization to be eligible for a grant under this subsection.

---

[143] P.L. 98-378, §5; 98 Stat.1305.

SOCIAL SECURITY ACT—§ 457(a)(2)(B)(i)

SUPPORT OBLIGATIONS

SEC. 456. [42 U.S.C. 656] (a)(1) The support rights assigned to the State pursuant to section 408(a)(3) or secured on behalf of a child receiving foster care maintenance payments shall constitute an obligation owed to such State by the individual responsible for providing such support. Such obligation shall be deemed for collection purposes to be collectible under all applicable State and local processes.

(2) The amount of such obligation shall be—

(A) the amount specified in a court order which covers the assigned support rights, or

(B) if there is no court order, an amount determined by the State in accordance with a formula approved by the Secretary.

(3) Any amounts collected from a noncustodial parent under the plan shall reduce, dollar for dollar, the amount of his obligation under subparagraphs (A) and (B) of paragraph (2).

(b) NONDISCHARGEABILITY.—A debt (as defined in section 101 of title 11 of the United States Code) owed under State law to a State (as defined in such section) or municipality (as defined in such section) that is in the nature of support and that is enforceable under this part is not released by a discharge in bankruptcy under title 11 of the United States Code[144].

DISTRIBUTION OF COLLECTED SUPPORT

SEC. 457. [42 U.S.C. 657] (a)[145] IN GENERAL.—Subject to subsections (d) and (e), an amount collected on behalf of a family as support by a State pursuant to a plan approved under this part shall be distributed as follows:

(1) FAMILIES RECEIVING ASSISTANCE.—In the case of a family receiving assistance from the State, the State shall—

(A) pay to the Federal Government the Federal share of the amount so collected; and

(B) retain, or distribute to the family, the State share of the amount so collected.

In no event shall the total of the amounts paid to the Federal Government and retained by the State exceed the total of the amounts that have been paid to the family as assistance by the State.

(2) FAMILIES THAT FORMERLY RECEIVED ASSISTANCE.—In the case of a family that formerly received assistance from the State:

(A) CURRENT SUPPORT PAYMENTS.—To the extent that the amount so collected does not exceed the amount required to be paid to the family for the month in which collected, the State shall distribute the amount so collected to the family.

(B) PAYMENTS OF ARREARAGES.—To the extent that the amount so collected exceeds the amount required to be paid to the family for the month in which collected, the State shall distribute the amount so collected as follows:

(i) DISTRIBUTION OF ARREARAGES THAT ACCRUED AFTER THE FAMILY CEASED TO RECEIVE ASSISTANCE.—

---

[144] See Vol. II, 11 U.S.C. 101 and 523.

[145] P.L. 109-171, §7301(b)(1)(A), amends subsection (a) in its entirety, **to be effective October 1, 2009.**

See Vol. II, P.L. 109-171, §7301(e), with respect to applicability and a State option to accelerate the effective date to a date not earlier than October 1, 2008.

426 SOCIAL SECURITY ACT—§ 457(a)(2)(B)(i)(I)

(I) PRE–OCTOBER 1997.—Except as provided in subclause (II), the provisions of this section as in effect and applied on the day before the date of the enactment of section 302 of the Personal Responsibility and Work Opportunity Reconciliation Act of 1996 (other than subsection (b)(1) (as so in effect))[146] shall apply with respect to the distribution of support arrearages that—

(aa) accrued after the family ceased to receive assistance, and

(bb) are collected before October 1, 1997.

(II) POST–SEPTEMBER 1997.—With respect to the amount so collected on or after October 1, 1997 (or before such date, at the option of the State)—

(aa) IN GENERAL.—The State shall first distribute the amount so collected (other than any amount described in clause (iv)) to the family to the extent necessary to satisfy any support arrearages with respect to the family that accrued after the family ceased to receive assistance from the State.

(bb) REIMBURSEMENT OF GOVERNMENTS FOR ASSISTANCE PROVIDED TO THE FAMILY.—After the application of division (aa) and clause (ii)(II)(aa) with respect to the amount so collected, the State shall retain the State share of the amount so collected, and pay to the Federal Government the Federal share (as defined in subsection (c)(2)) of the amount so collected, but only to the extent necessary to reimburse amounts paid to the family as assistance by the State.

(cc) DISTRIBUTION OF THE REMAINDER TO THE FAMILY.—To the extent that neither division (aa) nor division (bb) applies to the amount so collected, the State shall distribute the amount to the family.

(ii) DISTRIBUTION OF ARREARAGES THAT ACCRUED BEFORE THE FAMILY RECEIVED ASSISTANCE.—

(I) PRE–OCTOBER 2000.—Except as provided in subclause (II), the provisions of this section as in effect and applied on the day before the date of enactment of section 302 of the Personal Responsibility and Work Opportunity Reconciliation Act of 1996[147] (other than subsection (b)(1) (as so in effect)) shall apply with respect to the distribution of support arrearages that—

(aa) accrued before the family received assistance, and

(bb) are collected before October 1, 2000.

---

[146] August 22, 1996 is the date of enactment for P.L. 104-193.

[147] P.L. 104-193, §302(b), provided that the effective date for the amendments made by §302 shall be October 1, 1996, or earlier at the State's option.

(II) POST-SEPTEMBER 2000.—Unless, based on the report required by paragraph (5), the Congress determines otherwise, with respect to the amount so collected on or after October 1, 2000 (or before such date, at the option of the State)—

(aa) IN GENERAL.—The State shall first distribute the amount so collected (other than any amount described in clause (iv)) to the family to the extent necessary to satisfy any support arrearages with respect to the family that accrued before the family received assistance from the State.

(bb) REIMBURSEMENT OF GOVERNMENTS FOR ASSISTANCE PROVIDED TO THE FAMILY.—After the application of clause (i)(II)(aa) and division (aa) with respect to the amount so collected, the State shall retain the State share of the amount so collected, and pay to the Federal Government the Federal share (as defined in subsection (c)(2)) of the amount so collected, but only to the extent necessary to reimburse amounts paid to the family as assistance by the State.

(cc) DISTRIBUTION OF THE REMAINDER TO THE FAMILY.—To the extent that neither division (aa) nor division (bb) applies to the amount so collected, the State shall distribute the amount to the family.

(iii) DISTRIBUTION OF ARREARAGES THAT ACCRUED WHILE THE FAMILY RECEIVED ASSISTANCE.—In the case of a family described in this subparagraph, the provisions of paragraph (1) shall apply with respect to the distribution of support arrearages that accrued while the family received assistance.

(iv) AMOUNTS COLLECTED PURSUANT TO SECTION 464.—Notwithstanding any other provision of this section, any amount of support collected pursuant to section 464 shall be retained by the State to the extent past-due support has been assigned to the State as a condition of receiving assistance from the State, up to the amount necessary to reimburse the State for amounts paid to the family as assistance by the State. The State shall pay to the Federal Government the Federal share of the amounts so retained. To the extent the amount collected pursuant to section 464 exceeds the amount so retained, the State shall distribute the excess to the family.

(v) ORDERING RULES FOR DISTRIBUTIONS.—For purposes of this subparagraph, unless an earlier effective date is required by this section, effective October 1, 2000, the State shall treat any support arrearages collected, except for amounts collected pursuant to section 464, as accruing in the following order:

(I) To the period after the family ceased to receive assistance.

428   SOCIAL SECURITY ACT—§ 457(a)(2)(B)(v)(II)

(II) To the period before the family received assistance.

(III) To the period while the family was receiving assistance.

(3) FAMILIES THAT NEVER RECEIVED ASSISTANCE.—In the case of any other family, the State shall distribute to the family the portion of the amount so collected that remains after withholding any fee pursuant to section 454(6)(B)(ii).

(4) FAMILIES UNDER CERTAIN AGREEMENTS.—In the case of an amount collected for a family in accordance with a cooperative agreement under section 454(33), distribute the amount so collected pursuant to the terms of the agreement.

(5) STUDY AND REPORT.—Not later than October 1, 1999, the Secretary shall report to the Congress the Secretary's findings with respect to—

(A) whether the distribution of post-assistance arrearages to families has been effective in moving people off of welfare and keeping them off of welfare;

(B) whether early implementation of a pre-assistance arrearage program by some States has been effective in moving people off of welfare and keeping them off of welfare;

(C) what the overall impact has been of the amendments made by the Personal Responsibility and Work Opportunity Reconciliation Act of 1996[148] with respect to child support enforcement in moving people off of welfare and keeping them off of welfare; and

(D) based on the information and data the Secretary has obtained, what changes, if any, should be made in the policies related to the distribution of child support arrearages.

(6) STATE OPTION FOR APPLICABILITY.—Notwithstanding any other provision of this subsection, a State may elect to apply the rules described in clauses (i)(II), (ii)(II), and (v) of paragraph (2)(B) to support arrearages collected on and after October 1, 1998, and, if the State makes such an election, shall apply the provisions of this section, as in effect and applied on the day before the date of enactment of section 302 of the Personal Responsibility and Work Opportunity Reconciliation Act of 1996[149] (Public Law 104-193, 110 Stat. 2200), other than subsection (b)(1) (as so in effect), to amounts collected before October 1, 1998.

(7)[150] STATE OPTION TO PASS THROUGH ADDITIONAL SUPPORT WITH FEDERAL FINANCIAL PARTICIPATION.—

(A) FAMILIES THAT FORMERLY RECEIVED ASSISTANCE.— Notwithstanding paragraph (2), a State shall not be required to pay to the Federal Government the Federal share of an amount collected on behalf of a family that formerly received assistance from the State to the extent that the State pays the amount to the family.

---

[148] P.L. 104-193; 110 Stat. 2105.

[149] P.L. 104-193, §302(b), provided that the effective date for the amendments made by §302 shall be October 1, 1996, or earlier at the State's option.

[150] P.L. 109-171, §7301(b)(1)(B)(i), added paragraph (7), effective October 1, 2008.

P.L. 109-171, §7301(b)(1)(B)(iii), provides that **effective October 1, 2009, this paragraph (7) is redesignated as paragraph (6).**

SOCIAL SECURITY ACT—§ 457(c)(4)   429

(B) FAMILIES THAT CURRENTLY RECEIVE ASSISTANCE.—
(i) IN GENERAL.— Notwithstanding paragraph (1), in the case of a family that receives assistance from the State, a State shall not be required to pay to the Federal Government the Federal share of the excepted portion (as defined in clause (ii)) of any amount collected on behalf of such family during a month to the extent that—
(I) the State pays the excepted portion to the family; and
(II) the excepted portion is disregarded in determining the amount and type of assistance provided to the family under such program.
(ii) EXCEPTED PORTION DEFINED.—For purposes of this subparagraph, the term "excepted portion "means that portion of the amount collected on behalf of a family during a month that does not exceed $100 per month, or in the case of a family that includes 2 or more children, that does not exceed an amount established by the State that is not more than $200 per month.

(b)[151] CONTINUATION OF ASSIGNMENTS.—Any rights to support obligations, assigned to a State as a condition of receiving assistance from the State under part A and in effect on September 30, 1997 (or such earlier date, on or after August 22, 1996, as the State may choose), shall remain assigned after such date.

(c) DEFINITIONS.—As used in subsection (a):
(1) ASSISTANCE.—The term "assistance from the State" means—
(A) assistance under the State program funded under part A or under the State plan approved under part A of this title (as in effect on the day before the date of the enactment of the Personal Responsibility and Work Opportunity Reconciliation Act of 1996); and
(B) foster care maintenance payments under the State plan approved under part E of this title.
(2) FEDERAL SHARE.—The term "Federal share" means that portion of the amount collected resulting from the application of the Federal medical assistance percentage in effect for the fiscal year in which the amount is distributed.
(3) FEDERAL MEDICAL ASSISTANCE PERCENTAGE.—The term "Federal medical assistance percentage" means—
(A) 75 percent, in the case of Puerto Rico, the Virgin Islands, Guam, and American Samoa; or
(B) the Federal medical assistance percentage (as defined in section 1905(b), as such section was in effect on September 30, 1995) in the case of any other State.
(4) STATE SHARE.—The term "State share" means 100 percent minus the Federal share.

---

[151] P.L. 109-171, §7301(c), amends subsection (b) in its entirety, **to be effective October 1, 2009.** See Vol. II, P.L. 109-171, §7301(e), with respect to applicability and a State option to accelerate the effective date to a date not earlier than October 1, 2008.

430 SOCIAL SECURITY ACT—§ 457(c)(5)

(5)[152] CURRENT SUPPORT AMOUNT DEFINED.— The term "current support amount" means, with respect to amounts collected as support on behalf of a family, the amount designated as the monthly support obligation of the noncustodial parent in the order requiring the support or calculated by the State based on the order.

(d) GAP PAYMENTS NOT SUBJECT TO DISTRIBUTION UNDER THIS SECTION.—At State option, this section shall not apply to any amount collected on behalf of a family as support by the State (and paid to the family in addition to the amount of assistance otherwise payable to the family) pursuant to a plan approved under this part if such amount would have been paid to the family by the State under section 402(a)(28), as in effect and applied on the day before the date of the enactment of section 302 of the Personal Responsibility and Work Opportunity Reconciliation Act of 1996[153].

(e) Notwithstanding the preceding provisions of this section, amounts collected by a State as child support for months in any period on behalf of a child for whom a public agency is making foster care maintenance payments under part E—

(1) shall be retained by the State to the extent necessary to reimburse it for the foster care maintenance payments made with respect to the child during such period (with appropriate reimbursement of the Federal Government to the extent of its participation in the financing);

(2) shall be paid to the public agency responsible for supervising the placement of the child to the extent that the amounts collected exceed the foster care maintenance payments made with respect to the child during such period but not the amounts required by a court or administrative order to be paid as support on behalf of the child during such period; and the responsible agency may use the payments in the manner it determines will serve the best interests of the child, including setting such payments aside for the child's future needs or making all or a part thereof available to the person responsible for meeting the child's day-to-day needs; and

(3) shall be retained by the State, if any portion of the amounts collected remains after making the payments required under paragraphs (1) and (2), to the extent that such portion is necessary to reimburse the State (with appropriate reimbursement to the Federal Government to the extent of its participation in the financing) for any past foster care maintenance payments (or payments of assistance under the State program funded under part A) which were made with respect to the child (and with respect to which past collections have not previously been retained); and any balance shall be paid to the State agency responsible for supervising the placement of the child, for use by such agency in accordance with paragraph (2).

---

[152] P.L. 109-171, §7301(b)(2), adds this paragraph (5), **effective October 1, 2009**.
See Vol. II, P.L. 109-171, §7301(e), with respect to applicability and a State option to accelerate the effective date to a date not earlier than October 1, 2008.
[153] P.L. 104-193, §302(b), provided that the effective date for the amendments made by §302 shall be October 1, 1996, or earlier at the State's option.

SOCIAL SECURITY ACT—§ 458(b)(5) 431

INCENTIVE PAYMENTS TO STATES

SEC. 458. [42 U.S.C. 658a] (a) IN GENERAL.—In addition to any other payment under this part, the Secretary shall, subject to subsection (f), make an incentive payment to each State for each fiscal year in an amount determined under subsection (b).

(b) AMOUNT OF INCENTIVE PAYMENT.—

(1) IN GENERAL.—The incentive payment for a State for a fiscal year is equal to the incentive payment pool for the fiscal year, multiplied by the State incentive payment share for the fiscal year.

(2) INCENTIVE PAYMENT POOL.—

(A) IN GENERAL.—In paragraph (1), the term "incentive payment pool" means—

(i) $422,000,000 for fiscal year 2000;

(ii) $429,000,000 for fiscal year 2001;

(iii) $450,000,000 for fiscal year 2002;

(iv) $461,000,000 for fiscal year 2003;

(v) $454,000,000 for fiscal year 2004;

(vi) $446,000,000 for fiscal year 2005;

(vii) $458,000,000 for fiscal year 2006;

(viii) $471,000,000 for fiscal year 2007;

(ix) $483,000,000 for fiscal year 2008; and

(x) for any succeeding fiscal year, the amount of the incentive payment pool for the fiscal year that precedes such succeeding fiscal year, multiplied by the percentage (if any) by which the CPI for such preceding fiscal year exceeds the CPI for the second preceding fiscal year.

(B) CPI.—For purposes of subparagraph (A), the CPI for a fiscal year is the average of the Consumer Price Index for the 12-month period ending on September 30 of the fiscal year. As used in the preceding sentence, the term "Consumer Price Index" means the last Consumer Price Index for all-urban consumers published by the Department of Labor.

(3) STATE INCENTIVE PAYMENT SHARE.—In paragraph (1), the term "State incentive payment share" means, with respect to a fiscal year—

(A) the incentive base amount for the State for the fiscal year; divided by

(B) the sum of the incentive base amounts for all of the States for the fiscal year.

(4) INCENTIVE BASE AMOUNT.—In paragraph (3), the term "incentive base amount" means, with respect to a State and a fiscal year, the sum of the applicable percentages (determined in accordance with paragraph (6)) multiplied by the corresponding maximum incentive base amounts for the State for the fiscal year, with respect to each of the following measures of State performance for the fiscal year:

(A) The paternity establishment performance level.

(B) The support order performance level.

(C) The current payment performance level.

(D) The arrearage payment performance level.

(E) The cost–effectiveness performance level.

(5) MAXIMUM INCENTIVE BASE AMOUNT.—

432   SOCIAL SECURITY ACT—§ 458(b)(5)(A)

(A) IN GENERAL.—For purposes of paragraph (4), the maximum incentive base amount for a State for a fiscal year is—

(i) with respect to the performance measures described in subparagraphs (A), (B), and (C) of paragraph (4), the State collections base for the fiscal year; and

(ii) with respect to the performance measures described in subparagraphs (D) and (E) of paragraph (4), 75 percent of the State collections base for the fiscal year.

(B) DATA REQUIRED TO BE COMPLETE AND RELIABLE.—Notwithstanding subparagraph (A), the maximum incentive base amount for a State for a fiscal year with respect to a performance measure described in paragraph (4) is zero, unless the Secretary determines, on the basis of an audit performed under section 452(a)(4)(C)(i), that the data which the State submitted pursuant to section 454(15)(B) for the fiscal year and which is used to determine the performance level involved is complete and reliable.

(C) STATE COLLECTIONS BASE.—For purposes of subparagraph (A), the State collections base for a fiscal year is equal to the sum of—

(i) 2 times the sum of—

(I) the total amount of support collected during the fiscal year under the State plan approved under this part in cases in which the support obligation involved is required to be assigned to the State pursuant to part A or E of this title or title XIX; and

(II) the total amount of support collected during the fiscal year under the State plan approved under this part in cases in which the support obligation involved was so assigned but, at the time of collection, is not required to be so assigned; and

(ii) the total amount of support collected during the fiscal year under the State plan approved under this part in all other cases.

(6) DETERMINATION OF APPLICABLE PERCENTAGES BASED ON PERFORMANCE LEVELS.—

(A) PATERNITY ESTABLISHMENT.—

(i) DETERMINATION OF PATERNITY ESTABLISHMENT PERFORMANCE LEVEL.—The paternity establishment performance level for a State for a fiscal year is, at the option of the State, the IV-D paternity establishment percentage determined under section 452(g)(2)(A) or the statewide paternity establishment percentage determined under section 452(g)(2)(B).

(ii) DETERMINATION OF APPLICABLE PERCENTAGE.—The applicable percentage with respect to a State's paternity establishment performance level is as follows:

If the paternity establishment performance level is:		The applicable percentage is:
At least:	But less than:	
80%	....	100

SOCIAL SECURITY ACT—§ 458(b)(6)(A)(ii) 433

If the paternity establishment performance level is:		The applicable percentage is:
At least:	**But less than:**	
79%	80%	98
78%	79%	96
77%	78%	94
76%	77%	92
75%	76%	90
74%	75%	88
73%	74%	86
72%	73%	84
71%	72%	82
70%	71%	80
69%	70%	79
68%	69%	78
67%	68%	77
66%	67%	76
65%	66%	75
64%	65%	74
63%	64%	73
62%	63%	72
61%	62%	71
60%	61%	70
59%	60%	69
58%	59%	68
57%	58%	67
56%	57%	66
55%	56%	65
54%	55%	64
53%	54%	63
52%	53%	62
51%	52%	61
50%	51%	60
0%	50%	0.

Notwithstanding the preceding sentence, if the paternity establishment performance level of a State for a fiscal year is less than 50 percent but exceeds by at least 10 percentage points the paternity establishment perfor-

434 SOCIAL SECURITY ACT—§ 458(b)(6)(B)

mance level of the State for the immediately preceding fiscal year, then the applicable percentage with respect to the State's paternity establishment performance level is 50 percent.

(B) ESTABLISHMENT OF CHILD SUPPORT ORDERS.—

(i) DETERMINATION OF SUPPORT ORDER PERFORMANCE LEVEL.—The support order performance level for a State for a fiscal year is the percentage of the total number of cases under the State plan approved under this part in which there is a support order during the fiscal year.

(ii) DETERMINATION OF APPLICABLE PERCENTAGE.—The applicable percentage with respect to a State's support order performance level is as follows:

If the support order performance level is:		The applicable percentage is:
At least:	But less than:	
80%		100
79%	80%	98
78%	79%	96
77%	78%	94
76%	77%	92
75%	76%	90
74%	75%	88
73%	74%	86
72%	73%	84
71%	72%	82
70%	71%	80
69%	70%	79
68%	69%	78
67%	68%	77
66%	67%	76
65%	66%	75
64%	65%	74
63%	64%	73
62%	63%	72
61%	62%	71
60%	61%	70
59%	60%	69
58%	59%	68
57%	58%	67
56%	57%	66

SOCIAL SECURITY ACT—§ 458(b)(6)(C)(ii)   435

| If the support order performance level is: | | The applicable percentage is: |
At least:	But less than:	
55%	56%	65
54%	55%	64
53%	54%	63
52%	53%	62
51%	52%	61
50%	51%	60
0%	50%	0.

Notwithstanding the preceding sentence, if the support order performance level of a State for a fiscal year is less than 50 percent but exceeds by at least 5 percentage points the support order performance level of the State for the immediately preceding fiscal year, then the applicable percentage with respect to the State's support order performance level is 50 percent.

(C) COLLECTIONS ON CURRENT CHILD SUPPORT DUE.—

(i) DETERMINATION OF CURRENT PAYMENT PERFORMANCE LEVEL.—The current payment performance level for a State for a fiscal year is equal to the total amount of current support collected during the fiscal year under the State plan approved under this part divided by the total amount of current support owed during the fiscal year in all cases under the State plan, expressed as a percentage.

(ii) DETERMINATION OF APPLICABLE PERCENTAGE.—The applicable percentage with respect to a State's current payment performance level is as follows:

| If the support order performance level is: | | The applicable percentage is: |
At least:	But less than:	
80%		100
79%	80%	98
78%	79%	96
77%	78%	94
76%	77%	92
75%	76%	90
74%	75%	88
73%	74%	86
72%	73%	84
71%	72%	82
70%	71%	80

436 SOCIAL SECURITY ACT—§ 458(b)(6)(C)(ii)(cont)

If the support order performance level is:		The applicable percentage is:
At least:	But less than:	
69%	70%	79
68%	69%	78
67%	68%	77
66%	67%	76
65%	66%	75
64%	65%	74
63%	64%	73
62%	63%	72
61%	62%	71
60%	61%	70
59%	60%	69
58%	59%	68
57%	58%	67
56%	57%	66
55%	56%	65
54%	55%	64
53%	54%	63
52%	53%	62
51%	52%	61
50%	51%	60
49%	50%	59
48%	49%	58
47%	48%	57
46%	47%	56
45%	46%	55
44%	45%	54
43%	44%	53
42%	43%	52
41%	42%	51
40%	41%	50
0%	40%	0.

Notwithstanding the preceding sentence, if the current payment performance level of a State for a fiscal year is less than 40 percent but exceeds by at least 5 percentage points the current payment performance level of the

SOCIAL SECURITY ACT—§ 458(b)(6)(D)(ii) 437

State for the immediately preceding fiscal year, then the applicable percentage with respect to the State's current payment performance level is 50 percent.

(D) COLLECTIONS ON CHILD SUPPORT ARREARAGES.—

(i) DETERMINATION OF ARREARAGE PAYMENT PERFORMANCE LEVEL.—The arrearage payment performance level for a State for a fiscal year is equal to the total number of cases under the State plan approved under this part in which payments of past–due child support were received during the fiscal year and part or all of the payments were distributed to the family to whom the past–due child support was owed (or, if all past–due child support owed to the family was, at the time of receipt, subject to an assignment to the State, part or all of the payments were retained by the State) divided by the total number of cases under the State plan in which there is past–due child support, expressed as a percentage.

(ii) DETERMINATION OF APPLICABLE PERCENTAGE.—The applicable percentage with respect to a State's arrearage payment performance level is as follows:

If the support order performance level is:		The applicable percentage is:
At least:	But less than:	
80%		100
79%	80%	98
78%	79%	96
77%	78%	94
76%	77%	92
75%	76%	90
74%	75%	88
73%	74%	86
72%	73%	84
71%	72%	82
70%	71%	80
69%	70%	79
68%	69%	78
67%	68%	77
66%	67%	76
65%	66%	75
64%	65%	74
63%	64%	73
62%	63%	72

438 SOCIAL SECURITY ACT—§ 458(b)(6)(D)(ii)(cont)

If the support order performance level is:		The applicable percentage is:
At least:	**But less than:**	
61%	62%	71
60%	61%	70
59%	60%	69
58%	59%	68
57%	58%	67
56%	57%	66
55%	56%	65
54%	55%	64
53%	54%	63
52%	53%	62
51%	52%	61
50%	51%	60
49%	50%	59
48%	49%	58
47%	48%	57
46%	47%	56
45%	46%	55
44%	45%	54
43%	44%	53
42%	43%	52
41%	42%	51
40%	41%	50
0%	40%	0.

Notwithstanding the preceding sentence, if the arrearage payment performance level of a State for a fiscal year is less than 40 percent but exceeds by at least 5 percentage points the arrearage payment performance level of the State for the immediately preceding fiscal year, then the applicable percentage with respect to the State's arrearage payment performance level is 50 percent.

(E) COST–EFFECTIVENESS.—

(i) DETERMINATION OF COST-EFFECTIVENESS PERFORMANCE LEVEL.—The cost-effectiveness performance level for a State for a fiscal year is equal to the total amount collected during the fiscal year under the State plan approved under this part divided by the total amount expended during the fiscal year under the State plan, expressed as a ratio.

SOCIAL SECURITY ACT—§ 458(f)(2) 439

(ii) DETERMINATION OF APPLICABLE PERCENTAGE.—The applicable percentage with respect to a State's cost-effectiveness performance level is as follows:

| If the cost–effectiveness performance level is: | | The applicable percentage is: |
At least:	But less than:	
5.00		100
4.50	4.99	90
4.00	4.50	80
3.50	4.00	70
3.00	3.50	60
2.50	3.00	50
2.00	2.50	40
0.00	2.00	0

(c) TREATMENT OF INTERSTATE COLLECTIONS.—In computing incentive payments under this section, support which is collected by a State at the request of another State shall be treated as having been collected in full by both States, and any amounts expended by a State in carrying out a special project assisted under section 455(e) shall be excluded.

(d) ADMINISTRATIVE PROVISIONS.—The amounts of the incentive payments to be made to the States under this section for a fiscal year shall be estimated by the Secretary at/or before the beginning of the fiscal year on the basis of the best information available. The Secretary shall make the payments for the fiscal year, on a quarterly basis (with each quarterly payment being made no later than the beginning of the quarter involved), in the amounts so estimated, reduced or increased to the extent of any overpayments or underpayments which the Secretary determines were made under this section to the States involved for prior periods and with respect to which adjustment has not already been made under this subsection. Upon the making of any estimate by the Secretary under the preceding sentence, any appropriations available for payments under this section are deemed obligated.

(e) REGULATIONS.—The Secretary shall prescribe such regulations as may be necessary governing the calculation of incentive payments under this section, including directions for excluding from the calculations certain closed cases and cases over which the States do not have jurisdiction.

(f) REINVESTMENT.—A State to which a payment is made under this section shall expend the full amount of the payment to supplement, and not supplant, other funds used by the State—

(1) to carry out the State plan approved under this part; or

(2) for any activity (including cost-effective contracts with local agencies) approved by the Secretary, whether or not the expenditures for the activity are eligible for reimbursement under this part, which may contribute to improving the effectiveness or efficiency of the State program operated under this part.

440 SOCIAL SECURITY ACT—§ 458(f)(2)(cont)

CONSENT BY THE UNITED STATES TO INCOME WITHHOLDING, GARNISHMENT, AND SIMILAR PROCEEDINGS FOR ENFORCEMENT OF CHILD SUPPORT AND ALIMONY OBLIGATIONS

SEC. 459. [42 U.S.C. 659] (a) CONSENT TO SUPPORT ENFORCEMENT.—Notwithstanding any other provision of law (including section 207 of this Act and section 5301 of title 38, United States Code[154]), effective January 1, 1975, moneys (the entitlement to which is based upon remuneration for employment) due from, or payable by, the United States or the District of Columbia (including any agency, subdivision, or instrumentality thereof) to any individual, including members of the Armed Forces of the United States, shall be subject, in like manner and to the same extent as if the United States or the District of Columbia were a private person, to withholding in accordance with State law enacted pursuant to subsections (a)(1) and (b) of section 466 and regulations of the Secretary under such subsections, and to any other legal process brought, by a State agency administering a program under a State plan approved under this part or by an individual obligee, to enforce the legal obligation of the individual to provide child support or alimony.

(b) CONSENT TO REQUIREMENTS APPLICABLE TO PRIVATE PERSON.—With respect to notice to withhold income pursuant to subsection (a)(1) or (b) of section 466, or any other order or process to enforce support obligations against an individual (if the order or process contains or is accompanied by sufficient data to permit prompt identification of the individual and the moneys involved), each governmental entity specified in subsection (a) shall be subject to the same requirements as would apply if the entity were a private person, except as otherwise provided in this section.

(c) DESIGNATION OF AGENT; RESPONSE TO NOTICE OR PROCESS.—The head of each agency subject to this section shall—

(1) DESIGNATION OF AGENT.—

(A) designate an agent or agents to receive orders and accept service of process in matters relating to child support or alimony; and

(B) annually publish in the Federal Register the designation of the agent or agents, identified by title or position, mailing address, and telephone number.

(2) RESPONSE TO NOTICE OR PROCESS.—If an agent designated pursuant to paragraph (1) of this subsection receives notice pursuant to State procedures in effect pursuant to subsection (a)(1) or (b) of section 466, or is effectively served with any order, process, or interrogatory, with respect to an individual's child support or alimony payment obligations, the agent shall—

(A) as soon as possible (but not later than 15 days) thereafter, send written notice of the notice or service (together with a copy of the notice or service) to the individual at the duty station or last-known home address of the individual;

(B) within 30 days (or such longer period as may be prescribed by applicable State law) after receipt of a notice pur-

---

[154] See Vol. II, 38 U.S.C. 5301.

SOCIAL SECURITY ACT—§ 459(h)   441

suant to such State procedures, comply with all applicable provisions of section 466; and

(C) within 30 days (or such longer period as may be prescribed by applicable State law) after effective service of any other such order, process, or interrogatory, withhold available sums in response to the order or process, or answer the interrogatory.

(d) PRIORITY OF CLAIMS.—If a governmental entity specified in subsection (a) receives notice or is served with process, as provided in this section, concerning amounts owed by an individual for more than 1 person—

(1) support collection under section 466(b) must be given priority over any other process, as provided in section 466(b)(7);

(2) allocation of moneys due or payable to an individual among claimants under section 466(b) shall be governed by section 466(b) and the regulations prescribed under such section; and

(3) such moneys as remain after compliance with paragraphs (1) and (2) shall be available to satisfy any other such processes on a first-come, first-served basis, with any such process being satisfied out of such moneys as remain after the satisfaction of all such processes which have been previously served.

(e) NO REQUIREMENT TO VARY PAY CYCLES.—A governmental entity that is affected by legal process served for the enforcement of an individual's child support or alimony payment obligations shall not be required to vary its normal pay and disbursement cycle in order to comply with the legal process.

(f) RELIEF FROM LIABILITY.—

(1) Neither the United States, nor the government of the District of Columbia, nor any disbursing officer shall be liable with respect to any payment made from moneys due or payable from the United States to any individual pursuant to legal process regular on its face, if the payment is made in accordance with this section and the regulations issued to carry out this section.

(2) No Federal employee whose duties include taking actions necessary to comply with the requirements of subsection (a) with regard to any individual shall be subject under any law to any disciplinary action or civil or criminal liability or penalty for, or on account of, any disclosure of information made by the employee in connection with the carrying out of such actions.

(g) REGULATIONS.—Authority to promulgate regulations for the implementation of this section shall, insofar as this section applies to moneys due from (or payable by)—

(1) the United States (other than the legislative or judicial branches of the Federal Government) or the government of the District of Columbia, be vested in the President (or the designee of the President);

(2) the legislative branch of the Federal Government, be vested jointly in the President pro tempore of the Senate and the Speaker of the House of Representatives (or their designees), and

(3) the judicial branch of the Federal Government, be vested in the Chief Justice of the United States (or the designee of the Chief Justice).

(h) MONEYS SUBJECT TO PROCESS.—

442 SOCIAL SECURITY ACT—§ 459(h)(1)

(1) IN GENERAL.—Subject to paragraph (2), moneys payable to an individual which are considered to be based upon remuneration for employment, for purposes of this section—

(A) consist of—

(i) compensation payable for personal services of the individual, whether the compensation is denominated as wages, salary, commission, bonus, pay, allowances, or otherwise (including severance pay, sick pay, and incentive pay);

(ii) periodic benefits (including a periodic benefit as defined in section 228(h)(3)) or other payments—

(I) under the insurance system established by title II;

(II) under any other system or fund established by the United States which provides for the payment of pensions, retirement or retired pay, annuities, dependents' or survivors' benefits, or similar amounts payable on account of personal services performed by the individual or any other individual;

(III) as compensation for death under any Federal program;

(IV) under any Federal program established to provide "black lung" benefits; or

(V) by the Secretary of Veterans Affairs as compensation for a service-connected disability paid by the Secretary to a former member of the Armed Forces who is in receipt of retired or retainer pay if the former member has waived a portion of the retired or retainer pay in order to receive such compensation;

(iii) worker's compensation benefits paid or payable under Federal or State law;

(iv) benefits paid or payable under the Railroad Retirement System, and

(v) special benefits for certain World War II veterans payabable under title VIII; but

(B) do not include any payment—

(i) by way or reimbursement or otherwise, to defray expenses incurred by the individual in carrying out duties associated with the employment of the individual,

(ii) as allowances for members of the uniformed services payable pursuant to chapter 7 of title 37, United States Code[155], as prescribed by the Secretaries concerned (defined by section 101(5) of such title) as necessary for the efficient performance of duty; or

(iii) of periodic benefits under title 38, United States Code, except as provided in subparagraph (A)(ii)(V).

(2) CERTAIN AMOUNTS EXCLUDED.—In determining the amount of any moneys due from, or payable by, the United States to any individual, there shall be excluded amounts which—

(A) are owed by the individual to the United States;

---

[155] See Vol. II, 37 U.S.C. chapter 7 and §101(5).

SOCIAL SECURITY ACT—§ 459(i)(3)(A)   443

(B) are required by law to be, and are, deducted from the remuneration or other payment involved, including Federal employment taxes, and fines and forfeitures ordered by court-martial;

(C) are properly withheld for Federal, State, or local income tax purposes, if the withholding of the amounts is authorized or required by law and if amounts withheld are not greater than would be the case if the individual claimed all dependents to which he was entitled (the withholding of additional amounts pursuant to section 3402(i) of the Internal Revenue Code of 1986[156] may be permitted only when the individual presents evidence of a tax obligation which supports the additional withholding);

(D) are deducted as health insurance premiums;

(E) are deducted as normal retirement contributions (not including amounts deducted for supplementary coverage); or

(F) are deducted as normal life insurance premiums from salary or other remuneration for employment (not including amounts deducted for supplementary coverage).

(i) DEFINITIONS.—For purposes of this section—

(1) UNITED STATES.—The term "United States" includes any department, agency, or instrumentality of the legislative, judicial, or executive branch of the Federal Government, the United States Postal Service, the Postal Rate Commission[157] , any Federal corporation created by an Act of Congress that is wholly owned by the Federal Government, and the governments of the territories and possessions of the United States.

(2) CHILD SUPPORT.—The term "child support", when used in reference to the legal obligations of an individual to provide such support, means amounts required to be paid under a judgment, decree, or order, whether temporary, final, or subject to modification, issued by a court or an administrative agency of competent jurisdiction, for the support and maintenance of a child, including a child who has attained the age of majority under the law of the issuing State, or a child and the parent with whom the child is living, which provides for monetary support, health care, arrearages or reimbursement, and which may include other related costs and fees, interest and penalties, income withholding, attorney's fees, and other relief.

(3) ALIMONY.—

(A) IN GENERAL.—The term "alimony", when used in reference to the legal obligations of an individual to provide the same, means periodic payments of funds for the support and maintenance of the spouse (or former spouse) of the individual, and (subject to and in accordance with State law) includes separate maintenance, alimony pendente lite, maintenance, and spousal support, and includes attorney's fees, interest, and court costs when and to the extent that the same are expressly made recoverable as such pursuant to a decree,

---

[156] See Vol. II, P.L. 83-591, §3402(i).

[157] P.L. 109-435, §604(f), provided that "Whenever a reference is made in any provision of law (other than this Act or a provision of law amended by this Act), regulation, rule, document, or other record of the United States to the Postal Rate Commission, such reference shall be considered a reference to the Postal Regulatory Commission".

444   SOCIAL SECURITY ACT—§ 459(i)(3)(B)

order, or judgment issued in accordance with applicable State law by a court of competent jurisdiction.

(B) EXCEPTIONS.—Such term does not include—

(i) any child support; or

(ii) any payment or transfer of property or its value by an individual to the spouse or a former spouse of the individual in compliance with any community property settlement, equitable distribution of property, or other division of property between spouses of former spouses.

(4) PRIVATE PERSON.—The term "private person" means a person who does not have sovereign or other special immunity or privilege which causes the person not to be subject to legal process.

(5) LEGAL PROCESS.—The term "legal process" means any writ, order, summons, or other similar process in the nature of garnishment—

(A) which is issued by—

(i) a court or an administrative agency of competent jurisdiction in any State, territory, or possession of the United States;

(ii) a court or an administrative agency of competent jurisdiction in any foreign country with which the United States has entered into an agreement which requires the United States to honor the process; or

(iii) an authorized official pursuant to an order of such a court or an administrative agency of competent jurisdiction or pursuant to State or local law; and

(B) which is directed to, and the purpose of which is to compel, a governmental entity which holds moneys which are otherwise payable to an individual to make a payment from the moneys to another party in order to satisfy a legal obligation of the individual to provide child support or make alimony payments.

INTERNATIONAL SUPPORT ENFORCEMENT

SEC. 459A. [42 U.S.C. 659a] (a) AUTHORITY FOR DECLARATIONS.—

(1) DECLARATION.—The Secretary of State, with the concurrence of the Secretary of Health and Human Services, is authorized to declare any foreign country (or a political subdivision thereof) to be a foreign reciprocating country if the foreign country has established, or undertakes to establish, procedures for the establishment and enforcement of duties of support owed to obligees who are residents of the United States, and such procedures are substantially in conformity with the standards prescribed under subsection (b).

(2) REVOCATION.—A declaration with respect to a foreign country made pursuant to paragraph (1) may be revoked if the Secretaries of State and Health and Human Services determine that—

(A) the procedures established by the foreign country regarding the establishment and enforcement of duties of support have been so changed, or the foreign country's implementation of such procedures is so unsatisfactory, that such procedures do not meet the criteria for such a declaration; or

(B) continued operation of the declaration is not consistent with the purposes of this part.

(3) FORM OF DECLARATION.—A declaration under paragraph (1) may be made in the form of an international agreement, in connection with an international agreement or corresponding foreign declaration, or on a unilateral basis.

(b) STANDARDS FOR FOREIGN SUPPORT ENFORCEMENT PROCEDURES.—

(1) MANDATORY ELEMENTS.—Support enforcement procedures of a foreign country which may be the subject of a declaration pursuant to subsection (a)(1) shall include the following elements:

(A) The foreign country (or political subdivision thereof) has in effect procedures, available to residents of the United States—

(i) for establishment of paternity, and for establishment of orders of support for children and custodial parents; and

(ii) for enforcement of orders to provide support to children and custodial parents, including procedures for collection and appropriate distribution of support payments under such orders.

(B) The procedures described in subparagraph (A), including legal and administrative assistance, are provided to residents of the United States at no cost.

(C) An agency of the foreign country is designated as a Central Authority responsible for—

(i) facilitating support enforcement in cases involving residents of the foreign country and residents of the United States; and

(ii) ensuring compliance with the standards established pursuant to this subsection.

(2) ADDITIONAL ELEMENTS.—The Secretary of Health and Human Services and the Secretary of State, in consultation with the States, may establish such additional standards as may be considered necessary to further the purposes of this section.

(c) DESIGNATION OF UNITED STATES CENTRAL AUTHORITY.—It shall be the responsibility of the Secretary of Health and Human Services to facilitate support enforcement in cases involving residents of the United States and residents of foreign countries that are the subject of a declaration under this section, by activities including—

(1) development of uniform forms and procedures for use in such cases;

(2) notification of foreign reciprocating countries of the State of residence of individuals sought for support enforcement purposes, on the basis of information provided by the Federal Parent Locator Service; and

(3) such other oversight, assistance, and coordination activities as the Secretary may find necessary and appropriate.

(d) EFFECT ON OTHER LAWS.—State may enter into reciprocal arrangements for the establishment and enforcement of support obligations with foreign countries that are not the subject of a declaration pursuant to subsection (a), to the extent consistent with Federal law.

446 SOCIAL SECURITY ACT—§ 459A(d)(cont)

CIVIL ACTIONS TO ENFORCE SUPPORT OBLIGATIONS

Sec. 460. [42 U.S.C. 660] The district courts of the United States shall have jurisdiction, without regard to any amount in controversy, to hear and determine any civil action certified by the Secretary of Health and Human Services under section 452(a)(8) of this Act. A civil action under this section may be brought in any judicial district in which the claim arose, the plaintiff resides, or the defendant resides.

Sec. 461. [Repealed.[158]]

Sec. 462. [Repealed.[159]]

USE OF FEDERAL PARENT LOCATOR SERVICE IN CONNECTION WITH THE ENFORCEMENT OR DETERMINATION OF CHILD CUSTODY AND IN CASES OF PARENTAL KIDNAPING OF A CHILD

Sec. 463. [42 U.S.C. 663] (a) The Secretary shall enter into an agreement with every State under which the services of the Federal Parent Locator Service established under section 453 shall be made available to each State for the purpose of determining the whereabouts of any parent or child when such information is to be used to locate such parent or child for the purpose of—

(1) enforcing any State or Federal law with respect to the unlawful taking or restraint of a child; or

(2) making or enforcing a child custody or visitation determination.

(b) An agreement entered into under subsection (a) shall provide that the State agency described in section 454 will, under procedures prescribed by the Secretary in regulations, receive and transmit to the Secretary requests from authorized persons for information as to (or useful in determining) the whereabouts of any parent or child when such information is to be used to locate such parent or child for the purpose of—

(1) enforcing any State or Federal law with respect to the unlawful taking or restraint of a child; or

(2) making or enforcing a child custody or visitation determination.

(c) Information authorized to be provided by the Secretary under subsection (a), (b), (e), or (f) shall be subject to the same conditions with respect to disclosure as information authorized to be provided under section 453, and a request for information by the Secretary under this section shall be considered to be a request for information under section 453 which is authorized to be provided under such section. Only information as to the most recent address and place of employment of any parent or child shall be provided under this section.

(d) For purposes of this section—

(1) the term "custody or visitation determination" means a judgment, decree, or other order of a court providing for the custody or visitation of a child, and includes permanent and temporary orders, and initial orders and modification;

(2) the term "authorized person" means—

(A) any agent or attorney of any State having an agreement under this section, who has the duty or authority under the

---

[158] P.L. 104-193, §362(b)(1); 110 Stat. 2246.
[159] P.L. 104-193, §362(b)(1); 110 Stat. 2246.

SOCIAL SECURITY ACT—§ 464(a)(2)(A)   447

law of such State to enforce a child custody or visitation determination;

(B) any court having jurisdiction to make or enforce such a child custody or visitation determination, or any agent of such court; and

(C) any agent or attorney of the United States, or of a State having an agreement under this section, who has the duty or authority to investigate, enforce, or bring a prosecution with respect to the unlawful taking or restraint of a child.

(e) The Secretary shall enter into an agreement with the Central Authority designated by the President in accordance with section 7 of the International Child Abduction Remedies Act[160], under which the services of the Federal Parent Locator Service established under section 453 shall be made available to such Central Authority upon its request for the purpose of locating any parent or child on behalf of an applicant to such Central Authority within the meaning of section 3(1) of that Act. The Federal Parent Locator Service shall charge no fees for services requested pursuant to this subsection.

(f) The Secretary shall enter into an agreement with the Attorney General of the United States, under which the services of the Federal Parent Locator Service established under section 453 shall be made available to the Office of Juvenile Justice and Delinquency Prevention upon its request to locate any parent or child on behalf of such Office for the purpose of—

(1) enforcing any State or Federal law with respect to the unlawful taking or restraint of a child, or

(2) making or enforcing a child custody or visitation determination.

The Federal Parent Locator Service shall charge no fees for services requested pursuant to this subsection.

COLLECTION OF PAST-DUE SUPPORT FROM FEDERAL TAX REFUNDS

SEC. 464. [42 U.S.C. 664] (a)(1) Upon receiving notice from a State agency administering a plan approved under this part that a named individual owes past-due support which has been assigned to such State pursuant to section 408(a)(3) or section 471(a)(17), the Secretary of the Treasury shall determine whether any amounts, as refunds of Federal taxes paid, are payable to such individual (regardless of whether such individual filed a tax return as a married or unmarried individual). If the Secretary of the Treasury finds that any such amount is payable, he shall withhold from such refunds an amount equal to the past-due support, shall concurrently send notice to such individual that the withholding has been made (including in or with such notice a notification to any other person who may have filed a joint return with such individual of the steps which such other person may take in order to secure his or her proper share of the refund), and shall pay such amount to the State agency (together with notice of the individual's home address) for distribution in accordance with section 457. This subsection may be executed by the disbursing official of the Department of the Treasury.

(2)(A) Upon receiving notice from a State agency administering a plan approved under this part that a named individual owes past-

---

[160] See Vol. II, P.L. 100-300, §§3(1) and 7.

448 SOCIAL SECURITY ACT—§ 464(a)(2)(A)(cont)

due support[161] (as that term is defined for purposes of this paragraph under subsection (c)) which such State has agreed to collect under section 454(4)(A)(ii), and that the State agency has sent notice to such individual in accordance with paragraph (3)(A), the Secretary of the Treasury shall determine whether any amounts, as refunds of Federal taxes paid, are payable to such individual (regardless of whether such individual filed a tax return as a married or unmarried individual). If the Secretary of the Treasury finds that any such amount is payable, he shall withhold from such refunds an amount equal to such past-due support, and shall concurrently send notice to such individual that the withholding has been made, including in or with such notice a notification to any other person who may have filed a joint return with such individual of the steps which such other person may take in order to secure his or her proper share of the refund. The Secretary of the Treasury shall pay the amount withheld to the State agency, and the State shall pay to the Secretary of the Treasury any fee imposed by the Secretary of the Treasury to cover the costs of the withholding and any required notification. The State agency shall, subject to paragraph (3)(B), distribute such amount to or on behalf of the child to whom the support was owed in accordance with section 457. This subsection may be executed by the Secretary of the Department of the Treasury or his designee.

(B) This paragraph shall apply only with respect to refunds payable under section 6402 of the Internal Revenue Code of 1954[162] after December 31, 1985.

(3)(A) Prior to notifying the Secretary of the Treasury under paragraph (1) or (2) that an individual owes past-due support, the State shall send notice to such individual that a withholding will be made from any refund otherwise payable to such individual. The notice shall also (i) instruct the individual owing the past-due support of the steps which may be taken to contest the State's determination that past-due support is owed or the amount of the past-due support, and (ii) provide information, as may be prescribed by the Secretary of Health and Human Services by regulation in consultation with the Secretary of the Treasury, with respect to procedures to be followed, in the case of a joint return, to protect the share of the refund which may be payable to another person.

(B) If the Secretary of the Treasury determines that an amount should be withheld under paragraph (1) or (2), and that the refund from which it should be withheld is based upon a joint return, the Secretary of the Treasury shall notify the State that the withholding is being made from a refund based upon a joint return, and shall furnish to the State the names and addresses of each taxpayer filing such joint return. In the case of a withholding under paragraph (2), the State may delay distribution of the amount withheld until the State has been notified by the Secretary of the Treasury that the other person filing the joint return has received his or her proper share of the refund, but such delay may not exceed six months.

(C) If the other person filing the joint return with the named individual owing the past-due support takes appropriate action to se-

---

[161] P.L. 109-171, §7301(f)(1)(A), struck out "(as that term is defined for purposes of this paragraph under subsection (c))", effective October 1, 2007.
[162] See Vol. II, P.L. 83-591, §6402.

cure his or her proper share of a refund from which a withholding was made under paragraph (1) or (2), the Secretary of the Treasury shall pay such share to such other person. The Secretary of the Treasury shall deduct the amount of such payment from amounts subsequently payable to the State agency to which the amount originally withheld from such refund was paid.

(D) In any case in which an amount was withheld under paragraph (1) or (2) and paid to a State, and the State subsequently determines that the amount certified as past-due support was in excess of the amount actually owed at the time the amount withheld is to be distributed to or on behalf of the child, the State shall pay the excess amount withheld to the named individual thought to have owed the past-due support (or, in the case of amounts withheld on the basis of a joint return, jointly to the parties filing such return).

(b)(1) The Secretary of the Treasury shall issue regulations, approved by the Secretary of Health and Human Services, prescribing the time or times at which States must submit notices of past-due support, the manner in which such notices must be submitted, and the necessary information that must be contained in or accompany the notices. The regulations shall be consistent with the provisions of subsection (a)(3), shall specify the minimum amount of past-due support to which the offset procedure established by subsection (a) may be applied, and the fee that a State must pay to reimburse the Secretary of the Treasury for the full cost of applying the offset procedure, and shall provide that the Secretary of the Treasury will advise the Secretary of Health and Human Services, not less frequently than annually, of the States which have furnished notices of past-due support under subsection (a), the number of cases in each State with respect to which such notices have been furnished, the amount of support sought to be collected under this subsection by each State, and the amount of such collections actually made in the case of each State. Any fee paid to the Secretary of the Treasury pursuant to this subsection may be used to reimburse appropriations which bore all or part of the cost of applying such procedure.

(2) In the case of withholdings made under subsection (a)(2), the regulations promulgated pursuant to this subsection shall include the following requirements:

(A) The withholding shall apply only in the case where the State determines that the amount of the past-due support which will be owed at the time the withholding is to be made, based upon the pattern of payment of support and other enforcement actions being pursued to collect the past-due support, is equal to or greater than $500. The State may limit the $500 threshold amount to amounts of past-due support accrued since the time that the State first began to enforce the child support order involved under the State plan, and may limit the application of the withholding to past-due support accrued since such time.

(B) The fee which the Secretary of the Treasury may impose to cover the costs of the withholding and notification may not exceed $25 per case submitted.

450   SOCIAL SECURITY ACT—§ 464(b)(2)(B)(cont)

(c) In[163] this part the term "past-due support" means the amount of a delinquency, determined under a court order, or an order of an administrative process established under State law, for support and maintenance of a child (whether or not a minor)[164], or of a child (whether or not a minor)[165] and the parent with whom the child (whether or not a minor)[166] is living.[167]

ALLOTMENTS FROM PAY FOR CHILD AND SPOUSAL SUPPORT OWED BY MEMBERS OF THE UNIFORMED SERVICES ON ACTIVE DUTY

SEC. 465. [42 U.S.C. 665] (a)(1) In any case in which child support payments or child and spousal support payments are owed by a member of one of the uniformed services (as defined in section 101(3) of title 37, United States Code[168]) on active duty, such member shall be required to make allotments from his pay and allowances (under chapter 13 of title 37, United States Code) as payment of such support, when he has failed to make periodic payments under a support order that meets the criteria specified in section 303(b)(1)(A) of the Consumer Credit Protection Act[169] (15 U.S.C. 1673(b)(1)(A)) and the resulting delinquency in such payments is in a total amount equal to the support payable for two months or longer. Failure to make such payments shall be established by notice from an authorized person (as defined in subsection (b)) to the designated official in the appropriate uniformed service. Such notice (which shall in turn be given to the affected member) shall also specify the person to whom the allotment is to be payable. The amount of the allotment shall be the amount necessary to comply with the order (which, if the order so provides, may include arrearages as well as amounts for current support), except that the amount of the allotment, together with any other amounts withheld for support from the wages of the member, as a percentage of his pay from the uniformed service, shall not exceed the limits prescribed in sections 303(b) and (c) of the Consumer Credit Protection Act (15 U.S.C. 1673(b) and (c)). An allotment under this subsection shall be adjusted or discontinued upon notice from the authorized person.

(2) Notwithstanding the preceding provisions of this subsection, no action shall be taken to require an allotment from the pay and allowances of any member of one of the uniformed services under such provisions (A) until such member has had a consultation with a judge advocate of the service involved (as defined in section 801(13) of title 10, United States Code[170]), or with a judge advocate[171] (as defined in section 801(11) of such title)[172] in the case of the Coast Guard, or with a legal officer designated by the Secretary concerned (as defined

---

[163] P.L. 109-171, §7301(f)(1)(B)(i)(I), struck out "(1) Except as provided in paragraph (2), as used in" and substituted "In", effective October 1, 2007.

[164] P.L. 109-171, §7301(f)(1)(B)(i)(II), inserted "(whether or not a minor)", effective October 1, 2007.

[165] P.L. 109-171, §7301(f)(1)(B)(i)(II), inserted "(whether or not a minor)", effective October 1, 2007.

[166] P.L. 109-171, §7301(f)(1)(B)(i)(II), inserted "(whether or not a minor)", effective October 1, 2007.

[167] P.L. 109-171, §7301(f)(1)(B)(ii),struck out paragraphs (2) and (3), effective October 1, 2007. For paragraphs (2) and (3) as they formerly read, see Vol.II, Appendix J, Superseded Provisions, P.L. 109-171.

[168] See Vol. II, 37 U.S.C. 101(3).

[169] See Vol. II, P.L. 90-321, §303(b).

[170] See Vol. II, 10 U.S.C. 801(13).

[171] P.L. 109-241, §218(b)(2), struck out "law specialist" and substituted "judge advocate".

[172] As in original. P.L. 109-241, §218 (a)(1), struck out paragraph (11) of §801 of title 10, United States Code.

SOCIAL SECURITY ACT—§ 466(a)(2)   451

in section 101(5) of title 37, United States Code[173]) in any other case, in person, to discuss the legal and other factors involved with respect to the member's support obligation and his failure to make payments thereon, or (B) until 30 days have elapsed after the notice described in the second sentence of paragraph (1) is given to the affected member in any case where it has not been possible, despite continuing good faith efforts, to arrange such a consultation.

(b) For purposes of this section the term "authorized person" with respect to any member of the uniformed services means—

(1) any agent or attorney of a State having in effect a plan approved under this part who has the duty or authority under such plan to seek to recover any amounts owed by such member as child or child and spousal support (including, when authorized under the State plan, any official of a political subdivision); and

(2) the court which has authority to issue an order against such member for the support and maintenance of a child, or any agent of such court.

(c) The Secretary of Defense, in the case of the Army, Navy, Air Force, and Marine Corps, and the Secretary concerned (as defined in section 101(5) of title 37, United States Code[174]) in the case of each of the other uniformed services, shall each issue regulations applicable to allotments to be made under this section, designating the officials to whom notice of failure to make support payments, or notice to discontinue or adjust an allotment, should be given, prescribing the form and content of the notice and specifying any other rules necessary for such Secretary to implement this section.

REQUIREMENT OF STATUTORILY PRESCRIBED PROCEDURES TO IMPROVE
EFFECTIVENESS OF CHILD SUPPORT ENFORCEMENT

SEC. 466. [42 U.S.C. 666] (a) In order to satisfy section 454(20)(A), each State must have in effect laws requiring the use of the following procedures, consistent with this section and with regulations of the Secretary, to increase the effectiveness of the program which the State administers under this part:

(1)(A) Procedures described in subsection (b) for the withholding from income of amounts payable as support in cases subject to enforcement under the State plan.

(B) Procedures under which the income of a person with a support obligation imposed by a support order issued (or modified) in the State before January 1, 1994, if not otherwise subject to withholding under subsection (b), shall become subject to withholding as provided in subsection (b) if arrearages occur, without the need for a judicial or administrative hearing.

(2) Expedited administrative and judicial procedures (including the procedures specified in subsection (c)) for establishing paternity and for establishing, modifying, and enforcing support obligations. The Secretary may waive the provisions of this paragraph with respect to one or more political subdivisions within the State on the basis of the effectiveness and timeliness of support order issuance and enforcement or paternity establishment

[173] See Vol. II, 37 U.S.C. 101(5).
[174] See Vol. II, 37 U.S.C. 101(5).

452 SOCIAL SECURITY ACT—§ 466(a)(2)(cont)

within the political subdivision (in accordance with the general rule for exemptions under subsection (d)).

(3) Procedures under which the State child support enforcement agency shall request, and the State shall provide, that for the purpose of enforcing a support order under any State plan approved under this part—

(A) any refund of State income tax which would otherwise be payable to a noncustodial parent will be reduced, after notice has been sent to that noncustodial parent of the proposed reduction and the procedures to be followed to contest it (and after full compliance with all procedural due process requirements of the State), by the amount of any overdue support owed by such noncustodial parent;

(B) the amount by which such refund is reduced shall be distributed in accordance with section 457 in the case of overdue support assigned to a State pursuant to section 408(a)(3) or 471(a)(17), or, in any other case, shall be distributed, after deduction of any fees imposed by the State to cover the costs of collection, to the child or parent to whom such support is owed; and

(C) notice of the noncustodial parent's social security account number (or numbers, if he has more than one such number) and home address shall be furnished to the State agency requesting the refund offset, and to the State agency enforcing the order.

(4) LIENS.—Procedures under which—

(A) liens arise by operation of law against real and personal property for amounts of overdue support owed by a noncustodial parent who resides or owns property in the State; and

(B) the State accords full faith and credit to liens described in subparagraph (A) arising in another State, when the State agency, party, or other entity seeking to enforce such a lien complies with the procedural rules relating to recording or serving liens that arise within the State, except that such rules may not require judicial notice or hearing prior to the enforcement of such a lien.

(5) PROCEDURES CONCERNING PATERNITY ESTABLISHMENT.—

(A) ESTABLISHMENT PROCESS AVAILABLE FROM BIRTH UNTIL AGE 18.—

(i) Procedures which permit the establishment of the paternity of a child at any time before the child attains 18 years of age.

(ii) As of August 16, 1984, clause (i) shall also apply to a child for whom paternity has not yet been established or for whom a paternity action was brought but dismissed because a statute of limitations of less than 18 years was then in effect in the State.

(B) PROCEDURES CONCERNING GENETIC TESTING.—

(i) GENETIC TESTING REQUIRED IN CERTAIN CONTESTED CASES.—Procedures under which the State is required, in a contested paternity case (unless otherwise barred by State law) to require the child and all other parties (other than individuals found under section 454(29) to have good cause and other exceptions for refusing to cooperate) to submit to genetic tests upon the request of any such party, if the request is supported by a sworn statement by the party—

(I) alleging paternity, and setting forth facts establishing a reasonable possibility of the requisite sexual contact between the parties; or

(II) denying paternity, and setting forth facts establishing a reasonable possibility of the nonexistence of sexual contact between the parties.

(ii) OTHER REQUIREMENTS.—Procedures which require the State agency, in any case in which the agency orders genetic testing—

(I) to pay costs of such tests, subject to recoupment (if the State so elects) from the alleged father if paternity is established; and

(II) to obtain additional testing in any case if an original test result is contested, upon request and advance payment by the contestant.

(C) VOLUNTARY PATERNITY ACKNOWLEDGMENT.—

(i) SIMPLE CIVIL PROCESS.—Procedures for a simple civil process for voluntarily acknowledging paternity under which the State must provide that, before a mother and a putative father can sign an acknowledgment of paternity, the mother and the putative father must be given notice, orally, or through the use of video or audio equipment, and in writing, of the alternatives to, the legal consequences of, and the rights (including, if 1 parent is a minor, any rights afforded due to minority status) and responsibilities that arise from, signing the acknowledgment.

(ii) HOSPITAL–BASED PROGRAM.—Such procedures must include a hospital–based program for the voluntary acknowledgment of paternity focusing on the period immediately before or after the birth of a child.

(iii) PATERNITY ESTABLISHMENT SERVICES.—

(I) STATE–OFFERED SERVICES.—Such procedures must require the State agency responsible for maintaining birth records to offer voluntary paternity establishment services.

(II) REGULATIONS.—

(aa) SERVICES OFFERED BY HOSPITALS AND BIRTH RECORD AGENCIES.—The Secretary shall prescribe regulations governing voluntary paternity establishment services offered by hospitals and birth record agencies.

(bb) SERVICES OFFERED BY OTHER ENTITIES.—The Secretary shall prescribe regulations specifying the types of other entities that may offer voluntary paternity establishment services, and governing the provision of such services, which shall include a requirement that such an entity must use the same notice provisions used by, use the same materials used by, provide the personnel

454 SOCIAL SECURITY ACT—§ 466(a)(5)(C)(iv)

providing such services with the same training provided by, and evaluate the provision of such services in the same manner as the provision of such services is evaluated by, voluntary paternity establishment programs of hospitals and birth record agencies.

(iv) USE OF PATERNITY ACKNOWLEDGMENT AFFIDAVIT.—Such procedures must require the State to develop and use an affidavit for the voluntary acknowledgment of paternity which includes the minimum requirements of the affidavit specified by the Secretary under section 452(a)(7) for the voluntary acknowledgment of paternity, and to give full faith and credit to such an affidavit signed in any other State according to its procedures.

(D) STATUS OF SIGNED PATERNITY ACKNOWLEDGMENT.—

(i) INCLUSION IN BIRTH RECORDS.—Procedures under which the name of the father shall be included on the record of birth of the child of unmarried parents only if—

(I) the father and mother have signed a voluntary acknowledgment of paternity; or

(II) a court or an administrative agency of competent jurisdiction has issued an adjudication of paternity.

Nothing in this clause shall preclude a State agency from obtaining an admission of paternity from the father for submission in a judicial or administrative proceeding, or prohibit the issuance of an order in a judicial or administrative proceeding which bases a legal finding of paternity on an admission of paternity by the father and any other additional showing required by State law.

(ii) LEGAL FINDING OF PATERNITY.—Procedures under which a signed voluntary acknowledgment of paternity is considered a legal finding of paternity, subject to the right of any signatory to rescind the acknowledgment within the earlier of—

(I) 60 days; or

(II) the date of an administrative or judicial proceeding relating to the child (including a proceeding to establish a support order) in which the signatory is a party.

(iii) CONTEST.—Procedures under which, after the 60–day period referred to in clause (ii), a signed voluntary acknowledgment of paternity may be challenged in court only on the basis of fraud, duress, or material mistake of fact, with the burden of proof upon the challenger, and under which the legal responsibilities (including child support obligations) of any signatory arising from the acknowledgment may not be suspended during the challenge, except for good cause shown.

(E) BAR ON ACKNOWLEDGMENT RATIFICATION PROCEEDINGS.—Procedures under which judicial or administrative proceedings are not required or permitted to ratify an unchallenged acknowledgment of paternity.

SOCIAL SECURITY ACT—§ 466(a)(5)(M)   455

(F) ADMISSIBILITY OF GENETIC TESTING RE-
SULTS.—Procedures—

(i) requiring the admission into evidence, for purposes
of establishing paternity, of the results of any genetic
test that is—

(I) of a type generally acknowledged as reliable by
accreditation bodies designated by the Secretary;
and

(II) performed by a laboratory approved by such
an accreditation body;

(ii) requiring an objection to genetic testing results to
be made in writing not later than a specified number of
days before any hearing at which the results may be introduced into evidence (or, at State option, not later than
a specified number of days after receipt of the results);
and

(iii) making the test results admissible as evidence of
paternity without the need for foundation testimony or
other proof of authenticity or accuracy, unless objection
is made.

(G) PRESUMPTION OF PATERNITY IN CERTAIN
CASES.—Procedures which create a rebuttable or, at the
option of the State, conclusive presumption of paternity upon
genetic testing results indicating a threshold probability
that the alleged father is the father of the child.

(H) DEFAULT ORDERS.—Procedures requiring a default order to be entered in a paternity case upon a showing of service
of process on the defendant and any additional showing required by State law.

(I) NO RIGHT TO JURY TRIAL.—Procedures providing that
the parties to an action to establish paternity are not entitled
to a trial by jury.

(J) TEMPORARY SUPPORT ORDER BASED ON PROBABLE PATER-
NITY IN CONTESTED CASES.—Procedures which require that a
temporary order be issued, upon motion by a party, requiring the provision of child support pending an administrative
or judicial determination of parentage, if there is clear and
convincing evidence of paternity (on the basis of genetic tests
or other evidence).

(K) PROOF OF CERTAIN SUPPORT AND PATERNITY ESTABLISH-
MENT COSTS.—Procedures under which bills for pregnancy,
childbirth, and genetic testing are admissible as evidence
without requiring third–party foundation testimony, and
shall constitute prima facie evidence of amounts incurred
for such services or for testing on behalf of the child.

(L) STANDING OF PUTATIVE FATHERS.—Procedures ensuring that the putative father has a reasonable opportunity to
initiate a paternity action.

(M) FILING OF ACKNOWLEDGMENTS AND ADJUDICATIONS
IN STATE REGISTRY OF BIRTH RECORDS.—Procedures under
which voluntary acknowledgments and adjudications of
paternity by judicial or administrative processes are filed
with the State registry of birth records for comparison with
information in the State case registry.

456 SOCIAL SECURITY ACT—§ 466(a)(6)

(6) Procedures which require that a noncustodial parent give security, post a bond, or give some other guarantee to secure payment of overdue support, after notice has been sent to such noncustodial parent of the proposed action and of the procedures to be followed to contest it (and after full compliance with all procedural due process requirements of the State).

(7) REPORTING ARREARAGES TO CREDIT BUREAUS.—

(A) IN GENERAL.—Procedures (subject to safeguards pursuant to subparagraph (B)) requiring the State to report periodically to consumer reporting agencies (as defined in section 603(f) of the Fair Credit Reporting Act (15 U.S.C. 1681a(f)[175])) the name of any noncustodial parent who is delinquent in the payment of support, and the amount of overdue support owed by such parent.

(B) SAFEGUARDS.—Procedures ensuring that, in carrying out subparagraph (A), information with respect to a noncustodial parent is reported—

(i) only after such parent has been afforded all due process required under State law, including notice and a reasonable opportunity to contest the accuracy of such information; and

(ii) only to an entity that has furnished evidence satisfactory to the State that the entity is a consumer reporting agency (as so defined).

(8)(A) Procedures under which all child support orders not described in subparagraph (B) will include provision for withholding from income, in order to assure that withholding as a means of collecting child support is available if arrearages occur without the necessity of filing application for services under this part.

(B) Procedures under which all child support orders which are initially issued in the State on or after January 1, 1994, and are not being enforced under this part will include the following requirements:

(i) The income of a noncustodial parent shall be subject to withholding, regardless of whether support payments by such parent are in arrears, on the effective date of the order; except that such income shall not be subject to withholding under this clause in any case where (I) one of the parties demonstrates, and the court (or administrative process) finds, that there is good cause not to require immediate income withholding, or (II) a written agreement is reached between both parties which provides for an alternative arrangement.

(ii) The requirements of subsection (b)(1) (which shall apply in the case of each noncustodial parent against whom a support order is or has been issued or modified in the State, without regard to whether the order is being enforced under the State plan).

(iii) The requirements of paragraphs (2), (5), (6), (7), (8), (9), and (10) of subsection (b), where applicable.

---

[175] See Vol. II, P.L. 90-321, Title VI.

SOCIAL SECURITY ACT—§ 466(a)(10)(A)(ii)   457

(iv) Withholding from income of amounts payable as support must be carried out in full compliance with all procedural due process requirements of the State.

(9) Procedures which require that any payment or installment of support under any child support order, whether ordered through the State judicial system or through the expedited processes required by paragraph (2), is (on and after the date it is due)—

(A) a judgment by operation of law, with the full force, effect, and attributes of a judgment of the State, including the ability to be enforced,

(B) entitled as a judgment to full faith and credit in such State and in any other State, and

(C) not subject to retroactive modification by such State or by any other State;

except that such procedures may permit modification with respect to any period during which there is pending a petition for modification, but only from the date that notice of such petition has been given, either directly or through the appropriate agent, to the obligee or (where the obligee is the petitioner) to the obligor.

(10) REVIEW AND ADJUSTMENT OF SUPPORT ORDERS UPON REQUEST.—

(A) 3-YEAR CYCLE.—

(i) IN GENERAL.—Procedures under which every 3 years (or such shorter cycle as the State may determine), upon the request of either parent or[176] if there is an assignment under part A,[177] upon the request of the State agency under the State plan or of either parent, the State shall with respect to a support order being enforced under this part, taking into account the best interests of the child involved—

(I) review and, if appropriate, adjust the order in accordance with the guidelines established pursuant to section 467(a) if the amount of the child support award under the order differs from the amount that would be awarded in accordance with the guidelines;

(II) apply a cost–of–living adjustment to the order in accordance with a formula developed by the State; or

(III) use automated methods (including automated comparisons with wage or State income tax data) to identify orders eligible for review, conduct the review, identify orders eligible for adjustment, and apply the appropriate adjustment to the orders eligible for adjustment under any threshold that may be established by the State.

(ii) OPPORTUNITY TO REQUEST REVIEW OF ADJUST-MENT.—If the State elects to conduct the review under

---

[176] P.L. 109-171, §7302(a)(1), struck out "parent, or," and substituted "parent or", effective October 1, 2007.

[177] P.L. 109-171, §7302(a)(2), struck out "upon the request of the State agency under the State plan or of either parent,", effective October 1, 2007.

458 SOCIAL SECURITY ACT—§ 466(a)(10)(A)(iii)

subclause (II) or (III) of clause (i), procedures which permit either party to contest the adjustment, within 30 days after the date of the notice of the adjustment, by making a request for review and, if appropriate, adjustment of the order in accordance with the child support guidelines established pursuant to section 467(a).

(iii) NO PROOF OF CHANGE IN CIRCUMSTANCES NECESSARY IN 3–YEAR CYCLE REVIEW.—Procedures which provide that any adjustment under clause (i) shall be made without a requirement for proof or showing of a change in circumstances.

(B) PROOF OF SUBSTANTIAL CHANGE IN CIRCUMSTANCES NECESSARY IN REQUEST FOR REVIEW OUTSIDE 3–YEAR CYCLE.—Procedures under which, in the case of a request for a review, and if appropriate, an adjustment outside the 3–year cycle (or such shorter cycle as the State may determine) under clause (i), the State shall review and, if the requesting party demonstrates a substantial change in circumstances, adjust the order in accordance with the guidelines established pursuant to section 467(a).

(C) NOTICE OF RIGHT TO REVIEW.—Procedures which require the State to provide notice not less than once every 3 years to the parents subject to the order informing the parents of their right to request the State to review and, if appropriate, adjust the order pursuant to this paragraph. The notice may be included in the order.

(11) Procedures under which a State must give full faith and credit to a determination of paternity made by any other State, whether established through voluntary acknowledgment or through administrative or judicial processes.

(12) LOCATOR INFORMATION FROM INTERSTATE NETWORKS.—Procedures to ensure that all Federal and State agencies conducting activities under this part have access to any system used by the State to locate an individual for purposes relating to motor vehicles or law enforcement.

(13) RECORDING OF SOCIAL SECURITY NUMBERS IN CERTAIN FAMILY MATTERS.—Procedures requiring that the social security number of—

(A) any applicant for a professional license, driver's license, occupational license, recreational license, or marriage license be recorded on the application;

(B) any individual who is subject to a divorce decree, support order, or paternity determination or acknowledgment be placed in the records relating to the matter; and

(C) any individual who has died be placed in the records relating to the death and be recorded on the death certificate.

For purposes of subparagraph (A), if a State allows the use of a number other than the social security number to be used on the face of the document while the social security number is kept on file at the agency, the State shall so advise any applicants.

(14) HIGH–VOLUME, AUTOMATED ADMINISTRATIVE ENFORCEMENT IN INTERSTATE CASES.—

(A) IN GENERAL.—Procedures under which—

SOCIAL SECURITY ACT—§ 466(a)(15)(A) 459

(i) the State shall use high–volume automated administrative enforcement, to the same extent as used for intrastate cases, in response to a request made by another State to enforce support orders, and shall promptly report the results of such enforcement procedure to the requesting State;

(ii) the State may, by electronic or other means, transmit to another State a request for assistance in enforcing support orders through high–volume, automated administrative enforcement, which request—

(I) shall include such information as will enable the State to which the request is transmitted to compare the information about the cases to the information in the data bases of the State; and

(II) shall constitute a certification by the requesting State—

(aa) of the amount of support under an order the payment of which is in arrears; and

(bb) that the requesting State has complied with all procedural due process requirements applicable to each case;

(iii) if the State provides assistance to another State pursuant to this paragraph with respect to a case, neither State shall consider the case to be transferred to the caseload of such other State (but the assisting State may establish a corresponding case based on such other State's request for assistance); and

(iv) the State shall maintain records of—

(I) the number of such requests for assistance received by the State;

(II) the number of cases for which the State collected support in response to such a request; and

(III) the amount of such collected support.

(B) HIGH-VOLUME AUTOMATED ADMINISTRATIVE ENFORCEMENT.—In this part, the term "high-volume automated administrative enforcement" in interstate cases, means, on request of another State, the identification by a State, through automated data matches with financial institutions and other entities where assets may be found, of assets owned by persons who owe child support in other States, and the seizure of such assets by the State, through levy or other appropriate processes.

(15) PROCEDURES TO ENSURE THAT PERSONS OWING OVERDUE SUPPORT WORK OR HAVE A PLAN FOR PAYMENT OF SUCH SUPPORT.—Procedures under which the State has the authority, in any case in which an individual owes overdue support with respect to a child receiving assistance under a State program funded under part A, to issue an order or to request that a court or an administrative process established pursuant to State law issue an order that requires the individual to—

(A) pay such support in accordance with a plan approved by the court, or, at the option of the State, a plan approved by the State agency administering the State program under this part; or

(B) if the individual is subject to such a plan and is not incapacitated, participate in such work activities (as defined in section 407(d)) as the court, or, at the option of the State, the State agency administering the State program under this part, deems appropriate.

(16) AUTHORITY TO WITHHOLD OR SUSPEND LICENSES.—Procedures under which the State has (and uses in appropriate cases) authority to withhold or suspend, or to restrict the use of driver's licenses, professional and occupational licenses, and recreational and sporting licenses of individuals owing overdue support or failing, after receiving appropriate notice, to comply with subpoenas or warrants relating to paternity or child support proceedings.

(17) FINANCIAL INSTITUTION DATA MATCHES.—

(A) IN GENERAL.—Procedures under which the State agency shall enter into agreements with financial institutions doing business in the State—

(i) to develop and operate, in coordination with such financial institutions, and the Federal Parent Locator Service in the case of financial institutions doing business in two or more States, a data match system, using automated data exchanges to the maximum extent feasible, in which each such financial institution is required to provide for each calendar quarter the name, record address, social security number or other taxpayer identification number, and other identifying information for each noncustodial parent who maintains an account at such institution and who owes past–due support, as identified by the State by name and social security number or other taxpayer identification number; and

(ii) in response to a notice of lien or levy, encumber or surrender, as the case may be, assets held by such institution on behalf of any noncustodial parent who is subject to a child support lien pursuant to paragraph (4).

(B) REASONABLE FEES.—The State agency may pay a reasonable fee to a financial institution for conducting the data match provided for in subparagraph (A)(i), not to exceed the actual costs incurred by such financial institution.

(C) LIABILITY.—A financial institution shall not be liable under any Federal or State law to any person—

(i) for any disclosure of information to the State agency under subparagraph (A)(i);

(ii) for encumbering or surrendering any assets held by such financial institution in response to a notice of lien or levy issued by the State agency as provided for in subparagraph (A)(ii); or

(iii) for any other action taken in good faith to comply with the requirements of subparagraph (A).

(D) DEFINITIONS.—For purposes of this paragraph—

(i) FINANCIAL INSTITUTION.—The term "financial institution" has the meaning given to such term by section 469A(d)(1).

(ii) ACCOUNT.—The term "account" means a demand deposit account, checking or negotiable withdrawal order account, savings account, time deposit account, or money-market mutual fund account.

(18) ENFORCEMENT OF ORDERS AGAINST PATERNAL OR MATERNAL GRANDPARENTS.—Procedures under which, at the State's option, any child support order enforced under this part with respect to a child of minor parents, if the custodial parent of such child is receiving assistance under the State program under part A, shall be enforceable, jointly and severally, against the parents of the noncustodial parent of such child.

(19) HEALTH CARE COVERAGE.—Procedures under which—

(A) effective as provided in section 401(c)(3) of the Child Support Performance and Incentive Act of 1998, all child support orders enforced pursuant to this part shall include a provision for medical support for the child to be provided by either or both parents, and shall be enforced, where appropriate, through the use of the National Medical Support Notice promulgated pursuant to section 401(b) of the Child Support Performance and Incentive Act of 1998 (and referred to in section 609(a)(5)(C) of the Employee Retirement Income Security Act of 1974 in connection with group health plans covered under title I of such Act, in section 401(e) of the Child Support Performance and Incentive Act of 1998 in connection with State or local group health plans, and in section 401(f) of such Act in connection with church group health plans);

(B) unless alternative coverage is allowed for in any order of the court (or other entity issuing the child support order), in any case in which a parent is required under the child support order to provide such health care coverage and the employer of such parent is known to the State agency —

(i) the State agency uses the National Medical Support Notice to transfer notice of the provision for the health care coverage of the child to the employer;

(ii) within 20 business days after the date of the National Medical Support Notice, the employer is required to transfer the Notice, excluding the severable employer withholding notice described in section 401(b)(2)(C) of the Child Support Performance and Incentive Act of 1998, to the appropriate plan providing any such health care coverage for which the child is eligible;

(iii) in any case in which the parent is a newly hired employee entered in the State Directory of New Hires pursuant to section 653a(e) of this title, the State agency provides, where appropriate, the National Medical Support Notice, together with an income withholding notice issued pursuant to subsection (b), within two days after the date of the entry of such employee in such Directory; and

(iv) in any case in which the employment of the parent with any employer who has received a National Medical Support Notice is terminated, such employer is required to notify the State agency of such termination; and

(C) any liability of the obligated parent to such plan for employee contributions which are required under such plan for enrollment of the child is effectively subject to appropriate

462 SOCIAL SECURITY ACT—§ 466(a)(19)(C)(cont)

enforcement, unless the obligated parent contests such enforcement based on a mistake of fact.

all child support orders enforced pursuant to this part shall include a provision for the health care coverage of the child, and in the case in which a noncustodial parent provides such coverage and changes employment, and the new employer provides health care coverage, the State agency shall transfer notice of the provision to the employer, which notice shall operate to enroll the child in the noncustodial parent's health plan, unless the noncustodial parent contests the notice.

Notwithstanding section 454(20)(B), the procedures which are required under paragraphs (3), (4), (6), (7), and (15) need not be used or applied in cases where the State determines (using guidelines which are generally available within the State and which take into account the payment record of the noncustodial parent, the availability of other remedies, and other relevant considerations) that such use or application would not carry out the purposes of this part or would be otherwise inappropriate in the circumstances.

(b) The procedures referred to in subsection (a)(1)(A) (relating to the withholding from income of amounts payable as support) must provide for the following:

(1) In the case of each noncustodial parent against whom a support order is or has been issued or modified in the State, and is being enforced under the State plan, so much of such parent's income must be withheld, in accordance with the succeeding provisions of this subsection, as is necessary to comply with the order and provide for the payment of any fee to the employer which may be required under paragraph (6)(A), up to the maximum amount permitted under section 303(b) of the Consumer Credit Protection Act (15 U.S.C. 1673(b))[178]. If there are arrearages to be collected, amounts withheld to satisfy such arrearages, when added to the amounts withheld to pay current support and provide for the fee, may not exceed the limit permitted under such section 303(b), but the State need not withhold up to the maximum amount permitted under such section in order to satisfy arrearages.

(2) Such withholding must be provided without the necessity of any application therefor in the case of a child (whether or not eligible for assistance under a State program funded under part A) with respect to whom services are already being provided under the State plan under this part, and must be provided in accordance with this subsection on the basis of an application for services under the State plan in the case of any other child in whose behalf a support order has been issued or modified in the State. In either case such withholding must occur without the need for any amendment to the support order involved or for any further action (other than those actions required under this part) by the court or other entity which issued such order.

(3)(A) The income of a noncustodial parent shall be subject to such withholding, regardless of whether support payments by such parent are in arrears, in the case of a support order being enforced under this part that is issued or modified on or after the first day of the 25th month beginning after the date of the enact-

---

[178] See Vol. II, P.L. 90-321, §303(b).

SOCIAL SECURITY ACT—§ 466(b)(6)(A)(i)(I)   463

ment of this paragraph, on the effective date of the order; except that such income shall not be subject to such withholding under this subparagraph in any case where (i) one of the parties demonstrates, and the court (or administrative process) finds, that there is good cause not to require immediate income withholding, or (ii) a written agreement is reached between both parties which provides for an alternative arrangement.

(B) The income of a noncustodial parent shall become subject to such withholding, in the case of income not subject to withholding under subparagraph (A), on the date on which the payments which the noncustodial parent has failed to make under a support order are at least equal to the support payable for one month or, if earlier, and without regard to whether there is an arrearage, the earliest of—

(i) the date as of which the noncustodial parent requests that such withholding begin,

(ii) the date as of which the custodial parent requests that such withholding begin, if the State determines, in accordance with such procedures and standards as it may establish, that the request should be approved, or

(iii) such earlier date as the State may select.

(4)(A) Such withholding must be carried out in full compliance with all procedural due process requirements of the State, and the State must send notice to each noncustodial parent to whom paragraph (1) applies—

(i) that the withholding has commenced; and

(ii) of the procedures to follow if the noncustodial parent desires to contest such withholding on the grounds that the withholding or the amount withheld is improper due to a mistake of fact.

(B) The notice under subparagraph (A) of this paragraph shall include the information provided to the employer under paragraph (6)(A).

(5) Such withholding must be administered by the State through the State disbursement unit established pursuant to section 454B, in accordance with the requirements of section 454B.

(6)(A)(i) The employer of any absent parent to whom paragraph (1) applies, upon being given notice as described in clause (ii), must be required to withhold from such noncustodial parent's income the amount specified by such notice (which may include a fee, established by the State, to be paid to the employer unless waived by such employer) and pay such amount (after deducting and retaining any portion thereof which represents the fee so established) to the State disbursement unit within 7 business days after the date the amount would (but for this subsection) have been paid or credited to the employee, for distribution in accordance with this part. The employer shall withhold funds as directed in the notice, except that when an employer receives an income withholding order issued by another State, the employer shall apply the income withholding law of the State of the obligor's principal place of employment in determining—

(I) the employer's fee for processing an income withholding order;

464 SOCIAL SECURITY ACT—§ 466(b)(6)(A)(i)(II)

(II) the maximum amount permitted to be withheld from the obligor's income;

(III) the time periods within which the employer must implement the income withholding order and forward the child support payment;

(IV) the priorities for withholding and allocating income withheld for multiple child support obligees; and

(V) any withholding terms or conditions not specified in the order.

An employer who complies with an income withholding notice that is regular on its face shall not be subject to civil liability to any individual or agency for conduct in compliance with the notice.

(ii) The notice given to the employer shall be in a standard format prescribed by the Secretary, and contain only such information as may be necessary for the employer to comply with the withholding order.

(iii) As used in this subparagraph, the term "business day" means a day on which State offices are open for regular business.

(B) Methods must be established by the State to simplify the withholding process for employers to the greatest extent possible, including permitting any employer to combine all withheld amounts into a single payment to each appropriate agency or entity (with the portion thereof which is attributable to each individual employee being separately designated).

(C) The employer must be held liable to the State for any amount which such employer fails to withhold from income due an employee following receipt by such employer of proper notice under subparagraph (A), but such employer shall not be required to vary the normal pay and disbursement cycles in order to comply with this paragraph.

(D) Provision must be made for the imposition of a fine against any employer who—

(i) discharges from employment, refuses to employ, or takes disciplinary action against any noncustodial parent subject to income withholding required by this subsection because of the existence of such withholding and the obligations or additional obligations which it imposes upon the employer; or

(ii) fails to withhold support from income or to pay such amounts to the State disbursement unit in accordance with this subsection.

(7) Support collection under this subsection must be given priority over any other legal process under State law against the same income.

(8) For purposes of subsection (a) and this subsection, the term "income" means any periodic form of payment due to an individual, regardless of source, including wages, salaries, commissions, bonuses, worker's compensation, disability, payments pursuant to a pension or retirement program, and interest.

(9) The State must extend its withholding system under this subsection so that such system will include withholding from income derived within such State in cases where the applicable support orders were issued in other States, in order to assure that

child support owed by noncustodial parents in such State or any other State will be collected without regard to the residence of the child for whom the support is payable or of such child's custodial parent.

(10) Provision must be made for terminating withholding.

(11) Procedures under which the agency administering the State plan approved under this part may execute a withholding order without advance notice to the obligor, including issuing the withholding order through electronic means.

(c) EXPEDITED PROCEDURES.—The procedures specified in this subsection are the following:

(1) ADMINISTRATIVE ACTION BY STATE AGENCY.—Procedures which give the State agency the authority to take the following actions relating to establishment of paternity or to establishment, modification, or enforcement of support orders, without the necessity of obtaining an order from any other judicial or administrative tribunal, and to recognize and enforce the authority of State agencies of other States to take the following actions:

(A) GENETIC TESTING.—To order genetic testing for the purpose of paternity establishment as provided in section 466(a)(5).

(B) FINANCIAL OR OTHER INFORMATION.—To subpoena any financial or other information needed to establish, modify, or enforce a support order, and to impose penalties for failure to respond to such a subpoena.

(C) RESPONSE TO STATE AGENCY REQUEST.—To require all entities in the State (including for–profit, nonprofit, and governmental employers) to provide promptly, in response to a request by the State agency of that or any other State administering a program under this part, information on the employment, compensation, and benefits of any individual employed by such entity as an employee or contractor, and to sanction failure to respond to any such request.

(D) ACCESS TO INFORMATION CONTAINED IN CERTAIN RECORDS.—To obtain access, subject to safeguards on privacy and information security, and subject to the nonliability of entities that afford such access under this subparagraph, to information contained in the following records (including automated access, in the case of records maintained in automated data bases):

(i) Records of other State and local government agencies, including—

(I) vital statistics (including records of marriage, birth, and divorce);

(II) State and local tax and revenue records (including information on residence address, employer, income and assets);

(III) records concerning real and titled personal property;

(IV) records of occupational and professional licenses, and records concerning the ownership and control of corporations, partnerships, and other business entities;

(V) employment security records;

(VI) records of agencies administering public assistance programs;

(VII) records of the motor vehicle department; and

(VIII) corrections records.

(ii) Certain records held by private entities with respect to individuals who owe or are owed support (or against or with respect to whom a support obligation is sought), consisting of—

(I) the names and addresses of such individuals and the names and addresses of the employers of such individuals, as appearing in customer records of public utilities and cable television companies, pursuant to an administrative subpoena authorized by subparagraph (B); and

(II) information (including information on assets and liabilities) on such individuals held by financial institutions.

(E) CHANGE IN PAYEE.—In cases in which support is subject to an assignment in order to comply with a requirement imposed pursuant to part A, part E, or section 1912, or to a requirement to pay through the State disbursement unit established pursuant to section 454B, upon providing notice to obligor and obligee, to direct the obligor or other payor to change the payee to the appropriate government entity.

(F) INCOME WITHHOLDING.—To order income withholding in accordance with subsections (a)(1)(A) and (b).

(G) SECURING ASSETS.—In cases in which there is a support arrearage, to secure assets to satisfy any current support obligation and the arrearage by—

(i) intercepting or seizing periodic or lump–sum payments from—

(I) a State or local agency, including unemployment compensation, workers' compensation, and other benefits; and

(II) judgments, settlements, and lotteries;

(ii) attaching and seizing assets of the obligor held in financial institutions;

(iii) attaching public and private retirement funds; and

(iv) imposing liens in accordance with subsection (a)(4) and, in appropriate cases, to force sale of property and distribution of proceeds.

(H) INCREASE MONTHLY PAYMENTS.—For the purpose of securing overdue support, to increase the amount of monthly support payments to include amounts for arrearages, subject to such conditions or limitations as the State may provide.

Such procedures shall be subject to due process safeguards, including (as appropriate) requirements for notice, opportunity to contest the action, and opportunity for an appeal on the record to an independent administrative or judicial tribunal.

(2) SUBSTANTIVE AND PROCEDURAL RULES.—The expedited procedures required under subsection (a)(2) shall include the following rules and authority, applicable with respect to all proceedings

to establish paternity or to establish, modify, or enforce support orders:

    (A) LOCATOR INFORMATION; PRESUMPTIONS CONCERNING NOTICE.—Procedures under which—

        (i) each party to any paternity or child support proceeding is required (subject to privacy safeguards) to file with the State case registry upon entry of an order, and to update as appropriate, information on location and identity of the party, including social security number, residential and mailing addresses, telephone number, driver's license number, and name, address, and telephone number of employer; and

        (ii) in any subsequent child support enforcement action between the parties, upon sufficient showing that diligent effort has been made to ascertain the location of such a party, the court or administrative agency of competent jurisdiction shall may deem State due process requirements for notice and service of process to be met with respect to the party, upon delivery of written notice to the most recent residential or employer address filed with the State case registry pursuant to clause (i).

    (B) STATEWIDE JURISDICTION.—Procedures under which—

        (i) the State agency and any administrative or judicial tribunal with authority to hear child support and paternity cases exerts statewide jurisdiction over the parties; and

        (ii) in a State in which orders are issued by courts or administrative tribunals, a case may be transferred between local jurisdictions in the State without need for any additional filing by the petitioner, or service of process upon the respondent, to retain jurisdiction over the parties.

    (3) COORDINATION WITH ERISA.—Notwithstanding subsection (d) of section 514 of the Employee Retirement Income Security Act of 1974[179] (relating to effect on other laws), nothing in this subsection shall be construed to alter, amend, modify, invalidate, impair, or supersede subsections (a), (b), and (c) of such section 514 as it applies with respect to any procedure referred to in paragraph (1) and any expedited procedure referred to in paragraph (2), except to the extent that such procedure would be consistent with the requirements of section 206(d)(3) of such Act (relating to qualified domestic relations orders) or the requirements of section 609(a) of such Act (relating to qualified medical child support orders) if the reference in such section 206(d)(3) to a domestic relations order and the reference in such section 609(a) to a medical child support order were a reference to a support order referred to in paragraphs (1) and (2) relating to the same matters, respectively.

    (d) If a State demonstrates to the satisfaction of the Secretary, through the presentation to the Secretary of such data pertaining to caseloads, processing times, administrative costs, and average support collections, and such other data or estimates as the Secretary

---

[179] See Vol. II, P.L. 93-406, §514.

468 SOCIAL SECURITY ACT—§ 466(d)(cont)

may specify, that the enactment of any law or the use of any procedure or procedures required by or pursuant to this section will not increase the effectiveness and efficiency of the State child support enforcement program, the Secretary may exempt the State, subject to the Secretary's continuing review and to termination of the exemption should circumstances change, from the requirement to enact the law or use the procedure or procedures involved.

(e) For purposes of this section, the term "overdue support" means the amount of a delinquency pursuant to an obligation determined under a court order, or an order of an administrative process established under State law, for support and maintenance of a minor child which is owed to or on behalf of such child, or for support and maintenance of the noncustodial parent's spouse (or former spouse) with whom the child is living if and to the extent that spousal support (with respect to such spouse or former spouse) would be included for section 454(4). At the option of the State, overdue support may include amounts which otherwise meet the definition in the first sentence of this subsection but which are owed to or on behalf of a child who is not a minor child. The option to include support owed to children who are not minors shall apply independently to each procedure specified under this section.

(f) UNIFORM INTERSTATE FAMILY SUPPORT ACT.—In order to satisfy section 454(20)(A), on and after January 1, 1998, each State must have in effect the Uniform Interstate Family Support Act, as approved by the American Bar Association on February 9, 1993, and as in effect on August 22, 1996, including any amendments officially adopted as of such date by the National Conference of Commissioners on Uniform State Laws.

(g) LAWS VOIDING FRAUDULENT TRANSFERS.—In order to satisfy section 454(20)(A), each State must have in effect—

(1)(A) the Uniform Fraudulent Conveyance Act of 1981;

(B) the Uniform Fraudulent Transfer Act of 1984; or

(C) another law, specifying indicia of fraud which create a prima facie case that a debtor transferred income or property to avoid payment to a child support creditor, which the Secretary finds affords comparable rights to child support creditors; and

(2) procedures under which, in any case in which the State knows of a transfer by a child support debtor with respect to which such a prima facie case is established, the State must—

(A) seek to void such transfer; or

(B) obtain a settlement in the best interests of the child support creditor.

STATE GUIDELINES FOR CHILD SUPPORT AWARDS

SEC. 467. [42 U.S.C. 667] (a) Each State, as a condition for having its State plan approved under this part, must establish guidelines for child support award amounts within the State. The guidelines may be established by law or by judicial or administrative action, and shall be reviewed at least once every 4 years to ensure that their application results in the determination of appropriate child support award amounts.

(b)(1) The guidelines established pursuant to subsection (a) shall be made available to all judges and other officials who have the power to determine child support awards within such State.

SOCIAL SECURITY ACT—§ 469A(b)

(2) There shall be a rebuttable presumption, in any judicial or administrative proceeding for the award of child support, that the amount of the award which would result from the application of such guidelines is the correct amount of child support to be awarded. A written finding or specific finding on the record that the application of the guidelines would be unjust or inappropriate in a particular case, as determined under criteria established by the State, shall be sufficient to rebut the presumption in that case.

(c) The Secretary shall furnish technical assistance to the States for establishing the guidelines, and each State shall furnish the Secretary with copies of its guidelines.

ENCOURAGEMENT OF STATES TO ADOPT SIMPLE CIVIL PROCESS FOR VOLUNTARILY ACKNOWLEDGING PATERNITY AND A CIVIL PROCEDURE FOR ESTABLISHING PATERNITY IN CONTESTED CASES

SEC. 468. [42 U.S.C. 668] In the administration of the child support enforcement program under this part, each State is encouraged to establish and implement a civil procedure for establishing paternity in contested cases.

COLLECTION AND REPORTING OF CHILD SUPPORT ENFORCEMENT DATA

SEC. 469. [42 U.S.C. 669] (a) IN GENERAL.—With respect to each type of service described in subsection (b), the Secretary shall collect and maintain up-to-date statistics, by State, and on a fiscal year basis, on—

(1) the number of cases in the caseload of the State agency administering the plan approved under this part in which the service is needed; and

(2) the number of such cases in which the service has actually been provided.

(b) TYPES OF SERVICES.—The statistics required by subsection (a) shall be separately stated with respect to paternity establishment services and child support obligation establishment services.

(c) TYPES OF SERVICE RECIPIENTS.—The statistics required by subsection (a) shall be separately stated with respect to—

(1) recipients of assistance under a State program funded under part A or of payments or services under a State plan approved under part E; and

(2) individuals who are not such recipients.

(d) For purposes of subsection (a)(2), a service has actually been provided when the task described by the service has been accomplished.

NONLIABILITY FOR FINANCIAL INSTITUTIONS PROVIDING FINANCIAL RECORDS TO STATE CHILD SUPPORT ENFORCEMENT AGENCIES IN CHILD SUPPORT CASES

SEC. 469A. [42 U.S.C. 669a] (a) IN GENERAL.—Notwithstanding any other provision of Federal or State law, a financial institution shall not be liable under any Federal or State law to any person for disclosing any financial record of an individual to a State child support enforcement agency attempting to establish, modify, or enforce a child support obligation of such individual, or for disclosing any such record to the Federal Parent Locator Service pursuant to section 466(a)(17)(A).

(b) PROHIBITION OF DISCLOSURE OF FINANCIAL RECORD OBTAINED BY STATE CHILD SUPPORT ENFORCEMENT AGENCY.—A State child sup-

470 SOCIAL SECURITY ACT—§ 469A(b)(cont)

port enforcement agency which obtains a financial record of an individual from a financial institution pursuant to subsection (a) may disclose such financial record only for the purpose of, and to the extent necessary in, establishing, modifying, or enforcing a child support obligation of such individual.

(c) CIVIL DAMAGES FOR UNAUTHORIZED DISCLOSURE.—

(1) DISCLOSURE BY STATE OFFICER OR EMPLOYEE.—If any person knowingly, or by reason of negligence, discloses a financial record of an individual in violation of subsection (b), such individual may bring a civil action for damages against such person in a district court of the United States.

(2) NO LIABILITY FOR GOOD FAITH BUT ERRONEOUS INTERPRETATION.—No liability shall arise under this subsection with respect to any disclosure which results from a good faith, but erroneous, interpretation of subsection (b).

(3) DAMAGES.—In any action brought under paragraph (1), upon a finding of liability on the part of the defendant, the defendant shall be liable to the plaintiff in an amount equal to the sum of—

(A) the greater of—

(i) $1,000 for each act of unauthorized disclosure of a financial record with respect to which such defendant is found liable; or

(ii) the sum of—

(I) the actual damages sustained by the plaintiff as a result of such unauthorized disclosure; plus

(II) in the case of a willful disclosure or a disclosure which is the result of gross negligence, punitive damages; plus

(B) the costs (including attorney's fees) of the action.

(d) DEFINITIONS.—For purposes of this section—

(1) FINANCIAL INSTITUTION.—The term "financial institution" means—

(A) a depository institution, as defined in section 3(c) of the Federal Deposit Insurance Act (12 U.S.C. 1813(c));

(B) an institution-affiliated party, as defined in section 3(u) of such Act (12 U.S.C. 1813(u));

(C) any Federal credit union or State credit union, as defined in section 101 of the Federal Credit Union Act (12 U.S.C. 1752), including an institution-affiliated party of such a credit union, as defined in section 206(r) of such Act (12 U.S.C. 1786(r)); and

(D) any benefit association, insurance company, safe deposit company, money-market mutual fund, or similar entity authorized to do business in the State.

(2) FINANCIAL RECORD.—The term "financial record" has the meaning given such term in section 1101 of the Right to Financial Privacy Act of 1978[180] (12 U.S.C. 3401).

GRANTS TO STATES FOR ACCESS AND VISITATION PROGRAMS

SEC. 469B. [42 U.S.C. 669b] (a) IN GENERAL.—The Administration for Children and Families shall make grants under this section

---

[180] See Vol. II, P.L. 95-630, §1101.

SOCIAL SECURITY ACT—§ 470 471

to enable States to establish and administer programs to support and facilitate noncustodial parents' access to and visitation of their children, by means of activities including mediation (both voluntary and mandatory), counseling, education, development of parenting plans, visitation enforcement (including monitoring, supervision and neutral dropoff and pickup), and development of guidelines for visitation and alternative custody arrangements.

(b) AMOUNT OF GRANT.—The amount of the grant to be made to a State under this section for a fiscal year shall be an amount equal to the lesser of—

(1) 90 percent of State expenditures during the fiscal year for activities described in subsection (a); or

(2) the allotment of the State under subsection (c) for the fiscal year.

(c) ALLOTMENTS TO STATES.—

(1) IN GENERAL.—The allotment of a State for a fiscal year is the amount that bears the same ratio to $10,000,000 for grants under this section for the fiscal year as the number of children in the State living with only 1 biological parent bears to the total number of such children in all States.

(2) MINIMUM ALLOTMENT.—The Administration for Children and Families shall adjust allotments to States under paragraph (1) as necessary to ensure that no State is allotted less than—

(A) $50,000 for fiscal year 1997 or 1998; or

(B) $100,000 for any succeeding fiscal year.

(d) NO SUPPLANTATION OF STATE EXPENDITURES FOR SIMILAR ACTIVITIES.—A State to which a grant is made under this section may not use the grant to supplant expenditures by the State for activities specified in subsection (a), but shall use the grant to supplement such expenditures at a level at least equal to the level of such expenditures for fiscal year 1995.

(e) STATE ADMINISTRATION.—Each State to which a grant is made under this section—

(1) may administer State programs funded with the grant directly or through grants to or contracts with courts, local public agencies, or nonprofit private entities;

(2) shall not be required to operate such programs on a statewide basis; and

(3) shall monitor, evaluate, and report on such programs in accordance with regulations prescribed by the Secretary.

Part E—Federal Payments for Foster Care and Adoption Assistance[181]

PURPOSE: APPROPRIATION

SEC. 470. [42 U.S.C. 670] For the purpose of enabling each State to provide, in appropriate cases, foster care and transitional independent living programs for children who otherwise would have been eligible for assistance under the State's plan approved under part A (as such plan was in effect on June 1, 1995) and adoption assistance for

---

[181] See Vol. II, P.L. 104-193, §403, with respect to five-year limited eligibility of qualified aliens for Federal means-tested public benefit.

472 SOCIAL SECURITY ACT—§ 470(cont)

children with special needs, there are authorized to be appropriated for each fiscal year (commencing with the fiscal year which begins October 1, 1980) such sums as may be necessary to carry out the provisions of this part. The sums made available under this section shall be used for making payments to States which have submitted, and had approved by the Secretary, State plans under this part.

STATE PLAN FOR FOSTER CARE AND ADOPTION ASSISTANCE[182]

SEC. 471. [42 U.S.C. 671] (a) In order for a State to be eligible for payments under this part, it shall have a plan approved by the Secretary which—

(1) provides for foster care maintenance payments in accordance with section 472 and for adoption assistance in accordance with section 473;

(2) provides that the State agency responsible for administering the program authorized by subpart 1 of part B of this title shall administer, or supervise the administration of, the program authorized by this part;

(3) provides that the plan shall be in effect in all political subdivisions of the State, and, if administered by them, be mandatory upon them;

(4) provides that the State shall assure that the programs at the local level assisted under this part will be coordinated with the programs at the State or local level assisted under parts A and B of this title, under title XX of this Act, and under any other appropriate provision of Federal law;

(5) provides that the State will, in the administration of its programs under this part, use such methods relating to the establishment and maintenance of personnel standards on a merit basis as are found by the Secretary to be necessary for the proper and efficient operation of the programs, except that the Secretary shall exercise no authority with respect to the selection, tenure of office, or compensation of any individual employed in accordance with such methods;

(6) provides that the State agency referred to in paragraph (2) (hereinafter in this part referred to as the "State agency") will make such reports, in such form and containing such information as the Secretary may from time to time require, and comply with such provisions as the Secretary may from time to time find necessary to assure the correctness and verification of such reports;

(7) provides that the State agency will monitor and conduct periodic evaluations of activities carried out under this part;

(8) subject to subsection (c), provides safeguards which restrict the use of or disclosure of information concerning individuals assisted under the State plan to purposes directly connected with (A) the administration of the plan of the State approved under this part, the plan or program of the State under part A, B, or D of this title or under title I, V, X, XIV, XVI (as in effect in Puerto Rico, Guam, and the Virgin Islands), XIX, or XX, or the supplemental security income program established by title XVI, (B) any investigation, prosecution, or criminal or civil proceeding, con-

---

[182] See Vol. II, P.L. 110-351, §503, with respect to prohibition of Federal funding to unlawfully present individuals.

SOCIAL SECURITY ACT—§ 471(a)(12)

ducted in connection with the administration of any such plan or program, (C) the administration of any other Federal or federally assisted program which provides assistance, in cash or in kind, or services, directly to individuals on the basis of need, (D) any audit or similar activity conducted in connection with the administration of any such plan or program by any governmental agency which is authorized by law to conduct such audit or activity, and (E) reporting and providing information pursuant to paragraph (9) to appropriate authorities with respect to known or suspected child abuse or neglect; and the safeguards so provided shall prohibit disclosure, to any committee or legislative body (other than an agency referred to in clause (D) with respect to an activity referred to in such clause), of any information which identifies by name or address any such applicant or recipient; except that nothing contained herein shall preclude a State from providing standards which restrict disclosures to purposes more limited than those specified herein, or which, in the case of adoptions, prevent disclosure entirely;

(9) provides that the State agency will—

(A) report to an appropriate agency or official, known or suspected instances of physical or mental injury, sexual abuse or exploitation, or negligent treatment or maltreatment of a child receiving aid under part B or this part under circumstances which indicate that the child's health or welfare is threatened thereby; and

(B) provide such information with respect to a situation described in subparagraph (A) as the State agency may have;

(10)[183] provides for the establishment or designation of a State authority or authorities which shall be responsible for establishing and maintaining standards for foster family homes and child care institutions which are reasonably in accord with recommended standards of national organizations concerned with standards for such institutions or homes, including standards related to admission policies, safety, sanitation, and protection of civil rights, provides[184] that the standards so established shall be applied by the State to any foster family home or child care institution receiving funds under this part or part B of this title, and provides that a waiver of any such standard may be made only on a case-by-case basis for non-safety standards (as determined by the State) in relative foster family homes for specific children in care[185];

(11) provides for periodic review of the standards referred to in the preceding paragraph and amounts paid as foster care maintenance payments and adoption assistance to assure their continuing appropriateness;

(12) provides for granting an opportunity for a fair hearing before the State agency to any individual whose claim for benefits

---

[183] See Vol. II, P.L. 110-351, §104(b), with respect to a report on licensing standards for relatives.

[184] P.L. 110-351, §104(a)(1), struck out "and provides" and substituted "provides".

[185] P.L. 110-351, §104(a)(2), inserted ", and provides that a waiver of any such standard may be made only on a case-by-case basis for non-safety standards (as determined by the State) in relative foster family homes for specific children in care". For the effective date, see Vol. II, P.L. 110-351, §601.

available pursuant to this part is denied or is not acted upon with reasonable promptness;

(13) provides that the State shall arrange for a periodic and independently conducted audit of the programs assisted under this part and part B of this title, which shall be conducted no less frequently than once every three years;

(14) provides (A) specific goals (which shall be established by State law on or before October 1, 1982) for each fiscal year (commencing with the fiscal year which begins on October 1, 1983) as to the maximum number of children (in absolute numbers or as a percentage of all children in foster care with respect to whom assistance under the plan is provided during such year) who, at any time during such year, will remain in foster care after having been in such care for a period in excess of twenty-four months, and (B) a description of the steps which will be taken by the State to achieve such goals;

(15) provides that—

(A) in determining reasonable efforts to be made with respect to a child, as described in this paragraph, and in making such reasonable efforts, the child's health and safety shall be the paramount concern;

(B) except as provided in subparagraph (D), reasonable efforts shall be made to preserve and reunify families—

(i) prior to the placement of a child in foster care, to prevent or eliminate the need for removing the child from the child's home; and

(ii) to make it possible for a child to safely return to the child's home;

(C) if continuation of reasonable efforts of the type described in subparagraph (B) is determined to be inconsistent with the permanency plan for the child, reasonable efforts shall be made to place the child in a timely manner in accordance with the permanency plan (including, if appropriate, through an interstate placement) and to complete whatever steps are necessary to finalize the permanent placement of the child;

(D) reasonable efforts of the type described in subparagraph (B) shall not be required to be made with respect to a parent of a child if a court of competent jurisdiction has determined that—

(i) the parent has subjected the child to aggravated circumstances (as defined in State law, which definition may include but need not be limited to abandonment, torture, chronic abuse, and sexual abuse);

(ii) the parent has—

(I) committed murder (which would have been an offense under section 1111(a) of title 18, United States Code[186], if the offense had occurred in the special maritime or territorial jurisdiction of the United States) of another child of the parent;

(II) committed voluntary manslaughter (which would have been an offense under section 1112(a)

---

[186] See Vol. II, 18 U.S.C. 1111(a).

SOCIAL SECURITY ACT—§ 471(a)(19)   475

of title 18, United States Code[187], if the offense
had occurred in the special maritime or territorial
jurisdiction of the United States) of another child
of the parent;

(III) aided or abetted, attempted, conspired,
or solicited to commit such a murder or such a
voluntary manslaughter; or

(IV) committed a felony assault that results in
serious bodily injury to the child or another child of
the parent; or

(iii) the parental rights of the parent to a sibling have
been terminated involuntarily;

(E) if reasonable efforts of the type described in subparagraph (B) are not made with respect to a child as a result of
a determination made by a court of competent jurisdiction in
accordance with subparagraph (D)—

(i) a permanency hearing (as described in section
475(5)(C)), which considers in-State and out-of-State
permanent placement options for the child, shall be held
for the child within 30 days after the determination; and

(ii) reasonable efforts shall be made to place the child
in a timely manner in accordance with the permanency
plan, and to complete whatever steps are necessary to
finalize the permanent placement of the child; and

(F) reasonable efforts to place a child for adoption or with
a legal guardian, including identifying appropriate in-State
and out-of-State placements may be made concurrently with
reasonable efforts of the type described in subparagraph (B);

(16) provides for the development of a case plan (as defined in
section 475(1)) for each child receiving foster care maintenance
payments under the State plan and provides for a case review system which meets the requirements described in section 475(5)(B)
with respect to each such child;

(17) provides that, where appropriate, all steps will be taken,
including cooperative efforts with the State agencies administering the program funded under part A and plan approved under
part D, to secure an assignment to the State of any rights to support on behalf of each child receiving foster care maintenance payments under this part;

(18) not later than January 1, 1997, provides that neither the
State nor any other entity in the State that receives funds from
the Federal Government and is involved in adoption or foster care
placements may—

(A) deny to any person the opportunity to become an adoptive or a foster parent, on the basis of the race, color, or national origin of the person, or of the child, involved; or

(B) delay or deny the placement of a child for adoption or
into foster care, on the basis of the race, color, or national
origin of the adoptive or foster parent, or the child, involved;

(19) provides that the State shall consider giving preference to
an adult relative over a non-related caregiver when determining

---

[187] See Vol. II, 18 U.S.C. 1112(a).

476   SOCIAL SECURITY ACT—§ 471(a)(19)(cont)

a placement for a child, provided that the relative caregiver meets all relevant State child protection standards;

(20)(A) unless an election provided for in subparagraph (B) is made with respect to the State,[188] provides procedures for criminal records checks, including fingerprint-based checks of national crime information databases (as defined in section 534(e)(3)(A) of title 28, United States Code[189]), for any prospective foster or adoptive parent before the foster or adoptive parent may be finally approved for placement of a child regardless of whether foster care maintenance payments or adoption assistance payments are to be made on behalf of the child under the State plan under this part, including procedures requiring that—

(i) in any case involving a child on whose behalf such payments are to be made in which a record check reveals a felony conviction for child abuse or neglect, for spousal abuse, for a crime against children (including child pornography), or for a crime involving violence, including rape, sexual assault, or homicide, but not including other physical assault or battery, if a State finds that a court of competent jurisdiction has determined that the felony was committed at any time, such final approval shall not be granted; and

(ii) in any case involving a child on whose behalf such payments are to be made in which a record check reveals a felony conviction for physical assault, battery, or a drug-related offense, if a State finds that a court of competent jurisdiction has determined that the felony was committed within the past 5 years, such final approval shall not be granted; and

(B)[190] subparagraph (A) shall not apply to a State plan if, on or before September 30, 2005, the Governor of the State has notified the Secretary in writing that the State has elected to make subparagraph (A) inapplicable to the State, or if, on or before such date, the State legislature, by law, has elected to make subparagraph (A) inapplicable to the State;

(C)[191] provides that the State shall—

(i) check any child abuse and neglect registry maintained by the State for information on any prospective foster or adoptive parent and on any other adult living in the home of such a prospective parent, and request any other State in which any such prospective parent or other adult has resided in the preceding 5 years, to enable the State to check any

---

[188] P.L. 109-248, §152(b)(1), strikes out "unless an election provided for in subparagraph (B) is made with respect to the State,", effective October 1, 2008, as provided in §152(c)(2). See Vol. II, P.L. 109-248, §152(c)(3), which allows for a delay if state legislation is required.

[189] See Vol. II, 28 U.S.C. 534 (e)(3)(A).

[190] P.L. 109-248, §152(b)(2), struck out subparagraph (B) and provides for the redesignation of subparagraph (C), as added by P.L. 109-248, §152(a)(1)(B), as subparagraph (B), effective October 1, 2008, as provided in §152(c)(2). See Vol. II, P.L. 109-248, §152(c)(3), which allows for a delay if state legislation is required.

[191] P.L. 109-248, §152(a)(1)(B) , added this subparagraph (C) and P.L. 109-248, §152(b)(2), provides for the redesignation of this subparagraph (C) as subparagraph (B), effective October 1, 2008, as provided in §152(c)(2). See Vol. II, P.L. 109-248, §152(c)(3), which allows for a delay if state legislation is required. P.L. 110-351, §101(c)(2)(B)(i)(II), redesignates subparagraph (D), as added by P.L. 110-351, §101(c)(2)(A)(ii), as subparagraph (C); §101(c)(2)(B)(ii)), provides that the redesignation made by §101(c)(2)(B)(i)(II) shall take effect immediately after the amendments made by §152 of P.L. 109-248 take effect.

See Vol. II, P.L. 109-248, §152(c), with respect to the effective date, which allows for a delay if state legislation is required.

SOCIAL SECURITY ACT—§ 471(a)(21)(C)   477

child abuse and neglect registry maintained by such other State for such information, before the prospective foster or adoptive parent may be finally approved for placement of a child, regardless of whether foster care maintenance payments or adoption assistance payments are to be made on behalf of the child under the State plan under this part;

(ii) comply with any request described in clause (i) that is received from another State; and

(iii) have in place safeguards to prevent the unauthorized disclosure of information in any child abuse and neglect registry maintained by the State, and to prevent any such information obtained pursuant to this subparagraph from being used for a purpose other than the conducting of background checks in foster or adoptive placement cases; and[192]

(D)[193] provides procedures for criminal records checks, including fingerprint-based checks of national crime information databases (as defined in section 534(e)(3)(A) of title 28, United States Code), on any relative guardian, and for checks described in subparagraph (C)[194] of this paragraph on any relative guardian and any other adult living in the home of any relative guardian, before the relative guardian may receive kinship guardianship assistance payments on behalf of the child under the State plan under this part;

(21) provides for health insurance coverage (including, at State option, through the program under the State plan approved under title XIX) for any child who has been determined to be a child with special needs, for whom there is in effect an adoption assistance agreement (other than an agreement under this part) between the State and an adoptive parent or parents, and who the State has determined cannot be placed with an adoptive parent or parents without medical assistance because such child has special needs for medical, mental health, or rehabilitative care, and that with respect to the provision of such health insurance coverage—

(A) such coverage may be provided through 1 or more State medical assistance programs;

(B) the State, in providing such coverage, shall ensure that the medical benefits, including mental health benefits, provided are of the same type and kind as those that would be provided for children by the State under title XIX;

(C) in the event that the State provides such coverage through a State medical assistance program other than the program under title XIX, and the State exceeds its funding for services under such other program, any such

---

[192] P.L. 110-351, §101(c)(2)(A)(i), added "and".

[193] P.L. 110-351, §101(c)(2)(A)(ii), added subparagraph (D). For the effective date, see Vol. II, P.L. 110-351, §601.

P.L. 110-351, §101(c)(2)(B)(i)(II), redesignates this subparagraph (D) as subparagraph (C); §101(c)(2)(B)(ii)), provides that the redesignation made by §101(c)(2)(B)(i)(II) shall take effect immediately after the amendments made by §152 of P.L. 109-248 take effect.

See Vol. II, P.L. 109-248, §152(c), with respect to the effective date, which allows for a delay if state legislation is required.

[194] P.L. 110-351, §101(c)(2)(B)(i)(I), strikes out "(C)" and substitutes "(B)". P.L. 110-351, §101(c)(2)(B)(ii)), provides that this amendment made by §101(c)(2)(A)(i)(i) shall take effect immediately after the amendments made by §152 of P.L. 109-248 take effect.

See Vol. II, P.L. 109-248, §152(c), with respect to the effective date, which allows for a delay if state legislation is required.

478 SOCIAL SECURITY ACT—§ 471(a)(21)(C)(cont)

child shall be deemed to be receiving aid or assistance under the State plan under this part for purposes of section 1902(a)(10)(A)(i)(I); and

(D) in determining cost–sharing requirements, the State shall take into consideration the circumstances of the adopting parent or parents and the needs of the child being adopted consistent, to the extent coverage is provided through a State medical assistance program, with the rules under such program;

(22) provides that, not later than January 1, 1999, the State shall develop and implement standards to ensure that children in foster care placements in public or private agencies are provided quality services that protect the safety and health of the children;

(23) provides that the State shall not—

(A) deny or delay the placement of a child for adoption when an approved family is available outside of the jurisdiction with responsibility for handling the case of the child; or

(B) fail to grant an opportunity for a fair hearing, as described in paragraph (12), to an individual whose allegation of a violation of subparagraph (A) of this paragraph is denied by the State or not acted upon by the State with reasonable promptness,

(24) include a certification that, before a child in foster care under the responsibility of the State is placed with prospective foster parents, the prospective foster parents will be prepared adequately with the appropriate knowledge and skills to provide for the needs of the child and that such preparation will be continued, as necessary, after the placement of the child;

(25) provide that the State shall have in effect procedures for the orderly and timely interstate placement of children; and procedures implemented in accordance with an interstate compact, if incorporating with the procedures prescribed by paragraph (26), shall be considered to satisfy the requirement of this paragraph;

(26) provides that—

(A)(i) within 60 days after the State receives from another State a request to conduct a study of a home environment for purposes of assessing the safety and suitability of placing a child in the home, the State shall, directly or by contract—

(I) conduct and complete the study; and

(II) return to the other State a report on the results of the study, which shall address the extent to which placement in the home would meet the needs of the child; and

(ii) in the case of a home study begun on or before September 30, 2008, if the State fails to comply with clause (i) within the 60-day period as a result of circumstances beyond the control of the State (such as a failure by a Federal agency to provide the results of a background check, or the failure by any entity to provide completed medical forms, requested by the State at least 45 days before the end of the 60-day period), the State shall have 75 days to comply with clause (i) if the State documents the circumstances involved and certifies that completing the home study is in the best interests of the child; except that

SOCIAL SECURITY ACT—§ 471(a)(29)(C) 479

(iii) this subparagraph shall not be construed to require the State to have completed, within the applicable period, the parts of the home study involving the education and training of the prospective foster or adoptive parents;

(B) the State shall treat any report described in subparagraph (A) that is received from another State or an Indian tribe (or from a private agency under contract with another State) as meeting any requirements imposed by the State for the completion of a home study before placing a child in the home, unless, within 14 days after receipt of the report, the State determines, based on grounds that are specific to the content of the report, that making a decision in reliance on the report would be contrary to the welfare of the child; and

(C) the State shall not impose any restriction on the ability of a State agency administering, or supervising the administration of, a State program operated under a State plan approved under this part to contract with a private agency for the conduct of a home study described in subparagraph (A);[195]

(27) provides that, with respect to any child in foster care under the responsibility of the State under this part or part B and without regard to whether foster care maintenance payments are made under section 472 on behalf of the child, the State has in effect procedures for verifying the citizenship or immigration status of the child;[196]

(28)[197] at the option of the State, provides for the State to enter into kinship guardianship assistance agreements to provide kinship guardianship assistance payments on behalf of children to grandparents and other relatives who have assumed legal guardianship of the children for whom they have cared as foster parents and for whom they have committed to care on a permanent basis, as provided in section 473(d);[198]

(29)[199] provides that, within 30 days after the removal of a child from the custody of the parent or parents of the child, the State shall exercise due diligence to identify and provide notice to all adult grandparents and other adult relatives of the child (including any other adult relatives suggested by the parents), subject to exceptions due to family or domestic violence, that—

(A) specifies that the child has been or is being removed from the custody of the parent or parents of the child;

(B) explains the options the relative has under Federal, State, and local law to participate in the care and placement of the child, including any options that may be lost by failing to respond to the notice;

(C) describes the requirements under paragraph (10) of this subsection to become a foster family home and the ad-

---

[195] P.L. 110-351, §101(a)(1), struck out "and".
[196] P.L. 110-351, §101(a)(2), struck out the period and substituted "; and*".
*P.L. 110-351, §103(a)(1), struck out "and".
[197] P.L. 110-351, §101(a)(3), added paragraph (28). For the effective date, see Vol. II, P.L. 110-351, §601.
[198] P.L. 110-351, §103(a)(2), struck out the period and substituted "; and*".
*P.L. 110-351, §204(b)(1), struck out "and".
[199] P.L. 110-351, §103(a)(3), added paragraph (29). For the effective date, see Vol. II, P.L. 110-351, §601.

480   SOCIAL SECURITY ACT—§ 471(a)(29)(C)(cont)

ditional services and supports that are available for children placed in such a home; and

(D) if the State has elected the option to make kinship guardianship assistance payments under paragraph (28) of this subsection, describes how the relative guardian of the child may subsequently enter into an agreement with the State under section 473(d) to receive the payments;[200]

(30)[201] provides assurances that each child who has attained the minimum age for compulsory school attendance under State law and with respect to whom there is eligibility for a payment under the State plan is a full-time elementary or secondary school student or has completed secondary school, and for purposes of this paragraph, the term "elementary or secondary school student" means, with respect to a child, that the child is—

(A) enrolled (or in the process of enrolling) in an institution which provides elementary or secondary education, as determined under the law of the State or other jurisdiction in which the institution is located;

(B) instructed in elementary or secondary education at home in accordance with a home school law of the State or other jurisdiction in which the home is located;

(C) in an independent study elementary or secondary education program in accordance with the law of the State or other jurisdiction in which the program is located, which is administered by the local school or school district; or

(D) incapable of attending school on a full-time basis due to the medical condition of the child, which incapability is supported by regularly updated information in the case plan of the child;[202]

(31)[203] provides that reasonable efforts shall be made—

(A) to place siblings removed from their home in the same foster care, kinship guardianship, or adoptive placement, unless the State documents that such a joint placement would be contrary to the safety or well-being of any of the siblings; and

(B) in the case of siblings removed from their home who are not so jointly placed, to provide for frequent visitation or other ongoing interaction between the siblings, unless that State documents that frequent visitation or other ongoing interaction would be contrary to the safety or well-being of any of the siblings;[204]

---

[200] P.L. 110-351, §204(b)(2), struck out the period and substituted "; and*".
P.L. 110-351, §206(1), struck out "and".
[201] P.L. 110-351, §204(b)(3), added paragraph (30). For the effective date, see Vol. II, P.L. 110-351, §601.
[202] P.L. 110-351, §206(2), struck out the period and inserted "; and*".
P.L. 110-351, §301(c)(1)(A)(i), struck out "and".
[203] P.L. 110-351, §206(3), added paragraph (31). For the effective date, see Vol. II, P.L. 110-351, §601.
[204] P.L. 110-351, §301(c)(1)(A)(ii), struck out the period and inserted ";and*".
*P.L. 110-351, §403(1), struck out "and".

SOCIAL SECURITY ACT—§ 472(a)(2)(A)   481

(32)[205] provides that the State will negotiate in good faith with any Indian tribe, tribal organization or tribal consortium in the State that requests to develop an agreement with the State to administer all or part of the program under this part on behalf of Indian children who are under the authority of the tribe, organization, or consortium, including foster care maintenance payments on behalf of children who are placed in State or tribally licensed foster family homes, adoption assistance payments, and, if the State has elected to provide such payments, kinship guardianship assistance payments under section 473(d), and tribal access to resources for administration, training, and data collection under this part; and[206]

(33)[207] provides that the State will inform any individual who is adopting, or whom the State is made aware is considering adopting, a child who is in foster care under the responsibility of the State of the potential eligibility of the individual for a Federal tax credit under section 23 of the Internal Revenue Code of 1986.

(b) The Secretary shall approve any plan which complies with the provisions of subsection (a) of this section.

(c) USE OF CHILD WELFARE RECORDS IN STATE COURT PROCEEDINGS.—Subsection (a)(8) shall not be construed to limit the flexibility of a State in determining State policies relating to public access to court proceedings to determine child abuse and neglect or other court hearings held pursuant to part B of this part, except that such policies shall, at a minimum, ensure the safety and well-being of the child, parents, and family.

FOSTER CARE MAINTENANCE PAYMENTS PROGRAM[208]

SEC. 472. [42 U.S.C. 672] (a) IN GENERAL.—

(1) ELIGIBILITY.—Each State with a plan approved under this part shall make foster care maintenance payments on behalf of each child who has been removed from the home of a relative specified in section 406(a) (as in effect on July 16, 1996) into foster care if—

(A) the removal and foster care placement met, and the placement continues to meet, the requirements of paragraph (2); and

(B) the child, while in the home, would have met the AFDC eligibility requirement of paragraph (3).

(2) REMOVAL AND FOSTER CARE PLACEMENT REQUIREMENTS.—The removal and foster care placement of a child meet the requirements of this paragraph if—

(A) the removal and foster care placement are in accordance with—

---

[205] P.L. 110-351, §301(c)(1)(A)(iii), adds paragraph (32). P.L. 110-351, §301(f), provides that this amendment shall take effect **on October 1, 2009, without regard to whether the regulations required under subsecton (e)(1) have been promulgated by such date.**
See Vol. II, P.L. 110-351, §301(d), with respect to rules of construction and §301(e), with respect to regulations.
[206] P.L. 110-351, §403(2), struck out the period and substituted "; and*".
[207] P.L. 110-351, §403(3), added paragraph (33). For the effective date, see Vol. II, P.L. 110-351, §601.
[208] See Vol. II, P.L. 96-272, §102(e), with respect to the Secretary's report to Congress on the placement of children in foster care pursuant to certain voluntary agreements.

482 SOCIAL SECURITY ACT—§ 472(a)(2)(A)(i)

(i) a voluntary placement agreement entered into by a parent or legal guardian of the child who is the relative referred to in paragraph (1); or

(ii) a judicial determination to the effect that continuation in the home from which removed would be contrary to the welfare of the child and that reasonable efforts of the type described in section 471(a)(15) for a child have been made;

(B) the child's placement and care are the responsibility of—

(i) the State agency administering the State plan approved under section 471; or[209]

(ii) any other public agency with which the State agency administering or supervising the administration of the State plan has made an agreement which is in effect; and[210]

(iii)[211] an Indian tribe or a tribal organization (as defined in section 479B(a)) or a tribal consortium that has a plan approved under section 471 in accordance with section 479B; and

(C) the child has been placed in a foster family home or child-care institution.

(3) AFDC ELIGIBILITY REQUIREMENT.—

(A) IN GENERAL.—A child in the home referred to in paragraph (1) would have met the AFDC eligibility requirement of this paragraph if the child—

(i) would have received aid under the State plan approved under section 402 (as in effect on July 16, 1996) in the home, in or for the month in which the agreement was entered into or court proceedings leading to the determination referred to in paragraph (2)(A)(ii) of this subsection were initiated; or

(ii)(I) would have received the aid in the home, in or for the month referred to in clause (i), if application had been made therefor; or

(II) had been living in the home within 6 months before the month in which the agreement was entered into or the proceedings were initiated, and would have received the aid in or for such month, if, in such month, the child had been living in the home with the relative referred to in paragraph (1) and application for the aid had been made.

(B) RESOURCES DETERMINATION.—For purposes of subparagraph (A), in determining whether a child would have received aid under a State plan approved under section 402 (as in effect on July 16, 1996), a child whose resources (determined pursuant to section 402(a)(7)(B), as so in effect) have a combined value of not more than $10,000 shall be considered a child whose resources have a combined value

---

[209] P.L. 110-351, §301(a)(2)(A), strikes out "or", **to be effective October 1, 2009.**

[210] P.L. 110-351, §301(a)(2)(B), strikes out "and", and substitutes "or", **to be effective October 1, 2009.**

[211] P.L. 110-351, §301(a)(2)(C), adds clause (iii), **to be effective October 1, 2009.**

SOCIAL SECURITY ACT—§ 472(e) 483

of not more than $1,000 (or such lower amount as the State may determine for purposes of section 402(a)(7)(B)).

(4) ELIGIBILITY OF CERTAIN ALIEN CHILDREN.—Subject to title IV of the Personal Responsibility and Work Opportunity Reconciliation Act of 1996[212], if the child is an alien disqualified under section 245A(h) or 210(f) of the Immigration and Nationality Act[213] from receiving aid under the State plan approved under section 402 in or for the month in which the agreement described in paragraph (2)(A)(i) was entered into or court proceedings leading to the determination described in paragraph (2)(A)(ii) were initiated, the child shall be considered to satisfy the requirements of paragraph (3), with respect to the month, if the child would have satisfied the requirements but for the disqualification.

(b) Foster care maintenance payments may be made under this part only on behalf of a child described in subsection (a) of this section who is—

(1) in the foster family home of an individual, whether the payments therefor are made to such individual or to a public or private child-placement or child-care agency, or

(2) in a child-care institution, whether the payments therefor are made to such institution or to a public or private child-placement or child-care agency, which payments shall be limited so as to include in such payments only those items which are included in the term "foster care maintenance payments" (as defined in section 475(4)).

(c) For the purposes of this part, (1) the term "foster family home" means a foster family home for children which is licensed by the State in which it is situated or has been approved, by the agency of such State having responsibility for licensing homes of this type, as meeting the standards established for such licensing; and (2) the term "child-care institution" means a private child-care institution, or a public child-care institution which accommodates no more than twenty-five children, which is licensed by the State in which it is situated or has been approved, by the agency of such State responsible for licensing or approval of institutions of this type, as meeting the standards established for such licensing,[214] but the term shall not include detention facilities, forestry camps, training schools, or any other facility operated primarily for the detention of children who are determined to be delinquent.

(d) Notwithstanding any other provision of this title, Federal payments may be made under this part with respect to amounts expended by any State as foster care maintenance payments under this section, in the case of children removed from their homes pursuant to voluntary placement agreements as described in subsection (a), only if (at the time such amounts were expended) the State has fulfilled all of the requirements of section 422(b)(8).

(e) No Federal payment may be made under this part with respect to amounts expended by any State as foster care maintenance pay-

---

[212] See Vol. II, P.L. 104-193, §§400-435.

[213] See Vol. II, P.L. 82-414, §§210(f) and 245A(h).

[214] P.L. 110-351, §201(b), inserts "except, in the case of a child who has attained 18 years of age, the term shall include a supervised setting in which the individual is living independently, in accordance with such conditions as the Secretary shall establish in regulations," **to be effective October 1, 2010.**

484   SOCIAL SECURITY ACT—§ 472(e)(cont)

ments under this section, in the case of any child who was removed from his or her home pursuant to a voluntary placement agreement as described in subsection (a) and has remained in voluntary placement for a period in excess of 180 days, unless there has been a judicial determination by a court of competent jurisdiction (within the first 180 days of such placement) to the effect that such placement is in the best interests of the child.

(f) For the purposes of this part and part B of this title, (1) the term "voluntary placement" means an out-of-home placement of a minor, by or with participation of a State agency, after the parents or guardians of the minor have requested the assistance of the agency and signed a voluntary placement agreement; and (2) the term "voluntary placement agreement" means a written agreement, binding on the parties to the agreement, between the State agency, any other agency acting on its behalf, and the parents or guardians of a minor child which specifies, at a minimum, the legal status of the child and the rights and obligations of the parents or guardians, the child, and the agency while the child is in placement.

(g) In any case where—

(1) the placement of a minor child in foster care occurred pursuant to a voluntary placement agreement entered into by the parents or guardians of such child as provided in subsection (a), and

(2) such parents or guardians request (in such manner and form as the Secretary may prescribe) that the child be returned to their home or to the home of a relative,

the voluntary placement agreement shall be deemed to be revoked unless the State agency opposes such request and obtains a judicial determination, by a court of competent jurisdiction, that the return of the child to such home would be contrary to the child's best interests.

(h)(1) For purposes of titles XIX, any child with respect to whom foster care maintenance payments are made under this section is deemed to be a dependent child as defined in section 406 (as in effect as of July 16, 1996) and deemed to be a recipient of aid to families with dependent children under part A of this title (as so in effect). For purposes of title XX, any child with respect to whom foster care maintenance payments are made under this section is deemed to be a minor child in a needy family under a State program funded under part A of this title and is deemed to be a recipient of assistance under such part.

(2) For purposes of paragraph (1), a child whose costs in a foster family home or child care institution are covered by the foster care maintenance payments being made with respect to the child's minor parent, as provided in section 475(4)(B), shall be considered a child with respect to whom foster care maintenance payments are made under this section.

(i) ADMINISTRATIVE COSTS ASSOCIATED WITH OTHERWISE ELIGIBLE CHILDREN NOT IN LICENSED FOSTER CARE SETTINGS.—Expenditures by a State that would be considered administrative expenditures for purposes of section 474(a)(3) if made with respect to a child who was residing in a foster family home or childcare institution shall be so considered with respect to a child not residing in such a home or institution—

(1) in the case of a child who has been removed in accordance with subsection (a) of this section from the home of a relative spec-

SOCIAL SECURITY ACT—§ 473(a)(2)(A)(i)(I)   485

ified in section 406(a) (as in effect on July 16, 1996), only for expenditures—

(A) with respect to a period of not more than the lesser of 12 months or the average length of time it takes for the State to license or approve a home as a foster home, in which the child is in the home of a relative and an application is pending for licensing or approval of the home as a foster family home; or

(B) with respect to a period of not more than 1 calendar month when a child moves from a facility not eligible for payments under this part into a foster family home or child care institution licensed or approved by the State; and

(2) in the case of any other child who is potentially eligible for benefits under a State plan approved under this part and at imminent risk of removal from the home, only if—

(A) reasonable efforts are being made in accordance with section 471(a)(15) to prevent the need for, or if necessary to pursue, removal of the child from the home; and

(B) the State agency has made, not less often than every 6 months, a determination (or redetermination) as to whether the child remains at imminent risk of removal from the home.

ADOPTION AND GUARDIANSHIP[215] ASSISTANCE PROGRAM

SEC. 473. [42 U.S.C. 673] (a)(1)(A) Each State having a plan approved under this part shall enter into adoption assistance agreements (as defined in section 475(3)) with the adoptive parents of children with special needs.

(B) Under any adoption assistance agreement entered into by a State with parents who adopt a child with special needs, the State—

(i) shall make payments of nonrecurring adoption expenses incurred by or on behalf of such parents in connection with the adoption of such child, directly through the State agency or through another public or nonprofit private agency, in amounts determined under paragraph (3), and

(ii) in any case where the child meets the requirements of paragraph (2), may make adoption assistance payments to such parents, directly through the State agency or through another public or nonprofit private agency, in amounts so determined.

(2)(A) For purposes of paragraph (1)(B)(ii), a child meets the requirements of this paragraph if—

(i)[216] in the case of a child who is not an applicable child for the fiscal year (as defined in subsection (e)), the child—

(I)[217](aa[218])(AA[219]) was removed from the home of a relative specified in section 406(a) (as in effect on July 16, 1996) and placed in foster care in accordance with a voluntary placement agreement with respect to which

---

[215] P.L. 110-351, §101(c)(5), inserted "AND GUARDIANSHIP". For the effective date, see Vol. II, P.L. 110-351, §601.

[216] P.L. 110-351, §402(1)(A)(i)(VI), struck out "if the child)—" and substituted "if—" and this new clause (i). For the effective date, see Vol. II, P.L. 110-351, §601.

[217] P.L. 110-351, §402(1)(A)(i)(IV), redesignated the former clause (i) as subclause (I) and §402(1)(A)(i)(V) realigned the margin.

[218] P.L. 110-351, §402(1)(A)(i)(III), redesignated the former subclause (I) as item (aa) and §402(1)(A)(i)(V) realigned the margin.

[219] P.L. 110-351, §402(1)(A)(i)(I), redesignated the former item (aa) as subitem (AA) and §402(1)(A)(i)(V) realigned the margin.

486 SOCIAL SECURITY ACT—§ 473(a)(2)(A)(i)(I)(cont)

Federal payments are provided under section 474 (or section 403, as such section was in effect on July 16, 1996), or in accordance with a judicial determination to the effect that continuation in the home would be contrary to the welfare of the child; and

(BB)[220] met the requirements of section 472(a)(3) with respect to the home referred to in subitem (AA) of this item[221].

(bb)[222] meets all of the requirements of title XVI with respect to eligibility for supplemental security income benefits; or

(cc)[223] is a child whose costs in a foster family home or child-care institution are covered by the foster care maintenance payments being made with respect to the minor parent of the child as provided in section 475(4)(B); and

(II)[224] has been determined by the State, pursuant to subsection (c)(1)[225] of this section, to be a child with special needs; or[226]

(ii)[227] in the case of a child who is an applicable child for the fiscal year (as so defined), the child—

(I)(aa) at the time of initiation of adoption proceedings was in the care of a public or licensed private child placement agency or Indian tribal organization pursuant to—

(AA) an involuntary removal of the child from the home in accordance with a judicial determination to the effect that continuation in the home would be contrary to the welfare of the child; or

(BB) a voluntary placement agreement or voluntary relinquishment;

(bb) meets all medical or disability requirements of title XVI with respect to eligibility for supplemental security income benefits; or

(cc) was residing in a foster family home or child care institution with the child's minor parent, and the child's minor parent was in such foster family home or child care institution pursuant to—

(AA) an involuntary removal of the child from the home in accordance with a judicial determination to the effect that continuation in the home would be contrary to the welfare of the child; or

(BB) a voluntary placement agreement or voluntary relinquishment; and

---

[220] P.L. 110-351, §402(1)(A)(i)(I), redesignated the former item (bb) as subitem (BB) and §402(1)(A)(i)(V) realigned the margin.

[221] P.L. 110-351, §402(1)(A)(i)(II), struck out "item (aa) of this subclause" and substituted "subitem (AA) of this item".

[222] P.L. 110-351, §402(1)(A)(i)(III), redesignated the former subclause (II) as item (bb) and §402(1)(A)(i)(V) realigned the margin.

[223] P.L. 110-351, §402(1)(A)(i)(III), redesignated the former subclause (III) as item (cc).

[224] P.L. 110-351, §402(1)(A)(i)(IV), redesignated the former clause (i) as subclause (I) and §402(1)(A)(i)(V) realigned the margin.

[225] P.L. 110-351, §402(1)(A)(i)(VII)(aa), struck out "(c)" and substituted "(c)(i)".

[226] P.L. 110-351, §402(1)(A)(i)(VII)(bb), struck out the period and substituted "; or".

[227] P.L. 110-351, §402(1)(A)(i)(VIII), added this new clause (ii). For the effective date, see Vol. II, P.L. 110-351, §601.

SOCIAL SECURITY ACT—§ 473(a)(2)(C)(ii) 487

(II) has been determined by the State, pursuant to subsection (c)(2), to be a child with special needs.

(B) Section 472(a)(4) shall apply for purposes of subparagraph (A) of this paragraph, in any case in which the child is an alien described in such section.

(C) A child shall be treated as meeting the requirements of this paragraph for the purpose of paragraph (1)(B)(ii) if—

(i)[228] in the case of a child who is not an applicable child for the fiscal year (as defined in subsection (e)), the child—

(I)[229] meets the requirements of subparagraph (A)(i)(II)[230];

(II)[231] was determined eligible for adoption assistance payments under this part with respect to a prior adoption;

(III)[232] is available for adoption because—

(aa)[233] the prior adoption has been dissolved, and the parental rights of the adoptive parents have been terminated; or

(bb)[234] the child's adoptive parents have died; and

(IV)[235] fails to meet the requirements of subparagraph (A)(i)[236] but would meet such requirements if—

(aa)[237] the child were treated as if the child were in the same financial and other circumstances the child was in the last time the child was determined eligible for adoption assistance payments under this part; and

(bb)[238] the prior adoption were treated as never having occurred; or[239]

(ii)[240] in the case of a child who is an applicable child for the fiscal year (as so defined), the child meets the requirements of subparagraph (A)(ii)(II), is determined eligible for adoption assistance payments under this part with respect to a prior adoption (or who would have been determined eligible for such payments had the Adoption and Safe Families Act of 1997[241] been in effect at the time that such determination would have been made), and is available for adoption because the prior adoption has been dissolved and the parental rights of the adoptive parents have been terminated or because the child's adoptive parents have died.

---

[228] P.L. 110-351, §402(1)(A)(ii)(V), struck out "if the child—" and substituted "if—" and this new clause (i). For the effective date, see Vol. II, P.L. 110-351, §601.

[229] P.L. 110-351, §402(1)(A)(ii)(III), redesignated the former clause (i) as subclause (I) and §402(1)(A)(ii)(IV) realigned the margin.

[230] P.L. 110-351, §402(1)(A)(ii)(VI), struck out "(A)(ii)" and inserted "(A)(i)(II)".

[231] P.L. 110-351, §402(1)(A)(ii)(III), redesignated the former clause (ii) as subclause (II) and §402(1)(A)(ii)(IV) realigned the margin.

[232] P.L. 110-351, §402(1)(A)(ii)(III), redesignated the former clause (iii) as subclause (III) and §402(1)(A)(ii)(IV) realigned the margin.

[233] P.L. 110-351, §402(1)(A)(ii)(I), redesignated the former subclause (I) as item (aa) and §402(1)(A)(ii)(IV) realigned the margin.

[234] P.L. 110-351, §402(1)(A)(ii)(I), redesignated the former subclause (II) as item (bb) and §402(1)(A)(ii)(IV) realigned the margin.

[235] P.L. 110-351, §402(1)(A)(ii)(III), redesignated the former clause (iv) as subclause (IV) and §402(1)(A)(ii)(IV) realigned the margin.

[236] P.L. 110-351, §402(1)(A)(ii)(VII)(aa), struck out "(A)" and inserted "(A)(i)".

[237] P.L. 110-351, §402(1)(A)(ii)(II), redesignated the former subclause (I) as item (aa) and §402(1)(A)(ii)(IV) realigned the margin.

[238] P.L. 110-351, §402(1)(A)(ii)(II), redesignated the former subclause (II) as item (bb) and §402(1)(A)(ii)(IV) realigned the margin.

[239] P.L. 110-351, §402(1)(A)(ii)(VII)(bb), struck out the period and inserted a "; or".

[240] P.L. 110-351, §402(1)(A)(ii)(VIII), added clause (ii). For the effective date, see Vol. II, P.L. 110-351, §601.

[241] P.L. 105-89; 111 Stat. 2115.

488 SOCIAL SECURITY ACT—§ 473(a)(2)(D)

(D)[242] In determining the eligibility for adoption assistance payments of a child in a legal guardianship arrangement described in section 471(a)(28), the placement of the child with the relative guardian involved and any kinship guardianship assistance payments made on behalf of the child shall be considered never to have been made.

(3) The amount of the payments to be made in any case under clauses (i) and (ii) of paragraph (1)(B) shall be determined through agreement between the adoptive parents and the State or local agency administering the program under this section, which shall take into consideration the circumstances of the adopting parents and the needs of the child being adopted, and may be readjusted periodically, with the concurrence of the adopting parents (which may be specified in the adoption assistance agreement), depending upon changes in such circumstances. However, in no case may the amount of the adoption assistance payment made under clause (ii) of paragraph (1)(B) exceed the foster care maintenance payment which would have been paid during the period if the child with respect to whom the adoption assistance payment is made had been in a foster family home.

(4)[243] Notwithstanding the preceding paragraph, (A) no payment may be made to parents with respect to any child who has attained the age of eighteen (or, where the State determines that the child has a mental or physical handicap which warrants the continuation of assistance, the age of twenty-one), and (B) no payment may be made to parents with respect to any child if the State determines that the parents are no longer legally responsible for the support of the child or if the State determines that the child is no longer receiving any support from such parents. Parents who have been receiving adoption assistance payments under this section shall keep the State or local agency administering the program under this section informed of circumstances which would, pursuant to this subsection, make them ineligible for such assistance payments, or eligible for assistance payments in a different amount.

(5) For purposes of this part, individuals with whom a child (who has been determined by the State, pursuant to subsection (c), to be a child with special needs) is placed for adoption in accordance with applicable State and local law shall be eligible for such payments, during the period of the placement, on the same terms and subject to the same conditions as if such individuals had adopted such child.

(6)(A) For purposes of paragraph (1)(B)(i), the term "nonrecurring adoption expenses" means reasonable and necessary adoption fees, court costs, attorney fees, and other expenses which are directly related to the legal adoption of a child with special needs and which are not incurred in violation of State or Federal law.

(B) A State's payment of nonrecurring adoption expenses under an adoption assistance agreement shall be treated as an expenditure made for the proper and efficient administration of the State plan for purposes of section 474(a)(3)(E).

---

[242] P.L. 110-351, §101(c)(1)(B), added subparagraph (D). For the effective date, see Vol. II, P.L. 110-351, §601.

[243] P.L. 110-351, §201(c), amends paragraph (4), in its entirety, **to be effective October 1, 2010.**

SOCIAL SECURITY ACT—§ 473(c)

(7)[244](A) Notwithstanding any other provision of this subsection, no payment may be made to parents with respect to any applicable child for a fiscal year that—

(i) would be considered a child with special needs under subsection (c)(2);

(ii) is not a citizen or resident of the United States; and

(iii) was adopted outside of the United States or was brought into the United States for the purpose of being adopted.

(B) Subparagraph (A) shall not be construed as prohibiting payments under this part for an applicable child described in subparagraph (A) that is placed in foster care subsequent to the failure, as determined by the State, of the initial adoption of the child by the parents described in subparagraph (A).

(8)[245] A State shall spend an amount equal to the amount of savings (if any) in State expenditures under this part resulting from the application of paragraph (2)(A)(ii) to all applicable children for a fiscal year to provide to children or families any service (including post-adoption services) that may be provided under this part or part B.

(b)(1) For purposes of title XIX, any child who is described in paragraph (3) is deemed to be a dependent child as defined in section 406 (as in effect as of July 16, 1996) and deemed to be a recipient of aid to families with dependent children under part A of this title (as so in effect) in the State where such child resides.

(2) For purposes of title XX, any child who is described in paragraph (3) is deemed to be a minor child in a needy family under a State program funded under part A of this title and deemed to be a recipient of assistance under such part.

(3) A child described in this paragraph is any child—

(A)(i) who is a child described in subsection (a)(2), and

(ii) with respect to whom an adoption assistance agreement is in effect under this section (whether or not adoption assistance payments are provided under the agreement or are being made under this section), including any such child who has been placed for adoption in accordance with applicable State and local law (whether or not an interlocutory or other judicial decree of adoption has been issued),[246]

(B) with respect to whom foster care maintenance payments are being made under section 472, or[247]

(C)[248] with respect to whom kinship guardianship assistance payments are being made pursuant to subsection (d).

(4) For purposes of paragraphs (1) and (2), a child whose costs in a foster family home or child-care institution are covered by the foster care maintenance payments being made with respect to the child's minor parent, as provided in section 475(4)(B), shall be considered a child with respect to whom foster care maintenance payments are being made under section 472.

(c) For purposes of this section—

---

[244] P.L. 110-351, §402(1)(B), added paragraph (7). For the effective date, see Vol. II, P.L. 110-351, §601.

[245] P.L. 110-351, §402(1)(B), added paragraph (8). For the effective date, see Vol. II, P.L. 110-351, §601.

[246] P.L. 110-351, §101(f)(1), struck out "or".

[247] P.L. 110-351, §101(f)(2), struck out the period and inserted ", or".

[248] P.L. 110-351, §101(f)(3), added subparagraph (C). For the effective date, see Vol. II, P.L. 110-351, §601.

490   SOCIAL SECURITY ACT—§ 473(c)(1)

(1) in the case of a child who is not an applicable child for a fiscal year, the child shall not be considered a child with special needs unless[249]—

(A)[250] the State has determined that the child cannot or should not be returned to the home of his parents; and

(B)[251] the State had first determined (A) that there exists with respect to the child a specific factor or condition (such as his ethnic background, age, or membership in a minority or sibling group, or the presence of factors such as medical conditions or physical, mental, or emotional handicaps) because of which it is reasonable to conclude that such child cannot be placed with adoptive parents without providing adoption assistance under this section or medical assistance under title XIX, and (B) that, except where it would be against the best interests of the child because of such factors as the existence of significant emotional ties with prospective adoptive parents while in the care of such parents as a foster child, a reasonable, but unsuccessful, effort has been made to place the child with appropriate adoptive parents without providing adoption assistance under this section or medical assistance under title XIX; or[252]

(2)[253] in the case of a child who is an applicable child for a fiscal year, the child shall not be considered a child with special needs unless—

(A) the State has determined, pursuant to a criterion or criteria established by the State, that the child cannot or should not be returned to the home of his parents;

(B)(i) the State has determined that there exists with respect to the child a specific factor or condition (such as ethnic background, age, or membership in a minority or sibling group, or the presence of factors such as medical conditions or physical, mental, or emotional handicaps) because of which it is reasonable to conclude that the child cannot be placed with adoptive parents without providing adoption assistance under this section and medical assistance under title XIX; or

(ii) the child meets all medical or disability requirements of title XVI with respect to eligibility for supplemental security income benefits; and

(C) the State has determined that, except where it would be against the best interests of the child because of such factors as the existence of significant emotional ties with prospective adoptive parents while in the care of the parents as a foster child, a reasonable, but unsuccessful, effort has been made to place the child with appropriate adoptive parents without

---

[249] P.L. 110-351, §402(2)(B), struck out "this section, a child shall not be considered a child with special needs unless" and substituted "this section—" and a new paragraph (1). For the effective date, see Vol. II, P.L. 110-351, §601.

[250] P.L. 110-351, §402(2)(A), redesignated the former paragraph (1) as subparagraph (A) and realigned the margin.

[251] P.L. 110-351, §402(2)(A) , redesignated the former paragraph (2) as subparagraph (B) and realigned the margin.

[252] P.L. 110-351, §402(2)(C), struck out the period and inserted ", or".

[253] P.L. 110-351, §402(2)(D), added this paragraph (2). For the effective date, see Vol. II, P.L. 110-351, §601.

SOCIAL SECURITY ACT—§ 473(d) (3)(A)(i)(I) 491

providing adoption assistance under this section or medical assistance under title XIX.

(d) [254] KINSHIP GUARDIANSHIP ASSISTANCE PAYMENTS FOR CHILDREN.—

(1) KINSHIP GUARDIANSHIP ASSISTANCE AGREEMENT.—

(A) IN GENERAL.—In order to receive payments under section 474(a)(5), a State shall.—

(i) negotiate and enter into a written, binding kinship guardianship assistance agreement with the prospective relative guardian of a child who meets the requirements of this paragraph; and

(ii) provide the prospective relative guardian with a copy of the agreement.

(B) MINIMUM REQUIREMENTS.—The agreement shall specify, at a minimum.—

(i) the amount of, and manner in which, each kinship guardianship assistance payment will be provided under the agreement, and the manner in which the payment may be adjusted periodically, in consultation with the relative guardian, based on the circumstances of the relative guardian and the needs of the child;

(ii) the additional services and assistance that the child and relative guardian will be eligible for under the agreement;

(iii) the procedure by which the relative guardian may apply for additional services as needed; and

(iv) subject to subparagraph (D), that the State will pay the total cost of nonrecurring expenses associated with obtaining legal guardianship of the child, to the extent the total cost does not exceed $2,000.

(C) INTERSTATE APPLICABILITY.—The agreement shall provide that the agreement shall remain in effect without regard to the State residency of the relative guardian.

(D) NO EFFECT ON FEDERAL REIMBURSEMENT.—Nothing in subparagraph (B)(iv) shall be construed as affecting the ability of the State to obtain reimbursement from the Federal Government for costs described in that subparagraph.

(2) LIMITATIONS ON AMOUNT OF KINSHIP GUARDIANSHIP ASSISTANCE PAYMENT.—A kinship guardianship assistance payment on behalf of a child shall not exceed the foster care maintenance payment which would have been paid on behalf of the child if the child had remained in a foster family home.

(3) CHILD'S ELIGIBILITY FOR A KINSHIP GUARDIANSHIP ASSISTANCE PAYMENT.—

(A) IN GENERAL.—A child is eligible for a kinship guardianship assistance payment under this subsection if the State agency determines the following:

(i) The child has been—

(I) removed from his or her home pursuant to a voluntary placement agreement or as a result of a judicial determination to the effect that

---

[254] P.L. 110-351, §101(b), added subsection (d). For the effective date, see Vol. II, P.L. 110-351, §601.

492   SOCIAL SECURITY ACT—§ 473(d) (3)(A)(i)(I)(cont)

continuation in the home would be contrary to the welfare of the child; and

(II) eligible for foster care maintenance payments under section 472 while residing for at least 6 consecutive months in the home of the prospective relative guardian.

(ii) Being returned home or adopted are not appropriate permanency options for the child.

(iii) The child demonstrates a strong attachment to the prospective relative guardian and the relative guardian has a strong commitment to caring permanently for the child.

(iv) With respect to a child who has attained 14 years of age, the child has been consulted regarding the kinship guardianship arrangement.

(B) TREATMENT OF SIBLINGS.—With respect to a child described in subparagraph (A) whose sibling or siblings are not so described—

(i) the child and any sibling of the child may be placed in the same kinship guardianship arrangement, in accordance with section 471(a)(31), if the State agency and the relative agree on the appropriateness of the arrangement for the siblings; and

(ii) kinship guardianship assistance payments may be paid on behalf of each sibling so placed.

(e)[255] APPLICABLE CHILD DEFINED.—

(1) ON THE BASIS OF AGE.—

(A) IN GENERAL.—Subject to paragraphs (2) and (3), in this section, the term "applicable child" means a child for whom an adoption assistance agreement is entered into under this section during any fiscal year described in subparagraph (B) if the child attained the applicable age for that fiscal year before the end of that fiscal year.

(B) APPLICABLE AGE.—For purposes of subparagraph (A), the applicable age for a fiscal year is as follows:

In the case of fiscal year:	The applicable age is:
2010	16
2011	14
2012	12
2013	10
2014	8
2015	6
2016	4

---

[255] P.L. 110-351, §402(3), added subsection (e). For the effective date, see Vol. II, P.L. 110-351, §601.

SOCIAL SECURITY ACT—§ 473A(b)(2)(C)   493

In the case of fiscal year:	The applicable age is:
2017..........................	2
2018 or thereafter.....	any age.

(2) EXCEPTION FOR DURATION IN CARE.—Notwithstanding paragraph (1) of this subsection, beginning with fiscal year 2010, such term shall include a child of any age on the date on which an adoption assistance agreement is entered into on behalf of the child under this section if the child—

(A) has been in foster care under the responsibility of the State for at least 60 consecutive months; and

(B) (B) meets the requirements of subsection (a)(2)(A)(ii).

(3) EXCEPTION FOR MEMBER OF A SIBLING GROUP.—Notwithstanding paragraphs (1) and (2) of this subsection, beginning with fiscal year 2010, such term shall include a child of any age on the date on which an adoption assistance agreement is entered into on behalf of the child under this section without regard to whether the child is described in paragraph (2)(A) of this subsection if the child—

(A) is a sibling of a child who is an applicable child for the fiscal year under paragraph (1) or (2) of this subsection;

(B) is to be placed in the same adoption placement as an applicable child for the fiscal year who is their sibling; and

(C) meets the requirements of subsection (a)(2)(A)(ii).

ADOPTION INCENTIVE PAYMENTS

SEC. 473A. [42 U.S.C. 673b] (a) GRANT AUTHORITY.—Subject to the availability of such amounts as may be provided in advance in appropriations Acts for this purpose, the Secretary shall make a grant to each State that is an incentive-eligible State for a fiscal year in an amount equal to the adoption incentive payment payable to the State under this section for the fiscal year, which shall be payable in the immediately succeeding fiscal year.

(b) INCENTIVE–ELIGIBLE STATE.—A State is an incentive-eligible State for a fiscal year if—

(1) the State has a plan approved under this part for the fiscal year;

(2)(A) the number of foster child adoptions in the State during the fiscal year exceeds the base number of foster child adoptions for the State for the fiscal year;[256]

(B) the number of older child adoptions in the State during the fiscal year exceeds the base number of older child adoptions for the State for the fiscal year; or[257]

(C)[258] the State's foster child adoption rate for the fiscal year exceeds the highest ever foster child adoption rate determined for the State;

---

[256] P.L. 110-351, §401(e)(3)(A)(i), struck out "or".
[257] P.L. 110-351, §401(e)(3)(A)(ii), inserted "or".
[258] P.L. 110-351, §401(e)(3)(A)(iii), added subparagraph (C). For the effective date, see Vol. II, P.L. 110-351, §601.

494 SOCIAL SECURITY ACT—§ 473A(b)(3)

(3) the State is in compliance with subsection (c) for the fiscal year;

(4) [259]the State provides health insurance coverage to any child with special needs (as determined under section 473(c)) for whom there is in effect an adoption assistance agreement between a State and an adoptive parent or parents; and

(5) the fiscal year is any of fiscal years 2008 through 2012[260].

(c) DATA REQUIREMENTS.—

(1) IN GENERAL.—A State is in compliance with this subsection for a fiscal year if the State has provided to the Secretary the data described in paragraph (2)—

(A) for fiscal years 1995 through 1997 (or, if the first fiscal year for which the State seeks a grant under this section is after fiscal year 1998, the fiscal year that precedes such first fiscal year); and

(B) for each succeeding fiscal year that precedes the fiscal year.

(2) DETERMINATION OF NUMBERS OF ADOPTIONS BASED ON AFCARS DATA.—The Secretary shall determine the numbers of foster child adoptions, of special needs adoptions that are not older child adoptions, and of older child adoptions in a State during a fiscal year[261], and the foster child adoption rate for the state for the fiscal year[262] for purposes of this section, on the basis of data meeting the requirements of the system established pursuant to section 479, as reported by the State and approved by the Secretary by August 1 of the succeeding fiscal year.

(3) NO WAIVER OF AFCARS REQUIREMENTS.—This section shall not be construed to alter or affect any requirement of section 479 or of any regulation prescribed under such section with respect to reporting of data by States, or to waive any penalty for failure to comply with such a requirement.

(d) ADOPTION INCENTIVE PAYMENT.—

(1) IN GENERAL.—Except as provided in paragraph (2), the adoption incentive payment payable to a State for a fiscal year under this section shall be equal to the sum of—

(A) $4,000, multiplied by the amount (if any) by which the number of foster child adoptions in the State during the fiscal year exceeds the base number of foster child adoptions for the State for the fiscal year;

(B) $4,000[263], multiplied by the amount (if any) by which the number of special needs adoptions that are not older child adoptions in the State during the fiscal year exceeds the base number of special needs adoptions that are not older child adoptions for the State for the fiscal year; and

---

[259] P.L. 110-351, §401(a)(1), struck out "in the case of fiscal years 2001 through 2007," . For the effective date, see Vol. II, P.L. 110-351, §601.

[260] P..L. 110-351, §401(a)(2), struck out "1998 through 2007" and substituted "2008 through 2012". For the effective date, see Vol. II, P.L. 110-351, §601.

[261] P.L. 110-351, §401(a)(3), struck out "each of fiscal years 2002 through 2007" and substituted "a fiscal year". For the effective date, see Vol. II, P.L. 110-351, §601.

[262] P.L. 110-351, §401(e)(3)(B), inserted "and the foster child adoption rate for the State for the fiscal year ". For the effective date, see Vol. II, P.L. 110-351, §601.

[263] P.L. 110-351, §401(c)(1), struck out "$2,000" and substituted "$4,000". For the effective date, see Vol. II, P.L. 110-351, §601.

SOCIAL SECURITY ACT—§ 473A(d)(3)(B)(ii)(II)   495

(C) $8,000[264], multiplied by the amount (if any) by which the number of older child adoptions in the State during the fiscal year exceeds the base number of older child adoptions for the State for the fiscal year.

(2) PRO RATA ADJUSTMENT IF INSUFFICIENT FUNDS AVAILABLE.—For any fiscal year, if the total amount of adoption incentive payments otherwise payable under this section for a fiscal year exceeds the amount appropriated pursuant to subsection (h) for the fiscal year, the amount of the adoption incentive payment payable to each State under this section for the fiscal year shall be—

(A) the amount of the adoption incentive payment that would otherwise be payable to the State under this section for the fiscal year; multiplied by

(B) the percentage represented by the amount so appropriated for the fiscal year, divided by the total amount of adoption incentive payments otherwise payable under this section for the fiscal year.

(3)[265] INCREASED INCENTIVE PAYMENT FOR EXCEEDING THE HIGHEST EVER FOSTER CHILD ADOPTION RATE.—

(A) IN GENERAL.—If—

(i) for fiscal year 2009 or any fiscal year thereafter the total amount of adoption incentive payments payable under paragraph (1) of this subsection are less than the amount appropriated under subsection (h) for the fiscal year; and

(ii) a State's foster child adoption rate for that fiscal year exceeds the highest ever foster child adoption rate determined for the State, then the adoption incentive payment otherwise determined under paragraph (1) of this subsection for the State shall be increased, subject to subparagraph (C) of this paragraph, by the amount determined for the State under subparagraph (B) of this paragraph.

(B) AMOUNT OF INCREASE.—For purposes of subparagraph (A), the amount determined under this subparagraph with respect to a State and a fiscal year is the amount equal to the product of—

(i) $1,000; and

(ii) the excess of—

(I) the number of foster child adoptions in the State in the fiscal year; over

(II) the product (rounded to the nearest whole number) of—

(aa) the highest ever foster child adoption rate determined for the State; and

(bb) the number of children in foster care under the supervision of the State on the last day of the preceding fiscal year.

---

[264] P.L. 110-351, §401(c)(2), struck out "$4,000" and substituted "$8,000". For the effective date, see Vol. II, P.L. 110-351, §601.

[265] P.L. 110-351, §401(e)(1)(C), added paragraph (3). For the effective date, see Vol. II, P.L. 110-351, §601.

496 SOCIAL SECURITY ACT—§ 473A(d)(3)(C)

(C) PRO RATA ADJUSTMENT IF INSUFFICIENT FUNDS AVAILABLE.—For any fiscal year, if the total amount of increases in adoption incentive payments otherwise payable under this paragraph for a fiscal year exceeds the amount available for such increases for the fiscal year, the amount of the increase payable to each State under this paragraph for the fiscal year shall be—

(i) the amount of the increase that would otherwise be payable to the State under this paragraph for the fiscal year; multiplied by

(ii) the percentage represented by the amount so available for the fiscal year, divided by the total amount of increases otherwise payable under this paragraph for the fiscal year.

(e) 24-MONTH[266] AVAILABILITY OF INCENTIVE PAYMENTS.—Payments to a State under this section in a fiscal year shall remain available for use by the State for the 24-month period beginning with the month in which the payments are made[267].

(f) LIMITATIONS ON USE OF INCENTIVE PAYMENTS.—A State shall not expend an amount paid to the State under this section except to provide to children or families any service (including post-adoption services) that may be provided under part B or E. Amounts expended by a State in accordance with the preceding sentence shall be disregarded in determining State expenditures for purposes of Federal matching payments under sections 424, 434, and 474.

(g) DEFINITIONS.—As used in this section:

(1) FOSTER CHILD ADOPTION.—The term "foster child adoption" means the final adoption of a child who, at the time of adoptive placement, was in foster care under the supervision of the State.

(2) SPECIAL NEEDS ADOPTION.—The term "special needs adoption" means the final adoption of a child for whom an adoption assistance agreement is in effect under section 473.

(3) BASE NUMBER OF FOSTER CHILD ADOPTIONS.—The term "base number of foster child adoptions for a State" means, with respect to any fiscal year, the number of foster child adoptions in the State in fiscal year 2007.[268]

(4) BASE NUMBER OF SPECIAL NEEDS ADOPTIONS THAT ARE NOT OLDER CHILD ADOPTIONS.—The term "base number of special needs adoptions that are not older child adoptions[269] for a State" means, with respect to any fiscal year, the number of special

---

[266] P.L. 110-351, §401(d)(1), struck out "2-year" and substituted "24-Month". For the effective date, see Vol. II, P.L. 110-351, §601.

[267] P.L. 110-351, §401(d)(2), struck out "through the end of the succeeding fiscal year" and substituted "for the 24-month period beginning with the month in which the payments are made". For the effective date, see Vol. II, P.L. 110-351, §601.

[268] P.L. 110-351, §401(b)(1), struck out "means—" and subparagraphs (A) and (B) and substituted "means, with respect to any fiscal year, the number of foster child adoptions in the State in fiscal year 2007.". For the effective date, see Vol. II, P.L. 110-351, §601. For subparagraphs (A) and (B) as they formerly read, see Vol. II, Appendix J, Superseded Provisions, P.L. 110-351.

[269] P.L. 110-351, §401(b)(2(A), inserted "that are not older child adoptions". For the effective date, see Vol. II, P.L. 110-351, §601.

SOCIAL SECURITY ACT—§ 473A(i)   497

needs adoptions that are not older child adoptions in the State in fiscal year 2007.[270]

(5) Base number of older child adoptions.—The term "base number of older child adoptions for a State" means, with respect to any fiscal year, the number of older child adoptions in the State in fiscal year 2007.[271]

(6) Older child adoptions.—The term "older child adoptions" means the final adoption of a child who has attained 9 years of age if—

(A) at the time of the adoptive placement, the child was in foster care under the supervision of the State; or (B) an adoption assistance agreement was in effect under section 473 with respect to the child.

(7)[272] HIGHEST EVER FOSTER CHILD ADOPTION RATE.—The term "highest ever foster child adoption rate" means, with respect to any fiscal year, the highest foster child adoption rate determined for any fiscal year in the period that begins with fiscal year 2002 and ends with the preceding fiscal year.

(8)[273] FOSTER CHILD ADOPTION RATE.—The term "foster child adoption rate" means, with respect to a State and a fiscal year, the percentage determined by dividing—

(A) the number of foster child adoptions finalized in the State during the fiscal year; by

(B) the number of children in foster care under the supervision of the State on the last day of the preceding fiscal year.

(h) LIMITATIONS ON AUTHORIZATION OF APPROPRIATIONS.—

(1) IN GENERAL.—For grants under subsection (a), there are authorized to be appropriated to the Secretary—

(A) $20,000,000 for fiscal year 1999;

(B) $43,000,000 for fiscal year 2000;

(C) $20,000,000 for each of fiscal years 2001 through 2003, and

(D) $43,000,000 for each of fiscal years 2004 through 2013[274].

(2) AVAILABILITY.—Amounts appropriated under paragraph (1), or under any other law for grants under subsection (a), are authorized to remain available until expended, but not after fiscal year 2013[275].

(i) TECHNICAL ASSISTANCE.—

---

[270] P.L. 110-351, §401(b)(2)(B), struck out "means—" and subparagraphs (A) and (B) and substituted "means, with respect to any fiscal year, the number of special needs adoptions that are not older child adoptions in the State in fiscal year 2007.". For the effective date, see Vol. II, P.L. 110-351, §601. For subparagraphs (A) and (B) as they formerly read, see Vol. II, Appendix J, Superseded Provisions, P.L. 110-351.

[271] P.L. 110-351, §401(b)(3), struck out "means—" and subparagraphs (A) and (B) and substituted "means, with respect to any fiscal year, the number of older child adoptions in the State in fiscal year 2007.". For the effective date, see Vol. II, P.L. 110-351, §601. For subparagraphs (A) and (B) as they formerly read, see Vol. II, Appendix J, Superseded Provisions, P.L. 110-351.

[272] P.L. 110-351, §401(e)(2), added paragraph (7). For the effective date, see Vol. II, P.L. 110-351, §601.

[273] P.L. 110-351, §401(e)(2), added paragraph (8). For the effective date, see Vol. II, P.L. 110-351, §601.

[274] P..L. 110-351, §401(a)(4), struck out "2008" and substituted "2013". For the effective date, see Vol. II, P.L. 110-351, §601.

[275] P.L. 108-145, §3(a)(5)(B)(ii), struck out "2003" and substituted "2008*", effective October 1, 2003.

*P..L. 110-351, §401(a)(4), struck out "2008" and substituted "2013". For the effective date, see Vol. II, P.L. 110-351, §601.

498 SOCIAL SECURITY ACT—§ 473A(i)(1)

(1) IN GENERAL.—The Secretary may, directly or through grants or contracts, provide technical assistance to assist States and local communities to reach their targets for increased numbers of adoptions and, to the extent that adoption is not possible, alternative permanent placements, for children in foster care.

(2) DESCRIPTION OF THE CHARACTER OF THE TECHNICAL ASSISTANCE.—The technical assistance provided under paragraph (1) may support the goal of encouraging more adoptions out of the foster care system, when adoptions promote the best interests of children, and may include the following:

(A) The development of best practice guidelines for expediting termination of parental rights.

(B) Models to encourage the use of concurrent planning.

(C) The development of specialized units and expertise in moving children toward adoption as a permanency goal.

(D) The development of risk assessment tools to facilitate early identification of the children who will be at risk of harm if returned home.

(E) Models to encourage the fast tracking of children who have not attained 1 year of age into pre–adoptive placements.

(F) Development of programs that place children into pre-adoptive families without waiting for termination of parental rights.

(3) TARGETING OF TECHNICAL ASSISTANCE TO THE COURTS.—Not less than 50 percent of any amount appropriated pursuant to paragraph (4) shall be used to provide technical assistance to the courts.

(4) LIMITATIONS ON AUTHORIZATION OF APPROPRIATIONS.—To carry out this subsection, there are authorized to be appropriated to the Secretary of Health and Human Services not to exceed $10,000,000 for each of fiscal years 2004 through 2006.

TIMELY INTERSTATE HOME STUDY INCENTIVE PAYMENTS

SEC. 473B.[276] [42 U.S.C. 673c note] (a) GRANT AUTHORITY.—The Secretary shall make a grant to each State that is a home study incentive-eligible State for a fiscal year in an amount equal to the timely interstate home study incentive payment payable to the State under this section for the fiscal year, which shall be payable in the immediately succeeding fiscal year.

(b) HOME STUDY INCENTIVE–ELIGIBLE STATE.—A State is a home study incentive-eligible State for a fiscal year if—

(1) the State has a plan approved under this part for the fiscal year;

(2) the State is in compliance with subsection (c) for the fiscal year; and

(3) based on data submitted and verified pursuant to subsection (c), the State has completed a timely interstate home study during the fiscal year.

(c) DATA REQUIREMENTS.—

---

[276] P.L. 109-239, §4(b), added this section, effective October 1, 2006. P.L. 109-239, §4(c) provides that **"Effective October 1, 2010, section 473B of the Social Security Act is repealed."**

SOCIAL SECURITY ACT—§ 473B.(d)(3)(B)   499

(1) IN GENERAL.—A State is in compliance with this subsection for a fiscal year if the State has provided to the Secretary a written report, covering the preceding fiscal year, that specifies—

(A) the total number of interstate home studies requested by the State with respect to children in foster care under the responsibility of the State, and with respect to each such study, the identity of the other State involved;

(B) the total number of timely interstate home studies completed by the State with respect to children in foster care under the responsibility of other States, and with respect to each such study, the identity of the other State involved; and

(C) such other information as the Secretary may require in order to determine whether the State is a home study incentive-eligible State.

(2) VERIFICATION OF DATA.—In determining the number of timely interstate home studies to be attributed to a State under this section, the Secretary shall check the data provided by the State under paragraph (1) against complementary data so provided by other States.

(d) TIMELY INTERSTATE HOME STUDY INCENTIVE PAYMENTS.—

(1) IN GENERAL.—The timely interstate home study incentive payment payable to a State for a fiscal year shall be $1,500, multiplied by the number of timely interstate home studies attributed to the State under this section during the fiscal year, subject to paragraph (2).

(2) PRO RATA ADJUSTMENT IF INSUFFICIENT FUNDS AVAILABLE.—If the total amount of timely interstate home study incentive payments otherwise payable under this section for a fiscal year exceeds the total of the amounts made available pursuant to subsection (h) for the fiscal year (reduced (but not below zero) by the total of the amounts (if any) payable under paragraph (3) of this subsection with respect to the preceding fiscal year), the amount of each such otherwise payable incentive payment shall be reduced by a percentage equal to—

(A) the total of the amounts so made available (as so reduced); divided by

(B) the total of such otherwise payable incentive payments.

(3) APPROPRIATIONS AVAILABLE FOR UNPAID INCENTIVE PAYMENTS FOR PRIOR FISCAL YEARS.—

(A) IN GENERAL.—If payments under this section are reduced under paragraph (2) or subparagraph (B) of this paragraph for a fiscal year, then, before making any other payment under this section for the next fiscal year, the Secretary shall pay each State whose payment was so reduced an amount equal to the total amount of the reductions which applied to the State, subject to subparagraph (B) of this paragraph.

(B) PRO RATA ADJUSTMENT IF INSUFFICIENT FUNDS AVAILABLE.—If the total amount of payments otherwise payable under subparagraph (A) of this paragraph for a fiscal year exceeds the total of the amounts made available pursuant to subsection (h) for the fiscal year, the amount of each such payment shall be reduced by a percentage equal to—

500 SOCIAL SECURITY ACT—§ 473B.(d)(3)(B)(i)

(i) the total of the amounts so made available; divided by
(ii) the total of such otherwise payable payments.

(e) TWO-YEAR AVAILABILITY OF INCENTIVE PAYMENTS.—Payments to a State under this section in a fiscal year shall remain available for use by the State through the end of the next fiscal year.

(f) LIMITATIONS ON USE OF INCENTIVE PAYMENTS.—A State shall not expend an amount paid to the State under this section except to provide to children or families any service (including post-adoption services) that may be provided under part B or E. Amounts expended by a State in accordance with the preceding sentence shall be disregarded in determining State expenditures for purposes of Federal matching payments under sections 423, 434, and 474.

(g) DEFINITIONS.—In this section:

(1) HOME STUDY.—The term "home study" means an evaluation of a home environment conducted in accordance with applicable requirements of the State in which the home is located, to determine whether a proposed placement of a child would meet the individual needs of the child, including the child's safety, permanency, health, well-being, and mental, emotional, and physical development.

(2) INTERSTATE HOME STUDY.—The term "interstate home study" means a home study conducted by a State at the request of another State, to facilitate an adoptive or foster placement in the State of a child in foster care under the responsibility of the State.

(3) TIMELY INTERSTATE HOME STUDY.—The term "timely interstate home study" means an interstate home study completed by a State if the State provides to the State that requested the study, within 30 days after receipt of the request, a report on the results of the study. The preceding sentence shall not be construed to require the State to have completed, within the 30-day period, the parts of the home study involving the education and training of the prospective foster or adoptive parents.

(h) LIMITATIONS ON AUTHORIZATION OF APPROPRIATIONS.—

(1) IN GENERAL.—For payments under this section, there are authorized to be appropriated to the Secretary—

(A) $10,000,000 for fiscal year 2007;
(B) $10,000,000 for fiscal year 2008;
(C) $10,000,000 for fiscal year 2009; and
(D) $10,000,000 for fiscal year 2010.

(2) AVAILABILITY.—Amounts appropriated under paragraph (1) are authorized to remain available until expended.

PAYMENTS TO STATES; ALLOTMENTS TO STATES[277]

SEC. 474. [42 U.S.C. 674] (a) For each quarter beginning after September 30, 1980, each State which has a plan approved under this part shall be entitled to a payment equal to the sum of—

(1) an amount equal to the Federal medical assistance percentage (which shall be as defined in section 1905(b), in the case of a State other than the District of Columbia, or 70 percent, in the

---

[277] See Vol. II, P.L. 99-177, §256, with respect to treatment of foster care and adoption assistance programs.

SOCIAL SECURITY ACT—§ 474(a)(3)(B)   501

case of the District of Columbia)[278] of the total amount expended
during such quarter as foster care maintenance payments under
section 472 for children in foster family homes or child-care institutions[279]; plus

(2) an amount equal to the Federal medical assistance percentage (which shall be as defined in section 1905(b), in the case of a
State other than the District of Columbia, or 70 percent, in the
case of the District of Columbia)[280] of the total amount expended
during such quarter as adoption assistance payments under section 473 pursuant to adoption assistance agreements[281]; plus

(3) subject to section 472(i) an amount equal to the sum of the
following proportions of the total amounts expended during such
quarter as found necessary by the Secretary for the provision of
child placement services and for the proper and efficient administration of the State plan—

(A) 75 per centum of so much of such expenditures as are
for the training (including both short-and long-term training at educational institutions through grants to such institutions or by direct financial assistance to students enrolled
in such institutions) of personnel employed or preparing for
employment by the State agency or by the local agency administering the plan in the political subdivision,

(B)[282] 75 percent of so much of such expenditures (including
travel and per diem expenses) as are for the short-term training of current or prospective foster or adoptive parents or
relative guardians,[283] the members[284] of the staff of State-licensed or State-approved child care institutions providing
care, or State-licensed or State-approved child welfare agen-

---

[278] P.L. 110-275, §302(a), struck out "(as defined in section 1905(b))" and substituted "(which shall
be as defined in section 1905(b), in the case of a State other than the District of Columbia, or 70
percent, in the case of the District of Columbia)", effective October 1, 2008 and applicable to calendar
quarters beginning on and after that date.

[279] P.L. 110-351, §301(c)(2), inserts the following: "(or, with respect to such payments made during
such quarter under a cooperative agreement or contract entered into by the State and an Indian
tribe, tribal organization, or tribal consortium for the administration or payment of funds under this
part, an amount equal to the Federal medical assistance percentage that would apply under section
479B(d) (in this paragraph referred to as the 'tribal FMAP') if such Indian tribe, tribal organization,
or tribal consortium made such payments under a program operated under that section, unless the
tribal FMAP is less than the Federal medical assistance percentage that applies to the State)", **to
take effect on October 1, 2009, without regard to whether the regulations required under
subsection (e)(1) have been promulgated by such date.**
See Vol. II, P.L. 110-351, §301(d), with respect to some rules of construction and §301(e), with
respect to regulations.

[280] P.L. 110-275, §302(a), struck out "(as defined in section 1905(b))" and substituted "(which shall
be as defined in section 1905(b), in the case of a State other than the District of Columbia, or 70
percent, in the case of the District of Columbia)", effective October 1, 2008 and applicable to calendar
quarters beginning on and after that date.

[281] P.L. 110-351, §301(c)(2), inserts the following: "(or, with respect to such payments made during
such quarter under a cooperative agreement or contract entered into by the State and an Indian
tribe, tribal organization, or tribal consortium for the administration or payment of funds under this
part, an amount equal to the Federal medical assistance percentage that would apply under section
479B(d) (in this paragraph referred to as the 'tribal FMAP') if such Indian tribe, tribal organization,
or tribal consortium made such payments under a program operated under that section, unless the
tribal FMAP is less than the Federal medical assistance percentage that applies to the State)", **to
take effect on October 1, 2009, without regard to whether the regulations required under
subsection (e)(1) have been promulgated by such date.**
See Vol. II, P.L. 110-351, §301(d), with respect to some rules of construction and §301(e), with
respect to regulations.

[282] See Vol. II, P.L. 110-351, §203(b), with respect to the phase-in of expenditures based on the
amendments made by P.L. 110-351, §203(a).

[283] P.L. 110-351, §203(a)(1), inserted "or relative guardians". For the effective date, see Vol. II,
P.L. 110-351, §601.

[284] P.L. 110-351, §203(a)(2), struck out "and the members" and substituted ", the members".

502 SOCIAL SECURITY ACT—§ 474(a)(3)(B)(cont)

cies providing services,[285] to [286] children receiving assistance under this part, and members of the staff of abuse and neglect courts, agency attorneys, attorneys representing children or parents, guardians ad litem, or other court-appointed special advocates representing children in proceedings of such courts,[287] in ways that increase the ability of such current or prospective parents, guardians,[288] staff members, institutions, attorneys and advocates[289] to provide support and assistance to foster and adopted children, and children living with relative guardians[290] whether incurred directly by the State or by contract,

(C) 50 percent of so much of such expenditures as are for the planning, design, development, or installation of statewide mechanized data collection and information retrieval systems (including 50 percent of the full amount of expenditures for hardware components for such systems) but only to the extent that such systems—

(i) meet the requirements imposed by regulations promulgated pursuant to section 479(b)(2);

(ii) to the extent practicable, are capable of interfacing with the State data collection system that collects information relating to child abuse and neglect;

(iii) to the extent practicable, have the capability of interfacing with, and retrieving information from, the State data collection system that collects information relating to the eligibility of individuals under part A (for the purposes of facilitating verification of eligibility of foster children); and

(iv) are determined by the Secretary to be likely to provide more efficient, economical, and effective administration of the programs carried out under a State plan approved under part B or this part; and

(D) 50 percent of so much of such expenditures as are for the operation of the statewide mechanized data collection and information retrieval systems referred to in subparagraph (C); and

(E) one-half of the remainder of such expenditures; plus

(4) an amount equal to the amount (if any) by which—

(A) the lesser of—

(i) 80 percent of the amount expended by the State during the fiscal year in which the quarter occurs to carry out programs in accordance with the State application

---

[285] P.L. 110-351, §203(a)(3), inserted ", or State-licensed or State-approved child welfare agencies providiing services,". For the effective date, see Vol. II, P.L. 110-351, §601.

[286] P.L. 110-351, §203(a)(4), struck out "foster and adoptive". For the effective date, see Vol. II, P.L. 110-351, §601.

[287] P.L. 110-351, §203(a)(5), inserted "and members of the staff of abuse and neglect courts, agency attorneys, attorneys representing children or parents, guardians ad litem, or other court-appointed special advocates representing children in proceedings of such courts,". For the effective date, see Vol. II, P.L. 110-351, §601.

[288] P.L. 110-351, §203(a)(6), inserted "guardians,". For the effective date, see Vol. II, P.L. 110-351, §601.

[289] P.L. 110-351, §203(a)(7), struck out "and institutions" and substituted "institutions, attorneys, and advocates". For the effective date, see Vol. II, P.L. 110-351, §601.

[290] P.L. 110-351, §203(a)(8), inserted "and children living with relative guardians". For the effective date, see Vol. II, P.L. 110-351, §601.

SOCIAL SECURITY ACT—§ 474(b)(4)(C)   503

approved under section 477(b) for the period in which the quarter occurs (including any amendment that meets the requirements of section 477(b)(5)); or

(ii) the amount allotted to the State under section 477(c)(1) for the fiscal year in which the quarter occurs, reduced by the total of the amounts payable to the State under this paragraph for all prior quarters in the fiscal year; exceeds

(B) the total amount of any penalties assessed against the State under section 477(e) during the fiscal year in which the quarter occurs; plus[291]

(5)[292] an amount equal to the percentage by which the expenditures referred to in paragraph (2) of this subsection are reimbursed of the total amount expended during such quarter as kinship guardianship assistance payments under section 473(d) pursuant to kinship guardianship assistance agreements.

(b)(1) The Secretary shall, prior to the beginning of each quarter, estimate the amount to which a State will be entitled under subsection (a) for such quarter, such estimates to be based on (A) a report filed by the State containing its estimate of the total sum to be expended in such quarter in accordance with subsection (a), and stating the amount appropriated or made available by the State and its political subdivisions for such expenditures in such quarter, and if such amount is less than the State's proportionate share of the total sum of such estimated expenditures, the source or sources from which the difference is expected to be derived, (B) records showing the number of children in the State receiving assistance under this part, and (C) such other investigation as the Secretary may find necessary.

(2) The Secretary shall then pay to the State, in such installments as he may determine, the amounts so estimated, reduced or increased to the extent of any overpayment or underpayment which the Secretary determines was made under this section to such State for any prior quarter and with respect to which adjustment has not already been made under this subsection.

(3) The pro rata share to which the United States is equitably entitled, as determined by the Secretary, of the net amount recovered during any quarter by the State or any political subdivision thereof with respect to foster care and adoption assistance furnished under the State plan shall be considered an overpayment to be adjusted under this subsection.

(4)(A) Within 60 days after receipt of a State claim for expenditures pursuant to subsection (a), the Secretary shall allow, disallow, or defer such claim.

(B) Within 15 days after a decision to defer such a State claim, the Secretary shall notify the State of the reasons for the deferral and of the additional information necessary to determine the allowability of the claim.

(C) Within 90 days after receiving such necessary information (in readily reviewable form), the Secretary shall—

---

[291] P.L. 110-351, §101(c)(3)(A), inserted "; plus".

[292] P.L. 110-351, §101(c)(3)(B), added paragraph (5). For the effective date, see Vol. II, P.L. 110-351, §601.

504 SOCIAL SECURITY ACT—§ 474(b)(4)(C)(i)

(i) disallow the claim, if able to complete the review and determine that the claim is not allowable, or

(ii) in any other case, allow the claim, subject to disallowance (as necessary)—

(I) upon completion of the review, if it is determined that the claim is not allowable; or

(II) on the basis of findings of an audit or financial management review.

(c) AUTOMATED DATA COLLECTION EXPENDITURES.—The Secretary shall treat as necessary for the proper and efficient administration of the State plan all expenditures of a State necessary in order for the State to plan, design, develop, install, and operate data collection and information retrieval systems described in subsection (a)(3)(C), without regard to whether the systems may be used with respect to foster or adoptive children other than those on behalf of whom foster care maintenance payments or adoption assistance payments may be made under this part.

(d)(1) If, during any quarter of a fiscal year, a State's program operated under this part is found, as a result of a review conducted under section 1123A, or otherwise, to have violated paragraph (18) or (23) of section 471(a) with respect to a person or to have failed to implement a corrective action plan within a period of time not to exceed 6 months with respect to such violation, then, notwithstanding subsection (a) of this section and any regulations promulgated under section 1123A(b)(3), the Secretary shall reduce the amount otherwise payable to the State under this part, for that fiscal year quarter and for any subsequent quarter of such fiscal year, until the State program is found, as a result of a subsequent review under section 1123A, to have implemented a corrective action plan with respect to such violation, by—

(A) 2 percent of such otherwise payable amount, in the case of the 1st such finding for the fiscal year with respect to the State;

(B) 3 percent of such otherwise payable amount, in the case of the 2nd such finding for the fiscal year with respect to the State; or

(C) 5 percent of such otherwise payable amount, in the case of the 3rd or subsequent such finding for the fiscal year with respect to the State.

In imposing the penalties described in this paragraph, the Secretary shall not reduce any fiscal year payment to a State by more than 5 percent

(2) Any other entity which is in a State that receives funds under this part and which violates paragraph (18) or (23) of section 471(a) during a fiscal year quarter with respect to any person shall remit to the Secretary all funds that were paid by the State to the entity during the quarter from such funds.

(3)(A) Any individual who is aggrieved by a violation of section 471(a)(18) by a State or other entity may bring an action seeking relief from the State or other entity in any United States district court.

(B) An action under this paragraph may not be brought more than 2 years after the date the alleged violation occurred.

(4) This subsection shall not be construed to affect the application of the Indian Child Welfare Act of 1978.

SOCIAL SECURITY ACT—§ 475(1)(A)   505

(e) DISCRETIONARY GRANTS FOR EDUCATIONAL AND TRAINING VOUCHERS FOR YOUTHS AGING OUT OF FOSTER CARE.—From amounts appropriated pursuant to section 477(h)(2), the Secretary may make a grant to a State with a plan approved under this part, for a calendar quarter, in an amount equal to the lesser of—

(1) 80 percent of the amounts expended by the State during the quarter to carry out programs for the purposes described in section 477(a)(6); or

(2) the amount, if any, allotted to the State under section 477(c)(3) for the fiscal year in which the quarter occurs, reduced by the total of the amounts payable to the State under this subsection for such purposes for all prior quarters in the fiscal year.

(f)(1) If the Secretary finds that a State has failed to submit to the Secretary data, as required by regulation, for the data collection system implemented under section 479, the Secretary shall, within 30 days after the date by which the data was due to be so submitted, notify the State of the failure and that payments to the State under this part will be reduced if the State fails to submit the data, as so required, within 6 months after the date the data was originally due to be so submitted.

(2) If the Secretary finds that the State has failed to submit the data, as so required, by the end of the 6-month period referred to in paragraph (1) of this subsection, then, notwithstanding subsection (a) of this section and any regulations promulgated under section 1123A(b)(3), the Secretary shall reduce the amounts otherwise payable to the State under this part, for each quarter ending in the 6-month period (and each quarter ending in each subsequent consecutively occurring 6-month period until the Secretary finds that the State has submitted the data, as so required), by—

(A) 1/6 of 1 percent of the total amount expended by the State for administration of foster care activities under the State plan approved under this part in the quarter so ending, in the case of the 1st 6-month period during which the failure continues; or

(B) 1/4 of 1 percent of the total amount so expended, in the case of the 2nd or any subsequent such 6-month period.

(g)[293] For purposes of this part, after the termination of a demonstration project relating to guardianship conducted by a State under section 1130, the expenditures of the State for the provision, to children who, as of September 30, 2008, were receiving assistance or services under the project, of the same assistance and services under the same terms and conditions that applied during the conduct of the project, are deemed to be expenditures under the State plan approved under this part.

DEFINITIONS

SEC. 475. [42 U.S.C. 675] As used in this part or part B of this title:

(1) The term "case plan" means a written document which includes at least the following:

(A) A description of the type of home or institution in which a child is to be placed, including a discussion of the safety

---

[293] P.L. 110-351, §101(d), added subsection (g). For the effective date, see Vol. II, P.L. 110-351, §601.

506   SOCIAL SECURITY ACT—§ 475(1)(A)(cont)

and appropriateness of the placement and how the agency which is responsible for the child plans to carry out the voluntary placement agreement entered into or judicial determination made with respect to the child in accordance with section 472(a)(1).

(B) A plan for assuring that the child receives safe and proper care and that services are provided to the parents, child, and foster parents in order to improve the conditions in the parents' home, facilitate return of the child to his own safe home or the permanent placement of the child, and address the needs of the child while in foster care, including a discussion of the appropriateness of the services that have been provided to the child under the plan.

(C) The[294] health and education records of the child, including the most recent information available regarding[295]—

(i) the names and addresses of the child's health and educational providers;

(ii) the child's grade level performance;

(iii) the child's school record;

(iv)[296] a record of the child's immunizations;

(v)[297] the child's known medical problems;

(vi)[298] the child's medications; and

(vii)[299] any other relevant health and education information concerning the child determined to be appropriate by the State agency.

(D) Where appropriate, for a child age 16 or over, a written description of the programs and services which will help such child prepare for the transition from foster care to independent living.

(E) In the case of a child with respect to whom the permanency plan is adoption or placement in another permanent home, documentation of the steps the agency is taking to find an adoptive family or other permanent living arrangement for the child, to place the child with an adoptive family, a fit and willing relative, a legal guardian, or in another planned permanent living arrangement, and to finalize the adoption or legal guardianship. At a minimum, such documentation shall include child specific recruitment efforts such as the use of State, regional, and national adoption exchanges including electronic exchange systems to facilitate orderly and timely in-State and interstate placements.

---

[294] P.L. 109-239, §7(1)(A), struck out "To the extent available and accessible, the" and substituted "The", effective October 1, 2006. See Vol. II, P.L. 109-239, §14, with respect to applicability and the possible delay permitted if State legislation was required.

[295] P.L. 109-239, §7(1)(B), inserted "the most recent information available regarding", effective October 1, 2006. See Vol. II, P.L. 109-239, §14, with respect to applicability and the possible delay permitted if State legislation was required.

[296] P.L. 110-351, §204(a)(1)(A), struck out clause (iv) and redesignated the former clause (v) as clause (iv). For the effective date, see Vol. II, P.L. 110-351, §601. For clause (iv) as it formerly read, see Vol. II, Appendix J, Superseded Provisions, P.L. 110-351.

[297] P.L. 110-351, §204(a)(1)(A), redesignated the former clause (vi) as clause (v).

[298] P.L. 110-351, §204(a)(1)(A), redesignated the former clause (vii) as clause (vi).

[299] P.L. 110-351, §204(a)(1)(A), redesignated the former clause (viii) as clause (vii).

SOCIAL SECURITY ACT—§ 475(3)

(F)[300] In the case of a child with respect to whom the permanency plan is placement with a relative and receipt of kinship guardianship assistance payments under section 473(d), a description of—

(i) the steps that the agency has taken to determine that it is not appropriate for the child to be returned home or adopted;

(ii) the reasons for any separation of siblings during placement;

(iii) the reasons why a permanent placement with a fit and willing relative through a kinship guardianship assistance arrangement is in the child's best interests;

(iv) the ways in which the child meets the eligibility requirements for a kinship guardianship assistance payment;

(v) the efforts the agency has made to discuss adoption by the child's relative foster parent as a more permanent alternative to legal guardianship and, in the case of a relative foster parent who has chosen not to pursue adoption, documentation of the reasons therefor; and

(vi) the efforts made by the State agency to discuss with the child's parent or parents the kinship guardianship assistance arrangement, or the reasons why the efforts were not made.

(G)[301] A plan for ensuring the educational stability of the child while in foster care, including—

(i) assurances that the placement of the child in foster care takes into account the appropriateness of the current educational setting and the proximity to the school in which the child is enrolled at the time of placement; and

(ii)(I) an assurance that the State agency has coordinated with appropriate local educational agencies (as defined under section 9101 of the Elementary and Secondary Education Act of 1965) to ensure that the child remains in the school in which the child is enrolled at the time of placement; or

(II) if remaining in such school is not in the best interests of the child, assurances by the State agency and the local educational agencies to provide immediate and appropriate enrollment in a new school, with all of the educational records of the child provided to the school.

(2) The term "parents" means biological or adoptive parents or legal guardians, as determined by applicable State law.

(3) The term "adoption assistance agreement" means a written agreement, binding on the parties to the agreement, between the State agency, other relevant agencies, and the prospective adoptive parents of a minor child which at a minimum (A) specifies the nature and amount of any payments, services, and assistance

---

[300] P.L. 110-351, §101(c)(4), added subparagraph (F). For the effective date, see Vol. II, P.L. 110-351, §601.

[301] P.L. 110-351, §204(a)(1)(B), added subparagraph (G). For the effective date, see Vol. II, P.L. 110-351, §601.

508 SOCIAL SECURITY ACT—§ 475(3)(cont)

to be provided under such agreement, and (B) stipulates that the agreement shall remain in effect regardless of the State of which the adoptive parents are residents at any given time. The agreement shall contain provisions for the protection (under an interstate compact approved by the Secretary or otherwise) of the interests of the child in cases where the adoptive parents and child move to another State while the agreement is effective."

(4)(A) The term "foster care maintenance payments" means payments to cover the cost of (and the cost of providing) food, clothing, shelter, daily supervision, school supplies, a child's personal incidentals, liability insurance with respect to a child, reasonable[302] travel to the child's home for visitation, and reasonable travel for the child to remain in the school in which the child is enrolled at the time of placement[303]. In the case of institutional care, such term shall include the reasonable costs of administration and operation of such institution as are necessarily required to provide the items described in the preceding sentence

(B) In cases where—

(i) a child placed in a foster family home or child-care institution is the parent of a son or daughter who is in the same home or institution, and

(ii) payments described in subparagraph (A) are being made under this part with respect to such child,

the foster care maintenance payments made with respect to such child as otherwise determined under subparagraph (A) shall also include such amounts as may be necessary to cover the cost of the items described in that subparagraph with respect to such son or daughter.

(5) The term "case review system" means a procedure for assuring that—

(A) each child has a case plan designed to achieve placement in a safe setting that is the least restrictive (most family like) and most appropriate setting available and in close proximity to the parents' home, consistent with the best interest and special needs of the child, which—

(i) if the child has been placed in a foster family home or child-care institution a substantial distance from the home of the parents of the child, or in a State different from the State in which such home is located, sets forth the reasons why such placement is in the best interests of the child, and

(ii) if the child has been placed in foster care outside the State in which the home of the parents of the child is located, requires that, periodically, but not less frequently than every 6[304] months, a caseworker on the staff of the State agency of the State in which the home

---

[302] P.L. 110-351, §204(a)(2)(A), struck out "and reasonable" and substituted "reasonable".

[303] P.L. 110-351, §204(a)(2)(B), inserted ", and reasonable travel for the child to remain in the school in which the child is enrolled at the time of placement". For the effective date, see Vol. II, P.L. 110-351, §601.

[304] P.L. 109-239, §6(b), struck out "12" and substituted "6", effective October 1, 2006. See Vol. II, P.L. 109-239, §14, with respect to applicability and a possible delay permitted if State legislation is required.

SOCIAL SECURITY ACT—§ 475(5)(C)

of the parents of the child is located, of the State in which the child has been placed, or of a private agency under contract with either such State[305], visit such child in such home or institution and submit a report on such visit to the State agency of the State in which the home of the parents of the child is located,

(B) the status of each child is reviewed periodically but no less frequently than once every six months by either a court or by administrative review (as defined in paragraph (6)) in order to determine the safety of the child, the continuing necessity for and appropriateness of the placement, the extent of compliance with the case plan, and the extent of progress which has been made toward alleviating or mitigating the causes necessitating placement in foster care, and to project a likely date by which the child may be returned to and safely maintained in the home or placed for adoption or legal guardianship,

(C) with respect to each such child, (i) procedural safeguards will be applied, among other things, to assure each child in foster care under the supervision of the State of a permanency hearing to be held, in a family or juvenile court or another court (including a tribal court) of competent jurisdiction, or by an administrative body appointed or approved by the court, no later than 12 months after the date the child is considered to have entered foster care (as determined under subparagraph (F)) (and not less frequently than every 12 months thereafter during the continuation of foster care), which hearing shall determine the permanency plan for the child that includes whether, and if applicable when, the child will be returned to the parent, placed for adoption and the State will file a petition for termination of parental rights, or referred for legal guardianship, or (in cases where the State agency has documented to the State court a compelling reason for determining that it would not be in the best interests of the child to return home, be referred for termination of parental rights, or be placed for adoption, with a fit and willing relative, or with a legal guardian) placed in another planned permanent living arrangement, in the case of a child who will not be returned to the parent, the hearing shall consider in-State and out-of-State placement options, and, in the case of a child described in subparagraph (A)(ii), the hearing shall determine whether the out-of-State placement continues to be appropriate and in the best interests of the child, and, in the case of a child who has attained age 16, the services needed to assist the child to make the transition from foster care to independent living; (ii) procedural safeguards shall be applied with respect to parental rights pertaining to the removal of the child from the home of his parents, to a change in the child's placement, and to any determination

---

[305] P.L. 109-239, §6(a), struck out "or of the State in which such child has been placed" and substituted "of the State in which such child has been placed, or of a private agency under contract with either such State", effective October 1, 2006. See Vol. II, P.L. 109-239, §14, with respect to applicability and a possible delay permitted if State legislation is required.

510   SOCIAL SECURITY ACT—§ 475(5)(C)(cont)

affecting visitation privileges of parents; and (iii) procedural safeguards shall be applied to assure that in any permanency hearing held with respect to the child, including any hearing regarding the transition of the child from foster care to independent living, the court or administrative body conducting the hearing consults, in an age-appropriate manner, with the child regarding the proposed permanency or transition plan for the child;

(D) a child's health and education record (as described in paragraph (1)(A)) is reviewed and updated, and a copy of the record is[306] supplied to the foster parent or foster care provider with whom the child is placed, at the time of each placement of the child in foster care, and is supplied at no cost at the time the child leaves foster care if the child is leaving foster care by reason of having attained the age of majority under the State law[307];

(E) in the case of a child who has been in foster care under the responsibility of the State for 15 of the most recent 22 months, or, if a court of competent jurisdiction has determined a child to be an abandoned infant (as defined under State law) or has made a determination that the parent has committed murder of another child of the parent, committed voluntary manslaughter of another child of the parent, aided or abetted, attempted, conspired, or solicited to commit such a murder or such a voluntary manslaughter, or committed a felony assault that has resulted in serious bodily injury to the child or to another child of the parent, the State shall file a petition to terminate the parental rights of the child's parents (or, if such a petition has been filed by another party, seek to be joined as a party to the petition), and, concurrently, to identify, recruit, process, and approve a qualified family for an adoption, unless—

(i) at the option of the State, the child is being cared for by a relative;

(ii) a State agency has documented in the case plan (which shall be available for court review) a compelling reason for determining that filing such a petition would not be in the best interests of the child; or

(iii) the State has not provided to the family of the child, consistent with the time period in the State case plan, such services as the State deems necessary for the safe return of the child to the child's home, if reasonable efforts of the type described in section 471(a)(15)(B)(ii) are required to be made with respect to the child;

(F) a child shall be considered to have entered foster care on the earlier of—

---

[306] P.L. 109-239, §7(2)(A), inserted "a copy of the record is supplied", effective October 1, 2006. See Vol. II, P.L. 109-239, §14, with respect to applicability and the possible delay permitted if State legislation was required.

[307] P.L. 109-239, §7(2)(B), inserted ", and is supplied at no cost at the time the child leaves foster care if the child is leaving foster care by reason of having attained the age of majority under the State law", effective October 1, 2006. See Vol. II, P.L. 109-239, §14, with respect to applicability and the possible delay permitted if State legislation was required.

SOCIAL SECURITY ACT—§ 475(8)(A) 511

(i) the date of the first judicial finding that the child has been subjected to child abuse or neglect; or

(ii) the date that is 60 days after the date on which the child is removed from the home;[308]

(G) the foster parents (if any) of a child and any preadoptive parent or relative providing care for the child are provided with notice of, and a right[309] to be heard in, any proceeding [310] to be held with respect to the child, except that this subparagraph shall not be construed to require that any foster parent, preadoptive parent, or relative providing care for the child be made a party to such a proceeding[311] solely on the basis of such notice and right[312] to be heard; and[313]

(H)[314] during the 90-day period immediately prior to the date on which the child will attain 18 years of age, or such greater age as the State may elect under paragraph (8)(B)(iii), whether during that period foster care maintenance payments are being made on the child's behalf or the child is receiving benefits or services under section 477, a caseworker on the staff of the State agency, and, as appropriate, other representatives of the child provide the child with assistance and support in developing a transition plan that is personalized at the direction of the child, includes specific options on housing, health insurance, education, local opportunities for mentors and continuing support services, and work force supports and employment services, and is as detailed as the child may elect.

(6) The term "administrative review" means a review open to the participation of the parents of the child, conducted by a panel of appropriate persons at least one of whom is not responsible for the case management of, or the delivery of services to, either the child or the parents who are the subject of the review.

(7) The term "legal guardianship" means a judicially created relationship between child and caretaker which is intended to be permanent and self-sustaining as evidenced by the transfer to the caretaker of the following parental rights with respect to the child: protection, education, care and control of the person, custody of the person, and decisionmaking. The term "legal guardian" means the caretaker in such a relationship.

(8)[315](A) Subject to subparagraph (B), the term "child" means an individual who has not attained 18 years of age.

---

[308] P.L. 110-351, §202(1) struck out "and".

[309] P.L. 109-239, §8(a)(1), struck out "an opportunity" and substituted "a right", effective October 1, 2006. See Vol. II, P.L. 109-239, §14, with respect to applicability and the possible delay permitted if State legislation was required.

[310] P.L. 109-239, §8(a)(2), struck out "review or hearing" and substituted "proceeding", effective October 1, 2006. See Vol. II, P.L. 109-239, §14, with respect to applicability and the possible delay permitted if State legislation was required.

[311] P.L. 109-239, §8(a)(2), struck out "review or hearing" and substituted "proceeding", effective October 1, 2006. See Vol. II, P.L. 109-239, §14, with respect to applicability and the possible delay permitted if State legislation was required.

[312] P.L. 109-239, §8(a)(1), struck out "an opportunity" and substituted "a right", effective October 1, 2006. See Vol. II, P.L. 109-239, §14, with respect to applicability and the possible delay permitted if State legislation was required.

[313] P.L. 110-351, §202(2) struck out the period and inserted "; and".

[314] P.L. 110-351, §202(3), added subparagraph (H). For the effective date, see Vol. II, P.L. 110-351, §601.

[315] P.L. 110-351, §201(a), adds paragraph (8), **to be effective October 1, 2010.**

512 SOCIAL SECURITY ACT—§ 475(8)(B)

(B) At the option of a State, the term shall include an individual—

(i)(I) who is in foster care under the responsibility of the State;

(II) with respect to whom an adoption assistance agreement is in effect under section 473 if the child had attained 16 years of age before the agreement became effective; or

(III) with respect to whom a kinship guardianship assistance agreement is in effect under section 473(d) if the child had attained 16 years of age before the agreement became effective;

(ii) who has attained 18 years of age; (iii) who has not attained 19, 20, or 21 years of age, as the State may elect; and (iv) who is—

(iii) who has not attained 19, 20, or 21 years of age, as the State may elect; and

(iv) who is—

(I) completing secondary education or a program leading to an equivalent credential;

(II) enrolled in an institution which provides postsecondary or vocational education;

(III) participating in a program or activity designed to promote, or remove barriers to, employment;

(IV) employed for at least 80 hours per month; or

(V) incapable of doing any of the activities described in subclauses (I) through (IV) due to a medical condition, which incapability is supported by regularly updated information in the case plan of the child.

TECHNICAL ASSISTANCE; DATA COLLECTION AND EVALUATION

Sec. 476. [42 U.S.C. 676] (a) The Secretary may provide technical assistance to the States to assist them to develop the programs authorized under this part and shall periodically (1) evaluate the programs authorized under this part and part B of this title and (2) collect and publish data pertaining to the incidence and characteristics of foster care and adoptions in this country.

(b) Each State shall submit statistical reports as the Secretary may require with respect to children for whom payments are made under this part containing information with respect to such children including legal status, demographic characteristics, location, and length of any stay in foster care.

(c)[316] TECHNICAL ASSISTANCE AND IMPLEMENTATION SERVICES FOR TRIBAL PROGRAMS.—

(1) AUTHORITY.—The Secretary shall provide technical assistance and implementation services that are dedicated to improving services and permanency outcomes for Indian children and their families through the provision of assistance described in paragraph (2).

(2) ASSISTANCE PROVIDED.—

(A) IN GENERAL.—The technical assistance and implementation services shall be to—

---

[316] P.L. 110-351, §302, added subsection (c). For the effective date, see Vol. II, P.L. 110-351, §601.

(i) provide information, advice, educational materials, and technical assistance to Indian tribes and tribal organizations with respect to the types of services, administrative functions, data collection, program management, and reporting that are required under State plans under part B and this part;

(ii) assist and provide technical assistance to—

(I) Indian tribes, tribal organizations, and tribal consortia seeking to operate a program under part B or under this part through direct application to the Secretary under section 479B; and

(II) Indian tribes, tribal organizations, tribal consortia, and States seeking to develop cooperative agreements to provide for payments under this part or satisfy the requirements of section 422(b)(9) , 471(a)(32), or 477(b)(3)(G); and

(iii) subject to subparagraph (B), make one-time grants, to tribes, tribal organizations, or tribal consortia that are seeking to develop, and intend, not later than 24 months after receiving such a grant to submit to the Secretary a plan under section 471 to implement a program under this part as authorized by section 479B, that shall—

(I) not exceed $300,000; and

(II) be used for the cost of developing a plan under section 471 to carry out a program under section 479B, including costs related to development of necessary data collection systems, a cost allocation plan, agency and tribal court procedures necessary to meet the case review system requirements under section 475(5), or any other costs attributable to meeting any other requirement necessary for approval of such a plan under this part.

(B) GRANT CONDITION.—

(i) IN GENERAL.—As a condition of being paid a grant under subparagraph (A)(iii), a tribe, tribal organization, or tribal consortium shall agree to repay the total amount of the grant awarded if the tribe, tribal organization, or tribal consortium fails to submit to the Secretary a plan under section 471 to carry out a program under section 479B by the end of the 24-month period described in that subparagraph.

(ii) EXCEPTION.—The Secretary shall waive the requirement to repay a grant imposed by clause (i) if the Secretary determines that a tribe's, tribal organization's, or tribal consortium's failure to submit a plan within such period was the result of circumstances beyond the control of the tribe, tribal organization, or tribal consortium.

(C) IMPLEMENTATION AUTHORITY.—The Secretary may provide the technical assistance and implementation services described in subparagraph (A) either directly or through a grant or contract with public or private organizations knowl-

514   SOCIAL SECURITY ACT—§ 476(c)(3)

edgeable and experienced in the field of Indian tribal affairs and child welfare.

(3) APPROPRIATION.—There is appropriated to the Secretary, out of any money in the Treasury of the United States not otherwise appropriated, $3,000,000 for fiscal year 2009 and each fiscal year thereafter to carry out this subsection

JOHN H. CHAFEE FOSTER CARE INDEPENDENCE PROGRAM

SEC. 477. [42 U.S.C. 677] (a) PURPOSE.—The purpose of this section is to provide States with flexible funding that will enable programs to be designed and conducted—

(1) to identify children who are likely to remain in foster care until 18 years of age and to help these children make the transition to self-sufficiency by providing services such as assistance in obtaining a high school diploma, career exploration, vocational training, job placement and retention, training in daily living skills, training in budgeting and financial management skills, substance abuse prevention, and preventive health activities (including smoking avoidance, nutrition education, and pregnancy prevention);

(2) to help children who are likely to remain in foster care until 18 years of age receive the education, training, and services necessary to obtain employment;

(3) to help children who are likely to remain in foster care until 18 years of age prepare for and enter postsecondary training and education institutions;

(4) to provide personal and emotional support to children aging out of foster care, through mentors and the promotion of interactions with dedicated adults;

(5) to provide financial, housing, counseling, employment, education, and other appropriate support and services to former foster care recipients between 18 and 21 years of age to complement their own efforts to achieve self-sufficiency and to assure that program participants recognize and accept their personal responsibility for preparing for and then making the transition from adolescence to adulthood;[317]

(6) to make available vouchers for education and training, including postsecondary training and education, to youths who have aged out of foster care.; and[318]

(7)[319] to provide the services referred to in this subsection to children who, after attaining 16 years of age, have left foster care for kinship guardianship or adoption.

(b) APPLICATIONS.—

(1) IN GENERAL.—A State may apply for funds from its allotment under subsection (c) for a period of five consecutive fiscal years by submitting to the Secretary, in writing, a plan that meets the requirements of paragraph (2) and the certifications required by paragraph (3) with respect to the plan.

(2) STATE PLAN.—A plan meets the requirements of this paragraph if the plan specifies which State agency or agencies will

---

[317] P.L. 110-351, §101(e)(1)(A), struck out "and".

[318] P.L. 110-351, §101(e)(1)(B), struck out the period and inserted "; and".

[319] P.L. 110-351, §101(e)(1)(C), added paragraph (7). For the effective date, see Vol. II, P.L. 110-351, §601.

administer, supervise, or oversee the programs carried out under the plan, and describes how the State intends to do the following:

(A) Design and deliver programs to achieve the purposes of this section.

(B) Ensure that all political subdivisions in the State are served by the program, though not necessarily in a uniform manner.

(C) Ensure that the programs serve children of various ages and at various stages of achieving independence.

(D) Involve the public and private sectors in helping adolescents in foster care achieve independence.

(E) Use objective criteria for determining eligibility for benefits and services under the programs, and for ensuring fair and equitable treatment of benefit recipients.

(F) Cooperate in national evaluations of the effects of the programs in achieving the purposes of this section.

(3) CERTIFICATIONS.—The certifications required by this paragraph with respect to a plan are the following:

(A) A certification by the chief executive officer of the State that the State will provide assistance and services to children who have left foster care because they have attained 18 years of age, and who have not attained 21 years of age.

(B) A certification by the chief executive officer of the State that not more than 30 percent of the amounts paid to the State from its allotment under subsection (c) for a fiscal year will be expended for room or board for children who have left foster care because they have attained 18 years of age, and who have not attained 21 years of age.

(C) A certification by the chief executive officer of the State that none of the amounts paid to the State from its allotment under subsection (c) will be expended or room or board for any child who has not attained 18 years of age.

(D) A certification by the chief executive officer of the State that the State will use training funds provided under the program of Federal payments for foster care and adoption assistance to provide training to help foster parents, adoptive parents, workers in group homes, and case managers understand and address the issues confronting adolescents preparing for independent living, and will, to the extent possible, coordinate such training with the independent living program conducted for adolescents.

(E) A certification by the chief executive officer of the State that the State has consulted widely with public and private organizations in developing the plan and that the State has given all interested members of the public at least 30 days to submit comments on the plan.

(F) A certification by the chief executive officer of the State that the State will make every effort to coordinate the State programs receiving funds provided from an allotment made to the State under subsection (c) with other Federal and State programs for youth (especially transitional living youth projects funded under part B of title III of the Juvenile Justice and Delinquency Prevention Act of 1974), abstinence education programs, local housing programs, programs

516   SOCIAL SECURITY ACT—§ 477(b)(3)(F)(cont)

for disabled youth (especially sheltered workshops), and school-to-work programs offered by high schools or local workforce agencies.

(G) A certification by the chief executive officer of the State that each Indian tribe in the State has been consulted about the programs to be carried out under the plan; that there have been efforts to coordinate the programs with such tribes; and that[320] benefits and services under the programs will be made available to Indian children in the State on the same basis as to other children in the State.[321]

(H) A certification by the chief executive officer of the State that the State will ensure that adolescents participating in the program under this section participate directly in designing their own program activities that prepare them for independent living and that the adolescents accept personal responsibility for living up to their part of the program.

(I) A certification by the chief executive officer of the State that the State has established and will enforce standards and procedures to prevent fraud and abuse in the programs carried out under the plan.

(J) A certification by the chief executive officer of the State that the State educational and training voucher program under this section is in compliance with the conditions specified in subsection (i), including a statement describing methods the State will use—

(i) to ensure that the total amount of educational assistance to a youth under this section and under other Federal and Federally supported programs does not exceed the limitation specified in subsection (i)(5); and

(ii) to avoid duplication of benefits under this and any other Federal or Federally assisted benefit program.

(4) APPROVAL.—The Secretary shall approve an application submitted by a State pursuant to paragraph (1) for a period if—

(A) the application is submitted on or before June 30 of the calendar year in which such period begins; and

(B) the Secretary finds that the application contains the material required by paragraph (1).

(5) AUTHORITY TO IMPLEMENT CERTAIN AMENDMENTS; NOTIFICATION.—A State with an application approved under paragraph (4) may implement any amendment to the plan contained in the application if the application, incorporating the amendment, would be approvable under paragraph (4). Within 30 days after a State

---

[320] P.L. 110-351, §301(c)(1)(B)(i), strikes out "and that" and substitutes "that", **to be effective October 1, 2009.**

[321] P.L. 110-351, §301(c)(1)(B)(ii), strikes out the period and inserts the following: "; and that the State will negotiate in good faith with any Indian tribe, tribal organization, or tribal consortium in the State that does not receive an allotment under subsection (j)(4) for a fiscal year and that requests to develop an agreement with the State to administer, supervise, or oversee the programs to be carried out under the plan with respect to the Indian children who are eligible for such programs and who are under the authority of the tribe, organization, or consortium and to receive from the State an appropriate portion of the State allotment under subsection (c) for the cost of such administration, supervision, or oversight.", **to take effect on October 1, 2009 without regard to whether the regulations required under subsection (e)(1) have been promulgated by such date.**

See Vol. II, P.L. 110-351, §301(d), with respect to some rules of construction and §301(e), with respect to regulations.

SOCIAL SECURITY ACT—§ 477(d)(3)   517

implements any such amendment, the State shall notify the Secretary of the amendment.

(6) AVAILABILITY.—The State shall make available to the public any application submitted by the State pursuant to paragraph (1), and a brief summary of the plan contained in the application.

(c) ALLOTMENTS TO STATES.—

(1) GENERAL PROGRAM ALLOTMENT.—From the amount specified in subsection (h)(1) that remains after applying subsection (g)(2) for a fiscal year, the Secretary shall allot to each State with an application approved under subsection (b) for the fiscal year the amount which bears the ratio to such remaining amount equal to the State foster care ratio, as adjusted in accordance with paragraph (2).

(2) HOLD HARMLESS PROVISION.—

(A) IN GENERAL.—The Secretary shall allot to each State whose allotment for a fiscal year under paragraph (1) is less than the greater of $500,000 or the amount payable to the State under this section for fiscal year 1998, an additional amount equal to the difference between such allotment and such greater amount.

(B) RATABLE REDUCTION OF CERTAIN ALLOTMENTS.—In the case of a State not described in subparagraph (A) of this paragraph for a fiscal year, the Secretary shall reduce the amount allotted to the State for the fiscal year under paragraph (1) by the amount that bears the same ratio to the sum of the differences determined under subparagraph (A) of this paragraph for the fiscal year as the excess of the amount so allotted over the greater of $500,000 or the amount payable to the State under this section for fiscal year 1998 bears to the sum of such excess amounts determined for all such States.

(3) VOUCHER PROGRAM ALLOTMENT.—From the amount, if any, appropriated pursuant to subsection (h)(2) for a fiscal year, the Secretary may allot to each State with an application approved under subsection (b) for the fiscal year an amount equal to the State foster care ratio multiplied by the amount so specified.

(4) STATE FOSTER CARE RATIO.—In this subsection, the term "State foster care ratio"means the ratio of the number of children in foster care under a program of the State in the most recent fiscal year for which the information is available to the total number of children in foster care in all States for the most recent fiscal year.

(d) IN GENERAL.—

(1) IN GENERAL.—A State to which an amount is paid from its allotment under subsection (c) may use the amount in any manner that is reasonably calculated to accomplish the purposes of this section.

(2) NO SUPPLANTATION OF OTHER FUNDS AVAILABLE FOR SAME GENERAL PURPOSES.—The amounts paid to a State from its allotment under subsection (c) shall be used to supplement and not supplant any other funds which are available for the same general purposes in the State.

(3) TWO-YEAR AVAILABILITY OF FUNDS.—Payments made to a State under this section for a fiscal year shall be expended by the State in the fiscal year or in the succeeding fiscal year.

518 SOCIAL SECURITY ACT—§ 477(d)(4)

(4) REALLOCATION OF UNUSED FUNDS.—If a State does not apply for funds under this section for a fiscal year within such time as may be provided by the Secretary, the funds to which the State would be entitled for the fiscal year shall be reallocated to 1 or more other States on the basis of their relative need for additional payments under this section, as determined by the Secretary.

(e) PENALTIES.—

(1) USE OF GRANT IN VIOLATION OF THIS PART.—If the Secretary is made aware, by an audit conducted under chapter 75 of title 31, United States Code[322], or by any other means, that a program receiving funds from an allotment made to a State under subsection (c) has been operated in a manner that is inconsistent with, or not disclosed in the State application approved under subsection (b), the Secretary shall assess a penalty against the State in an amount equal to not less than 1 percent and not more than 5 percent of the amount of the allotment.

(2) FAILURE TO COMPLY WITH DATA REPORTING REQUIRE-MENT.—The Secretary shall assess a penalty against a State that fails during a fiscal year to comply with an information collection plan implemented under subsection (f) in an amount equal to not less than 1 percent and not more than 5 percent of the amount allotted to the State for the fiscal year.

(3) PENALTIES BASED ON DEGREE OF NONCOMPLIANCE.—The Secretary shall assess penalties under this subsection based on the degree of noncompliance.

(f) DATA COLLECTION AND PERFORMANCE MEASUREMENT.—

(1) IN GENERAL.—The Secretary, in consultation with State and local public officials responsible for administering independent living and other child welfare programs, child welfare advocates, Members of Congress, youth service providers, and researchers, shall—

(A) develop outcome measures (including measures of educational attainment, high school diploma, employment, avoidance of dependency, homelessness, nonmarital childbirth, incarceration, and high-risk behaviors) that can be used to assess the performance of States in operating independent living programs;

(B) identify data elements needed to track—

(i) the number and characteristics of children receiving services under this section;

(ii) the type and quantity of services being provided; and

(iii) State performance on the outcome measures; and

(C) develop and implement a plan to collect the needed information beginning with the second fiscal year beginning after the date of the enactment of this section.

(2) REPORT TO THE CONGRESS.—Within 12 months after the date of the enactment of this section, the Secretary shall submit to the Committee on Ways and Means of the House of Representatives and the Committee on Finance of the Senate a report detailing the plans and timetable for collecting from the States the information described in paragraph (1) and a proposal to impose

---

[322] See Vol. II, 31 U.S.C. chapter 75.

SOCIAL SECURITY ACT—§ 477(i)(4)   519

penalties consistent with paragraph (e)(2) on States that do not report data.

(g) EVALUATIONS.—

(1) GENERAL.—The Secretary shall conduct evaluations of such State programs funded under this section as the Secretary deems to be innovative or of potential national significance. The evaluation of any such program shall include information on the effects of the program on education, employment, and personal development. To the maximum extent practicable, the evaluations shall be based on rigorous scientific standards including random assignment to treatment and control groups. The Secretary is encouraged to work directly with State and local governments to design methods for conducting the evaluations, directly or by grant, contract, or cooperative agreement.

(2) FUNDING OF EVALUATIONS.—The Secretary shall reserve 1.5 percent of the amount specified in subsection (h) for a fiscal year to carry out, during the fiscal year, evaluation, technical assistance, performance measurement, and data collection activities related to this section, directly or through grants, contracts, or cooperative agreements with appropriate entities.

(h) LIMITATION ON AUTHORIZATION OF APPROPRIATIONS.—To carry out this section and for payments to States under section 474(a)(4), there are authorized to be appropriated to the Secretary for each fiscal year—

(1) $140,000,000, which shall be available for all purposes under this section; and

(2) an additional $60,000,000, which are authorized to be available for payments to States for education and training vouchers for youths who age out of foster care, to assist the youths to develop skills necessary to lead independent and productive lives.

(i) EDUCATIONAL AND TRAINING VOUCHERS.—The following conditions shall apply to a State educational and training voucher program under this section:

(1) Vouchers under the program may be available to youths otherwise eligible for services under the State program under this section.

(2) For purposes of the voucher program, youths who, after attaining 16 years of age, are adopted from, or enter kinship guardianship from, foster care[323] may be considered to be youths otherwise eligible for services under the State program under this section.

(3) The State may allow youths participating in the voucher program on the date they attain 21 years of age to remain eligible until they attain 23 years of age, as long as they are enrolled in a postsecondary education or training program and are making satisfactory progress toward completion of that program.

(4) The voucher or vouchers provided for an individual under this section—

---

[323] P.L. 110-351, §101(e)(2), struck out "adopted from foster care after attaining age 16" and substituted "who, after attaining 16 years of age, are adopted from, or enter kinship guardianship from, foster care". For the effective date, see Vol. II, P.L. 110-351, §601.

520 SOCIAL SECURITY ACT—§ 477(i)(4)(A)

(A) may be available for the cost of attendance at an institution of higher education, as defined in section 102 of the Higher Education Act of 1965[324]; and

(B) shall not exceed the lesser of $5,000 per year or the total cost of attendance, as defined in section 472 of that Act.

(5) The amount of a voucher under this section may be disregarded for purposes of determining the recipient's eligibility for, or the amount of, any other Federal or Federally supported assistance, except that the total amount of educational assistance to a youth under this section and under other Federal and Federally supported programs shall not exceed the total cost of attendance, as defined in section 472 of the Higher Education Act of 1965[325], and except that the State agency shall take appropriate steps to prevent duplication of benefits under this and other Federal or Federally supported programs.

(6) The program is coordinated with other appropriate education and training programs.

(j) [326] AUTHORITY FOR AN INDIAN TRIBE, TRIBAL ORGANIZATION, OR TRIBAL CONSORTIUM TO RECEIVE AN ALLOTMENT.—

(1) IN GENERAL.—An Indian tribe, tribal organization, or tribal consortium with a plan approved under section 479B, or which is receiving funding to provide foster care under this part pursuant to a cooperative agreement or contract with a State, may apply for an allotment out of any funds authorized by paragraph (1) or (2) (or both) of subsection (h) of this section.

(2) APPLICATION.—A tribe, organization, or consortium desiring an allotment under paragraph (1) of this subsection shall submit an application to the Secretary to directly receive such allotment that includes a plan which—

(A) satisfies such requirements of paragraphs (2) and (3) of subsection (b) as the Secretary determines are appropriate;

(B) contains a description of the tribe's, organization's, or consortium's consultation process regarding the programs to be carried out under the plan with each State for which a portion of an allotment under subsection (c) would be redirected to the tribe, organization, or consortium; and

(C) contains an explanation of the results of such consultation, particularly with respect to—

(i) determining the eligibility for benefits and services of Indian children to be served under the programs to be carried out under the plan; and

(ii) the process for consulting with the State in order to ensure the continuity of benefits and services for such children who will transition from receiving benefits and services under programs carried out under a State plan under subsection (b)(2) to receiving benefits and services under programs carried out under a plan under this subsection.

---

[324] See Vol. II, P.L. 89-329, §102.

[325] See Vol. II, P.L. 89-329, §472.

[326] P.L. 110-351, §301(b), adds subsection (j), **to be effective on October 1, 2009,** without regard to whether the regulations required under subsection (e)(1) have been promulgated by such date.

SOCIAL SECURITY ACT—§ 479(a)(1) 521

(3) PAYMENTS.—The Secretary shall pay an Indian tribe, tribal organization, or tribal consortium with an application and plan approved under this subsection from the allotment determined for the tribe, organization, or consortium under paragraph (4) of this subsection in the same manner as is provided in section 474(a)(4) (and, where requested, and if funds are appropriated, section 474(e)) with respect to a State, or in such other manner as is determined appropriate by the Secretary, except that in no case shall an Indian tribe, a tribal organization, or a tribal consortium receive a lesser proportion of such funds than a State is authorized to receive under those sections.

(4) ALLOTMENT.—From the amounts allotted to a State under subsection (c) of this section for a fiscal year, the Secretary shall allot to each Indian tribe, tribal organization, or tribal consortium with an application and plan approved under this subsection for that fiscal year an amount equal to the tribal foster care ratio determined under paragraph (5) of this subsection for the tribe, organization, or consortium multiplied by the allotment amount of the State within which the tribe, organization, or consortium is located. The allotment determined under this paragraph is deemed to be a part of the allotment determined under section 477(c) for the State in which the Indian tribe, tribal organization, or tribal consortium is located.

(5) TRIBAL FOSTER CARE RATIO.—For purposes of paragraph (4), the tribal foster care ratio means, with respect to an Indian tribe, tribal organization, or tribal consortium, the ratio of—

(A) the number of children in foster care under the responsibility of the Indian tribe, tribal organization, or tribal consortium (either directly or under supervision of the State), in the most recent fiscal year for which the information is available; to

(B) the sum of—

(i) the total number of children in foster care under the responsibility of the State within which the Indian tribe, tribal organization, or tribal consortium is located; and

(ii) the total number of children in foster care under the responsibility of all Indian tribes, tribal organizations, or tribal consortia in the State (either directly or under supervision of the State) that have a plan approved under this subsection.

RULE OF CONSTRUCTION

SEC. 478. [42 U.S.C. 678] Nothing in this part shall be construed as precluding State courts from exercising their discretion to protect the health and safety of children in individual cases, including cases other than those described in section 471(a)(15)(D).

COLLECTION OF DATA RELATING TO ADOPTION AND FOSTER CARE[327]

SEC. 479. [42 U.S.C. 679] (a)(1) Not later than 90 days after the date of the enactment of this subsection[328], the Secretary shall establish an

---

[327] See Vol. II, P.L. 99-509, §9442, with respect to the maternal and child health and adoption clearinghouse.

[328] October 21, 1986. [P.L. 99-509, §9443; 100 Stat. 2073]

522　　SOCIAL SECURITY ACT—§ 479(a)(1)(cont)

Advisory Committee on Adoption and Foster Care Information (in this section referred to as the "Advisory Committee") to study the various methods of establishing, administering, and financing a system for the collection of data with respect to adoption and foster care in the United States.

(2) The study required by paragraph (1) shall—

(A) identify the types of data necessary to—

(i) assess (on a continuing basis) the incidence, characteristics, and status of adoption and foster care in the United States, and

(ii) develop appropriate national policies with respect to adoption and foster care;

(B) evaluate the feasibility and appropriateness of collecting data with respect to privately arranged adoptions and adoptions arranged through private agencies without assistance from public child welfare agencies;

(C) assess the validity of various methods of collecting data with respect to adoption and foster care; and

(D) evaluate the financial and administrative impact of implementing each such method.

(3) Not later than October 1, 1987, the Advisory Committee shall submit to the Secretary and the Congress a report setting forth the results of the study required by paragraph (1) and evaluating and making recommendations with respect to the various methods of establishing, administering, and financing a system for the collection of data with respect to adoption and foster care in the United States.

(4)(A) Subject to subparagraph (B), the membership and organization of the Advisory Committee shall be determined by the Secretary.

(B) The membership of the Advisory Committee shall include representatives of—

(i) private, nonprofit organizations with an interest in child welfare (including organizations that provide foster care and adoption services),

(ii) organizations representing State and local governmental agencies with responsibility for foster care and adoption services,

(iii) organizations representing State and local governmental agencies with responsibility for the collection of health and social statistics,

(iv) organizations representing State and local judicial bodies with jurisdiction over family law,

(v) Federal agencies responsible for the collection of health and social statistics, and

(vi) organizations and agencies involved with privately arranged or international adoptions.

(5) After the date of the submission of the report required by paragraph (3), the Advisory Committee shall cease to exist.

(b)(1)(A) Not later than July 1, 1988, the Secretary shall submit to the Congress a report that—

(i) proposes a method of establishing, administering, and financing a system for the collection of data relating to adoption and foster care in the United States,

(ii) evaluates the feasibility and appropriateness of collecting data with respect to privately arranged adoptions and adoptions

SOCIAL SECURITY ACT—§ 479A(1)   523

arranged through private agencies without assistance from public child welfare agencies, and

(iii) evaluates the impact of the system proposed under clause (i) on the agencies with responsibility for implementing it.

(B) The report required by subparagraph (A) shall—

(i) specify any changes in law that will be necessary to implement the system proposed under subparagraph (A)(i), and

(ii) describe the type of system that will be implemented under paragraph (2) in the absence of such changes.

(2) Not later than December 31, 1988, the Secretary shall promulgate final regulations providing for the implementation of—

(A) the system proposed under paragraph (1)(A)(i), or

(B) if the changes in law specified pursuant to paragraph (1)(B)(i) have not been enacted, the system described in paragraph (1)(B)(ii).

Such regulations shall provide for the full implementation of the system not later than October 1, 1991.

(c) Any data collection system developed and implemented under this section shall—

(1) avoid unnecessary diversion of resources from agencies responsible for adoption and foster care;

(2) assure that any data that is collected is reliable and consistent over time and among jurisdictions through the use of uniform definitions and methodologies;

(3) provide comprehensive national information with respect to—

(A) the demographic characteristics of adoptive and foster children and their biological and adoptive or foster parents,

(B) the status of the foster care population (including the number of children in foster care, length of placement, type of placement, availability for adoption, and goals for ending or continuing foster care),

(C) the number and characteristics of—

(i) children placed in or removed from foster care,

(ii) children adopted or with respect to whom adoptions have been terminated, and

(iii) children placed in foster care outside the State which has placement and care responsibility, and

(D) the extent and nature of assistance provided by Federal, State, and local adoption and foster care programs and the characteristics of the children with respect to whom such assistance is provided; and

(4) utilize appropriate requirements and incentives to ensure that the system functions reliably throughout the United States.

ANNUAL REPORT

SEC. 479A. [42 U.S.C. 679b] The Secretary, in consultation with Governors, State legislatures, State and local public officials responsible for administering child welfare programs, and child welfare advocates, shall—

(1) develop a set of outcome measures (including length of stay in foster care, number of foster care placements, and number of adoptions) that can be used to assess the performance of States in

524 SOCIAL SECURITY ACT—§ 479A(1)(cont)

operating child protection and child welfare programs pursuant to parts B and E to ensure the safety of children;

(2) to the maximum extent possible, the outcome measures should be developed from data available from the Adoption and Foster Care Analysis and Reporting System;

(3) develop a system for rating the performance of States with respect to the outcome measures, and provide to the States an explanation of the rating system and how scores are determined under the rating system;

(4) prescribe such regulations as may be necessary to ensure that States provide to the Secretary the data necessary to determine State performance with respect to each outcome measure, as a condition of the State receiving funds under this part;

(5) on May 1, 1999, and annually thereafter, prepare and submit to the Congress a report on the performance of each State on each outcome measure, which shall examine the reasons for high performance and low performance and, where possible, make recommendations as to how State performance could be improved; and

(6) include in the report submitted pursuant to paragraph (5) for fiscal year 2007 or any succeeding fiscal year, State-by-State data on—

(A) the percentage of children in foster care under the responsibility of the State who were visited on a monthly basis by the caseworker handling the case of the child; and

(B) the percentage of the visits that occurred in the residence of the child.

PROGRAMS OPERATED BY INDIAN TRIBAL ORGANIZATIONS[329]

SEC. 479B. [42 U.S.C. 679c] (a) DEFINITIONS OF INDIAN TRIBE; TRIBAL ORGANIZATIONS.—In this section, the terms "Indian tribe" and "tribal organization" have the meanings given those terms in section 4 of the Indian Self-Determination and Education Assistance Act (25 U.S.C. 450b).

(b) AUTHORITY.— Except as otherwise provided in this section, this part shall apply in the same manner as this part applies to a State to an Indian tribe, tribal organization, or tribal consortium that elects to operate a program under this part and has a plan approved by the Secretary under section 471 in accordance with this section.

(c) PLAN REQUIREMENTS.—

(1) IN GENERAL.—An Indian tribe, tribal organization, or tribal consortium that elects to operate a program under this part shall include with its plan submitted under section 471 the following:

(A) FINANCIAL MANAGEMENT.—Evidence demonstrating that the tribe, organization, or consortium has not had any uncorrected significant or material audit exceptions under Federal grants or contracts that directly relate to the administration of social services for the 3-year period prior to the date on which the plan is submitted.

---

[329] P.L. 110-351, §301(a), adds §479B, **to take effect on October 1, 2009,** without regard to whether the regulations required under §301(e)(1) have been promulgated by such date.

See Vol. II, P.L. 110-351, §301(d), with respect to rules of construction and §301(e), with respect to regulations.

SOCIAL SECURITY ACT—§ 479B(c) (1)(D)   525

(B) SERVICE AREAS AND POPULATIONS.—For purposes of complying with section 471(a)(3), a description of the service area or areas and populations to be served under the plan and an assurance that the plan shall be in effect in all service area or areas and for all populations served by the tribe, organization, or consortium.

(C) ELIGIBILITY.—

(i) IN GENERAL.—Subject to clause (ii) of this subparagraph, an assurance that the plan will provide—

(I) foster care maintenance payments under section 472 only on behalf of children who satisfy the eligibility requirements of section 472(a);

(II) adoption assistance payments under section 473 pursuant to adoption assistance agreements only on behalf of children who satisfy the eligibility requirements for such payments under that section; and

(III) at the option of the tribe, organization, or consortium, kinship guardianship assistance payments in accordance with section 473(d) only on behalf of children who meet the requirements of section 473(d)(3).

(ii) SATISFACTION OF FOSTER CARE ELIGIBILITY REQUIREMENTS.—For purposes of determining whether a child whose placement and care are the responsibility of an Indian tribe, tribal organization, or tribal consortium with a plan approved under section 471 in accordance with this section satisfies the requirements of section 472(a), the following shall apply:

(I) USE OF AFFIDAVITS, ETC.—Only with respect to the first 12 months for which such plan is in effect, the requirement in paragraph (1) of section 472(a) shall not be interpreted so as to prohibit the use of affidavits or nunc pro tunc orders as verification documents in support of the reasonable efforts and contrary to the welfare of the child judicial determinations required under that paragraph.

(II) AFDC ELIGIBILITY REQUIREMENT.—The State plan approved under section 402 (as in effect on July 16, 1996) of the State in which the child resides at the time of removal from the home shall apply to the determination of whether the child satisfies section 472(a)(3).

(D) OPTION TO CLAIM IN-KIND EXPENDITURES FROM THIRD-PARTY SOURCES FOR NON-FEDERAL SHARE OF ADMINISTRATIVE AND TRAINING COSTS DURING INITIAL IMPLEMENTATION PERIOD.—Only for fiscal year quarters beginning after September 30, 2009, and before October 1, 2014, a list of the in-kind expenditures (which shall be fairly evaluated, and may include plants, equipment, administration, or services) and the third-party sources of such expenditures that the tribe, organization, or consortium may claim as part of the non-Federal share of administrative or training expenditures attributable to such quarters for purposes of receiving

526 SOCIAL SECURITY ACT—§ 479B(c) (1)(D)(i)

payments under section 474(a)(3). The Secretary shall permit a tribe, organization, or consortium to claim in-kind expenditures from third party sources for such purposes during such quarters subject to the following:

(i) NO EFFECT ON AUTHORITY FOR TRIBES, ORGANIZATIONS, OR CONSORTIA TO CLAIM EXPENDITURES OR INDIRECT COSTS TO THE SAME EXTENT AS STATES.—Nothing in this subparagraph shall be construed as preventing a tribe, organization, or consortium from claiming any expenditures or indirect costs for purposes of receiving payments under section 474(a) that a State with a plan approved under section 471(a) could claim for such purposes.

(ii) FISCAL YEAR 2010 OR 2011.—

(I) EXPENDITURES OTHER THAN FOR TRAINING.—With respect to amounts expended during a fiscal year quarter beginning after September 30, 2009, and before October 1, 2011, for which the tribe, organization, or consortium is eligible for payments under subparagraph (C), (D), or (E) of section 474(a)(3), not more than 25 percent of such amounts may consist of in-kind expenditures from third-party sources specified in the list required under this subparagraph to be submitted with the plan.

(II) TRAINING EXPENDITURES.—With respect to amounts expended during a fiscal year quarter beginning after September 30, 2009, and before October 1, 2011, for which the tribe, organization, or consortium is eligible for payments under subparagraph (A) or (B) of section 474(a)(3), not more than 12 percent of such amounts may consist of in-kind expenditures from third-party sources that are specified in such list and described in subclause (III).

(III) SOURCES DESCRIBED.—For purposes of subclause (II), the sources described in this subclause are the following:

(aa) A State or local government.

(bb) An Indian tribe, tribal organization, or tribal consortium other than the tribe, organization, or consortium submitting the plan.

(cc) A public institution of higher education.

(dd) A Tribal College or University (as defined in section 316 of the Higher Education Act of 1965 (20 U.S.C. 1059c)).

(ee) A private charitable organization.

(iii) FISCAL YEAR 2012, 2013, OR 2014.—

(I) IN GENERAL.—Except as provided in subclause (II) of this clause and clause (v) of this subparagraph, with respect to amounts expended during any fiscal year quarter beginning after September 30, 2011, and before October 1, 2014, for which the tribe, organization, or consortium is eligible for payments under any subparagraph of section 474(a)(3) of this Act, the only in-kind expenditures from third-party sources that may be claimed by the tribe, organization, or consortium for purposes of determining the non-Federal share of such expenditures (without regard to whether the expenditures are specified on the list required under this subparagraph to be submitted with the plan) are in-kind expenditures that are specified in regulations promulgated by the Secretary under section 301(e)(2) of the Fostering Connections to Success and Increasing Adoptions Act of 2008 and are from an applicable third-party source specified in such regulations, and do not exceed the applicable percentage for claiming such in-kind expenditures specified in the regulations.

(II) TRANSITION PERIOD FOR EARLY APPROVED TRIBES, ORGANIZATIONS, OR CONSORTIA.—Subject to clause (v), if the tribe, organization, or consortium is an early approved tribe, organization, or consortium (as defined in subclause (III) of this clause), the Secretary shall not require the tribe, organization, or consortium to comply with such regulations before October 1, 2013. Until the earlier of the date such tribe, organization, or consortium comes into compliance with such regulations or October 1, 2013, the limitations on the claiming of in-kind expenditures from third-party sources under clause (ii) shall continue to apply to such tribe, organization, or consortium (without regard to fiscal limitation) for purposes of determining the non-Federal share of amounts expended by the tribe, organization, or consortium during any fiscal year quarter that begins after September 30, 2011, and before such date of compliance or October 1, 2013, whichever is earlier.

(III) DEFINITION OF EARLY APPROVED TRIBE, ORGANIZATION, OR CONSORTIUM.—For purposes of subclause (II) of this clause, the term "early approved tribe, organization, or consortium" means an Indian tribe, tribal organization, or tribal consortium that had a plan approved under section 471 in accordance with this section for any quarter of fiscal year 2010 or 2011.

(iv) FISCAL YEAR 2015 AND THEREAFTER.—Subject to clause (v) of this subparagraph, with respect to amounts expended during any fiscal year quarter beginning after September 30, 2014, for which the tribe, organization, or consortium is eligible for payments under any subparagraph of section 474(a)(3) of this Act, in-kind expenditures from third-party sources may be claimed for purposes of determining the non-Federal share of expenditures under any subparagraph of such section 474(a)(3)

528   SOCIAL SECURITY ACT—§ 479B(c) (1)(D)(v)

only in accordance with the regulations promulgated by the Secretary under section 301(e)(2) of the Fostering Connections to Success and Increasing Adoptions Act of 2008.

(v) DEFINITION OF EARLY APPROVED TRIBE, ORGANIZATION, OR CONSORTIUM.—For purposes of subclause (II) of this clause, the term "early approved tribe, organization, or consortium" means an Indian tribe, tribal organization, or tribal consortium that had a plan approved under section 471 in accordance with this section for any quarter of fiscal year 2010 or 2011.

(I) in the case of any quarter of fiscal year 2012, 2013, or 2014, the limitations on claiming in-kind expenditures from third-party sources under clause (ii) of this subparagraph shall apply (without regard to fiscal limitation) for purposes of determining the non-Federal share of such expenditures; and

(II) in the case of any quarter of fiscal year 2015 or any fiscal year thereafter, no tribe, organization, or consortium may claim in-kind expenditures from third-party sources for purposes of determining the non-Federal share of such expenditures if a State with a plan approved under section 471(a) of this Act could not claim in-kind expenditures from third-party sources for such purposes.

(2) CLARIFICATION OF TRIBAL AUTHORITY TO ESTABLISH STANDARDS FOR TRIBAL FOSTER FAMILY HOMES AND TRIBAL CHILD CARE INSTITUTIONS.—For purposes of complying with section 471(a)(10), an Indian tribe, tribal organization, or tribal consortium shall establish and maintain a tribal authority or authorities which shall be responsible for establishing and maintaining tribal standards for tribal foster family homes and tribal child care institutions.

(3) CONSORTIUM.—The participating Indian tribes or tribal organizations of a tribal consortium may develop and submit a single plan under section 471 that meets the requirements of this section.

(d) DETERMINATION OF FEDERAL MEDICAL ASSISTANCE PERCENTAGE FOR FOSTER CARE MAINTENANCE AND ADOPTION ASSISTANCE PAYMENTS.—

(1) PER CAPITA INCOME.—For purposes of determining the Federal medical assistance percentage applicable to an Indian tribe, a tribal organization, or a tribal consortium under paragraphs (1), (2), and (5) of section 474(a), the calculation of the per capita income of the Indian tribe, tribal organization, or tribal consortium shall be based upon the service population of the Indian tribe, tribal organization, or tribal consortium, except that in no case shall an Indian tribe, a tribal organization, or a tribal consortium receive less than the Federal medical assistance percentage for any State in which the tribe, organization, or consortium is located.

(2) CONSIDERATION OF OTHER INFORMATION.—Before making a calculation under paragraph (1), the Secretary shall consider any information submitted by an Indian tribe, a tribal organization,

or a tribal consortium that the Indian tribe, tribal organization, or tribal consortium considers relevant to making the calculation of the per capita income of the Indian tribe, tribal organization, or tribal consortium.

(e) NONAPPLICATION TO COOPERATIVE AGREEMENTS AND CONTRACTS.—Any cooperative agreement or contract entered into between an Indian tribe, a tribal organization, or a tribal consortium and a State for the administration or payment of funds under this part that is in effect as of the date of enactment of this section shall remain in full force and effect, subject to the right of either party to the agreement or contract to revoke or modify the agreement or contract pursuant to the terms of the agreement or contract. Nothing in this section shall be construed as affecting the authority for an Indian tribe, a tribal organization, or a tribal consortium and a State to enter into a cooperative agreement or contract for the administration or payment of funds under this part.

(f) JOHN H. CHAFEE FOSTER CARE INDEPENDENCE PROGRAM.—Except as provided in section 477(j), subsection (b) of this section shall not apply with respect to the John H. Chafee Foster Care Independence Program established under section 477 (or with respect to payments made under section 474(a)(4) or grants made under section 474(e)).

(g) RULE OF CONSTRUCTION.—Nothing in this section shall be construed as affecting the application of section 472(h) to a child on whose behalf payments are paid under section 472, or the application of section 473(b) to a child on whose behalf payments are made under section 473 pursuant to an adoption assistance agreement or a kinship guardianship assistance agreement, by an Indian tribe, tribal organization, or tribal consortium that elects to operate a foster care and adoption assistance program in accordance with this section.

TITLE V—MATERNAL AND CHILD HEALTH SERVICES BLOCK GRANT[1]

TABLE OF CONTENTS OF TITLE[2]

		Page
Sec. 501.	Authorization of appropriations	531
Sec. 502.	Allotments to States and Federal set-aside	534
Sec. 503.	Payments to States	536
Sec. 504.	Use of allotment funds	537
Sec. 505.	Application for block grant funds	538
Sec. 506.	Reports and audits	540
Sec. 507.	Criminal penalty for false statements	544
Sec. 508.	Nondiscrimination	544
Sec. 509.	Administration of title and State programs	545
Sec. 510.	Separate program for abstinence education	546

AUTHORIZATION OF APPROPRIATIONS

SEC. 501. [42 U.S.C. 701] (a) To improve the health of all mothers and children consistent with the applicable health status goals and national health objectives established by the Secretary under the Public Health Service Act for the year 2000, there are authorized to be appropriated $850,000,000 for fiscal year 2001 and each fiscal year thereafter—

(1) for the purpose of enabling each State—

(A) to provide and to assure mothers and children (in particular those with low income or with limited availability of health services) access to quality maternal and child health services;

(B) to reduce infant mortality and the incidence of preventable diseases and handicapping conditions among children, to reduce the need for inpatient and long-term care services, to increase the number of children (especially preschool children) appropriately immunized against disease and the number of low income children receiving health assessments and follow-up diagnostic and treatment services, and otherwise to promote the health of mothers and infants by providing prenatal, delivery, and postpartum care for low income, at-risk pregnant women, and to promote the health of children by providing preventive and primary care services for low income children;

(C) to provide rehabilitation services for blind and disabled individuals under the age of 16 receiving benefits under title

---

[1] Title V of the Social Security Act is administered by the Health Resources and Services Administration, Public Health Service, Department of Health and Human Services.

Title V appears in the United States Code as §§701-710, subchapter V, chapter 7, Title 42.

Regulations of the Secretary of Health and Human Services relating to Title V are contained in chapter I, Title 42, and in subtitle A, Title 45, Code of Federal Regulations.

See Vol. II, P.L. 78-410, §317A(a) and (d), with respect to coordination required in lead poisoning prevention.

See Vol. II, P.L. 88-352, §601, with respect to prohibition against discrimination in federally assisted programs.

See Vol. II, P.L. 91-230, §612, with respect to assistance for education of children with disabilities and assistance under other Federal programs.

See Vol. II, P.L. 101-239, §6509, with respect to a maternal and child health handbook.

[2] This table of contents does not appear in the law.

532 SOCIAL SECURITY ACT—§ 501(a)(1)(C)(cont)

XVI, to the extent medical assistance for such services is not provided under title XIX; and

(D) to provide and to promote family-centered, community-based, coordinated care (including care coordination services, as defined in subsection (b)(3)) for children with special health care needs and to facilitate the development of community-based systems of services for such children and their families;

(2) for the purpose of enabling the Secretary (through grants, contracts, or otherwise) to provide for special projects of regional and national significance, research, and training with respect to maternal and child health and children with special health care needs (including early intervention training and services development), for genetic disease testing, counseling, and information development and dissemination programs, for grants (including funding for comprehensive hemophilia diagnostic treatment centers) relating to hemophilia without regard to age, and for the screening of newborns for sickle cell anemia, and other genetic disorders and follow-up services; and

(3) subject to section 502(b) for the purpose of enabling the Secretary (through grants, contracts, or otherwise) to provide for developing and expanding the following—

(A) maternal and infant health home visiting programs in which case management services as defined in subparagraphs (A) and (B) of subsection (b)(4), health education services, and related social support services are provided in the home to pregnant women or families with an infant up to the age one by an appropriate health professional or by a qualified nonprofessional acting under the supervision of a health care professional,

(B) projects designed to increase the participation of obstetricians and pediatricians under the program under this title and under state plans approved under title XIX,

(C) integrated maternal and child health service delivery systems (of the type described in section 1136 and using, once developed, the model application form developed under section 6506(a) of the Omnibus Budget Reconciliation Act of 1989[3]),

(D) maternal and child health centers which (i) provide prenatal, delivery, and postpartum care for pregnant women and preventive and primary care services for infants up to age one, and (ii) operate under the direction of a not-for-profit hospital,

(E) maternal and child health projects to serve rural populations, and

(F) outpatient and community based services programs (including day care services) for children with special health care needs whose medical services are provided primarily through inpatient institutional care.

Funds appropriated under this section may only be used in a manner consistent with the Assisted Suicide Funding Restriction Act of 1997.

(b) For purposes of this title:

---

[3] P.L. 101-239.

SOCIAL SECURITY ACT—§ 501(c)(2)

(1) The term "consolidated health programs" means the programs administered under the provisions of—

(A) this title (relating to maternal and child health and services for children with special health care needs),

(B) section 1615(c) of this Act (relating to supplemental security income for disabled children),

(C) sections 316 (relating to lead-based paint poisoning prevention programs), 1101(relating to genetic disease programs), 1121 (relating to sudden infant death syndrome programs) and 1131 (relating to hemophilia treatment centers) of the Public Health Service Act[4], and

(D) title VI[5] of the Health Services and Centers Amendments of 1978 (Public Law 95-626; relating to adolescent pregnancy grants),

as such provisions were in effect before the date of the enactment of the Maternal and Child Health Services Block Grant Act[6].

(2) The term "low income" means, with respect to an individual or family, such an individual or family with an income determined to be below the income official poverty line defined by the Office of Management and Budget and revised annually in accordance with section 673(2) of the Omnibus Budget Reconciliation Act of 1981[7].

(3) The term "care coordination services" means services to promote the effective and efficient organization and utilization of resources to assure access to necessary comprehensive services for children with special health care needs and their families.

(4) The term "case management services" means—

(A) with respect to pregnant women, services to assure access to quality prenatal, delivery, and postpartum care; and

(B) with respect to infants up to age one, services to assure access to quality preventive and primary care services.

(c)(1)(A) For the purpose of enabling the Secretary (through grants, contracts, or otherwise) to provide for special projects of regional and national significance for the development and support of family-to-family health information centers described in paragraph (2), there is appropriated to the Secretary, out of any money in the Treasury not otherwise appropriated—

(i) $3,000,000 for fiscal year 2007;

(ii) $4,000,000 for fiscal year 2008; and

(iii) $5,000,000 for fiscal year 2009.

(B) Funds appropriated or authorized to be appropriated under subparagraph (A) shall—

(i) be in addition to amounts appropriated under subsection (a) and retained under section 502(a)(1) for the purpose of carrying out activities described in subsection (a)(2); and

(ii) remain available until expended.

(2) The family-to-family health information centers described in this paragraph are centers that—

---

[4] P.L. 97-35, §2193(b)(1), repealed §§316, 1101, 1121, and 1131 of P.L. 78-410.
[5] P.L. 95-626, Title VI, was repealed by P.L. 97-35, §955(b); 95 Stat. 592.
[6] August 13, 1981 - P.L. 97-35, Title XXI, subtitle D; 95 Stat. 818.
[7] See Vol. II, P.L. 97-35, §673(2).

534 SOCIAL SECURITY ACT—§ 501(c)(2)(A)

(A) assist families of children with disabilities or special health care needs to make informed choices about health care in order to promote good treatment decisions, cost-effectiveness, and improved health outcomes for such children;

(B) provide information regarding the health care needs of, and resources available for, such children;

(C) identify successful health delivery models for such children;

(D) develop with representatives of health care providers, managed care organizations, health care purchasers, and appropriate State agencies, a model for collaboration between families of such children and health professionals;

(E) provide training and guidance regarding caring for such children;

(F) conduct outreach activities to the families of such children, health professionals, schools, and other appropriate entities and individuals; and

(G) are staffed—

(i) by such families who have expertise in Federal and State public and private health care systems; and

(ii) by health professionals.

(3) The Secretary shall develop family-to-family health information centers described in paragraph (2) in accordance with the following:

(A) With respect to fiscal year 2007, such centers shall be developed in not less than 25 States.

(B) With respect to fiscal year 2008, such centers shall be developed in not less than 40 States.

(C) With respect to fiscal year 2009 and each fiscal year thereafter, such centers shall be developed in all States.

(4) The provisions of this title that are applicable to the funds made available to the Secretary under section 502(a)(1) apply in the same manner to funds made available to the Secretary under paragraph (1)(A).

(5) For purposes of this subsection, the term "State" means each of the 50 States and the District of Columbia.

ALLOTMENTS TO STATES AND FEDERAL SET-ASIDE

SEC. 502. [42 U.S.C. 702] (a)(1) Of the amounts appropriated under section 501(a) for a fiscal year that are not in excess of $600,000,000, the Secretary shall retain an amount equal to 15 percent for the purpose of carrying out activities described in section 501(a)(2). The authority of the Secretary to enter into any contracts under this title is effective for any fiscal year only to such extent or in such amounts as are provided in appropriations Acts.

(2) For purposes of paragraph (1)—

(A) amounts retained by the Secretary for training shall be used to make grants to public or nonprofit private institutions of higher learning for training personnel for health care and related services for mothers and children; and

(B) amounts retained by the Secretary for research shall be used to make grants to, contracts with, or jointly financed cooperative agreements with, public or nonprofit institutions of higher learning and public or nonprofit private agencies and organizations engaged in research or in maternal and child health or programs for children with special health care needs for research

SOCIAL SECURITY ACT—§ 502(c)(1)(B)(ii)   535

projects relating to maternal and child health services or services for children with special health care needs which show promise of substantial contribution to the advancement thereof.

(3) No funds may be made available by the Secretary under this subsection or subsection (b) unless an application therefor has been submitted to, and approved by, the Secretary. Such application shall be in such form, be submitted in such manner, and contain and be accompanied by such information as the Secretary may specify. No such application may be approved unless it contains assurances that the applicant will use the funds provided only for the purposes specified in the approved application and will establish such fiscal control and fund accounting procedures as may be necessary to assure proper disbursement and accounting of Federal funds paid to the applicant under this title.

(b)(1)(A) Of the amounts appropriated under section 501(a) for a fiscal year in excess of $600,000,000 the Secretary shall retain an amount equal to 12 3/4 percent thereof for the projects described in subparagraphs (A) through (F) of section 501(a)(3).

(B) Any amount appropriated under section 501(a) for a fiscal year in excess of $600,000,000 that remains after the Secretary has retained the applicable amount (if any) under subparagraph (A) shall be retained by the Secretary in accordance with subsection (a) and allocated to the States in accordance with subsection (c).

(2)(A) Of the amounts retained for the purpose of carrying out activities described in section 501(a)(3)(A), (B), (C), (D) and (E), the Secretary shall provide preference to qualified applicants which demonstrate that the activities to be carried out with such amounts shall be in areas with a high infant mortality rate (relative to the average infant mortality rate in the United States or in the State in which the area is located).

(B) In carrying out activities described in section 501(a)(3)(D), the Secretary shall not provide for developing or expanding a maternal and child health center unless the Secretary has received satisfactory assurances that there will be applied, towards the costs of such development or expansion, non-Federal funds in an amount at least equal to the amount of funds provided under this title toward such development or expansion.

(c) From the remaining amounts appropriated under section 501(a) for any fiscal year that are not in excess of $600,000,000, the Secretary shall allot to each State which has transmitted an application for the fiscal year under section 505(a), an amount determined as follows:

(1) The Secretary shall determine, for each State—

(A)(i) the amount provided or allotted by the Secretary to the State and to entities in the State under the provisions of the consolidated health programs (as defined in section 501(b)(1)), other than for any of the projects or programs described in subsection (a), from appropriations for fiscal year 1981,

(ii) the proportion that such amount for that State bears to the total of such amounts for all the States, and

(B)(i) the number of low income children in the State, and

(ii) the proportion that such number of children for that State bears to the total of such numbers of children for all the States.

536　　SOCIAL SECURITY ACT—§ 502(c)(2)

(2) Each such State shall be allotted for each fiscal year an amount equal to the sum of—

(A) the amount of the allotment to the State under this subsection in fiscal year 1983, and

(B) the State's proportion (determined under paragraph (1)(B)(ii)) of the amount by which the allotment available under this subsection for all the States for that fiscal year exceeds the amount that was available under this subsection for allotment for all the States for fiscal year 1983.

(d)(1) To the extent that all the funds appropriated under this title for a fiscal year are not otherwise allotted to States either because all the States have not qualified for such allotments under section 505(a) for the fiscal year or because some States have indicated in their descriptions of activities under section 505(a) that they do not intend to use the full amount of such allotments, such excess shall be allotted among the remaining States in proportion to the amount otherwise allotted to such States for the fiscal year without regard to this paragraph.

(2) To the extent that all the funds appropriated under this title for a fiscal year are not otherwise allotted to States because some State allotments are offset under section 506(b)(2), such excess shall be allotted among the remaining States in proportion to the amount otherwise allotted to such States for the fiscal year without regard to this paragraph.

PAYMENTS TO STATES

SEC. 503. [42 U.S.C. 703] (a) From the sums appropriated therefor and the allotments available under section 502(c), the Secretary shall make payments as provided by section 6503(a) of title 31, United States Code[8] to each State provided such an allotment under section 502(c), for each quarter, of an amount equal to four-sevenths of the total of the sums expended by the State during such quarter in carrying out the provisions of this title.

(b) Any amount payable to a State under this title from allotments for a fiscal year which remains unobligated at the end of such year shall remain available to such State for obligation during the next fiscal year. No payment may be made to a State under this title from allotments for a fiscal year for expenditures made after the following fiscal year.

(c) The Secretary, at the request of a State, may reduce the amount of payments under subsection (a) by—

(1) the fair market value of any supplies or equipment furnished the State, and

(2) the amount of the pay, allowances, and travel expenses of any officer or employee of the Government when detailed to the State and the amount of any other costs incurred in connection with the detail of such officer or employee,

when the furnishing of supplies or equipment or the detail of an officer or employee is for the convenience of and at the request of the State and for the purpose of conducting activities described in section 505(a) on a temporary basis. The amount by which any payment is so reduced shall be available for payment by the Secretary of the

---

[8] See Vol. II, 31 U.S.C. 6503(a).

SOCIAL SECURITY ACT—§ 504(d)   537

costs incurred in furnishing the supplies or equipment or in detailing the personnel, on which the reduction of the payment is based, and the amount shall be deemed to be part of the payment and shall be deemed to have been paid to the State.

USE OF ALLOTMENT FUNDS

SEC. 504. [42 U.S.C. 704] (a) Except as otherwise provided under this section, a State may use amounts paid to it under section 503 for the provision of health services and related activities (including planning, administration, education, and evaluation and including payment of salaries and other related expenses of National Health Service Corps personnel) consistent with its application transmitted under section 505(a).

(b) Amounts described in subsection (a) may not be used for—

(1) inpatient services, other than inpatient services provided to children with special health care needs or to high-risk pregnant women and infants and such other inpatient services as the Secretary may approve;

(2) cash payments to intended recipients of health services;

(3) the purchase or improvement of land, the purchase, construction, or permanent improvement (other than minor remodeling) of any building or other facility, or the purchase of major medical equipment;

(4) satisfying any requirement for the expenditure of non-Federal funds as a condition for the receipt of Federal funds;

(5) providing funds for research or training to any entity other than a public or nonprofit private entity; or

(6) payment for any item or service (other than an emergency item or service) furnished—

(A) by an individual or entity during the period when such individual or entity is excluded under this title or title XVIII, XIX, or XX pursuant to section 1128, 1128A, 1156, or 1842(j)(2), or

(B) at the medical direction or on the prescription of a physician during the period when the physician is excluded under this title or title XVIII, XIX, or XX pursuant to section 1128, 1128A, 1156, or 1842(j)(2) and when the person furnishing such item or service knew or had reason to know of the exclusion (after a reasonable time period after reasonable notice has been furnished to the person).

The Secretary may waive the limitation contained in paragraph (3) upon the request of a State if the Secretary finds that there are extraordinary circumstances to justify the waiver and that granting the waiver will assist in carrying out this title.

(c) A State may use a portion of the amounts described in subsection (a) for the purpose of purchasing technical assistance from public or private entities if the State determines that such assistance is required in developing, implementing, and administering programs funded under this title.

(d) Of the amounts paid to a State under section 503 from an allotment for a fiscal year under section 502(c), not more than 10 percent may be used for administering the funds paid under such section.

538 SOCIAL SECURITY ACT—§ 504(d)(cont)

APPLICATION FOR BLOCK GRANT FUNDS

SEC. 505. [42 U.S.C. 705] (a) In order to be entitled to payments for allotments under section 502 for a fiscal year, a State must prepare and transmit to the Secretary an application (in a standardized form specified by the Secretary) that—

(1) contains a statewide needs assessment (to be conducted every 5 years) that shall identify (consistent with the health status goals and national health objectives referred to in section 501(a)) the need for—

(A) preventive and primary care services for pregnant women, mothers, and infants up to age one;

(B) preventive and primary care services for children; and

(C) services for children with special health care needs (as specified in section 501(a)(1)(D));

(2) includes for each fiscal year—

(A) a plan for meeting the needs identified by the state-wide needs assessment under paragraph (1); and

(B) a description of how the funds allotted to the State under section 502(c) will be used for the provision and coordination of services to carry out such plan that shall include—

(i) subject to paragraph (3), a statement of the goals and objectives consistent with the health status goals and national health objectives referred to in section 501(a) for meeting the needs specified in the State plan described in subparagraph (A);

(ii) an identification of the areas and localities in the State in which services are to be provided and coordinated;

(iii) an identification of the types of services to be provided and the categories or characteristics of individuals to be served; and

(iv) information the State will collect in order to prepare reports required under section 506(a);

(3) except as provided under subsection (b), provides that the State will use—

(A) at least 30 percent of such payment amounts for preventive and primary care services for children, and

(B) at least 30 percent of such payment amounts for services for children with special health care needs (as specified in section 501(a)(1)(D));

(4) provides that a State receiving funds for maternal and child health services under this title shall maintain the level of funds being provided solely by such State for maternal and child health programs at a level at least equal to the level that such State provided for such programs in fiscal year 1989; and

(5) provides that—

(A) the State will establish a fair method (as determined by the State) for allocating funds allotted to the State under this title among such individuals, areas, and localities identified under paragraph (1)(A) as needing maternal and child health services, and the State will identify and apply guidelines for the appropriate frequency and content of, and appropriate referral and followup with respect to, health care assessments and services financially assisted by the State under this title and methods for assuring quality assessments and services;

(B) funds allotted to the State under this title will only be used, consistent with section 508, to carry out the purposes of this title or to continue activities previously conducted under the consolidated health programs (described in section 501(b)(1));

(C) the State will use—

(i) special consideration (where appropriate) for the continuation of the funding of special projects in the State previously funded under this title (as in effect before August 31, 1981), and

(ii) a reasonable proportion (based upon the State's previous use of funds under this title) of such sums to carry out the purposes described in subparagraphs (A) through (D) of section 501(a)(1);

(D) if any charges are imposed for the provision of health services assisted by the State under this title, such charges (i) will be pursuant to a public schedule of charges, (ii) will not be imposed with respect to services provided to low income mothers or children, and (iii) will be adjusted to reflect the income, resources, and family size of the individual provided the services;

(E) the State agency (or agencies) administering the State's program under this title will provide for a toll-free telephone number (and other appropriate methods) for the use of parents to access information about health care providers and practitioners who provide health care services under this title and title XIX and about other relevant health and health-related providers and practitioners; and

(F) the State agency (or agencies) administering the State's program under this title will—

(i) participate in the coordination of activities between such program and the early and periodic screening, diagnostic, and treatment program under section 1905(a)(4)(B) (including the establishment of periodicity and content standards for early and periodic screening, diagnostic, and treatment services), to ensure that such programs are carried out without duplication of effort,

(ii) participate in the arrangement and carrying out of coordination agreements described in section 1902(a)(11) (relating to coordination of care and services available under this title and title XIX),

(iii) participate in the coordination of activities within the State with programs carried out under this title and related Federal grant programs (including supplemental food programs for mothers, infants, and children, related education programs, and other health, developmental disability, and family planning programs), and

(iv) provide, directly and through their providers and institutional contractors, for services to identify pregnant women and infants who are eligible for medical assistance under subparagraph (A) or (B) of section

540   SOCIAL SECURITY ACT—§ 505(a)(5)(F)(iv)(cont)

1902(l)(1) and, once identified, to assist them in applying for such assistance.

The application shall be developed by, or in consultation with, the State maternal and child health agency and shall be made public within the State in such manner as to facilitate comment from any person (including any Federal or other public agency) during its development and after its transmittal.

(b) The Secretary may waive the requirements under subsection (a)(3) that a State's application for a fiscal year provide for the use of funds for specific activities if for that fiscal year—

(1) the Secretary determines—

(A) on the basis of information provided in the State's most recent annual report submitted under section 506(a)(1), that the State has demonstrated an extraordinary unmet need for one of the activities described in subsection (a)(3), and

(B) that the granting of the waiver is justified and will assist in carrying out the purposes of this title; and

(2) the State provides assurances to the Secretary that the State will provide for the use of some amounts paid to it under section 503 for the activities described in subparagraphs (A) and (B) of subsection (a)(3) and specifies the percentages to be substituted in each of such subparagraphs.

REPORTS AND AUDITS

SEC. 506. [42 U.S.C. 706] (a)(1) Each State shall prepare and submit to the Secretary annual reports on its activities under this title. Each such report shall be prepared by, or in consultation with, the State maternal and child health agency. In order properly to evaluate and to compare the performance of different States assisted under this title and to assure the proper expenditure of funds under this title, such reports shall be in such standardized form and contain such information (including information described in paragraph (2)) as the Secretary determines (after consultation with the States) to be necessary (A) to secure an accurate description of those activities, (B) to secure a complete record of the purposes for which funds were spent, of the recipients of such funds,,[9] (C) to describe the extent to which the State has met the goals and objectives it set forth under section 505(a)(2)(B)(i) and the national health objectives referred to in section 501(a) and (D) to determine the extent to which funds were expended consistent with the State's application transmitted under section 505(a). Copies of the report shall be provided, upon request, to any interested public agency, and each such agency may provide its views on these reports to the Congress.

(2) Each annual report under paragraph (1) shall include the following information:

(A)(i) The number of individuals served by the State under this title (by class of individuals).

(ii) The proportion of each class of such individuals which has health coverage.

(iii) The types (as defined by the Secretary) of services provided under this title to individuals within each such class.

_____

[9] As in original.

(iv) The amounts spent under this title on each type of services, by class of individuals served.

(B) Information on the status of maternal and child health in the State, including—

(i) information (by county and by racial and ethnic group) on—

(I) the rate of infant mortality, and

(II) the rate of low-birth-weight births;

(ii) information (on a State-wide basis) on—

(I) the rate of maternal mortality,

(II) the rate of neonatal death,

(III) the rate of perinatal death,

(IV) the number of children with chronic illness and the type of illness,

(V) the proportion of infants born with fetal alcohol syndrome,

(VI) the proportion of infants born with drug dependency,

(VII) the proportion of women who deliver who do not receive prenatal care during the first trimester of pregnancy, and

(VIII) the proportion of children, who at their second birthday, have been vaccinated against each of measles, mumps, rubella, polio, diphtheria, tetanus, pertussis, Hib meningitis, and hepatitis B; and

(iii) information on such other indicators of maternal, infant, and child health care status as the Secretary may specify.

(C) Information (by racial and ethnic group) on—

(i) the number of deliveries in the State in the year, and

(ii) the number of such deliveries to pregnant women who were provided prenatal, delivery, or postpartum care under this title or were entitled to benefits with respect to such deliveries under the State plan under title XIX in the year.

(D) Information (by racial and ethnic group) on—

(i) the number of infants under one year of age who were in the State in the year, and

(ii) the number of such infants who were provided services under this title or were entitled to benefits under the State plan under title XIX or the State plan under title XXI at any time during the year.

(E) Information on the number of—

(i) obstetricians,

(ii) family practitioners,

(iii) certified family nurse practitioners,

(iv) certified nurse midwives,

(v) pediatricians, and

(vi) certified pediatric nurse practitioners,

who were licensed in the State in the year.

For purposes of subparagraph (A), each of the following shall be considered to be a separate class of individuals: pregnant women, infants up to age one, children with special health care needs, other children under age 22, and other individuals.

542 SOCIAL SECURITY ACT—§ 506(a)(3)

(3) The Secretary shall annually transmit to the Committee on Energy and Commerce of the House of Representatives and the Committee on Finance of the Senate a report that includes—

(A) a description of each project receiving funding under paragraph (2) or (3) of section 502(a), including the amount of Federal funds provided, the number of individuals served or trained, as appropriate, under the project, and a summary of any formal evaluation conducted with respect to the project;

(B) a summary of the information described in paragraph (2)(A) reported by States;

(C) based on information described in paragraph (2)(B) supplied by the States under paragraph (1), a compilation of the following measures of maternal and child health in the United States and in each State:

(i) Information on—

(I) the rate of infant mortality, and

(II) the rate of low-birth-weight births.

Information under this clause shall also be compiled by racial and ethnic group.

(ii) Information on—

(I) the rate of maternal mortality,

(II) the rate of neonatal death,

(III) the rate of perinatal death,

(IV) the proportion of infants born with fetal alcohol syndrome,

(V) the proportion of infants born with drug dependency,

(VI) the proportion of women who deliver who do not receive prenatal care during the first trimester of pregnancy, and

(VII) the proportion of children, who at their second birthday, have been vaccinated against each of measles, mumps, rubella, polio, diphtheria, tetanus, pertussis, Hib meningitis, and hepatitis B.

(iii) Information on such other indicators of maternal, infant, and child health care status as the Secretary has specified under paragraph (2)(B)(iii).

(iv) Information (by racial and ethnic group) on—

(I) the number of deliveries in the State in the year, and

(II) the number of such deliveries to pregnant women who were provided prenatal, delivery, or postpartum care under this title or were entitled to benefits with respect to such deliveries under the State plan under title XIX in the year;

(D) based on information described in subparagraphs (C), (D), and (E) of paragraph (2) supplied by the States under paragraph (1), a compilation of the following information in the United States and in each State:

(i) Information on—

(I) the number of deliveries in the year, and

(II) the number of such deliveries to pregnant women who were provided prenatal, delivery, or postpartum care under this title or were entitled to benefits with respect to such deliveries under a State plan under title XIX or the State plan under title XXI in the year.

Information under this clause shall also be compiled by racial and ethnic group.

(ii) Information on—

(I) the number of infants under one year of age in the year, and

(II) the number of such infants who were provided services under this title or were entitled to benefits under a State plan under title XIX at any time during the year.

Information under this clause shall also be compiled by racial and ethnic group.

(iii) Information on the number of—

(I) obstetricians,

(II) family practitioners,

(III) certified family nurse practitioners,

(IV) certified nurse midwives,

(V) pediatricians, and

(VI) certified pediatric nurse practitioners,

who were licensed in a State in the year; and

(E) an assessment of the progress being made to meet the health status goals and national health objectives referred to in section 501(a).

(b)(1) Each State shall, not less often than once every two years, audit its expenditures from amounts received under this title. Such State audits shall be conducted by an entity independent of the State agency administering a program funded under this title in accordance with the Comptroller General's standards for auditing governmental organizations, programs, activities, and functions and generally accepted auditing standards. Within 30 days following the completion of each audit report, the State shall submit a copy of that audit report to the Secretary.

(2) Each State shall repay to the United States amounts found by the Secretary, after notice and opportunity for a hearing to the State, not to have been expended in accordance with this title and, if such repayment is not made, the Secretary may offset such amounts against the amount of any allotment to which the State is or may become entitled under this title or may otherwise recover such amounts.

(3) The Secretary may, after notice and opportunity for a hearing, withhold payment of funds to any State which is not using its allotment under this title in accordance with this title. The Secretary may withhold such funds until the Secretary finds that the reason for the withholding has been removed and there is reasonable assurance that it will not recur.

(c) The State shall make copies of the reports and audits required by this section available for public inspection within the State.

(d)(1) For the purpose of evaluating and reviewing the block grant established under this title, the Secretary and the Comptroller General shall have access to any books, accounts, records, correspondence, or other documents that are related to such block grant, and that are in the possession, custody, or control of States, political subdivisions thereof, or any of their grantees.

544 SOCIAL SECURITY ACT—§ 506(d)(2)

(2) In conjunction with an evaluation or review under paragraph (1), no State or political subdivision thereof (or grantee of either) shall be required to create or prepare new records to comply with paragraph (1).

(3) For other provisions relating to deposit, accounting, reports, and auditing with respect to Federal grants to States, see section 6503(b) of title 31, United States Code[10].

CRIMINAL PENALTY FOR FALSE STATEMENTS

SEC. 507. [42 U.S.C. 707] (a) Whoever—
(1) knowingly and willfully makes or causes to be made any false statement or representation of a material fact in connection with the furnishing of items or services for which payment may be made by a State from funds allotted to the State under this title, or
(2) having knowledge of the occurrence of any event affecting his initial or continued right to any such payment conceals or fails to disclose such event with an intent fraudulently to secure such payment either in a greater amount than is due or when no such payment is authorized,
shall be fined not more than $25,000 or imprisoned for not more than five years, or both.

(b) For civil monetary penalties for certain submissions of false claims, see section 1128A of this Act.

NONDISCRIMINATION

SEC. 508. [42 U.S.C. 708] (a)(1) For the purpose of applying the prohibitions against discrimination on the basis of age under the Age Discrimination Act of 1975[11], on the basis of handicap under section 504 of the Rehabilitation Act of 1973[12], on the basis of sex under title IX of the Education Amendments of 1972[13], or on the basis of race, color, or national origin under title VI of the Civil Rights Act of 1964[14], programs and activities funded in whole or in part with funds made available under this title are considered to be programs and activities receiving Federal financial assistance.

(2) No person shall on the ground of sex or religion be excluded from participation in, be denied the benefits of, or be subjected to discrimination under, any program or activity funded in whole or in part with funds made available under this title.

(b) Whenever the Secretary finds that a State, or an entity that has received a payment from an allotment to a State under section 502(c), has failed to comply with a provision of law referred to in subsection (a)(1), with subsection (a)(2), or with an applicable regulation (including one prescribed to carry out subsection (a)(2)), he shall notify the chief executive officer of the State and shall request him to secure compliance. If within a reasonable period of time, not to exceed sixty days, the chief executive officer fails or refuses to secure compliance, the Secretary may—

---

[10] See Vol. II, 31 U.S.C. 6503(b).
[11] See Vol. II, P.L. 94-135, Title III [89 Stat. 728].
[12] See Vol. II, P.L. 93-112, §504.
[13] See Vol. II, P.L. 92-318, Title IX.
[14] See Vol. II, P.L. 88-352, Title VI.

SOCIAL SECURITY ACT—§ 509(a)(8)   545

(1) refer the matter to the Attorney General with a recommendation that an appropriate civil action be instituted,

(2) exercise the powers and functions provided by title VI of the Civil Rights Act of 1964[15], the Age Discrimination Act of 1975[16], or section 504 of the Rehabilitation Act of 1973[17], as may be applicable, or

(3) take such other action as may be provided by law.

(c) When a matter is referred to the Attorney General pursuant to subsection (b)(1), or whenever he has reason to believe that the entity is engaged in a pattern or practice in violation of a provision of law referred to in subsection (a)(1) or in violation of subsection (a)(2), the Attorney General may bring a civil action in any appropriate district court of the United States for such relief as may be appropriate, including injunctive relief.

ADMINISTRATION OF TITLE AND STATE PROGRAMS

SEC. 509. [42 U.S.C. 709] (a) The Secretary shall designate an identifiable administrative unit with expertise in maternal and child health within the Department of Health and Human Services, which unit shall be responsible for—

(1) the Federal program described in section 502(a);

(2) promoting coordination at the Federal level of the activities authorized under this title and under title XIX of this Act, especially early and periodic screening, diagnosis and treatment, related activities funded by the Departments of Agriculture and Education, and under health block grants and categorical health programs, such as immunizations, administered by the Secretary;

(3) disseminating information to the States in such areas as preventive health services and advances in the care and treatment of mothers and children;

(4) providing technical assistance, upon request, to the States in such areas as program planning, establishment of goals and objectives, standards of care, and evaluation and in developing consistent and accurate data collection mechanisms in order to report the information required under section 506(a)(2);

(5) in cooperation with the National Center for Health Statistics and in a manner that avoids duplication of data collection, collection, maintenance, and dissemination of information relating to the health status and health service needs of mothers and children in the United States;

(6) assisting in the preparation of reports to the Congress on the activities funded and accomplishments achieved under this title from the information required to be reported by the States under sections 505(a) and 506; and[18]

(7) assisting States in the development of care coordination services (as defined in section 501(b)(3)); and

(8) developing and making available to the State agency (or agencies) administering the State's program under this title a na-

---

[15] See Vol. II, P.L. 88-352, Title VI.
[16] See Vol. II, P.L. 93-66, §211(a)(1)(A).
[17] See Vol. II, P.L. 93-112, §504.
[18] As in original. "and" should probably not appear.

546 SOCIAL SECURITY ACT—§ 509(a)(8)(cont)

tional directory listing by State the toll-free numbers described in section 505(a)(5)(E).

(b) The State health agency of each State shall be responsible for the administration (or supervision of the administration) of programs carried out with allotments made to the State under this title, except that, in the case of a State which on July 1, 1967, provided for administration (or supervision thereof) of the State plan under this title (as in effect on such date) by a State agency other than the State health agency, that State shall be considered to comply[19] the requirement of this subsection if it would otherwise comply but for the fact that such other State agency administers (or supervises the administration of) any such program providing services for children with special health care needs.

SEPARATE PROGRAM FOR ABSTINENCE EDUCATION[20]

SEC. 510. [42 U.S.C. 710] (a) For the purpose described in subsection (b), the Secretary shall, for fiscal year 1998 and each subsequent fiscal year, allot to each State which has transmitted an application for the fiscal year under section 505(a) an amount equal to the product of—

(1) the amount appropriated in subsection (d) for the fiscal year; and

(2) the percentage determined for the State under section 502(c)(1)(B)(ii).

(b)(1) The purpose of an allotment under subsection (a) to a State is to enable the State to provide abstinence education, and at the option of the State, where appropriate, mentoring, counseling, and adult supervision to promote abstinence from sexual activity, with a focus on those groups which are most likely to bear children out-of-wedlock.

(2) For purposes of this section, the term "abstinence education" means an educational or motivational program which—

(A) has as its exclusive purpose, teaching the social, psychological, and health gains to be realized by abstaining from sexual activity;

(B) teaches abstinence from sexual activity outside marriage as the expected standard for all school age children;

(C) teaches that abstinence from sexual activity is the only certain way to avoid out-of-wedlock pregnancy, sexually transmitted diseases, and other associated health problems;

(D) teaches that a mutually faithful monogamous relationship in context of marriage is the expected standard of human sexual activity;

(E) teaches that sexual activity outside of the context of marriage is likely to have harmful psychological and physical effects;

(F) teaches that bearing children out-of-wedlock is likely to have harmful consequences for the child, the child's parents, and society;

(G) teaches young people how to reject sexual advances and how alcohol and drug use increases vulnerability to sexual advances; and

(H) teaches the importance of attaining self-sufficiency before engaging in sexual activity.

---

[19] As in original. Probably should be "comply with".
[20] See Vol. II, P.L. 109-432, §401, with respect to an extension of abstinence education program.

SOCIAL SECURITY ACT—§ 510(d)   547

(c)(1) Sections 503, 507, and 508 apply to allotments under subsection (a) to the same extent and in the same manner as such sections apply to allotments under section 502(c).

(2) Sections 505 and 506 apply to allotments under subsection (a) to the extent determined by the Secretary to be appropriate.

(d) For the purpose of allotments under subsection (a), there is appropriated, out of any money in the Treasury not otherwise appropriated, an additional $50,000,000 for each of the fiscal years 1998 through 2003. The appropriation under the preceding sentence for a fiscal year is made on October 1 of the fiscal year.

[TITLE VI—TEMPORARY STATE FISCAL RELIEF[1]]

---

[1] P.L. 108-27, §401(b), added this title to the Social Security Act, effective May 28, 2003.
Title VI, §601(g), as enacted by P.L. 108-27, provided that
"(g) REPEAL.—Effective as of October 1, 2004, this title is repealed."

TITLE VII—ADMINISTRATION[1]

TABLE OF CONTENTS OF TITLE[2]

		Page
Sec. 701.	Social Security Administration	551
Sec. 702.	Commissioner; Deputy Commissioner; Other Officers	551
Sec. 703.	Social Security Advisory Board	553
Sec. 704.	Administrative Duties of the Commissioner	556
Sec. 705.	Training grants for public welfare personnel	558
[Sec. 706.	Repealed.]	560
Sec. 707.	Grants for expansion and development of undergraduate and graduate programs	560
Sec. 708.	Delivery of benefit checks	560
Sec. 709.	Recommendations by Board of Trustees to remedy inadequate balances in the social security trust funds	561
Sec. 710.	Budgetary treatment of trust fund operations	562
Sec. 711.	Office of Rural Health Policy	562
Sec. 712.	Duties and authority of Secretary	563

SOCIAL SECURITY ADMINISTRATION

SEC. 701. [42 U.S.C. 901] (a) There is hereby established, as an independent agency in the executive branch of the Government, a Social Security Administration (in this title referred to as the "Administration").

(b) It shall be the duty of the Administration to administer the old-age, survivors, and disability insurance program under title II and the supplemental security income program under title XVI.

COMMISSIONER; DEPUTY COMMISSIONER; OTHER OFFICERS

Commissioner of Social Security

SEC. 702. [42 U.S.C. 902] (a)(1) There shall be in the Administration a Commissioner of Social Security (in this title referred to as the "Commissioner") who shall be appointed by the President, by and with the advice and consent of the Senate.

(2) The Commissioner shall be compensated at the rate provided for level I of the Executive Schedule.

(3) The Commissioner shall be appointed for a term of 6 years, except that the initial term of office for Commissioner shall terminate January 19, 2001. In any case in which a successor does not take office at the end of a Commissioner's term of office, such Commissioner may continue in office until the entry upon office of such a successor. A Commissioner appointed to a term of office after the commencement of such term may serve under such appointment only for the remainder of such term. An individual serving in the the office of Commissioner may be removed from office only pursuant to a finding by the President of neglect of duty or malfeasance in office.

---

[1] Title VII of the Social Security Act is administered by the Office of the Commissioner of Social Security.

Title VII appears in the United States Code as §§901-912 of subchapter VII, chapter 7, Title 42.

Regulations of the Social Security Administration relating to Title VII are contained in subtitle A and chapter II, Title 45, Code of Federal Regulations.

See Vol. II, 31 U.S.C. 6504-6505, with respect to intergovernmental cooperation.

See Vol. II, P.L. 88-352, §601, for prohibition against discrimination in federally assisted programs.

[2] This table of contents does not appear in the law.

552 SOCIAL SECURITY ACT—§ 702(a)(4)

(4) The Commissioner shall be responsible for the exercise of all powers and the discharge of all duties of the Administration, and shall have authority and control over all personnel and activities thereof.

(5) The Commissioner may prescribe such rules and regulations as the Commissioner determines necessary or appropriate to carry out the functions of the Administration. The regulations prescribed by the Commissioner shall be subject to the rulemaking procedures established under section 553 of title 5, United States Code[3].

(6) The Commissioner may establish, alter, consolidate, or discontinue such organizational units or components within the Administration as the Commissioner considers necessary or appropriate, except that this paragraph shall not apply with respect to any unit, component, or provision provided for by this Act.

(7) The Commissioner may assign duties, and delegate, or authorize successive redelegations of, authority to act and to render decisions, to such officers and employees of the Administration as the Commissioner may find necessary. Within the limitations of such delegations, redelegations, or assignments, all official acts and decisions of such officers and employees shall have the same force and effect as though performed or rendered by the Commissioner.

(8) The Commissioner and the Secretary of Health and Human Services (in this title referred to as the "Secretary") shall consult, on an ongoing basis, to ensure—

(A) the coordination of the programs administered by the Commissioner, as described in section 701, with the programs administered by the Secretary under titles XVIII and XIX of this Act; and

(B) that adequate information concerning benefits under such titles XVIII and XIX is available to the public.

Deputy Commissioner of Social Security

(b)(1) There shall be in the Administration a Deputy Commissioner of Social Security (in this title referred to as the Deputy Commissioner) who shall be appointed by the President, by and with the advice and consent of the Senate.

(2) The Deputy Commissioner shall be appointed for a term of 6 years, except that the initial term of office for the Deputy Commissioner shall terminate January 19, 2001. In any case in which a successor does not take office at the end of a Deputy Commissioner's term of office, such Deputy Commissioner may continue in office until the entry upon office of such a successor. A Deputy Commissioner appointed to a term of office after the commencement of such term may serve under such appointment only for the remainder of such term.

(3) The Deputy Commissioner shall be compensated at the rate provided for level II of the Executive Schedule.

(4) The Deputy Commissioner shall perform such duties and exercise such powers as the Commissioner shall from time to time assign or delegate. The Deputy Commissioner shall be Acting Commissioner of the Administration during the absence or disability of the Commissioner and, unless the President designates another officer of the

---

[3] See Vol. II, 5 U.S.C. 553.

SOCIAL SECURITY ACT—§ 703(b)(2)   553

Government as Acting Commissioner, in the event of a vacancy in the office of the Commissioner.

Chief Actuary

(c)(1) There shall be in the Administration a Chief Actuary, who shall be appointed by, and in direct line of authority to, the Commissioner. The Chief Actuary shall be appointed from individuals who have demonstrated, by their education and experience, superior expertise in the actuarial sciences. The Chief Actuary shall serve as the chief actuarial officer of the Administration, and shall exercise such duties as are appropriate for the office of the Chief Actuary and in accordance with professional standards of actuarial independence. The Chief Actuary may be removed only for cause.

(2) The Chief Actuary shall be compensated at the highest rate of basic pay for the Senior Executive Service under section 5382(b) of title 5, United States Code[4].

Chief Financial Officer

(d) There shall be in the Administration a Chief Financial Officer appointed by the Commissioner in accordance with section 901(a)(2) of title 31, United States Code[5].

Inspector General

(e) There shall be in the Administration an Inspector General appointed by the President, by and with the advice and consent of the Senate, in accordance with section 3(a) of the Inspector General Act of 1978.

SOCIAL SECURITY ADVISORY BOARD

Establishment of Board

SEC. 703. [42 U.S.C. 903] (a) There shall be established a Social Security Advisory Board (in this section referred to as the "Board").

(b) On and after the date the Commissioner takes office, the Board shall advise the Commissioner on policies related to the old-age, survivors, and disability insurance program under title II, the program of special benefits for certain World War II veterans under title VIII, and the supplemental security income program under title XVI. Specific functions of the Board shall include—

> (1) analyzing the Nation's retirement and disability systems and making recommendations with respect to how the old-age, survivors, and disability insurance program and the supplemental security income program, supported by other public and private systems, can most effectively assure economic security;

> (2) studying and making recommendations relating to the coordination of programs that provide health security with programs described in paragraph (1);

---

[4] See Vol. II, 5 U.S.C. 5382(b).
[5] See Vol. II, 31 U.S.C. 901(a)(2).

554   SOCIAL SECURITY ACT—§ 703(b)(3)

(3) making recommendations to the President and to the Congress with respect to policies that will ensure the solvency of the old-age, survivors, and disability insurance program, both in the short-term and the long-term;

(4) making recommendations with respect to the quality of service that the Administration provides to the public;

(5) making recommendations with respect to policies and regulations regarding the old-age, survivors, and disability insurance program and the supplemental security income program;

(6) increasing public understanding of the social security system;

(7) making recommendations with respect to a long-range research program and evaluation plan for the Administration;

(8) reviewing and assessing any major studies of social security as may come to the attention of the Board; and

(9) making recommendations with respect to such other matters as the Board determines to be appropriate.

Structure and Membership of the Board

(c)(1) The Board shall be composed of 7 members who shall be appointed as follows:

(A) 3 members shall be appointed by the President, by and with the advice and consent of the Senate. Not more than 2 of such members shall be from the same political party.

(B) 2 members (each member from a different political party) shall be appointed by the President pro tempore of the Senate with the advice of the Chairman and the Ranking Minority Member of the Senate Committee on Finance.

(C) 2 members (each member from a different political party) shall be appointed by the Speaker of the House of Representatives, with the advice of the Chairman and the Ranking Minority Member of the House Committee on Ways and Means.

(2) The members shall be chosen on the basis of their integrity, impartiality, and good judgment, and shall be individuals who are, by reason of their education, experience, and attainments, exceptionally qualified to perform the duties of members of the Board.

Terms of Appointment

(d) Each member of the Board shall serve for a term of 6 years, except that—

(1) a member appointed to a term of office after the commencement of such term may serve under such appointment only for the remainder of such term; and

(2) the terms of service of the members initially appointed under this section shall begin on October 1, 1994, and expire as follows:

(A) The terms of service of the members initially appointed by the President shall expire as designated by the President at the time of nomination, 1 each at the end of—

(i) 2 years;

(ii) 4 years; and

SOCIAL SECURITY ACT—§ 703(h)

(iii) 6 years.

(B) The terms of service of members initially appointed by the President pro tempore of the Senate shall expire as designated by the President pro tempore of the Senate at the time of nomination, 1 each at the end of—

(i) 3 years; and
(ii) 6 years.

(C) The terms of service of members initially appointed by the Speaker of the House of Representatives shall expire as designated by the Speaker of the House of Representatives at the time of nomination, 1 each at the end of—

(i) 4 years; and
(ii) 5 years.

Chairman

(e) A member of the Board shall be designated by the President to serve as Chairman for a term of 4 years, coincident with the term of the President, or until the designation of a successor.

Compensation, Expenses and Per Diem

(f) A member of the Board shall, for each day (including traveltime) during which the member is attending meetings or conferences of the Board or otherwise engaged in the business of the Board, be compensated at the daily rate of basic pay for level IV of the Executive Schedule. While serving on business of the Board away from their homes or regular places of business, members may be allowed travel expenses, including per diem in lieu of subsistence, as authorized by section 5703 of title 5, United States Code[6], for persons in the Government employed intermittently.

Meeting

(g)(1) The Board shall meet at the call of the Chairman (in consultation with the other members of the Board) not less than 4 times each year to consider a specific agenda of issues, as determined by the Chairman in consultation with the other members of the Board.

(2) Four members of the Board (not more than 3 of whom may be of the same political party) shall constitute a quorum for purposes of conducting business.

Federal Advisory Committee Act

(h) The Board shall be exempt from the provisions of the Federal Advisory Committee Act (5 U.S.C. App.).

---

[6] See Vol. II, 5 U.S.C. 5703.

556 SOCIAL SECURITY ACT—§ 703(i)

Personnel

(i) The Board shall, without regard to the provisions of title 5, United States Code, relating to the competitive service, appoint a Staff Director who shall be paid at a rate equivalent to a rate established for the Senior Executive Service under section 5382 of title 5, United States Code[7]. The Board shall appoint such additional personnel as the Board determines to be necessary to provide adequate support for the Board, and may compensate such additional personnel without regard to the provisions of title 5, United States Code, relating to the competitive service.

Authorization of Appropriations

(j) There are authorized to be appropriated, out of the Federal Disability Insurance Trust Fund, the Federal Old-Age and Survivors Insurance Trust Fund, and the general fund of the Treasury, such sums as are necessary to carry out the purposes of this section.

ADMINISTRATIVE DUTIES OF THE COMMISSIONER

Personnel

SEC. 704. [42 U.S.C. 904] (a)(1) The Commissioner shall appoint such additional officers and employees as the Commissioner considers necessary to carry out the functions of the Administration under this Act, and attorneys and experts may be appointed without regard to the civil service laws. Except as otherwise provided in the preceding sentence or in any other provision of law, such officers and employees shall be appointed, and their compensation shall be fixed, in accordance with title 5, United States Code.

(2) The Commissioner may procure the services of experts and consultants in accordance with the provisions of section 3109 of title 5, United States Code[8].

(3) Notwithstanding any requirements of section 3133 of title 5, United States Code, the Director of the Office of Personnel Management shall authorize for the Administration a total number of Senior Executive Service positions which is substantially greater than the number of such positions authorized in the Social Security Administration in the Department of Health and Human Services as of immediately before the date of the enactment of the Social Security Independence Program Improvements Act of 1994[9] to the extent that the greater number of such authorized positions is specified in the comprehensive work force plan as established and revised by the Commissioner under subsection (b)(2). The total number of such positions authorized for the Administration shall not at any time be less than the number of such authorized positions as of immediately before such date.

---

[7] See Vol. II, 5 U.S.C. 5382.
[8] See Vol. II, 5 U.S.C. 3109.
[9] August 15, 1994 [P.L. 103-296; 108 Stat. 1464]

Budgetary Matters

(b)(1)(A) The Commissioner shall prepare an annual budget for the Administration, which shall be submitted by the President to the Congress without revision, together with the President's annual budget for the Administration.

(B) The Commissioner shall include in the annual budget prepared pursuant to subparagraph (A) an itemization of the amount of funds required by the Social Security Administration for the fiscal year covered by the budget to support efforts to combat fraud committed by applicants and beneficiaries.

(2)(A) Appropriations requests for staffing and personnel of the Administration shall be based upon a comprehensive work force plan, which shall be established and revised from time to time by the Commissioner.

(B) Appropriations for administrative expenses of the Administration are authorized to be provided on a biennial basis.

Employment Restriction

(c) The total number of positions in the Administration (other than positions established under section 702) which—

(1) are held by noncareer appointees (within the meaning of section 3132(a)(7) of title 5, United States Code[10]) in the Senior Executive Service, or

(2) have been determined by the President or the Office of Personnel Management to be of a confidential, policy-determining, policy-making, or policy-advocating character and have been excepted from the competitive service thereby,

may not exceed at any time the equivalent of 20 full-time positions.

Seal of Office

(d) The Commissioner shall cause a seal of office to be made for the Administration of such design as the Commissioner shall approve. Judicial notice shall be taken of such seal.

Data Exchanges

(e)(1) Notwithstanding any other provision of law (including subsection (b), (o), (p), (q), (r), and (u) of section 552a of title 5, United States Code[11]—

(A) the Secretary shall disclose to the Commissioner any record or information requested in writing by the Commissioner for the purpose of administering any program administered by the Commissioner, if records or information of such type were disclosed to the Commissioner of Social Security in the Department of Health and Human Services under applicable rules, regulations, and procedures in effect before the date of the enactment of the Social Se-

---

[10] See Vol. II, 5 U.S.C. 3132(a)(7).
[11] See Vol. II, 5 U.S.C. 552a.

558   SOCIAL SECURITY ACT—§ 704(e)(1)(A)(cont)

curity Independence and Program Improvements Act of 1994[12]; and

(B) the Commissioner shall disclose to the Secretary or to any State any record or information requested in writing by the Secretary to be so disclosed for the purpose of administering any program administered by the Secretary, if records or information of such type were so disclosed under applicable rules, regulations, and procedures in effect before the date of the enactment of the Social Security Independence and Program Improvements Act of 1994.

(2) The Commissioner and the Secretary shall enter into an agreement under which the Commissioner provides the Secretary data concerning the quality of the services and information provided to beneficiaries of the programs under titles XVIII and XIX and the administrative services provided by the Social Security Administration in support of such programs. Such agreement shall stipulate the type of data to be provided and the terms and conditions under which the data are to be provided.

(3) The Commissioner and the Secretary shall periodically review the need for exchanges of information not referred to in paragraph (1) or (2) and shall enter into such agreements as may be necessary and appropriate to provide information to each other or to States in order to meet the programmatic needs of the requesting agencies.

(4)(A) Any disclosure from a system of records (as defined in section 552a(a)(5) of title 5, United States Code[13]) pursuant to this subsection shall be made as a routine use under subsection (b)(3) of section 552a of such title (unless otherwise authorized under such section 552a).

(B) Any computerized comparison of records, including matching programs, between the Commissioner and the Secretary shall be conducted in accordance with subsections (o), (p), (q), (r), and (u) of section 552a of title 5, United States Code.

(5) The Commissioner and the Secretary shall each ensure that timely action is taken to establish any necessary routine uses for disclosures required under paragraph (1) or agreed to pursuant to paragraph (3).

TRAINING GRANTS FOR PUBLIC WELFARE PERSONNEL

SEC. 705. [42 U.S.C. 906] (a) In order to assist in increasing the effectiveness and efficiency of administration of public assistance programs by increasing the number of adequately trained public welfare personnel available for work in public assistance programs, there are hereby authorized to be appropriated for the fiscal year ending June 30, 1963, the sum of $3,500,000, and for each fiscal year thereafter the sum of $5,000,000.

(b) Such portion of the sums appropriated pursuant to subsection (a) for any fiscal year as the Secretary may determine, but not in excess of $1,000,000 in the case of the fiscal year ending June 30, 1963, and $2,000,000 in the case of any fiscal year thereafter, shall be available for carrying out subsection (f). From the remainder of the sums so appropriated for any fiscal year, the Secretary shall make allotments to the States on the basis of (1) population, (2) relative need for

---

[12] August 15, 1994 [P.L. 103-296; 108 Stat.1464]
[13] See Vol. II, 5 U.S.C. 552a(a)(5).

trained public welfare personnel, particularly for personnel to provide self-support and self-care services, and (3) financial need.

(c) From each State's allotment under subsection (b), the Secretary shall from time to time pay to such State its costs of carrying out the purposes of this section through (1) grants to public or other nonprofit institutions of higher learning for training personnel employed or preparing for employment in public assistance programs, (2) special courses of study or seminars of short duration conducted for such personnel by experts hired on a temporary basis for the purpose, and (3) establishing and maintaining, directly or through grants to such institutions, fellowships or traineeships for such personnel at such institutions, with such stipends and allowances as may be permitted under regulations of the Secretary.

(d) Payments pursuant to subsection (c) shall be made in advance on the basis of estimates by the Secretary and adjustments may be made in future payments under this section to take account of overpayments or underpayments in amounts previously paid.

(e) The amount of any allotment to a State under subsection (b) for any fiscal year which the State certifies to the Secretary will not be required for carrying out the purposes of this section in such State shall be available for reallotment from time to time, on such dates as the Secretary may fix, to other States which the Secretary determines have need in carrying out such purposes for sums in excess of those previously allotted to them under this section and will be able to use such excess amounts during such fiscal year; such reallotments to be made on the basis provided in subsection (b) for the initial allotments to the States. Any amount so reallotted to a State shall be deemed part of its allotment under such subsection.

(f)(1) The portion of the sums appropriated for any fiscal year which is determined by the Secretary under the first sentence of subsection (b) to be available for carrying out this subsection shall be available to enable him to provide (A) directly or through grants to or contracts with public or nonprofit private institutions of higher learning, for training personnel who are employed or preparing for employment in the administration of public assistance programs, (B) directly or through grants to or contracts with public or nonprofit private agencies or institutions, for special courses of study or seminars of short duration (not in excess of one year) for training of such personnel, and (C) directly or through grants to or contracts with public or nonprofit private institutions of higher learning, for establishing and maintaining fellowships or traineeships for such personnel at such institutions, with such stipends and allowances as may be permitted by the Secretary.

(2) Payments under paragraph (1) may be made in advance on the basis of estimates by the Secretary, or may be made by way of reimbursement, and adjustments may be made in future payments under this subsection to take account of overpayments or underpayments in amounts previously paid.

(3) The Secretary may, to the extent he finds such action to be necessary, prescribe requirements to assure that any individual will repay the amount of his fellowship or traineeship received under this subsection to the extent such individual fails to serve, for the period prescribed by the Secretary, with a State or political subdivision thereof, or with the Federal Government, in connection with administration

560   SOCIAL SECURITY ACT—§ 705(f)(3)(cont)

of any State or local public assistance program. The Secretary may relieve any individual of his obligation to so repay, in whole or in part, whenever and to the extent that requirement of such repayment would, in his judgment, be inequitable or would be contrary to the purposes of any of the public welfare programs established by this Act.

SEC. 706. [Repealed.[14]]

GRANTS FOR EXPANSION AND DEVELOPMENT OF UNDERGRADUATE AND GRADUATE PROGRAMS

SEC. 707. [42 U.S.C. 908] (a) There is authorized to be appropriated $5,000,000 for the fiscal year ending June 30, 1969, and $5,000,000 for each of the three succeeding fiscal years, for grants by the Secretary to public or nonprofit private colleges and universities and to accredited graduate schools of social work or an association of such schools to meet part of the costs of development, expansion, or improvement of (respectively) undergraduate programs in social work and programs for the graduate training of professional social work personnel, including the costs of compensation of additional faculty and administrative personnel and minor improvements of existing facilities. Not less than one-half of the sums appropriated for any fiscal year under the authority of this subsection shall be used by the Secretary for grants with respect to undergraduate programs.

(b) In considering applications for grants under this section, the Secretary shall take into account the relative need in the States for personnel trained in social work and the effect of the grants thereon.

(c) Payment of grants under this section may be made (after necessary adjustments on account of previously made overpayments or underpayments) in advance or by way of reimbursement, and on such terms and conditions and in such installments, as the Secretary may determine.

(d) For purposes of this section—

(1) the term "graduate school of social work" means a department, school, division, or other administrative unit, in a public or nonprofit private college or university, which provides, primarily or exclusively, a program of education in social work and allied subjects leading to a graduate degree in social work;

(2) the term "accredited" as applied to a graduate school of social work refers to a school which is accredited by a body or bodies approved for the purpose by the Commissioner of Education or with respect to which there is evidence satisfactory to the Secretary that it will be so accredited within a reasonable time; and

(3) the term "nonprofit" as applied to any college or university refers to a college or university which is a corporation or association, or is owned and operated by one or more corporations or associations, no part of the net earnings of which inures, or may lawfully inure, to the benefit of any private shareholder or individual.

DELIVERY OF BENEFIT CHECKS

SEC. 708. [42 U.S.C. 909] (a) If the day regularly designated for the delivery of benefit checks under title II, title VIII or title XVI falls on a

---

[14] P.L. 103-296-296, §108(a)(2); 108 Stat. 1481.

SOCIAL SECURITY ACT—§ 709(b)(2)   561

Saturday, Sunday, or legal public holiday (as defined in section 6103 of title 5, United States Code[15] in any month, the benefit checks which would otherwise be delivered on such day shall be mailed for delivery on the first day preceding such day which is not a Saturday, Sunday, or legal public holiday (as so defined), without regard to whether the delivery of such checks would as a result have to be made before the end of the month for which such checks are issued.

(b) If more than the correct amount of payment under title II, title VIII or XVI is made to any individual as a result of the receipt of a benefit check pursuant to subsection (a) before the end of the month for which such check is issued, no action shall be taken (under section 204 or 1631(b) or otherwise) to recover such payment or the incorrect portion thereof.

(c) For purposes of computing the "OASDI trust fund ratio" under section 201(l), the "OASDI fund ratio" under section 215(i), and the "balance ratio" under section 709(b), benefit checks delivered before the end of the month for which they are issued by reason of subsection (a) of this section shall be deemed to have been delivered on the regularly designated delivery date.

RECOMMENDATIONS BY BOARD OF TRUSTEES TO REMEDY INADEQUATE
BALANCES IN THE SOCIAL SECURITY TRUST FUNDS

SEC. 709. [42 U.S.C. 910] (a) If the Board of Trustees of the Federal Old-Age and Survivors Insurance Trust Fund and the Federal Disability Insurance Trust Fund, the Federal Hospital Insurance Trust Fund, or the Federal Supplementary Medical Insurance Trust Fund determines at any time that the balance ratio of any such Trust Fund for any calendar year may become less than 20 percent, the Board shall promptly submit to each House of the Congress a report setting forth its recommendations for statutory adjustments affecting the receipts and disbursements of such Trust Fund necessary to maintain the balance ratio of such Trust Fund at not less than 20 percent, with due regard to the economic conditions which created such inadequacy in the balance ratio and the amount of time necessary to alleviate such inadequacy in a prudent manner. The report shall set forth specifically the extent to which benefits would have to be reduced, taxes under section 1401, 3101, or 3111 of the Internal Revenue Code of 1954[16] would have to be increased, or a combination thereof, in order to obtain the objectives referred to in the preceding sentence.

(b) For purposes of this section, the term "balance ratio" means, with respect to any calendar year in connection with any Trust Fund referred to in subsection (a), the ratio of—

(1) the balance in such Trust Fund as of the beginning of such year, including the taxes transferred under section 201(a) on the first day of such year and reduced by the outstanding amount of any loan (including interest thereon) theretofore made to such Trust Fund under section 201(l) or 1817(j), to

(2) the total amount which (for amounts which will be paid from the Federal Old-Age and Survivors Insurance Trust Fund and the Federal Disability Insurance Trust Fund, as estimated

---

[15] Legal public holidays which may affect check delivery are (1) New Year's Day [January 1], (2) Independence Day [July 4], and (3) Labor Day [first Monday in September].
[16] See Vol. II, P.L. 83-591, §§1401, 3101, and 3111.

562 SOCIAL SECURITY ACT—§ 709(b)(2)(cont)

by the Commissioner, and for amounts which will be paid from the Federal Hospital Insurance Trust and the Federal Supplementary Medical Insurance Trust Fund, as estimated by the Secretary) will be paid from such Trust Fund during such calendar year for all purposes authorized by section 201, 1817, or 1841 (as applicable), other than payments of interest on, or repayments of, loans under section 201(l) or 1817(j), but excluding any transfer payments between such Trust Fund and any other Trust Fund referred to in subsection (a) and reducing the amount of any transfers to the Railroad Retirement Account by the amount of any transfers into such Trust Fund from that Account.

BUDGETARY TREATMENT OF TRUST FUND OPERATIONS[17]

SEC. 710. [42 U.S.C. 911] (a) The receipts and disbursements of the Federal Old-Age and Survivors Insurance Trust Fund and the Federal Disability Insurance Trust Fund and the taxes imposed under sections 1401 and 3101 of the Internal Revenue Code of 1986[18] shall not be included in the totals of the budget of the United States Government as submitted by the President or of the congressional budget and shall be exempt from any general budget limitation imposed by statute on expenditures and net lending (budget outlays) of the United States Government.

(b) No provision of law enacted after the date of enactment of the Balanced Budget and Emergency Deficit Control Act of 1985[19] (other than a provision of an appropriation Act that appropriated funds authorized under the Social Security Act as in effect on the date of the enactment of the Balanced Budget and Emergency Deficit Control Act of 1985) may provide for payments from the general fund of the Treasury to any Trust Fund specified in subsection (a) or for payments from any such Trust Fund to the general fund of the Treasury.

OFFICE OF RURAL HEALTH POLICY

SEC. 711. [42 U.S.C. 912] (a) There shall be established in the Department of Health and Human Services (in this section referred to as the "Department") an Office of Rural Health Policy (in this section referred to as the "Office"). The Office shall be headed by a Director, who shall advise the Secretary on the effects of current policies and proposed statutory, regulatory, administrative, and budgetary changes in the programs established under titles XVIII and XIX on the financial viability of small rural hospitals, the ability of rural areas (and rural hospitals in particular) to attract and retain physicians and other health professionals, and access to (and the quality of) health care in rural areas.

(b) In addition to advising the Secretary with respect to the matters specified in subsection (a), the Director, through the Office, shall—

(1) oversee compliance with the requirements of section 1102(b) of this Act and section 4403 of the Omnibus Budget Reconciliation Act of 1987[20] (as such section pertains to rural health issues),

---

[17] See Vol. II, P.L. 93-344, §3(2), with respect to budget authority for fiscal year 1992 and subsequent fiscal years.
[18] See Vol. II, P.L. 83-591, §§1401 and 3101.
[19] December 12, 1985 [P.L. 99-177; 99 Stat. 1037]
[20] See Vol. II, P.L. 100-203, §4403.

SOCIAL SECURITY ACT—§ 712

(2) establish and maintain a clearinghouse for collecting and disseminating information on—

(A) rural health care issues, including rural mental health, rural infant mortality prevention, and rural occupational safety and preventive health promotion,

(B) research findings relating to rural health care, and

(C) innovative approaches to the delivery of health care in rural area, including programs providing community-based mental health services, pre-natal and infant care services, and rural occupational safety and preventive health education and promotion,

(3) coordinate the activities within the Department that relate to rural health care,

(4) provide information to the Secretary and others in the Department with respect to the activities, of other Federal departments and agencies, that relate to rural health care, including activities relating to rural mental health, rural infant mortality, and rural occupational safety and preventive health promotion, and

(5) administer grants, cooperative agreements, and contracts to provide technical assistance and other activities as necessary to support activities related to improving health care in rural areas.

DUTIES AND AUTHORITY OF SECRETARY

SEC. 712. [42 U.S.C. 913] The Secretary shall perform the duties imposed upon the Secretary by this Act. The Secretary is authorized to appoint and fix the compensation of such officers and employees, and to make such expenditures as may be necessary for carrying out the functions of the Secretary under this Act. The Secretary may appoint attorneys and experts without regard to the civil service laws.

TITLE VIII—SPECIAL BENEFITS FOR CERTAIN WORLD WAR II VETERANS[1]

TABLE OF CONTENTS OF TITLE[2]

		Page
Sec. 801.	Basic entitlement to benefits	565
Sec. 802.	Qualified individuals	565
Sec. 803.	Residence outside the United States	565
Sec. 804.	Disqualifications	566
Sec. 805.	Benefit amount	566
Sec. 806.	Applications and furnishing of information	566
Sec. 807.	Representative payees	567
Sec. 808.	Overpayments and underpayments	573
Sec. 809.	Hearings and review	574
Sec. 810.	Other administrative provisions	575
Sec. 810A.	Optional Federal administration of State recognition payments	576
Sec. 811.	Penalties for fraud	576
Sec. 812.	Definitions	577
Sec. 813.	Appropriations	579

BASIC ENTITLEMENT TO BENEFITS

SEC. 801. [42 U.S.C. 1001] Every individual who is a qualified individual under section 802 shall, in accordance with and subject to the provisions of this title, be entitled to a monthly benefit paid by the Commissioner of Social Security for each month after September 2000 (or such earlier month, if the Commissioner determines is administratively feasible) the individual resides outside the United States.

QUALIFIED INDIVIDUALS

SEC. 802. [42 U.S.C. 1002] Except as otherwise provided in this title, an individual—

(1) who has attained the age of 65 on or before the date of the enactment of this title;

(2) who is a World War II veteran;

(3) who is eligible for a supplemental security income benefit under title XVI for—

(A) the month in which this title is enacted; and

(B) the month in which the individual files an application for benefits under this title;

(4) whose total benefit income is less than 75 percent of the Federal benefit rate under title XVI;

(5) who has filed an application for benefits under this title; and

(6) who is in compliance with all requirements imposed by the Commissioner of Social Security under this title,

shall be a qualified individual for purposes of this title.

RESIDENCE OUTSIDE THE UNITED STATES

SEC. 803. [42 U.S.C. 1003] For purposes of section 801, with respect to any month, an individual shall be regarded as residing outside the

---

[1] Title VIII of the Social Security Act is administered by the Social Security Administration.

Title VIII appears in the United States Code, §§1001-1013, subchapter VIII, chapter 7, Title 42. See Vol. II, P.L. 88-352, §601, for prohibition against discrimination in Federally assisted programs.

[2] This table of contents does not appear in the law.

566 SOCIAL SECURITY ACT—§ 803(cont)

United States if, on the first day of the month, the individual so resides outside the United States.

DISQUALIFICATIONS

SEC. 804. [42 U.S.C. 1004] (a) IN GENERAL.—Notwithstanding section 802, an individual may not be a qualified individual for any month—

(1) that begins after the month in which the Commissioner of Social Security is notified by the Attorney General that the individual has been removed from the United States pursuant to section 237(a) or 212(a)(6)(A) of the Immigration and Nationality Act[3] and before the month in which the individual is lawfully admitted to the United States for permanent residence;

(2) during any part of which the individual is fleeing to avoid prosecution, or custody or confinement after conviction, under the laws of the United States or the jurisdiction within the United States from which the person has fled, for a crime, or an attempt to commit a crime, that is a felony under the laws of the place from which the individual has fled or, in jurisdictions that do not define crimes as felonies, is punishable by death or imprisonment for a term exceeding 1 year regardless of the actual sentence imposed;

(3) during any part of which the individual violates a condition of probation or parole imposed under Federal or State law; or

(4) during which the individual resides in a foreign country and is not a citizen or national of the United States if payments for such month to individuals residing in such country are withheld by the Treasury Department under section 3329 of title 31, United States Code[4].

(b) REQUIREMENT FOR ATTORNEY GENERAL.—For the purpose of carrying out subsection (a)(1), the Attorney General shall notify the Commissioner of Social Security as soon as practicable after the removal of any individual under section 237(a) or 212(a)(6)(A) of the Immigration and Nationality Act[5].

BENEFIT AMOUNT

SEC. 805. [42 U.S.C. 1005] The benefit under this title payable to a qualified individual for any month shall be in an amount equal to 75 percent of the Federal benefit rate under title XVI for the month, reduced by the amount of the qualified individual's benefit income for the month.

APPLICATIONS AND FURNISHING OF INFORMATION

SEC. 806. [42 U.S.C. 1006] (a) IN GENERAL.—The Commissioner of Social Security shall, subject to subsection (b), prescribe such requirements with respect to the filing of applications, the furnishing of information and other material, and the reporting of events and changes in circumstances, as may be necessary for the effective and efficient administration of this title.

(b) VERIFICATION REQUIREMENT.—The requirements prescribed by the Commissioner of Social Security under subsection (a) shall preclude any determination of entitlement to benefits under this title

---

[3] See Vol. II, P.L. 82-414, §§212(a)(6)(A) and 237(a).
[4] See Vol. II, P.L. 31 U.S.C. 3329.
[5] See Vol. II, P.L. 82-414, §§212(a)(6)(A) and 237(a).

SOCIAL SECURITY ACT—§ 807(b)(2)(D)   567

solely on the basis of declarations by the individual concerning qualifications or other material facts, and shall provide for verification of material information from independent or collateral sources, and the procurement of additional information as necessary in order to ensure that the benefits are provided only to qualified individuals (or their representative payees) in correct amounts.

REPRESENTATIVE PAYEES[6]

SEC. 807. [42 U.S.C. 1007] (a) IN GENERAL.—If the Commissioner of Social Security determines that the interest of any qualified individual under this title would be served thereby, payment of the qualified individual's benefit under this title may be made, regardless of the legal competency or incompetency of the qualified individual, either directly to the qualified individual, or for his or her use and benefit, to another person (the meaning of which term, for purposes of this section, includes an organization) with respect to whom the requirements of subsection (b) have been met (in this section referred to as the qualified individual's "representative payee"). If the Commissioner of Social Security determines that a representative payee has misused any benefit paid to the representative payee pursuant to this section, section 205(j), or section 1631(a)(2), the Commissioner of Social Security shall promptly revoke the person's designation as the qualified individual's representative payee under this subsection, and shall make payment to an alternative representative payee or, if the interest of the qualified individual under this title would be served thereby, to the qualified individual.

(b) EXAMINATION OF FITNESS OF PROSPECTIVE REPRESENTATIVE PAYEE.—

(1) Any determination under subsection (a) to pay the benefits of a qualified individual to a representative payee shall be made on the basis of—

(A) an investigation by the Commissioner of Social Security of the person to serve as representative payee, which shall be conducted in advance of the determination and shall, to the extent practicable, include a face-to-face interview with the person (or, in the case of an organization, a representative of the organization); and

(B) adequate evidence that the arrangement is in the interest of the qualified individual.

(2) As part of the investigation referred to in paragraph (1), the Commissioner of Social Security shall—

(A) require the person being investigated to submit documented proof of the identity of the person;

(B) in the case of a person who has a social security account number issued for purposes of the program under title II or an employer identification number issued for purposes of the Internal Revenue Code of 1986, verify the number;

(C) determine whether the person has been convicted of a violation of section 208, 811, or 1632;

(D) obtain information concerning whether such person has been convicted of any other offense under Federal or

---

[6] See Vol. II, P.L. 108-203, §103(a), with respect to a report evaluating existing procedures and reviews for the qualification of representative payees.

568 SOCIAL SECURITY ACT—§ 807(b)(2)(D)(cont)

State law which resulted in imprisonment for more than 1 year;

(E) obtain information concerning whether such person is a person described in section 804(a)(2); and

(F) determine whether payment of benefits to the person in the capacity as representative payee has been revoked or terminated pursuant to this section, section 205(j), or section 1631(a)(2)(A)(iii) by reason of misuse of funds paid as benefits under this title, title II, or XVI, respectively.

(3) Notwithstanding the provisions of section 552a of title 5, United States Code[7], or any other provision of Federal or State law (other than section 6103 of the Internal Revenue Code of 1986[8] and section 1106(c) of this Act), the Commissioner shall furnish any Federal, State, or local law enforcement officer, upon the written request of the officer, with the current address, social security account number, and photograph (if applicable) of any person investigated under this subsection, if the officer furnishes the Commissioner with the name of such person and such other identifying information as may reasonably be required by the Commissioner to establish the unique identity of such person, and notifies the Commissioner that—

(A) such person is described in section 804(a)(2),

(B) such person has information that is necessary for the officer to conduct the officer's official duties, and

(C) the location or apprehension of such person is within the officer's official duties.

(c) REQUIREMENT FOR MAINTAINING LISTS OF UNDESIRABLE PAYEES.—The Commissioner of Social Security shall establish and maintain lists which shall be updated periodically and which shall be in a form that renders such lists available to the servicing offices of the Social Security Administration. The lists shall consist of—

(1) the names and (if issued) social security account numbers or employer identification numbers of all persons with respect to whom, in the capacity of representative payee, the payment of benefits has been revoked or terminated under this section, section 205(j), or section 1631(a)(2)(A)(iii) by reason of misuse of funds paid as benefits under this title, title II, or XVI, respectively; and

(2) the names and (if issued) social security account numbers or employer identification numbers of all persons who have been convicted of a violation of section 208, 811, or 1632.

(d) PERSONS INELIGIBLE TO SERVE AS REPRESENTATIVE PAYEES.—

(1) IN GENERAL.—The benefits of a qualified individual may not be paid to any other person pursuant to this section if—

(A) the person has been convicted of a violation of section 208, 811, or 1632;

(B) except as provided in paragraph (2), payment of benefits to the person in the capacity of representative payee has been revoked or terminated under this section, section 205(j), or section 1631(a)(2)(A)(ii) by reason of misuse of funds paid as benefits under this title, title II, or title XVI, respectively;

---

[7] See Vol. II, 5 U.S.C.552a.
[8] See Vol. II, P.L. 83-591, §6103.

SOCIAL SECURITY ACT—§ 807(e)(1) 569

(C) except as provided in paragraph (2)(B), the person is a creditor of the qualified individual and provides the qualified individual with goods or services for consideration;

(D) such person has previously been convicted as described in subsection (b)(2)(D), unless the Commissioner determines that such payment would be appropriate notwithstanding such conviction; or

(E) such person is a person described in section 804(a)(2).

(2) EXEMPTIONS.—

(A) The Commissioner of Social Security may prescribe circumstances under which the Commissioner of Social Security may grant an exemption from paragraph (1) to any person on a case-by-case basis if the exemption is in the best interest of the qualified individual whose benefits would be paid to the person pursuant to this section.

(B) Paragraph (1)(C) shall not apply with respect to any person who is a creditor referred to in such paragraph if the creditor is—

(i) a relative of the qualified individual and the relative resides in the same household as the qualified individual;

(ii) a legal guardian or legal representative of the individual;

(iii) a facility that is licensed or certified as a care facility under the law of the political jurisdiction in which the qualified individual resides;

(iv) a person who is an administrator, owner, or employee of a facility referred to in clause (iii), if the qualified individual resides in the facility, and the payment to the facility or the person is made only after the Commissioner of Social Security has made a good faith effort to locate an alternative representative payee to whom payment would serve the best interests of the qualified individual; or

(v) a person who is determined by the Commissioner of Social Security, on the basis of written findings and pursuant to procedures prescribed by the Commissioner of Social Security, to be acceptable to serve as a representative payee.

(C) The procedures referred to in subparagraph (B)(v) shall require the person who will serve as representative payee to establish, to the satisfaction of the Commissioner of Social Security, that—

(i) the person poses no risk to the qualified individual;

(ii) the financial relationship of the person to the qualified individual poses no substantial conflict of interest; and

(iii) no other more suitable representative payee can be found.

(e) DEFERRAL OF PAYMENT PENDING APPOINTMENT OF REPRESENTATIVE PAYEE.—

(1) IN GENERAL.—Subject to paragraph (2), if the Commissioner of Social Security makes a determination described in the first sentence of subsection (a) with respect to any qualified individ-

570 SOCIAL SECURITY ACT—§ 807(e)(2)

ual's benefit and determines that direct payment of the benefit to the qualified individual would cause substantial harm to the qualified individual, the Commissioner of Social Security may defer (in the case of initial entitlement) or suspend (in the case of existing entitlement) direct payment of the benefit to the qualified individual, until such time as the selection of a representative payee is made pursuant to this section.

(2) TIME LIMITATION.—

(A) IN GENERAL.—Except as provided in subparagraph (B), any deferral or suspension of direct payment of a benefit pursuant to paragraph (1) shall be for a period of not more than 1 month.

(B) EXCEPTION IN THE CASE OF INCOMPETENCY.—Subparagraph (A) shall not apply in any case in which the qualified individual is, as of the date of the Commissioner of Social Security's determination, legally incompetent under the laws of the jurisdiction in which the individual resides.

(3) PAYMENT OF RETROACTIVE BENEFITS.—Payment of any benefits which are deferred or suspended pending the selection of a representative payee shall be made to the qualified individual or the representative payee as a single sum or over such period of time as the Commissioner of Social Security determines is in the best interest of the qualified individual.

(f) HEARING.—Any qualified individual who is dissatisfied with a determination by the Commissioner of Social Security to make payment of the qualified individual's benefit to a representative payee under subsection (a) of this section or with the designation of a particular person to serve as representative payee shall be entitled to a hearing by the Commissioner of Social Security to the same extent as is provided in section 809(a), and to judicial review of the Commissioner of Social Security's final decision as is provided in section 809(b).

(g) NOTICE REQUIREMENTS.—

(1) IN GENERAL.—In advance, to the extent practicable, of the payment of a qualified individual's benefit to a representative payee under subsection (a), the Commissioner of Social Security shall provide written notice of the Commissioner's initial determination to so make the payment. The notice shall be provided to the qualified individual, except that, if the qualified individual is legally incompetent, then the notice shall be provided solely to the legal guardian or legal representative of the qualified individual.

(2) SPECIFIC REQUIREMENT.—Any notice required by paragraph (1) shall be clearly written in language that is easily understandable to the reader, shall identify the person to be designated as the qualified individual's representative payee, and shall explain to the reader the right under subsection (f) of the qualified individual or of the qualified individual's legal guardian or legal representative—

(A) to appeal a determination that a representative payee is necessary for the qualified individual;

(B) to appeal the designation of a particular person to serve as the representative payee of the qualified individual; and

SOCIAL SECURITY ACT—§ 807(i)(A)   571

(C) to review the evidence upon which the designation is based and to submit additional evidence.

(h) ACCOUNTABILITY MONITORING.—

(1) IN GENERAL.—In any case where payment under this title is made to a person other than the qualified individual entitled to the payment, the Commissioner of Social Security shall establish a system of accountability monitoring under which the person shall report not less often than annually with respect to the use of the payments. The Commissioner of Social Security shall establish and implement statistically valid procedures for reviewing the reports in order to identify instances in which persons are not properly using the payments.

(2) SPECIAL REPORTS.—Notwithstanding paragraph (1), the Commissioner of Social Security may require a report at any time from any person receiving payments on behalf of a qualified individual, if the Commissioner of Social Security has reason to believe that the person receiving the payments is misusing the payments.

(3) AUTHORITY TO REDIRECT DELIVERY OF BENEFIT PAYMENTS WHEN A REPRESENTATIVE PAYEE FAILS TO PROVIDE REQUIRED ACCOUNTING.—In any case in which the person described in paragraph (1) or (2) receiving benefit payments on behalf of a qualified individual fails to submit a report required by the Commissioner of Social Security under paragraph (1) or (2), the Commissioner may, after furnishing notice to such person and the qualified individual, require that such person appear in person at a United States Government facility designated by the Social Security Administration as serving the area in which the qualified individual resides in order to receive such benefit payments.

(4) MAINTAINING LISTS OF PAYEES.—The Commissioner of Social Security shall maintain lists which shall be updated periodically of—

(A) the name, address, and (if issued) the social security account number or employer identification number of each representative payee who is receiving benefit payments pursuant to this section, section 205(j), or section 1631(a)(2); and

(B) the name, address, and social security account number of each individual for whom each representative payee is reported to be providing services as representative payee pursuant to this section, section 205(j), or section 1631(a)(2).

(5) MAINTAINING LISTS OF AGENCIES.—The Commissioner of Social Security shall maintain lists, which shall be updated periodically, of public agencies and community-based nonprofit social service agencies which are qualified to serve as representative payees pursuant to this section and which are located in the jurisdiction in which any qualified individual resides.

(i) RESTITUTION.—In any case where the negligent failure of the Commissioner of Social Security to investigate or monitor a representative payee results in misuse of benefits by the representative payee, the Commissioner of Social Security shall make payment to the qualified individual or the individual's alternative representative payee of an amount equal to the misused benefits. In any case in which a representative payee that—

(A) is not an individual; or

572 SOCIAL SECURITY ACT—§ 807(i)(B)

(B) is an individual who, for any month during a period when misuse occurs, serves 15 or more individuals who are beneficiaries under this title, title II, title XVI, or any combination of such titles;

misuses all or part of an individual's benefit paid to such representative payee, the Commissioner of Social Security shall pay to the beneficiary or the beneficiary's alternative representative payee an amount equal to the amount of such benefit so misused. The provisions of this paragraph are subject to the limitations of subsection (l)(2). The Commissioner of Social Security shall make a good faith effort to obtain restitution from the terminated representative payee.

(j) MISUSE OF BENEFITS.—For purposes of this title, misuse of benefits by a representative payee occurs in any case in which the representative payee receives payment under this title for the use and benefit of another person under this title and converts such payment, or any part thereof, to a use other than for the use and benefit of such person. The Commissioner of Social Security may prescribe by regulation the meaning of the term "use and benefit" for purposes of this subsection.

(k) PERIODIC ONSITE REVIEW.—

(1) IN GENERAL.—In addition to such other reviews of representative payees as the Commissioner of Social Security may otherwise conduct, the Commissioner may provide for the periodic onsite review of any person or agency that receives the benefits payable under this title (alone or in combination with benefits payable under title II or title XVI) to another individual pursuant to the appointment of such person or agency as a representative payee under this section, section 205(j), or section 1631(a)(2) in any case in which—

(A) the representative payee is a person who serves in that capacity with respect to 15 or more such individuals; or

(B) the representative payee is an agency that serves in that capacity with respect to 50 or more such individuals.

(2) REPORT.—Within 120 days after the end of each fiscal year, the Commissioner shall submit to the Committee on Ways and Means of the House of Representatives and the Committee on Finance of the Senate a report on the results of periodic onsite reviews conducted during the fiscal year pursuant to paragraph (1) and of any other reviews of representative payees conducted during such fiscal year in connection with benefits under this title. Each such report shall describe in detail all problems identified in such reviews and any corrective action taken or planned to be taken to correct such problems, and shall include—

(A) the number of such reviews;

(B) the results of such reviews;

(C) the number of cases in which the representative payee was changed and why;

(D) the number of cases involving the exercise of expedited, targeted oversight of the representative payee by the Commissioner conducted upon receipt of an allegation of misuse of funds, failure to pay a vendor, or a similar irregularity;

(E) the number of cases discovered in which there was a misuse of funds;

SOCIAL SECURITY ACT—§ 808(a)(1) 573

(F) how any such cases of misuse of funds were dealt with by the Commissioner;

(G) the final disposition of such cases of misuse of funds, including any criminal penalties imposed; and

(H) such other information as the Commissioner deems appropriate.

(l) LIABILITY FOR MISUSED AMOUNTS.—

(1) IN GENERAL.—In addition to such other reviews of representative payees as the Commissioner of Social Security may otherwise conduct, the Commissioner may provide for the periodic onsite review of any person or agency that receives the benefits payable under this title (alone or in combination with benefits payable under title II or title XVI) to another individual pursuant to the appointment of such person or agency as a representative payee under this section, section 205(j), or section 1631(a)(2) in any case in which—

(A) the representative payee is a person who serves in that capacity with respect to 15 or more such individuals; or

(B) the representative payee is an agency that serves in that capacity with respect to 50 or more such individuals.

(2) REPORT.—Within 120 days after the end of each fiscal year, the Commissioner shall submit to the Committee on Ways and Means of the House of Representatives and the Committee on Finance of the Senate a report on the results of periodic onsite reviews conducted during the fiscal year pursuant to paragraph (1) and of any other reviews of representative payees conducted during such fiscal year in connection with benefits under this title. Each such report shall describe in detail all problems identified in such reviews and any corrective action taken or planned to be taken to correct such problems, and shall include—

(A) the number of such reviews;

(B) the results of such reviews;

(C) the number of cases in which the representative payee was changed and why;

(D) the number of cases involving the exercise of expedited, targeted oversight of the representative payee by the Commissioner conducted upon receipt of an allegation of misuse of funds, failure to pay a vendor, or a similar irregularity;

(E) the number of cases discovered in which there was a misuse of funds;

(F) how any such cases of misuse of funds were dealt with by the Commissioner;

(G) the final disposition of such cases of misuse of funds, including any criminal penalties imposed; and

(H) such other information as the Commissioner deems appropriate.

OVERPAYMENTS AND UNDERPAYMENTS

SEC. 808. [42 U.S.C. 1008] (a) IN GENERAL.—Whenever the Commissioner of Social Security finds that more or less than the correct amount of payment has been made to any person under this title, proper adjustment or recovery shall be made, as follows:

(1) With respect to payment to a person of more than the correct amount, the Commissioner of Social Security shall decrease

574 SOCIAL SECURITY ACT—§ 808(a)(1)(cont)

any payment under this title to which the overpaid person (if a qualified individual) is entitled, or shall require the overpaid person or his or her estate to refund the amount in excess of the correct amount, or, if recovery is not obtained under these two methods, shall seek or pursue recovery by means of reduction in tax refunds based on notice to the Secretary of the Treasury, as authorized under section 3720A of title 31[9].

(2) With respect to payment of less than the correct amount to a qualified individual who, at the time the Commissioner of Social Security is prepared to take action with respect to the underpayment—

(A) is living, the Commissioner of Social Security shall make payment to the qualified individual (or the qualified individual's representative payee designated under section 807) of the balance of the amount due the underpaid qualified individual.

(B) is deceased, the balance of the amount due shall revert to the general fund of the Treasury.

(b) WAIVER OF RECOVERY OF OVERPAYMENT.—In any case in which more than the correct amount of payment has been made, there shall be no adjustment of payments to, or recovery by the United States from, any person who is without fault if the Commissioner of Social Security determines that the adjustment or recovery would defeat the purpose of this title or would be against equity and good conscience.

(c) LIMITED IMMUNITY FOR DISBURSING OFFICERS.—A disbursing officer may not be held liable for any amount paid by the officer if the adjustment or recovery of the amount is waived under subsection (b), or adjustment under subsection (a) is not completed before the death of the qualified individual against whose benefits deductions are authorized.

(d) AUTHORIZED COLLECTION PRACTICES.—

(1) IN GENERAL.—With respect to any delinquent amount, the Commissioner of Social Security may use the collection practices described in sections 3711(e), 3716, and 3718 of title 31, United States Code[10], as in effect on October 1, 1994.

(2) DEFINITION.—For purposes of paragraph (1), the term "delinquent amount" means an amount—

(A) in excess of the correct amount of the payment under this title; and

(B) determined by the Commissioner of Social Security to be otherwise unrecoverable under this section from a person who is not a qualified individual under this title.

(e) AUTHORIZED COLLECTION PRACTICES.—For provisions relating to the cross-program recovery of overpayments made under programs administered by the Commissioner of Social Security, see section 1147.

HEARINGS AND REVIEW

SEC. 809. [42 U.S.C. 1009] (a) HEARINGS.—

(1) IN GENERAL.—The Commissioner of Social Security shall make findings of fact and decisions as to the rights of any individ-

---

[9] See Vol. II, 31 U.S.C. 3720A.
[10] See Vol. II, 31 U.S.C. 3711(e), 3716, and 3718.

ual applying for payment under this title. The Commissioner of Social Security shall provide reasonable notice and opportunity for a hearing to any individual who is or claims to be a qualified individual and is in disagreement with any determination under this title with respect to entitlement to, or the amount of, benefits under this title, if the individual requests a hearing on the matter in disagreement within 60 days after notice of the determination is received, and, if a hearing is held, shall, on the basis of evidence adduced at the hearing affirm, modify, or reverse the Commissioner of Social Security's findings of fact and the decision. The Commissioner of Social Security may, on the Commissioner of Social Security's own motion, hold such hearings and conduct such investigations and other proceedings as the Commissioner of Social Security deems necessary or proper for the administration of this title. In the course of any hearing, investigation, or other proceeding, the Commissioner may administer oaths and affirmations, examine witnesses, and receive evidence. Evidence may be received at any hearing before the Commissioner of Social Security even though inadmissible under the rules of evidence applicable to court procedure. The Commissioner of Social Security shall specifically take into account any physical, mental, educational, or linguistic limitation of the individual (including any lack of facility with the English language) in determining, with respect to the entitlement of the individual for benefits under this title, whether the individual acted in good faith or was at fault, and in determining fraud, deception, or intent.

(2) EFFECT OF FAILURE TO TIMELY REQUEST REVIEW.—A failure to timely request review of an initial adverse determination with respect to an application for any payment under this title or an adverse determination on reconsideration of such an initial determination shall not serve as a basis for denial of a subsequent application for any payment under this title if the applicant demonstrates that the applicant failed to so request such a review acting in good faith reliance upon incorrect, incomplete, or misleading information, relating to the consequences of reapplying for payments in lieu of seeking review of an adverse determination, provided by any officer or employee of the Social Security Administration.

(3) NOTICE REQUIREMENTS.—In any notice of an adverse determination with respect to which a review may be requested under paragraph (1), the Commissioner of Social Security shall describe in clear and specific language the effect on possible entitlement to benefits under this title of choosing to reapply in lieu of requesting review of the determination.

(b) JUDICIAL REVIEW.—The final determination of the Commissioner of Social Security after a hearing under subsection (a)(1) shall be subject to judicial review as provided in section 205(g) to the same extent as the Commissioner of Social Security's final determinations under section 205.

OTHER ADMINISTRATIVE PROVISIONS

SEC. 810. [42 U.S.C. 1010] (a) REGULATIONS AND ADMINISTRATIVE ARRANGEMENTS.—The Commissioner of Social Security may prescribe

576   SOCIAL SECURITY ACT—§ 810(a)(cont)

such regulations, and make such administrative and other arrangements, as may be necessary or appropriate to carry out this title.

(b) PAYMENT OF BENEFITS.—Benefits under this title shall be paid at such time or times and in such installments as the Commissioner of Social Security determines are in the interests of economy and efficiency.

(c) ENTITLEMENT REDETERMINATIONS.—An individual's entitlement to benefits under this title, and the amount of the benefits, may be redetermined at such time or times as the Commissioner of Social Security determines to be appropriate.

(d) SUSPENSION AND TERMINATION OF BENEFITS.—Regulations prescribed by the Commissioner of Social Security under subsection (a) may provide for the suspension and termination of entitlement to benefits under this title as the Commissioner determines is appropriate.

OPTIONAL FEDERAL ADMINISTRATION OF STATE RECOGNITION PAYMENTS

SEC. 810A. [42 U.S.C. 1010a] (a) IN GENERAL.—The Commissioner of Social Security may enter into an agreement with any State (or political subdivision thereof) that provides cash payments on a regular basis to individuals entitled to benefits under this title under which the Commissioner of Social Security shall make such payments on behalf of such State (or subdivision).

(b) AGREEMENT TERMS.—

(1) IN GENERAL.—Such agreement shall include such terms as the Commissioner of Social Security finds necessary to achieve efficient and effective administration of both this title and the State program.

(2) FINANCIAL TERMS.—Such agreement shall provide for the State to pay the Commissioner of Social Security, at such times and in such installments as the parties may specify—

(A) an amount equal to the expenditures made by the Commissioner of Social Security pursuant to such agreement as payments to individuals on behalf of such State; and

(B) an administration fee to reimburse the administrative expenses incurred by the Commissioner of Social Security in making payments to individuals on behalf of the State.

(c) SPECIAL DISPOSITION OF ADMINISTRATION FEES.—Administration fees, upon collection, shall be credited to a special fund established in the Treasury of the United States for State recognition payments for certain World War II veterans. The amounts so credited, to the extent and in the amounts provided in advance in appropriations Acts, shall be available to defray expenses incurred in carrying out this title.

PENALTIES FOR FRAUD

SEC. 811. [42 U.S.C. 1011] (a) IN GENERAL.—Whoever—

(1) knowingly and willfully makes or causes to be made any false statement or representation of a material fact in an application for benefits under this title;

(2) at any time knowingly and willfully makes or causes to be made any false statement or representation of a material fact for use in determining any right to the benefits;

(3) having knowledge of the occurrence of any event affecting—

(A) his or her initial or continued right to the benefits; or

SOCIAL SECURITY ACT—§ 812(1) 577

(B) the initial or continued right to the benefits of any other individual in whose behalf he or she has applied for or is receiving the benefit, conceals or fails to disclose the event with an intent fraudulently to secure the benefit either in a greater amount or quantity than is due or when no such benefit is authorized; or

(4) having made application to receive any such benefit for the use and benefit of another and having received it, knowingly and willfully converts the benefit or any part thereof to a use other than for the use and benefit of the other individual, shall be fined under title 18, United States Code, imprisoned not more than 5 years, or both.

(b) COURT ORDER FOR RESTITUTION.—

(1) IN GENERAL.—Any Federal court, when sentencing a defendant convicted of an offense under subsection (a), may order, in addition to or in lieu of any other penalty authorized by law, that the defendant make restitution to the Commissioner of Social Security, in any case in which such offense results in—

(A) the Commissioner of Social Security making a benefit payment that should not have been made, or

(B) an individual suffering a financial loss due to the defendant's violation of subsection (a) in his or her capacity as the individual's representative payee appointed pursuant to section 807(i).

(2) RELATED PROVISIONS.—Sections 3612, 3663, and 3664 of title 18, United States Code[11], shall apply with respect to the issuance and enforcement of orders of restitution under this subsection. In so applying such sections, the Commissioner of Social Security shall be considered the victim.

(3) STATED REASONS FOR NOT ORDERING RESTITUTION.—If the court does not order restitution, or orders only partial restitution, under this subsection, the court shall state on the record the reasons therefor.

(4) RECEIPT OF RESTITUTION PAYMENTS.—

(A) IN GENERAL.—Except as provided in subparagraph (B), funds paid to the Commissioner of Social Security as restitution pursuant to a court order shall be deposited as miscellaneous receipts in the general fund of the Treasury.

(B) PAYMENT TO THE INDIVIDUAL.—In the case of funds paid to the Commissioner of Social Security pursuant to paragraph (1)(B), the Commissioner of Social Security shall certify for payment to the individual described in such paragraph an amount equal to the lesser of the amount of the funds so paid or the individual's outstanding financial loss as described in such paragraph, except that such amount may be reduced by any overpayment of benefits owed under this title, title II, or title XVI by the individual.

DEFINITIONS

SEC. 812. [42 U.S.C. 1012] In this title:

(1) WORLD WAR II VETERAN.—The term "World War II veteran" means a person who—

---

[11] See Vol. II, 18 U.S.C. 3612, 3663, and 3664.

578 SOCIAL SECURITY ACT—§ 812(1)(A)

(A) served during World War II—
(i) in the active military, naval, or air service of the United States during World War II; or
(ii) in the organized military forces of the Government of the Commonwealth of the Philippines, while the forces were in the service of the Armed Forces of the United States pursuant to the military order of the President dated July 26, 1941, including among the military forces organized guerrilla forces under commanders appointed, designated, or subsequently recognized by the Commander in Chief, Southwest Pacific Area, or other competent authority in the Army of the United States, in any case in which the service was rendered before December 31, 1946; and
(B) was discharged or released therefrom under conditions other than dishonorable—
(i) after service of 90 days or more; or
(ii) because of a disability or injury incurred or aggravated in the line of active duty.

(2) WORLD WAR II.—The term "World War II" means the period beginning on September 16, 1940, and ending on July 24, 1947.

(3) SUPPLEMENTAL SECURITY INCOME BENEFIT UNDER TITLE XVI.—The term "supplemental security income benefit under title XVI", except as otherwise provided, includes State supplementary payments which are paid by the Commissioner of Social Security pursuant to an agreement under section 1616(a) of this Act or section 212(b) of Public Law 93-66[12].

(4) FEDERAL BENEFIT RATE UNDER TITLE XVI.—The term "Federal benefit rate under title XVI" means, with respect to any month, the amount of the supplemental security income cash benefit (not including any State supplementary payment which is paid by the Commissioner of Social Security pursuant to an agreement under section 1616(a) of this Act or section 212(b) of Public Law 93-66) payable under title XVI for the month to an eligible individual with no income.

(5) UNITED STATES.—The term "United States" means, notwithstanding section 1101(a)(1), only the 50 States, the District of Columbia, and the Commonwealth of the Northern Mariana Islands.

(6) BENEFIT INCOME.—The term "benefit income" means any recurring payment received by a qualified individual as an annuity, pension, retirement, or disability benefit (including any veterans' compensation or pension, workmen's compensation payment, old-age, survivors, or disability insurance benefit, railroad retirement annuity or pension, and unemployment insurance benefit), but only if a similar payment was received by the individual from the same (or a related) source during the 12-month period preceding the month in which the individual files an application for benefits under this title.

---

[12] See Vol. II, P.L. 93-66, §212(b).

SOCIAL SECURITY ACT—§ 813 579

APPROPRIATIONS

SEC. 813. [42 U.S.C. 1013] There are hereby appropriated for fiscal year 2000 and subsequent fiscal years, out of any funds in the Treasury not otherwise appropriated, such sums as may be necessary to carry out this title.

TITLE IX—MISCELLANEOUS PROVISIONS RELATING TO EMPLOYMENT SECURITY[1]

TABLE OF CONTENTS OF TITLE[2]

		Page
Sec. 901.	Employment security administration account	581
Sec. 902.	Transfers to Federal unemployment account and report to Congress	586
Sec. 903.	Amounts transferred to State accounts	587
Sec. 904.	Unemployment Trust Fund	591
Sec. 905.	Extended unemployment compensation account	593
Sec. 906.	Unemployment compensation research program	595
Sec. 907.	Personnel training	595
Sec. 908.	Advisory Council on Unemployment Compensation	596
Sec. 909.	Federal Employees Compensation Account	597
Sec. 910.	Borrowing between Federal accounts	597

EMPLOYMENT SECURITY ADMINISTRATION ACCOUNT

Establishment of Account

SEC. 901. [42 U.S.C. 1101] (a) There is hereby established in the Unemployment Trust Fund an employment security administration account.

Appropriations to Account

(b)(1) There is hereby appropriated to the Unemployment Trust Fund for credit to the employment security administration account, out of any moneys in the Treasury not otherwise appropriated, for the fiscal year ending June 30, 1961, and for each fiscal year thereafter, an amount equal to 100 per centum of the tax (including interest, penalties, and additions to the tax) received during the fiscal year under the Federal Unemployment Tax Act[3] and covered into the Treasury.

(2) The amount appropriated by paragraph (1) shall be transferred at least monthly from the general fund of the Treasury to the Unemployment Trust Fund and credited to the employment security administration account. Each such transfer shall be based on estimates made by the Secretary of the Treasury of the amounts received in the Treasury. Proper adjustments shall be made in the amounts subsequently transferred, to the extent prior estimates (including estimates

---

[1] Title IX of the Social Security Act is administered by the Department of Labor.

Title IX appears in the United States Code as §§1101–1110, subchapter IX, chapter 7, Title 42.

Regulations of the Secretary of Labor relating to Title IX are contained in chapter V, Title 20, Code of Federal Regulations.

P.L. 109-91, §203, provides that "The Secretary of Labor may prescribe any operating instructions or regulations necessary to carry out this title and any amendment made by this title." (P.L. 109-91, Title II, Assistance relating to Unemployment).

See Vol. II, 31 U.S.C. 6504-6505, with respect to intergovernmental cooperation.

See Vol. II, P.L. 88-352, §601, for prohibition against discrimination in federally assisted programs.

See Vol. II, P.L. 93-618, §§221-249, with respect to adjustment assistance for workers.

See Vol. II, P.L. 100-203, §9151, with respect to the determination of the amount of the Federal share of certain extended benefits.

[2] This table of contents does not appear in the law.

[3] The "Federal Unemployment Tax Act" is in §§3301-3311 of P.L. 83-591. See Vol. II, P.L. 83-591.

582 SOCIAL SECURITY ACT—§ 901(b)(2)(cont)

for the fiscal year ending June 30, 1960) were in excess of or were less than the amounts required to be transferred.

(3) The Secretary of the Treasury is directed to pay from time to time from the employment security administration account into the Treasury, as repayments to the account for refunding internal revenue collections, amounts equal to all refunds made after June 30, 1960, of amounts received as tax under the Federal Unemployment Tax Act (including interest on such refunds).

Administrative Expenditures

(c)(1) There are hereby authorized to be made available for expenditure out of the employment security administration account for the fiscal year ending June 30, 1971, and for each fiscal year thereafter—

(A) such amounts (not in excess of the applicable limit provided by paragraph (3) and, with respect to clause (ii), not in excess of the limit provided by paragraph (4)) as the Congress may deem appropriate for the purpose of—

(i) assisting the States in the administration of their unemployment compensation laws as provided in title III (including administration pursuant to agreements under any Federal unemployment compensation law),

(ii) the establishment and maintenance of systems of public employment offices in accordance with the Act of June 6, 1933,[4] as amended (29 U.S.C., secs. 49–49n), and

(iii) carrying into effect section 4103 of title 38 of the United States Code[5];

(B) such amounts (not in excess of the limit provided by paragraph (4) with respect to clause (iii)) as the Congress may deem appropriate for the necessary expenses of the Department of Labor for the performance of its functions under—

(i) this title and titles III and XII of this Act,

(ii) the Federal Unemployment Tax Act,

(iii) the provisions of the Act of June 6, 1933, as amended,

(iv) chapter 41 (except section 4103) of title 38 of the United States Code, and

(v) any Federal unemployment compensation law.

The term "necessary expenses" as used in this subparagraph (B) shall include the expense of reimbursing a State for salaries and other expenses of employees of such State temporarily assigned or detailed to duty with the Department of Labor and of paying such employees for travel expenses, transportation of household goods, and per diem in lieu of subsistence while away from their regular duty stations in the State, at rates authorized by law for civilian employees of the Federal Government.

(2) The Secretary of the Treasury is directed to pay from the employment security administration account into the Treasury as miscellaneous receipts the amount estimated by him which will be expended during a three-month period by the Treasury Department for the performance of its functions under—

---

[4] See Vol. II, P.L. 73-30.
[5] See Vol. II, Title 38 U.S.C. 4103.

SOCIAL SECURITY ACT—§ 901(c)(5)(B)   583

(A) this title and titles III and XII of this Act, including the expenses of banks for servicing unemployment benefit payment and clearing accounts which are offset by the maintenance of balances of Treasury funds with such banks,

(B) the Federal Unemployment Tax Act, and

(C) any Federal unemployment compensation law with respect to which responsibility for administration is vested in the Secretary of Labor.

If it subsequently appears that the estimates under this paragraph in any particular period were too high or too low, appropriate adjustments shall be made by the Secretary of the Treasury in future payments.

(3)(A) For purposes of paragraph (1)(A), the limitation on the amount authorized to be made available for any fiscal year after June 30, 1970, is, except as provided in subparagraph (B) and in the second sentence of section 901(f)(3)(A), an amount equal to 95 percent of the amount estimated and set forth in the budget of the United States Government for such fiscal year as the amount by which the net receipts during such year under the Federal Unemployment Tax Act will exceed the amount transferred under section 905(b) during such year to the extended unemployment compensation account.

(B) The limitation established by subparagraph (A) is increased by any unexpended amount retained in the employment security administration account in accordance with section 901(f)(2)(B).

(C) Each estimate of net receipts under this paragraph shall be based upon a tax rate of 0.6 percent.

(4) For purposes of paragraphs (1)(A)(ii) and (1)(B)(iii) the amount authorized to be made available out of the employment security administration account for any fiscal year after June 30, 1972, shall reflect the proportion of the total cost of administering the system of public employment offices in accordance with the Act of June 6, 1933[6], as amended, and of the necessary expenses of the Department of Labor for the performance of its functions under the provisions of such Act, as the President determines is an appropriate charge to the employment security administration account, and reflects in his annual budget for such year. The President's determination, after consultation with the Secretary, shall take into account such factors as the relationship between employment subject to State laws and the total labor force in the United States, the number of claimants and the number of job applicants, and such other factors as he finds relevant.

(5)(A) There are authorized to be appropriated out of the employment security administration account to carry out program integrity activities, in addition to any amounts available under paragraph (1)(A)(i)—

(i) $89,000,000 for fiscal year 1998;
(ii) $91,000,000 for fiscal year 1999;
(iii) $93,000,000 fiscal year 2000;
(iv) $96,000,000 for fiscal year 2001; and
(v) $98,000,000 for fiscal year 2002.

(B) In any fiscal year in which a State receives funds appropriated pursuant to this paragraph, the State shall expend a proportion of

---

[6] See Vol. II, P.L. 73-30.

584 SOCIAL SECURITY ACT—§ 901(c)(5)(B)(cont)

the funds appropriated pursuant to paragraph (1)(A)(i) to carry out program integrity activities that is not less than the proportion of the funds appropriated under such paragraph that was expended by the State to carry out program integrity activities in fiscal year 1997.

(C) For purposes of this paragraph, the term "program integrity activities" means initial claims review activities, eligibility review activities, benefit payments control activities, and employer liability auditing activities.

Additional Tax Attributable to Reduced Credits

(d)(1) The Secretary of the Treasury is directed to transfer from the employment security administration account—

(A) To the Federal unemployment account, an amount equal to the amount by which—

(i) 100 per centum of the additional tax received under the Federal Unemployment Tax Act with respect to any State by reason of the reduced credits provisions of section 3302(c)(3) of such Act and covered into the Treasury for the repayment of advances made to the State under section 1201, exceeds

(ii) the amount transferred to the account of such State pursuant to subparagraph (B) of this paragraph.

Any amount transferred pursuant to this subparagraph shall be credited against, and shall operate to reduce, that balance of advances, made under section 1201 to the State, with respect to which employers paid such additional tax.

(B) To the account (in the Unemployment Trust Fund) of the State with respect to which employers paid such additional tax, an amount equal to the amount by which such additional tax received and covered into the Treasury exceeds that balance of advances, made under section 1201 to the State, with respect to which employers paid such additional tax.

(2) Transfers under this subsection shall be as of the beginning of the month succeeding the month in which the moneys were credited to the employment security administration account pursuant to subsection (b)(2).

Revolving Fund

(e)(1) There is hereby established in the Treasury a revolving fund which shall be available to make the advances authorized by this subsection. There are hereby authorized to be appropriated, without fiscal year limitation, to such revolving fund such amounts as may be necessary for the purposes of this section.

(2) The Secretary of the Treasury is directed to advance from time to time from the revolving fund to the employment security administration account such amounts as may be necessary for the purposes of this section. If the net balance in the employment security administration account as of the beginning of any fiscal year equals 40 percent of the amount of the total appropriation by the Congress out of the employment security administration account for the preceding fiscal year, no advance may be made under this subsection during such fiscal year.

SOCIAL SECURITY ACT—§ 901(f)(3)(B)   585

(3) Advances to the employment security administration account made under this subsection shall bear interest until repaid at a rate equal to the average rate of interest (computed as of the end of the calendar month next preceding the date of such advance) borne by all interest-bearing obligations of the United States then forming a part of the public debt; except that where such average rate is not a multiple of one-eighth of 1 per centum, the rate of interest shall be the multiple of one-eighth of 1 per centum next lower than such average rate.

(4) Advances to the employment security administration account made under this subsection, plus interest accrued thereon, shall be repaid by the transfer from time to time, from the employment security administration account to the revolving fund, of such amounts as the Secretary of the Treasury, in consultation with the Secretary of Labor, determines to be available in the employment security administration account for such repayment. Any amount transferred as a repayment under this paragraph shall be credited against, and shall operate to reduce, any balance of advances (plus accrued interest) repayable under this subsection.

Determination of Excess and Amount To Be Retained in Employment Security Administration Account

(f)(1) The Secretary of the Treasury shall determine as of the close of each fiscal year (beginning with the fiscal year ending June 30, 1961) the excess in the employment security administration account.

(2) The excess in the employment security administration account as of the close of any fiscal year is the amount by which the net balance in such account as of such time (after the application of section 902(b) and section 901(f)(3)(C)) exceeds the net balance in the employment security administration account as of the beginning of that fiscal year (including the fiscal year for which the excess is being computed) for which the net balance was higher than as of the beginning of any other such fiscal year.

(3)(A) The excess determined as provided in paragraph (2) as of the close of any fiscal year after June 30, 1972, shall be retained (as of the beginning of the succeeding fiscal year) in the employment security administration account until the amount in such account is equal to 40 percent of the amount of the total appropriation by the Congress out of the employment security administration account for the fiscal year for which the excess is determined. Three-eighths of the amount in the employment security administration account as of the beginning of any fiscal year after June 30, 1972, or $150 million, whichever is the lesser, is authorized to be made available for such fiscal year pursuant to subsection (c)(1) for additional costs of administration due to an increase in the rate of insured unemployment for a calendar quarter of at least 15 percent over the rate of insured unemployment for the corresponding calendar quarter in the immediately preceding year.

(B) If the entire amount of the excess determined as provided in paragraph (2) as of the close of any fiscal year after June 30, 1972, is not retained in the employment security administration account, there shall be transferred (as of the beginning of the succeeding fiscal year) to the extended unemployment compensation account the bal-

586   SOCIAL SECURITY ACT—§ 901(f)(3)(B)(cont)

ance of such excess or so much thereof as is required to increase the amount in the extended unemployment compensation account to the limit provided in section 905(b)(2).

(C) If as of the close of any fiscal year after June 30, 1972, the amount in the extended unemployment compensation account exceeds the limit provided in section 905(b)(2), such excess shall be transferred to the employment security administration account as of the close of such fiscal year.

(4) For the purposes of this section, the net balance in the employment security administration account as of any time is the amount in such account as of such time reduced by the sum of—

(A) the amounts then subject to transfer pursuant to subsection (d), and

(B) the balance of advances (plus interest accrued thereon) then repayable to the revolving fund established by subsection (e).

The net balance in the employment security administration account as of the beginning of any fiscal year shall be determined after the disposition of the excess in such account as of the close of the preceding fiscal year.

Transfers For Calendar Years 1988, 1989, and 1990

(g)(1) With respect to calendar years 1988, 1989, and 1990, the Secretary of the Treasury shall transfer from the employment security administration account—

(A) to the Federal unemployment account an amount equal to 50 percent of the amount of tax received under section 3301(1) of the Federal Unemployment Tax Act[7] which is attributable to the difference in the tax rates between paragraphs (1) and (2) of such section; and

(B) to the extended unemployment compensation account an amount equal to 50 percent of such amount of tax received.

(2) Transfers under this subsection shall be as of the beginning of the month succeeding the month in which the moneys were credited to the employment security administration account pursuant to subsection (b)(2) with respect to wages paid during such calendar years.

TRANSFERS TO FEDERAL UNEMPLOYMENT ACCOUNT AND REPORT TO CONGRESS

Transfers to Federal Unemployment Account

SEC. 902. [42 U.S.C. 1102] (a) Whenever the Secretary of the Treasury determines pursuant to section 901(f) that there is an excess in the employment security administration account as of the close of any fiscal year and the entire amount of such excess is not retained in the employment security administration account or transferred to the extended unemployment compensation account as provided in section 901(f)(3), there shall be transferred (as of the beginning of the succeeding fiscal year) to the Federal unemployment account the balance of such excess or so much thereof as is required to increase the amount

---

[7] See Vol. II, P.L. 83-591, §3301(1).

in the Federal unemployment account to whichever of the following is the greater:

(1) $550 million, or

(2) the amount (determined by the Secretary of Labor and certified by him to the Secretary of the Treasury) equal to 0.5 percent of the total wages subject (determined without any limitation on amount) to contributions under all State unemployment compensation laws for the calendar year ending during the fiscal year for which the excess is determined.

Transfers to Employment Security Administration Account

(b) The amount, if any, by which the amount in the Federal unemployment account as of the close of any fiscal year exceeds the greater of the amounts specified in paragraphs (1) and (2) of subsection (a) shall be transferred to the employment security administration account as of the close of such fiscal year.

Report to the Congress

(c) Whenever the Secretary of Labor has reason to believe that in the next fiscal year the employment security administration account will reach the limit provided for such account in section 901(f)(3)(A), and the Federal unemployment account will reach the limit provided for such account in section 902(a), and the extended unemployment compensation account will reach the limit provided for such account in section 905(b)(2), he shall, after consultation with the Secretary of the Treasury, so report to the Congress with a recommendation for appropriate action by the Congress.

AMOUNTS TRANSFERRED TO STATE ACCOUNTS

In General

SEC. 903. [42 U.S.C. 1103] (a)(1) If as of the close of any fiscal year after the fiscal year ending June 30, 1972, the amount in the extended unemployment compensation account has reached the limit provided in section 905(b)(2) and the amount in the Federal unemployment account has reached the limit provided in section 902(a) and all advances and interest pursuant to section 905(d) and section 1203 have been repaid, and there remains in the employment security administration account any amount over the amount provided in section 901(f)(3)(A), such excess amount, except as provided in subsection (b), shall be transferred (as of the beginning of the succeeding fiscal year) to the accounts of the States in the Unemployment Trust Fund.

(2) Each State's share of the funds to be transferred under this subsection as of any October 1—

(A) shall be determined by the Secretary of Labor and certified by such Secretary to the Secretary of the Treasury before such date, and

(B) shall bear the same ratio to the total amount to be so transferred as—

588 SOCIAL SECURITY ACT—§ 903(a)(2)(B)(i)

(i) the amount of wages subject to tax under section 3301 of the Internal Revenue Code of 1986[8] during the preceding calendar year which are determined by the Secretary of Labor to be attributable to the State, bears to

(ii) the total amount of wages subject to such tax during such year.

Limitations on Transfers

(b)(1) If the Secretary of Labor finds that on October 1 of any fiscal year—

(A) a State is not eligible for certification under section 303, or

(B) the law of a State is not approvable under section 3304 of the Federal Unemployment Tax Act,

then the amount available for transfer to such State's account shall, in lieu of being so transferred, be transferred to the Federal unemployment account as of the beginning of such October 1. If, during the fiscal year beginning on such October 1, the Secretary of Labor finds and certifies to the Secretary of the Treasury that such State is eligible for certification under section 303, that the law of such State is approvable under such section 3304, or both, the Secretary of the Treasury shall transfer such amount from the Federal unemployment account to the account of such State. If the Secretary of Labor does not so find and certify to the Secretary of the Treasury before the close of such fiscal year then the amount which was available for transfer to such State's account as of October 1 of such fiscal year shall (as of the close of such fiscal year) become unrestricted as to use as part of the Federal unemployment account.

(2) The amount which, but for this paragraph, would be transferred to the account of a State under subsection (a) or paragraph (1) of this subsection shall be reduced (but not below zero) by the balance of advances made to the State under section 1201. The sum by which such amount is reduced shall—

(A) be transferred to or retained in (as the case may be) the Federal unemployment account, and

(B) be credited against, and operate to reduce—

(i) first, any balance of advances made before the date of the enactment of the Employment Security Act of 1960[9] to the State under section 1201, and

(ii) second, any balance of advances made on or after such date to the State under section 1201.

Use of Transferred Amounts

(c)(1) Except as provided in paragraph (2), amounts transferred to the account of a State pursuant to subsections (a) and (b) shall be used only in the payment of cash benefits to individuals with respect to their unemployment, exclusive of expenses of administration.

(2) A State may, pursuant to a specific appropriation made by the legislative body of the State, use money withdrawn from its account

---

[8] See Vol. II, P.L. 83-591, §3301.
[9] Enacted on September 13, 1960, [Title V of P.L. 86-778; 74 Stat. 970].

SOCIAL SECURITY ACT—§ 903(d)(1)   589

in the payment of expenses incurred by it for the administration of its unemployment compensation law and public employment offices if and only if—

(A) the purposes and amounts were specified in the law making the appropriation,

(B) the appropriation law did not authorize the obligation of such money after the close of the two-year period which began on the date of enactment of the appropriation law,

(C) the money is withdrawn and the expenses are incurred after such date of enactment,

(D)(i) the appropriation law limits the total amount which may be obligated under such appropriation at any time to an amount which does not exceed, at any such time, the amount by which—

(I) the aggregate of the amounts transferred to the account of such State pursuant to subsections (a) and (b), exceeds

(II) the aggregate of the amounts used by the State pursuant to this subsection and charged against the amounts transferred to the account of such State, and

(ii) for purposes of clause (i), amounts used by a State for administration shall be chargeable against transferred amounts at the exact time the obligation is entered into, and

(E) the use of the money is accounted for in accordance with standards established by the Secretary of Labor.

(3)(A) If—

(i) amounts transferred to the account of a State pursuant to subsections (a) and (b) of this section were used in payment of unemployment benefits to individuals; and

(ii) the Governor of such State submits a request to the Secretary of Labor that such amounts be restored under this paragraph,

then the amounts described in clause (i) shall be restored to the status of funds transferred under subsections (a) and (b) of this section which have not been used by eliminating any charge against amounts so transferred for the use of such amounts in the payment of unemployment benefits.

(B) Subparagraph (A) shall apply only to the extent that the amounts described in clause (i) of such subparagraph do not exceed the amount then in the State's account.

(C) Subparagraph (A) shall not apply if the State has a balance of advances made to its account under title XII of this Act.

(D) If the Secretary of Labor determines that the requirements of this paragraph are met with respect to any request, the Secretary shall notify the Governor of the State that such requirements are met with respect to such request and the amount restored under this paragraph. Such restoration shall be as of the first day of the first month following the month in which the notification is made.

Special Transfer in Fiscal Year 2002

(d)(1) The Secretary of the Treasury shall transfer (as of the date determined under paragraph (5)) from the Federal unemployment account to the account of each State in the Unemployment Trust Fund

590 SOCIAL SECURITY ACT—§ 903(d)(1)(cont)

the amount determined with respect to such State under paragraph (2).

(2)(A) The amount to be transferred under this subsection to a State account shall (as determined by the Secretary of Labor and certified by such Secretary to the Secretary of the Treasury) be equal to—

(i) the amount which would have been required to have been transferred under this section to such account at the beginning of fiscal year 2002 if—

(I) section 209(a)(1) of the Temporary Extended Unemployment Compensation Act of 2002 had been enacted before the close of fiscal year 2001, and

(II) section 5402 of Public Law 105-33 (relating to increase in Federal unemployment account ceiling) had not been enacted, minus

(ii) the amount which was in fact transferred under this section to such account at the beginning of fiscal year 2002.

(B) Notwithstanding the provisions of subparagraph (A)—

(i) the aggregate amount transferred to the States under this subsection may not exceed a total of $8,000,000,000; and

(ii) all amounts determined under subparagraph (A) shall be reduced ratably, if and to the extent necessary in order to comply with the limitation under clause (i).

(3)(A) Except as provided in paragraph (4), amounts transferred to State account pursuant to this subsection may be used only in the payment of cash benefits—

(i) to individuals with respect to their unemployment, and

(ii) which are allowable under subparagraph (B) or (C).

(B)(i) At the option of the State, cash benefits under this paragraph may include amounts which shall be payable as—

(I) regular compensation, or

(II) additional compensation, upon the exhaustion of any temporary extended unemployment compensation (if such State has entered into an agreement under the Temporary Extended Unemployment Compensation Act of 2002), for individuals eligible for regular compensation under the unemployment compensation law of such State.

(ii) Any additional compensation under clause (i) may not be taken into account for purposes of any determination relating to the amount of any extended compensation for which an individual might be eligible.

(C)(i) At the option of the State, cash benefits under this paragraph may include amounts which shall be payable to 1 or more categories of individuals not otherwise eligible for regular compensation under the unemployment compensation law of such State, including those described in clause (iii).

(ii) The benefits paid under this subparagraph to any individual may not, for any period of unemployment, exceed the maximum amount of regular compensation authorized under the unemployment compensation law of such State for that same period, plus any additional compensation (described in subparagraph (B)(i)) which could have been paid with respect to that amount.

(iii) The categories of individuals described in this clause include the following:

SOCIAL SECURITY ACT—§ 904(b)   591

(I) Individuals who are seeking, or available for, only part-time (and not full-time) work.

(II) Individuals who would be eligible for regular compensation under the unemployment compensation law of such State under an alternative base period.

(D) Amounts transferred to a State account under this subsection may be used in the payment of cash benefits to individuals only for weeks of unemployment beginning after the date of enactment of this subsection.

(4) Amounts transferred to a State account under this subsection may be used for the administration of its unemployment compensation law and public employment offices (including in connection with benefits described in paragraph (3) and any recipients thereof), subject to the same conditions as set forth in subsection (c)(2) (excluding subparagraph (B) thereof, and deeming the reference to "subsections (a) and (b)" in subparagraph (D) thereof to include this subsection).

(5) Transfers under this subsection shall be made within 10 days after the date of enactment of this paragraph.

(e) SPECIAL TRANSFER IN FISCAL YEAR 2006.—Not later than 10 days after the date of the enactment of this subsection, the Secretary of the Treasury shall transfer from the Federal unemployment account—

(1) $15,000,000 to the account of Alabama in the Unemployment Trust Fund;

(2) $400,000,000 to the account of Louisiana in the Unemployment Trust Fund; and

(3) $85,000,000 to the account of Mississippi in the Unemployment Trust Fund.

UNEMPLOYMENT TRUST FUND

Establishment, etc.

SEC. 904. [42 U.S.C. 1104] (a) There is hereby established in the Treasury of the United States a trust fund to be known as the "Unemployment Trust Fund", hereinafter in this title called the "Fund". The Secretary of the Treasury is authorized and directed to receive and hold in the Fund all moneys deposited therein by a State agency from a State unemployment fund, or by the Railroad Retirement Board to the credit of the railroad unemployment insurance account or the railroad unemployment insurance administration fund, or otherwise deposited in or credited to the Fund or any account therein. Such deposit may be made directly with the Secretary of the Treasury, with any depositary[10] designated by him for such purpose, or with any Federal Reserve Bank.

Investments

(b) It shall be the duty of the Secretary of the Treasury to invest such portion of the Fund as is not, in his judgment, required to meet current withdrawals. Such investment may be made only in interest-bearing obligations of the United States or in obligations guaran-

---
[10] As in original. Possibly should be "depository".

592   SOCIAL SECURITY ACT—§ 904(b)(cont)

teed as to both principal and interest by the United States. For such purpose such obligations may be acquired (1) on original issue at the issue price, or (2) by purchase of outstanding obligations at the market price. The purposes for which obligations of the United States may be issued under chapter 31 of title 31, United States Code, are hereby extended to authorize the issuance at par of special obligations exclusively to the Fund. Such special obligations shall bear interest at a rate equal to the average rate of interest, computed as of the end of the calendar month next preceding the date of such issue, borne by all interest-bearing obligations of the United States then forming part of the public debt; except that where such average rate is not a multiple of one-eighth of 1 per centum, the rate of interest of such special obligations shall be the multiple of one-eighth of 1 per centum next lower than such average rate. Obligations other than such special obligations may be acquired for the Fund only on such terms as to provide an investment yield not less than the yield which would be required in the case of special obligations if issued to the Fund upon the date of such acquisition. Advances made to the Federal unemployment account pursuant to section 1203 shall not be invested.

Sale or Redemption of Obligations

(c) Any obligations acquired by the Fund (except special obligations issued exclusively to the Fund) may be sold at the market price, and such special obligations may be redeemed at par plus accrued interest.

Treatment of Interest and Proceeds

(d) The interest on, and the proceeds from the sale or redemption of, any obligations held in the Fund shall be credited to and form a part of the Fund.

Separate Book Accounts

(e) The Fund shall be invested as a single fund, but the Secretary of the Treasury shall maintain a separate book account for each State agency, the employment security administration account, the Federal unemployment account, the railroad unemployment insurance account, and the railroad unemployment insurance administration fund and shall credit quarterly (on March 31, June 30, September 30, and December 31, of each year) to each account, on the basis of the average daily balance of such account, a proportionate part of the earnings of the Fund for the quarter ending on such date. For the purpose of this subsection, the average daily balance shall be computed—

(1) in the case of any State account, by reducing (but not below zero) the amount in the account by the balance of advances made to the State under section 1201, and

(2) in the case of the Federal unemployment account—

(A) by adding to the amount in the account the aggregate of the reductions under paragraph (1), and

(B) by subtracting from the sum so obtained the balance of advances made under section 1203 to the account.

SOCIAL SECURITY ACT—§ 905(b)(2)   593

Payments to State Agencies and Railroad Retirement Board

(f) The Secretary of the Treasury is authorized and directed to pay out of the Fund to any State agency such amount as it may duly requisition, not exceeding the amount standing to the account of such State agency at the time of such payment. The Secretary of the Treasury is authorized and directed to make such payments out of the railroad unemployment insurance account for the payment of benefits, and out of the railroad unemployment insurance administration fund for the payment of administrative expenses, as the Railroad Retirement Board may duly certify, not exceeding the amount standing to the credit of such account or such fund, as the case may be, at the time of such payment.

Federal Unemployment Account

(g) There is hereby established in the Unemployment Trust Fund a Federal unemployment account.

EXTENDED UNEMPLOYMENT COMPENSATION ACCOUNT[11]

Establishment of Account

SEC. 905. [42 U.S.C. 1105] (a) There is hereby established in the Unemployment Trust Fund an extended unemployment compensation account. For the purposes provided for in section 904(e), such account shall be maintained as a separate book account.

Transfers to Account

(b)(1) Except as provided in paragraph (3), the Secretary of the Treasury shall transfer (as of the close of each month) from the employment security administration account to the extended unemployment compensation account established by subsection (a), an amount (determined by such Secretary) equal to 20 percent of the amount by which—

(A) the transfers to the employment security administration account pursuant to section 901(b)(2) during such month, exceed

(B) the payments during such month from the employment security administration account pursuant to section 901(b)(3) and (d).

If for any such month the payments referred to in subparagraph (B) exceed the transfers referred to in subparagraph (A), proper adjustments shall be made in the amounts subsequently transferred.

(2) Whenever the Secretary of the Treasury determines pursuant to section 901(f) that there is an excess in the employment security administration account as of the close of any fiscal year beginning after June 30, 1972, there shall be transferred (as of the beginning of the succeeding fiscal year) to the extended unemployment compensation account the total amount of such excess or so much thereof as is

---

[11] See Vol. II, P.L. 97-248, §604(a), with respect to an appropriation of funds to assist States in meeting administrative costs.

594 SOCIAL SECURITY ACT—§ 905(b)(2)(cont)

required to increase the amount in the extended unemployment compensation account to whichever of the following is the greater:

(A) $750,000,000, or

(B) the amount (determined by the Secretary of Labor and certified by him to the Secretary of the Treasury) equal to 0.5 percent of the total wages subject (determined without any limitation on amount) to contributions under all State unemployment compensation laws for the calendar year ending during the fiscal year for which the excess is determined.

(3) The Secretary of the Treasury shall make no transfer pursuant to paragraph (1) as of the close of any month if he determines that the amount in the extended unemployment compensation account is equal to (or in excess of) the limitation provided in paragraph (2).

Transfers to State Accounts

(c) Amounts in the extended unemployment compensation account shall be available for transfer to the accounts of the States in the Unemployment Trust Fund as provided in section 204(e) of the Federal-State Extended Unemployment Compensation Act of 1970[12].

Advances to Extended Unemployment Compensation Account and Repayment

(d) There are hereby authorized to be appropriated, without fiscal year limitation, to the extended unemployment compensation account, as repayable advances, such sums as may be necessary to carry out the purposes of the Federal-State Extended Unemployment Compensation Act of 1970. Amounts appropriated as repayable advances shall be repaid by transfers from the extended unemployment compensation account to the general fund of the Treasury, at such times as the amount in the extended unemployment compensation account is determined by the Secretary of the Treasury, in consultation with the Secretary of Labor, to be adequate for such purpose. Repayments under the preceding sentence shall be made whenever the Secretary of the Treasury (after consultation with the Secretary of Labor) determines that the amount then in the account exceeds the amount necessary to meet the anticipated payments from the account during the next 3 months. Any amount transferred as a repayment under this subsection shall be credited against, and shall operate to reduce, any balance of advances repayable under this subsection. Amounts appropriated as repayable advances for purposes of this subsection shall bear interest at a rate equal to the average rate of interest, computed as of the end of the calendar month next preceding the date of such advance, borne by all interest bearing obligations of the United States then forming part of the public debt; except that in cases in which such average rate is not a multiple of one-eighth of 1 percent, the rate of interest shall be the multiple of one-eighth of 1 percent next lower than such average rate.

---

[12] See Vol. II, P.L. 91-373.

SOCIAL SECURITY ACT—§ 907(b)   595

UNEMPLOYMENT COMPENSATION RESEARCH PROGRAM

SEC. 906. [42 U.S.C. 1106] (a) The Secretary of Labor shall—

(1) establish a continuing and comprehensive program of research to evaluate the unemployment compensation system. Such research shall include, but not be limited to, a program of factual studies covering the role of unemployment compensation under varying patterns of unemployment including those in seasonal industries, the relationship between the unemployment compensation and other social insurance programs, the effect of State eligibility and disqualification provisions, the personal characteristics, family situations, employment background and experience of claimants, with the results of such studies to be made public; and

(2) establish a program of research to develop information (which shall be made public) as to the effect and impact of extending coverage to excluded groups with first attention to agricultural labor.

(b) To assist in the establishment and provide for the continuation of the comprehensive research program relating to the unemployment compensation system, there are hereby authorized to be appropriated for the fiscal year ending June 30, 1971, and for each fiscal year thereafter, such sums, not to exceed $8,000,000, as may be necessary to carry out the purposes of this section. From the sums authorized to be appropriated by this subsection the Secretary may provide for the conduct of such research through grants or contracts.

PERSONNEL TRAINING

SEC. 907. [42 U.S.C. 1107] (a) In order to assist in increasing the effectiveness and efficiency of administration of the unemployment compensation program by increasing the number of adequately trained personnel, the Secretary of Labor shall—

(1) provide directly, through State agencies, or through contracts with institutions of higher education or other qualified agencies, organizations, or institutions, programs and courses designed to train individuals to prepare them, or improve their qualifications, for service in the administration of the unemployment compensation program, including claims determinations and adjudication, with such stipends and allowances as may be permitted under regulations of the Secretary;

(2) develop training materials for and provide technical assistance to the State agencies in the operation of their training programs;

(3) under such regulations as he may prescribe, award fellowships and traineeships to persons in the Federal-State employment security agencies, in order to prepare them or improve their qualifications for service in the administration of the unemployment compensation program.

(b) The Secretary may, to the extent that he finds such action to be necessary, prescribe requirements to assure that any person receiving a fellowship, traineeship, stipend or allowance shall repay the costs thereof to the extent that such person fails to serve in the Federal-State employment security program for the period prescribed by the Secretary. The Secretary may relieve any individual of his obliga-

596 SOCIAL SECURITY ACT—§ 907(b)(cont)

tion to so repay, in whole or in part, whenever and to the extent that such repayment would, in his judgment, be inequitable or would be contrary to the purposes of any of the programs established by this section.

(c) The Secretary, with the concurrence of the State, may detail Federal employees to State unemployment compensation administration and the Secretary may concur in the detailing of State employees to the United States Department of Labor for temporary periods for training or for purposes of unemployment compensation administration, and the provisions of section 507 of the Elementary and Secondary Education Act of 1965[13] (79 Stat. 27) or any more general program of interchange enacted by a law amending, supplementing, or replacing section 507 shall apply to any such assignment.

(d) There are hereby authorized to be appropriated for the fiscal year ending June 30, 1971, and for each fiscal year thereafter such sums, not to exceed $5,000,000, as may be necessary to carry out the purposes of this section.

ADVISORY COUNCIL ON UNEMPLOYMENT COMPENSATION

SEC. 908. [42 U.S.C. 1108] (a) ESTABLISHMENT.—Not later than February 1, 1992, and every 4th year thereafter, the Secretary of Labor shall establish an advisory council to be known as the Advisory Council on Unemployment Compensation (referred to in this section as the "Council").

(b) FUNCTION.—It shall be the function of each Council to evaluate the unemployment compensation program, including the purpose, goals, countercyclical effectiveness, coverage, benefit adequacy, trust fund solvency, funding of State administrative costs, administrative efficiency, and any other aspects of the program and to make recommendations for improvement.

(c) MEMBERS.—

(1) IN GENERAL.—Each Council shall consist of 11 members as follows:

(A) 5 members appointed by the President, to include representatives of business, labor, State government, and the public.

(B) 3 members appointed by the President pro tempore of the Senate, in consultation with the Chairman and ranking member of the Committee on Finance of the Senate.

(C) 3 members appointed by the Speaker of the House of Representative, in consultation with the Chairman and ranking member of the Committee on Ways and Means of the House of Representatives.

(2) QUALIFICATIONS.—In appointing members under subparagraphs (B) and (C) of paragraph (1), the President pro tempore of the Senate and the Speaker of the House of Representatives shall each appoint—

(A) 1 representative of the interests of business,

(B) 1 representative of the interests of labor, and

---

[13] See, instead, Vol. II, 5 U.S.C. 3371-3376. [P.L. 89-10, 79 Stat. 27, §507 was classified to 20 U.S.C. 867. P.L. 91-230, §143(a)(3), redesignated §507 as §553; §553 was classified to 20 U.S.C. 869b. P.L. 91-648, 81 Stat. 1909, §403, repealed §553, effective January 5, 1971. P.L. 91-648, §402, approved January 5, 1971, amended chapter 33 of Title 5, U.S.C., to include 5 U.S.C. 3371-3376, "Subchapter VI, Assignments to and from States".]

SOCIAL SECURITY ACT—§ 910(a)(1) 597

(C) 1 representative of the interests of State governments.

(3) VACANCIES.—A vacancy in any Council shall be filled in the manner in which the original appointment was made.

(4) Chairman.—The President shall appoint the Chairman of the Council from among its members.

(d) STAFF AND OTHER ASSISTANCE.—

(1) IN GENERAL.—Each council may engage any technical assistance (including actuarial services) required by the Council to carry out its functions under this section.

(2) ASSISTANCE FROM SECRETARY OF LABOR.—The Secretary of Labor shall provide each Council with any staff, office facilities, and other assistance, and any data prepared by the Department of Labor, required by the Council to carry out its functions under this section.

(e) COMPENSATION.—Each member of any Council—

(1) shall be entitled to receive compensation at the rate of pay for level V of the Executive Schedule under section 5316 of title 5, United States Code, for each day (including travel time) during which such member is engaged in the actual performance of duties vested in the Council, and

(2) while engaged in the performance of such duties away from such member's home or regular place of business, shall be allowed travel expenses (including per diem in lieu of subsistence) as authorized by section 5703 of title 5, United States Code, for persons in the Government employed intermittently.

(f) REPORT.—

(1) IN GENERAL.—Not later than February 1 of the third year following the year in which any Council is required to be established under subsection (a), the Council shall submit to the President and the Congress a report setting forth the findings and recommendations of the Council as a result of its evaluation of the unemployment compensation program under this section.

(2) REPORT OF FIRST COUNCIL.—The Council shall include in its report required to be submitted by February 1, 1995, the Council's findings and recommendations with respect to determining eligibility for extended unemployment benefits on the basis of unemployment statistics for regions, States, or subdivisions of States.

FEDERAL EMPLOYEES COMPENSATION ACCOUNT

SEC. 909. [42 U.S.C. 1109] There is hereby established in the Unemployment Trust Fund a Federal Employees Compensation Account which shall be used for the purposes specified in section 8509 of title 5, United States Code. For the purposes provided for in section 904(e), such account shall be maintained as a separate book account.

BORROWING BETWEEN FEDERAL ACCOUNTS

SEC. 910. [42 U.S.C. 1110] (a) IN GENERAL.—Whenever the Secretary of the Treasury (after consultation with the Secretary of Labor) determines that—

(1) the amount in the employment security administration account, Federal unemployment account, or extended unemployment compensation account, is insufficient to meet the anticipated payments from the account,

598 SOCIAL SECURITY ACT—§ 910(a)(2)

(2) such insufficiency may cause such account to borrow from the general fund of the Treasury, and

(3) the amount in any other such account exceeds the amount necessary to meet the anticipated payments from such other account,

the Secretary shall transfer to the account referred to in paragraph (1) from the account referred to paragraph (3)[14] an amount equal to the insufficiency determined under paragraph (1) (or, if less, the excess determined under paragraph (3)).

(b) TREATMENT OF ADVANCE.—Any amount transferred under subsection (a)—

(1) shall be treated as a noninterest-bearing repayable advance, and

(2) shall not be considered in computing the amount in any account for purposes of the application of sections 901(f)(2), 902(b), and 905(b).

(c) REPAYMENT.—Whenever the Secretary of the Treasury (after consultation with the Secretary of Labor) determines that the amount in the account to which an advance is made under subsection (a) exceeds the amount necessary to meet the anticipated payments from the account, the Secretary shall transfer from the account to the account from which the advance was made an amount equal to the lesser of the amount so advanced or such excess.

---

[14] As in original. Probably should read "in paragraph (3)".

[TITLE X—GRANTS TO STATES FOR AID TO THE BLIND[1]]

TABLE OF CONTENTS OF TITLE[2]

		Page
Sec. 1001.	Appropriation	599
Sec. 1002.	State plans for aid to the blind	599
Sec. 1003.	Payment to States	601
Sec. 1004.	Operation of State plans	603
Sec. 1005.	Administration	603
Sec. 1006.	Definition	603

APPROPRIATION

SEC. 1001. [42 U.S.C. 1201] For the purpose of enabling each State to furnish financial assistance, as far as practicable under the conditions in such State, to needy individuals who are blind, there is hereby authorized to be appropriated for each fiscal year a sum sufficient to carry out the purposes of this title. The sums made available under this section shall be used for making payments to States which have submitted, and had approved by the Secretary of Health, Education, and Welfare, State plans for aid to the blind.

STATE PLANS FOR AID TO THE BLIND

SEC. 1002. [42 U.S.C. 1202] (a) A State plan for aid to the blind must (1) except to the extent permitted by the Secretary with respect to services, provide that it shall be in effect in all political subdivisions of the State, and, if administered by them, be mandatory upon them; (2) provide for financial participation by the State; (3) either provide for the establishment or designation of a single State agency to administer the plan, or provide for the establishment or designation of a single State agency to supervise the administration of the plan; (4) provide (A) for granting an opportunity for a fair hearing before the State agency to any individual whose claim for aid to the blind is denied or is not acted upon with reasonable promptness, and (B) that if the State plan is administered in each of the political subdivisions

---

[1] P.L. 92-603, §303, *repealed* Title X, effective January 1, 1974, *except* with respect to Puerto Rico, Guam, and the Virgin Islands.

Title X of the Social Security Act is administered by the Department of Health and Human Services. The Office of Family Assistance, administers benefit payments under Title X. The Administration for Public Services, Office of Human Development Services, administers social services under Title X.

Title X appears in the United States Code as §§1201-1206, subchapter X, chapter 7, Title 42.

Regulations of the Secretary of Health and Human Services relating to Title X are contained in subtitle A and chapter XIII, Title 45, Code of Federal Regulations.

The Commonwealth of the Northern Marianas may elect to initiate a Title X social services program if it chooses; see Vol. II, Appendix, P.L. 94-241, [Covenant to Establish Northern Mariana Islands], approved March 24, 1976.

See Vol. II, 31 U.S.C. 6504-6505, with respect to intergovernmental cooperation; and 31 U.S.C. 7501-7507, with respect to uniform audit requirements for State and local governments receiving Federal financial assistance.

See Vol. II, P.L. 82-183, §618, for the "Jenner Amendment", which prohibits denial of grants-in-aid under certain conditions.

See Vol. II, P.L. 88-352, §601, for prohibition against discrimination in federally assisted programs.

See Vol. II, P.L. 89-97, §121(b), with respect to restrictions on payment to a State receiving payments under Title XIX.

[2] This table of contents does not appear in the law.

600 SOCIAL SECURITY ACT—§ 1002(a)(cont)

of the State by a local agency and such local agency provides a hearing at which evidence may be presented prior to a hearing before the State agency, such local agency may put into effect immediately upon issuance its decision upon the matter considered at such hearing; (5) provide (A) such methods of administration (including after January 1, 1940, methods relating to the establishment and maintenance of personnel standards on a merit basis, except that the Secretary shall exercise no authority with respect to the selection, tenure of office, and compensation of any individual employed in accordance with such methods) as are found by the Secretary to be necessary for the proper and efficient operation of the plan[3], and (B) for the training and effective use of paid subprofessional staff, with particular emphasis on the full-time or part-time employment of recipients and other persons of low-income, as community service aides, in the administration of the plan and for the use of nonpaid or partially paid volunteers in a social service volunteer program in providing services to applicants and recipients and in assisting any advisory committees established by the State agency; (6) provide that the State agency will make such reports, in such form and containing such information, as the Secretary may from time to time require, and comply with such provisions as the Secretary may from time to time find necessary to assure the correctness and verification of such reports; and (7) provide that no aid will be furnished any individual under the plan with respect to any period with respect to which he is receiving old-age assistance under the State plan approved under section 2 of this Act or assistance under a State program funded under Part A of title IV; (8) provide that the State agency shall, in determining need, take into consideration any other income and resources of the individual claiming aid to the blind, as well as any expenses reasonably attributable to the earning of any such income, except that, in making such determination, the State agency (A) shall disregard the first $85 per month of earned income, plus one-half of earned income in excess of $85 per month, (B) shall, for a period not in excess of twelve months, and may, for a period not in excess of thirty-six months, disregard such additional amounts of other income and resources, in the case of an individual who has a plan for achieving self-support approved by the State agency, as may be necessary for the fulfillment of such plan, and (C) may, before disregarding the amounts referred to in clauses (A) and (B), disregard not more than $7.50 of any income;[4] (9) provide safeguards which permit the use or disclosure of information concerning applicants or recipients only (A) to public officials who require such information in connection with their official duties, or (B) to other persons for purposes directly connected with the administration of the State plan;[5] (10) provide that, in determining whether an individual is blind, there shall be an examination by a physician skilled in diseases of the eye or by an optometrist, whichever the individual may select; (11) effective July 1, 1951, provide that all individuals wishing to make application for aid to the blind shall have opportunity to do so, and that aid to the

---

[3] P.L. 91-648, §208(a)(3)(D), transferred to the U.S. Civil Service Commission, effective March 6, 1971, all powers, functions, and duties of the Secretary under subparagraph (A).

[4] See Vol. II, Appendix K, Income and Resource Exclusions, for a list of provisions from Federal laws regarding exclusions from income and resources.

[5] See Vol. II, P.L. 82-183, §618, for the "Jenner Amendment" prohibiting denial of grants-in-aid under certain conditions.

SOCIAL SECURITY ACT—§ 1003(a)(2)   601

blind shall be furnished with reasonable promptness to all eligible individuals; (12) effective July 1, 1953, provide, if the plan includes payments to individuals in private or public institutions, for the establishment or designation of a State authority or authorities which shall be responsible for establishing and maintaining standards for such institutions; (13) provide a description of the services (if any) which the State agency makes available (using whatever internal organizational arrangement it finds appropriate for this purpose) to applicants for and recipients of aid to the blind to help them attain self-support or self-care, including a description of the steps taken to assure, in the provision of such services, maximum utilization of other agencies providing similar or related services; and (14) provide that information is requested and exchanged for purposes of income and eligibility verification in accordance with a State system which meets the requirements of section 1137 of this Act.

(b) The Secretary shall approve any plan which fulfills the conditions specified in subsection (a), except that he shall not approve any plan which imposes, as a condition of eligibility for aid to the blind under the plan—

(1) Any residence requirement which excludes any resident of the State who has resided therein five years during the nine years immediately preceding the application for aid and has resided therein continuously for one year immediately preceding the application; or

(2) Any citizenship requirement which excludes any citizen of the United States.

At the option of the State, the plan may provide that manuals and other policy issuances will be furnished to persons without charge for the reasonable cost of such materials, but such provision shall not be required by the Secretary as a condition for the approval of such plan under this title. In the case of any State (other than Puerto Rico and the Virgin Islands) which did not have on January 1, 1949, a State plan for aid to the blind approved under this title, the Secretary shall approve a plan of such State for aid to the blind for purposes of this title, even though it does not meet the requirements of clause (8) of subsection (a) of this section, if it meets all other requirements of this title for an approved plan for aid to the blind; but payments under section 1003 shall be made, in the case of any such plan, only with respect to expenditures thereunder which would be included as expenditures for the purposes of section 1003 under a plan approved under this section without regard to the provisions of this sentence.

PAYMENT TO STATES

Sec. 1003. [42 U.S.C. 1203] (a) From the sums appropriated therefor, the Secretary of the Treasury shall pay to each State which has an approved plan for aid to the blind, for each quarter, beginning with the quarter commencing October 1, 1958—

(1) [Stricken.[6]]

(2) in the case of Puerto Rico, the Virgin Islands, and Guam, an amount equal to one-half of the total of the sums expended during such quarter as aid to the blind under the State plan, not counting so much of any expenditure with respect to any month

---

[6] P.L. 97-35, §2184(c)(2)(A); 95 Stat. 817.

602   SOCIAL SECURITY ACT—§ 1003(a)(2)(cont)

as exceeds $37.50 multiplied by the total number of recipients of aid to the blind for such month; and

(3) in the case of any State, an amount equal to 50 percent of the total amounts expended during such quarter as found necessary by the Secretary for the proper and efficient administration of the State plan.

(b) The method of computing and paying such amounts shall be as follows:

(1) The Secretary of Health, Education, and Welfare shall, prior to the beginning of each quarter, estimate the amount to be paid to the State for such quarter under the provisions of subsection (a), such estimate to be based on (A) a report filed by the State containing its estimate of the total sum to be expended in such quarter in accordance with the provisions of such subsection, and stating the amount appropriated or made available by the State and its political subdivisions for such expenditures in such quarter, and if such amount is less than the State's proportionate share of the total sum of such estimated expenditures, the source or sources from which the difference is expected to be derived, (B) records showing the number of blind individuals in the State, and (C) such other investigation as the Secretary may find necessary.

(2) The Secretary of Health, Education, and Welfare shall then certify to the Secretary of the Treasury the amount so estimated by the Secretary of Health, Education, and Welfare, (A) reduced or increased, as the case may be, by any sum by which he finds that his estimate for any prior quarter was greater or less than the amount which should have been paid to the State under subsection (a) for such quarter, and (B) reduced by a sum equivalent to the pro rata share to which the United States is equitably entitled, as determined by the Secretary of Health, Education, and Welfare, of the net amount recovered during a prior quarter by the State or any political subdivision thereof with respect to aid to the blind furnished under the State plan; except that such increases or reductions shall not be made to the extent that such sums have been applied to make the amount certified for any prior quarter greater or less than the amount estimated by the Secretary of Health, Education, and Welfare for such prior quarter: *Provided*, That any part of the amount recovered from the estate of a deceased recipient which is not in excess of the amount expended by the State or any political subdivision thereof for the funeral expenses of the deceased shall not be considered as a basis for reduction under clause (B) of this paragraph.

(3) The Secretary of the Treasury shall thereupon, through the Division of Disbursement[7] of the Treasury Department, and prior to audit or settlement by the General Accounting Office[8], pay to the State, at the time or times fixed by the Secretary of Health, Education, and Welfare, the amounts so certified.

---

[7] As in original. The Division of Disbursement was consolidated in the Fiscal Service of the Treasury Department by Reorganization Plan No. III, §1(a), effective June 30, 1940 (54 Stat. 1231).

[8] P.l. 108-271, §8(B), provided that "Any reference to the General Accounting Office in any law, rule, regulation, certificate, directive, instruction, or other official paper in force on the date of enactment of this Act (July 7, 2004) shall be considered to refer and apply to the Government Accountability Office."

SOCIAL SECURITY ACT—§ 1006(2)   603

OPERATION OF STATE PLANS

SEC. 1004. [42 U.S.C. 1204] In the case of any State plan for aid to the blind which has been approved by the Secretary of Health, Education, and Welfare, if the Secretary, after reasonable notice and opportunity for hearing to the State agency administering or supervising the administration of such plan, finds—

(1) that the plan has been so changed as to impose any residence or citizenship requirement prohibited by section 1002(b), or that in the administration of the plan any such prohibited requirement is imposed, with the knowledge of such State agency, in a substantial number of cases; or

(2) that in the administration of the plan there is a failure to comply substantially with any provision required by section 1002(a) to be included in the plan;

the Secretary shall notify such State agency that further payments will not be made to the State (or, in his discretion, that payments will be limited to categories under or parts of the State plan not affected by such failure) until the Secretary is satisfied that such prohibited requirement is no longer so imposed, and that there is no longer any such failure to comply. Until he is so satisfied he shall make no further payments to such State (or shall limit payments to categories under or parts of the State plan not affected by such failure).

ADMINISTRATION

SEC. 1005. [42 U.S.C. 1205] There is hereby authorized to be appropriated for the fiscal year ending June 30, 1936, the sum of $30,000, for all necessary expenses of the Board in administering the provisions of this title.

DEFINITION

SEC. 1006. [42 U.S.C. 1206] For the purposes of this title, the term "aid to the blind" means money payments to blind individuals who are needy, but does not include any such payments to or care in behalf of any individual who is an inmate of a public institution (except as a patient in a medical institution) or any individual who is a patient in an institution for tuberculosis or mental diseases. Such term also includes payments which are not included within the meaning of such term under the preceding sentence, but which would be so included except that they are made on behalf of such a needy individual to another individual who (as determined in accordance with standards prescribed by the Secretary) is interested in or concerned with the welfare of such needy individual, but only with respect to a State whose State plan approved under section 1002 includes provision for—

(1) determination by the State agency that such needy individual has, by reason of his physical or mental condition, such inability to manage funds that making payments to him would be contrary to his welfare and, therefore, it is necessary to provide such aid through payments described in this sentence;

(2) making such payments only in cases in which such payments will, under the rules otherwise applicable under the State plan for determining need and the amount of aid to the blind to be paid (and in conjunction with other income and resources), meet

604 SOCIAL SECURITY ACT—§ 1006(2)(cont)

all the need[9] of the individuals with respect to whom such payments are made;

(3) undertaking and continuing special efforts to protect the welfare of such individual and to improve, to the extent possible, his capacity for self-care and to manage funds;

(4) periodic review by such State agency of the determination under paragraph (1) to ascertain whether conditions justifying such determination still exist, with provision for termination of such payments if they do not and for seeking judicial appointment of a guardian or other legal representative, as described in section 1111, if and when it appears that such action will best serve the interests of such needy individual; and

(5) opportunity for a fair hearing before the State agency on the determination referred to in paragraph (1) for any individual with respect to whom it is made.

At the option of a State (if its plan approved under this title so provides), such term (i) need not include money payments to an individual who has been absent from such State for a period in excess of 90 consecutive days (regardless of whether he has maintained his residence in such State during such period) until he has been present in such State for 30 consecutive days in the case of such an individual who has maintained his residence in such State during such period or 90 consecutive days in the case of any other such individual, and (ii) may include rent payments made directly to a public housing agency on behalf of a recipient or a group or groups of recipients of aid under such plan.

---

[9] As in original. Probably should be "needs".

TITLE XI—GENERAL PROVISIONS, PEER REVIEW, AND ADMINISTRATIVE SIMPLIFICATION[1]

TABLE OF CONTENTS OF TITLE[2]

Page

Part A—General Provisions

Sec. 1101.	Definitions	607
Sec. 1102.	Rules and regulations	610
Sec. 1103.	Separability	610
Sec. 1104.	Reservation of power	610
Sec. 1105.	Short title	610
Sec. 1106.	Disclosure of information in possession of agency	611
Sec. 1107.	Penalty for fraud	613
Sec. 1108.	Additional grants to Puerto Rico, the Virgin Islands, Guam, and American Samoa; limitation on total payments	614
Sec. 1109.	Amounts disregarded not to be taken into account in determining eligibility of other individuals	616
Sec. 1110.	Cooperative research or demonstration projects	617
Sec. 1111.	Public assistance payments to legal representatives	619
Sec. 1112.	Medical care guides and reports for public assistance and medical assistance	619
Sec. 1113.	Assistance for United States citizens returned from foreign countries	619
Sec. 1114.	Appointment of Advisory Council and other advisory groups	620
Sec. 1115.	Demonstration projects	622
Sec. 1116.	Administrative and judicial review of certain administrative determinations	625
Sec. 1117.	Appointment of the Administrator and Chief Actuary of the Centers for Medicare and Medicaid Services	627
Sec. 1118.	Alternative Federal payment with respect to public assistance expenditures	627
Sec. 1119.	Federal participation in payments for repairs to home owned by recipient of aid or assistance	628
Sec. 1120.	Approval of certain projects	628
Sec. 1121.	Uniform reporting systems for health services facilities and organizations	628
Sec. 1122.	Limitation on Federal participation for capital expenditures	629
Sec. 1123.	Effect of failure to carry out State plan	633
Sec. 1123A.	Reviews of child and family services programs, and of foster care and adoption assistance programs, for conformity with State plan requirements	633
Sec. 1124.	Disclosure of ownership and related information	635
Sec. 1124A.	Disclosure requirements for other providers under part B of Medicare	636
Sec. 1125.	Issuance of subpenas by Comptroller General	637

---

[1] Title XI of the Social Security Act is administered by the Department of Health and Human Services and by the Department of Labor.

Title XI appears in the United States Code as §§1301-1320d-8, subchapter XI, chapter 7, Title 42.

Regulations of the Secretary of Health and Human Services relating to Title XI are contained in chapter III, Title 20, in chapters I, II, and IV, Title 42, and in subtitle A and chapters I, III, and XIII, Title 45, Code of Federal Regulations. Regulations of the Secretary of Labor relating to Title XI are contained in chapter V, Title 20, and subtitle A, Title 29, Code of Federal Regulations.

See Vol. II, P.L. 88-352, §601, for prohibition against discrimination in federally assisted programs.

See Vol. II, P.L. 100-204, §724(d), with respect to furnishing information to the United States Commission on Improving the Effectiveness of the United Nations; and §725(b), with respect to the detailing of Government personnel.

See Vol. II, P.L. 100-235, §§5-8, with respect to responsibilities of each Federal agency for computer systems security and privacy.

[2] This table of contents does not appear in the law.

605

606 SOCIAL SECURITY ACT—TITLE XI(cont)

Sec. 1126.	Disclosure by institutions, organizations, and agencies of owners and certain other individuals who have been convicted of certain offenses	638
Sec. 1127.	Adjustments in SSI benefits on account of retroactive benefits under Title II	638
Sec. 1128.	Exclusion of certain individuals and entities from participation in medicare and State health care programs	639
Sec. 1128A.	Civil monetary penalties	648
Sec. 1128B.	Criminal penalties for acts involving Federal health care programs	655
Sec. 1128C.	Fraud and abuse control program	659
Sec. 1128D.	Guidance regarding application of health care fraud and abuse sanctions	661
Sec. 1128E.	Health care fraud and abuse data collection program	664
Sec. 1128F.	Coordination of Medicare and Medicaid Surety Bond Provisions	666
Sec. 1129.	Civil monetary penalties and assessments for Titles II, VIII, and XVI	667
Sec. 1129A.	Administrative procedure for imposing penalties for false or misleading statements	671
Sec. 1129B.	Attempts to interfere with administration of social security act	672
Sec. 1130.	Demonstration projects	673
Sec. 1130A.	Effect of failure to carry out State plan	675
Sec. 1131.	Notification of social security claimant with respect to deferred vested benefits	675
Sec. 1132.	Period within which certain claims must be filed	676
Sec. 1133.	Applicants or recipients under public assistance programs not to be required to make election respecting certain veterans' benefits	676
Sec. 1134.	Nonprofit hospital philanthropy	677
Sec. 1135.	Authority to waive requirements during national emergencies	677
Sec. 1136.	Exclusion of representatives and health care providers convicted of violations from participation in social security programs	681
Sec. 1137.	Income and eligibility verification system	683
Sec. 1138.	Hospital protocols for organ procurement and standards for organ procurement agencies	688
Sec. 1139.	National Commission on Children	690
Sec. 1140.	Prohibition of misuse of symbols, emblems, or names in reference to social security or medicare	694
Sec. 1141.	Blood donor locator service	696
Sec. 1142.	Research on outcomes of health care services and procedures	699
Sec. 1143.	Social security account statements	703
Sec. 1144.	Outreach efforts to increase awareness of the availability of medicare cost–sharing and subsidies for low-income individuals under title xviii	705
Sec. 1145.	Protection of social security and medicare trust funds	708
Sec. 1146.	Public disclosure of certain information on hospital financial interest and referral patterns	709
Sec. 1147.	Cross-program recovery of overpayments from benefits	709
Sec. 1148.	The ticket to work and self-sufficiency program	710
Sec. 1149.	Work incentives outreach program	720
Sec. 1150.	State grants for work incentives assistance to disabled beneficiaries	724

Part B—PEER REVIEW OF THE UTILIZATION AND QUALITY OF HEALTH CARE SERVICES

Sec. 1151.	Purpose	725
Sec. 1152.	Definition of utilization and quality control peer review organization	725
Sec. 1153.	Contracts with utilization and quality control peer review organizations	726
Sec. 1154.	Functions of peer review organizations	730
Sec. 1155.	Right to hearing and judicial review	737

SOCIAL SECURITY ACT—§ 1101(a)(2)

607

Sec. 1156.	Obligations of health care practitioners and providers of health care services; sanctions and penalties; hearings and review	737
Sec. 1157.	Limitation on liability	739
Sec. 1158.	Application of this part to certain State programs receiving Federal financial assistance	740
Sec. 1159.	Authorization for use of certain funds to administer the provisions of this part	740
Sec. 1160.	Prohibition against disclosure of information	740
Sec. 1161.	Annual reports	742
Sec. 1162.	Exemptions for religious nonmedical health care institutions	743
Sec. 1163.	Medical officers in American Samoa, the Northern Mariana Islands, and the Trust Territory of the Pacific Islands to be included in the utilization and quality control peer review program	743

Part C—Administrative Simplification

Sec. 1171.	Definitions	743
Sec. 1172.	General requirements for adoption of standards	745
Sec. 1173.	Standards for information transactions and data elements	746
Sec. 1174.	Timetables for adoption of standards	748
Sec. 1175.	Requirements	749
Sec. 1176.	General penalty for failure to comply with requirements and standards	750
Sec. 1177.	Wrongful disclosure of individually identifiable health information	751
Sec. 1178.	Effect on State law	751
Sec. 1179.	Processing payment transactions by financial institutions	752
Sec. 1180.	Application of HIPPA regulations to genetic information	753

Part A—General Provisions

DEFINITIONS

SEC. 1101. [42 U.S.C. 1301] (a) When used in this Act—

(1) The term "State", except where otherwise provided, includes the District of Columbia and the Commonwealth of Puerto Rico, and when used in titles IV, V, VII, XI, XIX, and XXI includes the Virgin Islands and Guam. Such term when used in titles III, IX, and XII also includes the Virgin Islands. Such term when used in title V and in part B of this title also includes American Samoa, the Northern Mariana Islands, and the Trust Territory of the Pacific Islands. Such term when used in titles XIX and XXI also includes the Northern Mariana Islands and American Samoa. In the case of Puerto Rico, the Virgin Islands, and Guam, titles I, X, and XIV, and title XVI (as in effect without regard to the amendment made by section 301 of the Social Security Amendments of 1972[3]) shall continue to apply, and the term "State" when used in such titles (but not in title XVI as in effect pursuant to such amendment after December 31, 1973) includes Puerto Rico, the Virgin Islands, and Guam. Such term when used in title XX also includes the Virgin Islands, Guam, American Samoa, and the Northern Mariana Islands. Such term when used in title IV also includes American Samoa.

(2) The term "United States" when used in a geographical sense means, except where otherwise provided, the States.

---

[3] P.L. 92-603, §301, added Title XVI, Supplemental Security Income for the Aged, Blind, and Disabled.

608   SOCIAL SECURITY ACT—§ 1101(a)(3)

(3) The term "person" means an individual, a trust or estate, a partnership, or a corporation.

(4) The term "corporation" includes associations, joint-stock companies, and insurance companies.

(5) The term "shareholder" includes a member in an association, joint-stock company, or insurance company.

(6) The term "Secretary", except when the context otherwise requires, means the Secretary of Health and Human Services.

(7) The terms "physician" and "medical care" and "hospitalization" include osteopathic practitioners or the services of osteopathic practitioners and hospitals within the scope of their practice as defined by State law.

(8)(A) The "Federal percentage" for any State (other than Puerto Rico, the Virgin Islands, and Guam) shall be 100 per centum less the State percentage; and the State percentage shall be that percentage which bears the same ratio to 50 per centum as the square of the per capita income of such State bears to the square of the per capita income of the United States; except that the Federal percentage shall in no case be less than 50 per centum or more than 65 per centum.

(B) The Federal percentage for each State (other than Puerto Rico, the Virgin Islands, and Guam) shall be promulgated by the Secretary between October 1 and November 30 of each year, on the basis of the average per capita income of each State and of the United States for the three most recent calendar years for which satisfactory data are available from the Department of Commerce. Such promulgation shall be conclusive for each of the four quarters in the period beginning October 1 next succeeding such promulgation: *Provided*, That the Secretary shall promulgate such percentages as soon as possible after the enactment of the Social Security Amendments of 1958[4], which promulgation shall be conclusive for each of the eleven quarters in the period beginning October 1, 1958, and ending with the close of June 30, 1961.

(C) The term "United States" means (but only for purposes of subparagraphs (A) and (B) of this paragraph) the fifty States and the District of Columbia.

(D) Promulgations made before satisfactory data are available from the Department of Commerce for a full year on the per capita income of Alaska shall prescribe a Federal percentage for Alaska of 50 per centum and, for purposes of such promulgations, Alaska shall not be included as part of the "United States". Promulgations made thereafter but before per capita income data for Alaska for a full three-year period are available from the Department of Commerce shall be based on satisfactory data available therefrom for Alaska for such one full year or, when such data are available for a two-year period, for such two years.

(9) The term "shared health facility" means any arrangement whereby—

(A) two or more health care practitioners practice their professions at a common physical location;

---

[4] August 28, 1958 [P.L. 85-840; 72 Stat. 1013].

SOCIAL SECURITY ACT—§ 1101(d)

(B) such practitioners share (i) common waiting areas, examining rooms, treatment rooms, or other space, (ii) the services of supporting staff, or (iii) equipment;

(C) such practitioners have a person (who may himself be a practitioner)—

(i) who is in charge of, controls, manages, or supervises substantial aspects of the arrangement or operation for the delivery of health or medical services at such common physical location, other than the direct furnishing of professional health care services by the practitioners to their patients; or

(ii) who makes available to such practitioners the services of supporting staff who are not employees of such practitioners;

and who is compensated in whole or in part, for the use of such common physical location or support services pertaining thereto, on a basis related to amounts charged or collected for the services rendered or ordered at such location or on any basis clearly unrelated to the value of the services provided by the person; and

(D) at least one of such practitioners received payments on a fee-for-service basis under titles XVIII and XIX in an amount exceeding $5,000 for any one month during the preceding 12 months or in an aggregate amount exceeding $40,000 during the preceding 12 months;

except that such term does not include a provider of services (as defined in section 1861(u) of this Act), a health maintenance organization (as defined in section 1301(a) of the Public Health Service Act[5]), a hospital cooperative shared services organization meeting the requirements of section 501(e) of the Internal Revenue Code of 1954[6], or any public entity.

(10) The term "Administration" means the Social Security Administration, except where the context requires otherwise.

(b) The terms "includes" and "including" when used in a definition contained in this Act shall not be deemed to exclude other things otherwise within the meaning of the term defined.

(c) Whenever under this Act or any Act of Congress, or under the law of any State, an employer is required or permitted to deduct any amount from the remuneration of an employee and to pay the amount deducted to the United States, a State, or any political subdivision thereof, then for the purposes of this Act the amount so deducted shall be considered to have been paid to the employee at the time of such deduction.

(d) Nothing in this Act shall be construed as authorizing any Federal official, agent, or representative, in carrying out any of the provisions of this Act, to take charge of any child over the objection of either of the parents of such child, or of the person standing in loco parentis to such child.

---

[5] See Vol. II, P.L. 78-410, §1301(a).

[6] See Vol. II, P.L. 83-591, §501(e).

P.L. 99-514, §2, provides, except when inappropriate, that any reference to the Internal Revenue Code of 1954 shall include a reference to the Internal Revenue Code of 1986.

610 SOCIAL SECURITY ACT—§ 1101(d)(cont)

RULES AND REGULATIONS

SEC. 1102. [42 U.S.C. 1302] (a) The Secretary of the Treasury, the Secretary of Labor, and the Secretary of Health and Human Services, respectively, shall make and publish such rules and regulations, not inconsistent with this Act, as may be necessary to the efficient administration of the functions with which each is charged under this Act.

(b)(1) Whenever the Secretary publishes a general notice of proposed rulemaking for any rule or regulation proposed under title XVIII, title XIX, or part B of this title that may have a significant impact on the operations of a substantial number of small rural hospitals, the Secretary shall prepare and make available for public comment an initial regulatory impact analysis. Such analysis shall describe the impact of the proposed rule or regulation on such hospitals and shall set forth, with respect to small rural hospitals, the matters required under section 603 of title 5, United States Code, to be set forth with respect to small entities. The initial regulatory impact analysis (or a summary) shall be published in the Federal Register at the time of the publication of general notice of proposed rulemaking for the rule or regulation.

(2) Whenever the Secretary promulgates a final version of a rule or regulation with respect to which an initial regulatory impact analysis is required by paragraph (1), the Secretary shall prepare a final regulatory impact analysis with respect to the final version of such rule or regulation. Such analysis shall set forth, with respect to small rural hospitals, the matters required under section 604 of title 5, United States Code, to be set forth with respect to small entities. The Secretary shall make copies of the final regulatory impact analysis available to the public and shall publish, in the Federal Register at the time of publication of the final version of the rule or regulation, a statement describing how a member of the public may obtain a copy of such analysis.

(3) If a regulatory flexibility analysis is required by chapter 6 of title 5, United States Code[7], for a rule or regulation to which this subsection applies, such analysis shall specifically address the impact of the rule or regulation on small rural hospitals.

SEPARABILITY

SEC. 1103. [42 U.S.C. 1303] If any provision of this Act, or the application thereof to any person or circumstance, is held invalid, the remainder of the Act and the application of such provision to other persons or circumstances shall not be affected thereby.

RESERVATION OF POWER

SEC. 1104. [42 U.S.C. 1304] The right to alter, amend, or repeal any provision of this Act is hereby reserved to the Congress.

SHORT TITLE

SEC. 1105. [42 U.S.C. 1305] This Act may be cited as the "Social Security Act".

---

[7] See Vol. II, 5 U.S.C. 603 and 604.

SOCIAL SECURITY ACT—§ 1106(b)   611

DISCLOSURE OF INFORMATION IN POSSESSION OF AGENCY[8]

SEC. 1106. [42 U.S.C. 1306] (a)(1) No disclosure of any return or portion of a return (including information returns and other written statements) filed with the Commissioner of Internal Revenue under title VIII of the Social Security Act[9] or under subchapter E of chapter 1 or subchapter A of chapter 9 of the Internal Revenue Code[10], or under regulations made under authority thereof, which has been transmitted to the head of the applicable agency by the Commissioner of Internal Revenue, or of any file, record, report, or other paper, or any information, obtained at any time by the head of the applicable agency or by any officer or employee of the applicable agency in the course of discharging the duties of the head of the applicable agency under this Act, and no disclosure of any such file, record, report, or other paper, or information, obtained at any time by any person from the head of the applicable agency or from any officer or employee of the applicable agency, shall be made except as the head of the applicable agency may by regulations prescribe and except as otherwise provided by Federal law. Any person who shall violate any provision of this section shall be deemed guilty of a felony and, upon conviction thereof, shall be punished by a fine not exceeding $10,000 for each occurrence of a violation, or by imprisonment not exceeding 5 years, or both.

(2) For purposes of this subsection and subsection (b), the term "applicable agency" means—

(A) the Social Security Administration, with respect to matter transmitted to or obtained by such Administration or matter disclosed by such Administration, or

(B) the applicable agency, with respect to matter transmitted to or obtained by such Department or matter disclosed by such Department.

(b) Requests for information, disclosure of which is authorized by regulations prescribed pursuant to subsection (a) of this section, and requests for services, may, subject to such limitations as may be prescribed by the head of the applicable agency to avoid undue interference with his functions under this Act, be complied with if the agency, person, or organization making the request agrees to pay for the information or services requested in such amount, if any (not exceeding the cost of furnishing the information or services), as may be determined

---

[8] See Vol. II, 5 U.S.C. 552, with respect to information available to the public from agencies; and 5 U.S.C. 8347(m)(3), with respect to disclosure of information to the Office of Personnel Management.

See Vol. II, 38 U.S.C. 5317 and 5318 with respect to Veterans' Benefits information.

See Vol. II, P.L. 83-591, §6103(l)(1), with respect to disclosure of returns and return information by the Secretary of the Treasury to the Social Security Administration; and §7213(a)(1), with respect to the penalty for unauthorized disclosure of that tax return information.

See Vol. II, P.L. 97-253, §307(f), with respect to supplying information about civil service annuitants.

See Vol. II, P.L.106-169, §209, with respect to State data exchanges.

[9] The reference to Title VIII of the Social Security Act refers to the Title VIII-Taxes with Respect to Employment-that was omitted from the Act as superseded by the provisions of the Internal Revenue code of 1939 and the Internal Revenue code of 1986. However, the provisions of §205 still apply with regard to tax return information provided under Title VIII of the Act prior to its repeal.

P.L. 76-1, §4, 53 Stat.1 repealed the former Title VIII, effective February 11, 1939. The substance of Title VIII was then included in the Internal Revenue Code of 1039 at §§1400-1425. Currently, the substance of the former Title VIII may be found at §§3101-3126 (Subtitle C-Employment Taxes; Chapter 21-Federal Insurance Contributions Act). See Vol. II, P.L. 83-591, §§3101-3126.

[10] P.L. 76-1. Should refer, instead, to P.L. 83-591, Subtitles A and C.

612   SOCIAL SECURITY ACT—§ 1106(b)(cont)

by the head of the applicable agency. Payments for information or services furnished pursuant to this section shall be made in advance or by way of reimbursement, as may be requested by the head of the applicable agency, and shall be deposited in the Treasury as a special deposit to be used to reimburse the appropriations (including authorizations to make expenditures from the Federal Old-Age and Survivors Insurance Trust Fund, the Federal Disability Insurance Trust Fund, the Federal Hospital Insurance Trust Fund, and the Federal Supplementary Medical Insurance Trust Fund) for the unit or units of the applicable agency which furnished the information or services. Notwithstanding the preceding provisions of this subsection, requests for information made pursuant to the provisions of part D of title IV of this Act for the purpose of using Federal records for locating parents shall be complied with and the cost incurred in providing such information shall be paid for as provided in such part D of title IV.

(c) Notwithstanding sections 552 and 552a of title 5, United States Code[11], or any other provision of law, whenever the Commissioner of Social Security or the Secretary determines that a request for information is made in order to assist a party in interest (as defined in section 3 of the Employee Retirement Income Security Act of 1974[12] (29 U.S.C. 1002)) with respect to the administration of an employee benefit plan (as so defined), or is made for any other purpose not directly related to the administration of the program or programs under this Act to which such information relates, such Commissioner or Secretary may require the requester to pay the full cost, as determined by the such Commissioner or Secretary, of providing such information.

(d) Notwithstanding any other provision of this section, in any case in which—

> (1) information regarding whether an individual is shown on the records of the Commissioner of Social Security as being alive or deceased is requested from the Commissioner for purposes of epidemiological or similar research which the Commissioner in consultation with the Secretary of Health and Human Services finds may reasonably be expected to contribute to a national health interest, and
>
> (2) the requester agrees to reimburse the Commissioner for providing such information and to comply with limitations on safeguarding and rerelease or redisclosure of such information as may be specified by the Commissioner,

the Commissioner shall comply with such request, except to the extent that compliance with such request would constitute a violation of the terms of any contract entered into under section 205(r).

(e) Notwithstanding any other provision of this section the Secretary shall make available to each State agency operating a program under title XIX and shall, subject to the limitations contained in subsection (e)[13], make available for public inspection in readily accessible form and fashion, the following official reports (not including, however, references to any internal tolerance rules and practices that may be contained therein, internal working papers or other informal mem-

---

[11] See Vol. II, 5 U.S.C. 552 and 552a.
[12] See Vol. II, P.L. 93-406, §3.
[13] As in original. Probably should be "subsection (f)".

SOCIAL SECURITY ACT—§ 1107(b)   613

oranda) dealing with the operation of the health programs established by titles XVIII and XIX—

(1) individual contractor performance reviews and other formal evaluations of the performance of carriers, intermediaries, and State agencies, including the reports of follow-up reviews;

(2) comparative evaluations of the performance of such contractors, including comparisons of either overall performance or of any particular aspect of contractor operation; and

(3) program validation survey reports and other formal evaluations of the performance of providers of services, including the reports of follow-up reviews, except that such reports shall not identify individual patients, individual health care practitioners, or other individuals.

(f) No report described in subsection (e) shall be made public by the Secretary or the State title XIX agency until the contractor or provider of services whose performance is being evaluated has had a reasonable opportunity (not exceeding 60 days) to review such report and to offer comments pertinent parts of which may be incorporated in the public report; nor shall the Secretary be required to include in any such report information with respect to any deficiency (or improper practice or procedures) which is known by the Secretary to have been fully corrected, within 60 days of the date such deficiency was first brought to the attention of such contractor or provider of services, as the case may be.

PENALTY FOR FRAUD[14]

SEC. 1107. [42 U.S.C. 1307] (a) Whoever, with the intent to defraud any person, shall make or cause to be made any false representation concerning the requirements of this Act, of chapter 2, 21, or 23 of the Internal Revenue Code of 1954[15], or of any provision of subtitle F of such Code which corresponds (within the meaning of section 7852(b) of such Code[16]) to a provision contained in subchapter E of chapter 9 of the Internal Revenue Code of 1939[17], or of any rules or regulations issued thereunder, knowing such representations to be false, shall be deemed guilty of a misdemeanor, and, upon conviction thereof, shall be punished by a fine not exceeding $1,000, or by imprisonment not exceeding one year, or both.

(b) Whoever, with the intent to elicit information as to the social security account number, date of birth, employment, wages, or benefits of any individual (1) falsely represents to the Commissioner of Social Security or the Secretary that he is such individual, or the wife, husband, widow, widower, divorced wife, divorced husband, surviving divorced wife, surviving divorced husband, surviving divorced mother, surviving divorced father, child, or parent of such individual, or the duly authorized agent of such individual, or of the wife, husband, widow, widower, divorced wife, divorced husband, surviving divorced wife, surviving divorced husband, surviving divorced mother, surviving divorced father, child, or parent of such individual, or (2) falsely represents to any person that he is an employee or agent of the

---

[14] See Vol. II, 18 U.S.C. 1028, with respect to penalties relating to use of identification documents.
[15] P.L. 83-591.
[16] See Vol. II, P.L. 83-591.
[17] P.L. 76-1.

614   SOCIAL SECURITY ACT—§ 1107(b)(cont)

United States, shall be deemed guilty of a felony and, upon conviction thereof, shall be punished by a fine not exceeding $10,000 for each recurrence of a violation or by imprisonment not exceeding 5 years or both.

ADDITIONAL GRANTS TO PUERTO RICO, THE VIRGIN ISLANDS, GUAM, AND AMERICAN SAMOA; LIMITATION ON TOTAL PAYMENTS

SEC. 1108. [42 U.S.C. 1308] (a) LIMITATION ON TOTAL PAYMENTS TO EACH TERRITORY.—

(1) IN GENERAL.—Notwithstanding any other provision of this Act (except for paragraph (2) of this subsection), the total amount certified by the Secretary of Health and Human Services under titles I, X, XIV, and XVI, under parts A and E of title IV, and under subsection (b) of this section, for payment to any territory for a fiscal year shall not exceed the ceiling amount for the territory for the fiscal year.

(2) CERTAIN PAYMENTS DISREGARDED.—Paragraph (1) of this subsection shall be applied without regard to any payment made under section 403(a)(2), 403(a)(4), 403(a)(5), 406, or 413(f).

(b) ENTITLEMENT TO MATCHING GRANT[18].—

(1) IN GENERAL.—Each territory shall be entitled to receive from the Secretary for each fiscal year a grant in an amount equal to 75 percent of the amount (if any) by which—

(A) the total expenditures of the territory during the fiscal year under the territory programs funded under parts A and E of title IV, including any amount paid to the State under part A of title IV that is transferred in accordance with section 404(d) and expended under the program to which transferred; exceeds

(B) the sum of—

(i) the amount of the family assistance grant payable to the territory without regard to section 409; and

(ii) the total amount expended by the territory during fiscal year 1995 pursuant to parts A and F of title IV (as so in effect), other than for child care.

(2) APPROPRIATION.—Out of any money in the Treasury of the United States not otherwise appropriated, there are appropriated for fiscal years 1997 through 2003, such sums as are necessary for grants under this paragraph.

(c) DEFINITIONS.—As used in this section:

(1) TERRITORY.—The term "territory" means Puerto Rico, the Virgin Islands, Guam, and American Samoa.

(2) CEILING AMOUNT.—The term "ceiling amount" means, with respect to a territory and a fiscal year, the mandatory ceiling amount with respect to the territory, reduced for the fiscal year in accordance with subsection (e), and reduced by the amount of any penalty imposed on the territory under any provision of law specified in subsection (a) during the fiscal year.

(3) FAMILY ASSISTANCE GRANT.—The term "family assistance grant" has the meaning given such term by section 403(a)(1)(B).

---

[18] See Vol. II, P.L. 109-171, §7101(a), with respect to the extension of the temporary assistance for needy families block grant program.

SOCIAL SECURITY ACT—§ 1108(f)(4)   615

(4) MANDATORY CEILING AMOUNT.—The term "mandatory ceiling amount" means—
 (A) $107,255,000 with respect to Puerto Rico;
 (B) $4,686,000 with respect to Guam;
 (C) $3,554,000 with respect to the Virgin Islands; and
 (D) $1,000,000 with respect to American Samoa.
(5) TOTAL AMOUNT EXPENDED BY THE TERRITORY.—The term "total amount expended by the territory"—
 (A) does not include expenditures during the fiscal year from amounts made available by the Federal Government; and
 (B) when used with respect to fiscal year 1995, also does not include—
  (i) expenditures during fiscal year 1995 under subsection (g) or (i) of section 402 (as in effect on September 30, 1995); or
  (ii) any expenditures during fiscal year 1995 for which the territory (but for section 1108, as in effect on September 30, 1995) would have received reimbursement from the Federal Government.
(d) AUTHORITY TO TRANSFER FUNDS TO CERTAIN PROGRAMS.—A territory to which an amount is paid under subsection (b) of this section may use the amount in accordance with section 404(d).
(e) [Stricken.[19]]
(f) Subject to subsection (g) and section 1935(a)(1)(B), the total amount certified by theSecretary under title XIX with respect to a fiscal year for payment to—
 (1) Puerto Rico shall not exceed (A) $116,500,000 for fiscal year 1994 and (B) for each succeeding fiscal year the amount provided in this paragraph for the preceding fiscal year increased by the percentage increase in the medical care component of the consumer price index for all urban consumers (as published by the Bureau of Labor Statistics) for the twelve-month period ending in March preceding the beginning of the fiscal year, rounded to the nearest $100,000;
 (2) the Virgin Islands shall not exceed (A) $3,837,500 for fiscal year 1994, and (B) for each succeeding fiscal year the amount provided in this paragraph for the preceding fiscal year increased by the percentage increase referred to in paragraph (1)(B), rounded to the nearest $10,000;
 (3) Guam shall not exceed (A) $3,685,000 for fiscal year 1994, and (B) for each succeeding fiscal year the amount provided in this paragraph for the preceding fiscal year increased by the percentage increase referred to in paragraph (1)(B), rounded to the nearest $10,000;
 (4) Northern Mariana Islands shall not exceed (A) $1,110,000 for fiscal year 1994, and (B) for each succeeding fiscal year the amount provided in this paragraph for the preceding fiscal year increased by the percentage increase referred to in paragraph (1)(B), rounded to the nearest $10,000; and

---

[19] P.L. 105-33, §5512(c); 111 Stat. 619.

616 SOCIAL SECURITY ACT—§ 1108(f)(5)

(5) American Samoa shall not exceed (A) $2,140,000 for fiscal year 1994, and (B) for each succeeding fiscal year the amount provided in this paragraph for the preceding fiscal year increased by the percentage increase referred to in paragraph (1)(B), rounded to the nearest $10,000.

(g) MEDICAID PAYMENTS TO TERRITORIES FOR FISCAL YEAR 1998 AND THEREAFTER.—

(1) FISCAL YEAR1998.—With respect to fiscal year 1998, the amounts otherwise determined for Puerto Rico, the Virgin Islands, Guam, the Northern Mariana Islands, and American Samoa under subsection (f) for such fiscal year shall be increased by the following amounts:

(A) For Puerto Rico, $30,000,000.

(B) For the Virgin Islands, $750,000.

(C) For Guam, $750,000.

(D) For the Northern Mariana Islands, $500,000.

(E) For American Samoa, $500,000.

(2) FISCAL YEAR 1999 AND THEREAFTER.—Notwithstanding subsection (f), and subject to paragraph (3).

(3) FISCAL YEARS 2006 AND 2007 FOR CERTAIN INSULAR AREAS—The amounts otherwise determined under this subsection for Puerto Rico, the Virgin Islands, Guam, the Northern Mariana Islands, and American Samoa for fiscal year 2006 and fiscal year 2007 shall be increased by the following amounts:

(A) For Puerto Rico, $12,000,000 for fiscal year 2006 and $12,000,000 for fiscal year 2007.

(B) For the Virgin Islands, $2,500,000 for fiscal year 2006 and $5,000,000 for fiscal year 2007.

(C) For Guam, $2,500,000 for fiscal year 2006 and $5,000,000 for fiscal year 2007.

(D) For the Northern Mariana Islands, $1,000,000 for fiscal year 2006 and $2,000,000 for fiscal year 2007.

(E) For American Samoa, $2,000,000 for fiscal year 2006 and $4,000,000 for fiscal year 2007.

Such amounts shall not be taken into account in applying paragraph (2) for fiscal year 2007 but shall be taken into account in applying such paragraph for fiscal year 2008 and subsequent fiscal years.

AMOUNTS DISREGARDED NOT TO BE TAKEN INTO ACCOUNT IN
DETERMINING ELIGIBILITY OF OTHER INDIVIDUALS

SEC. 1109. [42 U.S.C. 1309] Any amount which is disregarded (or set aside for future needs) in determining the eligibility of and amount of the aid or assistance for any individual under a State plan approved under title I, X, XIV, XVI, or XIX, shall not be taken into consideration in determining the eligibility of and amount of aid or assistance for any other individual under a State plan approved under any other of such titles.

SOCIAL SECURITY ACT—§ 1110(b)(1)

COOPERATIVE RESEARCH OR DEMONSTRATION PROJECTS[20]

SEC. 1110. [42 U.S.C. 1310] (a)(1) There are hereby authorized to be appropriated for the fiscal year ending June 30, 1957, $5,000,000 and for each fiscal year thereafter such sums as the Congress may determine for (A) making grants to States and public and other organizations and agencies for paying part of the cost of research or demonstration projects such as those relating to the prevention and reduction of dependency, or which will aid in effecting coordination of planning between private and public welfare agencies or which will help improve the administration and effectiveness of programs carried on or assisted under the Social Security Act and programs related thereto, and (B) making contracts or jointly financed cooperative arrangements with States and public and other organizations and agencies for the conduct of research or demonstration projects relating to such matters.

(2) No contract or jointly financed cooperative arrangement shall be entered into, and no grant shall be made, under paragraph (1), until the Secretary (or the Commissioner, with respect to any jointly financed cooperative agreement or grant concerning titles II or XVI) obtains the advice and recommendations of specialists who are competent to evaluate the proposed projects as to soundness of their design, the possibilities of securing productive results, the adequacy of resources to conduct the proposed research or demonstrations, and their relationship to other similar research or demonstrations already completed or in process.

(3) Grants and payments under contracts or cooperative arrangements under paragraph (1) may be made either in advance or by way of reimbursement, as may be determined by the Secretary (or the Commissioner, with respect to any jointly financed cooperative agreement or grant concerning title II or XVI); and shall be made in such installments and on such conditions as the Secretary (or the Commissioner, as applicable) finds necessary to carry out the purposes of this subsection.

(b)(1) The Commissioner is authorized to waive any of the requirements, conditions, or limitations of title XVI (or to waive them only for specified purposes, or to impose additional requirements, conditions, or limitations) to such extent and for such period as the Commissioner finds necessary to carry out one or more experimental, pilot, or demonstration projects which, in the Commissioner's judgment, are likely to assist in promoting the objectives or facilitate the administration of such title. Any costs for benefits under or administration of any such project (including planning for the project and the review and evaluation of the project and its results), in excess of those that would have been incurred without regard to the project, shall be met by the Commissioner from amounts available to the Commissioner for this purpose from appropriations made to carry out such title. The costs of any such project which is carried out in coordination with one or more related projects under other titles of this Act shall be allocated among the appropriations available for such projects and any Trust Funds involved, in a manner determined by the Commissioner with

---

[20] See Vol. II, P.L. 99-272, §9215, with respect to the extension of approval of certain Medicare municipal health services demonstration projects.

618 SOCIAL SECURITY ACT—§ 1110(b)(1)(cont)

respect to the old-age, survivors, and disability insurance programs under title II and the supplemental security income program under title XVI, and by the Secretary with respect to other titles of this Act, taking into consideration the programs (or types of benefit) to which the project (or part of a project) is most closely related or which the project (or part of a project) is intended to benefit. If, in order to carry out a project under this subsection, the Commissioner requests a State to make supplementary payments (or the Commissioner makes them pursuant to an agreement under section 1616) to individuals who are not eligible therefor, or in amounts or under circumstances in which the State does not make such payments, the Commissioner shall reimburse such State for the non-Federal share of such payments from amounts appropriated to carry out title XVI. If, in order to carry out a project under this subsection, the Secretary requests a State to provide medical assistance under its plan approved under title XIX to individuals who are not eligible therefor, or in amounts or under circumstances in which the State does not provide such medical assistance, the Secretary shall reimburse such State for the non-Federal share of such assistance from amounts appropriated to carry out title XVI, which shall be provided by the Commissioner to the Secretary for this purpose.

(2) With respect to the participation of recipients of supplemental security income benefits in experimental, pilot, or demonstration projects under this subsection—

(A) the Commissioner is not authorized to carry out any project that would result in a substantial reduction in any individual's total income and resources as a result of his or her participation in the project;

(B) the Commissioner may not require any individual to participate in a project; and the Commissioner shall assure (i) that the voluntary participation of individuals in any project is obtained through informed written consent which satisfies the requirements for informed consent established by the Commissioner for use in any experimental, pilot, or demonstration project in which human subjects are at risk, and (ii) that any individual's voluntary agreement to participate in any project may be revoked by such individual at any time;

(C) the Commissioner shall, to the extent feasible and appropriate, include recipients who are under age 18 as well as adult recipients; and

(D) the Commissioner shall include in the projects carried out under this section such experimental, pilot, or demonstration projects as may be necessary to ascertain the feasibility of treating alcoholics and drug addicts to prevent the onset of irreversible medical conditions which may result in permanent disability, including programs in residential care treatment centers.

(c)(1) In addition to the amount otherwise appropriated in any other law to carry out subsection (a) for fiscal year 2004, up to $8,500,000 is authorized and appropriated and shall be used by the Commissioner of Social Security under this subsection for purposes of conducting a statistically valid survey to determine how payments made to individuals, organizations, and State or local government agencies that are representative payees for benefits paid under title II or XVI are

SOCIAL SECURITY ACT—§ 1113(a)(3)   619

being managed and used on behalf of the beneficiaries for whom such benefits are paid.

(2) Not later than 18 months after the date of enactment of this subsection, the Commissioner of Social Security shall submit a report on the survey conducted in accordance with paragraph (1) to the Committee on Ways and Means of the House of Representatives and the Committee on Finance of the Senate.

PUBLIC ASSISTANCE PAYMENTS TO LEGAL REPRESENTATIVES

SEC. 1111. [42 U.S.C. 1311] For purposes of titles I, X, XIV, and XVI, and part A of title IV, payments on behalf of an individual, made to another person who has been judicially appointed, under the law of the State in which such individual resides, as legal representative of such individual for the purpose of receiving and managing such payments (whether or not he is such individual's legal representative for other purposes), shall be regarded as money payments to such individual.

MEDICAL CARE GUIDES AND REPORTS FOR PUBLIC ASSISTANCE AND
MEDICAL ASSISTANCE

SEC. 1112. [42 U.S.C. 1312] In order to assist the States to extend the scope and content, and improve the quality, of medical care and medical services for which payments are made to or on behalf of needy and low-income individuals under this Act and in order to promote better public understanding about medical care and medical assistance for needy and low-income individuals, the Secretary shall develop and revise from time to time guides or recommended standards as to the level, content, and quality of medical care and medical services for the use of the States in evaluating and improving their public assistance medical care programs and their programs of medical assistance; shall secure periodic reports from the States on items included in, and the quantity of, medical care and medical services for which expenditures under such programs are made; and shall from time to time publish data secured from these reports and other information necessary to carry out the purposes of this section.

ASSISTANCE FOR UNITED STATES CITIZENS RETURNED FROM FOREIGN
COUNTRIES

SEC. 1113. [42 U.S.C. 1313] (a)(1) The Secretary is authorized to provide temporary assistance to citizens of the United States and to dependents of citizens of the United States, if they (A) are identified by the Department of State as having returned, or been brought, from a foreign country to the United States because of the destitution of the citizen of the United States or the illness of such citizen or any of his dependents or because of war, threat of war, invasion, or similar crisis, and (B) are without available resources.

(2) Except in such cases or classes of cases as are set forth in regulations of the Secretary, provision shall be made for reimbursement to the United States by the recipients of the temporary assistance to cover the cost thereof.

(3) The Secretary may provide assistance under paragraph (1) directly or through utilization of the services and facilities of appropriate public or private agencies and organizations, in accordance with agreements providing for payment, in advance or by way of reimburse-

620 SOCIAL SECURITY ACT—§ 1113(a)(3)(cont)

ment, as may be determined by the Secretary, of the cost thereof. Such cost shall be determined by such statistical, sampling, or other method as may be provided in the agreement.

(b) The Secretary is authorized to develop plans and make arrangements for provision of temporary assistance within the United States to individuals specified in subsection (a)(1). Such plans shall be developed and such arrangements shall be made after consultation with the Secretary of State, the Attorney General, and the Secretary of Defense. To the extent feasible, assistance provided under subsection (a) shall be provided in accordance with the plans developed pursuant to this subsection, as modified from time to time by the Secretary.

(c) For purposes of this section, the term "temporary assistance" means money payments, medical care, temporary billeting, transportation, and other goods and services necessary for the health or welfare of individuals (including guidance, counseling, and other welfare services) furnished to them within the United States upon their arrival in the United States and for such period after their arrival, not exceeding ninety days, as may be provided in regulations of the Secretary; except that assistance under this section may be furnished beyond such ninety-day period in the case of any citizen or dependent upon a finding by the Secretary that the circumstances involved necessitate or justify the furnishing of assistance beyond such period in that particular case.

(d) The total amount of temporary assistance provided under this section shall not exceed $1,000,000 during any fiscal year beginning after September 30, 2003, except that, in the case of fiscal year 2006, the total amount of such assistance provided during that fiscal year shall not exceed $6,000000.

(e)(1) The Secretary may accept on behalf of the United States gifts, in cash or in kind, for use in carrying out the program established under this section. Gifts in the form of cash shall be credited to the appropriation account from which this program is funded, in addition to amounts otherwise appropriated, and shall remain available until expended.

(2) Gifts accepted under paragraph (1) shall be available for obligation or other use by the United States only to the extent and in the amounts provided in appropriation Acts.

APPOINTMENT OF ADVISORY COUNCIL AND OTHER ADVISORY GROUPS[21]

SEC. 1114. [42 U.S.C. 1314] (a) The Secretary shall, during 1964, appoint an Advisory Council on Public Welfare for the purpose of reviewing the administration of the public assistance and child welfare services programs for which funds are appropriated pursuant to this Act and making recommendations for improvement of such administration, and reviewing the status of and making recommendations with respect to the public assistance programs for which funds are so appropriated, especially in relation to the old-age, survivors, and disability insurance program, with respect to the fiscal capacities of the States and the Federal Government, and with respect to any other matters bearing on the amount and proportion of the Federal and

---

[21] See Vol. II, P.L. 92-463, §§2–15, approved October 6, 1972, with respect to provisions governing the operations of advisory committees.

See Vol. II, P.L. 103-432, §232, with respect to measurement and reporting of welfare receipt.

SOCIAL SECURITY ACT—§ 1114(h)(1)   621

State shares in the public assistance and child welfare services programs.

(b) The Council shall be appointed by the Secretary without regard to the provisions of title 5, United States Code, governing appointments in the competitive service and shall consist of twelve persons who shall, to the extent possible, be representatives of employers and employees in equal numbers, representatives of State or Federal agencies concerned with the administration or financing of the public assistance and child welfare services programs, representatives of nonprofit private organizations concerned with social welfare programs, other persons with special knowledge, experience, or qualifications with respect to such programs, and members of the public.

(c) The Council is authorized to engage such technical assistance as may be required to carry out its functions, and the Secretary shall, in addition, make available to the Council such secretarial, clerical, and other assistance and such pertinent data prepared by the Department of Health and Human Services as it may require to carry out such functions.

(d) The Council shall make a report of its findings and recommendations (including recommendations for changes in the provisions of the Social Security Act) to the Secretary, such report to be submitted not later than July 1, 1966, after which date such Council shall cease to exist.

(e) The Secretary shall also from time to time thereafter appoint an Advisory Council on Public Welfare, with the same functions and constituted in the same manner as prescribed for the Advisory Council in the preceding subsections of this section. Each Council so appointed shall report its findings and recommendations, as prescribed in subsection (d), not later than July 1 of the second year after the year in which it is appointed, after which date such Council shall cease to exist.

(f) The Secretary may also appoint, without regard to the provisions of title 5, United States Code, governing appointments in the competitive service, such advisory committees as he may deem advisable to advise and consult with him in carrying out any of his functions under this Act. The Secretary shall report to the Congress annually on the number of such committees and on the membership and activities of each such committee.

(g) Members of the Council or of any advisory committee appointed under this section who are not regular full-time employees of the United States shall, while serving on business of the Council or any such committee, be entitled to receive compensation at rates fixed by the Secretary, but not exceeding $75 per day, including travel time; and while so serving away from their homes or regular places of business, they may be allowed travel expenses, including per diem in lieu of subsistence, as authorized by section 5703 of title 5, United States Code[22], for persons in Government service employed intermittently.

(h)(1) Any member of the Council or any advisory committee appointed under this Act, who is not a regular full-time employee of the United States, is hereby exempted, with respect to such appointment, from the operation of sections 203, 205, and 209 of title 18, United

_____
[22] See Vol. II, 5 U.S.C. 5703.

622   SOCIAL SECURITY ACT—§ 1114(h)(1)(cont)

States Code[23], except as otherwise specified in paragraph (2) of this subsection.

(2) The exemption granted by paragraph (1) shall not extend—

(A) to the receipt or payment of salary in connection with the appointee's Government service from any source other than the employer of the appointee at the time of his appointment, or

(B) during the period of such appointment, to the prosecution or participation in the prosecution, by any person so appointed, of any claim against the Government involving any matter with which such person, during such period, is or was directly connected by reason of such appointment.

DEMONSTRATION PROJECTS

SEC. 1115. [42 U.S.C. 1315] (a) In the case of any experimental, pilot, or demonstration project which, in the judgment of the Secretary, is likely to assist in promoting the objectives of title I, X, XIV, XVI, or XIX, or part A or D of title IV, in a State or States—

(1) the Secretary may waive compliance with any of the requirements of section 2, 402, 454, 1002, 1402, 1602, or 1902, as the case may be, to the extent and for the period he finds necessary to enable such State or States to carry out such project, and

(2)(A) costs of such project which would not otherwise be included as expenditures under section 3, 455, 1003, 1403, 1603, or 1903, as the case may be, and which are not included as part of the costs of projects under section 1110, shall, to the extent and for the period prescribed by the Secretary, be regarded as expenditures under the State plan or plans approved under such title, or for administration of such State plan or plans, as may be appropriate, and

(B) costs of such project which would not otherwise be a permissable use of funds under part A of title IV and which are not included as part of the costs of projects under section 1110, shall to the extent and for the period prescribed by the Secretary, be regarded as a permissable use of funds under such part.

In addition, not to exceed $4,000,000 of the aggregate amount appropriated for payments to States under such titles for any fiscal year beginning after June 30, 1967, shall be available, under such terms and conditions as the Secretary may establish, for payments to States to cover so much of the cost of such projects as is not covered by payments under such titles and is not included as part of the cost of projects for purposes of section 1110.

(b) In the case of any experimental, pilot, or demonstration project undertaken under subsection (a) to assist in promoting the objectives of part D of title IV, the project—

(1) must be designed to improve the financial well-being of children or otherwise improve the operation of the child support program;

(2) may not permit modifications in the child support program which would have the effect of disadvantaging children in need of support; and

(3) must not result in increased cost to the Federal Government under part A of such title.

---

[23] See Vol. II, 18 U.S.C. 203, 205, and 209.

(c)(1)(A) The Secretary shall enter into agreements with up to 8 States submitting applications under this subsection for the purpose of conducting demonstration projects in such States to test and evaluate the use, with respect to individuals who received aid under part A of title IV in the preceding month (on the basis of the unemployment of the parent who is the principal earner), of a number greater than 100 for the number of hours per month that such individuals may work and still be considered to be unemployed for purposes of section 407. If any State submits an application under this subsection for the purpose of conducting a demonstration project to test and evaluate the total elimination of the 100-hour rule, the Secretary shall approve at least one such application.

(B) If any State with an agreement under this subsection so requests, the demonstration project conducted pursuant to such agreement may test and evaluate the complete elimination of the 100-hour rule and of any other durational standard that might be applied in defining unemployment for purposes of determining eligibility under section 407.

(2) Notwithstanding section 402(a)(1), a demonstration project conducted under this subsection may be conducted in one or more political subdivisions of the State.

(3) An agreement under this subsection shall be entered into between the Secretary and the State agency designated under section 402(a)(3). Such agreement shall provide for the payment of aid under the applicable State plan under part A of title IV as though section 407 had been modified to reflect the definition of unemployment used in the demonstration project but shall also provide that such project shall otherwise be carried out in accordance with all of the requirements and conditions of section 407 (and, except as provided in paragraph (2), any related requirements and conditions under part A of title IV).

(4) A demonstration project under this subsection may be commenced any time after September 30, 1990, and shall be conducted for such period of time as the agreement with the Secretary may provide; except that, in no event may a demonstration project under this section be conducted after September 30, 1995.

(5)(A) Any State with an agreement under this subsection shall evaluate the comparative cost and employment effects of the use of the definition of unemployment in its demonstration project under this section by use of experimental and control groups comprised of a random sample of individuals receiving aid under section 407 and shall furnish the Secretary with such information as the Secretary determines to be necessary to evaluate the results of the project conducted by the State.

(B) The Secretary shall report the results of the demonstration projects conducted under this subsection to the Congress not later than 6 months after all such projects are completed.

(e)(1)[24] The provisions of this subsection shall apply to the extension of any State-wide comprehensive demonstration project (in this subsection referred to as "waiver project") for which a waiver of compliance with requirements of title XIX is granted under subsection (a).

---

[24] As in original. P.L. 105-33, §4757, added subsection (e), effective August 5, 1997. No subsection (d) has been enacted.

624   SOCIAL SECURITY ACT—§ 1115(e)(2)

(2) During the 6-month period ending 1 year before the date the waiver under subsection (a) with respect to a waiver project would otherwise expire, the chief executive officer of the State which is operating the project may submit to the Secretary a written request for an extension, of up to 3 years, of the project.

(3) If the Secretary fails to respond to the request within 6 months after the date it is submitted, the request is deemed to have been granted.

(4) If such a request is granted, the deadline for submittal of a final report under the waiver project is deemed to have been extended until the date that is 1 year after the date the waiver project would otherwise have expired.

(5) The Secretary shall release an evaluation of each such project not later than 1 year after the date of receipt of the final report.

(6) Subject to paragraphs (4) and (7), the extension of a waiver project under this subsection shall be on the same terms and conditions (including applicable terms and conditions relating to quality and access of services, budget neutrality, data and reporting requirements, and special population protections) that applied to the project before its extension under this subsection.

(7) If an original condition of approval of a waiver project was that Federal expenditures under the project not exceed the Federal expenditures that would otherwise have been made, the Secretary shall take such steps as may be necessary to ensure that, in the extension of the project under this subsection, such condition continues to be met. In applying the previous sentence, the Secretary shall take into account the Secretary's best estimate of rates of change in expenditures at the time of the extension.

(f) An application by the chief executive officer of a State for an extension of a waiver project the State is operating under an extension under subsection (e) (in this subsection referred to as the "waiver project") shall be submitted and approved or disapproved in accordance with the following:

(1) The application for an extension of the waiver project shall be submitted to the Secretary at least 120 days prior to the expiration of the current period of the waiver project.

(2) Not later than 45 days after the date such application is received by the Secretary, the Secretary shall notify the State if the Secretary intends to review the terms and conditions of the waiver project. A failure to provide such notification shall be deemed to be an approval of the application.

(3) Not later than 45 days after the date a notification is made in accordance with paragraph (2), the Secretary shall inform the State of proposed changes in the terms and conditions of the waiver project. A failure to provide such information shall be deemed to be an approval of the application.

(4) During the 30-day period that begins on the date information described in paragraph (3) is provided to a State, the Secretary shall negotiate revised terms and conditions of the waiver project with the State.

(5)(A) Not later than 120 days after the date an application for an extension of the waiver project is submitted to the Secretary (or such later date agreed to by the chief executive officer of the State), the Secretary shall—

SOCIAL SECURITY ACT—§ 1116(a)(3)   625

(i) approve the application subject to such modifications in the terms and conditions—

(I) as have been agreed to by the Secretary and the State; or

(II) in the absence of such agreement, as are determined by the Secretary to be reasonable, consistent with the overall objectives of the waiver project, and not in violation of applicable law; or

(ii) disapprove the application.

(B) A failure by the Secretary to approve or disapprove an application submitted under this subsection in accordance with the requirements of subparagraph (A) shall be deemed to be an approval of the application subject to such modifications in the terms and conditions as have been agreed to (if any) by the Secretary and the State.

(6) An approval of an application for an extension of a waiver project under this subsection shall be for a period not to exceed 3 years.

(7) An extension of a waiver project under this subsection shall be subject to the final reporting and evaluation requirements of paragraphs (4) and (5) of subsection (e) (taking into account the extension under this subsection with respect to any timing requirements imposed under those paragraphs).

ADMINISTRATIVE AND JUDICIAL REVIEW OF CERTAIN ADMINISTRATIVE
DETERMINATIONS

SEC. 1116. [42 U.S.C. 1316] (a)(1) Whenever a State plan is submitted to the Secretary by a State for approval under title I, X, XIV, XVI, or XIX, he shall, not later than 90 days after the date the plan is submitted to him, make a determination as to whether it conforms to the requirements for approval under such title. The 90 day period provided herein may be extended by written agreement of the Secretary and the affected State.

(2) Any State dissatisfied with a determination of the Secretary under paragraph (1) with respect to any plan may, within 60 days after it has been notified of such determination, file a petition with the Secretary for reconsideration of the issue of whether such plan conforms to the requirements for approval under such title. Within 30 days after receipt of such a petition, the Secretary shall notify the State of the time and place at which a hearing will be held for the purpose of reconsidering such issue. Such hearing shall be held not less than 20 days nor more than 60 days after the date notice of such hearing is furnished to such State, unless the Secretary and such State agree in writing to holding the hearing at another time. The Secretary shall affirm, modify, or reverse his original determination within 60 days of the conclusion of the hearing.

(3) Any State which is dissatisfied with a final determination made by the Secretary on such a reconsideration or a final determination of the Secretary under section 4, 1004, 1404, 1604, or 1904 may, within 60 days after it has been notified of such determination, file with the United States court of appeals for the circuit in which such State is located a petition for review of such determination. A copy of the petition shall be forthwith transmitted by the clerk of the court to the Secretary. The Secretary thereupon shall file in the court the record

626 SOCIAL SECURITY ACT—§ 1116(a)(3)(cont)

of the proceedings on which he based his determination as provided in section 2112 of title 28, United States Code[25].

(4) The findings of fact by the Secretary, if supported by substantial evidence, shall be conclusive; but the court, for good cause shown, may remand the case to the Secretary to take further evidence, and the Secretary may thereupon make new or modified findings of fact and may modify his previous action, and shall certify to the court the transcript and record of the further proceedings. Such new or modified findings of fact shall likewise be conclusive if supported by substantial evidence.

(5) The court shall have jurisdiction to affirm the action of the Secretary or to set it aside, in whole or in part. The judgment of the court shall be subject to review by the Supreme Court of the United States upon certiorari or certification as provided in section 1254 of title 28, United States Code[26].

(b) For the purposes of subsection (a), any amendment of a State plan approved under title I, X, XIV, XVI, or XIX, may, at the option of the State, be treated as the submission of a new State plan.

(c) Action pursuant to an initial determination of the Secretary described in subsection (a) shall not be stayed pending reconsideration, but in the event that the Secretary subsequently determines that his initial determination was incorrect he shall certify restitution forthwith in a lump sum of any funds incorrectly withheld or otherwise denied.

(d) Whenever the Secretary determines that any item or class of items on account of which Federal financial participation is claimed under title I, X, XIV, XVI, [27] shall be disallowed for such participation, the State shall be entitled to and upon request shall receive a reconsideration of the disallowance.

(e)[28](1) Whenever the Secretary determines that any item or class of items on account of which Federal financial participation is claimed under title XIX shall be disallowed for such participation, the State shall be entitled to and upon request shall receive a reconsideration of the disallowance, provided that such request is made during the 60-day period that begins on the date the State receives notice of the disallowance.

(2)(A) A State may appeal a disallowance of a claim for federal financial participation under title XIX by the Secretary, or an unfavorable reconsideration of a disallowance, during the 60-day period that begins on the date the State receives notice of the disallowance or of the unfavorable reconsideration, in whole or in part, to the Departmental Appeals Board, established in the Department of Health and Human Services (in this paragraph referred to as the "Board"), by filing a notice of appeal with the Board.

(B) The Board shall consider a State's appeal of a disallowance of such a claim (or of an unfavorable reconsideration of a disallowance) on the basis of such documentation as the State may submit and as the Board may require to support

---

[25] See Vol. II, 28 U.S.C. 2112.
[26] See Vol. II, 28 U.S.C. 1254.
[27] P.L. 110-275, §204(b), struck out "or XIX," effective July 15, 2008.
[28] P.L. 110-275, §204(a), added subsection (e), effective July 15, 2008 and applicable to any disallowance of a claim for Federal financial participation under title XIX of the Social Security Act (42 U.S.C. 1396 et seq.) made on or after such date or during the 60-day period prior to such date.

the final decision of the Board. In deciding whether to uphold a disallowance of such a claim or any portion thereof, the Board shall be bound by all applicable laws and regulations and shall conduct a thorough review of the issues, taking into account all relevant evidence. The Board's decision of an appeal under subparagraph (A) shall be the final decision of the Secretary and shall be subject to reconsideration by the Board only upon motion of either party filed during the 60-day period that begins on the date of the Board's decision or to judicial review in accordance with subparagraph (C).

(C) A State may obtain judicial review of a decision of the Board by filing an action in any United States District Court located within the appealing State (or, if several States jointly appeal the disallowance of claims for Federal financial participation under section 1903, in any United States District Court that is located within any State that is a party to the appeal) or the United States District Court for the District of Columbia. Such an action may only be filed—

(i) if no motion for reconsideration was filed within the 60-day period specified in subparagraph (B), during such 60- day period; or

(ii) if such a motion was filed within such period, during the 60-day period that begins on the date of the Board's decision on such motion.

APPOINTMENT OF THE ADMINISTRATOR AND CHIEF ACTUARY OF THE
CENTERS FOR MEDICARE AND MEDICAID SERVICES

SEC. 1117. [42 U.S.C. 1317] (a) The Administrator of the Health Care Financing Administration shall be appointed by the President by and with the advice and consent of the Senate.

(b)(1) There is established in the Health Care Financing Administration the position of Chief Actuary. The Chief Actuary shall be appointed by, and in direct line of authority to, the Administrator of such Administration. The Chief Actuary shall be appointed from among individuals who have demonstrated, by their education and experience, superior expertise in the actuarial sciences. The Chief Actuary shall exercise such duties as are appropriate for the office of the Chief Actuary and in accordance with professional standards of actuarial independence. The Chief Actuary may be removed only for cause.

(2) The Chief Actuary shall be compensated at the highest rate of basic pay for the Senior Executive Service under section 5382(b) of title 5, United States Code[29].

(3) In the office of the Chief Actuary there shall be an actuary whose duties relate exclusively to the programs under parts C and D of title XVIII and related provisions of such title.

ALTERNATIVE FEDERAL PAYMENT WITH RESPECT TO PUBLIC ASSISTANCE
EXPENDITURES

SEC. 1118. [42 U.S.C. 1318] In the case of any State which has in effect a plan approved under title XIX for any calendar quarter, the total of the payments to which such State is entitled for such quarter, and for each succeeding quarter in the same fiscal year (which for

---

[29] See Vol. II, 5 U.S.C. 5382(b).

628 SOCIAL SECURITY ACT—§ 1118(cont)

purposes of this section means the 4 calendar quarters ending with September 30), under paragraphs (1) and (2) of sections 3(a), 1003(a), 1403(a), and 1603(a) shall, at the option of the State, be determined by application of the Federal medical assistance percentage (as defined in section 1905), instead of the percentages provided under each such section, to the expenditures under its State plans approved under titles I, X, XIV, and XVI, which would be included in determining the amounts of the Federal payments to which such State is entitled under such sections, but without regard to any maximum on the dollar amounts per recipient which may be counted under such sections. For purposes of the preceding sentence, the term "Federal medical assistance percentage" shall, in the case of Puerto Rico, the Virgin Islands, and Guam, mean 75 per centum.

FEDERAL PARTICIPATION IN PAYMENTS FOR REPAIRS TO HOME OWNED
BY RECIPIENT OF AID OR ASSISTANCE

SEC. 1119. [42 U.S.C. 1319] In the case of an expenditure for repairing the home owned by an individual who is receiving aid or assistance, other than medical assistance to the aged, under a State plan approved under title I, X, XIV, or XVI, if—

(1) the State agency or local agency administering the plan approved under such title has made a finding (prior to making such expenditure) that (A) such home is so defective that continued occupancy is unwarranted, (B) unless repairs are made to such home, rental quarters will be necessary for such individual, and (C) the cost of rental quarters to take care of the needs of such individual (including his spouse living with him in such home and any other individual whose needs were taken into account in determining the need of such individual) would exceed (over such time as the Secretary may specify) the cost of repairs needed to make such home habitable together with other costs attributable to continued occupancy of such home, and

(2) no such expenditures were made for repairing such home pursuant to any prior finding under this section,

the amount paid to any such State for any quarter under section 3(a), 1003(a), 1403(a), or 1603(a) shall be increased by 50 per centum of such expenditures, except that the excess above $500 expended with respect to any one home shall not be included in determining such expenditures.

APPROVAL OF CERTAIN PROJECTS

SEC. 1120. [42 U.S.C. 1320] No payment shall be made under this Act with respect to any experimental, pilot, demonstration, or other project all or any part of which is wholly financed with Federal funds made available under this Act (without any State, local, or other non-Federal financial participation) unless such project shall have been personally approved by the Secretary or Under Secretary of Health and Human Services.

UNIFORM REPORTING SYSTEMS FOR HEALTH SERVICES FACILITIES AND
ORGANIZATIONS

SEC. 1121. [42 U.S.C. 1320a] (a) For the purposes of reporting the cost of services provided by, of planning, and of measuring and comparing the efficiency of and effective use of services in, hospitals,

SOCIAL SECURITY ACT—§ 1122(a) 629

skilled nursing facilities, intermediate care facilities, home health agencies, health maintenance organizations, and other types of health services facilities and organizations to which payment may be made under this Act, the Secretary shall establish by regulation, for each such type of health services facility or organization, a uniform system for the reporting by a facility or organization of that type of the following information:

(1) The aggregate cost of operation and the aggregate volume of services.

(2) The costs and volume of services for various functional accounts and subaccounts.

(3) Rates, by category of patient and class of purchaser.

(4) Capital assets, as defined by the Secretary, including (as appropriate) capital funds, debt service, lease agreements used in lieu of capital funds, and the value of land, facilities, and equipment.

(5) Discharge and bill data.

The uniform reporting system for a type of health services facility or organization shall provide for appropriate variation in the application of the system to different classes of facilities or organizations within that type and shall be established, to the extent practicable, consistent with the cooperative system for producing comparable and uniform health information and statistics described in section 306(e)(1) of the Public Health Service Act[30]. In reporting under such a system, hospitals shall employ such chart of accounts, definitions, principles, and statistics as the Secretary may prescribe in order to reach a uniform reconciliation of financial and statistical data for specified uniform reports to be provided to the Secretary.

(b) The Secretary shall—

(1) monitor the operation of the systems established under subsection (a);

(2) assist with and support demonstrations and evaluations of the effectiveness and cost of the operation of such systems and encourage State adoption of such systems; and

(3) periodically revise such systems to improve their effectiveness and diminish their cost.

(c) The Secretary shall provide information obtained through use of the uniform reporting systems described in subsection (a) in a useful manner and format to appropriate agencies and organizations, including health systems agencies (designated under section 1515 of the Public Health Service Act) and State health planning and development agencies (designated under section 1521 of such Act), as may be necessary to carry out such agencies' and organizations' functions.

LIMITATION ON FEDERAL PARTICIPATION FOR CAPITAL EXPENDITURES

SEC. 1122. [42 U.S.C. 1320a–1] (a) The purpose of this section is to assure that Federal funds appropriated under titles XVIII and XIX are not used to support unnecessary capital expenditures made by or on behalf of health care facilities which are reimbursed under any of such titles and that, to the extent possible, reimbursement under such titles shall support planning activities with respect to health services and facilities in the various States.

---

[30] See Vol. II, P.L. 78-410, §306 (e)(1).

630   SOCIAL SECURITY ACT—§ 1122(a)(cont)

(b) The Secretary, after consultation with the Governor (or other chief executive officer) and with appropriate local public officials, shall make an agreement with any State which is able and willing to do so under which a designated planning agency (which shall be an agency described in clause (ii) of subsection (d)(1)(B) that has a governing body or advisory board at least half of whose members represent consumer interests) will—

(1) make, and submit to the Secretary together with such supporting materials as he may find necessary, findings and recommendations with respect to capital expenditures proposed by or on behalf of any health care facility in such State within the field of its responsibilities,

(2) receive from other agencies described in clause (ii) of subsection (d)(1)(B), and submit to the Secretary together with such supporting material as he may find necessary, the findings and recommendations of such other agencies with respect to capital expenditures proposed by or on behalf of health care facilities in such State within the fields of their respective responsibilities, and

(3) establish and maintain procedures pursuant to which a person proposing any such capital expenditure may appeal a recommendation by the designated agency and will be granted an opportunity for a fair hearing by such agency or person other than the designated agency as the Governor (or other chief executive officer) may designate to hold such hearings,

whenever and to the extent that the findings of such designated agency or any such other agency indicate that any such expenditure is not consistent with the standards, criteria, or plans developed pursuant to the Public Health Service Act[31] to meet the need for adequate health care facilities in the area covered by the plan or plans so developed.

(c) The Secretary shall pay any such State from the general fund in the Treasury, in advance or by way of reimbursement as may be provided in the agreement with it (and may make adjustments in such payments on account of overpayments or underpayments previously made), for the reasonable cost of performing the functions specified in subsection (b).

(d)(1) Except as provided in paragraph (2), if the Secretary determines that—

(A) neither the planning agency designated in the agreement described in subsection (b) nor an agency described in clause (ii) of subparagraph (B) of this paragraph had been given notice of any proposed capital expenditure (in accordance with such procedure or in such detail as may be required by such agency) at least 60 days prior to obligation for such expenditure; or

(B)(i) the planning agency so designated or an agency so described had received such timely notice of the intention to make such capital expenditure and had, within a reasonable period after receiving such notice and prior to obligation for such expenditure, notified the person proposing such expenditure that the expenditure would not be in conformity with the standards, criteria, or plans developed by such agency or any other agency described

---

[31] P.L. 78-410.

SOCIAL SECURITY ACT—§ 1122(e) 631

in clause (ii) for adequate health care facilities in such State or in the area for which such other agency has responsibility, and

(ii) the planning agency so designated had, prior to submitting to the Secretary the findings referred to in subsection (b)—

(I) consulted with, and taken into consideration the findings and recommendations of, the State planning agencies established pursuant to sections 314(a) and 604(a) of the Public Health Service Act[32] (to the extent that either such agency is not the agency so designated) as well as the public or nonprofit private agency or organization responsible for the comprehensive regional, metropolitan area, or other local area plan or plans referred to in section 314(b) of the Public Health Service Act and covering the area in which the health care facility proposing such capital expenditure is located (where such agency is not the agency designated in the agreement), or, if there is no such agency, such other public or nonprofit private agency or organization (if any) as performs, as determined in accordance with criteria included in regulations, similar functions, and

(II) granted to the person proposing such capital expenditure an opportunity for a fair hearing with respect to such findings;

then, for such period as he finds necessary in any case to effectuate the purpose of this section, he shall, in determining the Federal payments to be made under titles XVIII and XIX with respect to services furnished in the health care facility for which such capital expenditure is made, not include any amount which is attributable to depreciation, interest on borrowed funds, a return on equity capital (in the case of proprietary facilities), or other expenses related to such capital expenditure. With respect to any organization which is reimbursed on a per capita or a fixed fee or negotiated rate basis, in determining the Federal payments to be made under titles XVIII and XIX, the Secretary shall exclude an amount which in his judgment is a reasonable equivalent to the amount which would otherwise be excluded under this subsection if payment were to be made on other than a per capita or a fixed fee or negotiated rate basis.

(2) If the Secretary, after submitting the matters involved to the advisory council established or designated under subsection (i), determines that an exclusion of expenses related to any capital expenditure of any health care facility would discourage the operation or expansion of such facility which has demonstrated to his satisfaction proof of capability to provide comprehensive health care services (including institutional services) efficiently, effectively, and economically, or would otherwise be inconsistent with the effective organization and delivery of health services or the effective administration of title XVIII or XIX, he shall not exclude such expenses pursuant to paragraph (1).

(e) Where a person obtains under lease or comparable arrangement any facility or part thereof, or equipment for a facility, which would have been subject to an exclusion under subsection (d) if the person had acquired it by purchase, the Secretary shall (1) in computing such person's rental expense in determining the Federal payments to be made under titles XVIII and XIX with respect to services furnished in

---

[32] See Vol. II, P.L. 78-410, §§314(a) and 604(a).

632 SOCIAL SECURITY ACT—§ 1122(e)(cont)

such facility, deduct the amount which in his judgment is a reasonable equivalent of the amount that would have been excluded if the person had acquired such facility or such equipment by purchase, and (2) in computing such person's return on equity capital deduct any amount deposited under the terms of the lease or comparable arrangement.

(f) Any person dissatisfied with a determination by the Secretary under this section may within six months following notification of such determination request the Secretary to reconsider such determination. A determination by the Secretary under this section shall not be subject to administrative or judicial review.

(g) For the purposes of this section, a "capital expenditure" is an expenditure which, under generally accepted accounting principles, is not properly chargeable as an expense of operation and maintenance and which (1) exceeds $600,000 (or such lesser amount as the State may establish), (2) changes the bed capacity of the facility with respect to which such expenditure is made, or (3) substantially changes the services of the facility with respect to which such expenditure is made. For purposes of clause (1) of the preceding sentence, the cost of the studies, surveys, designs, plans, working drawings, specifications, and other activities essential to the acquisition, improvement, expansion, or replacement of the plant and equipment with respect to which such expenditure is made shall be included in determining whether such expenditure exceeds the dollar amount specified in clause (1).

(h) The provisions of this section shall not apply to a religious non-medical health care institution (as defined in section 1861(ss)(1)).

(i)(1) The Secretary shall establish a national advisory council, or designate an appropriate existing national advisory council, to advise and assist him in the preparation of general regulations to carry out the purposes of this section and on policy matters arising in the administration of this section, including the coordination of activities under this section with those under other parts of this Act or under other Federal or federally assisted health programs.

(2) The Secretary shall make appropriate provision for consultation between and coordination of the work of the advisory council established or designated under paragraph (1) and the Federal Hospital Council, the National Advisory Health Council, the Health Insurance Benefits Advisory Council, and other appropriate national advisory councils with respect to matters bearing on the purposes and administration of this section and the coordination of activities under this section with related Federal health programs.

(3) If an advisory council is established by the Secretary under paragraph (1), it shall be composed of members who are not otherwise in the regular full-time employ of the United States, and who shall be appointed by the Secretary without regard to the civil service laws from among leaders in the fields of the fundamental sciences, the medical sciences, and the organization, delivery, and financing of health care, and persons who are State or local officials or are active in community affairs or public or civic affairs or who are representative of minority groups. Members of such advisory council, while attending meetings of the council or otherwise serving on business of the council, shall be entitled to receive compensation at rates fixed by the Secretary, but not exceeding the maximum rate specified at the time of such service for grade GS-18 in section 5332 of title 5, United States Code, including traveltime, and while away from their homes or regular places of

SOCIAL SECURITY ACT—§ 1123A(b)   633

business they may also be allowed travel expenses, including per diem in lieu of subsistence, as authorized by section 5703 of such title 5[33] for persons in the Government service employed intermittently.

(j) A capital expenditure made by or on behalf of a health care facility shall not be subject to review pursuant to this section if 75 percent of the patients who can reasonably be expected to use the service with respect to which the capital expenditure is made will be individuals enrolled in an eligible organization as defined in section 1876(b), and if the Secretary determines that such capital expenditure is for services and facilities which are needed by such organization in order to operate efficiently and economically and which are not otherwise readily accessible to such organization because—

(1) the facilities do not provide common services at the same site (as usually provided by the organization),

(2) the facilities are not available under a contract of reasonable duration,

(3) full and equal medical staff privileges in the facilities are not available,

(4) arrangements with such facilities are not administratively feasible, or

(5) the purchase of such services is more costly than if the organization provided the services directly.

EFFECT OF FAILURE TO CARRY OUT STATE PLAN

SEC. 1123. [42 U.S.C. 1320a–2] In an action brought to enforce a provision of the Social Security Act, such provision is not to be deemed unenforceable because of its inclusion in a section of the Act requiring a State plan or specifying the required contents of a State plan. This section is not intended to limit or expand the grounds for determining the availability of private actions to enforce State plan requirements other than by overturning any such grounds applied in Suter v. Artist M., 112 S. Ct. 1360 (1992), but not applied in prior Supreme Court decisions respecting such enforceability: *Provided*, however, That this section is not intended to alter the holding in Suter v. Artist M. that section 471(a)(15) of the Act is not enforceable in a private right of action.

REVIEWS OF CHILD AND FAMILY SERVICES PROGRAMS, AND OF FOSTER CARE AND ADOPTION ASSISTANCE PROGRAMS, FOR CONFORMITY WITH STATE PLAN REQUIREMENTS

SEC. 1123A. [42 U.S.C. 1320a–1a] (a) IN GENERAL.—The Secretary, in consultation with the State agencies administering the State programs under parts B and E of title IV, shall promulgate regulations for the review of such programs to determine whether such programs are in substantial conformity with—

(1) State plan requirements under such parts B and E,

(2) implementing regulations promulgated by the Secretary, and

(3) the relevant approved State plans.

(b) ELEMENTS OF REVIEW SYSTEM.—The regulations referred to in subsection (a) shall—

---

[33] See Vol. II, 5 U.S.C. 5703.

634 SOCIAL SECURITY ACT—§ 1123A(b)(1)

(1) specify the timetable for conformity reviews of State programs, including—

(A) an initial review of each State program;

(B) a timely review of a State program following a review in which such program was found not to be in substantial conformity; and

(C) less frequent reviews of State programs which have been found to be in substantial conformity, but such regulations shall permit the Secretary to reinstate more frequent reviews based on information which indicates that a State program may not be in conformity;

(2) specify the requirements subject to review (which shall include determining whether the State program is in conformity with the requirement of section 471(a)(27)), and the criteria to be used to measure conformity with such requirements and to determine whether there is a substantial failure to so conform;

(3) specify the method to be used to determine the amount of any Federal matching funds to be withheld (subject to paragraph (4)) due to the State program's failure to so conform, which ensures that—

(A) such funds will not be withheld with respect to a program, unless it is determined that the program fails substantially to so conform;

(B) such funds will not be withheld for a failure to so conform resulting from the State's reliance upon and correct use of formal written statements of Federal law or policy provided to the State by the Secretary; and

(C) the amount of such funds withheld is related to the extent of the failure to so conform; and

(4) require the Secretary, with respect to any State program found to have failed substantially to so conform—

(A) to afford the State an opportunity to adopt and implement a corrective action plan, approved by the Secretary, designed to end the failure to so conform;

(B) to make technical assistance available to the State to the extent feasible to enable the State to develop and implement such a corrective action plan;

(C) to suspend the withholding of any Federal matching funds under this section while such a corrective action plan is in effect; and

(D) to rescind any such withholding if the failure to so conform is ended by successful completion of such a corrective action plan.

(c) PROVISIONS FOR ADMINISTRATIVE AND JUDICIAL REVIEW.—The regulations referred to in subsection (a) shall—

(1) require the Secretary, not later than 10 days after a final determination that a program of the State is not in conformity, to notify the State of—

(A) the basis for the determination; and

(B) the amount of the Federal matching funds (if any) to be withheld from the State;

(2) afford the State an opportunity to appeal the determination to the Departmental Appeals Board within 60 days after receipt

SOCIAL SECURITY ACT—§ 1124(a)(2)(C)   635

of the notice described in paragraph (1), (or, if later after failure to continue or to complete a corrective action plan); and

(3) afford the State an opportunity to obtain judicial review of an adverse decision of the Board, within 60 days after the State receives notice of the decision of the Board, by appeal to the district court of the United States for the judicial district in which the principal or headquarters office of the agency responsible for administering the program is located.

DISCLOSURE OF OWNERSHIP AND RELATED INFORMATION[34]

SEC. 1124. [42 U.S.C. 1320a–3] (a)(1) The Secretary shall by regulation or by contract provision provide that each disclosing entity (as defined in paragraph (2)) shall—

(A) as a condition of the disclosing entity's participation in, or certification or recertification under, any of the programs established by titles V, XVIII, and XIX, or

(B) as a condition for the approval or renewal of a contract or agreement between the disclosing entity and the Secretary or the appropriate State agency under any of the programs established under titles V, XVIII, and XIX,

supply the Secretary or the appropriate State agency with full and complete information as to the identity of each person with an ownership or control interest (as defined in paragraph (3)) in the entity or in any subcontractor (as defined by the Secretary in regulations) in which the entity directly or indirectly has a 5 per centum or more ownership interest and supply the Secretary with the[35] both the employer identification number (assigned pursuant to section 6109 of the Internal Revenue Code of 1986[36]) and social security account number (assigned under section 205(c)(2)(B)) of the disclosing entity, each person with an ownership or control interest (as defined in subsection (a)(3)), and any subcontractor in which the entity directly or indirectly has a 5 percent or more ownership interest.

(2) As used in this section, the term "disclosing entity" means an entity which is—

(A) a provider of services (as defined in section 1861(u), other than a fund), an independent clinical laboratory, a renal disease facility, a managed care entity, as defined in section 1932(a)(1)(B), or a health maintenance organization (as defined in section 1301(a) of the Public Health Service Act[37]);

(B) an entity (other than an individual practitioner or group of practitioners) that furnishes, or arranges for the furnishing of, items or services with respect to which payment may be claimed by the entity under any plan or program established pursuant to title V or under a State plan approved under title XIX; or

(C) a carrier or other agency or organization that is acting as a fiscal intermediary or agent with respect to one or more providers of services (for purposes of part A or part B of title XVIII, or both, or for purposes of a State plan approved under title XIX) pursuant to (i) an agreement under section 1816, (ii) a contract un-

---

[34] See Vol. II, P.L. 78-410, §1318, with respect to financial disclosure by health maintenance organizations.
[35] As in original. The word "the" probably should not appear.
[36] See Vol. II, P.L. 83-591, §6109.
[37] See Vol. II, P.L. 78-410, §1301(a).

636   SOCIAL SECURITY ACT—§ 1124(a)(2)(C)(cont)

der section 1842, or (iii) an agreement with a single State agency administering or supervising the administration of a State plan approved under title XIX.

(3) As used in this section, the term "person with an ownership or control interest" means, with respect to an entity, a person who—

(A)(i) has directly or indirectly (as determined by the Secretary in regulations) an ownership interest of 5 per centum or more in the entity; or

(ii) is the owner of a whole or part interest in any mortgage, deed of trust, note, or other obligation secured (in whole or in part) by the entity or any of the property or assets thereof, which whole or part interest is equal to or exceeds 5 per centum of the total property and assets of the entity; or

(B) is an officer or director of the entity, if the entity is organized as a corporation; or

(C) is a partner in the entity, if the entity is organized as a partnership.

(b) To the extent determined to be feasible under regulations of the Secretary, a disclosing entity shall also include in the information supplied under subsection (a)(1), with respect to each person with an ownership or control interest in the entity, the name of any other disclosing entity with respect to which the person is a person with an ownership or control interest.

DISCLOSURE REQUIREMENTS FOR OTHER PROVIDERS UNDER PART B OF MEDICARE

SEC. 1124A. [42 U.S.C. 1320a–3a] (a) DISCLOSURE REQUIRED TO RECEIVE PAYMENT.—No payment may be made under part B of title XVIII for items or services furnished by any disclosing part B provider unless such provider has provided the Secretary with full and complete information—

(1) on the identity of each person with an ownership or control interest in the provider or in any subcontractor (as defined by the Secretary in regulations) in which the provider directly or indirectly has a 5 percent or more ownership interest;

(2) with respect to any person identified under paragraph (1) or any managing employee of the provider—

(A) on the identity of any other entities providing items or services for which payment may be made under title XVIII with respect to which such person or managing employee is a person with an ownership or control interest at the time such information is supplied or at any time during the 3-year period ending on the date such information is supplied, and

(B) as to whether any penalties, assessments, or exclusions have been assessed against such person or managing employee under section 1128, 1128A, or 1128B; and

(3) including the employer identification number (assigned pursuant to section 6109 of the Internal Revenue Code of 1986[38]) and social security account number (assigned under section 205(c)(2)(B)) of the disclosing part B provider and any person, managing employee, or other entity identified or described under paragraph (1) or (2).

---

[38] See Vol. II, P.L. 83-591, §6109.

SOCIAL SECURITY ACT—§ 1125(a) 637

(b) UPDATES TO INFORMATION SUPPLIED.—A disclosing part B provider shall notify the Secretary of any changes or updates to the information supplied under subsection (a) not later than 180 days after such changes or updates take effect.

(c) VERIFICATION.—

(1) TRANSMITTAL BY HHS.—The Secretary shall transmit—

(A) to the Commissioner of Social Security information concerning each social security account number (assigned under section 205(c)(2)(B)), and

(B) to the Secretary of the Treasury information concerning each employer identification number (assigned pursuant to section 6109 of the Internal Revenue Code of 1986),

supplied to the Secretary pursuant to subsection (a)(3) or section 1124(c) to the extent necessary for verification of such information in accordance with paragraph (2).

(2) VERIFICATION.—The Commissioner of Social Security and the Secretary of the Treasury shall verify the accuracy of, or correct, the information supplied by the Secretary to such official pursuant to paragraph (1), and shall report such verifications or corrections to the Secretary.

(3) FEES FOR VERIFICATION.—The Secretary shall reimburse the Commissioner and Secretary of the Treasury, at a rate negotiated between the Secretary and such official, for the costs incurred by such official in performing the verification and correction services described in this subsection.

(d) DEFINITIONS.—FOR PURPOSES OF THIS SECTION—

(1) the term "disclosing part B provider" means any entity receiving payment on an assignment-related basis (or, for purposes of subsection (a)(3), any entity receiving payment) for furnishing items or services for which payment may be made under part B of title XVIII, except that such term does not include an entity described in section 1124(a)(2);

(2) the term "managing employee" means, with respect to a provider, a person described in section 1126(b); and

(3) the term "person with an ownership or control interest" means, with respect to a provider—

(A) a person described in section 1124(a)(3), or

(B) a person who has one of the 5 largest direct or indirect ownership or control interests in the provider.

ISSUANCE OF SUBPENAS BY COMPTROLLER GENERAL

SEC. 1125. [42 U.S.C. 1320a–4] (a) For the purpose of any audit, investigation, examination, analysis, review, evaluation, or other function authorized by law with respect to any program authorized under this Act, the Comptroller General of the United States shall have power to sign and issue subpenas to any person requiring the production of any pertinent books, records, documents, or other information. Subpenas so issued by the Comptroller General shall be served by anyone authorized by him (1) by delivering a copy thereof to the person named therein, or (2) by registered mail or by certified mail addressed to such person at his last dwelling place or principal place of business. A verified return by the person so serving the subpena setting forth the manner of service, or, in the case of service by registered mail or

638 SOCIAL SECURITY ACT—§ 1125(a)(cont)

by certified mail, the return post office receipt therefor signed by the person so served, shall be proof of service.

(b) In case of contumacy by, or refusal to obey a subpena issued pursuant to subsection (a) of this section and duly served upon, any person, any district court of the United States for the judicial district in which such person charged with contumacy or refusal to obey is found or resides or transacts business, upon application by the Comptroller General, shall have jurisdiction to issue an order requiring such person to produce the books, records, documents, or other information sought by the subpena; and any failure to obey such order of the court may be punished by the court as a contempt thereof. In proceedings brought under this subsection, the Comptroller General shall be represented by attorneys employed in the General Accounting Office[39] or by counsel whom he may employ without regard to the provisions of title 5, United States Code, governing appointments in the competitive service, and the provisions of chapter 51 and subchapters III and VI of chapter 53 of such title, relating to classification and General Schedule pay rates.

(c) No personal medical record in the possession of the General Accounting Office shall be subject to subpena or discovery proceedings in a civil action.

DISCLOSURE BY INSTITUTIONS, ORGANIZATIONS, AND AGENCIES OF OWNERS AND CERTAIN OTHER INDIVIDUALS WHO HAVE BEEN CONVICTED OF CERTAIN OFFENSES

SEC. 1126. [42 U.S.C. 1320a–5] (a) As a condition of participation in or certification or recertification under the programs established by titles XVIII, and XIX, any hospital, nursing facility, or other entity (other than an individual practitioner or group of practitioners) shall be required to disclose to the Secretary or to the appropriate State agency the name of any person that is a person described in subparagraphs (A) and (B) of section 1128(b)(8). The Secretary or the appropriate State agency shall promptly notify the Inspector General in the Department of Health and Human Services of the receipt from any entity of any application or request for such participation, certification, or recertification which discloses the name of any such person, and shall notify the Inspector General of the action taken with respect to such application or request.

(b) For the purposes of this section, the term "managing employee" means, with respect to an entity, an individual, including a general manager, business manager, administrator, and director, who exercises operational or managerial control over the entity, or who directly or indirectly conducts the day-to-day operations of the entity.

ADJUSTMENTS IN SSI BENEFITS ON ACCOUNT OF RETROACTIVE BENEFITS UNDER TITLE II

SEC. 1127. [42 U.S.C. 1320a–6] (a) Notwithstanding any other provision of this Act, in any case where an individual—

(1) is entitled to benefits under title II that were not paid in the months in which they were regularly due; and

---

[39] P.L. 108-271, §8(b), provided that "Any reference to the General Accounting Office in any law, rule, regulation, certificate, directive, instruction, or other official paper in force on the date of enactment of this Act (July 7, 2004) shall be considered to refer and apply to the Government Accountability Office."

SOCIAL SECURITY ACT—§ 1128(a)(3) 639

(2) is an individual or eligible spouse eligible for supplemental security income benefits for one or more months in which the benefits referred to in clause (1) were regularly due,

then any benefits under title II that were regularly due in such month or months, or supplemental security income benefits for such month or months, which are due but have not been paid to such individual or eligible spouse shall be reduced by an amount equal to so much of the supplemental security income benefits, whether or not paid retroactively, as would not have been paid or would not be paid with respect to such individual or spouse if he had received such benefits under title II in the month or months in which they were regularly due. A benefit under title II shall not be reduced pursuant to the preceding sentence to the extent that any amount of such benefit would not otherwise be available for payment in full of the maximum fee which may be recovered from such benefit by an attorney pursuant to subsection (a)(4) or (b) of section 206.

(b) For purposes of this section, the term "supplemental security income benefits" means benefits paid or payable by the Commissioner of Social Security under title XVI, including State supplementary payments under an agreement pursuant to section 1616(a) or an administration agreement under section 212(b) of Public Law 93-66[40].

(c) From the amount of the reduction made under subsection (a), the Commissioner of Social Security shall reimburse the State on behalf of which supplementary payments were made for the amount (if any) by which such State's expenditures on account of such supplementary payments for the month or months involved exceeded the expenditures which the State would have made (for such month or months) if the individual had received the benefits under title II at the times they were regularly due. An amount equal to the portion of such reduction remaining after reimbursement of the State under the preceding sentence shall be covered into the general fund of the Treasury.

EXCLUSION OF CERTAIN INDIVIDUALS AND ENTITIES FROM
PARTICIPATION IN MEDICARE AND STATE HEALTH CARE PROGRAMS

SEC. 1128. [42 U.S.C. 1320a–7] (a) MANDATORY EXCLUSION.—The Secretary shall exclude the following individuals and entities from participation in any Federal health care program (as defined in section 1128B(f)):

(1) Conviction of program-related crimes.—Any individual or entity that has been convicted of a criminal offense related to the delivery of an item or service under title XVIII or under any State health care program.

(2) Conviction relating to patient abuse.—Any individual or entity that has been convicted, under Federal or State law, of a criminal offense relating to neglect or abuse of patients in connection with the delivery of a health care item or service.

(3) FELONY CONVICTION RELATING TO HEALTH CARE FRAUD.—Any individual or entity that has been convicted for an offense which occurred after the date of the enactment of the Health Insurance Portability and Accountability Act of 1996[41],

---

[40] See Vol. II, P.L. 93-66, §212(b).
[41] August 21, 1996 [P.L. 104-191; 110 Stat.1936].

640 SOCIAL SECURITY ACT—§ 1128(a)(4)

under Federal or State law, in connection with the delivery of a health care item or service or with respect to any act or omission in a health care program (other than those specifically described in paragraph (1)) operated by or financed in whole or in part by any Federal, State, or local government agency, of a criminal offense consisting of a felony relating to fraud, theft, embezzlement, breach of fiduciary responsibility, or other financial misconduct.

(4) FELONY CONVICTION RELATING TO CONTROLLED SUBSTANCE.—Any individual or entity that has been convicted for an offense which occurred after the date of the enactment of the Health Insurance Portability and Accountability Act of 1996, under Federal or State law, of a criminal offense consisting of a felony relating to the unlawful manufacture, distribution, prescription, or dispensing of a controlled substance.

(b) PERMISSIVE EXCLUSION.—The Secretary may exclude the following individuals and entities from participation in any Federal health care program (as defined in section 1128B(f)):

(1) CONVICTION RELATING TO FRAUD.—Any individual or entity that has been convicted for an offense which occurred after the date of the enactment of the Health Insurance Portability and Accountability Act of 1996, under Federal or State law—

(A) of a criminal offense consisting of a misdemeanor relating to fraud, theft, embezzlement, breach of fiduciary responsibility, or other financial misconduct—

(i) in connection with the delivery of a health care item or service, or

(ii) with respect to any act or omission in a health care program (other than those specifically described in subsection (a)(1)) operated by or financed in whole or in part by any Federal, State, or local government agency; or

(B) of a criminal offense relating to fraud, theft, embezzlement, breach of fiduciary responsibility, or other financial misconduct with respect to any act or omission in a program (other than a health care program) operated by or financed in whole or in part by any Federal, State, or local government agency.

(2) Conviction relating to obstruction of an investigation.—Any individual or entity that has been convicted, under Federal or State law, in connection with the interference with or obstruction of any investigation into any criminal offense described in paragraph (1) or in subsection (a).

(3) Misdemeanor conviction relating to controlled substance.—Any individual or entity that has been convicted, under Federal or State law, of a criminal offense consisting of a misdemeanor relating to the unlawful manufacture, distribution, prescription, or dispensing of a controlled substance.

(4) LICENSE REVOCATION OR SUSPENSION.—ANY INDIVIDUAL OR ENTITY—

(A) whose license to provide health care has been revoked or suspended by any State licensing authority, or who otherwise lost such a license or the right to apply for or renew such a license, for reasons bearing on the individual's or entity's professional competence, professional performance, or financial integrity, or

(B) who surrendered such a license while a formal disciplinary proceeding was pending before such an authority and the proceeding concerned the individual's or entity's professional competence, professional performance, or financial integrity.

(5) EXCLUSION OR SUSPENSION UNDER FEDERAL OR STATE HEALTH CARE PROGRAM.—Any individual or entity which has been suspended or excluded from participation, or otherwise sanctioned, under—

(A) any Federal program, including programs of the Department of Defense or the Department of Veterans Affairs, involving the provision of health care, or

(B) a State health care program,

for reasons bearing on the individual's or entity's professional competence, professional performance, or financial integrity.

(6) CLAIMS FOR EXCESSIVE CHARGES OR UNNECESSARY SERVICES AND FAILURE OF CERTAIN ORGANIZATIONS TO FURNISH MEDICALLY NECESSARY SERVICES.—Any individual or entity that the Secretary determines—

(A) has submitted or caused to be submitted bills or requests for payment (where such bills or requests are based on charges or cost) under title XVIII or a State health care program containing charges (or, in applicable cases, requests for payment of costs) for items or services furnished substantially in excess of such individual's or entity's usual charges (or, in applicable cases, substantially in excess of such individual's or entity's costs) for such items or services, unless the Secretary finds there is good cause for such bills or requests containing such charges or costs;

(B) has furnished or caused to be furnished items or services to patients (whether or not eligible for benefits under title XVIII or under a State health care program) substantially in excess of the needs of such patients or of a quality which fails to meet professionally recognized standards of health care;

(C) is—

(i) a health maintenance organization (as defined in section 1903(m)) providing items and services under a State plan approved under title XIX, or

(ii) an entity furnishing services under a waiver approved under section 1915(b)(1),

and has failed substantially to provide medically necessary items and services that are required (under law or the contract with the State under title XIX) to be provided to individuals covered under that plan or waiver, if the failure has adversely affected (or has a substantial likelihood of adversely affecting) these individuals; or

(D) is an entity providing items and services as an eligible organization under a risk–sharing contract under section 1876 and has failed substantially to provide medically necessary items and services that are required (under law or such contract) to be provided to individuals covered under the

642 SOCIAL SECURITY ACT—§ 1128(b)(6)(D)(cont)

risk–sharing contract, if the failure has adversely affected (or has a substantial likelihood of adversely affecting) these individuals.

(7) FRAUD, KICKBACKS, AND OTHER PROHIBITED ACTIVITIES.—Any individual or entity that the Secretary determines has committed an act which is described in section 1128A, 1128B, or 1129.

(8) ENTITIES CONTROLLED BY A SANCTIONED INDIVIDUAL.—Any entity with respect to which the Secretary determines that a person—

(A)(i) who has a direct or indirect ownership or control interest of 5 percent or more in the entity or with an ownership or control interest (as defined in section 1124(a)(3)) in that entity,

(ii) who is an officer, director, agent, or managing employee (as defined in section 1126(b)) of that entity; or

(iii) who was described in clause (i) but is no longer so described because of a transfer of ownership or control interest, in anticipation of (or following) a conviction, assessment, or exclusion described in subparagraph (B) against the person, to an immediate family member (as defined in subsection (j)(1)) or a member of the household of the person (as defined in subsection (j)(2)) who continues to maintain an interest described in such clause—

is a person—

(B)(i) who has been convicted of any offense described in subsection (a) or in paragraph (1), (2), or (3) of this subsection;

(ii) against whom a civil monetary penalty has been assessed under section 1128A or 1129; or

(iii) who has been excluded from participation under a program under title XVIII or under a State health care program.

(9) FAILURE TO DISCLOSE REQUIRED INFORMATION.—Any entity that did not fully and accurately make any disclosure required by section 1124, section 1124A, or section 1126.

(10) FAILURE TO SUPPLY REQUESTED INFORMATION ON SUBCONTRACTORS AND SUPPLIERS.—Any disclosing entity (as defined in section 1124(a)(2)) that fails to supply (within such period as may be specified by the Secretary in regulations) upon request specifically addressed to the entity by the Secretary or by the State agency administering or supervising the administration of a State health care program—

(A) full and complete information as to the ownership of a subcontractor (as defined by the Secretary in regulations) with whom the entity has had, during the previous 12 months, business transactions in an aggregate amount in excess of $25,000, or

(B) full and complete information as to any significant business transactions (as defined by the Secretary in regulations), occurring during the five–year period ending on the date of such request, between the entity and any wholly owned supplier or between the entity and any subcontractor.

(11) FAILURE TO SUPPLY PAYMENT INFORMATION.—Any individual or entity furnishing items or services for which payment may be made under title XVIII or a State health care program that

fails to provide such information as the Secretary or the appropriate State agency finds necessary to determine whether such payments are or were due and the amounts thereof, or has refused to permit such examination of its records by or on behalf of the Secretary or that agency as may be necessary to verify such information.

(12) FAILURE TO GRANT IMMEDIATE ACCESS.—Any individual or entity that fails to grant immediate access, upon reasonable request (as defined by the Secretary in regulations) to any of the following:

(A) To the Secretary, or to the agency used by the Secretary, for the purpose specified in the first sentence of section 1864(a) (relating to compliance with conditions of participation or payment).

(B) To the Secretary or the State agency, to perform the reviews and surveys required under State plans under paragraphs (26), (31), and (33) of section 1902(a) and under section 1903(g).

(C) To the Inspector General of the Department of Health and Human Services, for the purpose of reviewing records, documents, and other data necessary to the performance of the statutory functions of the Inspector General.

(D) To a State medicaid fraud control unit (as defined in section 1903(q)), for the purpose of conducting activities described in that section.

(13) FAILURE TO TAKE CORRECTIVE ACTION.—Any hospital that fails to comply substantially with a corrective action required under section 1886(f)(2)(B).

(14) DEFAULT ON HEALTH EDUCATION LOAN OR SCHOLARSHIP OBLIGATIONS.—Any individual who the Secretary determines is in default on repayments of scholarship obligations or loans in connection with health professions education made or secured, in whole or in part, by the Secretary and with respect to whom the Secretary has taken all reasonable steps available to the Secretary to secure repayment of such obligations or loans, except that (A) the Secretary shall not exclude pursuant to this paragraph a physician who is the sole community physician or sole source of essential specialized services in a community if a State requests that the physician not be excluded, and (B) the Secretary shall take into account, in determining whether to exclude any other physician pursuant to this paragraph, access of beneficiaries to physician services for which payment may be made under title XVIII or XIX.

(15) INDIVIDUALS CONTROLLING A SANCTIONED ENTITY.—

(A) Any individual—

(i) who has a direct or indirect ownership or control interest in a sanctioned entity and who knows or should know (as defined in section 1128A(i)(6)) of the action constituting the basis for the conviction or exclusion described in subparagraph (B); or

(ii) who is an officer or managing employee (as defined in section 1126(b)) of such an entity.

(B) For purposes of subparagraph (A), the term "sanctioned entity" means an entity—

644 SOCIAL SECURITY ACT—§ 1128(b)(15)(B)(i)

(i) that has been convicted of any offense described in subsection (a) or in paragraph (1), (2), or (3) of this subsection; or

(ii) that has been excluded from participation under a program under title XVIII or under a State health care program.

(c) NOTICE, EFFECTIVE DATE, AND PERIOD OF EXCLUSION.—

(1) An exclusion under this section or under section 1128A shall be effective at such time and upon such reasonable notice to the public and to the individual or entity excluded as may be specified in regulations consistent with paragraph (2).

(2)(A) Except as provided in subparagraph (B), such an exclusion shall be effective with respect to services furnished to an individual on or after the effective date of the exclusion.

(B) Unless the Secretary determines that the health and safety of individuals receiving services warrants the exclusion taking effect earlier, an exclusion shall not apply to payments made under title XVIII or under a State health care program for—

(i) inpatient institutional services furnished to an individual who was admitted to such institution before the date of the exclusion, or

(ii) home health services and hospice care furnished to an individual under a plan of care established before the date of the exclusion,

until the passage of 30 days after the effective date of the exclusion.

(3)(A) The Secretary shall specify, in the notice of exclusion under paragraph (1) and the written notice under section 1128A, the minimum period (or, in the case of an exclusion of an individual under subsection (b)(12) or in the case described in subparagraph (G), the period) of the exclusion.

(B) Subject to subparagraph (G), in the case of an exclusion under subsection (a), the minimum period of exclusion shall be not less than five years, except that, upon the request of the administrator of a Federal health care program (as defined in section 1128B(f)) who determines that the exclusion would impose a hardship on individuals entitled to benefits under part A of title XVIII or enrolled under part B of such title, or both, the Secretary may, after consulting with the Inspector General of the Department of Health and Human Services, waive the exclusion under subsection (a)(1), (a)(3), or (a)(4) with respect to that program in the case of an individual or entity that is the sole community physician or sole source of essential specialized services in a community. The Secretary's decision whether to waive the exclusion shall not be reviewable.

(C) In the case of an exclusion of an individual under subsection (b)(12), the period of the exclusion shall be equal to the sum of—

(i) the length of the period in which the individual failed to grant the immediate access described in that subsection, and

(ii) an additional period, not to exceed 90 days, set by the Secretary.

(D) Subject to subparagraph (G), in the case of an exclusion of an individual or entity under paragraph (1), (2), or (3) of subsection (b), the period of the exclusion shall be 3 years, unless

SOCIAL SECURITY ACT—§ 1128(d)(3)(B)(i)   645

the Secretary determines in accordance with published regulations that a shorter period is appropriate because of mitigating circumstances or that a longer period is appropriate because of aggravating circumstances.

(E) In the case of an exclusion of an individual or entity under subsection (b)(4) or (b)(5), the period of the exclusion shall not be less than the period during which the individual's or entity's license to provide health care is revoked, suspended, or surrendered, or the individual or the entity is excluded or suspended from a Federal or State health care program.

(F) In the case of an exclusion of an individual or entity under subsection (b)(6)(B), the period of the exclusion shall be not less than 1 year.

(G) In the case of an exclusion of an individual under subsection (a) based on a conviction occurring on or after the date of the enactment of this subparagraph, if the individual has (before, on, or after such date) been convicted—

(i) on one previous occasion of one or more offenses for which an exclusion may be effected under such subsection, the period of the exclusion shall be not less than 10 years, or

(ii) on 2 or more previous occasions of one or more offenses for which an exclusion may be effected under such subsection, the period of the exclusion shall be permanent.

(d) NOTICE TO STATE AGENCIES AND EXCLUSION UNDER STATE HEALTH CARE PROGRAMS.—

(1) Subject to paragraph (3), the Secretary shall exercise the authority under this section and section 1128A in a manner that results in an individual's or entity's exclusion from all the programs under title XVIII and all the State health care programs in which the individual or entity may otherwise participate.

(2) The Secretary shall promptly notify each appropriate State agency administering or supervising the administration of each State health care program (and, in the case of an exclusion effected pursuant to subsection (a) and to which section 304(a)(5) of the Controlled Substances Act[42] may apply, the Attorney General)—

(A) of the fact and circumstances of each exclusion effected against an individual or entity under this section or section 1128A, and

(B) of the period (described in paragraph (3)) for which the State agency is directed to exclude the individual or entity from participation in the State health care program.

(3)(A) Except as provided in subparagraph (B), the period of the exclusion under a State health care program under paragraph (2) shall be the same as any period of exclusion under title XVIII.

(B)(i) The Secretary may waive an individual's or entity's exclusion under a State health care program under paragraph (2) if the Secretary receives and approves a request for the waiver with respect to the individual or entity from the State agency administering or supervising the administration of the program.

---

[42] See Vol. II, P.L. 91-513, 304(a)(5).

646 SOCIAL SECURITY ACT—§ 1128(d)(3)(B)(ii)

(ii) A State health care program may provide for a period of exclusion which is longer than the period of exclusion under title XVIII.

(e) NOTICE TO STATE LICENSING AGENCIES.—The Secretary shall—

(1) promptly notify the appropriate State or local agency or authority having responsibility for the licensing or certification of an individual or entity excluded (or directed to be excluded) from participation under this section or section 1128A, of the fact and circumstances of the exclusion,

(2) request that appropriate investigations be made and sanctions invoked in accordance with applicable State law and policy, and

(3) request that the State or local agency or authority keep the Secretary and the Inspector General of the Department of Health and Human Services fully and currently informed with respect to any actions taken in response to the request.

(f) NOTICE, HEARING, AND JUDICIAL REVIEW.—

(1) Subject to paragraph (2), any individual or entity that is excluded (or directed to be excluded) from participation under this section is entitled to reasonable notice and opportunity for a hearing thereon by the Secretary to the same extent as is provided in section 205(b), and to judicial review of the Secretary's final decision after such hearing as is provided in section 205(g), except that, in so applying such sections and section 205(l), any reference therein to the Commissioner of Social Security or the Social Security Administration shall be considered a reference to the Secretary or the Department of Health and Human Services, respectively.

(2) Unless the Secretary determines that the health or safety of individuals receiving services warrants the exclusion taking effect earlier, any individual or entity that is the subject of an adverse determination under subsection (b)(7) shall be entitled to a hearing by an administrative law judge (as provided under section 205(b)) on the determination under subsection (b)(7) before any exclusion based upon the determination takes effect.

(3) The provisions of section 205(h) shall apply with respect to this section and sections 1128A, 1129, and 1156 to the same extent as it is applicable with respect to title II, except that, in so applying such section and section 205(l), any reference therein to the Commissioner of Social Security shall be considered a reference to the Secretary.

(g) APPLICATION FOR TERMINATION OF EXCLUSION.—

(1) An individual or entity excluded (or directed to be excluded) from participation under this section or section 1128A may apply to the Secretary, in the manner specified by the Secretary in regulations and at the end of the minimum period of exclusion provided under subsection (c)(3) and at such other times as the Secretary may provide, for termination of the exclusion effected under this section or section 1128A.

(2) The Secretary may terminate the exclusion if the Secretary determines, on the basis of the conduct of the applicant which occurred after the date of the notice of exclusion or which was unknown to the Secretary at the time of the exclusion, that—

SOCIAL SECURITY ACT—§ 1128(j)(2)   647

(A) there is no basis under subsection (a) or (b) or section 1128A(a) for a continuation of the exclusion, and

(B) there are reasonable assurances that the types of actions which formed the basis for the original exclusion have not recurred and will not recur.

(3) The Secretary shall promptly notify each appropriate State agency administering or supervising the administration of each State health care program (and, in the case of an exclusion effected pursuant to subsection (a) and to which section 304(a)(5) of the Controlled Substances Act[43] may apply, the Attorney General) of the fact and circumstances of each termination of exclusion made under this subsection.

(h) DEFINITION OF STATE HEALTH CARE PROGRAM.—For purposes of this section and sections 1128A and 1128B, the term "State health care program" means—

(1) a State plan approved under title XIX,

(2) any program receiving funds under title V or from an allotment to a State under such title,

(3) any program receiving funds under title XX or from an allotment to a State under such title, or

(4) a State child health plan approved under title XXI.

(i) CONVICTED DEFINED.—For purposes of subsections (a) and (b), an individual or entity is considered to have been "convicted" of a criminal offense—

(1) when a judgment of conviction has been entered against the individual or entity by a Federal, State, or local court, regardless of whether there is an appeal pending or whether the judgment of conviction or other record relating to criminal conduct has been expunged;

(2) when there has been a finding of guilt against the individual or entity by a Federal, State, or local court;

(3) when a plea of guilty or nolo contendere by the individual or entity has been accepted by a Federal, State, or local court; or

(4) when the individual or entity has entered into participation in a first offender, deferred adjudication, or other arrangement or program where judgment of conviction has been withheld.

(j) DEFINITION OF IMMEDIATE FAMILY MEMBER AND MEMBER OF HOUSEHOLD.—For purposes of subsection (b)(8)(A)(iii):

(1) The term "immediate family member" means, with respect to a person—

(A) the husband or wife of the person;

(B) the natural or adoptive parent, child, or sibling of the person;

(C) the stepparent, stepchild, stepbrother, or stepsister of the person;

(D) the father–, mother–, daughter–, son–, brother–, or sister–in–law of the person;

(E) the grandparent or grandchild of the person; and

(F) the spouse of a grandparent or grandchild of the person.

(2) The term "member of the household" means, with respect to any person, any individual sharing a common abode as part of a single family unit with the person, including domestic employees

---

[43] See Vol. II, P.L. 91-513, 304(a)(5).

648   SOCIAL SECURITY ACT—§ 1128(j)(2)(cont)

and others who live together as a family unit, but not including a roomer or boarder.

CIVIL MONETARY PENALTIES

SEC. 1128A. [42 U.S.C. 1320a–7a] (a) Any person (including an organization, agency, or other entity, but excluding a beneficiary, as defined in subsection (i)(5)) that—

(1) knowingly presents or causes to be presented to an officer, employee, or agent of the United States, or of any department or agency thereof, or of any State agency (as defined in subsection (i)(1)), a claim (as defined in subsection (i)(2)) that the Secretary determines—

(A) is for a medical or other item or service that the person knows or should know was not provided as claimed, including any person who engages in a pattern or practice of presenting or causing to be presented a claim for an item or service that is based on a code that the person knows or should know will result in a greater payment to the person than the code the person knows or should know is applicable to the item or service actually provided,

(B) is for a medical or other item or service and the person knows or should know the claim is false or fraudulent,

(C) is presented for a physician's service (or an item or service incident to a physician's service) by a person who knows or should know that the individual who furnished (or supervised the furnishing of) the service—

(i) was not licensed as a physician,

(ii) was licensed as a physician, but such license had been obtained through a misrepresentation of material fact (including cheating on an examination required for licensing), or

(iii) represented to the patient at the time the service was furnished that the physician was certified in a medical specialty by a medical specialty board when the individual was not so certified,

(D) is for a medical or other item or service furnished during a period in which the person was excluded from the program under which the claim was made pursuant to a determination by the Secretary under this section or under section 1128, 1156, 1160(b) (as in effect on September 2, 1982), 1862(d) (as in effect on the date of the enactment of the Medicare and Medicaid Patient and Program Protection Act of 1987[44]), or 1866(b) or as a result of the application of the provisions of section 1842(j)(2), or

(E) is for a pattern of medical or other items or services that a person knows or should know are not medically necessary;

(2) knowingly presents or causes to be presented to any person a request for payment which is in violation of the terms of (A) an assignment under section 1842(b)(3)(B)(ii), or (B) an agreement with a State agency (or other requirement of a State plan under title XIX) not to charge a person for an item or service in excess of the amount permitted to be charged, or (C) an agreement to be

---

[44] August 18, 1987 [P.L. 100-93; 101 Stat. 680].

a participating physician or supplier under section 1842(h)(1), or (D) an agreement pursuant to section 1866(a)(1)(G);

(3) knowingly gives or causes to be given to any person, with respect to coverage under title XVIII of inpatient hospital services subject to the provisions of section 1886, information that he knows or should know is false or misleading, and that could reasonably be expected to influence the decision when to discharge such person or another individual from the hospital;

(4) in the case of a person who is not an organization, agency, or other entity, is excluded from participating in a program under title XVIII or a State health care program in accordance with this subsection or under section 1128 and who, at the time of a violation of this subsection—

    (A) retains a direct or indirect ownership or control interest in an entity that is participating in a program under title XVIII or a State health care program, and who knows or should know of the action constituting the basis for the exclusion; or

    (B) is an officer or managing employee (as defined in section 1126(b)) of such an entity;

(5) offers to or transfers remuneration to any individual eligible for benefits under title XVIII of this Act, or under a State health care program (as defined in section 1128(h)) that such person knows or should know is likely to influence such individual to order or receive from a particular provider, practitioner, or supplier any item or service for which payment may be made, in whole or in part, under title XVIII, or a State health care program (as so defined);

(6) arranges or contracts (by employment or otherwise) with an individual or entity that the person knows or should know is excluded from participation in a Federal health care program (as defined in section 1128B(f)), for the provision of items or services for which payment may be made under such a program; or

(7) commits an act described in paragraph (1) or (2) of section 1128B(b)

shall be subject, in addition to any other penalties that may be prescribed by law, to a civil money penalty of not more than $10,000 for each item or service (or, in cases under paragraph (3), $15,000 for each individual with respect to whom false or misleading information was given; in cases under paragraph (4), $10,000 for each day the prohibited relationship occurs; or in cases under paragraph (7), $50,000 for each such act). In addition, such a person shall be subject to an assessment of not more than 3 times the amount claimed for each such item or service in lieu of damages sustained by the United States or a State agency because of such claim (or, in cases under paragraph (7), damages of not more than 3 times the total amount of remuneration offered, paid, solicited, or received, without regard to whether a portion of such remuneration was offered, paid, solicited, or received for a lawful purpose). In addition the Secretary may make a determination in the same proceeding to exclude the person from participation in the Federal health care programs (as defined in section 1128B(f)(1))and to direct the appropriate State agency to exclude the person from participation in any State health care program.

650   SOCIAL SECURITY ACT—§ 1128A(a)(7)(cont)

(b)(1) If a hospital or a critical access hospital knowingly makes a payment, directly or indirectly, to a physician as an inducement to reduce or limit services provided with respect to individuals who—

(A) are entitled to benefits under part A or part B of title XVIII or to medical assistance under a State plan approved under title XIX, and

(B) are under the direct care of the physician,

the hospital or a critical access hospital shall be subject, in addition to any other penalties that may be prescribed by law, to a civil money penalty of not more than $2,000 for each such individual with respect to whom the payment is made.

(2) Any physician who knowingly accepts receipt of a payment described in paragraph (1) shall be subject, in addition to any other penalties that may be prescribed by law, to a civil money penalty of not more than $2,000 for each individual described in such paragraph with respect to whom the payment is made.

(3)(A) Any physician who executes a document described in subparagraph (B) with respect to an individual knowing that all of the requirements referred to in such subparagraph are not met with respect to the individual shall be subject to a civil monetary penalty of not more than the greater of—

(i) $5,000, or

(ii) three times the amount of the payments under title XVIII for home health services which are made pursuant to such certification.

(B) A document described in this subparagraph is any document that certifies, for purposes of title XVIII, that an individual meets the requirements of section 1814(a)(2)(C) or 1835(a)(2)(A) in the case of home health services furnished to the individual.

(c)(1) The Secretary may initiate a proceeding to determine whether to impose a civil money penalty, assessment, or exclusion under subsection (a) or (b) only as authorized by the Attorney General pursuant to procedures agreed upon by them. The Secretary may not initiate an action under this section with respect to any claim, request for payment, or other occurrence described in this section later than six years after the date the claim was presented, the request for payment was made, or the occurrence took place. The Secretary may initiate an action under this section by serving notice of the action in any manner authorized by Rule 4 of the Federal Rules of Civil Procedure[45].

(2) The Secretary shall not make a determination adverse to any person under subsection (a) or (b) until the person has been given written notice and an opportunity for the determination to be made on the record after a hearing at which the person is entitled to be represented by counsel, to present witnesses, and to cross-examine witnesses against the person.

(3) In a proceeding under subsection (a) or (b) which—

(A) is against a person who has been convicted (whether upon a verdict after trial or upon a plea of guilty or nolo contendere) of a Federal crime charging fraud or false statements, and

(B) involves the same transaction as in the criminal action,

---

[45] See Vol. II, Federal Rules of Civil Procedure.

the person is estopped from denying the essential elements of the criminal offense.

(4) The official conducting a hearing under this section may sanction a person, including any party or attorney, for failing to comply with an order or procedure, failing to defend an action, or other misconduct as would interfere with the speedy, orderly, or fair conduct of the hearing. Such sanction shall reasonably relate to the severity and nature of the failure or misconduct. Such sanction may include—

(A) in the case of refusal to provide or permit discovery, drawing negative factual inferences or treating such refusal as an admission by deeming the matter, or certain facts, to be established,

(B) prohibiting a party from introducing certain evidence or otherwise supporting a particular claim or defense,

(C) striking pleadings, in whole or in part,

(D) staying the proceedings,

(E) dismissal of the action,

(F) entering a default judgment,

(G) ordering the party or attorney to pay attorneys' fees and other costs caused by the failure or misconduct, and

(H) refusing to consider any motion or other action which is not filed in a timely manner.

(d) In determining the amount or scope of any penalty, assessment, or exclusion imposed pursuant to subsection (a) or (b), the Secretary shall take into account—

(1) the nature of claims and the circumstances under which they were presented,

(2) the degree of culpability, history of prior offenses, and financial condition of the person presenting the claims, and

(3) such other matters as justice may require.

(e) Any person adversely affected by a determination of the Secretary under this section may obtain a review of such determination in the United States Court of Appeals for the circuit in which the person resides, or in which the claim was presented, by filing in such court (within sixty days following the date the person is notified of the Secretary's determination) a written petition requesting that the determination be modified or set aside. A copy of the petition shall be forthwith transmitted by the clerk of the court to the Secretary, and thereupon the Secretary shall file in the Court the record in the proceeding as provided in section 2112 of title 28, United States Code[46]. Upon such filing, the court shall have jurisdiction of the proceeding and of the question determined therein, and shall have the power to make and enter upon the pleadings, testimony, and proceedings set forth in such record a decree affirming, modifying, remanding for further consideration, or setting aside, in whole or in part, the determination of the Secretary and enforcing the same to the extent that such order is affirmed or modified. No objection that has not been urged before the Secretary shall be considered by the court, unless the failure or neglect to urge such objection shall be excused because of extraordinary circumstances. The findings of the Secretary with respect to questions of fact, if supported by substantial evidence on the record considered as a whole, shall be conclusive. If any party shall apply to the court for leave to adduce additional evidence and shall show

---

[46] See Vol. II, 28 U.S.C. 2112.

652 SOCIAL SECURITY ACT—§ 1128A(e)(cont)

to the satisfaction of the court that such additional evidence is material and that there were reasonable grounds for the failure to adduce such evidence in the hearing before the Secretary, the court may order such additional evidence to be taken before the Secretary and to be made a part of the record. The Secretary may modify his findings as to the facts, or make new findings, by reason of additional evidence so taken and filed, and he shall file with the court such modified or new findings, which findings with respect to questions of fact, if supported by substantial evidence on the record considered as a whole, shall be conclusive, and his recommendations, if any, for the modification or setting aside of his original order. Upon the filing of the record with it, the jurisdiction of the court shall be exclusive and its judgment and decree shall be final, except that the same shall be subject to review by the Supreme Court of the United States, as provided in section 1254 of title 28, United States Code[47].

(f) Civil money penalties and assessments imposed under this section may be compromised by the Secretary and may be recovered in a civil action in the name of the United States brought in United States district court for the district where the claim was presented, or where the claimant resides, as determined by the Secretary. Amounts recovered under this section shall be paid to the Secretary and disposed of as follows:

(1)(A) In the case of amounts recovered arising out of a claim under title XIX, there shall be paid to the State agency an amount bearing the same proportion to the total amount recovered as the State's share of the amount paid by the State agency for such claim bears to the total amount paid for such claim.

(B) In the case of amounts recovered arising out of a claim under an allotment to a State under title V, there shall be paid to the State agency an amount equal to three-sevenths of the amount recovered.

(2) Such portion of the amounts recovered as is determined to have been paid out of the trust funds under sections 1817 and 1841 shall be repaid to such trust funds.

(3) With respect to amounts recovered arising out of a claim under a Federal health care program (as defined in section 1128B(f)), the portion of such amounts as is determined to have been paid by the program shall be repaid to the program, and the portion of such amounts attributable to the amounts recovered under this section by reason of the amendments made by the Health Insurance Portability and Accountability Act of 1996[48] (as estimated by the Secretary) shall be deposited into the Federal Hospital Insurance Trust Fund pursuant to section 1817(k)(2)(C).

(4) The remainder of the amounts recovered shall be deposited as miscellaneous receipts of the Treasury of the United States.
The amount of such penalty or assessment, when finally determined, or the amount agreed upon in compromise, may be deducted from any sum then or later owing by the United States or a State agency to the person against whom the penalty or assessment has been assessed.

(g) A determination by the Secretary to impose a penalty, assessment, or exclusion under subsection (a) or (b) shall be final upon the

---

[47] See Vol. II, 28 U.S.C. 1254.
[48] P.L. 104-191.

expiration of the sixty-day period referred to in subsection (e). Matters that were raised or that could have been raised in a hearing before the Secretary or in an appeal pursuant to subsection (e) may not be raised as a defense to a civil action by the United States to collect a penalty, assessment, or exclusion assessed under this section.

(h) Whenever the Secretary's determination to impose a penalty, assessment, or exclusion under subsection (a) or (b) becomes final, he shall notify the appropriate State or local medical or professional organization, the appropriate State agency or agencies administering or supervising the administration of State health care programs (as defined in section 1128(h)), and the appropriate utilization and quality control peer review organization, and the appropriate State or local licensing agency or organization (including the agency specified in section 1864(a) and 1902(a)(33)) that such a penalty, assessment, or exclusion has become final and the reasons therefor.

(i) For the purposes of this section:

(1) The term "State agency" means the agency established or designated to administer or supervise the administration of the State plan under title XIX of this Act or designated to administer the State's program under title V or title XX of this Act.

(2) The term "claim" means an application for payments for items and services under a Federal health care program (as defined in section 1128B(f)).

(3) The term "item or service" includes (A) any particular item, device, medical supply, or service claimed to have been provided to a patient and listed in an itemized claim for payment, and (B) in the case of a claim based on costs, any entry in the cost report, books of account or other documents supporting such claim.

(4) The term "agency of the United States" includes any contractor acting as a fiscal intermediary, carrier, or fiscal agent or any other claims processing agent for a Federal health care program (as so defined).

(5) The term "beneficiary" means an individual who is eligible to receive items or services for which payment may be made under a Federal health care program (as so defined) but does not include a provider, supplier, or practitioner.

(6) The term "remuneration" includes the waiver of coinsurance and deductible amounts (or any part thereof), and transfers of items or services for free or for other than fair market value. The term "remuneration" does not include—

(A) the waiver of coinsurance and deductible amounts by a person, if—

(i) the waiver is not offered as part of any advertisement or solicitation;

(ii) the person does not routinely waive coinsurance or deductible amounts; and

(iii) the person—

(I) waives the coinsurance and deductible amounts after determining in good faith that the individual is in financial need; or

(II) fails to collect coinsurance or deductible amounts after making reasonable collection efforts;

654 SOCIAL SECURITY ACT—§ 1128A(i)(6)(B)

(B) subject to subsection (n), any permissible practice described in any subparagraph of section 1128B(b)(3) or in regulations issued by the Secretary;

(C) differentials in coinsurance and deductible amounts as part of a benefit plan design as long as the differentials have been disclosed in writing to all beneficiaries, third party payers, and providers, to whom claims are presented and as long as the differentials meet the standards as defined in regulations promulgated by the Secretary not later than 180 days after the date of the enactment of the Health Insurance Portability and Accountability Act of 1996[49];

(D) incentives given to individuals to promote the delivery of preventive case as determined by the Secretary in regulations so promulgated; or

(D)[50] a reduction in the copayment amount for covered OPD services under section 1833(t)(5)(B).

(7) The term "should know" means that a person, with respect to information—

(A) acts in deliberate ignorance of the truth or falsity of the information; or

(B) acts in reckless disregard of the truth or falsity of the information,

and no proof of specific intent to defraud is required.

(j)(1) The provisions of subsections (d) and (e) of section 205 shall apply with respect to this section to the same extent as they are applicable with respect to title II. The Secretary may delegate the authority granted by section 205(d) (as made applicable to this section) to the Inspector General of the Department of Health and Human Services for purposes of any investigation under this section.

(2) The Secretary may delegate authority granted under this section and under section 1128 to the Inspector General of the Department of Health and Human Services.

(k) Whenever the Secretary has reason to believe that any person has engaged, is engaging, or is about to engage in any activity which makes the person subject to a civil monetary penalty under this section, the Secretary may bring an action in an appropriate district court of the United States (or, if applicable, a United States court of any territory) to enjoin such activity, or to enjoin the person from concealing, removing, encumbering, or disposing of assets which may be required in order to pay a civil monetary penalty if any such penalty were to be imposed or to seek other appropriate relief.

(l) A principal is liable for penalties, assessments, and an exclusion under this section for the actions of the principal's agent acting within the scope of the agency.

(m)(1) For purposes of this section, with respect to a Federal health care program not contained in this Act, references to the Secretary in this section shall be deemed to be references to the Secretary or Administrator of the department or agency with jurisdiction over such program and references to the Inspector General of the Department of Health and Human Services in this section shall be deemed to be

---

[49] August 21, 1996 [P.L. 104-191; 110 Stat.1936].

[50] As in original. P.L. 105-33, §4523(c)(3), added this second subparagraph (D), effective August 5, 1997.

SOCIAL SECURITY ACT—§ 1128B(a)(3)   655

references to the Inspector General of the applicable department or agency.

(2)(A) The Secretary and Administrator of the departments and agencies referred to in paragraph (1) may include in any action pursuant to this section, claims within the jurisdiction of other Federal departments or agencies as long as the following conditions are satisfied:

(i) The case involves primarily claims submitted to the Federal health care programs of the department or agency initiating the action.

(ii) The Secretary or Administrator of the department or agency initiating the action gives notice and an opportunity to participate in the investigation to the Inspector General of the department or agency with primary jurisdiction over the Federal health care programs to which the claims were submitted.

(B) If conditions specified in subparagraph (A) are fulfilled, the Inspector General of the department or agency initiating the action is authorized to exercise all powers granted under the Inspector General Act of 1978 (5 U.S.C. App.) with respect to the claims submitted to the other departments or agencies to the same manner and extent as provided in that Act with respect to claims submitted to such departments or agencies.

(n)(1) Subparagraph (B) of subsection (i)(6) shall not apply to a practice described in paragraph (2) unless—

(A) the Secretary, through the Inspector General of the Department of Health and Human Services, promulgates a rule authorizing such a practice as an exception to remuneration; and

(B) the remuneration is offered or transferred by a person under such rule during the 2-year period beginning on the date the rule is first promulgated.

(2) A practice described in this paragraph is a practice under which a health care provider or facility pays, in whole or in part, premiums for medicare supplemental policies for individuals entitled to benefits under part A of title XVIII pursuant to section 226A.

CRIMINAL PENALTIES FOR ACTS INVOLVING FEDERAL HEALTH CARE PROGRAMS[51]

SEC. 1128B. [42 U.S.C. 1320a–7b] (a) Whoever—

(1) knowingly and willfully makes or causes to be made any false statement or representation of a material fact in any application for any benefit or payment under a Federal health care program (as defined in subsection (f)),

(2) at any time knowingly and willfully makes or causes to be made any false statement or representation of a material fact for use in determining rights to such benefit or payment,

(3) having knowledge of the occurrence of any event affecting (A) his initial or continued right to any such benefit or payment, or (B) the initial or continued right to any such benefit or payment of any other individual in whose behalf he has applied for or is receiving such benefit or payment, conceals or fails to disclose such event with an intent fraudulently to secure such benefit or

---

[51] See Vol. II, 18 U.S.C. 1028, with respect to penalties relating to use of identification documents.

656 SOCIAL SECURITY ACT—§ 1128B(a)(3)(cont)

payment either in a greater amount or quantity than is due or when no such benefit or payment is authorized,

(4) having made application to receive any such benefit or payment for the use and benefit of another and having received it, knowingly and willfully converts such benefit or payment or any part thereof to a use other than for the use and benefit of such other person,

(5) presents or causes to be presented a claim for a physician's service for which payment may be made under a Federal health care program and knows that the individual who furnished the service was not licensed as a physician, or

(6) for a fee knowingly and willfully counsels or assists an individual to dispose of assets (including by any transfer in trust) in order for the individual to become eligible for medical assistance under a State plan under title XIX, if disposing of the assets results in the imposition of a period of ineligibility for such assistance under section 1917(c),

shall (i) in the case of such a statement, representation, concealment, failure, or conversion by any person in connection with the furnishing (by that person) of items or services for which payment is or may be made under the program, be guilty of a felony and upon conviction thereof fined not more than $25,000 or imprisoned for not more than five years or both, or (ii) in the case of such a statement, representation, concealment, failure, conversion, or provision of counsel or assistance by any other person be guilty of a misdemeanor and upon conviction thereof fined not more than $10,000 or imprisoned for not more than one year, or both. In addition, in any case where an individual who is otherwise eligible for assistance under a Federal health care program is convicted of an offense under the preceding provisions of this subsection, the administrator of such program may at its option (notwithstanding any other provision of such program) limit, restrict, or suspend the eligibility of that individual for such period (not exceeding one year) as it deems appropriate; but the imposition of a limitation, restriction, or suspension with respect to the eligibility of any individual under this sentence shall not affect the eligibility of any other person for assistance under the plan, regardless of the relationship between that individual and such other person.

(b)(1) Whoever knowingly and willfully solicits or receives any remuneration (including any kickback, bribe, or rebate) directly or indirectly, overtly or covertly, in cash or in kind—

(A) in return for referring an individual to a person for the furnishing or arranging for the furnishing of any item or service for which payment may be made in whole or in part under a Federal health care program, or

(B) in return for purchasing, leasing, ordering, or arranging for or recommending purchasing, leasing, or ordering any good, facility, service, or item for which payment may be made in whole or in part under Federal health care program,

shall be guilty of a felony and upon conviction thereof, shall be fined not more than $25,000 or imprisoned for not more than five years, or both.

(2) Whoever knowingly and willfully offers or pays any remuneration (including any kickback, bribe, or rebate) directly or indirectly,

SOCIAL SECURITY ACT—§ 1128B(b)(3)(F) 657

overtly or covertly, in cash or in kind to any person to induce such person—

(A) to refer an individual to a person for the furnishing or arranging for the furnishing of any item or service for which payment may be made in whole or in part under a Federal health care program, or

(B) to purchase, lease, order, or arrange for or recommend purchasing, leasing, or ordering any good, facility, service, or item for which payment may be made in whole or in part under a Federal health care program,

shall be guilty of a felony and upon conviction thereof, shall be fined not more than $25,000 or imprisoned for not more than five years, or both.

(3) Paragraphs (1) and (2) shall not apply to—

(A) a discount or other reduction in price obtained by a provider of services or other entity under title XVIII or a State health care program if the reduction in price is properly disclosed and appropriately reflected in the costs claimed or charges made by the provider or entity under title XVIII or a State health care program;

(B) any amount paid by an employer to an employee (who has a bona fide employment relationship with such employer) for employment in the provision of covered items or services;

(C) any amount paid by a vendor of goods or services to a person authorized to act as a purchasing agent for a group of individuals or entities who are furnishing services reimbursed under title XVIII or a State health care program if—

(i) the person has a written contract, with each such individual or entity, which specifies the amount to be paid the person, which amount may be a fixed amount or a fixed percentage of the value of the purchases made by each such individual or entity under the contract, and

(ii) in the case of an entity that is a provider of services (as defined in section 1861(u)), the person discloses (in such form and manner as the Secretary requires) to the entity and, upon request, to the Secretary the amount received from each such vendor with respect to purchases made by or on behalf of the entity;

(D) a waiver of any coinsurance under part B of title XVIII by a Federally qualified health care center with respect to an individual who qualifies for subsidized services under a provision of the Public Health Service Act[52];

(E) any payment practice specified by the Secretary in regulations promulgated pursuant to section 14(a) of the Medicare and Medicaid Patient and Program Protection Act of 1987[53] or in regulations under section 1860D-3(a)(6)

(F) any remuneration between an organization and an individual or entity providing items or services, or a combination thereof, pursuant to a written agreement between the organization and the individual or entity if the organization is an eligible organization under section 1876 or if the written agreement, through a

---

[52] P.L. 78-410.
[53] P.L. 100-93.

658   SOCIAL SECURITY ACT—§ 1128B(b)(3)(F)(cont)

risk-sharing arrangement, places the individual or entity at substantial financial risk for the cost or utilization of the items or services, or a combination thereof, which the individual or entity is obligated to provide;

(G) the waiver or reduction by pharmacies (including pharmacies of the Indian Health Service, Indian tribes, tribal organizations, and urban Indian organizations) of any cost-sharing imposed under part D of title XVIII, if the conditions described in clauses (i) through (iii) of section 1128A(i)(6)(A) are met with respect to the waiver or reduction (except that, in the case of such a waiver or reduction on behalf of a subsidy eligible individual (as defined in section 1860D-14(a)(3)), section 1128A(i)(6)(A) shall be applied without regard to clauses (ii) and (iii) of that section); and

(H)[54] any remuneration between a health center entity described under clause (i) or (ii) of section 1905(l)(2)(B) and any individual or entity providing goods, items, services, donations, loans, or a combination thereof, to such health center entity pursuant to a contract, lease, grant, loan, or other agreement, if such agreement contributes to the ability of the health center entity to maintain or increase the availability, or enhance the quality, of services provided to a medically underserved population served by the health center entity.

(c) Whoever knowingly and willfully makes or causes to be made, or induces or seeks to induce the making of, any false statement or representation of a material fact with respect to the conditions or operation of any institution, facility, or entity in order that such institution, facility, or entity may qualify (either upon initial certification or upon recertification) as a hospital, critical access hospital, skilled nursing facility, nursing facility, intermediate care facility for the mentally retarded, or other entity (including an eligible organization under section 1876(b)) for which certification is required under title XVIII or a State health care program (as defined in section 1128(h)), or with respect to information required to be provided under section 1124A, shall be guilty of a felony and upon conviction thereof shall be fined not more than $25,000 or imprisoned for not more than five years, or both.

(d) Whoever knowingly and willfully—

(1) charges, for any service provided to a patient under a State plan approved under title XIX, money or other consideration at a rate in excess of the rates established by the State, (or, in the case of services provided to an individual enrolled with a medicaid managed care organization under title XIX under a contract under section 1903(m) or under a contractual, referral, or other arrangement under such contract, at a rate in excess of the rate permitted under such contract), or

(2) charges, solicits, accepts, or receives, in addition to any amount otherwise required to be paid under a State plan approved under title XIX, any gift, money, donation, or other consideration (other than a charitable, religious, or philanthropic contribution from an organization or from a person unrelated to the patient)—

---

[54] See Vol. II, P.L. 108-173, §431(b), with respect to rulemaking for exception for health center entity arrangements.

SOCIAL SECURITY ACT—§ 1128C(a)(2) 659

(A) as a precondition of admitting a patient to a hospital, nursing facility, or intermediate care facility for the mentally retarded, or

(B) as a requirement for the patient's continued stay in such a facility,

when the cost of the services provided therein to the patient is paid for (in whole or in part) under the State plan,

shall be guilty of a felony and upon conviction thereof shall be fined not more than $25,000 or imprisoned for not more than five years, or both.

(e) Whoever accepts assignments described in section 1842(b)(3)(B)(ii) or agrees to be a participating physician or supplier under section 1842(h)(1) and knowingly, willfully, and repeatedly violates the term of such assignments or agreement, shall be guilty of a misdemeanor and upon conviction thereof shall be fined not more than $2,000 or imprisoned for not more than six months, or both.

(f) For purposes of this section, the term "Federal health care program" means—

(1) any plan or program that provides health benefits, whether directly, through insurance, or otherwise, which is funded directly, in whole or in part, by the United States Government (other than the health insurance program under chapter 89 of title 5, United States Code[55]); or

(2) any State health care program, as defined in section 1128(h).

FRAUD AND ABUSE CONTROL PROGRAM

SEC. 1128C. [42 U.S.C. 1320a–7c] (a) ESTABLISHMENT OF PROGRAM.—

(1) IN GENERAL.—Not later than January 1, 1997, the Secretary, acting through the Office of the Inspector General of the Department of Health and Human Services, and the Attorney General shall establish a program—

(A) to coordinate Federal, State, and local law enforcement programs to control fraud and abuse with respect to health plans,

(B) to conduct investigations, audits, evaluations, and inspections relating to the delivery of and payment for health care in the United States,

(C) to facilitate the enforcement of the provisions of sections 1128, 1128A, and 1128B and other statutes applicable to health care fraud and abuse,

(D) to provide for the modification and establishment of safe harbors and to issue advisory opinions and special fraud alerts pursuant to section 1128D, and

(E) to provide for the reporting and disclosure of certain final adverse actions against health care providers, suppliers, or practitioners pursuant to the data collection system established under section 1128E.

(2) COORDINATION WITH HEALTH PLANS.—In carrying out the program established under paragraph (1), the Secretary and the Attorney General shall consult with, and arrange for the sharing of data with representatives of health plans.

---

[55] See Vol. II, 5 U.S.C. chapter 89.

660 SOCIAL SECURITY ACT—§ 1128C(a)(3)

(3) GUIDELINES.—
(A) IN GENERAL.—The Secretary and the Attorney General shall issue guidelines to carry out the program under paragraph (1). The provisions of sections 553, 556, and 557 of title 5, United States Code, shall not apply in the issuance of such guidelines.
(B) INFORMATION GUIDELINES.—
(i) IN GENERAL.—Such guidelines shall include guidelines relating to the furnishing of information by health plans, providers, and others to enable the Secretary and the Attorney General to carry out the program (including coordination with health plans under paragraph (2)).
(ii) CONFIDENTIALITY.—Such guidelines shall include procedures to assure that such information is provided and utilized in a manner that appropriately protects the confidentiality of the information and the privacy of individuals receiving health care services and items.
(iii) QUALIFIED IMMUNITY FOR PROVIDING INFORMATION.—The provisions of section 1157(a) (relating to limitation on liability) shall apply to a person providing information to the Secretary or the Attorney General in conjunction with their performance of duties under this section.
(4) ENSURING ACCESS TO DOCUMENTATION.—The Inspector General of the Department of Health and Human Services is authorized to exercise such authority described in paragraphs (3) through (9) of section 6 of the Inspector General Act of 1978 (5 U.S.C. App.) as necessary with respect to the activities under the fraud and abuse control program established under this subsection.
(5) AUTHORITY OF INSPECTOR GENERAL.—Nothing in this Act shall be construed to diminish the authority of any Inspector General, including such authority as provided in the Inspector General Act of 1978 (5 U.S.C. App.).
(b) ADDITIONAL USE OF FUNDS BY INSPECTOR GENERAL.—
(1) REIMBURSEMENTS FOR INVESTIGATIONS.—The Inspector General of the Department of Health and Human Services is authorized to receive and retain for current use reimbursement for the costs of conducting investigations and audits and for monitoring compliance plans when such costs are ordered by a court, voluntarily agreed to be the payor, or otherwise.
(2) CREDITING.—Funds received by the Inspector General under paragraph (1) as reimbursement for costs of conducting investigations shall be deposited to the credit of the appropriation from which initially paid, or to appropriations for similar purposes currently available at the time of deposit, and shall remain available for obligation for 1 year from the date of the deposit of such funds.
(c) HEALTH PLAN DEFINED.—For purposes of this section, the term "health plan" means a plan or program that provides health benefits, whether directly, through insurance, or otherwise, and includes—
(1) a policy of health insurance;
(2) a contract of a service benefit organization; and
(3) a membership agreement with a health maintenance organization or other prepaid health plan.

SOCIAL SECURITY ACT—§ 1128D(a)(2)(A)   661

GUIDANCE REGARDING APPLICATION OF HEALTH CARE FRAUD AND ABUSE SANCTIONS

SEC. 1128D. [42 U.S.C. 1320a–7d] (a) SOLICITATION OF PUBLICATION OF MODIFICATIONS TO EXISTING SAFE HARBORS AND NEW SAFE HARBORS.—

(1) IN GENERAL.—

(A) SOLICITATION OF PROPOSALS FOR SAFE HARBORS.—Not later than January 1, 1997, and not less than annually thereafter, the Secretary shall publish a notice in the Federal Register soliciting proposals, which will be accepted during a 60–day period, for—

(i) modifications to existing safe harbors issued pursuant to section 14(a) of the Medicare and Medicaid Patient and Program Protection Act of 1987[56] (42 U.S.C. 1320a–7b note);

(ii) additional safe harbors specifying payment practices that shall not be treated as a criminal offense under section 1128B(b) and shall not serve as the basis for an exclusion under section 1128(b)(7);

(iii) advisory opinions to be issued pursuant to subsection (b);and

(iv) special fraud alerts to be issued pursuant to subsection (c).

(B) PUBLICATION OF PROPOSED MODIFICATIONS AND PROPOSED ADDITIONAL SAFE HARBORS.—After considering the proposals described in clauses (i) and (ii) of subparagraph (A), the Secretary, in consultation with the Attorney General, shall publish in the Federal Register proposed modifications to existing safe harbors and proposed additional safe harbors, if appropriate, with a 60–day comment period. After considering any public comments received during this period, the Secretary shall issue final rules modifying the existing safe harbors and establishing new safe harbors, as appropriate.

(C) REPORT.—The Inspector General of the Department of Health and Human Services (in this section referred to as the "Inspector General") shall, in an annual report to Congress or as part of the year–end semiannual report required by section 5 of the Inspector General Act of 1978 (5 U.S.C. App.), describe the proposals received under clauses (i) and (ii) of subparagraph (A) and explain which proposals were included in the publication described in subparagraph (B), which proposals were not included in that publication, and the reasons for the rejection of the proposals that were not included.

(2) CRITERIA FOR MODIFYING AND ESTABLISHING SAFE HARBORS.—In modifying and establishing safe harbors under paragraph (1)(B), the Secretary may consider the extent to which providing a safe harbor for the specified payment practice may result in any of the following:

(A) An increase or decrease in access to health care services.

---

[56] P.L. 100-93.

662 SOCIAL SECURITY ACT—§ 1128D(a)(2)(B)

(B) An increase or decrease in the quality of health care services.

(C) An increase or decrease in patient freedom of choice among health care providers.

(D) An increase or decrease in competition among health care providers.

(E) An increase or decrease in the ability of health care facilities to provide services in medically underserved areas or to medically underserved populations.

(F) An increase or decrease in the cost to Federal health care programs (as defined in section 1128B(f)).

(G) An increase or decrease in the potential overutilization of health care services.

(H) The existence or nonexistence of any potential financial benefit to a health care professional or provider which may vary based on their decisions of—

(i) whether to order a health care item or service; or

(ii) whether to arrange for a referral of health care items or services to a particular practitioner or provider.

(I) Any other factors the Secretary deems appropriate in the interest of preventing fraud and abuse in Federal health care programs (as so defined).

(b) ADVISORY OPINIONS.—

(1) ISSUANCE OF ADVISORY OPINIONS.—The Secretary, in consultation with the Attorney General, shall issue written advisory opinions as provided in this subsection.

(2) MATTERS SUBJECT TO ADVISORY OPINIONS.—The Secretary shall issue advisory opinions as to the following matters:

(A) What constitutes prohibited remuneration within the meaning of section 1128B(b) or section 1128A(i)(6).

(B) Whether an arrangement or proposed arrangement satisfies the criteria set forth in section 1129B(b)(3) for activities which do not result in prohibited remuneration.

(C) Whether an arrangement or proposed arrangement satisfies the criteria which the Secretary has established, or shall establish by regulation for activities which do not result in prohibited remuneration.

(D) What constitutes an inducement to reduce or limit services to individuals entitled to benefits under title XVIII or title XIX within the meaning of section 1128A(b).

(E) Whether any activity or proposed activity constitutes grounds for the imposition of a sanction under section 1128, 1128A, or 1128B.

(3) MATTERS NOT SUBJECT TO ADVISORY OPINIONS.—Such advisory opinions shall not address the following matters:

(A) Whether the fair market value shall be, or was paid or received for any goods, services or property.

(B) Whether an individual is a bona fide employee within the requirements of section 3121(d)(2) of the Internal Revenue Code of 1986[57].

(4) EFFECT OF ADVISORY OPINIONS.—

---

[57] See Vol. II, P.L. 83-591, §3121(d)(2).

SOCIAL SECURITY ACT—§ 1128D(c)(1)(B)   663

(A) BINDING AS TO SECRETARY AND PARTIES IN-VOLVED.—Each advisory opinion issued by the Secretary shall be binding as to the Secretary and the party or parties requesting the opinion.

(B) FAILURE TO SEEK OPINION.—The failure of a party to seek an advisory opinion may not be introduced into evidence to prove that the party intended to violate the provisions of sections 1128, 1128A, or 1128B.

(5) REGULATIONS.—

(A) IN GENERAL.—Not later than 180 days after the date of the enactment of this section, the Secretary shall issue regulations to carry out this section. Such regulations shall provide for—

(i) the procedure to be followed by a party applying for an advisory opinion;

(ii) the procedure to be followed by the Secretary in responding to a request for an advisory opinion;

(iii) the interval in which the Secretary shall respond;

(iv) the reasonable fee to be charged to the party requesting an advisory opinion; and

(v) the manner in which advisory opinions will be made available to the public.

(B) SPECIFIC CONTENTS.—Under the regulations promulgated pursuant to subparagraph (A)—

(i) the Secretary shall be required to issue to a party requesting an advisory opinion by not later than 60 days after the request is received; and

(ii) the fee charged to the party requesting an advisory opinion shall be equal to the costs incurred by the Secretary in responding to the request.

(6) APPLICATION OF SUBSECTION.—This subsection shall apply to requests for advisory opinions made on or after the date which is 6 months after the date of enactment[58] of this section.

(c) SPECIAL FRAUD ALERTS.—

(1) IN GENERAL.—

(A) REQUEST FOR SPECIAL FRAUD ALERTS.—Any person may present, at any time, a request to the Inspector General for a notice which informs the public of practices which the Inspector General considers to be suspect or of particular concern under the Medicare program under title XVIII or a State health care program, as defined in section 1128(h) (in this subsection referred to as a "special fraud alert").

(B) ISSUANCE AND PUBLICATION OF SPECIAL FRAUD ALERTS.—Upon receipt of a request described in subparagraph (A), the Inspector General shall investigate the subject matter of the request to determine whether a special fraud alert should be issued. If appropriate, the Inspector General shall issue a special fraud alert in response to the request. All special fraud alerts issued pursuant to this subparagraph shall be published in the Federal Register.

---

[58] August 21, 1996 [P.L. 104-191, §205].

664   SOCIAL SECURITY ACT—§ 1128D(c)(2)

(2) CRITERIA FOR SPECIAL FRAUD ALERTS.—In determining whether to issue a special fraud alert upon a request described in paragraph (1), the Inspector General may consider—

(A) whether and to what extent the practices that would be identified in the special fraud alert may result in any of the consequences described in subsection (a)(2); and

(B) the volume and frequency of the conduct that would be identified in the special fraud alert.

HEALTH CARE FRAUD AND ABUSE DATA COLLECTION PROGRAM

SEC. 1128E. [42 U.S.C. 1320a–7e] (a) GENERAL PURPOSE.—Not later than January 1, 1997, the Secretary shall establish a national health care fraud and abuse data collection program for the reporting of final adverse actions (not including settlements in which no findings of liability have been made) against health care providers, suppliers, or practitioners as required by subsection (b), with access as set forth in subsection (c), and shall maintain a database of the information collected under this section.

(b) REPORTING OF INFORMATION.—

(1) IN GENERAL.—Each Government agency and health plan shall report any final adverse action (not including settlements in which no findings of liability have been made) taken against a health care provider, supplier, or practitioner.

(2) INFORMATION TO BE REPORTED.—The information to be reported under paragraph (1) includes:

(A) The name and TIN (as defined in section 7701(a)(41) of the Internal Revenue Code of 1986[59]) of any health care provider, supplier, or practitioner who is the subject of a final adverse action.

(B) The name (if known) of any health care entity with which a health care provider, supplier, or practitioner, who is the subject of a final adverse action, is affiliated or associated.

(C) The nature of the final adverse action and whether such action is on appeal.

(D) A description of the acts or omissions and injuries upon which the final adverse action was based, and such other information as the Secretary determines by regulation is required for appropriate interpretation of information reported under this section.

(3) CONFIDENTIALITY.—In determining what information is required, the Secretary shall include procedures to assure that the privacy of individuals receiving health care services is appropriately protected.

(4) TIMING AND FORM OF REPORTING.—The information required to be reported under this subsection shall be reported regularly (but not less often than monthly) and in such form and manner as the Secretary prescribes. Such information shall first be required to be reported on a date specified by the Secretary.

(5) TO WHOM REPORTED.—The information required to be reported under this subsection shall be reported to the Secretary.

(6) SANCTIONS FOR FAILURE TO REPORT.—

---

[59] See Vol. II, P.L. 83-591, §7701(a)(41).

SOCIAL SECURITY ACT—§ 1128E(g)(1)(A)   665

(A) HEALTH PLANS.—Any health plan that fails to report information on an adverse action required to be reported under this subsection shall be subject to a civil money penalty of not more than $25,000 for each such adverse action not reported. Such penalty shall be imposed and collected in the same manner as civil money penalties under subsection (a) of section 1128A are imposed and collected under that section.

(B) GOVERNMENTAL AGENCIES.—The Secretary shall provide for a publication of a public report that identifies those Government agencies that have failed to report information on adverse actions as required to be reported under this subsection.

(c) DISCLOSURE AND CORRECTION OF INFORMATION.—

(1) DISCLOSURE.—With respect to the information about final adverse actions (not including settlements in which no findings of liability have been made) reported to the Secretary under this section with respect to a health care provider, supplier, or practitioner, the Secretary shall, by regulation, provide for—

(A) disclosure of the information, upon request, to the health care provider, supplier, or licensed practitioner, and

(B) procedures in the case of disputed accuracy of the information.

(2) CORRECTIONS.—Each Government agency and health plan shall report corrections of information already reported about any final adverse action taken against a health care provider, supplier, or practitioner, in such form and manner that the Secretary prescribes by regulation.

(d) ACCESS TO REPORTED INFORMATION.—

(1) AVAILABILITY.—The information in the database maintained under this section shall be available to Federal and State government agencies and health plans pursuant to procedures that the Secretary shall provide by regulation.

(2) FEES FOR DISCLOSURE.—The Secretary may establish or approve reasonable fees for the disclosure of information in such database (other than with respect to requests by Federal agencies). The amount of such a fee shall be sufficient to recover the full costs of operating the database. Such fees shall be available to the Secretary or, in the Secretary's discretion to the agency designated under this section to cover such costs.

(e) PROTECTION FROM LIABILITY FOR REPORTING.—No person or entity, including the agency designated by the Secretary in subsection (b)(5) shall be held liable in any civil action with respect to any report made as required by this section, without knowledge of the falsity of the information contained in the report.

(f) COORDINATION WITH NATIONAL PRACTITIONER DATA BANK.—The Secretary shall implement this section in such a manner as to avoid duplication with the reporting requirements established for the National Practitioner Data Bank under the Health Care Quality Improvement Act of 1986 (42 U.S.C. 11101 et seq.).

(g) DEFINITIONS AND SPECIAL RULES.—For purposes of this section:

(1) FINAL ADVERSE ACTION.—

(A) IN GENERAL.—The term "final adverse action" includes:

666 SOCIAL SECURITY ACT—§ 1128E(g)(1)(A)(i)

(i) Civil judgments against a health care provider, supplier, or practitioner in Federal or State court related to the delivery of a health care item or service.

(ii) Federal or State criminal convictions related to the delivery of a health care item or service.

(iii) Actions by Federal or State agencies responsible for the licensing and certification of health care providers, suppliers, and licensed health care practitioners, including—

(I) formal or official actions, such as revocation or suspension of a license (and the length of any such suspension), reprimand, censure or probation,

(II) any other loss of license or the right to apply for, or renew, a license of the provider, supplier, or practitioner, whether by operation of law, voluntary surrender, non–renewability, or otherwise, or

(III) any other negative action or finding by such Federal or State agency that is publicly available information.

(iv) Exclusion from participation in Federal or State health care programs (as defined in sections 1128B(f) and 1128(h), respectively).

(v) Any other adjudicated actions or decisions that the Secretary shall establish by regulation.

(B) EXCEPTION.—The term does not include any action with respect to a malpractice claim.

(2) PRACTITIONER.—The terms "licensed health care practitioner", "licensed practitioner", and "practitioner" mean, with respect to a State, an individual who is licensed or otherwise authorized by the State to provide health care services (or any individual who, without authority holds himself or herself out to be so licensed or authorized).

(3) GOVERNMENT AGENCY.—The term "Government agency" shall include:

(A) The Department of Justice.

(B) The Department of Health and Human Services.

(C) Any other Federal agency that either administers or provides payment for the delivery of health care services, including, but not limited to the Department of Defense and the Department of Veterans Affairs.

(D) State law enforcement agencies.

(E) State medicaid fraud control units.

(F) Federal or State agencies responsible for licensing and certification of health care providers and licensed health care practitioners.

(4) HEALTH PLAN.—The term "health plan" has the meaning given such term by section 1128C(c).

(5) DETERMINATION OF CONVICTION.—For purposes of paragraph (1), the existence of a conviction shall be determined under paragraphs (1) through (4) of section 1128(i).

COORDINATION OF MEDICARE AND MEDICAID SURETY BOND PROVISIONS

SEC. 1128F. [42 U.S.C. 1320a–7f] In the case of a home health agency that is subject to a surety bond requirement under title XVIII

SOCIAL SECURITY ACT—§ 1129(a)(3) 667

and title XIX, the surety bond provided to satisfy the requirement under one such title shall satisfy the requirement under the other such title so long as the bond applies to guarantee return of overpayments under both such titles.

CIVIL MONETARY PENALTIES AND ASSESSMENTS FOR TITLES II, VIII, AND XVI

SEC. 1129. [42 U.S.C. 1320a–8] (a)(1) Any person (including an organization, agency, or other entity) who—

(A) makes, or causes to be made, a statement or representation of a material fact, for use in determining any initial or continuing right to or the amount of monthly insurance benefits under title II or benefits or payments under title VIII or XVI, that the person knows or should know is false or misleading,

(B) makes such a statement or representation for such use with knowing disregard for the truth, or

(C) omits from a statement or representation for such use, or otherwise withholds disclosure of, a fact which the person knows or should know is material to the determination of any initial or continuing right to or the amount of monthly insurance benefits under title II or benefits or payments under title VIII or XVI, if the person knows, or should know, that the statement or representation with such omission is false or misleading or that the withholding of such disclosure is misleading,

shall be subject to, in addition to any other penalties that may be prescribed by law, a civil money penalty of not more than $5,000 for each such statement or representation or each receipt of such benefits or payments while withholding disclosure of such fact. Such person also shall be subject to an assessment, in lieu of damages sustained by the United States because of such statement or representation or because of such withholding of disclosure of a material fact, of not more than twice the amount of benefits or payments paid as a result of such a statement or representation or such a withholding of disclosure. In addition, the Commissioner of Social Security may make a determination in the same proceeding to recommend that the Secretary exclude, as provided in section 1128, such a person who is a medical provider or physician from participation in the programs under title XVIII.

(2) For purposes of this section, a material fact is one which the Commissioner of Social Security may consider in evaluating whether an applicant is entitled to benefits under title II or title VIII, or eligible for benefits or payments under title XVI.

(3) Any person (including an organization, agency, or other entity) who, having received, while acting in the capacity of a representative payee pursuant to section 205(j), 807, or 1631(a)(2), a payment under title II, VIII, or XVI for the use and benefit of another individual, converts such payment, or any part thereof, to a use that such person knows or should know is other than for the use and benefit of such other individual shall be subject to, in addition to any other penalties that may be prescribed by law, a civil money penalty of not more than $5,000 for each such conversion. Such person shall also be subject to an assessment, in lieu of damages sustained by the United States resulting from the conversion, of not more than twice the amount of any payments so converted.

668 SOCIAL SECURITY ACT—§ 1129(a)(3)(cont)

(b)(1) The Commissioner of Social Security may initiate a proceeding to determine whether to impose a civil money penalty or assessment, or whether to recommend exclusion under subsection (a) only as authorized by the Attorney General pursuant to procedures agreed upon by the Commissioner of Social Security and the Attorney General. The Commissioner of Social Security may not initiate an action under this section with respect to any violation described in subsection (a) later than 6 years after the date the violation was committed. The Commissioner of Social Security may initiate an action under this section by serving notice of the action in any manner authorized by Rule 4 of the Federal Rules of Civil Procedure[60].

(2) The Commissioner of Social Security shall not make a determination adverse to any person under this section until the person has been given written notice and an opportunity for the determination to be made on the record after a hearing at which the person is entitled to be represented by counsel, to present witnesses, and to cross-examine witnesses against the person.

(3) In a proceeding under this section which—

   (A) is against a person who has been convicted (whether upon a verdict after trial or upon a plea of guilty or nolo contendere) of a Federal or State crime; and

   (B) involves the same transaction as in the criminal action;
the person is estopped from denying the essential elements of the criminal offense.

(4) The official conducting a hearing under this section may sanction a person, including any party or attorney, for failing to comply with an order or procedure, for failing to defend an action, or for such other misconduct as would interfere with the speedy, orderly, or fair conduct of the hearing. Such sanction shall reasonably relate to the severity and nature of the failure or misconduct. Such sanction may include—

   (A) in the case of refusal to provide or permit discovery, drawing negative factual inference or treating such refusal as an admission by deeming the matter, or certain facts, to be established;

   (B) prohibiting a party from introducing certain evidence or otherwise supporting a particular claim or defense;

   (C) striking pleadings, in whole or in part;

   (D) staying the proceedings;

   (E) dismissal of the action;

   (F) entering a default judgment;

   (G) ordering the party or attorney to pay attorney's fees and other costs caused by the failure or misconduct; and

   (H) refusing to consider any motion or other action which is not filed in a timely manner.

(c) In determining pursuant to subsection (a) the amount or scope of any penalty or assessment, or whether to recommend and exclusion, the Commissioner of Social Security shall take into account—

   (1) the nature of the statements, representations, or actions referred to in subsection (a) and the circumstances under which they occurred;

   (2) the degree of culpability, history of prior offenses, and financial condition of the person committing the offense; and

   (3) such other matters as justice may require.

---

[60] See Vol. II, Federal Rules of Civil Procedure, Rule 4.

SOCIAL SECURITY ACT—§ 1129(e)(1)(A)　　　　669

(d)(1) Any person adversely affected by a determination of the Commissioner of Social Security under this section may obtain a review of such determination in the United States Court of Appeals for the circuit in which the person resides, or in which the statement or representation referred to in subsection (a) was made, by filing in such court (within 60 days following the date the person is notified of the Commissioner's determination) a written petition requesting that the determination be modified or set aside. A copy of the petition shall be forthwith transmitted by the clerk of the court to the Commissioner of Social Security, and thereupon the Commissioner of Social Security shall file in the court the record in the proceeding as provided in section 2112 of title 28, United States Code[61]. Upon such filing, the court shall have jurisdiction of the proceeding and of the question determined therein, and shall have the power to make and enter upon the pleadings, testimony, and proceedings set forth in such record a decree affirming, modifying, remanding for further consideration, or setting aside, in whole or in part, the determination of the Commissioner of Social Security and enforcing the same to the extent that such order is affirmed or modified. No objection that has not been urged before the Commissioner of Social Security shall be considered by the court, unless the failure to neglect to urge such objection shall be excused because of extraordinary circumstances.

(2) The findings of the Commissioner of Social Security with respect to questions of fact, if supported by substantial evidence on the record considered as a whole, shall be conclusive in the review described in paragraph (1). If any party shall apply to the court for leave to adduce additional evidence and shall show to the satisfaction of the court that such additional evidence is material and that there were reasonable grounds for the failure to adduce such evidence in the hearing before the Commissioner of Social Security, the court may order such additional evidence to be taken before the Commissioner of Social Security and to be made a part of the record. The Commissioner of Social Security may modify such findings as to the facts, or make new findings, by reason of additional evidence so taken and filed, and the Commissioner of Social Security shall file with the court such modified or new findings, which findings with respect to questions of fact, if supported by substantial evidence on the record considered as a whole shall be conclusive, and the Commissioner's recommendations, if any, for the modification or setting aside of the Commissioner's original order.

(3) Upon the filing of the record and the Commissioner's original or modified order with the court, the jurisdiction of the court shall be exclusive and its judgment and decree shall be final, except that the same shall be subject to review by the Supreme Court of the United States, as provided in section 1254 of title 28, United States Code[62].

(e)(1) Civil money penalties and assessments imposed under this section may be compromised by the Commissioner of Social Security and may be recovered—

　　(A) in a civil action in the name of the United States brought in United States district court for the district where the, violation occurred or where the person resides, as determined by the Commissioner of Social Security.

---

[61] See Vol. II, 28 U.S.C. 2112.
[62] See Vol. II, 28 U.S.C. 1254.

670 SOCIAL SECURITY ACT—§ 1129(e)(1)(B)

(B) by means of reduction in tax refunds to which the person is entitled, based on notice to the Secretary of the Treasury as permitted under section 3720A of title 31, United States Code[63];

(C)(i) by decrease of any payment of monthly insurance benefits under title II, notwithstanding section 207,

(ii) by decrease of any payment under title VIII to which the person is entitled, or

(iii) by decrease of any payment under title XVI for which the person is eligible, notwithstanding section 207, as made applicable to title XVI by reason of section 1631(d)(1);

(D) by authorities provided under the Debt Collection Act of 1982, as amended, to the extent applicable to debts arising under the Social Security Act;

(E) by deduction of the amount of such penalty or assessment, when finally determined, or the amount agreed upon in comprise, from any sum then or later owing by the United States to the person against whom the penalty or assessment has been assessed; or

(F) by any combination of the foregoing.

(2) Amounts recovered under this section shall be recovered under by the Commissioner of Social Security and shall be disposed of as follows:

(A) In the case of amounts recovered arising out of a determination relating to title II, the amounts shall be transferred to the Managing Trustee of the Federal Old-Age and Survivors Insurance Trust Fund or the Federal Disability Insurance Trust Fund, as determined appropriate by the Secretary, and such amounts shall be deposited by the Managing Trustee into such Trust Fund.

(B) In the case of any other amounts recovered under this section, the amounts shall be deposited by the Commissioner of Social Security into the general fund of the Treasury as miscellaneous receipts.

(f) A determination pursuant to subsection (a) by the Commissioner of Social Security to impose a penalty or assessment, or to recommend an exclusion shall be final upon the expiration of the 60-day period referred to in subsection (d). Matters that were raised or that could have been raised in a hearing before the Commissioner of Social Security or in an appeal pursuant to subsection (d) may not be raised as a defense to a civil action by the United States to collect a penalty or assessment imposed under this section.

(g) Whenever the Commissioner's determination to impose a penalty or assessment under this section with respect to a medical provider or physician becomes final, the Commissioner shall notify the Secretary of the final determination and the reasons therefor, and the Secretary shall then notify the entities described in section 1128A(h) of such final determination.

(h) Whenever the Commissioner of Social Security has reason to believe that any person has engaged, is engaging, or is about to engage in any activity which makes the person subject to a civil monetary penalty under this section, the Commissioner of Social Security may bring action in an appropriate district court of the United States (or, if applicable, a United States court of any territory) to enjoin such activ-

---

[63] See Vol. II, 31 U.S.C. 3720A.

ity, or to enjoin the person from concealing, removing, encumbering, or disposing of assets which may be required in order to pay a civil monetary penalty and assessment if any such penalty were to be imposed or to seek other appropriate relief.

(i)(1) The provisions of subsections (d) and (e) of section 205 shall apply with respect to this section to the same extent as they are applicable with respect to title II. The Commissioner of Social Security may delegate the authority granted by section 205(d) (as made applicable to this section) to the Inspector General for purposes of any investigation under this section.

(2) The Commissioner of Social Security may delegate authority granted under this section to the Inspector General.

(j) For purposes of this section, the term "State agency", shall have the same meaning as in section 1128A(i)(1).

(k) A principal is liable for penalties and assessments under subsection (a), and for an exclusion under section 1128 based on a recommendation under subsection (a), for the actions of the principal's agent acting within the scope of the agency.

(l) As soon as the Inspector General, Social Security Administration, has reason to believe that fraud was involved in the application of an individual for monthly insurance benefits under title II or for benefits under title VIII or XVI, the Inspector General shall make available to the Commissioner of Social Security information identifying the individual, unless a United States attorney, or equivalent State prosecutor, with jurisdiction over potential or actual related criminal cases, certifies, in writing, that there is a substantial risk that making the information so available in a particular investigation or redetermining the eligibility of the individual for such benefits would jeopardize the criminal prosecution of any person who is a subject of the investigation from which the information is derived.

ADMINISTRATIVE PROCEDURE FOR IMPOSING PENALTIES FOR FALSE OR MISLEADING STATEMENTS

SEC. 1129A. [42 U.S.C. 1320a–8a] (a) IN GENERAL.—Any person who—

> (1) makes, or causes to be made, a statement or representation of a material fact, for use in determining any initial or continuing right to or the amount of monthly insurance benefits under title II or benefits or payments under title VIII or XVI, that the person knows or should know is false or misleading,

> (2) makes such a statement or representation for such use with knowing disregard for the truth, or

> (3) omits from a statement or representation for such use, or otherwise withholds disclosure of, a fact which the person knows or should know is material to the determination of any initial or continuing right to or the amount of monthly insurance benefits under title II or benefits or payments under title VIII or XVI, if the person knows, or should know, that the statement or representation with such omission is false or misleading or that the withholding of such disclosure is misleading,

shall be subject to, in addition to any other penalties that may be prescribed by law, a penalty described in subsection (b) to be imposed by the Commissioner of Social Security.

(b) PENALTY.—The penalty described in this subsection is—

672 SOCIAL SECURITY ACT—§ 1129A(b)(1)

(1) nonpayment of benefits under title II that would otherwise be payable to the person; and

(2) ineligibility for cash benefits under title XVI,

for each month that begins during the applicable period described in subsection (c).

(c) DURATION OF PENALTY.—The duration of the applicable period, with respect to a determination by the Commissioner under subsection (a) that a person has engaged in conduct described in subsection (a), shall be—

(1) six consecutive months, in the case of the first such determination with respect to the person;

(2) twelve consecutive months, in the case of the second such determination with respect to the person; and

(3) twenty-four consecutive months, in the case of the third or subsequent such determination with respect to the person.

(d) EFFECT ON OTHER ASSISTANCE.—A person subject to a period of nonpayment of benefits under title II or ineligibility for title XVI benefits by reason of this section nevertheless shall be considered to be eligible for and receiving such benefits, to the extent that the person would be receiving or eligible for such benefits but for the imposition of the penalty, for purposes of—

(1) determination of the eligibility of the person for benefits under titles XVIII and XIX; and

(2) determination of the eligibility or amount of benefits payable under title II or XVI to another person.

(e) DEFINITION.—In this section, the term "benefits under title VIII or XVI" includes State supplementary payments made by the Commissioner pursuant to an agreement under section 810A or 1616(a) of this Act or section 212(b) of Public Law 93-66[64], as the case may be.

(f) CONSULTATIONS.—The Commissioner of Social Security shall consult with the Inspector General of the Social Security Administration regarding initiating actions under this section.

ATTEMPTS TO INTERFERE WITH ADMINISTRATION OF SOCIAL SECURITY ACT

SEC. 1129B. [42 U.S.C. 1320a-8b] Whoever corruptly or by force or threats of force (including any threatening letter or communication) attempts to intimidate or impede any officer, employee, or contractor of the Social Security Administration (including any State employee of a disability determination service or any other individual designated by the Commissioner of Social Security) acting in an official capacity to carry out a duty under this Act, or in any other way corruptly or by force or threats of force (including any threatening letter or communication) obstructs or impedes, or attempts to obstruct or impede, the due administration of this Act, shall be fined not more than $5,000, imprisoned not more than 3 years, or both, except that if the offense is committed only by threats of force, the person shall be fined not more than $3,000, imprisoned not more than 1 year, or both. In this subsection, the term "threats of force" means threats of harm to the officer or employee of the United States or to a contractor of the Social Security Administration, or to a member of the family of such an officer or employee or contractor.

---

[64] See Vol. II, P.L. 93-406, §212(b).

DEMONSTRATION PROJECTS

SEC. 1130. [42 U.S.C. 1320a–9] (a) AUTHORITY TO APPROVE DEMONSTRATION PROJECTS.—

(1) IN GENERAL.—The Secretary may authorize States to conduct demonstration projects pursuant to this section which the Secretary finds are likely to promote the objectives of part B or E of title IV.

(2) LIMITATION.—The Secretary may authorize not more than 10 demonstration projects under paragraph (1) in each of fiscal years 1998 through 2003.

(3) CERTAIN TYPES OF PROPOSALS REQUIRED TO BE CONSIDERED.—

(A) If an appropriate application therefor is submitted, the Secretary shall consider authorizing a demonstration project which is designed to identify and address barriers that result in delays to adoptive placements for children in foster care.

(B) If an appropriate application therefor is submitted, the Secretary shall consider authorizing a demonstration project which is designed to identify and address parental substance abuse problems that endanger children and result in the placement of children in foster care, including through the placement of children with their parents in residential treatment facilities (including residential treatment facilities for post-partum depression) that are specifically designed to serve parents and children together in order to promote family reunification and that can ensure the health and safety of the children in such placements.

(C) If an appropriate application therefor is submitted, the Secretary shall consider authorizing a demonstration project which is designed to address kinship care.

(4) LIMITATION ON ELIGIBILITY.—The Secretary may not authorize a State to conduct a demonstration project under this section if the State fails to provide health insurance coverage to any child with special needs (as determined under section 473(c)) for whom there is in effect an adoption assistance agreement between a State and an adoptive parent or parents.

(5) REQUIREMENT TO CONSIDER EFFECT OF PROJECT ON TERMS AND CONDITIONS OF CERTAIN COURT ORDERS.—In considering an application to conduct a demonstration project under this section that has been submitted by a State in which there is in effect a court order determining that the State's child welfare program has failed to comply with the provisions of part B or E of title IV, or with the Constitution of the United States, the Secretary shall take into consideration the effect of approving the proposed project on the terms and conditions of the court order related to the failure to comply.

(b) WAIVER AUTHORITY.—The Secretary may waive compliance with any requirement of part B or E of title IV which (if applied) would prevent a State from carrying out a demonstration project under this section or prevent the State from effectively achieving the purpose of such a project, except that the Secretary may not waive—

(1) any provision of section 422(b)(8), or section 479; or

674 SOCIAL SECURITY ACT—§ 1130(b)(2)

(2) any provision of such part E, to the extent that the waiver would impair the entitlement of any qualified child or family to benefits under a State plan approved under such part E.

(c) TREATMENT AS PROGRAM EXPENDITURES.—For purposes of parts B and E of title IV, the Secretary shall consider the expenditures of any State to conduct a demonstration project under this section to be expenditures under subpart 1 or 2 of such part B, or under such part E, as the State may elect.

(d) DURATION OF DEMONSTRATION.—A demonstration project under this section may be conducted for not more than 5 years, unless in the judgment of the Secretary, the demonstration project should be allowed to continue.

(e) APPLICATION.—Any State seeking to conduct a demonstration project under this section shall submit to the Secretary an application, in such form as the Secretary may require, which includes—

(1) a description of the proposed project, the geographic area in which the proposed project would be conducted, the children or families who would be served by the proposed project, and the services which would be provided by the proposed project (which shall provide, where appropriate, for random assignment of children and families to groups served under the project and to control groups);

(2) a statement of the period during which the proposed project would be conducted;

(3) a discussion of the benefits that are expected from the proposed project (compared to a continuation of activities under the approved plan or plans of the State);

(4) an estimate of the costs or savings of the proposed project;

(5) a statement of program requirements for which waivers would be needed to permit the proposed project to be conducted;

(6) a description of the proposed evaluation design; and

(7) such additional information as the Secretary may require.

(f) EVALUATIONS; REPORT.—Each State authorized to conduct a demonstration project under this section shall—

(1) obtain an evaluation by an independent contractor of the effectiveness of the project, using an evaluation design approved by the Secretary which provides for—

(A) comparison of methods of service delivery under the project, and such methods under a State plan or plans, with respect to efficiency, economy, and any other appropriate measures of program management;

(B) comparison of outcomes for children and families (and groups of children and families) under the project, and such outcomes under a State plan or plans, for purposes of assessing the effectiveness of the project in achieving program goals; and

(C) any other information that the Secretary may require; and

(2) provide interim and final evaluation reports to the Secretary, at such times and in such manner as the Secretary may require.

(g) COST NEUTRALITY.—The Secretary may not authorize a State to conduct a demonstration project under this section unless the Secretary determines that the total amount of Federal funds that will be

SOCIAL SECURITY ACT—§ 1131(a)(3)(B)   675

expended under (or by reason of) the project over its approved term (or such portion thereof or other period as the Secretary may find appropriate) will not exceed the amount of such funds that would be expended by the State under the State plans approved under parts B and E of title IV if the project were not conducted.

EFFECT OF FAILURE TO CARRY OUT STATE PLAN

SEC. 1130A. [42 U.S.C. 1320a–10] In an action brought to enforce a provision of the Social Security Act, such provision is not to be deemed unenforceable because of its inclusion in a section of the Act requiring a State plan or specifying the required contents of a State plan. This section is not intended to limit or expand the grounds for determining the availability of private actions to enforce State plan requirements other than by overturning any such grounds applied in Suter v. Artist M., 112 S. Ct. 1360 (1992), but not applied in prior Supreme Court decisions respecting such enforceability: *Provided*, however, That this section is not intended to alter the holding in Suter v. Artist M. that section 471(a)(15) of the Act is not enforceable in a private right of action.

NOTIFICATION OF SOCIAL SECURITY CLAIMANT WITH RESPECT TO DEFERRED VESTED BENEFITS

SEC. 1131. [42 U.S.C. 1320b–1] (a) Whenever—
(1) the Commissioner of Social Security makes a finding of fact and a decision as to—
(A) the entitlement of any individual to monthly benefits under section 202, 223, or 228, or
(B) the entitlement of any individual to a lump-sum death payment payable under section 202(i) on account of the death of any person to whom such individual is related by blood, marriage, or adoption, or
(2) the Commissioner of Social Security makes a finding of fact and a decision as to the entitlement under section 226 of any individual to hospital insurance benefits under part A of title XVIII, or
(3) the Commissioner of Social Security is requested to do so—
(A) by any individual with respect to whom the Commissioner of Social Security holds information obtained under section 6057 of the Internal Revenue Code of 1954[65], or
(B) in the case of the death of the individual referred to in subparagraph (A), by the individual who would be entitled to payment under section 204(d) of this Act,
the Commissioner of Social Security shall transmit to the individual referred to in paragraph (1) or (2) or the individual making the request under paragraph (3) any information, as reported by the employer, regarding any deferred vested benefit transmitted to the Commissioner of Social Security pursuant to such section 6057 with respect to the individual referred to in paragraph (1), (2), or (3)(A) or the person on whose wages and self-employment income entitlement (or claim of entitlement) is based.

---

[65] See Vol. II, P.L. 83-591, §6057.

676   SOCIAL SECURITY ACT—§ 1131(a)(3)(B)(cont)

(b)(1) For purposes of section 201(g)(1), expenses incurred in the administration of subsection (a) shall be deemed to be expenses incurred for the administration of title II.

(2) There are hereby authorized to be appropriated to the Federal Old-Age and Survivors Insurance Trust Fund for each fiscal year (commencing with the fiscal year ending June 30, 1974) such sums as the Commissioner of Social Security deems necessary on account of additional administrative expenses resulting from the enactment of the provisions of subsection (a).

PERIOD WITHIN WHICH CERTAIN CLAIMS MUST BE FILED

SEC. 1132. [42 U.S.C. 1320b–2] (a) Notwithstanding any other provision of this Act (but subject to subsection (b)), any claim by a State for payment with respect to an expenditure made during any calendar quarter by the State—

(1) in carrying out a State plan approved under title I, IV, X, XIV, XVI, XIX, or XX of this Act, or

(2) under any other provision of this Act which provides (on an entitlement basis) for Federal financial participation in expenditures made under State plans or programs,

shall be filed (in such form and manner as the Secretary shall by regulations prescribe) within the two-year period which begins on the first day of the calendar quarter immediately following such calendar quarter; and payment shall not be made under this Act on account of any such expenditure if claim therefor is not made within such two-year period; except that this subsection shall not be applied so as to deny payment with respect to any expenditure involving court-ordered retroactive payments or audit exceptions, or adjustments to prior year costs.

(b) The Secretary shall waive the requirement imposed under subsection (a) with respect to the filing of any claim if he determines (in accordance with regulations) that there was good cause for the failure by the State to file such claim within the period prescribed under subsection (a). Any such waiver shall be only for such additional period of time as may be necessary to provide the State with a reasonable opportunity to file such claim. A failure to file a claim within such time period which is attributable to neglect or administrative inadequacies shall be deemed not to be for good cause.

APPLICANTS OR RECIPIENTS UNDER PUBLIC ASSISTANCE PROGRAMS NOT TO BE REQUIRED TO MAKE ELECTION RESPECTING CERTAIN VETERANS' BENEFITS

SEC. 1133. [42 U.S.C. 1320b–3] (a) Notwithstanding any other provision of law (but subject to subsection (b)), no individual who is an applicant for or recipient of aid or assistance under a State plan approved under title I, X, XIV, or XVI, or of benefits under the Supplemental Security Income program established by title XVI shall—

(1) be required, as a condition of eligibility for (or of continuing to receive) such aid, assistance, or benefits, to make an election under section 306 of the Veterans' and Survivors' Pension Improvement Act of 1978[66] with respect to pension paid by the Secretary of Veterans Affairs, or

---

[66] See Vol. II, P.L. 95-588, §306.

SOCIAL SECURITY ACT—§ 1135(a)(1)   677

(2) by reason of failure or refusal to make such an election, be denied (or suffer a reduction in the amount of) such aid, assistance, or benefits.

(b) The provisions of subsection (a) shall be applicable only with respect to an individual, who is an applicant for or recipient of aid, assistance, or benefits described in subsection (a), during a period with respect to which there is in effect—

(1) in case such individual is an applicant for or recipient of aid or assistance under a State plan referred to in subsection (a), in the State having such plan, or

(2) in case such individual is an applicant for or recipient of benefits under the Supplemental Security Income program established by title XVI, in the State in which the individual applies for or receives such benefits,

a State plan for medical assistance, approved under title XIX, under which medical assistance is available to such individual only for periods for which such individual is a recipient of aid, assistance, or benefits described in subsection (a).

NONPROFIT HOSPITAL PHILANTHROPY

SEC. 1134. [42 U.S.C. 1320b–4] For purposes of determining, under titles XVIII and XIX of this Act, the reasonable costs of services provided by nonprofit hospitals or critical access hospitals, the following items shall not be deducted from the operating costs of such hospitals or critical access hospitals:

(1) A grant, gift, or endowment, or income therefrom, which is to or for such a hospital and which has not been designated by the donor for paying any specific operating costs.

(2) A grant or similar payment which is to such a hospital, which was made by a governmental entity, and which is not available under the terms of the grant or payment for use as operating funds.

(3) Those types of donor designated grants and gifts (including grants and similar payments which are made by a governmental entity), and income therefrom, which the Secretary determines, in the best interests of needed health care, should be encouraged.

(4) The proceeds from the sale or mortgage of any real estate or other capital asset of such a hospital, which real estate or asset the hospital acquired through gift or grant, if such proceeds are not available for use as operating funds under the terms of the gift or grant.

Paragraph (4) shall not apply to the recovery of the appropriate share of depreciation when gains or losses are realized from the disposal of depreciable assets.

AUTHORITY TO WAIVE REQUIREMENTS DURING NATIONAL EMERGENCIES

SEC. 1135. [42 U.S.C. 1320b–5] (a) PURPOSE.—The purpose of this section is to enable the Secretary to ensure to the maximum extent feasible, in any emergency area and during an emergency period (as defined in subsection (g)(1))—

(1) that sufficient health care items and services are available to meet the needs of individuals in such area enrolled in the programs under titles XVIII, XIX, and XXI; and

(2) that health care providers (as defined in subsection (g)(2)) that furnish such items and services in good faith, but that are unable to comply with one or more requirements described in subsection (b), may be reimbursed for such items and services and exempted from sanctions for such noncompliance, absent any determination of fraud or abuse.

(b) SECRETARIAL AUTHORITY.—To the extent necessary to accomplish the purpose specified in subsection (a), the Secretary is authorized, subject to the provisions of this section, to temporarily waive or modify the application of, with respect to health care items and services furnished by a health care provider (or classes of health care providers) in any emergency area (or portion of such an area) during any portion of an emergency period, the requirements of titles XVIII, XIX, or XXI, or any regulation thereunder (and the requirements of this title other than this section, and regulations thereunder, insofar as they relate to such titles), pertaining to—

(1)(A) conditions of participation or other certification requirements for an individual health care provider or types of providers,

(B) program participation and similar requirements for an individual health care provider or types of providers, and

(C) pre-approval requirements;

(2) requirements that physicians and other health care professionals be licensed in the State in which they provide such services, if they have equivalent licensing in another State and are not affirmatively excluded from practice in that State or in any State a part of which is included in the emergency area;

(3) actions under section 1867 (relating to examination and treatment for emergency medical conditions and women in labor) for—

(A) a transfer of an individual who has not been stabilized in violation of subsection (c) of such section if the transfer arises out of the circumstances of the emergency;

(B) the direction or relocation of an individual to receive medical screening in an alternative location—

(i) pursuant to an appropriate State emergency preparedness plan; or

(ii) in the case of a public health emergency described in subsection (g)(1)(B) that involves a pandemic infectious disease, pursuant to a State pandemic preparedness plan or a plan referred to in clause (i), whichever is applicable in the State;

(4) sanctions under section 1877(g) (relating to limitations on physician referral);

(5) deadlines and timetables for performance of required activities, except that such deadlines and timetables may only be modified, not waived;

(6) limitations on payments under section 1851(i) for health care items and services furnished to individuals enrolled in a Medicare+Choice plan by health care professionals or facilities not included under such plan; and

(7) sanctions and penalties that arise from the noncompliance with the following requirements (as promulgated under the au-

SOCIAL SECURITY ACT—§ 1135(d)(1)(C) 679

thority of section 264(c) of the Health Insurance Portability and Accountability Act of 1996[67] (42 U.S.C. 1320d-2 note)—

(A) section 164.510 of title 45, Code of Federal Regulations, relating to—

(i) requirements to obtain a patient's agreement to speak with family members or friends; and

(ii) the requirement to honor a request to opt out of the facility directory;

(B) section 164.520 of such title, relating to the requirement to distribute a notice; or

(C) section 164.522 of such title, relating to—

(i) the patient's right to request privacy restrictions; and

(ii) the patient's right to request confidential communications.

Insofar as the Secretary exercises authority under paragraph (6) with respect to individuals enrolled in a Medicare+Choice plan, to the extent possible given the circumstances, the Secretary shall reconcile payments made on behalf of such enrollees to ensure that the enrollees do not pay more than would be required had they received services from providers within the network of the plan and may reconcile payments to the organization offering the plan to ensure that such organization pays for services for which payment is included in the capitation payment it receives under part C of title XVIII. A waiver or modification provided for under paragraph (3) or (7) shall only be in effect if such actions are taken in a manner that does not discriminate among individuals on the basis of their source of payment or of their ability to pay, and, except in the case of a waiver or modification to which the fifth sentence of this subsection applies, shall be limited to a 72-hour period beginning upon implementation of a hospital disaster protocal. A waiver or modification under such paragraph (7) shall be withdrawn after such period and the provider shall comply with the requirements under such paragraph for any patient still under the care of the provider. If a public health emergency described in subsection (g)(1)(B) involves a pandemic infectious disease (such as pandemic influenza), the duration of a waiver or modification under paragraph (3) shall be determined in accordance with subsection (e) as such subsection applies to public health emergencies.

(c) AUTHORITY FOR RETROACTIVE WAIVER.—A waiver or modification of requirements pursuant to this section may, at the Secretary's discretion, be made retroactive to the beginning of the emergency period or any subsequent date in such period specified by the Secretary.

(d) CERTIFICATION TO CONGRESS.—The Secretary shall provide a certification and advance written notice to the Congress at least two days before exercising the authority under this section with respect to an emergency area. Such a certification and notice shall include—

(1) a description of—

(A) the specific provisions that will be waived or modified;

(B) the health care providers to whom the waiver or modification will apply;

(C) the geographic area in which the waiver or modification will apply; and

---

[67] See Vol. II, P.L. 104-191, §264(c).

680 SOCIAL SECURITY ACT—§ 1135(d)(1)(D)

(D) the period of time for which the waiver or modification will be in effect; and

(2) a certification that the waiver or modification is necessary to carry out the purpose specified in subsection (a).

(e) DURATION OF WAIVER.—

(1) IN GENERAL.—A waiver or modification of requirements pursuant to this section terminates upon—

(A) the termination of the applicable declaration of emergency or disaster described in subsection (g)(1)(A);

(B) the termination of the applicable declaration of public health emergency described in subsection (g)(1)(B); or

(C) subject to paragraph (2), the termination of a period of 60 days from the date the waiver or modification is first published (or, if applicable, the date of extension of the waiver or modification under paragraph (2)).

(2) EXTENSION OF 60-DAY PERIODS.—The Secretary may, by notice, provide for an extension of a 60-day period described in paragraph (1)(C) (or an additional period provided under this paragraph) for additional period or periods (not to exceed, except as subsequently provided under this paragraph, 60 days each), but any such extension shall not affect or prevent the termination of a waiver or modification under subparagraph (A) or (B) of paragraph (1).

(f) REPORT TO CONGRESS.—Within one year after the end of the emergency period in an emergency area in which the Secretary exercised the authority provided under this section, the Secretary shall report to the Congress regarding the approaches used to accomplish the purposes described in subsection (a), including an evaluation of such approaches and recommendations for improved approaches should the need for such emergency authority arise in the future.

(g) DEFINITIONS.—For purposes of this section:

(1) EMERGENCY AREA; EMERGENCY PERIOD.—An "emergency area" is a geographical area in which, and an "emergency period" is the period during which, there exists—

(A) an emergency or disaster declared by the President pursuant to the National Emergencies Act[68] or the Robert T. Stafford Disaster Relief and Emergency Assistance Act[69]; and

(B) a public health emergency declared by the Secretary pursuant to section 319 of the Public Health Service Act.

(2) HEALTH CARE PROVIDER.—The term "health care provider" means any entity that furnishes health care items or services, and includes a hospital or other provider of services, a physician or other health care practitioner or professional, a health care facility, or a supplier of health care items or services.

---

[68] P.L. 94-412.
[69] P.L. 93-288.

EXCLUSION OF REPRESENTATIVES AND HEALTH CARE PROVIDERS CONVICTED OF VIOLATIONS FROM PARTICIPATION IN SOCIAL SECURITY PROGRAMS

SEC. 1136. [42 U.S.C. 1320b–6] (a) IN GENERAL.—The Commissioner of Social Security shall exclude from participation in the social security programs any representative or health care provider—

(1) who is convicted of a violation of section 208 or 1632 of this Act;

(2) who is convicted of any violation under title 18, United States Code, relating to an initial application for or continuing entitlement to, or amount of, benefits under title II of this Act, or an initial application for or continuing eligibility for, or amount of, benefits under title XVI of this Act; or

(3) who the Commissioner determines has committed an offense described in section 1129(a)(1) of this Act.

(b) NOTICE, EFFECTIVE DATE, AND PERIOD OF EXCLUSION.—

(1) An exclusion under this section shall be effective at such time, for such period, and upon such reasonable notice to the public and to the individual excluded as may be specified in regulations consistent with paragraph (2).

(2) Such an exclusion shall be effective with respect to services furnished to any individual on or after the effective date of the exclusion. Nothing in this section may be construed to preclude, in determining disability under title II or title XVI, consideration of any medical evidence derived from services provided by a health care provider before the effective date of the exclusion of the health care provider under this section.

(3)(A) The Commissioner shall specify, in the notice of exclusion under paragraph (1), the period of the exclusion.

(B) Subject to subparagraph (C), in the case of an exclusion under subsection (a), the minimum period of exclusion shall be 5 years, except that the Commissioner may waive the exclusion in the case of an individual who is the sole source of essential services in a community. The Commissioner's decision whether to waive the exclusion shall not be reviewable.

(C) In the case of an exclusion of an individual under subsection (a) based on a conviction or a determination described in subsection (a)(3) occurring on or after the date of the enactment of this section, if the individual has (before, on, or after such date of the enactment) been convicted, or if such a determination has been made with respect to the individual—

(i) on one previous occasion of one or more offenses for which an exclusion may be effected under such subsection, the period of the exclusion shall be not less than 10 years; or

(ii) on two or more previous occasions of one or more offenses for which an exclusion may be effected under such subsection, the period of the exclusion shall be permanent.

(c) NOTICE TO STATE AGENCIES.—The Commissioner shall promptly notify each appropriate State agency employed for the purpose of making disability determinations under section 221 or 1633(a)—

(1) of the fact and circumstances of each exclusion effected against an individual under this section; and

682 SOCIAL SECURITY ACT—§ 1136(c)(2)

(2) of the period (described in subsection (b)(3)) for which the State agency is directed to exclude the individual from participation in the activities of the State agency in the course of its employment.

(d) NOTICE TO STATE LICENSING AGENCIES.—The Commissioner shall—

(1) promptly notify the appropriate State or local agency or authority having responsibility for the licensing or certification of an individual excluded from participation under this section of the fact and circumstances of the exclusion;

(2) request that appropriate investigations be made and sanctions invoked in accordance with applicable State law and policy; and

(3) request that the State or local agency or authority keep the Commissioner and the Inspector General of the Social Security Administration fully and currently informed with respect to any actions taken in response to the request.

(e) NOTICE, HEARING, AND JUDICIAL REVIEW.—

(1) Any individual who is excluded (or directed to be excluded) from participation under this section is entitled to reasonable notice and opportunity for a hearing thereon by the Commissioner to the same extent as is provided in section 205(b), and to judicial review of the Commissioner's final decision after such hearing as is provided in section 205(g).

(2) The provisions of section 205(h) shall apply with respect to this section to the same extent as it is applicable with respect to title II.

(f) APPLICATION FOR TERMINATION OF EXCLUSION.—

(1) An individual excluded from participation under this section may apply to the Commissioner, in the manner specified by the Commissioner in regulations and at the end of the minimum period of exclusion provided under subsection (b)(3) and at such other times as the Commissioner may provide, for termination of the exclusion effected under this section.

(2) The Commissioner may terminate the exclusion if the Commissioner determines, on the basis of the conduct of the applicant which occurred after the date of the notice of exclusion or which was unknown to the Commissioner at the time of the exclusion, that—

(A) there is no basis under subsection (a) for a continuation of the exclusion; and

(B) there are reasonable assurances that the types of actions which formed the basis for the original exclusion have not recurred and will not recur.

(3) The Commissioner shall promptly notify each State agency employed for the purpose of making disability determinations under section 221 or 1633(a) of the fact and circumstances of each termination of exclusion made under this subsection.

(g) AVAILABILITY OF RECORDS OF EXCLUDED REPRESENTATIVES AND HEALTH CARE PROVIDERS.—Nothing in this section shall be construed to have the effect of limiting access by any applicant or beneficiary under title II or XVI, any State agency acting under section 221 or 1633(a), or the Commissioner to records maintained by any representative or health care provider in connection with services provided to

SOCIAL SECURITY ACT—§ 1137(a)(1)   683

the applicant or beneficiary prior to the exclusion of such representative or health care provider under this section.

(h) REPORTING REQUIREMENT.—Any representative or health care provider participating in, or seeking to participate in, a social security program shall inform the Commissioner, in such form and manner as the Commissioner shall prescribe by regulation, whether such representative or health care provider has been convicted of a violation described in subsection (a).

(i) DELEGATION OF AUTHORITY.—The Commissioner may delegate authority granted by this section to the Inspector General.

(j) DEFINITIONS.—For purposes of this section:

(1) EXCLUDE.—The term "exclude" from participation means—

(A) in connection with a representative, to prohibit from engaging in representation of an applicant for, or recipient of, benefits, as a representative payee under section 205(j) or section 1631(a)(2)(A)(ii), or otherwise as a representative, in any hearing or other proceeding relating to entitlement to benefits; and

(B) in connection with a health care provider, to prohibit from providing items or services to an applicant for, or recipient of, benefits for the purpose of assisting such applicant or recipient in demonstrating disability.

(2) SOCIAL SECURITY PROGRAM.—The term "social security programs" means the program providing for monthly insurance benefits under title II, and the program providing for monthly supplemental security income benefits to individuals under title XVI (including State supplementary payments made by the Commissioner pursuant to an agreement under section 1616(a) of this Act or section 212(b) of Public Law 93-66)[70].

(3) CONVICTED.—An individual is considered to have been "convicted" of a violation—

(A) when a judgment of conviction has been entered against the individual by a Federal, State, or local court, except if the judgment of conviction has been set aside or expunged;

(B) when there has been a finding of guilt against the individual by a Federal, State, or local court;

(C) when a plea of guilty or nolo contendere by the individual has been accepted by a Federal, State, or local court; or

(D) when the individual has entered into participation in a first offender, deferred adjudication, or other arrangement or program where judgment of conviction has been withheld.

INCOME AND ELIGIBILITY VERIFICATION SYSTEM[71]

SEC. 1137. [42 U.S.C. 1320b–7] (a) In order to meet the requirements of this section, a State must have in effect an income and eligibility verification system which meets the requirements of subsection (d) and under which—

(1) the State shall require, as a condition of eligibility for benefits under any program listed in subsection (b), that each applicant for or recipient of benefits under that program furnish to the State his social security account number (or numbers, if he

---

[70] See Vol. II, P.L. 93-66, §212(b).

[71] See Vol. II, P.L. 103-432, §232, with respect to measurement and reporting of welfare receipt.

684   SOCIAL SECURITY ACT—§ 1137(a)(1)(cont)

has more than one such number), and the State shall utilize such account numbers in the administration of that program so as to enable the association of the records pertaining to the applicant or recipient with his account number;

(2) wage information from agencies administering State unemployment compensation laws available pursuant to section 3304(a)(16) of the Internal Revenue Code of 1954[72], wage information reported pursuant to paragraph (3) of this subsection, and wage, income, and other information from the Social Security Administration and the Internal Revenue Service available pursuant to section 6103(l)(7) of such Code[73], shall be requested and utilized to the extent that such information may be useful in verifying eligibility for, and the amount of, benefits available under any program listed in subsection (b), as determined by the Secretary of Health and Human Services (or, in the case of the unemployment compensation program, by the Secretary of Labor, or, in the case of the supplemental nutrition assistance program[74], by the Secretary of Agriculture);

(3) employers (as defined in section 453A(a)(2)(B)) (including State and local governmental entities and labor organizations) in such State are required, effective September 30, 1988, to make quarterly wage reports to a State agency (which may be the agency administering the State's unemployment compensation law) except that the Secretary of Labor (in consultation with the Secretary of Health and Human Services and the Secretary of Agriculture) may waive the provisions of this paragraph if he determines that the State has in effect an alternative system which is as effective and timely for purposes of providing employment related income and eligibility data for the purposes described in paragraph (2), and except that no report shall be filed with respect to an employee of a State or local agency performing intelligence or counterintelligence functions, if the head of such agency has determined that filing such a report could endanger the safety of the employee or compromise an ongoing investigation or intelligence mission, and except that in the case of wage reports with respect to domestic service employment, a State may permit employers (as so defined) that make returns with respect to such employment on a calendar year basis pursuant to section 3510 of the Internal Revenue Code of 1986 to make such reports on an annual basis;

(4) the State agencies administering the programs listed in subsection (b) adhere to standardized formats and procedures established by the Secretary of Health and Human Services (in consultation with the Secretary of Agriculture) under which—

> (A) the agencies will exchange with each other information in their possession which may be of use in establishing or verifying eligibility or benefit amounts under any other such program;

---

[72] See Vol. II, P.L. 83-591, §3304(a).
[73] See Vol. II, P.L. 83-591, §6103(l).
[74] P.L. 110-246, §4002(b)(1)(A), struck out "food stamp program" and substituted "supplemental nutrition assistance program", effective October 1, 2008. P.L. 110-234, §4002(b)(1)(A), which made the same amendment, was repealed, effective May 22, 2008 pursuant to P.L. 110-246, §4(a).

SOCIAL SECURITY ACT—§ 1137(b)(3)   685

(B) such information shall be made available to assist in the child support program under part D of title IV of this Act, and to assist the Secretary of Health and Human Services in establishing or verifying eligibility or benefit amounts under titles II and XVI of this Act, but subject to the safeguards and restrictions established by the Secretary of the Treasury with respect to information released pursuant to section 6103(l) of the Internal Revenue Code of 1954[75] and

(C) the use of such information shall be targeted to those uses which are most likely to be productive in identifying and preventing ineligibility and incorrect payments, and no State shall be required to use such information to verify the eligibility of all recipients;

(5) adequate safeguards are in effect so as to assure that—

(A) the information exchanged by the State agencies is made available only to the extent necessary to assist in the valid administrative needs of the program receiving such information, and the information released pursuant to section 6103(l) of the Internal Revenue Code of 1954 is only exchanged with agencies authorized to receive such information under such section 6103(l); and

(B) the information is adequately protected against unauthorized disclosure for other purposes, as provided in regulations established by the Secretary of Health and Human Services, or, in the case of the unemployment compensation program, the Secretary of Labor, or, in the case of the supplemental nutrition assistance program[76], the Secretary of Agriculture, or in the case of information released pursuant to section 6103(l) of the Internal Revenue Code of 1954, the Secretary of the Treasury;

(6) all applicants for and recipients of benefits under any such program shall be notified at the time of application, and periodically thereafter, that information available through the system will be requested and utilized; and

(7) accounting systems are utilized which assure that programs providing data receive appropriate reimbursement from the programs utilizing the data for the costs incurred in providing the data.

(b) The programs which must participate in the income and eligibility verification system are—

(1) any State program funded under part A of title IV of this Act;

(2) the medicaid program under title XIX of this Act;

(3) the unemployment compensation program under section 3304 of the Internal Revenue Code of 1954[77];

---

[75] See Vol. II, P.L. 83-591, §6103(l).

[76] P.L. 110-246, §4002(b)(1)(A), struck out "food stamp program" and substituted "supplemental nutrition assistance program", effective October 1, 2008. P.L. 110-234, §4002(b)(1)(A), which made the same amendment, was repealed, effective May 22, 2008 pursuant to P.L. 110-246, §4(a).

[77] See Vol. II, P.L. 83-591, §3304.

686 SOCIAL SECURITY ACT—§ 1137(b)(4)

(4) the supplemental nutrition assistance program[78] under the Food and Nutrition Act of 2008[79]; and

(5) any State program under a plan approved under title I, X, XIV, or XVI of this Act.

(c)(1) In order to protect applicants for and recipients of benefits under the programs identified in subsection (b), or under the supplemental security income program under title XVI, from the improper use of information obtained from the Secretary of the Treasury under section 6103(l)(7)(B) of the Internal Revenue Code of 1954[80], no Federal, State, or local agency receiving such information may terminate, deny, suspend, or reduce any benefits of an individual until such agency has taken appropriate steps to independently verify information relating to—

(A) the amount of the asset or income involved,

(B) whether such individual actually has (or had) access to such asset or income for his own use, and

(C) the period or periods when the individual actually had such asset or income.

(2) Such individual shall be informed by the agency of the findings made by the agency on the basis of such verified information, and shall be given an opportunity to contest such findings, in the same manner as applies to other information and findings relating to eligibility factors under the program.

(d) The requirements of this subsection, with respect to an income and eligibility verification system of a State, are as follows:

(1)(A) The State shall require, as a condition of an individual's eligibility for benefits under a program listed in subsection (b), a declaration in writing, under penalty of perjury—

(i) by the individual,

(ii) in the case in which eligibility for program benefits is determined on a family or household basis, by any adult member of such individual's family or household (as applicable), or

(iii) in the case of an individual born into a family or household receiving benefits under such program, by any adult member or such family or household no later than the next redetermination of eligibility of such family or household following the birth of such individual,

stating whether the individual is a citizen or national of the United States, and, if that individual is not a citizen or national of the United States, that the individual is in a satisfactory immigration status.

(B) In this subsection, in the case of the program described in subsection (b)(4)—

(i) any reference to the State shall be considered a reference to the State agency, and

---

[78] P.L. 110-246, §4002(b)(1)(A), struck out "food stamp program" and substituted "supplemental nutrition assistance program", effective October 1, 2008. P.L. 110-234, §4002(b)(1)(A), which made the same amendment, was repealed, effective May 22, 2008 pursuant to P.L. 110-246, §4(a).

[79] P.L. 88-525.

P.L. 110-246, §4002(b)(1)(B), struck out "Food Stamp Act of 1977" and substituted "Food and Nutrition Act of 2008", effective October 1, 2008. P.L. 110-234, §4002(b)(1)(B), which made the same amendment, was repealed, effective May 22, 2008 pursuant to P.L. 110-246, §4(a).

[80] See Vol. II, P.L. 83-591, §6103(l)(7)(B).

SOCIAL SECURITY ACT—§ 1137(d)(4)(B)(ii)

(ii) any reference to an individual's eligibility for benefits under the program shall be considered a reference to the individual's eligibility to participate in the program as a member of a household, and

(iii) the term "satisfactory immigration status" means an immigration status which does not make the individual ineligible for benefits under the applicable program.

(2) If such an individual is not a citizen or national of the United States, there must be presented either—

(A) alien registration documentation or other proof of immigration registration from the Immigration and Naturalization Service that contains the individual's alien admission number or alien file number (or numbers if the individual has more than one number), or

(B) such other documents as the State determines constitutes reasonable evidence indicating a satisfactory immigration status.

(3) If the documentation described in paragraph (2)(A) is presented, the State shall utilize the individual's alien file or alien admission number to verify with the Immigration and Naturalization Service the individual's immigration status through an automated or other system (designated by the Service for use with States) that—

(A) utilizes the individual's name, file number, admission number, or other means permitting efficient verification, and

(B) protects the individual's privacy to the maximum degree possible.

(4) In the case of such an individual who is not a citizen or national of the United States, if, at the time of application for benefits, the statement described in paragraph (1) is submitted but the documentation required under paragraph (2) is not presented or if the documentation required under paragraph (2)(A) is presented but such documentation is not verified under paragraph (3)—

(A) the State—

(i) shall provide a reasonable opportunity to submit to the State evidence indicating a satisfactory immigration status, and

(ii) may not delay, deny, reduce, or terminate the individual's eligibility for benefits under the program on the basis of the individual's immigration status until such a reasonable opportunity has been provided; and

(B) if there are submitted documents which the State determines constitutes reasonable evidence indicating such status—

(i) the State shall transmit to the Immigration and Naturalization Service either photostatic or other similar copies of such documents, or information from such documents, as specified by the Immigration and Naturalization Service, for official verification,

(ii) pending such verification, the State may not delay, deny, reduce, or terminate the individual's eligibility for benefits under the program on the basis of the individual's immigration status, and

688   SOCIAL SECURITY ACT—§ 1137(d)(4)(B)(iii)

(iii) the State shall not be liable for the consequences of any action, delay, or failure of the Service to conduct such verification.

(5) If the State determines, after complying with the requirements of paragraph (4), that such an individual is not in a satisfactory immigration status under the applicable program—

(A) the State shall deny or terminate the individual's eligibility for benefits under the program, and

(B) the applicable fair hearing process shall be made available with respect to the individual.

(e) Each Federal agency responsible for administration of a program described in subsection (b) shall not take any compliance, disallowance, penalty, or other regulatory action against a State with respect to any error in the State's determination to make an individual eligible for benefits based on citizenship or immigration status—

(1) if the State has provided such eligibility based on a verification of satisfactory immigration status by the Immigration and Naturalization Service,

(2) because the State, under subsection (d)(4)(A)(ii), was required to provide a reasonable opportunity to submit documentation,

(3) because the State, under subsection (d)(4)(B)(ii), was required to wait for the response of the Immigration and Naturalization Service to the State's request for official verification of the immigration status of the individual, or

(4) because of a fair hearing process described in subsection (d)(5)(B).

(f) Subsections (a)(1) and (d) shall not apply with respect to aliens seeking medical assistance for the treatment of an emergency medical condition under section 1903(v)(2).

HOSPITAL PROTOCOLS FOR ORGAN PROCUREMENT AND STANDARDS FOR
ORGAN PROCUREMENT AGENCIES

SEC. 1138. [42 U.S.C. 1320b–8] (a)(1) The Secretary shall provide that a hospital or critical access hospital meeting the requirements of title XVIII or XIX may participate in the program established under such title only if—

(A) the hospital or critical access hospital establishes written protocols for the identification of potential organ donors that—

(i) assure that families of potential organ donors are made aware of the option of organ or tissue donation and their option to decline,

(ii) encourage discretion and sensitivity with respect to the circumstances, views, and beliefs of such families, and

(iii) require that such hospital's designated organ procurement agency (as defined in paragraph (3)(B)) is notified of potential organ donors;

(B) in the case of a hospital in which organ transplants are performed, the hospital is a member of, and abides by the rules and requirements of, the Organ Procurement and Transplantation Network established pursuant to section 372 of the Public

SOCIAL SECURITY ACT—§ 1138(a)(3)(B)   689

Health Service Act[81] (in this section referred to as the "Network"); and

(C) the hospital or critical access hospital has an agreement (as defined in paragraph (3)(A)) only with such hospital's designated organ procurement agency.

(2)(A) The Secretary shall grant a waiver of the requirements under subparagraphs (A)(iii) and (C) of paragraph (1) to a hospital or critical access hospital desiring to enter into an agreement with an organ procurement agency other than such hospital's designated organ procurement agency if the Secretary determines that—

(i) the waiver is expected to increase organ donation; and

(ii) the waiver will assure equitable treatment of patients referred for transplants within the service area served by such hospital's designated organ procurement agency and within the service area served by the organ procurement agency with which the hospital seeks to enter into an agreement under the waiver.

(B) In making a determination under subparagraph (A), the Secretary may consider factors that would include, but not be limited to—

(i) cost effectiveness;

(ii) improvements in quality;

(iii) whether there has been any change in a hospital's designated organ procurement agency due to a change made on or after December 28, 1992, in the definitions for metropolitan statistical areas (as established by the Office of Management and Budget); and

(iv) the length and continuity of a hospital's relationship with an organ procurement agency other than the hospital's designated organ procurement agency;

except that nothing in this subparagraph shall be construed to permit the Secretary to grant a waiver that does not meet the requirements of subparagraph (A).

(C) Any hospital or critical access hospital seeking a waiver under subparagraph (A) shall submit an application to the Secretary containing such information as the Secretary determines appropriate.

(D) The Secretary shall—

(i) publish a public notice of any waiver application received from a hospital or critical access hospital under this paragraph within 30 days of receiving such application; and

(ii) prior to making a final determination on such application under subparagraph (A), offer interested parties the opportunity to submit written comments to the Secretary during the 60-day period beginning on the date such notice is published.

(3) For purposes of this subsection—

(A) the term "agreement" means an agreement described in section 371(b)(3)(A) of the Public Health Service Act[82] ;

(B) the term "designated organ procurement agency" means, with respect to a hospital or critical access hospital, the organ procurement agency designated pursuant to subsection (b) for the service area in which such hospital is located; and

---

[81] See Vol. II, P.L. 78-410, §372.
[82] See Vol. II, P.L. 78-410, §371(b).

690   SOCIAL SECURITY ACT—§ 1138(a)(3)(C)

(C) the term "organ" means a human kidney, liver, heart, lung, pancreas, and any other human organ or tissue specified by the Secretary for purposes of this subsection.

(b)(1) The Secretary shall provide that payment may be made under title XVIII or XIX with respect to organ procurement costs attributable to payments made to an organ procurement agency only if the agency—

(A)(i) is a qualified organ procurement organization (as described in section 371(b) of the Public Health Service Act[83]) that is operating under a grant made under section 371(a) of such Act, or (ii) has been certified or recertified by the Secretary within the previous 2 years (4 years if the Secretary determines appropriate for an organization on the basis of its past practices) as meeting the standards to be a qualified organ procurement organization (as so described);

(B) meets the requirements that are applicable under such title for organ procurement agencies;

(C) meets performance-related standards prescribed by the Secretary;

(D) is a member of, and abides by the rules and requirements of, the Network;

(E) allocates organs, within its service area and nationally, in accordance with medical criteria and the policies of the Network; and

(F) is designated by the Secretary as an organ procurement organization payments to which may be treated as organ procurement costs for purposes of reimbursement under such title.

(2) The Secretary may not designate more than one organ procurement organization for each service area (described in section 371(b)(1)(E) of the Public Health Service Act) under paragraph (1)(F).

NATIONAL COMMISSION ON CHILDREN

SEC. 1139. [42 U.S.C. 1320b–9] (a)(1)[84] There is hereby established a commission to be known as the National Commission on Children (in this section referred to as the "Commission").

(b)(1) The Commission shall consist of—

(A) 12 members to be appointed by the President,

(B) 12 members to be appointed by the Speaker of the House of Representatives, and

(C) 12 members to be appointed by the President pro tempore of the Senate.

(2) The President, the Speaker, and the President pro tempore shall each appoint as members of the Commission—

(A) 4 individuals who—

(i) are representatives of organizations providing services to children,

(ii) are involved in activities on behalf of children, or

(iii) have engaged in academic research with respect to the problems and needs of children,

---

[83] See Vol. II, P.L. 78-410, §371(b).
[84] As in original. No paragraph (a)(2) has been enacted.

SOCIAL SECURITY ACT—§ 1139(d)(2)(B)   691

(B) 4 individuals who are elected or appointed public officials (at the Federal, State, or local level) involved in issues and programs relating to children, and

(C) 4 individuals who are parents or representatives of parents or parents' organizations.

(3) The appointments made pursuant to subparagraphs (B) and (C) of paragraph (1) shall be made in consultation with the chairmen of committees of the House of Representatives and the Senate, respectively, having jurisdiction over relevant Federal programs.

(c)(1) It shall be the duty and function of the Commission to serve as a forum on behalf of the children of the Nation and to conduct the studies and issue the report required by subsection (d).

(2) The Commission (and any committees that it may form) shall conduct public hearings in different geographic areas of the country, both urban and rural, in order to receive the views of a broad spectrum of the public on the status of the Nation's children and on ways to safeguard and enhance the physical, mental, and emotional well-being of all of the children of the Nation, including those with physical or mental disabilities, and others whose circumstances deny them a full share of the opportunities that parents of the Nation may rightfully expect for their children.

(3) The Commission shall receive testimony from individuals, and from representatives of public and private organizations and institutions with an interest in the welfare of children, including educators, health care professionals, religious leaders, providers of social services, representatives of organizations with children as members, elected and appointed public officials, and from parents and children speaking in their own behalf.

(d) The Commission shall submit to the President, and to the Committees on Finance and Labor and Human Resources of the Senate and the Committees on Ways and Means, Education and Labor, and Energy and Commerce of the House of Representatives, an interim report no later than March 31, 1990, and a final report no later than March 31, 1991, setting forth recommendations with respect to the following subjects:

(1) Questions relating to the health of children that the Commission shall address include—

(A) how to reduce infant mortality,

(B) how to reduce the number of low-birth-weight babies,

(C) how to reduce the number of children with chronic illnesses and disabilities,

(D) how to improve the nutrition of children,

(E) how to promote the physical fitness of children,

(F) how to ensure that pregnant women receive adequate prenatal care,

(G) how to ensure that all children have access to both preventive and acute care health services, and

(H) how to improve the quality and availability of health care for children.

(2) Questions relating to social and support services for children and their parents that the Commission shall address include—

(A) how to prevent and treat child neglect and abuse,

(B) how to provide help to parents who seek assistance in meeting the problems of their children,

692 SOCIAL SECURITY ACT—§ 1139(d)(2)(C)

(C) how to provide counseling services for children,

(D) how to strengthen the family unit,

(E) how children can be assured of adequate care while their parents are working or participating in education or training programs,

(F) how to improve foster care and adoption services,

(G) how to reduce drug and alcohol abuse by children and youths, and

(H) how to reduce the incidence of teenage pregnancy.

(3) Questions relating to education that the Commission shall address include—

(A) how to encourage academic excellence for all children at all levels of education,

(B) how to use preschool experiences to enhance educational achievement,

(C) how to improve the qualifications of teachers,

(D) how schools can better prepare the Nation's youth to compete in the labor market,

(E) how parents and schools can work together to help children achieve success at each step of the academic ladder,

(F) how to encourage teenagers to complete high school and remain in school to fulfill their academic potential,

(G) how to address the problems of drug and alcohol abuse by young people,

(H) how schools might lend support to efforts aimed at reducing the incidence of teenage pregnancy, and

(I) how schools might better meet the special needs of children who have physical or mental handicaps.

(4) Questions relating to income security that the Commission shall address include—

(A) how to reduce poverty among children,

(B) how to ensure that parents support their children to the fullest extent possible through improved child support collection services, including services on behalf of children whose parents are unmarried, and

(C) how to ensure that cash assistance to needy children is adequate.

(5) Questions relating to tax policy that the Commission shall address include—

(A) how to assure the equitable tax treatment of families with children,

(B) the effect of existing tax provisions, including the dependent care tax credit, the earned income tax credit, and the targeted jobs tax credit, on children living in poverty,

(C) whether the dependent care tax credit should be refundable and the effect of such a policy,

(D) whether the earned income tax credit should be adjusted for family size and the effect of such a policy, and

(E) whether there are other tax-related policies which would reduce poverty among children.

(6) In addition to addressing the questions specified in paragraphs (1) through (5), the Commission shall—

(A) seek to identify ways in which public and private organizations and institutions can work together at the community level to identify deficiencies in existing services for families and children and to develop recommendations to ensure that the needs of families and children are met, using all available resources, in a coordinated and comprehensive manner, and

(B) assess the existing capacities of agencies to collect and analyze data on the status of children and on relevant programs, identify gaps in the data collection system, and recommend ways to improve the collection of data and the coordination among agencies in the collection and utilization of data.

The reports required by this subsection shall be based upon the testimony received in the hearings conducted pursuant to subsection (c), and upon other data and findings developed by the Commission.

(e)(1)(A) Members of the Commission shall first be appointed not later than 60 days after the date of the enactment of this section[85], for terms ending on March 31, 1991.

(B) A vacancy in the Commission shall not affect its powers, but shall be filled in the same manner as the vacant position was first filled.

(2) The Commission shall elect one of its members to serve as Chairman of the Commission. The Chairman shall be a nonvoting member of the Commission.

(3) A majority of the members of the Commission shall constitute a quorum for the transaction of business.

(4)(A) The Commission shall meet at the call of the Chairman, or at the call of a majority of the members of the Commission.

(B) The Commission shall meet not less than 4 times during the period beginning with the date of the enactment of this section and ending with September 30, 1990.

(5) Decisions of the Commission shall be according to the vote of a simple majority of those present and voting at a properly called meeting.

(6) Members of the Commission shall serve without compensation, but shall be reimbursed for travel, subsistence, and other necessary expenses incurred in the performance of their duties as members of the Commission.

(f)(1) The Commission shall appoint an Executive Director of the Commission. In addition to the Executive Director, the Commission may appoint and fix the compensation of such personnel as it deems advisable. Such appointments and compensation may be made without regard to title 5, United States Code, that govern appointments in the competitive services, and the provisions of chapter 51 and subchapter III of chapter 53 of such title that relate to classifications and the General Schedule pay rates.

(2) The Commission may procure such temporary and intermittent services of consultants under section 3109(b) of title 5, United States Code[86], as the Commission determines to be necessary to carry out the duties of the Commission.

(g) In carrying out its duties, the Commission, or any duly organized committee thereof, is authorized to hold such hearings, sit and

---

[85] December 22, 1987 [P.L. 100-203; 101 Stat. 1330-316].
[86] See Vol. II, 5 U.S.C. 3109(b).

694   SOCIAL SECURITY ACT—§ 1139(g)(cont)

act at such times and places, and take such testimony, with respect to matters for which it has a responsibility under this section, as the Commission or committee may deem advisable.

(h)(1) The Commission may secure directly from any department or agency of the United States such data and information as may be necessary to carry out its responsibilities.

(2) Upon request of the Commission, any such department or agency shall furnish any such data or information.

(i) The General Services Administration shall provide to the Commission, on a reimbursable basis, such administrative support services as the Commission may request.

(j) There are authorized to be appropriated through fiscal year 1991, such sums as may be necessary to carry out this section for each of fiscal years 1989 and 1990.

(k)(1) The Commission is authorized to accept donations of money, property, or personal services. Funds received from donations shall be deposited in the Treasury in a separate fund created for this purpose. Funds appropriated for the Commission and donated funds may be expended for such purposes as official reception and representation expenses, public surveys, public service announcements, preparation of special papers, analyses, and documentaries, and for such other purposes as determined by the Commission to be in furtherance of its mission to review national issues affecting children.

(2) For purposes of Federal income, estate, and gift taxation, money and other property accepted under paragraph (1) of this subsection shall be considered as a gift or bequest to or for the use of the United States.

(3) Expenditure of appropriated and donated funds shall be subject to such rules and regulations as may be adopted by the Commission and shall not be subject to Federal procurement requirements.

(l) The Commission is authorized to conduct such public surveys as it deems necessary in support of its review of national issues affecting children and, in conducting such surveys, the Commission shall not be deemed to be an "agency" for the purpose of section 3502 of title 44, United States Code[87].

PROHIBITION OF MISUSE OF SYMBOLS, EMBLEMS, OR NAMES IN REFERENCE TO SOCIAL SECURITY OR MEDICARE

SEC. 1140. [42 U.S.C. 1320b–10] (a)(1) No person may use, in connection with any item constituting an advertisement, solicitation, circular, book, pamphlet, or other communication, or a play, motion picture, broadcast, telecast, or other production, alone or with other words, letters, symbols, or emblems—

    (A) the words "Social Security", "Social Security Account", "Social Security System", "Social Security Administration", "Medicare", "Centers for Medicare and Medicaid Services", "Department of Health and Human Services", "Health and Human Services", "Supplemental Security Income Program", or "Medicaid", the letters "SSA", "CMS", "DHHS", "HHS", or "SSI", or any other combination or variation of such words or letters, or

    (B) a symbol or emblem of the Social Security Administration, Centers for Medicare and Medicaid Services, or Department of

---

[87] See Vol. II, 44 U.S.C. 3502.

SOCIAL SECURITY ACT—§ 1140(a)(4)(B)   695

Health and Human Services (including the design of, or a reasonable facsimile of the design of, the social security card issued pursuant to section 205(c)(2)(F), or the Medicare card the check used for payment of benefits under title II, or envelopes or other stationery used by the Social Security Administration, Centers for Medicare and Medicaid Services, or Department of Health and Human Services) or any other combination or variation of such symbols or emblems,

in a manner which such person knows or should know would convey, or in a manner which reasonably could be interpreted or construed as conveying, the false impression that such item is approved, endorsed, or authorized by the Social Security Administration, the Centers for Medicare and Medicaid Services, or the Department of Health and Human Services or that such person has some connection with, or authorization from, the Social Security Administration, the Centers for Medicare and Medicaid Services, or the Department of Health and Human Services. The preceding provisions of this subsection shall not apply with respect to the use by any agency or instrumentality of a State or political subdivision of a State of any words or letters which identify an agency or instrumentality of such State or of a political subdivision of such State or the use by any such agency or instrumentality of any symbol or emblem of an agency or instrumentality of such State or a political subdivision of such State.

(2)(A) No person may, for a fee, reproduce, reprint, or distribute any item consisting of a form, application, or other publication of the Social Security Administration unless such person has obtained specific, written authorization for such activity in accordance with regulations which the Commissioner of Social Security shall prescribe.

(B) No person may, for a fee, reproduce, reprint, or distribute any item consisting of a form, application, or other publication of the Department of Health and Human Services unless such person has obtained specific, written authorization for such activity in accordance with regulations which the Secretary shall prescribe.

(3) Any determination of whether the use of one or more words, letters, symbols, or emblems (or any combination or variation thereof) in connection with an item described in paragraph (1) or the reproduction, reprinting, or distribution of an item described in paragraph (2) is a violation of this subsection shall be made without regard to any inclusion in such item (or any so reproduced, reprinted, or distributed copy thereof) of a disclaimer of affiliation with the United States Government or any particular agency or instrumentality thereof.

(4)(A) No person shall offer, for a fee, to assist an individual to obtain a product or service that the person knows or should know is provided free of charge by the Social Security Administration unless, at the time the offer is made, the person provides to the individual to whom the offer is tendered a notice that—

(i) explains that the product or service is available free of charge from the Social Security Administration, and

(ii) complies with standards prescribed by the Commissioner of Social Security respecting the content of such notice and its placement, visibility, and legibility.

(B) Subparagraph (A) shall not apply to any offer—

696   SOCIAL SECURITY ACT—§ 1140(a)(4)(B)(i)

(i) to serve as a claimant representative in connection with a claim arising under subchapter II of this chapter, subchapter VIII of this chapter, or subchapter XVI of this chapter; or

(ii) to prepare, or assist in the preparation of, an individual's plan for achieving self-support under subchapter XVI of this chapter.

(b) The Commissioner or the Secretary (as applicable) may, pursuant to regulations, impose a civil money penalty not to exceed—

(1) except as provided in paragraph (2), $5,000, or

(2) in the case of a violation consisting of a broadcast or telecast, $25,000,

against any person for each violation by such person of subsection (a). In the case of any items referred to in subsection (a)(1) consisting of pieces of mail, each such piece of mail which contains one or more words, letters, symbols, or emblems in violation of subsection (a) shall represent a separate violation. In the case of any item referred to in subsection (a)(2), the reproduction, reprinting, or distribution of such item shall be treated as a separate violation with respect to each copy thereof so reproduced, reprinted, or distributed.

(c)(1) The provisions of section 1128A (other than subsections (a), (b), (f), (h), and (i) and the first sentence of subsection (c)) shall apply to civil money penalties under subsection (b) in the same manner as such provisions apply to a penalty or proceeding under section 1128A(a).

(2) Penalties imposed against a person under subsection (b) may be compromised by the Commissioner or the Secretary (as applicable) and may be recovered in a civil action in the name of the United States brought in the district court of the United States for the district in which the violation occurred or where the person resides, has its principal office, or may be found, as determined by the Commissioner or the Secretary (as applicable). Amounts recovered under this section shall be paid to the Secretary and shall be deposited as miscellaneous receipts of the Treasury of the United States, except that (A) to the extent that such amounts are recovered under this section as penalties imposed for misuse of words, letters, symbols, or emblems relating to the Social Security Administration, such amounts shall be deposited into the Federal Old-Age and Survivors Insurance Trust Fund, and (B) to the extent that such amounts are recovered under this section as penalties imposed for misuse of words, letters, symbols, or emblems relating to the Department of Health and Human Services, such amounts shall be deposited into the Federal Hospital Insurance Trust Fund or the Federal Supplementary Medical Insurance Trust Fund, as appropriate. The amount of such penalty when finally determined, or the amount agreed upon in compromise, may be deducted from any sum then or later owing by the United States to the person against whom the penalty has been imposed.

(d) The preceding provisions of this section may be enforced through the Office of the Inspector General of the Social Security Administration or the Office of the Inspector General of the Department of Health and Human Services (as appropriate).

BLOOD DONOR LOCATOR SERVICE

SEC. 1141. [42 U.S.C. 1320b–11] (a) IN GENERAL.—The Commissioner of Social Security shall establish and conduct a Blood Donor Locator Service, which shall be used to obtain and transmit to any authorized person (as defined in subsection (h)(1)) the most recent mailing address of any blood donor who, as indicated by the donated blood or products derived therefrom or by the history of the subsequent use of such blood or blood products, has or may have the virus for acquired immune deficiency syndrome, in order to inform such donor of the possible need for medical care and treatment.

(b) PROVISION OF ADDRESS INFORMATION.—Whenever the Commissioner of Social Security receives a request, filed by an authorized person (as defined in subsection (h)(1)), for the mailing address of a donor described in subsection (a) and the Commissioner of Social Security is reasonably satisfied that the requirements of this section have been met with respect to such request, the Commissioner of Social Security shall promptly undertake to provide the requested address information from—

(1) the files and records maintained by the Social Security Administration, and

(2) such files and records obtained pursuant to section 6103(m)(6) of the Internal Revenue Code of 1986[88] as the Commissioner of Social Security considers necessary to comply with such request.

(c) MANNER AND FORM OF REQUESTS.—A request for address information under this section shall be filed in such manner and form as the Commissioner of Social Security shall by regulation prescribe, shall include the blood donor's social security account number, and shall be accompanied or supported by such documents as the Commissioner of Social Security may determine to be necessary.

(d) PROCEDURES AND SAFEGUARDS.—Any authorized person shall, as a condition for receiving address information from the Blood Donor Locator Service—

(1) establish and maintain, to the satisfaction of the Commissioner of Social Security, a system for standardizing records with respect to any request, the reason for such request, and the date of such request made by or of it and any disclosure of address information made by or to it,

(2) establish and maintain, to the satisfaction of the Commissioner of Social Security, a secure area or place in which such address information and all related blood donor records shall be stored,

(3) restrict, to the satisfaction of the Commissioner of Social Security, access to the address information and related blood donor records only to persons whose duties or responsibilities require access and to whom disclosure may be made under the provisions of this section,

(4) provide such other safeguards which the Commissioner of Social Security determines (and which the Commissioner of Social Security prescribes in regulations) to be necessary or appropriate to protect the confidentiality of the address information and related blood donor records,

(5) furnish a report to the Commissioner of Social Security, at such time and containing such information as the Commissioner of Social Security may prescribe, which describes the procedures established and utilized by the authorized person for ensuring

---

[88] See Vol. II, P.L. 83-591, §6103(m)(6).

698 SOCIAL SECURITY ACT—§ 1141(d)(5)(cont)

the confidentiality of address information and related blood donor records required under this subsection, and

(6) destroy such address information and related blood donor records, upon completion of their use in providing the notification for which the information was obtained, so as to make such information and records undisclosable.

If the Commissioner of Social Security determines that any authorized person has failed to, or does not, meet the requirements of this subsection, the Commissioner of Social Security may, after any proceedings for review established under subsection (f), take such actions as are necessary to ensure such requirements are met, including refusing to disclose address information to such authorized person until the Commissioner of Social Security determines that such requirements have been or will be met. In the case of any authorized person who discloses any address information received pursuant to this section or any related blood donor records to any agent, this subsection shall apply to such authorized person and each such agent (except that, in the case of an agent, any report to the Commissioner of Social Security or other action with respect to the Commissioner of Social Security shall be made or taken through such authorized person). The Commissioner of Social Security shall destroy all related blood donor records in the possession of the Social Security Administration upon completion of their use in transmitting mailing addresses as required under subsection (a), so as to make such records undisclosable.

(e) ARRANGEMENTS WITH STATE AGENCIES AND AUTHORIZED PERSONS.—The Commissioner of Social Security, in carrying out the Commissioner's duties and functions under this section, shall enter into arrangements

(1) with State agencies to accept and to transmit to the Commissioner of Social Security requests for address information under this section and to accept and to transmit such information to authorized persons, and

(2) with State agencies and authorized persons otherwise to cooperate with the Commissioner of Social Security in carrying out the purposes of this section.

(f) PROCEDURES FORI ADMINISTRATIVE REVIEW.—The Commissioner of Social Security shall by regulation prescribe procedures which provide for administrative review of any determination that any authorized person has failed to meet the requirements of this section.

(g) UNAUTHORIZED DISCLOSURE OF INFORMATION.—Paragraphs (1), (2), and (3) of section 7213(a) of the Internal Revenue Code of 1986[89] shall apply with respect to the unauthorized willful disclosure to any person of address information or related blood donor records acquired or maintained by or under the Commissioner of Social Security, or pursuant to this section by any authorized person, or of information derived from any such address information or related blood donor records, in the same manner and to the same extent as such paragraphs apply with respect to unauthorized disclosures of return and return information described in such paragraphs. Paragraph (4) of section 7213(a) of such Code shall apply with respect to the willful offer of any item of material value in exchange for

---

[89] See Vol. II, P.L. 83-591, §7213(a)(1), (2), and (3).

SOCIAL SECURITY ACT—§ 1142(a)(1)(B)   699

any such address information or related blood donor record in the same manner and to the same extent as such paragraph applies with respect to offers (in exchange for any return or return information) described in such paragraph.

(h) DEFINITIONS.—for purposes of this section—

(1) AUTHORIZED PERSON.—The term "authorized person" means—

(A) any agency of a State (or of a political subdivision of a State) which has duties or authority under State law relating to the public health or otherwise has the duty or authority under State law to regulate blood donations, and

(B) any entity engaged in the acceptance of blood donations which is licensed or registered by the Food and Drug Administration in connection with the acceptance of such blood donations, and which, in accordance with such regulations as may be prescribed by the Commissioner of Social Security, provides for—

(i) the confidentiality of any address information received pursuant to this section and related blood donor records,

(ii) blood donor notification procedures for individuals with respect to whom such information is requested and a finding has been made that they have or may have the virus for acquired immune deficiency syndrome, and

(iii) counseling services for such individuals who have been found to have such virus.

(2) RELATED BLOOD DONOR RECORD.—The term "related blood donor record" means any record, list, or compilation which indicates, directly or indirectly, the identity of any individual with respect to whom a request for address information has been made pursuant to this section.

(3) STATE.—The term "State" includes the District of Columbia, the Commonwealth of Puerto Rico, the Virgin Islands, Guam, the Commonwealth of the Northern Marianas, and the Trust Territory of the Pacific Islands.

RESEARCH ON OUTCOMES OF HEALTH CARE SERVICES AND PROCEDURES

SEC. 1142. [42 U.S.C. 1320b–12] (a) DATE CERTAIN ESTABLISHMENT OF PROGRAM.—

(1) IN GENERAL.—The Secretary, acting through the Administrator for Health Care Policy and Research[90], shall—

(A) conduct and support research with respect to the outcomes, effectiveness, and appropriateness of health care services and procedures in order to identify the manner in which diseases, disorders, and other health conditions can most effectively and appropriately be prevented, diagnosed, treated, and managed clinically; and

(B) assure that the needs and priorities of the program under title XVIII are appropriately reflected in the development and periodic review and updating (through the process

---

[90] PL. 106-129, §2(b)(2), provided that any reference to the Administrator for Health Care Policy and Research is deemed to be a reference to the Director of the Agency for Health Care and Quality.

700 SOCIAL SECURITY ACT—§ 1142(a)(1)(B)(cont)

set forth in section 913 of the Public Health Service Act[91]) of treatment-specific or condition-specific practice guidelines for clinical treatments and conditions in forms appropriate for use in clinical practice, for use in educational programs, and for use in reviewing quality and appropriateness of medical care.

(2) EVALUATIONS OF ALTERNATIVE SERVICES AND PROCEDURES.—In carrying out paragraph (1), the Secretary shall conduct or support evaluations of the comparative effects, on health and functional capacity, of alternative services and procedures utilized in preventing, diagnosing, treating, and clinically managing diseases, disorders, and other health conditions.

(3) INITIAL GUIDELINES.—

(A) In carrying out paragraph (1)(B) of this subsection, and section 912(d) of the Public Health Service Act[92], the Secretary shall, by not later than January 1, 1991, assure the development of an initial set of the guidelines specified in paragraph (1)(B) that shall include not less than 3 clinical treatments or conditions that—

(i)(I) account for a significant portion of expenditures under title XVIII; and

(II) have a significant variation in the frequency or the type of treatment provided; or

(ii) otherwise meet the needs and priorities of the program under title XVIII, as set forth under subsection (b)(3).

(B)(i) The Secretary shall provide for the use of guidelines developed under subparagrah[93] (A) to improve the quality, effectiveness, and appropriateness of care provided under title XVIII. The Secretary shall determine the impact of such use on the quality, appropriateness, effectiveness, and cost of medical care provided under such title and shall report to the Congress on such determination by not later than January 1, 1993.

(ii) For the purpose of carrying out clause (i), the Secretary shall expend, from the amounts specified in clause (iii), $1,000,000 for fiscal year 1990 and $1,500,000 for each of the fiscal years 1991 and 1992.

(iii) For each fiscal year, for purposes of expenditures required in clause (ii)—

(I) 60 percent of an amount equal to the expenditure involved is appropriated from the Federal Hospital Insurance Trust Fund (established under section 1817); and

---

[91] See Vol. II, P.L. 78-410, for the current §913. [P.L. 106-129, amended the former §913 of the Public Health Service Act in its entirety, effective December 6, 1999. The original reference to §913 was omitted in the general amendment of Title IX by P.L. 106-129, §2(a), Dec. 6, 1999, 113 Stat. 1653. Section 2(a) of P.L.106-129 enacted a new §913.]

[92] P.L. 106-129, amended Title IX of the Public Health Service Act in its entirety, effective December 6, 1999. Until then, P.L. 78-410, §912(d) read "(d) DATE CERTAIN FOR INITIAL GUIDELINES AND STANDARDS.—The Administrator, by not later than January 1, 1991, shall assure the development of an initial set of guidelines, standards, performance measures, and review criteria under subsection (a) that includes not less than 3 clinical treatments or conditions described in section 1142(a)(3) of the Social Security Act."

[93] As in original; should be "subparagraph".

SOCIAL SECURITY ACT—§ 1142(c)(1)   701

(II) 40 percent of an amount equal to the expenditure involved is appropriated from the Federal Supplementary Medical Insurance Trust Fund (established under section 1841).

(b) PRIORITIES.—

(1) IN GENERAL.—The Secretary shall establish priorities with respect to the diseases, disorders, and other health conditions for which research and evaluations are to be conducted or supported under subsection (a). In establishing such priorities, the Secretary shall, with respect to a disease, disorder, or other health condition, consider the extent to which—

(A) improved methods of prevention, diagnosis, treatment, and clinical management can benefit a significant number of individuals;

(B) there is significant variation among physicians in the particular services and procedures utilized in making diagnoses and providing treatments or there is significant variation in the outcomes of health care services or procedures due to different patterns of diagnosis or treatment;

(C) the services and procedures utilized for diagnosis and treatment result in relatively substantial expenditures; and

(D) the data necessary for such evaluations are readily available or can readily be developed.

(2) PRELIMINARY ASSESSMENTS.—For the purpose of establishing priorities under paragraph (1), the Secretary may, with respect to services and procedures utilized in preventing, diagnosing, treating, and clinically managing diseases, disorders, and other health conditions, conduct or support assessments of the extent to which—

(A) rates of utilization vary among similar populations for particular diseases, disorders, and other health conditions;

(B) uncertainties exist on the effect of utilizing a particular service or procedure; or

(C) inappropriate services and procedures are provided.

(3) RELATIONSHIP WITH MEDICARE PROGRAM.—In establishing priorities under paragraph (1) for research and evaluation, and under section 914(a) of the Public Health Service Act[94] for the agenda under such section, the Secretary shall assure that such priorities appropriately reflect the needs and priorities of the program under title XVIII, as set forth by the Administrator of the Centers for Medicare and Medicaid Services.

(c) METHODOLOGIES AND CRITERIA FOR EVALUATIONS.—For the purpose of facilitating research under subsection (a), the Secretary shall—

(1) conduct and support research with respect to the improvement of methodologies and criteria utilized in conducting research with respect to outcomes of health care services and procedures;

---

[94] See Vol. II, P.L. 78-410, for the current §914(a). [P.L. 106-129, amended the former §914 of the Public Health Service Act in its entirety, effective December 6, 1999. The original reference to §914 was omitted in the general amendment of Title IX by P.L. 106-129, §2(a), Dec. 6, 1999, 113 Stat. 1653. Section 2(a) of P.L. 106-129 enacted a new §914.]

702 SOCIAL SECURITY ACT—§ 1142(c)(2)

(2) conduct and support reviews and evaluations of existing research findings with respect to such treatment or conditions;

(3) conduct and support reviews and evaluations of the existing methodologies that use large data bases in conducting such research and shall develop new research methodologies, including data-based methods of advancing knowledge and methodologies that measure clinical and functional status of patients, with respect to such research;

(4) provide grants and contracts to research centers, and contracts to other entities, to conduct such research on such treatment or conditions, including research on the appropriate use of prescription drugs;

(5) conduct and support research and demonstrations on the use of claims data and data on clinical and functional status of patients in determining the outcomes, effectiveness, and appropriateness of such treatment; and

(6) conduct and support supplementation of existing data bases, including the collection of new information, to enhance data bases for research purposes, and the design and development of new data bases that would be used in outcomes and effectiveness research.

(d) STANDARDS FOR DATABASES.—In carrying out this section, the Secretary shall develop—

(1) uniform definitions of data to be collected and used in describing a patient's clinical and functional status;

(2) common reporting formats and linkages for such data; and

(3) standards to assure the security, confidentiality, accuracy, and appropriate maintenance of such data.

(e) DISSEMINATION OF RESEARCH FINDINGS AND GUIDELINES.—

(1) IN GENERAL.—The Secretary shall provide for the dissemination of the findings of research and the guidelines described in subsection (a), and for the education of providers and others in the application of such research findings and guidelines.

(2) COOPERATIVE EDUCATIONAL ACTIVITIES.—In disseminating findings and guidelines under paragraph (1), and in providing for education under such paragraph, the Secretary shall work with professional associations, medical specialty and subspecialty organizations, and other relevant groups to identify and implement effective means to educate physicians, other providers, consumers, and others in using such findings and guidelines, including training for physician managers within provider organizations.

(f) EVALUATIONS.—The Secretary shall conduct and support evaluations of the activities carried out under this section to determine the extent to which such activities have had an effect on the practices of physicians in providing medical treatment, the delivery of health care, and the outcomes of health care services and procedures.

(g) RESEARCH WITH RESPECT TO DISSEMINATION.—The Secretary may conduct or support research with respect to improving methods of disseminating information on the effectiveness and appropriateness of health care services and procedures.

(h) REPORT TO CONGRESS.—Not later than February 1 of each of the years 1991 and 1992, and of each second year thereafter, the Secretary shall report to the Congress on the progress of the activities under this

SOCIAL SECURITY ACT—§ 1143(a)(2)(C)   703

section during the preceding fiscal year (or preceding 2 fiscal years, as appropriate), including the impact of such activities on medical care (particularly medical care for individuals receiving benefits under title XVIII).

(i) AUTHORIZATION OF APPROPRIATIONS.—

(1) IN GENERAL.—There are authorized to be appropriated to carry out this section—

(A) $50,000,000 for fiscal year 1990;
(B) $75,000,000 for fiscal year 1991;
(C) $110,000,000 for fiscal year 1992;
(D) $148,000,000 for fiscal year 1993; and
(E) $185,000,000 for fiscal year 1994.

(2) SPECIFICATIONS.—For the purpose of carrying out this section, for each of the fiscal years 1990 through 1992 an amount equal to two-thirds of the amounts authorized to be appropriated under paragraph (1), and for each of the fiscal years 1993 and 1994 an amount equal to 70 percent of such amounts, are to be appropriated in the following proportions from the following trust funds:

(A) 60 percent from the Federal Hospital Insurance Trust Fund (established under section 1817).

(B) 40 percent from the Federal Supplementary Medical Insurance Trust Fund (established under section 1841).

(3) ALLOCATIONS.—

(A) For each fiscal year, of the amounts transferred or otherwise appropriated to carry out this section, the Secretary shall reserve appropriate amounts for each of the purposes specified in clauses (i) through (iv) of subparagraph (B).

(B) The purposes referred to in subparagraph (A) are—

(i) the development of guidelines, standards, performance measures, and review criteria;
(ii) research and evaluation;
(iii) data-base standards and development; and
(iv) education and information dissemination.

SOCIAL SECURITY ACCOUNT STATEMENTS

Provision Upon Request

SEC. 1143. [42 U.S.C. 1320b–13] (a)(1) Beginning not later than October 1, 1990, the Commissioner of Social Security shall provide upon the request of an eligible individual a social security account statement (hereinafter referred to as the "statement").

(2) Each statement shall contain—

(A) the amount of wages paid to and self-employment income derived by the eligible individual as shown by the records of the Commissioner at the date of the request;

(B) an estimate of the aggregate of the employer, employee, and self-employment contributions of the eligible individual for old-age, survivors, and disability insurance as shown by the records of the Commissioner on the date of the request;

(C) a separate estimate of the aggregate of the employer, employee, and self-employment contributions of the eligible individual for hospital insurance as shown by the records of the Commissioner on the date of the request;

704 SOCIAL SECURITY ACT—§ 1143(a)(2)(D)

(D) an estimate of the potential monthly retirement, disability, survivor, and auxiliary benefits payable on the eligible individual's account together with a description of the benefits payable under the medicare program of title XVIII; and

(E) in the case of an eligible individual described in paragraph (3)(C)(ii), an explanation, in language calculated to be understood by the average eligible individual, of the operation of the provisions under sections 202(k)(5) and 215(a)(7) and an explanation of the maximum potential effects of such provisions on the eligible individual's monthly retirement, survivor, and auxiliary benefits.

(3) For purposes of this section, the term "eligible individual" means an individual —

(A) who has a social security account number,

(B) who has attained age 25 or over, and

(C)(i) who has wages or net earnings from self-employment, or (ii) with respect to whom the Commissioner has information that the pattern of wages or self-employment income indicate a likelihood of noncovered employment.

Notice to Eligible Individuals

(b) The Commissioner shall, to the maximum extent practicable, take such steps as are necessary to assure that eligible individuals are informed of the availability of the statement described in subsection (a).

Mandatory Provision of Statements

(c)(1) By not later than September 30, 1995, the Commissioner shall provide a statement to each eligible individual who has attained age 60 by October 1, 1994, and who is not receiving benefits under title II and for whom a current mailing address can be determined through such methods as the Commissioner determines to be appropriate. In fiscal years 1995 through 1999 the Commissioner shall provide a statement to each eligible individual who attains age 60 in such fiscal years and who is not receiving benefits under title II and for whom a current mailing address can be determined through such methods as the Commissioner determines to be appropriate. The Commissioner shall provide with each statement to an eligible individual notice that such statement is updated annually and is available upon request.

(2) Beginning not later than October 1, 1999, the Commissioner shall provide a statement on an annual basis to each eligible individual who is not receiving benefits under title II and for whom a mailing address can be determined through such methods as the Commissioner determines to be appropriate. With respect to statements provided to eligible individuals who have not attained age 50, such statements need not include estimates of monthly retirement benefits. However, if such statements provided to eligible individuals who have not attained age 50 do not include estimates of retirement benefit amounts, such statements shall include a description of the benefits (including auxiliary benefits) that are available upon retirement.

Disclosure to Governmental Employees of Effect of Noncovered Employment

(d)(1) In the case of any individual commencing employment on or after January 1, 2005, in any agency or instrumentality of any State (or political subdivision thereof, as defined in section 218(b)(2)) in a position in which service performed by the individual does not constitute "employment" as defined in section 210, the head of the agency or instrumentality shall ensure that, prior to the date of the commencement of the individual's employment in the position, the individual is provided a written notice setting forth an explanation, in language calculated to be understood by the average individual, of the maximum effect on computations of primary insurance amounts (under section 215(a)(7)) and the effect on benefit amounts (under section 202(k)(5)) of monthly periodic payments or benefits payable based on earnings derived in such service. Such notice shall be in a form which shall be prescribed by the Commissioner of Social Security.

(2) The written notice provided to an individual pursuant to paragraph (1) shall include a form which, upon completion and signature by the individual, would constitute certification by the individual of receipt of the notice. The agency or instrumentality providing the notice to the individual shall require that the form be completed and signed by the individual and submitted to the agency or instrumentality and to the pension, annuity, retirement, or similar fund or system established by the governmental entity involved responsible for paying the monthly periodic payments or benefits, before commencement of service with the agency or instrumentality.

OUTREACH EFFORTS TO INCREASE AWARENESS OF THE AVAILABILITY OF MEDICARE COST–SHARING AND SUBSIDIES FOR LOW-INCOME INDIVIDUALS UNDER TITLE XVIII

SEC. 1144. [42 U.S.C. 1320b–14] (a) OUTREACH.—

(1) IN GENERAL.—The Commissioner of Social Security (in this section referred to as the "Commissioner") shall conduct outreach efforts to—

(A) identify individuals entitled to benefits under the medicare program under title XVIII who may be eligible for medical assistance for payment of the cost of medicare cost–sharing under the medicaid program pursuant to sections 1902(a)(10)(E) and 1933 for the transitional assistance under section 1869D-31(f), or for premium and cost-sharing subsidies under section 1860D-14; and

(B) notify such individuals of the availability of such medical assistance program, and subsidies under such sections.

(2) CONTENT OF NOTICE.—Any notice furnished under paragraph (1) shall state that eligibility for medicare cost–sharing assistance, the transitional assistance under section 1860D-31(f), or premium and cost-sharing subsidies under section 1860D-14 under such sections is conditioned upon—

(A) the individual providing to the State information about income and resources (in the case of an individual residing in a State that imposes an assets test for eligibility for medicare cost-sharing under the medicaid program); and

(B) meeting the applicable eligibility criteria.

706　　SOCIAL SECURITY ACT—§ 1144(a)(2)(B)(cont)

(b) COORDINATION WITH STATES.—
　　(1) IN GENERAL.—In conducting the outreach efforts under this section, the Commissioner shall—
　　　　(A) furnish the agency of each State responsible for the administration of the medicaid program and any other appropriate State agency with information consisting of the name and address of individuals residing in the State that the Commissioner determines may be eligible for medical assistance for payment of the cost of medicare cost-sharing under the medicaid program pursuant to sections 1902(a)(10)(E) and 1933, for transitional assistance under section 1860D-31(f), or for premium and cost-sharing subsidies for low-income individuals under section 1860D-14; and
　　　　(B) update any such information not less frequently than once per year.
　　(2) INFORMATION IN PERIODIC UPDATES.—The periodic updates described in paragraph (1)(B) shall include information on individuals who are or may be eligible for the medical assistance, program, and subsidies described in paragraph (1)(A) because such individuals have experienced reductions in benefits under title II.
　(c)[95] ASSISTANCE WITH MEDICARE SAVINGS PROGRAM AND LOW-INCOME SUBSIDY PROGRAM APPLICATIONS.—
　　(1) DISTRIBUTION OF APPLICATIONS AND INFORMATION TO INDIVIDUALS WHO ARE POTENTIALLY ELIGIBLE FOR LOW-INCOME SUBSIDY PROGRAM.—For each individual who submits an application for low-income subsidies under section 1860D–14, requests an application for such subsidies, or is otherwise identified as an individual who is potentially eligible for such subsidies, the Commissioner shall do the following:
　　　　(A) Provide information describing the low-income subsidy program under section 1860D–14 and the Medicare Savings Program (as defined in paragraph (7)). In accordance with paragraph (3), transmit data from such an application for purposes of initiating an application for benefits under the Medicare Savings Program.
　　　　(B) Provide an application for enrollment under such low-income subsidy program (if not already received by the Commissioner).
　　　　(C) In accordance with paragraph (3), transmit data from such an application for purposes of initiating an application for benefits under the Medicare Savings Program.
　　　　(D) Provide information on how the individual may obtain assistance in completing such application and an application under the Medicare Savings Program, including information on how the individual may contact the State health insurance assistance program (SHIP).
　　　　(E) Make the application described in subparagraph (B) and the information described in subparagraphs (A) and (D) available at local offices of the Social Security Administration.
　　(2) TRAINING PERSONNEL IN EXPLAINING BENEFIT PROGRAMS AND ASSISTING IN COMPLETING LIS APPLICATION.—The Commis-

---

[95] P.L. 110-275, §113(a), adds this subsection (c), **to be effective January 1, 2010.**

sioner shall provide training to those employees of the Social Security Administration who are involved in receiving applications for benefits described in paragraph (1)(B) in order that they may promote beneficiary understanding of the low-income subsidy program and the Medicare Savings Program in order to increase participation in these programs. Such employees shall provide assistance in completing an application described in paragraph (1)(B) upon request.

(3) TRANSMITTAL OF DATA TO STATES.—Beginning on January 1, 2010, with the consent of an individual completing an application for benefits described in paragraph (1)(B), the Commissioner shall electronically transmit to the appropriate State Medicaid agency data from such application, as determined by the Commissioner, which transmittal shall initiate an application of the individual for benefits under the Medicare Savings Program with the State Medicaid agency. In order to ensure that such data transmittal provides effective assistance for purposes of State adjudication of applications for benefits under the Medicare Savings Program, the Commissioner shall consult with the Secretary, after the Secretary has consulted with the States, regarding the content, form, frequency, and manner in which data (on a uniform basis for all States) shall be transmitted under this subparagraph.

(4) COORDINATION WITH OUTREACH.—The Commissioner shall coordinate outreach activities under this subsection in connection with the low-income subsidy program and the Medicare Savings Program.

(5) REIMBURSEMENT OF SOCIAL SECURITY ADMINISTRATION ADMINISTRATIVE COSTS.—

(A) INITIAL MEDICARE SAVINGS PROGRAM COSTS; ADDITIONAL LOW-INCOME SUBSIDY COSTS.—

(i) INITIAL MEDICARE SAVINGS PROGRAM COSTS.—There are hereby appropriated to the Commissioner to carry out this subsection, out of any funds in the Treasury not otherwise appropriated, $24,100,000. The amount appropriated under ths[96] clause shall be available on October 1, 2008, and shall remain available until expended.

(ii) ADDITIONAL AMOUNT FOR LOW-INCOME SUBSIDY ACTIVITIES.—There are hereby appropriated to the Commissioner, out of any funds in the Treasury not otherwise appropriated, $24,800,000 for fiscal year 2009 to carry out low-income subsidy activities under section 1860D–14 and the Medicare Savings Program (in accordance with this subsection), to remain available until expended. Such funds shall be in addition to the Social Security Administration's Limitation on Administrative Expenditure appropriations for such fiscal year.

(B) SUBSEQUENT FUNDING UNDER AGREEMENTS.—

(i) IN GENERAL.—Effective for fiscal years beginning on or after October 1, 2010, the Commissioner and the Secretary shall enter into an agreement which shall pro-

---

[96] As in original. Should be "this".

708 SOCIAL SECURITY ACT—§ 1144(c)(5)(B)(i)(I)

vide funding (subject to the amount appropriated under clause (ii)) to cover the administrative costs of the Commissioner's activities under this subsection. Such agreement shall—

(I) provide funds to the Commissioner for the full cost of the Social Security Administration's work related to the Medicare Savings Program required under this section;

(II) provide such funding quarterly in advance of the applicable quarter based on estimating methodology agreed to by the Commissioner and the Secretary; and require an annual accounting and reconciliation of the actual costs incurred and funds provided under this subsection.

(III) require an annual accounting and reconciliation of the actual costs incurred and funds provided under this subsection.

(ii) APPROPRIATION.—There are hereby appropriated to the Secretary solely for the purpose of providing payments to the Commissioner pursuant to an agreement specified in clause (i) that is in effect, out of any funds in the Treasury not otherwise appropriated, not more than $3,000,000 for fiscal year 2011 and each fiscal year thereafter.

(C) LIMITATION.—In no case shall funds from the Social Security Administration's Limitation on Administrative Expenses be used to carry out activities related to the Medicare Savings Program. For fiscal years beginning on or after October 1, 2010, no such activities shall be undertaken by the Social Security Administration unless the agreement specified in subparagraph (B) is in effect and full funding has been provided to the Commissioner as specified in such subparagraph.

(6) GAO ANALYSIS AND REPORT.—

(A) ANALYSIS.—The Comptroller General of the United States shall prepare an analysis of the impact of this subsection—

(i) in increasing participation in the Medicare Savings Program, and on States and the Social Security Administration.

(ii) on States and the Social Security Administration.

(B) REPORT.—Not later than January 1, 2012, the Comptroller General shall submit to Congress, the Commissioner, and the Secretary a report on the analysis conducted under subparagraph (A).

(7) MEDICARE SAVINGS PROGRAM DEFINED.—For purposes of this subsection, the term "Medicare Savings Program" means the program of medical assistance for payment of the cost of medicare cost-sharing under the Medicaid program pursuant to sections 1902(a)(10)(E) and 1933.

PROTECTION OF SOCIAL SECURITY AND MEDICARE TRUST FUNDS

SEC. 1145. [42 U.S.C. 1320b–15] (a) IN GENERAL.—No officer or employee of the United States shall—

SOCIAL SECURITY ACT—§ 1147(b)(1)(B)(ii)   709

(1) delay the deposit of any amount into (or delay the credit of any amount to) any Federal fund or otherwise vary from the normal terms, procedures, or timing for making such deposits or credits,

(2) refrain from the investment in public debt obligations of amounts in any Federal fund, or

(3) redeem prior to maturity amounts in any Federal fund which are invested in public debt obligations for any purpose other than the payment of benefits or administrative expenses from such Federal fund.

(b) PUBLIC DEBT OBLIGATION.—For purposes of this section, the term "public debt obligation" means any obligation subject to the public debt limit established under section 3101 of title 31, United States Code[97].

(c) FEDERAL FUND.—For purposes of this section, the term "Federal fund" means—

(1) the Federal Old–Age and Survivors Insurance Trust Fund;

(2) the Federal Disability Insurance Trust Fund;

(3) the Federal Hospital Insurance Trust Fund; and

(4) the Federal Supplementary Medical Insurance Trust Fund.

PUBLIC DISCLOSURE OF CERTAIN INFORMATION ON HOSPITAL FINANCIAL INTEREST AND REFERRAL PATTERNS

SEC. 1146. [42 U.S.C. 1320b–16] The Secretary shall make available to the public, in a form and manner specified by the Secretary, information disclosed to the Secretary pursuant to section 1866(a)(1)(S).

CROSS-PROGRAM RECOVERY OF OVERPAYMENTS FROM BENEFITS

SEC. 1147. [42 U.S.C. 1320b–17] (a) IN GENERAL.—Subject to subsection (b), whenever the Commissioner of Social Security determines that more than the correct amount of any payment has been made to a person under a program described in subsection (e), the Commissioner of Social Security may recover the amount incorrectly paid by decreasing any amount which is payable to such person under any other program specified in that subsection.

(b) LIMITATION APPLICABLE TO CURRENT BENEFITS.—

(1) IN GENERAL.—In carrying out subsection (a), the Commissioner of Social Security may not decrease the monthly amount payable to an individual under a program described in subsection (e) that is paid when regularly due—

(A) in the case of benefits under title II or VIII, by more than 10 percent of the amount of the benefit payable to the person for that month under such title; and

(B) in the case of benefits under title XVI, by an amount greater than the lesser of—

(i) the amount of the benefit payable to the person for that month; or

(ii) an amount equal to 10 percent of the person's income for that month (including such monthly benefit but excluding payments under title II when recovery is also made from title II payments and excluding income excluded pursuant to section 1612(b)).

---

[97] See Vol. II, 31 U.S.C. 3101.

710 SOCIAL SECURITY ACT—§ 1147(b)(2)

(2) EXCEPTION.—Paragraph (1) shall not apply if—
(A) the person or the spouse of the person was involved in willful misrepresentation or concealment of material information in connection with the amount incorrectly paid; or
(B) the person so requests.

(c) NO EFFECT ON ELIGIBILITY OR BENEFIT AMOUNT UNDER TITLE VIII OR XVI.—In any case in which the Commissioner of Social Security takes action in accordance with subsection (a) to recover an amount incorrectly paid to any person, neither that person, nor (with respect to the program described in subsection (e)(3)) any individual whose eligibility for benefits under such program or whose amount of such benefits, is determined by considering any part of that person's income, shall, as a result of such action—
(1) become eligible for benefits under the program described in paragraph (2) or (3) of subsection (e); or
(2) if such person or individual is otherwise so eligible, become eligible for increased benefits under such program.

(d) INAPPLICABILITY OF PROHIBITION AGAINST ASSESSMENT AND LEGAL PROCESS.—Section 207 shall not apply to actions taken under the provisions of this section to decrease amounts payable under titles II and XVI.

(e) PROGRAMS DESCRIBED.—The programs described in this subsection are the following:
(1) The old-age, survivors, and disability insurance benefits program under title II.
(2) The special benefits for certain World War II veterans program under title VIII.
(3) The supplemental security income benefits program under title XVI (including, for purposes of this section, State supplementary payments paid by the Commissioner pursuant to an agreement under section 1616(a) of this Act or section 212(b) of Public Law 93-66[98]).

THE TICKET TO WORK AND SELF-SUFFICIENCY PROGRAM[99]

SEC. 1148. [42 U.S.C. 1320b–19] (a) IN GENERAL.—The Commissioner shall establish a Ticket to Work and Self-Sufficiency Program, under which a disabled beneficiary may use a ticket to work and self-sufficiency issued by the Commissioner in accordance with this section to obtain employment services, vocational rehabilitation services, or other support services from an employment network which is of the beneficiary's choice and which is willing to provide such services to such beneficiary.

(b) TICKET SYSTEM.—
(1) DISTRIBUTION OF TICKETS.—The Commissioner may issue a ticket to work and self-sufficiency to disabled beneficiaries for participation in the Program.
(2) ASSIGNMENT OF TICKETS.—A disabled beneficiary holding a ticket to work and self-sufficiency may assign the ticket to any

---

[98] See Vol. II, P.L. 93-66, §212(b).

[99] See Vol. II, P.L. 106-170, §2, with respect to Congress's findings and purposes with regard to providing assistance to individuals with disabilities to lead productive work lives; §101(d), with respect to the graduated implementation of the Ticket to Work and Self-Sufficiency Program; §101(e), with respect to specific regulations required to implement the amendments made by §101; and §101(f) with respect to the Ticket to Work and Work Incentives Advisory Panel.

employment network of the beneficiary's choice which is serving under the Program and is willing to accept the assignment.

(3) TICKET TERMS.—A ticket issued under paragraph (1) shall consist of a document which evidences the Commissioner's agreement to pay (as provided in paragraph (4)) an employment network, which is serving under the Program and to which such ticket is assigned by the beneficiary, for such employment services, vocational rehabilitation services, and other support services as the employment network may provide to the beneficiary.

(4) PAYMENTS TO EMPLOYMENT NETWORKS.—The Commissioner shall pay an employment network under the Program in accordance with the outcome payment system under subsection (h)(2) or under the outcome-milestone payment system under subsection (h)(3) (whichever is elected pursuant to subsection (h)(1)). An employment network may not request or receive compensation for such services from the beneficiary.

(c) STATE PARTICIPATION.—

(1) IN GENERAL.—Each State agency administering or supervising the administration of the State plan approved under title I of the Rehabilitation Act of 1973 (29 U.S.C. 720 et seq.)[100] may elect to participate in the Program as an employment network with respect to a disabled beneficiary. If the State agency does elect to participate in the Program, the State agency also shall elect to be paid under the outcome payment system or the outcome-milestone payment system in accordance with subsection (h)(1). With respect to a disabled beneficiary that the State agency does not elect to have participate in the Program, the State agency shall be paid for services provided to that beneficiary under the system for payment applicable under section 222(d) and subsections (d) and (e) of section 1615. The Commissioner shall provide for periodic opportunities for exercising such elections.

(2) EFFECT OF PARTICIPATION BY STATE AGENCY.—

(A) STATE AGENCIES PARTICIPATING.—In any case in which a State agency described in paragraph (1) elects under that paragraph to participate in the Program, the employment services, vocational rehabilitation services, and other support services which, upon assignment of tickets to work and self-sufficiency, are provided to disabled beneficiaries by the State agency acting as an employment network shall be governed by plans for vocational rehabilitation services approved under title I of the Rehabilitation Act of 1973 (29 U.S.C. 720 et seq.)[101].

(B) STATE AGENCIES ADMINISTERING MATERNAL AND CHILD HEALTH SERVICES PROGRAMS.—Subparagraph (A) shall not apply with respect to any State agency administering a program under title V of this Act.

(3) AGREEMENTS BETWEEN STATE AGENCIES AND EMPLOYMENT NETWORKS.—State agencies and employment networks shall enter into agreements regarding the conditions under which services will be provided when an individual is referred by an employment network to a State agency for services. The Commis-

---

[100] P.L. 93-112.
[101] P.L. 93-112.

712   SOCIAL SECURITY ACT—§ 1148(c)(3)(cont)

sioner shall establish by regulations the timeframe within which such agreements must be entered into and the mechanisms for dispute resolution between State agencies and employment networks with respect to such agreements.

(d) RESPONSIBILITIES OF THE COMMISSIONER.—

(1) SELECTION AND QUALIFICATIONS OF PROGRAM MANAGERS.—The Commissioner shall enter into agreements with 1 or more organizations in the private or public sector for service as a program manager to assist the Commissioner in administering the Program. Any such program manager shall be selected by means of a competitive bidding process, from among organizations in the private or public sector with available expertise and experience in the field of vocational rehabilitation or employment services.

(2) TENURE, RENEWAL, AND EARLY TERMINATION.—Each agreement entered into under paragraph (1) shall provide for early termination upon failure to meet performance standards which shall be specified in the agreement and which shall be weighted to take into account any performance in prior terms. Such performance standards shall include—

(A) measures for ease of access by beneficiaries to services; and

(B) measures for determining the extent to which failures in obtaining services for beneficiaries fall within acceptable parameters, as determined by the Commissioner.

(3) PRECLUSION FROM DIRECT PARTICIPATION IN DELIVERY OF SERVICES IN OWN SERVICE AREA.—Agreements under paragraph (1) shall preclude—

(A) direct participation by a program manager in the delivery of employment services, vocational rehabilitation services, or other support services to beneficiaries in the service area covered by the program manager's agreement; and

(B) the holding by a program manager of a financial interest in an employment network or service provider which provides services in a geographic area covered under the program manager's agreement.

(4) SELECTION OF EMPLOYMENT NETWORKS.—

(A) IN GENERAL.—The Commissioner shall select and enter into agreements with employment networks for service under the Program. Such employment networks shall be in addition to State agencies serving as employment networks pursuant to elections under subsection (c).

(B) ALTERNATE PARTICIPANTS.—In any State where the Program is being implemented, the Commissioner shall enter into an agreement with any alternate participant that is operating under the authority of section 222(d)(2) in the State as of the date of the enactment of this section and chooses to serve as an employment network under the Program.

(5) TERMINATION OF AGREEMENTS WITH EMPLOYMENT NETWORKS.—The Commissioner shall terminate agreements with employment networks for inadequate performance, as determined by the Commissioner.

(6) QUALITY ASSURANCE.—The Commissioner shall provide for such periodic reviews as are necessary to provide for effective

quality assurance in the provision of services by employment networks. The Commissioner shall solicit and consider the views of consumers and the program manager under which the employment networks serve and shall consult with providers of services to develop performance measurements. The Commissioner shall ensure that the results of the periodic reviews are made available to beneficiaries who are prospective service recipients as they select employment networks. The Commissioner shall ensure that the periodic surveys of beneficiaries receiving services under the Program are designed to measure customer service satisfaction.

(7) DISPUTE RESOLUTION.—The Commissioner shall provide for a mechanism for resolving disputes between beneficiaries and employment networks, between program managers and employment networks, and between program managers and providers of services. The Commissioner shall afford a party to such a dispute a reasonable opportunity for a full and fair review of the matter in dispute.

(e) PROGRAM MANAGERS.—

(1) IN GENERAL.—A program manager shall conduct tasks appropriate to assist the Commissioner in carrying out the Commissioner's duties in administering the Program.

(2) RECRUITMENT OF EMPLOYMENT NETWORKS.—A program manager shall recruit, and recommend for selection by the Commissioner, employment networks for service under the Program. The program manager shall carry out such recruitment and provide such recommendations, and shall monitor all employment networks serving in the Program in the geographic area covered under the program manager's agreement, to the extent necessary and appropriate to ensure that adequate choices of services are made available to beneficiaries. Employment networks may serve under the Program only pursuant to an agreement entered into with the Commissioner under the Program incorporating the applicable provisions of this section and regulations thereunder, and the program manager shall provide and maintain assurances to the Commissioner that payment by the Commissioner to employment networks pursuant to this section is warranted based on compliance by such employment networks with the terms of such agreement and this section. The program manager shall not impose numerical limits on the number of employment networks to be recommended pursuant to this paragraph.

(3) FACILITATION OF ACCESS BY BENEFICIARIES TO EMPLOYMENT NETWORKS.—A program manager shall facilitate access by beneficiaries to employment networks. The program manager shall ensure that each beneficiary is allowed changes in employment networks without being deemed to have rejected services under the Program. When such a change occurs, the program manager shall reassign the ticket based on the choice of the beneficiary. Upon the request of the employment network, the program manager shall make a determination of the allocation of the outcome or milestone-outcome payments based on the services provided by each employment network. The program manager shall establish and maintain lists of employment networks available to beneficiaries and shall make such lists generally available to the public. The program manager shall ensure that all information

714   SOCIAL SECURITY ACT—§ 1148(e)(4)

provided to disabled beneficiaries pursuant to this paragraph is
provided in accessible formats.

(4) ENSURING AVAILABILITY OF ADEQUATE SERVICES.—The program manager shall ensure that employment services, vocational rehabilitation services, and other support services are provided to beneficiaries throughout the geographic area covered under the program manager's agreement, including rural areas.

(5) REASONABLE ACCESS TO SERVICES.—The program manager shall take such measures as are necessary to ensure that sufficient employment networks are available and that each beneficiary receiving services under the Program has reasonable access to employment services, vocational rehabilitation services, and other support services. Services provided under the Program may include case management, work incentives planning, supported employment, career planning, career plan development, vocational assessment, job training, placement, follow-up services, and such other services as may be specified by the Commissioner under the Program. The program manager shall ensure that such services are available in each service area.

(f) EMPLOYMENT NETWORKS.—

(1) QUALIFICATIONS FOR EMPLOYMENT NETWORKS.—

(A) IN GENERAL.—Each employment network serving under the Program shall consist of an agency or instrumentality of a State (or a political subdivision thereof) or a private entity, that assumes responsibility for the coordination and delivery of services under the Program to individuals assigning to the employment network tickets to work and self-sufficiency issued under subsection (b).

(B) ONE-STOP DELIVERY SYSTEMS.—An employment network serving under the Program may consist of a one-stop delivery system established under subtitle B of title I of the Workforce Investment Act of 1998 (29 U.S.C. 2811 et seq.).

(C) COMPLIANCE WITH SELECTION CRITERIA.—No employment network may serve under the Program unless it meets and maintains compliance with both general selection criteria (such as professional and educational qualifications, where applicable) and specific selection criteria (such as substantial expertise and experience in providing relevant employment services and supports).

(D) SINGLE OR ASSOCIATED PROVIDERS ALLOWED.—An employment network shall consist of either a single provider of such services or of an association of such providers organized so as to combine their resources into a single entity. An employment network may meet the requirements of subsection (e)(4) by providing services directly, or by entering into agreements with other individuals or entities providing appropriate employment services, vocational rehabilitation services, or other support services.

(2) REQUIREMENTS RELATING TO PROVISION OF SERVICES.—Each employment network serving under the Program shall be required under the terms of its agreement with the Commissioner to—

(A) serve prescribed service areas; and

SOCIAL SECURITY ACT—§ 1148(g)(1)(C)(iv)   715

(B) take such measures as are necessary to ensure that employment services, vocational rehabilitation services, and other support services provided under the Program by, or under agreements entered into with, the employment network are provided under appropriate individual work plans that meet the requirements of subsection (g).

(3) ANNUAL FINANCIAL REPORTING.—Each employment network shall meet financial reporting requirements as prescribed by the Commissioner.

(4) PERIODIC OUTCOMES REPORTING.—Each employment network shall prepare periodic reports, on at least an annual basis, itemizing for the covered period specific outcomes achieved with respect to specific services provided by the employment network. Such reports shall conform to a national model prescribed under this section. Each employment network shall provide a copy of the latest report issued by the employment network pursuant to this paragraph to each beneficiary upon enrollment under the Program for services to be received through such employment network. Upon issuance of each report to each beneficiary, a copy of the report shall be maintained in the files of the employment network. The program manager shall ensure that copies of all such reports issued under this paragraph are made available to the public under reasonable terms.

(g) INDIVIDUAL WORK PLANS.—

(1) REQUIREMENTS.—Each employment network shall—

(A) take such measures as are necessary to ensure that employment services, vocational rehabilitation services, and other support services provided under the Program by, or under agreements entered into with, the employment network are provided under appropriate individual work plans that meet the requirements of subparagraph (C);

(B) develop and implement each such individual work plan, in partnership with each beneficiary receiving such services, in a manner that affords such beneficiary the opportunity to exercise informed choice in selecting an employment goal and specific services needed to achieve that employment goal;

(C) ensure that each individual work plan includes at least—

(i) a statement of the vocational goal developed with the beneficiary, including, as appropriate, goals for earnings and job advancement;

(ii) a statement of the services and supports that have been deemed necessary for the beneficiary to accomplish that goal;

(iii) a statement of any terms and conditions related to the provision of such services and supports; and

(iv) a statement of understanding regarding the beneficiary's rights under the Program (such as the right to retrieve the ticket to work and self-sufficiency if the beneficiary is dissatisfied with the services being provided by the employment network) and remedies available to the individual, including information on the availability of advocacy services and assistance in resolving disputes

716   SOCIAL SECURITY ACT—§ 1148(g)(1)(C)(iv)(cont)

through the State grant program authorized under section 1150;

(D) provide a beneficiary the opportunity to amend the individual work plan if a change in circumstances necessitates a change in the plan; and

(E) make each beneficiary's individual work plan available to the beneficiary in, as appropriate, an accessible format chosen by the beneficiary.

An individual work plan established pursuant to this subsection shall be treated, for purposes of section 51(d)(6)(B)(i) of the Internal Revenue Code of 1986, as an individualized written plan for employment under a State plan for vocational rehabilitation services approved under the Rehabilitation Act of 1973.

(2) EFFECTIVE UPON WRITTEN APPROVAL.—A beneficiary's individual work plan shall take effect upon written approval by the beneficiary or a representative of the beneficiary and a representative of the employment network that, in providing such written approval, acknowledges assignment of the beneficiary's ticket to work and self-sufficiency.

(h) EMPLOYMENT NETWORK PAYMENT SYSTEMS.—

(1) ELECTION OF PAYMENT SYSTEM BY EMPLOYMENT NETWORKS.—

(A) IN GENERAL.—The Program shall provide for payment authorized by the Commissioner to employment networks under either an outcome payment system or an outcome-milestone payment system. Each employment network shall elect which payment system will be utilized by the employment network, and, for such period of time as such election remains in effect, the payment system so elected shall be utilized exclusively in connection with such employment network (except as provided in subparagraph (B)).

(B) NO CHANGE IN METHOD OF PAYMENT FOR BENEFICIARIES WITH TICKETS ALREADY ASSIGNED TO THE EMPLOYMENT NETWORKS.—Any election of a payment system by an employment network that would result in a change in the method of payment to the employment network for services provided to a beneficiary who is receiving services from the employment network at the time of the election shall not be effective with respect to payment for services provided to that beneficiary and the method of payment previously selected shall continue to apply with respect to such services.

(2) OUTCOME PAYMENT SYSTEM.—

(A) IN GENERAL.—The outcome payment system shall consist of a payment structure governing employment networks electing such system under paragraph (1)(A) which meets the requirements of this paragraph.

(B) PAYMENTS MADE DURING OUTCOME PAYMENT PERIOD.—The outcome payment system shall provide for a schedule of payments to an employment network, in connection with each individual who is a beneficiary, for each month, during the individual's outcome payment period, for which benefits (described in paragraphs (3) and (4) of subsection (k)) are not payable to such individual because of work or earnings.

(C) COMPUTATION OF PAYMENTS TO EMPLOYMENT NETWORK.—The payment schedule of the outcome payment system shall be designed so that—

(i) the payment for each month during the outcome payment period for which benefits (described in paragraphs (3) and (4) of subsection (k)) are not payable is equal to a fixed percentage of the payment calculation base for the calendar year in which such month occurs; and

(ii) such fixed percentage is set at a percentage which does not exceed 40 percent.

(3) OUTCOME–MILESTONE PAYMENT SYSTEM.—

(A) IN GENERAL.—The outcome–milestone payment system shall consist of a payment structure governing employment networks electing such system under paragraph (1)(A) which meets the requirements of this paragraph.

(B) EARLY PAYMENTS UPON ATTAINMENT OF MILESTONES IN ADVANCE OF OUTCOME PAYMENT PERIODS.—The outcome-milestone payment system shall provide for 1 or more milestones, with respect to beneficiaries receiving services from an employment network under the Program, that are directed toward the goal of permanent employment. Such milestones shall form a part of a payment structure that provides, in addition to payments made during outcome payment periods, payments made prior to outcome payment periods in amounts based on the attainment of such milestones.

(C) LIMITATION ON TOTAL PAYMENTS TO EMPLOYMENT NETWORK.—The payment schedule of the outcome milestone payment system shall be designed so that the total of the payments to the employment network with respect to each beneficiary is less than, on a net present value basis (using an interest rate determined by the Commissioner that appropriately reflects the cost of funds faced by providers), the total amount to which payments to the employment network with respect to the beneficiary would be limited if the employment network were paid under the outcome payment system.

(4) DEFINITIONS.—In this subsection:

(A) PAYMENT CALCULATION BASE.—The term "payment calculation base" means, for any calendar year—

(i) in connection with a title II disability beneficiary, the average disability insurance benefit payable under section 223 for all beneficiaries for months during the preceding calendar year; and

(ii) in connection with a title XVI disability beneficiary (who is not concurrently a title II disability beneficiary), the average payment of supplemental security income benefits based on disability payable under title XVI (excluding State supplementation) for months during the preceding calendar year to all beneficiaries who have attained 18 years of age but have not attained 65 years of age.

(B) OUTCOME PAYMENT PERIOD.—The term "outcome payment period" means, in connection with any individual who had assigned a ticket to work and self-sufficiency to an employment network under the Program, a period—

(i) beginning with the first month, ending after the date on which such ticket was assigned to the employment network, for which benefits (described in paragraphs (3) and (4) of subsection (k)) are not payable to such individual by reason of engagement in substantial gainful activity or by reason of earnings from work activity; and

(ii) ending with the 60th month (consecutive or otherwise), ending after such date, for which such benefits are not payable to such individual by reason of engagement in substantial gainful activity or by reason of earnings from work activity.

(5) PERIODIC REVIEW AND ALTERATIONS OF PRESCRIBED SCHEDULES.—

(A) PERCENTAGES AND PERIODS.—The Commissioner shall periodically review the percentage specified in paragraph (2)(C), the total payments permissible under paragraph (3)(C), and the period of time specified in paragraph (4)(B) to determine whether such percentages, such permissible payments, and such period provide an adequate incentive for employment networks to assist beneficiaries to enter the workforce, while providing for appropriate economies. The Commissioner may alter such percentage, such total permissible payments, or such period of time to the extent that the Commissioner determines, on the basis of the Commissioner's review under this paragraph, that such an alteration would better provide the incentive and economies described in the preceding sentence.

(B) NUMBER AND AMOUNTS OF MILESTONE PAYMENTS.—The Commissioner shall periodically review the number and amounts of milestone payments established by the Commissioner pursuant to this section to determine whether they provide an adequate incentive for employment networks to assist beneficiaries to enter the workforce, taking into account information provided to the Commissioner by program managers, the Ticket to Work and Work Incentives Advisory Panel established by section 101(f) of the Ticket to Work and Work Incentives Improvement Act of 1999, and other reliable sources. The Commissioner may from time to time alter the number and amounts of milestone payments initially established by the Commissioner pursuant to this section to the extent that the Commissioner determines that such an alteration would allow an adequate incentive for employment networks to assist beneficiaries to enter the workforce. Such alteration shall be based on information provided to the Commissioner by program managers, the Ticket to Work and Work Incentives Advisory Panel established by section 101(f) of the Ticket to Work and Work

SOCIAL SECURITY ACT—§ 1148(j)(1)(B)   719

Incentives Improvement Act of 1999[102], or other reliable sources.

(C) REPORT ON THE ADEQUACY OF INCENTIVES.—The Commissioner shall submit to the Congress not later than 36 months after the date of the enactment of the Ticket to Work and Work Incentives Improvement Act of 1999 a report with recommendations for a method or methods to adjust payment rates under subparagraphs (A) and (B), that would ensure adequate incentives for the provision of services by employment networks of—

(i) individuals with a need for ongoing support and services;

(ii) individuals with a need for high–cost accommodations;

(iii) individuals who earn a subminimum wage; and

(iv) individuals who work and receive partial cash benefits.

The Commissioner shall consult with the Ticket to Work and Work Incentives Advisory Panel established under section 101(f) of the Ticket to Work and Work Incentives Improvement Act of 1999 during the development and evaluation of the study. The Commissioner shall implement the necessary adjusted payment rates prior to full implementation of the Ticket to Work and Self-Sufficiency Program.

(i) SUSPENSION OF DISABILITY REVIEWS.—During any period for which an individual is using, as defined by the Commissioner, a ticket to work and self-sufficiency issued under this section, the Commissioner (and any applicable State agency) may not initiate a continuing disability review or other review under section 221 of whether the individual is or is not under a disability or a review under title XVI similar to any such review under section 221.

(j) AUTHORIZATIONS.—

(1) PAYMENTS TO EMPLOYMENT NETWORKS.—

(A) TITLE II DISABILITY BENEFICIARIES.—There are authorized to be transferred from the Federal Old-Age and Survivors Insurance Trust Fund and the Federal Disability Insurance Trust Fund each fiscal year such sums as may be necessary to make payments to employment networks under this section. Money paid from the Trust Funds under this section with respect to title II disability beneficiaries who are entitled to benefits under section 223 or who are entitled to benefits under section 202(d) on the basis of the wages and self-employment income of such beneficiaries, shall be charged to the Federal Disability Insurance Trust Fund, and all other money paid from the Trust Funds under this section shall be charged to the Federal Old-Age and Survivors Insurance Trust Fund.

(B) TITLE XVI DISABILITY BENEFICIARIES.—Amounts authorized to be appropriated to the Social Security Administration under section 1601 (as in effect pursuant to the amendments made by section 301 of the Social Security Amendments of 1972) shall include amounts necessary to carry out

---

[102] See Vol. II, P.L. 106-170, §101(f).

720 SOCIAL SECURITY ACT—§ 1148(j)(2)

the provisions of this section with respect to title XVI disability beneficiaries.

(2) ADMINISTRATIVE EXPENSES.—The costs of administering this section (other than payments to employment networks) shall be paid from amounts made available for the administration of title II and amounts made available for the administration of title XVI, and shall be allocated among such amounts as appropriate.

(k) DEFINITIONS.—In this section:

(1) COMMISSIONER.—The term "Commissioner" means the Commissioner of Social Security.

(2) DISABLED BENEFICIARY.—The term "disabled beneficiary" means a title II disability beneficiary or a title XVI disability beneficiary.

(3) TITLE II DISABILITY BENEFICIARY.—The term "title II disability beneficiary" means an individual entitled to disability insurance benefits under section 223 or to monthly insurance benefits under section 202 based on such individual's disability (as defined in section 223(d)). An individual is a title II disability beneficiary for each month for which such individual is entitled to such benefits.

(4) TITLE XVI DISABILITY BENEFICIARY.—The term "title XVI disability beneficiary" means an individual eligible for supplemental security income benefits under title XVI on the basis of blindness (within the meaning of section 1614(a)(2)) or disability (within the meaning of section 1614(a)(3)). An individual is a title XVI disability beneficiary for each month for which such individual is eligible for such benefits.

(5) SUPPLEMENTAL SECURITY INCOME BENEFIT.—The term "supplemental security income benefit under title XVI" means a cash benefit under section 1611 or 1619(a), and does not include a State supplementary payment, administered federally or otherwise.

(l) REGULATIONS.—Not later than 1 year after the date of the enactment of the Ticket to Work and Work Incentives Improvement Act of 1999, the Commissioner shall prescribe such regulations as are necessary to carry out the provisions of this section.

WORK INCENTIVES OUTREACH PROGRAM

SEC. 1149. [42 U.S.C. 1320b–20] (a) ESTABLISHMENT.—

(1) IN GENERAL.—The Commissioner, in consultation with the Ticket to Work and Work Incentives Advisory Panel established under section 101(f) of the Ticket to Work and Work Incentives Improvement Act of 1999[103], shall establish a community-based work incentives planning and assistance program for the purpose of disseminating accurate information to disabled beneficiaries on work incentives programs and issues related to such programs.

(2) GRANTS, COOPERATIVE AGREEMENTS, CONTRACTS, AND OUTREACH.—Under the program established under this section, the Commissioner shall—

(A) establish a competitive program of grants, cooperative agreements, or contracts to provide benefits planning and assistance, including information on the availability of pro-

---

[103] See Vol. II, P.L. 106-170, §101(f).

tection and advocacy services, to disabled beneficiaries, including individuals participating in the Ticket to Work and Self-Sufficiency Program established under section 1148, the program established under section 1619, and other programs that are designed to encourage disabled beneficiaries to work;

(B) conduct directly, or through grants, cooperative agreements, or contracts, ongoing outreach efforts to disabled beneficiaries (and to the families of such beneficiaries) who are potentially eligible to participate in Federal or State work incentive programs that are designed to assist disabled beneficiaries to work, including—

(i) preparing and disseminating information explaining such programs; and

(ii) working in cooperation with other Federal, State, and private agencies and nonprofitorganizations that serve disabled beneficiaries, and with agencies and organizations that focus on vocational rehabilitation and work-related training and counseling;

(C) establish a corps of trained, accessible, and responsive work incentives specialists within the Social Security Administration who will specialize in disability work incentives under titles II and XVI for the purpose of disseminating accurate information with respect to inquiries and issues relating to work incentives to—

(i) disabled beneficiaries;

(ii) benefit applicants under titles II and XVI; and

(iii) individuals or entities awarded grants under subparagraphs (A) or (B); and

(D) provide—

(i) training for work incentives specialists and individuals providing planning assistance described in subparagraph (C); and

(ii) technical assistance to organizations and entities that are designed to encourage disabled beneficiaries to return to work.

(3) COORDINATION WITH OTHER PROGRAMS.—The responsibilities of the Commissioner established under this section shall be coordinated with other public and private programs that provide information and assistance regarding rehabilitation services and independent living supports and benefits planning for disabled beneficiaries including the program under section 1619, the plans for achieving self-support program (PASS), and any other Federal or State work incentives programs that are designed to assist disabled beneficiaries, including educational agencies that provide information and assistance regarding rehabilitation, school-to-work programs, transition services (as defined in, and provided in accordance with, the Individuals with Disabilities Education Act (20 U.S.C. 1400 et seq.)), a one-stop delivery system established under subtitle B of title I of the Workforce Investment Act of 1998 (29 U.S.C. 2811 et seq.), and other services.

(b) CONDITIONS.—

(1) SELECTION OF ENTITIES.—

(A) APPLICATION.—An entity shall submit an application for a grant, cooperative agreement, or contract to provide

722   SOCIAL SECURITY ACT—§ 1149(b)(1)(B)

benefits planning and assistance to the Commissioner at such time, in such manner, and containing such information as the Commissioner may determine is necessary to meet the requirements of this section.

(B) STATEWIDENESS.—The Commissioner shall ensure that the planning, assistance, and information described in paragraph (2) shall be available on a statewide basis.

(C) ELIGIBILITY OF STATES AND PRIVATE ORGANIZATIONS.—

(i) IN GENERAL.—The Commissioner may award a grant, cooperative agreement, or contract under this section to a State or a private agency or organization (other than Social Security Administration Field Offices and the State agency administering the State medicaid program under title XIX, including any agency or entity described in clause (ii), that the Commissioner determines is qualified to provide the planning, assistance, and information described in paragraph (2)).

(ii) AGENCIES AND ENTITIES DESCRIBED.—The agencies and entities described in this clause are the following:

(I) Any public or private agency or organization (including Centers for Independent Living established under title VII of the Rehabilitation Act of 1973 (29 U.S.C. 796 et seq.)[104], protection and advocacy organizations, client assistance programs established in accordance with section 112 of the Rehabilitation Act of 1973 (29 U.S.C. 732)[105], and State Developmental Disabilities Councils established in accordance with section 124 of the Developmental Disabilities Assistance and Bill of Rights Act (42 U.S.C. 6024)) that the Commissioner determines satisfies the requirements of this section.

(II) The State agency administering the State program funded under part A of title IV.

(D) EXCLUSION FOR CONFLICT OF INTEREST.—The Commissioner may not award a grant, cooperative agreement, or contract under this section to any entity that the Commissioner determines would have a conflict of interest if the entity were to receive a grant, cooperative agreement, or contract under this section.

(2) SERVICES PROVIDED.—A recipient of a grant, cooperative agreement, or contract to provide benefits planning and assistance shall select individuals who will act as planners and provide information, guidance, and planning to disabled beneficiaries on the—

(A) availability and interrelation of any Federal or State work incentives programs designed to assist disabled beneficiaries that the individual may be eligible to participate in;

(B) adequacy of any health benefits coverage that may be offered by an employer of the individual and the extent to

---

[104] P.L. 93-112.
[105] P.L. 93-112.

SOCIAL SECURITY ACT—§ 1149(d) 723

which other health benefits coverage may be available to the individual; and

(C) availability of protection and advocacy services for disabled beneficiaries and how to access such services.

(3) AMOUNT OF GRANTS, COOPERATIVE AGREEMENTS, OR CONTRACTS.—

(A) BASED ON POPULATION OF DISABLED BENEFICIARIES.—Subject to subparagraph (B), the Commissioner shall award a grant, cooperative agreement, or contract under this section to an entity based on the percentage of the population of the State where the entity is located who are disabled beneficiaries.

(B) LIMITATIONS.—

(i) PER GRANT.—No entity shall receive a grant, cooperative agreement, or contract under this section for a fiscal year that is less than $50,000 or more than $300,000.

(ii) TOTAL AMOUNT FOR ALL GRANTS, COOPERATIVE AGREEMENTS, AND CONTRACTS.—The total amount of all grants, cooperative agreements, and contracts awarded under this section for a fiscal year may not exceed $23,000,000.

(4) ALLOCATION OF COSTS.—The costs of carrying out this section shall be paid from amounts made available for the administration of title II and amounts made available for the administration of title XVI, and shall be allocated among those amounts as appropriate.

(c) DEFINITIONS.—In this section:

(1) COMMISSIONER.—The term "Commissioner" means the Commissioner of Social Security.

(2) DISABLED BENEFICIARY.—The term "disabled beneficiary" means an individual—

(A) who is a disabled beneficiary as defined in section 1148(k)(2) of this Act;

(B) who is receiving a cash payment described in section 1616(a) of this Act or a supplementary payment described in section 212(a)(3) of Public Law 93-66 (without regard to whether such payment is paid by the Commissioner pursuant to an agreement under section 1616(a) of this Act or under section 212(b) of Public Law 93-66)[106];

(C) who, pursuant to section 1619(b) of this Act, is considered to be receiving benefits under title XVI of this Act; or

(D) who is entitled to benefits under part A of title XVIII of this Act by reason of the penultimate sentence of section 226(b) of this Act.

(d) AUTHORIZATION OF APPROPRIATIONS.—There are authorized to be appropriated to carry out this section $23,000,000 for each of the fiscal years 2000 through 2009.

---

[106] See Vol. II, P.L. 93-66, §212.

724   SOCIAL SECURITY ACT—§ 1149(d)(cont)

STATE GRANTS FOR WORK INCENTIVES ASSISTANCE TO DISABLED
BENEFICIARIES

SEC. 1150. [42 U.S.C. 1320b–21] (a) IN GENERAL.—Subject to subsection (c), the Commissioner may make payments in each State to the protection and advocacy system established pursuant to part C of title I of the Developmental Disabilities Assistance and Bill of Rights Act (42 U.S.C. 6041 et seq.) for the purpose of providing services to disabled beneficiaries.

(b) SERVICES PROVIDED.—Services provided to disabled beneficiaries pursuant to a payment made under this section may include—

(1) information and advice about obtaining vocational rehabilitation and employment services; and

(2) advocacy or other services that a disabled beneficiary may need to secure, maintain, or regain gainful employment.

(c) APPLICATION.—In order to receive payments under this section, a protection and advocacy system shall submit an application to the Commissioner, at such time, in such form and manner, and accompanied by such information and assurances as the Commissioner may require.

(d) AMOUNT OF PAYMENTS.—

(1) IN GENERAL.—Subject to the amount appropriated for a fiscal year for making payments under this section, a protection and advocacy system shall not be paid an amount that is less than—

(A) in the case of a protection and advocacy system located in a State (including the District of Columbia and Puerto Rico) other than Guam, American Samoa, the United States Virgin Islands, and the Commonwealth of the Northern Mariana Islands, the greater of—

(i) $100,000; or

(ii) $1/3$ of 1 percent of the amount available for payments under this section; and

(B) in the case of a protection and advocacy system located in Guam, American Samoa, the United States Virgin Islands, and the Commonwealth of the Northern Mariana Islands, $50,000.

(2) INFLATION ADJUSTMENT.—For each fiscal year in which the total amount appropriated to carry out this section exceeds the total amount appropriated to carry out this section in the preceding fiscal year, the Commissioner shall increase each minimum payment under subparagraphs (A) and (B) of paragraph (1) by a percentage equal to the percentage increase in the total amount so appropriated to carry out this section.

(e) ANNUAL REPORT.—Each protection and advocacy system that receives a payment under this section shall submit an annual report to the Commissioner and the Ticket to Work and Work Incentives Advisory Panel established under section 101(f) of the Ticket to Work and Work Incentives Improvement Act of 1999[107] on the services provided to individuals by the system.

(f) FUNDING.—

(1) ALLOCATION OF PAYMENTS.—Payments under this section shall be made from amounts made available for the administra-

---

[107] See Vol. II, P.L. 106-170, §101(f)(2).

SOCIAL SECURITY ACT—§ 1152(1)(A)

tion of title II and amounts made available for the administration of title XVI, and shall be allocated among those amounts as appropriate.

(2) CARRYOVER.—Any amounts allotted for payment to a protection and advocacy system under this section for a fiscal year shall remain available for payment to or on behalf of the protection and advocacy system until the end of the succeeding fiscal year.

(g) DEFINITIONS.—In this section:

(1) COMMISSIONER.—The term "Commissioner" means the Commissioner of Social Security.

(2) DISABLED BENEFICIARY.—The term "disabled beneficiary" has the meaning given that term in section 1148(k)(2).

(3) PROTECTION AND ADVOCACY SYSTEM.—The term "protection and advocacy system" means a protection and advocacy system established pursuant to part C of title I of the Developmental Disabilities Assistance and Bill of Rights Act (42 U.S.C. 6041 et seq.).

(h) AUTHORIZATION OF APPROPRIATIONS.—There are authorized to be appropriated to carry out this section $7,000,000 for each of the fiscal years 2000 through 2009.

Part B—PEER REVIEW OF THE UTILIZATION AND QUALITY OF HEALTH CARE SERVICES[108]

PURPOSE

SEC. 1151. [42 U.S.C. 1320c] The purpose of this part is to establish the contracting process which the Secretary must follow pursuant to the requirements of section 1862(g) of this Act, including the definition of the utilization and quality control peer review organizations with which the Secretary shall contract, the functions such peer review organizations are to perform, the confidentiality of medical records, and related administrative matters to facilitate the carrying out of the purposes of this part.

DEFINITION OF UTILIZATION AND QUALITY CONTROL PEER REVIEW ORGANIZATION

SEC. 1152. [42 U.S.C. 1320c–1] The term "utilization and quality control peer review organization" means an entity which—

(1)(A) is composed of a substantial number of the licensed doctors of medicine and osteopathy engaged in the practice of medicine or surgery in the area and who are representative of the practicing physicians in the area, designated by the Secretary under section 1153, with respect to which the entity shall perform services under this part, or (B) has available to it, by arrangement or otherwise, the services of a sufficient number of licensed doctors of medicine or osteopathy engaged in the practice of medicine or surgery in such area to assure that adequate peer

---

[108] See Vol. II, P.L. 99-509, §9353(a)(4), with respect to contracts for small-area analysis.

See Vol. II, P.L. 100-203, §4091(a)(1), with respect to the one-time extensions to permit staggering of contract expiration dates; and §4094(e), with respect to the telecommunications demonstration projects.

See Vol. II, P.L. 108-173, §109(d), with respect to an Institute of Medicine study of quality improvement organizations.

726 SOCIAL SECURITY ACT—§ 1152(1)(A)(cont)

review of the services provided by the various medical specialties and subspecialties can be assured;

(2) is able, in the judgment of the Secretary, to perform review functions required under section 1154 in a manner consistent with the efficient and effective administration of this part and to perform reviews of the pattern of quality of care in an area of medical practice where actual performance is measured against objective criteria which define acceptable and adequate practice; and

(3) has at least one individual who is a representative of consumers on its governing body.

CONTRACTS WITH UTILIZATION AND QUALITY CONTROL PEER REVIEW ORGANIZATIONS

SEC. 1153. [42 U.S.C. 1320c–2] (a)(1) The Secretary shall establish throughout the United States geographic areas with respect to which contracts under this part will be made. In establishing such areas, the Secretary shall use the same areas as established under section 1152 of this Act as in effect immediately prior to the date of the enactment of the Peer Review Improvement Act of 1982[109], but subject to the provisions of paragraph (2).

(2) As soon as practicable after the date of the enactment of the Peer Review Improvement Act of 1982, the Secretary shall consolidate such geographic areas, taking into account the following criteria:

(A) Each State shall generally be designated as a geographic area for purposes of paragraph (1).

(B) The Secretary shall establish local or regional areas rather than State areas only where the volume of review activity or other relevant factors (as determined by the Secretary) warrant such an establishment, and the Secretary determines that review activity can be carried out with equal or greater efficiency by establishing such local or regional areas. In applying this subparagraph the Secretary shall take into account the number of hospital admissions within each State for which payment may be made under title XVIII or a State plan approved under title XIX, with any State having fewer than 180,000 such admissions annually being established as a single statewide area, and no local or regional area being established which has fewer than 60,000 total hospital admissions (including public and private pay patients) under review annually, unless the Secretary determines that other relevant factors warrant otherwise.

(C) No local or regional area shall be designated which is not a self-contained medical service area, having a full spectrum of services, including medical specialists' services.

(b)(1) The Secretary shall enter into a contract with a utilization and quality control peer review organization for each area established under subsection (a) if a qualified organization is available in such area and such organization and the Secretary have negotiated a proposed contract which the Secretary determines will be carried out by such organization in a manner consistent with the efficient and effective administration of this part. If more than one such qualified organization meets the requirements of the preceding sentence, priority

---

[109] September 3, 1982 [P.L. 97-248, Title I, Subtitle C; 96 Stat. 381].

SOCIAL SECURITY ACT—§ 1153(c)(4)   727

shall be given to any such organization which is described in section 1152(1)(A).

(2)(A) Prior to November 15, 1984, the Secretary shall not enter into a contract under this part with any entity which is, or is affiliated with (through management, ownership, or common control), an entity (other than a self-insured employer) which directly or indirectly makes payments to any practitioner or provider whose health care services are reviewed by such entity or would be reviewed by such entity if it entered into a contract with the Secretary under this part. For purposes of this paragraph, an entity shall not be considered to be affiliated with another entity which makes payments (directly or indirectly) to any practitioner or provider, by reason of management, ownership, or common control, if the management, ownership, or common control consists only of members of the governing board being affiliated (through management, ownership, or common control) with a health maintenance organization or competitive medical plan which is an "eligible organization" as defined in section 1876(b).

(B) If, after November 14, 1984, the Secretary determines that there is no other entity available for an area with which the Secretary can enter into a contract under this part, the Secretary may then enter into a contract under this part with an entity described in subparagraph (A) for such area if such entity otherwise meets the requirements of this part.

(3)(A) The Secretary shall not enter into a contract under this part with any entity which is, or is affiliated with (through management, ownership, or common control), a health care facility, or association of such facilities, within the area served by such entity or which would be served by such entity if it entered into a contract with the Secretary under this part.

(B) For purposes of subparagraph (A), an entity shall not be considered to be affiliated with a health care facility or association of facilities by reason of management, ownership, or common control if the management, ownership, or common control consists only of not more than 20 percent of the members of the governing board of the entity being affiliated (through management, ownership, or common control) with one or more of such facilities or associations.

(c) Each contract with an organization under this section shall provide that—

(1) the organization shall perform the functions set forth in section 1154(a), or may subcontract for the performance of all or some of such functions (and for purposes of paragraphs (2) and (3) of subsection (b), a subcontract under this paragraph shall not constitute an affiliation with the subcontractor);

(2) the Secretary shall have the right to evaluate the quality and effectiveness of the organization in carrying out the functions specified in the contract;

(3) the contract shall be for an initial term of three years and shall be renewable on a triennial basis thereafter;

(4) if the Secretary intends not to renew a contract, he shall notify the organization of his decision at least 90 days prior to the expiration of the contract term, and shall provide the organization an opportunity to present data, interpretations of data, and other information pertinent to its performance under the con-

728 SOCIAL SECURITY ACT—§ 1153(c)(4)(cont)

tract, which shall be reviewed in a timely manner by the Secretary;

(5) the organization may terminate the contract upon 90 days notice to the Secretary;

(6) the Secretary may terminate the contract prior to the expiration of the contract term upon 90 days notice to the organization if the Secretary determines that—

(A) the organization does not substantially meet the requirements of section 1152; or

(B) the organization has failed substantially to carry out the contract or is carrying out the contract in a manner inconsistent with the efficient and effective administration of this part, but only after such organization has had an opportunity to submit data and have such data reviewed by the panel established under subsection (d);

(7) the Secretary shall include in the contract negotiated objectives against which the organization's performance will be judged, and negotiated specifications for use of regional norms, or modifications thereof based on national norms, for performing review functions under the contract; and

(8) reimbursement shall be made to the organization on a monthly basis, with payments for any month being made not later than 15 days after the close of such month.

In evaluating the performance of utilization and quality control peer review organizations under contracts under this part, the Secretary shall place emphasis on the performance of such organizations in educating providers and practitioners (particularly those in rural areas) concerning the review process and criteria being applied by the organization.

(d)(1) Prior to making any termination under subsection (c)(6)(B), the Secretary must provide the organization with an opportunity to provide data, interpretations of data, and other information pertinent to its performance under the contract. Such data and other information shall be reviewed in a timely manner by a panel appointed by the Secretary, and the panel shall submit a report of its findings to the Secretary in a timely manner. The Secretary shall make a copy of the report available to the organization.

(2) The Secretary may accept or not accept the findings of the panel. After the panel has submitted a report with respect to an organization, the Secretary may, with the concurrence of the organization, amend the contract to modify the scope of the functions to be carried out by the organization, or in any other manner. The Secretary may terminate a contract under the authority of subsection (c)(6)(B) upon 90 days notice after the panel has submitted a report, or earlier if the organization so agrees.

(3) A panel appointed by the Secretary under this subsection shall consist of not more than five individuals, each of whom shall be a member of a utilization and quality control peer review organization having a contract with the Secretary under this part. While serving on such panel individuals shall be paid at a per diem rate not to exceed the current per diem equivalent at the time that service on the panel is rendered for grade GS-18 under section 5332 of title 5, United States Code. Appointments shall be made without regard to title 5, United States Code.

SOCIAL SECURITY ACT—§ 1153(i)(2)(A)   729

(4) During the period after the Secretary has given notice of intent to terminate a contract, and prior to the time that the Secretary enters into a contract with another utilization and quality control peer review organization, the Secretary may transfer review responsibilities of the organization under the contract being terminated to another utilization and quality control peer review organization, or to an intermediary or carrier having an agreement under section 1816 or a contract under section 1842.

(e)(1) Except as provided in paragraph (2), contracting authority of the Secretary under this section may be carried out without regard to any provision of law relating to the making, performance, amendment, or modification of contracts of the United States as the Secretary may determine to be inconsistent with the purposes of this part. The Secretary may use different contracting methods with respect to different geographical areas.

(2) If a peer review organization with a contract under this section is required to carry out a review function in addition to any function required to be carried out at the time the Secretary entered into or renewed the contract with the organization, the Secretary shall, before requiring such organization to carry out such additional function, negotiate the necessary contractual modifications, including modifications that provide for an appropriate adjustment (in light of the cost of such additional function) to the amount of reimbursement made to the organization.

(f) Any determination by the Secretary to terminate or not to renew a contract under this section shall not be subject to judicial review.

(g) The Secretary shall provide that fiscal intermediaries furnish to peer review organizations, each month on a timely basis, data necessary to initiate the review process under section 1154(a) on a timely basis. If the Secretary determines that a fiscal intermediary is unable to furnish such data on a timely basis, the Secretary shall require the hospital to do so.

(h)(1) The Secretary shall publish in the Federal Register any new policy or procedure adopted by the Secretary that affects substantially the performance of contract obligations under this section not less than 30 days before the date on which such policy or procedure is to take effect. This paragraph shall not apply to the extent it is inconsistent with a statutory deadline.

(2) The Secretary shall publish in the Federal Register the general criteria and standards used for evaluating the efficient and effective performance of contract obligations under this section and shall provide opportunity for public comment with respect to such criteria and standards.

(3) The Secretary shall regularly furnish each peer review organization with a contract under this section with a report that documents the performance of the organization in relation to the performance of other such organizations.

(i)(1) Notwithstanding any other provision of this section, the Secretary shall not renew a contract with any organization that is not an in-State organization (as defined in paragraph (3)) unless the Secretary has first complied with the requirements of paragraph (2).

(2)(A) Not later than six months before the date on which a contract period ends with respect to an organization that is not an in-State organization, the Secretary shall publish in the Federal Register—

730   SOCIAL SECURITY ACT—§ 1153(i)(2)(A)(i)

(i) the date on which such period ends; and
(ii) the period of time in which an in-State organization may submit a proposal for the contract ending on such date.
(B) If one or more qualified in-State organizations submits a proposal within the period of time specified under subparagraph (A)(ii), the Secretary shall not automatically renew the current contract on a noncompetitive basis, but shall provide for competition for the contract in the same manner as a new contract under subsection (b).
(3) For purposes of this subsection, an in-State organization is an organization that has its primary place of business in the State in which review will be conducted (or, which is owned by a parent corporation the headquarters of which is located in such State).

FUNCTIONS OF PEER REVIEW ORGANIZATIONS

SEC. 1154. [42 U.S.C. 1320c–3] (a) Any utilization andquality control peer review organization entering into a contract with the Secretary under this part must perform the following functions:
(1) The organization shall review some or all of the professional activities in the area, subject to the terms of the contract and subject to the requirements of subsection (d), of physicians and other health care practitioners and institutional and noninstitutional providers of health care services in the provision of health care services and items for which payment may be made (in whole or in part) under title XVIII (including where payment is made for such services to eligible organizations pursuant to contracts under section 1876, to Medicare Advantage organizations pursuant to contracts under part C, and to prescription drug sponsors pursuant to contracts under part D) for the purpose of determining whether—
(A) such services and items are or were reasonable and medically necessary and whether such services and items are not allowable under subsection (a)(1) or (a)(9) of section 1862;
(B) the quality of such services meets professionally recognized standards of health care; and
(C) in case such services and items are proposed to be provided in a hospital or other health care facility on an inpatient basis, such services and items could, consistent with the provision of appropriate medical care, be effectively provided more economically on an outpatient basis or in an inpatient health care facility of a different type.
If the organization performs such reviews with respect to a type of health care practitioner other than medical doctors, the organization shall establish procedures for the involvement of health care practitioners of that type in such reviews.
(2) The organization shall determine, on the basis of the review carried out under subparagraphs (A), (B), and (C) of paragraph (1), whether payment shall be made for services under title XVIII. Such determination shall constitute the conclusive determination on those issues for purposes of payment under title XVIII, except that payment may be made if—
(A) such payment is allowed by reason of section 1879;
(B) in the case of inpatient hospital services or extended care services, the peer review organization determines that additional time is required in order to arrange for postdis-

SOCIAL SECURITY ACT—§ 1154(a)(3)(E)(i)   731

charge care, but payment may be continued under this sub-paragraph for not more than two days, but only in the case where the provider of such services did not know and could not reasonably have been expected to know (as determined under section 1879) that payment would not otherwise be made for such services under title XVIII prior to notification by the organization under paragraph (3);

(C) such determination is changed as the result of any hearing or review of the determination under section 1155; or

(D) such payment is authorized under section 1861(v)(1)(G).

The organization shall identify cases for which payment should not be made by reason of paragraph (1)(B) only through the use of criteria developed pursuant to guidelines established by the Secretary.

(3)(A) Subject to subparagraphs (B) and (D), whenever the organization makes a determination that any health care services or items furnished or to be furnished to a patient by any practitioner or provider are disapproved, the organization shall promptly notify such patient and the agency or organization responsible for the payment of claims under title XVIII of this Act of such determination.

(B) The notification under subparagraph (A) with respect to services or items disapproved by reason of subparagraph (A) or (C) of paragraph (1) shall not occur until 20 days after the date that the organization has—

(i) made a preliminary notification to such practitioner or provider of such proposed determination, and

(ii) provided such practitioner or provider an opportunity for discussion and review of the proposed determination.

(C) The discussion and review conducted under subparagraph (B)(ii) shall not affect the rights of a practitioner or provider to a formal reconsideration of a determination under this part (as provided under section 1155).

(D) The notification under subparagraph (A) with respect to services or items disapproved by reason of paragraph (1)(B) shall not occur until after—

(i) the organization has notified the practitioner or provider involved of the determination and of the practitioner's or provider's right to a formal reconsideration of the determination under section 1155, and

(ii) if the provider or practitioner requests such a reconsideration, the organization has made such a reconsideration.

If a provider or practitioner is provided a reconsideration, such reconsideration shall be in lieu of any subsequent reconsideration to which the provider or practitioner may be otherwise entitled under section 1155, but shall not affect the right of a beneficiary from seeking reconsideration under such section of the organization's determination (after any reconsideration requested by the provider or physician under clause (ii)).

(E)(i) In the case of services and items provided by a physician that were disapproved by reason of paragraph (1)(B), the notice to the patient shall state the following: "In the judgment of the peer review organization, the medical care received was not acceptable

732   SOCIAL SECURITY ACT—§ 1154(a)(3)(E)(i)(cont)

under the medicare program. The reasons for the denial have been discussed with your physician."

(ii) In the case of services or items provided by an entity or practitioner other than a physician, the Secretary may substitute the entity or practitioner which provided the services or items for the term "physician" in the notice described in clause (i).

(4)(A) The organization shall, after consultation with the Secretary, determine the types and kinds of cases (whether by type of health care or diagnosis involved, or whether in terms of other relevant criteria relating to the provision of health care services) with respect to which such organization will, in order to most effectively carry out the purposes of this part, exercise review authority under the contract. The organization shall notify the Secretary periodically with respect to such determinations. Each peer review organization shall provide that a reasonable proportion of its activities are involved with reviewing, under paragraph (1)(B), the quality of services and that a reasonable allocation of such activities is made among the different cases and settings (including post-acute-care settings, ambulatory settings, and health maintenance organizations). In establishing such allocation, the organization shall consider (i) whether there is reason to believe that there is a particular need for reviews of particular cases or settings because of previous problems regarding quality of care, (ii) the cost of such reviews and the likely yield of such reviews in terms of number and seriousness of quality of care problems likely to be discovered as a result of such reviews, and (iii) the availability and adequacy of alternative quality review and assurance mechanisms.

(B) The contract of each organization shall provide for the review of services (including both inpatient and outpatient services) provided by eligible organizations pursuant to a risk-sharing contract under section 1876 (or that is subject to review under section 1882(t)(3)) for the purpose of determining whether the quality of such services meets professionally recognized standards of health care, including whether appropriate health care services have not been provided or have been provided in inappropriate settings and whether individuals enrolled with an eligible organization have adequate access to health care services provided by or through such organization (as determined, in part, by a survey of individuals enrolled with the organization who have not yet used the organization to receive such services). The contract of each organization shall also provide that with respect to health care provided by a health maintenance organization or competitive medical plan under section 1876, the organization shall maintain a beneficiary outreach program designed to apprise individuals receiving care under such section of the role of the peer review system, of the rights of the individual under such system, and of the method and purposes for contacting the organization. The previous two sentences shall not apply with respect to a contract year if another entity has been awarded a contract under subparagraph (C). Under the contract the level of effort expended by the organization on reviews under this subparagraph shall be equivalent, on a per enrollee basis, to the level of effort expended by the organ-

SOCIAL SECURITY ACT—§ 1154(a)(6)(A)(ii)   733

ization on utilization and quality reviews performed with respect to individuals not enrolled with an eligible organization.

(C) The Secretary may provide, by contract under competitive procurement procedures on a State-by-State basis in up to 25 States, for the review described in subparagraph (B) by an appropriate entity (which may be a peer review organization described in that subparagraph). In selecting among States in which to conduct such competitive procurement procedures, the Secretary may not select States which, as a group, have more than 50 percent of the total number of individuals enrolled with eligible organizations under section 1876. Under a contract with an entity under this subparagraph—

(i) the entity must be, or must meet all the requirements under section 1152 to be, a utilization and quality control peer review organization (other than the ability to perform review functions under this section that are not described in subparagraph (B)),

(ii) the contract must meet the requirement of section 1153(b)(3), and

(iii) the level of effort expended under the contract shall be, to the extent practicable, not less than the level of effort that would otherwise be required under the third sentence of subparagraph (B) if this subparagraph did not apply.

(5) The organization shall consult with nurses and other professional health care practitioners (other than physicians described in section 1861(r)(1)) and with representatives of institutional and noninstitutional providers of health care services, with respect to the organization's responsibility for the review under paragraph (1) of the professional activities of such practitioners and providers.

(6)(A) The organization shall, consistent with the provisions of its contract under this part, apply professionally developed norms of care, diagnosis, and treatment based upon typical patterns of practice within the geographic area served by the organization as principal points of evaluation and review, taking into consideration national norms where appropriate. Such norms with respect to treatment for particular illnesses or health conditions shall include—

(i) the types and extent of the health care services which, taking into account differing, but acceptable, modes of treatment and methods of organizing and delivering care, are considered within the range of appropriate diagnosis and treatment of such illness or health condition, consistent with professionally recognized and accepted patterns of care; and

(ii) the type of health care facility which is considered, consistent with such standards, to be the type in which health care services which are medically appropriate for such illness or condition can most economically be provided.

As a component of the norms described in clause (i) or (ii), the organization shall take into account the special problems associated with delivering care in remote rural areas, the availability of service alternatives to inpatient hospitalization, and other appropriate factors (such as the distance from a patient's residence to the site of care, family support, availability of proximate alterna-

734   SOCIAL SECURITY ACT—§ 1154(a)(6)(B)

tive sites of care, and the patient's ability to carry out necessary or prescribed self-care regimens) that could adversely affect the safety or effectiveness of treatment provided on an outpatient basis.

(B) The organization shall—

(i) offer to provide, several times each year, for a physician representing the organization to meet (at a hospital or at a regional meeting) with medical and administrative staff of each hospital (the services of which are reviewed by the organization) respecting the organization's review of the hospital's services for which payment may be made under title XVIII, and

(ii) publish (not less often than annually) and distribute to providers and practitioners whose services are subject to review a report that describes the organization's findings with respect to the types of cases in which the organization has frequently determined that (I) inappropriate or unnecessary care has been provided, (II) services were rendered in an inappropriate setting, or (III) services did not meet professionally recognized standards of health care.

(7) The organization, to the extent necessary and appropriate to the performance of the contract, shall—

(A)(i) make arrangements to utilize the services of persons who are practitioners of, or specialists in, the various areas of medicine (including dentistry, optometry, and podiatry, or other types of health care, which persons shall, to the maximum extent practicable, be individuals engaged in the practice of their profession within the area served by such organization; and

(ii) in the case of psychiatric and physical rehabilitation services, make arrangements to ensure that (to the extent possible) initial review of such services be made by a physician who is trained in psychiatry or physical rehabilitation (as appropriate).[110]

(B) undertake such professional inquiries either before or after, or both before and after, the provision of services with respect to which such organization has a responsibility for review which in the judgment of such organization will facilitate its activities;

(C) examine the pertinent records of any practitioner or provider of health care services providing services with respect to which such organization has a responsibility for review under paragraph (1); and

(D) inspect the facilities in which care is rendered or services are provided (which are located in such area) of any practitioner or provider of health care services providing services with respect to which such organization has a responsibility for review under paragraph (1).

(8) The organization shall perform such duties and functions and assume such responsibilities and comply with such other requirements as may be required by this part or under regulations

---

[110] Punctuation as in original.

SOCIAL SECURITY ACT—§ 1154(a)(14)   735

of the Secretary promulgated to carry out the provisions of this part or as may be required to carry out section 1862(a)(15).

(9)(A) The organization shall collect such information relevant to its functions, and keep and maintain such records, in such form as the Secretary may require to carry out the purposes of this part, and shall permit access to and use of any such information and records as the Secretary may require for such purposes, subject to the provisions of section 1160.

(B) If the organization finds, after reasonable notice to and opportunity for discussion with the physician or practitioner concerned, that the physician or practitioner has furnished services in violation of section 1156(a) and the organization determines that the physician or practitioner should enter into a corrective action plan under section 1156(b)(1), the organization shall notify the State board or boards responsible for the licensing or disciplining of the physician or practitioner of its finding and of any action taken as a result of the finding.

(10) The organization shall coordinate activities, including information exchanges, which are consistent with economical and efficient operation of programs among appropriate public and private agencies or organizations including—

(A) agencies under contract pursuant to sections 1816 and 1842 of this Act;

(B) other peer review organizations having contracts under this part; and

(C) other public or private review organizations as may be appropriate.

(11) The organization shall make available its facilities and resources for contracting with private and public entities paying for health care in its area for review, as feasible and appropriate, of services reimbursed by such entities.

(12)   [Stricken.[111]]

(13) Notwithstanding paragraph (4), the organization shall perform the review described in paragraph (1) with respect to early readmission cases to determine if the previous inpatient hospital services and the post-hospital services met professionally recognized standards of health care. Such reviews may be performed on a sample basis if the organization and the Secretary determine it to be appropriate. In this paragraph, an "early readmission case" is a case in which an individual, after discharge from a hospital, is readmitted to a hospital less than 31 days after the date of the most recent previous discharge.

(14) The organization shall conduct an appropriate review of all written complaints about the quality of services (for which payment may otherwise be made under title XVIII) not meeting professionally recognized standards of health care, if the complaint is filed with the organization by an individual entitled to benefits for such services under such title (or a person acting on the individual's behalf). The organization shall inform the individual (or representative) of the organization's final disposition of the complaint. Before the organization concludes that the quality of services does not meet professionally recognized standards

---

[111] P.L. 103-432, §156(a)(2)(A)(i); 108 Stat. 4440.

736 SOCIAL SECURITY ACT—§ 1154(a)(14)(cont)

of health care, the organization must provide the practitioner or person concerned with reasonable notice and opportunity for discussion.

(15) During each year of the contract entered into under section 1153(b), the organization shall perform significant on-site review activities, including on-site review in at least 20 percent of the rural hospitals in the organization's area.

(16) The organization shall provide for a review and report to the Secretary when requested by the Secretary under section 1867(d)(3). The organization shall provide reasonable notice of the review to the physician and hospital involved. Within the time period permitted by the Secretary, the organization shall provide a reasonable opportunity for discussion with the physician and hospital involved, and an opportunity for the physician and hospital to submit additional information, before issuing its report to the Secretary under such section.

(17) The organization shall execute its responsibilities under subparagraphs (A) and (B) of paragraph (1) by offering to providers, practitioners, Medicare Advantage organizations offering Medicare Advantage plans under part C, and prescription drug sponsors offering prescription drug plans under part D quality improvement assistance pertaining to prescription drug therapy. For purposes of this part and title XVIII, the functions described in this paragraph shall be treated as a review function.

(b)(1) No physician shall be permitted to review—

(A) health care services provided to a patient if he was directly responsible for providing such services; or

(B) health care services provided in or by an institution, organization, or agency, if he or any member of his family has, directly or indirectly, a significant financial interest in such institution, organization, or agency.

(2) For purposes of this subsection, a physician's family includes only his spouse (other than a spouse who is legally separated from him under a decree of divorce or separate maintenance), children (including legally adopted children), grandchildren, parents, and grandparents.

(c) No utilization and quality control peer review organization shall utilize the services of any individual who is not a duly licensed doctor of medicine, osteopathy, dentistry, optometry, or podiatry to make final determinations of denial decisions in accordance with its duties and functions under this part with respect to the professional conduct of any other duly licensed doctor of medicine, osteopathy, dentistry, optometry, or podiatry, or any act performed by any duly licensed doctor of medicine, osteopathy, dentistry, optometry, or podiatry in the exercise of his profession.

(d) Each contract under this part shall require that the utilization and quality control peer review organization's review responsibility pursuant to subsection (a)(1) will include review of all ambulatory surgical procedures specified pursuant to section 1833(i)(1)(A) which are performed in the area, or, at the discretion of the Secretary a sample of such procedures.

(e)(1) If—

(A) a hospital has determined that a patient no longer requires inpatient hospital care, and

SOCIAL SECURITY ACT—§ 1156(a)(3) 737

(B) the attending physician has agreed with the hospital's determination,
the hospital may provide the patient (or the patient's representative) with a notice (meeting conditions prescribed by the Secretary under section 1879) of the determination.

(2)-(4) [Stricken.[112]]

(f) The Secretary, in consultation with appropriate experts, shall identify methods that would be available to assist peer review organizations (under subsection (a)(4)) in identifying those cases which are more likely than others to be associated with a quality of services which does not meet professionally recognized standards of health care.

RIGHT TO HEARING AND JUDICIAL REVIEW

SEC. 1155. [42 U.S.C. 1320c–4] Any beneficiary who is entitled to benefits under title XVIII, and, subject to section 1154(a)(3)(D), any practitioner or provider, who is dissatisfied with a determination made by a contracting peer review organization in conducting its review responsibilities under this part, shall be entitled to a reconsideration of such determination by the reviewing organization. Where the reconsideration is adverse to the beneficiary and where the matter in controversy is $200 or more, such beneficiary shall be entitled to a hearing by the Secretary (to the same extent as beneficiaries under title II are entitled to a hearing by the Commissioner of Social Security under section 205(b)). For purposes of the preceding sentence, subsection (l) of section 205 shall apply, except that any reference in such subsection to the Commissioner of Social Security or the Social Security Administration shall be deemed a reference to the Secretary or the Department of Health and Human Services, respectively. Where the amount in controversy is $2,000 or more, such beneficiary shall be entitled to judicial review of any final decision relating to a reconsideration described in this subsection.

OBLIGATIONS OF HEALTH CARE PRACTITIONERS AND PROVIDERS OF
HEALTH CARE SERVICES; SANCTIONS AND PENALTIES; HEARINGS AND
REVIEW

SEC. 1156. [42 U.S.C. 1320c–5] (a) It shall be the obligation of any health care practitioner and any other person (including a hospital or other health care facility, organization, or agency) who provides health care services for which payment may be made (in whole or in part) under this Act, to assure, to the extent of his authority that services or items ordered or provided by such practitioner or person to beneficiaries and recipients under this Act—

(1) will be provided economically and only when, and to the extent, medically necessary;

(2) will be of a quality which meets professionally recognized standards of health care; and

(3) will be supported by evidence of medical necessity and quality in such form and fashion and at such time as may reasonably be required by a reviewing peer review organization in the exercise of its duties and responsibilities.

---

[112] P.L. 106-554, Appendix F, [title V, §521(c)]; 114 Stat. 2763, 2763A-543.

(b)(1) If after reasonable notice and opportunity for discussion with the practitioner or person concerned, and, if appropriate, after the practitioner or person has been given a reasonable opportunity to enter into and complete a corrective action plan (which may include remedial education) agreed to by the organization, and has failed successfully to complete such plan, any organization having a contract with the Secretary under this part determines that such practitioner or person has—

(A) failed in a substantial number of cases substantially to comply with any obligation imposed on him under subsection (a), or

(B) grossly and flagrantly violated any such obligation in one or more instances,

such organization shall submit a report and recommendations to the Secretary. If the Secretary agrees with such determination, the Secretary (in addition to any other sanction provided under law) may exclude (permanently or for such period as the Secretary may prescribe, except that such period may not be less than 1 year) such practitioner or person from eligibility to provide services under this Act on a reimbursable basis. If the Secretary fails to act upon the recommendations submitted to him by such organization within 120 days after such submission, such practitioner or person shall be excluded from eligibility to provide services on a reimbursable basis until such time as the Secretary determines otherwise.

(2) A determination made by the Secretary under this subsection to exclude a practitioner or person shall be effective on the same date and in the same manner as an exclusion from participation under the programs under this Act becomes effective under section 1128(c), and shall (subject to the minimum period specified in the second sentence of paragraph (1)) remain in effect until the Secretary finds and gives reasonable notice to the public that the basis for such determination has been removed and that there is reasonable assurance that it will not recur.

(3) In lieu of the sanction authorized by paragraph (1), the Secretary may require that (as a condition to the continued eligibility of such practitioner or person to provide such health care services on a reimbursable basis) such practitioner or person pays to the United States, in case such acts or conduct involved the provision or ordering by such practitioner or person of health care services which were medically improper or unnecessary, an amount not in excess of up to $10,000 for each instance of the medically improper or unnecessary services so provided. Such amount may be deducted from any sums owing by the United States (or any instrumentality thereof) to the practitioner or person from whom such amount is claimed.

(4) Any practitioner or person furnishing services described in paragraph (1) who is dissatisfied with a determination made by the Secretary under this subsection shall be entitled to reasonable notice and opportunity for a hearing thereon by the Secretary to the same extent as is provided in section 205(b), and to judicial review of the Secretary's final decision after such hearing as is provided in section 205(g).

(5) Before the Secretary may effect an exclusion under paragraph (2) in the case of a provider or practitioner located in a rural health professional shortage area or in a county with a population of less than 70,000, the provider or practitioner adversely affected by the determination is entitled to a hearing before an administrative law judge

SOCIAL SECURITY ACT—§ 1157(c)   739

(described in section 205(b)) respecting whether the provider or practitioner should be able to continue furnishing services to individuals entitled to benefits under this Act, pending completion of the administrative review procedure under paragraph (4). If the judge does not determine, by a preponderance of the evidence, that the provider or practitioner will pose a serious risk to such individuals if permitted to continue furnishing such services, the Secretary shall not effect the exclusion under paragraph (2) until the provider or practitioner has been provided reasonable notice and opportunity for an administrative hearing thereon under paragraph (4).

(6) When the Secretary effects an exclusion of a physician under paragraph (2), the Secretary shall notify the State board responsible for the licensing of the physician of the exclusion.

(c) It shall be the duty of each utilization and quality control peer review organization to use such authority or influence it may possess as a professional organization, and to enlist the support of any other professional or governmental organization having influence or authority over health care practitioners and any other person (including a hospital or other health care facility, organization, or agency) providing health care services in the area served by such review organization, in assuring that each practitioner or person (referred to in subsection (a)) providing health care services in such area shall comply with all obligations imposed on him under subsection (a).

LIMITATION ON LIABILITY

SEC. 1157. [42 U.S.C. 1320c–6] (a) Notwithstanding any other provision of law, no person providing information to any organization having a contract with the Secretary under this part shall be held, by reason of having provided such information, to have violated any criminal law, or to be civilly liable under any law of the United States or of any State (or political subdivision thereof) unless—

(1) such information is unrelated to the performance of the contract of such organization; or

(2) such information is false and the person providing it knew, or had reason to believe, that such information was false.

(b) No organization having a contract with the Secretary under this part and no person who is employed by, or who has a fiduciary relationship with, any such organization or who furnishes professional services to such organization, shall be held by reason of the performance of any duty, function, or activity required or authorized pursuant to this part or to a valid contract entered into under this part, to have violated any criminal law, or to be civilly liable under any law of the United States or of any State (or political subdivision thereof) provided due care was exercised in the performance of such duty, function, or activity.

(c) No doctor of medicine or osteopathy and no provider (including directors, trustees, employees, or officials thereof) of health care services shall be civilly liable to any person under any law of the United States or of any State (or political subdivision thereof) on account of any action taken by him in compliance with or reliance upon professionally developed norms of care and treatment applied by an organization under contract pursuant to section 1153 operating in the area where such doctor of medicine or osteopathy or provider took such action; but only if—

740   SOCIAL SECURITY ACT—§ 1157(c)(1)

(1) he takes such action in the exercise of his profession as a doctor of medicine or osteopathy or in the exercise of his functions as a provider of health care services; and

(2) he exercised due care in all professional conduct taken or directed by him and reasonably related to, and resulting from, the actions taken in compliance with or reliance upon such professionally accepted norms of care and treatment.

(d) The Secretary shall make payment to an organization under contract with him pursuant to this part, or to any member or employee thereof, or to any person who furnishes legal counsel or services to such organization, in an amount equal to the reasonable amount of the expenses incurred, as determined by the Secretary, in connection with the defense of any suit, action, or proceeding brought against such organization, member, or employee related to the performance of any duty or function under such contract by such organization, member, or employee.

APPLICATION OF THIS PART TO CERTAIN STATE PROGRAMS RECEIVING FEDERAL FINANCIAL ASSISTANCE

SEC. 1158. [42 U.S.C. 1320c–7] (a) A State plan approved under title XIX of this Act may provide that the functions specified in section 1154 may be performed in an area by contract with a utilization and quality control peer review organization that has entered into a contract with the Secretary in accordance with the provisions of section 1862(g).

(b) In the event a State enters into a contract in accordance with subsection (a), the Federal share of the expenditures made to the contracting organization for its costs in the performance of its functions under the State plan shall be 75 percent (as provided in section 1903(a)(3)(C)).

AUTHORIZATION FOR USE OF CERTAIN FUNDS TO ADMINISTER THE PROVISIONS OF THIS PART

SEC. 1159. [42 U.S.C. 1320c–8] Expenses incurred in the administration of the contracts described in section 1862(g) shall be payable from—

(1) funds in the Federal Hospital Insurance Trust Fund; and

(2) funds in the Federal Supplementary Medical Insurance Trust Fund,

in such amounts from each of such Trust Funds as the Secretary shall deem to be fair and equitable after taking into consideration the expenses attributable to the administration of this part with respect to each of such programs. The Secretary shall make such transfers of moneys between such Trust Funds as may be appropriate to settle accounts between them in cases where expenses properly payable from one such Trust Fund have been paid from the other such Trust Fund.

PROHIBITION AGAINST DISCLOSURE OF INFORMATION

SEC. 1160. [42 U.S.C. 1320c–9] (a) An organization, in carrying out its functions under a contract entered into under this part, shall not be a Federal agency for purposes of the provisions of section 552 of title 5, United States Code[113] (commonly referred to as the Freedom of Information Act). Any data or information acquired by any such

---

[113] See Vol. II, 5 U.S.C. 552.

SOCIAL SECURITY ACT—§ 1160(b)(2)   741

organization in the exercise of its duties and functions shall be held
in confidence and shall not be disclosed to any person except—
    (1) to the extent that may be necessary to carry out the purposes
of this part,
    (2) in such cases and under such circumstances as the Secre-
tary shall by regulations provide to assure adequate protection of
the rights and interests of patients, health care practitioners, or
providers of health care, or
    (3) in accordance with subsection (b).
  (b) An organization having a contract with the Secretary under
this part shall provide in accordance with procedures and safeguards
established by the Secretary, data and information—
    (1) which may identify specific providers or practitioners as may
be necessary—
        (A) to assist Federal and State agencies recognized by the
    Secretary as having responsibility for identifying and inves-
    tigating cases or patterns of fraud or abuse, which data and
    information shall be provided by the peer review organization
    to any such agency at the request of such agency relating to
    a specific case or pattern;
        (B) to assist appropriate Federal and State agencies recog-
    nized by the Secretary as having responsibility for identifying
    cases or patterns involving risks to the public health, which
    data and information shall be provided by the peer review or-
    ganization to any such agency—
            (i) at the discretion of the peer review organization, at
        the request of such agency relating to a specific case or
        pattern with respect to which such agency has made a
        finding, or has a reasonable belief, that there may be a
        substantial risk to the public health, or
            (ii) upon a finding by, or the reasonable belief of, the
        peer review organization that there may be a substantial
        risk to the public health;
        (C) to assist appropriate State agencies recognized by the
    Secretary as having responsibility for licensing or certifica-
    tion of providers or practitioners or to assist national accred-
    itation bodies acting pursuant to section 1865 in accrediting
    providers for purposes of meeting the conditions described in
    title XVIII, which data and information shall be provided by
    the peer review organization to any such agency or body at
    the request of such agency or body relating to a specific case
    or to a possible pattern of substandard care, but only to the
    extent that such data and information are required by the
    agency or body to carry out its respective function which is
    within the jurisdiction of the agency or body under State law
    or under section 1865; and
        (D) to provide notice in accordance with section
    1154(a)(9)(B);
    (2) to assist the Secretary, and such Federal and State agencies
recognized by the Secretary as having health planning or related
responsibilities under Federal or State law (including health systems agencies and State health planning and development agencies), in carrying out appropriate health care planning and related activities, which data and information shall be provided in

742   SOCIAL SECURITY ACT—§ 1160(b)(2)(cont)

such format and manner as may be prescribed by the Secretary
or agreed upon by the responsible Federal and State agencies and
such organization, and shall be in the form of aggregate statistical data (without explicitly identifying any individual) on a geographic, institutional, or other basis reflecting the volume and
frequency of services furnished, as well as the demographic characteristics of the population subject to review by such organization.
The penalty provided in subsection (c) shall not apply to the disclosure of any information received under this subsection, except that
such penalty shall apply to the disclosure (by the agency receiving
such information) of any such information described in paragraph (1)
unless such disclosure is made in a judicial, administrative, or other
formal legal proceeding resulting from an investigation conducted by
the agency receiving the information. An organization may require
payment of a reasonable fee for providing information under this subsection in response to a request for such information.
  (c) It shall be unlawful for any person to disclose any such information described in subsection (a) other than for the purposes provided
in subsections (a) and (b), and any person violating the provisions of
this section shall, upon conviction, be fined not more than $1,000, and
imprisoned for not more than 6 months, or both, and shall be required
to pay the costs of prosecution.
  (d) No patient record in the possession of an organization having
a contract with the Secretary under this part shall be subject to subpoena or discovery proceedings in a civil action. No document or other
information produced by such an organization in connection with its
deliberations in making determinations under section 1154(a)(1)(B)
or 1156(a)(2) shall be subject to subpoena or discovery in any administrative or civil proceeding; except that such an organization shall
provide, upon request of a practitioner or other person adversely affected by such a determination, a summary of the organization's findings and conclusions in making the determination.
  (e) For purposes of this section and section 1157, the term "organization with a contract with the Secretary under this part" includes an
entity with a contract with the Secretary under section 1154(a)(4)(C).

ANNUAL REPORTS

  SEC. 1161. [42 U.S.C. 1320c–10] The Secretary shall submit to the
Congress not later than April 1 of each year, a full and complete report
on the administration, impact, and cost of the program under this part
during the preceding fiscal year, including data and information on—
    (1) the number, status, and service areas of all utilization and
  quality control peer review organizations participating in the program;
    (2) the number of health care institutions and practitioners
  whose services are subject to review by such organizations, and
  the number of beneficiaries and recipients who received services
  subject to such review during such year;
    (3) the various methods of reimbursement utilized in contracts
  under this part, and the relative efficiency of each such method
  of reimbursement;

SOCIAL SECURITY ACT—§ 1171(5)   743

(4) the imposition of penalties and sanctions under this title for violations of law and for failure to comply with the obligations imposed by this part;

(5) the total costs incurred under titles XVIII and XIX of this Act in the implementation and operation of all procedures required by such titles for the review of services to determine their medical necessity, appropriateness of use, and quality; and

(6) descriptions of the criteria upon which decisions are made, and the selection and relative weights of such criteria.

EXEMPTIONS FOR RELIGIOUS NONMEDICAL HEALTH CARE INSTITUTIONS

SEC. 1162. [42 U.S.C. 1320c–11] The provisions of this part shall not apply with respect to a religious nonmedical health care institution (as defined in section 1861(ss)(1)).

MEDICAL OFFICERS IN AMERICAN SAMOA, THE NORTHERN MARIANA ISLANDS, AND THE TRUST TERRITORY OF THE PACIFIC ISLANDS TO BE INCLUDED IN THE UTILIZATION AND QUALITY CONTROL PEER REVIEW PROGRAM

SEC. 1163. [42 U.S.C 1320c–12] For purposes of applying this part to American Samoa, the Northern Mariana Islands, and the Trust Territory of the Pacific Islands, individuals licensed to practice medicine in those places shall be considered to be physicians and doctors of medicine.

Part C—Administrative Simplification

DEFINITIONS

SEC. 1171. [42 U.S.C. 1320d] For purposes of this part:

(1) CODE SET.—The term "code set" means any set of codes used for encoding data elements, such as tables of terms, medical concepts, medical diagnostic codes, or medical procedure codes.

(2) HEALTH CARE CLEARINGHOUSE.—The term "health care clearinghouse" means a public or private entity that processes or facilitates the processing of nonstandard data elements of health information into standard data elements.

(3) HEALTH CARE PROVIDER.—The term "health care provider" includes a provider of services (as defined in section 1861(u)), a provider of medical or other health services (as defined in section 1861(s)), and any other person furnishing health care services or supplies.

(4) HEALTH INFORMATION.—The term "health information" means any information, whether oral or recorded in any form or medium, that—

(A) is created or received by a health care provider, health plan, public health authority, employer, life insurer, school or university, or health care clearinghouse; and

(B) relates to the past, present, or future physical or mental health or condition of an individual, the provision of health care to an individual, or the past, present, or future payment for the provision of health care to an individual.

(5) HEALTH PLAN.—The term "health plan" means an individual or group plan that provides, or pays the cost of, medical care

744 SOCIAL SECURITY ACT—§ 1171(5)(cont)

(as such term is defined in section 2791 of the Public Health Service Act[114]). Such term includes the following, and any combination thereof:

(A) A group health plan (as defined in section 2791(a) of the Public Health Service Act), but only if the plan—

(i) has 50 or more participants (as defined in section 3(7) of the Employee Retirement Income Security Act of 1974[115]); or

(ii) is administered by an entity other than the employer who established and maintains the plan.

(B) A health insurance issuer (as defined in section 2791(b) of the Public Health Service Act).

(C) A health maintenance organization (as defined in section 2791(b) of the Public Health Service Act[116]).

(D) Part A, B, or C of the Medicare program under title XVIII.

(E) The medicaid program under title XIX.

(F) A Medicare supplemental policy (as defined in section 1882(g)(1)).

(G) A long-term care policy, including a nursing home fixed indemnity policy (unless the Secretary determines that such a policy does not provide sufficiently comprehensive coverage of a benefit so that the policy should be treated as a health plan).

(H) An employee welfare benefit plan or any other arrangement which is established or maintained for the purpose of offering or providing health benefits to the employees of 2 or more employers.

(I) The health care program for active military personnel under title 10, United States Code.

(J) The veterans health care program under chapter 17 of title 38, United States Code.

(K) The Civilian Health and Medical Program of the Uniformed Services (CHAMPUS), as defined in section 1072(4) of title 10, United States Code.

(L) The Indian health service program under the Indian Health Care Improvement Act (25 U.S.C. 1601 et seq.)[117].

(M) The Federal Employees Health Benefit Plan under chapter 89 of title 5, United States Code.

(6) INDIVIDUALLY IDENTIFIABLE HEALTH INFORMATION.—The term "individually identifiable health information" means any information, including demographic information collected from an individual, that—

(A) is created or received by a health care provider, health plan, employer, or health care clearinghouse; and

(B) relates to the past, present, or future physical or mental health or condition of an individual, the provision of health care to an individual, or the past, present, or future payment for the provision of health care to an individual, and—

---

[114] See Vol. II, P.L. 78-410, §2791(a).
[115] See Vol. II, P.L. 93-406, §3(7).
[116] See Vol. II, P.L. 78-410, §2791(b).
[117] P.L. 94-437.

SOCIAL SECURITY ACT—§ 1172(c)(3)   745

(i) identifies the individual; or
(ii) with respect to which there is a reasonable basis to believe that the information can be used to identify the individual.
(7) STANDARD.—The term "standard", when used with reference to a data element of health information or a transaction referred to in section 1173(a)(1), means any such data element or transaction that meets each of the standards and implementation specifications adopted or established by the Secretary with respect to the data element or transaction under sections 1172 through 1174.
(8) STANDARD SETTING ORGANIZATION.—The term "standard setting organization" means a standard setting organization accredited by the American National Standards Institute, including the National Council for Prescription Drug Programs, that develops standards for information transactions, data elements, or any other standard that is necessary to, or will facilitate, the implementation of this part.

GENERAL REQUIREMENTS FOR ADOPTION OF STANDARDS

SEC. 1172. [42 U.S.C. 1320d–1] (a) APPLICABILITY.—Any standard adopted under this part shall apply, in whole or in part, to the following persons:
(1) A health plan.
(2) A health care clearinghouse.
(3) A health care provider who transmits any health information in electronic form in connection with a transaction referred to in section 1173(a)(1).
(b) REDUCTION OF COSTS.—Any standard adopted under this part shall be consistent with the objective of reducing the administrative costs of providing and paying for health care.
(c) ROLE OF STANDARD SETTING ORGANIZATIONS.—
(1) IN GENERAL.—Except as provided in paragraph (2), any standard adopted under this part shall be a standard that has been developed, adopted, or modified by a standard setting organization.
(2) SPECIAL RULES.—
(A) DIFFERENT STANDARDS.—The Secretary may adopt a standard that is different from any standard developed, adopted, or modified by a standard setting organization, if—
(i) the different standard will substantially reduce administrative costs to health care providers and health plans compared to the alternatives; and
(ii) the standard is promulgated in accordance with the rulemaking procedures of subchapter III of chapter 5 of title 5, United States Code.
(B) NO STANDARD BY STANDARD SETTING ORGANIZATION.—If no standard setting organization has developed, adopted, or modified any standard relating to a standard that the Secretary is authorized or required to adopt under this part—
(i) paragraph (1) shall not apply; and
(ii) subsection (f) shall apply.
(3) CONSULTATION REQUIREMENT.—

746 SOCIAL SECURITY ACT—§ 1172(c)(3)(A)

(A) IN GENERAL.—A standard may not be adopted under this part unless—

(i) in the case of a standard that has been developed, adopted, or modified by a standard setting organization, the organization consulted with each of the organizations described in subparagraph (B) in the course of such development, adoption, or modification; and

(ii) in the case of any other standard, the Secretary, in complying with the requirements of subsection (f), consulted with each of the organizations described in subparagraph (B) before adopting the standard.

(B) ORGANIZATIONS DESCRIBED.—The organizations referred to in subparagraph (A) are the following:

(i) The National Uniform Billing Committee.

(ii) The National Uniform Claim Committee.

(iii) The Workgroup for Electronic Data Interchange.

(iv) The American Dental Association.

(d) IMPLEMENTATION SPECIFICATIONS.—The Secretary shall establish specifications for implementing each of the standards adopted under this part.

(e) PROTECTION OF TRADE SECRETS.—Except as otherwise required by law, a standard adopted under this part shall not require disclosure of trade secrets or confidential commercial information by a person required to comply with this part.

(f) ASSISTANCE TO THE SECRETARY.—In complying with the requirements of this part, the Secretary shall rely on the recommendations of the National Committee on Vital and Health Statistics established under section 306(k) of the Public Health Service Act (42 U.S.C. 242k(k)), and shall consult with appropriate Federal and State agencies and private organizations. The Secretary shall publish in the Federal Register any recommendation of the National Committee on Vital and Health Statistics regarding the adoption of a standard under this part.

(g) APPLICATION TO MODIFICATIONS OF STANDARDS.—This section shall apply to a modification to a standard (including an addition to a standard) adopted under section 1174(b) in the same manner as it applies to an initial standard adopted under section 1174(a).

STANDARDS FOR INFORMATION TRANSACTIONS AND DATA ELEMENTS

SEC. 1173. [42 U.S.C. 1320d–2] (a) STANDARDS TO ENABLE ELECTRONIC EXCHANGE.—

(1) IN GENERAL.—The Secretary shall adopt standards for transactions, and data elements for such transactions, to enable health information to be exchanged electronically, that are appropriate for—

(A) the financial and administrative transactions described in paragraph (2); and

(B) other financial and administrative transactions determined appropriate by the Secretary, consistent with the goals of improving the operation of the health care system and reducing administrative costs.

(2) TRANSACTIONS.—The transactions referred to in paragraph (1)(A) are transactions with respect to the following:

(A) Health claims or equivalent encounter information.

SOCIAL SECURITY ACT—§ 1173(d)(1)(B) 747

(B) Health claims attachments.
(C) Enrollment and disenrollment in a health plan.
(D) Eligibility for a health plan.
(E) Health care payment and remittance advice.
(F) Health plan premium payments.
(G) First report of injury.
(H) Health claim status.
(I) Referral certification and authorization.

(3) ACCOMMODATION OF SPECIFIC PROVIDERS.—The standards adopted by the Secretary under paragraph (1) shall accommodate the needs of different types of health care providers.

(b) UNIQUE HEALTH IDENTIFIERS.—

(1) IN GENERAL.—The Secretary shall adopt standards providing for a standard unique health identifier for each individual, employer, health plan, and health care provider for use in the health care system. In carrying out the preceding sentence for each health plan and health care provider, the Secretary shall take into account multiple uses for identifiers and multiple locations and specialty classifications for health care providers.

(2) USE OF IDENTIFIERS.—The standards adopted under paragraph (1) shall specify the purposes for which a unique health identifier may be used.

(c) CODE SETS.—

(1) IN GENERAL.—The Secretary shall adopt standards that—

(A) select code sets for appropriate data elements for the transactions referred to in subsection (a)(1) from among the code sets that have been developed by private and public entities; or

(B) establish code sets for such data elements if no code sets for the data elements have been developed.

(2) DISTRIBUTION.—The Secretary shall establish efficient and low-cost procedures for distribution (including electronic distribution) of code sets and modifications made to such code sets under section 1174(b).

(d) SECURITY STANDARDS FOR HEALTH INFORMATION.—

(1) SECURITY STANDARDS.—The Secretary shall adopt security standards that—

(A) take into account—

(i) the technical capabilities of record systems used to maintain health information;

(ii) the costs of security measures;

(iii) the need for training persons who have access to health information;

(iv) the value of audit trails in computerized record systems; and

(v) the needs and capabilities of small health care providers and rural health care providers (as such providers are defined by the Secretary); and

(B) ensure that a health care clearinghouse, if it is part of a larger organization, has policies and security procedures which isolate the activities of the health care clearinghouse with respect to processing information in a manner that prevents unauthorized access to such information by such larger organization.

748   SOCIAL SECURITY ACT—§ 1173(d)(2)

(2) SAFEGUARDS.—Each person described in section 1172(a) who maintains or transmits health information shall maintain reasonable and appropriate administrative, technical, and physical safeguards—

(A) to ensure the integrity and confidentiality of the information;

(B) to protect against any reasonably anticipated—

(i) threats or hazards to the security or integrity of the information; and

(ii) unauthorized uses or disclosures of the information; and

(C) otherwise to ensure compliance with this part by the officers and employees of such person.

(e) ELECTRONIC SIGNATURE.—

(1) STANDARDS.—The Secretary, in coordination with the Secretary of Commerce, shall adopt standards specifying procedures for the electronic transmission and authentication of signatures with respect to the transactions referred to in subsection (a)(1).

(2) EFFECT OF COMPLIANCE.—Compliance with the standards adopted under paragraph (1) shall be deemed to satisfy Federal and State statutory requirements for written signatures with respect to the transactions referred to in subsection (a)(1).

(f) TRANSFER OF INFORMATION AMONG HEALTH PLANS.—The Secretary shall adopt standards for transferring among health plans appropriate standard data elements needed for the coordination of benefits, the sequential processing of claims, and other data elements for individuals who have more than one health plan.

TIMETABLES FOR ADOPTION OF STANDARDS

SEC. 1174. [42 U.S.C. 1320d–3] (a) INITIAL STANDARDS.—The Secretary shall carry out section 1173 not later than 18 months after the date of the enactment of the Health Insurance Portability and Accountability Act of 1996[118], except that standards relating to claims attachments shall be adopted not later than 30 months after such date.

(b) ADDITIONS AND MODIFICATIONS TO STANDARDS.—

(1) IN GENERAL.—Except as provided in paragraph (2), the Secretary shall review the standards adopted under section 1173, and shall adopt modifications to the standards (including additions to the standards), as determined appropriate, but not more frequently than once every 12 months. Any addition or modification to a standard shall be completed in a manner which minimizes the disruption and cost of compliance.

(2) SPECIAL RULES.—

(A) FIRST 12-MONTH PERIOD.—Except with respect to additions and modifications to code sets under subparagraph (B), the Secretary may not adopt any modification to a standard adopted under this part during the 12-month period beginning on the date the standard is initially adopted, unless the Secretary determines that the modification is necessary in order to permit compliance with the standard.

(B) ADDITIONS AND MODIFICATIONS TO CODE SETS.—

---

[118] The date of enactment for P.L. 104-191 was August 21, 1996 [P.L. 104-191; 110 Stat. 1998].

SOCIAL SECURITY ACT—§ 1175(b)(1)(B)   749

(i) IN GENERAL.—The Secretary shall ensure that procedures exist for the routine maintenance, testing, enhancement, and expansion of code sets.

(ii) ADDITIONAL RULES.—If a code set is modified under this subsection, the modified code set shall include instructions on how data elements of health information that were encoded prior to the modification may be converted or translated so as to preserve the informational value of the data elements that existed before the modification. Any modification to a code set under this subsection shall be implemented in a manner that minimizes the disruption and cost of complying with such modification.

REQUIREMENTS

SEC. 1175. [42 U.S.C. 1320d–4] (a) CONDUCT OF TRANSACTIONS BY PLANS.—

(1) IN GENERAL.—If a person desires to conduct a transaction referred to in section 1173(a)(1) with a health plan as a standard transaction—

(A) the health plan may not refuse to conduct such transaction as a standard transaction;

(B) the insurance plan may not delay such transaction, or otherwise adversely affect, or attempt to adversely affect, the person or the transaction on the ground that the transaction is a standard transaction; and

(C) the information transmitted and received in connection with the transaction shall be in the form of standard data elements of health information.

(2) SATISFACTION OF REQUIREMENTS.—A health plan may satisfy the requirements under paragraph (1) by—

(A) directly transmitting and receiving standard data elements of health information; or

(B) submitting nonstandard data elements to a health care clearinghouse for processing into standard data elements and transmission by the health care clearinghouse, and receiving standard data elements through the health care clearinghouse.

(3) TIMETABLE FOR COMPLIANCE.—Paragraph (1) shall not be construed to require a health plan to comply with any standard, implementation specification, or modification to a standard or specification adopted or established by the Secretary under sections 1172 through 1174 at any time prior to the date on which the plan is required to comply with the standard or specification under subsection (b).

(b) COMPLIANCE WITH STANDARDS.—

(1) INITIAL COMPLIANCE.—

(A) IN GENERAL.—Not later than 24 months after the date on which an initial standard or implementation specification is adopted or established under sections 1172 and 1173, each person to whom the standard or implementation specification applies shall comply with the standard or specification.

(B) SPECIAL RULE FOR SMALL HEALTH PLANS.—In the case of a small health plan, paragraph (1) shall be applied by

750   SOCIAL SECURITY ACT—§ 1175(b)(1)(B)(cont)

substituting "36 months" for "24 months". For purposes of this subsection, the Secretary shall determine the plans that qualify as small health plans.

(2) COMPLIANCE WITH MODIFIED STANDARDS.—If the Secretary adopts a modification to a standard or implementation specification under this part, each person to whom the standard or implementation specification applies shall comply with the modified standard or implementation specification at such time as the Secretary determines appropriate, taking into account the time needed to comply due to the nature and extent of the modification. The time determined appropriate under the preceding sentence may not be earlier than the last day of the 180-day period beginning on the date such modification is adopted. The Secretary may extend the time for compliance for small health plans, if the Secretary determines that such extension is appropriate.

(3) CONSTRUCTION.—Nothing in this subsection shall be construed to prohibit any person from complying with a standard or specification by—

(A) submitting nonstandard data elements to a health care clearinghouse for processing into standard data elements and transmission by the health care clearinghouse; or

(B) receiving standard data elements through a health care clearinghouse.

GENERAL PENALTY FOR FAILURE TO COMPLY WITH REQUIREMENTS AND STANDARDS

SEC. 1176. [42 U.S.C. 1320d–5] (a) GENERAL PENALTY.—

(1) IN GENERAL.—Except as provided in subsection (b), the Secretary shall impose on any person who violates a provision of this part a penalty of not more than $100 for each such violation, except that the total amount imposed on the person for all violations of an identical requirement or prohibition during a calendar year may not exceed $25,000.

(2) PROCEDURES.—The provisions of section 1128A (other than subsections (a) and (b) and the second sentence of subsection (f)) shall apply to the imposition of a civil money penalty under this subsection in the same manner as such provisions apply to the imposition of a penalty under such section 1128A.

(b) LIMITATIONS.—

(1) OFFENSES OTHERWISE PUNISHABLE.—A penalty may not be imposed under subsection (a) with respect to an act if the act constitutes an offense punishable under section 1177.

(2) NONCOMPLIANCE NOT DISCOVERED.—A penalty may not be imposed under subsection (a) with respect to a provision of this part if it is established to the satisfaction of the Secretary that the person liable for the penalty did not know, and by exercising reasonable diligence would not have known, that such person violated the provision.

(3) FAILURES DUE TO REASONABLE CAUSE.—

(A) IN GENERAL.—Except as provided in subparagraph (B), a penalty may not be imposed under subsection (a) if—

(i) the failure to comply was due to reasonable cause and not to willful neglect; and

SOCIAL SECURITY ACT—§ 1178(a)(2) 751

(ii) the failure to comply is corrected during the 30-day period beginning on the first date the person liable for the penalty knew, or by exercising reasonable diligence would have known, that the failure to comply occurred.

(B) EXTENSION OF PERIOD.—

(i) NO PENALTY.—The period referred to in subparagraph (A)(ii) may be extended as determined appropriate by the Secretary based on the nature and extent of the failure to comply.

(ii) ASSISTANCE.—If the Secretary determines that a person failed to comply because the person was unable to comply, the Secretary may provide technical assistance to the person during the period described in subparagraph (A)(ii). Such assistance shall be provided in any manner determined appropriate by the Secretary.

(4) REDUCTION.—In the case of a failure to comply which is due to reasonable cause and not to willful neglect, any penalty under subsection (a) that is not entirely waived under paragraph (3) may be waived to the extent that the payment of such penalty would be excessive relative to the compliance failure involved.

WRONGFUL DISCLOSURE OF INDIVIDUALLY IDENTIFIABLE HEALTH INFORMATION

SEC. 1177. [42 U.S.C. 1320d–6] (a) OFFENSE.—A person who knowingly and in violation of this part—

(1) uses or causes to be used a unique health identifier;

(2) obtains individually identifiable health information relating to an individual; or

(3) discloses individually identifiable health information to another person,

shall be punished as provided in subsection (b).

(b) PENALTIES.—A person described in subsection (a) shall—

(1) be fined not more than $50,000, imprisoned not more than 1 year, or both;

(2) if the offense is committed under false pretenses, be fined not more than $100,000, imprisoned not more than 5 years, or both; and

(3) if the offense is committed with intent to sell, transfer, or use individually identifiable health information for commercial advantage, personal gain, or malicious harm, be fined not more than $250,000, imprisoned not more than 10 years, or both.

EFFECT ON STATE LAW

SEC. 1178. [42 U.S.C. 1320d–7] (a) GENERAL EFFECT.—

(1) GENERAL RULE.—Except as provided in paragraph (2), a provision or requirement under this part, or a standard or implementation specification adopted or established under sections 1172 through 1174, shall supersede any contrary provision of State law, including a provision of State law that requires medical or health plan records (including billing information) to be maintained or transmitted in written rather than electronic form.

(2) EXCEPTIONS.—A provision or requirement under this part, or a standard or implementation specification adopted or estab-

752 SOCIAL SECURITY ACT—§ 1178(a)(2)(A)

lished under sections 1172 through 1174, shall not supersede a contrary provision of State law, if the provision of State law—
    (A) is a provision the Secretary determines—
        (i) is necessary—
            (I) to prevent fraud and abuse;
            (II) to ensure appropriate State regulation of insurance and health plans;
            (III) for State reporting on health care delivery or costs; or
            (IV) for other purposes; or
        (ii) addresses controlled substances; or
    (B) subject to section 264(c)(2) of the Health Insurance Portability and Accountability Act of 1996[119], relates to the privacy of individually identifiable health information.
    (b) PUBLIC HEALTH.—Nothing in this part shall be construed to invalidate or limit the authority, power, or procedures established under any law providing for the reporting of disease or injury, child abuse, birth, or death, public health surveillance, or public health investigation or intervention.
    (c) STATE REGULATORY REPORTING.—Nothing in this part shall limit the ability of a State to require a health plan to report, or to provide access to, information for management audits, financial audits, program monitoring and evaluation, facility licensure or certification, or individual licensure or certification.

PROCESSING PAYMENT TRANSACTIONS BY FINANCIAL INSTITUTIONS

    SEC. 1179. [42 U.S.C. 1320d–8] To the extent that an entity is engaged in activities of a financial institution (as defined in section 1101 of the Right to Financial Privacy Act of 1978), or is engaged in authorizing, processing, clearing, settling, billing, transferring, reconciling, or collecting payments, for a financial institution, this part, and any standard adopted under this part, shall not apply to the entity with respect to such activities, including the following:
    (1) The use or disclosure of information by the entity for authorizing, processing, clearing, settling, billing, transferring, reconciling or collecting, a payment for, or related to, health plan premiums or health care, where such payment is made by any means, including a credit, debit, or other payment card, an account, check, or electronic funds transfer.
    (2) The request for, or the use of disclosure of, information by the entity with respect to a payment described in paragraph (1)—
        (A) for transferring receivables;
        (B) for auditing;
        (C) in connection with—
            (i) a customer dispute; or
            (ii) an inquiry from, or to, a customer;
        (D) in a communication to a customer of the entity regarding the customer's transactions, payment card, account, check, or electronic funds transfer;
        (E) for reporting to consumer reporting agencies; or
        (F) for complying with—
            (i) a civil or criminal subpoena; or

---

[119] See Vol. II, P.L. 104-191, §264(c)(2).

SOCIAL SECURITY ACT—§ 1180(c) 753

(ii) a Federal or State law regulating the entity.

APPLICATION OF HIPPA REGULATIONS TO GENETIC INFORMATION[120]

SEC. 1180. [42 U.S.C. 1320d–9] (a) IN GENERAL.—The Secretary shall revise the HIPAA privacy regulation (as defined in subsection (b)) so it is consistent with the following:

(1) Genetic information shall be treated as health information described in section 1171(4)(B).

(2) The use or disclosure by a covered entity that is a group health plan, health insurance issuer that issues health insurance coverage, or issuer of a medicare supplemental policy of protected health information that is genetic information about an individual for underwriting purposes under the group health plan, health insurance coverage, or medicare supplemental policy shall not be a permitted use or disclosure.

(b) DEFINITIONS.—For purposes of this section:

(1) GENETIC INFORMATION; GENETIC TEST; FAMILY MEMBER.—The terms "genetic information""genetic test"and "family member" have the meanings given such terms in section 2791 of the Public Health Service Act (42 U.S.C. 300gg–91)[121], as amended by the Genetic Information Nondiscrimination Act of 2007.

(2) GROUP HEALTH PLAN; HEALTH INSURANCE COVERAGE; MEDICARE SUPPLEMENTAL POLICY .—The terms "group health plan"and "health insurance coverage" have the meanings given such terms in section 2791 of the Public Health Service Act (42 U.S.C. 300gg–91)[122], and the term "medicare supplemental policy" has the meaning given such term in section 1882(g).

(3) HIPAA PRIVACY REGULATION.—The term "HIPPA privacy regulation" means the regulations promulgated by the Secretary under this part and section 264 of the Health Insurance Portability and Accountability Act of 1996 (42 U.S.C. 1320d–2 note) [123].

(4) UNDERWRITING PURPOSES.—The term "underwriting purposes" means, with respect to a group health plan, health insurance coverage, or a medicare supplemental policy—

(A) rules for, or determination of, eligibility (including enrollment and continued eligibility) for, or determination of, benefits under the plan, coverage, or policy;

(B) the computation of premium or contribution amounts under the plan, coverage, or policy;

(C) the application of any pre-existing condition exclusion under the plan, coverage, or policy; and

(D) other activities related to the creation, renewal, or replacement of a contract of health insurance or health benefits

(c) PROCEDURE.—The revisions under subsection (a) shall be made by notice in the Federal Register published not later than 60 days after the date of the enactment of this section and shall be effective upon publication, without opportunity for any prior public comment,

---

[120] P.L. 110-233, §105(a), adds this section, **to be effective May 21, 2009.**
See Vol. II, P.L. 110-233, §105(b)(1), with respect to the deadline for issuing final regulations.
[121] See Vol. II, P.L. 78-410, §2791.
[122] See Vol. II, P.L. 78-410, §2791.
[123] See Vol. II, P.L. 104-191, §264.

754   SOCIAL SECURITY ACT—§ 1180(c)(cont)

but may be revised, consistent with this section, after opportunity for public comment.

(d) ENFORCEMENT.—In addition to any other sanctions or remedies that may be available under law, a covered entity that is a group health plan, health insurance issuer, or issuer of a medicare supplemental policy and that violates the HIPAA privacy regulation (as revised under subsection (a) or otherwise) with respect to the use or disclosure of genetic information shall be subject to the penalties described in sections 1176 and 1177 in the same manner and to the same extent that such penalties apply to violations of this part.

TITLE XII—ADVANCES TO STATE UNEMPLOYMENT FUNDS[1]

TABLE OF CONTENTS OF TITLE[2]

		Page
Sec. 1201.	Advances to State unemployment funds	755
Sec. 1202.	Repayment by States of advances to State unemployment funds	756
Sec. 1203.	Advances to Federal unemployment account	759
Sec. 1204.	Definition of Governor	759

ADVANCES TO STATE UNEMPLOYMENT FUNDS[3]

SEC. 1201. [42 U.S.C. 1321] (a)(1) Advances shall be made to the States from the Federal unemployment account in the Unemployment Trust Fund as provided in this section, and shall be repayable, with interest to the extent provided in section 1202(b), in the manner provided in sections 901(d)(1), 903(b)(2), and 1202. An advance to a State for the payment of compensation in any 3-month period may be made if—

(A) the Governor of the State applies therefor no earlier than the first day of the month preceding the first month of such 3-month period, and

(B) he furnishes to the Secretary of Labor his estimate of the amount of an advance which will be required by the State for the payment of compensation in each month of such 3-month period.

(2) In the case of any application for an advance under this section to any State for any 3-month period, the Secretary of Labor shall—

(A) determine the amount (if any) which he finds will be required by such State for the payment of compensation in each month of such 3-month period, and

(B) certify to the Secretary of the Treasury the amount (not greater than the amount estimated by the Governor of the State) determined under subparagraph (A).

The aggregate of the amounts certified by the Secretary of Labor with respect to any 3-month period shall not exceed the amount which the Secretary of the Treasury reports to the Secretary of Labor is available in the Federal unemployment account for advances with respect to each month of such 3-month period.

(3) For purposes of this subsection—

(A) an application for an advance shall be made on such forms, and shall contain such information and data (fiscal and otherwise) concerning the operation and administration of the State unemployment compensation law, as the Secretary of Labor deems necessary or relevant to the performance of his duties under this title,

---

[1] Title XII of the Social Security Act is administered by the Department of Labor.

Title XII appears in the United States Code as §§1321-1324, subchapter XII, chapter 7, Title 42.

Regulations of the Secretary of Labor relating to Title XII are contained in chapter V, Title 20, Code of Federal Regulations.

See Vol. II, P.L. 88-352, §601, for prohibition against discrimination in Federally assisted programs.

[2] This table of contents does not appear in the law.

[3] See Vol. II, P.L. 83-591, §3302(c)(3), with respect to advances to a State or State agency.

See Vol. II, P.L. 96-499, §1025, with respect to withholding certification of State unemployment laws.

755

756 SOCIAL SECURITY ACT—§ 1201(a)(3)(B)

(B) the amount required by any State for the payment of compensation in any month shall be determined with due allowance for contingencies and taking into account all other amounts that will be available in the State's unemployment fund for the payment of compensation in such month, and

(C) the term "compensation" means cash benefits payable to individuals with respect to their unemployment, exclusive of expenses of administration.

(b) The Secretary of the Treasury shall, prior to audit or settlement by the General Accounting Office[4], transfer in monthly installments from the Federal unemployment account to the account of the State in the Unemployment Trust Fund the amount certified under subsection (a) by the Secretary of Labor (but not exceeding that portion of the balance in the Federal unemployment account at the time of the transfer which is not restricted as to use pursuant to section 903(b)(1)). The amount of any monthly installment so transferred shall not exceed the amount estimated by the State to be required for the payment of compensation for the month with respect to which such installment is made.

REPAYMENT BY STATES OF ADVANCES TO STATE UNEMPLOYMENT FUNDS

SEC. 1202. [42 U.S.C. 1322] (a) The Governor of any State may at any time request that funds be transferred from the account of such State to the Federal unemployment account in repayment of part or all of that balance of advances, made to such State under section 1201, specified in the request. The Secretary of Labor shall certify to the Secretary of the Treasury the amount and balance specified in the request; and the Secretary of the Treasury shall promptly transfer such amount in reduction of such balance.

(b)(1) Except as otherwise provided in this subsection, each State shall pay interest on any advance made to such State under section 1201. Interest so payable with respect to periods during any calendar year shall be at the rate determined under paragraph (4) for such calendar year.

(2) No interest shall be required to be paid under paragraph (1) with respect to any advance or advances made during any calendar year if—

(A) such advances are repaid in full before the close of September 30 of the calendar year in which the advances were made,

(B) no other advance was made to such State under section 1201 during such calendar year and after the date on which the repayment of the advances was completed, and

(C) such State meets funding goals, established under regulations issued by the Secretary of Labor, relating to the accounts of the States in the Unemployment Trust Fund.

(3)(A) Interest payable under paragraph (1) which was attributable to periods during any fiscal year shall be paid by the State to the Secretary of the Treasury prior to the first day of the following fiscal year. If interest is payable under paragraph (1) on any advance (hereinafter in this subparagraph referred to as the "first advance") by reason of an-

---

[4] P.L. 108-271, §8(b), provided that "Any reference to the General Accounting Office in any law, rule, regulation, certificate, directive, instruction, or other official paper in force on the date of enactment of this Act (July 7, 2004) shall be considered to refer and apply to the Government Accountability Office."

other advance made to such State after September 30 of the calendar year in which the first advance was made, interest on such first advance attributable to periods before such September 30 shall be paid not later than the day after the date on which the other advance was made.

(B) Notwithstanding subparagraph (A), in the case of any advance made during the last 5 months of any fiscal year, interest on such advance attributable to periods during such fiscal year shall not be required to be paid before the last day of the succeeding taxable year. Any interest the time for payment of which is deferred by the preceding sentence shall bear interest in the same manner as if it were an advance made on the day on which it would have been required to be paid but for this subparagraph.

(C)(i) In the case of any State which meets the requirements of clause (ii) for any calendar year, any interest otherwise required to be paid under this subsection during such calendar year shall be paid as follows—

(I) 25 percent of the amount otherwise required to be paid on or before any day during such calendar year shall be paid on or before such day; and

(II) 25 percent of the amount otherwise required to be paid on or before such day shall be paid on or before the corresponding day in each of the 3 succeeding calendar years.

No interest shall accrue on such deferred interest.

(ii) A State meets the requirements of this clause for any calendar year if the rate of insured unemployment (as determined for purposes of section 203 of the Federal-State Extended Unemployment Compensation Act of 1970[5]) under the State law of the period consisting of the first 6 months of the preceding calendar year equaled or exceeded 7.5 percent.

(4) The interest rate determined under this paragraph with respect to any calendar year is a percentage (but not in excess of 10 percent) determined by dividing—

(A) the aggregate amount credited under section 904(e) to State accounts on the last day of the last calendar quarter of the immediately preceding calendar year, by

(B) the aggregate of the average daily balances of the State accounts for such quarter as determined under section 904(e).

(5) Interest required to be paid under paragraph (1) shall not be paid (directly or indirectly) by a State from amounts in its unemployment fund. If the Secretary of Labor determines that any State action results in the paying of such interest directly or indirectly (by an equivalent reduction in State unemployment taxes or otherwise) from such unemployment fund, the Secretary of Labor shall not certify such State's unemployment compensation law under section 3304 of the Internal Revenue Code of 1954[6]. Such noncertification shall be made in accordance with section 3304(c) of such Code.

(6)(A) For purposes of paragraph (2), any voluntary repayment shall be applied against advances made under section 1201 on the last made first repaid basis. Any other repayment of such an advance shall be applied against advances on a first made first repaid basis.

---

[5] See Vol. II, P.L. 91-373, §203.
[6] See Vol. II., P.L. 83-591, §3304.

758 SOCIAL SECURITY ACT—§ 1202(b)(6)(B)

(B) For purposes of this paragraph, the term "voluntary repayment" means any repayment made under subsection (a).

(7) This subsection shall only apply to advances made on or after April 1, 1982.

(8)(A) With respect to interest due under this section on September 30 of 1983, 1984, or 1985 (other than interest previously deferred under paragraph (3)(C)), a State may pay 80 percent of such interest in four annual installments of at least 20 percent beginning with the year after the year in which it is otherwise due, if such State meets the criteria of subparagraph (B). No interest shall accrue on such deferred interest.

(B) To meet the criteria of this subparagraph a State must—

(i) have taken no action since October 1, 1982, which would reduce its net unemployment tax effort or the net solvency of its unemployment system (as determined for purposes of section 3302(f) of the Internal Revenue Code of 1954[7]); and

(ii)(I) have taken an action (as certified by the Secretary of Labor) after March 31, 1982, which would have increased revenue liabilities and decreased benefits under the State's unemployment compensation system (hereinafter referred to as a "solvency effort") by a combined total of the applicable percentage (as compared to such revenues and benefits as would have been in effect without such State action) for the calendar year for which the deferral is requested; or

(II) have had, for taxable year 1982, an average unemployment tax rate which was equal to or greater than 2.0 percent of the total of the wages (as determined without any limitation on amount) attributable to such State subject to contribution under the State unemployment compensation law with respect to such taxable year.

In the case of the first year for which there is a deferral (over a 4-year period) of the interest otherwise payable for such year, the applicable percentage shall be 25 percent. In the case of the second such year, the applicable percentage shall be 35 percent. In the case of the third such year, the applicable percentage shall be 50 percent.

(C)(i) The base year is the first year for which deferral under this provision is requested and subsequently granted. The Secretary of Labor shall estimate the unemployment rate for the base year. To determine whether a State meets the requirements of subparagraph (B)(ii)(I), the Secretary of Labor shall determine the percentage by which the benefits and taxes in the base year with the application of the action referred to in subparagraph (B)(ii)(I) are lower or greater, as the case may be, than such benefits and taxes would have been without the application of such action. In making this determination, the Secretary shall deem the application of the action referred to in subparagraph (B)(ii)(I) to have been effective for the base year to the same extent as such action is effective for the year following the year for which the deferral is sought. Once a deferral is approved under clause (ii)(I) of subparagraph (B) a State must continue to maintain its solvency effort. Failure to do so shall result in the State being required to make immediate payment of all deferred interest.

_____

[7] See Vol. II, P.L. 83-591, §3302(f).

SOCIAL SECURITY ACT—§ 1204

759

(ii) Increases in the taxable wage base from $6,000 to $7,000 or increases after 1984 in the maximum tax rate to 5.4 percent shall not be counted for purposes of meeting the requirement of subparagraph (B).

(D) In the case of a State which produces a solvency effort of 50 percent, 80 percent, and 90 percent rather than the 25 percent, 35 percent, and 50 percent required under subparagraph (B), the interest shall be computed at an interest rate which is 1 percentage point less than the otherwise applicable interest rate.

(9) Any interest otherwise due from a State on September 30 of a calendar year after 1982 may be deferred (and no interest shall accrue on such deferred interest) for a grace period of not to exceed 9 months if, for the most recent 12-month period for which data are available before the date such interest is otherwise due, the State had an average total unemployment rate of 13.5 percent or greater.

(c) Interest paid by States in accordance with this section shall be credited to the Federal unemployment account established by section 904(g) in the Unemployment Trust Fund.

ADVANCES TO FEDERAL UNEMPLOYMENT ACCOUNT

SEC. 1203. [42 U.S.C. 1323] There are hereby authorized to be appropriated to the Federal unemployment account, as repayable advances, such sums as may be necessary to carry out the purposes of this title. Amounts appropriated as repayable advances shall be repaid by transfers from the Federal unemployment account to the general fund of the Treasury, at such times as the amount in the Federal unemployment account is determined by the Secretary of the Treasury, in consultation with the Secretary of Labor, to be adequate for such purpose. Any amount transferred as a repayment under this section shall be credited against, and shall operate to reduce, any balance of advances repayable under this section. Whenever, after the application of sections 901(f)(3) and 902(a) with respect to the excess in the employment security administration account as of the close of any fiscal year, there remains any portion of such excess, so much of such remainder as does not exceed the balance of advances made pursuant to this section shall be transferred to the general fund of the Treasury and shall be credited against, and shall operate to reduce, such balance of advances. Amounts appropriated as repayable advances for purposes of this subsection shall bear interest at a rate equal to the average rate of interest, computed as of the end of the calendar month next preceding the date of such advance, borne by all interest bearing obligations of the United States then forming part of the public debt; except that in cases in which such average rate is not a multiple of one-eighth of 1 percent, the rate of interest shall be the multiple of one-eighth of 1 percent next lower than such average rate.

DEFINITION OF GOVERNOR

SEC. 1204. [42 U.S.C. 1324] When used in this title, the term "Governor" includes the Commissioners[8] of the District of Columbia.

---

[8] P.L. 93-198, §711, abolished the office of Commissioner of the District of Columbia and §421 replaced it with the office of Mayor of the District of Columbia.

[TITLE XIII—RECONVERSION UNEMPLOYMENT BENEFITS FOR SEAMEN[1]]

---

[1] P.L. 79-719 (60 Stat. 978, approved August 10, 1946), §306, added Title XIII to the Social Security Act.

P.L. 98-369, §2663(f), repealed Title XIII, effective July 18, 1984, but this amendment shall not be construed as changing or affecting any right, liability, status, or interpretation which existed under this provision before that date.

[TITLE XIV—GRANTS TO STATES FOR AID TO THE PERMANENTLY AND TOTALLY DISABLED[1]]

TABLE OF CONTENTS OF TITLE[2]

		Page
Sec. 1401.	Appropriation	763
Sec. 1402.	State plans for aid to the permanently and totally disabled	763
Sec. 1403.	Payment to States	765
Sec. 1404.	Operation of State plans	766
Sec. 1405.	Definition	767

APPROPRIATION

SEC. 1401. [42 U.S.C. 1351] For the purpose of enabling each State to furnish financial assistance, as far as practicable under the conditions in such State, to needy individuals eighteen years of age and older who are permanently and totally disabled, there is hereby authorized to be appropriated for each fiscal year a sum sufficient to carry out the purposes of this title. The sums made available under this section shall be used for making payments to States which have submitted, and had approved by the Administrator, State plans for aid to the permanently and totally disabled.

STATE PLANS FOR AID TO THE PERMANENTLY AND TOTALLY DISABLED

SEC. 1402. [42 U.S.C. 1352] (a) A State plan for aid to the permanently and totally disabled must (1) except to the extent permitted by the Secretary with respect to services, provide that it shall be in effect in all political subdivisions of the State, and, if administered by them, be mandatory upon them; (2) provide for financial participation by the State; (3) either provide for the establishment or designation of a single State agency to administer the plan, or provide for the establishment or designation of a single State agency to supervise the administration of the plan; (4) provide (A) for granting an opportunity for a fair hearing before the State agency to any individual whose claim for aid to the permanently and totally disabled is denied or is not acted upon with reasonable promptness, and (B) that if the State plan is administered in each of the political subdivisions of the State

---

[1] P.L. 92-603, §303, *repealed* Title XIV, effective January 1, 1974, *except* with respect to Puerto Rico, Guam, and the Virgin Islands. The Commonwealth of the Northern Marianas may elect to initiate a Title XIV social services program if it chooses; see Vol. II, P.L. 94-241, [Covenant to Establish a Commonwealth of the Northern Marianas].

Title XIV of the Social Security Act is administered by the Department of Health and Human Services. The Office of Family Assistance, Family Support Administration, administers benefit payments under Title XIV. The Office of Human Development Services administers social services under Title XIV.

Title XIV appears in the United States Code as §§1351-1355, subchapter XIV, chapter 7, Title 42.

Regulations of the Secretary of Health and Human Services relating to Title XIV are contained in chapter 1, Title 42, and subtitle A and chapter XIII, Title 45, Code of Federal Regulations.

See Vol. II, 31 U.S.C. 6504-6505 with respect to intergovernmental cooperation.

See Vol. II, 31 U.S.C. 7501-7507 with respect to uniform audit requirements for State and local governments receiving Federal financial assistance.

See Vol. II, P.L. 82-183, §618, for the "Jenner Amendment", which prohibits denial of grants-in-aid under certain conditions.

See Vol. II, P.L. 88-352, §601, for prohibition against discrimination in Federally assisted programs.

See Vol. II, P.L. 89-97, §121(b), with respect to restrictions on payment to a State receiving payments under Title XIX.

[2] This table of contents does not appear in the law.

764   SOCIAL SECURITY ACT—§ 1402(a)(cont)

by a local agency and such local agency provides a hearing at which evidence may be presented prior to a hearing before the State agency, such local agency may put into effect immediately upon issuance its decision upon the matter considered at such hearing; (5) provide (A) such methods of administration (including methods relating to the establishment and maintenance of personnel standards on a merit basis, except that the Secretary shall exercise no authority with respect to the selection, tenure of office, and compensation of any individual employed in accordance with such methods) as are found by the Secretary to be necessary for the proper and efficient operation of the plan[3], and (B) for the training and effective use of paid subprofessional staff, with particular emphasis on the full-time or part-time employment of recipients and other persons of low income, as community service aides, in the administration of the plan and for the use of nonpaid or partially paid volunteers in a social service volunteer program in providing services to applicants and recipients and in assisting any advisory committees established by the State agency; (6) provide that the State agency will make such reports, in such form and containing such information, as the Secretary may from time to time require, and comply with such provisions as the Secretary may from time to time find necessary to assure the correctness and verification of such reports; (7) provide that no aid will be furnished any individual under the plan with respect to any period with respect to which he is receiving old-age assistance under the State plan approved under section 2 of this Act, assistance under a State program funded under part A of title IV or aid to the blind under the State plan approved under section 1002 of this Act; (8) provide that the State agency shall, in determining need, take into consideration any other income and resources of an individual claiming aid to the permanently and totally disabled, as well as any expenses reasonably attributable to the earning of any such income; except that, in making such determination, (A) the State agency may disregard not more than $7.50 of any income, (B) of the first $80 per month of additional income which is earned the State agency may disregard not more than the first $20 thereof plus one-half of the remainder, and (C) the State agency may, for a period not in excess of 36 months, disregard such additional amounts of other income and resources, in the case of an individual who has a plan for achieving self-support approved by the State agency, as may be necessary for the fulfillment of such plan, but only with respect to the part or parts of such period during substantially all of which he is actually undergoing vocational rehabilitation;[4] (9) provide safeguards which permit the use or disclosure of information concerning applicants or recipients only (A) to public officials who require such information in connection with their official duties, or (B) to other persons for purposes directly connected with the administration of the State plan;[5] (10) provide that all individuals wishing to make application for aid to the permanently and totally disabled shall have opportunity to do so, and that aid to the permanently and totally disabled

---

[3] P.L. 91-648, §208(a)(3)(D), transferred to the U.S. Civil Service Commission, effective March 6, 1971, all powers, functions, and duties of the Secretary under subparagraph (A).

[4] See Vol. II, Appendix K, Income and Resource Exclusions, for a list of provisions from Federal laws regarding exclusions from income and resources.

[5] See Vol. II, P.L. 82-183, §618, for the "Jenner Amendment", with respect to denial of grants-in-aid under certain conditions.

SOCIAL SECURITY ACT—§ 1403(b)   765

shall be furnished with reasonable promptness to all eligible individuals; (11) effective July 1, 1953, provide, if the plan includes payments to individuals in private or public institutions, for the establishment or designation of a State authority or authorities which shall be responsible for establishing and maintaining standards for such institutions; (12) provide a description of the services (if any) which the State agency makes available (using whatever internal organizational arrangement it finds appropriate for this purpose) to applicants for and recipients of aid to the permanently and totally disabled to help them attain self-support or self-care, including a description of the steps taken to assure, in the provision of such services, maximum utilization of other agencies providing similar or related services; and (13) provide that information is requested and exchanged for purposes of income and eligibility verification in accordance with a State system which meets the requirements of section 1137 of this Act.

(b) The Secretary shall approve any plan which fulfills the conditions specified in subsection (a), except that he shall not approve any plan which imposes, as a condition of eligibility for aid to the permanently and totally disabled under the plan—

> (1) Any residence requirement which excludes any resident of the State who has resided therein five years during the nine years immediately preceding the application for aid to the permanently and totally disabled and has resided therein continuously for one year immediately preceding the application;

> (2) Any citizenship requirement which excludes any citizen of the United States.

At the option of the State, the plan may provide that manuals and other policy issuances will be furnished to persons without charge for the reasonable cost of such materials, but such provision shall not be required by the Secretary as a condition for the approval of such plan under this title.

PAYMENT TO STATES

SEC. 1403. [42 U.S.C. 1353] (a) From the sums appropriated therefor, the Secretary of the Treasury shall pay to each State which has an approved plan for aid to the permanently and totally disabled, for each quarter, beginning with the quarter commencing October 1, 1958—

> (1) [Stricken.[6]]

> (2) in the case of Puerto Rico, the Virgin Islands, and Guam, an amount equal to one-half of the total of the sums expended during such quarter as aid to the permanently and totally disabled under the State plan, not counting so much of any expenditure with respect to any month as exceeds $37.50 multiplied by the total number of recipients of aid to the permanently and totally disabled for such month; and

> (3) in the case of any State, an amount equal to 50 percent of the total amounts expended during such quarter as found necessary by the Secretary for the proper and efficient administration of the State plan.

(b) The method of computing and paying such amounts shall be as follows:

---

[6] P.L. 97-35, §2184(c)(2)(A); 95 Stat. 817.

766 SOCIAL SECURITY ACT—§ 1403(b)(1)

(1) The Administrator shall, prior to the beginning of each quarter, estimate the amount to be paid to the State for such quarter under the provisions of subsection (a), such estimate to be based on (A) a report filed by the State containing its estimate of the total sum to be expended in such quarter in accordance with the provisions of such subsection, and stating the amount appropriated or made available by the State and its political subdivisions for such expenditures in such quarter, and if such amount is less than the State's proportionate share of the total sum of such estimated expenditures, the source or sources from which the difference is expected to be derived, (B) records showing the number of permanently and totally disabled individuals in the State, and (C) such other investigation as the Administrator may find necessary.

(2) The Administrator shall then certify to the Secretary of the Treasury the amount so estimated by the Administrator, (A) reduced or increased, as the case may be, by any sum by which he finds that his estimate for any prior quarter was greater or less than the amount which should have been paid to the State under subsection (a) for such quarter, and (B) reduced by a sum equivalent to the pro rata share to which the United States is equitably entitled, as determined by the Administrator, of the net amount recovered during a prior quarter by the State or any political subdivision thereof with respect to aid to the permanently and totally disabled furnished under the State plan; except that such increases or reductions shall not be made to the extent that such sums have been applied to make the amount certified for any prior quarter greater or less than the amount estimated by the Administrator for such prior quarter: *Provided* , That any part of the amount recovered from the estate of a deceased recipient which is not in excess of the amount expended by the State or any political subdivision thereof for the funeral expenses of the deceased shall not be considered as a basis for reduction under clause (B) of this paragraph.

(3) The Secretary of the Treasury shall thereupon, through the Fiscal Service of the Treasury Department, and prior to audit or settlement by the General Accounting Office[7], pay to the State, at the time or times fixed by the Administrator, the amount so certified.

OPERATION OF STATE PLANS

SEC. 1404. [42 U.S.C. 1354] In the case of any State plan for aid to the permanently and totally disabled which has been approved by the Secretary of Health, Education, and Welfare, if the Secretary after reasonable notice and opportunity for hearing to the State agency administering or supervising the administration of such plan, finds—

(1) that the plan has been so changed as to impose any residence or citizenship requirement prohibited by section 1402(b), or that in the administration of the plan any such prohibited re-

---

[7] P.L. 108-271, §8(b), provided that "Any reference to the General Accounting Office in any law, rule, regulation, certificate, directive, instruction, or other official paper in force on the date of enactment of this Act (July 7, 2004) shall be considered to refer and apply to the Government Accountability Office."

SOCIAL SECURITY ACT—§ 1405(4) 767

quirement is imposed, with the knowledge of such State agency, in a substantial number of cases; or

(2) that in the administration of the plan there is a failure to comply substantially with any provision required by section 1402(a) to be included in the plan;

the Secretary shall notify such State agency that further payments will not be made to the State (or, in his discretion, that payments will be limited to categories under or parts of the State plan not affected by such failure) until he is satisfied that such prohibited requirement is no longer so imposed, and that there is no longer any such failure to comply. Until he is so satisfied he shall make no further payments to such State (or shall limit payments to categories under or parts of the State plan not affected by such failure).

DEFINITION

Sec. 1405. [42 U.S.C. 1355] For the purposes of this title, the term "aid to the permanently and totally disabled" means money payments to needy individuals eighteen years of age or older who are permanently and totally disabled, but does not include any such payments to or care in behalf of any individual who is an inmate of a public institution (except as a patient in a medical institution) or any individual who is a patient in an institution for tuberculosis or mental diseases. Such term also includes payments which are not included within the meaning of such term under the preceding sentence, but which would be so included except that they are made on behalf of such a needy individual to another individual who (as determined in accordance with standards prescribed by the Secretary) is interested in or concerned with the welfare of such needy individual, but only with respect to a State whose State plan approved under section 1402 includes provision for—

(1) determination by the State agency that such needy individual has, by reason of his physical or mental condition, such inability to manage funds that making payments to him would be contrary to his welfare and, therefore, it is necessary to provide such aid through payments described in this sentence;

(2) making such payments only in cases in which such payments will, under the rules otherwise applicable under the State plan for determining need and the amount of aid to the permanently and totally disabled to be paid (and in conjunction with other income and resources), meet all the need[8] of the individuals with respect to whom such payments are made;

(3) undertaking and continuing special efforts to protect the welfare of such individual and to improve, to the extent possible, his capacity for self-care and to manage funds;

(4) periodic review by such State agency of the determination under paragraph (1) to ascertain whether conditions justifying such determination still exist, with provision for termination of such payments if they do not and for seeking judicial appointment of a guardian or other legal representative, as described in section 1111, if and when it appears that such action will best serve the interests of such needy individual; and

---

[8] As in original. Should be "needs".

768 SOCIAL SECURITY ACT—§ 1405(5)

(5) opportunity for a fair hearing before the State agency on the determination referred to in paragraph (1) for any individual with respect to whom it is made.

At the option of a State (if its plan approved under this title so provides), such term (i) need not include money payments to an individual who has been absent from such State for a period in excess of ninety consecutive days (regardless of whether he has maintained his residence in such State during such period) until he has been present in such State for thirty consecutive days in the case of such an individual who has maintained his residence in such State during such period or ninety consecutive days in the case of any other such individual, and (ii) may include rent payments made directly to a public housing agency on behalf of a recipient or a group or groups of recipients of aid under such plan.

[TITLE XV—UNEMPLOYMENT COMPENSATION FOR FEDERAL EMPLOYEES[1]]

---

[1] P.L. 83-767 (68 Stat. 1130, approved September 1, 1954), §4(a), added Title XV to the Social Security Act.

P.L. 89-554 (80 Stat. 378, approved September 6, 1966), §8, repealed Title XV. Now see 5 U.S.C. 8501 et seq. (may be found in Vol. II).

[TITLE XVI—GRANTS TO STATES FOR AID TO THE AGED, BLIND, OR DISABLED[1]]

TABLE OF CONTENTS OF TITLE[2]

		Page
Sec. 1601.	Appropriation	771
Sec. 1602.	State plans for aid to the aged, blind, or disabled	771
Sec. 1603.	Payments to States	775
Sec. 1604.	Operation of State plans	776
Sec. 1605.	Definitions	776

APPROPRIATION

SEC. 1601. [42 U.S.C. 1381 note] For the purpose of enabling each State, as far as practicable under the conditions in such State, to furnish financial assistance to needy individuals who are 65 years of age or over, are blind, or are 18 years of age or over and permanently and totally disabled, there is hereby authorized to be appropriated for each fiscal year a sum sufficient to carry out the purposes of this title. The sums made available under this section shall be used for making payments to States which have submitted, and had approved by the Secretary of Health, Education, and Welfare, State plans for aid to the aged, blind, or disabled.

STATE PLANS FOR AID TO THE AGED, BLIND, OR DISABLED

SEC. 1602. [42 U.S.C. 1382 note] (a) A State plan for aid to the aged, blind, or disabled, must—

(1) except to the extent permitted by the Secretary with respect to services, provide that it shall be in effect in all political subdivisions of the State, and, if administered by them, be mandatory upon them;

(2) provide for financial participation by the State;

(3) either provide for the establishment or designation of a single State agency to administer the plan, or provide for the establishment or designation of a single State agency to supervise the administration of the plan;

---

[1] This Title XVI of the Social Security Act is administered by the Department of Health and Human Services. The Office of Family Assistance, Family Support Administration, administers benefit payments under this Title XVI. The Office of Human Development Services administers social services under this Title XVI.

This Title XVI appears in the United States Code as §§1381 note -1385 note, subchapter XVI, chapter 7, Title 42.

Regulations of the Secretary of Health and Human Services with respect to this Title XVI are contained in subtitle A and chapter XIII, Title 45, Code of Federal Regulations.

P.L. 92-603, §§301 and 303, *repealed* this title effective January 1, 1974, except with respect to Guam, Puerto Rico, and the Virgin Islands. The Commonwealth of the Northern Marianas may elect to initiate a Title XVI social services program if it chooses.

See Vol. II, 31 U.S.C. 6504-6505 with respect to intergovernmental cooperation and 31 U.S.C. 7501-7507 with respect to uniform audit requirements for State and local governments receiving Federal financial assistance.

See Vol. II, P.L. 82-183, §618, for the "Jenner Amendment", with respect to prohibition against denial of grants-in-aid under certain conditions.

See Vol. II, P.L. 88-352, §601, with respect to prohibition against discrimination in federally assisted programs.

See Vol. II, P.L. 89-97, §121(b), with respect to restrictions on payment to a State receiving payments under Title XIX.

[2] This table of contents does not appear in the law.

772 SOCIAL SECURITY ACT—§ 1602(a)(4)

(4) provide (A) for granting an opportunity for a fair hearing before the State agency to any individual whose claim for aid or assistance under the plan is denied or is not acted upon with reasonable promptness, and (B) that if the State plan is administered in each of the political subdivisions of the State by a local agency and such local agency provides a hearing at which evidence may be presented prior to a hearing before the State agency, such local agency may put into effect immediately upon issuance its decision upon the matter considered at such hearing;

(5) provide (A) such methods of administration (including methods relating to the establishment and maintenance of personnel standards on a merit basis, except that the Secretary shall exercise no authority with respect to the selection, tenure of office, and compensation of any individual employed in accordance with such methods) as are found by the Secretary to be necessary for the proper and efficient operation of the plan[3], and (B) for the training and effective use of paid subprofessional staff, with particular emphasis on the full-time or part-time employment of recipients and other persons of low income, as community service aides, in the administration of the plan and for the use of nonpaid or partially paid volunteers in a social service volunteer program in providing services to applicants and recipients and in assisting any advisory committees established by the State agency;

(6) provide that the State agency will make such reports, in such form and containing such information, as the Secretary may from time to time require, and comply with such provisions as the Secretary may from time to time find necessary to assure the correctness and verification of such reports;

(7) provide safeguards which permit the use or disclosure of information concerning applicants or recipients only (A) to public officials who require such information in connection with their official duties, or (B) to other persons for purposes directly connected with the administration of the State plan;

(8) provide that all individuals wishing to make application for aid or assistance under the plan shall have opportunity to do so, and that such aid or assistance shall be furnished with reasonable promptness to all eligible individuals;

(9) provide, if the plan includes aid or assistance to or on behalf of individuals in private or public institutions, for the establishment or designation of a State authority or authorities which shall be responsible for establishing and maintaining standards for such institutions;

(10) provide a description of the services (if any) which the State agency makes available (using whatever internal organizational arrangement it finds appropriate for this purpose) to applicants for or recipients of aid or assistance under the plan to help them attain self-support or self-care, including a description of the steps taken to assure, in the provision of such services, maximum utilization of other agencies providing similar or related services;

---

[3] P.L. 91-648, §208(a)(3)(D), transferred to the U.S. Civil Service Commission, effective March 6, 1971, all powers, functions, and duties of the Secretary under subparagraph (A).

SOCIAL SECURITY ACT—§ 1602(a)(15)   773

(11) provide that no aid or assistance will be furnished any individual under the plan with respect to any period with respect to which he is receiving assistance under the State plan approved under title I or aid under a State program funded under part A of title IV or under title X or XIV;

(12) provide that, in determining whether an individual is blind, there shall be an examination by a physician skilled in the diseases of the eye or by an optometrist, whichever the individual may select;

(13) include reasonable standards, consistent with the objectives of this title, for determining eligibility for and the extent of aid or assistance under the plan;

(14) provide that the State agency shall, in determining need for aid to the aged, blind, or disabled, take into consideration any other income and resources of an individual claiming such aid, as well as any expenses reasonably attributable to the earning of any such income; except that, in making such determination with respect to any individual—

(A) if such individual is blind, the State agency (i) shall disregard the first $85 per month of earned income plus one-half of earned income in excess of $85 per month, and (ii) shall, for a period not in excess of 12 months, and may, for a period not in excess of 36 months, disregard such additional amounts of other income and resources, in the case of any such individual who has a plan for achieving self-support approved by the State agency, as may be necessary for the fulfillment of such plan,

(B) if such individual is not blind but is permanently and totally disabled, (i) of the first $80 per month of earned income, the State agency may disregard not more than the first $20 thereof plus one-half of the remainder, and (ii) the State agency may, for a period not in excess of 36 months, disregard such additional amounts of other income and resources, in the case of any such individual who has a plan for achieving self-support approved by the State agency, as may be necessary for the fulfillment of such plan, but only with respect to the part or parts of such period during substantially all of which he is actually undergoing vocational rehabilitation,

(C) if such individual has attained age 65 and is neither blind nor permanently and totally disabled, of the first $80 per month of earned income the State agency may disregard not more than the first $20 thereof plus one-half of the remainder, and

(D) the State agency may, before disregarding the amounts referred to above in this paragraph (14), disregard not more than $7.50 of any income;[4] and

(15) provide that information is requested and exchanged for purposes of income and eligibility verification in accordance with a State system which meets the requirements of section 1137 of this Act.

---

[4] See Vol. II, Appendix K, Income and Resource Exclusions, for a list of provisions from Federal laws regarding exclusions from income and resources.

774 SOCIAL SECURITY ACT—§ 1602(a)(15)(cont)

Notwithstanding paragraph (3), if on January 1, 1962, and on the date on which a State submits its plan for approval under this title, the State agency which administered or supervised the administration of the plan of such State approved under title X was different from the State agency which administered or supervised the administration of the plan of such State approved under title I and the State agency which administered or supervised the administration of the plan of such State approved under title XIV, the State agency which administered or supervised the administration of such plan approved under title X may be designated to administer or supervise the administration of the portion of the State plan for aid to the aged, blind, or disabled which relates to blind individuals and a separate State agency may be established or designated to administer or supervise the administration of the rest of such plan; and in such case the part of the plan which each such agency administers, or the administration of which each such agency supervises, shall be regarded as a separate plan for purposes of this title.

(b) The Secretary shall approve any plan which fulfills the conditions specified in subsection (a), except that he shall not approve any plan which imposes, as a condition of eligibility for aid or assistance under the plan—

(1) an age requirement of more than sixty-five years; or

(2) any residence requirement which excludes any resident of the State who has resided therein five years during the nine years immediately preceding the application for such aid and has resided therein continuously for one year immediately preceding the application,[5] ; or

(3) any citizenship requirement which excludes any citizen of the United States.

At the option of the State, the plan may provide that manuals and other policy issuances will be furnished to persons without charge for the reasonable cost of such materials, but such provision shall not be required by the Secretary as a condition for the approval of such plan under this title. In the case of any State to which the provisions of section 344 of the Social Security Act Amendments of 1950[6] were applicable on January 1, 1962, and to which the sentence of section 1002(b) following paragraph (2) thereof is applicable on the date on which its State plan for aid to the aged, blind, or disabled was submitted for approval under this title, the Secretary shall approve the plan of such State for aid to the aged, blind, or disabled for purposes of this title, even though it does not meet the requirements of paragraph (14) of subsection (a), if it meets all other requirements of this title for an approved plan for aid to the aged, blind, or disabled; but payments under section 1603 shall be made, in the case of any such plan, only with respect to expenditures thereunder which would be included as expenditures for the purposes of section 1603 under a plan approved under this section without regard to the provisions of this sentence.

(c) Subject to the last sentence of subsection (a), nothing in this title shall be construed to permit a State to have in effect with respect to any period more than one State plan approved under this title.

---

[5] As in original. Comma should be stricken.
[6] P.L. 87-543, §136(b); 76 Stat. 197, repealed §344, effective July 25, 1962.

PAYMENTS TO STATES

SEC. 1603. [42 U.S.C. 1383 note] (a) From the sums appropriated therefor, the Secretary shall pay to each State which has a plan approved under this title, for each quarter, beginning with the quarter commencing October 1, 1962—

(1) [Stricken.[7]]

(2) in the case of Puerto Rico, the Virgin Islands, and Guam, an amount equal to—

(A) one-half of the total of the sums expended during such quarter as aid to the aged, blind, or disabled under the State plan, not counting so much of any expenditure with respect to any month as exceeds $37.50 multiplied by the total number of recipients of aid to the aged, blind, or disabled for such month; plus

(B) one-half of the amount by which such expenditures exceed the maximum which may be counted under clause[8] (A), not counting so much of any expenditure with respect to any month as exceeds the product of $45 multiplied by the total number of such recipients of aid to the aged, blind, or disabled for such month; and

(3) [Stricken.[9]]

(4) in the case of any State, an amount equal to 50 percent of the total amounts expended during such quarter as found necessary by the Secretary for the proper and efficient administration of the State plan.

(b)(1) Prior to the beginning of each quarter, the Secretary shall estimate the amount to which a State will be entitled under subsection (a) for such quarter, such estimates to be based on (A) a report filed by the State containing its estimate of the total sum to be expended in such quarter in accordance with the provisions of such subsection, and stating the amount appropriated or made available by the State and its political subdivisions for such expenditures in such quarter, and if such amount is less than the State's proportionate share of the total sum of such estimated expenditures, the source or sources from which the difference is expected to be derived, and (B) such other investigation as the Secretary may find necessary.

(2) The Secretary shall then pay, in such installments as he may determine, to the State the amount so estimated, reduced or increased to the extent of any overpayment or underpayment which the Secretary determines was made under this section to such State for any prior quarter and with respect to which adjustment has not already been made under this subsection.

(3) The pro rata share to which the United States is equitably entitled, as determined by the Secretary, of the net amount recovered during any quarter by the State or any political subdivision thereof with respect to aid or assistance furnished under the State plan, but excluding any amount of such aid or assistance recovered from the estate of a deceased recipient which is not in excess of the amount expended by the State or any political subdivision thereof for the fu-

---

[7] P.L. 97-35, §2184(d)(5)(A); 95 Stat. 818.

[8] As in original. Possibly, should be "subparagraph".

[9] P.L. 97-35, §2184(d)(5)(A); 95 Stat. 818.

776 SOCIAL SECURITY ACT—§ 1603(b)(3)(cont)

neral expenses of the deceased, shall be considered an overpayment to be adjusted under this subsection.

(4) Upon the making of any estimate by the Secretary under this subsection, any appropriations available for payments under this section shall be deemed obligated.

OPERATION OF STATE PLANS

SEC. 1604. [42 U.S.C. 1384 note] If the Secretary, after reasonable notice and opportunity for hearing to the State agency administering or supervising the administration of the State plan approved under this title, finds—

(1) that the plan has been so changed that it no longer complies with the provisions of section 1602; or

(2) that in the administration of the plan there is a failure to comply substantially with any such provision;

the Secretary shall notify such State agency that further payments will not be made to the State (or, in his discretion, that payments will be limited to categories under or parts of the State plan not affected by such failure), until the Secretary is satisfied that there will no longer be any such failure to comply. Until he is so satisfied he shall make no further payments to such State (or shall limit payments to categories under or parts of the State plan not affected by such failure).

DEFINITIONS

SEC. 1605. [42 U.S.C. 1385 note] (a)[10] For purposes of this title, the term "aid to the aged, blind, or disabled" means money payments to needy individuals who are 65 years of age or older, are blind, or are 18 years of age or over and permanently and totally disabled, but such term does not include—

(1) any such payments to or care in behalf of any individual who is an inmate of a public institution (except as a patient in a medical institution); or

(2) any such payments to or care in behalf of any individual who has not attained 65 years of age and who is a patient in an institution for tuberculosis or mental diseases.

Such term also includes payments which are not included within the meaning of such term under the preceding sentence, but which would be so included except that they are made on behalf of such a needy individual to another individual who (as determined in accordance with standards prescribed by the Secretary) is interested in or concerned with the welfare of such needy individual, but only with respect to a State whose State plan approved under section 1602 includes provision for—

(A) determination by the State agency that such needy individual has, by reason of his physical or mental condition, such inability to manage funds that making payments to him would be contrary to his welfare and, therefore, it is necessary to provide such aid through payments described in this sentence;

(B) making such payments only in cases in which such payments will, under the rules otherwise applicable under the State plan for determining need and the amount of aid to the aged, blind, or disabled to be paid (and in conjunction with other in-

---

[10] As in original; "(a)" should be stricken.

SOCIAL SECURITY ACT—§ 1605(a)(2)(E)   777

come and resources), meet all the need[11] of the individuals with respect to whom such payments are made;

(C) undertaking and continuing special efforts to protect the welfare of such individual and to improve, to the extent possible, his capacity for self-care and to manage funds;

(D) periodic review by such State agency of the determination under clause[12] (A) to ascertain whether conditions justifying such determination still exist, with provision for termination of such payments if they do not and for seeking judicial appointment of a guardian or other legal representative, as described in section 1111, if and when it appears that such action will best serve the interests of such needy individual; and

(E) opportunity for a fair hearing before the State agency on the determination referred to in clause[13] (A) for any individual with respect to whom it is made.

At the option of a State (if its plan approved under this title so provides), such term (i) need not include money payments to an individual who has been absent from such State for a period in excess of ninety consecutive days (regardless of whether he has maintained his residence in such State during such period) until he has been present in such State for thirty consecutive days in the case of such an individual who has maintained his residence in such State during such period or ninety consecutive days in the case of any other such individual, and (ii) may include rent payments made directly to a public housing agency on behalf of a recipient or a group or groups of recipients of aid under such plan.

---

[11] As in original. Should be "needs".
[12] As in original. Possibly, should be "subparagraph".
[13] As in original. Possibly, should be "subparagraph".

TITLE XVI—SUPPLEMENTAL SECURITY INCOME FOR THE AGED, BLIND, AND DISABLED[1]

TABLE OF CONTENTS OF TITLE[2]

		Page
Sec. 1601.	Purpose; appropriations	780
Sec. 1602.	Basic eligibility for benefits	780

Part A—Determination of Benefits

Sec. 1611.	Eligibility for and amount of benefits	780
Sec. 1612.	Income	789
Sec. 1613.	Resources	795
Sec. 1614.	Meaning of terms	802
Sec. 1615.	Rehabilitation services for blind and disabled individuals	809
Sec. 1616.	Optional State supplementation	810
Sec. 1617.	Cost–of–living adjustments in benefits	814
Sec. 1618.	Operation of State supplementation programs	814
Sec. 1619.	Benefits for individuals who perform substantial gainful activity despite severe medical impairment	817
Sec. 1620.	Medical and social services for certain handicapped persons	819
Sec. 1621.	Attribution of sponsor's income and resources to aliens	821

Part B—Procedural and General Provisions

Sec. 1631.	Payments and procedures	823
Sec. 1632.	Penalties for fraud	851
Sec. 1633.	Administration	852
Sec. 1634.	Determinations of medicaid eligibility	853
Sec. 1635.	Outreach program for children	855
Sec. 1636.	Treatment referrals for individuals with an alcoholism or drug addiction condition	855
Sec. 1637.	Annual report on program	855

---

[1] This Title XVI of the Social Security Act is administered by the Social Security Administration.

This Title XVI appears in the United States Code as §§1381-1383f, subchapter XVI, chapter 7, Title 42.

Regulations with respect to this Title XVI are contained in chapter III, Title 20, Code of Federal Regulations.

P.L. 94-241, §1 (§502 of Covenant to Establish a Commonwealth of the Northern Mariana Islands in Political Union with the United States of America), approved March 24, 1976, provides that this Title XVI is applicable to the Northern Mariana Islands.

See Vol. II, P.L. 88-352, §601, for prohibition against discrimination in federally assisted programs.

See Vol. II, 31 U.S.C. 3720 and 3720A, with respect to collection of payments due to Federal agencies.

See Vol. II, P.L. 88-352, §601, for prohibition against discrimination in Federally assisted programs.

See Vol. II, P.L. 88-525, §11(i), with respect to the acceptance by social security offices of applications for participation in the food stamp program from recipients of supplemental security income.

See Vol. II, P.L. 100-203, §9117, with respect to the demonstration program to assist homeless individuals.

See Vol. II, P.L. 100-204, §724(d), with respect to furnishing information to the United States Commission on Improving the Effectiveness of the United Nations; and §725(b), with respect to the detailing of Government personnel.

See Vol. II, P.L. 100-235, §§5-8, with respect to responsibilities of each Federal agency for computer systems security and privacy.

See Vol. II, P.L. 100-690, §5301(a)(1)(C) and (d)(1)(B), with respect to benefits of drug traffickers and possessors.

See Vol. II, P.L. 103-296, §206(g), with respect to annual reports on reviews of OASDI and SSI cases.

[2] This table of contents does not appear in the law.

779

780 SOCIAL SECURITY ACT—TITLE XVI(cont)

PURPOSE; APPROPRIATIONS

SEC. 1601. [42 U.S.C. 1381] For the purpose of establishing a national program to provide supplemental security income to individuals who have attained age 65 or are blind or disabled, there are authorized to be appropriated sums sufficient to carry out this title.

BASIC ELIGIBILITY FOR BENEFITS

SEC. 1602. [42 U.S.C. 1381a] Every aged, blind, or disabled individual who is determined under part A to be eligible on the basis of his income and resources shall, in accordance with and subject to the provisions of this title, be paid benefits by the Commissioner of Social Security.

Part A—Determination of Benefits

ELIGIBILITY FOR AND AMOUNT OF BENEFITS[3]

Definition of Eligible Individual

SEC. 1611. [42 U.S.C. 1382] (a)(1) Each aged, blind, or disabled individual who does not have an eligible spouse and—

(A) whose income, other than income excluded pursuant to section 1612(b), is at a rate of not more than $1,752 (or, if greater, the amount determined under section 1617) for the calendar year 1974 or any calendar year thereafter, and

(B) whose resources, other than resources excluded pursuant to section 1613(a), are not more than (i) in case such individual has a spouse with whom he is living, the applicable amount determined under paragraph (3)(A), or (ii) in case such individual has no spouse with whom he is living, the applicable amount determined under paragraph (3)(B),

shall be an eligible individual for purposes of this title.

(2) Each aged, blind, or disabled individual who has an eligible spouse and—

(A) whose income (together with the income of such spouse), other than income excluded pursuant to section 1612(b), is at a rate of not more than $2,628 (or, if greater, the amount determined under section 1617) for the calendar year 1974, or any calendar year thereafter, and

(B) whose resources (together with the resources of such spouse), other than resources excluded pursuant to section 1613(a), are not more than the applicable amount determined under paragraph (3)(A),

shall be an eligible individual for purposes of this title.

(3)(A) The dollar amount referred to in clause (i) of paragraph (1)(B), and in paragraph (2)(B), shall be $2,250 prior to January 1, 1985, and shall be increased to $2,400 on January 1, 1985, to $2,550 on January 1, 1986, to $2,700 on January 1, 1987, to $2,850 on January 1, 1988, and to $3,000 on January 1, 1989.

(B) The dollar amount referred to in clause (ii) of paragraph (1)(B), shall be $1,500 prior to January 1, 1985, and shall be increased to

---

[3] See Vol. II, P.L. 93-66, §211, with respect to supplemental security income benefits for essential persons.

SOCIAL SECURITY ACT—§ 1611(c)(3)

781

$1,600 on January 1, 1985, to $1,700 on January 1, 1986, to $1,800 on January 1, 1987, to $1,900 on January 1, 1988, and to $2,000 on January 1, 1989.

Amounts of Benefits[4]

(b)(1) The benefit under this title for an individual who does not have an eligible spouse shall be payable at the rate of $1,752 (or, if greater, the amount determined under section 1617) for the calendar year 1974 and any calendar year thereafter, reduced by the amount of income, not excluded pursuant to section 1612(b), of such individual.

(2) The benefit under this title for an individual who has an eligible spouse shall be payable at the rate of $2,628 (or, if greater, the amount determined under section 1617) for the calendar year 1974 and any calendar year thereafter, reduced by the amount of income, not excluded pursuant to section 1612(b), of such individual and spouse.

Period for Determination of Benefits

(c)(1) An individual's eligibility for a benefit under this title for a month shall be determined on the basis of the individual's (and eligible spouse's, if any) income, resources, and other relevant characteristics in such month, and, except as provided in paragraphs (2), (3), (4), (5), and (6), the amount of such benefit shall be determined for such month on the basis of income and other characteristics in the first or, if the Commissioner of Social Security so determines, second month preceding such month. Eligibility for and the amount of such benefits shall be redetermined at such time or times as may be provided by the Commissioner of Social Security.

(2) The amount of such benefit for the month in which an application for benefits becomes effective (or, if the Commissioner of Social Security so determines, for such month and the following month) and for any month immediately following a month of ineligibility for such benefits (or, if the Commissioner of Social Security so determines, for such month and the following month) shall—

    (A) be determined on the basis of the income of the individual and the eligible spouse, if any, of such individual and other relevant circumstances in such month; and

    (B) in the case of the first month following a period of ineligibility in which eligibility is restored after the first day of such month, bear the same ratio to the amount of the benefit which would have been payable to such individual if eligibility had been restored on the first day of such month as the number of days in such month including and following the date of restoration of eligibility bears to the total number of days in such month.

(3) For purposes of this subsection, an increase in the benefit amount payable under title II (over the amount payable in the preceding month, or, at the election of the Commissioner of Social Security, the second preceding month) to an individual receiving benefits under this title shall be included in the income used to determine the benefit under this title of such individual for any month which is—

---

[4] See Vol. II, Appendices A and B, for Cost-of-Living Increase information.

782   SOCIAL SECURITY ACT—§ 1611(c)(3)(A)

(A) the first month in which the benefit amount payable to such individual under this title is increased pursuant to section 1617, or

(B) at the election of the Commissioner of Social Security, the month immediately following such month.

(4)(A) Notwithstanding paragraph (3), if the Commissioner of Social Security determines that reliable information is currently available with respect to the income and other circumstances of an individual for a month (including information with respect to a class of which such individual is a member and information with respect to scheduled cost-of-living adjustments under other benefit programs), the benefit amount of such individual under this title for such month may be determined on the basis of such information.

(B) The Commissioner of Social Security shall prescribe by regulation the circumstances in which information with respect to an event may be taken into account pursuant to subparagraph (A) in determining benefit amounts under this title.

(5) Notwithstanding paragraphs (1) and (2), any income which is paid to or on behalf of an individual in any month pursuant to (A) a State program funded under part A of title IV, (B) section 472 of this Act (relating to foster care assistance), (C) section 412(e) of the Immigration and Nationality Act (relating to assistance for refugees), (D) section 501(a) of Public Law 96-422 (relating to assistance for Cuban and Haitian entrants), or (E) the Act of November 2, 1921 (42 Stat. 208)[5], as amended (relating to assistance furnished by the Bureau of Indian Affairs), shall be taken into account in determining the amount of the benefit under this title of such individual (and his eligible spouse, if any) only for that month, and shall not be taken into account in determining the amount of the benefit for any other month.

(6) The dollar amount in effect under subsection (b) as a result of any increase in benefits under this title by reason of section 1617 shall be used to determine the value of any in-kind support and maintenance required to be taken into account in determining the benefit payable under this title to an individual (and the eligible spouse, if any, of the individual) for the 1st 2 months for which the increase in benefits applies.

(7) For purposes of this subsection, an application of an individual for benefits under this title shall be effective on the later of—

(A) the first day of the month following the date such application is filed, or

(B) the first day of the month following the date such individual becomes eligible for such benefits with respect to such application.

(8) The Commissioner of Social Security may waive the limitations specified in subparagraphs (A) and (B) of subsection (e)(1) on an individual's eligibility and benefit amount for a month (to the extent either such limitation is applicable by reason of such individual's presence throughout such month in a hospital, extended care facility, nursing home, or intermediate care facility) if such waiver would promote the individual's removal from such institution or facility. Upon waiver of such limitations, the Commissioner of Social Security shall apply, to the month preceding the month of removal, or, if the Commissioner of

---

[5] See Vol. II, P.L. 82-414, §412(e), P.L. 96-422, §501(a), and P.L. 67-85, the Act of November 2, 1921.

SOCIAL SECURITY ACT—§ 1611(e)(1)(B)(i)   783

Social Security so determines, the two months preceding the month of removal, the benefit rate that is appropriate to such individual's living arrangement subsequent to his removal from such institution or facility.

(9)(A) Notwithstanding paragraphs (1) and (2), any nonrecurring income which is paid to an individual in the first month of any period of eligibility shall be taken into account in determining the amount of the benefit under this title of such indiviudal (and his eligible spouse, if any) only for that month, shall not be taken into account in determining the amount of the benefit for any other month.

(B) For purposes of subparagraph (A), payments to an individual in varying amounts from the same or similar source for the same or similar purpose shall not be considered to be nonrecurring income.

(10) For purposes of this subsection, renumeration for service performed as a member of a uniformed service may be treated as received in the month in which it was earned, if the Commissioner of Social Security determines that such treatment would promote the economical and efficient adminstration of the program authorized by this title.

Special Limits on Gross Income

(d) The Commissioner of Social Security may prescribe the circumstances under which, consistently with the purposes of this title, the gross income from a trade or business (including farming) will be considered sufficiently large to make an individual ineligible for benefits under this title. For purposes of this subsection, the term "gross income" has the same meaning as when used in chapter 1 of the Internal Revenue Code of 1954[6].

Limitation on Eligibility of Certain Individuals

(e)(1)(A) Except as provided in subparagraphs (B), (C), (D), (E), and (G), no person shall be an eligible individual or eligible spouse for purposes of this title with respect to any month if throughout such month he is an inmate of a public institution.

(B) In any case where an eligible individual or his eligible spouse (if any) is, throughout any month (subject to subparagraph (G)), in a medical treatment facility receiving payments (with respect to such individual or spouse) under a State plan approved under title XIX, or an eligible individual is a child described in section 1614(f)(2)(B), or, in the case of an eligible individual who is a child under the age of 18, receiving payments (with respect to such individual) under any health insurance policy issued by a private provider of such insurance the benefit under this title for such individual for such month shall be payable (subject to subparagraph (E))—

> (i) at a rate not in excess of $360 per year (reduced by the amount of any income not excluded pursuant to section 1612(b)) in the case of an individual who does not have an eligible spouse;

---

[6] See Vol. II, P.L. 83-591, §62.
    P.L. 99-514, §2, provides, except when inappropriate, any reference to the Internal Revenue Code of 1954 shall include a reference to the Internal Revenue Code of 1986.

784 SOCIAL SECURITY ACT—§ 1611(e)(1)(B)(ii)

(ii) in the case of an individual who has an eligible spouse, if only one of them is in such a facility throughout such month, at a rate not in excess of the sum of—

(I) the rate of $360 per year (reduced by the amount of any income, not excluded pursuant to section 1612(b), of the one who is in such facility), and

(II) the applicable rate specified in subsection (b)(1) (reduced by the amount of any income, not excluded pursuant to section 1612(b), of the other); and

(iii) at a rate not in excess of $720 per year (reduced by the amount of any income not excluded pursuant to section 1612(b)) in the case of an individual who has an eligible spouse, if both of them are in such a facility throughout such month.

For purposes of this subsection, a medical treatment facility that provides services described in section 1917(c)(1)(C) shall be considered to be receiving payments with respect to an individual under a State plan approved under title XIX during any period of ineligibility of such individual provided for under the State plan pursuant to section 1917(c).

(C) As used in subparagraph (A), the term "public institution" does not include a publicly operated community residence which serves no more than 16 residents.[7]

(D) A person may be an eligible individual or eligible spouse for purposes of this title with respect to any month throughout which he is a resident of a public emergency shelter for the homeless (as defined in regulations which shall be prescribed by the Commissioner of Social Security); except that no person shall be an eligible individual or eligible spouse by reason of this subparagraph more than 6 months in any 9-month period.

(E) Notwithstanding subparagraphs (A) and (B), any individual who—

(i)(I) is an inmate of a public institution, the primary purpose of which is the provision of medical or psychiatric care, through-out any month as described in subparagraph (A), or

(II) is in a medical treatment facility throughout any month as described in subparagraph (B),

(ii) was eligible under section 1619(a) or (b) for the month preceding such month, and

(iii) under an agreement of the public institution or the medical treatment facility is permitted to retain any benefit payable by reason of this subparagraph,

may be an eligible individual or eligible spouse for purposes of this title (and entitled to a benefit determined on the basis of the rate applicable under subsection (b)) for the month referred to in subclause (I) or (II) of clause (i) and, if such subclause still applies, for the succeeding month.

(F) An individual who is an eligible individual or an eligible spouse for a month by reason of subparagraph (E) shall not be treated as being eligible under section 1619(a) or (b) for such month for purposes of clause (ii) of such subparagraph.

---

[7] See Vol. II, P.L. 96-598, §4, with respect to the Boundary County Restorium, Bonner's Ferry, Idaho.

SOCIAL SECURITY ACT—§ 1611(e)(1)(I)(i)(II)   785

(G) A person may be an eligible individual or eligible spouse for purposes of this title, and subparagraphs (A) and (B) shall not apply, with respect to any particular month throughout which he or she is an inmate of a public institution the primary purpose of which is the provision of medical or psychiatric care, or is in a medical treatment facility receiving payments (with respect to such individual or spouse) under a State plan approved under title XIX or, in the case of an individual who is a child under the age of 18, under any health insurance policy issued by a private provider of such insurance, if it is determined in accordance with subparagraph (H) or (J) that—

 (i) such person's stay in that institution or facility (or in that institution or facility and one or more other such institutions or facilities during a continuous period of institutionalization) is likely (as certified by a physician) not to exceed 3 months, and the particular month involved is one of the first 3 months throughout which such person is in such an institution or facility during a continuous period of institutionalization; and

 (ii) such person needs to continue to maintain and provide for the expenses of the home or living arrangement to which he or she may return upon leaving the institution or facility.

The benefit of any person under this title (including State supplementation if any) for each month to which this subparagraph applies shall be payable, without interruption of benefit payments and on the date the benefit involved is regularly due, at the rate that was applicable to such person in the month prior to the first month throughout which he or she is in the institution or facility.

(H) The Commissioner of Social Security shall establish procedures for the determinations required by clauses (i) and (ii) of subparagraph (G), and may enter into agreements for making such determinations (or for providing information or assistance in connection with the making of such determinations) with appropriate State and local public and private agencies and organizations. Such procedures and agreements shall include the provision of appropriate assistance to individuals who, because of their physical or mental condition, are limited in their ability to furnish the information needed in connection with the making of such determinations.

(I)(i) The Commissioner shall enter into an agreement, with any interested State or local institution comprising a jail, prison, penal institution, or correctional facility, or with any other interested State or local institution a purpose of which is to confine individuals as described in section 202(x)(1)(A)(ii)[8], under which—

 (I) the institution shall provide to the Commissioner, on a monthly basis and in a manner specified by the Commissioner, the names, social security account numbers, dates of birth, confinement commencement dates, and, to the extent available to the institution, such other identifying information concerning the inmates of the institution as the Commissioner may require for the purpose of carrying out this paragraph and the other provisions of this title; and

 (II) the Commissioner shall pay to any such institution, with respect to each individual who receives in the month

---

[8] The reference to §202(x)(1)(A)(ii) shall be deemed a reference to such §202(x)(1)(A)(ii) as amended by P.L. 106-170, §402(b)(1)(C).

786   SOCIAL SECURITY ACT—§ 1611(e)(1)(I)(i)(II)(cont)

preceding the first month throughout which such individual is an inmate of the jail, prison, penal institution, or correctional facility that furnishes information respecting such individual pursuant to subclause (I), or is confined in the institution (that so furnishes such information) as described in section 202(x)(1)(A)(ii), a benefit under this title for such preceding month, and who is determined by the Commissioner to be ineligible for benefits under this title by reason of confinement based on the information provided by such institution, $400 (subject to reduction under clause (ii)) if the institution furnishes the information described in subclause (I) to the Commissioner within 30 days after the date such individual becomes an inmate of such institution, or $200 (subject to reduction under clause (ii)) if the institution furnishes such information after 30 days after such date but within 90 days after such date.

(ii) The dollar amounts specified in clause (i)(II) shall be reduced by 50 percent if the Commissioner is also required to make a payment to the institution with respect to the same individual under an agreement entered into under section 202(x)(3)(B).

(iii) The Commissioner shall maintain, and shall provide on a reimbursable basis, information obtained pursuant to agreements entered into under clause (i) to any Federal or federally-assisted cash, food, or medical assistance program for eligibility and other administrative purposes under such program.

(iv) Payments to institutions required by clause (i)(II) shall be made from funds otherwise available for the payment of benefits under this title and shall be treated as direct spending for purposes of the Balanced Budget and Emergency Deficit Control Act of 1985.

(J) For the purpose of carrying out this paragraph, the Commissioner of Social Security shall conduct periodic computer matches with data maintained by the Secretary of Health and Human Services under title XVIII or XIX. The Secretary shall furnish to the Commissioner, in such form and manner and under such terms as the Commissioner and the Secretary shall mutually agree, such information as the Commissioner may request for this purpose. Information obtained pursuant to such a match may be substituted for the physician's certification otherwise required under subparagraph (G)(i).

(2) No person shall be an eligible individual or eligible spouse for purposes of this title if, after notice to such person by the Commissioner of Social Security that it is likely that such person is eligible for any payments of the type enumerated in section 1612(a)(2)(B), such person fails within 30 days to take all appropriate steps to apply for and (if eligible) obtain any such payments.

(3) Notwithstanding anything to the contrary in the criteria being used by the Commissioner of Social Security in determining when a husband and wife are to be considered two eligible individuals for purposes of this title and when they are to be considered an eligible individual with an eligible spouse, the State agency administering or supervising the administration of a State plan under any other program under this Act may (in the administration of such plan) treat a husband and wife living in the same medical treatment facility described in paragraph (1)(B) as though they were an eligible individual with his or her eligible spouse for purposes of this title (rather than two eligible individuals), after they have continuously lived in the same

SOCIAL SECURITY ACT—§ 1611(e)(5)(B)   787

such facility for 6 months, if treating such husband and wife as two eligible individuals would prevent either of them from receiving benefits or assistance under such plan or reduce the amount thereof.

(4)(A) No person shall be considered an eligible individual or eligible spouse for purposes of this title with respect to any month if during such month the person is—

(i) fleeing to avoid prosecution, or custody or confinement after conviction, under the laws of the place from which the person flees, for a crime, or an attempt to commit a crime, which is a felony under the laws of the place from which the person flees, or, in jurisdictions that do not define crimes as felonies, is punishable by death or imprisonment for a term exceeding 1 year regardless of the actual sentence imposed; or

(ii) violating a condition of probation or parole imposed under Federal or State law.

(B) Notwithstanding subparagraph (A), the Commissioner shall, for good cause shown, treat the person referred to in subparagraph (A) as an eligible individual or eligible spouse if the Commissioner determines that—

(i) a court of competent jurisdiction has found the person not guilty of the criminal offense, dismissed the charges relating to the criminal offense, vacated the warrant for arrest of the person for the criminal offense, or issued any similar exonerating order (or taken similar exonerating action), or

(ii) the person was erroneously implicated in connection with the criminal offense by reason of identity fraud.

(C) Notwithstanding subparagraph (A), the Commissioner may, for good cause shown based on mitigating circumstances, treat the person referred to in subparagraph (A) as an eligible individual or eligible spouse if the Commissioner determines that—

(i) the offense described in subparagraph (A)(i) or underlying the imposition of the probation or parole described in subparagraph (A)(ii) was nonviolent and not drug-related, and

(ii) in the case of a person who is not considered an eligible individual or eligible spouse pursuant to subparagraph (A)(ii), the action that resulted in the violation of a condition of probation or parole was nonviolent and not drug-related.

(5) Notwithstanding any other provision of law (other than section 6103 of the Internal Revenue Code of 1986[9] and section 1106(c) of this Act), the Commissioner shall furnish any Federal, State, or local law enforcement officer, upon the written request of the officer, with the current address, Social Security number, and photograph (if applicable) of any recipient of benefits under this title, if the officer furnishes the Commissioner with the name of the recipient, and other identifying information as reasonably required by the Commissioner to establish the unique identity of the recipient, and notifies the Commissioner that—

(A) the recipient is described in clause (i) or (ii) of paragraph (4)(A);

(B) the location or apprehension of the recipient is within the officer's official duties.

---

[9] See Vol. II, P.L. 83-591, §6103.

788 SOCIAL SECURITY ACT—§ 1611(f)

Suspension of Payments to Individuals Who Are Outside the United States

(f)(1) Notwithstanding any other provision of this title, no individual (other than a child described in section 1614(a)(1)(B)(ii)) shall be considered an eligible individual for purposes of this title for any month during all of which such individual is outside the United States (and no person shall be considered the eligible spouse of an individual for purposes of this title with respect to any month during all of which such person is outside the United States). For purposes of the preceding sentence, after an individual has been outside the United States for any period of 30 consecutive days, he shall be treated as remaining outside the United States until he has been in the United States for a period of 30 consecutive days.

(2) For a period of not more than 1 year, the first sentence of paragraph (1) shall not apply to any individual who—

(A) was eligible to receive a benefit under this title for the month immediately preceding the first month during all of which the individual was outside the United States; and

(B) demonstrates to the satisfaction of the Commissioner of Social Security that the absence of the individual from the United States will be—

(i) for not more than 1 year; and

(ii) for the purposes of conducting studies as part of an educational program that is—

(I) designed to substantially enhance the ability of the individual to engage in gainful employment;

(II) sponsored by a school, college, or university in the United States; and

(III) not available to the individual in the United States.

Certain Individuals Deemed To Meet Resources Test

(g) In the case of any individual or any individual and his spouse (as the case may be) who—

(1) received aid or assistance for December 1973 under a plan of a State approved under title I, X, XIV, or XVI,

(2) has, since December 31, 1973, continuously resided in the State under the plan of which he or they received such aid or assistance for December 1973, and

(3) has, since December 31, 1973, continuously been (except for periods not in excess of six consecutive months) an eligible individual or eligible spouse with respect to whom supplemental security income benefits are payable,

the resources of such individual or such individual and his spouse (as the case may be) shall be deemed not to exceed the amount specified in sections 1611(a)(1)(B) and 1611(a)(2)(B) during any period that the resources of such individual or such individual and his spouse (as the case may be) does not exceed the maximum amount of resources specified in the State plan, as in effect for October 1972, under which he or they received such aid or assistance for December 1973.

SOCIAL SECURITY ACT—§ 1612(a)(1)(C)   789

Certain Individuals Deemed To Meet Income Test

(h) In determining eligibility for, and the amount of, benefits payable under this section in the case of any individual or any individual and his spouse (as the case may be) who—

(1) received aid or assistance for December 1973 under a plan of a State approved under title X or XVI,

(2) is blind under the definition of that term in the plan, as in effect for October 1972, under which he or they received such aid or assistance for December 1973,

(3) has, since December 31, 1973, continuously resided in the State under the plan of which he or they received such aid or assistance for December 1973, and

(4) has, since December 31, 1973, continuously been (except for periods not in excess of six consecutive months) an eligible individual or an eligible spouse with respect to whom supplemental security income benefits are payable,

there shall be disregarded an amount equal to the greater of (A) the maximum amount of any earned or unearned income which could have been disregarded under the State plan, as in effect for October 1972, under which he or they received such aid or assistance for December 1973, and (B) the amount which would be required to be disregarded under section 1612 without application of this subsection.

Application and Review Requirements for Certain Individuals

(i) For application and review requirements affecting the eligibility of certain individuals, see section 1631(j).

INCOME

Meaning of Income

SEC. 1612. [42 U.S.C. 1382a] (a) For purposes of this title, income means both earned income and unearned income; and—

(1) earned income means only—

(A) wages as determined under section 203(f)(5)(C) but without the application of section 210(j)(3) (and, in the case of cash remuneration paid for service as a member of a uniformed service (other than payments described in paragraph (2)(H) of this subsection or subsection (b)(20)), without regard to the limitations contained in section 209(d))[10];

(B) net earnings from self-employment, as defined in section 211 (without the application of the second and third sentences following subsection (a)(11), the last paragraph of subsection (a), and section 210(j)(3)), including earnings for services described in paragraphs (4), (5), and (6) of subsection (c);

(C) remuneration received for services performed in a sheltered workshop or work activities center; and

---

[10] P.L. 110-245, §201(a), inserted "(and, in the case of cash remuneration paid for service as a member of a uniformed service (other than payments described in paragraph (2)(H) of this subsection or subsection (b)(20)), without regard to the limitations contained in section 209(d))", effective with respect to benefits payable for months beginning after 60 days after June 17, 2008.

790 SOCIAL SECURITY ACT—§ 1612(a)(1)(D)

(D) any royalty earned by an individual in connection with any publication of the work of the individual, and that portion of any honorarium which is received for services rendered; and

(2) unearned income means all other income, including—

(A) support and maintenance furnished in cash or kind; except that (i) in the case of any individual (and his eligible spouse, if any) living in another person's household and receiving support and maintenance in kind from such person, the dollar amounts otherwise applicable to such individual (and spouse) as specified in subsections (a) and (b) of section 1611 shall be reduced by 33 1/3 percent in lieu of including such support and maintenance in the unearned income of such individual (and spouse) as otherwise required by this subparagraph, (ii) in the case of any individual or his eligible spouse who resides in a nonprofit retirement home or similar nonprofit institution, support and maintenance shall not be included to the extent that it is furnished to such individual or such spouse without such institution receiving payment therefor (unless such institution has expressly undertaken an obligation to furnish full support and maintenance to such individual or spouse without any current or future payment therefor) or payment therefor is made by another nonprofit organization, and (iii) support and maintenance shall not be included and the provisions of clause (i) shall not be applicable in the case of any individual (and his eligible spouse, if any) for the period which begins with the month in which such individual (or such individual and his eligible spouse) began to receive support and maintenance while living in a residential facility (including a private household) maintained by another person and ends with the close of the month in which such individual (or such individual and his eligible spouse) ceases to receive support and maintenance while living in such a residential facility (or, if earlier, with the close of the seventeenth month following the month in which such period began), if, not more than 30 days prior to the date on which such individual (or such individual and his eligible spouse) began to receive support and maintenance while living in such a residential facility, (I) such individual (or such individual and his eligible spouse) were residing in a household maintained by such individual (or by such individual and others) as his or their own home, (II) there occurred within the area in which such household is located (and while such individual, or such individual and his spouse, were residing in the household referred to in subclause (I)) a catastrophe on account of which the President declared a major disaster to exist therein for purposes of the Disaster Relief and Emergency Assistance Act[11], and (III) such individual declares that he (or he and his eligible spouse) ceased to continue living in the household referred to in subclause (II) because of such catastrophe;

---

[11] P.L. 93-288.

SOCIAL SECURITY ACT—§ 1612(b)(1)   791

(B) any payments received as an annuity, pension, retirement, or disability benefit, including veterans' compensation and pensions, workmen's compensation payments, old-age, survivors, and disability insurance benefits, railroad retirement annuities and pensions, and unemployment insurance benefits;

(C) prizes and awards;

(D) payments to the individual occasioned by the death of another person, to the extent that the total of such payments exceeds the amount expended by such individual for purposes of the deceased person's last illness and burial;

(E) support and alimony payments, and (subject to the provisions of subparagraph (D) excluding certain amounts expended for purposes of a last illness and burial) gifts (cash or otherwise) and inheritances;

(F) rents, dividends, interest, and royalties not described in paragraph (1)(E);[12]

(G) any earnings of, and additions to, the corpus of a trust established by an individual (within the meaning of section 1613(e)), of which the individual is a beneficiary, to which section 1613(e) applies, and, in the case of an irrevocable trust, with respect to which circumstances exist under which a payment from the earnings or additions could be made to or for the benefit of the individual; and[13]

(H)[14] payments to or on behalf of a member of a uniformed service for housing of the member (and his or her dependents, if any) on a facility of a uniformed service, including payments provided under section 403 of title 37, United States Code[15], for housing that is acquired or constructed under subchapter IV of chapter 169 of title 10 of such Code[16], or any related provision of law, and any such payments shall be treated as support and maintenance in kind subject to subparagraph (A) of this paragraph.

Exclusions From Income[17]

(b) In determining the income of an individual (and his eligible spouse) there shall be excluded—

(1) subject to limitations (as to amount or otherwise) prescribed by the Commissioner of Social Security, if such individual is under the age of 22 and is, as determined by the Commissioner of Social Security, a student regularly attending a school, college, or university, or a course of vocational or technical training designed to prepare him for gainful employment, the earned income of such individual;

---

[12] P.L. 110-245, §201(b)(1)(A), struck out "and".

[13] P.L. 110-245, §201(b)(1)(B), struck out the period and substituted "; and".

[14] P.L. 110-245, §201(b)(1)(C), added subparagraph (H), effective with respect to benefits payable for months beginning after 60 days after June 17, 2008.

[15] See Vol. II, 37 U.S.C. 403.

[16] See Vol. II, 10 U.S.C. Chapter 169, subchapter IV.

[17] See Vol. II, Appendix K, Income and Resource Exclusions, for a list of provisions from Federal laws regarding exclusions from income and resources.

792 SOCIAL SECURITY ACT—§ 1612(b)(2)

(2)(A) the first $240 per year (or proportionately smaller amounts for shorter periods) of income (whether earned or unearned) other than income which is paid on the basis of the need of the eligible individual, and

(B) monthly (or other periodic) payments received by any individual, under a program established prior to July 1, 1973 (or any program established prior to such date but subsequently amended so as to conform to State or Federal constitutional standards), if (i) such payments are made by the State of which the individual receiving such payments is a resident, (ii) eligibility of any individual for such payments is not based on need and is based solely on attainment of age 65 or any other age set by the State and residency in such State by such individual, and (iii) on or before September 30, 1985, such individual (I) first becomes an eligible individual or an eligible spouse under this title, and (II) satisfies the twenty-five-year residency requirement of such program as such program was in effect prior to January 1, 1983;

(3) in any calendar quarter, the first—

(A) $60 of unearned income, and

(B) $30 of earned income,

of such individual (and such spouse, if any) which, as determined in accordance with criteria, prescribed by the Commissioner of Social Security, is received too infrequently or irregularly to be included;

(4)(A) if such individual (or such spouse) is blind (and has not attained age 65, or received benefits under this title (or aid under a State plan approved under section 1002 or 1602) for the month before the month in which he attained age 65), (i) the first $780 per year (or proportionately smaller amounts for shorter periods) of earned income not excluded by the preceding paragraphs of this subsection, plus one-half of the remainder thereof, (ii) an amount equal to any expenses reasonably attributable to the earning of any income, and (iii) such additional amounts of other income, where such individual has a plan for achieving self-support approved by the Commissioner of Social Security, as may be necessary for the fulfillment of such plan,

(B) if such individual (or such spouse) is disabled but not blind (and has not attained age 65, or received benefits under this title (or aid under a State plan approved under section 1402 or 1602) for the month before the month in which he attained age 65), (i) the first $780 per year (or proportionately smaller amounts for shorter periods) of earned income not excluded by the preceding paragraphs of this subsection, (ii) such additional amounts of earned income of such individual, if such individual's disability is sufficiently severe to result in a functional limitation requiring assistance in order for him to work, as may be necessary to pay the costs (to such individual) of attendant care services, medical devices, equipment, prostheses, and similar items and services (not including routine drugs or routine medical services unless such drugs or services are necessary for the control of the disabling condition) which are necessary (as determined by the Commissioner of Social Security in regulations) for that purpose, whether or not such assistance is also needed to enable him to carry out his normal daily functions, except that the amounts to be excluded shall

SOCIAL SECURITY ACT—§ 1612(b)(13)   793

be subject to such reasonable limits as the Commissioner of Social Security may prescribe, (iii) one-half of the amount of earned income not excluded after the application of the preceding provisions of this subparagraph, and (iv) such additional amounts of other income, where such individual has a plan for achieving self-support approved by the Commissioner of Social Security, as may be necessary for the fulfillment of such plan, or

(C) if such individual (or such spouse) has attained age 65 and is not included under subparagraph (A) or (B), the first $780 per year (or proportionately smaller amounts for shorter periods) of earned income not excluded by the preceding paragraphs of this subsection, plus one–half of the remainder thereof;

(5) any amount received from any public agency as a return or refund of taxes paid on real property or on food purchased by such individual (or such spouse);

(6) assistance, furnished to or on behalf of such individual (and spouse), which is based on need and furnished by any State or political subdivision of a State;

(7) any portion of any grant, scholarship, fellowship, or gift (or portion of a gift) used to pay the cost of tuition and fees at any educational (including technical or vocational education) institution;

(8) home produce of such individual (or spouse) utilized by the household for its own consumption;

(9) if such individual is a child, one-third of any payment for his support received from an absent parent;

(10) any amounts received for the foster care of a child who is not an eligible individual but who is living in the same home as such individual and was placed in such home by a public or nonprofit private child-placement or child-care agency;

(11) assistance received under the Disaster Relief and Emergency Assistance Act[18] or other assistance provided pursuant to a Federal statute on account of a catastrophe which is declared to be a major disaster by the President;

(12) interest income received on assistance funds referred to in paragraph (11) within the 9-month period beginning on the date such funds are received (or such longer periods as the Commissioner of Social Security shall by regulations prescribe in cases where good cause is shown by the individual concerned for extending such period);

(13) any support or maintenance assistance furnished to or on behalf of such individual (and spouse if any) which (as determined under regulations of the Commissioner of Social Security by such State agency as the chief executive officer of the State may designate) is based on need for such support or maintenance, including assistance received to assist in meeting the costs of home energy (including both heating and cooling), and which is (A) assistance furnished in kind by a private nonprofit agency, or (B) assistance furnished by a supplier of home heating oil or gas, by an entity providing home energy whose revenues are primarily derived on a rate-of-return basis regulated by a State or Federal governmental entity, or by a municipal utility providing home energy;

---

[18] See Vol. II, P.L. 93-288.

794 SOCIAL SECURITY ACT—§ 1612(b)(14)

(14) assistance paid, with respect to the dwelling unit occupied by such individual (or such individual and spouse), under the United States Housing Act of 1937[19], the National Housing Act[20], section 101 of the Housing and Urban Development Act of 1965[21], title V of the Housing Act of 1949[22], or section 202(h) of the Housing Act of 1959 [23];

(15) the value of any commercial transportation ticket, for travel by such individual (or spouse) among the 50 States, the District of Columbia, the Commonwealth of Puerto Rico, the Virgin Islands, Guam, American Samoa, and the Northern Mariana Islands, which is received as a gift by such individual (or such spouse) and is not converted to cash;

(16) interest accrued on the value of an agreement entered into by such individual (or such spouse) representing the purchase of a burial space excluded under section 1613(a)(2)(B), and left to accumulate;

(17) any amount received by such individual (or such spouse) from a fund established by a State to aid victims of crime;

(18) relocation assistance provided by a State or local government to such individual (or such spouse), comparable to assistance provided under title II of the Uniform Relocation Assistance and Real Property Acquisitions Policies Act of 1970 which is subject to the treatment required by section 216 of such Act[24];

(19) any refund of Federal income taxes made to such individual (or such spouse) by reason of section 32 of the Internal Revenue Code of 1986[25] (relating to earned income tax credit), and any payment made to such individual (or such spouse) by an employer under section 3507 of such Code[26] (relating to advance payment of earned income credit);

(20) special pay received pursuant to section 310 of title 37, United States Code[27];

(21) the interest or other earnings on any account established and maintained in accordance with section 1631(a)(2)(F);

(22) any gift to, or for the benefit of, an individual who has not attained 18 years of age and who has a life-threatening condition, from an organization described in section 501(c)(3) of the Internal Revenue Code of 1986 which is exempt from taxation under section 501(a) of such Code[28]—

(A) in the case of an in-kind gift, if the gift is not converted to cash; or

(B) in the case of a cash gift, only to the extent that the total amount excluded from the income of the individual pursuant to this paragraph in the calendar year in which the gift is made does not exceed $2,000;[29]

---

[19] See Vol. II, P.L. 75-412.
[20] See Vol. II, P.L. 73-479.
[21] See Vol. II, P.L. 89-117.
[22] See Vol. II, P.L. 81-171.
[23] See Vol. II, P.L. 86-372.
[24] See Vol. II, P.L. 91-646, §216.
[25] See Vol. II, P.L. 83-591, §32.
[26] See Vol. II, P.L. 83-591, §3507.
[27] See Vol. II, 37 U.S.C. 310.
[28] See Vol. II, P.L. 83-591, §501.
[29] P.L. 110-245, §202(a)(1), struck out "and".

SOCIAL SECURITY ACT—§ 1613(a)(4)   795

(23) interest or dividend income from resources—
    (A) not excluded under section 1613(a), or
    (B) excluded pursuant to Federal law other than sections 1613(a);[30]

(24)[31] any annuity paid by a State to the individual (or such spouse) on the basis of the individual's being a veteran (as defined in section 101 of title 38, United States Code[32]), and blind, disabled, or age; and[33]

(25)[34] any benefit (whether cash or in-kind) conferred upon (or paid on behalf of) a participant in an AmeriCorps position approved by the Corporation for National and Community Service under section 123 of the National and Community Service Act of 1990 (42 U.S.C. 12573)[35].

RESOURCES

Exclusions From Resources[36]

SEC. 1613. [42 U.S.C. 1382b] (a) In determining the resources of an individual (and his eligible spouse, if any) there shall be excluded—

(1) the home (including the land that appertains thereto);

(2)(A) household goods, personal effects, and an automobile, to the extent that their total value does not exceed such amount as the Commissioner of Social Security determines to be reasonable; and

(B) the value of any burial space or agreement (including any interest accumulated thereon) representing the purchase of a burial space (subject to such limits as to size or value as the Commissioner of Social Security may by regulation prescribe) held for the purpose of providing a place for the burial of the individual, his spouse, or any other member of his immediate family;

(3) other property which is so essential to the means of self-support of such individual (and such spouse) as to warrant its exclusion, as determined in accordance with and subject to limitations prescribed by the Commissioner of Social Security, except that the Commissioner of Social Security shall not establish a limitation on property (including the tools of a tradesperson and the machinery and livestock of a farmer) that is used in a trade or business or by such individual as an employee;

(4) such resources of an individual who is blind or disabled and who has a plan for achieving self-support approved by the Commissioner of Social Security, as may be necessary for the fulfillment of such plan;

---

[30] P.L. 110-245, §202(a)(2), struck out the period and substituted "; and".
P.L. 110-245, §203(1), struck out "and".

[31] P.L. 110-245, §202(a)(3), added paragraph (24), effective with respect to benefits payable for months beginning after 60 days after June 17, 2008.

[32] See Vol. II, 38 U.S.C. 101(2).

[33] P.L. 110-245, §203(2), struck out the period and substituted "; and".

[34] P.L. 110-245, §203(3), added paragraph (25), effective with respect to benefits payable for months beginning after 60 days after June 17, 2008.

[35] See Vol. II, P.L. 101-610, §123.

[36] See Vol. II, Appendix K, Income and Resource Exclusions, for a list of provisions from Federal laws regarding exclusions from income and resources.

796   SOCIAL SECURITY ACT—§ 1613(a)(5)

(5) in the case of Natives of Alaska, shares of stock held in a Regional or a Village Corporation, during the period of twenty years in which such stock is inalienable, as provided in section 7(h) and section 8(c) of the Alaska Native Claims Settlement Act[37];

(6) assistance referred to in section 1612(b)(11) for the 9-month period beginning on the date such funds are received (or for such longer period as the Commissioner of Social Security shall by regulations prescribe in cases where good cause is shown by the individual concerned for extending such period); and, for purposes of this paragraph, the term "assistance" includes interest thereon which is excluded from income under section 1612(b)(12);

(7) any amount received from the United States which is attributable to underpayments of benefits due for one or more prior months, under this title or title II, to such individual (or spouse) or to any other person whose income is deemed to be included in such individual's (or spouse's) income for purposes of this title; but the application of this paragraph in the case of any such individual (and eligible spouse if any), with respect to any amount so received from the United States, shall be limited to the first 9 months following the month in which such amount is received, and written notice of this limitation shall be given to the recipient concurrently with the payment of such amount;[38]

(8) the value of assistance referred to in section 1612(b)(14), paid with respect to the dwelling unit occupied by such individual (or such individual and spouse);

(9) for the 9-month period beginning after the month in which received, any amount received by such individual (or such spouse) from a fund established by a State to aid victims of crime, to the extent that such individual (or such spouse) demonstrates that such amount was paid as compensation for expenses incurred or losses suffered as a result of a crime;

(10) for the 9-month period beginning after the month in which received, relocation assistance provided by a State or local government to such individual (or such spouse), comparable to assistance provided under title II of the Uniform Relocation Assistance and Real Property Acquisitions Policies Act of 1970 which is subject to the treatment required by section 216 of such Act[39];

(11) for the 9-month period beginning after the month in which received—

(A) notwithstanding section 203 of the Economic Growth and Tax Relief Reconciliation Act of 2001, any refund of Federal income taxes made to such individual (or such spouse) under section 24 of the Internal Revenue Code of 1986 (relating to child tax credit) by reason of subsection (d) thereof; and

(B) any refund of Federal income taxes made to such individual (or such spouse) by reason of section 32 of the Internal Revenue Code of 1986 (relating to earned income tax credit), and any payment made to such individual (or such spouse)

---

[37] See Vol. II, P.L. 92-203, §§7(h) and 8(c).
[38] See Vol. II, P.L. 101-508, §5041(1), with respect to notification of certain individuals eligible to receive retroactive benefits.
[39] See Vol. II, P.L. 91-646, §216.

SOCIAL SECURITY ACT—§ 1613(b)(1)   797

by an employer under section 3507 of such Code[40] (relating to advance payment of earned income credit);

(12) any account, including accrued interest or other earnings thereon, established and maintained in accordance with section 1631(a)(2)(F);

(13) any gift to, or for the benefit of, an individual who has not attained 18 years of age and who has a life-threatening condition, from an organization described in section 501(c)(3) of the Internal Revenue Code of 1986 which is exempt from taxation under section 501(a) of such Code[41]—

(A) in the case of an in-kind gift, if the gift is not converted to cash; or

(B) in the case of a cash gift, only to the extent that the total amount excluded from the resources of the individual pursuant to this paragraph in the calendar year in which the gift is made does not exceed $2,000;

(14) for the 9-month period beginning after the month in which received, any amount received by such individual (or spouse) or any other person whose income is deemed to be included in such individual's (or spouse's) income for purposes of this title as restitution for benefits under this title, title II, or title VIII that a representative payee of such individual (or spouse) or such other person under section 205(j), 807, or 1631(a)(2) has misused;[42]

(15) for the 9-month period beginning after the month in which received, any grant, scholarship, fellowship, or gift (or portion of a gift) used to pay the cost of tuition and fees at any educational (including technical or vocational education) institution; and[43]

(16)[44] for the month of receipt and every month thereafter, any annuity paid by a State to the individual (or such spouse) on the basis of the individual's being a veteran (as defined in section 101 of title 38, United States Code[45]), and blind, disabled, or aged.

In determining the resources of an individual (or eligible spouse) an insurance policy shall be taken into account only to the extent of its cash surrender value; except that if the total face value of all life insurance policies on any person is $1,500 or less, no part of the value of any such policy shall be taken into account.

Disposition of Resources

(b)(1) The Commissioner of Social Security shall prescribe the period or periods of time within which, and the manner in which, various kinds of property must be disposed of in order not to be included in determining an individual's eligibility for benefits. Any portion of the individual's benefits paid for any such period shall be conditioned upon such disposal; and any benefits so paid shall (at the time of the disposal) be considered overpayments to the extent they would not

---

[40] See Vol. II, P.L. 83-591, §§32 and 3507.
[41] See Vol. II, P.L. 83-591, §501.
[42] P.L. 110-245, §202(b)(1), struck "and".
[43] P.L. 110-245, §202(b)(2), struck out the period and substituted "; and".
[44] P..L. 110-245, §202(b)(3), added paragraph (16), effective with respect to benefits payable for months beginning after 60 days after June 17, 2008.
[45] See Vol. II, 38 U.S.C. 101(2).

798 SOCIAL SECURITY ACT—§ 1613(b)(1)(cont)

have been paid had the disposal occurred at the beginning of the period for which such benefits were paid.

(2) Notwithstanding the provisions of paragraph (1), the Commissioner of Social Security shall not require the disposition of any real property for so long as it cannot be sold because (A) it is jointly owned (and its sale would cause undue hardship, due to loss of housing, for the other owner or owners), (B) its sale is barred by a legal impediment, or (C) as determined under regulations issued by the Commissioner of Social Security, the owner's reasonable efforts to sell it have been unsuccessful.

Disposal of Resources for Less Than Fair Market Value

(c)(1)(A)(i) If an individual or the spouse of an individual disposes of resources for less than fair market value on or after the look-back date described in clause (ii)(I), the individual is ineligible for benefits under this title for months during the period beginning on the date described in clause (iii) and equal to the number of months calculated as provided in clause (iv).

(ii)(I) The look-back date described in this subclause is a date that is 36 months before the date described in subclause (II).

(II) The date described in this subclause is the date on which the individual applies for benefits under this title or, if later, the date on which the individual (or the spouse of the individual) disposes of resources for less than fair market value.

(iii) The date described in this clause is the first day of the first month in or after which resources were disposed of for less than fair market value and which does not occur in any other period of ineligibility under this paragraph.

(iv) The number of months calculated under this clause shall be equal to—

(I) the total, cumulative uncompensated value of all resources so disposed of by the individual (or the spouse of the individual) on or after the look-back date described in clause (ii)(I); divided by

(II) the amount of the maximum monthly benefit payable under section 1611(b), plus the amount (if any) of the maximum State supplementary payment corresponding to the State's payment level applicable to the individual's living arrangement and eligibility category that would otherwise be payable to the individual by the Commissioner pursuant to an agreement under section 1616(a) of this Act or section 212(b) of Public Law 93-66[46], for the month in which occurs the date described in clause (ii)(II),

rounded, in the case of any fraction, to the nearest whole number, but shall not in any case exceed 36 months.

(B)(i) Notwithstanding subparagraph (A), this subsection shall not apply to a transfer of a resource to a trust if the portion of the trust attributable to the resource is considered a resource available to the individual pursuant to subsection (e)(3) (or would be so considered but for the application of subsection (e)(4)).

---

[46] See Vol. II, P.L. 93-66, §212(b).

SOCIAL SECURITY ACT—§ 1613(c)(1)(C)(iii)(II)   799

(ii) In the case of a trust established by an individual or an individual's spouse (within the meaning of subsection (e)), if from such portion of the trust, if any, that is considered a resource available to the individual pursuant to subsection (e)(3) (or would be so considered but for the application of subsection (e)(4)) or the residue of the portion on the termination of the trust—

(I) there is made a payment other than to or for the benefit of the individual; or

(II) no payment could under any circumstance be made to the individual,

then, for purposes of this subsection, the payment described in clause (I) or the foreclosure of payment described in clause (II) shall be considered a transfer of resources by the individual or the individual's spouse as of the date of the payment or foreclosure, as the case may be.

(C) An individual shall not be ineligible for benefits under this title by reason of the application of this paragraph to a disposal of resources by the individual or the spouse of the individual, to the extent that—

(i) the resources are a home and title to the home was transferred to—

(I) the spouse of the transferor;

(II) a child of the transferor who has not attained 21 years of age, or is blind or disabled;

(III) a sibling of the transferor who has an equity interest in such home and who was residing in the transferor's home for a period of at least 1 year immediately before the date the transferor becomes an institutionalized individual; or

(IV) a son or daughter of the transferor (other than a child described in subclause (II)) who was residing in the transferor's home for a period of at least 2 years immediately before the date the transferor becomes an institutionalized individual, and who provided care to the transferor which permitted the transferor to reside at home rather than in such an institution or facility;

(ii) the resources—

(I) were transferred to the transferor's spouse or to another for the sole benefit of the transferor's spouse;

(II) were transferred from the transferor's spouse to another for the sole benefit of the transferor's spouse;

(III) were transferred to, or to a trust (including a trust described in section 1917(d)(4)) established solely for the benefit of, the transferor's child who is blind or disabled; or

(IV) were transferred to a trust (including a trust described in section 1917(d)(4)) established solely for the benefit of an individual who has not attained 65 years of age and who is disabled;

(iii) a satisfactory showing is made to the Commissioner of Social Security (in accordance with regulations promulgated by the Commissioner) that—

(I) the individual who disposed of the resources intended to dispose of the resources either at fair market value, or for other valuable consideration;

(II) the resources were transferred exclusively for a purpose other than to qualify for benefits under this title; or

800 SOCIAL SECURITY ACT—§ 1613(c)(1)(C)(iii)(III)

(III) all resources transferred for less than fair market value have been returned to the transferor; or

(iv) the Commissioner determines, under procedures established by the Commissioner, that the denial of eligibility would work an undue hardship as determined on the basis of criteria established by the Commissioner.

(D) For purposes of this subsection, in the case of a resource held by an individual in common with another person or persons in a joint tenancy, tenancy in common, or similar arrangement, the resource (or the affected portion of such resource) shall be considered to be disposed of by the individual when any action is taken, either by the individual or by any other person, that reduces or eliminates the individual's ownership or control of such resource.

(E) In the case of a transfer by the spouse of an individual that results in a period of ineligibility for the individual under this subsection, the Commissioner shall apportion the period (or any portion of the period) among the individual and the individual's spouse if the spouse becomes eligible for benefits under this title.

(F) For purposes of this paragraph—

(i) the term "benefits under this title" includes payments of the type described in section 1616(a) of this Act and of the type described in section 212(b) of Public Law 93-66[47];

(ii) the term "institutionalized individual" has the meaning given such term in section 1917(e)(3); and

(iii) the term "trust" has the meaning given such term in subsection (e)(6)(A) of this section.

(2)(A) At the time an individual (and the individual's eligible spouse, if any) applies for benefits under this title, and at the time the eligibility of an individual (and such spouse, if any) for such benefits is redetermined, the Commissioner of Social Security shall—

(i) inform such individual of the provisions of paragraph (1) section 1917(c) providing for a period of ineligibility for benefits under this title and title XIX, respectively, for individuals who make certain dispositions of resources for less than fair market value, and inform such individual that information obtained pursuant to clause (ii) will be made available to the State agency administering a State plan under title XIX (as provided in subparagraph (B)); and

(ii) obtain from such individual information which may be used in determining whether or not a period of ineligibility for such benefits would be required by reason of paragraph (1) or section 1917(c).

(B) The Commissioner of Social Security shall make the information obtained under subparagraph (1)(A)(ii) available, on request, to any State agency administering a State plan approved under title XIX.

Funds Set Aside for Burial Expenses

(d)(1) In determining the resources of an individual, there shall be excluded an amount, not in excess of $1,500 each with respect to such individual and his spouse (if any), that is separately identifiable and

---

[47] See Vol. II, P.L. 93-66, §212(b).

SOCIAL SECURITY ACT—§ 1613(e)(3)(A) 801

has been set aside to meet the burial and related expenses of such individual or spouse.

(2) The amount of $1,500, referred to in paragraph (1), with respect to an individual shall be reduced by an amount equal to (A) the total face value of all insurance policies on his life which are owned by him or his spouse and the cash surrender value of which has been excluded in determining the resources of such individual or of such individual and his spouse, and (B) the total of any amounts in an irrevocable trust (or other irrevocable arrangement) available to meet the burial and related expenses of such individual or his spouse.

(3) If the Commissioner of Social Security finds that any part of the amount excluded under paragraph (1) was used for purposes other than those for which it was set aside in cases where the inclusion of any portion of the amount would cause the resources of such individual, or of such individual and spouse, to exceed the limits specified in paragraph (1) or (2) (whichever may be applicable) of section 1611(a), the Commissioner shall reduce any future benefits payable to the eligible individual (or to such individual and his spouse) by an amount equal to such part.

(4) The Commissioner of Social Security may provide by regulations that whenever an amount set aside to meet burial and related expenses is excluded under paragraph (1) in determining the resources of an individual, any interest earned or accrued on such amount (and left to accumulate), and any appreciation in the value of prepaid burial arrangements for which such amount was set aside, shall also be excluded (to such extent and subject to such conditions or limitations as such regulations may prescribe) in determining the resources (and the income) of such individual.

Trusts

(e)(1) In determining the resources of an individual, paragraph (3) shall apply to a trust (other than a trust described in paragraph (5)) established by the individual.

(2)(A) For purposes of this subsection, an individual shall be considered to have established a trust if any assets of the individual (or of the individual's spouse) are transferred to the trust other than by will.

(B) In the case of an irrevocable trust to which are transferred the assets of an individual (or of the individual's spouse) and the assets of any other person, this subsection shall apply to the portion of the trust attributable to the assets of the individual (or of the individual's spouse).

(C) This subsection shall apply to a trust without regard to—
    (i) the purposes for which the trust is established;
    (ii) whether the trustees have or exercise any discretion under the trust;
    (iii) any restrictions on when or whether distributions may be made from the trust; or
    (iv) any restrictions on the use of distributions from the trust.

(3)(A) In the case of a revocable trust established by an individual, the corpus of the trust shall be considered a resource available to the individual.

802   SOCIAL SECURITY ACT—§ 1613(e)(3)(B)

(B) In the case of an irrevocable trust established by an individual, if there are any circumstances under which payment from the trust could be made to or for the benefit of the individual (or of the individual's spouse), the portion of the corpus from which payment to or for the benefit of the individual (or of the individual's spouse) could be made shall be considered a resource available to the individual.

(4) The Commissioner of Social Security may waive the application of this subsection with respect to an individual if the Commissioner determines that such application would work an undue hardship (as determined on the basis of criteria established by the Commissioner) on the individual.

(5) This subsection shall not apply to a trust described in subparagraph (A) or (C) of section 1917(d)(4).

(6) For purposes of this subsection—

(A) the term "trust" includes any legal instrument or device that is similar to a trust;

(B) the term "corpus" means, with respect to a trust, all property and other interests held by the trust, including accumulated earnings and any other addition to the trust after its establishment (except that such term does not include any such earnings or addition in the month in which the earnings or addition is credited or otherwise transferred to the trust); and

(C) the term "asset" includes any income or resource of the individual (or of the individual's spouse), including—

(i) any income excluded by section 1612(b);

(ii) any resource otherwise excluded by this section; and

(iii) any other payment or property to which the individual (or of the individual's spouse) is entitled but does not receive or have access to because of action by—

(I) the individual or spouse;

(II) a person or entity (including a court) with legal authority to act in place of, or on behalf of, the individual or spouse; or

(III) a person or entity (including a court) acting at the direction of, or on the request of, the individual or spouse.

MEANING OF TERMS

Aged, Blind, or Disabled Individual

SEC. 1614. [42 U.S.C. 1382c] (a)(1) For purposes of this title, the term "aged, blind, or disabled individual" means an individual who—

(A) is 65 years of age or older, is blind (as determined under paragraph (2)), or is disabled (as determined under paragraph (3)), and

(B)(i) is a resident of the United States, and is either (I) a citizen or (II) an alien lawfully admitted for permanent residence or otherwise permanently residing in the United States under color of law (including any alien who is lawfully present in the United States as a result of the application of the provisions of section 212(d)(5) of the Immigration and Nationality Act[48]), or

---

[48] See Vol. II, P.L. 82-414, §212(d)(5).

SOCIAL SECURITY ACT—§ 1614(a)(3)(E)   803

(ii) is a child who is a citizen of the United States, and who is living with a parent of the child who is a member of the Armed Forces of the United States assigned to permanent duty ashore outside the United States.

(2) An individual shall be considered to be blind for purposes of this title if he has central visual acuity of 20/200 or less in the better eye with the use of a correcting lens. An eye which is accompanied by a limitation in the fields of vision such that the widest diameter of the visual field subtends an angle no greater than 20 degrees shall be considered for purposes of the first sentence of this subsection as having a central visual acuity of 20/200 or less. An individual shall also be considered to be blind for purposes of this title if he is blind as defined under a State plan approved under title X or XVI as in effect for October 1972 and received aid under such plan (on the basis of blindness) for December 1973, so long as he is continuously blind as so defined.

(3)(A) Except as provided in subparagraph (C), an individual shall be considered to be disabled for purposes of this title if he is unable to engage in any substantial gainful activity by reason of any medically determinable physical or mental impairment which can be expected to result in death or which has lasted or can be expected to last for a continuous period of not less than twelve months.

(B) For purposes of subparagraph (A), an individual shall be determined to be under a disability only if his physical or mental impairment or impairments are of such severity that he is not only unable to do his previous work but cannot, considering his age, education, and work experience, engage in any other kind of substantial gainful work which exists in the national economy, regardless of whether such work exists in the immediate area in which he lives, or whether a specific job vacancy exists for him, or whether he would be hired if he applied for work. For purposes of the preceding sentence (with respect to any individual), "work which exists in the national economy" means work which exists in significant numbers either in the region where such individual lives or in several regions of the country.

(C)(i) An individual under the age of 18 shall be considered disabled for the purposes of this title if that individual has a medically determinable physical or mental impairment, which results in marked and severe functional limitations, and which can be expected to result in death or which has lasted or can be expected to last for a continuous period of not less than 12 months.

(ii) Notwithstanding clause (i), no individual under the age of 18 who engages in substantial gainful activity (determined in accordance with regulations prescribed pursuant to subparagraph (E)) may be considered to be disabled.

(D) For purposes of this paragraph, a physical or mental impairment is an impairment that results from anatomical, physiological, or psychological abnormalities which are demonstrable by medically acceptable clinical and laboratory diagnostic techniques.

(E) The Commissioner of Social Security shall by regulations prescribe the criteria for determining when services performed or earnings derived from services demonstrate an individual's ability to engage in substantial gainful activity. In determining whether an individual is able to engage in substantial gainful activity by reason of his earnings, where his disability is sufficiently severe to result in a

804   SOCIAL SECURITY ACT—§ 1614(a)(3)(E)(cont)

functional limitation requiring assistance in order for him to work, there shall be excluded from such earnings an amount equal to the cost (to such individual) of any attendant care services, medical devices, equipment, prostheses, and similar items and services (not including routine drugs or routine medical services unless such drugs or services are necessary for the control of the disabling condition) which are necessary (as determined by the Commissioner of Social Security in regulations) for that purpose, whether or not such assistance is also needed to enable him to carry out his normal daily functions; except that the amounts to be excluded shall be subject to such reasonable limits as the Commissioner of Social Security may prescribe. Notwithstanding the provisions of subparagraph (B), an individual whose services or earnings meet such criteria shall be found not to be disabled. The Commissioner of Social Security shall make determinations under this title with respect to substantial gainful activity, without regard to the legality of the activity.

(F) Notwithstanding the provisions of subparagraphs (A) through (D), an individual shall also be considered to be disabled for purposes of this title if he is permanently and totally disabled as defined under a State plan approved under title XIV or XVI as in effect for October 1972 and received aid under such plan (on the basis of disability) for December 1973 (and for at least one month prior to July 1973), so long as he is continuously disabled as so defined.

(G) In determining whether an individual's physical or mental impairment or impairments are of a sufficient medical severity that such impairment or impairments could be the basis of eligibility under this section, the Commissioner of Social Security shall consider the combined effect of all of the individual's impairments without regard to whether any such impairment, if considered separately, would be of such severity. If the Commissioner of Social Security does find a medically severe combination of impairments, the combined impact of the impairments shall be considered throughout the disability determination process.

(H)(i) In making determinations with respect to disability under this title, the provisions of sections 221(h), 221(k), and 223(d)(5) shall apply in the same manner as they apply to determinations of disability under title II.

(ii)(I) Not less frequently than once every 3 years, the Commissioner shall review in accordance with paragraph (4) the continued eligibility for benefits under this title of each individual who has not attained 18 years of age and is eligible for such benefits by reason of an impairment (or combination of impairments) which is likely to improve (or, at the option of the Commissioner, which is unlikely to improve).

(II) A representative payee of a recipient whose case is reviewed under this clause shall present, at the time of review, evidence demonstrating that the recipient is, and has been, receiving treatment, to the extent considered medically necessary and available, of the condition which was the basis for providing benefits under this title.

(III) If the representative payee refuses to comply without good cause with the requirements of subclause (II), the Commissioner of Social Security shall, if the Commissioner determines it is in the best interest of the individual, promptly suspend payment of benefits to the representative payee, and provide for payment of benefits to an alternative representative payee of the individual or, of the interest of the individual under this title would be served thereby, to the individual.

(IV) Subclause (II) shall not apply to the representative payee of any individual with respect to whom the Commissioner determines such application would be inappropriate or unnecessary. In making such determination, the Commissioner shall take into consideration the nature of the individual's impairment (or combination of impairments). Section 1631(c) shall not apply to a finding by the Commissioner that the requirements of subclause (II) should not apply to an individual's representative payee.

(iii) If an individual is eligible for benefits under this title by reason of disability for the month preceding the month in which the individual attains the age of 18 years, the Commissioner shall redetermine such eligibility—

(I) by applying the criteria used in determining initial eligibility for individuals who are age 18 or older; and

(II) either during the 1-year period beginning on the individual's 18th birthday or, in lieu of a continuing disability review, whenever the Commissioner determines that an individual's case is subject to a redetermination under this clause.

With respect to any redetermination under this clause, paragraph (4) shall not apply.

(iv)(I) Except as provided in subclause (VI), not later than 12 months after the birth of an individual, the Commissioner shall review in accordance with paragraph (4) the continuing eligibility for benefits under this title by reason of disability of such individual whose low birth weight is a contributing factor material to the Commissioner's determination that the individual is disabled.

(II) A review under subclause (I) shall be considered a substitute for a review otherwise required under any other provision of the subparagraph during that 12-month period.

(III) A representative payee of a recipient whose case is reviewed under this clause shall present, at the time of review, evidence demonstrating that the recipient is, and has been, receiving treatment, to the extent considered medically necessary and available, of the condition which was the basis for providing benefits under this title.

(IV) If the representative payee refuses to comply without good cause with the requirements of subclause (III), the Commissioner of Social Security shall, if the Commissioner determines it is in the best interest of the individual, promptly suspend payment of benefits to the representative payee, and provide for payment of benefits to an alternative representative payee of the individual or, if the interest of the individual under this title would be served thereby, to the individual.

(V) Subclause (III) shall not apply to the representative payee of any individual with respect to whom the Commissioner determines such application would be inappropriate or unnecessary. In making such determination, the Commissioner shall take into consideration the nature of the individual's impairment (or combination of impairments). Section 1631(c) shall not apply to a finding by the Commissioner that the requirements of subclause (III) should not apply to an individual's representative payee.

806   SOCIAL SECURITY ACT—§ 1614(a)(3)(H)(iv)(VI)

(VI) Subclause (I) shall not apply in the case of an individual described in that subclause who, at the time of the individual's initial disability determination, the Commissioner determines has an impairment that is not expected to improve within 12 months after the birth of that individual, and who the Commissioner schedules for a continuing disability review at a date that is after the individual attains 1 year of age.

(I) In making any determination under this title with respect to the disability of an individual who has not attained the age of 18 years and to whom section 221(h) does not apply, the Commissioner of Social Security shall make reasonable efforts to ensure that a qualified pediatrician or other individual who specializes in a field of medicine appropriate to the disability of the individual (as determined by the Commissioner of Social Security) evaluates the case of such individual.

(J) Notwithstanding subparagraph (A), an individual shall not be considered to be disabled for purposes of this title if alcoholism or drug addiction would (but for this subparagraph) be a contributing factor material to the Commissioner's determination that the individual is disabled.

(4) A recipient of benefits based on disability under this title may be determined not to be entitled to such benefits on the basis of a finding that the physical or mental impairment on the basis of which such benefits are provided has ceased, does not exist, or is not disabling only if such finding is supported by—

(A) in the case of an individual who is age 18 or older—

(i) substantial evidence which demonstrates that—

(I) there has been any medical improvement in the individual's impairment or combination of impairments (other than medical improvement which is not related to the individual's ability to work), and

(II) the individual is now able to engage in substantial gainful activity; or

(ii) substantial evidence (except in the case of an individual eligible to receive benefits under section 1619) which—

(I) consists of new medical evidence and a new assessment of the individual's residual functional capacity, and demonstrates that—

(aa) although the individual has not improved medically, he or she is nonetheless a beneficiary of advances in medical or vocational therapy or technology (related to the individual's ability to work), and

(bb) the individual is now able to engage in substantial gainful activity, or

(II) demonstrates that—

(aa) although the individual has not improved medically, he or she has undergone vocational therapy (related to the individual's ability to work), and

(bb) the individual is now able to engage in substantial gainful activity; or

(iii) substantial evidence which demonstrates that, as determined on the basis of new or improved diagnostic tech-

SOCIAL SECURITY ACT—§ 1614(b)   807

niques or evaluations, the individual's impairment or combination of impairments is not as disabling as it was considered to be at the time of the most recent prior decision that he or she was under a disability or continued to be under a disability, and that therefore the individual is able to engage in substantial gainful activity; or

(B) In the case of an individual who is under the age of 18—

(i) substantial evidence which demonstrates that there has been medical improvement in the individual's impairment or combination of impairments, and that such impairment or combination of impairments no longer results in marked and severe functional limitations; or

(ii) substantial evidence which demonstrates that, as determined on the basis of new or improved diagnostic techniques or evaluations, the individual's impairment or combination of impairments, is not as disabling as it was considered to be at the time of the most recent prior decision that the individual was under a disability or continued to be under a disability, and such impairment or combination of impairments does not result in marked and severe functional limitations; or

(C) in the case of any individual, substantial evidence (which may be evidence on the record at the time any prior determination of the entitlement to benefits based on disability was made, or newly obtained evidence which relates to that determination) which demonstrates that a prior determination was in error.

Nothing in this paragraph shall be construed to require a determination that an individual receiving benefits based on disability under this title is entitled to such benefits if the prior determination was fraudulently obtained or if the individual is engaged in substantial gainful activity, cannot be located, or fails, without good cause, to cooperate in a review of his or her entitlement or to follow prescribed treatment which would be expected (i) to restore his or her ability to engage in substantial gainful activity, or (ii) in the case of an individual under the age of 18, to eliminate or improve the individal's impairment or combination of impairments so that it no longer results in marked and severe functional limitations. Any determination under this paragraph shall be made on the basis of all the evidence available in the individual's case file, including new evidence concerning the individual's prior or current condition which is presented by the individual or secured by the Commissioner of Social Security. Any determination made under this paragraph shall be made on the basis of the weight of the evidence and on a neutral basis with regard to the individual's condition, without any initial inference as to the presence or absence of disability being drawn from the fact that the individual has previously been determined to be disabled.

Eligible Spouse

(b) For purposes of this title, the term "eligible spouse" means an aged, blind, or disabled individual who is the husband or wife of another aged, blind, or disabled individual, and who, in a month, is living with such aged, blind, or disabled individual on the first day of the

808 SOCIAL SECURITY ACT—§ 1614(b)(cont)

month or, in any case in which either spouse files an application for benefits, on the first day of the month following the date the application is filed, or, in any case in which either spouse requests restoration of eligibility under this title during the month, at the time the request is filed. If two aged, blind, or disabled individuals are husband and wife as described in the preceding sentence, only one of them may be an "eligible individual" within the meaning of section 1611(a).

Definition of Child

(c) For purposes of this title, the term "child" means an individual who is neither married nor (as determined by the Commissioner of Social Security) the head of a household, and who is (1) under the age of eighteen, or (2) under the age of twenty-two and (as determined by the Commissioner of Social Security) a student regularly attending a school, college, or university, or a course of vocational or technical training designed to prepare him for gainful employment.

Determination of Marital Relationships

(d) In determining whether two individuals are husband and wife for purposes of this title, appropriate State law shall be applied; except that—

(1) if a man and woman have been determined to be husband and wife under section 216(h)(1) for purposes of title II they shall be considered (from and after the date of such determination or the date of their application for benefits under this title, whichever is later) to be husband and wife for purposes of this title, or

(2) if a man and woman are found to be holding themselves out to the community in which they reside as husband and wife, they shall be so considered for purposes of this title notwithstanding any other provision of this section.

United States

(e) For purposes of this title, the term "United States", when used in a geographical sense, means the 50 States and the District of Columbia.

Income and Resources of Individuals Other Than Eligible Individuals and Eligible Spouses

(f)(1) For purposes of determining eligibility for and the amount of benefits for any individual who is married and whose spouse is living with him in the same household but is not an eligible spouse, such individual's income and resources shall be deemed to include any income and resources of such spouse, whether or not available to such individual, except to the extent determined by the Commissioner of Social Security to be inequitable under the circumstances.

(2)(A) For purposes of determining eligibility for and the amount of benefits for any individual who is a child under age 18, such individ-

SOCIAL SECURITY ACT—§ 1615(d)   809

ual's income and resources shall be deemed to include any income and resources of a parent of such individual (or the spouse of such a parent) who is living in the same household as such individual, whether or not available to such individual, except to the extent determined by the Commissioner of Social Security to be inequitable under the circumstances.

(B) Subparagraph (A) shall not apply in the case of any child who has not attained the age of 18 years who—

(i) is disabled;

(ii) received benefits under this title, pursuant to section 1611(e)(1)(B), while in an institution described in section 1611(e)(1)(B);

(iii) is eligible for medical assistance under a State home care plan approved by the Secretary under the provisions of section 1915(c) relating to waivers, or authorized under section 1902(e)(3); and

(iv) but for this subparagraph, would not be eligible for benefits under this title.

(3) For purposes of determining eligibility for and the amount of benefits for any individual who is an alien, such individual's income and resources shall be deemed to include the income and resources of his sponsor and such sponsor's spouse (if such alien has a sponsor) as provided in section 1621. Any such income deemed to be income of such individual shall be treated as unearned income of such individual.

(4) For purposes of paragraphs (1) and (2), a spouse or parent (or spouse of such a parent) who is absent from the household in which the individual lives due solely to a duty assignment as a member of the Armed Forces on active duty shall, in the absence of evidence to the contrary, be deemed to be living in the same household as the individual.

REHABILITATION SERVICES FOR BLIND AND DISABLED INDIVIDUALS

SEC. 1615. [42 U.S.C. 1382d] (a) In the case of any blind or disabled individual who—

(1) has not attained age 16; and

(2) with respect to whom benefits are paid under this title,

the Commissioner of Social Security shall make provision for referral of such individual to the appropriate State agency administering the State program under title V.

(b) [Repealed.[49]]

(c) [Repealed.[50]]

(d) The Commissioner of Social Security is authorized to reimburse the State agency administering or supervising the administration of a State plan for vocational rehabilitation services approved under title I of the Rehabilitation Act of 1973 for the costs incurred under such plan in the provision of rehabilitation services to individuals who are referred for such services pursuant to subsection (a)(1), in cases where the furnishing of such services results in the performance by such individuals of substantial gainful activity for a continuous period of nine months, (2) in cases where such individuals receive benefits as a re-

---

[49] P.L. 97-35, §2193(c)(8)(B); 95 Stat. 828.
[50] P.L. 106-170, §101(b)(2)(B); 113 Stat. 1874.

810 SOCIAL SECURITY ACT—§ 1615(d)(cont)

sult of section 1631(a)(6) (except that no reimbursement under this subsection shall be made for services furnished to any individual receiving such benefits for any period after the close of such individual's ninth consecutive month of substantial gainful activity or the close of the month with which his or her entitlement to such benefits ceases, whichever first occurs), and (3) in cases where such individuals, without good cause, refuse to continue to accept vocational rehabilitation services or fail to cooperate in such a manner as to preclude their successful rehabilitation. The determination that the vocational rehabilitation services contributed to the successful return of an individual to substantial gainful activity, the determination that an individual, without good cause, refused to continue to accept vocational rehabilitation services or failed to cooperate in such a manner as to preclude successful rehabilitation, and the determination of the amount of costs to be reimbursed under this subsection shall be made by the Commissioner of Social Security in accordance with criteria determined by the Commissioner in the same manner as under section 222(d)(1).

(e) The Commissioner of Social Security may reimburse the State agency described in subsection (d) for the costs described therein incurred in the provision of rehabilitation services—

(1) for any month for which an individual received—

(A) benefits under section 1611 or 1619(a);

(B) assistance under section 1619(b); or

(C) a federally administered State supplementary payment under section 1616 of this Act or section 212(b) of Public Law 93-66[51]; and

(2) for any month before the 13th consecutive month for which an individual, for a reason other than cessation of disability or blindness, was ineligible for—

(A) benefits under section 1611 or 1619(a);

(B) assistance under section 1619(b); or

(C) a federally administered State supplementary payment under section 1616 of this Act or section 212(b) of Public Law 93-66[52].

OPTIONAL STATE SUPPLEMENTATION[53]

SEC. 1616. [42 U.S.C. 1382e] (a) Any cash payments which are made by a State (or political subdivision thereof) on a regular basis to individuals who are receiving benefits under this title or who would but for their income be eligible to receive benefits under this title, as assistance based on need in supplementation of such benefits (as determined by the Commissioner of Social Security), shall be excluded under section 1612(b)(6) in determining the income of such individuals for purposes of this title and the Commissioner of Social Security and such State may enter into an agreement which satisfies subsection (b) under which the Commissioner of Social Security will, on behalf of such State (or subdivision) make such supplementary payments to all such individuals.

---

[51] See Vol. II, P.L. 93-66, §212(b).

[52] See Vol. II, P.L. 93-66, §212(b).

[53] See Vol. II, P.L. 93-233, §8, with respect to the eligibility of supplemental security recipients to increases to include the bonus value of certain benefits.

SOCIAL SECURITY ACT—§ 1616(d)(2)(A)   811

(b) Any agreement between the Commissioner of Social Security and a State entered into under subsection (a) shall provide—
  (1) that such payments will be made (subject to subsection (c)) to all individuals residing in such State (or subdivision) who are receiving benefits under this title, and
  (2) such other rules with respect to eligibility for or amount of the supplementary payments, and such procedural or other general administrative provisions, as the Commissioner of Social Security finds necessary (subject to subsection (c)) to achieve efficient and effective administration of both the program which the Commissioner conducts under this title and the optional State supplementation.
At the option of the State (but subject to paragraph (2) of this subsection), the agreement between the Commissioner of Social Security and such State entered into under subsection (a) shall be modified to provide that the Commissioner of Social Security will make supplementary payments, on and after an effective date to be specified in the agreement as so modified, to individuals receiving benefits determined under section 1611(e)(1)(B).

(c)(1) Any State (or political subdivision) making supplementary payments described in subsection (a) may at its option impose as a condition of eligibility for such payments, and include in the State's agreement with the Commissioner of Social Security under such subsection, a residence requirement which excludes individuals who have resided in the State (or political subdivision) for less than a minimum period prior to application for such payments.

(2) Any State (or political subdivision), in determining the eligibility of any individual for supplementary payments described in subsection (a), may disregard amounts of earned and unearned income in addition to other amounts which it is required or permitted to disregard under this section in determining such eligibility, and shall include a provision specifying the amount of any such income that will be disregarded, if any.

(3) Any State (or political subdivision) making supplementary payments described in subsection (a) shall have the option of making such payments to individuals who receive benefits under this title under the provisions of section 1619, or who would be eligible to receive such benefits but for their income.[54]

(d)(1) Any State which has entered into an agreement with the Commissioner of Social Security under this section which provides that the Commissioner of Social Security will, on behalf of the State (or political subdivision), make the supplementary payments to individuals who are receiving benefits under this title (or who would but for their income be eligible to receive such benefits), shall, in accordance with paragraph (5)[55], pay to the Commissioner of Social Security an amount equal to the expenditures made by the Commissioner of Social Security as such supplementary payments, plus an administration fee assessed in accordance with paragraph (2) and any additional services fee charged in accordance with paragraph (3).

(2)(A) The Commissioner of Social Security shall assess each State an administration fee in an amount equal to—

---

[54] See Vol. II, P.L. 96-265, §201(e), with respect to the maintenance of separate accounts.
[55] See Vol. II, P.L. 92-603, §401(d), with respect to phaseout of the hold harmless provision.

812 SOCIAL SECURITY ACT—§ 1616(d)(2)(A)(i)

(i) the number of supplementary payments made by the Commissioner of Social Security on behalf of the State under this section for any month in a fiscal year; multiplied by

(ii) the applicable rate for the fiscal year.

(B) As used in subparagraph (A), the term "applicable rate" means—

(i) for fiscal year 1994, $1.67;

(ii) for fiscal year 1995, $3.33;

(iii) for fiscal year 1996, $5.00;

(iv) for fiscal year 1997, $5.00;

(v) for fiscal year 1998, $6.20;

(vi) for fiscal year 1999, $7.60;

(vii) for fiscal year 2000, $7.80;

(viii) for fiscal year 2001, $8.10;

(ix) for fiscal year 2002, $8.50; and

(x) for fiscal year 2003 and each succeeding fiscal year—

(I) the applicable rate in the preceding fiscal year, increased by the percentage, if any, by which the Consumer Price Index for the month of June of the calendar year of the increase exceeds the Consumer Price Index for the month of June of the calendar year preceding the calendar year of the increase, and rounded to the nearest whole cent; or

(II) such different rate as the Commissioner determines is appropriate for the State.

(C) Upon making a determination under subparagraph (B)(x)(II), the Commissioner of Social Security shall promulgate the determination in regulations, which may take into account the complexity of administering the State's supplementary payment program.

(D) All fees assessed pursuant to this paragraph shall be transferred to the Commissioner of Social Security at the same time that amounts for such supplementary payments are required to be so tranferred.

(3)(A) The Commissioner of Social Security may charge a State an additional services fee if, at the request of the State, the Commissioner of Social Security provides additional services beyond the level customarily provided, in the administration of State supplementary payments pursuant to this section.

(B) The additional services fee shall be in an amount that the Commissioner of Social Security determines is necessary to cover all costs (including indirect costs) incurred by the Federal Government in furnishing the additional services referred to in subparagraph (A).

(4)(A) The first $5 of each administration fee assessed pursuant to paragraph (2), upon collection, shall be deposited in the general fund of the Treasury of the United States as miscellaneous receipts.

(B) That portion of each administration fee in excess of $5, and 100 percent of each additional services fee charged pursuant to paragraph (3), upon collection for fiscal year 1998 and each subsequent fiscal year, shall be credited to a special fund established in the Treasury of the United States for State supplementary payment fees. The amounts so credited, to the extent and in the amounts provided in advance in appropriations Acts, shall be available to defray expenses incurred in carrying out this title and related laws.[56]

---

[56] See Vol. II, P.L. 105-78, §516(b)(2), with respect to limitations on authorization of appropriations.

SOCIAL SECURITY ACT—§ 1616(e)(4) 813

(5)(A)(i) Any State which has entered into an agreement with the Commissioner of Social Security under this section shall remit the payments and fees required under this subsection with respect to monthly benefits paid to individuals under this title no later than—

(I) the business day preceding the date that the Commissioner pays such monthly benefits; or

(II) with respect to such monthly benefits paid for the month that is the last month of the State's fiscal year, the fifth business day following such date.

(ii) The Commissioner may charge States a penalty in an amount equal to 5 percent of the payment and the fees due if the remittance is received after the date required by clause (i).

(B) The Cash Management Improvement Act of 1990 shall not apply to any payments or fees required under this subsection that are paid by a State before the date required by subparagraph (A)(i).

(C) Notwithstanding subparagraph (A)(i), the Commissioner may make supplementary payments on behalf of a State with funds appropriated for payment of benefits under this title, and subsequently to be reimbursed for such payments by the State at such times as the Commissioner and State may agree. Such authority may be exercised only if extraordinary circumstances affecting a State's ability to make payment when required by subparagraph (A)(i) are determined by the Commissioner to exist.

(e)(1) Each State shall establish or designate one or more State or local authorities which shall establish, maintain, and insure the enforcement of standards for any category of institutions, foster homes, or group living arrangements in which (as determined by the State) a significant number of recipients of supplemental security income benefits is residing or is likely to reside. Such standards shall be appropriate to the needs of such recipients and the character of the facilities involved, and shall govern such matters as admission policies, safety, sanitation, and protection of civil rights.

(2) Each State shall annually make available for public review a summary of the standards established pursuant to paragraph (1), and shall make available to any interested individual a copy of such standards, along with the procedures available in the State to insure the enforcement of such standards and a list of any waivers of such standards and any violations of such standards which have come to the attention of the authority responsible for their enforcement.

(3) Each State shall certify annually to the Commissioner of Social Security that it is in compliance with the requirements of this subsection.

(4) Payments made under this title with respect to an individual shall be reduced by an amount equal to the amount of any supplementary payment (as described in subsection (a)) or other payment made by a State (or political subdivision thereof) which is made for or on account of any medical or any other type of remedial care provided by an institution of the type described in paragraph (1) to such individual as a resident or an inpatient of such institution if such institution is not approved as meeting the standards described in such paragraph by the appropriate State or local authorities.

814   SOCIAL SECURITY ACT—§ 1616(e)(4)(cont)

COST–OF–LIVING ADJUSTMENTS IN BENEFITS[57]

SEC. 1617. [42 U.S.C. 1382f] (a) Whenever benefit amounts under title II are increased by any percentage effective with any month as a result of a determination made under section 215(i)—

(1) each of the dollar amounts in effect for such month under subsections (a)(1)(A), (a)(2)(A), (b)(1), and (b)(2) of section 1611, and subsection (a)(1)(A) of section 211 of Public Law 93-66[58] , as specified in such subsections or as previously increased under this section, shall be increased by the amount (if any) by which—

(A) the amount which would have been in effect for such month under such subsection but for the rounding of such amount pursuant to paragraph (2), exceeds

(B) the amount in effect for such month under such subsection; and

(2) the amount obtained under paragraph (1) with respect to each subsection shall be further increased by the same percentage by which benefit amounts under title II are increased for such month, or, if greater (in any case where the increase under title II was determined on the basis of the wage increase percentage rather than the CPI increase percentage), the percentage by which benefit amounts under title II would be increased for such month if the increase had been determined on the basis of the CPI increase percentage, (and rounded, when not a multiple of $12, to the next lower multiple of $12), effective with respect to benefits for months after such month.

(b) The new dollar amounts to be in effect under section 1611 of this title and under section 211 of Public Law 93-66 by reason of subsection (a) of this section shall be published in the Federal Register together with, and at the same time as, the material required by section 215(i)(2)(D) to be published therein by reason of the determination involved.

(c) Effective July 1, 1983—

(1) each of the dollar amounts in effect under subsections (a)(1)(A) and (b)(1) of section 1611, as previously increased under this section, shall be increased by $240 (and the dollar amount in effect under subsection (a)(1)(A) of section 211 of Public Law 93-66, as previously so increased, shall be increased by $120); and

(2) each of the dollar amounts in effect under subsections (a)(2)(A) and (b)(2) of section 1611, as previously increased under this section, shall be increased by $360.

OPERATION OF STATE SUPPLEMENTATION PROGRAMS

SEC. 1618. [42 U.S.C. 1382g] (a) In order for any State which makes supplementary payments of the type described in section 1616(a) (including payments pursuant to an agreement entered into under section 212(a) of Public Law 93-66[59]), on or after June 30, 1977, to be eligible for payments pursuant to title XIX with respect to expenditures for any calendar quarter which begins—

(1) after June 30, 1977, or, if later,

---

[57] See Vol. II, Appendixes A and B, for Cost-of-Living Increase information.
[58] See Vol. II, P.L. 93-66, §211.
[59] See Vol. II, P.L. 93-66, §212(a).

SOCIAL SECURITY ACT—§ 1618(e)(1)   815

(2) after the calendar quarter in which it first makes such supplementary payments,

such State must have in effect an agreement with the Commissioner of Social Security whereby the State will—

(3) continue to make such supplementary payments, and

(4) maintain such supplementary payments at levels which are not lower than the levels of such payments in effect in December 1976, or, if no such payments were made in that month, the levels for the first subsequent month in which such payments were made.

(b)(1) The Commissioner of Social Security shall not find that a State has failed to meet the requirements imposed by paragraph (4) of subsection (a) with respect to the levels of its supplementary payments for a particular month or months if the State's expenditures for such payments in the twelve-month period (within which such month or months fall) beginning on the effective date of any increase in the level of supplemental security income benefits pursuant to section 1617 are not less than its expenditures for such payments in the preceding twelve-month period.

(2) For purposes of determining under paragraph (1) whether a State's expenditures for supplementary payments in the 12-month period beginning on the effective date of any increase in the level of supplemental security income benefits are not less than the State's expenditures for such payments in the preceding 12-month period, the Commissioner of Social Security, in computing the State's expenditures, shall disregard, pursuant to a 1-time election of the State, all expenditures by the State for retroactive supplementary payments that are required to be made in connection with the retroactive supplemental security income benefits referred to in section 5041 of the Omnibus Budget Reconciliation Act of 1990[60].

(c) Any State which satisfies the requirements of this section solely by reason of subsection (b) for a particular month or months in any 12-month period (described in such subsection) ending on or after June 30, 1982, may elect, with respect to any month in any subsequent 12-month period (so described), to apply subsection (a)(4) as though the reference to December 1976 in such subsection were a reference to the month of December which occurred in the 12-month period immediately preceding such subsequent period.

(d) The Commissioner of Social Security shall not find that a State has failed to meet the requirements imposed by paragraph (4) of subsection (a) with respect to the levels of its supplementary payments for any portion of the period July 1, 1980, through June 30, 1981, if the State's expenditures for such payments in that twelve-month period were not less than its expenditures for such payments for the period July 1, 1976, through June 30, 1977 (or, if the State made no supplementary payments in the period July 1, 1976, through June 30, 1977, the expenditures for the first twelve-month period extending from July 1 through June 30 in which the State made such payments).

(e)(1) For any particular month after March 1983, a State which is not treated as meeting the requirements imposed by paragraph (4) of

---

[60] P.L. 101-508.

816   SOCIAL SECURITY ACT—§ 1618(e)(1)(cont)

subsection (a) by reason of subsection (b) shall be treated as meeting such requirements if and only if—

(A) the combined level of its supplementary payments (to recipients of the type involved) and the amounts payable (to or on behalf of such recipients) under section 1611(b) of this Act and section 211(a)(1)(A) of Public Law 93-66[61], for that particular month,

is not less than—

(B) the combined level of its supplementary payments (to recipients of the type involved) and the amounts payable (to or on behalf of such recipients) under section 1611(b) of this Act and section 211(a)(1)(A) of Public Law 93-66[62], for March 1983, increased by the amount of all cost-of-living adjustments under section 1617 (and any other benefit increases under this title) which have occurred after March 1983 and before that particular month.

(2) In determining the amount of any increase in the combined level involved under paragraph (1)(B) of this subsection, any portion of such amount which would otherwise be attributable to the increase under section 1617(c) shall be deemed instead to be equal to the amount of the cost-of-living adjustment which would have occurred in July 1983 (without regard to the 3-percent limitation contained in section 215(i)(1)(B)) if section 111 of the Social Security Amendments of 1983[63] had not been enacted.

(f) The Commissioner of Social Security shall not find that a State has failed to meet the requirements imposed by subsection (a) with respect to the levels of its supplementary payments for the period January 1, 1984, through December 31, 1985, if in the period January 1, 1986, through December 31, 1986, its supplementary payment levels (other than to recipients of benefits determined under section 1611(e)(1)(B)) are not less than those in effect in December 1976, increased by a percentage equal to the percentage by which payments under section 1611(b) of this Act and section 211(a)(1)(A) of Public Law 93-66 have been increased as a result of all adjustments under section 1617(a) and (c) which have occurred after December 1976 and before February 1986.

(g) In order for any State which makes supplementary payments of the type described in section 1616(a) (including payments pursuant to an agreement entered into under section 212(a) of Public Law 93-66[64]) to recipients of benefits determined under section 1611(e)(1)(B), on or after October 1, 1987, to be eligible for payments pursuant to title XIX with respect to any calendar quarter which begins—

(1) after October 1, 1987, or, if later

(2) after the calendar quarter in which it first makes such supplementary payments to recipients of benefits so determined,

such State must have in effect an agreement with the Commissioner of Social Security whereby the State will—

(3) continue to make such supplementary payments to recipients of benefits so determined, and

(4) maintain such supplementary payments to recipients of benefits so determined at levels which assure (with respect to

---

[61] See Vol. II, P.L. 93-66, §211(a)(1)(A).
[62] See Vol. II, P.L. 93-66, §211(a)(1)(A).
[63] P.L. 98-21.
[64] See Vol. II, P.L. 93-66, §212(a).

SOCIAL SECURITY ACT—§ 1619(b)(1) 817

any particular month beginning with the month in which this subsection is first effective) that—

(A) the combined level of such supplementary payments and the amounts payable to or on behalf of such recipients under section 1611(e)(1)(B) for that particular month,

is not less than—

(B) the combined level of such supplementary payments and the amounts payable to or on behalf of such recipients under section 1611(e)(1)(B) for October 1987 (or, if no such supplementary payments were made for that month, the combined level for the first subsequent month for which such payments were made), increased—

(i) in a case to which clause (i) of such section 1611(e)(1)(B) applies or (with respect to the individual or spouse who is in the hospital, home, or facility involved) to which clause (ii) of such section applies, by $5, and

(ii) in a case to which clause (iii) of such section 1611(e)(1)(B) applies, by $10.

BENEFITS FOR INDIVIDUALS WHO PERFORM SUBSTANTIAL GAINFUL ACTIVITY DESPITE SEVERE MEDICAL IMPAIRMENT[65]

SEC. 1619. [42 U.S.C. 1382h] (a)(1) Except as provided in section 1631(j), any individual who was determined to be an eligible individual (or eligible spouse) by reason of being under a disability and was eligible to receive benefits under section 1611 (or a federally administered State supplementary payment) for a month and whose earnings in a subsequent month exceed the amount designated by the Commissioner of Social Security ordinarily to represent substantial gainful activity shall qualify for a monthly benefit under this subsection for such subsequent month (which shall be in lieu of any benefit under section 1611) equal to an amount determined under section 1611(b)(1) (or, in the case of an individual who has an eligible spouse, under section 1611(b)(2)), and for purposes of title XIX shall be considered to be receiving supplemental security income benefits under this title, for so long as—

(A) such individual continues to have the disabling physical or mental impairment on the basis of which such individual was found to be under a disability; and

(B) the income of such individual, other than income excluded pursuant to section 1612(b), is not equal to or in excess of the amount which would cause him to be ineligible for payments under section 1611 and such individual meets all other non-disability-related requirements for eligibility for benefits under this title.

(2) The Commissioner of Social Security shall make a determination under paragraph (1)(A) with respect to an individual not later than 12 months after the first month for which the individual qualifies for a benefit under this subsection.

(b)(1) Except as provided in section 1631(j), for purposes of title XIX, any individual who was determined to be a blind or disabled individual eligible to receive a benefit under section 1611 or any federally administered State supplementary payment for a month and

---

[65] See Vol. II, P.L. 96-265, §201(e), with respect to the maintenance of separate accounts.

818 SOCIAL SECURITY ACT—§ 1619(b)(1)(cont)

who in a subsequent month is ineligible for benefits under this title (and for any federally administered State supplementary payments) because of his or her income shall, nevertheless, be considered to be receiving supplemental security income benefits for such subsequent month provided that the Commissioner of Social Security determines under regulations that—

(A) such individual continues to be blind or continues to have the disabling physical or mental impairment on the basis of which he was found to be under a disability and, except for his earnings, meets all non-disability-related requirements for eligibility for benefits under this title;

(B) the income of such individual would not, except for his earnings and increases pursuant to section 215(i) in the level of monthly insurance benefits to which the individual is entitled under title II that occur while such individual is considered to be receiving supplemental security income benefits by reason of this subsection, be equal to or in excess of the amount which would cause him to be ineligible for payments under section 1611(b) (if he were otherwise eligible for such payments);

(C) the termination of eligibility for benefits under title XIX would seriously inhibit his ability to continue his employment; and

(D) such individual's earnings are not sufficient to allow him to provide for himself a reasonable equivalent of the benefits under this title (including any federally administered State supplementary payments), benefits under title XIX, and publicly funded attendant care services (including personal care assistance), which would be available to him in the absence of such earnings.

(2)(A) Determinations made under paragraph (1)(D) shall be based on information and data updated no less frequently than annually.

(B) In determining an individual's earnings for purposes of paragraph (1)(D), there shall be excluded from such earnings an amount equal to the sum of any amounts which are or would be excluded under clauses (ii) and (iv) of section 1612(b)(4)(B) (or under clauses (ii) and (iii) of section 1612(b)(4)(A)) in determining his or her income.

(3) In the case of a State that exercises the option under section 1902(f), any individual who—

(A)(i) qualifies for a benefit under subsection (a), or

(ii) meets the requirements of paragraph (1); and

(B) was eligible for medical assistance under the State plan approved under title XIX in the month immediately preceding the first month in which the individual qualified for a benefit under such subsection or met such requirements,

shall remain eligible for medical assistance under such plan for so long as the individual qualifies for a benefit under such subsection or meets such requirements.

(c) Subsection (a)(2) and section 1631(j)(2)(A) shall not be construed, singly or jointly, to require more than 1 determination during any 12-month period with respect to the continuing disability or blindness of an individual.

(d) The Commissioner of Social Security and the Secretary of Education shall jointly develop and disseminate information, and establish training programs for staff personnel, with respect to the potential availability of benefits and services for disabled individuals under

SOCIAL SECURITY ACT—§ 1620(b)(3)   819

the provisions of this section. The Commissioner of Social Security shall provide such information to individuals who are applicants for and recipients of benefits based on disability under this title and shall conduct such programs for the staffs of the district offices of the Social Security Administration. The Secretary of Education shall conduct such programs for the staffs of the State Vocational Rehabilitation agencies, and in cooperation with such agencies shall also provide such information to other appropriate individuals and to public and private organizations and agencies which are concerned with rehabilitation and social services or which represent the disabled.

MEDICAL AND SOCIAL SERVICES FOR CERTAIN HANDICAPPED PERSONS

SEC. 1620. [42 U.S.C. 1382i] (a) There are authorized to be appropriated such sums as may be necessary to establish and carry out a 3-year Federal-State pilot program to provide medical and social services for certain handicapped individuals in accordance with this section.

(b)(1) The total sum of $18,000,000 shall be allotted to the States for such program by the Commissioner of Social Security, during the period beginning September 1, 1981, and ending September 30, 1984, as follows:

(A) The total sum of $6,000,000 shall be allotted to the States for the fiscal year ending September 30, 1982 (which for purposes of this section shall include the month of September 1981).

(B) The total sum of $6,000,000, plus any amount remaining available (after the application of paragraph (4)) from the allotment made under subparagraph (A), shall be allotted to the States for the fiscal year ending September 30, 1983.

(C) The total sum of $6,000,000, plus any amount remaining available (after the application of paragraph (4)) from the allotments made under subparagraphs (A) and (B), shall be allotted to the States for the fiscal year ending September 30, 1984.

(2) The allotment to each State from the total sum allotted under paragraph (1) for any fiscal year shall bear the same ratio to such total sum as the number of individuals in such State who are over age 17 and under age 65 and are receiving supplemental security income benefits as disabled individuals in such year (as determined by the Commissioner of Social Security on the basis of the most recent data available) bears to the total number of such individuals in all the States. For purposes of the preceding sentence, the term "supplemental security income benefits" includes payments made pursuant to an agreement under section 1616(a) of this Act or under section 212(b) of Public Law 93-66[66].

(3) At the beginning of each fiscal year in which the pilot program under this section is in effect, each State that does not intend to use the allotment to which it is entitled for such year (or any allotment which was made to it for a prior fiscal year), or that does not intend to use the full amount of any such allotment, shall certify to the Commissioner of Social Security the amount of such allotment which it does not intend to use, and the State's allotment for the fiscal year (or years) involved shall thereupon be reduced by the amount so certified.

---

[66] See Vol. II, P.L. 93-66, §212(b).

820 SOCIAL SECURITY ACT—§ 1620(b)(4)

(4) The portion of the total amount available for allotment for any particular fiscal year under paragraph (1) which is not allotted to States for that year by reason of paragraph (3) (plus the amount of any reductions made at the beginning of such year in the allotments of States for prior fiscal years under paragraph (3)) shall be reallocated in such manner as the Commissioner of Social Security may determine to be appropriate to States which need, and will use, additional assistance in providing services to severely handicapped individuals in that particular year under their approved plans. Any amount reallocated to a State under this paragraph for use in a particular fiscal year shall be treated for purposes of this section as increasing such State's allotment for that year by an equivalent amount.

(c) In order to participate in the pilot program and be eligible to receive payments for any period under subsection (d), a State (during such period) must have a plan, approved by the Commissioner of Social Security as meeting the requirements of this section, which provides medical and social services for severely handicapped individuals whose earnings are above the level which ordinarily demonstrates an ability to engage in substantial gainful activity and who are not receiving benefits under section 1611 or 1619 or assistance under a State plan approved under section 1902, and which—

(1) declares the intent of the State to participate in the pilot program;

(2) designates an appropriate State agency to administer or supervise the administration of the program in the State;

(3) describes the criteria to be applied by the State in determining the eligibility of any individual for assistance under the plan and in any event requires a determination by the State agency to the effect that (A) such individual's ability to continue his employment would be significantly inhibited without such assistance and (B) such individual's earnings are not sufficient to allow him to provide for himself a reasonable equivalent of the cash and other benefits that would be available to him under this title and titles XIX and XX in the absence of those earnings;

(4) describes the process by which the eligibility of individuals for such assistance is to be determined (and such process may not involve the performance of functions by any State agency or entity which is engaged in making determinations of disability for purposes of disability insurance or supplemental security income benefits except when the use of a different agency or entity to perform those functions would not be feasible);

(5) describes the medical and social services to be provided under the plan;

(6) describes the manner in which the medical and social services involved are to be provided and, if they are not to be provided through the State's medical assistance and social services programs under titles XIX and XX (with the Federal payments being made under subsection (d) of this section rather than under those titles), specifies the particular mechanisms and procedures to be used in providing such services; and

(7) contains such other provisions as the Commissioner of Social Security may find to be necessary or appropriate to meet the requirements of this section or otherwise carry out its purpose.

SOCIAL SECURITY ACT—§ 1621(b)(1)(A)   821

(d)(1) From its allotment under subsection (b) for any fiscal year (and any amounts remaining available from allotments made to it for prior fiscal years), the Commissioner of Social Security shall from time to time pay to each State which has a plan approved under subsection (c) an amount equal to 75 per centum of the total sum expended under such plan (including the cost of administration of such plan) in providing medical and social services to severely handicapped individuals who are eligible for such services under the plan.

(2) The method of computing and making payments under this section shall be as follows:

(A) The Commissioner of Social Security shall, prior to each period for which a payment is to be made to a State, estimate the amount to be paid to the State for such period under the provisions of this section.

(B) From the allotment available therefor, the Commissioner of Social Security shall pay the amount so estimated, reduced or increased, as the case may be, by any sum (not previously adjusted under this subsection) by which the Commissioner finds that the Commissioner's estimate of the amount to be paid the State for any prior period under this section was greater or less than the amount which should have been paid to the State for such period under this section.

(e) Within nine months after the date of the enactment of this section[67], the Commissioner of Social Security shall prescribe and publish such regulations as may be necessary or appropriate to carry out the pilot program and otherwise implement this section.

(f) Each State participating in the pilot program under his section shall from time to time report to the Commissioner of Social Security on the operation and results of such program in that State, with particular emphasis upon the work incentive effects of the program. On or before October 1, 1983, the Commissioner of Social Security shall submit to the Congress a report on the program, incorporating the information contained in the State reports along with the Commissioner's findings and recommendations.

ATTRIBUTION OF SPONSOR'S INCOME AND RESOURCES TO ALIENS

SEC. 1621. [42 U.S.C. 1382j] (a) For purposes of determining eligibility for and the amount of benefits under this title for an individual who is an alien, the income and resources of any person who (as a sponsor of such individual's entry into the United States) executed an affidavit of support or similar agreement with respect to such individual, and the income and resources of the sponsor's spouse, shall be deemed to be the income and resources of such individual (in accordance with subsections (b) and (c)) for a period of 3 years after the individual's entry into the United States. Any such income deemed to be income of such individual shall be treated as unearned income of such individual.

(b)(1) The amount of income of a sponsor (and his spouse) which shall be deemed to be the unearned income of an alien for any year shall be determined as follows:

(A) The total yearly rate of earned and unearned income (as determined under section 1612(a)) of such sponsor and such spon-

---

[67] This section was enacted June 9, 1980 (P.L. 96-265; 94 Stat. 446, 448).

sor's spouse (if such spouse is living with the sponsor) shall be determined for such year.

(B) The amount determined under subparagraph (A) shall be reduced by an amount equal to (i) the maximum amount of the Federal benefit under this title for such year which would be payable to an eligible individual who has no other income and who does not have an eligible spouse (as determined under section 1611(b)(1)), plus (ii) one-half of the amount determined under clause (i) multiplied by the number of individuals who are dependents of such sponsor (or such sponsor's spouse if such spouse is living with the sponsor), other than such alien and such alien's spouse.

(C) The amount of income which shall be deemed to be unearned income of such alien shall be at a yearly rate equal to the amount determined under subparagraph (B). The period for determination of such amount shall be the same as the period for determination of benefits under section 1611(c).

(2) The amount of resources of a sponsor (and his spouse) which shall be deemed to be the resources of an alien for any year shall be determined as follows:

(A) The total amount of the resources (as determined under section 1613) of such sponsor and such sponsor's spouse (if such spouse is living with the sponsor) shall be determined.

(B) The amount determined under subparagraph (A) shall be reduced by an amount equal to (i) the applicable amount determined under section 1611(a)(3)(B) in the case of a sponsor who has no spouse with whom he is living, or (ii) the applicable amount determined under section 1611(a)(3)(A) in the case of a sponsor who has a spouse with whom he is living.

(C) The resources of such sponsor (and spouse) as determined under subparagraphs (A) and (B) shall be deemed to be resources of such alien in addition to any resources of such alien.

(c) In determining the amount of income of an alien during the period of 3 years after such alien's entry into the United States, the reduction in dollar amounts otherwise required under section 1612(a)(2)(A)(i) shall not be applicable if such alien is living in the household of a person who is a sponsor (or such sponsor's spouse) of such alien, and is receiving support and maintenance in kind from such sponsor (or spouse), nor shall support or maintenance furnished in cash or kind to an alien by such alien's sponsor (to the extent that it reflects income or resources which were taken into account in determining the amount of income and resources to be deemed to the alien under subsection (a) or (b)) be considered to be income of such alien under section 1612(a)(2)(A).

(d)(1) Any individual who is an alien shall, during the period of 3 years after entry into the United States, in order to be an eligible individual or eligible spouse for purposes of this title, be required to provide to the Commissioner of Social Security such information and documentation with respect to his sponsor as may be necessary in order for the Commissioner of Social Security to make any determination required under this section, and to obtain any cooperation from such sponsor necessary for any such determination. Such alien shall also be required to provide to the Commissioner of Social Security such information and documentation as the Commissioner of Social Security

SOCIAL SECURITY ACT—§ 1631(a)(1)

823

may request and which such alien or his sponsor provided in support of such alien's immigration application.

(2) The Commissioner of Social Security shall enter into agreements with the Secretary of State and the Attorney General whereby any information available to such persons and required in order to make any determination under this section will be provided by such persons to the Commissioner of Social Security, and whereby such persons shall inform any sponsor of an alien, at the time such sponsor executes an affidavit of support or similar agreement, of the requirements imposed by this section.

(e) Any sponsor of an alien, and such alien, shall be jointly and severally liable for an amount equal to any overpayment made to such alien during the period of 3 years after such alien's entry into the United States, on account of such sponsor's failure to provide correct information under the provisions of this section, except where such sponsor was without fault, or where good cause for such failure existed. Any such overpayment which is not repaid to the Commissioner of Social Security or recovered in accordance with section 1631(b) shall be withheld from any subsequent payment to which such alien or such sponsor is entitled under any provision of this Act.

(f)(1) The provisions of this section shall not apply with respect to any individual who is an "aged, blind, or disabled individual" for purposes of this title by reason of blindness (as determined under section 1614(a)(2)) or disability (as determined under section 1614(a)(3)), from and after the onset of the impairment, if such blindness or disability commenced after the date of such individual's admission into the United States for permanent residence.

(2) The provisions of this section shall not apply with respect to any alien who is—

(A) admitted to the United States as a result of the application, prior to April 1, 1980, of the provisions of section 203(a)(7) of the Immigration and Nationality Act[68];

(B) admitted to the United States as a result of the application, after March 31, 1980, of the provisions of section 207(c)(1) of such Act;

(C) paroled into the United States as a refugee under section 212(d)(5) of such Act[69]; or

(D) granted political asylum by the Attorney General.

Part B—Procedural and General Provisions

PAYMENTS AND PROCEDURES[70]

Payment of Benefits

SEC. 1631. [42 U.S.C. 1383] (a)(1) Benefits under this title shall be paid at such time or times and (subject to paragraph (10)) in such installments as will best effectuate the purposes of this title, as determined under regulations (and may in any case be paid less frequently than monthly where the amount of the monthly benefit would not exceed $10).

---

[68] See Vol. II, P.L. 82-414, §203(a)(7).
[69] See Vol. II, P.L. 82-414, §§207(c)(1) and 212(d).
[70] See Vol. II, P.L. 90-321, §913(2), with respect to electronic fund transfers.

824   SOCIAL SECURITY ACT—§ 1631(a)(2)

(2)(A)(i) Payments of the benefit of any individual may be made to any such individual or to the eligible spouse (if any) of such individual or partly to each.

(ii)(I) Upon a determination by the Commissioner of Social Security that the interest of such individual would be served thereby, such payments shall be made, regardless of the legal competency or incompetency of the individual or eligible spouse, to another individual, or an organization, with respect to whom the requirements of subparagraph (B) have been met (in this paragraph referred to as such individual's "representative payee") for the use and benefit of the individual or eligible spouse.

(II) In the case of an individual eligible for benefits under this title by reason of disability, the payment of such benefits shall be made to a representative payee if the Commissioner of Social Security determines that such payment would serve the interest of the individual because the individual also has an alcoholism or drug addiction condition (as determined by the Commissioner) and the individual is incapable of managing such benefits.

(iii) If the Commissioner of Social Security or a court of competent jurisdiction determines that the representative payee of an individual or eligible spouse has misused any benefits which have been paid to the representative payee pursuant to clause (ii) or section 205(j)(1) or 807, the Commissioner of Social Security shall promptly terminate payment of benefits to the representative payee pursuant to this subparagraph, and provide for payment of benefits to an alternative representative payee of the individual or eligible spouse or, if the interest of the individual under this title would be served thereby, to the individual or eligible spouse.

(iv) For purposes of this paragraph, misuse of benefits by a representative payee occurs in any case in which the representative payee receives payment under this title for the use and benefit of another person and converts such payment, or any part thereof, to a use other than for the use and benefit of such other person. The Commissioner of Social Security may prescribe by regulation the meaning of the term "use and benefit" for purposes of this clause.

(B)(i) Any determination made under subparagraph (A) for payment of benefits to the representative payee of an individual or eligible spouse shall be made on the basis of—

(I) an investigation by the Commissioner of Social Security of the person to serve as representative payee, which shall be conducted in advance of such payment, and shall, to the extent practicable, include a face-to-face interview with such person; and

(II) adequate evidence that such payment is in the interest of the individual or eligible spouse (as determined by the Commissioner of Social Security in regulations).

(ii) As part of the investigation referred to in clause (i)(I), the Commissioner of Social Security shall—

(I) require the person being investigated to submit documented proof of the identity of such person, unless information establishing such identity was submitted with an application for benefits under title II, title VIII, or this title;

(II) verify the social security account number (or employer identification number) of such person;

SOCIAL SECURITY ACT—§ 1631(a)(2)(B)(v)(IV)   825

(III) determine whether such person has been convicted of a violation of section 208, 811, or 1632;

(IV) obtain information concerning whether the person has been convicted of any other offense under Federal or State law which resulted in imprisonment for more than 1 year;

(V) obtain information concerning whether such person is a person described in section 1611(e)(4)(A); and

(VI) determine whether payment of benefits to such person has been terminated pursuant to subparagraph (A)(iii), whether the designation of such person as a representative payee has been revoked pursuant to section 807(a), and whether certification of payment of benefits to such person has been revoked pursuant to section 205(j), by reason of misuse of funds paid as benefits under title II, title VIII, or this title.

(iii) Benefits of an individual may not be paid to any other person pursuant to subparagraph (A)(ii) if—

(I) such person has previously been convicted as described in clause (ii)(III);

(II) except as provided in clause (iv), payment of benefits to such person pursuant to subparagraph (A)(ii) has previously been terminated as described in clause (ii)(VI), the designation of such person as a representative payee has been revoked pursuant to section 807(a), or certification of payment of benefits to such person under section 205(j) has previously been revoked as described in section 205(j)(2)(B)(i)(VI);

(III) except as provided in clause (v), such person is a creditor of such individual who provides such individual with goods or services for consideration;

(IV) the person has previously been convicted as described in clause (ii)(IV) of this subparagraph, unless the Commissioner determines that the payment would be appropriate notwithstanding the conviction; or

(V) such person is a person described in section 1611(e)(4)(A).

(iv) The Commissioner of Social Security shall prescribe regulations under which the Commissioner of Social Security may grant an exemption from clause (iii)(II) to any person on a case-by-case basis if such exemption would be in the best interest of the individual or eligible spouse whose benefits under this title would be paid to such person pursuant to subparagraph (A)(ii).

(v) Clause (iii)(III) shall not apply with respect to any person who is a creditor referred to therein if such creditor is—

(I) a relative of such individual if such relative resides in the same household as such individual;

(II) a legal guardian or legal representative of such individual;

(III) a facility that is licensed or certified as a care facility under the law of a State or a political subdivision of a State;

(IV) a person who is an administrator, owner, or employee of a facility referred to in subclause (III) if such individual resides in such facility, and the payment of benefits under this title to such facility or such person is made only after good faith efforts have been made by the local servicing office of the Social Security Administration to locate an alternative representative payee to whom the payment of such benefits would serve the best interests of such individual; or

826   SOCIAL SECURITY ACT—§ 1631(a)(2)(B)(v)(V)

(V) an individual who is determined by the Commissioner of Social Security, on the basis of written findings and under procedures which the Commissioner of Social Security shall prescribe by regulation, to be acceptable to serve as a representative payee.

(vi) The procedures referred to in clause (v)(V) shall require the individual who will serve as representative payee to establish, to the satisfaction of the Commissioner of Social Security, that—

(I) such individual poses no risk to the beneficiary;

(II) the financial relationship of such individual to the beneficiary poses no substantial conflict of interest; and

(III) no other more suitable representative payee can be found.

(vii) In the case of an individual described in subparagraph (A)(ii)(II), when selecting such individual's representative payee, preference shall be given to—

(I) a certified community-based nonprofit social service agency (as defined in subparagraph (I));

(II) a Federal, State, or local government agency whose mission is to carry out income maintenance, social service, or health care-related activities;

(III) a State or local government agency with fiduciary responsibilities; or

(IV) a designee of an agency (other than of a Federal agency) referred to in the preceding subclauses of this clause, if the Commissioner of Social Security deems it appropriate,

unless the Commissioner of Social Security determines that selection of a family member would be appropriate.

(viii) Subject to clause (ix), if the Commissioner of Social Security makes a determination described in subparagraph (A)(ii) with respect to any individual's benefit and determines that direct payment of the benefit to the individual would cause substantial harm to the individual, the Commissioner of Social Security may defer (in the case of initial entitlement) or suspend (in the case of existing entitlement) direct payment of such benefit to the individual, until such time as the selection of a representative payee is made pursuant to this subparagraph.

(ix)(I) Except as provided in subclause (II), any deferral or suspension of direct payment of a benefit pursuant to clause (viii) shall be for a period of not more than 1 month.

(II) Subclause (I) shall not apply in any case in which the individual or eligible spouse is, as of the date of the Commissioner's determination, legally incompetent, under the age of 15 years, or described in subparagraph (A)(ii)(II).

(x) Payment pursuant to this subparagraph of any benefits which are deferred or suspended pending the selection of a representative payee shall be made to the individual, or to the representative payee upon such selection, as a single sum or over such period of time as the Commissioner of Social Security determines is in the best interests of the individual entitled to such benefits.

(xi) Any individual who is dissatisfied with a determination by the Commissioner of Social Security to pay such individual's benefits to a representative payee under this title, or with the designation of a particular person to serve as representative payee, shall be entitled to a hearing by the Commissioner of Social Security, and to judicial

SOCIAL SECURITY ACT—§ 1631(a)(2)(C)(ii)   827

review of the Commissioner's final decision, to the same extent as is provided in subsection (c).

(xii) In advance of the first payment of an individual's benefit to a representative payee under subparagraph (A)(ii), the Commissioner of Social Security shall provide written notice of the Commissioner's initial determination to make any such payment. Such notice shall be provided to such individual, except that, if such individual—

(I) is under the age of 15,

(II) is an unemancipated minor under the age of 18, or

(III) is legally incompetent,

then such notice shall be provided solely to the legal guardian or legal representative of such individual.

(xiii) Any notice described in clause (xii) shall be clearly written in language that is easily understandable to the reader, shall identify the person to be designated as such individual's representative payee, and shall explain to the reader the right under clause (xi) of such individual or of such individual's legal guardian or legal representative—

(I) to appeal a determination that a representative payee is necessary for such individual,

(II) to appeal the designation of a particular person to serve as the representative payee of such individual, and

(III) to review the evidence upon which such designation is based and submit additional evidence.

(xiv) Notwithstanding the provisions of section 552a of title 5, United States Code[71], or any other provision of Federal or State law (other than section 6103 of the Internal Revenue Code of 1986[72] and section 1106(c) of this Act), the Commissioner shall furnish any Federal, State, or local law enforcement officer, upon the written request of the officer, with the current address, social security account number, and photograph (if applicable) of any person investigated under this subparagraph, if the officer furnishes the Commissioner with the name of such person and such other identifying information as may reasonably be required by the Commissioner to establish the unique identity of such person, and notifies the Commissioner that—

(I) such person is described in section 1611(e)(4)(A),

(II) such person has information that is necessary for the officer to conduct the officer's official duties, and

(III) the location or apprehension of such person is within the officer's official duties

(C)(i) In any case where payment is made under this title to a representative payee of an individual or spouse, the Commissioner of Social Security shall establish a system of accountability monitoring whereby such person shall report not less often than annually with respect to the use of such payments. The Commissioner of Social Security shall establish and implement statistically valid procedures for reviewing such reports in order to identify instances in which such persons are not properly using such payments.

(ii) Clause (i) shall not apply in any case where the representative payee is a State institution. In such cases, the Commissioner of Social Security shall establish a system of accountability monitoring for institutions in each State.

---

[71] See Vol. II, 5 U.S.C. 552a.
[72] See Vol. II, P.L. 83-591, §6103.

828   SOCIAL SECURITY ACT—§ 1631(a)(2)(C)(iii)

(iii) Clause (i) shall not apply in any case where the individual entitled to such payment is a resident of a Federal institution and the representative payee is the institution.

(iv) Notwithstanding clauses (i), (ii), and (iii), the Commissioner of Social Security may require a report at any time from any representative payee, if the Commissioner of Social Security has reason to believe that the representative payee is misusing such payments.

(v) In any case in which the person described in clause (i) or (iv) receiving payments on behalf of another fails to submit a report required by the Commissioner of Social Security under clause (i) or (iv), the Commissioner may, after furnishing notice to the person and the individual entitled to the payment, require that such person appear in person at a field office of the Social Security Administration serving the area in which the individual resides in order to receive such payments.

(D)(i) Except as provided in the next sentence, a qualified organization may collect from an individual a monthly fee for expenses (including overhead) incurred by such organization in providing services performed as such individual's representative payee pursuant to subparagraph (A)(ii) if the fee does not exceed the lesser of—

(I) 10 percent of the monthly benefit involved, or

(II) $25.00 per month ($50.00 per month in any case in which an individual is described in subparagraph (A)(ii)(II).

A qualified organization may not collect a fee from an individual for any month with respect to which the Commissioner of Social Security or a court of competent jurisdiction has determined that the organization misused all or part of the individual's benefit, and any amount so collected by the qualified organization for such month shall be treated as a misused part of the individual's benefit for purposes of subparagraphs (E) and (F). The Commissioner of Social Security shall adjust annually (after 1995) each dollar amount set forth in subclause (II) of this clause under procedures providing for adjustments in the same manner and to the same extent as adjustments are provided for under the procedures used to adjust benefit amounts under section 215(i)(2)(A), except that any amount so adjusted that is not a multiple of $1.00 shall be rounded to the nearest multiple of $1.00. Any agreement providing for a fee in excess of the amount permitted under this clause shall be void and shall be treated as misuse by the organization of such individual's benefits.

(ii) For purposes of this subparagraph, the term "qualified organization" means any State or local government agency whose mission is to carry out income maintenance, social service, or health care-related activities, any State or local government agency with fiduciary responsibilities, or any certified community-based nonprofit social service agency (as defined in subparagraph (I)), if the agency, in accordance with any applicable regulations of the Commissioner of Social Security—

(I) regularly provides services as a representative payee pursuant to subparagraph (A)(ii) or section 205(j)(4) or 807 concurrently to 5 or more individuals; and

(II) demonstrates to the satisfaction of the Commissioner of Social Security that such agency is not otherwise a creditor of any such individual.

SOCIAL SECURITY ACT—§ 1631(a)(2)(F)(i)(II)   829

The Commissioner of Social Security shall prescribe regulations under which the Commissioner of Social Security may grant an exception from subclause (II) for any individual on a case-by-case basis if such exception is in the best interests of such individual.

(iii) Any qualified organization which knowingly charges or collects, directly or indirectly, any fee in excess of the maximum fee prescribed under clause (i) or makes any agreement, directly or indirectly, to charge or collect any fee in excess of such maximum fee, shall be fined in accordance with title 18, United States Code, or imprisoned not more than 6 months, or both.

(iv) In the case of an individual who is no longer eligible for benefits under this title but to whom any amount of past-due benefits under this title has not been paid, for purposes of clause (i), any amount of such past-due benefits payable in any month shall be treated as a monthly benefit referred to in clause (i)(I).

(E) RESTITUTION.—In cases where the negligent failure of the Commissioner of Social Security to investigate or monitor a representative payee results in misuse of benefits by the representative payee, the Commissioner of Social Security shall make payment to the beneficiary or the beneficiary's representative payee of an amount equal to such misused benefits. In any case in which a representative payee that—

(i) is not an individual (regardless of whether it is a "qualified organization" within the meaning of subparagraph (D)(ii)); or

(ii) is an individual who, for any month during a period when misuse occurs, serves 15 or more individuals who are beneficiaries under this title, title II, title VIII, or any combination of such titles;

misuses all or part of an individual's benefit paid to such representative payee, the Commissioner of Social Security shall pay to the beneficiary or the beneficiary's alternative representative payee an amount equal to the amount of such benefit so misused. The provisions of this subparagraph are subject to the limitations of subparagraph (H)(ii). The Commissioner of Social Security shall make a good faith effort to obtain restitution from the terminated representative payee.

(F)(i)(I) Each representative payee of an eligible individual under the age of 18 who is eligible for the payment of benefits described in subclause (II) shall establish on behalf of such individual an account in a financial institution into which such benefits shall be paid, and shall thereafter maintain such account for use in accordance with clause (ii).

(II) Benefits described in this subclause are past-due monthly benefits under this title (which, for purposes of this subclause, include State supplementary payments made by the Commissioner pursuant to an agreement under section 1616 or section 212(b) of Public Law 93-66) in an amount (after any withholding by the Commissioner for reimbursement to a State for interim assistance under subsection (g) and payment of attorney fees under subsection (d)(2)(B)) that exceeds the product of—

(aa) 6, and

(bb) the maximum monthly benefit payable under this title to an eligible individual.

830 SOCIAL SECURITY ACT—§ 1631(a)(2)(F)(ii)

(ii)(I) A representative payee shall use funds in the account established under clause (i) to pay for allowable expenses described in subclause (II).

(II) An allowable expense described in this subclause is an expense for—

(aa) education or job skills training;
(bb) personal needs assistance;
(cc) special equipment
(dd) housing modification
(ee) medical treatment;
(ff) therapy or rehabilitation; or
(gg) any other item or service that the Commissioner determines to be appropriate;

provided that such expense benefits such individual and, in the case of an expense described in item (bb), (cc), (dd), (ff), or (gg), is related to the impairment (or combination of impairments) of such individual.

(III) The use of funds from an account established under clause (i) in any manner not authorized by this clause—

(aa) by a representative payee shall be considered a misapplication of benefits for all purposes of this paragraph, and any representative payee who knowingly misapplies benefits from such an account shall be liable to the Commissioner in an amount equal to the total amount of such benefits; and

(bb) by an eligible individual who is his or her own payee shall be considered a misapplication of benefits for all purposes of this paragraph and in any case in which the individual knowingly misapplies benefits from such an account, the Commissioner shall reduce future benefits payable to such individual (or to such individual and his spouse) by an amount equal to the total amount of such benefits so misapplied.

(IV) This clause shall continue to apply to funds in the account after the child has reached age 18, regardless of whether benefits are paid directly to the beneficiary or through a representative payee.

(iii) The representative payee may deposit into the account established under clause (i) any other funds representing past due benefits under this title to the eligible individual, provided that the amount of such past due benefits is equal to or exceeds the maximum monthly benefit payable under this title to an eligible individual (including State supplementary payments made by the Commissioner pursuant to an agreement under section 1616 or section 212(b) of Public Law 93-66[73]).

(iv) The Commissioner of Social Security shall establish a system for accountability monitoring whereby such representative payee shall report, at such time and in such manner as the Commissioner shall require, on activity respecting funds in the account established pursuant to clause (i).

(G)(i) In addition to such other reviews of representative payees as the Commissioner of Social Security may otherwise conduct, the Commissioner shall provide for the periodic onsite review of any person or agency that receives the benefits payable under this title (alone or in combination with benefits payable under title II or title VIII) to another individual pursuant to the appointment of the person or agency

---

[73] See Vol. II, P.L. 93-66, §212(b).

SOCIAL SECURITY ACT—§ 1631(a)(2)(I)   831

as a representative payee under this paragraph, section 205(j), or section 807 in any case in which—

(I) the representative payee is the person who serves in the capacity with respect to 15 or more such individuals;

(II) the representative payee is a certified community-based nonprofit social service agency (as defined in subparagraph (I) of this paragraph or section 205(j)(10)); or

(III) the representative payee is an agency (other than an agency described in subclause (II)) that serves in that capacity with respect to 50 or more such individuals.

(ii) Within 120 days after the end of each fiscal year, the Commissioner shall submit to the Committee on Ways and Means of the House of Representatives and the Committee on Finance of the Senate a report on the results of periodic onsite reviews conducted during the fiscal year pursuant to clause (i) and of any other reviews of representative payees conducted during such fiscal year in connection with benefits under this title. Each such report shall describe in detail all problems identified in the reviews and any corrective action taken or planned to be taken to correct the problems, and shall include-

(I) the number of the reviews;

(II) the results of such reviews;

(III) the number of cases in which the representative payee was changed and why;

(IV) the number of cases involving the exercise of expedited, targeted oversight of the representative payee by the Commissioner conducted upon receipt of an allegation of misuse of funds, failure to pay a vendor, or a similar irregularity;

(V) the number of cases discovered in which there was a misuse of funds;

(VI) how any such cases of misuse of funds were dealt with by the Commissioner;

(VII) the final disposition of such cases of misuse of funds, including any criminal penalties imposed; and

(VIII) such other information as the Commissioner deems appropriate.

(H)(i) If the Commissioner of Social Security or a court of competent jurisdiction determines that a representative payee that is not a Federal, State, or local government agency has misused all or part of an individual's benefit that was paid to the representative payee under this paragraph, the representative payee shall be liable for the amount misused, and the amount (to the extent not repaid by the representative payee) shall be treated as an overpayment of benefits under this title to the representative payee for all purposes of this Act and related laws pertaining to the recovery of the overpayments. Subject to clause (ii), upon recovering all or any part of the amount, the Commissioner shall make payment of an amount equal to the recovered amount to such individual or such individual's alternative representative payee.

(ii) The total of the amount paid to such individual or such individual's alternative representative payee under clause (i) and the amount paid under subparagraph (E) may not exceed the total benefit amount misused by the representative payee with respect to such individual.

(I) For purposes of this paragraph, the term "certified community-based nonprofit social service agency" means a community-based non-

832   SOCIAL SECURITY ACT—§ 1631(a)(2)(I)(cont)

profit social service agency which is in compliance with requirements, under regulations which shall be prescribed by the Commissioner, for annual certification to the Commissioner that it is bonded in accordance with requirements specified by the Commissioner and that it is licensed in each State in which it serves as a representative payee (if licensing is available in the State) in accordance with requirements specified by the Commissioner. Any such annual certification shall include a copy of any independent audit on the agency which may have been performed since the previous certification.

(3) The Commissioner of Social Security may by regulations establish ranges of incomes within which a single amount of benefits under this title shall apply.

(4) The Commissioner of Social Security—

(A) may make to any individual initially applying for benefits under this title who is presumptively eligible for such benefits for the month following the date the application is filed and who is faced with financial emergency a cash advance against such benefits, including any federally-administered State supplementary payments, in an amount not exceeding the monthly amount that would be payable to an eligible individual with no other income for the first month of such presumptive eligibility, which shall be repaid through proportionate reductions in such benefits over a period of not more than 6 months; and

(B) may pay benefits under this title to an individual applying for such benefits on the basis of disability or blindness for a period not exceeding 6 months prior to the determination of such individual's disability or blindness, if such individual is presumptively disabled or blind and is determined to be otherwise eligible for such benefits, and any benefits so paid prior to such determination shall in no event be considered overpayments for purposes of subsection (b) solely because such individual is determined not to be disabled or blind.

(5) Payment of the benefit of any individual who is an aged, blind, or disabled individual solely by reason of blindness (as determined under section 1614(a)(2)) or disability (as determined under section 1614(a)(3)), and who ceases to be blind or to be under such disability, shall continue (so long as such individual is otherwise eligible) through the second month following the month in which such blindness or disability ceases.

(6) Notwithstanding any other provision of this title, payment of the benefit of any individual who is an aged, blind, or disabled individual solely by reason of blindness (as determined under section 1614(a)(2)) or disability (as determined under section 1614(a)(3)) shall not be terminated or suspended because the blindness or other physical or mental impairment, on which the individual's eligibility for such benefit is based, has or may have ceased, if—

(A) such individual is participating in a program consisting of the Ticket to Work and Self-Sufficiency Program under section 1148 or another program of vocational rehabilitation services, employment services, or other support services approved by the Commissioner of Social Security, and,

(B) the Commissioner of Social Security determines that the completion of such program, or its continuation for a specified period of time, will increase the likelihood that such individual may (following his participation in such program) be permanently removed from the blindness and disability benefit rolls.

(7)(A) In any case where—

(i) an individual is a recipient of benefits based on disability or blindness under this title,

(ii) the physical or mental impairment on the basis of which such benefits are payable is found to have ceased, not to have existed, or to no longer be disabling, and as a consequence such individual is determined not to be entitled to such benefits, and

(iii) a timely request for review or for a hearing is pending with respect to the determination that he is not so entitled,

such individual may elect (in such manner and form and within such time as the Commissioner of Social Security shall by regulations prescribe) to have the payment of such benefits continued for an additional period beginning with the first month beginning after the date of the enactment of this paragraph for which (under such determination) such benefits are no longer otherwise payable, and ending with the earlier of (I) the month preceding the month in which a decision is made after such a hearing, or (II) the month preceding the month in which no such request for review or a hearing is pending.

(B)(i) If an individual elects to have the payment of his benefits continued for an additional period under subparagraph (A), and the final decision of the Commissioner of Social Security affirms the determination that he is not entitled to such benefits, any benefits paid under this title pursuant to such election (for months in such additional period) shall be considered overpayments for all purposes of this title, except as otherwise provided in clause (ii).

(ii) If the Commissioner of Social Security determines that the individual's appeal of his termination of benefits was made in good faith, all of the benefits paid pursuant to such individual's election under subparagraph (A) shall be subject to waiver consideration under the provisions of subsection (b)(1).

(C) The provisions of subparagraphs (A) and (B) shall apply with respect to determinations (that individuals are not entitled to benefits) which are made on or after the date of the enactment of this paragraph[74], or prior to such date but only on the basis of a timely request for review or for a hearing.

(8)(A) In any case in which an administrative law judge has determined after a hearing as provided in subsection (c) that an individual is entitled to benefits based on disability or blindness under this title and the Commissioner of Social Security has not issued the Commissioner's final decision in such case within 110 days after the date of the administrative law judge's determination, such benefits shall be currently paid for the months during the period beginning with the month in which such 110-day period expires and ending with the month in which such final decision is issued.

(B) For purposes of subparagraph (A), in determining whether the 110-day period referred to in subparagraph (A) has elapsed, any period of time for which the action or inaction of such individual or such individual's representative without good cause results in the delay in the issuance of the Commissioner's final decision shall not be taken

---

[74] This paragraph was enacted October 9, 1984. [P.L. 98-460, §7(b); 98 Stat. 1083]

834   SOCIAL SECURITY ACT—§ 1631(a)(8)(B)(cont)

into account to the extent that such period of time exceeds 20 calendar days.

(C) Any benefits currently paid under this title pursuant to this paragraph (for the months described in subparagraph (A)) shall not be considered overpayments for any purposes of this title, unless payment of such benefits was fraudulently obtained.

(9) Benefits under this title shall not be denied to any individual solely by reason of the refusal of the individual to accept an amount offered as compensation for a crime of which the individual was a victim.

(10)(A) If an individual is eligible for past-due monthly benefits under this title in an amount that (after any withholding for reimbursement to a State for interim assistance under subsection (g) and payment of attorney fees under subsection (d)(2)(B)) equals or exceeds the product of—

(i) 3, and

(ii) the maximum monthly benefit payable under this title to an eligible individual (or, if appropriate, to an eligible individual and eligible spouse),

then the payment of such past-due benefits (after any such reimbursement to a State and payment of attorney fees under subsection (d)(2)(B)) shall be made in installments as provided in subparagraph (B).

(B)(i) The payment of past-due benefits subject to this subparagraph shall be made in not to exceed 3 installments that are made at 6-month intervals.

(ii) Except as provided in clause (iii), the amount of each of the first and second installments may not exceed an amount equal to the product of clauses (i) and (ii) of subparagraph (A).

(iii) In the case of an individual who has—

(I) outstanding debt attributable to—

(aa) food,

(bb) clothing,

(cc) shelter, or

(dd) medically necessary services, supplies or equipment, or medicine; or

(II) current expenses or expenses anticipated in the near term attributable to—

(aa) medically necessary services, supplies or equipment, or medicine, or

(bb) the purchase of a home, and

such debt or expenses are not subject to reimbursement by a public assistance program, the Secretary under title XVIII, a State plan approved under title XIX, or any private entity legally liable to provide payment pursuant to an insurance policy, pre–paid plan, or other arrangement, the limitation specified in clause (ii) may be exceeded by an amount equal to the total of such debt and expenses.

(C) This paragraph shall not apply to any individual who, at the time of the Commissioner's determination that such individual is eligible for the payment of past-due monthly benefits under this title—

(i) is afflicted with a medically determinable impairment that is expected to result in death within 12 months; or

SOCIAL SECURITY ACT—§ 1631(b)(1)(B) 835

(ii) is ineligible for benefits under this title and the Commissioner determines that such individual is likely to remain ineligible for the next 12 months.

(D) For purposes of this paragraph, the term "benefits under this title" includes supplementary payments pursuant to an agreement for Federal administration under section 1616(a), and payments pursuant to an agreement entered into under section 212(b) of Public Law 93-66.

Overpayments and Underpayments

(b)(1)(A) Whenever the Commissioner of Social Security finds that more or less than the correct amount of benefits has been paid with respect to any individual, proper adjustment or recovery shall, subject to the succeeding provisions of this subsection, be made by appropriate adjustments in future payments to such individual or by recovery from such individual or his eligible spouse (or from the estate of either) or by payment to such individual or his eligible spouse, or, if such individual is deceased, by payment—

(i) to any surviving spouse of such individual, whether or not the individual's eligible spouse, if (within the meaning of the first sentence of section 202(i)) such surviving husband or wife was living in the same household with the individual at the time of his death or within the 6 months immediately preceding the month of such death, or

(ii) if such individual was a disabled or blind child who was living with his parent or parents at the time of his death or within the 6 months immediately preceding the month of such death, to such parent or parents.

(B) The Commissioner of Social Security (i) shall make such provision as the Commissioner finds appropriate in the case of payment of more than the correct amount of benefits with respect to an individual with a view to avoiding penalizing such individual or his eligible spouse who was without fault in connection with the overpayment, if adjustment or recovery on account of such overpayment in such case would defeat the purposes of this title, or be against equity and good conscience, or (because of the small amount involved) impede efficient or effective administration of this title, and (ii) shall in any event make the adjustment or recovery (in the case of payment of more than the correct amount of benefits), in the case of an individual or eligible spouse receiving monthly benefit payments under this title (including supplementary payments of the type described in section 1616(a) and payments pursuant to an agreement entered into under section 212(a) of Public Law 93-66[75]), in amounts which in the aggregate do not exceed (for any month) the lesser of (I) the amount of his or their benefit under this title for that month or (II) an amount equal to 10 percent of his or their income for that month (including such benefit but excluding payments under title II when recovery is made from title II payments pursuant to section 1147 and excluding income excluded pursuant to section 1612(b)), and in the case of an individual or eligible spouse to whom a lump sum is payable under this title (including un-

---

[75] See Vol. II, P.L. 93-66, §212(a).

836   SOCIAL SECURITY ACT—§ 1631(b)(1)(B)(cont)

der section 1616(a) of this Act or under an agreement entered into under section 212(a) of Public Law 93-66) shall, as at least one means of recovering such overpayment, make the adjustment or recovery from the lump sum payment in an amount equal to not less than the lesser of the amount of the overpayment or the lump sum payment, unless fraud, willful misrepresentation, or concealment of material information was involved on the part of the individual or spouse in connection with the overpayment, or unless the individual requests that such adjustment or recovery be made at a higher or lower rate and the Commissioner of Social Security determines that adjustment or recovery at such rate is justified and appropriate. The availability (in the case of an individual who has been paid more than the correct amount of benefits) of procedures for adjustment or recovery at a limited rate under clause (ii) of the preceding sentence shall not, in and of itself, prevent or restrict the provision (in such case) of more substantial relief under clause (i) of such sentence.

(2) Notwithstanding any other provision of this section, when any payment of more than the correct amount is made to or on behalf of an individual who has died, and such payment—

(A) is made by direct deposit to a financial institution;

(B) is credited by the financial institution to a joint account of the deceased individual and another person; and

(C) such other person is the surviving spouse of the deceased individual, and was eligible for a payment under this title (including any State supplementation payment paid by the Commissioner of Social Security) as an eligible spouse (or as either member of an eligible couple) for the month in which the deceased individual died,

the amount of such payment in excess of the correct amount shall be treated as a payment of more than the correct amount to such other person. If any payment of more than the correct amount is made to a representative payee on behalf of an individual after the individual's death, the representative payee shall be liable for the repayment of the overpayment, and the Commissioner of Social Security shall establish an overpayment control record under the social security account number of the representative payee.

(3) If any overpayment with respect to an individual (or an individual and his or her spouse) is attributable solely to the ownership or possession by such individual (and spouse if any) of resources having a value which exceeds the applicable dollar figure specified in paragraph (1)(B) or (2)(B) of section 1611(a) by $50 or less, such individual (and spouse if any) shall be deemed for purposes of the second sentence of paragraph (1) to have been without fault in connection with the overpayment, and no adjustment or recovery shall be made under the first sentence of such paragraph, unless the Commissioner of Social Security finds that the failure of such individual (and spouse if any) to report such value correctly and in a timely manner was knowing and willful.

(4)(A) With respect to any delinquent amount, the Commissioner of Social Security may use the collection practices described in sections 3711(f), 3716, 3717, and 3718 of title 31, United States Code, and in

SOCIAL SECURITY ACT—§ 1631(c)(1)(A)   837

section 5514 of title 5, United States Code[76], all as in effect immediately after the enactment of the Debt Collection Improvement Act of 1996[77].

(B) For purposes of subparagraph (A), the term "delinquent amount" means an amount—

(i) in excess of the correct amount of payment under this title;

(ii) paid to a person after such person has attained 18 years of age; and

(iii) determined by the Commissioner of Social Security, under regulations, to be otherwise unrecoverable under this section after such person ceases to be a beneficiary under this title.

(5) For payments for which adjustments are made by reason of a retroactive payment of benefits under title II, see section 1127.

(6) For provisions relating to the cross-program recovery of overpayments made under programs administered by the Commissioner of Social Security, see section 1147.

Hearings and Review

(c)(1)(A) The Commissioner of Social Security is directed to make findings of fact, and decisions as to the rights of any individual applying for payment under this title. Any such decision by the Commissioner of Social Security which involves a determination of disability and which is in whole or in part unfavorable to such individual shall contain a statement of the case, in understandable language, setting forth a discussion of the evidence, and stating the Commissioner's determination and the reason or reasons upon which it is based. The Commissioner of Social Security shall provide reasonable notice and opportunity for a hearing to any individual who is or claims to be an eligible individual or eligible spouse and is in disagreement with any determination under this title with respect to eligibility of such individual for benefits, or the amount of such individual's benefits, if such individual requests a hearing on the matter in disagreement within sixty days after notice of such determination is received, and, if a hearing is held, shall, on the basis of evidence adduced at the hearing affirm, modify, or reverse the Commissioner's findings of fact and such decision. The Commissioner of Social Security is further authorized, on the Commissioner's own motion, to hold such hearings and to conduct such investigations and other proceedings as the Commissioner may deem necessary or proper for the administration of this title. In the course of any hearing, investigation, or other proceeding, the Commissioner may administer oaths and affirmations, examine witnesses, and receive evidence. Evidence may be received at any hearing before the Commissioner of Social Security even though inadmissible under the rules of evidence applicable to court procedure. The Commissioner of Social Security shall specifically take into account any physical, mental, educational, or linguistic limitation of such individual (including any lack of facility with the English language) in determining, with respect to the eligibility of such individual for benefits

---

[76] See Vol. II, 31 U.S.C. 3711(f), 3716, 3717 and 3718.
See Vol. II, 5 U.S.C. 5514.
[77] The date of enactment for the Debt Collection Improvement Act of 1996, §31001 of P.L. 104-134 was April 26, 1996.

838   SOCIAL SECURITY ACT—§ 1631(c)(1)(A)(cont)

under this title, whether such individual acted in good faith or was at fault, and in determining fraud, deception, or intent.

(B)(i) A failure to timely request review of an initial adverse determination with respect to an application for any payment under this title or an adverse determination on reconsideration of such an initial determination shall not serve as a basis for denial of a subsequent application for any payment under this title if the applicant demonstrates that the applicant, or any other individual referred to in subparagraph (A), failed to so request such a review acting in good faith reliance upon incorrect, incomplete, or misleading information, relating to the consequences of reapplying for payments in lieu of seeking review of an adverse determination, provided by any officer or employee of the Social Security Administration or any State agency acting under section 221.

(ii) In any notice of an adverse determination with respect to which a review may be requested under subparagraph (A), the Commissioner of Social Security shall describe in clear and specific language the effect on possible eligibility to receive payments under this title of choosing to reapply in lieu of requesting review of the determination.

(2) Determination on the basis of such hearing, except to the extent that the matter in disagreement involves a disability (within the meaning of section 1614(a)(3)), shall be made within ninety days after the individual requests the hearing as provided in paragraph (1).

(3) The final determination of the Commissioner of Social Security after a hearing under paragraph (1) shall be subject to judicial review as provided in section 205(g) to the same extent as the Commissioner's final determinations under section 205.

Procedures; Prohibitions of Assignments; Representation of Claimants

(d)(1) The provisions of section 207 and subsections (a), (d), and (e) of section 205 shall apply with respect to this part to the same extent as they apply in the case of title II.

(2)[78](A) The provisions of section 206 (other than subsections (a)(4) and (d) thereof) shall apply to this part to the same extent as they apply in the case of title II, except that such section shall be applied—

(i) by substituting in subparagraphs (A)(ii)(I) and (D)(i) of subsection (a)(2), the phrase "(as determined before any applicable reduction under section 1631(g), and reduced by the amount of any reduction in benefits under this title or title II made pursuant to section 1127(a))" for the parenthetical phrase contained therein;

(ii) by substituting, in subsections (a)(2)(B) and (b)(1)(B)(i), the phrase "paragraph (7)(A) or (8)(A) of section 1631(a) or the requirements of due process of law" for the phrase "subsection (g) or (h) of section 223";

(iii) by substituting, in subsection (a)(2)(C)(i), the phrase "under title II" for the phrase "under title XVI";

---

[78] See Vol. II, P.L. 108-203, §302, with respect to the temporary extension of attorney fee payment system to Title XVI claims; §303, with respect to a nationwide demonstration project providing for extension of fee withholding procedures to non-attorney representatives; and §304, with respect to a GAO study regarding the fee payment process for claimant representatives.

SOCIAL SECURITY ACT—§ 1631(d)(2)(C)(iii)   839

(iv) by substituting, in subsection (b)(1)(A), the phrase "pay the amount of such fee" for the phrase "certify the amount of such fee for payment" and by striking, in subsection (b)(1)(A), the phrase "or certified for payment"; and

(v) by substituting, in subsection (b)(1)(B)(ii), the phrase "deemed to be such amounts as determined before any applicable reduction under section 1631(g), and reduced by the amount of any reduction in benefits under this title or title II made pursuant to section 1127(a)" for the phrase "determined before any applicable reduction under section 1127(a))".

(B) Subject to subparagraph (C), if the claimant is determined to be entitled to past-due benefits under this title and the person representing the claimant is an attorney, the Commissioner of Social Security shall pay out of such past-due benefits to such attorney an amount equal to the lesser of—

(i) so much of the maximum fee as does not exceed 25 percent of such past-due benefits (as determined before any applicable reduction under section 1631(g) and reduced by the amount of any reduction in benefits under this title or title II pursuant to section 1127(a)), or

(ii) the amount of past-due benefits available after any applicable reductions under sections 1631(g) and 1127(a).

(C)(i) Whenever a fee for services is required to be paid to an attorney from a claimant's past-due benefits pursuant to subparagraph (B), the Commissioner shall impose on the attorney an assessment calculated in accordance with clause (ii).

(ii)(I) The amount of an assessment under clause (i) shall be equal to the product obtained by multiplying the amount of the representative's fee that would be required to be paid by subparagraph (B) before the application of this subparagraph, by the percentage specified in subclause (II), except that the maximum amount of the assessment may not exceed $75. In the case of any calendar year beginning after the amendments made by section 302 of the Social Security Protection Act of 2003 take effect[79], the dollar amount specified in the preceding sentence (including a previously adjusted amount) shall be adjusted annually under the procedures used to adjust benefit amounts under section 215(i)(2)(A)(ii), except such adjustment shall be based on the higher of $75 or the previously adjusted amount that would have been in effect for December of the preceding year, but for the rounding of such amount pursuant to the following sentence. Any amount so adjusted that is not a multiple of $1 shall be rounded to the next lowest multiple of $1, but in no case less than $75.

(II) The percentage specified in this subclause is such percentage rate as the Commissioner determines is necessary in order to achieve full recovery of the costs of determining and approving fees to attorneys from the past-due benefits of claimants, but not in excess of 6.3 percent.

(iii) The Commissioner may collect the assessment imposed on an attorney under clause (i) by offset from the amount of the fee otherwise required by subparagraph (B) to be paid to the attorney from a claimant's past-due benefits.

---

[79] See Vol. II, P.L. 108-203, §302(c).

840   SOCIAL SECURITY ACT—§ 1631(d)(2)(C)(iv)

(iv) An attorney subject to an assessment under clause (i) may not, directly or indirectly, request or otherwise obtain reimbursement for such assessment from the claimant whose claim gave rise to the assessment.

(v) Assessments on attorneys collected under this subparagraph shall be deposited as miscellaneous receipts in the general fund of the Treasury.

(vi) The assessments authorized under this subparagraph shall be collected and available for obligation only to the extent and in the amount provided in advance in appropriations Acts. Amounts so appropriated are authorized to remain available until expended, for administrative expenses in carrying out this title and related laws.

(D) The Commissioner of Social Security shall notify each claimant in writing, together with the notice to such claimant of an adverse determination, of the options for obtaining attorneys to represent individuals in presenting their cases before the Commissioner of Social Security. Such notification shall also advise the claimant of the availability to qualifying claimants of legal services organizations which provide legal services free of charge.

Applications and Furnishing of Information[80]

(e)(1)(A) The Commissioner of Social Security shall, subject to subparagraph (B) and subsection (j), prescribe such requirements with respect to the filing of applications, the suspension or termination of assistance, the furnishing of other data and material, and the reporting of events and changes in circumstances, as may be necessary for the effective and efficient administration of this title.

(B)(i) The requirements prescribed by the Commissioner of Social Security pursuant to subparagraph (A) shall require that eligibility for benefits under this title will not be determined solely on the basis of declarations by the applicant concerning eligibility factors or other relevant facts, and that relevant information will be verified from independent or collateral sources and additional information obtained as necessary in order to assure that such benefits are only provided to eligible individuals (or eligible spouses) and that the amounts of such benefits are correct. For this purpose and for purposes of federally administered supplementary payments of the type described in section 1616(a) of this Act (including payments pursuant to an agreement entered into under section 212(a) of Public Law 93-66[81]), the Commissioner of Social Security shall, as may be necessary, request and utilize information available pursuant to section 6103(l)(7) of the Internal Revenue Code of 1954[82], and any information which may be available from State systems under section 1137 of this Act, and shall comply with the requirements applicable to States (with respect to information available pursuant to section 6103(l)(7)(B) of such Code) under subsections (a)(6) and (c) of such section 1137.

---

[80] See Vol. II, P.L. 88-525, §11(i), with respect to inquiry into the need for food stamps.
See Vol. II, P.L. 95-630, §§1101-1121, with respect to an individual's right to financial privacy.
[81] See Vol. II, P.L. 93-66, §212(a).
[82] See Vol. II, P.L. 83-591, §6107)(l)(7).

SOCIAL SECURITY ACT—§ 1631(e)(1)(B)(ii)(V)   841

(ii)[83](I) The Commissioner of Social Security may require each applicant for, or recipient of, benefits under this title to provide authorization by the applicant or recipient (or by any other person whose income or resources are material to the determination of the eligibility of the applicant or recipient for such benefits) for the Commissioner to obtain (subject to the cost reimbursement requirements of section 1115(a) of the Right to Financial Privacy Act) from any financial institution (within the meaning of section 1101(1) of such Act) any financial record (within the meaning of section 1101(2) of such Act[84]) held by the institution with respect to the applicant or recipient (or any such other person) whenever the Commissioner determines the record is needed in connection with a determination with respect to such eligibility or the amount of such benefits.

(II) Notwithstanding section 1104(a)(1) of the Right to Financial Privacy Act[85], an authorization provided by an applicant or recipient (or any other person whose income or resources are material to the determination of the eligibility of the applicant or recipient) pursuant to subclause (I) of this clause shall remain effective until the earliest of—

> (aa) the rendering of a final adverse decision on the applicant's application for eligibility for benefits under this title;
> (bb) the cessation of the recipient's eligibility for benefits under this title; or
> (cc) the express revocation by the applicant or recipient
(or such other person referred to in subclause (I)) of the authorization, in a written notification to the Commissioner.

(III)(aa) An authorization obtained by the Commissioner of Social Security pursuant to this clause shall be considered to meet the requirements of the Right to Financial Privacy Act for purposes of section 1103(a) of such Act, and need not be furnished to the financial institution, notwithstanding section 1104(a) of such Act.

(bb) The certification requirements of section 1103(b) of the Right to Financial Privacy Act[86] shall not apply to requests by the Commissioner of Social Security pursuant to an authorization provided under this clause.

(cc) A request by the Commissioner pursuant to an authorization provided under this clause is deemed to meet the requirements of section 1104(a)(3) of the Right to Financial Privacy Act and the flush language of section 1102 of such Act[87].

(IV) The Commissioner shall inform any person who provides authorization pursuant to this clause of the duration and scope of the authorization.

(V) If an applicant for, or recipient of, benefits under this title (or any such other person referred to in subclause (I)) refuses to provide, or revokes, any authorization made by the applicant or recipient for the Commissioner of Social Security to obtain from any financial institution any financial record, the Commissioner may, on that basis,

---

[83] See Vol. II, P.L. 110-90, §4, with respect to the extension of the SSI Web-based Asset Demonstration Project to the Medicaid program.
[84] See Vol. II, P.L. 95-630, §§1101(1), 1102(2), and 1115(a).
[85] See Vol. II, P.L. 95-630, §1104(a)(1).
[86] See Vol. II, P.L. 95-630, §1103(b).
[87] See Vol. II, P.L. 95-630, §§1102(a)(3) and 1104(a)(3).

842   SOCIAL SECURITY ACT—§ 1631(e)(1)(B)(ii)(V)(cont)

determine that the applicant or recipient is ineligible for benefits under this title.

(C) For purposes of making determinations under section 1611(e), the requirements prescribed by the Commissioner of Social Security pursuant to subparagraph (A) of this paragraph shall require each administrator of a nursing home, extended care facility, or intermediate care facility, within 2 weeks after the admission of any eligible individual or eligible spouse receiving benefits under this title, to transmit to the Commissioner a report of the admission.

(2) In case of the failure by any individual to submit a report of events and changes in circumstances relevant to eligibility for or amount of benefits under this title as required by the Commissioner of Social Security under paragraph (1), or delay by any individual in submitting a report as so required, the Commissioner of Social Security (in addition to taking any other action the Commissioner may consider appropriate under paragraph (1)) shall reduce any benefits which may subsequently become payable to such individual under this title by—

(A) $25 in the case of the first such failure or delay,

(B) $50 in the case of the second such failure or delay, and

(C) $100 in the case of the third or a subsequent such failure or delay,

except where the individual was without fault or good cause for such failure or delay existed.

(3) The Commissioner of Social Security shall provide a method of making payments under this title to an eligible individual who does not reside in a permanent dwelling or does not have a fixed home or mailing address.

(4) A translation into English by a third party of a statement made in a foreign language by an applicant for or recipient of benefits under this title shall not be regarded as reliable for any purpose under this title unless the third party, under penalty of perjury—

(A) certifies that the translation is accurate; and

(B) discloses the nature and scope of the relationship between the third party and the applicant or recipient, as the case may be.

(5) In any case in which it is determined to the satisfaction of the Commissioner of Social Security that an individual failed as of any date to apply for benefits under this title by reason of misinformation provided to such individual by any officer or employee of the Social Security Administration relating to such individual's eligibility for benefits under this title, such individual shall be deemed to have applied for such benefits on the later of—

(A) the date on which such misinformation was provided to such individual, or

(B) the date on which such individual met all requirements for entitlement to such benefits (other than application therefor).

(6) In any case in which an individual visits a field office of the Social Security Administration and represents during the visit to an officer or employee of the Social Security Administration in the office that the individual's visit is occasioned by—

(A) the receipt of a notice from the Social Security Administration indicating a time limit for response by the individual, or

(B) the theft, loss, or nonreceipt of a benefit payment under this title, the Commissioner of Social Security shall ensure that the individual is granted a face-to-face interview at the office with an officer or employee of the Social Security Administration before the close of business on the day of the visit.

(7)(A)(i) The Commissioner of Social Security shall immediately redetermine the eligibility of an individual for benefits under this title if there is reason to believe that fraud or similar fault was involved in the application of the individual for such benefits, unless a United States attorney, or equivalent State prosecutor, with jurisdiction over potential or actual related criminal cases, certifies, in writing, that there is a substantial risk that such action by the Commissioner of Social Security with regard to recipients in a particular investigation would jeopardize the criminal prosecution of a person involved in a suspected fraud.

(ii) When redetermining the eligibility, or making an initial determination of eligibility, of an individual for benefits under this title, the Commissioner of Social Security shall disregard any evidence if there is reason to believe that fraud or similar fault was involved in the providing of such evidence.

(B) For purposes of subparagraph (A), similar fault is involved with respect to a determination if—

(i) an incorrect or incomplete statement that is material to the determination is knowingly made; or

(ii) information that is material to the determination is knowingly concealed.

(C) If, after redetermining the eligibility of an individual for benefits under this title, the Commissioner of Social Security determines that there is insufficient evidence to support such eligibility, the Commissioner of Social Security may terminate such eligibility and may treat benefits paid on the basis of such insufficient evidence as overpayments.

(8)(A) The Commissioner of Social Security shall request the Immigration and Naturalization Service or the Centers for Disease Control to provide the Commissioner of Social Security with whatever medical information, identification information, and employment history either such entity has with respect to any alien who has applied for benefits under title XVI to the extent that the information is relevant to any determination relating to eligibility for such benefits under title XVI.

(B) Subparagraph (A) shall not be construed to prevent the Commissioner of Social Security from adjudicating the case before receiving such information.

(9) Notwithstanding any other provision of law, the Commissioner shall, at least 4 times annually and upon request of the Immigration and Naturalization Service (hereafter in this paragraph referred to as the "Service"), furnish the Service with the name and address of, and other identifying information on, any individual who the Commissioner knows is not lawfully present in the United States, and shall ensure that each agreement entered into under section 1616(a) with a State provides that the State shall furnish such information at such times with respect to any individual who the State knows is not lawfully present in the United States.

844 SOCIAL SECURITY ACT—§ 1631(f)

Furnishing of Information by Other Agencies[88]

(f) The head of any Federal agency shall provide such information as the Commissioner of Social Security needs for purposes of determining eligibility for or amount of benefits, or verifying other information with respect thereto.

Reimbursement to States for Interim Assistance Payments

(g)(1) Notwithstanding subsection (d)(1) and subsection (b) as it relates to the payment of less than the correct amount of benefits, the Commissioner of Social Security may, upon written authorization by an individual, withhold benefits due with respect to that individual and may pay to a State (or a political subdivision thereof if agreed to by the Commissioner of Social Security and the State) from the benefits withheld an amount sufficient to reimburse the State (or political subdivision) for interim assistance furnished on behalf of the individual by the State (or political subdivision).

(2) For purposes of this subsection, the term "benefits" with respect to any individual means supplemental security income benefits under this title, and any State supplementary payments under section 1616 or under section 212 of Public Law 93-66[89] which the Commissioner of Social Security makes on behalf of a State (or political subdivision thereof), that the Commissioner of Social Security has determined to be due with respect to the individual at the time the Commissioner of Social Security makes the first payment of benefits with respect to the period described in clause (A) or (B) of paragraph (3). A cash advance made pursuant to subsection (a)(4)(A) shall not be considered as the first payment of benefits for purposes of the preceding sentence.

(3) For purposes of this subsection, the term "interim assistance" with respect to any individual means assistance financed from State or local funds and furnished for meeting basic needs (A) during the period, beginning with the month following the month in which the individual filed an application for benefits (as defined in paragraph (2)), for which he was eligible for such benefits, or (B) during the period beginning with the first month for which the individual's benefits (as defined in paragraph (2)) have been terminated or suspended if the individual was subsequently found to have been eligible for such benefits.

(4) In order for a State to receive reimbursement under the provisions of paragraph (1), the State shall have in effect an agreement with the Commissioner of Social Security which shall provide—

> (A) that if the Commissioner of Social Security makes payment to the State (or a political subdivision of the State as provided for under the agreement) in reimbursement for interim assistance (as defined in paragraph (3)) for any individual in an amount greater than the reimbursable amount authorized by paragraph (1), the State (or political subdivision) shall pay to the individual the balance of such payment in excess of the reimbursable amount as expeditiously as possible, but in any event within ten working days or a shorter period specified in the agreement; and

---

[88] See Vol. II, P.L. 95-630, §§1101-1121, with respect to an individual's right to financial privacy.
[89] See Vol. II, P.L. 93-66, §212.

SOCIAL SECURITY ACT—§ 1631(i)(2)   845

    (B) that the State will comply with such other rules as the Commissioner of Social Security finds necessary to achieve efficient and effective administration of this subsection and to carry out the purposes of the program established by this title, including protection of hearing rights for any individual aggrieved by action taken by the State (or political subdivision) pursuant to this subsection.

    (5) The provisions of subsection (c) shall not be applicable to any disagreement concerning payment by the Commissioner of Social Security to a State pursuant to the preceding provisions of this subsection nor the amount retained by the State (or political subdivision).

Payment of Certain Travel Expenses[90]

    (h) The Commissioner of Social Security shall pay travel expenses, either on an actual cost or commuted basis, to individuals for travel incident to medical examinations requested by the Commissioner of Social Security in connection with disability determinations under this title, and to parties, their representatives, and all reasonably necessary witnesses for travel within the United States (as defined in section 1614(e)) to attend reconsideration interviews and proceedings before administrative law judges with respect to any determination under this title. The amount available under the preceding sentence for payment for air travel by any person shall not exceed the coach fare for air travel between the points involved unless the use of first-class accommodations is required (as determined under regulations of the Commissioner of Social Security) because of such person's health condition or the unavailability of alternative accommodations; and the amount available for payment for other travel by any person shall not exceed the cost of travel (between the points involved) by the most economical and expeditious means of transportation appropriate to such person's health condition, as specified in such regulations. The amount available for payment under this subsection for travel by a representative to attend an administrative proceeding before an administrative law judge or other adjudicator shall not exceed the maximum amount allowable under this subsection for such travel originating within the geographic area of the office having jurisdiction over such proceeding.

Payment to States With Respect to Certain Unnegotiated Checks

    (i)(1) The Secretary of the Treasury shall, on a monthly basis, notify the Commissioner of Social Security of all benefit checks issued under this title which include amounts representing State supplementary payments as described in paragraph (2) and which have not been presented for payment within one hundred and eighty days after the day on which they were issued.

    (2) The Commissioner of Social Security shall from time to time determine the amount representing the total of the State supplementary payments made pursuant to agreements under section 1616(a) of this

---

[90] See Vol. II, P.L. 102-394; 106 Stat.1807, with respect to limitation on administrative expenses.

846 SOCIAL SECURITY ACT—§ 1631(i)(2)(cont)

Act and under section 212(b) of Public Law 93-66[91] which is included in all such benefit checks not presented for payment within one hundred and eighty days after the day on which they were issued, and shall pay each State (or credit each State with) an amount equal to that State's share of all such amount. Amounts not paid to the States shall be returned to the appropriation from which they were originally paid.

(3) The Commissioner of Social Security, upon notice from the Secretary of the Treasury under paragraph (1), shall notify any State having an agreement described in paragraph (2) of all such benefit checks issued under that State's agreement which were not presented for payment within one hundred and eighty days after the day on which they were issued.

(4) The Commissioner of Social Security shall, to the maximum extent feasible, investigate the whereabouts and eligibility of the individuals whose benefit checks were not presented for payment within one hundred and eighty days after the day on which they were issued.

Application and Review Requirements for Certain Individuals

(j)(1) Notwithstanding any provision of section 1611 or 1619, any individual who—

(A) was an eligible individual (or eligible spouse) under section 1611 or was eligible for benefits under or pursuant to section 1619, and

(B) who, after such eligibility, is ineligible for benefits under or pursuant to both such sections for a period of 12 consecutive months (or 24 consecutive months, in the case of such an individual whose ineligibility for benefits under or pursuant to both such sections is a result of being called to active duty pursuant to section 12301(d) or 12302 of title 10, United States Code[92], or section 502(f) of title 32, United States Code[93])

may not thereafter become eligible for benefits under or pursuant to either such section until the individual has reapplied for benefits under section 1611 and been determined to be eligible for benefits under such section, or has filed a request for reinstatement of eligibility under subsection (p)(2) and been determined to be eligible for reinstatement.

(2)(A) Notwithstanding any provision of section 1611 or section 1619 (other than subsection (c) thereof), any individual who was eligible for benefits pursuant to section 1619(b), and who—

(i)(I) on the basis of the same impairment on which his or her eligibility under such section 1619(b) was based becomes eligible (other than pursuant to a request for reinstatement under subsection (p)) for benefits under section 1611 or 1619(a) for a month that follows a period during which the individual was ineligible for benefits under sections 1611 and 1619(a), and

(II) has earned income (other than income excluded pursuant to section 1612(b)) for any month in the 12-month period preceding such month that is equal to or in excess of the amount that

---

[91] See Vol. II, P.L. 93-66, §212.
[92] See Vol. II, 10 U.S.C. 12301(d) and 12302.
[93] See Vol. II, 32 U.S.C. 502(f).

SOCIAL SECURITY ACT—§ 1631(l)(1)

847

would cause him or her to be ineligible for payments under section 1611(b) for that month (if he or she were otherwise eligible for such payments); or

(ii)(I) on the basis of the same impairment on which his or her eligibility under such section 1619(b) was based becomes eligible under section 1619(b) for a month that follows a period during which the individual was ineligible under section 1611 and section 1619, and

(II) has earned income (other than income excluded pursuant to section 1612(b)) for such month or for any month in the 12-month period preceding such month that is equal to or in excess of the amount that would cause him or her to be ineligible for payments under section 1611(b) for that month (if he or she were otherwise eligible for such payments);

shall, upon becoming eligible (as described in clause (i)(I) or (ii)(I)), be subject to a prompt review of the type described in section 1614(a)(4).

(B) If the Commissioner of Social Security determines pursuant to a review required by subparagraph (A) that the impairment upon which the eligibility of an individual is based has ceased, does not exist, or is not disabling, such individual may not thereafter become eligible for a benefit under or pursuant to section 1611 or section 1619 until the individual has reapplied for benefits under section 1611 and been determined to be eligible for benefits under such section.

Notifications to Applicants and Recipients

(k) The Commissioner of Social Security shall notify an individual receiving benefits under section 1611 on the basis of disability or blindness of his or her potential eligibility for benefits under or pursuant to section 1619—

(1) at the time of the initial award of benefits to the individual under section 1611 (if the individual has attained the age of 18 at the time of such initial award), and

(2) at the earliest time after an initial award of benefits to an individual under section 1611 that the individual's earned income for a month (other than income excluded pursuant to section 1612(b)) is $200 or more, and periodically thereafter so long as such individual has earned income (other than income so excluded) of $200 or more per month.

Special Notice to Blind Individuals with Respect to Hearings and Other Official Actions

(l)(1) In any case where an individual who is applying for or receiving benefits under this title on the basis of blindness is entitled (under subsection (c) or otherwise) to receive notice from the Commissioner of Social Security of any decision or determination made or other action taken or proposed to be taken with respect to his or her rights under this title, such individual shall at his or her election be entitled either (A) to receive a supplementary notice of such decision, determination, or action, by telephone, within 5 working days after the initial notice is mailed, (B) to receive the initial notice in the form of a certified letter, or (C) to receive notification by some alternative procedure

848   SOCIAL SECURITY ACT—§ 1631(l)(1)(cont)

established by the Commissioner of Social Security and agreed to by the individual.

(2) The election under paragraph (1) may be made at any time; but an opportunity to make such an election shall in any event be given (A) to every individual who is an applicant for benefits under this title on the basis of blindness, at the time of his or her application, and (B) to every individual who is a recipient of such benefits on the basis of blindness, at the time of each redetermination of his or her eligibility. Such an election, once made by an individual, shall apply with respect to all notices of decisions, determinations, and actions which such individual may thereafter be entitled to receive under this title until such time as it is revoked or changed.

Pre-release Procedures for Institutionalized Persons

(m) The Commissioner of Social Security shall develop a system under which an individual can apply for supplemental security income benefits under this title prior to the discharge or release of the individual from a public institution.

Concurrent SSI and Food Stamp Applications by Institutionalized Individuals

(n) The Commissioner of Social Security and the Secretary of Agriculture shall develop a procedure under which an individual who applies for supplemental security income benefits under this section shall also be permitted to apply at the same time for participation in the supplemental nutrition assistance program[94] authorized under the Food and Nutrition Act of 2008[95] (7 U.S.C. 2011 et seq.).

Notice Requirements

(o) The Commissioner of Social Security shall take such actions as are necessary to ensure that any notice to one or more individuals issued pursuant to this title by the Commissioner of Social Security or by a State agency—
    (1) is written in simple and clear language, and
    (2) includes the address and telephone number of the local office
of the Social Security Administration which serves the recipient. In the case of any such notice which is not generated by a local servicing office, the requirements of paragraph (2) shall be treated as satisfied if such notice includes the address of the local office of the Social Security Administration which services the recipient of the notice and a telephone number through which such office can be reached.

---

[94] P.L. 110-246, §4002(b)(1)(A), struck out "food stamp program"; and substituted "supplemental nutrition assistance program", effective October 1, 2008.
    P.L. 110-234, §4002(b)(1)(A), which made the same amendment was repealed, effective May 22, 2008 pursuant to P.L. 110-246, §4(a).
[95] P.L. 88-525.
    P.L. 110-246, §4002(b)(1)(B), struck out "Food Stamp Act"; and substituted "Food and Nutrition Act of 2008", effective October 1, 2008.
    P.L. 110-234, §4002(b)(1)(B), which made the same amendment was repealed, effective May 22, 2008 pursuant to P.L. 110-246, §4(a).

SOCIAL SECURITY ACT—§ 1631(p)(4)(B)(ii)   849

(p)(1)(A) Eligibility for benefits under this title shall be reinstated in any case where the Commissioner determines that an individual described in subparagraph (B) has filed a request for reinstatement meeting the requirements of paragraph (2)(A) during the period prescribed in subparagraph (C). Reinstatement of eligibility shall be in accordance with the terms of this subsection.

(B) An individual is described in this subparagraph if—

(i) prior to the month in which the individual files a request for reinstatement—

(I) the individual was eligible for benefits under this title on the basis of blindness or disability pursuant to an application filed therefor; and

(II) the individual thereafter was ineligible for such benefits due to earned income (or earned and unearned income) for a period of 12 or more consecutive months;

(ii) the individual is blind or disabled and the physical or mental impairment that is the basis for the finding of blindness or disability is the same as (or related to) the physical or mental impairment that was the basis for the finding of blindness or disability that gave rise to the eligibility described in clause (i);

(iii) the individual's blindness or disability renders the individual unable to perform substantial gainful activity; and

(iv) the individual satisfies the nonmedical requirements for eligibility for benefits under this title.

(C)(i) Except as provided in clause (ii), the period prescribed in this subparagraph with respect to an individual is 60 consecutive months beginning with the month following the most recent month for which the individual was eligible for a benefit under this title (including section 1619) prior to the period of ineligibility described in subparagraph (B)(i)(II).

(ii) In the case of an individual who fails to file a reinstatement request within the period prescribed in clause (i), the Commissioner may extend the period if the Commissioner determines that the individual had good cause for the failure to so file.

(2)(A)(i) A request for reinstatement shall be filed in such form, and containing such information, as the Commissioner may prescribe.

(ii) A request for reinstatement shall include express declarations by the individual that the individual meets the requirements specified in clauses (ii) through (iv) of paragraph (1)(B).

(B) A request for reinstatement filed in accordance with subparagraph (A) may constitute an application for benefits in the case of any individual who the Commissioner determines is not eligible for reinstated benefits under this subsection.

(3) In determining whether an individual meets the requirements of paragraph (1)(B)(ii), the provisions of section 1614(a)(4) shall apply.

(4)(A) Eligibility for benefits reinstated under this subsection shall commence with the benefit payable for the month following the month in which a request for reinstatement is filed.

(B)(i) Subject to clause (ii), the amount of the benefit payable for any month pursuant to the reinstatement of eligibility under this subsection shall be determined in accordance with the provisions of this title.

(ii) The benefit under this title payable for any month pursuant to a request for reinstatement filed in accordance with paragraph (2) shall

850   SOCIAL SECURITY ACT—§ 1631(p)(4)(B)(ii)(cont)

be reduced by the amount of any provisional benefit paid to such individual for such month under paragraph (7).

(C) Except as otherwise provided in this subsection, eligibility for benefits under this title reinstated pursuant to a request filed under paragraph (2) shall be subject to the same terms and conditions as eligibility established pursuant to an application filed therefor.

(5) Whenever an individual's eligibility for benefits under this title is reinstated under this subsection, eligibility for such benefits shall be reinstated with respect to the individual's spouse if such spouse was previously an eligible spouse of the individual under this title and the Commissioner determines that such spouse satisfies all the requirements for eligibility for such benefits except requirements related to the filing of an application. The provisions of paragraph (4) shall apply to the reinstated eligibility of the spouse to the same extent that they apply to the reinstated eligibility of such individual.

(6) An individual to whom benefits are payable under this title pursuant to a reinstatement of eligibility under this subsection for twenty–four months (whether or not consecutive) shall, with respect to benefits so payable after such twenty-fourth month, be deemed for purposes of paragraph (1)(B)(i)(I) to be eligible for such benefits on the basis of an application filed therefor.

(7)(A) An individual described in paragraph (1)(B) who files a request for reinstatement in accordance with the provisions of paragraph (2)(A) shall be eligible for provisional benefits payable in accordance with this paragraph, unless the Commissioner determines that the individual does not meet the requirements of paragraph (1)(B)(i) or that the individual's declaration under paragraph (2)(A)(ii) is false. Any such determination by the Commissioner shall be final and not subject to review under paragraph (1) or (3) of subsection (c).

(B)(i) Except as otherwise provided in clause (ii), the amount of a provisional benefit for a month shall equal the amount of the monthly benefit that would be payable to an eligible individual under this title with the same kind and amount of income.

(ii) If the individual has a spouse who was previously an eligible spouse of the individual under this title and the Commissioner determines that such spouse satisfies all the requirements of section 1614(b) except requirements related to the filing of an application, the amount of a provisional benefit for a month shall equal the amount of the monthly benefit that would be payable to an eligible individual and eligible spouse under this title with the same kind and amount of income.

(C)(i) Provisional benefits shall begin with the month following the month in which a request for reinstatement is filed in accordance with paragraph (2)(A).

(ii) Provisional benefits shall end with the earliest of—

(I) the month in which the Commissioner makes a determination regarding the individual's eligibility for reinstated benefits;

(II) the fifth month following the month for which provisional benefits are first payable under clause (i); or

(III) the month in which the Commissioner determines that the individual does not meet the requirements of paragraph (1)(B)(i) or that the individual's declaration made in accordance with paragraph (2)(A)(ii) is false.

SOCIAL SECURITY ACT—§ 1632(b)(2)

(D) In any case in which the Commissioner determines that an individual is not eligible for reinstated benefits, any provisional benefits paid to the individual under this paragraph shall not be subject to recovery as an overpayment unless the Commissioner determines that the individual knew or should have known that the individual did not meet the requirements of paragraph (1)(B).

(8) For purposes of this subsection other than paragraph (7), the term "benefits under this title" includes State supplementary payments made pursuant to an agreement under section 1616(a) of this Act or section 212(b) of Public Law 93-66[96].

PENALTIES FOR FRAUD[97]

SEC. 1632. [42 U.S.C. 1383a] (a) Whoever—

(1) knowingly and willfully makes or causes to be made any false statement or representation of a material fact in any application for any benefit under this title,

(2) at any time knowingly and willfully makes or causes to be made any false statement or representation of a material fact for use in determining rights to any such benefit,

(3) having knowledge of the occurrence of any event affecting (A) his initial or continued right to any such benefit, or (B) the initial or continued right to any such benefit of any other individual in whose behalf he has applied for or is receiving such benefit, conceals or fails to disclose such event with an intent fraudulently to secure such benefit either in a greater amount or quantity than is due or when no such benefit is authorized, or

(4) having made application to receive any such benefit for the use and benefit of another and having received it, knowingly and willfully converts such benefit or any part thereof to a use other than for the use and benefit of such other person,

shall be fined under title 18, United States Code, imprisoned not more than 5 years, or both

(b)(1) Any Federal court, when sentencing a defendant convicted of an offense under subsection (a), may order, in addition to or in lieu of any other penalty authorized by law, that the defendant make restitution to the Commissioner of Social Security, in any case in which such offense results in—

(A) the Commissioner of Social Security making a benefit payment that should not have been made, or

(B) an individual suffering a financial loss due to the defendant's violation of subsection (a) in his or her capacity as the individual's representative payee appointed pursuant to section 1631(a)(2).

(2) Sections 3612, 3663, and 3664 of title 18, United States Code[98], shall apply with respect to the issuance and enforcement of orders of restitution under this subsection. In so applying such sections, the Commissioner of Social Security shall be considered the victim.

---

[96] See Vol. II, P.L. 93-66, §212(b).

[97] See Vol. II, 18 U.S.C. 1028 and 1738, with respect to penalties relating to use of identification documents.

[98] See Vol. II, 18 U.S.C. 3612, 3663 and 3664.

852 SOCIAL SECURITY ACT—§ 1632(b)(3)

(3) If the court does not order restitution, or orders only partial restitution, under this subsection, the court shall state on he record the reasons therefor.

(4)(A) Except as provided in subparagraph (B), funds paid to the Commissioner of Social Security as restitution pursuant to a court order shall be deposited as miscellaneous receipts in the general fund of the Treasury.

(B) In the case of funds paid to the Commissioner of Social Security pursuant to paragraph (1)(B), the Commissioner of Social Security shall certify for payment to the individual described in such paragraph an amount equal to the lesser of the amount of the funds so paid or the individual's outstanding financial loss as described in such paragraph, except that such amount may be reduced by any overpayment of benefits owed under this title, title II, or title VIII by the individual.

(c) Any person or entity convicted of a violation of subsection (a) of this section or section 208 may not be certified as a representative payee under section 1631(a)(2).

ADMINISTRATION

SEC. 1633. [42 U.S.C. 1383b] (a) Subject to subsection (b), the Commissioner of Social Security may make such administrative and other arrangements (including arrangements for the determination of blindness and disability under section 1614(a)(2) and (3) in the same manner and subject to the same conditions as provided with respect to disability determinations under section 221) as may be necessary or appropriate to carry out the Commissioner's functions under this title.

(b) In determining, for purposes of this title, whether an individual is blind, there shall be an examination of such individual by a physician skilled in the diseases of the eye or by an optometrist, whichever the individual may select.

(c)(1) In any case in which the Commissioner of Social Security initiates a review under this title, similar to the continuing disability reviews authorized for purposes of title II under section 221(i), the Commissioner of Social Security shall notify the individual whose case is to be reviewed in the same manner as required under section 221(i)(4).

(2) For suspension of continuing disability reviews and other reviews under this title similar to reviews under section 221 in the case of an individual using a ticket to work and self-sufficiency, see section 1148(i).

(d) The Commissioner of Social Security shall establish by regulation criteria for time limits and other criteria related to individuals' plans for achieving self-support, that take into account—

(1) the length of time that the individual will need to achieve the individual's employment goal (within such reasonable period as the Commissioner of Social Security may establish); and

(2) other factors determined by the Commissioner of Social Security to be appropriate.

(e)(1) The Commissioner of Social Security shall review determinations, made by State agencies pursuant to subsection (a) in connection with applications for benefits under this title on the basis of blindness or disability, that individuals who have attained 18 years of age are blind or disabled as of a specified onset date. The Commissioner of

SOCIAL SECURITY ACT—§ 1634(b)(2)(B)   853

Social Security shall review such a determination before any action is taken to implement the determination.

(2)(A) In carrying out paragraph (1), the Commissioner of Social Security shall review—

(i) at least 20 percent of all determinations referred to in paragraph (1) that are made in fiscal year 2006;

(ii) at least 40 percent of all such determinations that are made in fiscal year 2007; and

(iii) at least 50 percent of all such determinations that are made in fiscal year 2008 or thereafter.

(B) In carrying out subparagraph (A), the Commissioner of Social Security shall, to the extent feasible, select for review the determinations which the Commissioner of Social Security identifies as being the most likely to be incorrect.

DETERMINATIONS OF MEDICAID ELIGIBILITY[99]

SEC. 1634. [42 U.S.C. 1383c] (a) The Commissioner of Social Security may enter into an agreement with any State which wishes to do so under which the Commissioner will determine eligibility for medical assistance in the case of aged, blind, or disabled individuals under such State's plan approved under title XIX. Any such agreement shall provide for payments by the State, for use by the Commissioner of Social Security in carrying out the agreement, of an amount equal to one-half of the cost of carrying out the agreement, but in computing such cost with respect to individuals eligible for benefits under this title, the Commissioner of Social Security shall include only those costs which are additional to the costs incurred in carrying out this title.

(b)(1) An eligible disabled widow or widower (described in paragraph (2)) who is entitled to a widow's or widower's insurance benefit based on a disability for any month under section 202(e) or (f) but is not eligible for benefits under this title in that month, and who applies for the protection of this subsection under paragraph (3), shall be deemed for purposes of title XIX to be an individual with respect to whom benefits under this title are paid in that month if he or she—

(A) has been continuously entitled to such widow's or widower's insurance benefits from the first month for which the increase described in paragraph (2)(C) was reflected in such benefits through the month involved, and

(B) would be eligible for benefits under this title in the month involved if the amount of the increase described in paragraph (2)(C) in his or her widow's or widower's insurance benefits, and any subsequent cost-of-living adjustments in such benefits under section 215(i), were disregarded.

(2) For purposes of paragraph (1), the term "eligible disabled widow or widower" means an individual who—

(A) was entitled to a monthly insurance benefit under title II for December 1983,

(B) was entitled to a widow's or widower's insurance benefit based on a disability under section 202(e) or (f) for January 1984 and with respect to whom a benefit under this title was paid in that month, and

---

[99] See Vol. II, P.L. 94-566, §503, with respect to preservation of medicaid eligibility.

854 SOCIAL SECURITY ACT—§ 1634(b)(2)(C)

(C) because of the increase in the amount of his or her widow's or widower's insurance benefits which resulted from the amendments made by section 134 of the Social Security Amendments of 1983 (Public Law 98-21[100]) (eliminating the additional reduction factor for disabled widows and widowers under age 60), was ineligible for benefits under this title in the first month in which such increase was paid to him or her (and in which a retroactive payment of such increase for prior months was not made).

(3) This subsection shall only apply to an individual who files a written application for protection under this subsection, in such manner and form as the Commissioner of Social Security may prescribe, no later than July 1, 1988.

(4) For purposes of this subsection, the term "benefits under this title" includes payments of the type described in section 1616(a) or of the type described in section 212(a) of Public Law 93-66[101].

(c) If any individual who has attained the age of 18 and is receiving benefits under this title on the basis of blindness or a disability which began before he or she attained the age of 22—

(1) becomes entitled, on or after the effective date of this subsection, to child's insurance benefits which are payable under section 202(d) on the basis of such disability or to an increase in the amount of the child's insurance benefits which are so payable, and

(2) ceases to be eligible for benefits under this title because of such child's insurance benefits or because of the increase in such child's insurance benefits,

such individual shall be treated for purposes of title XIX as receiving benefits under this title so long as he or she would be eligible for benefits under this title in the absence of such child's insurance benefits or such increase.[102]

(d)(1) This subsection applies with respect to any person who—

(A) applies for and obtains benefits under subsection (e) or (f) of section 202 (or under any other subsection of section 202 if such person is also eligible for benefits under such subsection (e) or (f)) being then not entitled to hospital insurance benefits under part A of title XVIII, and

(B) is determined to be ineligible (by reason of the receipt of such benefits under section 202) for supplemental security income benefits under this title or for State supplementary payments of the type described in section 1616(a) (or payments of the type described in section 212(a) of Public Law 93-66).

(2) For purposes of title XIX, each person with respect to whom this subsection applies—

(A) shall be deemed to be a recipient of supplemental security income benefits under this title if such person received such a benefit for the month before the month in which such person began to receive a benefit described in paragraph (1)(A), and

(B) shall be deemed to be a recipient of State supplementary payments of the type referred to in section 1616(a) of this Act (or payments of the type described in section 212(a) of Public Law 93-66) if such person received such a payment for the month be-

---

[100] P.L. 98-21; 97 Stat. 97.
[101] See Vol. II, P.L. 93-66, §212(a).
[102] See Vol. II, P.L. 99-643, §6(b), with respect to State determinations.

SOCIAL SECURITY ACT—§ 1637(a)(4)   855

fore the month in which such person began to receive a benefit described in paragraph (1)(A),
for so long as such person (i) would be eligible for such supplemental security income benefits, or such State supplementary payments (or payments of the type described in section 212(a) of Public Law 93-66[103]), in the absence of benefits described in paragraph (1)(A), and (ii) is not entitled to hospital insurance benefits under part A of title XVIII.

OUTREACH PROGRAM FOR CHILDREN

SEC. 1635. [42 U.S.C. 1383d] (a) ESTABLISHMENT.—The Commissioner of Social Security shall establish and conduct an ongoing program of outreach to children who are potentially eligible for benefits under this title by reason of disability or blindness.

(b) REQUIREMENTS.—Under this program, the Commissioner of Social Security shall—

(1) aim outreach efforts at populations for whom such efforts would be most effective; and

(2) work in cooperation with other Federal, State, and private agencies, and nonprofit organizations, which serve blind or disabled individuals and have knowledge of potential recipients of supplemental security income benefits, and with agencies and organizations (including school systems and public and private social service agencies) which focus on the needs of children.

TREATMENT REFERRALS FOR INDIVIDUALS WITH AN ALCOHOLISM OR DRUG ADDICTION CONDITION

SEC. 1636. [42 U.S.C. 1383e] In the case of any individual whose benefits under this title are paid to a representative payee pursuant to section 1631(a)(2)(A)(ii)(II), the Commissioner of Social Security shall refer such individual to the appropriate State agency administering the State plan for substance abuse treatment services approved under subpart II of part B of title XIX of the Public Health Service Act[104] (42 U.S.C. 300x-21 et seq.).

ANNUAL REPORT ON PROGRAM

SEC. 1637. [42 U.S.C. 1383f] (a) Not later than May 30 of each year, the Commissioner of Social Security shall prepare and deliver a report annually to the President and the Congress regarding the program under this title, including—

(1) a comprehensive description of the program;

(2) historical and current data on allowances and denials, including number of applications and allowance rates for initial determinations, reconsideration determinations, administrative law judge hearings, appeals council reviews, and Federal court decisions;

(3) historical and current data on characteristics of recipients and program costs, by recipient group (aged, blind, disabled adults, and disabled children);

(4) historical and current data on prior enrollment by recipients in public benefit programs, including State programs funded un-

---

[103] See Vol. II, P.L. 93-66, §212(a).
[104] P.L. 78-410.

SOCIAL SECURITY ACT—§ 1637(a)(4)(cont)

der part A of title IV of the Social Security Act and State general assistance programs;

(5) projections of future number of recipients and program costs, through at least 25 years;

(6) number of redeterminations and continuing disability reviews, and the outcomes of such redeterminations and reviews;

(7) data on the utilization of work incentives;

(8) detailed information on administrative and other program operation costs;

(9) summaries of relevant research undertaken by the Social Security Administration, or by other researchers;

(10) State supplementation program operations;

(11) a historical summary of statutory changes to this title; and

(12) such other information as the Commissioner deems useful.

(b) Each member of the Social Security Advisory Board shall be permitted to provide an individual report, or a joint report if agreed, of views of the program under this title, to be included in the annual report required under this section.

TITLE XVII—GRANTS FOR PLANNING COMPREHENSIVE ACTION TO COMBAT MENTAL RETARDATION[1]

TABLE OF CONTENTS OF TITLE[2]

		Page
Sec. 1701.	Authorization of appropriations	857
Sec. 1702.	Grants to States	857
Sec. 1703.	Applications	858
Sec. 1704.	Payments	858

AUTHORIZATION OF APPROPRIATIONS

SEC. 1701. [42 U.S.C. 1391] For the purpose of assisting the States (including the District of Columbia, the Commonwealth of Puerto Rico, the Virgin Islands, Guam, and American Samoa) to plan for and take other steps leading to comprehensive State and community action to combat mental retardation, there is authorized to be appropriated the sum of $2,200,000. There are also authorized to be appropriated, for assisting such States in initiating the implementation and carrying out of planning and other steps to combat mental retardation, $2,750,000 for the fiscal year ending June 30, 1966, and $2,750,000 for the fiscal year ending June 30, 1967.

GRANTS TO STATES

SEC. 1702. [42 U.S.C. 1392] The sums appropriated pursuant to the first sentence of section 1701 shall be available for grants to States by the Secretary during the fiscal year ending June 30, 1964, and the succeeding fiscal year; and the sums appropriated pursuant to the second sentence of such section for the fiscal year ending June 30, 1966, shall be available for such grants during such year and the next two fiscal years, and sums appropriated pursuant thereto for the fiscal year ending June 30, 1967, shall be available for such grants during such year and the succeeding fiscal year. Any such grant to a State, which shall not exceed 75 per centum of the cost of the planning and related activities involved, may be used by it to determine what action is needed to combat mental retardation in the State and the resources available for this purpose, to develop public awareness of the mental retardation problem and of the need for combating it, to coordinate State and local activities relating to the various aspects of mental retardation and its prevention, treatment, or amelioration, and to plan other activities leading to comprehensive State and community action to combat mental retardation.

---

[1] Title XVII of the Social Security Act is administered by the Rehabilitation Services Administration, Office of Special Education and Rehabilitative Services, Department of Education.

Title XVII appears in the United States Code as §§1391-1394, subchapter XVII, chapter 7, Title 42.

No regulations have been promulgated for Title XVII.

Title XVII was added to the Social Security Act by P.L. 88-156, "Maternal and Child Health and Mental Retardation Planning Amendments of 1963", §5 (77 Stat. 273, 275), effective October 24, 1963; however, it now is inactive.

[2] This table of contents does not appear in the law.

858 SOCIAL SECURITY ACT—§ 1702(cont)

APPLICATIONS

SEC. 1703. [42 U.S.C. 1393] In order to be eligible for a grant under section 1702, a State must submit an application therefor which—

(1) designates or establishes a single State agency, which may be an interdepartmental agency, as the sole agency for carrying out the purposes of this title;

(2) indicates the manner in which provision will be made to assure full consideration of all aspects of services essential to planning for comprehensive State and community action to combat mental retardation, including services in the fields of education, employment, rehabilitation, welfare, health, and the law, and services provided through community programs for and institutions for the mentally retarded;

(3) sets forth its plans for expenditure of such grant, which plans provide reasonable assurance of carrying out the purposes of this title;

(4) provides for submission of a final report of the activities of the State agency in carrying out the purposes of this title, and for submission of such other reports, in such form and containing such information, as the Secretary[3] may from time to time find necessary for carrying out the purposes of this title and for keeping such records and affording such access thereto as he may find necessary to assure the correctness and verification of such reports; and

(5) provides for such fiscal control and fund accounting procedures as may be necessary to assure proper disbursement of and accounting for funds paid to the State under this title.

PAYMENTS

SEC. 1704. [42 U.S.C. 1394] Payment of grants under this title may be made (after necessary adjustment on account of previously made underpayments or overpayments) in advance or by way of reimbursement, and in such installments and on such conditions, as the Secretary may determine.

---

[3] P.L. 88-156, §6, provides that the term "Secretary" means the Secretary of Health, Education, and Welfare [now Secretary of Health and Human Services].

CPSIA information can be obtained at www.ICGtesting.com
Printed in the USA
LVOW082317071111
253961LV00004B/191/P